D1475211

MAGNETIC RECORDING TECHNOLOGY

Other McGraw-Hill Reference Books of Interest

Handbooks

Avallone and Baumeister • MARK'S STANDARD HANDBOOK FOR MECHANICAL ENGINEERS

Benson • AUDIO ENGINEERING HANDBOOK

Benson • TELEVISION ENGINEERING HANDBOOK

Coombs • PRINTED CIRCUITS HANDBOOK

Coombs • BASIC ELECTRONIC INSTRUMENT HANDBOOK

Croft and Summers • AMERICAN ELECTRICIANS' HANDBOOK

Di Giacomo • VLSI HANDBOOK

Fink and Beaty • STANDARD HANDBOOK FOR ELECTRICAL ENGINEERS

Fink and Christiansen • ELECTRONIC ENGINEERS' HANDBOOK

Harper • HANDBOOK OF ELECTRONIC SYSTEMS DESIGN

Harper • HANDBOOK OF THICK FILM HYBRID MICROELECTRONICS

Harper • HANDBOOK OF WIRING, CABLING, AND INTERCONNECTING FOR ELECTRONICS

Hicks • STANDARD HANDBOOK OF ENGINEERING CALCULATIONS

Inglis • ELECTRONIC COMMUNICATIONS HANDBOOK

Juran and Gryna • JURAN'S QUALITY CONTROL HANDBOOK

Kaufman and Seidman • HANDBOOK OF ELECTRONICS CALCULATIONS

Kurtz • HANDBOOK OF ENGINEERING ECONOMICS

Stout • MICROPROCESSOR APPLICATIONS HANDBOOK

Stout and Kaufman • HANDBOOK OF MICROCIRCUIT DESIGN AND APPLICATION

Stout and Kaufman • HANDBOOK OF OPERATIONAL AMPLIFIER CIRCUIT DESIGN

Tuma • ENGINEERING MATHEMATICS HANDBOOK

Williams • DESIGNER'S HANDBOOK OF INTEGRATED CIRCUITS

Williams and Taylor • ELECTRONIC FILTER DESIGN HANDBOOK

Dictionaries

DICTIONARY OF COMPUTERS

DICTIONARY OF ELECTRICAL AND ELECTRONIC ENGINEERING

DICTIONARY OF ENGINEERING

DICTIONARY OF SCIENTIFIC AND TECHNICAL TERMS

Markus • ELECTRONICS DICTIONARY

Other

Luther • DIGITAL VIDEO IN THE PC ENVIRONMENT

Mee and Daniel • MAGNETIC STORAGE HANDBOOK

Philips • COMPACT DISC INTERACTIVE

MAGNETIC RECORDING TECHNOLOGY

C. Denis Mee Editor

Los Gatos, California

Eric D. Daniel Editor

Redwood City, California

Second Edition

McGRAW-HILL

New York San Francisco Washington, D.C. Auckland Bogotá
Caracas Lisbon London Madrid Mexico City Milan
Montreal Paris San Juan Singapore
Sydney Tokyo Toronto

Library of Congress Cataloging-in-Publication Data

Magnetic recording technology / editors, C. Denis Mee, Eric D. Daniel
— 2nd ed.
    p.   cm.
    Rev. ed. of: Magnetic recording handbook. c1990.
    Includes bibliographical references and index.
    ISBN 0-07-041276-6 (hc)
    1. Magnetic recorders and recording. I. Mee, C. Denis.
II. Daniel, Eric D. III. Series: Magnetic recording handbook.
TK7881.6.M25   1995
621.39'76—dc20   95-44642
                                                      CIP

Second edition of Part 1 of *Magnetic Recording Handbook,* © 1990.

McGraw-Hill

A Division of The **McGraw-Hill** Companies

Copyright © 1996, 1990 by The McGraw-Hill Companies, Inc. All rights
reserved. Printed in the United States of America. Except as permitted
under the United States Copyright Act of 1976, no part of this publication
may be reproduced or distributed in any form or by any means, or stored in a
database or retrieval system, without the prior written permission of the
publisher.

1 2 3 4 5 6 7 8 9 0 DOC/DOC 9 0 0 9 8 7 6

ISBN 0-07-041276-6

*The sponsoring editor for this book was Stephen S. Chapman, and the
production supervisor was Suzanne W. B. Rapcavage. It was set in Times
Roman by Huron Valley Graphics, Ann Arbor, Michigan.*

Printed and bound by R. R. Donnelley & Sons Company.

This book is printed on acid-free paper.

McGraw-Hill books are available at special quantity discounts to use as
premiums and sales promotions, or for use in corporate training
programs. For more information, please write to the Director of Special
Sales, McGraw-Hill, 11 West 19th Street, New York, NY 10011. Or
contact your local bookstore.

*To order or receive additional information on these or any other
McGraw-Hill titles, in the United States please call 1-800-822-8158.
In other countries, contact your local McGraw-Hill representative.*   **BC15XXA**

Information contained in this work has been obtained by The
McGraw-Hill Companies, Inc. ("McGraw-Hill") from sources
believed to be reliable. However, neither McGraw-Hill nor its
authors guarantees the accuracy or completeness of any information published herein and neither McGraw-Hill nor its authors shall be responsible for any errors, omissions, or damages
arising out of use of this information. This work is published
with the understanding that McGraw-Hill and its authors are
supplying information but are not attempting to render engineering or other professional services. If such services are required, the assistance of an appropriate professional should be
sought.

To the memory of Eberhard Köster, author of the chapter on Particulate Media, who died in August, 1995.

C. Denis Mee
Eric D. Daniel

September, 1995

CONTENTS

ABOUT THE EDITORS

C. Denis Mee spent nearly three decades with IBM, where he specialized in advanced storage technologies, magneto-optical storage, bubbles, magnetic recording heads, media, and recording technologies for computer rigid disks. He was appointed an IBM Fellow in 1983. He retired from IBM in 1993.

Eric D. Daniel worked with Memorex Corporation for 17 years on a wide variety of magnetic recording media, including computer, instrumentation, video and audio tapes, computer rigid, and flexible disks. He is a former Fellow of Memorex, and has a total of more than 40 years' experience in magnetic recording research and development.

CONTRIBUTORS

Thomas C. Arnoldussen *IBM Corporation, San Jose, Calif.*

Bharat Bhushan *Ohio State University, Columbus, Ohio*

Dan S. Bloomberg *Xerox Corporation, Palo Alto, Calif.*

G. A. Neville Connell *Xerox Corporation, Palo Alto, Calif.*

Eric D. Daniel *Redwood City, Calif.*

Robert E. Jones *Carnegie-Mellon University, Pittsburgh, Pa.*

Eberhard Köster *Frankenthal, Germany*

John C. Mallinson *Belmont, Calif.*

Masud Mansuripur *University of Arizona, Tucson, Ariz.*

C. Denis Mee *Los Gatos, Calif.*

Barry K. Middleton *Manchester University, Manchester, England*

James E. Monson *Harvey Mudd College, Claremont, Calif.*

Ching Tsang *IBM Corporation, San Jose, Calif.*

Jiang-Gang Zhu *University of Minnesota, Minneapolis, Minn.*

FOREWORD

Magnetic Recording Technology is an updated and substantially expanded version of Part I of the *Magnetic Recording Handbook* published in 1990. A similarly extensive revision of Part II of that work will be published separately under the title *Magnetic Storage Handbook*.

The major additions and revisions that have gone into *Magnetic Recording Technology* are highlighted below:

Film Recording Media. This now rates a separate chapter to reflect the fact that deposited film media have now virtually taken over from particulate media for data recording on hard disks, and have gained significant entry in video and other tape applications.

Micromagnetics of Film Media. This is a completely new chapter included to cover this increasingly important aspect of film media technology.

Magnetoresistive Heads. A new author has contributed a section devoted to this subject in the chapter on *Recording Heads*. This section gives a greatly expanded treatment to reflect the rapidly increasing importance of magnetoresistive heads in high-performance hard-disk drives and other data storage applications.

Tribology of the Head-Medium Interface. This is an entirely new chapter covering the critical interface between the head and the medium, with particular emphasis on tribology.

Recording Limitations. This chapter has been largely rewritten. It includes a more rigorous treatment of noise theory, and a closer examination of the impact of magnetoresistive read heads on recording system limitations.

Magnetooptical Recording. Several sections have been added by a new author, covering advances in the design and analyses of recording media and heads. New multilayer media are described which are capable of direct overwrite and very high resolution recording.

Other chapters of *Magnetic Recording Technology* required less extensive revision. However, where significant technological advances have occurred in recent years, these are covered by the inclusion of the relevant new data, text, and references.

PREFACE

The purpose of this book, *Magnetic Recording Technology*, is to provide a single reference that covers the many scientific and engineering disciplines of magnetic recording. The book is organized in the following way:

This book is concerned with establishing the underlying technologies that are common to all forms of magnetic recording. Separate chapters treat the processes by which recording and reproduction take place; the materials, design, and fabrication of media; the materials, design, and fabrication of heads; the limit on performance due to noise, interference, and distortion; the key magnetic and recording measurement techniques that have evolved; the mechanical interface between the head and medium that is of critical importance in all but optically addressed media; and, finally, reversible optical recording in which the signals are recorded thermomagnetically then reproduced magnetooptically. It is some eight years since the publication of the first of the books that form the basis of the current work. The preface written at that time remarked on the rapid growth of the information-storage industry and the position occupied by magnetic recording as the dominant non-static memory technology. In the intervening years the industry has grown at an accelerated pace, but magnetic recording remains ubiquitous as the technology of choice for reversible, low-cost information storage. The versatility of magnetic recording is still unmatched in providing different storage media formats—tapes, stripes, cards, flexible disks, as well as hard disks—a capability that makes magnetic recording uniquely adaptable to a wide variety of data, video, and audio applications, both at the business and consumer levels.

Optical recording has gained strong acceptance in certain read-only, hard-disk applications where removability (the easy replacement of one disk with another) is the overriding requirement. Major examples are, in the order in which large-scale commercial development occurred, the *Compact Disc* for prerecorded audio, the *CD ROM* for computer applications, and disks for prerecorded digital-video programs are in the offing. Considerable research has been directed toward developing reversible optical recording devices which would expand the applications of optically-addressed storage products. One approach uses media in which recording takes place by optically induced phase changes which, at least to a limited extent, are reversible. The other approach, magnetooptical recording, provides unlimited reversibility by recording thermomagnetically and reading back magnetooptically. Longstanding research has led to commercially viable magnetooptical disk products for computer storage and audio applications. This technology is also capable of sustained improvements in storage density which can be expected to lead to lower-cost products. The combination of inexpensive, large-capacity, rewritable optical disks, which may be removed from the drive, will make this form of storage an increasingly viable contender for future computer and consumer applications. Magnetooptical recording falls within the category "magnetic recording" and is therefore treated extensively in these books.

With the exception of magnetooptical recording, all magnetic recording products employ the same basic inductive-recording technology which has been developed over the last 40 to 60 years. The technology has improved immensely as understanding has been gained of the underlying physics of the recording and reproducing processes. Advances in recording materials and processes for fabricating components have also contributed in a major way to extending the performance of magnetic recording technology into different industries. Costs have continued to go down as means have been developed to pack more information reliably into a given storage space or to replace existing devices with ones smaller and less expensive to fabricate. A useful measure of such advances is the annual increase in areal storage density—the quantity of information that can be stored in a given area of the surface of a recording medium. For example, in the case of rigid disks, the areal storage density over the last eight years has risen by a factor of 25, equivalent to an astonishing average annual increase of approximately 50 percent, with no sign of peaking out in the immediate future.

The bulk of the research and development that has made this rate of progress possible has been carried out in the magnetic recording industry. During the past eight years, however, a surge in research activities in magnetic recording and related fields has occurred in the U.S.A. through the formation of nine research centers at universities throughout the country. Not only have these university centers accelerated the progress in materials, components, and systems for information storage, they have also provided a steady stream of trained graduates who have carried this progress to industry.

The purpose of this book, *Magnetic Recording Technology*, and the companion volume, *Magnetic Storage Handbook,* to be published later, is to provide definitive, comprehensive, up-to-date reference material for use by anyone engaged in the research, development, or manufacturing of information storage products based on magnetic recording.

Magnetic Recording Technology. This book covers the underlying technologies that are common to the various forms of magnetic recording, from the physics of the recording and reproducing processes to the tribology of the head-medium interface. The book should be of particular value to the students and staff at the University Storage Research Centers and to their counterparts engaged in research and advanced development within industry.

Magnetic Storage Handbook. This book covers the more practical aspects of magnetic recording, including the major applications and products used for storing computer data, and video and audio signals in analog and digital form. It will be useful to the student as a reference book, but its main purpose is to provide the scientists and engineers in industry with a single source of information on the major applications of magnetic recording, and the related storage products.

SI (Système International D'Unités) units are used throughout. Where other units (such as cgs) are widely used, values expressed in these units are listed in parentheses.

A comprehensive treatise on magnetic recording is possible only by combining the knowledge of many talented people. We greatly appreciate the dedicated efforts of the authors who have contributed their reviews of each branch of the subject and have cooperated in producing an in-depth coverage of this multi-disciplined field. We are also grateful to a number of external reviewers who assisted in our attempt to produce a uniform and up-to-date coverage of the subject matter.

C. Denis Mee
Eric D. Daniel

LIST OF ABBREVIATIONS AND SYMBOLS

Abbreviations

AFM	atomic force microscope
APD	avalanche photo diode
CNR	carrier-to-noise ratio
DRAW	direct read after write
EPR-4	extended partial response, Class 4
FM	frequency modulation
HPF	hot pressed ferrite
LSB	least significant bit
ME	metal evaporated
MFM	magnetic force microscope
MP	metal particle
MSB	most significant bit
NEP	noise-equivalent power
NOP	non-contact optical profiler
NPR	noise-power ratio
PBS	polarizing beam splitter
PET	polyethylene teraphthalate
PMMA	polymethyl methacrylate
SCF	single crystal ferrite
SFD	switching field distribution
SNR	signal-to-noise ratio
STM	scanning tunneling microscope
TEM	transmission electron microscope
THD	third harmonic distortion
VSM	vibrating sample magnetometer

Symbols

A	area; exchange energy constant; exchange stiffness
a	acceleration; arctangent transition parameter; lattice constant
A_c	cross-sectional area of head core
A_g	cross-sectional area of head gap
a_x	transition parameter for longitudinal magnetization
a_y	transition parameter for perpendicular magnetization
B	half-amplitude (0-peak) of zig-zag pattern; magnetic induction (flux density)
b	base-film thickness; bit length; radius of particle; space between magnetoresistive head shields; width of guard band

B_g	air-gap flux density	E	energy; Young's modulus
B_m	maximum induction (flux density)	e	charge of electron; head output voltage
b_p	critical particle radius for superparamagnetic behavior	E_a	anisotropy energy
		e_b	back emf
		E_d	demagnetizing energy
B_r	remanent induction (flux density)	E_e	exchange energy
		E_f	Fermi energy
B_s	saturation induction (flux density)	E_h	external magnetic field energy
b_0	particle radius for single-domain behavior	E_k	magnetocrystalline energy
		E_{ms}	magnetoelastic energy
C	capacitance; capacity (bytes)	e_n	noise output voltage
		e_s	signal output voltage
c	average length per turn in magnet coil; damping constant	E_t	total energy
		e_x	output from longitudinal magnetization
C_i	specific heat per unit volume of layer i	e_y	output from perpendicular magnetization
		F	force
C_r	crosstalk	f	focal length; frequency
		f_c	carrier frequency
D	data rate; delay factor; recording density; width of domain wall	f_{max}	maximum recorded frequency
		f_s	signal frequency
d	head-to-medium spacing	f_0	Larmor frequency
		$F(\theta)$	particle orientation factor
D_a	areal density (b/mm^2)	G	gain; Green's function
D_c	recording density for maximum resolution	g	gap length
		g_{eff}	effective gap length
d_{eff}	effective head-to-medium spacing	H	magnetic field
		h	reduced magnetic field; stripe height of magnetoresistive head
D_l	linear (bit) density (b/mm)		
d_l	lens diameter	H_a	total anisotropy field
D_r	recording density (fr/mm)	H_{appl}	applied field (e.g., of magnetometer)
D_t	track density (t/mm)	H_b	bias field
		H_c	coercivity
d_0	minimum stable domain diameter spacing corresponding to nominal "in-contact" conditions	h_c	reduced coercivity (H_c/H_a)
		H_d	demagnetizing field
		H_g	deep gap field
		H_k	magnetocrystalline anisotropy field
D_{50}	linear density at which the output falls 50%	H_m	shape anisotropy field; maximum (applied) field
$D_{(i)}$	thermal diffusivity of magnetooptical film ($\{i\} = f$) and dielectric ($\{i\} = d$)	H_{mrx}, H_{mry}	sensitivity-function fields for a magnetoresistive head
		H_r	remanence coercivity

h_r	reduced remanence coercivity (H_c/H_a)	K_{eff}	effective uniaxial anisotropy constant
H_{rx}, H_{ry}	fields from a ring head (Karlqvist equations)	K_p	figure of merit including laser power tolerance
H_t	total field ($H_{appl} + H_d$)	K_r	figure of merit for rotating power
H_u	effective field seen by spin-up electrons due to spin-orbit effect	K_u	uniaxial anisotropy constant
H_0	particle switching (nucleation) field	k_x	position gain constant
		K_0, K_1, K_2	crystalline anisotropy constants
h_0	reduced nucleation field (H_0/H_a)	k_1, k_2, k_3	spring constants
$H_{0.25}$	reverse field required to switch 25% of particles after saturation [$M_r(H_{0.25})/M_r(\infty) = 0.5$]	$K_\perp$	perpendicular anisotropy constant
		$K(H_1, H_2)$	Preisach distribution function
$H_{0.5}$	dc field in ideal anhysteresis required to obtain one-half saturation [$M_{ar}(H_{0.5})/M_{ar}(\infty) = 0.5$]	L	inductance; inductance of voice coil; length of dipole; length of head poles; orbital angular momentum quantum number
$H_{0.75}$	reverse field required to switch 75% of particles after saturation [$M_r(H_{0.75})/M_r(\infty) = -0.5$]	l	length of head magnetic circuit; length of particle
		l_c	length of head core
H_1	positive field axis of the Preisach diagram	L_d	spacing loss
H_2	negative field axis of the Preisach diagram	$L_{dif}(t)$	approximate thickness of dielectric layer heated in time t
I	intensity of electron beam; Laplace transform of current	L_g	gap loss
		L_δ	thickness loss
i	current	$L_{\{i\}}$	thickness of magnetic layer ($\{i\} = f$), overlayer ($\{i\} = o$), and intermediate layer ($\{i\} = i$)
i_n	total noise current		
i_{ne}	electronic noise current	M	magnetization; mass
i_{nt}	thermal noise current	m	dipole magnetic moment; mass; mass of electron; particle magnetic moment; reduced magnetization [$M(H)/M(\infty)$]
$I(r)$	light intensity at radius r		
$I_{\{i\}}$	intensity of magnetooptical radiation from semi-infinite ($\{i\} = s$) or quadrilayer ($\{i\} = q$) sample		
		m_{ar}	reduced anhysteretic magnetization, $M_{ar}(H)/M_{ar}(\infty)$
J	exchange integral; moment of inertia; total angular momentum quantum number	m_B	Bohr magneton
		M_d	dc demagnetizing remanent magnetization
j	$\sqrt{-1}$		
J_{ij}	exchange integral between nearest neighbor atoms i and j	M_r	remanent magnetization (remanence)
		m_r	reduced remanent magnetization [$M_r(H)/M_r(\infty)$]
K	magnetic anisotropy constant	M_s	saturation magnetization
k	Boltzmann constant; wave number ($2\pi/\lambda$)	M_{sb}	saturation magnetization of bulk material

M_0	peak value of sine-wave magnetization; value of magnetization in between transitions
$M(H)$	magnetization in a field H
$M(H_m)$	magnetization in a field of maximum value H_m
$M_r(H)$	remanent magnetization after applying a field H
$M_r(H_m)$	remanent magnetization after applying a field of maximum value H_m
$M_r(\infty)$	saturation remanent magnetization (retentivity)
N	demagnetization factor; number of atoms per unit volume; number of particles per unit volume
n	index of number of tracks; number of turns; refractive index
N_A	numerical aperture
N_a	demagnetization factor along a axis of an ellipsoid
N_b	demagnetization factor along b axis of an ellipsoid
N_c	demagnetization factor along c axis of an ellipsoid
N_{eff}	effective demagnetization factor used for deskewing hysteresis loop
N_h	number of turns on head
N_l	number of turns on coil
$N_d(E)$	density of spin-down states at energy E
$N_u(E)$	density of spin-up states at energy E
$\mathbf{n}^+$	complex refractive index for right circularly polarized light
$\mathbf{n}^-$	complex refractive index for left circularly polarized light
$n_{\{i\}}$	refractive index of overlayer ($\{i\} = o$), or intermediate layer ($\{i\} = i$)
P	average laser power on each detector; normalized pressure (p/p_a); power; print-to-signal ratio
p	pole-tip length; volumetric packing density
p_a	ambient (atmospheric) pressure
P, P_e	power dissipated
P_i	laser power incident on medium
P_s	optical signal power on each detector
P_{shot}	optical shot noise power on each detector
p_{25}	pulse width at 25% amplitude
p_{50}	pulse width at 50% amplitude
Q	head parameter in calculating transition length
R	data rate; reflectivity; reluctance; resolution; resistance
r	radial coordinate; radius
r_b	e^{-1} intensity radius of laser beam
R_c	reluctance of core
R_e	resolution
R_g	reluctance of gap
r_{ij}	distance between nearest neighbor atoms i and j
r_x	ordinary (unconverted) reflected amplitude for linear polarization x
r_y	magnetooptical (converted) reflected amplitude for linear polarization y for incident polarization x
R_0	base resistance of magnetoresistive head
r_+	reflected amplitude for right circularly polarized light
r_-	reflected amplitude for left circularly polarized light
$r_{\{i\}}$	complex Fresnel coefficient ($\{i\} = x, y, +$ or $-$)
S	element of surface; remanence squareness $[M_r(H)/M_s]$; signal normalized to zero-peak signal from saturated region; spin angular momentum quantum number; synchronization pattern
s	distance between head and permeable layer
S_{sat}	zero-to-peak signal from a saturated region

S_{trans}	normalized zero-to-peak signal from an isolated transition
$S*$	coercivity squareness factor
$S(H)$	remanence squareness in an applied field H
$S(H_m)$	remanence squareness in an applied field of maximum value H_m
T	data period; temperature; tension; thickness of pole in a single-pole head; torque
t	magnetoresistive sensor thickness; time; total thickness of medium including substrate; track spacing
T_c	Curie temperature
T_{comp}	compensation temperature
t_{min}	minimum track spacing
U	magnetostatic potential
U_0	magnetostatic potential between pole tips
V	head-to-medium velocity; output voltage
v	particle volume; volume
v_p	critical volume for superparamagnetic behavior
W	full-width-at-half-maximum of Gaussian read beam; work
w	head width; track width; written mark width
w_{eff}	effective track width
w_h	width of head
W_i	strength of single ion anisotropy of atom of type i
w_r	read track width
w_t	tape width
w_w	write track width
X	normalized coordinate (x/B)
X_i	atomic fraction of atom of type i
Y	normalized coordinate (y/L)
Z	atomic number; impedance
Z_{ij}	number of j atoms that are nearest neighbors of atom i
α	absorption coefficient; angle of polarizer; coefficient of thermal expansion; direction cosine
α_a	coefficient of thermal expansion of arm
β	angle; bandwidth; direction cosine
γ	angle; direction cosine
Δh_r	switching field distribution
ΔT	change in temperature
Δw	side fringe width
δ	depth of focus; eddy current penetration depth; stripe width in transmission line theory; thickness of a domain wall; thickness of a magnetic medium
δ_f	thickness of base film
δ_w	domain wall width parameter; side fringe width of read head
δw_w	side fringe width of write head
$\epsilon(\omega)$	complex dielectric tensor (at frequency ω)
ζ	fraction of heat residing in magnetic film
η	efficiency; quantum efficiency
η_k	polar Kerr ellipticity
θ	angular coordinate
Θ_c	Curie temperature
θ_h	half-angle of lens
θ_k	polar Kerr rotation
θ_s	maximum Kerr rotation in system
κ	thermal conductivity
λ	characteristic length in transmission line theory; magnetostriction coefficient; wavelength
λ_c	critical wavelength for maximum resolution
λ_{min}	minimum recordable wavelength
λ_s	magnetostriction coefficient
μ	coefficient of friction; relative magnetic permeability
μ_r	relative permeability
μ'	real permeability
μ''	imaginary permeability
μ_0	magnetic permeability of vacuum
ν	frequency; Poisson's ratio

ξ	polarizing beam splitter efficiency	τ_d	penetration diffusion time
ρ	base resistivity of magnetoresistive head; density; resistivity	τ_e	electrical time constant
		τ_{eq}	time constant to reach uniform film temperature
ρ_m	magnetic pole volume density	τ_{lat}	lateral diffusion time
		τ_m	time constant of magnet
σ	standard deviation; stress	Φ	magnetic flux
σ_m	magnetic pole surface density	ϕ	angular coordinate; magnetic flux; physical rotation of polarizing beam splitter
σ_r, σ_s	stresses along polar coordinates	χ	constant relating fluctuations in anisotropy to average anisotropy; magnetic susceptibility
σ_s	specific magnetic moment (saturation moment per unit mass)		
		χ_{ar}	anhysteretic susceptibility
$\sigma(\omega)$	complex conductivity tensor (at angular frequency ω)	χ_0	initial reversible susceptibility
τ	time constant	ω	angular frequency ($2\pi f$)

CHAPTER 1
INTRODUCTION

Eric D. Daniel
Redwood City, California

C. Denis Mee
Los Gatos, California

This chapter provides a simple nonmathematical review of magnetic recording principles and introduces some of the more frequently used terms. It also gives an indication of the variety of configurations and applications of magnetic recording, and outlines the direction and focus of present and future research and development efforts. The primary purpose is to provide a reader, relatively new to magnetic recording, with the background required to assimilate the more specialized chapters that follow. The introductory material may also assist readers skilled in some, but not all, of the various aspects of magnetic recording to put their specialties in perspective and expand their interests.

Since this introduction does not include a tutorial review of the principles of magnetism, a reader lacking a background in magnetism should consult one of the standard texts (Brown, 1978; Chikazumi and Charap, 1978; Wohlfarth, 1980–1982). For additional review and general reading in magnetic recording, reference can be made to a limited number of books or collections of key papers (Hoagland, 1963; Mee, 1964; Masumoto, 1977; Camras, 1985; White, 1985; Mallinson, 1993; Bertram, 1994; Jorgensen, 1995) and to a published set of review articles (Arnoldussen, 1986; Bate, 1986; Bertram, 1986; Jeffers, 1986; Wood, 1986).

1.1 MAGNETIC RECORDING CHARACTERISTICS

1.1.1 Properties of a Permanent Magnet

A permanent magnet is composed of a ferromagnetic or ferrimagnetic material that has the property of staying magnetized in a given direction after the field that created this magnetization is removed. This property is displayed by a hysteresis loop, such as that shown in Fig. 1.1*a,* in which the magnetization M is plotted against the applied field H (Chikazumi and Charap, 1978). The magnetization is not a unique function of the field but depends on the direction and magnitude of

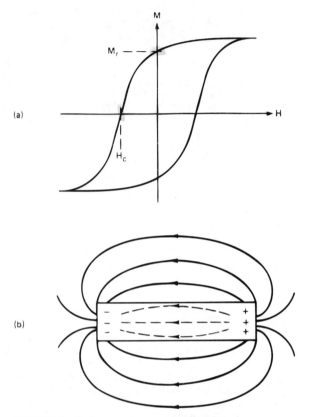

FIGURE 1.1   Basic properties of a permanent magnet. (*a*) Hysteresis loop showing remanent magnetization M_r and coercivity H_c; (*b*) bar magnet showing surface poles and the fields these poles produce outside (full lines) and inside (dashed lines) the bar.

previous applied fields. There are two important parameters of the loop: first, the remanent magnetization M_r, the magnetization that remains after the field is removed; second, the coercivity H_c, the reverse field required to reduce the magnetization to zero. The remanent magnetization indicates the extent to which the magnet stays magnetized after the applied field is removed; the coercivity expresses the degree to which the magnet resists being demagnetized. The product $M_r H_c$ measures the strength of the magnet.

The external and internal fields of a bar magnet are sketched in Fig. 1.1*b*. If it is assumed that the magnetization of the bar is approximately uniform, the magnetic poles are surface poles on the left and right faces. The field is directed from the positive to the negative pole faces. That portion of the field that lies within the bar opposes the magnetization and constitutes a demagnetizing field H_d. As the strength of this field approaches that of the coercivity (it cannot exceed it), progressively larger losses in remnant magnetization occur.

The strength of the demagnetizing field is primarily dependent upon the geometry of the magnet, and can be expressed in terms of the demagnetization factor (Chikazumi, 1978; Wohlfarth, 1980).

Demagnetization field

$$N = \frac{-H_d}{M} \tag{1.1}$$

Magnetization

Except in certain geometries (ellipsoids), N varies throughout the body of the magnet, but simple arguments can be based on considering a mean value for a bar magnet. Two extremes are of interest. If the bar is made increasingly long in the x direction, as in Fig. 1.2a, the demagnetizing factor N_x in this direction decreases and eventually approaches zero, while the factors N_y and N_z in the y and z directions approach 0.5. If the bar is made increasingly short in the x direction and the dimensions in the y and z directions expanded, as in Fig. 1.2b, N_x approaches a maximum value of 1 ($H_d = -M_x$) in the central region, while N_y and N_z tend to zero.

1.1.2 Basic Processes in Magnetic Recording

In principle, a magnetic recording medium consists of a permanent magnet configured so that a pattern of remanent magnetization can be formed along the length of a single track, or a number of parallel tracks, defined on its surface. Recording (or writing) takes place by causing relative motion between the medium and a recording transducer. A simple, one-track example is given in Fig. 1.3a. The medium is in

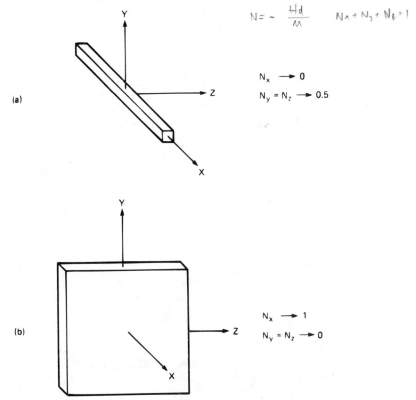

$$N = -\frac{H_d}{M} \qquad N_x + N_y + N_z = 1$$

$N_x \longrightarrow 0$

$N_y = N_z \longrightarrow 0.5$

(a)

(b)

$N_x \longrightarrow 1$

$N_y = N_z \longrightarrow 0$

FIGURE 1.2 Demagnetizing factors of bar magnets of square cross section and different length-to-width ratios. (a) A long, thin bar; (b) a wide, thin sheet. The condition $N_x + N_y + N_z = 1$ always applies.

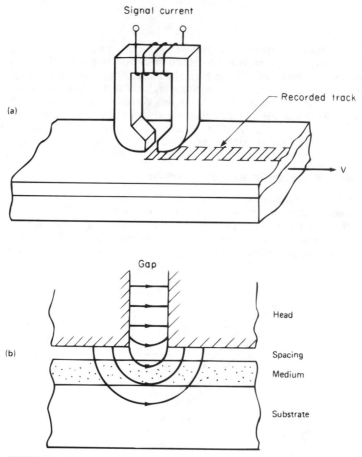

FIGURE 1.3   Illustration of the recording process using a single-track ring head. (*a*)
Three-dimensional view; (*b*) cross section showing the magnetic field from the gap.

the form of a magnetic layer supported on a nonmagnetic substrate. The transducer, or recording head, is a ring-shaped electromagnet with a gap at the surface
facing the medium. When the head is fed with a current representing the signal to
be recorded, the fringing field from the gap magnetizes the medium as shown in
Fig. 1.3*b*. For a constant medium velocity, the spatial variations in remanent magnetization along the length of the medium reflect the temporal variations in the head
current, and constitute a recording of the signal. In the ordinary way the recording
process is highly nonlinear because it relies on hysteresis.

The recorded magnetization creates a pattern of external and internal fields analogous, in the simplest case, to a series of contiguous bar magnets. When the recorded
medium is passed over the same head, or a reproducing head of similar construction,
at the same velocity, the flux emanating from the medium surface is intercepted by
the head core, and a voltage is induced in the coil proportional to the rate of change of
this flux. The voltage is not an exact replica of the recording signal, but it constitutes a
reproduction of it in that information describing the recording signal can be obtained
from this voltage by appropriate electrical processing.

In between recording and reproduction, the recorded signal can be stored indefinitely, provided the medium is not exposed to magnetic fields comparable in strength to those used in recording. At any time, however, a recording that is no longer required can be erased by means of a strong field applied by the same head as that used for recording, by a separate erase head, or by a bulk eraser that subjects the medium, in its entirety, to a 50- or 60-Hz field. After erasure, the medium is ready for a new recording. Overwriting an old signal with a new one, without a separate erase step, is adequate in many circumstances. Overwriting has to be used when only a single head is available for writing and reading.

The recording and reproducing processes will be described more fully later in this Introduction and are analyzed in detail in Chap. 2.

1.1.3   Media Configurations

With the exception of some early wire recorders, all magnetic recorders use media in the form of a magnetic layer (sometimes two layers) supported by a nonmagnetic substrate. The magnetic material of the medium may be a coating made of magnetic particles held in a plastic binder (Bate, 1986), or it may consist of a deposited film of metal or oxide (Arnoldussen, 1986). The traditional particulate material is a type of ferrimagnetic iron oxide, gamma ferric oxide, in the form of small, needle-shaped particles. Other magnetic particles, including metal particles, have been subsequently introduced to improve the performance of particulate media. Most deposited metal films use alloys made predominantly of cobalt, and have the advantage of having a much higher magnetization than particulate media, coupled with the facility of making the magnetic layer very thin. Coercivity is important in media for much the same reasons as it is in permanent magnets, and has tended to increase, particularly in recent years. Such increases have been necessitated by the development of more sophisticated recording devices with shorter minimum recorded wave-lengths and consequently larger demagnetizing fields.

One of the advantages of magnetic recording is that it can be readily adapted to use many configurations of the recording media. Media using plastic film as a substrate are used mainly in the form of tapes and flexible disks, but also appear in a variety of card and sheet configurations coated over the whole surface, or in a magnetic stripe coated on a portion of the surface. Media using metal or ceramic substrates have been made in the form of drums and rigid disks. Tapes vary in width from less than 4 to over 50 mm, and in length from a cartridge roll of less than 1 m to a reel of over 3000 m. Flexible disks vary in diameter from about 75 to 200 mm. Rigid disks range from 32 to about 360 mm, and up to a dozen double-sided disks are rotated on a single spindle.

The properties, materials, design, and fabrication of particulate and deposited-film magnetic media are discussed in detail in Chaps. 3, 4, and 5.

1.1.4   Head Configurations

There is great variety in the design and composition of heads and in the way they interface with media (Jeffers, 1986). The medium may be moved in nominal contact with fixed heads, or moved past a head, supported by an air bearing, which maintains a controlled spacing between the surfaces of the medium and the head. Heads may also be embedded in a rotating cylinder in contact with a moving medium, so that the heads scan across the medium at high velocity. A head may contain a single element and record or reproduce a single track, or it may contain many elements and record many tracks simultaneously. Reproduction may take place using an inductive head like the ring-shaped structure of Fig. 1.3. Inductive heads can also be made where a thin main pole is on the magnetic side of the medium, while an energized auxiliary pole is on the substrate side.

It is also possible to design heads that respond to magnetic flux rather than to its rate of change. Such flux-sensing heads use galvanomagnetic effects in which the magnetic field causes a change in electrical field (the Hall effect) or in resistance (magnetoresistance), or make use of the principle of the flux gate. Magnetoresistance reading heads have found widespread application in magnetic tape and rigid-disk drives. Finally, optical beams may be used to record on a heat-sensitive magnetic medium (thermomagnetic recording), and to reproduce such a recording using Kerr or Faraday rotation effects (magnetooptic reproduction) (Meiklejohn, 1986).

A variety of magnetic materials is used in making heads. Laminated, high-permeability metals are the traditional means of making the core, and are still used when the coercivity of the medium demands a high recording field from the head. Ferrite cores have the advantages of greater ease of fabrication and better wear characteristics. For rigid-disk and certain other applications, semiconductor techniques have been adapted to make heads by depositing multilayer films. Such film heads are particularly suited to applications where smallness of size is dictated or where many-element multitrack operation is required. Up to 100 head elements have been built in a single stack using film fabrication technology.

Details of the properties, materials, design, and fabrication of heads are given in Chap. 6. Magnetooptic recording is treated in Chap. 10.

1.1.5 Recording Signals

Magnetic recording is used to store many different types of signals. Analog recording of sound was the first and is still a major application. Audio recording involves relatively low-frequency signals and low medium speeds, but is demanding in terms of linearity and signal-to-noise ratio. Digital recording of encoded computer data on disk and tape recorders has evolved as another major use. Rigid-disk drives use high signal frequencies coupled with high medium speeds, and emphasize small access times together with high data reliability. A third large application area is video recording, the recording of visual images in the form of video signals, for professional or consumer use. The high video frequencies are normally recorded using frequency-modulation (FM) encoding, and high head-to-medium velocities are obtained by the use of scanning-head drums. Instrumentation recording covers a wide range of applications and may use any of the recording techniques described above.

The trend is to use digital encoding to record all types of signals because, in principle, it allows original signals to be reconstructed perfectly through the use of error detection and correction schemes. Digital audio is already used widely for professional purposes and is available for consumer use. Active development and standardization is under way for professional and consumer digital video recording.

As depicted in Fig. 1.4, there are essentially three types of signals used in magnetic recording. The linearity required in analog recording is obtained by using ac bias. This consists of a high-frequency current which is added to the signal current in the record head and, in effect, replaces normal hysteretic magnetization of the medium with a linear process known as *anhysteretic magnetization* (Westmijze, 1953b). In digital recording, a coded series of reversals in the direction of magnetization, or transitions, constitutes the recorded signal. Reproduction is effected by reconstructing the pattern by, for example, detecting "zero crossings" in the reproduced waveform. The situation in FM video recording is similar, except that the positions of the zero crossings are modulated by the video signal.

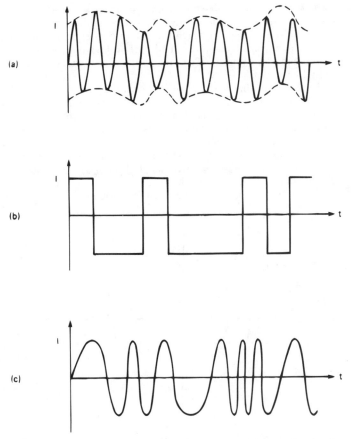

FIGURE 1.4 Three types of recording signal current. (*a*) An analog signal to which a high-frequency ac bias is added; (*b*) a binary digital signal; (*c*) a frequency-modulated signal.

The way in which the signals are processed before and after recording differs greatly according to the application (Wood, 1986). However, the underlying magnetic recording process, in which the temporal variations of a signal or its encoded version are presented by spatial variations in magnetization along a recorded track, is common to all applications. This process, together with the inductive reproducing process, is expressed in elementary but general terms in the introductory review given here.

1.2 MAGNETIC RECORDING PRINCIPLES

1.2.1 Recording Field

There are two distinct types of inductive head: the ring head (such as that of Fig. 1.3), in which the recording field is the leakage field from the gap, and the single-pole (or probe) head, in which the recording field spreads out from the tip of a thin energized pole. The essential characteristics of these recording fields can be grasped by considering idealized models in which the length of the gap or the thickness of the single pole is infinitesimally small, and all other relevant dimensions, including the width of the head, are infinite. The last assumption reduces the problem to a two-dimensional one.

The field from the idealized ring head is shown diagrammatically in Fig. 1.5a. The lines of force are semicircles about the gap centerline. When an element of the recording medium passes over the head at a distance y, it experiences a field that starts from the perpendicular direction, rotates to a longitudinally directed maximum in the central plane of the gap, and then rotates toward the opposite perpendicular direction while falling to zero. The field vector follows the circular locus shown in Fig. 1.5b, where the diameter of the circle is inversely proportional to y.

The corresponding field from the idealized single-pole head is shown in Fig. 1.6a. The field contours spread radially outward from the pole tip, and the direction

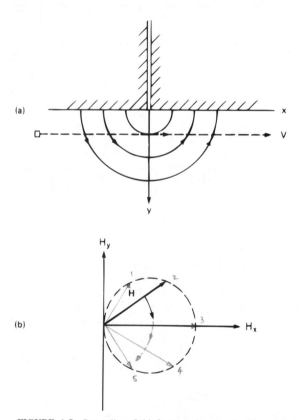

FIGURE 1.5   Recording field from a ring head with semi-infinite pole dimensions and an infinitesimally short gap. (a) Cross section of the pole tips showing the lines of force and the passage of an element of medium through the field at a spacing y; (b) the locus of the vector field H experienced by the element of medium.

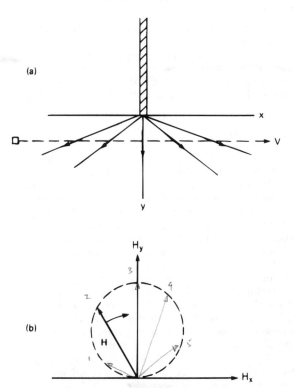

FIGURE 1.6 Recording field from a single-pole head with a pole of infinite depth and infinitesimal thickness. (*a*) Cross section of the pole tip showing the lines of force and the passage of an element of medium through the field at a spacing *y*; (*b*) locus of the vector field *H* experienced by the element of medium. (The pole is assumed to be uniformly wound with a coil, or energized inductively by a nearby auxiliary pole.)

of the field experienced by an element of medium now rotates from longitudinal, through perpendicular, to longitudinal in the opposite sense. The locus of the field vector is again circular, but the center is now on the *y* axis, as shown in Fig. 1.6*b*.

An important conclusion is that either type of head gives rise to a rotating recording field that has both longitudinal and perpendicular components, and hence will tend to induce a recorded magnetization that has both longitudinal and perpendicular components (Tjaden and Leyten, 1964). Generally, the ring head promotes longitudinal, and the single-pole head perpendicular, components of field and magnetization. At small separations and high fields, the reverse situation can occur; the final magnetization is determined in the trailing region, where the element of medium exits the head field, rather than in the region of maximum field strength.

In practical forms of the ring head, the gap *g* is of finite length, and the poles are also finite in length. These dimensions complicate, but do not change, the basic nature of the head-field distribution except at very close spacings for which $y \ll g$ (Westmijze, 1953*a;* Karlqvist, 1954). In practical forms of the single-pole head, the thickness *T* of the pole is finite, which has an effect analogous to that of the gap in a ring head. Also, an efficient single-pole head must provide a low-reluctance return path for the flux, a path which, ideally, is situated on the other side of the recording medium opposite the main pole. This return path may consist of a large auxiliary pole, a high-permeability underlayer, or a combination of these. The field distribution is modified, particularly close to the auxiliary pole or underlayer, by an emphasis of the perpendicular component (Iwasaki and Nakamura, 1977).

1.2.2 Medium Anisotropy

The direction of the recorded magnetization is also strongly influenced by the magnetic anisotropy of the medium. For example, a common type of medium consists of acicular (needle-shaped) particles with their long dimensions oriented parallel to the longitudinal direction during manufacture (Bate, 1986). Such a medium exhibits uniaxial anisotropy in that it has a much higher remanent magnetization in the longitudinal direction than in any other direction. It will therefore favor longitudinal recording, in which the magnetization is directed along the length of the track. Alloy films may also be made in such a way that the preferred directions of magnetization lie in the plane of the film, although the anisotropy in the plane is usually multiaxial rather than uniaxial (Arnoldussen, 1986).

Conversely, media can be made which favor magnetization normal to the plane. Thus, certain alloy films may be designed to have a crystal orientation and grain structure that produce uniaxial anisotropy perpendicular to the plane of the film (Iwasaki and Ouchi, 1978). Also, suitable particles can be oriented so that their easy axes lie perpendicular to the plane of a medium (Fujiwara, 1985). Either type of medium favors perpendicular recording, particularly if the perpendicular anisotropy field H_k is strong enough to counter the demagnetizing field associated with a medium in the form of a thin layer ($H_k > M_r$).

A third type of medium can be made, for example, using particles which individually have many (six or eight) different easy directions of magnetization (Jeschke, 1954; Lemke, 1979). If the shape anisotropy associated with a finite thickness is ignored, such a medium is intrinsically isotropic. The direction of its recorded magnetization is dominated by the geometry of the head-field distribution rather than by the magnetic properties of the medium.

1.2.3 Longitudinal Recording

The combination of a ring head and a medium having longitudinal anisotropy tends to produce a recorded magnetization which is predominantly longitudinal. This combination has been the one used traditionally, and it still dominates all major analog and digital applications. Ideally, the pattern of magnetization created by a square-wave recording signal would be like that shown in Fig. 1.7a. If the square wave has a fundamental frequency f, and the medium moves with velocity V, the recorded pattern can be characterized by the wavelength

$$\lambda = \frac{V}{f} \tag{1.2}$$

by the bit length

$$b = \frac{\lambda}{2} \tag{1.3}$$

or by the linear density

$$D = \frac{2f}{V} \tag{1.4}$$

measured in flux reversals per millimeter (fr/mm).

Figure 1.7a represents a low-density recording. The bulk of the flux created by the magnetization reversals returns outside the medium, and the demagnetizing field is small. At higher densities, Fig. 1.7b, the demagnetizing field and the loss in magnetization associated with it become progressively larger. Eventually, the transitions lose their sharpness and the recorded pattern approaches a sine wave corresponding to the fundamental of the square wave that represents the recording signal. In the central plane of the medium, the demagnetization factor at high densities approaches the limiting value $N = 1$, and the demagnetizing field approaches the value $H_d = -M_0$, where M_0 is the demagnetized value of the magnetization between transitions, or the peak value if the magnetization is sinusoidal. At the surface of the medium, however, the demagnetization factor approaches the limiting value $N = 0.5$, and the demagnetizing field approaches the value $H_d = -0.5M_0$, one-half the field limit in the central plane (Wallace, 1951; Westmijze, 1953b). In Sec. 1.2.5 on reproduction it is shown that, as the recording density increases, the

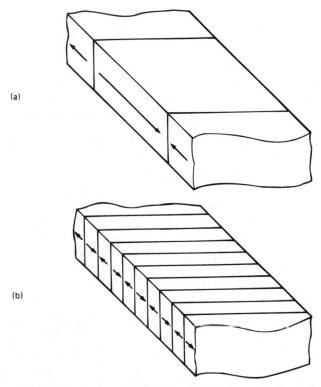

FIGURE 1.7 Longitudinally recorded magnetization at (a) a low and (b) a high density.

useful flux supplied to the reproducing head comes from a progressively shallow layer immediately beneath the surface. It can therefore be argued that the demagnetization conditions at the surface of a medium of appreciable thickness are of dominant importance compared with those in the center.

1.2.4 Perpendicular Recording

The corresponding situation for a medium with perpendicular anisotropy is illustrated in Fig. 1.8. In the central plane of the medium the demagnetization conditions are the reverse of what they were for longitudinal recording. At the low density shown in Fig. 1.8a, the demagnetization factor in the perpendicular direction approaches the maximum value $N = 1$, corresponding to $H_d = -M_0$. At a high density, shown in Fig. 1.8b, the demagnetization factor and the demagnetizing field approach zero. From this central-plane analysis it would appear that perpendicular recording should be the ideal mode to use for high-density recording (Iwasaki and Nakamura, 1977). If, however, the demagnetization factor is evaluated at the surface rather than at the center, the limiting value is $N = 0.5$, corresponding to a demagnetizing field of $H_d = -0.5M_0$, exactly the same as for longitudinal recording (Wallace 1951; Westmijze, 1953b). Therefore, at densities so high that conditions near the surface rather than in the central plane are of paramount importance, the

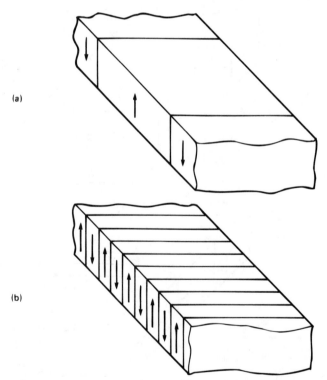

(a)

(b)

FIGURE 1.8 Perpendicularly recorded magnetization at (a) a low and (b) a high density.

effects of demagnetization in perpendicular recording should be little different from those in longitudinal recording (Westmijze, 1953b; Mallinson and Bertram, 1984).

Such arguments are on too limited a basis to warrant arriving at definitive conclusions concerning the relative merits of the longitudinal and perpendicular modes of recording. More complete analyses need to take into account a variety of complex macromagnetic and micromagnetic considerations. Important macromagnetic factors include the finite head-field gradients and demagnetization effects during the recording process; the keeping effect of heads (particularly large-pole ring heads) in modifying demagnetization fields; the enhancement of perpendicular recording media made possible by the use of a high-permeability underlayer; and, perhaps most difficult of all, the nonlinear nature and directional properties of the hysteresis loops of the media. The more important micromagnetic factors include the precise structure of the magnetic boundary defining a transition, and the way in which a relatively thick perpendicular medium is magnetically "switched" throughout its depth.

Work is proceeding along these lines using a variety of analytical, computer-modeling, and experimental techniques (e.g., Iwasaki, 1984; Middleton and Wright, 1982; Beardsley, 1982a, 1982b; Bromley, 1983; Weilinga, 1983; Tong et al., 1984; Bertram, 1994). The results are described and discussed extensively in Chap. 2, and specific aspects related to media, heads, recording limitations, and measurements are covered in Chaps. 3 to 9.

1.2.5 Reproduction

Reproduction with a magnetic head is insensitive to the direction of the recorded magnetization. The head reacts to the flux emerging from the surface of the medium, but the vectorial nature of the magnetization that created this flux cannot be deduced from the head response. Thus, for example, a ring head is just as adept at reproducing a perpendicular recording as a longitudinal one. Another simplifying fact is that, unlike the recording process, the reproducing process is linear. Therefore, it is possible to deduce the response to complex waveforms from considering sine waves.

For the present purpose, attention is confined to an inductive ring head. If an efficient head of this type makes perfect contact with the medium, and all the available flux ϕ is collected, the voltage induced in a coil of N turns is

$$e = -N \frac{d\phi}{dt} = -NV \frac{d\phi}{dx} \tag{1.5}$$

where the x direction is down the track. If the flux (or a Fourier component of it) is sinusoidal and written as $\phi \cos (2\pi x/\lambda)$, the peak voltage in the coil becomes

$$E = -\frac{2\pi NV\phi}{\lambda} = -2\pi N\phi f \tag{1.6}$$

and is proportional to frequency.

Further information concerning the response of the head can be obtained from a knowledge of the field distribution of the head when energized, by applying the principle of reciprocity (Westmijze, 1953a). One of the key results—and it applies to any type of reproducing head—is that the head output falls off exponentially with the spacing that exists accidentally, or purposely, between the active surfaces of the head and the medium. Thus

$$\frac{e_d}{e_0} = \exp\left(-\frac{2\pi d}{\lambda}\right) \tag{1.7}$$

where the subscripts denote a spacing of d and a spacing of zero. The severity of this spacing loss increases rapidly with decreasing wavelength, and can be conveniently calculated by expressing the loss as $54.6d/\lambda$ in decibels (Wallace, 1951). The spacing loss is always of critical significance in magnetic recording, and often is the dominant cause of loss at high densities.

A further aspect of the spacing loss is that it applies also to the spacing between the head and elementary layers positioned beneath the surface of the medium. A deeper elementary layer becomes less capable of contributing significantly to the short-wavelength, or high-density, output. Consequently, at very high densities, virtually all the output comes from a thin layer near the surface, when the medium has a thickness which is an appreciable fraction of the wavelength (Wallace, 1951).

So far, it has been assumed that the head gap length is infinitesimal. When it is finite, it is the source of another, aperture-type of loss, the gap loss, that produces a null in the reproducing response as the wavelength approaches the gap length (Lübeck, 1937; Westmijze, 1953a). In practice, gap loss is one of the easier losses to control, except when the same head has to be used for recording and reproducing. A similar (usually larger) loss is associated with the finite thickness of the pole in a single-pole head when it is used for reproducing.

1.3   PRACTICAL CONSTRAINTS

1.3.1   Noise and Interference

All magnetic recorders produce unwanted signals in the form of noise and interference, and these impose limitations on the achievable performance. This subject is covered extensively in Chap. 8 and receives only brief mention here. Essentially, there are two major sources of noise: the medium and the reproducing head (electronics noise is usually negligible). Medium noise arises from the fact that no medium is magnetically homogeneous. Particulate media are obviously discontinuous, and create noise in accordance with the number, density, size, and spatial distribution of the particles (Mann, 1957; Mallinson, 1969; Daniel, 1972). Deposited-film media are inhomogeneous because they possess a grain structure, or because irregular domains are formed to minimize the energy at transition boundaries (Baugh et al., 1983; Belk et al., 1985). The major head noise arises from the fact that any head possesses an impedance, and the real part of this impedance gives rise to noise of thermal origin. Other forms of head noise are associated with magnetic domain changes (Barkhausen noise) or magnetostriction effects ("rubbing" noise).

Interference—the appearance of signals other than those intended—arises in many ways, such as cross-talk between different elements in a multitrack head; incomplete erasure of a previously recorded signal; track misregistration when a head scans a track on successive occasions; and print-through, the magnetic transfer of signals between the layers in a stored reel of tape. Which effect is the most serious depends on the type of recorder and the application. In most analog recorders, medium noise is dominant, but reproducing head noise will become more significant as signal frequencies go up and track widths diminish. Medium noise is also the dominant form of noise in digital disk drives, but, currently, interference due to track misregistration constitutes a more serious limitation than noise. Print-through is of consequence only in the analog recording of audio signals.

1.3.2 Head-Medium Interface

Magnetic recording involves mechanical motion between the media and heads, and, as intimated above, the spacing between these components must be made critically small. This combination imposes stringent demands upon the surface characteristics of media and heads: their flatness, smoothness, freedom from asperities, frictional properties, and mutual capability to resist wear.

In the great majority of recorders using flexible media, the heads and media are run nominally in contact in order to reduce spacing losses to the values required for high-density performance at practical head-media speeds. The head material, profile, and surface integrity are critical properties in achieving adequate head life and avoiding undue wear of the medium. The corresponding properties of the medium are, if anything, more critical, because they must be maintained over an enormously larger surface area. Particulate media have the advantage that the magnetic and tribological properties can be controlled independently, through the choice of particle and the choice of plastic binder and additives.

In rigid-disk drives the problem is approached differently. The head is mounted on a slider which flies above the rotating disk, and provides an air bearing which, in principle, avoids wear entirely (Gross et al., 1980). Early air bearings were formed by designing the slider to create hydrodynamic pressure and weighting the head to achieve a flying height of about 20 μm. Modern bearings are designed to be self-adjusting and to fly at a height of 0.05 μm or less. In practice, wear is not entirely eliminated by the use of a flying head. Durability to occasional head-medium contacts at full velocity is required in addition to the slower-speed contact which occurs when the head takes off or lands during the starting and stopping the disk rotation. Because of these requirements, the disk magnetic layers are protected by lubricant or protective overcoat layers. Such layers are typically required when metal-film media are used, but their thickness must be small with respect to the flying height in order to avoid excessive spacing loss.

A detailed discussion of the head-medium interface, with particular emphasis on the rigid-disk interface, is given in Chap. 7.

1.4 RECORDING TECHNOLOGY EMPHASIS

1.4.1 Areal Density

Magnetic recording research and development efforts will continue to be aimed toward achieving higher areal density by a combination of increases in linear and track densities (Mallinson, 1985). Increases in linear density will require improvements in materials and recording techniques, and controlled miniaturization of the key recording components. Increases in track density will require advances in media properties, narrow-track head design, and head-positioning technology. Some of the areas that are expected to receive emphasis are outlined below.

1.4.2 Head and Media Developments

Sophisticated methods of head fabrication will continue to be developed for ferrite, metal, and composite head structures. In particular, the use of deposition techniques, similar to those used in the semiconductor industry, is an attractive means to achieving some of the miniaturization goals, and applications of film heads can be expected to dominate. This technology has also spurred renewed interest in flux-sensing read heads, particularly those relying upon the use of a thin magnetoresistance element. Such heads give larger reproduce signals than inductive heads, particularly at lower head-to-medium speeds. This higher sensitivity can be used to offset the lower signal flux available when track density is increased.

Media developments cover a broad range of materials and processes. Iron oxide remains the dominant magnetic ingredient of particulate media, but the higher magnetization of metal particles makes them advantageous for certain high-areal-density applications. Deposited-metal-film media have even higher magnetization potential, and a high-output amplitude can be obtained from a very thin layer, which is favorable at high linear and track densities. Problems associated with early metal film media, such as durability and corrosion, have been solved. As a result, sputtered metal-film rigid disks have almost completely displaced particulate disks. Likewise, evaporated metal-film tapes are used in consumer recording products demanding use of the highest density technology.

The dimensions of head magnetic elements and the recorded transitions in media have decreased to the point where micromagnetic structure and switching mechanisms can no longer be ignored. Grain size in ferrite-head poles, domain effects in film-head poles, and micromagnetic irregularities in recorded transition boundaries are becoming of critical concern. Further advances in head and media materials and design will be assisted by a better understanding of, and ability to control, domain-level phenomena.

1.4.3 Recording Modes

The dominant mode of recording has been to magnetize the medium predominantly in the longitudinal direction. Early attempts to record in the perpendicular direction failed because the media used would not readily support such magnetization (Hoagland, 1958). The situation was changed in the mid-1970s by the introduction of a cobalt-chromium medium which possesses the requisite properties favoring magnetization in the perpendicular direction (Iwasaki and Ouchi, 1978). Subsequently, the interest in exploring the perpendicular mode for high-density recording increased rapidly and, for some years, this area of study attracted magnetic recording research activities worldwide (Iwasaki, 1980). These activities include work on particulate as well as single- and double-layer metal-film media, and the study of various types of single-pole head with an auxiliary pole on the same or the opposite side.

Despite these research efforts, the practical implementation of perpendicular recording has been slow, and some of the fundamental aspects of this mode of recording are still not fully understood. Once again, a stronger emphasis at the micromagnetic level will be required before the potential of this mode of recording can be fully assessed, and perpendicular media and heads optimized.

1.4.4 Optical Recording

In terms of linear density, magnetic recording is ahead of optical recording. Moreover, the linear density of optical recording is limited by the wavelength of the light source. Therefore, short of developing a short-wavelength laser (e.g., by frequency doubling), magnetic recording's lead in linear density will lengthen. With respect to track density, however, optical recording is ahead of magnetic recording. The advantages of optical recording stem from the capability to maintain a useful signal-to-noise ratio down to very narrow track widths, together with the wide bandwidth with which the beam position can be servoed. The adoption of magnetooptical recording and reproducing techniques to disk storage application is receiving increasing emphasis. It offers an instant large increase in track density and, despite the lower linear density, can result in a net increase in areal density. The principles and technology of magnetooptical recording are described in Chap. 10. This advantage will, however, be eroded as the conventional forms of magnetic recording continue their spectacular advance.

REFERENCES

Arnoldussen, T. C., "Thin Film Recording Media," *Proc. IEEE,* **74** (1986).

Bate, G., "Particulate Recording Media," *Proc. IEEE,* **74** (1986).

Baugh, R. A., E. S. Murdock, and B. R. Najarajan, "Measurement of Noise in Magnetic Media," *IEEE Trans. Magn.,* **MAG-19,** 1722 (1983).

Beardsley, I. A., "Effect of Particle Orientation on High Density Recording," *IEEE Trans. Magn.,* **MAG-18,** 1191 (1982*a*).

Beardsley, I. A., "Self-Consistent Recording Model for Perpendicular Recording," *J. Appl. Phys.* **53,** 2582 (1982*b*).

Belk, N. R., P. K. George, and G. S. Mowry, "Noise in High Performance Thin-Film Longitudinal Magnetic Recording Media," *IEEE Trans. Magn.,* **MAG-21,** 1350 (1985).

Bertram, H. N., "Fundamentals of the Magnetic Recording Process," *Proc. IEEE,* **74** (1986).

Bertram, H. N., *Theory of Magnetic Recording,* Cambridge University Press, 1994.

Bromley, D. J., "A Comparison of Vertical and Longitudinal Magnetic Recording Based on Analytical Models," *IEEE Trans. Magn.,* **MAG-19,** 2239 (1983).

Brown, W. F., *Micromagnetics,* Krieger, New York, 1978.

Camras, M., *Magnetic Tape Recording,* Van Nostrand Reinhold, New York, 1985.

Camras, M., *Magnetic Recording Handbook,* Van Nostrand Reinhold, New York, 1988.

Chikazumi, S., and S. H. Charap, *Physics of Magnetism,* Krieger, New York, 1978.

Daniel, E. D., "Tape Noise in Audio Recording," *J. Audio Eng. Soc.,* **20,** 92 (1972).

Fujiwara, T., "Barium Ferrite Media for Perpendicular Recording," *IEEE Trans. Magn.* **MAG-21,** 1480 (1985).

Gross, W. A., L. Matsch, V. Castelli, A. Eshel, T. Vohr, and M. Wilamann, *Fluid Film Lubrication,* Wiley, New York, 1980.

Hoagland, A. S., "High-Resolution Magnetic Recording Structures," *IBM J. Res. Dev.,* **2,** 91 (1958).

Hoagland, A. S., *Digital Magnetic Recording,* Wiley, New York, 1963.

Iwasaki, S., "Perpendicular Magnetic Recording—Evolution and Future," *IEEE Trans. Magn.,* **MAG-20,** 607 (1984).

Iwasaki, S., and Y. Nakamura, "An Analysis of the Magnetization Mode for High Density Magnetic Recording," *IEEE Trans. Magn.,* **MAG-13,** 1272 (1977).

Iwasaki, S., and K. Ouchi, "Co-Cr Recording Films with Perpendicular Magnetic Anisotropy," *IEEE Trans. Magn.* **MAG-14,** 849 (1978).

Jeffers, F., "High Density Magnetic Recording Heads," *Proc. IEEE,* **74,** 1540 (1986).

Jeschke, J. C., East German Patent 8684, 1954.

Jorgensen, F., *The Complete Handbook of Magnetic Recording,* 4th ed. TAB Books, Blue Ridge Summit, Penn., 1995.

Karlqvist, O., "Calculation of the Magnetic Field in the Ferromagnetic Layer of a Magnetic Drum," *Trans. R. Inst Technol. (Stockholm),* **86,** 3 (1954).

Lemke, J. U., "Ultra-High Density Recording with New Heads and Tapes," *IEEE Trans. Magn.,* **MAG-15,** 1561 (1979).

Lübeck, H., "Magnetische Schallaufzeichrung mit Filmen und Ringkopfen," *Akust. Z.,* **2,** 273 (1937).

Mallinson, J. C., "The Maximum Signal-to-Noise Ratio of a Tape Recorder," *IEEE Trans. Magn.,* **MAG-5,** 182 (1969).

Mallinson, J. C., "The Next Decade in Magnetic Recording," *IEEE Trans. Magn.,* **MAG-21,** 1217 (1985).

Mallinson, J. C., *The Foundations of Magnetic Recording,* Academic, San Diego, 1987.

Mallinson, J. C., *The Foundations of Magnetic Recording,* Academic, San Diego, 2nd. Ed., 1993.

Mallinson, J. C., and H. N. Bertram, "Theoretical and Experimental Comparison of the Longitudinal and Vertical Modes of Magnetic Recording," *IEEE Trans. Magn.,* **MAG-20,** 461 (1984).

Mann, P. A., "Das Rauschen eines Magnettonbandes," *Arch. Elek. Ubertragung.* **11,** 97 (1957).

Masumoto, M., *Magnetic Recording* (in Japanese), Kyoritsu, Tokyo, 1977.

Mee, C. D., *The Physics of Magnetic Recording,* North-Holland, Amsterdam, 1964.

Meiklejohn, W. H. "Magnetooptics, A High Density Magnetic Recording Technology," *Proc. IEEE,* **74,** 1570 (1986).

Middleton, B. K., and C. D. Wright, "Perpendicular Recording," *IERE Conf. Proc.,* **54,** 181 (1982).

Tjaden, D. L. A., and J. Leyten, "A 5000:1 Scale Model of the Magnetic Recording Process," *Philips Tech. Rev.,* **25,** 319 (1964).

Tong, H. C., R. Ferrier, P. Chang, J. Tzeng, and K. L. Parker, "The Micromagnetics of Thin-Film Disk Recording Tracks," *IEEE Trans. Magn.,* **MAG-20,** 1831 (1984).

Wallace, R. L., "The Reproduction of Magnetically Recorded Signals," *Bell Syst. Tech. J.,* **30,** 1145 (1951).

Weilinga, T., "Investigations on Perpendicular Magnetic Recording," Thesis, Twente Univ. Technol., the Netherlands, 1983.

Westmijze, W. K., "Studies in Magnetic Recording," *Philips Res. Rep.,* **8,** 161 (1953a).

Westmijze, W. K., "Studies in Magnetic Recording," *Philips Res. Rep.,* **8,** 245 (1953b).

White, R. M., *Introduction to Magnetic Recording,* IEEE Press, New York, 1985.

Wohlfarth, E. P., *Ferromagnetic Materials,* North-Holland, Amsterdam, 1980–1982, vols. I–IV.

Wood, R., "Magnetic Recording Systems," *Proc. IEEE,* **74,** 1557 (1986).

CHAPTER 2
RECORDING AND REPRODUCING PROCESSES

Barry K. Middleton

Manchester University, Manchester, England

The aim of this chapter is to describe the contributions of the record and reproduce processes to the observed output voltage waveforms. Although the first of these processes is complex in the extreme and defies explanation in anything approaching a rigorous way, much has been learned with simplified models, and the essential quantities controlling the recording process appear to have been identified. The line taken here will be to follow these simpler models and to discuss their limitations and indicate the achievements of the more rigorous works. In contrast, the reproduce process is well understood, and good agreement between theory and experiment has been obtained. This is partly because the reproduce process is easily described mathematically and partly because measurable voltages are generated through the reproduce process and so reveal its character directly.

A number of books have covered the topics of this chapter (Hoagland, 1963; Mee, 1964; Sebestyen, 1973; Jorgensen, 1980; Bertram, 1994), but progress continues and new outlooks need to be presented. Emphasis will be placed upon laying a foundation for the understanding of recent advances in magnetic recording by attempting to complement and extend the available literature.

This chapter will deal first with the reproducing process, for the reasons already outlined, and then consider nonlinear and linear, or ac-biased, recording.

2.1 THE REPRODUCING PROCESS

In this section the process by which voltages are generated in the coils of heads of various structures is described. The response to magnetization components directed parallel to the surfaces of the recording media and the recorded tracks, and in directions perpendicular to the surface, will be considered under the broad headings of longitudinal and perpendicular recording.

The treatment here covers both longitudinal and perpendicular recording and makes appropriate comparisons between the two. However, in reference to experimental results, there is substantial information available for longitudinal recording but less relating to perpendicular recording, and so a truly balanced approach to the two aspects of the reproduce process is difficult to achieve.

Section 2.1.1 deals with the reciprocity formulas which form the basis of all the calculations of the output voltages generated by recorded magnetization patterns in the media.

2.1.1   The Basis of Reproduce Theory: Reciprocity

Figure 2.1a and b shows the basic geometrical situation as a medium moves past a ring head and a single-pole head, respectively. The diagrams show how the chosen coordinate system applies to both head structures equally well and is potentially suitable for any head structure. Let us begin by assuming the heads produce field components $H_x(x, y, z)$ and $H_y(x, y, z)$ in the x and y directions. Then, for media with x and y components M_x and M_y of magnetization, the corresponding output voltages e_x and e_y at time t can be derived using the principle of reciprocity (Westmijze, 1953; Mee, 1964; Sebestyen, 1973); and this procedure is carried out in Appendix I. The result is

$$e_x(\bar{x}) = -\mu_0 V \int_{-\omega/2}^{+\omega/2} dz \int_{d}^{d+\delta} dy \int_{-\infty}^{+\infty} \frac{dM_x(x - \bar{x})}{d\bar{x}} \frac{H_x(x, y, z)}{i} dx \qquad (2.1a)$$

$$e_y(\bar{x}) = -\mu_0 V \int_{-\omega/2}^{+\omega/2} dz \int_{d}^{d+\delta} dy \int_{-\infty}^{+\infty} \frac{dM_y(x - \bar{x})}{d\bar{x}} \frac{H_y(x, y, z)}{i} dx \qquad (2.1b)$$

where μ_0 = permeability of free space
$\bar{x} = Vt$
V = tape velocity
i = current in head coil that produces above-mentioned field
     components
d = spacing of head from medium of thickness δ
w = track width

The above formulas may be simplified when the track width w is much larger than other dimensions in the system, whence it may be assumed that there is no variation of magnetization with the z dimension. Thus, Eqs. (2.1a) and (2.1b) may be simplified to

$$e_x(\bar{x}) = -\mu_0 V w \int_{d}^{d+\delta} dy \int_{-\infty}^{+\infty} \frac{dM_x(x - \bar{x})}{d\bar{x}} \frac{H_x(x, y)}{i} dx \qquad (2.2a)$$

$$e_y(\bar{x}) = -\mu_0 V w \int_{d}^{d+\delta} dy \int_{-\infty}^{+\infty} \frac{dM_y(x - \bar{x})}{d\bar{x}} \frac{H_y(x, y)}{i} dx \qquad (2.2b)$$

These equations form the basis for the study of the reproduce process and are often referred to simply as the *reciprocity formulas*. Also the occurrence in the same equations of head-field distributions means that they are often termed *head sensitivity functions*. However, some discussions of the relevant mathematical forms of magnetization and head fields are necessary to be able to proceed with any calculations, and these will be considered in the following sections.

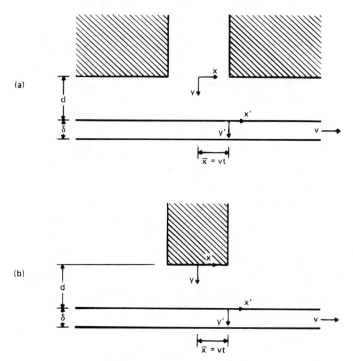

(a)

(b)

FIGURE 2.1 Definition of symbols and dimensions employed. The axes z and z' are directed into the paper.

2.1.2 Reproduction with a Ring Head

The schematic forms of the head-field distributions H_x and H_y are shown in Fig. 2.2, and a detailed consideration of them is given in Chap. 6. However, space is provided for a brief review of their form in view of their significance to the record process, which will be discussed later, as well as to the reproduce process currently being considered.

For the ring head the field distributions have been determined precisely by a number of workers. For distances from the head of $y > g/2$, the longitudinal and perpendicular field components are sufficiently accurately given by the expressions (Karlqvist, 1954)

$$H_x = \frac{H_g}{\pi} \left(\arctan \frac{g/2 + x}{y} + \arctan \frac{g/2 - x}{y} \right) \tag{2.3a}$$

$$H_y = \frac{-H_g}{2\pi} \ln \frac{(g/2 + x)^2 + y^2}{(g/2 - x)^2 + y^2} \tag{2.3b}$$

where H_g is the field in the gap, and g is the gap length. Figure 2.3 shows the variations of H_x and H_y as functions of spacing as determined from Eqs. (2.3a) and (2.3b). These may be compared with more detailed results from rigorous computations shown in Chap. 6. It can be seen that the precise results differ from those of

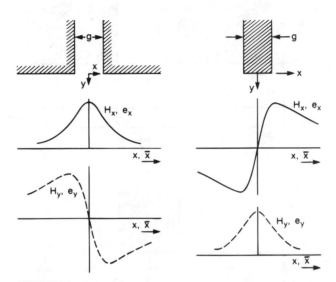

FIGURE 2.2   General form of field distributions for (*a*) a ring head and (*b*) a single-pole head.

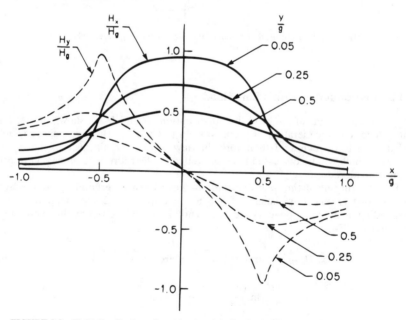

FIGURE 2.3   Field distributions for a ring head derived using Karlqvist's equations.

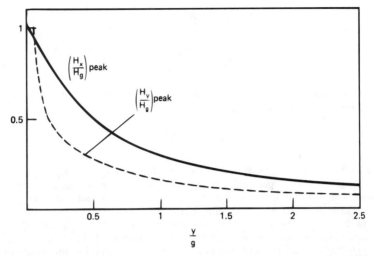

FIGURE 2.4 Reduced field amplitudes as a function of reduced separation: $(H_x/H_g)_{peak}$ = longitudinal component; $(H_y/H_g)_{peak}$ = perpendicular component.

Eqs. (2.3) at small separations from the head where peaks in H_x appear near to the gap edges. These departures can be expressed analytically by correction terms (Fan, 1961; Wilton, 1990), which simply add to Eqs. (2.3a) and (2.3b). The values of these terms are easily calculable (Fan, 1961; Baird, 1980; Middleton and Davies, 1984; Wilton, 1990) to give precise results if needed.

The variations of the peak amplitudes of the head fields are shown in Fig. 2.4 as functions of reduced head-to-medium separation. The peak field values can be shown using Eqs. (2.3) to be given by

$$H_x(0, y) = \frac{2H_g}{\pi} \arctan \frac{g}{2y} \tag{2.4a}$$

$$H_y(x_0, y) = \frac{-H_g}{2\pi} \ln \frac{(g/2 + x_0)^2 + y^2}{(g/2 - x_0)^2 + y^2} \tag{2.4b}$$

where
$$x_0^2 = \left(\frac{g}{2}\right)^2 + y^2 \tag{2.4c}$$

The distances $\pm x_0$ represent the positions of the maxima and minima of the field distribution H_y, and so $2x_0$ is a measure of its "width." It can be shown that $2x_0$ is also the width of the field distribution H_x at 50 percent of peak amplitude. Calling this p_{50}, for reasons which will become obvious later, leads to

$$p_{50} = 2\left[\left(\frac{g}{2}\right)^2 + y^2\right]^{1/2} \tag{2.5}$$

This quantity is plotted in Fig. 2.5 as a function of reduced spacing y/g.

At large separations or, conversely, when head gaps are short, Eqs. (2.3) reduce to the simple forms

$$H_x = \frac{H_g g}{\pi} \frac{y}{x^2 + y^2} \tag{2.6a}$$

$$H_y = \frac{-H_g g}{\pi} \frac{x}{x^2 + y^2} \tag{2.6b}$$

An approximation for the head gap field can be obtained from a simple consideration of the magnetic circuit of the heads, leading to

$$H_g = \frac{ni}{g + lA_g/\mu A_c} \tag{2.7}$$

where n is the number of turns in the head coil, l is the length of the magnetic circuit of the head of relative permeability μ, and A_g and A_c are, respectively, the cross-sectional area of the head magnetic circuit at the gap and the average cross-sectional area for the whole magnetic circuit.

With the determination of H_g, the dependence of head field on head gap can be examined. The variation of reduced head field, given by Eqs. (2.4a) and (2.7), is shown plotted against reduced gap in Fig. 2.6 for finite and infinite values of head permeability. The role of head geometry as determined by the quantity $lA_g/\mu A_c$ is an important factor in controlling head-field amplitudes, and obviously its magnitude needs to be kept as small as possible for fields to be highest. The same quantity will, at a later stage, also be shown to have a role in determining reproduced pulse amplitudes.

2.1.3 Output Voltage Waveforms

2.1.3.1 *Special Cases.* In digital recording the magnetization in the medium is changed in as short a distance as possible along the recorded track to allow the

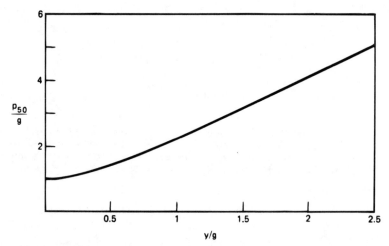

FIGURE 2.5 Width of field distribution, and also pulse width, as a function of reduced separation.

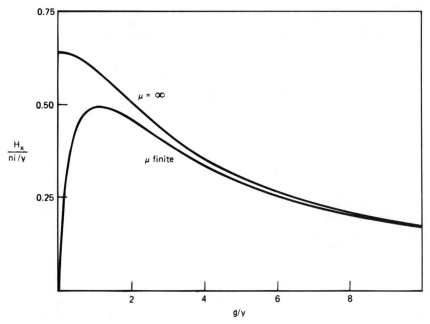

FIGURE 2.6 Reduced field amplitude as a function of reduced gap for infinite- and finite-permeability heads: $\mu = \infty$, $lA_g/\mu A_c = 0$; μ finite, $lA_g/\mu A_c = 0.2$.

maximum number of transitions per unit distance. In the ideal case, the magnetization would undergo a step change from its maximum value in one sense to its maximum value in the opposite sense. Considering a step change from a value of $-M_r$ to $+M_r$ in the x component of magnetization M_x, where M_r is the remnant magnetization, would cause Eq. (2.2a) to reduce to (Eldridge, 1960; Teer, 1961; Mee, 1964)

$$e_x(\bar{x}) = -2\mu_0 VwM_r \int_d^{d+\delta} \frac{H_x(\bar{x}, y)}{i}\, dy \qquad (2.8a)$$

Similarly, a change of the same magnitude in the components of magnetization M_y directed normal to the plane would result in an output voltage easily derived from Eq. (2.2b) as

$$e_y(\bar{x}) = -2\mu_0 VwM_r \int_d^{d+\delta} \frac{H_y(\bar{x}, y)}{i}\, dy \qquad (2.8b)$$

When the recording media are thin, the integrations in Eqs. (2.8a) and (2.8b) may be dispensed with and the results become

$$e_x(\bar{x}) = -2\mu_0 VwM_r\delta\, \frac{H_x(\bar{x}, y)}{i} \qquad (2.9a)$$

$$e_y(\bar{x}) = -2\mu_0 VwM_r\delta\, \frac{H_y(\bar{x}, y)}{i} \qquad (2.9b)$$

Thus the output voltage waveforms are identical in shape to those of the head-field distributions. Therefore, the shapes of the pulses, their amplitudes, and their widths have already been shown as functions of spacing and gap in Figs. 2.3 to 2.6; and the reason for introducing the quantity p_{50} should now be clear. In all cases it is apparent that spacing is an extremely important parameter and that it must be minimized to maintain pulse amplitudes as high and widths as small as possible.

Another special case is of particular interest. It can be demonstrated by taking Eq. (2.2a) for a thin film and considering the situation when the length of the head-field distribution becomes so short as to approach a delta function. Then

$$e_x(\bar{x}) \propto \frac{dM_x(\bar{x})}{dx} \tag{2.10}$$

This is perfect readback since there are no losses introduced by the reproduce head, and the output is proportional to the magnetization gradient in the recording medium. This prediction is very useful in that it impresses the need for high magnetization gradients, and this implies short magnetization transition lengths between neighboring levels of magnetization. In reality the predicted situation is never quite achieved but is best approached with very short gaps in good contact with very thin recording media.

2.1.3.2 Sine-Wave Recording.
Many of the features of the reproduce process are most adequately demonstrated by considering the voltage waveforms generated in a reproduce head by a sinusoidal variation of magnetization in the medium. Many of the early works dealing with the reproduce process in longitudinal recording (Westmijze, 1953; Fan, 1961; Wang, 1966) confronted this problem, and the works are in substantial agreement in their predictions.

Consider the magnetization to be given by

$$M_x(x) = M_0 \sin kx \tag{2.11}$$

where k is the wave number, $2\pi/\lambda$ and λ is the wavelength. Substitution of this and H_x given by Karlqvist into the reciprocity formula results in

$$e(\bar{x}) = - \mu_o VwMl_0 \, \frac{H_g g}{i} \, k\delta \, [e^{-kd}]\left[\frac{1 - e^{-k\delta}}{k\delta} \right]\left[\frac{\sin{(kg/2)}}{kg/2} \right] \cos k\bar{x} \tag{2.12}$$

The above equation is presented in a form which is intended to highlight the important features of the reproduce process. The terms in the square brackets are all known as *loss terms* and in general have values of less than unity, the smallness being a measure of the loss introduced. These terms will now be considered in detail.

The first term is the spacing loss

$$L_d = e^{-kd} \tag{2.13}$$

and this shows that the output falls exponentially with the ratio of spacing to wavelength (Wallace, 1951). By taking logarithms of both sides of Eq. (2.13), it can be shown that the loss amounts to 54.6 dB per wavelength of spacing between head and medium. Equation (2.13) is plotted in Fig. 2.7 as a function of d/λ.

The second term to be considered is the thickness loss

$$L_\delta = \frac{1 - e^{-k\delta}}{k\delta} \tag{2.14}$$

This is also plotted in Fig. 2.7, where it is seen not to be such a severe source of deterioration of the signal as that due to spacing, but its importance should not be diminished.

The third term is the gap loss term (Lübeck, 1937)

$$L_g = \frac{\sin (kg/2)}{kg/2} \tag{2.15}$$

and it is plotted in Fig. 2.8 as a function of g/λ. Its value passes through a null at $\lambda = g$, and at multiples of x thereafter. However, Eq. (2.12) was derived using a head-field distribution which is approximate, and so Eq. (2.15) itself is approximate. Repeating the calculations for an exact head-field distribution leads to the same result as before except that the gap loss term is modified to [Fan, 1961]

$$L'_g = \frac{\sin (kg/2)}{kg/2} \left[1 + \sum_{n=1}^{\infty} \frac{A_n}{U} \frac{n(-1)^n 4\pi}{4 - (4\pi n/kg)^2} \right] \tag{2.16}$$

where the coefficients A_n/U in the summation were originally given as far as the term $n = 3$ (Fan, 1961) but have more recently been evaluated as far as $n = 6$ (Baird, 1980; Wilton, 1990) and checked experimentally as far as $n = 3$ (Dinnis et al., 1992). The corresponding variation of gap loss with wavelength is also shown in Fig. 2.8, where it is seen that the first null in the output is shifted from $\lambda = g$. The new location can be estimated by taking the first term in the summation (i.e., that involving $A_1/U = -0.08054$) and determining the value of λ/g for which the loss term goes to zero. The null occurs when

$$\lambda = \frac{g}{0.88} \tag{2.17}$$

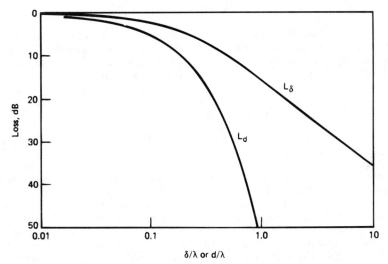

FIGURE 2.7 Thickness loss L_δ and separation loss L_d as functions of reduced thickness and reduced spacing, respectively.

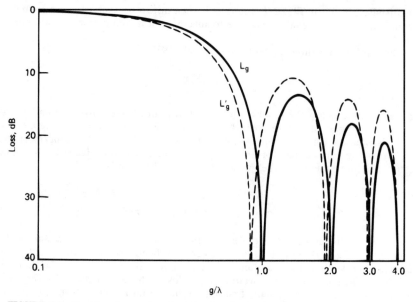

FIGURE 2.8 Gap loss L_g as a function of reduced gap length g/λ. Curve L_g, approximate expression; curve L'_g, accurate expression.

This result was first produced using calculations based upon a conformal mapping solution of the head-field distribution (Westmijze, 1953). Another way of stating the result is that the "effective" gap length, g_{eff}, is some 14 percent higher than the physical gap length. Replacing g by g_{eff} in Eq. (2.15) gives a simple and accurate approximation to the gap loss in the range $\lambda > g_{eff}$.

2.1.3.3   Finite Transition Lengths.   To investigate the output voltages arising from transitions of finite length, it is necessary to assume that the magnetization distributions take on a particularly convenient mathematical form. For the x and y components of magnetization, these are assumed to be (Miyata and Hartel, 1959)

$$M_x = \frac{2}{\pi} M_0 \arctan \frac{x'}{a_x} \tag{2.18a}$$

$$M_y = \frac{2}{\pi} M_0 \arctan \frac{x'}{a_y} \tag{2.18b}$$

where a_x and a_y are the transition length parameters for longitudinal and perpendicular recording, respectively, and where the magnetization changes from a value $-M_0$ to $+M_0$ over the transition. These distributions are shown in Fig. 2.9, where a tangent through the origin of the curve shows that the transition lengths might reasonably be quoted as πa_x or πa_y for the two different components of magnetization. The output voltage characteristics are now most conveniently considered separately for the hypothetical cases of purely longitudinal and purely perpendicular recording.

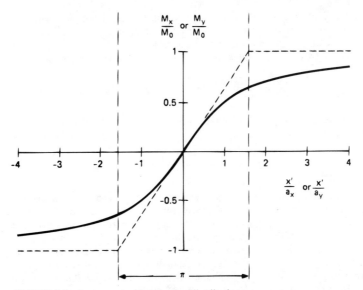

FIGURE 2.9 Arctangent magnetization distributions.

Longitudinal Recording. The output voltage waveforms in longitudinal record-ing are obtained by substitution from Eq. (2.18a) into the reciprocity formula and by using Appendix II to obtain

$$e_x(\bar{x}) = \frac{-2\mu_0 VwH_g M_0}{\pi i} \int_d^{d+\delta} \left(\arctan \frac{g/2 + \bar{x}}{a_x + y} + \arctan \frac{g/2 - \bar{x}}{a_x + y} \right) dy \quad (2.19)$$

Upon completion of the y integration, the total output voltage is given by

$$\begin{aligned}
e_x(\bar{x}) = \frac{-\mu_0 VwH_g M_0}{\pi i} \Bigg[&2(a_x + d + \delta) \left(\arctan \frac{g/2 + \bar{x}}{a_x + d + \delta} + \arctan \frac{g/2 - \bar{x}}{a_x + d + \delta} \right) \\
&- 2(a_x + d) \left(\arctan \frac{g/2 + \bar{x}}{a_x + d} + \arctan \frac{g/2 - \bar{x}}{a_x + d} \right) \\
&+ \left(\frac{g}{2} + \bar{x} \right) \ln \frac{(a_x + d + \delta)^2 + (g/2 + \bar{x})^2}{(a_x + d)^2 + (g/2 + \bar{x})^2} \\
&+ \left(\frac{g}{2} - \bar{x} \right) \ln \frac{(a_x + d + \delta)^2 + (g/2 - \bar{x})^2}{(a_x + d)^2 + (g/2 - \bar{x})^2} \Bigg]
\end{aligned} \quad (2.20)$$

This equation has been obtained previously (Speliotis and Morrison, 1966a; Potter, 1970; Middleton and Davies, 1984), and it can be used to investigate the factors controlling the amplitudes and widths of pulses. While it is easy to find pulse amplitude by putting $\bar{x} = 0$, it is not possible to find a simple formula for pulse width. Therefore, it is more convenient to consider certain limiting cases which provide a useful insight into the replay process.

For replay from a thin film in which $\delta \ll d$, Eq. (2.19) reduces to

$$e_x(\bar{x}) = \frac{-2\mu_0 VwH_g M_0\delta}{\pi i}\left(\arctan\frac{g/2 + \bar{x}}{a_x + d} + \arctan\frac{g/2 - \bar{x}}{a_x + d}\right) \quad (2.21)$$

By comparing this with the Karlqvist expressions for the head-field distribution, it is apparent that

$$e_x(\bar{x}) = \frac{-2\mu_0 VwM_0\delta}{i} H_x(\bar{x}, a_x + d) \quad (2.22)$$

This states that the output voltage waveform follows the same form as the head-field distribution except that the distance from the head surface $y\ (= d)$ is replaced by $a_x + d$. Therefore, the general characteristics of the output waveform are shown in Figs. 2.3 to 2.6, with the requirement that y is replaced by $a_x + d$.

Equation (2.22) is not limited in validity to the approximate head-field distribution of Eq. (2.3a) but applies for exact head-field distributions. This can be verified by comparing reproduced pulse shapes with detailed computations of exact field distributions (Middleton and Davies, 1984). Figure 2.10a shows the experimental pulse shapes obtained for long-gap heads used in contact recording, while Fig. 2.10b shows the same heads used in conjunction with an increased head-to-tape spacing. In the first case the pulses shows the "double-humped" feature discussed earlier, while at the larger spacing the pulse takes a form satisfactorily covered by the simple Karlqvist formula. The medium used was a chemically deposited cobalt film in which uniformity of magnetization through its thickness is a reasonable assumption. This is in line with the assumption leading up to the derivation of the relevant formulas, and so detailed comparisons between theory and experiment reveal good agreement for a range of $(a_x + d)/g$.

Returning to Eq. (2.21) and putting $\bar{x} = 0$ provides the pulse amplitude $e_x(0)$ as

$$e_x(0) = \frac{-4\mu_0 VwH_g M_0\delta}{\pi i}\arctan\frac{g/2}{a_x + d} \quad (2.23)$$

and this can be used to provide predictions suitable for comparison with experiment. Figure 2.11 shows experimental results obtained from pulses reproduced from an evaporated cobalt film medium. Output is displayed as a function of spacing d, introduced by adding spacers between head and medium, to which is

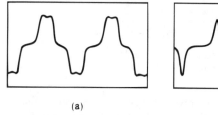

(a)   (b)

FIGURE 2.10 Observed output pulses for (a) contact reproduction with a 51-μm-gap ring head and (b) reproduction with the same head and a toal spacing of 5.8 μm (*Middleton and Davies, 1984*).

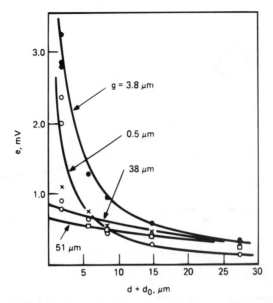

FIGURE 2.11   Pulse amplitudes as functions of spacing $d + d_o$ for gap lengths of 0.5, 3.8, 38, and 51 μm. The points are experimental and the lines theoretical. The film had H_c = 41 kA/m (510 Oe), δ = 0.2 μm, and M_r = 800 kA/m (800 emu/cm³) (*Middleton and Davies, 1984*).

added an effective spacing d_0 shown to be present in the experiments on contact recording (Bonyhard et al., 1966). Relevant properties of the medium and head, given in the figure captions, were used to obtain the theoretical curves. In all cases it was necessary to multiply the calculated outputs by a factor of 0.6 to obtain the results shown. This quantity is a form of head efficiency, which to some extent explains the losses and leakages of flux in the magnetic circuit of the head. The figures confirm the need for small values of spacing d (and a_x) to maintain highest outputs.

The variation of pulse amplitude with gap length is shown in Fig. 2.12. The results were obtained on the same medium as used earlier and the curve is derived using Eq. (2.23). The latter gives satisfactory results and the overall agreement between theory and experiment is confirmed. The graph shows the way in which a reduced gap length causes a general rise in pulse amplitude until the losses of the head gap circuit cause a sudden drop of amplitude at small values of gap length.

Pulse widths are also very much of interest, and these can be obtained from Eq. (2.21). For example, solving the equations $e_x(0)/2 = e_x(\bar{x})$ and $e_x(0)/4 = e_x(\bar{x})$ leads to values of $\bar{x}$, which, when doubled, give the pulse widths at 50 and 25 percent of pulse amplitude, respectively. Thus p_{50} and p_{25} are given by

$$p_{50} = 2\left[\left(\frac{g}{2}\right)^2 + (a_x + d)^2\right]^{1/2} \qquad (2.24a)$$

and

$$p_{25} = \left[\frac{2(a_x + d)g^2}{[(a_x + d)^2 + (g/2)^2]^{1/2} - (a_x + d)} - (a_x + d)^2 + g^2\right]^{1/2} \qquad (2.24b)$$

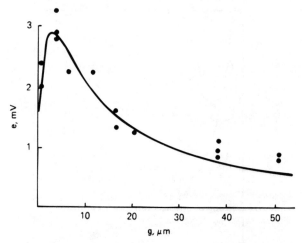

FIGURE 2.12 Pulse amplitude as a function of gap length. Points are for observations on the medium of Fig. 2.11, and curves are theoretical (*Middleton and Davies, 1984*).

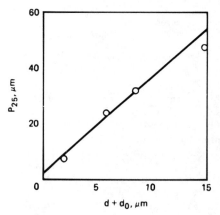

FIGURE 2.13 Pulse width as a function of total spacing ($d + d_o$). The points are for the medium of Fig. 2.11, and the curve is theoretical (*Middleton and Davies, 1984*).

The variation of p_{25} with total head-to-tape spacing is shown in Fig. 2.13 along with appropriate predictions from Eq. (2.24b). The experimental points are for a thin metallic medium which was separated from the reproducing heads by thin plastic spacers. Figure 2.14 shows the variations of pulse width caused by heads of different gaps. The line is the prediction derived from Eq. (2.24a), agreement being good in all cases. All graphs emphasize the need to keep spacings and gaps to a minimum.

While it has proved possible to test the validity of the thin-film approximations, it has not proved possible to verify the predictions of the full formula of Eq. (2.20). This is because magnetizations are never so simply described as in Eq. (2.18a), and their forms are complicated functions of distances into the media and are not sufficiently well known to be able to calculate expected output voltages. Further there is often a difference between the effective depth of recording and the medium thickness, and a detailed consideration of thickness losses is not easily made.

The anticipated role of medium thickness is most easily demonstrated by taking the short-gap approximation to the integrand of Eq. (2.19) and then integrating over y to obtain

$$e_x(\bar{x}) = \frac{-\mu_0 V w H_g M_0 g}{\pi i} \ln \frac{(a_x + d + \delta)^2 + \bar{x}^2}{(a_x + d)^2 + \bar{x}^2} \tag{2.25}$$

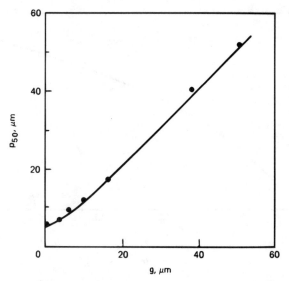

FIGURE 2.14 Pulse width as a function of gap length. The points are for the medium of Fig. 2.11, and the curve is theoretical (*Middleton and Davies, 1984*).

The amplitude of this pulse is obtained by putting $\bar{x} = 0$ in the above equation, while its width at 50 percent of peak amplitude can be derived in the manner described earlier as

$$p_{50} = 2[(a_x + d)(a_x + d + \delta)]^{1/2} \tag{2.26}$$

This equation, when viewed alongside Eq. (2.24a), has led to a suggestion that the following is a suitable approximation for the width of pulses in the general case (Middleton, 1966):

$$p_{50} = 2\left[\left(\frac{g}{2}\right)^2 + (a_x + d)(a_x + d + \delta)\right]^{1/2} \tag{2.27}$$

Figure 2.15a and b shows reduced pulse amplitude, derived from Eq. (2.25), and reduced pulse width, from Eq. (2.26), plotted as functions of reduced medium thickness $\delta/(a_x + d)$. Increasing medium thickness increases pulse amplitude and pulse width; but it should be pointed out that the parameter a_x is also a function of medium thickness, and so its influence is, in reality, more complex than might appear at first sight. Nevertheless it is reasonable to conclude that small thicknesses are needed if pulse widths are to be kept as short as possible.

Perpendicular Recording. The calculations in this section follow the form of those in the previous one. Thus to obtain the output voltage in perpendicular recording it is necessary to substitute from Eqs. (2.3b) and (2.18b) into Eq. (2.2b) and evaluate the integrals (see Appendix II). Thus

$$e_y(\bar{x}) = \frac{-\mu_0 V w H_g M_0}{\pi i} \int_d^{d+\delta} \ln \frac{(g/2 + \bar{x})^2 + (a_y + y)^2}{(g/2 - \bar{x})^2 + (a_y + y)^2} \, dy \tag{2.28}$$

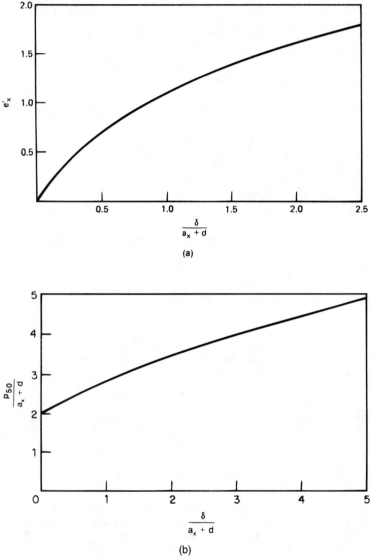

FIGURE 2.15 (*a*) Reduced output and (*b*) pulse width for longitudinal recording as functions of reduced medium thickness.

and completion of the y integration gives

$$e_y(\bar{x}) = \frac{-\mu_0 VwH_g M_0}{\pi i} \left[(a_y + d + \delta)\ln \frac{(a_y + d + \delta)^2 + (g/2 + \bar{x})^2}{(a_y + d + \delta)^2 + (g/2 - \bar{x})^2} \right.$$

$$\left. - (a_y + d)\ln \frac{(a_y + d)^2 + (g/2 + \bar{x})^2}{(a_y + d)^2 + (g/2 - \bar{x})^2} \right.$$

$$+ 2 \left(\frac{g}{2} + \bar{x}\right)\left(\arctan\frac{a_y + d + \delta}{g/2 + \bar{x}} - \arctan\frac{a_y + d}{g/2 + \bar{x}}\right)$$

$$+ 2 \left(\frac{g}{2} - \bar{x}\right)\left(\arctan\frac{a_y + d}{g/2 - \bar{x}} - \arctan\frac{a_y + d + \delta}{g/2 - \bar{x}}\right)\Bigg] \qquad (2.29)$$

It is not easy to visualize the shape of this pulse directly from this equation; therefore, as in the case of longitudinal recording, particular and revealing cases are sought.

Consider first the case of thin recording media ($\delta \ll d$) in which the integration over y in Eq. (2.28) can be avoided. The output voltage is given by

$$e_y(\bar{x}) = - \frac{\mu_0 V w H_g M_0 \delta}{\pi i} \ln \frac{(g/2 + \bar{x})^2 + (a_y + d)^2}{(g/2 - \bar{x})^2 + (a_y + d)^2} \qquad (2.30)$$

Comparison of this with Eq. (2.3b) shows that

$$e_y(\bar{x}) = \frac{\mu_0 V w M_0 \delta}{\pi i} H_y(\bar{x}, a_y + d) \qquad (2.31)$$

Therefore, in similar vein to the case of longitudinal recording, the output voltage waveform is identical in shape to that of the head field, and is shown in Fig. 2.3 to have what is often termed a *bimodal* form; that is, it is positive- and negative-going at different times. Experimental pulse shapes obtained for reproduction by ring heads from thin films of sputtered Co-Cr are shown in Fig. 2.16. The waveforms are very much of the form indicated in that the amplitudes of the positive- and negative-going parts of the pulses are roughly equal. However, observed waveforms often do not exhibit the same type of symmetry since the positive- and negative-going parts do not have the same amplitudes. The cause of the latter is thought to be considerable departures of the magnetization distributions from that assumed in Eq. (2.18b), as discussed in Sec. 2.2.3 below. This makes it difficult to investigate the replay process in the same detail as was done for longitudinal recording, and the limited availability of experimental results in this area somewhat reflects this difficulty. Returning to Eq. (2.30) it can be shown that the minimum and maximum of the output pulse occur at

$$\bar{x} = \bar{x}_0 = \pm \left[\left(\frac{g}{2}\right)^2 + (a_y + d)^2\right]^{1/2} \qquad (2.32)$$

which leads to a *peak-to-peak* distance p_{p-p} of

$$p_{p-p} = 2 \left[\left(\frac{g}{2}\right)^2 + (a_y + d)^2\right]^{1/2} \qquad (2.33)$$

FIGURE 2.16 The general shape of reproduced pulses obtained in perpendicular recording.

By comparing Eq. (2.33) with Eq. (2.24a) it can be seen that p_{50} and p_{p-p} coincide and that the graph of p_{50} (Fig. 2.5) applies equally well for p_{p-p}. Therefore pulse widths for longitudinal recording and peak-to-peak distances for perpendicular recording are comparable quantities and both can be termed *pulse widths*.

To investigate the influence of medium thickness, it is convenient to take the narrow-gap approximation to Eq. (2.28) and carry out the y integration. The result is

$$e_y(\bar{x}) = -\frac{2\mu_0 VwH_g M_0 g}{\pi i}\left(\arctan\frac{\bar{x}}{a_y+d} - \arctan\frac{\bar{x}}{a_y+d+\delta}\right) \quad (2.34)$$

Again this is a bimodal pulse with minimum and maximum at

$$\bar{x} = \bar{x}_0 = \pm[(a_y+d)(a_y+d+\delta)]^{1/2} \quad (2.35)$$

for which the pulse width is

$$P_{50} = 2[(a_y+d)(a_y+d+\delta)]^{1/2} \quad (2.36)$$

This formula for pulse width is identical to that in longitudinal recording.

The amplitude of the voltage waveform is obtained by substituting $\bar{x} = \bar{x}_0$ in Eq. (2.34) to obtain

$$e_y(\bar{x}_0) = -\frac{2\mu_0 VwH_g M_0 g}{\pi i}\left(\arctan\sqrt{\frac{a_y+d+\delta}{a_y+d}}\right.$$

$$\left. - \arctan\sqrt{\frac{a_y+d}{a_y+d+\delta}}\right) \quad (2.37)$$

The variation of reduced pulse amplitude,

$$e'_y = -\frac{e_y}{2\mu_0 VwH_g M_0 g/\pi i}$$

with reduced medium thickness $\delta/(a_y+d)$, derived from Eq. (2.37), is shown in Fig. 2.17. As expected, increasing medium thickness results in higher output.

The comments made earlier about the experimentally observed pulse shapes indicate the difficulty of comparing the above formulas with observations. Pulse shapes are related to the detail of the magnetization distributions, and so it is

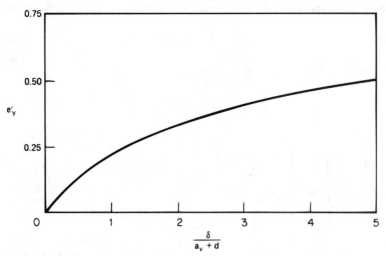

FIGURE 2.17 Reduced pulse amplitude as a function of reduced medium thickness for perpendicular recording.

necessary to consider the reproducing process along with recording theory; this is done in Sec. 2.2.

Reproduction with a single-pole head can be studied in just the same way as reproduction with a ring head. However, there is no need to work through a complete set of new calculations for the following reason. It was shown earlier that there is a general similarity between head-field components produced by ring and single-pole heads. In particular, H_x for the ring head and H_y for the single-pole head are similar, and so it can be expected, in view of Eqs. (2.22) and (2.31), that the output waveforms arising from longitudinal components of magnetization and a ring head are similar to those arising from perpendicular components of magnetization and a single-pole head (see Fig. 2.2). Hence all the equations covered under the discussion of longitudinal recording applying to a ring head also apply to perpendicular recording with a single-pole head (Middleton and Wright, 1982). A similar analogy could be made with respect to the reproduction of perpendicular components of magnetization with a ring head and longitudinal components of magnetization and a single-pole head. The only difference to take into account when applying the equations to a single-pole head is to note that H_g in Eq. (2.7) no longer refers to a gap-surface field but is a field at the tip of the single pole.

2.1.4   Recording at High Densities: Pulse Superposition

When the linear density of information in a recording medium is increased, a number of additional considerations come into play. First, the magnetization transitions in the medium are brought into proximity and interact, and, second, the reproduced pulses overlap. The process by which interactions between neighboring transitions occur in the medium is complex and is usually expressed in terms of changes of transition widths (Melbye and Chi, 1978; Barany and Bertram, 1987; Armstrong et al., 1991). This contrasts with the process of reproduction where pulses from neighboring transitions are simply summed by the reproduce head. As a first approximation to dealing with the pulse crowding situation, it is usually assumed that it is valid simply to superpose and sum isolated pulse waveforms at appropriate spacings to obtain the resultant voltage waveform. This process is known as *linear superposition* (Hoagland, 1963; Mallinson and Steele, 1969; Tjaden, 1973).

In mathematical terminology, pulse superposition simply states that the total voltage $e_t(\bar{x})$ is, for pulses of alternate polarity separated by a distance $\lambda/2$, given by

$$e_t(\bar{x}) = \sum_n (-1)^n e\left(\bar{x} + \frac{n\lambda}{2} \right) \tag{2.38}$$

where the values of n employed in the summation determine the recorded pattern. Generally there are two consequences of pulse crowding: the first is that the amplitudes of the pulses are altered; the second is that the positioning of the peaks of the pulses are shifted, leading to a phenomenon known as *peak shift*. Peak shift is a form of *intersymbol interference,* a term often employed in discussions of recording system behavior.

The effects of pulse crowding in longitudinal recording are illustrated in Fig. 2.18. This shows pulse shapes of the type predicted by Eq. (2.25) crowded together in the way suggested by Eq. (2.38). In Fig. 2.18b the pulses are clearly isolated. At the density shown in Fig. 2.18c the pulses are beginning to overlap, and it can be seen that each detracts from its neighbor and causes a reduction of pulse ampli-

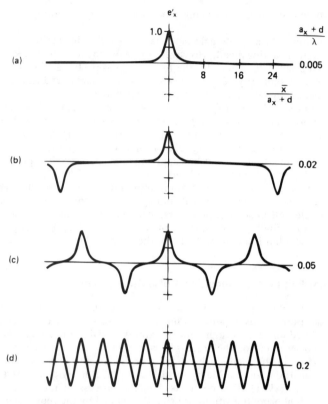

FIGURE 2.18 Predicted output waveforms for longitudinal recording at various reduced densities $(a_z + d)/\lambda$ (*Middleton and Wright, 1982*).

tudes. By the time the configuration in Fig. 2.18d is reached, the resultant waveform looks rather like a cosine wave of amplitude considerably reduced from that of the isolated pulses. Further increases of density continue to reduce the amplitude of this waveform.

In perpendicular recording, the pulses according to Eq. (2.30) are crowded together in the manner of Eq. (2.38) and are shown in Fig. 2.19. The isolated pulse shape, shown in Fig. 2.19a, has a particularly long "tail" which results in overlapping of pulses even at low densities (Fig. 2.19b). In perpendicular recording, the interaction of pulses is initially constructive, and in Fig. 2.19b, c, and d the peak amplitudes rise above those of the isolated pulses. At higher densities than those shown in Fig. 2.19d, however, the amplitude of the wave, which now resembles a sine wave, decreases rapidly.

The above results are encapsulated in Fig. 2.20, which shows the variation of output amplitude plotted as a function of reduced linear density. The predictions are given for short-gap heads for a reason to become apparent below. The output from longitudinal recording falls monotonically with increasing density, while that for perpendicular recording rises to a low peak and then falls. The fall of amplitude with density is identical at high densities for both modes of recording, provided the transition lengths are identical.

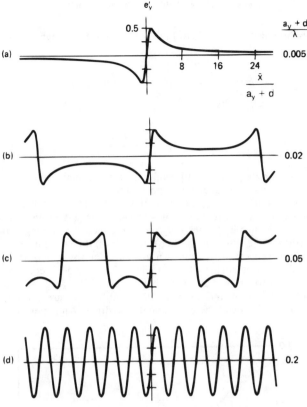

FIGURE 2.19 Predicted output waveforms in perpendicular recording as a function of reduced densities $(a_y + d)/\lambda$ (*Middleton and Wright, 1982*).

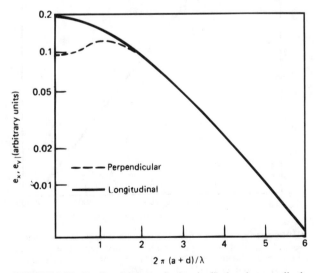

FIGURE 2.20 Predicted outputs for longitudinal and perpendicular recording as a function of reduced density $(a_x + d)/\lambda$ or $(a_y + d)/\lambda$.

It should be noted that the axes of Fig. 2.20 are log-linear, which implies at high densities

$$e_x(0) \propto \exp \frac{-2\pi(a_x + d)}{\lambda} \tag{2.39a}$$

and

$$e_y(0) \propto \exp \frac{-2\pi(a_y + d)}{\lambda} \tag{2.39b}$$

These equations can be obtained by summing the original waveforms using Eq. (2.38) and taking the short-wavelength approximations.

Experimental results which demonstrate the validity of Eq. (2.39a) for longitudinal recording are shown in Fig. 2.21. These results were taken on an instrumentation tape recorder using a high-coercivity recording medium moving with a velocity of 0.76 m/s (Middleton, 1982). At higher frequencies, the straight line satisfies Eq. (2.39a), and measurement of its slope can yield a value for $a_x + d$: the appropriate value is quoted. Graphs such as that in Fig. 2.21 provide a convenient way of investigating values for $a_x + d$ and have been used widely (e.g., Mallinson, 1975; Middleton, 1982; Bertram and Fielder, 1983), although care must be taken to correct for gap losses in any of the experimental readings. An experimental curve of

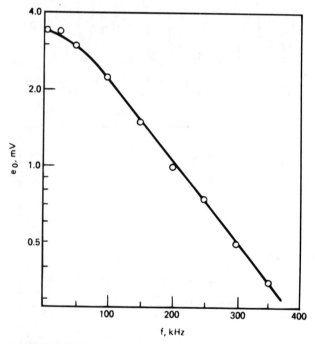

FIGURE 2.21 Observed output as a function of frequency for longitudinal recording using an instrumentation deck with tape of coercivity 52 kA/m (650 Oe) moving at 0.76 m/s. The value of $a_x + d$, determined from its slope, is 0.90 μm (*Middleton, 1982*).

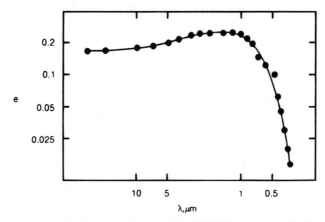

FIGURE 2.22 Output amplitude (arbitrary units) as a function of packing density for perpendicular recording with ring heads on a Co-Cr medium (Hokkyo et al., 1982). The properties of the medium were M_s = 400 kA/m (400 emu/cm³), H_c = 32kA/m (400 Oe), and δ = 0.5 μm.

output against density for perpendicular recording on a Co-Cr film is shown in Fig. 2.22 (Hokkyo et al., 1982). Its general form is as expected, with the initial rise of output occurring before the fall as density increases.

The other consequence of pulse crowding, peak shift, is illustrated in Fig. 2.23. Two pulses, whose shapes are shown as if they are isolated, have their peaks separated by a distance b. When they are summed in the reproduce head, the net output is shown by the broken curve. This summing process, based upon assuming the linear superposition of isolated pulse shapes, results in a waveform with peaks shifted from

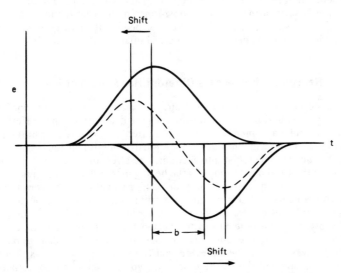

FIGURE 2.23 Schematic diagram showing the superposition of two isolated pulse shapes to give reduced output and peak shift.

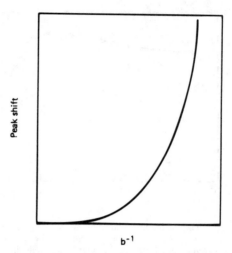

FIGURE 2.24 Peak shift as a function of packing density for the two-pulse arrangement of Fig. 2.23. Scales on axes are arbitrary.

the positions of the original pulses. The extent of the shift is expected to vary with density as shown in Fig. 2.24. Curves of this form have been observed (e.g., Morrison and Speliotis, 1967; Bertram and Fielder, 1983), although the magnitude of the peak shift tends to be less than that predicted by linear pulse superposition (Bertram and Fielder, 1983). This is because, during the recording process, the demagnetizing field from the previously recorded transition tends to augment the record field, and leads to a transition positioned to give reduced peak shift on reproduction.

In perpendicular recording, the analogous quantity to the peak shift of longitudinal recording is shift in the crossover position. This can be demonstrated graphically in a manner similar to that displayed for peak shift, and graphs of shift as a function of density can be derived which are similar to that in Fig. 2.24.

2.1.5 The Reproduce Process for Different Head Geometries

The reproduce heads used in practical circumstances do not always conform to a reasonable approximation to the semi-infinite pole head for which the Karlqvist and Fan formulas can be assumed to apply. More often the dimension p of the pole tips shown in Fig. 2.25a has a magnitude comparable to other dimensions in the recording system and so needs to be taken into account. The effect of reducing p is to bring the outer edges of the head near enough to the head gap to influence the fields produced by the head and, consequently, the output voltage waveforms on reproduction.

The x components of fields produced by thin-pole heads have been computed (Westmijze, 1953; Potter et al., 1971) and are shown in Fig. 2.25b. The predicted effect of shortening the pole tips is to shorten the head-field distribution and to cause it to have negative excursions. In view of the earlier discussions on the reproduce process, it could be expected that the output pulse shapes should show this feature, and indeed this is the case (Valstyn and Shew, 1973). Experimental results are shown in Fig. 2.25c for a long- and a 2-μm-pole head. The corresponding amplitude-versus-density curve is shown in Fig. 2.26. The narrowing of pulses causes a lifting of the high-density outputs over and above what is expected for the

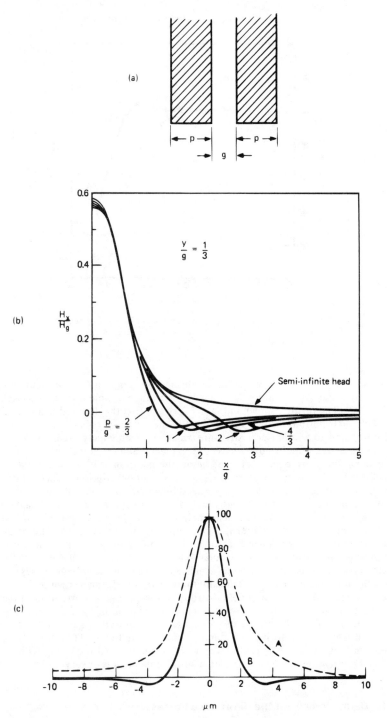

FIGURE 2.25 Finite-pole-tip heads (*a*) definition of symbols; (*b*) computed head-field shapes (Potter et al., 1971); (*c*) observed pulse shapes for (curve *A*) long- and (curve *B*) short-pole heads normalized for equal amplitude (*Valstyn and Shew, 1973*).

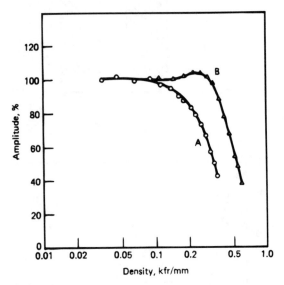

FIGURE 2.26 Observations of outputs as a function of density for (curve A) a long-pole head and (curve B) a narrow-pole head (*Valstyn and Shew, 1973*).

long-pole head. This basic result was confirmed by comparing theoretical and experimental curves of output against density for a range of pole dimensions (Kakehi et al., 1982). The results, shown in Fig. 2.27, reveal that the detailed features of the head-field distribution result in undulations in the output-versus-density curve.

Turning now to another pole structure which has been widely used, consider Fig. 2.28. Here a single main pole for record is placed above the recording medium, while an auxiliary drive pole is placed below the medium. Although a full description of this head structure is given in Chap. 6, a brief description of its operation is given here. The auxiliary pole is magnetized by a current in its coil and produces a low-amplitude but widespread field which penetrates the medium and magnetizes the main pole above the medium. The main pole then produces a localized field of sufficiently high strength to alter the magnetization in the medium. The resulting field distribution is a significant factor in determining output voltage waveforms, particularly when using a film of cobalt-chromium which has a soft nickel-iron backing layer (Iwasaki et al., 1979). In such a case the output voltage pulses should follow the form of the head-field distributions. The waveforms shown in Fig. 2.28*b* were compared with computed field distributions to give good correlation. In addition, the corresponding pulse-crowding curves are shown in Fig. 2.28*c;* the nulls in the output arise from the effects of pole length, as opposed to gap length of a ring head, and were shown to be easily and accurately predicted. Therefore, the predicted similarity between output waveforms for longitudinal recording with a ring head and perpendicular recording with a single-pole head is observed.

2.1.6 Deductions from the Reproduce Process

The previous section has shown that by fitting Eq. (2.39*a*) to the roll-off curve at high packing densities it is possible to determine a value for the quantity $(a_x + d)$.

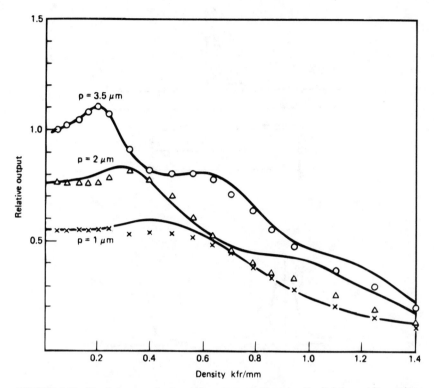

FIGURE 2.27 The influence of pole width on output versus density. Points are observations, and the lines are the result of calculations (*Kakehi et al., 1982*).

As mentioned previously this is now commonly done and values for $(a_x + d)$ are widely quoted. However, more information can be gleaned by careful fitting of mathematical expressions over the whole of the packing density range available to obtain values not only of $(a_x + d)$ but also δ and M_0 (Middleton and Jack-Kee, 1982; Loze et al., 1990). This process is made easy by the fact that closed form expressions are available for output versus packing density when individual pulse shapes are substituted into Eq. (2.38) and summed (Middleton et al., 1995).

Values of $(a_x + d)$, δ, and M_0 obtained for experimental roll-off curves are shown in Figs. 2.29, 2.30 and 2.31 for a particulate medium. All the quantities are seen to be strong functions of record current, with particularly δ and M_0 showing considerable variations. It is only to be expected that the depth of recording δ (rather than thickness) and M_0 should increase with increasing head field and that $(a_x + d)$ should show a minimum at the record current which gives rise to highest head field gradient.

Figs. 2.29, 2.30 and 2.31 also show values for the parameters obtained by methods employing spectral analysis and FFTs of wave forms (Loze et al., 1990). Parameters can also be obtained by considering only the amplitude of the fundamental of the output wave, rather than its total value, and consistent results have been shown to be easily obtained this way (Armstrong et al., 1991; Chan and Middleton, 1994).

All these methods depend on the validity of linear superposition if they are to produce consistent results. This they seem to do and it is further evidence of the

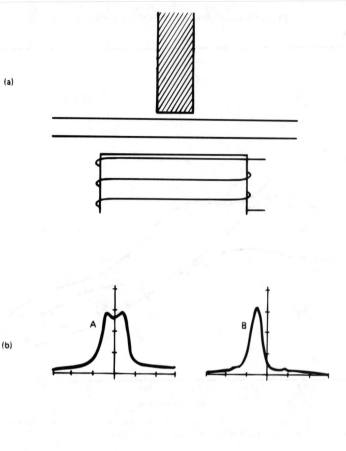

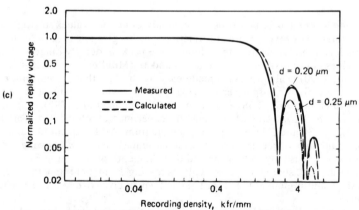

FIGURE 2.28 Perpendicular recording. (*a*) Main pole and auxiliary pole arrangement for perpendicular recording; (*b*) isolated pulse shapes reproduced by (curve *A*) poles of 2.0-μm and (curve *B*) 0.9-μm widths in contact with double-layer Co-Cr/Ni-Fe media (1.9 μm/per division); (*c*) output amplitude as a function of density (*Iwasaki et al., 1981*).

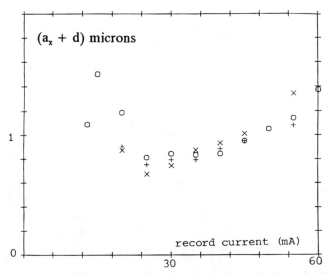

FIGURE 2.29 Experimental results of $(a_x + d)$ as a function record current amplitude for a particulate medium (Ampex 721) using wide band instrumentation heads (*Loze et al. 1990*). + from roll-off curves, x from spectrum analyser measurements, ○ from FFTs.

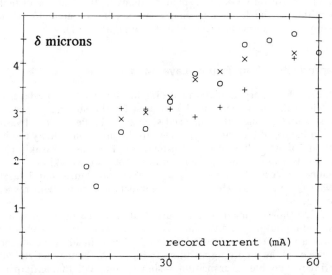

FIGURE 2.30 Experimental results for δ as a function of record current amplitude for a particulate medium (Ampex 721) using wideband instrumentation heads (*Loze et al., 1990*). + from roll-off curves, x from spectrum analyser measurements, ○ from FFTs.

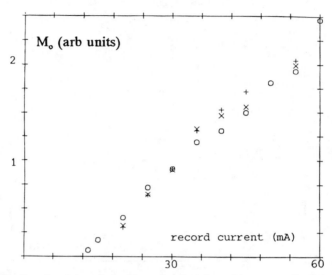

FIGURE 2.31 Experimental results for M_o as a function of record current amplitude for a particulate medium (Ampex 721) using wideband instrumentation heads (Loze et al., 1990). + from roll-off curves, x from spectrum analyser measurements, o from FFTs.

success of superposition theory in explaining many of the features of high-density recording, although the limitations caused by non-linear interactions can be observed in appropriate circumstances (Armstrong et al., 1991).

2.1.7 Reproduction from Double-Layer Media

Much of the work on perpendicular recording has involved double-layer recording media, in which the high-coercivity layers used for the storage process have thin underlayers of high-permeability material such as Ni-Fe Permalloy (Iwasaki et al., 1979). The influence of the underlayer is multifold but for simplicity can be categorized in terms of its influence on head-field distributions (Iwasaki, 1980, 1984; Mallinson and Bertram, 1984b), the recording process (Iwasaki et al., 1983), and the reproduce process (Yamamori et al., 1981; Nakamura and Iwasaki, 1982; Lopez, 1983; Quak, 1983). Here a few comments are made with respect to the reproduce process.

Figure 2.32a shows a magnetization distribution in a single-layer medium and the corresponding outputs at different wavelengths. The voltage waveforms can be considered as arising from the flux induced in the replay head by the magnetic poles on both surfaces of the recording medium. In Fig. 2.32b the magnetization distribution occurring in a double-layer medium is shown along with that anticipated for the underlayer. The latter is thought to offer means for the achievement of flux closure at the lower surface, thereby leaving magnetic poles only on the top surface of the medium. Figure 2.33 shows the effect of this on the variation of output with packing density (Yamamori et al., 1981). The output for a single-layer medium is a strong function of medium thickness, whereas the output for the double-layer medium is virtually independent of thickness since the influence of the lower side of the medium has been removed.

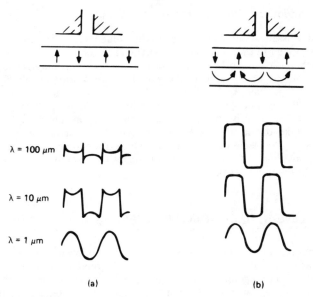

FIGURE 2.32 Output waveforms for perpendicular recording for (*a*) single Co-Cr and (*b*) double-layer media, Co-Cr on Ni-Fe, as a function of wavelength. Recording head—single-pole design; reproducing head—ring design.

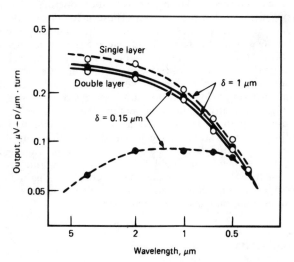

FIGURE 2.33 Output amplitudes as a function of wavelength for perpendicular recording on single- and double-layer (underlayer of 1 μm) Co-Cr media (*Yamamori et al., 1981*).

2.1.8   Reproduction with Magnetoresistive Heads

The heads discussed so far have all been of the inductive variety; that is, the output voltages developed in their coils are proportional to the rate of change of the flux induced in the cores. Such heads are not the only types available; there are also flux-sensitive heads which, as their name implies, are sensitive to the flux induced within them rather than its rate of change. Of these, the magnetoresistive head has been most widely studied and is considered fully in Chap. 6. With regard to the operation of a flux-sensitive head, it is sufficient to say at this stage that potential distributions take on the role of head sensitivity functions and replace the field distributions in the reciprocity formulas. Once the potential distributions are known, it is possible to determine output voltages (Cole et al., 1974; Potter, 1974; Davies and Middleton, 1975).

2.2   NONLINEAR RECORDING PROCESSES

The nonlinear recording process is one of great complexity and does not yield easily to rigorous analysis. Nevertheless, much has been learned about the primary factors involved in determining the nature of the process from the study of simplified models. In this section such simplified models will be presented and their successes and limitations discussed.

As a lead-in to this topic, consider a medium moving from left to right, first past a record head and then past a reproduce head. Any element of the medium that has passed the record head has been subjected to a complex history of head fields of varying amplitude and direction. The picture is further complicated by the existence of demagnetizing fields within the medium. These fields modify the field experienced by the medium during the record process. They remain present in the medium as it moves away from the record head, causing the written magnetization to change. They are also present as the medium moves under the reproduce head, thus causing a further change. Any precise model of magnetic recording therefore needs, as a whole, to take into account the vector nature of the recording process, the role of demagnetizing fields, and the various stages of the process which take place before a signal is finally produced in the reproduce head.

In most media, the particles are oriented in the direction of motion, thus encouraging longitudinal magnetization. When the medium is thin, the demagnetizing factor of the medium in a direction normal to its plane is large, causing large normal components of the demagnetizing field and discouraging normal components of magnetization. In this situation, it is possible to consider longitudinal recording solely in terms of longitudinal components of head field and magnetization. In cases where the medium is not thin, such an approach is invalid.

2.2.1   Longitudinal Recording

Consider the longitudinal recording process (Fig. 2.34) where a head field of negative polarity is shown being applied to a medium previously magnetized to a level $+ M_r$. The applied longitudinal field has its highest magnitude directly below the head gap, causing the magnetization to take on a value of $-M_r$. This means that to the right of the gap the magnetization undergoes a change from negative values to positive values and therefore a magnetization transition has been recorded.

At the center of the transition, $M_x = 0$, and this state of magnetization is

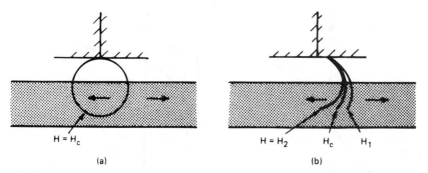

FIGURE 2.34 Head-field contours. (a) Contour of $H_z = H_c$ below a narrow-gap ring head; (b) contours for $H_x = H_1$ and $H_x = H_2$.

achieved when the field in the medium is equal to the coercivity. Using the short-gap approximation, the locus of the points at which $H_x = H_c$ is found by setting

$$H_c = \frac{H_g g}{\pi} \frac{y}{x^2 + y^2} \tag{2.40}$$

Reordering of this equation leads to

$$x^2 + \left(y - \frac{1}{2} \frac{H_g g}{H_c \pi} \right)^2 = \frac{1}{4} \left(\frac{H_g g}{H_c \pi} \right)^2 \tag{2.41}$$

which is the equation of a circle. This result implies that constant field contours are circular, as shown in Fig. 2.34a (Bauer and Mee, 1961). Thus the position of the transition center will vary with spacing from the head and, in a thick medium, will be a variable through its depth. In thin media the variations may be considered sufficiently small to be negligible.

The nature of the transition can be studied by assuming that the major change of the magnetization takes place over the field range H_1 to H_2 (Fig. 2.35). In a similar fashion to that used for the drawing of the field contours for the coercivity it is possible to obtain the contours for $H_x = H_1$ and $H_x = H_2$. These lines then display the boundaries of the transition and so give a visual picture of the form of the recorded transition as shown in Fig. 2.34b.

Should a more detailed representation of the variation of magnetization within a transition be required, the techniques illustrated in Fig. 2.35 are appropriate. The figure shows the head-field distribution at the time of recording, the hysteresis loop of the medium, and the means of tracing from the first to the second diagram to find the magnetization variation with position in the medium. This procedure can be applied to different head fields and hysteresis loop shapes. An analytical approach to the same problem can be made by assuming a mathematical form for the hysteresis loop $M(H)$. Then, since the field distribution $H = H_x(x, y)$ is known, the magnetization distribution $M(H)$ in the transition is given by

$$M_x(x) = M(H_x(x, y)) \tag{2.42}$$

which is the mathematical equivalent of the result obtained using the graphical technique. The magnetization gradient, or recorded pulse, is given by

$$\frac{dM_x}{dx} = \frac{dM(H_x)}{dH_x} \frac{dH_x}{dx} \tag{2.43}$$

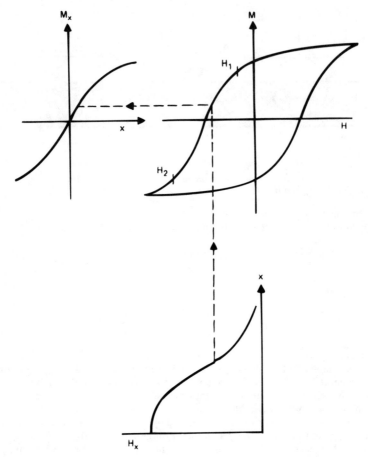

FIGURE 2.35 Scheme showing how recorded magnetizations can be determined for given media hysteresis and head-field distributions.

This formula says that the magnetization gradient is proportional to the product of the slope of the side of the hysteresis loop and the head-field gradient. Hence the requirements for short transition lengths are for rectangular hysteresis loops and high head-field gradients.

To improve the theory and make it more realistic it is necessary to take into account the demagnetizing fields H_d within the recording medium. These add to the applied head field to produce a total field, H_t, and can be taken into account by rewriting Eq. (2.43) as

$$\frac{dM_x}{dx} = \frac{dM(H_t)}{dH_t}\frac{dH_t}{dx} \tag{2.44a}$$

where

$$\frac{dH_t}{dx} = \frac{dH_x}{dx} + \frac{dH_d}{dx} \tag{2.44b}$$

Unfortunately, a complete solution of the equations requires the use of iterative, numerical methods since the magnetization gradient, which we need to calculate, is itself needed for the calculation of H_d. Therefore, to progress with the analytical approach, it is necessary to use an approximate method for solving the equations. The one adopted here is that proposed by Williams and Comstock (1972) but modified and developed in some detail by Maller and Middleton (1973, 1974). This basic method was developed for studies on thin media, which is the focus of the ensuing discussion.

Redrawing the hysteresis loop with more detail, as in Fig. 2.36a, permits a more satisfactory discussion of the recording process. Assuming the medium is initially magnetized, as before, to $+M_r$, the application of a head field of negative sense changes the magnetization according to the left-hand side of the major hysteresis loop, which is assumed to have the form

$$M(H) = \frac{2M_s}{\pi} \arctan \left(\frac{H + H_c}{H_c} \tan \frac{\pi S}{2} \right) \qquad (2.45)$$

where $S = M_r/M_s$ is the remanence squareness. The center of the transition is assumed to be positioned at point H_1 on the hysteresis loop since the removal of the corresponding element of the medium away from the head field leaves it with zero magnetization. This process, termed *relaxation,* will now be described.

When an element of the recorded magnetization distribution leaves the vicinity of the record head field, it relaxes to a new value by moving along one of the curves marked B to end up at some position along the curve C of Fig. 2.36a. The latter is determined by the levels of magnetization allowed by the demagnetizing fields in the medium. When this new distribution is transported under the reproduce head, there is a further readjustment of the magnetization. This arises because the high-permeability reproduce head has induced within it image charges of opposite sign to those in the recording medium. The image charges produce fields in the recording medium that reduce the demagnetizing field therein and so alter the magnetization. This process takes place along the lines marked D, and it is the final magnetization values on these lines that generate the output voltage in the reproduce head.

By way of explanation of curve C of Fig. 2.36, an arctangent magnetization distribution such as that shown in Fig. 2.37a gives rise to a demagnetization field H_d which is plotted in Fig. 2.37b. Each position x' in the medium is associated with unique values of the magnetization and demagnetization fields, and when these are plotted against each other, they give rise to curve C.

The calculations presented here are for the particular case of rectangular hysteresis loops shown in Fig. 2.36b for which $S = 1$. In such cases the sides of the hysteresis loops are vertical and so their slopes are infinite. Substituting $dM/dH = \infty$ in Eq. (2.44) leads to

$$\frac{dH_x}{dx} = - \frac{dHi_d}{dx} \qquad (2.46)$$

The left-hand side of Eq. (2.46) can be evaluated by taking the short-gap approximation for the head field from Eq. (2.6a) and optimizing H_g to produce the highest field gradient at the center of the transition, that is, at $H_x = H_1 = H_c$. The result is [†]

$$\frac{dH_x}{dx} = \frac{H_c}{y} \qquad (2.47)$$

[†]The head-field gradient H_c/y is the optimum value whereas earlier versions of this chapter and many works in the literature use a near-optimal value of $\sqrt{3}H_c/2y$.

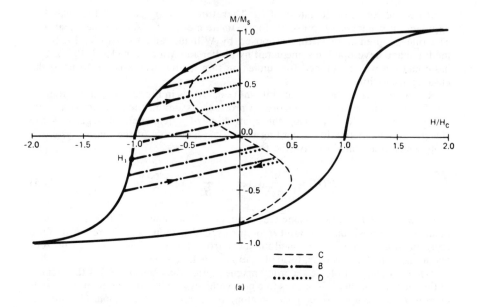

(a)

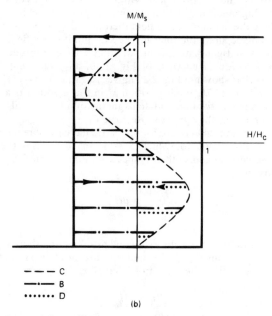

(b)

FIGURE 2.36 Assumed form of hysteresis loop shapes. (*a*) $S < 1$; (*b*) $S = 1$. Curve *B*—demagnetization after removal of applied field; curve *C*—demagnetizing field as a function of magnetization, and curve *D*—remagnetization under replay head (*Maller and Middleton, 1973*).

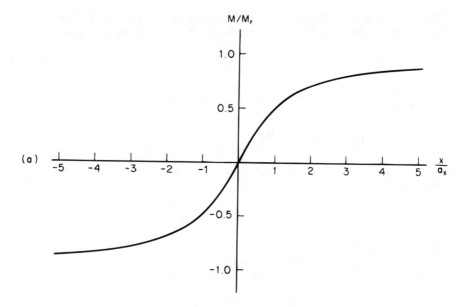

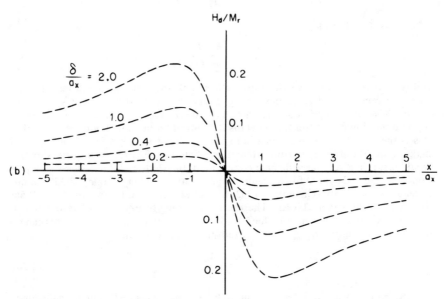

FIGURE 2.37 Arctangent transition. (*a*) Magnetization; (*b*) demagnetization field along the center plane of media of various thicknesses.

The demagnetizing field in the recorded transition can be calculated only by assuming a form for the recorded magnetization distribution. The form assumed here is

$$M_x = \frac{2}{\pi} M_r \arctan \frac{x}{a_x} \tag{2.48}$$

for which the self-demagnetizing field can be calculated using the results of Appendix III. Thus

$$H_{dx} = -\frac{1}{2\pi} \iint \frac{\partial M_x(x')}{\partial x'} \frac{x - x'}{(x - x')^2 + (y - y')^2} \, dx' \, dy' \tag{2.49}$$

and substitution from Eq. (2.48) and evaluation for the center plane of the medium results in

$$H_{dx} = -\frac{2}{\pi} M_r \left(\arctan \frac{x}{a_x} - \arctan \frac{x}{a_x + \delta/2} \right) \tag{2.50}$$

which takes the form shown in Fig. 2.37.

The magnetization gradient at the center of the transition and the center plane of the medium ($y = d + \delta/2$) is now determined to be

$$\frac{dH_{dx}}{dx} = -\frac{M_r \delta}{\pi} \frac{1}{a_x(a_x + \delta/2)} \tag{2.51}$$

Substituting this along with dH_x/dx from Eq. (2.47) into Eq. (2.46) and evaluating leads to a transition length of

$$a_x = -\frac{\delta}{4} + \left(\frac{\delta^2}{16} + \frac{M_r \delta y}{\pi H_c} \right)^{1/2} \tag{2.52}$$

which, for thin films, becomes

$$a_x = \left(\frac{M_r \delta d}{\pi H_c} \right)^{1/2} \tag{2.53}$$

If this transition is long, it suffers no further demagnetization when it moves away from the record head since the demagnetization curves B have zero slope (Fig. 2.36b). A similar situation occurs on replay, and a_x given by Eq. (2.53) is the value of the transition parameter that governs the output voltage. It should be noted that this is the shortest possible transition since the head field has been optimized to make it so. Should the transition length predicted by Eq. (2.53) be very short, it would result in a very large demagnetizing field. Inspection of the hysteresis loop of Fig. 2.36b reveals that, for a stable magnetization, demagnetizing fields cannot exceed the coercivity (Chapman, 1963; Davies et al., 1965; Bonyhard et al., 1966; Speliotis and Morrison, 1966a). Therefore, according to Eq. (2.50), there will be a minimum value of the transition length allowed by demagnetization, and this can be determined by letting $H_{d,max} = H_c$. For thin films, this leads to

$$a_d = \frac{M_r \delta}{2\pi H_c} \tag{2.54}$$

The reduced transition lengths caused by writing losses (a_x/δ) and by demagnetization (a_d/δ) are plotted in Fig. 2.38 as functions of $M_r/4\pi H_c$ for different values of

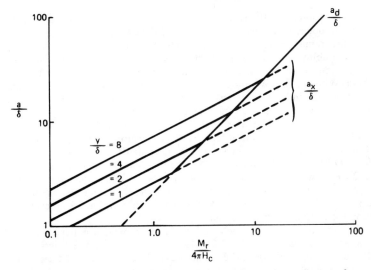

FIGURE 2.38 Reduced transition length a/δ for longitudinal recording as a function of $M_r/4\pi H_c$. Squareness $S = 1$.

y/δ. Two regimes of behavior can be identified corresponding to square root and linear dependency, and these are symptomatic of record demagnetization and self-demagnetization, respectively. For hysteresis loop squareness other than unity, the transition lengths differ at different parts of the record-demagnetization-reproduce cycle. As an example, consider the results for wide-gap heads shown in Fig. 2.39

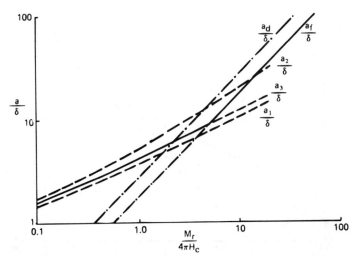

FIGURE 2.39 Predicted transition lengths for longitudinal recording at the instant of recording (a_1/δ), after relaxation (a_2/δ), and after remagnetization (a_3/δ) as functions of $M_r/4\pi H_c$. Also shown are the transition lengths after demagnetization (a_d/δ) and after remagnetization (a_f/δ) [$M_r/M_s = 0.8$, $(y + \delta/2)/\delta = 2.0$] (*Maller and Middleton, 1973*).

(Maller and Middleton, 1973). In the figure, a_1/δ represents the transition length under the influence of record head field, a_2/δ the demagnetized transition length, and a_3/δ the remagnetized transition length as it appears under the reproduce head. The implications are that short transition lengths are created under the record head and that these lengthen as they move away from the influence of the head field. When they move under the reproduce head, the reduction of demagnetizing fields results in a shorter transition. Of particular note is that the lengthening of the transitions due to relaxation and the shortening due to remagnetization almost compensate, making the final length close to the written one. At large values of $M_r/4\pi H_c$, the transition lengths are determined not by the write process but by demagnetization. In this case a_d/δ is the transition length after removal from the vicinity of the record head and a_f/δ is the final value under the reproduce head. Figure 2.39 shows the two basic regimes of record and replay demagnetization, although the picture is slightly more complicated than that shown in Fig. 2.38. These regimes have been confirmed by others employing more precise numerical modeling (Speliotis, 1972; Tjaden and Tercic, 1975).

On the experimental side, much has been done to provide experimental data and to fit theory to it (Davies et al., 1965; Bonyhard et al., 1966; Speliotis and Morrison, 1966a, 1966b; Speliotis, 1972; Tjaden and Tercic, 1975). The selected results shown in Fig. 2.40 are deduced from measurements of pulse lengths from cobalt films, using the replay theory presented here (Maller and Middleton, 1974). The basic features of the theory are confirmed.

In addition to considerations based on bulk properties, it is known that there is fine detail in recorded transitions which is of importance. This is illustrated diagrammatically in Fig. 2.41a, which shows a transition of arctangent form, and in Fig. 2.41b, which attempts to show that the transition in metallic films takes the form of a domain wall disposed in zig-zag or sawtooth fashion (Dressler and Judy, 1974). The available experimental evidence suggests that the transition length l defined by

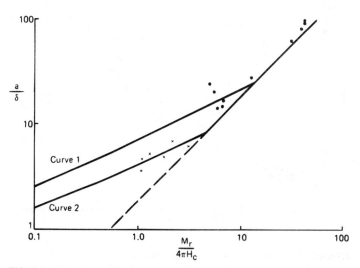

FIGURE 2.40   Observed transition lengths for film media as a function of $M_r/4\pi H_c$. The lines represent predictions. Curve 1: $(d + \delta/2)/\delta = 7.3$, $M_r/M_s = 0.95$. Curve 2: $(d + \delta/2)/\delta = 2.0$, $M_r/M_s = 0.8$ (*Maller and Middleton, 1973, 1974*).

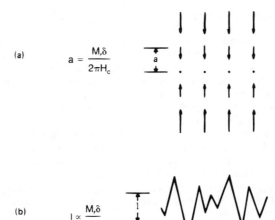

(a) $a = \dfrac{M_r\delta}{2\pi H_c}$

(b) $l \propto \dfrac{M_r\delta}{H_c}$

FIGURE 2.41 Schematic representation of (*a*) the assumed form of the magnetization at a transition and (*b*) the observed shape of the transition.

the average sawtooth amplitude in Fig. 2.41*b* varies as (Dressler and Judy, 1974; Yoshida et al., 1983; Gronau et al., 1983)

$$l \propto \frac{M_r\delta}{H_c} \tag{2.55}$$

It is perhaps fortunate that this should have the same form as Eq. (2.54), the formula for transition lengths caused by self-demagnetization when the fine detail of the transitions is ignored.

Attempts have been made to develop recording theory in thin films for transitions having sawtooth shapes (Muller and Murdock 1987; Middleton et al., 1988; Middleton and Miles, 1991). When the sawteeth are of uniform size their widths *l*, which are equivalent to πa, are very close to those derived using 'arctangent theory' of the type mentioned in this work. The relationship (2.55) is obtained in the self demagnetization limited case and a square root relationship in the record limited case. Extension of the theory to more realistic structures with distributions of sawtooth widths has produced distributions which are of the right form when compared with observations (Arnoldussen and Tong, 1986; Middleton and Miles, 1991). Such knowledge is important to the understanding of noise, which is considered elsewhere in this book.

In summarizing the lessons to be learned from the theory, it should be borne in mind that the treatment given here applies solely for thin films and is relevant to thicker, particulate media with less certainty. Nevertheless, for all media, it is necessary to keep M_r/H_c and δ small in order to achieve sharp transitions. This requirement has led to continued developments toward thinner media of higher coercivity. The other major requirement is that hysteresis loop squareness should be high, although considerations of low noise performance may contradict this (see Chap. 4 and 5).

2.2.2 Perpendicular Recording

In perpendicular recording the medium has a preferred orientation, or easy axis, in a direction normal to its plane so as to encourage components of magnetization in that direction (Iwasaki and Takemura, 1975; Iwasaki and Nakamura, 1977; Iwasaki, 1984). A typical recording medium consists of a sputtered film of cobalt-chromium having high anisotropy (anisotropy field $H_k > M_s$) and easy axis normal to its plane (Iwasaki and Ouchi, 1978). Suppose the head field is magnetizing the medium in an upward direction against a background of downward magnetization. Just as in longitudinal recording, the shape of the head-field distribution is important and needs to be taken into account in considering the recording process.

The model of the recording process to be described is simply an adaptation of that used earlier for longitudinal recording in thin-film media: two variations on the theme exist in the literature (Middleton and Wright, 1982; Bromley, 1983). As in the longitudinal case, the recorded transition lengths are determined by solution of the equation

$$\frac{dM_y}{dx} = \frac{dM(H_t)}{dH_t} \left(\frac{dH_y}{dx} + \frac{dH_d}{dx} \right) \tag{2.56}$$

in which the use of the y subscript denotes the consideration given to perpendicular components. For rectangular hysteresis loops, the slopes of their sides, dM/dH, is infinite, and

$$\frac{dH_y}{dx} = - \frac{dH_d}{dx} \tag{2.57}$$

To aid in obtaining the solution of this equation for a ring head, the maximum field gradient existing at the center of the transition at $H_y = H_c$ can be shown, using the short-gap head-field approximation, to be

$$\frac{dH_y}{dx} = 0.3 \frac{H_c}{y} \tag{2.58}$$

which is less than one-third of that given for the x component of the field. The other quantity needed is the demagnetizing field H_{dy}, which can be evaluated only when the magnetization distribution is known. Assuming an arctangent transition of the type

$$M_y(x) = \frac{2M_0}{\pi} \arctan \frac{x}{a_y} \tag{2.59}$$

where M_0 is the magnitude of the magnetization for each side of the transition, and using this in conjunction with the results of Appendix III leads to an expression for the demagnetizing field in the midplane of the recording medium

$$H_d = - \frac{2M_0}{\pi} \arctan \frac{x}{a_y + \delta/2} \tag{2.60}$$

Differentiation of this gives the field gradient, which, at the center of the transition, is

$$\frac{dH_d}{dx} = - \frac{2M_0}{\pi} \frac{1}{a_y + \delta/2} \tag{2.61}$$

Substitution of this and Eq. (2.58) into Eq. (2.57) leads to an expression for transition width

$$a_y = \frac{2}{0.3\pi} \frac{M_0}{H_c} \left(d + \frac{\delta}{2} \right) - \frac{\delta}{2} \tag{2.62}$$

To complete the equation, it is necessary to consider the value of M_0. In the case when $M_r < H_c$, demagnetization is limited and $M_0 = M_r$. For most practical cases, however, $M_r > H_c$, and consideration needs to be given to the effect of demagnetization. Equation (2.60) shows that at large values of x (distant from the transition), the demagnetizing field takes on a value $-M_0$. However, as in the case of longitudinal recording, a finite magnetization can be maintained only if the demagnetizing field does not exceed H_c. Thus the magnetization is limited to a value of $M_0 = H_c$, and use of this in Eq. (2.62) leads to

$$a_{yr} = \frac{2}{0.3\pi} \left(d + \frac{\delta}{2} \right) - \frac{\delta}{2} \tag{2.63}$$

The subscript r has been added to indicate that this solution applies to a ring head. The message of Eq. (2.63) is that head-to-tape spacing is a primary factor in determining transition length and that medium magnetic properties, such as M_r and H_c, make no contribution.

With regard to recording with a single-pole head, the considerations are the same as those already expounded for a ring head except that the head field, and therefore the head-field gradient, has a different value. Assuming that the y component of the field of a single-pole head takes the same mathematical form as the x component of the field of a ring head, the maximum head-field gradient that can occur at $H = H_c$ is given by

$$\frac{dH_y}{dx} = \frac{H_c}{y} \tag{2.64}$$

Using Eq. (2.64) along with Eq. (2.61) in Eq. (2.57) leads to a predicted transition width of

$$a_{yp} = \frac{2}{\pi} \frac{M_0}{H_c} \left(d + \frac{\delta}{2} \right) - \frac{\delta}{2} \tag{2.65}$$

The use of the extra subscript is to denote single-pole or probe head. Again, unless $M_r < H_c$ it is appropriate to make $M_0 = H_c$, and so

$$a_{yp} = \frac{2}{\pi} \left(d + \frac{\delta}{2} \right) - \frac{\delta}{2} \tag{2.66}$$

Here, once again, neither M_r nor H_c figures in the equation, and the head-to-medium separation is a primary factor.

Transition lengths for longitudinal and perpendicular recording are shown in Fig. 2.42 as a function of medium thickness for various head-to-medium spacings. A number of deductions may be made from this figure. First, perpendicular recording is much more sensitive to variations in head-to-medium spacing than is longitudinal recording, and reduced spacings would lead to shorter transitions regardless of which head was used. Second, perpendicular recording with a single-pole head is much more favorable than with a ring head. Third, longitudinal recording produces

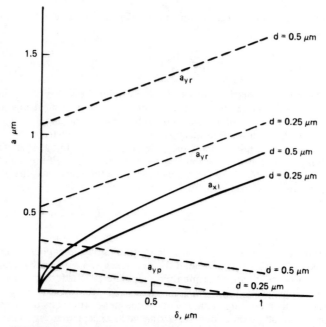

FIGURE 2.42 Predicted transition lengths as functions of media thickness for different spacing, based on balancing the field gradients at the midplane (*Middleton and Wright, 1982*).

short transitions only in very thin media. An alternative approach is to base the analysis on solving Eq. (2.56) at the surface rather than at the midplane of the medium. The corresponding results are plotted in Fig. 2.43. The conclusions are similar to those listed above except that, as expected, the dependence of transition length on medium thickness is much reduced. The fragility of these calculations is obvious when comparing Figs. 2.42 and 2.43.

On the experimental front no data have been provided on transition lengths. However, with transition lengths independent of M_r and H_c it is to be expected that the output voltage levels according to Eqs. (2.30) and (2.31) should be proportional to the product $M_0\delta$, that is, $H_c\delta$. Experimental results taken from cobalt-chromium films (Fig. 2.44) reveal the anticipated linear dependencies on H_c and δ (Hokkyo et al., 1982).

2.2.3 Record Theory for Thick Media

The theory so far developed only applies to thin media where recorded transition widths and locations do not vary through the depths of the media. Considerable development of it needs to take place if it is to apply to thick media and the basis for such a development is now given (Middleton et al., 1993).

Consider Fig. 2.45 where a thick medium of thickness D is shown moving to the right past a wide gap recording head. For means of computation the medium is split into N thin layers of thickness δ where $N\delta = D$. Using the superscript n to indicate

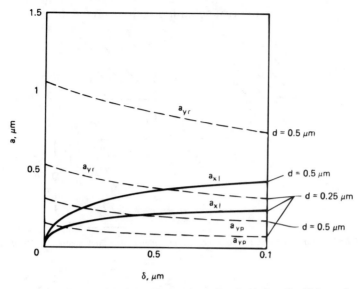

FIGURE 2.43 Predicted transition lengths as functions of media thickness for different spacing, based on balancing the field gradients at the surface.

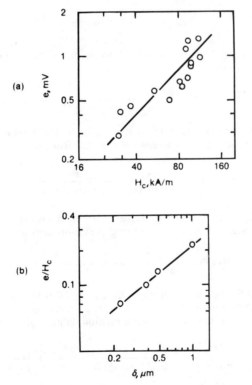

FIGURE 2.44 Observations of output amplitude as functions of (a) H_c (1.2 kfr/mm, $\delta = 1$ μm) and (b) δ (67 fr/mm, $M_s = 400$ kA/m) for perpendicular recording (*Suzuki and Iwasaki, 1982; Hokkyo et al., 1982*).

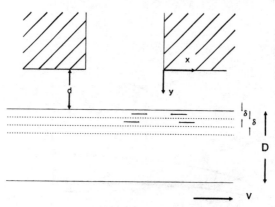

FIGURE 2.45 Coordinate system and discretization scheme for a thick medium *(Middleton et al., 1993)*.

the layer number increasing from the top surface near to the head, the magnetisation in a transition in the nth layer is taken to be

$$M_{xn} = -\frac{2}{\pi} M_{on} \arctan \frac{x}{a_{xn}} \tag{2.67}$$

The corresponding demagnetising field produced by the nth layer is of the form (Bonyhard et al., 1966)

$$H_d = \frac{M_{on}}{\pi} \delta \frac{x}{(a_{xn} + |y - y_n|)^2 + x^2} \tag{2.68}$$

where $|y-y_n|$ is distance above or below the nth layer. The total demagnetising field experienced by the nth layer as a result of the field from all of the layers is

$$H_{dn} = \frac{\delta}{\pi} \sum_{i=1}^{N} \frac{M_{on} x}{(a_{xn} + |i - n|\delta)^2 + x^2} \tag{2.69}$$

Adding this to the field produced by a 'Karlqvist' head with very wide gap, which is given in the mid plane of the nth layer using the co-ordinate system of Fig. 2.45, by

$$H_x(x,y) = \frac{H_g}{\pi} \left\{ \frac{\pi}{2} - \arctan \frac{x}{d + (n - \frac{1}{2}) \delta} \right\} \tag{2.70}$$

leads to the total field in the medium. Taking $H_g = 2H_c$ it is easily deduced that the middle of the transitions will be at $x = o$ in all layers of the medium and that applying Eq. (2.44) to the nth layer the transition width is given by

$$\frac{2}{\pi} \frac{M_{on}}{a_{xn}} = \chi_1 \left\{ \frac{H_g}{\pi} \frac{1}{d + (n-\frac{1}{2}) \delta} - \frac{M_o \delta}{\pi} \sum_{i=1}^{N} \frac{1}{(a_i + |i - n|\delta)^2} \right\} \tag{2.71}$$

where χ_1 is the slope of the hysteresis loop at $H = H_c$. Equations (2.71) are a set of simultaneous equations defining the transition widths in N layers of the medium.

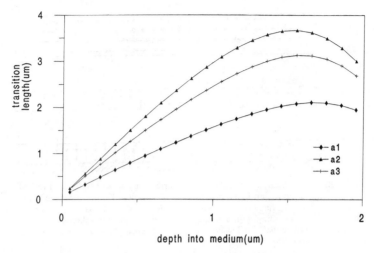

FIGURE 2.46   Transition width parameters a_1, a_2, and a_3 as functions of depth in a particulate medium of thickness 2μm (*Middleton et al., 1993*).

Computed values of a_{xn}, labelled a_1, are shown in Fig. 2.46 as a function of depth into the medium. Also shown are values of transition width after it has moved away from the record head, a_2, and after it moves under the reproduce head; a_3. a_2 and a_3 are easily derived by continuing the derivation started in this section in the manner of the derivations in (2.2.1).

It is to be noted that transition widths vary considerably through the depths of the media and when record fields other than $H_g = 2H_c$ and wide gaps are used so do transition locations and M_{on} (Dinnis, 1993). This approach therefore provides a means of investigating recorded distributions in other than thin media and has been applied to thick media (Dinnis et al., 1993; Dinnis 1993; Wei et al., 1994), multilayers (Dinnis et al., 1993) and metal evaporated tapes which have easy directions pointing out of the media planes (Stupp et al., 1993).

2.2.4   Self-Consistent Modeling

It has been realized for some time that there exist not only longitudinal components of magnetization in longitudinal recording but also perpendicular components (Wallace, 1951; Westmijze, 1953). Evidence for this became available as a result of large-scale physical modeling of the record and replay processes (Tjaden and Leyten, 1964), and more recently as a result of numerical modeling (Potter and Beardsley, 1980). A typical magnetization distribution arising from the latter work is shown in Fig. 2.47*a* and is a result of considering the vector nature of the record process. The modeling employs a vector hysteresis model of recording media (Ortenburger and Potter, 1979) based on an assembly of noninteracting fine particles having their easy axes distributed in three dimensions. The passage of the media through time-varying head fields is considered, along with fully self-consistent, point-by-point determination of the magnetization distribution. These involve calculations of the demagnetizing field for each magnetization distribution, along with procedures to ensure that, in each case, the magnetization and total field

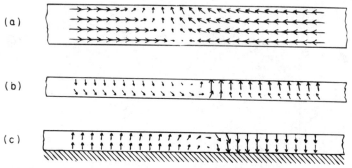

FIGURE 2.47 Predicted magnetization distributions in (*a*) longitudinal recording by a ring head of gap 1 μm on a medium of thickness 1 μm, (*b*) perpendicular recording by a ring head of gap 1 μm on a medium of thickness 0.5 μm, and (*c*) perpendicular recording with a single-pole head on a medium thickness 0.5 μm and with a soft magnetic underlayer (*Potter and Beardsley, 1980*).

within the medium conform to its hysteresis loop. Predictions have been produced not only for longitudinal recording but also for perpendicular recording with ring heads (Fig. 2.47*b*) and single-pole heads (Fig. 2.47*c*). While these calculations have exposed the complexity of the true situations, and the limitations of the simple models described earlier, they have not thrown doubt on the basic qualitative predictions of the role of media and head properties. Further, there will remain considerable problems with numerical modeling in that particle-particle interactions in the recording media are not yet fully taken into account (Ortenburger and Potter, 1979; Potter and Beardsley, 1980) and the modeling process is often sensitive to details of the loop models (Beardsley, 1982*a*). Nevertheless the numerical computations have provided what are probably the best attempts so far at modeling the recording process.

The complexity of these calculations can be somewhat reduced by neglecting the effects of demagnetizing fields during the record process. The much simplified modeling procedures provide useful insights into the nature of magnetic recording (Bertram, 1984*a*, 1984*b*) and are justified by experiments which revealed demagnetization-free recording in situations where head-to-tape spacing is small (Bertram and Niedermeyer, 1982).

In numerical modeling of perpendicularly oriented cobalt-chromium films (Beardsley, 1982*b*), it was found necessary to restrict the calculations to only uniform magnetization through the media thickness in order to obtain agreement between the calculations and experimental results. This may indicate a strong role for exchange interactions in metallic media which needs further investigation. This assumption of uniformity has led to the development of simpler analytical modeling procedures as will now be described.

Consider a medium initially magnetized to saturation in the negative sense by a large field applied in a direction normal to its plane. After the removal of the field, the medium is left with a magnetization of $-H_c$, as already described. The process by which magnetization is recorded into such a medium by the application of perpendicular components of head fields can then be derived with precision subject to a number of initial simplifying assumptions (Wielinga et al., 1983; Middleton and Wright, 1984; Lopez, 1984). The general thrust of these works is contained in the following discussion.

The application of a head field having perpendicular components in the positive sense is assumed to generate only perpendicular components of magnetization, the high anisotropy of the medium discouraging longitudinal components. Provided that the applied field is not so large as to magnetize the medium beyond the vertical side of the hysteresis loop, the total field at any point in the medium must be equal to the coercivity, and therefore

$$H_c = H_y(x, y) + H_d(x, y) \tag{2.72}$$

This equation defines the magnetization distribution since $H_d(x, y)$ is calculated from it. Solution of Eq. (2.72) in closed form is possible for the particular case of uniform magnetization through the depth of the medium. This is a reasonable assumption in strongly coupled media such as metallic films and leads to (Middleton and Wright, 1984)

$$M_y(x) = H_y(x, d) - H_c \tag{2.73}$$

where the magnetization in the medium is related to the head field along its top surface. Such a result provides a simple picture of the recording process.

By use of the Karlqvist approximation, the distributions recorded by a ring head have been predicted (Wright and Middleton, 1984) and the corresponding outputs calculated. The results are shown in Fig. 2.48a and b. The shapes of these outputs are similar to those observed experimentally and show the correct dependence on record current amplitude. The basic theory has been extended with minor modifications to cope with recording on media having hysteresis loops with sides of finite slope and on double-layer media (Lopez, 1984; Wright and Middleton, 1985). However these calculations are of limited generality since they apply for field amplitudes less than those needed to saturate the media when transitions adopt more complicated forms (Beardsley, 1982b) due to demagnetization effects.

To progress with the analytical modeling of the generalized recording process, it is necessary to obtain from the detailed numerical predictions, or large-scale modeling (Tjaden and Leyten, 1964; Monson et al., 1981), some pointers as to the essential features of either the record process itself or the recorded distributions. These might allow some simplifications to the modeling procedures which may make analytical approaches tractable. One feature which is already apparent is that the recorded transitions are all shaped round the contour $H = H_c$, where H is the total applied head field (Ortenburger and Potter, 1979; Fayling, 1982). Allying this to a second point that the recorded magnetization follows the vector head-field distribution (Bertram, 1984a) allows some insights into the nature of the processes and opens up avenues of attack for analytical work.

2.2.5   Media Orientations

Generally, the recording processes are never purely longitudinal or purely perpendicular but are always a mixture of the two. This applies even when the media are well oriented, but is particularly evident in unoriented media or in media having little or no bulk anisotropy. Media have been produced from particles having multiaxial symmetries, and their hysteresis properties show that they are essentially isotropic, and have a high remanence squareness in all directions (Jeschke, 1954; Krones, 1960). Detailed experimental and theoretical work confirmed suspicions that both longitudinal and perpendicular components of magnetization play a role in determining the outputs and that the latter may be active in keeping outputs high at short wavelengths (Lemke, 1979, 1982).

The process of recording on media of differing orientations has been investi-

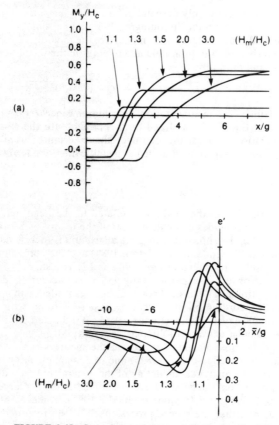

FIGURE 2.48 Strongly coupled perpendicular media. (*a*) Magnetization distributions predicted to occur as a result of recording with a ring head. (*b*) Corresponding reproduced waveforms induced in a ring head. H_m is the peak perpendicular field experienced by the medium (*Wright and Middleton, 1984*).

gated using self-consistent iterative modeling techniques (Beardsley, 1982*a*). In these computations a model was developed for a system of particles of differing anisotropies constrained to different orientations. Some of the results are shown in Fig. 2.49, where output voltage is related to packing density for particles which are (1) longitudinally oriented, (2) perpendicularly oriented, and (3) isotropically oriented. The longitudinally oriented medium gives the highest output at long wavelengths; then the output falls off steadily at shorter wavelengths. The perpendicularly oriented medium starts off at long wavelengths with a low output, but the output at short wavelengths is somewhat higher than for the longitudinal medium. The output from the isotropic medium is low at long and intermediate wavelengths, and at short wavelengths its output is intermediate between the outputs for longitudinal and perpendicular recording, as might be expected from intuitive reasoning. In the short-wavelength region, the difference between the three types of media does not appear to be large.

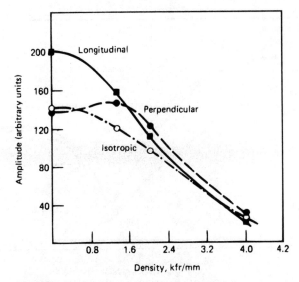

FIGURE 2.49 Predicted outputs for longitudinal, isotropic, and perpendicular particulate recording media (*after Beardsley, 1982a*).

2.2.6 Performance of Various Media and Modes of Recording

The preceding sections have discussed recording processes and how these are influenced by the magnetic properties of media and the properties of recording heads. Various features of recording processes have been identified, and these have been studied both qualitatively and quantitatively.

In longitudinal recording it has been shown that it is necessary to keep the ratio M_r/H_c of the recording media as low as possible, and to keep the media thin if transition widths are to be narrow and linear densities high. Head-to-tape spacings must also be kept small and, in regard to perpendicular recording, small spacing is the overriding requirement. A comparison of the potential of any media or mode of recording requires that all the variables be defined and the conditions under which the measurements taken or predictions made be specified. However, useful and realistic comparison is obtained by examining the best available experimental data rather than dealing in predictions, however good the theory.

Data have been assembled of the output performance obtained experimentally on various media in laboratories. These results (Mallinson and Bertram, 1984a; Mallinson, 1985), which include only calibrated data, show that there is little difference in attainable output levels for longitudinal recording and for perpendicular recording on metallic media having coercivities in the range 64 to 72 kA/m (800 to 900 Oe). This basic result has been repeated (Stubbs et al., 1985), and the results are shown in Fig. 2.50. Four types of media were investigated with the same short-gap ring head, and there was virtually no difference between recording on a longitudinal Co-Ni medium and recording on Co-Cr with or without a soft magnetic underlayer. Figure 2.50 also shows that signal levels hold up well to extremely high densities and that a considerable potential for achieving high densities exists with all media.

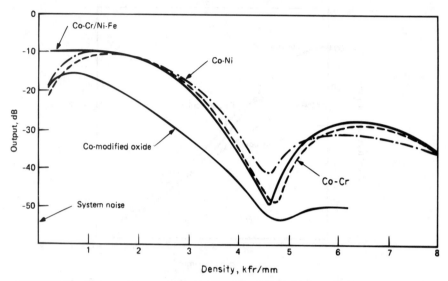

FIGURE 2.50 Output voltages as a function of packing density for recording longitudinally on Co-Ni-plated media and perpendicularly on single- and double-layer Co-Cr media. The output for a cobalt-modified oxide is also shown (*Stubbs et al., 1985*).

2.3 LINEAR RECORDING

So far this chapter has dealt with digital recording wherein the requirement is to be able to detect either of two stable states of magnetization in a recording medium, or the difference between these states. There is no requirement for a linear relationship between the level of magnetization in the recording medium and the recording signal. Linear recording brings with it a need for a linear recording process, and this itself creates a need for recording media which show a linear relationship between their magnetizations and the applied field. The latter conditions are created by the use of what is termed *biased recording,* in which an additional field, termed a *bias field,* is present along with the field intended for the recording of the signal. This section deals with the influence of the bias field on the magnetization and recording processes.

Recording with ac bias is well known as the basic process used in analog audio recording systems, and it also has a range of uses in instrumentation recording. Useful reviews of the physics of ac-bias recording exist in the literature (e.g., Westmijze, 1953; Mee, 1964).

This section proceeds with a discussion of the basic hysteretic and anhysteretic properties of magnetic recording media. This is followed by a consideration of the behavior of interacting fine-particle arrays partly as a means of explaining the earlier hysteresis properties and partly as a lead-in to the study of the recording process. However, the understanding of particle interactions is still limited. Finally the process of ac-bias recording is discussed in detail.

2.3.1 Hysteresis Properties of Recording Media

It is appropriate to begin with a discussion of the magnetic hysteresis properties of media as they are observed experimentally. This will provide a factual basis before discussion of the less certain area of interpreting these properties in terms of the behavior of individual particles and the nature of particle arrays. This discussion will center on the remanent magnetization curves which contrast with the hysteresis curves previously referenced. In hysteresis curves, it is usual to plot the instantaneous magnetization developed in the presence of an applied field as a function of that field, whereas the remanence curves show the magnetization remaining after removal of the field as a function of that field. There must be a strong connection between the two sets of curves, and indeed it is possible to trace out the remanence curves once a family of hysteresis curves is available.

Consider the application of a unidirectional magnetic field to a sample of medium which had previously been subject to an alternating field of decreasing amplitude so as to leave it in the demagnetized state. The variation of remanent magnetization with applied field is shown in Fig. 2.51. Also shown is the variation of magnetization with field when the specimen had previously been subject to a saturating field in the reverse direction. The curves are modified when an ac-bias field is present in addition to the unidirectional fields (Daniel and Levine, 1960a). The influence of the bias field is greatest when its amplitude is appropriately chosen to diminish the hysteretic processes present in unbiased magnetization and to produce what are termed *anhysteretic magnetization processes*. Figure 2.52 was obtained as a result of the application to a previously demagnetized sample of an alternating field, whose amplitude was reduced to zero prior to the reduction of the unidirectional field ("ideal" anhysteresis). It shows the variation of remanent magnetization

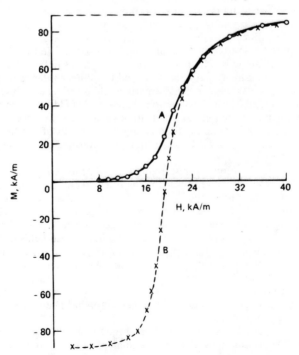

FIGURE 2.51 Remanent magnetization as a function of field strength for (curve *A*) an ac-demagnetized and (curve *B*) a negatively saturated γ-Fe$_2$O$_3$ medium (*Daniel and Levine, 1960a*).

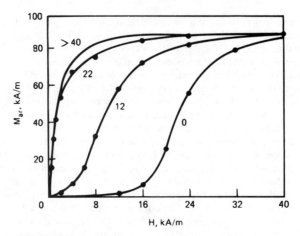

FIGURE 2.52 Anhysteretic remanent magnetization as a function of dc-field strength for different values of alternating-field amplitude in kA/m (*Daniel and Levine, 1960a*).

with unidirectional field amplitude, with the peak ac-field amplitude as a parameter. Providing that the latter is reduced sufficiently slowly, so that the medium experiences a sufficient number of cycles, the curves are fully reproducible. The curve for zero alternating-field amplitude is identical to that already considered in Fig. 2.51, but the influence of the additional ac fields is drastic. Most notable is the fact that, when the magnitude of the bias field approaches that of the remanence coercivity, this field alone is sufficient to cause the particles in the medium to switch and so little extra unidirectional field is needed to influence the remanent state of magnetization of the particles as the alternating field is reduced. Consequently, the magnetization is a rapidly varying function of applied dc field and is, in fact, a linear function of field up to quite high magnetization values. On the lower parts of these curves the susceptibility of the medium is high. As a result of the linearizing process, the curves cease to show hysteresis and so are termed *anhysteretic magnetization curves.*

In the recording situation the linearizing effect of the ac bias, as illustrated by these graphs, is a necessary requirement for linear recording. The experimental procedure adopted does not quite correspond to practical ac-bias recording as will now be described. It is true that when an element of a recording medium passes under a recording head it experiences the combined influence of unidirectional and ac fields, but as it passes away from the recording head, both fields decrease at the same time and at the same rate. Consequently, different curves are required, and these have been plotted under the new conditions of simultaneously reducing fields (Daniel and Levine, 1960a). The results are given in Fig. 2.53 and show how the curves steepen to reach a maximum slope as the ac field is increased and thereafter suffer a decreasing slope. This mode of magnetization has been termed "modified" anhysteretic magnetization.

The initial susceptibilities for the ideal and modified anhysteretic processes are shown in Fig. 2.54 as functions of ac-bias-field amplitude. In the ideal anhysteretic process the susceptibility approaches asymptotically a maximum value, whereas in the modified process there is a maximum value at a finite value of bias field. The

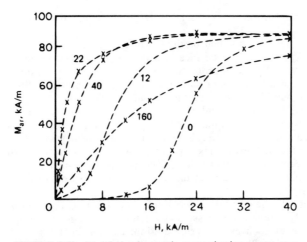

FIGURE 2.53 Modified anhysteretic magnetization curves as a function of dc-field strength for different values of alternating-field amplitude in kA/m (*Daniel and Levine, 1960a*).

occurrence of this maximum implies that optimum conditions must exist during the recording process.

2.3.2 Fine-Particle Assemblies

Particulate recording media consist of assemblies of fine particles of magnetic material which are subject to interactions, and the problems of understanding and modeling the behavior of particulate media are substantial. These interactions, however, are very important in recording and strongly influence the

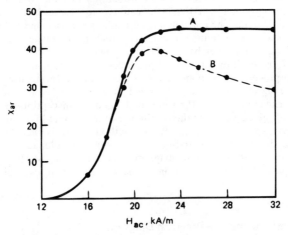

FIGURE 2.54 Initial susceptibilities for (curve *A*) ideal anhysteretic magnetization and (curve *B*) modified anhysteretic magnetization (*Daniel and Levine, 1960a*).

resulting magnetization achieved in anhysteretic magnetization and in ac-bias recording.

The properties of individual particles when observed in isolation are complex and do not fit easily alongside idealized modes of reversal (Knowles, 1981). In addition, individual particle properties differ considerably from one another, and the properties of assemblies of particles vary considerably from the properties of the individual particles making up the assemblies. These differences arise because of interparticle interactions and also because of variations in particle properties, orientations, and spatial positioning within the recording media. Overall, this represents a difficult, many-bodied problem in solid-state physics, and the attempts that have been made at solving this type of problem are necessarily simplified and somewhat approximate. Nevertheless, some progress has been made using various avenues of approach, and a brief discussion of some aspects of these approaches will now be given.

Beginning with the properties of individual particles, there is considerable background of study of reversal processes in particles having regular geometries. Possible reversal processes such as coherent rotation, curling, buckling, and fanning are discussed in detail in Chap. 3. Simple models of the hysteresis properties of particle assemblies in the form of recording media have been developed by summing the individual loops of particles of varying orientations and switching fields (Ortenburger and Potter, 1979). However, such approaches neglect the effects of interparticle interactions, which are known to be important, and further improvements in modeling are needed in this respect. The use of computers for determining the effects of interactions in particle arrays is now commonplace (e.g., Chantrell et al., 1984).

With regard to anhysteresis, progress has been made on the modeling in the sense that interactions have been taken into account, albeit in rather simplified arrangements. Generally, modeling has involved the use of Monte Carlo methods to treat systems of interacting fine particles which are disposed on lattices of particular shapes (Bertram, 1971; Chantrell et al., 1984). The particles are assumed to be ellipsoids of revolution arranged in chains with their long axes parallel to one another and pointing along the direction of the applied fields. Each particle is given a switching field according to a Gaussian probability distribution, and placed randomly within the lattice. The lattice is then subject to a large, but decaying, ac field in addition to a dc field. The particle magnetizations are assumed to "freeze" when the total local static fields reduce in value to equal the switching field of the particles. The local fields are given by $H_t = H_{dc} + H_{int}$, where H_{dc} is the externally applied dc field and H_{int} is the interaction field produced by magnetically frozen particles. This modeling process leads to anhysteresis curves of the form shown in Fig. 2.55. Two curves are shown: one for equally sized particles and one for a distribution of particle sizes. The curves are of the right shape, and the susceptibilities, as provided by the slopes of the curves near the origin, are of a reasonable order of magnitude compared with experimental data. While methods such as the above provide a means of modeling particle assemblies, they are not developed to a point where they can be applied with ease to the magnetic recording process. The problems arise with the complexity of the interaction fields, which demand excessive computing capacities.

2.3.3   Interactions and the Preisach Diagram

A means of graphic representation of the role of interaction fields is available in the form of the Preisach diagram, which has proved particularly useful (Preisach,

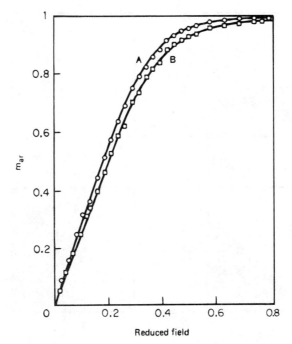

FIGURE 2.55 Predicted anhysteretic magnetization curves: (curve *A*) particles with identical volume, and (curve *B*) particles with a volume distribution (*Chantrell et al., 1984*).

1935). Although this oversimplifies the system, it has provided an insight into the behavior of particle assemblies and its use will now be described.

As a lead-in to this topic, consider two particles subject to interaction fields which are positive and negative, respectively, along their easy axes and which possess rectangular hysteresis loops. Figure 2.56*b* and *c* shows how the hysteresis loops are shifted according to the sense of the interactions. Obviously the particles are now much more easily switched by externally applied fields of interaction-field polarity, and so the interactions can be expected to influence measurable parameters.

In particle assemblies, the interaction field experienced by any one particle arises from the effects of all the other particles, and so is a complicated function of particle properties and geometries. The interaction field may be in any direction,

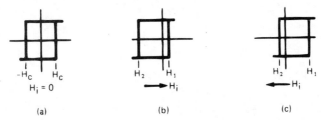

FIGURE 2.56 Effect of (*a*) zero, (*b*) positive, and (*c*) negative interaction fields on the hysteresis loops of single-domain particles.

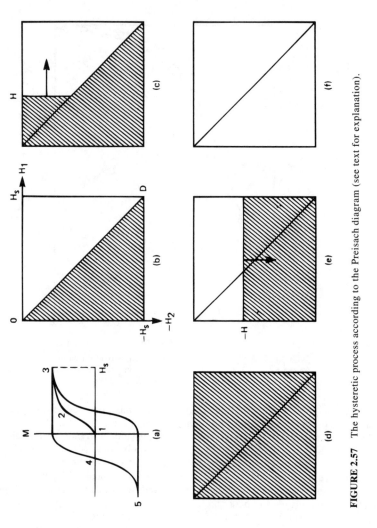

FIGURE 2.57   The hysteretic process according to the Preisach diagram (see text for explanation).

and this may alter the mode of magnetization reversal in the particle and therefore its intrinsic switching field. If it is possible to ignore the effects of the vector nature of the interactions, and just consider interaction and switching fields in one dimension, then it is possible to display the effects of the interaction fields in a graphical manner on what is known as the Preisach diagram. In one form of the diagram shown in Fig. 2.57, positive switching fields H_1 are plotted on the horizontal axis while negative switching fields H_2 are plotted on the vertical axis (Néel, 1955; Daniel and Levine, 1960a; Bate, 1962). Thus any particle occupies one point on the diagram and all the particles of an assembly appear on the diagram. The behavior of the assembly corresponding to a wide range of field histories and suitable examples can be portrayed as described below. An alternative form of this diagram plots H_i against H_c (Schwantke, 1958; Woodward and Della Torre, 1960). The two diagrams contain the same basic information, but are rotated through 45° with respect to one another.

Now consider the application of the Preisach diagram to explain the hysteresis process. Positively magnetized particles are indicated on the diagram by shaded areas; unshaded areas are occupied by negatively magnetized particles. The diagrams are shown bounded by $|H_1| = |H_2| = H_s$, where H_s is the maximum switching field (the field required to saturate the assembly). Figure 2.57b shows particles on the Preisach diagram which have been subject to demagnetization by an ac field of reducing amplitude. This has ensured that those particles experiencing positive interaction fields are left in a positive state of magnetization whereas those experiencing a negative interaction field are left in a negative state of magnetization. Thus, provided the distribution of points about the diagonal OD axis is symmetrical, the material has zero net magnetization. The application of a positive field H means that all particles which satisfy the condition $H \geq H_1$ will be switched to the positive sense of magnetization. This process is shown on the Preisach diagram indicated in Fig. 2.57c. All particles to the left of the vertical line $H_1 = H$ are switched to the positive sense of magnetization while those to the right remain magnetized in the negative sense. The total magnetization of the sample depends on the density distribution of the particles on the diagram but at this stage represents the magnetization 2 shown in Fig. 2.57a. Increasing the field moves the switching boundary to the right, as indicated by the arrow, causing more of the medium to be switched until the sample is saturated in the positive sense, Fig. 2.57d, and this state is represented by region 3 on the hysteresis loop. When the applied field is reduced from the value needed for saturation switching, the magnetization is determined by the horizontal line shown in Fig. 2.57e as it sweeps from top to bottom. Figure 2.57f shows the situation corresponding to negative saturation.

The ideal anhysteretic processes can be displayed in a similar way. Figure 2.58a shows the result of the application of successive fields of positive and negative polarity of decreasing amplitude, starting with a large positive field. In the presence of a constant dc field H_{dc}, the application of successive fields of positive and negative polarity of decreasing amplitude eventually results in the picture shown in Fig. 2.58b. When the steps in the reduction of the field become infinitesimal, the diagram becomes that shown in Fig. 2.58c for which the corresponding magnetization can be obtained if the density distribution of particles is known. In the modified anhysteresis, the diagrams are shown in Fig. 2.59a and b for finite and infinitesimal field decrements.

In all these cases the processes of magnetization can be portrayed and therein lies the value of the Preisach diagram. To enable determination of the magnetization at any stage of any of the processes depicted, it is necessary to have a knowledge of the density distribution of magnetizations of the particles. Sample distribu-

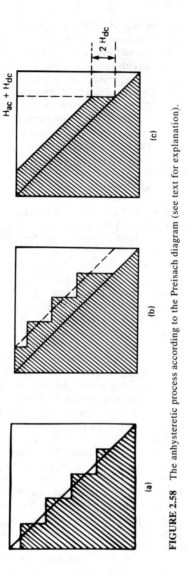

FIGURE 2.58   The anhysteretic process according to the Preisach diagram (see text for explanation).

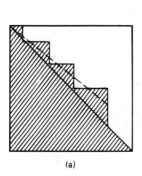
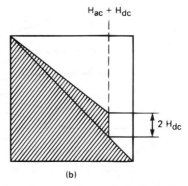

FIGURE 2.59 The modified anhysteretic process according to the Preisach diagram (see text for explanation).

tions have been measured (Biorci and Pescetti, 1958; Daniel and Levine, 1960b; Woodward and Della Torre, 1960, 1961; Bate, 1962), and when they conform to simple mathematical forms, the magnetizations can be calculated analytically. Despite such apparent simplicity of use, the diagram may be open to question regarding its stability during the process of magnetization change. For example, the process of reversal of magnetization in one or more particles will cause the interactions experienced by all the other particles in the assembly to change. This would imply that the Preisach diagram should change, although experiments seem to indicate a surprisingly large measure of stability of the diagram (Bate, 1962).

More formal attempts have been made to quantify the effects of interactions, although the cases studied so far fall considerably short of modeling realistic recording media. For example, the hysteresis loops of interacting pairs of particles have been studied in some detail in the case where the interaction fields are in either the positive or negative senses of the particle axes (Néel, 1958). Less restrictive computations have been given involving arbitrary positioning of particles (Bertram and Mallinson, 1969, 1970) and larger arrays of particles (Moskovitz and Della Torre, 1967; Soohoo and Ramachandran, 1974). In the latter work, the spatial positioning of particles was shown to be particularly important in an attempt to characterize the behavior of particle arrays. In view of the haphazard arrangement of particles in a recording medium, it must be conceded that the works mentioned above provide but a starting point for a more accurate modeling of the recording process.

2.3.4 Linear Recording Theory

The anhysteretic process has been shown to provide linear magnetization curves and so is employed in analog recording, where fidelity of transfer is an essential requirement. In biased recording systems, it is necessary to adjust the amplitude of both bias and signal fields to achieve the required linearity. From the considerations given earlier, it is clear that bias fields must be large and that, to avoid distortions, signal fields must be kept small and on a restricted part of the magnetization curve. When the medium has a rectangular hysteresis loop, the effect of the bias is to alternate the sense of the magnetization of the particles as long as its magnitude is above the coercivity, but when its magnitude falls below the coercivity, the particle

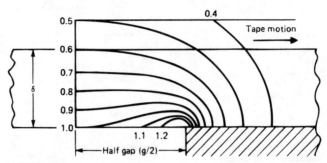

FIGURE 2.60   Total field contours near the gap of a record head (*Bertram, 1975*).

magnetizations become frozen into certain directions. The resulting medium magnetization is proportional to the signal-field amplitude, assuming that the signal is of much lower frequency than the bias. This simple description can be envisaged as a basis for the explanation of the linear recording process (Westmijze, 1953; Daniel and Levine, 1960*b*; Tjaden and Leyten, 1964; Bertram, 1974, 1975).

Consider Fig. 2.60, which shows the contours of constant total field amplitude around a record-head gap. These have been calculated using the Karlqvist approximations and are shown to penetrate a medium moving from left-to-right past the head and in contact with it. If it is supposed that the contour labeled 0.6 is where the total field equals the coercivity, this element of tape will have its magnetization continuously reversed as long as it remains inside the contour, but frozen as it passes outside the contour. Once the magnetization is frozen, it will have a value determined by the susceptibility χ_{ar} associated with the anhysteresis curve corresponding to

$$M_x(x) = \chi_{ar} H_x(x) \tag{2.74}$$

It is assumed that the resultant field is effective in the biasing process, but that only the x component of signal field contributes to the output since the susceptibility is large in this, the orientation, direction but is low in a direction normal to it. To investigate the variation of magnetization with depth into the tape, it can be shown that H_x varies almost linearly with y along the coercivity contour and so takes the form

$$H_x(x) = \frac{y}{\delta} H_x(\delta) \tag{2.75}$$

and this result, in combination with Eq. (2.74), leads to a flux in the reproduce head of

$$\phi_0 = \mu_0 w \chi_{ar} \delta H_x(\delta) \frac{1 - e^{-k\delta}(1 + k\delta)}{(k\delta)^2} \tag{2.76}$$

where $k = 2\pi/\lambda$ is the wave number. The variation of this flux with reduced wave number $k\delta$ is shown in Fig. 2.61. For the purpose of comparison, the results obtained by considering only x components of bias field, which lead to x components of magnetization having constant amplitude through the depth of the tape, are also shown. The experimental results follow very closely the predictions obtained using vector fields, and diverge considerably from those using longitudinal fields. Thus

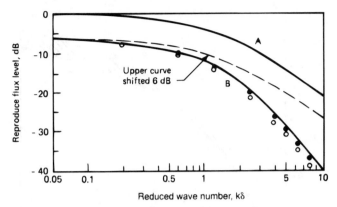

FIGURE 2.61 Reproduced flux as a function of a reduced wave number for biased sine-wave recording: (curve *A*) considering only the longitudinal component of bias field; (curve *B*) considering the resultant bias field (*Bertram, 1975*).

the need for vector modeling is confirmed for linear as well as nonlinear recording processes.

Following on from Eq. (2.76), it is to be anticipated that the output-signal amplitude should be proportional to record-signal amplitude, and this is known to be true when recording is at low levels. Attempts to record large signals on tapes lead, however, to distortions in the output waveform, and so output levels need to be specified along with a measure of nonlinear distortion. The cause of distortion can be appreciated by referring to observations which show that a wide range of magnetic media satisfies a universal anhysteretic magnetization curve, provided the parameters of the curve are properly specified (Köster, 1975). Figure 2.62 shows the reduced anhysteretic magnetization $m_{ar} = M_{ar}/M_r$ as a function of reduced field $h = H/H_{0.5}$, where $H_{0.5}$ is the field required to make $m_{ar} = 0.5$. The experimental points all fall within the shaded area and can be fitted closely by a single empirical curve. The initial part of the curve is linear, with a normalized susceptibility $m_{ar}/h = 0.57$. An empirical expression evaluated for sinusoidal inputs leads to a predicted linearity, equivalent to less than 3 percent third harmonic distortion, being maintained up to $m = 0.5$, or 50 percent of saturation. Such predictions are confirmed by experiment (Köster, 1975). The initial susceptibility, defined by $x_{ar} = dM_{ar}/dH$, can be shown from Eq. (2.74) to be proportional to M_r. Substitution of this into Eq. (2.76) yields an output voltage, for a specified level of distortion, proportional to $M_r\delta$. This relationship has also been confirmed experimentally (Köster, 1975; van Winsum, 1984).

Regarding the optimization of bias to produce maximum signal amplitude, consider first the dependence of depth of recording into the medium and its relation to head field. In the theory outlined above, the bias field should be large enough to allow the coercivity contour of the head field to penetrate through to the back layer of the medium (Bertram, 1975). When the bias field is larger or smaller, it can be shown to produce lower outputs. Second, the influence of bias field on the initial susceptibility of the modified anhysteretic curves is to cause it to have a maximum at a particular value of bias field near to the coercivity. Thus, on both counts, a direct and linear relationship between optimum bias level and coercivity could be

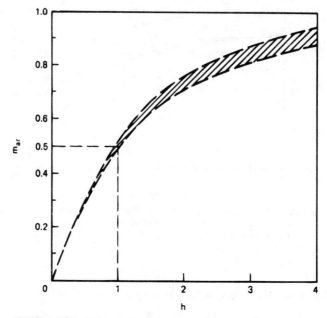

FIGURE 2.62 Universal anhysteretic magnetization curve derived from experimental results on a range of tapes. The shaded area accommodates all the experimental data from a wide variety of media (*after Köster, 1975*).

anticipated. Such a relationship has been both predicted and observed (Fujiwara, 1979; van Winsum, 1984).

APPENDIX I THE REPRODUCING PROCESS: RECIPROCITY

Consider two coils (1, 2) linked by a mutual inductance L_m. A current i_1 in coil 1 will cause a flux ϕ_2 to thread coil 2 given by

$$\phi_2 = L_m i_1 \tag{2.77a}$$

In a similar way, the flux ϕ_1 threading coil 1 as a result of a current i_2 in coil 2 is given by

$$\phi_1 = L_m i_2 \tag{2.77b}$$

The reciprocal relationships portrayed by the above equations are an example of the principle of reciprocity and are used here as a starting point for the derivation of expressions for the output voltages generated in the coils of reproduce heads.

In the above equations, the mutual inductance is a common factor, and so

$$\frac{\phi_1}{i_2} = \frac{\phi_2}{i_1} \tag{2.78}$$

Now take coil 1 to represent the coil of the reproduce head and coil 2 to carry a solenoidal current representing a magnetized element of the recording medium. Then, considering only x components of the head field $H_x(x, y)$, the flux ϕ_2 is given by

$$\phi_2 = \mu_0 H_x(x, y) \, dy \, dz \qquad (2.79)$$

where $dy \, dz$ is the area enclosed by coil 2. The current i_2 represents the x component of the magnetization, at point x' in the medium, via

$$i_2 = M_x(x')dx' \qquad (2.80a)$$

$$i_2 = M_x(x - \bar{x})dx \qquad (2.80b)$$

Use of this and Eq. (2.79) in Eq. (2.78) and manipulation of the resulting equation gives the flux in the reproduce-head coil as

$$\phi_1 = \mu_0 M_x(x - \bar{x}) \frac{H_x(x, y)}{i_1} \, dx \, dy \, dz \qquad (2.81)$$

Integration over the total volume of the recording medium leads to the total flux in the head coil

$$\phi_1 = \mu_0 \int_{-\infty}^{+\infty} \int_d^{d+\delta} \int_{-\infty}^{+\infty} M_x(x - \bar{x}) \frac{H_x(x, y)}{i_1} \, dx \, dy \, dz \qquad (2.82)$$

Noting that the reproduced voltage e_x is related to the flux by

$$e_x = -\frac{d\phi}{dt} \qquad (2.83)$$

leads to an output voltage of

$$e_x(\bar{x}) = -\mu_0 V \int_{-\infty}^{+\infty} \int_d^{d+\delta} \int_{-\infty}^{+\infty} \frac{dM_x(x - \bar{x})}{d\bar{x}} \frac{H_x(x, y)}{i_1} \, dx \, dy \, dz \qquad (2.84)$$

where the quantity $H_x(x, y)/i_1$ is the head field per unit current in the head winding should it be energized.

In a similar way, the output voltage arising from y components of magnetization in the medium is

$$e_y(\bar{x}) = -\mu_0 V \int_{-\infty}^{+\infty} \int_d^{d+\delta} \int_{-\infty}^{+\infty} \frac{dM_y(x - \bar{x})}{d\bar{x}} \frac{H_y(x, y)}{i_1} \, dx \, dy \, dz \qquad (2.85)$$

APPENDIX II   STANDARD INTEGRALS

The following are standard integrals needed to complete certain integrations in the main text:

$$\int_{-\infty}^{+\infty} \frac{1}{c^2 + (\bar{x} - x)^2} \left(\arctan \frac{a + x}{y} + \arctan \frac{a - x}{y} \right) dx$$

$$= \frac{\pi}{c}\left(\arctan \frac{a + \bar{x}}{c + y} + \arctan \frac{a - \bar{x}}{c + y}\right) \tag{2.86}$$

$$\int_{-\infty}^{+\infty} \frac{b^2}{x^2 + b^2} \ln[(x - a)^2 + c^2]\, dx = \pi b \ln[a^2 + (b + c)^2] \tag{2.87}$$

$$\int_{-\infty}^{+\infty} \arctan \frac{x}{y} \frac{1}{c^2 + (b - x)^2}\, dx = \frac{\pi}{c} \arctan \frac{b}{c + y} \tag{2.88}$$

APPENDIX III   DEMAGNETIZING FIELDS

In a magnetic material, there is no divergence of the induction B. The latter can be expressed as

$$\mathbf{B} = \mu_0(\mathbf{H} + \mathbf{M}) \tag{2.89}$$

while the condition of zero divergence is signified by

$$\nabla \cdot \mathbf{B} = 0 \tag{2.90}$$

Combining these two equations gives

$$\nabla \cdot \mathbf{H} = -\nabla \cdot \mathbf{M} \tag{2.91}$$

In magnetic field problems it is usual to express the field in terms of the gradient of a potential ϕ; i.e.,

$$\mathbf{H} = -\nabla \phi \tag{2.92}$$

so that introduction of it into Eq. (2.91) produces a version of Poisson's equation, namely,

$$\nabla^2 \phi = \nabla \cdot \mathbf{M} \tag{2.93}$$

wherein the quantity $-\nabla \cdot \mathbf{M}$ takes on the significance of a magnetic charge density. Solution of Poisson's equation takes the form

$$\phi(r) = -\frac{1}{4\pi}\int_{V'} \frac{\nabla \cdot \mathbf{M}}{|r - r'|}\, dV' - \frac{1}{4\pi}\int_{A'} \frac{\sigma_m(r')}{|r - r'|}\, dA' \tag{2.94}$$

where the first term is the potential arising from the volume charges within the magnetic material, with the integration taking place over all these charges, while the second term is the potential arising from surface charges $\sigma_m(r')$, with the integration taking place over all the relevant surfaces of the material. The surface charge density can be obtained from

$$\sigma_m(r') = \mathbf{M} \cdot \mathbf{n} \tag{2.95}$$

where $\mathbf{n}$ is the outward normal to the surface.
    Following from Eq. (2.94) the demagnetizing field is

$$H_d(r) = -\frac{1}{4\pi}\int_{V'} \frac{\nabla \cdot \mathbf{M}}{|r - r'|^2}\, dV' + \frac{1}{4\pi}\int_{A'} \frac{\sigma_m(r')}{|r - r'|^2}\, dA' \tag{2.96}$$

Use of the above equation in any generalized way is extremely difficult. However, certain particular cases of interest in this work are now discussed.

First, consider a magnetization which has only x components varying with the x dimension and giving rise to no surface charges. Then

$$\nabla \cdot \mathbf{M} = \frac{dM_x}{dx} \tag{2.97}$$

Use of this in Eq. (2.96) would give rise to a field having, in general, x, y, and z components. Considering only the x components yields

$$H_{dx}(x, y, z) = - \frac{1}{4\pi} \iiint \frac{dM_x}{dx'} \frac{(x - x') \, dx' \, dy' dz'}{|(x - x')^2 + (y - y')^2 + (z - z')^2|^{3/2}} \tag{2.98}$$

and when the transverse dimension is so large that the integration over z' may take place from $-\infty$ to $+\infty$, Eq. (2.98) becomes

$$H_{dx}(x, y) = - \frac{1}{2\pi} \iint \frac{dM_x}{dx} \frac{(x - x') \, dx' \, dy'}{(x - x')^2 + (y - y')^2} \tag{2.99}$$

The second case occurs when there are no volume charges and only y components of magnetization. Then $dM_y/dy = 0$, but there are surface charges of magnitude M_y. The y component of magnetic field is then, using Eq. (2.96),

$$H_{dy}(x, y, z) = \frac{1}{4\pi} \iint M_y \frac{(y - y') \, dx' \, dz'}{|(x - x')^2 + (y - y')^2 + (z - z')^2|^{3/2}} \tag{2.100}$$

Again, when the z dimension is infinite, this becomes

$$H_{dy}(x, y) = \frac{1}{2\pi} \int M_y \frac{(y - y') \, dx'}{(x - x')^2 + (y - y')^2} \tag{2.101}$$

REFERENCES

Armstrong, A. J., H. N. Bertram, R. D. Barndt, and J. K. Wolf, "Nonlinear Effects in High-Density Tape Recording," *IEEE Trans. Magn.* **MAG-27,** 4366, (1991).

Arnoldussen, T. C., and H. C. Tong, "Zigzag Transition Profiles, Noise and Correlation Statistics in Highly Oriented Longitudinal Thin Film Media," *IEEE Trans. Magn.* **MAG-22,** 889 (1986).

Baird, A. W., "An Evaluation and Approximation of the Fan Equations Describing Magnetic Fields Near Recording Heads," *IEEE Trans. Magn.,* **MAG-16,** 1350 (1980).

Barany, A. M., and H. N. Bertram, "Transition Position and Amplitude Fluctuation Model for Longitudinal Thin Film Media," *IEEE Trans. Magn.* **MAG-23,** 2374 (1987).

Bate, G., "Statistical Stability of the Preisach Diagram for Particles of Gamma-Ferric-Oxide," *J. Appl. Phys.,* **33,** 263 (1962).

Bauer, B. B., and C. D. Mee, "A New Model for Magnetic Recording," *IRE Trans. Audio,* **AU-9,** 139 (1961).

Beardsley, I. A., "Effect of Particle Orientation on High Density Recording," *IEEE Trans. Magn.,* **MAG-18,** 1191 (1982*a*).

Beardsley, I. A., "Self Consistent Recording Model for Perpendicularly Oriented Media, *J. Appl. Phys.,* **53,** 2582 (1982*b*).

Bertram, H. N., "Monte Carlo Calculation of Magnetic Anhysteresis," *J. Phys.*, **32**, 684 (1971).

Bertram, H. N., "Long Wavelength AC Bias Recording Theory," *IEEE Trans. Magn.*, **MAG-10**, 1039 (1974).

Bertram, H. N., "Wavelength Response in AC Biased Recording," *IEEE Trans. Magn.*, **MAG-11**, 1176 (1975).

Bertram, H. N., "Geometric Effects in the Magnetic Recording Process," *IEEE Trans. Magn.*, **MAG-20**, 468 (1984*a*).

Bertram, H. N., "The Effect of Angular Dependence of the Particle Nucleation Field on the Magnetic Recording Process," *IEEE Trans. Magn.*, **MAG-20**, 2094 (1984*b*).

Bertram, H. N., "Theory of Magnetic Recording," Cambridge University Press (1994).

Bertram, H. N., and L. D. Fielder, "Amplitude and Bit Shift Spectra Comparisons in Thin Metallic Media," *IEEE Trans. Magn.*, **MAG-19**, 1605 (1983).

Bertram, H. N., and J. C. Mallinson, "Theoretical Coercivity Field for an Interacting Anisotropic Dipole Pair of Arbitrary Bond Angle," *J. Appl. Phys.*, **40**, 1301 (1969).

Bertram, H. N., and J. C. Mallinson, "Switching Dynamics for an Interacting Anisotropic Dipole Pair of Arbitrary Bond Angle," *J. Appl. Phys.*, **41**, 1102 (1970).

Bertram, H. N., and R. Niedermeyer, "The Effect of Spacing on Demagnetization in Magnetic Recording," *IEEE Trans. Magn.*, **MAG-18**, 1206 (1982).

Biorci, A., and D. Pescetti, "An Analytical Theory of the Behavior of Ferromagnetic Materials," *Il Nuovo Cimento*, **7**, 829 (1958).

Bonyhard, P. I., A. V. Davies, and B. K. Middleton, "A Theory of Digital Magnetic Recording on Metallic Films" *IEEE Trans. Magn.*, **MAG-2**, 1 (1966).

Bromley, D. J., "A Comparison of Vertical and Longitudinal Magnetic Recording Based on Analytical Models," *IEEE Trans. Magn.*, **MAG-19**, 2239 (1983).

Chan, S. W. C., and B. K. Middleton, "Some Characteristics of VHS Tapes Used in Digital Recording," *IEE Conf. Publ.*, **402** 54 (1994).

Chantrell, R. W., A. Lyberatos, and E. P. Wohlfarth, "Anhysteretic Properties of Interacting Magnetic Tape Particles," *J. Appl. Phys.*, **55**, 2223 (1984).

Chapman, D. W., "Theoretical Limit on Digital Magnetic Recording Density," *Proc. IEEE*, **51**, 394 (1963).

Cole, R. W., R. I. Potter, C. C. Lin, K. L. Deckert, and E. P. Valstyn, "Numerical Analysis of the Shielded Magneto-Resistive Head," *IBM J. Res. Dev.*, **18**, 551 (1974).

Daniel, E. D., and I. Levine, "Experimental and Theoretical Investigation of the Magnetic Properties of Iron Oxide Recording Tape," *J. Acoust. Soc. Am.*, **32**, 1 (1960*a*).

Daniel, E. D., and I. Levine, "Determination of the Recording Performance of a Tape from its Magnetic Properties," *J. Acoust. Soc. Am.*, **32**, 258 (1960*b*).

Davies, A. V., and B. K. Middleton, "The Resolution of Vertical Magneto-Resistive Readout Heads," *IEEE Trans. Magn.*, **MAG-11**, 1689 (1975).

Davies, A. V., B. K. Middleton, and A. C. Tickle, "Digital Recording Properties of Evaporated Cobalt Films," *IEEE Trans. Magn.*, **MAG-1**, 344 (1965).

Dinnis, A. K., "The Modelling of the Digital Recording Process on Thick Media," PhD, Thesis, University of Manchester, England (1993).

Dinnis, A. K., B. K. Middleton, and J. J. Miles, "Characteristics of Magnetic Recording Heads," Meas. Sci. Technol., **3** 362 (1992).

Dinnis, A. K., B. K. Middleton, and J. J. Miles, "Theory of Longitudinal Digital Magnetic Recording on Thick Media," J. Mag. Magn. Mat., **120**, 149 (1993).

Dressler, D. D., and J. H. Judy, "A Study of Digitally Recorded Transitions in Thin Magnetic Films," *IEEE Trans. Magn.*, **MAG-10**, 674 (1974).

Eldridge, D. F., "Magnetic Recording and Reproduction of Pulses," *IRE Trans. Audio*, **7**, 141 (1960).

Fan, G. J., "A Study of the Playback Process of a Magnetic Ring Head," *IBM J. Res. Dev.,* **5,** 321 (1961).

Fayling, R. E., "Studies of the 'Magnetization Region' of a Ring-Type Head," *IEEE Trans. Magn.,* **MAG-18,** 1212 (1982).

Fujiwara, T., "Non-Linear Distortion in Long Wavelength AC Bias Recording," *IEEE Trans. Magn.,* **MAG-15,** 894 (1979).

Gronau, M., H. Goeke, D. Schuffler, and S. Sprenger, "Correlation Between Domain Wall Properties and Material Parameters in Amorphous SmCo Films," *IEEE Trans. Magn.,* **MAG-19,** 1653 (1983).

Hoagland, A. S., *Digital Magnetic Recording,* Wiley, New York, 1963.

Hokkyo, J., K. Hayakawa, I. Saito, S. Satake, K. Shirane, N. Honda, T. Shimamura, and T. Saito, "Reproducing Characteristics of Perpendicular Magnetic Recording," *IEEE Trans. Magn.,* **MAG-18,** 1203 (1982).

Iwasaki, S., "Perpendicular Magnetic Recording," *IEEE Trans. Magn.,* **MAG-16,** 71 (1980).

Iwasaki, S., "Perpendicular Magnetic Recording—Evolution and Future," *IEEE Trans. Magn.,* **MAG-20,** 607 (1984).

Iwasaki, S., and Y. Nakamura, "An Analysis for the Magnetization Mode for High Density Magnetic Recording," *IEEE Trans. Magn.,* **MAG-13,** 1272 (1977).

Iwasaki, S., and K. K. Ouchi, "CoCr Recording Films with Perpendicular Magnetic Anisotropy," *IEEE Trans. Magn.,* **MAG-14,** 849 (1978).

Iwasaki, S., and K. Takemura, "An Analysis for the Circular Mode of Magnetization in Short-Wavelength Recording," *IEEE Trans. Magn.,* **MAG-11,** 1173 (1975).

Iwasaki, S., Y. Nakamura, and K. Ouchi, "Perpendicular Magnetic Recording with a Composite Anisotropy Film," *IEEE Trans. Magn.,* **MAG-15,** 1456 (1979).

Iwasaki, S., Y. Nakamura, and H. Muraoka, "Wavelength Response of Perpendicular Magnetic Recording," *IEEE Trans. Magn.,* **MAG-17,** 2535 (1981).

Iwasaki, S., D. E. Speliotis, and Y. Yamamoto, "Head-to-Media Spacing Losses in Perpendicular Recording," *IEEE Trans. Magn.,* **MAG-19,** 1626 (1983).

Jeschke, J. C., East German Patent 8684, 1954.

Jorgensen, F., *The Complete Handbook of Magnetic Recording,* TAB Books, Blue Ridge Summit, Penn., 1980.

Kakehi, A., M. Oshiki, T. Aikawa, M. Sasaki, and T. Kozai, "A Thin Film Head for High Density Recording," *IEEE Trans. Magn.,* **MAG-18,** 1131 (1982).

Karlqvist, O., "Calculation of the Magnetic Field in the Ferromagnetic Layer of a Magnetic Drum," *Trans. R. Inst. Technol. (Stockholm),* **86,** 3 (1954).

Knowles, J. E., "Measurements on Single Magnetic Particles," *IEEE Trans. Magn.,* **MAG-14,** 858 (1978).

Knowles, J. E., "Magnetic Properties of Individual Acicular Particles," *IEEE Trans. Magn.,* **MAG-17,** 3008 (1981).

Köster, E., "A Contribution to Anhysteretic Remanence and AC Bias Recording," *IEEE Trans. Magn.,* **MAG-11,** 1185 (1975).

Krones, F., *Technik der Magnetspeicher,* Springer, Berlin, 1960, p. 474.

Lemke, J. U., "Ultra-High Density Recording with New Heads and Tapes," *IEEE Trans. Magn.,* **MAG-15,** 1561 (1979).

Lemke, J. U., "An Isotropic Particulate Medium with Additive Hilbert and Fourier Field Components," *J. Appl. Phys.,* **53,** 2361 (1982).

Lopez, O., "Reproducing Vertically Recorded Information—Double Layer Media," *IEEE Trans. Magn.,* **MAG-19,** 1614 (1983).

Lopez, O., "Analytic Calculation of Write Induced Separation Losses," *IEEE Trans. Magn.,* **MAG-20,** 715 (1984).

Loze, M. K., B. K. Middleton, A. Ryley, and C. D. Wright, 'A Comparison of Various Methods for Characterising the Head-Medium Interface in Digital Magnetic Recording', *IEEE Trans. Magn.*, **MAG-26**, 147 (1990).

Lübeck, H., "Megnetische Schallaufzeichrung mit Filmen und Ringkopfen," *Akust. Z.*, **2**, 273 (1937).

Maller, V. A. J., and B. K. Middleton, "A Simplified Model of the Writing Process in Saturation Magnetic Recording, "*IERE Conf. Proc.*, **26**, 137 (1973).

Maller, V. A. J., and B. K. Middleton, "A Simplified Model of the Writing Process in Saturation Magnetic Recording," *Radio Electron, Eng.*, **44**, 281 (1974).

Mallinson, J. C., "A Unified View of High Density Digital Recording Theory," *IEEE Trans. Magn.*, **MAG-11**, 1166 (1975).

Mallinson, J. C., "The Next Decade in Magnetic Recording," *IEEE Trans. Magn.*, **MAG-21**, 1217 (1985).

Mallinson, J. C., and C. W. Steele, "Theory of Linear Superposition in Tape Recording," *IEEE Trans. Magn.*, **MAG-5**, 886 (1969).

Mallinson, J. C., and H. N. Bertram, "Theoretical and Experimental Comparison of the Longitudinal and Vertical Modes of Magnetic Recording," *IEEE Trans. Magn.*, **MAG-20**, 461 (1984*a*).

Mallinson, J. C., and H. N. Bertram, "On the Characteristics of Pole-Keeper Head Fields," *IEEE Trans. Magn.*, **MAG-20**, 721 (1984*b*).

Mee, C. D., *The Physics of Magnetic Recording,* North-Holland, Amsterdam, 1964.

Melbye, H. E., and C. S. Chi, "Non-linearities in High Density Digital Recording," *IEEE Trans. Magn.*, **MAG-14**, 746 (1978).

Middleton, B. K., "The Dependence of Recording Characteristics of Thin Metal Tapes on Their Magnetic Properties and on the Replay Head," *IEEE Trans. Magn.*, **MAG-2**, 225 (1966).

Middleton, B. K., "Performance of a Recording Channel," *IERE Conf. Proc.*, **54**, 137 (1982).

Middleton, B. K., and A. V. Davies, "Gap Effects in Head Field Distributions and the Replay Process in Longitudinal Recording," *IERE Conf. Proc.*, **59**, 27 (1984).

Middleton, B. K., A. K. Dinnis, and J. J. Miles, "Digital Recording Theory for Thick Media," *IEEE Trans. Magn.*, **29**, 2286 (1993).

Middleton, B. K., J. J. Miles, and R. H. Noyau, "The Digital Recording Properties of Thin Film Media Having Sawtooth Magnetisation Transitions," *IEEE Trans. Magn.*, **24**, 3099 (1988).

Middleton, B. K., and J. J. Miles, "Recorded Magnetisation Distributions in Thin Film Media," *IEEE Trans. Magn.*, **27**, 4954 (1991).

Middleton, B. K., and J. J. Miles, "Sawtooth Magnetisation Transitions and the Digital Recording Properties of Thin Film Recording Media," *IEEE Conf. Proc. No. 319*, 20 (1991).

Middleton, B. K., and T. Jack-Kee, "Performance of Digital Magnetic Recording Channels Subject to Noise and Drop-outs," *Rad, Elec. Eng.*, **53**, 393 (1983).

Middleton, B. K., C. D. Wright, S. R. Cumpson, and J. J. Miles, "Output Waveforms in the Replay Process in Digital Magnetic Recording," *IEEE Trans. Magn.*, **31** (1995).

Middleton, B. K., and C. D. Wright, "Perpendicular Recording," *IERE Conf. Proc.*, **54**, 181 (1982).

Middleton, B. K., and C. D. Wright, "The Perpendicular Recording Process," *IEEE Trans. Magn.*, **MAG-20**, 458 (1984).

Miyata, J. J., and R. R. Hartel, "The Recording and Reproduction of Signals on Magnetic Medium Using Saturation-type Recording," *IRE Trans. Elect. Comp.*, **EC-8**, 159 (1959).

Monson, J. E., R. Fung, and A. S. Hoagland, "Large Scale Model Studies of Vertical Recording," *IEEE Trans. Magn.*, **MAG-17**, 2541 (1981).

Morrison, J. R., and D. E. Speliotis, "Study of Peak Shift in Thin Recording Surfaces," *IEEE Trans. Magn.*, **MAG-3**, 208 (1967).

Moskovitz, R., and E. Della Torre, "Hysteretic Magnetic Dipole Interaction Model," *IEEE Trans. Magn.,* **MAG-3,** 579 (1967).

Muller, M. W., and E. S. Murdock, "Williams-Comstock Type Model for Sawtooth Transitions in Thin Film Media," *IEEE Trans. Magn.,* **MAG-23,** 2368 (1987).

Nakamura, Y., and S. Iwasaki, "Reproducing Characteristics of Perpendicular Magnetic Head," *IEEE Trans. Magn.,* **MAG-18,** 1167 (1982).

Néel, L., "Some Theoretical Aspects of Rock Magnetism," *Philos. Mag. Suppl. (Adv. Phys.)* **4,** 191 (1955).

Néel, L., "Sur les Éffets de Couplage entre Grains Ferromagnetique Doués Hysteresis," *C. R. Acad. Sci. (Paris),* **246,** 2313 (1958).

Ortenburger, I. B., and R. I. Potter, "A Self-Consistent Calculation of the Transition Zone in Thick Particulate Media," *J. Appl. Phys.,* **50,** 2393 (1979).

Potter, R. I., "Analysis of Saturation Magnetic Recording Based on Arctangent Magnetization Transitions," *J. Appl. Phys.,* **41,** 1647 (1970).

Potter, R. I., "Digital Magnetic Recording Theory," *IEEE Trans. Magn.,* **MAG-10,** 502 (1974).

Potter, R. I., and I. A. Beardsley, "Self-Consistent Computer Calculations for Perpendicular Magnetic Recording," *IEEE Trans. Magn.,* **MAG-16,** 967 (1980).

Potter, R. I., R. J. Schmulian, and K. Hartmann, "Fringe Field and Readback Voltage Computations for Finite Pole-Tip Length Recording Heads," *IEEE Trans. Magn.,* **MAG-7,** 689 (1971).

Preisach, F., "Magnetic After-Effect," *Z. Phys.,* **94,** 277 (1935).

Quak, D., "Influence of the Layer Thickness of a Double Layer Medium on the Reproduced Signal in Perpendicular Recording," *IEEE Trans. Magn.,* **MAG-19,** 1502 (1983).

Satake, S., K. Hayakawa, J. Hokkyo, and T. Simamura, "Field Theory of Twin Pole Head and a Computer Simulation Model for a Perpendicular Recording," *IECE Tech. Group Meeting Magn. Rec.,* **MR77-26,** 33 (1977).

Schwantke, G., "Der Aufsprechvongang beim Magnetton ver fahren in Preisach-Darstellung," *Frequenz,* **12,** 383 (1958).

Sebestyen, L. E., *Digital Magnetic Tape Recording for Computer Applications,* Chapman and Hall, London, 1973.

Soohoo, R. F., and K. Ramachandran, "Switching Dynamics of an Assembly of Interacting Anisotropic Ferromagnetic Particles," *AIP Conf. Proc.,* **18,** 1098 (1974).

Speliotis, D. E., "Digital Recording Theory," *Ann. N.Y. Acad. Sci.,* **189,** 21 (1972).

Speliotis, D. E., and J. Morrison, "A Theoretical Analysis of Saturation Magnetic Recording," *IBM J. Res. Dev.,* **10,** 233 (1966a).

Speliotis, D. E., and J. R. Morrison, "Correlation between Magnetic and Recording Properties of Thin Surfaces," *IEEE Trans. Magn.,* **MAG-2,** 208 (1966b).

Stubbs, D. P., J. W. Whisler, C. D. Moe, and J. Skorjanec, "Ring Head Recording on Perpendicular Media: Output Spectra for CoCr and CoCr/CoNi Media," *J. Appl. Phys.,* **57,** 3970 (1985).

Stupp, S. E., B. K. Middleton, V. A. Virkorsky, and J. J. Miles, "Theory of Recording on Media with Arbitrary Easy Axis Orientation," *IEEE Trans. Magn.,* **29,** 3984 (1993).

Suzuki, T., and S. Iwasaki, "Magnetization Transitions in Perpendicular Magnetic Recording," *IEEE Trans. Magn.,* **MAG-18,** 769 (1982).

Teer, K., "Investigation of the Magnetic Recording Process with Step Functions," *Philips Res. Rep.,* **16,** 469 (1961).

Tjaden, D. L. A., "Some Notes on Superposition in Digital Magnetic Recording," *IEEE Trans. Magn.,* **MAG-9,** 331 (1973).

Tjaden, D. L. A., and J. Leyten, "A 5000:1 Scale Model of the Magnetic Recording Process," *Philips Tech. Rev.,* **25,** 319 (1964).

Tjaden, D. L. A., and E. J. Tercic, "Theoretical and Experimental Investigations of Digital Magnetic Recording on Thin Media," *Philips Res. Rep.*, **30**, 120 (1975).

Valstyn, E. P., and L. F. Shew, "Performance of Single-Turn Film Heads," *IEEE Trans. Magn.*, **MAG-9**, 317 (1973).

van Winsum, J. A., "Effect of Orientation Ratio and Powder Properties on Anhysteretic Linearity of Magnetic Tape Coatings," *IEEE Trans. Magn.*, **MAG-20**, 87 (1984).

Wallace, R. L., "The Reproduction of Magnetically Recorded Signals," *Bell Syst. Tech. J.*, **30**, 1145 (1951).

Wang, H. S. C., "Gap Loss Function of Certain Critical Parameters in Magnetic Data Recording Instruments and Storage Systems," *Rev. Sci. Inst.*, **37**, 1124 (1966).

Wei, D., H. N. Bertram, and F. Jeffers, "A Simplified Model of High Density Tape Recording," *IEEE Trans. Magn.*, **30**, 2739 (1994).

Westmijze, W. K., "Studies on Magnetic Recording," *Philips Res. Rep.*, **8**, 161 (1953).

Wielinga, T., J. H. J. Fluitman, and J. C. Lodder, "Perpendicular Standstill Recording in CoCr Films," *IEEE Trans. Magn.*, **MAG-19**, 94 (1983).

Williams, M. L., and R. L. Comstock, "An Analytical Model of the Write Process in Digital Magnetic Recording," *A.I.P. Conf. Proc.*, **5**, 738 (1972).

Wilton, D. T., "Comparison of Ring and Pole Head Magnetic Fields," *IEEE Trans. Magn.*, **26**, 1229 (1990).

Wohlfarth, E. P., "A Review of the Problem of Fine Particle Interactions with Special Reference to Magnetic Recording," *J. Appl. Phys.*, **35**, 783 (1976).

Woodward, J. G., and E. Della Torre, "Particle Interaction in Magnetic Recording Tapes," *J. Appl. Phys.*, **31**, 56 (1960).

Woodward, J. G., and E. Della Torre, "Particle Interaction in Magnetic Recording Tapes," *J. Appl. Phys.*, **32**, 126 (1961).

Wright, C. D., and B. K. Middleton, "The Perpendicular Record and Replay Processes," *IERE Conf. Proc.*, **59**, 9 (1984).

Wright, C. D., and B. K. Middleton, "Analytical Modeling of Perpendicular Recording," *IEEE Trans. Magn.*, **MAG-21**, 1398 (1985).

Yamamori, K., R. Nishikawa, T. Asano, and T. Fujiwara, "Perpendicular Magnetic Recording Performance of Double Layer Media," *IEEE Trans. Magn.*, **MAG-17**, 2538 (1981).

Yoshida, K., T. Okuwaki, N. Osakake, H. Tanabe, Y. H. Onuchi, T. Matsuda, K. Shinagawa, A. Tonomura, and H. Fujiwara, "Observation of Recorded Magnetization Patterns by Electron Holography," *IEEE Trans. Magn.*, **MAG-19**, 1600 (1983).

CHAPTER 3
PARTICULATE MEDIA

Eberhard Köster
Frankenthal, Germany

3.1   TYPES OF RECORDING MEDIA

Historically, magnetic recording media evolved from metal wires and tapes to magnetic oxide particles held in an organic binder and carried by a polymer tape substrate. This design of recording medium has the advantage that the substrate and the magnetic layer can be independently optimized. Furthermore, the magnetic layer itself can be tailored for optimum magnetic and mechanical properties by adjustment of the magnetic particles and the binder system. Particulate recording tape continues to be the dominant tape medium, with countless refinements introduced over the last several decades. As computer use grew, a new need arose for rapid access to stored data. The sequential access of information stored on tape was too slow for many applications. Plated metal films on spinning drums were used for a time. A read-write head could quickly be moved to any spot on the drum, providing improved access speed at the expense of storage capacity. The use of rotating rigid disks replaced drum storage since they could be more easily coated, and disks can be stacked and recorded on two sides, thus increasing the volume storage capacity compared with drums. Although metal and oxide films were considered for disk media in the early 1960s, particulate media dominated the disk as well as the tape industry. With the appearance of mini- and microcomputers, a third form of magnetic storage grew to major proportions, namely the flexible (floppy) disk. This serves the role of providing rugged, low-cost, transportable storage with relatively high capacity and rapid access. Again particulate technology is dominant.

Although particulate magnetic coatings have been the mainstay of media technology, it is generally recognized that the highest storage densities can be achieved by using metal films. Although film media are taking over a broad portion of the marketplace, and dominate the rigid disk application, film and particulate media will coexist for some time.

3.1.1   Storage Formats

Magnetic media of the three general types (tape, rigid disks, and flexible disks) have played major roles in the storage of information. Applications using magnetic stripes and cards also continue in special areas. Tape is the oldest form and remains an important medium today. Its main use in computer applications is for archival storage and mass memory systems. Tape media are, however, central to most audio, video, and instrumentation recording applications. These three recording applications have historically used linear or frequency-modulation techniques for recording analog information on a tape, in contrast to the digital information stored by a computer tape. Audio, video, and instrumentation recorders are, however, evolving toward the use of digital techniques, so that computer and noncomputer requirements are converging.

The second major class of media, the rigid disk, is designed to provide rapid access to data files which need to be called up frequently. Rigid-disk drives are designed to operate at high rotational speeds, typically in the range of 3000 to 8000 rpm, to minimize the "latency time" which elapses before a piece of data passes the head again. These drives are also operated continuously to eliminate the time for getting up to speed. Rigid substrates are needed for such high-speed operation to avoid hazardous mechanical resonances as well as mechanical distortion of the disk. Because of the high speed and rigidity of the disk, the head is designed to "fly" above the disk surface (on the order of 0.05 μm in advanced drives). Flying the head minimizes disk and head wear, which would severely shorten the life of the file if continuous head-disk contact were permitted. Tapes and flexible disks can tolerate such contact because of the slower speeds, mechanical compliance of the media, and lower duty cycles.

The flexible disk, like the rigid disk, permits direct access to data files. The substrate material is essentially the same as is used for tapes, only thicker. A magnetic coating is applied to both sides of a polyester base out of which disks are stamped and then packaged in a protective envelope. Flexible disks are not capable of as high a track density as rigid media, yet they fill a very significant need for easily transportable, direct-access storage of moderate capacity and low cost. The primary market niche is for personal computers, where rapid access is important but instant access unnecessary. The flexible disk also serves as a very convenient means of distributing programs and data.

3.1.2 Substrates

Standard substrate materials for recording media are biaxially oriented polyethylene terephthalate for flexible media and high-purity aluminum-(4–5%) magnesium alloys for rigid disks. Other substrate materials being explored include polyimides and polyimide-polyamide copolymers for flexible media, and glass and ceramics for rigid disks. New flexible media substrate development stems from the need for improved dimensional and thermal stability. Ultraviolet and electron-beam cross-polymerization of substrate materials is being explored, as well as laminated structures. The efforts to develop new rigid substrate materials originate in the need for smoother, more uniform surfaces to allow closer head-to-media spacings, as well as reduced substrate-induced noise and dropouts. Glass and ceramics have been considered for many years, but have only recently appeared in a disk product (sub-3-in diameter). Besides the cost, the main concern has been possible brittle fracture during file assembly or operation. Nevertheless, the ability to obtain extremely fine surface finishes on such substrates gives them continued appeal, especially for small disk, low-flying-height applications.

3.1.3 Particulate Media

The most commonly used magnetic media are particles of gamma ferric oxide. These are normally acicular, with a saturation magnetization of about 350 kA/m (emu/cm^3). When diluted by an organic binder to a volume fraction of 20 to 45 percent, the coating magnetization is accordingly smaller. The coercivity of a coating is in the range 23 to 32 kA/m (290 to 400 Oe) if the acicular particles are aligned by a magnetic field during the coating process, and smaller if the particles are randomly oriented. Tape and rigid-disk applications generally call for particle alignment to improve the recording properties. Flexible disks, on the other hand, are obliged to use random orientation, so that large web substrates can be coated, from which the disks are subsequently stamped.

Other particles that are being used for more advanced applications include cobalt-modified γ-Fe_2O_3, chromium dioxide, metal particles and barium ferrite. The properties which are sought in these particles are higher coercivity, smaller particle size, or higher magnetization. The chief advantage of γ-Fe_2O_3 is its proven long-term stability. Often the alternative particles are accompanied by thermal or chemical instabilities which can compromise their advantages and limit their application.

In addition to magnetic particles, nonmagnetic particles such as Al_2O_3 are often added to the coating to improve the tape or disk abrasion resistance. Their use can, however, lead to noise and magnetic or mechanical defects. Liquid or solid lubricants are also commonly used to reduce friction and wear.

3.1.4 Requirements of Magnetic Recording Media

Regardless of the application (audio, video, or data) and the type of recording (analog or digital pulse), the direction of progress is toward higher information density. In some system designs, linear density (along the recording track) may be favored for optimization, while in others, track density (number of tracks per width of tape or band of disk) may be favored. However, at a more global level it is higher areal density or even volume density which is the goal.

Digital pulse recording is a convenient format for evaluating the potential storage density of a medium. In this mode of recording, information is written as magnetization reversals along a track, which are read back as electrical pulses in the windings of an inductive head. The sharper the reversals, the slimmer the pulses and the greater the linear density capability. As the reversals are written closer, they destructively interfere with each other, causing the readback pulse to diminish in amplitude and shift in position. At sufficiently close spacing the distinction between sinusoidal and pulse recording vanishes. Hence pulse width is a good measure of linear information density capability, for pulse or sinusoidal recording.

The sharpness of a magnetic transition in a longitudinal medium is found to be proportional to an expression of the form $(M_r\delta/H_c)^n$, where M_r is the remanent magnetization, δ is the magnetic coating thickness, H_c is the coercivity, and n is between 0.5 and 1 (see Chap. 2). In any event, small pulse lengths and high linear density call for small $M_r\delta$ and/or high H_c, but the former diminishes the signal amplitude, while the latter limits the ability of the head to write on the medium. The choice of magnetization, thickness, and coercivity therefore depends on the linear density design goals and cannot be made without considering the head design and practical head-to-medium spacing.

Designing for high linear density cannot be the sole objective. Track density and adequate signal must also be considered. Signal amplitude is proportional to the track width as well as $M_r\delta$. If the linear density is increased by reducing $M_r\delta$, the track width needs to be increased (and track density decreased) to maintain a given signal level. In this sense, linear density and track density are traded against each other, unless the minimum required signal can be lowered by reducing noise. On the other hand, raising the linear density by increasing H_c does not suffer this trade-off. Similarly, decreasing the head-to-medium spacing allows simultaneous increases in linear and track densities.

Over the years, most of the areal density gains have been achieved by a combination of lowering system noise, decreasing coating thickness, and reducing flying height (for rigid disks). This is because for $\gamma\text{-}Fe_2O_3$, the primary recording medium, M_r and H_c are substantially fixed by materials properties and pigment-loading constraints. For this reason, as practical limits of coating thickness, flying height, and noise reduction are approached, it becomes more important to explore the use of alternative particles and deposited films with higher coercivities and magnetizations.

Besides the basic magnetic requirements outlined above, the most important properties needed in advanced media are of a mechanical nature. Substrate and coating surfaces must be smooth to reduce noise in all media and to reduce head-to-medium spacing on rigid disks. Mechanical wear resistance is highly important for all types of media, but especially so for thin films or thin particulate coatings. Magnetic uniformity in film media may be governed by compositional or grain size uniformity, which is the counterpart to pigment dispersion uniformity in particulate coatings; in both cases inhomogeneities result in noise. Gains in these mechanical areas can be ranked equal in importance to gains in magnetic properties.

3.2 PARTICLE MAGNETIZATION AND ANISOTROPY

3.2.1 Magnetization

The spontaneous magnetization of ferromagnetic or ferrimagnetic materials is one of the two fundamentals of any magnetic material used for magnetic recording. The other is the magnetic anisotropy, which allows some of the magnetization acquired in an applied field to remain even after the field is removed. The remanent magnetization, or remanence, constitutes the basis for a magnetic storage device.

As an intrinsic bulk property, the spontaneous magnetization is the parallel alignment of the uncompensated magnetic spin moments of ferromagnetic elements such as iron, cobalt, and nickel, or of the metal ions in ferromagnetic compounds such as chromium dioxide or europium sulfide. The ferrimagnetic oxides have a more complicated magnetic structure. For many ferrites the crystal structure is inverse spinel, which can be described by a unit cell with a cubic close packing of 32 oxygen ions in which di- and trivalent metal ions occupy certain interstices. Each unit cell contains eight $[MFe_2O_4]$, where M is a divalent metal ion. The trivalent iron ions occupy eight tetrahedral and eight octahedral sites with an antiferromagnetic alignment, that is, with opposite direction of their spin moments. Their resultant magnetic moment is zero, and only the divalent ions which are located on eight additional octahedral sites contribute to the spontaneous magnetization. Thus, the magnetic moment decreases in steps of one unit from five to one Bohr magnetons in the order of Mn, Fe, Co, Ni, and Cu as divalent ions in the spinel ferrites. Another group of ferrites has a hexagonal lattice of oxygen ions with some ions substituted by Ba, Sr, Pb, or Ca ions; they may also contain interstitial divalent ions.

The spontaneous alignment of the spin moments is due to quantum-mechanical exchange forces (Smit and Wijn, 1959; Kneller, 1962; Chikazumi, 1964; Tebble and Craig, 1969). Any deviation from this alignment gives rise to an increase of the free exchange-energy density

$$F_A = A \left(\frac{d\phi}{dx}\right)^2 \tag{3.1}$$

where A is the exchange-energy constant, which is of the order 10^{-11} J/m (10^{-6} erg/cm), and $d\phi/dx$ is the gradient of the angle ϕ between the individual spins. At zero absolute temperature, the spontaneous magnetization is given by the number of uncompensated Bohr magnetons. At higher temperatures the parallel alignment of the spins is increasingly disturbed by thermal fluctuations. Thus, the spontaneous magnetization, given by the mean value of the spin moments in zero field, decreases monotonically with increasing temperature until it becomes zero at the Curie temperature. This is shown in Fig. 3.1 for various magnetic materials. In mixed ferrites, the different sublattices may have different rates of fall of the spontaneous magnetization, leading to an intermediate compensation point with zero magnetization. In Table 3.1, the spontaneous magnetization of various bulk materials is listed, together with other intrinsic room temperature properties of interest.

In slowly varying magnetic fields, no further basic differences between ferro-

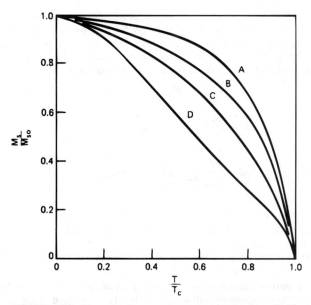

FIGURE 3.1 Normalized spontaneous magnetization M_s/M_0, where M_0 is the spontaneous magnetization 0°K, versus normalized temperature T/T_c, where T_c is the Curie temperature, for (curve A) ferromagnetic metals, (curve B) Fe_3O_4, (curve C) $CoFe_2O_3$, and (curve D) $BaFe_{12}O_{19}$.

TABLE 3.1 Spontaneous Magnetization M_{sb}, Curie temperature T_c, Constants of Magnetocrystalline Anisotropy K_1 and K_2, Magnetocrystalline Anisotropy Field H_k, and Saturation Magnetorestriction λ_s of Various Magnetic Materials at Room Temperature

Material	M_{sb}, kA/m (emu/cm^3)	T_c, °K	K_1, 10^3 J/m^3 (10^4 erg/cm^3)	K_2, 10^3 J/m^3 (10^4 erg/cm^3)	H_k, kA/m (4π Oe)	λ_s 10^{-6}
Fe	1710	1043	45	20	42	−4
Fe 30 at % Co	1900	1223	30	18	25	45
Co	1430	1393	430	120	479	−100
Fe$_4$N	1385	761				
Ni	483	658	−4.5	2.3	4.6	−36
CrO$_2$	480	387	22	4	73	3
Fe$_3$O$_4$	480	858	−11	−2.8	20	40
γ-Fe$_2$O$_3$	350	870	−4.6		21	−5
CoFe$_2$O$_4$	425	793	200		749	−110
BaFe$_{12}$O$_{19}$	380	728	330		1380	10

and ferrimagnetic materials are observed. In ac fields, the electric conductivity of the ferrites, which is several orders of magnitude lower, can be significant. However, the importance of conductivity is diminished when the material is in the form of fine particles well dispersed in a dielectric binder with few electrically conducting bridges between them.

The magnetization M is expressed in magnetic moment per unit volume, kA/m (emu/cm^3), or more conveniently in the case of porous material or powders, in magnetic moment per unit mass σ, A · m^2/kg (emu/g). In the latter case, or when the powder is dispersed in a liquid binder which is later solidified, as is the case with particulate recording media, the saturation magnetization M_s and the magnetization M are given, respectively, by

$$M_s = \frac{M_{sb}}{v_{tot}} \sum_i v_i = pM_{sb} \tag{3.2}$$

$$M = \frac{M_{sb}}{v_{tot}} \sum_i v_i \cos \theta_i = pM_{sb} \langle \cos \theta \rangle_{av} \tag{3.3}$$

where v_i = volume of the ith particle
θ = angle between magnetization and field directions
v_{tot} = total volume of sample
p = volumetric packing fraction of the magnetic particles

The saturation magnetization of the bulk material M_{sb} is introduced in distinction to the mean value of M_s of systems of fine particles. It is assumed in Eq. (3.3) that the magnetization is uniform in each particle, an assumption which is discussed in Sec. 3.2.4. The saturation magnetization, as usually measured in high magnetic fields, is equal to the spontaneous magnetization only at temperatures low compared to the Curie temperature. Near the Curie point, the spins are partially reoriented in the magnetic field, thus leading to a saturation magnetization which is higher than the spontaneous magnetization.

If the particle dimensions are decreased to the order of the lattice parameter, the spontaneous magnetization may be particle-size-dependent. From an extensive discussion of theoretical and experimental results (Jacobs and Bean, 1963) it appears, however, that for particle diameters down to 2 nm, the spontaneous magnetization does not significantly differ from the bulk value. Smaller particles are not important for consideration for magnetic recording media.

3.2.2 Local Anisotropies

The spin-orbit coupling of the electrons leads to energetically preferred orientations of the magnetic moments in the crystal lattice, and the symmetry of these orientations is reflected in the resulting magnetocrystalline anisotropy. While the spontaneous magnetization is a cooperative phenomenon, the magnetocrystalline anisotropy is a local effect, where each spin senses the local crystal-lattice symmetry (Birss, 1965). Consequently, lattice defects which introduce local variations of the crystal lattice symmetry can lead to an induced anisotropy. Interstitials, vacancies, or foreign atoms may diffuse under the influence of a magnetization distribution which is aligned by an applied field or stress, particularly at elevated temperatures. Such diffusion leads to a regular arrangement of the defects, resulting in an extrinsic form of uniaxial magnetocrystalline anisotropy.

The dependence of the free magnetocrystalline energy density F_k on the direction of the magnetization can be expressed in appropriate coordinates. The direction cosines α_1, α_2, α_3 are suitable for multiaxial cubic symmetry:

$$F_k = K_1(\alpha_1^2 \alpha_2^2 + \alpha_2^2 \alpha_3^2 + \alpha_1^2 \alpha_3^2) + K_2(\alpha_1^2 \alpha_2^2 \alpha_3^2) + \ldots \tag{3.4}$$

For the uniaxial anisotropy found with hexagonal and tetragonal lattice structures, F_k is expressed in terms of the angle ϕ of rotation from the preferred axis:

$$F_k = K_1 \sin^2 \phi + K_2 \sin^4 \phi \tag{3.5}$$

The magnetocrystalline energy constants K_1 and K_2 are expressed as energy densities in joules per cubic meter (J/m^3). They usually change much more rapidly with increasing temperature than the spontaneous magnetization.

The minima of Eqs. (3.4) and (3.5) represent the preferred, or easy, directions of magnetization. The maximum field necessary to rotate the magnetization from one easy direction into another is the anisotropy field H_k. This may be looked at as the magnetic field needed to produce a small initial rotation from the equilibrium direction (Chikazumi, 1964):

$$H_k = \frac{d^2 F(\phi)}{\mu_0 M_{sb} \, d\phi^2} \tag{3.6}$$

(Here, as with other energy equations in SI units, $\mu_0 M_{sb}$ has to be replaced by M_{sb} for use with cgs units.) The easy direction and the anisotropy fields of the most important configurations are shown in Table 3.2. The initial magnetic susceptibility due to rotation of the magnetization is inversely proportional to H_k.

A deformation of the crystal lattice changes its symmetry. This introduces an additional anisotropy, with a consequent change in the direction of the magnetization. Conversely, a change of the magnetization is accompanied by a fractional

TABLE 3.2 Easy Directions and Anisotropy Fields H_k for Various Combinations of the Constants of Magnetocrystalline Anisotropy K_1 and K_2

K_1	K_2	Easy directions	$\mu_0 H_k M_{sb}$
	(a) Cubic Anisotropy		
>0	$-\infty < K_2 < -9K_1$	$\langle 111 \rangle$	$-\frac{4}{3} K_1 - \frac{4}{9} K_2$
>0	$-9K_1 < K_2 < \infty$	$\langle 100 \rangle$	$2\,K_1$
<0	$-\infty < K_2 < \frac{9}{4}|K_1|$	$\langle 111 \rangle$	$-\frac{4}{3} K_1 - \frac{4}{9} K_2$
<0	$\frac{9}{4}|K_1| < K_2 < 9|K_1|$	$\langle 110 \rangle$	$K_1 + \frac{1}{2} K_2$
<0	$9|K_1| < K_2 < \infty$	$\langle 110 \rangle$	$-2K_1$
	(b) Uniaxial Anisotropy		
	$K_1 + K_2 > 0$	$\langle 001 \rangle$	$2K_1 + 4K_2$
	$K_1 + K_2 < 0$	Basal plane	0

SOURCE: Bozorth (1936).

change in length, $\lambda = \Delta l/l$, which is known as *magnetostriction*. The magnetostriction is directionally dependent in a similar way to the magnetocrystalline anisotropy. With an isotropic orientation distribution of crystal grains or particles, the free anisotropy energy density under the influence of an uniaxial stress σ has the form

$$F_\sigma = \tfrac{3}{2}\lambda_s \sigma \sin^2 \phi \tag{3.7}$$

in which λ_s is the saturation magnetostriction. This description of the uniaxial stress anisotropy is a sufficient approximation for many problems. More details on magnetostriction are given in review publications (Lee, 1955; Birss, 1959).

Another severe change of symmetry occurs at internal or free surfaces of the magnetic material, where the environment of the surface atoms has a lower symmetry than that of the crystal lattice. This may become of importance if the particles are small enough to have a comparable number of atoms in the volume and at the surface. For instance, in a cube of a face-centered cubic (FCC) crystal having a length of 10 lattice parameters, about one-third of the atoms are surface atoms. This fraction rapidly decreases with increasing dimensions. The surface atoms sense a uniaxial anisotropy perpendicular to the surface of the order of 0.1 to 1.0 J/m^2 (0.1 to 1.0×10^3 erg/cm^2) (Néel, 1954; Jacobs and Bean, 1963). This surface anisotropy has been used to explain the increase of coercivity of gamma ferric oxide by cobalt surface adsorption (Tokuoka et al., 1977), and may give rise to an anomalous increase in coercivity of iron oxide particles coated with sodium polyphosphate (Itoh et al., 1977). The experimental evidence of this anisotropy is still very much under discussion (Morrish and Haneda, 1983).

Exchange anisotropy is another kind of surface anisotropy which is located, for example, at the phase boundary between a ferro- or ferrimagnet and an antiferromagnet. It has been discovered on cobalt particles with an antiferromagnetic cobalt monoxide surface layer (Meiklejohn and Bean, 1956). The exchange coupling of the last plane of the magnetically fixed antiferromagnetic lattice to the first ferro- or ferrimagnetic lattice plane leads to unidirectional or vector anisotropy. This acts like a dc-bias field that displaces the hysteresis loop (Meiklejohn and Bean, 1956) and leads to a finite anhysteretic magnetization in zero external field (Köster and Steck, 1976).

3.2.3 Magnetostatic Anisotropies

The change of the normal component of the magnetization at the surface of a particle leads to an external as well as to an internal field with an associated energy density. The internal field is oppositely directed to the originating magnetization M, and hence is called the *demagnetizing field H_d*. For convenience, demagnetization is described by a geometrical shape factor N:

$$H_d = -NM \qquad (3.8)$$

For the general ellipsoid, with major semiaxes a, b, and c, N can be directly calculated (Osborn, 1945). In the SI unit system, the sum of the demagnetization factors of the three major axes is $N_a + N_b + N_c = 1$, whereas it is $N_a + N_b + N_c = 4\pi$ in the cgs unit system. Of particular interest is the rotational ellipsoid with $a > b = c$, which is the most convenient mathematical model to describe the elongated particles used in most magnetic recording media. With parallel rotation of the magnetization, the difference in demagnetizing field energy perpendicular and longitudinal to the particle axis constitutes the uniaxial shape-anisotropy energy density F_m. The easy axis coincides with the particle axis. The energy density varies with the angle ϕ between the magnetization and the particle axis as follows:

$$F_m = \tfrac{1}{2}\,\mu_0 M_{sb}^2 (N_b - N_a)\sin^2\phi \qquad (3.9)$$

The corresponding anisotropy field is

$$H_m = (N_b - N_a)M_{sb} \qquad (3.10)$$

The difference between the magnetization factors perpendicular and longitudinal to the particle axis, $N_b - N_a$, increases steeply with the axial ratio a/b of the particles, as shown in Fig. 3.2. Consequently, in almost all cases of fine-particle magnetism, shape anisotropy is highly significant. In fact, up to recently it has been the intention of research and application to rely predominantly on shape anisotropy. An advantage is that H_m is directly proportional to M_{sb}, which shows little temperature dependence in the vicinity of room temperature for the materials in use. In contrast, the magnetocrystalline anisotropy field of most of the materials available is strongly dependent on temperature. Further, the frequently used demagnetizing criterion M_r/H_c (remanence divided by coercivity) is independent of temperature for shape anisotropy.

Another form of magnetostatic anisotropy is the interaction anisotropy which occurs with a linear chain of isotropic magnetic spheres (Jacobs and Bean, 1955). This leads to a preferred direction of magnetization along the chain axis. The maximum anisotropy field corresponds to uniform parallel rotation of the magnetization in an infinite chain of contacting spheres. It amounts to $0.3M_{sb}$ ($1.2\,\pi M_{sb}$ in cgs units), and is smaller than the maximum shape-anisotropy field of $0.5M_{sb}$ ($2\pi M_{sb}$) for infinite cylinders.

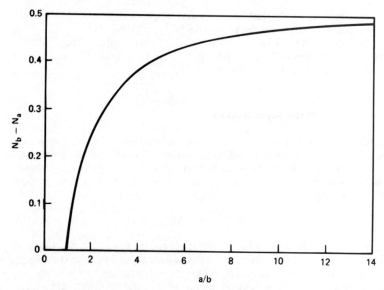

FIGURE 3.2 Difference of demagnetizing factors, $N_b - N_a$, of rotational ellipsoids with major semiaxes $a > b = c$ as a function of the axial ratio a/b.

3.2.4 Single-Domain Particles

Consider a large ferromagnetic crystal which is magnetized to saturation in a strong magnetic field H (positive direction). When the field is reversed continuously, the magnetization M is also reversed. It is usually not zero at zero field but has a finite value, the saturation remanance $M_r(\infty)$ and changes sign in a field $-H_c$, where H_c is the coercivity. For moderate crystalline anisotropies, H_c is found to be much smaller than the magnetocrystalline anisotropy field H_k. This is because the magnetization is not rotated spatially in unison in the volume of the crystal. Instead, it is rotated locally in thin sheets which are moved through the crystal, the domain walls. These walls separate domains with uniform magnetization oriented along the preferred axes of magnetization, but with different directions in neighboring domains. The magnetocrystalline anisotropy energy to be overcome for magnetization reversal is reduced to that in the domain walls. This reduction is at the expense of exchange energy, which enters through the angles between the spin vectors in the domain wall. The total energy of the crystal is further minimized by the reduction of the external field energy through the formation of the alternately magnetized domains. The overall minimization of external field, magnetocrystalline, and exchange energies leads to a certain geometric configuration and number of domains. The thickness of the domain wall, satisfying equilibrium between exchange and magnetocrystalline anisotropies, is of the order of

$$\delta = 5 \sqrt{\frac{A}{K}} \tag{3.11}$$

With $A \approx 10^{-11}$ J/m (10^{-6} erg/cm) and $K_1 = -4.6 \times 10^3$ J/m³ (-4.6×10^4 erg/cm³) for gamma ferric oxide, the domain wall thickness is 200 nm. For iron, the thickness is

70 nm. The domain structure of large crystals, various types of domains and domain walls, wall displacement, and the physical mechanisms of "wall friction," which control the coercivity, are fairly well understood (Kneller, 1962; Chikazumi, 1964; Craik and Tebble, 1965).

If the size of the crystal becomes sufficiently small, there is a critical particle size below which nonuniform magnetization configurations will no longer be stable, at least in zero external magnetic field. From discussions of critical particle dimensions for this to happen (Wohlfarth, 1963; Mee, 1964; Kneller, 1969), it appears that Eq. (3.11) represents a reasonable limit for predominant magnetocrystalline anisotropy. Throughout this chapter we use the definition of a single-domain particle in the following sense: nonuniform modes of magnetization reversal are admitted provided the magnetization is uniform through the volume of the particles in zero external field. This definition encompasses the situation where this condition is slightly violated by the fields from surface irregularities, which are deviations from the ideal ellipsoid. Such surface irregularities result in a mean magnetization in the easy direction, at zero external field, which is smaller than M_{sb} and must be taken into account in considerations of the remanence of particle systems.

3.2.5 Magnetization Processes. The basic mode of magnetization reversal for single-domain particles is uniform rotation of the magnetization (Stoner and Wohlfarth, 1948). The magnetization curves for particles with uniaxial anisotropy are shown in Fig. 3.3 for various angles θ between the easy direction of magnetization (the particle major axes in the case of shape anisotropy), and the applied field

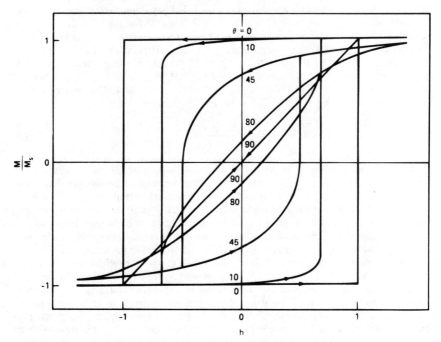

FIGURE 3.3 Magnetization M/M_s versus reduced applied field $h = H/H_a$, calculated for a uniaxial particle reversing its magnetization by uniform rotation. The parameter θ is the angle between field and particle axes (*Stoner and Wohlfarth, 1948*).

direction. The strong influence of particle orientation on the shape of the magnetization curve is evident. For $\theta = 0$, the normalized coercivity $h_c = H_c/H_a$ equals unity, where H_a stands for any of the uniaxial anisotropy fields described earlier. The coercivity decreases rapidly with increasing θ. At angles less than 45° it is controlled by irreversible and reversible magnetization changes but, at angles greater than 45°, by reversible rotation only. Here, the reduced coercivity is given by the equation

$$h_c = \frac{1}{2} \sin 2\theta \qquad\qquad (3.12)$$

In order to distinguish between the processes, it is useful to define the switching field H_0, or reduced switching field $h_0 = H_0/H_a$, for irreversible magnetization reversal. In the range of angles $\theta \leq 45°$, $h_c = h_0$. At angles $\theta > 45°$, h_c continues to decrease with increasing θ, while h_0 starts to increase again. At $\theta = 90°$, $h_c = 0$ and $h_0 = 1$. Owing to the angular variation of h_c and h_0, an assembly of identical particles with a distribution in particle-axis orientations has a distribution of both quantities. A random distribution of orientations leads to a reduced coercivity of $h_c = 0.479$, and to a reduced remanence coercivity of $h_r = H_r/H_a = 0.529$. The remanence coercivity H_r is a measure of the mean switching field, and is defined as the reverse field applied after saturation which reduces the remanent magnetization to zero. The reduced saturation remanence, called *remanence squareness* $S = M_r(\infty)/M_s$, of the random assembly becomes $S = \langle \cos \theta \rangle_{av} = 0.5$.

Magnetization curves $M(H)$ of assemblies of typical elongated single-domain, gamma ferric oxide particles are shown in Fig. 3.4. They demonstrate the characteristic hysteresis of magnetically hard materials. The curve for partially aligned particles has a higher saturation remanence $M_r(\infty)$, and a steeper slope at coercivity H_c, than the curve for randomly oriented particles. The distribution of switching fields can be characterized by the field $H_{0.25}$, where 25 percent of the particles have their magnetization reversed after saturation $[M_r(H_{0.25})/M_r(\infty) = 0.5]$, and $H_{0.75}$, where 75 percent of the particles are reversed $[M_r(H_{0.75})/M_r(\infty) = -0.5]$. The switching-field distribution is then expressed by the normalized quantity:

$$\Delta h_r = \frac{H_{0.75} - H_{0.25}}{H_r} \qquad\qquad (3.13)$$

This type of measurement is shown in Fig. 3.4, where $M_d(H)$ is the remanence acquired after saturation in the positive field direction and successive application of a dc field in the negative direction. For random distribution of particle axes of identical single-domain particles with uniaxial anisotropy and with uniform magnetization reversal, Δh_r amounts to 0.13. In summary, any particle orientation distribution deviating from the mathematically parallel alignment usually leads to a coercivity smaller than the anisotropy field H_a, a distribution in switching fields, and a saturation remanence smaller than M_s. In addition, particles with a distribution of the anisotropy field H_a further broaden the switching-field distribution. This may be due either to a distribution of the axial ratio a/b, and consequently of the shape-anisotropy field, or to a distribution of the magnetocrystalline anisotropy of the individual particles. The latter may be caused by unevenly distributed dopants that strongly influence the magnetocrystalline anisotropy, such as cobalt in iron oxide or cobalt and titanium in barium ferrite particles. For practical purposes, another parameter for characterizing the switching-field distribution, the *coercivity squareness S**, has been introduced. As shown in Fig. 3.4, S^* can be conveniently obtained

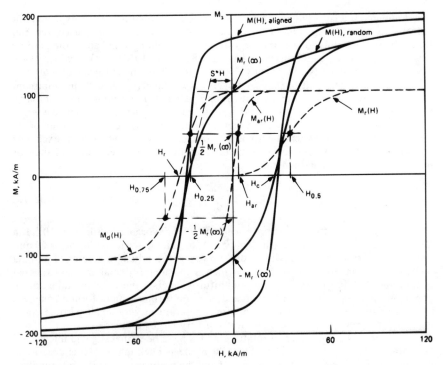

FIGURE 3.4 Magnetization $M(H)$, remanence $M_r(H)$, dc demagnetizing remanence $M_d(H)$, and anhysteretic remanence $M_{ar}(H)$ of a sample of randomly oriented $\gamma\text{-Fe}_2\text{O}_3$ particles. For the same particles, partially aligned, $M(H)$ is also included.

from the intersection of the slope of the magnetization curve $M(H)$ at the coercivity point $M(H_c) = 0$,

$$\frac{dM(H)}{dH} = \frac{M_r(\infty)}{H_c(1 - S^*)} \tag{3.14}$$

with the line $M = M_r(\infty)$. The quantity $1 - S^*$ almost equals Δh_r, since the contributions by reversal magnetization processes to $1 - S^*$ cancel each other. Other characterizations of the switching-field distribution, like the half-pulse width of the differentiated magnetization curve, or H_r/H_c, very much depend on reversible magnetization processes and may be used only if the angular distribution of the particle axes is kept constant (Köster, 1984).

The theoretical predictions for magnetization reversal by uniform rotation have been experimentally verified in cases with predominant magnetocrystalline anisotropy $H_k \gg M_{sb}$. Single-domain barium ferrite particles in the size range of 0.1 to 0.3 μm can be prepared by a flux method. These exhibit as a random assembly the theoretical values of $H_r = 0.529(H_k + H_m) = 530$ kA/m (6660 Oe), and $\Delta h_r = 0.13$, within the uncertainty of the data. Other examples are chromium dioxide doped with iridium (Kullmann et al., 1984b), and cobalt-doped gamma ferric oxide (Köster, 1972), both in the remanence coercivity range of 300 kA/m (3800 Oe). However, for predominant shape anisotropy, $H_k \ll M_{sb}$, much lower coercivities and a much broader switching-field distribution are obtained than expected for uniform rotation. For gamma ferric oxide, which is the most widely used material for magnetic recording media, the largest switching field H_0 found along the particle axis in a single particle measurement has been 84 kA/m (1050 Oe) (Knowles, 1984). The theoretical value is 156 kA/m (1960 Oe) for shape anisotropy with $a/b = 7$.

In fact, uniform rotation almost never occurs in particles with predominant shape anisotropy. Instead, the magnetization is reversed in a nonuniform fashion by trading long-range magnetostatic field energy against short-range exchange energy. This necessitates that the particle dimensions are large enough to accommodate incremental angles between the spins without introducing too high an exchange energy. Consequently, this reversal mode is strongly size-dependent, and there is indeed a critical particle diameter

$$2b_0 = 2 \left(\frac{4\pi A}{\mu_0 M_{sb}^2} \right)^{1/2} \tag{3.15}$$

above which nonuniform rotation is energetically favorable. With $A \approx 10^{11}$ J/m (10^{-6} erg/cm) and $M_{sb} = 350$ kA/m (emu/cm^3) for gamma ferric oxide, $2b_0 \approx 60$ nm. For iron, $2b_0 \approx 12$ nm. Experimentally, however, the critical diameter of gamma ferric oxide seems to be about 15 nm, which is considerably smaller than expected (Eagle and Mallinson, 1967). The nonuniform reversal mode which takes place above this critical diameter can be considered as a form of nonuniform magnetization reversal intermediate between uniform rotation in very small particles, and local nonuniform rotation in domain walls of very large particles.

Three models of nonuniform rotation modes have been investigated intensively (Wohlfarth, 1963; Kneller, 1969). The first mode is buckling, which is a periodic fluctuation of the magnetization direction from the particle axis. This mode involves magnetostatic field and exchange energy. The second mode is curling, which is best described by a bundle of twisted wires along the particle axis. It avoids any magnetostatic field energy but involves exchange energy. The third mode is fanning, described by a chain of spheres in which the angles between magnetization and chain axis for neighboring spheres are of opposite sign. This mode relies on magnetostatic energy and excludes exchange energy. With the reduced particle radius $b/b_0 > 0$, the switching field in the case of buckling in an infinite circular cylinder becomes

$$H_0 = 0.645 M_{sb} \left(\frac{b}{b_0} \right)^{-2/3} \tag{3.16}$$

while for curling in rotational ellipsoids,

$$H_0 = \left[0.5k \left(\frac{b}{b_0} \right)^{-2} - N_a \right] M_{sb} \tag{3.17}$$

Here k is a numerical factor, which increases monotonically with decreasing axial ratio a/b, from $k = 1.08$ for $a/b = \infty$ (infinite cylinder) to $k = 1.39$ for $a/b = 1$ (sphere). In a formal sense, N_b, the demagnetization factor perpendicular to the particle axis in Eq. (3.10), is reduced with increasing particle diameter. In the case of fanning, which is independent of particle diameter, the maximum nucleation field of an infinite chain of contacting spheres is reduced from $0.3M_{sb}$ for uniform rotation to values between $0.08M_{sb}$ and $0.125M_{sb}$. The reversal mode for a given cylinder radius is always the one with the least switching field H_0. For the magnetic particles used in magnetic recording media, b/b_0 has values between 2 and 4. Consequently, curling or fanning are the most likely modes to occur. Fanning may apply only if the particles are distinctively subdivided in crystallites, separated by boundaries, with little or no exchange coupling.

In reality, none of the above models seems to apply strictly, since the particle shape in general deviates considerably from the ideal ellipsoid, and offers additional sites for nucleation of magnetization reversal. Experimentally, the coercivity tends to be proportional to the inverse particle diameter rather than the inverse squared diameter as predicted for the curling mode. On the other hand, the coercivity is not independent of particle diameter as expected for fanning. This is demonstrated in Fig. 3.5, where the coercivity of gamma ferric oxide and chromium dioxide powder samples is plotted versus the inverse mean particle diameter. The two sets of data are not directly comparable because $2b$ has been determined from electron micrographs for the γ-Fe_2O_3 particles, and from x-ray analysis for the CrO_2 particles. Apparently some nonuniform mode of magnetization reversal takes place which involves less exchange energy, and consequently is less dependent on particle diameter, than curling. But the reversal mechanism is not solely dependent on magnetic interactions, and therefore independent of particle diameter, as with fanning. Recently, a mode of pseudo-curling or buckling has been proposed (Knowles, 1984). Instead of occurring simultaneously everywhere in the particle volume, as is the case with the above models, the switching is thought to start at one tip of an elongated particle and move through the particle in the fashion of falling dominoes.

Actual recording media always have a distribution of the direction of the particle axes, and the angular dependence of the coercivity must be considered. Further interest arises from the fact that the magnetic head field close to the head surface rotates from a longitudinal direction in the gap zone to a perpendicular direction over the pole piece. This process becomes of increasing interest in short-wavelength recording. Both the reduced coercivity h_c, and the switching field h_0, of infinitely long cylinders are plotted in Fig. 3.6 for the curling model as a function of the angle θ between the particle axis and the applied field direction. Similar curves are expected for the buckling or fanning modes. The parameter is the reduced cylinder radius b/b_0. The magnetocrystalline anisotropy is assumed to be negligible. As has

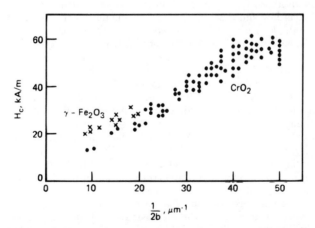

FIGURE 3.5 Coercivity H_c as a function of the inverse of the mean particle diameter $2b$ of isotropic powder samples of gamma ferric iron oxide and chromium dioxide (*Steck, 1985*).

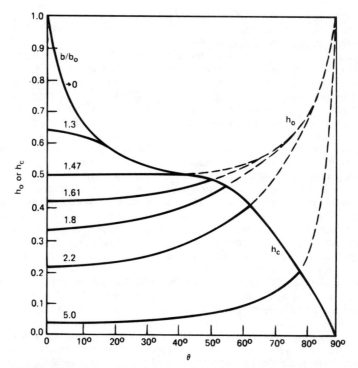

FIGURE 3.6 Reduced coercivity $h_c = H_c/H_a$, and reduced switching field h_o $= H_0/H_a$, of infinite cylinders ($H_a = 0.5M_s$) as a function of the angle θ between the field and the cylinder axis. The parameter is the reduced cylinder radius b/b_0 (*after Shtrikman and Treves, 1959*).

already been discussed for the mode of uniform rotation (curve for $b/b_0 \rightarrow 0$ in Fig. 3.6), h_c and h_0 at low and medium angles coincide until a critical angle is reached. Above this angle, h_c is controlled by reversible magnetization rotation according to Eq. (3.12) and becomes zero for $\theta = 90°$. The switching field increases further and is controlled by uniform rotation when the respective curves in Fig. 3.6 join the curve for uniform rotation. Experimental data are shown in Fig. 3.7. Here, the coercivity H_c and the remanence coercivity H_r of samples of gamma ferric oxide, chromium dioxide, and iron particles with different degrees of particle alignment, measured longitudinal and transverse to the direction of alignment, are plotted as a function of the mean angle of particle orientation $\langle\theta\rangle_{av} = \arccos S$. At low values of $\langle\theta\rangle_{av}$, $H_r \approx H_c$, as expected. At larger $\langle\theta\rangle_{av}$, $H_r > H_c$. The rate of increase of H_r at large values of $\langle\theta\rangle_{av}$ is far less than expected from the curling model, while H_c indeed tends to zero according to Eq. (3.12). Measurements of H_c and H_r on samples of aligned particles as a function of sample rotation (Bate, 1980) more prominently exhibit the maximum of H_c in Fig. 3.7.

The switching-field distribution of an isotropic particle assembly of identical particles is expected to increase with increasing b/b_0, from $\Delta h_r = 0.13$ for uniform rotation to $\Delta h_r = 0.56$ for $b/b_0 = 3$ of the curling mode, as shown in Fig. 3.8. Here, Δh_r is plotted versus b/b_0 for particle assemblies with various degrees of particle alignment. An azimuth-invariant distribution function for θ is assumed of the form

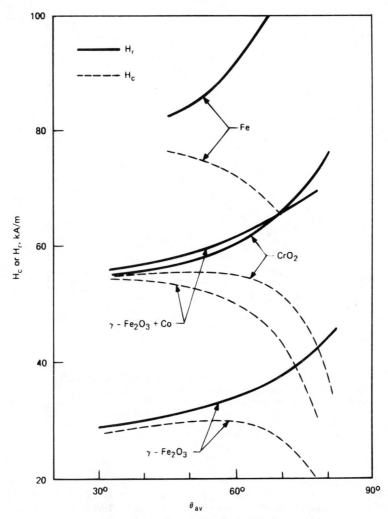

FIGURE 3.7 Coercivity H_c and remanence coercivity H_r versus the average angle, $\langle\theta\rangle_{av} = \arccos S$, of particle alignment $[S = M_r(\infty)/M_s]$, for iron, gamma ferric iron oxide, and chromium dioxide particles.

$\exp(\alpha\cos^2\theta)\sin\theta$, where α is the orientation parameter (Bertram, 1976). A lower value of b/b_0 means a higher coercivity, and also a lower switching-field distribution as shown in Fig. 3.9. Here, Δh_r of numerous isotropic powder samples of gamma ferric oxide, chromium dioxide, and iron particles is plotted as a function of the remanence coercivity H_r. The curves are shifted in proportion to the saturation magnetization of the respective materials and, in the case of chromium dioxide, in addition by the magnetocrystalline anisotropy field. With increasing alignment of identical particles, that is, with increasing S, Δh_r is expected to decrease to zero for $S \to 1$, as is indicated in Fig. 3.10. Here, Δh_r is shown as a function of the squareness

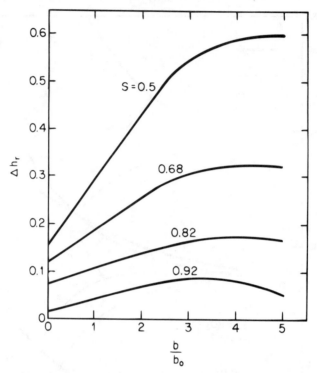

FIGURE 3.8 The parameter Δh_r for the switching-field distribution, calculated for various degrees of particle orientation, that is, for various values of the normalized saturation remanence S as a function of the reduced cylinder radius b/b_0. An azimuth invariant distribution function of the orientation angle θ of infinite cylinders has been used of the form exp $(\alpha \cos^2 \theta) \sin \theta$ used *(Bertram, 1976)*.

S for the reduced radii $b/b_0 = 2$ and $b/b_0 = 4$, together with measurements on samples of particles with different degrees of alignment made from a number of magnetic materials. Contrary to theory, the experimental data tend to a finite value of Δh_r for $S \rightarrow 1$. This is due to a distribution of particle diameters and a consequent distribution of switching fields, even for mathematically aligned particles. Assuming a triangular distribution for b/b_0, the experimental data in Fig. 3.10 can be quite well described by the curling model (Bertram, 1976).

3.2.6 Mixed Anisotropies and Saturation Remanence

So far, only one type of magnetic anisotropy has been considered at a time. In the case of collinear uniaxial shape and magnetocrystalline anisotropies, Eq. (3.17) extends to

$$H_0 = H_k + \left[\frac{k}{2} \left(\frac{b}{b_0} \right)^{-2} - N_a \right] M_{sb} \tag{3.18}$$

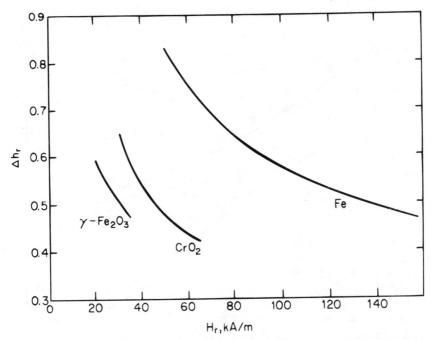

FIGURE 3.9 Switching-field distribution Δh_r as a function of remanence coercivity H_r for isotropic powder samples with a volumetric packing fraction of $p = 0.25$ of gamma ferric oxide, chromium dioxide, and iron particles. The curves represent the mean value of over 20 samples of each material with a standard deviation of 4 to 7 percent.

where the two anisotropies are simply additive. The magnetization curves of particles with cubic anisotropy are more complicated than those for uniaxial anisotropy (Johnson and Brown, 1961). Thus, the coercivity value

$$H_c = 0.32H_k \tag{3.19}$$

as given by Néel (1947) for an isotropic assembly of cubic particles may not apply in all cases, although it serves well for predominant magnetocrystalline anisotropy (Köster, 1972). Magnetization curves of an elongated single-domain particle, with a $\langle 111 \rangle$ fiber texture parallel to the long axis, and with $\langle 111 \rangle$ easy directions of magnetocrystalline anisotropy, have also been considered (Johnson and Brown, 1959). It has been found that the existence of collinear shape and magnetocrystalline easy axes does not raise the coercivity under all circumstances. In general, the situation of mixed anisotropies is little understood.

In the case of multiaxial anisotropies, the reduced saturation remanence, or squareness S, for isotropic particle assemblies increases monotonically with the number n of easy axes, from $S = 0.5$ for $n = 1$ (uniaxial anisotropy) to $S = 0.83$ for $n = 3$ (magnetocrystalline anisotropy with $K_1 > 0$), and to $S = 0.87$ for $n = 4$ (magnetocrystalline anisotropy with $K_1 < 0$) (Gans, 1932; Wohlfarth and Tonge, 1957; Tonge and Wohlfarth, 1958). The transition from $n = 1$ to $n = 3$ can be directly observed by measuring the temperature dependence of S for elongated cobalt-doped gamma ferric oxide particles (Sec. 3.2.2).

During the manufacturing process of particulate media, a step of compression

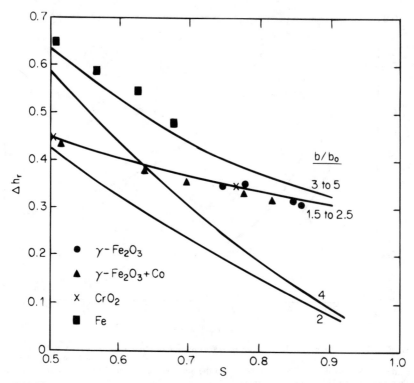

FIGURE 3.10 The parameter Δh_r for the switching-field distribution of iron, gamma ferric iron oxide, cobalt-modified gamma ferric iron oxide, and chromium dioxide particles of different degrees of particle alignment as a function of the remanence squareness S. The solid curves represent theoretical values for infinite cylinders of different reduced radii b/b_0, either constant in value or having a triangular distribution, calculated under the same conditions as in Fig. 3.8.

such as calendering is usually involved, which may introduce a more planar distribution of the particle axes. It is therefore of interest to note that for a planar isotropic distribution of uniaxial single-domain particles, $S = 2/\pi$, a value larger than $S = 0.5$ which results from an isotropic spatial distribution. Attempts have been made to differentiate between a spatial and a planar distribution of particle axes in magnetic tape samples (Bate and Williams, 1978; Bertram, 1978). It appears that the angular distribution is close to cylindrical around the direction of alignment, although some results are difficult to interpret because the remanence squareness of the individual particles along their axes is not necessarily unity. Their irregular shape, or spin canting at the surface (Morrish and Haneda, 1983), may cause local deviations from the otherwise uniform spin alignment and consequently a squareness smaller than unity. Thus, for isotropic powder samples, S is often below 0.5, and typically has a value of 0.47. For this reason the orientation ratio M_{rx}/M_{rz} is often used, instead of the squareness S, to characterize the degree of particle alignment. Here M_{rx} is the saturation remanence in the direction of particle alignment and M_{rz} is the saturation remanence transverse to the particle alignment. The orientation ratio is independent of the effect of nonuniform spin alignment which enters equally in M_{rx} and M_{rz}.

3.2.7 Magnetostatic Particle Interactions

In the previous sections, it has been assumed that the particles in an assembly are independent. In practice, magnetostatic interactions will mutually influence their magnetization reversal. The maximum average interaction-field energy density is of the order of $0.25p\mu_0M^2$, where $p = M_s/M_{sb}$ is the volumetric packing fraction of the particles. If shape anisotropy dominates $(K_1 \ll \mu_0M_{sb}^2)$, the energy density of the particles in the magnetostatic interaction field may have the same order of magnitude as the maximum shape-anisotropy energy density $F_{m_2} = 0.25 \ \mu_0M_{sb}^2$. Only for predominant magnetocrystalline anisotropy $(K_1 \gg \mu_0M_{sb}^2)$, the magnetostatic interactions may be negligible. The anhysteretic remanence $M_{ar}(H)$, which is acquired after application of a dc field H simultaneously with a slowly decreasing ac field H' of sufficiently high initial amplitude, $H' > H_0$, is directly controlled by the interaction fields. Here, the ac field serves to overcome the energy barriers that prevent irreversible magnetization changes from occurring in H alone, and $M_{ar}(H) = M_r(\infty)$ for $H > 0$ for independent particles if thermal fluctuation effects can be neglected. In practice, the presence of magnetostatic interaction effects dictates that $M_{ar}(H)$ has a finite slope; that is, the initial anhysteretic susceptibility $\chi_{ar} = dM_{ar}(H)/dH$ is finite. The anhysteretic remanence is a single-valued, odd function of the applied dc field (Fig. 3.4), and is thus used as the basic process for linearization of the recording channel in ac-bias recording (Chap. 2). Apart from this, the anhysteretic remanence is a useful tool for the study of interaction effects.

Another interesting measure of the interaction fields can be drawn from remanence curves. The static remanence curve $M_r(H)$ can be measured after ac demagnetization and successive application of a dc field H, with $m_r(H) = M_r(H)/M_r(\infty)$. The dc demagnetizing remanence $M_d(H)$ is acquired after saturation in one direction and successive application of a dc field in the opposite direction with $m_d(H) = M_d(H)/M_r(\infty)$. For independent uniaxial particles, the two remanence curves are interrelated as

$$m_d(H) = 1 - 2m_r(H) \tag{3.20}$$

When particles interact, this condition is not obeyed. According to Eq. (3.20), the field $H_{0.5}$ for irreversibly reversing 50 percent of the particles $[m_r(H_{0.5}) = 0.5]$ and the remanence coercivity H_r $[m_d(H_r) = 0]$ should be identical. In practice, $H_r < H_{0.5}$ (Fig. 3.4). For oriented gamma ferric oxide media, this difference amounts to 2 to 4 kA/m (25 to 50 Oe) or about 10 percent of H_r.

Different theoretical models for the interaction problems have been investigated. They are based on cooperative phenomena in Ewing-type models, on statistical considerations of pair models and their extension, the Preisach diagram, on statistical thermodynamical considerations, and on mean-field concepts. Most of these theories have not been advanced enough to give direct relations between the static and the anhysteretic magnetic magnetization parameters. The Preisach diagram (Chap. 2) is a powerful tool in describing the interaction-field distribution and its influence on various remanence curves. Also, a dynamic mean-field theory (Kneller, 1968, 1969, 1980) leads to a relationship between the initial anhysteretic susceptibility and the spontaneous magnetization M_{sb}, the volumetric packing fraction p, the remanence squareness S, and the remanence coercivity H_r:

$$\chi_{ar} = \frac{0.5p(1 - p)M_{sb}^2}{H_r^2(1 - S^2)} \tag{3.21}$$

The distribution of switching fields is not incorporated but, by empirical replacement of the numerical factor 0.5 by 0.27, good agreement with experiment is obtained. This theoretical approach can be extended to thermoremanent magnetization, the magnetization acquired after cooling in a dc field from temperatures above, to temperatures below, the Curie temperature.

The dc field can be normalized by writing $h = H/H_{ar}$, where H_{ar} is the field for which the anhysteretic remanence equals half the saturation remanence. The reduced anhysteretic remanence m_{ar} is then experimentally found to follow an almost universal curve versus h for tape samples with partially aligned particles, $0.70 \leq S \leq 0.87$, of the form (Köster, 1975)

$$m_{ar} = 0.569h - 0.0756h^3 + 0.0065h^5 \qquad (3.22)$$

for $h < 2$. Consequently, up to 50 percent of $M_r(\infty)$ can be utilized in ac-bias recording with less than 3 percent third harmonic distortion, independent of the magnetic material used or of the magnetic media preparation. The third-order factor in Eq. (3.22) varies from -0.095 for $S = 0.6$ to -0.063 for $S = 0.9$ in a systematic magnetic tape series, thus indicating the role of the distribution of the switching fields in the degree of linearity of the anhysteretic magnetization curve. The mean-field approach predicts that $H_{ar} = H_{0.5} - H_r$; this difference is directly related to χ_{ar} according to Eq. (3.22) with $h \to 0$:

$$(H_{0.5} - H_r) = \frac{0.569\, M_r(\infty)}{\chi_{ar}} \qquad (3.23)$$

The particle interactions not only cause a shift of $H_{0.5}$ and H_r but also reduce these properties with increasing p. There have been many attempts to calculate this dependence rigorously. They lead to equations with various exponents of p near unity, which are almost impossible to discriminate experimentally. In addition, if shape anisotropy is dominant, there may be an increase of the critical radius b_0 for uniform rotation which is expected to be proportional to $b_0(0)(1 - p)^{-1/2}$. This would reduce the rate of decrease of H_r with p (Kneller, 1969). With these questions open to discussion, it seems still legitimate to use Néel's formula

$$H_r(p) = H_{r,\mathrm{cryst}} + H_{r,\mathrm{shape}}(0)(1 - p) \qquad (3.24)$$

for which experimental examples are given in Fig. 3.11. Here, H_c and H_r are plotted for increasingly compacted iron, gamma ferric oxide, and chromium dioxide powders as a function of p. Equation (3.24) holds likewise for H_r and H_c. It appears, although still questioned (Huisman, 1982), that the contribution by the magnetocrystalline anisotropy, as a local effect to H_c and H_r, is independent of the long-range interaction fields and hence of the packing fraction p (Morrish and Yu, 1955). In fair agreement with the expected values, the experimental curves of Fig. 3.11 extrapolate to coercivities of 7 kA/m for iron, 6 kA/m for gamma ferric oxide, and 27 kA/m for chromium dioxide (88, 75, and 340 Oe, respectively). Thus, the magnetocrystalline contribution has been added in Eq. (3.24) to the original equation by Néel (Wohlfarth, 1963; Kneller, 1969).

The magnetostatic interactions also change the saturation remanence. A simple model of mean interaction fields predicts an increase of the remanence squareness S with increasing packing fraction p (Wohlfarth, 1955; Köster, 1970; Bertram and Bhatia, 1973). This is shown in Fig. 3.12, where the squareness of an isotropic sample of gamma ferric oxide particles, with a mean value of the axial ratio $a/b = 7$, is plotted as a function of p together with the theoretical curve (see also Smaller and

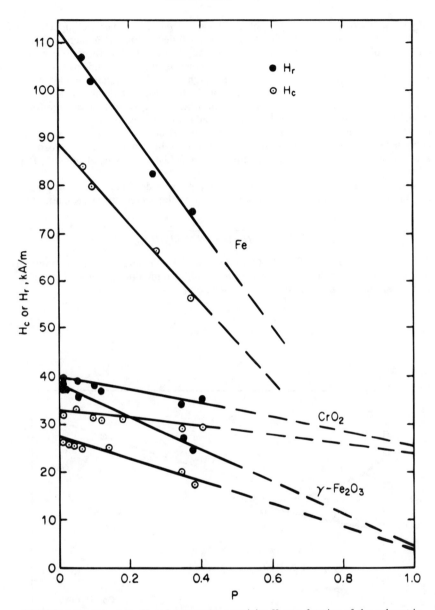

FIGURE 3.11 Coercivity H_c and remanence coercivity H_r as a function of the volumetric packing fraction p for isotropic assemblies of iron, gamma ferric iron oxide, and chromium dioxide particles.

Newman, 1970). The initial value of $S < 0.5$ at low p is due to particle imperfections as discussed before. Contradicting results of S decreasing with increasing densification of gamma ferric oxide powders may be due to the formation of flux-closing clusters. The increase of S with p, which is more pronounced for smaller values of a/b, also serves to explain the high remanence squareness of cobalt-phosphorus thin films. Such films are thought to consist of highly packed cobalt crystallites, more or less isolated from each other with respect to exchange forces, by phosphorus segregation in the grain boundaries. The parameter Δh_r, as defined earlier, is also plotted in Fig. 3.12. It is found to decrease with increasing p, in corroboration with the rather low value of the highly packed cobalt-phosphorus film. Generally, the magnetostatic interaction fields tend to level out all effects which rely on magnetostatic energy.

Finally, the initial reversible susceptibility χ_0 of an ac-demagnetized isotropic powder sample can be shown to increase owing to particle interactions (Köster, 1970):

$$\chi_0(p) = \frac{2pM_{sb}}{3H_a\,[1 - pN_b\,(\frac{2}{3}\,M_{sb}/H_a)]} \tag{3.25}$$

This equation allows the field H_a to be determined independently of the ambiguity of the nucleation of the magnetization reversal, provided the demagnetization factor N_b perpendicular to the particle axis is known:

$$H_a = \frac{2}{3}\,pM_{sb}\left(\frac{1}{\chi_0} + N_b\right) \tag{3.26}$$

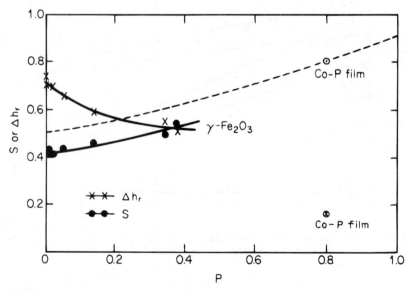

FIGURE 3.12 Remanence squareness S and the parameter Δh_r for the switching-field distribution versus the volumetric packing fraction p, for an isotropic assembly of gamma ferric iron oxide particles. The dashed curve has been calculated for infinite cylinders. Data for a cobalt-phosphorus film are included.

Equation (3.26) may be written as

$$\frac{2}{3}\frac{1}{\chi_0} = \frac{H_a}{pM_{sb}} - \frac{2}{3}N_b \tag{3.27}$$

giving the opportunity to determine H_a/M_{sb} and N_b from plotting $1/\chi_0$ as a function of $1/p$ for a series of differently compacted powder samples. In addition, the temperature dependence of χ_0 indicates whether shape anisotropy alone, or shape plus magnetocrystalline anisotropy, is present since, according to Eq. (3.25), χ_0 is independent of temperature for shape anisotropy alone ($H_a \propto M_{sb}$). This analysis may fail, as is the case with chromium dioxide, if the magnetocrystalline anisotropy field H_k happens to have the same temperature dependence as the spontaneous magnetization, instead of decreasing as usual more rapidly with temperature (Köster, 1970; Flanders, 1983).

3.2.8 Thermal Fluctuations

In analogy to Brownian movement, thermal energy causes fluctuations in the magnetization of a particle as a whole. The magnetization may be reversed statistically, as a time and temperature effect, if the total anisotropy energy of the particle, vK, is of the order of the thermal energy kT. Here, v is the volume of the particle, k is the Boltzmann constant, T is the absolute temperature, and K stands for any of the anisotropy energy density constants. This behavior is called *superparamagnetism* because the complete magnetic moments of the particles act like the individual spin moments of paramagnetic materials. There is a critical volume v_p given by

$$v_p = \ln(2tf_0)\,\frac{2kT}{\mu_0 M_{sb}H_a} \tag{3.28}$$

below which superparamagnetism exists (Wohlfarth, 1963). Here t is the time period of observation (duration of measurement), $f_0 = 10^9\,s^{-1}$ is the Larmor frequency, and H_a is the total anisotropy field. The latter may have to be replaced by the switching field H_0 of the particles or, consequently, by the remanence coercivity H_r, as the mean switching field of the sample under investigation. This has been done in order to calculate an upper limit of v_p for $t = 100$ s and $t = 300°K$ of gamma ferric oxide, of chromium dioxide, and of iron particles. The results are listed in Table 3.3 together with typical mean particle volumes of these materials. The implication of this effect for magnetic recording is that, even for $v > v_p$, the remanence may not be stable with time and temperature since

$$M_r\left(t, \frac{v}{v_p}\right) = M_r(0)\exp\left[-(2tf_0)^{1-v/v_p}\right] \tag{3.29}$$

and

$$H_c\left(\frac{v}{v_p}\right) = H_c(0)\left[1 - \left(\frac{v_p}{v}\right)^{1/2}\right] \tag{3.30}$$

Equation (3.29) is illustrated in Fig. 3.13 for $t = 100$ s (static measurement) and for spherical Co-Fe particles. The remanence increases very rapidly with increasing

TABLE 3.3 Critical Volume v_p and Critical Particle Diameter $2b_p$ for Superparamagnetic Behavior, Average Particle Volume $\langle v \rangle_{av}$, and Average Particle Diameter $\langle 2b \rangle_{av}$

Material	v_p, $10^{-4} \mu m^3$	$2b_p$, nm	$\langle v \rangle_{av}$, $10^{-4} \mu m^3$	$\langle 2b \rangle_{av}$, nm
$\gamma\text{-Fe}_2\text{O}_3$	0.2	15	2–25	30–70
CrO_2	0.09	11	1–10	25–52
Fe†	0.01	6	0.6–1	20–25

†Iron particles with $a/b = 7$.

particle dimensions, from zero at $v = v_p$ to its maximum value $M_r(0)$ which is practically stable at $v > 4v_p$. The influence of thermal fluctuations on H_c according to Eq. (3.30) is also shown in Fig. 3.13. They lead to a parabolic increase of H_c, from $H_c = 0$ at v_p to its maximum value $H_c(0)$ at relatively large volumes $v > 100v_p$. Before this happens, however, nonuniform magnetization reversal, or even multi-

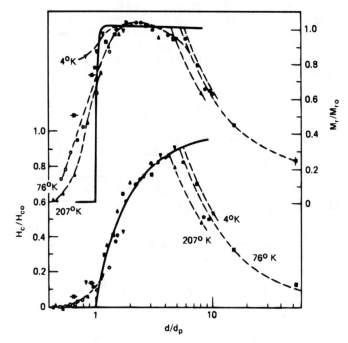

FIGURE 3.13 Coercivity H_c and saturation remanence $M_r(\infty)$ of isotropic assemblies of essentially spherical Co-Fe particles as a function of the reduced particle diameter d/d_p, where d_p is the critical diameter for superparamagnetic behavior. The parameter is the temperature of measurements. The solid curves are calculated from Eqs. (3.29) and (3.30) (*Kneller and Luborsky, 1963*).

TABLE 3.4 Time Factor $\ln (2tf_0)$ in Eq. (3.28) under Various Conditions of Magnetic Media Application

Application	t	$\ln (2tf_0)$
Archival storage	100 years	43
Static measurement	100 s	26
50- or 60-Hz measurement	20 ms	17
Audio ac-bias recording	$10\mu s$	10
Video recording	100 ns	5

domain behavior, sets in, which reduces H_c with increasing particle size. For optimum coercivity, a particle size must be chosen which is just before the peak on the right-hand side of the coercivity-versus-particle-size curve. This implies that the coercivity always depends on the speed of the magnetic field change during measurement, because v_p depends on t according to Eq. (3.28). In Table 3.4, the critical factor $\ln (2tf_0)$ is listed for various conditions of magnetic media application. It varies by a factor of less than 10 for a factor of 10^{17} in t. Although this reduces the impact of the time factor on the value of the coercivity, it has long been observed that H_c of gamma ferric oxide, for instance, as measured in a 50- or 60-Hz loop tracer is 5 to 10 percent higher than H_c as measured statically in a vibrating sample magnetometer (see also Sharrock, 1984). For chromium dioxide particles, this difference can be as high as 20 percent and consequently, the static coercivity of chromium dioxide magnetic tapes usually is 10 to 20 percent lower than that of cobalt-modified gamma ferric oxide tapes designed for the same application. This behavior is probably linked to the low exchange constant of CrO_2, as evidenced by its low Curie temperature. It has been shown that with a finite exchange constant, thermal fluctuations will always generate non-uniform magnetization reversals and lower the coercivity of acicular particles by more than the simplified theory outlined above predicts (Braun and Bertram, 1994).

Under the bias of a small applied field, $H \ll H_a$, the magnetization of particles which are only slightly larger than v_p can be reversed, and a remanence is acquired which depends on time and temperature. This effect is known in analog audio recording as print-through from one layer to another in a roll of tape (Sec. 3.2.4).

3.3 PREPARATION AND PROPERTIES OF PARTICLES

3.3.1 Preparation of Magnetic Particles

Ideally, to assure good magnetic and dispersibility properties, fine magnetic particles should be prepared by a direct precipitation process. This is in order to obtain isolated particles with smooth surfaces. In addition, they should resemble the ideal ellipsoid on which all theoretical considerations regarding the magnetization reversal processes are based. Unfortunately, gamma ferric oxide, γ-Fe_2O_3 (synthetic maghemite), the most widely used magnetic recording material, is metastable and can be prepared only by oxidation of ferrous oxide, Fe_3O_4 (synthetic magnetite). To make

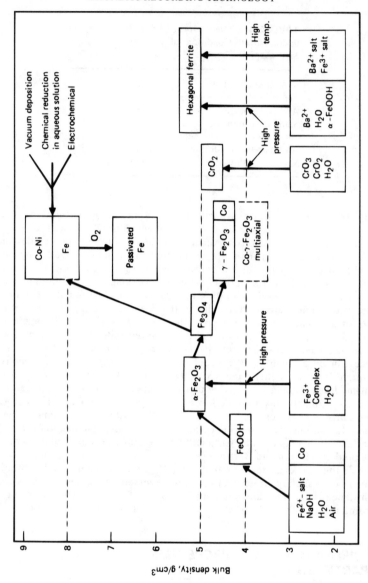

FIGURE 3.14 Stages of preparation and bulk density of magnetic particles.

things even more complicated, Fe_3O_4, because of its cubic lattice structure, cannot be directly prepared as elongated particles. Magnetite can be directly precipitated only with isometric shape, which allows a maximum coercivity of an isotropic powder sample, after oxidation to γ-Fe_2O_3, of about 15 kA/m (190 Oe). The coercivity is controlled by magnetocrystalline and shape anisotropy in about equal parts.

The preparation steps of various magnetic particle materials (Bate, 1980) are shown in Fig. 3.14 in terms of the achieved bulk density. First, needle-shaped iron oxide-hydroxide, FeOOH, is grown from a solution of iron salts and then dehydrated to the nonmagnetic modification α-Fe_2O_3 (synthetic hematite), which in turn is being reduced to Fe_3O_4. The oxide-hydroxide has three different acicular modifications which lead to γ-Fe_2O_3 particles of different morphological properties. Their principal methods of preparation and the reactions leading to γ-Fe_2O_3 are shown in Fig. 3.15. The orthorhombic α-FeOOH (synthetic goethite) has been mostly used so far. It consists of particles which often have a fibrous structure (Fig. 3.16a). The tetragonal β-FeOOH (synthetic akageneite) can be made in well-defined needles (Fig. 3.17c) which, however, consist of hollow tubes which collapse in the dehydration and reduction processes to particles with ill-defined shape. Thus, β-FeOOH is not in commercial use for the preparation of fine magnetic particles. Synthetic lepidocrocite (γ-FeOOH) again is orthorhombic and forms preferably bundles of particles which are conserved through all stages of the preparation process (Fig. 3.16c and d).

The restructuring of the crystal lattice that takes place in the solid-state reactions of the dehydration and reduction processes leads to Fe_3O_4 and consequently to γ-Fe_2O_3 particles with a rather irregular shape containing many pores (Fig. 3.16b and d). These deficiencies can be reduced to some extent by a direct hydrothermal synthesis of α-Fe_2O_3 from trivalent iron complexes under high pressure (Matsumoto, 1980). The directly precipitated α-Fe_2O_3 has a very dense structure and a well-defined shape (see Fig. 3.17a for particles made by a similar method). The final γ-Fe_2O_3, however (Fig. 3.17b), has some pores and irregularities at the surface as well. This is because, although the dehydration step has been eliminated, there is still material transport connected with the ensuing reduction and oxidation processes.

In order to assure well-crystallized particles with large coercivities, the dehydration and reduction processes need temperatures up to 750°C, which may cause the particles to form aggregates by sintering. Since this must be avoided at all costs, the FeOOH, or the directly precipitated α-Fe_2O_3 particles, are coated with organic or inorganic substances. Sometimes, elements such as P, Si, Al, or Sn are added in the preparation of FeOOH for this purpose, or for controlling the particle geometry. Indeed, most of the art of influencing the size and axial ratio of the magnetic particles takes place in the stage of seed formation and precipitation of the nonmagnetic precursor FeOOH.

The reduction process can be performed with hydrogen or organic substances such as oils of various kinds. The final oxidation should take place at temperatures below 350°C, because the ferrimagnetic γ-Fe_2O_3 will increasingly be transformed to the antiferromagnetic α-Fe_2O_3 at higher temperatures. The pseudomorphic transformation from orthorhombic FeOOH to the inverse spinel structure of Fe_3O_4, and finally to the defect spinel structure of γ-Fe_2O_3, leads to polycrystalline particles with a predominantly $\langle 110 \rangle$ fiber axis parallel to the long axis of the particles. The intermediate product of partially oxidized Fe_3O_4, $(\gamma$-$Fe_2O_3)_x(Fe_3O_4)_{1-x}$ (synthetic berthollide), which can have a slightly higher coercivity than γ-Fe_2O_3, is simply produced by interrupting the oxidation process at the desired value of x.

After the oxidation process, iron oxide powder batches are usually mechanically

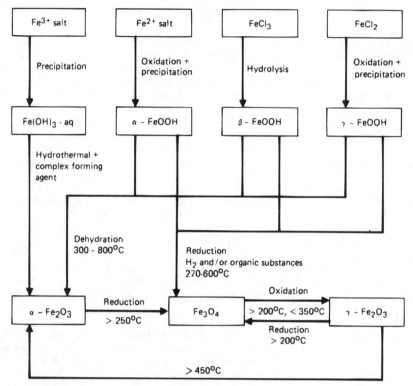

FIGURE 3.15 Principal methods of preparation and reactions for gamma ferric oxide particles.

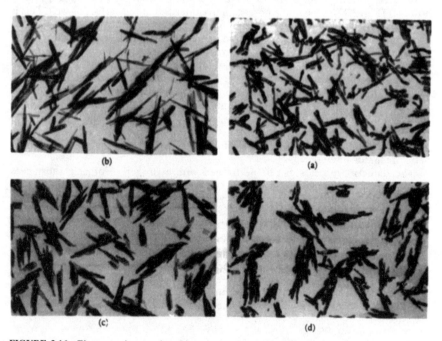

FIGURE 3.16 Electron micrographs of iron hydroxide and gamma ferric oxide particles: (a) α-FeOOH; (b) γ-Fe$_2$O$_3$ made from (a); (c) γ-FeOOH; (d) γ-Fe$_2$O$_3$ made from (c).

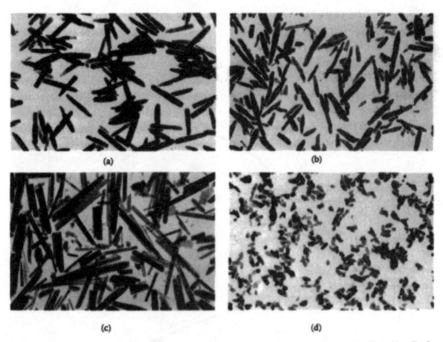

FIGURE 3.17 Electron micrographs of particles. (*a*) Directly synthesized α-Fe$_2$O$_3$; (*b*) γ-Fe$_2$O$_3$ made from (*a*); (*c*) β-FeOOH; (*d*) Co-doped γ-Fe$_2$O$_3$ with multiaxial magnetic anisotropy.

treated by tumbling in large drums or pressing between steel rolls, or by other means. Apart from the improved handling of powders with a higher apparent density, the mechanical treatment or densification also improves the dispersibility of the particles, as indicated in Fig. 3.18, possibly by a breaking up of agglomerates. Here the orientation ratio, the gloss of the as-coated and dried dispersion, and its coercivity are plotted as a function of the apparent density. Gloss is the reflectivity of the coating which is measured in this instance under an angle of incidence of 85°. It represents a convenient figure of merit for the homogeneity of particle dispersion. While the orientation ratio and the gloss indicate a maximum of dispersibility at a density of about 0.7 g/cm^3, the decreasing coercivity signals an increasing mechanical damage of the particles at higher degrees of densification. Sometimes, the particles are simultaneously treated with dispersants during this mechanical process to promote better dispersibility.

The substitution of a small amount of cobalt ions for iron ions causes a large increase of the magnetocrystalline anisotropy, as was initially shown for Fe$_3$O$_4$ (Bickford et al., 1956). Similarly, the magnetocrystalline anisotropy of γ-Fe$_2$O$_3$ can be increased by cobalt substitution, with a corresponding increase of the coercivity of the γ-Fe$_2$O$_3$ particles. Gamma ferric oxide with cobalt ions evenly distributed in the volume of the particles is made either by adding cobalt salts in the solution before the precipitation of the FeOOH, or by precipitation of cobalt hydroxide on the already formed FeOOH particles. The conversion process secures the homogeneous diffusion of the cobalt ions into the volume of the particles. The Co substitution causes a multiaxial magnetic anisotropy of the particles which can be used for the preparation of isotropic recording media. Such media have been suggested for a

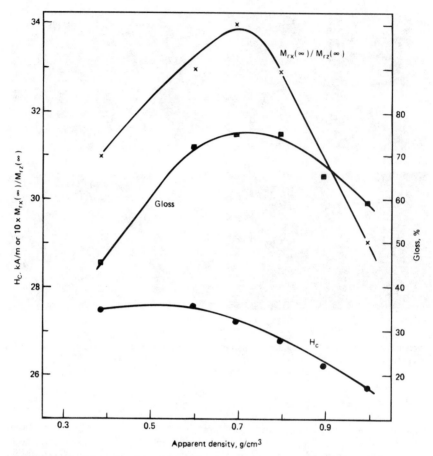

FIGURE 3.18 Orientation factor $M_{rx}(\infty)/M_{rz}(\infty)$, coercivity H_c, and gloss of as-coated and dried dispersion, versus the apparent density of γ-Fe$_2$O$_3$ particles after different degrees of densification (*Jakusch, 1984*).

combined longitudinal and perpendicular recording (Lemke, 1982). These particles either are cubic in shape, or have a low axial ratio a/b of about 2 (Fig. 3.17d). The latter are a compromise between a dominant multiaxial anisotropy with a pronounced temperature dependence of coercivity and remanence, and a dominant uniaxial anisotropy with a less pronounced temperature dependence of the magnetic properties. In the preparation process of this type of particle, the content of Fe^{2+} ions must be kept as low as possible because, in the presence of Fe^{2+} ions, an induced uniaxial anisotropy tends to be developed which reduces the squareness. This is shown in Fig. 3.19, where S is plotted versus the amount of Fe^{2+} present, for a constant amount of 5.5 wt % Co. It is of interest to note that, simultaneously with a decreasing S, the switching-field distribution Δh_r becomes larger, another reason to keep the Fe^{2+} content as low as possible.

The modification of γ-Fe$_2$O$_3$ with Co exclusively at the particle surface almost completely conserves the uniaxial magnetic anisotropy of γ-Fe$_2$O$_3$. This approach is

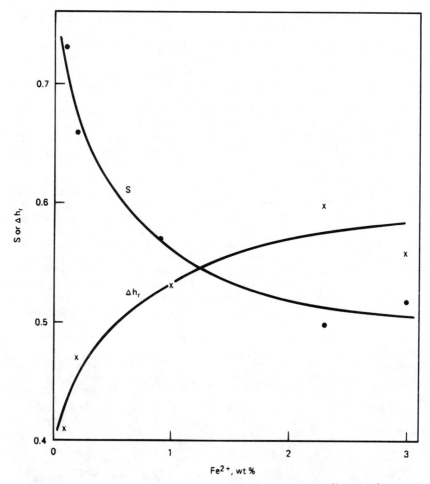

FIGURE 3.19 Remanence squareness S and switching-field distribution Δh_r versus the amount of Fe^{2+} ions present in volume-doped $\gamma\text{-}Fe_2O_3$ particles with an axial ratio of $a/b = 2$ (*Steck, 1985*).

currently most widely used in order to increase the coercivity of gamma ferric oxide particles beyond the value of 32 kA/m (400 Oe) achievable for pure gamma ferric oxide. These surface-modified particles are prepared by precipitation of cobalt hydroxide, with or without the presence of Fe^{2+} ions from an aqueous solution, and by a subsequent annealing of the dry powder (Schönfinger et al., 1972; Umeki et al., 1974; Shimizu et al., 1975). This annealing step must be controlled carefully in order to avoid diffusion of the Co or Fe^{2+} ions far into the volume of the particles (Witherell, 1984). An interesting dry process of preparing Co-modified $\gamma\text{-}Fe_2O_3$ is the pyrolytic decomposition of Co organometallic vapor on the surface of Fe_3O_4 particles in a fluid-bed reactor (Monteil and Dougier, 1980).

Carrying the reduction of FeOOH beyond Fe_3O_4 leads to a further increase of the bulk density to that of the pure metal (Fig. 3.14). This step is even more sensitive to sintering effects, making a protective surface treatment of the FeOOH precursor mandatory in order to obtain well-defined particles like those shown in Fig. 3.20a. Sintering is aggravated because the FeOOH particles must be chosen to be even smaller than those for the preparation of γ-Fe_2O_3. For instance, the specific surface area may be up to 100 m^2/g instead of up to 60 m^2/g. This is in order to obtain reasonable values of coercivity for iron or iron-cobalt particles, since the critical radius b_0 of iron for uniform magnetization reversal is about five times smaller than that of γ-Fe_2O_3 (Sec. 3.2). With pure iron, coercivities of up to about 160 kA/m (2000 Oe) have been obtained. The high specific surface area of the iron particles makes them pyrophoric, and they must be passivated by a controlled oxidation of their surface. In practice, about 50 percent of a particle's volume is oxidized with a kernel of pure iron. Consequently, the bulk density is lowered as indicated in Fig. 3.14.

The methods for a direct synthesis of metal particles, such as evaporation of the metal in an inert gas atmosphere (Tasaki et al., 1979), chemical reduction with borohydride (Oppegard, 1961), and electrochemical deposition (Luborsky, 1961), are not in commercial use. Some time ago, there was some interest in metal particles with intermediate coercivities which may be obtained by reducing the spontaneous magnetization. For this purpose, the iron can be alloyed to some extent with nickel by coprecipitation from Fe and Ni salts when starting from FeOOH. An easier method is by the precipitation of nickel hydroxide onto the already formed FeOOH particles. An evaporation method can also be used. Another way of reducing the spontaneous magnetization is the formation of Fe_4N by heating Fe particles

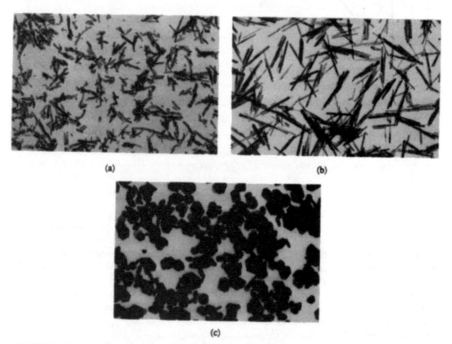

(a)   (b)

(c)

FIGURE 3.20   Electron micrographs of (a) iron particles, (b) CrO_2 particles, and (c) $BaFe_{12}O_{19}$ platelets.

in a mixture of hydrogen and ammonia (Tasaki et al., 1981). Iron carbonitrides ($Fe_4N_xC_{1-x}$), prepared by a similar process, have been claimed to be more stable to oxidation than Fe_4N (Andriamandroso et al., 1984). Another route for reducing the coercivity is the reduction of the axial ratio of the particles. An increase of particle diameter at constant axial ratio is not feasible, since the increased particle volume leads to prohibitive noise characteristics.

Chromium dioxide can be directly synthesized in a hydrothermal process at pressures between 3 and 7×10^6 Pa (4 to 10×10^6 lb/in^2) by reaction of CrO_3 with a Cr (III)-oxide. The particle size and its axial ratio are controlled by adding small amounts of Fe, Te, and Sb as doping elements. This process leads to perfectly crystallized, elongated particles (Fig. 3.20b). The addition of Fe and Ir increases the magnetocrystalline anisotropy of CrO_2. The reduction in size by the addition of antimony is illustrated in Fig. 3.21, where lines of constant specific surface area are drawn in a plot of Sb versus Fe content. Here Sb effectively increases the specific surface area; that is, it reduces the particle size and consequently its radius. The radius controls the contribution of shape anisotropy to the overall coercivity. The addition of Fe increases the coercivity through an increase of magnetocrystalline anisotropy as shown by Fig. 3.22, where lines of constant coercivity are drawn in the same diagram of Sb versus Fe content (Chen et al., 1984).

Since CrO_2 is a chemically oxidizing substance, the particles are made to have a

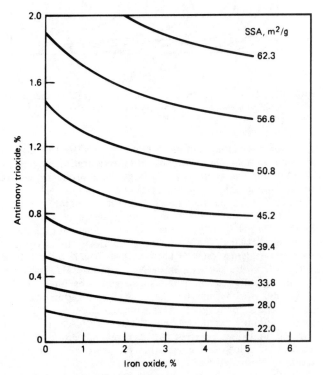

FIGURE 3.21 The specific surface area (SSA) that results from varying the percentages of antimony trioxide and iron oxide in the preparation of chromium dioxide particles (*Chen et al., 1984*).

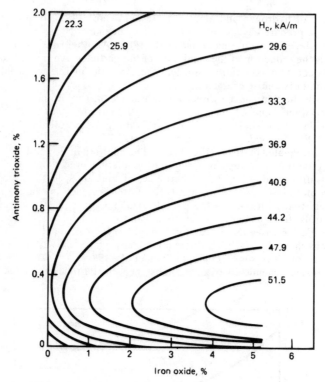

FIGURE 3.22 The coercivity H_c that results by varying the percentages of antimony trioxide and iron oxide in the preparation of chromium dioxide particles (*Chen et al., 1984*).

thin protective layer, for example, of orthorhombic CrOOH. This layer reduces the overall specific saturation magnetization but not the saturation magnetization of the kernel which controls the coercivity. In large-scale production, CrO_2 with a coercivity of up to about 72 kA/m (900 Oe) can be prepared.

The hexagonal ferrites, in particular barium ferrite, are of interest for perpendicular magnetic recording because they can be precipitated by various processes as hexagonal platelets (Fig. 3.20c). Their easy axis of magnetization is parallel to the c axis, which is perpendicular to the plane of the platelets. The possible preparation methods are precipitation in a NaCl-KCl flux, hydrothermal synthesis from $Ba(OH)_2$ with α-FeOOH, or from $Ba(NO_3)_2$ with $Fe(NO_3)_3$ and NaOH, and quenching of a $BaO + B_2O_3 + Fe_2O_3$ melt to an amorphous glass with subsequent crystallization by annealing. Only the hydrothermal and the glass crystallization processes are presently in commercial use for magnetic recording particles. Since the coercivity of barium ferrite can be as high as 480 kA/m (6000 Oe), it is usually reduced by adding e.g. Co, Ni, Sn, Zn, or Ti in order to be used in magnetic recording (Smit and Wijn, 1959; Kubo et al., 1982). Needle-shaped barium ferrite can also be made by a pseudomorphic reaction of elongated FeOOH particles as used for the preparation of γ-Fe_2O_3 particles with Na_2CO_3 (Takada et al., 1970). The c axis as the easy direction of magnetocrystalline anisotropy is perpendicular to the particle axis. A review of preparation methods is given by Hibst (1982).

TABLE 3.5 Specific Saturation Magnetization σ_s, Bulk Density ρ, Coercivity H_c, Mean Particle Volume $\langle v \rangle_{av}$, and Specific Surface Area (SSA) of Isotropic Powder Samples†

Material	σ_s, A·m²/kg (emu/g)	ρ, g/cm³	H_c, kA/m (4π Oe)	$\langle v \rangle_{av}$, 10^{-4} μm³	SSA, m²/g
Fe alloyed with Co	125–170	5.4	75–160	<1	35–60
Fe₄N, Fe-Ni	110–120	5.8	55–90	<1	35–50
CrO₂	76–84	4.8	25–75	0.8–10††	18–40
γ-Fe₂O₃	73–75	4.8	20–32	1–25	12–35
γ-Fe₂O₃ + Co	70–75	4.8	30–75	0.7–10	16–50
BaFe₁₂₋₂ₓCoₓTiₓO₁₉	55–65	5.3	50–150	<1	25–70

†With a volumetric packing fraction of $p = 0.25$.
††Total volume including nonmagnetic surface layer.

The magnetic powder properties for the materials discussed in this section are given in Table 3.5, together with their bulk density, range of specific surface area, and particle volumes.

3.3.2 Iron Oxides

The first experimental magnetic tapes were made with carbonyl-iron particles of more than 1 μm in diameter, and the first commercial audio tapes were produced with equant Fe_3O_4 and, later, with equant γ-Fe_2O_3 particles. Elongated γ-Fe_2O_3 particles were introduced in 1954 and are still most widely used in magnetic recording. Gamma ferric oxide combines the advantages of being chemically and structurally stable, and has a magnetic anisotropy which is dominated by shape. The particles tend to consist of individual crystallites with a $\langle 110 \rangle$ fiber axis parallel to the particle axis with other orientations occurring as well (Gustard and Vriend, 1969). Both magnetocrystalline and shape anisotropy seem to be additive, with a contribution of the magnetocrystalline anisotropy to the coercivity of about 6 kA/m (75 Oe) (Eagle and Mallinson, 1967; Köster, 1970). The crystallite size plays an important role because it degrades the magnetic properties of the particles if it becomes smaller than the particle diameter. This is demonstrated to the extreme by the data in Fig. 3.23 (Berkowitz et al., 1968). Here, the specific saturation magnetization σ_s and the coercivity H_c are plotted as a function of the crystallite size. With decreasing crystallite size, σ_s is reduced by nonmagnetic grain boundaries approximately 0.6 nm thick. Simultaneously, the crystallites become more sensitive to thermal fluctuations. The coercivity has a typical maximum as a function of crystallite size as discussed earlier. Consequently, the print-through effect in analog audio recording increases with decreasing crystallite size (Tochihara et al., 1970).

The particle size, or more precisely its volume v, has been reduced considerably over the years from over 30×10^{-4} to about 2×10^{-4} μm³ in order to reduce the noise of the recording media. The corresponding reduction of the particle diameter results in a more uniform reversal of magnetization. This leads to an increase of coercivity from below 20 to more than 32 kA/m (250 to 400 Oe), and a decrease of the switching-field distribution Δh_r from 0.6 to 0.5. These data are for an isotropic

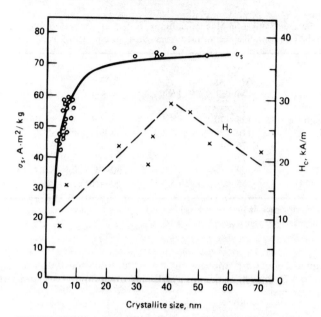

FIGURE 3.23 Specific saturation magnetization σ_s and coercivity H_c as a function of the crystallite size of elongated γ-Fe_2O_3 particles (*Berkowitz et al., 1968*).

powder sample with a volumetric packing fraction of $p = 0.25$. Unfortunately, the effect of thermal fluctuations, and consequently print-through, become more prominent with smaller particle volumes. A decrease in the distribution of particle volumes and larger crystallite sizes have helped to keep the print-through signals at reasonable values.

The use of γ-FeOOH as a precursor for γ-Fe_2O_3 was introduced commercially in 1970. The advantages are a better degree of orientation and a higher volumetric packing compared to particles made from the α-FeOOH used previously (Gustard and Wright, 1972). These improvements have been attributed to bundlelike aggregates of parallel particles. The remanence squareness can be increased from 0.72 to 0.85, and the volumetric packing fraction from 0.35 to 0.45. Consequently, the saturation remanence of audio tapes can be improved from about 95 to 135 kA/m (emu/cm^3). Meanwhile, the particles made from α-FeOOH were improved by carefully avoiding any sintering effects. Recently, particles based on a direct hydrothermal precipitation of α-Fe_2O_3 (Matsumoto, 1980) were introduced which are similar to the particles made from α-FeOOH, but which lead to about 10 percent higher saturation remanence under the same preparation conditions.

Magnetite Fe_3O_4 has the intrinsic advantage of a 37 percent higher spontaneous magnetization than γ-Fe_2O_3. It has, however, been little used in magnetic recording media owing to relatively high print-through signals and the precautions necessary to guard against partial oxidation during the medium manufacturing process. The intermediate state, $(\gamma$-$Fe_2O_3)_x(Fe_3O_4)_{1-x}$, has a maximum in coercivity at $x = 0.85$, which can be as much as 30 percent larger than that of the corresponding γ-Fe_2O_3 particles. However, these nonstoichiometric iron oxides suffer from prohibitive aging effects, even at room temperature, due to a directional pair-ordering effect of divalent iron ions (Imaoka, 1965; Chikazumi, 1974). Whether this divalent pair-ordering effect, or vacancy ordering, or even stress anisotropy, is the origin of the increased coercivity is still under discussion (Kishimoto, 1979; Kaneko, 1980; Kojima and Hanada, 1980). They recently gained some acceptance, however, as precursors for cobalt-modified iron oxides.

3.3.3 Cobalt-Modified Iron Oxides

It has been known for some time that the coercivity of γ-Fe$_2$O$_3$ is increased by introducing cobalt ions which replace trivalent iron ions on octahedral sites and simultaneously fill octahedral site vacancies (Jeschke, 1954; Khalafalla and Morrish, 1972). Since the cobalt ions have a large positive magnetocrystalline anisotropy, the $\langle 100 \rangle$ axes are easy directions of magnetization. Two of them are at 45° and one at 90° to the $\langle 110 \rangle$ fiber axis, which is the easy direction of the shape anisotropy. Consequently, for an isotropic powder sample, the remanence squareness increases from 0.5 for unmodified γ-Fe$_2$O$_3$, to 0.83 for dominating magnetocrystalline anisotropy. In close accordance with theoretical considerations (Tonge and Wohlfarth, 1958), the transition from dominating shape anisotropy to dominating multiaxial magnetocrystalline anisotropy occurs at $H_k/H_m = 1.16$ (Köster, 1972). The strong temperature dependence of the magnetocrystalline anisotropy thus leads to a temperature dependence of S (Speliotis et al., 1964). This is demonstrated in Fig. 3.24, where remanence squareness S and remanence coercivity H_r are plotted as a function of temperature. While γ-Fe$_2$O$_3$ (sample A) shows almost no variation of S and H_r in the temperature range from 140 to 420°K, Sample C, with 2.5 wt % Co in the particle volume, has a sharp increase of both quantities below 370°K. For particles (sample D) which have an axial ratio of 2 instead of the usual value of 7, S is much higher at room temperature, and H_r has a much more pronounced temperature dependence. The continuous increase of H_r in the curves of Fig. 3.24 indicates that shape and magnetocrystalline anisotropy add constructively to H_r, although their easy axes do not coincide. The particles of sample D behave more like multiaxial particles and are candidates for use in isotropic recording media (Lemke, 1982). However, such particles show strong temperature dependence of their magnetic properties. Also, reductions of recorded signals may occur after repeated use because of the high magnetostriction effects associated with cobalt ions. These defects may limit extensive commercial use of these particles.

Although it has raised interest since the early days of magnetic recording (Krones, 1960), cobalt-substituted Fe$_3$O$_4$ or $(\gamma$-Fe$_2$O$_3)_x$(Fe$_3$O$_4)_{1-x}$ has been little used in magnetic recording. Such materials suffer from the same defects described in the previous section for the unmodified materials. Furthermore, Co in $(\gamma$-Fe$_2$O$_3)_x$(Fe$_3$O$_4)_{1-x}$ develops large induced anisotropies after aging in external fields (Kamiya et al., 1980). This leads to recording signals which cannot be erased after prolonged storage, because they are permanently "recorded" by locally induced anisotropies.

Because of the pronounced temperature dependence of their magnetic parameters, little commercial use has been seen for γ-Fe$_2$O$_3$ with Co ions diffused throughout the particle volume. A breakthrough occurred, however, with the idea to adsorb cobalt ions at the particle surface (Schönfinger et al., 1972; Umeki et al., 1974). A strong anisotropy energy of the order of 1.5×10^5 J/m^3 (1.5×10^6 erg/cm^3) is reported to be found at the particle surface which inhibits the nucleation of magnetization reversal at any irregularities (Tokuoka et al., 1977). Thus, the shape anisotropy as given by Eq. (3.16) can be more fully utilized, and the coercivity is

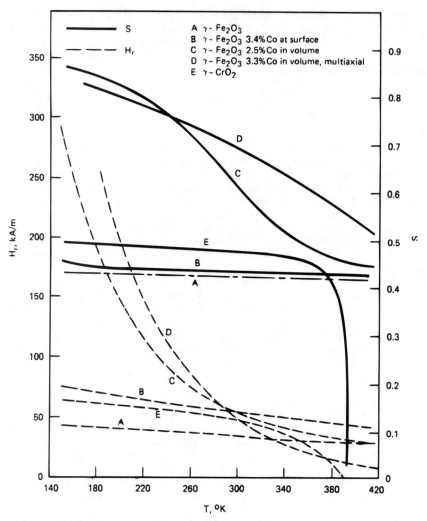

FIGURE 3.24 Remanence squareness S and remanence coercivity H_r as a function of temperature T for isotropic samples of (curve A) elongated $\gamma\text{-Fe}_2\text{O}_3$ particles, (curve B) the same with 3.4% Co concentrated at the particle surface, (curve C) the same with 2.5% Co evenly distributed in the particle volume, (curve D) almost equant $\gamma\text{-Fe}_2\text{O}_3$ particles with 3.3% Co evenly distributed in the particle volume, and (curve E) elongated CrO_2 particles.

raised to about 42 kA/m (530 Oe) without an increase of its temperature dependence. For this to happen, the additional anisotropy at the particle surface need only be above a certain threshold of the order of the magnetostatic energy 0.25 $\mu_0 M_{sb}^2 = 3.8 \times 10^4$ J/m^3 ($\pi M_{sb}^2 = 3.8 \times 10^5$ erg/cm^3) in order to prevent local demagnetizing fields from nucleating magnetization reversal at the surface. The coercivity increases proportionally to the amount of Co adsorbed until about 2 wt % of Co. Above this point, H_c stays at a constant value and the specific saturation magnetization starts to decrease (Tokuoka et al., 1977). The annealing step involved in the preparation of these particles makes it likely that, up to 2% Co concentration, the Co ions are incorporated into the iron oxide lattice at the particle surface. Thus, a thin layer of cobalt-modified iron oxide may be formed which has a high anisotropy energy density. Consequently, attempts were made to increase the thickness of this layer by depositing onto the particles Co^{2+} and Fe^{2+} ions simultaneously (Shimizu et al., 1975). A similar increase of coercivity, proportional to the amount of cobalt added, has been found without an increase of its temperature dependence. Thus, sample B in Fig. 3.24 exhibits little more temperature dependence of S and H_r than γ-Fe_2O_3 itself, although it has the same room temperature value of $H_r = 55$ kA/m (690 Oe) as sample C with the Co evenly distributed in the particle volume. The coercivity and specific saturation magnetization increase continuously with the amount of added Co and Fe ions in contrast with the Co-adsorbed type. This and the observed increase in particle size suggests the formation of a shell of cobalt-modified iron oxide around the γ-Fe_2O_3 particle. Beyond a coercivity of about 60 kA/m (750 Oe), the particles increasingly lose their uniaxial anisotropy, and, consequently, their magnetic parameters become increasingly temperature-dependent (Kishimoto et al., 1981). This indicates that beyond this coercivity, cobalt-modified iron oxide, with its cubic magnetocrystalline anisotropy, dominates the nucleation of magnetization reversal, an effect which seems to be retarded by an induced anisotropy with the easy axis of magnetization parallel to the particle axis. Recent developments use Fe(II)-rich precursor particles for the modification process, leading to particles with a slightly increased specific magnetization. In addition, these particles are advantageous for certain applications due to their almost black color and lower electrical resistivity.

3.3.4 Chromium Dioxide

Chromium dioxide (CrO_2) particles are single-crystal needles with a tetragonal rutile structure, unique metallic low resistivity, and deep black color. The easy direction of magnetocrystalline anisotropy has been reported either as parallel to the c axis, which is parallel to the particle axis (Rodbell, 1966), or inclined by 40° to the c axis (Cloud et al., 1962). The remanence coercivity H_r of a spatially isotropic particle assembly is expected to be $H_r = 0.529 H_k = 38.6$ kA/m (485 Oe) for uniaxial magnetocrystalline anisotropy, and $H_r = 0.529(N_b - N_a)M_{sb} = 0.23 M_{sb} = 110.4$ kA/m (1387 Oe) for shape anisotropy ($a/b = 6$) and uniform magnetization reversal. If the axes of easy magnetization coincide, both contributions add to give $H_r = 149$ kA/m (1872 Oe). In the case of CrO_2 made with 0.15 wt % Sb and 0.25 wt % Fe, a value of $H_r = 54.8$ kA/m (689 Oe) has been measured, extrapolated to zero volumetric packing fraction. This value can be separated into a contribution by magnetocrystalline anisotropy of 21.2 kA/m $= 0.29 H_k$, and a contribution by shape anisotropy of 33.6 kA/m $= 0.07 M_{sb}$ (Köster, 1973). The value for shape anisotropy may be attributed to a typical reduced particle radius of $b/b_0 = 3$. There is, however, no obvious explanation for the rather small contribution of magnetocrystalline anisotropy, unless the easy axis of magnetocrystalline anisotropy is indeed assumed to be inclined with respect to the c axis. In the case of 40° of inclination, a contribution of $0.3 H_k$ can be calculated, together with an equilibrium position of the magnetization direction in zero field of about 10° off the c axis. Whether this is evidence enough against collinear magnetocrystalline and shape anisotropy in CrO_2 particles is still open to discussion.

The temperature dependence of the magnetocrystalline anisotropy energy density of CrO_2 is about equal to that of M_{sb}^2, over a wide range; therefore H_d/M_s is almost independent of temperature up to about 80°C. Beyond this temperature it drops at an increasing rate to zero at the Curie temperature, typically 125°C (Rodbell, 1966; Köster, 1973). This is equally true for the inverse demagnetization criterion H_c/M_r and for the remanence squareness (curve E in Fig. 3.24), thus making CrO_2 a viable material for magnetic recording in spite of its relatively low Curie temperature.

The coercivity of CrO_2 can be controlled not only by the particle radius (already shown in Fig. 3.5) but also by its magnetocrystalline anisotropy. In Fig. 3.25, the magnetocrystalline anisotropy field H_k, and Curie temperature T_c, are plotted as a function of the amount of Fe added. Values as high as $H_k = 160$ kA/M (2000 Oe) have been achieved. An even more dramatic increase of H_k is found by using Ir additives in the hydrothermal synthesis of CrO_2 which increase the spin-orbit cou-

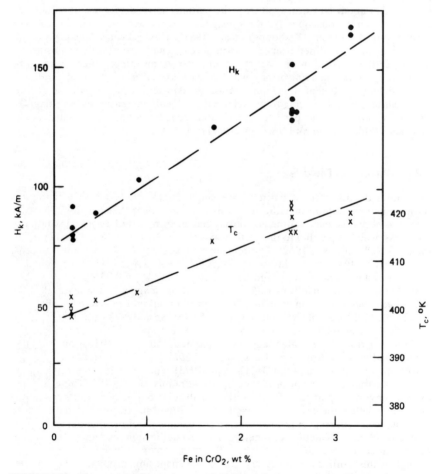

FIGURE 3.25 Magnetocrystalline anisotropy field H_k and Curie temperature T_c versus the amount of iron in chromium dioxide particles.

pling constants (Maestro et al., 1982). Values of H_k up to 580 kA/m (7300 Oe) are possible, and the remanence coercivity H_r can almost equal $0.529H_k$, the value expected for magnetization reversal by uniform rotation (Kullmann et al., 1984b). Apart from this rather expensive possibility, it has been possible to obtain coercivities of up to 72 kA/m (900 Oe) in production quantities.

Chromium dioxide particles can be made in very small sizes, with mean particle volumes of the order of 10^{-4} μm^3, using the direct hydrothermal precipitation process. This partially explains a marked difference between coercivities measured statically, and the coercivity in the rapidly changing fields as experienced in magnetic recording. Thus, depending on the type of magnetic recording application, the 55 kA/m cited above is equivalent to about 62 to 70 kA/m (780 to 880 Oe) in cobalt-modified iron particles of larger particle size.

The almost perfect shape of CrO_2 particles enables them to be well aligned, with a reduced saturation remanence as high as $S = 0.9$. The more irregularly shaped cobalt-modified iron oxide particles have a lesser degree of particle alignment. They may, however, have about the same value of S due to some multiaxial anisotropy contribution of the cobalt ions.

3.3.5 Metal Particles

Iron particles, as prepared from various FeOOH precursors, consist of a kernel of 50 to 70 vol % metal with a shell of ill-defined magnetic iron oxides which on top of this may be covered with non-magnetic, anti-sintering coatings. The magnetostatic energy and nucleation fields for magnetization in this situation can be analyzed theoretically, based on a model of coaxial prolate spheroids (Stavn and Morrish, 1979). It was found that the coercivity is almost unaltered by the magnetic oxide shell, and determined by the shape anisotropy of the iron kernel only. Thus, the maximum possible coercivity of a powder sample of infinite cylinders with a volumetric packing fraction of 0.25 is 307 kA/m (3860 Oe). So far, values have been obtained of up to 160 kA/m (2000 Oe). The contribution of magnetocrystalline anisotropy may be neglected, since its contribution to H_c amounts to only 13 kA/m (163 Oe) (Fig. 3.11). The specific saturation magnetization σ_s of the particles is reduced to 125 to 170 A · m²/kg (125 to 170 emu/g) and the bulk density to 5.4. to 6.0 g/cm³ because of the surface oxide shell. Consequently, magnetic recording media made of iron particles have a saturation remanence of about 240 kA/m (emu/cm³).

Apart from the application in high-coercivity recording media, attempts have been made to utilize the higher saturation magnetization in existing audio and video recording systems which are designed for coercivities between 45 and 60 kA/m (560 and 750 Oe). In order to achieve these low coercivities, however, the particle diameter, which controls H_c, and consequently the particle volume, becomes too large for reasonable noise values. In addition, the switching-field distribution Δh_r increases with decreasing H_c due to a less uniform magnetization reversal mode. Consequently, a compromise solution has been evolved by keeping the particle dimensions constant and reducing the saturation magnetization. This is achieved by alloying with Ni or by forming Fe_4N.

The metal particles obtained by condensation of vapor in an inert gas atmosphere (Tasaki et al., 1979) are spherical, and form linear chains similar to those obtained by the reduction of metal salts with borohydride (Oppegard et al., 1961), or the decomposition of metal carbonyls (Thomas, 1966). Using the evaporation method, a coercivity range of 55 to 180 kA/m (700 to 2300 Oe) has been achieved by alloying with Ni or Co, and keeping the particle diameter constant at approximately

20 nm (Tasaki et al., 1983). The specific saturation magnetization has been varied correspondingly, from 110 to 200 A · m^2/kg (110 to 200 emu/g).

3.3.6 Barium Ferrite

Barium ferrite (BaFe$_{12}$O$_{19}$), as such, is of little use for magnetic recording since its intrinsic anisotropy field $H_a = (2K_1/\mu_0 M_{sb}) - M_{sb} = 1000$ kA/m (13,000 Oe) is extremely high. Shape and magnetocrystalline anisotropy are orthogonal, and contribute with opposite sign to the anisotropy field. This is because the easy direction of magnetocrystalline anisotropy is perpendicular to the plain of the thin hexagonal barium ferrite platelets. The resulting remanence coercivity for uniform magnetization reversal is given by $H_r = 0.529 H_a$, or 530 kA/m (6660 Oe). This value is indeed found with particles in the size range of 0.1 to 0.3 μm, as precipitated in a NaCl flux. Increased interest has been raised for this type of material through the possible use in recording media for perpendicular recording. The idea is to orient the platelets flat in the plane of the recording media, thus having an easy direction of magnetization perpendicular to the plane. The magnetocrystalline anisotropy can be lowered through the substitution of the Ba^{2+} or Fe^{3+} ions by di- or trivalent ions, together with a reduction in M_{sb} and T_c. A more drastic reduction in anisotropy is produced using Co with Ti, or Zn with Ti, in BaMe$_x^{2+}$ Me$_x^{4+}$ Fe$_{12-2x}$O$_{19}$, as a combined substitution of the trivalent iron ions. Here Me^{2+} and Me^{4+} stand for the di- and tetravalent substitution ions, respectively. This type of substitution dramatically reduces H_k, and leads to an easy plane of magnetization perpendicular to the c axis, for $x > 1.2$ and $x > 0.3$ for the Co-Ti and Zn-Ti substitution, respectively. Thus, little saturation magnetization is lost in varying H_c over the whole range from almost zero to the maximum possible value. Generally, barium ferrite suffers from a relatively low specific magnetization. This can be increased by coating the platelets with a layer of cubic spinel, using a process similar to the surface modification of iron oxide with cobalt. Oriented barium ferrite media show extremely narrow switching field distributions. It is possible to obtain very high linear recording densities even at relatively low coercivities (Speliotis, 1988).

3.3.7 Morphological and Physicochemical Aspects

So far, only the mean particle dimensions have been addressed. Particle length and particle diameter are both subject to a distribution function, as illustrated in Fig. 3.26. Here, the normalized particle count is plotted versus particle diameter $2b$, using a Gaussian distribution as an approximation for the measured histograms. Representative samples of γ-Fe$_2$O$_3$, CrO$_2$, and Fe particles have been chosen. Similar distributions exist for the particle length. The characteristic feature of these distribution functions is an increase in the standard deviation, as well as a shift of the distribution curve, with increasing mean particle dimensions. The most conveniently measured quantity for characterization of the mean particle size is its specific surface area, and this is widely used. It scales quite well with the particle size and varies from 16 m^2/g for sample A of Fig. 3.26 to 48 m^2/g for sample F. Some caution has to be applied when using the specific surface area as a measure for particle volume. Measured areas are influenced by the axial ratio a/b, by the bulk density, and in particular by pores in the particles. Such factors can lead to misinterpretations of the specific surface area data, particularly for metal particles.

The typical shapes of various representatives of magnetic fine particles have

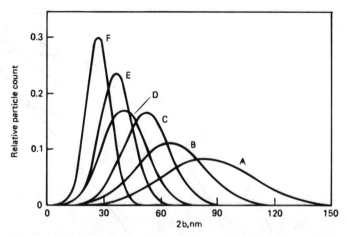

FIGURE 3.26 Normalized particle count versus particle diameter $2b$ for (curve A) γ-Fe_2O_3 particles (SSA = 16 m^2/g) as used in computer tapes or floppy disks, (curve B) Fe_2O_3 particles (SSA = 20 m^2/g), (curve C) γ-Fe_2O_3 particles (SSA = 24 m^2/g), (curve D) CrO_2 particles (SSA = 27 m^2/g) as used in audio cassette tapes (curve E) Co-modified γ-Fe_2O_3 (SSA = 36 m^2/g) and (curve F) Fe particles (SSA = 48 m^2/g) as used for video tapes (*Jakusch, 1984*).

been shown in Figs. 3.16, 3.17, and 3.20. It is common experience that particles with irregularly shaped surfaces yield less perfect degrees of alignment than those with smooth surfaces, such as CrO_2. This is due to a steric, frictionlike interference between the particles. The magnetic torque of the field applied for alignment increases proportionally to the volume v of the particles. Also, the friction between the particles increases with particle volume at a rate between $v^{1/3}$ and $v^{2/3}$. For these reasons, larger particles usually yield a better degree of alignment than smaller particles. Thus γ-Fe_2O_3 made from γ-FeOOH, which exists in the form of bundles of particles that rotate as a single-particle unit, gives a much better degree of alignment than the more individual particles made from α-FeOOH. In addition, large particles lend themselves to a higher volumetric packing fraction than small particles, an effect which again is connected with the surface-to-volume ratio (Patton, 1979).

The mechanical energy needed to disperse the particles in a binder solution, apart from depending on the degree of agglomeration produced in the synthesis of the particles, increases with decreasing particle size. This is demonstrated in Fig. 3.27, where the gloss of the as-coated and dried dispersion is plotted versus the milling time for the same particles used for Fig. 3.26. With increasing specific surface area, a longer milling time is needed to obtain the optimum gloss value (Patton, 1979). On the other hand, smaller particles yield a smoother final dispersion, as is indicated by the larger final gloss value. Exceptions from this general trend are γ-Fe_2O_3 particles made from γ-FeOOH (curve B), and CrO_2 particles (curve D), which are more easily dispersed than other particles of comparable size (curves A and C).

When considering the concentration of particles in a magnetic coating, one has to distinguish between the pigment-volume concentration and the packing fraction introduced earlier. The former is the volume occupied by the particles as related to

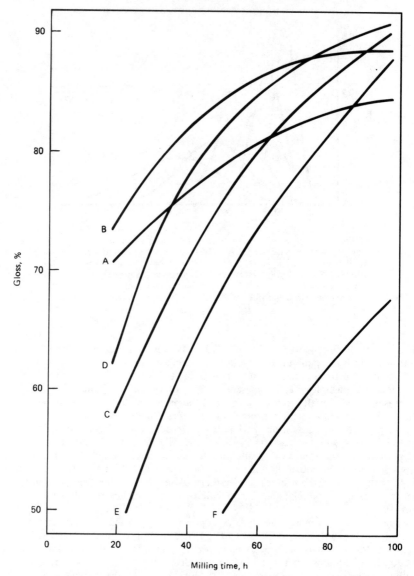

FIGURE 3.27 Gloss versus milling time for the same powder samples as in Fig. 3.26: (curve A) through (curve C) γ-Fe$_2$O$_3$, (curve D) CrO$_2$, (curve E) Co-modified γ-Fe$_2$O$_3$, and (curve F) Fe particles (*Jakusch, 1984*).

the nonvolatile components of a dispersion. The latter is related to the nonmagnetic volume of the coating (Patton, 1979). At low concentrations, both are identical since the particles are embedded in a continuous matrix of binder and additives. At higher pigment-volume concentrations, typically above a critical value of 0.3, the packing fraction increases more slowly and finally stays at a maximum value inde-

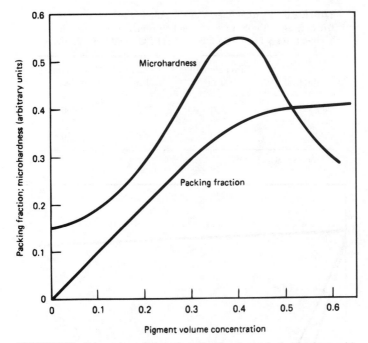

FIGURE 3.28 Schematic variation of packing fraction and microhardness with pigment-volume concentration of an as-dried coating.

pendent of the pigment-volume concentration. The closest packing of the particles is approached, and the magnetic coating increasingly contains pores (Huisman and Rasenberg, 1984). This situation is illustrated schematically in Fig. 3.28, where the packing fraction of the particles is shown versus the pigment-volume concentration. Usually, a pigment-volume concentration slightly above the critical value is chosen to exploit the compressive effect of the calendering and to obtain the highest possible saturation remanence (Rasenberg and Huisman, 1984). For iron oxide and chromium dioxide pigments, this amounts to a pigment-volume concentration of 0.45 to 0.55, and for metal pigments of 0.35 to 0.45. In comparison, the maximum values of the packing fraction are about 0.47 and 0.37, respectively. The lower values for metal pigments are accounted for by their smaller particle volume; that is, the critical volume concentration and the packing fraction usually decrease with decreasing particle volume. On the other hand, both can be considerably influenced by the dispersant used. An upper usable limit for the pigment-volume concentration is governed by the weakening of the bonds between the particles in the magnetic coating caused by increasing porosity. Below the critical particle-volume concentration, the particles act like a filler that leads to increased mechanical wear resistance. Above the critical value, the mechanical strength is weakened by the porosity of the coating (Dasgupta, 1984; Huisman and Rasenberg, 1984). This effect is shown in Fig. 3.28 in terms of the microhardness of the coating.

The effect of the dispersants in the milling process depends on the chemical nature of the surface of the particles (Sugihara et al., 1980), the dispersant, and the binder system used. The chemical nature of the surface of the particles can be

TABLE 3.6 Wetting Energy of Ethanol as a Proton Donor, Dioxane as a Proton Acceptor, and Nitromethane with a Dipole Moment, for γ-Fe_2O_3, Co-Modified γ-Fe_2O_3, and CrO_2 Particles

Material	Ethyl alcohol, mJ/m^2	Dioxane, mJ/m^2	Nitromethane, mJ/m^2
γ-Fe_2O_3	260	350	460
γ-Fe_2O_3 + Co	390	340	310
CrO_2	670	350	310

SOURCE: Jakusch (1984).

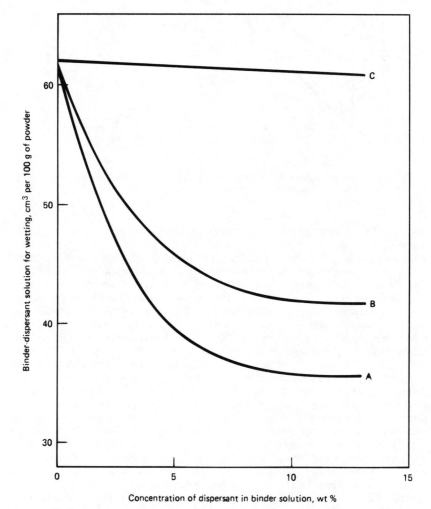

FIGURE 3.29 Amount of binder-dispersant solution needed for the wetting of γ-Fe_2O_3 powder as a function of concentration of dispersant in the binder solution for (curve A) phosphate ester, (curve B) lecithin, and (curve C) silicone oil (*Jakusch, 1984*).

investigated by measuring the wetting energy of test substances such as ethyl alcohol as a proton donor, dioxane as a proton acceptor, and nitromethane as a molecule with a dipole moment. The differences in wetting energies of the three test substances using typical γ-Fe_2O_3 and Co-modified γ-Fe_2O_3 particles are listed in Table 3.6. These data confirm the general experience that unmodified γ-Fe_2O_3 has an acidic surface character and polar characteristics which are reduced by the Co-modification process taking place in an alkaline solution. Surprisingly, CrO_2 exhibits a strong proton-donor adsorption which is not fully understood. The wetting energy can also be used to select suitable dispersants, and the isothermal curve of adsorption can be used to determine the amount of dispersant needed. A combination of both measurements can be performed in a flow calorimeter with the chosen solvent. The results obtained, however, have to be confirmed, or be adjusted, by tests with the binder system in the real formulation. The reason for this is a possible competitive adsorption of the binder and the dispersant on the surface of the particles (Jaycock, 1981). The adsorption characteristics of various binder systems have been studied, for example, on Co-modified γ-Fe_2O_3 particles, by a method of magnetic rotation of the particles in the binder solution (Sumiya et al., 1984). Another measure for the efficiency of a dispersant is the amount of binder solution containing the dispersant needed to just wet a given amount of powder, a method similar to the oil adsorption test. In Fig. 3.29, the critical amount of the solution is plotted versus the amount of dispersants for a γ-Fe_2O_3 powder and various dispersants. The less binder dispersant solution needed, the better the efficiency of the dispersant. The optimum amount of dispersant is indicated by the transition from a rapid decrease to a constant value of binder-dispersant solution needed. The lubricant included in Fig. 3.29 (curve *C*) is not supposed to be adsorbed at the surface of the particles and, hence, has no influence on the dispersibility properties. The intersection of the curves with the ordinate in Fig. 3.29 is equivalent to the oil absorption, a widely used test for the degree of densification of the powder (Patton, 1979).

3.4 MEDIA PREPARATION

3.4.1 Binder, Additives, and Dispersion

In order to form a cohesive and durable magnetic coating of defined thickness and surface structure, the particles are well dispersed in a polymeric binder, together with solvents, dispersants, lubricants, antistatic agents, and, if necessary, fillers for improved mechanical wear resistance or light absorption. The principles and operations are similar to those used in the paint industry. The dispersion is then coated onto the substrate, dried, and given a surface finish which, for flexible media, comprises a compression by calendering. If applicable, the particles are oriented after coating by a strong magnetic field, applied while the coating is still wet.

The binder is expected to lend itself to a high volumetric packing fraction of the particles and, in combination with the particles as a filler, must have high flexibility, high elasticity, high wear resistance, and low friction on metal or plastic surfaces. These partially contradictory requirements often make it necessary to use mixtures of compatible polymers and plasticizers. For instance, polymers with a lower molecular weight lead to smoother dispersions, with a higher volumetric packing fraction of the particles, but are less wear-resistant and show higher friction values. Thus, cross-linking or radiation curing after dispersion and coating is often used to improve these properties. For flexible recording media including nonmagnetic backcoats, the following groups of organic polymers may be used:

Copolymers of vinyl chloride

Copolymers of vinylidene chloride

Polyvinyl formal

Polyvinyl acetate resins

Acrylate and methacrylate resins

Combinations of polyether with OH groups with polyesters and polyisocyanates

Soluble polyurethane elastomers

Modified cellulose derivatives

Epoxy and phenoxy resins

Polyamides

In recent years, polyurethane binder systems have received the greatest interest (Mihalik, 1983; Williams and Markusch, 1983). For the cross-linking of polymers, polyfunctional isocyanates, melamine-formaldehyde or urea-formaldehyde condensation products of low molecular weight may be used. More recently, electron-beam curing has come into use (Brown et al., 1983). For better adhesion of the coating, the substrate is often precoated with polyvinylidene chloride copolymerizates or polyester.

The solvent, or solvent system, selected for a chosen binder system is one that most economically holds the solubles in solution and maintains the magnetic particle dispersion. It should be reasonably fast-drying, although too rapid an evaporation rate can cause problems in the coating and the drying process. Thus, combinations of solvents having different boiling points are often used. Typical solvents are as follows:

Methyl ethyl ketone

Methyl isobutyl ketone

Cyclohexanone

Tetrahydrofuran

Dioxane

N-methyl pyrrolidone

N-dimethyl formamide

Toluene as an inexpensive diluent

Rigid disks, with thermostable metal substrates, are usually coated with a reactive binder system which cures at temperatures up to 250°C. These are phenol-formaldehyde resins, urea-formaldehyde resins, epoxy resins sometimes together with amine or acidic anhydride hardeners, or polyvinyl acetate resins and silicone resins. These well-hardening resins are essential for the polishing and lapping process which is used to finish the coated disks with respect to coating thickness and surface flatness.

The main steps of preparing a dispersion are wetting and disagglomeration of the particles, stabilization, and final letdown with binder solution to the appropriate viscosity for the coating operation. The most important properties of the liquid for the wetting process are a low contact angle between liquid and solid and a low viscosity. It can thus be advantageous to perform the wetting with the solvent alone. In addition, the low-viscosity solvent may break up bonds between the particles through the Rehbinder effect (Parfitt, 1981).

In contrast to many paint manufacturing procedures, the particles must not be damaged during the dispersion process when magnetic pigments are used. The agglomerates need mechanical energy to break them up. This is introduced by the impact and shear forces in ball mills, sand mills, or kneaders, but care must be taken to maintain the mechanical integrity of the particles. This is done by controlling the milling charge and the time, temperature, and viscosity of the slurry. Usually a high viscosity in the range of 0.2 to 0.6 Pa·s (200 to 600 cP) is used to make use of the shear forces. This is achieved by adding only a part of the binder solution of the final formulation. The effect of milling time is shown in Fig. 3.30, in terms of the gloss of the as-coated, calendered tape surface, the saturation remanence, the coercivity, and the ac-bias noise as well as the print-through of the calendered tape. The detrimental effect of overmilling is evident and, in this particular case of γ-Fe$_2$O$_3$ made from γ-FeOOH, a milling time of 40 h in a ball mill is sufficient. In general, the milling time in ball mills can be between 20 and 200 h, depending on the magnetic pigment, the molecular weight of the binder, the dispersant, the viscosity of the slurry, the size and type of the balls, and the equipment used. Nowadays, continuously working sand mills are most widely used (Wheeler, 1981; Missenbach, 1983).

In order to achieve a stable dispersion, it is necessary to prevent flocculation and sedimentation. To this end, the magnetic particles must be enveloped by a stabilizing agent that prevents further intimate contact between them. This is partially accomplished by the organic polymer molecules of the binder system. These have polar groups and form an adsorbed layer on the particles with a tail or loop configuration. The stabilizing action is given by entropic effects which depend on the thickness of the adsorbed layer, the structure of the molecules, and the configuration of the polar groups. In addition, active dispersants of low molecular weight with hydrophobic and hydrophilic groups are used. The hydrophobic groups usually consist of a hydrocarbon chain with 6 to 30 C atoms. The hydrophilic groups, which react with the particle surface, are either ionic or have a dipole moment. Ionic dispersants may be anionic, such as carboxylates, sulfonates, and phosphates, or cationic, such as quaternary ammonium salts, alcanol ammonium salts, or imidazolinium salts. Amphoteric dispersants are betaines, amino oxides, and aminocarbon acids. Nonionic dispersants typically consist of arylpolyglycol ether, polyglycol ester, polyglycol amides, or polyalcohols. All dispersants must be carefully selected and their amount chosen with respect to the surface chemistry of the particles and the binder system used.

After dispersion, the remaining binder solution and solvent of the formulation are added, together with lubricants that assure good tape life. Extreme uses include still-framing in video where the same area of tape is scanned some 3600 times/per minute, or in computer tape application where the tape is subjected to repeated start and stop applications. The basic idea is that the lubricant forms a monomolecular layer on the surface of the magnetic coating, and is continuously replenished by diffusion from within the magnetic layer after wearing off during use. This necessitates a delicate balance between wear at too low a concentration, and deposits on the heads at too high a concentration of the lubricant. Silicone oils, substituted silicone oils, fatty acids, fatty acid esters, fluor polyether stearates, and natural or synthetic hydrocarbons in amounts of 1 to 6 wt % of the nonvolatile substances are used. Sometimes solid lubricants such as carbon black or polyfluor hydrocarbon are added. In addition, antistatic agents such as polyalkylene ether or

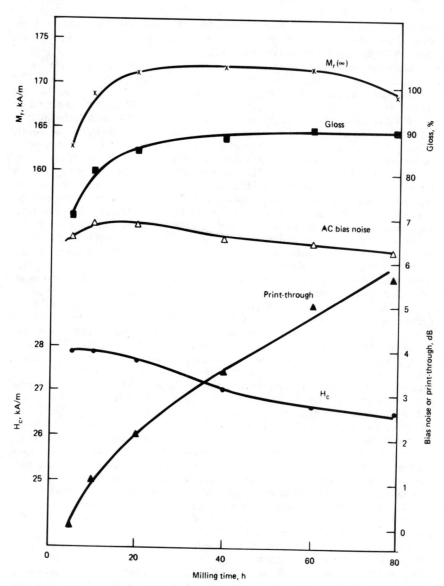

FIGURE 3.30 Gloss of the as-coated and dried dispersion, saturation remanence $M_r(\infty)$, coercivity H_c, ac-bias noise, and print-through signal of the calendered coating as a function of milling time for γ-Fe_2O_3 particles. For noise and print-through a relative scale has been used. The difference of 1 dB is indicated in the drawing (*Jakusch, 1984*).

quarternary ammonium salts are added to keep the resistivity of the magnetic coating in an acceptable level below 10^{11} Ω per square. Often carbon black is added as a conductive filler for this purpose as well (Burgess, 1983).

Nonmagnetic fillers like silicic acid, carborundum, alumina, chromium trioxide, or alpha ferric oxide are often added in small amounts in order to improve the wear resistance and frictional properties of the magnetic coating, as well as to obtain a cleaning action of the head surface by the surface of the magnetic coating. These fillers typically have a size range from 0.2 to 1 μm in diameter. For back coats with a defined surface roughness, which often are necessary for good tape winding characteristics in professional applications, carbon black and silicic acid below a size of 0.1 μm in diameter are most frequently used.

3.4.2 Tape and Disk Substrates

The substrates for particulate magnetic recording media are almost exclusively films of polyethylene terephthalate (polyester) for flexible media, and aluminum disks for rigid media. The polyester films are produced by extrusion and subsequent stretching to the necessary film thickness. According to the ratio of the degree of stretching in the longitudinal to that in the transverse direction, a distinction is drawn between balanced films for which the above ratio is about unity, and tensilized films which have a ratio of about 3. The latter have a tensile strength at an elongation of 5 percent of the order of 150 N/mm^2 (20×10^3 lb/in^2), which is about twice that of balanced films. Tensilized film is usually used in the thickness range below 10 μm. A final annealing step is employed at temperatures between 200 and 250°C, but some shrinkage may still take place at elevated temperatures. This leads to dimensional instabilities for flexible-disk applications. After exposure to 72°C, an initially circular track can become elliptic at room temperature, with a deformation of about 0.3 percent or 180 μm on a track radius of 60 mm (Greenberg et al., 1977). This behavior severely limits the application for high-density recording. Another example is helical-scan video recording, where a shrinkage after recording of 0.1 percent may occur at elevated temperatures. This causes a distortion of the video picture due to a mismatch of the line synchronization. Additional annealing steps after calendering are often added to reduce these possible distortions. Alternatively, other substrate materials, such as polyimides and polyimide-polyamide copolymers, have been explored for better dimensional stability.

Other important properties of the polyester films are their surface smoothness and their resistance to wear. Both are related to avoiding defects in the final magnetic coating which may cause local signal reductions (dropouts). For good winding and handling properties, films below 20-μm thickness must have a certain surface roughness which is produced by inorganic and, more recently, by organic fillers. Agglomerates of filler particles can lead to asperities of 5 to 30 μm in diameter and up to 2 μm in height. Thus, the control of size distribution of the filler is of great importance and determines the quality of the film for high-density recording. Another solution is to coextrude one formulation with, and one without, a filler. This leads to a film which is almost optically flat on one side but has a defined structure on the other side (Holloway, 1983). The high electrical surface resistance of about 10^{16} Ω per square leads to electrostatic surface charges which can cause difficulties in handling the films. In many applications it is therefore necessary to include a conductive back coating on magnetic recording tapes.

For rigid disks, aluminum disks of 1.3- and 1.9-mm thickness and 95- to 356-mm diameter are used. Glass, ceramics, and plastic substrates have often been dis-

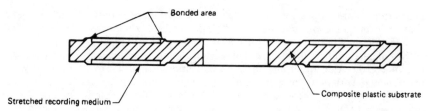

FIGURE 3.31   Schematic cross section of a rigid disk in combination with a stretched, web-coated medium.

cussed but so far have not been used in products. A combination of flexible- and rigid-disk technology has been suggested. It consists of an injection-molded composite plastic substrate with raised edges at the inner and outer diameters of the disk (Fig. 3.31). A web-coated, flexible media is isotropically stretched and bonded to the raised edges. This results in a compliant surface with a 250-μm gap between the substrate and the media (Knudsen, 1985). For aluminum disks, raw sheet made of an aluminum-magnesium alloy is punched into disks with an inner hold. Apart from an annealing step for improved flatness, the finishing processes include diamond turning, polishing, and lapping in order to meet the necessary dimensional and surface specifications. Typical specifications are an axial runout below 75 μm, a waviness below 0.5 μm, and a surface roughness below 0.03 μm. For improved adhesion of the magnetic coating and corrosion protection, the surface may be treated by a chromate process.

3.4.3   Coating and Orienting

In the production of flexible recording media, the coating takes place between an unwind and a rewind station that must have precise tension controls in order to handle substrate films as thin as 6 μm, and as wide as 1.5 m, at coating speeds as high as 5 m/s. The master rolls of length of the order of 5000 m are usually changed without interruption of the coating process. The coating head applies a coating, about 4 to 10 times as thick as the dry coating, uniformly over the width of the substrate web with tolerances of generally ±5 percent. There are a number of different types of coating systems (Landskroener, 1983). One is gravure coating (Fig. 3.32a), where small grooves in a roll pick up the dispersion and transfer it to the substrate film in contact. This has the advantage of giving a very uniform average coating thickness, but the disadvantage of needing a postsmoothing of the discontinuous coating pattern. Gravure coating also has the disadvantages of a restricted viscosity range and a fixed coating thickness for a given gravure roll. Knife coating (Fig. 3.32b) is much more flexible. Here the substrate web runs on a backing roll under a knife edge set at a defined distance from the film, and this determines the thickness of the coating. Modern extrusion knife coaters are closed units which are pressure-fed. Their advantages are their low cost and their ability to coat wide thickness ranges. The disadvantage of knife coaters is the critical adjustment of the straightness of the knife edge for a uniform coating thickness across the web. In a reverse roll coater (Fig. 3.32c), the dispersion is applied in excess by a nozzle onto a roll, the thickness being determined by a metering roll, and either transferred directly from that roll, or via a second coating roll, onto the film substrate, which is held by a compliant backing roll. The coating roll rotates in opposite direction to the movement of the film substrate. Application and metering can also be performed with a knife coater. The reverse roll

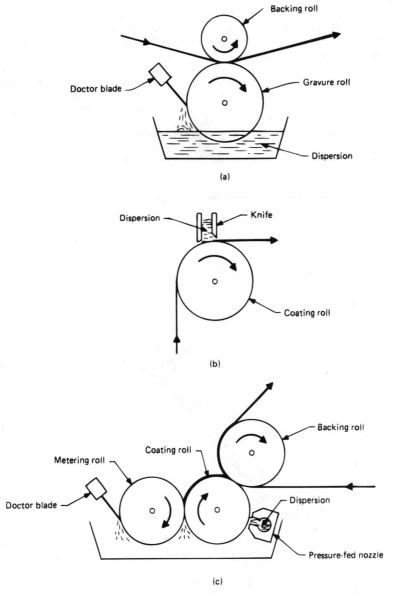

FIGURE 3.32 Coating systems: (*a*) gravure, (*b*) knife, and (*c*) reverse roll coating.

coater is very demanding as to the precision of the rolls and their respective relative velocities. Other coaters are based on the extrusion of the dispersion through the slotted opening of an extrusion die onto the film substrate. Before coating, the dispersion is carefully filtered with filter systems that effectively will remove particles as small as 3 to 5 μm. In case of cross-linked magnetic coatings, the reactive agent is mixed into the dispersion shortly before coating.

Directly after the coating operation, unless a magnetically isotropic medium is desired as is the case for flexible disks, a field parallel to the web transport direction is applied for the alignment of the particles. The preferred configuration of the magnetic pole pieces of permanent-magnet or electromagnet circuits is one of opposing poles on both sides of the web which have no perpendicular field component in the center plane. Naturally, attracting poles are used if an orientation perpendicular to the recording media is desired, for which a special ac-field method has been reported (Ohtsubo et al., 1984). It is of importance that the alignment, or orienting, field is large enough to reverse the magnetization of the particles such that they need only to be rotated by angles less than 90°. In Fig. 3.33, the degree of particle alignment as measured by the orientation factor $M_{rx}(\infty)/M_{rz}(\infty)$ is plotted versus the applied field. Here, $M_{rx}(\infty)$ is the reduced saturation remanence parallel, and

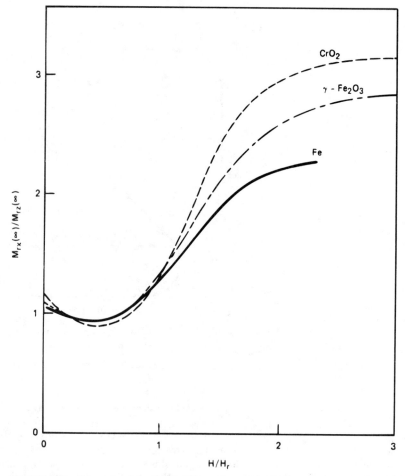

FIGURE 3.33   Orientation factor $M_{rx}(\infty)/M_{rz}(\infty)$ of gamma ferric oxide, chromium dioxide, and iron particles as a function of the reduced orientation field H/H_r. The quantity H_r is the remanence coercivity of the powder at a volumetric packing fraction of $p = 0.25$.

$M_{rz}(\infty)$ the saturation remanence transverse, to the direction of alignment. Alignment takes place only when the field approaches the remanence coercivity H_r of the particles. At fields higher than $3 \times H_r$ no further improvement in alignment is obtained. Instead, the dragging force of the magnetic field on the particles leads to disturbances of the magnetic coating. It is of great importance that no reverse field exists at the end of the magnet configuration, since field strengths as low as a few kiloamperes per meter (tens of oersteds) can destroy the state of particle alignment. Special designs use antennae of high permeability (Fig. 3.34a), or a low-field solenoid at the end of the magnet configuration (Fig. 3.34b), in order to compensate any field opposing the direction of the field of alignment. Opposing electromagnets have been designed with two air gaps that produce two consecutive orienting fields of equal magnitude, but of opposite

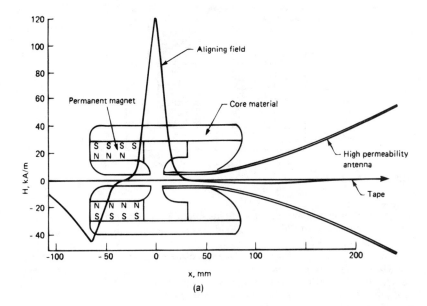

(a)

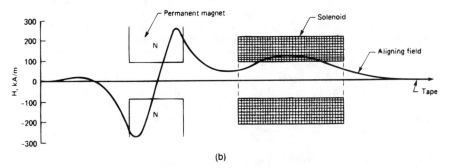

(b)

FIGURE 3.34 Orienting systems. (*a*) High-permeability antennae for the reduction of reverse field (*Bate and Dunn, 1980*), (*b*) opposing poles with a solenoid for the compensation of reverse field (*Sumiya et al., 1983*), and (*c*) double-gap electromagnet (*Köster et al., 1983*).

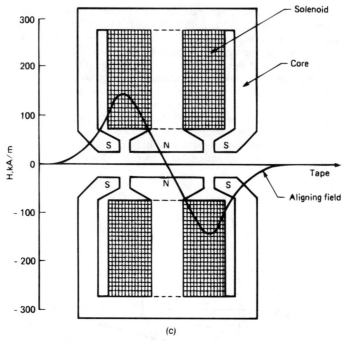

FIGURE 3.34   (*Continued*)

sign, thus eliminating any negative fields outside the magnetic configuration (Fig. 3.34*c*). The duration of the aligning field may become of importance if it is less than 50 ms (Newman, 1978).

The drying of the coating takes place in a closed unit at temperatures between 60 and 100°C. For environmental protection, the solvent vapor is either burned or recycled by adsorption on active charcoal (Landskroener, 1983). Sequential coaters with several coating and drying stations are in use for the application of precoatings, multiple recording layers, and back coatings.

In the production of rigid disks, the aluminum disk can be coated in various ways. However, of all methods tried so far, such as spray coating, dip coating, and fluid-bed coating, spin coating has emerged as the dominant method. After the substrate is rinsed with a solvent at low rotational speeds, the dispersion is applied and distributed over the substrate surface in ample quantity. The substrate is then accelerated to high rotational speeds for the spin-off of the surplus dispersion. The viscosity and flow characteristics of the dispersion determine the thickness and thickness profile of the final coating. The latter usually is an increase of thickness going from inside to outside of the substrate. The alignment of the particles in a circumferential direction takes place at low rotational speeds shortly before drying sets (Meijers, 1983).

3.4.4   Surface Finish and Slitting

The dried magnetic coating usually is not completely solid, but has a compressible spongelike structure. Consequently, in flexible recording media, the dried web is calendered between a highly polished steel roll, and a compliant roll having a paper, fabric, or plastic surface. The linear pressure can be as high as 3×10^5 N/m, and the steel roll temperature as high as 90°C. Usually several alternating steel and compliant rolls are combined in a row for high-speed operation. While the dispersion techniques and their theoretical background are based on the experience of the paint industry, the calendering process has been borrowed from the paper industry (Sharpe et al., 1978). The most important effect of calendering is to smooth the surface of the magnetic coating which, for high-density recording, should have a peak-to-valley roughness of less than 0.1 μm. Such highly smooth surfaces are not without problems. In conjunction with equally smooth recording heads, guiding elements, or drums, "blocking" or "slip-stick" phenomena can occur which can cause severe functional problems. Here, a careful compromise between short-wavelength response and frictional properties must be maintained.

Flexible disks, after calendering and punching, are submitted to a burnishing process where surface asperities are removed with ceramic rolls or with polishing tape. Rigid disks cannot be calendered. The curing of the thermosetting resins at temperatures up to 250°C, however, leads to a contraction of the coating and a corresponding densification. The surface finish of rigid disks is achieved by polishing and lapping the hardened magnetic coating. In a final step, rigid disks, and sometimes flexible disks, are lubricated by applying perfluoroalkyl polyether diluted in a fluorocarbon solvent. It is thought to be adsorbed in the pores of the magnetic coating, thus securing a thin surface layer of the lubricant even after repeated use (Lindner and Mee, 1982).

The slitting of magnetic tape is extremely critical. The abrasive nature of the magnetic particles and the tough characteristics of the polyester substrate make it difficult to obtain sharply cut edges. The use of hardened rotary-shear blades and a constant monitoring of the slitting process is important, as well as a careful and precise guidance and tensioning of slit tapes.

3.4.5 Surface Defects

Any deviation from an ideal flat surface of the magnetic recording layer may be seen as a surface defect. Long-wavelength undulations of the order of 0.1 to 10 mm in length usually contribute to multiplicative (modulation) noise. They may be caused by structures originating in the coating process that depend on the rheological properties of the dispersion, such as striations in the case of knife and reverse roll coating, or replicas of the structure of the gravure roll. Other long-wavelength variations may develop during the calendering process. Here, the compliant rolls must be as smooth as possible, and the line pressure and temperature of the rolls must be kept at a level just necessary to obtain the desired compression. Homogeneous rolls, cast from elastomeric compounds, can give better results with respect to modulation noise than composite compliant rolls made from paper or felt sheets (Mills et al., 1975).

Asperities or holes several tens of micrometers in dimension give rise to a signal reduction (dropout) or an extra signal (drop-in) of short duration. In tape or flexible-disk applications, asperities are the most common type of defect because they cause a spacing between the head and the recording surface that extends far beyond the lateral size of the defect, due to a tent effect (Alstad and Haynes, 1978). Asperities generally cause dropouts unless the asperity is magnetic and causes a spike signal (drop-in) when it passes the reproduce gap (Lee and Papin, 1982). Additives in the film substrate, and shedded film or foreign particles on the sub-

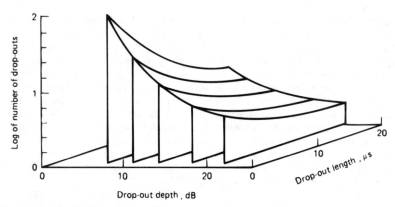

FIGURE 3.35 Number of dropouts of a home video tape as a function of dropout depth and length (recorded wavelength 1μm, track width 22 μm).

strate, can cause surface defects. In a magnetic coating, agglomerates of magnetic or foreign particles may give rise to asperities. After the coating and drying process, shedded film or foreign particles may be firmly pressed onto the magnetic coating during calendering. If these particles break off again at a later stage, sharp indentations occur which may cause additional signal losses and drop-ins. Scratches are another source of defects that occur if hard foreign particles are caught by the recording head, or by any guiding element, and damage the recording surface. A typical distribution of drop-outs in home video recording is shown in Fig. 3.35 as a function of the amount of dropout depth and length. The distribution increases markedly toward small dropouts in depth and length.

With rigid disks, scratches and holes in the aluminum substrate caused by handling are one possible source of defects. Holes in the magnetic coating may be due to wetting problems, or to agglomerates, as well as to foreign particles that have been broken away in the final polishing process. Microcracks can occur during the spin coating and particle alignment process as a result of unfavorable rheological properties of the dispersion. Finally, radial scratches on the polished coating may lead to dropout and drop-in signals.

3.5 STABILITY OF MEDIA

3.5.1 Mechanical Stability

The wear of the magnetic recording layer, or that of the recording head, is not easily amenable to precise theoretical or experimental analysis. It depends on the ill-defined geometrical configuration of the contact area. Additional factors are the intrinsic material properties such as yield stress or hardness, the microstructural properties such as porosity or grain structure, the environmental conditions such as temperature and humidity, and, last but not least, the frictional coefficient as influenced by the lubricant employed. Basically, the shear stress must not be allowed to exceed the yield stress, a condition which is usually obeyed. However, because of asperities or local sharp edges of the head, as well as magnetic or additive particles sticking out of the magnetic recording layer, much higher stresses are present locally which cause mutual erosion to take place, aided by increased local friction and heating effects.

Early in the development of rigid disks, alumina particles in the micrometer size range were incorporated in the magnetic coating as a supporting protection against the flying head damaging the magnetic layer in the event of head-disk interferences. Similarly, the trend to increasingly smaller particles in audio and video recording tapes makes it necessary to incorporate larger particles, often of nonmagnetic ferrite, into the magnetic layer. These serve as supporting posts for the head, thus reducing the shear forces on the magnetic coating. The same route has been taken with flexible disks. Obviously, a reasonable compromise between the mutual wear of head and coating must be found. This means making a compromise between wear of the head and a cleaning action of the tape that prevents clogging of the head. While head wear usually occurs gradually, the wear of the magnetic coating often starts with a loss of lubricant on its surface, followed by a cohesive failure of the coating. Then comes an avalanche effect of cohesive and adhesive failure caused by the debris of the previous erosion. Foreign materials like dust particles may cause the same effect. The cohesive strength of the coating depends not only on the yield stress of the binder system but also on the strength of the interaction between the binder and the particles. Finally, the adhesive strength of the coating on the substrate is of equal importance. With these properties carefully adjusted, modern magnetic recording media show extremely high wear resistance. For instance, over 100 million revolutions are achieved in flexible-disk applications, corresponding to 200 years of average use; and over 1 h of still-frame video application is possible, with rotating heads continuously running on the same track with a head-to-medium velocity of several meters per second. The wear rate of γ-Fe_2O_3 and CrO_2 particles on head materials of various hardness follows the known linear decrease of abrasivity with increasing relative hardness of the test body, and the steep increase of the wear rate at relative humidities above 70 percent (Mayer, 1974). In addition, the relative wear rates of γ-Fe_2O_3 and CrO_2 tapes depend on the binder system, the degree of cross-linking, the lubricant, and the size of the particles.

Another mechanical effect that can reduce the reliability of recording media is stick-slip and, in its worst manifestation, blocking. Stick-slip is usually due to a high coefficient of friction and leads to an irregular transport of the magnetic medium, with consequent frequency modulation of the recorded signal. Blocking can cause the complete standstill of sensitive tape transports, or leads to heads adhering immovably to a disk surface. A similar phenomenon of occasional blocking is called *stiction,* and this can be the initial step of the wear process of recording media (Chin and Mee, 1983). These effects may occur if the surfaces of the head or guide elements and of the recording layer are too smoothly polished, and is aggravated by high humidity and temperature. To avoid stick-slip or blocking, the frictional properties must be controlled by introducing and maintaining a defined microtexture of the surfaces involved. This is in conflict with the desired close proximity between head and recording layer. Further, the lubricant and adsorbents play important roles in controlling the coefficient of friction, which tends to be smaller at high pigment-volume concentrations (Miyoshi and Buckley, 1984).

The relaxation of a pack of tape wound on a reel is of concern in the archival storage of computer tapes, and in the shipment and use of tape, such as packs of audio cassette tape intended for use in high-speed duplication. The prolonged storage of a reel of tape leads to a relaxation of the stress in the tape pack caused by creep of the substrate film. This can lead to a destructive tape slippage (cinching) during wind or rewind, or to complete disintegration of a tape pack. Further, an increase of temperature above the winding temperature increases the stress and the resulting pressure in the tape pack. These effects occur because of the differential expansion of pack and hub and the anisotropic thermal expansion coefficient of the polyester substrate film. The stress relaxation of the polyester film and plastic flow of the magnetic coating lead to an increased tendency for pack disintegration once the tape has been returned to the operating environment. A decrease of humidity leads to similar effects due to a hygroscopic contraction of the pack relative to the hub (Bertram and Eshel, 1979).

3.5.2 Magnetic Stability

The printing of recorded signals from one layer of a wound reel of magnetic recording tape to another has already been mentioned in context with thermal fluctuation effects. It is commonly known as print-through, and is caused by reversals of magnetization, in the presence of the signal field from an adjacent layer, of particles whose volume is only slightly larger than the critical volume v_p for super-paramagnetic behavior. The range of volume v of the particles affected is given by Eq. (3.30) if the apparent coercivity is set equal to the signal field. For a given signal field, this range extends from v_p to a fixed multiple of v_p. Hence, if v_p increases with the elapsed time of observation t, or with the temperature T according to Eq. (3.28), the volume of the affected particles increases as well. If we assume a locally uniform distribution function of particle volumes, or just a linearized part of a real distribution function, the total volume of all particles involved, and consequently the printed signal, is proportional to v_p. Thus, following Eq. (3.28), the printed magnetization and its related print-through signal are proportional to the logarithm of the time of exposure to the printing field, and proportional to the storage temperature. The strength of the printing field for a given recorded magnetic flux is wavelength-dependent, and passes through a maximum whose location depends on the thickness of the base film δ_f, and the thickness of the magnetic coating δ, as

$$\lambda_{max} = 2\pi(\delta + \delta_f) \tag{3.31}$$

where λ_{max} is the wavelength of maximum print-through signal at a given recorded magnetic flux. The corresponding print-through signal is proportional to $\delta/(\delta + \delta_f)$. The details of these experimentally established print-through effects are fairly well understood (Tochihara et al., 1970; Bertram et al., 1980). The printed magnetization can be erased in low magnetic fields and is usually reduced by stress effects; that is, its final level depends to some extent on the mechanical construction of the recorder.

As mentioned earlier, an induced anisotropy is possible in the system $(\gamma\text{-}Fe_2O_3)_x(Fe_3O_4)_{1-x}$, with or without Co-modification, which leads to irreversible changes of the magnetic properties with time and temperature. This effect is also a cause for print-through signals and may, in addition, have serious consequences with respect to the ease of erasure of recorded tapes (Salmon et al., 1979). It is thought to be due to a migration and ordering of cation vacancies, and divalent iron ions, which lower the free-energy density of the magnetization state of each particle according to the magnetization distribution given by the recorded signal. Hence, the recorded magnetization pattern is "frozen" into the recording medium and cannot be erased even with the highest dc field or in a bulk eraser. Therefore, this behavior is called "memory" effect. It is demonstrated in Fig. 3.36 for a series of audio recording tapes made from $\gamma\text{-}Fe_2O_3$ particles with a surface Co modification using different amounts of Fe^{2+} ions. Immediately after recording, all tapes have a posterasure signal of about $-70\,dB$, independent of the Fe^{2+} or Co^{2+} content, and independent of the coercivity.

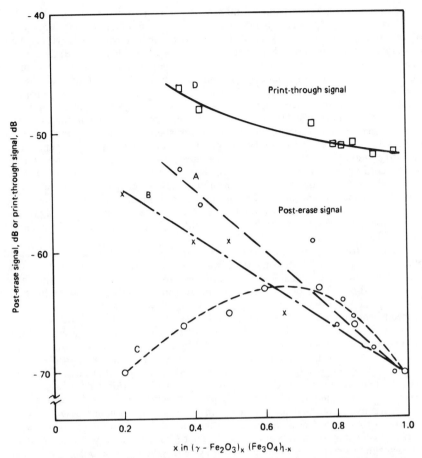

FIGURE 3.36 Posterasure signal as a function of x in $(\gamma\text{-}Fe_2O_3)_x(Fe_3O_4)_{1-x}$ of audio recording tapes made from surface Co-modified iron oxide particles. Measurements were made after storing a signal recorded to saturation remanence at 65°C for various times, then erasing in an ac field of initial amplitude 133 kA/m (1670 Oe). (Curve A) 1.5 wt % Co, 3 days' storage; (curve B) 1.5 wt % Co, 24 h storage; (curve C) particles without Co, 24 h storage. The print-through signal of tape A is shown with curve D.

After storage of the recorded tapes for 4 days at 54°C, the posterasure signal increases as much as 20 dB for $x = 0.3$ in $(\gamma\text{-}Fe_2O_3)_x(Fe_3O_4)_{1-x}$. In addition, the increase of print-through signal with Fe^{2+} content is shown in Fig. 3.36 for this tape series. The memory effect can be simulated in a vibrating-sample magnetometer by applying an ac field which continuously decreases to zero from an initial value of 133 kA/m (1670 Oe) (Fig. 3.36). The samples were stored in the state of saturation remanence for 24 h at 65°C and subsequently erased. The particles containing no Co ions show a maximum in the posterasure signal at an x value of about 0.7 (Salmon et al., 1979), while the particles containing 1.5 wt % Co have a linear increase of the posterasure signal with increasing Fe^{2+} content. Similar measurement indicate that tapes made from CrO_2 particles can be more easily erased than those made from $\gamma\text{-}Fe_2O_3$ and even more so than those made from Co-modified γ-Fe$_2$O$_3$ particles (Manly, 1976). The above magnetometer measurements suggest the existence of an exchange anisotropy of the gamma ferric oxide kernel coupled to a cobalt-ferrite shell with a magnetocrystalline anisotropy field that can be as high as 749 kA/m (9400 Oe), and whose magnetization can be reversed only in fields much larger than the erase field applied in the experiments. The exchange anisotropy may lead to an anhysteretic magnetization in an ac-erase field, caused by the biasing effect of the exchange anisotropy. A similar effect occurs in the Co-CoO exchange anisotropy system (Köster and Steck, 1976). For a memory effect to occur, the direction of magnetization of the iron oxide kernel must be transferred to the cobalt-ferrite shell. This may occur at elevated temperatures where, due to its small volume and the reduced magnetocrystalline anisotropy field, thermal fluctuation effects cause the cobalt-ferrite shell to be magnetized according to the magnetization of the iron oxide kernel. However, this possible effect, which may contribute to print-through signals as well, needs further investigation. The chance of an induced anisotropy being produced by the mechanical rearrangement of particles at elevated temperatures in the plastic binder as a possible source for a nonerasable signal is minute, although it cannot be totally excluded (Manly, 1976).

Magnetostriction effects can lead to a reduction in signal level after repeated playback of a recorded tape, or after a head-disk interference in rigid-disk application. The reduction of signal level is proportional to the logarithm of the number of passes, to the tension of the tape, to the reciprocal of the wavelength of the recording, and to the constant of magnetostriction (Woodward, 1982). The loss is caused by the combined action of the bending stresses around tape guide elements, or to the shear stresses in disk application, together with the demagnetizing fields of the magnetization transitions (Izawa, 1984). In addition, there is a correlation in magnitude to the print-through effect which suggests that the same particles of low magnetic anisotropy energy are involved. The significant contribution of the demagnetizing fields is shown in Fig. 3.37, where the signal loss after twenty passes on an audio recorder is shown to be inversely proportional to the recorded wavelength. The figure also shows that the signal loss increases in the sequence CrO$_2$, γ-Fe$_2$O$_3$, γ-Fe$_2$O$_3$ with surface Co modification, in the same order as the increase in magnetostriction constant (Flanders et al., 1979). There exists the interesting possibility of a zero magnetostriction composition in the system $(\gamma\text{-Fe}_2\text{O}_3)_x(\text{Fe}_3\text{O}_4)_{1-x}$, as a result of the compensation of the negative magnetostriction of γ-Fe$_2$O$_3$ or of Co-modified γ-Fe$_2$O$_3$, and the positive magnetostriction of Fe$_3$O$_4$ (Flanders, 1979).

3.5.3 Chemical Stability

Many of the polymeric binders used for magnetic recording media are susceptible to a degradation by hydrolysis, which can lead to the tapes becoming sticky or even shedding gummy and tacky materials. This effect is accelerated by an increase in temperature and humidity (Bertram and Chuddihy, 1982). For archival storage, the conditions of 18°C and 40 percent relative humidity have been recommended, with tight limits on fluctuations in order to keep the stress relaxation as low as possible.

Corrosion may play a role in the use of aluminum-disk substrates. With chromate treatment of the substrate surface, however, no problems are encountered in practical use. Similarly, the stabilization of metal or chromium dioxide particles effectively prevents any sizable signal degradation under reasonable storage conditions.

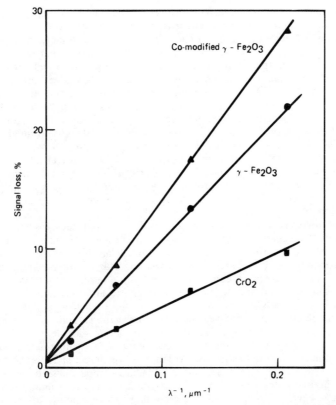

FIGURE 3.37 Signal loss after 20 passes on an audio recorder as a function of the recorded wavelength λ for tapes made with (1) CrO_2, (2) γ-Fe_2O_3, and (3) Co-modified γ-Fe_2O_3 particles.

3.6 PARTICULATE MEDIA APPLICATIONS

3.6.1 Audio Tapes

The requirements for analog audio tapes are strongly influenced by the anhysteretic recording process which is employed for linearization and noise reduction. The long-wavelength sensitivity of audio tapes is determined by the anhysteretic susceptibility. The key properties of audio tapes are the sensitivity, the frequency response, the signal-to-noise ratio (dynamic range), and the print-through. Equally important are modulation noise, dropouts, and wear resistance, properties associated with the mechanical homogeneity of the medium.

In order to ensure tape and recorder compatibility, a careful standardization has been established with internationally accepted reference tapes that set the ac bias and the signal current as well as the equalization. Thus, the range of permissible coercivity, of remanence, and of thickness is limited within about 10 percent.

A fine-tuning has to be made with respect to the degree of particle alignment which controls the remanence squareness, and with respect to the switching-field distribution (Köster et al., 1981). Coating thicknesses much larger than twice the recording head gap length are not favorable for the balance between long- and short-wavelength output. Typical values are 10 μm for reel-to-reel and 5 μm for compact cassette tape. Once the magnetic tape parameters are properly set at long wavelengths, the surface smoothness and the switching-field distribution primarily determine the frequency response. The response should be somewhat positive rather than negative with respect to the reference tape. The main focus of product improvement is on the reduction of the particulate noise through a reduction in particle size. Smaller particles mean a larger number of particles per unit volume, to which the signal-to-noise power ratio at long wavelengths is directly proportional. This route is limited by the print-through signal, which must be kept below a certain level, but progress can be made by changes in the preparation of the magnetic particles with respect to their morphology and their size distribution.

Major improvements in signal-to-noise ratio and frequency response through higher values of coercivity and remanence, or through a significantly smoother coating surface, require a new standardization. Therefore, there are now four different standards in existence for compact cassette recorders, apart from the standards for reel-to-reel machines. Historically, the latter have changed with the reductions made in tape speed. The cassette standards differ in coercivity, which has been increased successively in order to improve short-wavelength output. The increases in coercivity also involved increases in specific saturation moment of the particles from gamma ferric oxide, through chromium dioxide, to iron. Typical values of saturation remanence $M_r(\infty)$, coercivity H_c, switching-field distribution Δh_r, and number of particles per unit volume N, are shown in Table 3.7 for home reel-to-reel, as well as IEC I, II, and IV standard compact cassette audio tapes.

Only the first outer 1 or 2 μm of the magnetic coating contribute to the short-wavelength signal in compact cassette recording, which employs a tape speed of 47.5 mm/s. Therefore, it is of value to decouple the long- and short-wavelength recording by using a double-layer tape. Such tapes allow separate optimization of the outer layer for short, and the inner layer for long, wavelengths. Typically, the coercivity of the outer layer is 1.5 times that of the inner layer. This technique was first introduced for the IEC III standard, but is now successfully used in tape products meeting all four compact cassette standards. The next logical steps were to use smaller particles in the outer layer and larger ones in the inner layer for a better compromise between noise and print-through, with the coercivities of the layers being the same or having the ratio mentioned above.

The tapes for digitally encoded audio recording very much resemble those which are used for video recording application, and will be discussed in the following section.

3.6.2 Instrumentation and Video Tapes

Instrumentation and video tapes have in common that they are much more demanding in surface smoothness, and in low error rates, than analog audio tapes. They differ in their way of application. Instrumentation tape is moved over a multiple-track head, as in professional audio or computer tape applications. Video tape has to withstand narrow-track heads, which are mounted on a drum that runs at a circumferential speed of the order of 4 m/s. Thus, the mechanical wear

TABLE 3.7 Magnetic Material, Saturation Remanence $M_r(\infty)$, Coercivity H_c, Switching-Field Distribution Δh_r, and Number of Particles per Unit Volume, N, of Various Particulate Magnetic Recording Media

Application	Material	$M_r(\infty)$, kA/m (emu/cm³)	H_c, kA/m (4π Oe)	Δh_r	N, $10^3/\mu m^3$
Reel-to-reel audio tape	γ-Fe_2O_3	100–120	23–28	0.30–0.35	0.3
Audio tape IEC I	γ-Fe_2O_3	120–140	27–32	0.25–0.35	0.6
Audio tape IEC II	CrO_2	120–140	38–42	0.25–0.35	1.4
	γ-Fe_2O_3 + Co	120–140	45–52	0.25–0.35	0.6
Audio tape IEC IV	Fe	230–260	80–95	0.30–0.37	3
Professional video tape	Fe	240	110–125	0.32	4
	CrO_2	110	42	0.3	1.5
	γ-Fe_2O_3 + Co	90	52	0.35	1
Home video tape	CrO_2	110	44–58	0.35	2
	γ-Fe_2O_3 + Co	105	52–74	0.35	2
	Fe	220	110–125	0.38	4
Instrumentation tape	γ-Fe_2O_3	90	27	0.35	0.6
	γ-Fe_2O_3 + Co	105	56	0.50	0.8
Computer tape	γ-Fe_2O_3	87	23	0.30	0.16
	γ-Fe_2O_3 + Co	90	44	0.33	0.8
	CrO_2	120	40	0.29	1.4
	Fe	220	110–125	0.38	4
Flexible disk	γ-Fe_2O_3	56	27	0.34	0.3
	γ-Fe_2O_3 + Co	60	50	0.34	0.5
	Ba-ferrite	56	58	0.4	1.5
Computer disk	γ-Fe_2O_3	56	26–30	0.30	0.3
	γ-Fe_2O_3 + Co	60	44–55	0.30	0.5

situation, and consequently the formulation of the magnetic coatings, are quite different.

Instrumentation and 2-in-wide video tapes are designed for professional tape recorders based on standards which were established some 30 years ago. Consequently, these tapes historically relied on rather conservative gamma ferric oxide particles, except that instrumentation tapes have now been supplemented by tapes with a higher coercivity (Table 3.9). Also, the 1-in professional video recorders, which succeeded the 2-in recorders, use tapes with modern chromium dioxide or cobalt-modified gamma iron oxide particles. These tapes have intermediate remanence and coercivity values. Surface homogeneity and few dropouts are the key properties, in addition to the usual requirements with respect to wear and friction. In 1987 the 1/2-in Betacam SF System™ was introduced into the professional market. In order to cope with a recording wavelength as small as 0.6 μm, metal (Fe-) particles are used.

The half-inch home video tapes must meet a delicate balance between providing the surface smoothness needed for a good signal-to-noise ratio, without causing blocking of the tape on its path through the cassette housing and the recorder. The video color information is recorded separately in a frequency band below the luminance channel. Recording takes place anhysteretically with the luminance signal providing the bias field. Consequently, all parameters mentioned for audiotapes are applicable and must be properly adjusted in order to comply with the standard set by the recorder system. Further, the same long-wavelength surface inhomogeneities which are mentioned in Sec. 3.4 may contribute to an undue modulation of the color signal.

Next-generation camera-type or improved-quality home video, digitally encoded audio, and professional video recording systems are expected to go to wavelengths of less than 0.5 μm. This asks for the high remanence and coercivity values which are found with metal particle tapes. Barium ferrite platelets, oriented for perpendicular recording (Fujiwara, 1983), lend themselves to an extremely flat frequency response which may result in similar output levels as those of metal-particle tapes at the target wavelengths below 0.5 μm. However, it appears that metal-particle tapes will play an important role in this area of application. The main rival is metal-film evaporated tape which is more adapted to such short wavelengths because its magnetic coating has a thickness less than half of the recorded wavelength. The same approach is employed for particulate tape coatings with a thickness of below 0.5 μm (Köster, 1993). Typical data of different types of video tapes are listed in Table 3.7.

3.6.3 Computer Tapes and Flexible Disks

The standards of the reel-to-reel computer tape date back to the early sixties. Progress took place in the recording densities of the tape drives, which imposed increasingly stringent demands on surface smoothness and low dropout rates, but with little else changing. In the mid '80s a cartridge-type tape drive was developed, using a chromium dioxide tape for much higher track and longitudinal recording densities. The corresponding magnetic tape data are shown in Table 3.7. A number of smaller, low-end cassette and cartridge drives are now being used, and are evolving to use higher coercivity oxide and metal particle media. Great importance is attached to the archival behavior of computer tapes and tape reels (Bertram and Eshel, 1979) and computer tape cartridges.

For more than a decade, flexible disks have constituted an important means of peripheral data storage for small computer applications. Apart from rigid disks, the flexible disk is the most prominent example of a recording process which, ideally, employs full saturation of the magnetic coating throughout its thickness at all wavelengths. This is different from analog video recording, where the magnetic coating has a thickness of approximately 4 μm, and the record current is adjusted for maximum output for the shortest wavelength used. This implies that the magnetic coating is only magnetized through a depth of about 0.5 μm, half the recorded wavelength. In most types of tape recording, previously written information can be erased with an additional erase head before writing new data. This is rather difficult to implement in disk configurations. Therefore, the thickness of the magnetic coating of flexible disks must be less than half the shortest recorded wavelength. This leads to a coating thickness δ of the most advanced, smaller-size flexible disks of about 1 μm. This must be accurately controlled within 10 percent in order to assure the specified frequency response, usually called *resolution* in digital data recording. With gamma ferric oxide particles, and a volumetric packing fraction of about 0.4, the saturation remanence $M_r(\infty)$ of flexible disks is limited to values of about 70 kA/m (emu/em^3). Thus the remanent flux per unit track width, $\mu_0 M_r(\infty)\delta$, has been reduced with increasing linear recording density through reductions of δ. The flux has decreased from 280 nWb/m (mMx/cm) of the first flexible disks, to 120 nWb/m (12 Mx/m) of the 3.5-inch-diameter flexible-disk cartridge, and may soon be as low as 70 nWb/m (mMx/cm). Rigid-disk media run as low as 55 nWb/m (mMx/cm).

Consequently, the linear recording density limit of particulate media disks is determined, not only by the thinnest coating thickness that can be made, but also by the minimum signal level needed. It is of interest to note that similar flux levels are encountered in video recording. The magnetic particles used are predominantly made of gamma ferric oxide which, more recently, has a cobalt surface modification for higher coercivities. Metal particles have been used for higher signal levels at thin coating thicknesses. Barium ferrite may also be used for such applications.

In contrast to magnetic tape media, care must be taken in the coating process of flexible-disk web material that the particle axes are randomly distributed in the plane of the coating; otherwise a circumferential signal modulation occurs. In addition, any other surface structures along the direction of coating must be eliminated, since the head regularly travels transverse to them, a situation that may lead to dropouts and extra signals. Abrasion and wear play an important role because the head may run on one track for many repeated times. Finally, a certain light absorption is specified which is not that easily met, since the drive manufacturers tend to use infrared light diodes in the index hole detection circuit. Typical magnetic properties are listed in Table 3.7.

3.6.4 Rigid Disks

The properties of rigid disks are centered around the conditions needed for the low-flying recording head whose height above the disk may be 0.05 μm or less. On the one hand, it is necessary to provide a superfine surface finish and lubrication for interference-free flying, as well as good short-wavelength recording characteristics. On the other hand, it is essential to avoid stiction between disk and head that may prevent the drive spindle from turning after a standstill. Traditionally, disks used a magnetic coating of typically 0.7-μm thickness composed of elongated gamma ferric iron particles, which were oriented circumferentially, and whose coercivity was pushed to the limit of the available ferrite-head fields by surface-cobalt modification. The magnetic data are given in Table 3.7. Particulate rigid-disks are now confined to applications using large diameter disks. Since future disk drives will use smaller diameter metal film disks (Chap. 4), there is little future interest in particulate disks.

3.6.5 Other Applications for Particulate Media

There is a wealth of special applications of particulate recording media, in the form of cards, sheets, and stripes, that covers applications such as suburban traffic tickets, credit and access cards, accounting sheets, point-of-sale registration labels, word processing, and many more. Most of them constitute low-density recording modes with moderate requirements with respect to the magnetic recording media.

REFERENCES

Alstad, J. K., and M. K. Haynes, "Asperity Heights on Magnetic Tape Derived from Measured Signal Drop Out Lengths," *IEEE Trans. Magn.,* **MAG-14,** 749 (1978).

Andriamandroso, D., G. Demazean, M. Pouchard, and P. Hagenmuller, "New Ferromagnetic Materials for Magnetic Recording: The Iron Carbon Nitrides," *J. Solid State Chem.,* **54,** 54 (1984).

Bate, G., and J. A. Williams, "The Cylindrical Symmetry of the Angular Distribution of Particles in Magnetic Tape," *IEEE Trans. Magn., **MAG-14,*** 869 (1978).

Bate, G., *Ferromagnetic Materials,* ed., E. P. Wohlfarth, N. Holland Publ., Amsterdam, 1980, pp. 381–507.

Berkowitz, A. E., W. J. Schuele, and P. J. Flanders, "Interference of Crystallite Size on the Magnetic Properties of Acicular γ-Fe$_2$O$_3$ Particles," *J. Appl. Phys.,* **39,** 1261 (1968).

Bertram, H. N., Private Communication (1976).

Bertram, H. N., "Anisotropy of Well Oriented γ-Fe$_2$O$_3$ Magnetic Tapes," *AIP Conf. Proc.,* **18,** 1113 (1978).

Bertram, H. N., and A. Bhatia, "The Effect of Interactions on the Saturation Remanence of Particulate Assemblies, *IEEE Trans. Magn., **MAG-9,*** 127 (1973).

Bertram, H. N., and E. F. Chuddihy, "Kinetics of the Humid Ageing of Magnetic Recording Tape," *IEEE Trans. Magn., **MAG-18,*** 993 (1982).

Bertram, H. N., and A. Eshel, "Recording Media Archival Attributes (Magnetic)," Final Rep. Contract, AFSC Rome Air Dev. Center, No. F30602:78:C-0181, 1979.

Bertram, N., M. Stafford, and D. Mills, "The Print Through Phenomenon (Magnetic Recording), *J. Audio Eng. Soc.,* **28,** 690 (1980).

Bickford, L. R., J. M. Brownlow, and R. F. Penoyer, "Magnetocrystalline Anisotropy in Cobalt Substituted Magnetic Single Crystals," *Proc. Inst. Elec. Eng. (London),* **104B,** 238 (1956).

Birss, R. R., "The Saturation Magnetization of Ferromagnetics," *Adv. Phys.,* **8,** 252 (1959).

Birss, R. R., *Symmetry and Magnetism,* North-Holland, Amsterdam, 1965.

Bozorth, R. M., "Determination of Ferromagnetic Anisotropy in Single Crystals and in Polycrystalline Sheets," *Phys. Rev.,* **50,** 1076 (1936).

Braun, H. B., and H. N. Bertram, "Coercivity Reduction in an Elongated Ferromagnetic Single-Domain Particle," to be published in *J. Appl. Phys.,* **65,** (1994).

Brown, W. H., R. E. Ansel, L. Laskin, and S. R. Schmid, "Electron Beam Curing of Magnetic Media Coatings," *Proc. Symp. Magn. Media Mfg. Meth.,* MMIS, Chicago, 1983.

Burgess, K. A., "The Role of Carbon Black in Magnetic Media," *Proc. Symp. Magn. Media Mfg. Meth.,* MMIS, Chicago, 1983.

Chen, H. Y., D. M. Hiller, J. E. Hudson, and C. J. A. Westenbroek, "Advances in Properties and Manufacturing of Chromium Dioxide," *IEEE Trans. Magn., **MAG-20,*** 24 (1984).

Chikazumi, S., *Physics of Magnetism,* Wiley, New York, 1964.

Chin, C., and P. B. Mee, "Striction at the Winchester Head-Disk Interface," *IEEE Trans. Magn., **MAG-19,*** 1659 (1983).

Cloud, W. H., D. S. Schreiber, and K. R. Babcock, "X-Ray and Magnetic Structure of CrO$_2$ Single Crystals," *J. Appl. Phys.,* **33,** 1193 (1962).

Craik, D. J., and R. S. Tebble, *Ferromagnetism and Ferromagnetic Domains,* North-Holland, Amsterdam, 1965.

Dasgupta, S., "Characterization of Magnetic Dispersions: Rheological, Mechanical and Magnetic Properties," *IEEE Trans. Magn., **MAG-20,*** 7 (1984).

Eagle, D. F., and J. C. Mallinson, "On the Coercivity of Fe$_2$O$_3$ Particles," *J. Appl. Phys.,* **38,** 995 (1967).

Flanders, P. J., "Stress-Induced Playback Loss and Switching Field Reduction in Recording Materials," *J. Appl. Phys.,* **50,** 2390 (1979).

Flanders, P. J., "The Temperature Dependence of the Reduced Anisotropy in Magnetic Recording Particles," *IEEE Trans. Magn., **MAG-19,*** 2683 (1983).

Flanders, P. J., G. Kaganowicz, and Y. Takei, "Magnetostriction and Stress-Induced Playback Loss in Magnetic Tapes," *IEEE Trans. Magn., **MAG-15,*** 1065 (1979).

Fujiwara, T., "Barium Ferrite Particulate Tapes for Perpendicular Magnetic Recording," *Symp. Magn. Media Mfg. Meth.,* Honolulu, Hawaii, 1983.

Gans, R., "Über das Verhalten isotroper Ferromagnetika," *Ann. Phys.*, **15**, 28 (1932).

Greenberg, H. J., R. L. Stephens, and F. E. Talke, "Dimensional Stability of 'Floppy' Disks," *IEEE Trans. Magn.*, **MAG-13**, 1397 (1977).

Gustard, B., and H. Vriend, "A Study of the Orientation of Magnetic Particles in γFe_2O_3 and CrO_2 Recording Tapes Using an X-Ray Pole Figure Technique," *IEEE Trans. Magn.*, **MAG-5**, 326 (1969).

Gustard, B., and M. R. Wright, "A New γ-Fe_2O_3 Particle Exhibiting Improved Orientation," *IEEE Trans. Magn.*, **MAG-8**, 426 (1972).

Hibst, H., "Hexagonal Ferrites from Melts and Ageous Solutions, Magnetic Recording Media," *Angew. Chem. Int. Ed. Engl.*, **21**, 270 (1982).

Holloway, A. J., "Polyester Film, Surface Definition and Control," *Symp. Magn. Media Mfg. Meth.*, Honolulu, Hawaii, 1983.

Huisman, H. F., "Particle Interactions and H_c: An Experimental Approach," *IEEE Trans. Magn.*, **MAG-18**, 1095 (1982).

Huisman, H. F., and C. J. F. M. Rasenberg, "Mercury Porosimetry Analysis of Magnetic Coatings," *IEEE Trans. Magn.*, **MAG-20**, 13 (1984).

Imaoka, Y., "Ageing Effects of Ferromagnetic Iron Oxides," *J. Electrochem. Soc.*, Japan, **33**, 1 (1965).

Itoh, F., M. Satou, and Y. Yamazuki, "Anomalous Increase of Coercivity in Iron Oxide Powder Coated with Sodium Polyphosphate," *IEEE Trans. Magn.*, **MAG-13**, 1385 (1977).

Izawa, F., "Theoretical Study on Stress-Induced Demagnetization in Magnetic Recording Media," *IEEE Trans. Magn.*, **MAG-20**, 523 (1984).

Jacobs, I. S., and C. P. Bean, "An Approach to Elongated Fine Particle Magnets," *Phys. Rev.*, **100**, 1060 (1955).

Jacobs, I. S., and C. P. Bean, *Magnetism,* Academic Press, New York, 1963, vol. III, p. 271.

Jakusch, H., Private Communication (1984).

Jaycock, M. J., *Dispersion of Powders in Liquids,* 3d ed., Applied Science, London, 1981, p. 51.

Jeschke, J., "Verfahren zur Herstellung hartmagnetischer γ-Ferrite für Magnettonbänder," *Bild Ton,* **7**, 318 (1954).

Johnson, C. E., and W. F. Brown, Jr., "Stoner Wohlfarth Calculation on Particles with Both Magnetocrystalline and Shape Anisotropy," *J. Appl. Phys.*, **30S**, 320 (1959).

Johnson, C. E., and W. F. Brown, Jr., "Theoretical Magnetization Curves for Particles with Cubic Anisotropy," *J. Appl. Phys.*, **32S**, 243 (1961).

Kaneko, M., "Change in Coercivity of γ-Fe_2O_3-Fe_3O_4 Solid Solutions with Magnetostrictive Anisotropy," *IEEE Trans. Magn.*, **MAG-16**, 1319 (1980).

Khalafalla, D., and A. H. Morrish, "Investigation of Ferrimagnetic Cobalt-Doped Gamma-Ferric Oxide Micropowders," *J. Appl. Phys.*, **43**, 624 (1972).

Kishimoto, M., "Effect of Fe^{2+} Content on the Instability of Coercivity of Cobalt-Substituted Acicular Iron Oxides," *IEEE Trans. Magn.*, **MAG-15**, 905 (1979).

Kishimoto, M., S. Kitaoha, H. Andoh, M. Amemiya, and F. Hayama, "On the Coercivity of Cobalt-Ferrite Epitaxial Iron Oxide," *IEEE Trans. Magn.*, **MAG-17**, 3029 (1981).

Kneller, E., *Ferromagnetismus,* Springer-Verlag, Berlin, 1962.

Kneller, E., *Handbuch der Physik,* Springer-Verlag, Berlin, 1966, band XVIII/2, p. 438.

Kneller, E., "Magnetic Interaction Effects in Fine Particle Assemblies and Thin Films," *J. Appl. Phys.*, **39**, 945 (1968).

Kneller, E., *Magnetism and Metallurgy,* Academic Press, New York, 1969, vol. I, p. 365.

Kneller, E., "Static and Anhysteretic Magnetic Properties of Tapes," *IEEE Trans. Magn.*, **MAG-16**, 36 (1980).

Kneller, E., and F. E. Luborsky, "Particle Size Dependence of Coercivity and Remanence of Single Domain Particles," *J. Appl. Phys.*, **34**, 656 (1963).

Knowles, J. E., "The Measurement of The Anisotropy Field of Single Tape Particles," *IEEE Trans. Magn.,* **MAG-20,** 84 (1984).

Knudsen, J. K., "Stretched Surface Recording Disk for Use with a Flying Head," *IEEE Trans. Magn.,* **MAG-21,** 2588 (1985).

Kojima, H., and K. Hanada, "Origin of Coercivity Changes during the Oxidation of Fe_3O_4 to γ-Fe_2O_3," *IEEE Trans. Magn.,* **MAG-16,** 11 (1980).

Köster, E., "Reversible Susceptibility of an Assembly of Single Domain Particles and Their Magnetic Anisotropy," *J. Appl. Phys.,* **41,** 3332 (1970).

Köster, E., "Magnetic Anisotropy of Cobalt-Doped Gamma Ferric Oxide," *IEEE Trans. Magn.,* **MAG-8,** 428 (1972).

Köster, E., "Temperature Dependence of Magnetic Properties of Chromium-Dioxide and Cobalt-Doped Gamma-Ferric-Oxide Particles," *IERE Conf. Proc.,* **26,** 213 (1973).

Köster, E., "A Contribution to Anhysteretic Remanence and AC Bias Recording," *IEEE Trans. Magn.,* **MAG-11,** 1185 (1975).

Köster, E., "Recommendation of a Simple and Universally Applicable Method for Measuring the Switching Field Distribution of Magnetic Recording Media," *IEEE Trans. Magn.,* **MAG-20,** 81 (1984).

Köster, E., "Trends in Magnetic Recording Media," *J. Magnetism and Magnetic Materials,* **120,** 1C (1993).

Köster, E., and W. Steck, "Anhysteretic Growth of Exchange Fixed Remanent States," *IEEE Trans. Magn.,* **MAG-12,** 755 (1976).

Köster, E., H. Jakusch, and U. Kullmann, "Switching Field Distribution and AC Bias Recording," *IEEE Trans. Magn.,* **MAG-17,** 2550 (1981).

Köster, E., P. Deigner, P. Schäfer, K. Uhl, and R. Falk, "Device for Magnetically Orienting and Magnetizable Particles of Magnetic Recording Media in a Preferred Direction," U.S. Patent 0043,822,44, 1983.

Kubo, O., T. Ido, and H. Yokoyama, "Properties of Ba-Ferrite Particles for Perpendicular Magnetic Recording Media," *IEEE Trans. Magn.,* **MAG-18,** 1122 (1982).

Kullmann, U., E. Köster, and B. Meyer, "Magnetic Anisotropy of Ir-Doped CrO_2," *IEEE Trans. Magn.,* **MAG-20,** 742 (1984*b*).

Landskroener, P. A., "Conventional Coating Methods," *Symp. Magn. Media Mfg. Meth.,* Honolulu, Hawaii, 1983.

Lee, E. W., "Magnetostriction and Magnetochemical Effects," *Rep. Prog. Phys.,* **18,** 184 (1955).

Lee, T. D., and P. A. Papin, "Analysis of Dropouts in Video Tapes," *IEEE Trans. Magn.,* **MAG-18,** 1092 (1982).

Lemke, J. U., "An Isotropic Particulate Medium with Additive Hilbert and Fourier Field Components," *J. Appl. Phys.,* **53,** 2561 (1982).

Lindner, R. E., and P. B. Mee, "ESCA Determination of Fluorocarbon Lubricant Film Thickness on Magnetic Disk Media," *IEEE Trans. Magn.,* **MAG-18,** 1073 (1982).

Luborsky, F. E., "Development of Elongated Particle Magnets," *J. Appl. Phys.,* **32S,** 171 (1961).

Maestro, P., D. Andriamandroso, G. Demazean, M. Pouchard, and P. Hagenmuller, "New Improvements of CrO_2-Related Magnetic Recording Materials," *IEEE Trans. Magn.,* **MAG-18,** 1000 (1982).

Manly, W. A., Jr., "Erasure of Signals on Magnetic Recording Media," *IEEE Trans. Magn.,* **MAG-12,** 758 (1976).

Matsumoto, S., T. Koga, F. Fukai, and S. Nakatani, "Production of Acicular Ferric Oxide," U.S. Patent 4,202,871, 1980.

Mayer, D. H., "On the Abrasivity of γ-Fe_2O_3 and CrO_2 Magnetic Tapes," *IEEE Trans. Magn.,* **MAG-10,** 657 (1974).

Mee, C. D., *The Physics of Magnetic Recording,* North-Holland, Amsterdam, 1964.

Meijers, F. B., "Rigid Disk Coating Parameters," *Symp. Magn. Media Mfg. Meth.*, Honolulu, Hawaii, 1983.

Meiklejohn, W. H., "New Magnetic Anisotropy," *Phys. Rev.*, **105**, 904 (1957).

Meiklejohn, W. H., and C. P. Bean, "New Magnetic Anisotropy," *Phys. Rev.*, **102**, 1413 (1956).

Mihalik, R. S., "The Relationship between Polyurethane Binders and Various Binder Additives and Modifiers," *Symp. Magn. Media Mfg. Meth.*, Honolulu, Hawaii, 1983.

Mills, D., H. Kristensen, and V. Santos, "Control of Modulation Noise in Magnetic Recording Tape," *52d AES Convention*, Reprint No. 1084, 1975.

Missenbach, F. S., "Premixing, Milling, Filtering and Related Procedures," *Symp. Magn. Media Mfg. Meth.*, Honolulu, Hawaii, 1983.

Miyoshi, K., and D. H. Buckley, *Tribology and Mechanics of Magnetic Storage Systems*, American Society of Lubrication Engineers, Park Ridge, Illinois, 1984, p. 13.

Monteil, J. B., and P. Dougier, "A New Preparation Process of Cobalt Modified Iron Oxide," *Proc. Int. Conf. Ferrites*, 532 (1980).

Morrish, A. H., and K. Haneda, "Surface Magnetic Properties of Fine Particles," *J. Magn. Magn. Mater.*, **35**, 105 (1983).

Morrish, A. H., and S. P. Yu, "Dependence of the Coercive Force on the Density of Some Iron Oxide Powers," *J. Appl. Phys.*, **26**, 1049 (1955).

Néel, L., "Propriétés d'un Ferromagnétic Cubique en Grain Fines," *C. R. Acad. Sci. Paris*, **224**, 1488 (1947).

Néel, L., "Anisotropie Magnetique Superficielle et Structurelle d'Orientation," *J. Phys. Radium*, **15**, 225 (1954).

Newman, J. J., "Orientation of Magnetic Particles Assemblies," *IEEE Trans. Magn.*, **MAG-14**, 866 (1978).

Ohtsubo, A., Y. Satoh, T. Masuko, M. Hirama, and E. Abe, "A Perpendicular Orientation of a Coated Particulate Medium by an AC-Demagnetization Process," *IEEE Trans. Magn.*, **MAG-20**, 751 (1984).

Oppegard, A. L., F. J. Darnell, and H. C. Miller, "Magnetic Properties of Single Domain Iron and Iron-Cobalt Particles Prepared by Boronhydride Reduction," *J. Appl. Phys.*, **32S**, 184 (1961).

Osborn, J. A., "Demagnetizing Factors of the General Ellipsoid," *Phys. Rev.*, **67**, 351 (1945).

Parfitt, G. D., *Dispersion of Powder in Liquids*, 3d ed., Applied Science, London, 1981, p. 1.

Patton, T. C., *Paint Flow and Pigment Dispersion*, 2d ed., Wiley, New York, 1979.

Rasenberg, C. J. F. M., and H. F. Huisman, "Measurement of the Critical Pigment Volume Concentration of Particulate Magnetic Tape," *IEEE Trans. Magn.*, **MAG-20**, 748 (1984).

Rodbell, D. S., "Magnetocrystalline Anisotropy of Single Crystal CrO_2," *J. Phys. Soc. Jpn.*, **21**, 1224 (1966).

Salmon, O. N., R. E. Fayling, G. E. Gurr, and V. H. Halling, "Thermodynamics of Post-Erasure Signal Effects in γ-Fe_2O_3 Magnetic Recording Tapes," *IEEE Trans. Magn.*, **MAG-15**, 1315 (1979).

Schönfinger, E., M. Schwarzmann, and E. Köster, "Verfahren zur Herstellung von kobaltdotiertem γ-Eisen(III)-Oxiden," West German Patent 002243231, 1972.

Sharpe, J., T. Sutherst, and E. Cooper, "Machine Calendering," Technical Division of the British Paper and Board Industry Federation, London, 1978.

Sharrock, M. P., "Particle-Size Effects on the Switching Behavior of Uniaxial and Multiaxial Magnetic Recording Materials," *IEEE Trans. Magn.*, **MAG-20**, 754 (1984).

Shimizu, S., N. Umeki, T. Ubeori, N. Horiishi, Y. Okuda, Y. Yuhara, H. Kosaka, A. Takedoi, and K. Yaguchi, Japanese Patents 753,7667 and 753,7668, 1975.

Shtrikman, S., and D. Treves, "The Coercive Force and Rotational Hysteresis of Elongated Ferromagnetic Particles," *J. Phys. Radium*, **20**, 286 (1959).

Smaller, P., and J. S. Newman, "The Effect of Interactions of the Magnetic Properties of a Particulate Medium," *IEEE Trans. Magn.,* **MAG-6,** 804 (1970).

Smit, J., and H. P. J. Wijn, *Ferrites,* Wiley, New York, 1959.

Speliotis, D. E., "Magnetization Reversal in Ba-Ferrite Particulate Media," *J. Appl. Phys.,* **63,** 3432 (1988).

Stavn, M. J., and A. H. Morrish, "Magnetization of a Two-Component Stoner-Wohlfarth Particle," *IEEE Trans. Magn.,* **MAG-15,** 1235 (1979).

Steck, W., "Preparation and Properties of Particles for Magnetic Recording," *J. Phys. (Paris) Collogne C6 Suppl.,* **46,** C6-33 (1985).

Stoner, E. C., and E. P. Wohlfarth, "A Mechanism of Magnetic Hysteresis in Heterogeneous Alloys," *Philos. Trans. R. Soc. London,* **A240,** 599 (1948).

Sugihara, H., Y. Taketoni, T. Uehori, and Y. Imaoka, "The Behavior of Surface Hydroxyl Group of Magnetic Iron Oxide Particles," *Proc. Int. Conf. Ferrites,* 545 (1980).

Sumiya, K., S. Watatani, F. Hayama, K. Hakamae, and T. Matsumoto, "The Orientation of Magnetic Particles for High Density Recording," *J. Magn. Magn. Mater.,* **31–34,** 937 (1983).

Sumiya, K., N. Hirayama, F. Hayama, and T. Matsumoto, "Determination of Dispersability and Stability of Magnetic Paint by Rotation-Vibration Method," *IEEE Trans. Magn.,* **MAG-20,** 745 (1984).

Takada, T., Y. Ikeda, H. Yoshinaga, and Y. Bando, "A New Preparation Method of the Oriented Ferrite Magnets," *Proc. Int. Conf. Ferrites,* 275 (1970).

Tasaki, A., M. Ota, S. Kashu, and C. Hayashi, "Metal Tapes Using Ultra Fine Powder Prepared by Gas Evaporation Method," *IEEE Trans. Magn.,* **MAG-15,** 1540 (1979).

Tasaki, A., K. Tagawa, E. Kita, S. Harada, and T. Kusunose, "Recording Tapes Using Iron Nitride Fine Powder," *IEEE Trans. Magn.,* **MAG-17,** 3026 (1981).

Tasaki, A., N. Saegusa, and M. Ota, "Ultra Fine Magnetic Metal Particles—Research in Japan," *IEEE Trans. Magn.,* **MAG-19,** 1731 (1983).

Tebble, R. S., and D. J. Craik, *Magnetic Materials,* Wiley, New York, 1969.

Thomas, J. R., "Preparation and Magnetic Properties of Colloidal Cobalt Particles," *J. Appl. Phys.,* **37,** 2914 (1966).

Tochihara, S., Y. Imaoka, and M. Namikawa, "Accidental Printing Effect of Magnetic Recording Tapes Using Ultrafine Particles of Acicular γ-Fe$_2$O$_3$," *IEEE Trans. Magn.,* **MAG-6,** 808 (1970).

Tokuoka, Y., S. Umeki, and Y. Imaoka, "Anisotropy of Cobalt-Adsorbed γ-Fe$_2$O$_3$ Particles," *J. Phys. Suppl.,* **38,** 337 (1977).

Tonge, D. G., and E. P. Wohlfarth, "The Remanent Magnetization of Single Domain Ferromagnetic Particles: II. Mixed Uniaxial and Cubic Anisotropies," *Philos. Mag.,* **3,** 536 (1958).

Umeki, S., S. Saito, and Y. Imaoka, "A New High Coercive Magnetic Particle for Recording Tape," *IEEE Trans. Magn.,* **MAG-10,** 655 (1974).

Wheeler, D. A., *Dispersion of Powders and Liquids,* 3d ed., Applied Science, London, 1981, p. 327.

Williams, J. L., and P. H. Markusch, "The Chemistry of Isocyanates and Polyurethanes," *Symp. Magn. Media Mfg. Meth.,* Honolulu, Hawaii, 1983.

Williams, M. L., and R. L. Comstock, "An Analytic Model of the Write Process in Digital Magnetic Recording," *AIP Conf. Proc. Magn. Magn. Mater.,* **5,** 738 (1971).

Witherell, F. E., "Surface and Near-Surface Chemical Analysis of Cobalt-Treated Iron Oxide," *IEEE Trans. Magn.,* **MAG-20,** 739 (1984).

Wohlfarth, E. P., "The Effect of Particle Interaction on Coercive Forces of Ferromagnetic Micropowders," *Proc. R. Soc. London,* **A-232,** 208 (1955).

Wohlfarth, E. P., *Magnetism,* Academic Press, New York, 1963, vol. III, p. 351.

Wohlfarth, E. P., and D. G. Tonge, "The Remanent Magnetization of Single Domain Ferromagnetic Particles," *Philos. Mag.,* **2,** 1333 (1957).

Woodward, J. G., "Stress Demagnetization in Videotapes," *IEEE Trans. Magn.,* **MAG-18,** 1812 (1982).

CHAPTER 4
FILM MEDIA

Thomas C. Arnoldussen
IBM Corporation, San Jose, California

Thin magnetic films which have been explored for recording media are usually cobalt-based alloys, sputtered iron oxide being the principal exception. The cobalt alloys often possess a hexagonal crystal structure in which magnetocrystalline anisotropy aids in achieving a high coercivity. These films have been electroplated, chemically plated, evaporated, and sputtered. Most of the past work has focused on longitudinal media in which the easy axis of magnetization lies in the plane of the film. Such films range in thickness from 15 to 200 nm. Cobalt-chromium sputtered alloys have received attention for perpendicular media in which the easy axis is normal to the film plane.

The saturation magnetization of deposited films can range from as low as 240 kA/m (emu/cm^3) for sputtered γ-Fe$_2$O$_3$ to over 1000 kA/m for cobalt-iron alloys. The coercivity can range from under 32 to 240 kA/m (400 to 3000 Oe), depending on the deposition process and the material. The chief advantage of deposited films is the higher magnetization, which allows the use of thinner recording layers while maintaining signal amplitude. Thin recording layers lead to a better-defined magnetization reversal and consequently to higher recording densities. Film technology also makes possible the tailoring of magnetic properties to meet specific design requirements. Unlike a particulate coating, whose magnetic properties are largely determined by the type of particle used, a film of a given composition can be made to be isotropic or anisotropic, of high or low coercivity, of in-plane or perpendicular easy axis, by modifying the deposition process or substrate preparation.

Film media, because they are thin, require nonmagnetic processing or coating layers which are unnecessary with particulate media. In rigid-disk media, for example, an underlayer is usually deposited on the substrate first to improve the impact resistance of the total structure, and an overcoat is applied after the magnetic layer to provide abrasion resistance. Nonmagnetic wear or load-bearing particles cannot be used as with particulate coatings. Similarly, lubricant cannot be retained in a thin solid film as it can in an organic resin particulate coating. Therefore, new concepts in lubrication or elimination of lubricant are necessary for film media.

4.1 MAGNETIC PROPERTIES OF DEPOSITED FILMS

The magnetic films discussed here fall into the category of hard magnetic materials. Such materials require relatively large applied fields to become magnetized or to have their magnetization direction reversed. Once magnetized by an applied field, these materials retain a substantial fraction of their saturation magnetization after the applied field is removed. These are the properties required of a recording medium which will not easily lose written information as a result of stray external magnetic fields or internal demagnetizing fields. Such films are in contrast with soft magnetic films used in recording heads, where low coercivity, low magnetic remanence, and high permeability are required.

Much of the discussion of magnetic properties in Chap. 3 (such as ferromagnetic exchange coupling, crystalline anisotropy, shape anisotropy, magnetostriction) applies also to films and bulk materials. The reader is referred to that chapter for these defining concepts and equations. Here we will focus on how these properties are manifested in films.

4.1.1 Magnetization

Saturation magnetization is usually considered to be an intrinsic property of the material. For a given composition of a metal alloy, the saturation magnetization M_s will be nearly the same for a film alloy as for a bulk alloy. Provided that the film and bulk materials have the same local atomic ordering and compositional homogeneity, deviations of film magnetization from that of the bulk should occur only when the several atomic layers associated with the surface (or interface between films) constitute a substantial fraction of the total film thickness. Such effects are due to changes in local atomic ordering at the surface and consequently changes in the ferromagnetic coupling. For very thin films, thermal fluctuations can also reduce the magnetization.

More commonly, deviations of measured film from bulk magnetization are observed even for films many atomic layers thick. In reality, what is measured is an effective, or average, magnetization. While true surface atomic ordering effects may be negligible, interfacial composition variations may be significant. Oxidation of a surface or interdiffusion at an interface can cause appreciable changes in the measured effective saturation magnetization. Similarly, deposited films often possess nonequilibrium, microcrystalline structures and solute distributions which can yield magnetizations somewhat different from bulk materials of the same nominal composition. For example, certain stainless-steel alloys are weakly magnetic in bulk form, but films sputtered from such bulk materials may be strongly ferromagnetic. The opposite can also occur. Finally, films have varying degrees of surface roughness associated with them, which may be large compared with the film nominal thickness (for example, 5 to 10 nm roughness on a film of thickness 20 to 50 nm). Such roughness can lead to lower effective magnetization values for films, because of the inability to measure the film volume accurately.

Saturation magnetization may be considered an intrinsic property of a material, with due attention paid to the qualifications mentioned above. Remanent magnetization M_r is an extrinsic property. The magnetization remaining after a saturating field is removed depends very much on the microstructure, film thickness, the nature of the substrate on which the film is deposited, and the conditions of the film deposition process itself. In continuous films, irreversible magnetization changes may occur by domain nucleation and wall motion. In addition, when the magnetic anisotropies of crystallites in a film are not uniformly oriented in the applied field direction, saturation magnetization is achieved by a final reversible rotation of magnetization in the individual grains. This phenomenon occurs at applied fields ranging from about 20 percent greater than the coercivity to several times the coercivity. When the field is removed, the magnetization relaxes by rotation to a lower value determined by quantum mechanical exchange, crystalline anisotropy, and magnetostatic coupling between individual grains. The ratio $S = M_r/M_s$ is called the *remanence squareness.*

4.1.2 Magnetic Anisotropies

The mechanisms of magnetic anisotropy described in Chap. 3 are equally operative in deposited films. However, it is much more difficult, in practice, to isolate the individual contributions of magnetocrystalline, magnetostrictive, and magnetostatic anisotropies for polycrystalline films than for particulate recording media.

Magnetocrystalline anisotropy, which arises from spin-orbit coupling, is of prime importance in determining the magnetic behavior of a single (hypothetically isolated) grain, and may thus be a starting point in characterizing a polycrystalline film. However, in real polycrystalline films, this anisotropy may not be the sole mechanism governing magnetization direction and reversal phenomena. It may not even be the most important mechanism. Most metal-film media consist of cobalt-based alloys, and consequently possess a magnetocrystalline anisotropy derived from the hexagonal structure of cobalt. In some preparations of longitudinal media, an effort is made to grow a cobalt-based film with the hexagonal c axis oriented in the plane of the film, inasmuch as the c axis corresponds to the magnetocrystalline easy axis. In perpendicular Co-Cr recording media, a c axis perpendicular to the film plane is sought.

Individual magnetic grains are always in close enough proximity to experience strong magnetostatic coupling, provided that grain boundaries disrupt stronger exchange coupling. To the extent that exchange coupling across grain boundaries exists, free magnetic charge and magnetostatic coupling are diminished. Either of these coupling mechanisms has the effect of causing groups of neighboring grains to act, more or less, in unison. If magnetocrystalline anisotropies of individual grains are nearly aligned, magnetostatic coupling will tend to enhance this predominant anisotropy.

When exchange coupling is disrupted across a grain boundary, a single grain can be approximated as a magnetic dipole, whose field is given by the following expression:

$$\mathbf{H} = \frac{m}{4\pi L}\left[\frac{(x - L/2)\mathbf{x} + y\mathbf{y}}{[(x - L/2)^2 + y^2]^{3/2}} - \frac{(x + L/2)\mathbf{x} + y\mathbf{y}}{[(x + L/2)^2 + y^2]^{3/2}} \right] \tag{4.1}$$

Here m is the dipole magnetic moment and L is the dipole length. The dipole is shown oriented in the x direction in Fig. 4.1, where $\mathbf{x}$ and $\mathbf{y}$ are unit vectors. This equation permits a first-order estimation of magnetostatic coupling between grains. For a disk-shaped grain with in-plane magnetization, L may be taken to be approximately the grain diameter and m is roughly $(\pi L^2 \delta/4)M_s$, where δ is the film thickness.

Setting $y = 0$ in Eq. (4.1) gives the magnetostatic field collinear with the dipole, which would tend to align an adjacent dipole. Setting $x = 0$ gives the field

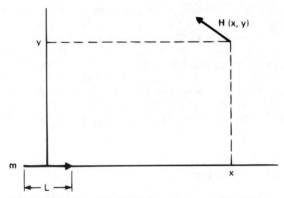

FIGURE 4.1   Magnetic field H (x, y) due to a magnetic dipole of magnitude m and length L, oriented in the x direction, and positioned at the origin.

antiparallel to the dipole, favoring antiparallel alignment of adjacent grains. The collinear alignment field falls off slightly faster than the antiparallel alignment field with increasing spacing, but the collinear field is always larger (5:1 for adjacent grains and 2:1 for large separations). Thus for two crystallites which have no strong easy axes of their own, alignment of the grains is favored. However, for a two-dimensional uniform array of grains, the multiple magnetostatic interaction fields do not lead to an overall alignment of magnetization. Instead, local fluctuations lead neighboring grains to form a cluster with a net alignment, due to minimization of magnetostatic energy. The cluster-to-cluster alignments remain random. Factors which can initiate or dominate local cluster alignment include statistical fluctuations of the following: anisotropy energies of individual grains, geometric local arrangement of grains, grain size, and orientation. This is further discussed in Section 3.1.5 on magnetization reversal and in Chap. 5.

In addition to coupling magnetic grains, magnetostatic energy can itself introduce strong anisotropies. Such anisotropy is usually referred to as *local shape anisotropy*. In films, individual grains have anisotropies derived from their shapes, quite analogous to those described earlier for particles. The shape of a grain can be the result of the natural growth habit of a particular crystal structure, but it is more often controlled by the specific conditions under which the film is deposited. In vacuum evaporation, or low-pressure sputtering, the angle at which incident atoms impinge on the substrate can strongly influence the growth morphology of the crystallites and their shape anisotropy. However conditions such as deposition rate, substrate temperature, alloy composition, substrate material, and surface conditions can also affect such grain shape anisotropies. For example, oblique incidence evaporation of metal films can produce strong shape anisotropy, with the easy axis parallel or perpendicular to the incident vapor stream, depending on the angle of incidence. This effect is enhanced by increased deposition rates, but it is somewhat diminished by increased substrate temperature, because the adatom surface mobility and the deposition rate are competing effects.

Local shape anisotropy may arise from the local arrangement of crystallites as well as the morphology of individual grains. Grains which, themselves, might be isotropic, yield very strong anisotropies when arranged in a linear chain during the growth process. This condition can also occur under certain conditions in oblique-angle evaporation. In films where the deposition process has induced the formation of such chains in a preferred direction, the center-to-center spacing of grains within a chain is essentially one grain diameter, while parallel chains tend to have separations which are about 10 percent larger. When magnetostatic interaction energies are computed, assuming that the center-to-center grain spacing between chains is only 5 to 10 percent larger than the center-to-center grain spacing within a chain, a strong anisotropy is produced with magnetization aligned in the direction of the chains.

In addition to magnetocrystalline and magnetostatic (shape) anisotropies, magnetostriction is a third major source of anisotropy. Magnetostriction refers to the interaction of magnetic and elastic properties of a material. The mechanical nature of conventional recording systems makes magnetostrictive properties of a medium generally undesirable, because unpredictable mechanical stresses occur during operation, and these can degrade the recorded signal integrity. So while magnetostriction can be used intentionally to induce magnetic anisotropy, it is difficult to control and seldom used. More will be said about this subject in the next section, where it is treated as a problem to control rather than a useful property in media design.

Before leaving the topic of anisotropy, mention should be made of an induced anisotropy which does not fit neatly into one of the above categories. This induced anisotropy results from applying a magnetic field during the growth of a film, or applying a field during a postdeposition anneal. The applied field affects the motion of atoms during growth or anneal. This atomic migration can result in a local ordering of magnetic species, vacancies, or other point defects, akin to magnetocrystalline anisotropy but not necessarily accompanied by long-range crystallographic order. Thus it is a spin-orbit coupling effect like crystalline anisotropy and not really a different physical mechanism. Atomic migration under an applied field, say during an anneal, can also induce grain growth, growth of precipitates, or defect ordering in a preferred direction. Again, this is not a distinct physical mechanism, but rather a technique to produce or enhance shape or magnetocrystalline anisotropies.

4.1.3 Magnetostriction

Magnetostriction, referred to in the previous section, can be even more critical in deposited films than in particulate media. The mechanical compliance of an organic binder in particulate coatings tends to mitigate stress effects on magnetic particles, whereas continuous films experience the full effect of any stresses. While accurate descriptions and measurements of magnetostriction are possible in single-crystal materials, the situation is more ambiguous for polycrystalline film structures.

Magnetostriction in a single crystal can involve one or more anisotropy directions. In a polycrystalline film, such anisotropies become averaged over the various crystallographic orientations taken by the grains. These orientations may be random or preferred, depending on the materials and the deposition conditions. Moreover, the finer the grain structure, the greater will be the effect of grain boundaries in determining the composite magnetostriction coefficients of a sample. Simple schemes for averaging the magnetostriction coefficients over all crystallite orientations in a film have been used, but they generally invoke assumptions of uniform stress or uniform strain and ignore grain boundary effects. The complexity of real film structures makes such exercises of little practical value. Besides the polycrystalline nature of film recording media, the fact that they are always multilayered structures makes a general formulation of magnetostriction problem intractable. Each layer contributes to the overall stress of the structure, and the stress may vary spatially.

Despite the difficulty in calculating magnetostrictive effects in polycrystalline multilayered media, the phenomenon is extremely important in media design. When theoretical calculation is impractical, empirical correlation with process parameters can be very useful. In deposition processes like sputtering, the built-in stresses depend on sufficiently many variables (rate, substrate temperature, sputtering pressure, substrate bias, and film thickness, to name some of the more important ones) that the final stresses, and consequent magnetic characteristics, will show some degree of random fluctuation. It is best to choose materials whose measured single-crystal magnetostriction coefficients are as low as possible, since this will minimize process control problems. Magnetostriction and its composition dependence are further discussed under magnetic and mechanical instabilities later in this chapter (Sec. 4.3).

4.1.4 Film Media Classification

Film recording media are often discussed in terms of the process used to deposit the magnetic layer, for example, plated, evaporated, or sputtered. This is a limiting perspective, since the fabrication of a multilayered film disk or tape often involves different processes for undercoats or overcoats from those used for the magnetic layer, such as a plated magnetic film and a sputtered overcoat.

The approach used here will be to classify and discuss the various types of film media according to more generic properties, which reflect their functional application and probable micromagnetic characteristics. The broadest division is between longitudinal recording media, where the magnetization vectors lie predominantly in the plane of the film, and perpendicular media, where the magnetization is predominantly perpendicular to the film plane. Most of the recording industry's attention in the past has been directed at materials and processes for longitudinally recorded media, and these will appropriately receive the most attention here. Beginning in the late 1970s, increased attention was given to perpendicular recording, with the principal media using sputtered Co-Cr alloys. This activity peaked in the 1980s and, while work continues, it is not a mainstream recording technology.

There is little need for defining subclassifications of perpendicular media. However, the richly varied history of longitudinal media warrants further categorization. In this area the broadest division is between metal and nonmetal (chiefly iron oxide) magnetic films. The second level of classification for longitudinal media will be according to whether the macroscopic magnetic properties are isotropic or anisotropic (that is, possess a preferred orientation) in the plane of the film. With only minor possible exceptions, all magnetically hard films used for recording media possess one or more types of anisotropy at the level of a single grain, local chains of grains, or clusters of grains. However, at the macroscopic level (about 1 μm and larger) films may appear to be isotropic or anisotropic, depending on the manner in which they are deposited or the manner in which the substrate is prepared. Except for what may be termed *accidental anisotropies,* plated films and most sputtered films fall in the isotropic category. The most notable anisotropic films are produced by oblique-incidence evaporation of metals or by annealing in the presence of an applied field. Anisotropic polishing texture on the substrate or anisotropically deposited underlayers can also induce a magnetic anisotropy in sputtered films which would otherwise be isotropic (Arnoldussen et al., 1984; Teng and Ballard, 1986;

Abe and Nishihara, 1986; Haines, 1987; Seagle et al., 1987; Simpson et al., 1987; Uchinami et al., 1987).

4.1.5 Magnetization Reversal and Noise

Control of the magnetization reversal process in a medium is of central importance, because information is recorded by inducing total or partial reversals via the recording head field. Coercivity determines a film's ability to withstand demagnetizing fields. It is a key magnetic parameter in determining linear information density in longitudinally magnetized films, and signal amplitude in perpendicularly magnetized films. But coercivity only describes the average behavior of all the crystallites in a film during the reversal process. Beyond controlling the average field at which magnetization switches, the film media designer must be concerned with the microscopic configuration in which the grains of the film are magnetized after a reversal is written. This micromagnetic structure is a key determinant of media noise.

Magnetization reversal in thin films may occur in three conceptually distinct ways: (1) individual grains undergo reversal independently; (2) local groups of grains, which are magnetically coupled to one another, undergo reversal in unison but independently of other clusters; (3) grains which are coupled over long range form magnetic domains, and reversal occurs by movement of domain walls. In real films more than one of these modes may be operative. In mode 1 coercivity is determined by the magnetocrystalline anisotropy in a grain, the grain shape, and the stress state. In mode 2 the factors in mode 1 apply, as well as the type of grain coupling within a cluster. In mode 3 wall energy controls coercivity and is affected by magnetocrystalline anisotropy, magnetostatic energy at the wall, stress variations, film roughness, and compositional irregularities. Numerous models have been formulated on the basis of these three modes of reversal, some analytic and some numerical, to describe micromagnetic structures, hysteretic properties, or to describe recorded information and noise sources (Néel, 1955; Middelhoek, 1963; Freiser, 1979; Hughes, 1983; Muller and Murdock, 1987; Zhang et al., 1988; Victora, 1987; Zhu and Bertram, 1988a; Zhu and Bertram, 1988b; Arnoldussen et al., 1991; Arnoldussen and Nunnelley, 1992). The details of all these models will not be elaborated here, but the focus will be on the implications of these different reversal modes. See Chap. 5 for a more thorough discussion.

The single most important reason for considering film media in preference to particulate coatings is the possibility of achieving higher effective magnetization. This can yield higher readback signals, or allow thinner films with the attendant recording benefits to lower thickness losses. Higher signals can increase the signal-to-noise ratio if media noise is insignificant compared with other noise sources in a recording system. If, however, head and electronic noise is sufficiently low, media noise sources must be considered when evaluating the relative merit of different media. In fact media noise has become the dominant concern in advanced media design.

Longitudinal Recording Media. In particulate media the intrinsic (ac-erased) signal-to-noise power ratio is proportional to the particle density, if the particles are well dispersed and act independently. Following this line of thought, if the grains of continuous films were uncoupled, such films might be expected to show higher signal-to-noise ratios since they have smaller and more densely packed grains. Longitudinally recorded metal films are indeed low in noise at low recording densities, but the noise increases with write frequency. This noise is related to the micromagnetic structure of the written magnetization reversals, and intergranular coupling is a key factor. The noise power in thin metal film media typically rises linearly with recording density at low densities, which is evidence that the observed noise is associated with the transitions themselves. The noise per transition is constant and the total noise is therefore proportional to the rate at which transitions are written. However, at higher densities the noise in some films rises at a supralinear rate as bit spacing becomes comparable with transition length. Finally the noise passes through a weak maximum and decreases at the highest densities, as seen in Fig. 4.2 (Baugh et al., 1983).

An early transition noise model (Belk et al., 1985) proposed that the transition noise could be explained by random pulse shifts (ignoring pulse shape variations). At low recording densities such noise would increase linearly with recording density (for that matter, random pulse shape or amplitude variations would also produce this effect). However, they proposed that at higher densities zigzag domain boundaries of adjacent transitions would shift so as to avoid each other. This type of adjacent transition correlation would predict a supralinear rise in noise at close transition spacing. While mathematically sound, this mechanism is not physically plausible. Analysis of Lorentz electron micrographs of recorded tracks (Arnoldussen and Tong, 1986) showed the existence of significant amplitude noise in addition to pulse shifting, and evidence that the walls of adjacent transitions tend to attract each other at close spacing, which is magnetically more plausible than avoidance. They proposed that at close bit spacing this random attraction of opposite polarity nearest neighbor transitions increased the variance of the transition width, introducing additional noise beyond whatever amplitude and pulse shift noise was present at low densities. This has become known as percolation. Thus the supralinear behavior was attributed to the transitions becoming noisier at close spacing, rather than a modulation effect. The decrease in noise at still higher densities was attributed to partial erasure of previously written bits by the record head. Analysis of noise spectra (Madrid and Wood, 1986) also leads to the conclusion that

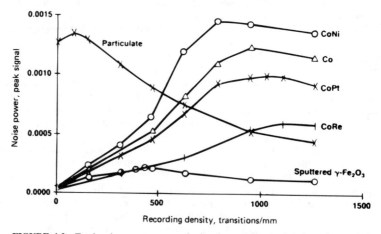

FIGURE 4.2 Total noise-power per peak-signal squared as a function of recorded magnetization reversal density, for several thin-film media and one particulate medium. The increase of noise with recording density for the metal media indicates that the noise is associated with the magnetization reversals themselves (*Baugh et al., 1983*).

the supralinear increase of noise results from the transitions becoming intrinsically noisier. Noise autocorrelation studies (Tang, 1986) and time domain noise analysis (Moon et al., 1988; Arnoldussen et al., 1993) corroborate that noise due to pulse shape variations dominates over pulse shift noise at high recording densities.

Longitudinal metal film media behave almost diametrically opposite to particulate media with regard to noise. Particulates tend to show the greatest noise in the dc-erased state and lowest when bulk ac-erased, while films show greatest noise in the bulk ac-erased condition (Ferrier et al., 1988). This may be understood intuitively as follows. When dc-erased, a film is (virtually) a single large domain with (virtually) no flux leakage from its surface. There are therefore no sources of signal or noise. Just as signal is written by using an external field to create a disruption in the flux continuity in the film, so are noise sources *created* by the action of an external field. When a film is bulk ac-erased, the external field breaks up the "single-domain" into a sea of randomly directed small "domains" of a characteristic size distribution. Each of these small "domains" acts as a noise source. Here the term "domain" is used in a loose sense: either a true domain in a film with strong exchange coupling between grains or a cluster of magnetostatically coupled grains with little, if any, exchange coupling between grains.

When a signal is being recorded as magnetization reversals, an intermediate state results. Between transitions the media is essentially dc-erased, single domain, relatively noise-free. In the vicinity of the recorded transitions, where average magnetization across the track width is passing through zero, the media takes on some of the character of a bulk ac-erased state. Although the average magnetization across a track tends toward zero at the center of a transition, discrete domains or clusters of coupled grains retain a net large magnetization, but tend to be randomly directed, with a characteristic size distribution related to the bulk ac-erased state. It is this randomness of "domain" direction and size in the vicinity of the transition which gives rise to *transition noise*.

By high resolution magnetic imaging of recorded tracks on a film medium, the statistical properties and therefore the media noise can be characterized (Arnoldussen and Tong, 1986; Ferrier et al., 1988). Conversely, key micromagnetic parameters can be inferred through recording and readback measurements via a formalism described for particulate media (Nunnelley et al., 1987), but applicable to films as well (Arnoldussen, 1992). Making the approximation of a zero-gap head and zero-thickness medium, neither of which essentially affects the result, the signal-to-noise ratio (SNR) due only to the medium can be calculated and related to test stand measurements. The voltage noise-squared spectrum (Arnoldussen, 1992) can be written as

$$V_{ns}^2(k) \approx (N\epsilon v \mu_o)^2 \times 2\pi k_1 (M_r\delta)^2 \ \frac{W \langle w_c^2 \rangle}{\langle w_c \rangle} \times k^2 a^2 e^{-2k(a+d)} \qquad (4.2)$$

An arctangent transition shape and an inductive head are assumed, again with little effect on the final result. N = number of coil turns on the head; ϵ = head efficiency; v = disk velocity; μ_o = permeability of free space; M_r = remanent magnetization of the medium; δ = medium thickness; W = trackwidth; w_c = correlation width of noise sources (width, in cross-track direction, of features like zigzag or vortex transition boundaries); and $\langle . . . \rangle$ denotes an ensemble average. The spatial angular frequency, k, is 2π divided by wavelength; and k_1 is the fundamental frequency of the square-wave pattern recorded. The effective magnetic head-medium spacing is d and a is the arctangent transition parameter. The mean-squared noise voltage is given by $(\frac{1}{2}\pi)$ times the integral of this equation from $k = 0$ to infinity (assuming an effectively infinite bandwidth detector). Under the same conditions the zero-to-peak signal voltage of an isolated transition is

$$V_{sg,peak} \approx (Nev\mu_o)\ (W\delta)\ \left(\frac{2M_r}{\pi}\right)\left(\frac{1}{a+d}\right) \tag{4.3}$$

The peak (isolated pulse) signal to rms noise written at a linear density $D = k_1/\pi$ is then given by

$$\frac{V_{sg,peak}}{V_{ns,rms}} \approx \frac{4}{\pi}\left[\frac{W\langle w_c\rangle}{\langle w_c{}^2\rangle}\frac{(d+a)}{a^2 k_1}\right]^{1/2} \tag{4.4}$$

Inasmuch as noise in film media is not stationary, but concentrated in the transitions, the most appropriate condition for which to compute the SNR is for the transition spacing just equal to the transition length (πa), or $k_1 = 1/a$. At this point, if we assume $d = 2a$ and $\langle w_c{}^2\rangle/\langle w_c\rangle = 0.01W$, the above SNR = 27 dB, typical of actual measurements. Going the other way, measurement of SNR, W, and d combined with a modeled estimate of a permits w_c to be inferred. The above expression may be subtly deceptive, as it appears that the SNR improves with increasing magnetic spacing d. The SNR is proportional to $(a + d)/a^2$, and a is roughly proportional to $d^{1/2}$, so that at a given linear density k_1/π SNR slightly increases with decreasing d, which is intuitively understandable. Under the condition that $k_1 = 1/a$, however, it appears that SNR degrades as d decreases. This is because the density at which the SNR is being evaluated increases with decreasing d, which means that for equal noise per transition the total noise increases. If, instead, we compute the ratio of isolated pulse peak amplitude to noise per transition density, a more appropriate measure, we obtain

$$\frac{V_{sg,peak}}{V_{ns,rms}/\sqrt{D}} \approx \frac{4}{\pi\sqrt{\pi}}\left[\frac{W\langle w_c\rangle}{\langle w_c{}^2\rangle}\frac{(d+a)}{a^2}\right]^{1/2} \tag{4.5}$$

This form shows that (for $a \propto d^{1/2}$), the transition noisiness decreases and signal to noise within a transition increases as magnetic spacing decreases.

It is clear from the above expressions that the track width W and the width of micromagnetic fluctuations w_c are the primary determinants of media SNR. Secondarily, longer transitions decrease SNR, but we can expect transition lengths and widths of micromagnetic features to be somewhat correlated. It is important to understand what controls these domain or cluster size distributions.

The remanent magnetization of metal films ranges from 300 to 1000 kA/m (emu/cm^3) compared with about 300 kA/m for magnetic oxide particles, and the grains in a metal film are far more densely packed than the particles in a particulate coating. Thus, while magnetic interactions between particles are significant and affect the switching properties of a particulate coating, even stronger interactions occur in metal-film layers. In a continuous metal film, high-magnetization grains will be coupled to one another by strong magnetostatic forces or by even stronger exchange forces or both. In either case, domains (or clusters of grains which tend to act as a unit) are formed by the strong interaction in continuous media.

The existence of domains or coupled grain clusters may be expected to alter the nature of magnetization reversal and therefore the recording process. In particulate coatings, the major questions of magnetization reversal relate to the physics of relatively isolated particle reversal. In continuous films, the nature of isolated grain magnetization reversal is only one aspect of the process. Beyond the individual grain, account must be taken of the intergranular coupling and the energetics and dynamics of "domain" nucleation and growth. In real films, these factors are influenced by the interaction of the magnetic layer with the substrate, roughness in various layers, defects, and so on.

Magnetization reversal and magnetic microstructure of recording patterns involve minimization of magnetostatic, magnetocrystalline, and exchange energies. Today's supercomputers and fast workstations have enabled significant understanding of these topics. Chapter 5 describes this type of modeling in detail. Prior to such computer simulation, simple mathematical and physical models produced important qualitative insight into the nature of micromagnetic behavior. Without much elaboration, some of these earlier efforts are mentioned here for historical perspective.

Néel approximated a 180° wall as an elliptical cylinder (Néel, 1955). Within the wall, the magnetization rotated from parallel to the wall in one direction to parallel in the opposite direction. He calculated the wall energy and dimensions by minimizing the sum of exchange, magnetocrystalline anisotropy, and demagnetization energies as a function of film thickness. Magnetization rotating out of the film plane is termed a Bloch wall and rotation in the plane has been termed a Néel wall. Middelhoek applied such calculations to walls in permalloy, including cross-tie walls as well (Middelhoek, 1963). Both of these works were directed at soft magnetic films and 180° walls parallel to the magnetization.

Magnetization reversals in magnetically hard films used for recording media are 180°, but with the "wall" running perpendicular to the dominant magnetization direction. Such a "wall" is unstable because of high demagnetization energy. Stability is achieved by spreading the magnetic charge over a larger region than defined by a wall. In a strongly oriented film this results in a zigzag wall structure as seen in Fig. 4.3. Both zigzag structures and even more complex vortex reversals have been observed in recorded transitions (Daval and Randet, 1970; Dressler and Judy, 1974; Chen, 1981; Tong et al., 1984). Freiser formulated an analytical model for zigzag wall boundaries (Freiser, 1979), though his focus was on their occasional existence in soft magnetic films, not recording media. An interesting conceptual framework, this model was not particularly useful for modeling recorded transitions, in part because a recorded transition length is very much dependent on the gradient of the head write field (Hsieh et al., 1974; Kullmann et al., 1984a). A very successful write field gradient model (Williams and Comstock, 1971) predicted the average transition length so well that it continues to be useful for recording predictions, even today. However, this model provided no insight into the micromagnetic structure and therefore no insight into noise mechanisms. More recently, the 2-dimensional model has been extended to 3D for narrow track modeling (Arnoldussen et al., 1991) and has been adapted to describe average zigzag microstructures (Muller and Murdock, 1987; Zhang et al., 1988). Yet none of these contribute to modeling noise in media because they contain no statistical randomness.

For the medium shown in Fig. 4.3, the arctangent transition model has been shown to accurately predict the central slope of the trackwidth-averaged transition profile, even though this transition was shown to be more like an error function than an arctangent (Arnoldussen and Tong, 1986). This suggests that use of simple transition functions like arctangents in analytical modeling of the recording process remains valid for applications like nominal pulse amplitude, linear deterministic peak shift, and resolution. Moreover, analytical arctangent and error functions have been used to describe some aspects of transition noise (Barany and Bertram, 1987; Arnoldussen and Nunnelley, 1992).

The microscopic origins of media noise have been much better described by numerical computer simulation models.

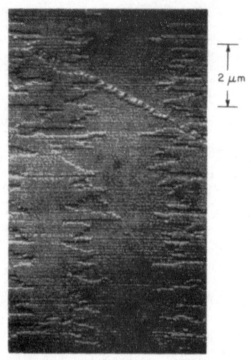

FIGURE 4.3 A portion of a recorded track showing two magnetization reversals written by a film head on an obliquely evaporated Fe-Co-Cr film medium, which is highly oriented in the direction of the track. For the medium, H_c = 40 kA/m (500 Oe), M_r = 900 kA/m (emu/cm^3), and film thickness is about 35 nm. The texture lines, running from top to bottom in the track direction, are from the substrate (*Photo courtesy of H. C. Tong*).

Magnetization reversal, which is the essence of the recording process, may proceed by domain nucleation and wall motion or by irreversible rotation. When the latter occurs, it probably proceeds in a cooperative manner, where clusters of grains undergo simultaneous rotation due to magnetic coupling. This has been demonstrated by means of a large-scale mechanical model, in which an array of pivoting magnets was shown to reverse its orientation in clusters (Reimer, 1964). In the 1980s computer simulations became a viable technique for exploring such behavior. The first of these (Hughes, 1983) considered the magnetostatic coupling of randomly oriented magnetic grains which were isolated from each other by nonmagnetic grain boundaries, characteristic of plated Co-(Ni)-P films as well as many sputtered Co-X-Cr films. In this model the width of the grain boundaries determined the degree of magnetostatic coupling. Random magnetocrystalline anisotropy directions were assigned to hexagonal cells representing individual grains. The magnetization configuration was solved as a magnetostatic problem. The simulation demonstrated that greater coupling produces greater remanent and coercive squareness ratios, but lower coercivities. Moreover, simulation of a recorded magnetization transition produced irregular transition boundaries which, in this case, were more associated with the boundary of magnetostatically coupled grain clusters (Fig. 4.4) than with dispersion of magnetic charge alone.

Hughes concluded that formation of these clusters of coupled grains should limit recording density, because a broader transition is forced by large clusters, and that noise will also be increased by virtue of forming large clusters. Since smaller clusters meant weaker intergranular coupling and lower squareness hysteresis loops, Hughes speculated that relatively low squareness media are to be sought for high density, low noise applications. This was in contrast to conventional wisdom that a significant advantage of film media is the possibility of achieving much squarer hysteresis than in particulate coatings, as illustrated in Fig. 4.5.

Following Hughes' work, modeling of magnetic films rose to yet a higher level of sophistication through use of ultrafast supercomputers or parallel processor computers (Victora, 1987; Zhu and Bertram, 1988a; Zhu and Bertram, 1988b; Mansuripur and McDaniel, 1988). Like Hughes' model, these simulations operate on arrays of cells representing crystallite grains, assign magnetization and anisotropies to individual cells, include the local magnetostatic field due to other cells (all or at least a large number of near neighbors), and proceed to an energy minimization. Unlike Hughes', they generally can include exchange coupling between grains using an effective exchange constant, and they all set up the problem using Landau-Lifshitz(-Gilbert) dynamic equations of motion, described in Chap. 5.

With such a model Victora obtained excellent quantitative agreement between calculated and measured torque curves for obliquely evaporated Co-Ni films (Victora, 1987). For uniaxial anisotropy films (Zhu and Bertram, 1988a), domain structures were generated which are qualitatively similar to actual domain structures seen by Lorentz electron microscopy (Chen, 1981; Tong et al., 1984; Arnoldussen and Tong, 1986). Modeled recording transitions were found to be much noisier when exchange coupling between grains was assumed than for zero intergranular exchange even when the problem was set up to maintain similar average transition profiles (Zhu and Bertram, 1988b). Although Hughes did not specifically treat intergranular exchange coupling, his conjecture about the relationship between coupling and squareness and transition noise were corroborated by Zhu and Bertram.

Not only have the theoretical treatments concurred that noise in film media increases with increasing hysteretic squareness, but this notion has been confirmed experimentally as well (Natarajan and Murdock, 1988; Sanders et al., 1989). Figure 4.6 shows noise (normalized by isolated signal pulse amplitude) versus S^* for a variety of cobalt alloy films along with some sputtered γ-Fe_2O_3 films. The striking

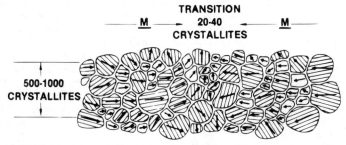

FIGURE 4.4 Schematic illustration of recorded transition on a polycrystalline film (*Hughes, 1983*).

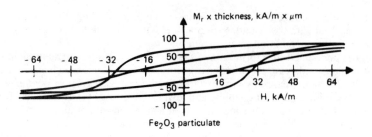

Fe₂O₃ particulate

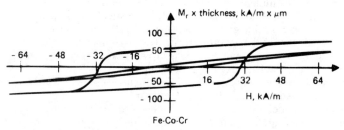

Fe-Co-Cr

FIGURE 4.5 Comparison of hysteresis loops of a typical iron oxide, oriented acicular particle coating (top), and those of a highly oriented, obliquely evaporated Fe-Co-Cr film (bottom). In both cases the larger, squarer loop is for the easy axis and the narrower loop is for the transverse direction. Isotropic media hysteresis loops resemble the easy axis loop of this figure, regardless of direction (*Rossi et al., 1984*).

correlation between squareness and noise invites the conclusion that low S^* is most desirable for recording. But one must keep in mind the entire recording system before drawing conclusions. The lower S^* is, the higher will be the head field required to saturate the medium. Too low a squareness could lead to difficulty in overwriting, producing a new noise source (residual old data) which is as detrimental as the media noise. Media with S^* slightly below the knee of the curve in Fig. 4.6 might be a suitable compromise. Also keep in mind that, while Fig. 4.6 shows a clear correlation, there is considerable scatter. Thus low noise and high S^* are not mutually exclusive.

Dynamic micromagnetic computer models should be capable of modeling the effects of defects and media inhomogeneities on magnetization reversal and noise, although there has not yet been extensive work along these lines. However, this would appear to be an extremely important area of study, because certain types of inhomogeneities are precisely the factors used in media fabrication to control coercivity, orientation, and noise. Namely, substrate roughness can produce high coercivity not directly related to magnetocrystalline anisotropy (Soohoo, 1981), and controlled circumferential substrate texture can induce a preferred orientation in the magnetic film (Arnoldussen et al., 1984; Rossi et al., 1984; Teng and Ballard, 1986; Abe and Nishihara, 1986; Haines, 1987; Seagle et al., 1987; Simpson et al., 1987; Uchinami et al., 1987).

Perpendicular Recording Media. Continuous film perpendicular recording media might also be expected to exhibit cooperative magnetic behavior, but whether

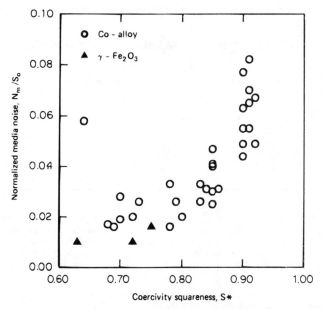

FIGURE 4.6 Rms media noise voltage, N_m, for a linear density of 3000 transitions/mm normalized by the zero-to-peak isolated pulse amplitude S_0 versus coercivity squareness S^* (*Sanders et al., 1989*).

domain formation and wall motion occur seems to depend on the film preparation conditions. There are two principal models to describe the nature of film perpendicular media, mainly focusing on Co-Cr alloys. One model treats the film as a continuum, forming stripe domains similar to those in bubble materials. The other treats the columnar grains (or multigrains) isolated by nonmagnetic grain boundaries, which have been observed in Co-Cr alloys, as relatively independent particles. The stripe domain model may be applicable for low-Cr-content films. However, under conditions leading to nonmagnetic grain boundary formation, such as increased chromium or oxygen, the particle model may be more realistic, because nonmagnetic grain boundaries can degrade or disrupt any exchange coupling between grains.

With regard to determining linear recording density, it probably makes little difference whether a perpendicular anisotropy film undergoes magnetization reversal by either particlelike switching or reverse domain nucleation and wall motion. However, the micromagnetic structure of a recorded pattern, and therefore media noise, may depend on the mode of reversal. Experimental evidence supporting both models suggests that the mode of magnetization reversal depends on the detailed film deposition conditions.

Perpendicular recording media are generally recognized as supporting more stable high-density recording patterns than longitudinal media, because magnetostatic demagnetizing fields decrease as perpendicular reversals are spaced closer together, whereas they increase for closely spaced longitudinal reversals. This same phenomenon favors smaller micromagnetic granularity in perpendicular media, and therefore potentially lower noise. Figure 4.7*a* depicts a longitudinally oriented film uniformly magnetized in the positive direction along a recording track, except for a small reversely oriented region. The long regions to either side of the reversed

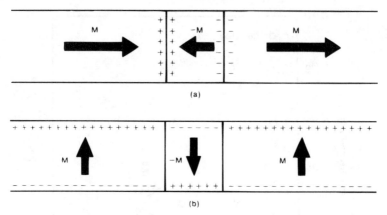

FIGURE 4.7 (*a*) Longitudinally oriented film, uniformly magnetized from left to right except for a small reversed region. Demagnetization field due to adjacent regions makes the reversed region thermodynamically unstable. (*b*) Perpendicularly oriented film, uniformly magnetized from bottom to top except for a small reversed region. Magnetostatic fields due to adjacent regions tend to stabilize the reversed region.

region exert a strong demagnetizing field on the reversed region, favoring the annihilation of the reversed portion. If exchange coupling is operative across grain boundaries, extra energy is required to support the reversed domain because of the 180° reversal of spin direction across the wall. These facts mean that the growth of longer domains at the expense of shorter ones is thermodynamically favored in longitudinal media.

In Fig. 4.7*b*, a perpendicularly oriented film is shown uniformly magnetized upward, except for a small reversed region. As with the longitudinal film, exchange coupling across grain boundaries means that energy must be added to the system to create the reversed domain, because of the creation of 180° domain walls. However, magnetostatic energy is lowered by creation of the reversed region. This then favors the formation of short domains at the expense of long domains along the track direction, leading to increased granularity. If the domain model applies, the smallest magnetic unit is a domain size determined by the balance between the magnetostatic energy decrease and the increase in wall energy due to exchange energy. If the particle model applies, the smallest magnetic unit is the grain or multigrain constituting the quasiparticle. At any rate, exchange forces drive toward the formation of shorter domain wall length and larger domains for both longitudinal and perpendicular films. However, magnetostatic forces drive toward shorter domains in perpendicular media and longer domains in longitudinal media. This suggests the possibility of lower media noise for perpendicular media, particularly for fine-grained media exhibiting particlelike behavior rather than domain behavior. Noise measurements on perpendicular Co-Cr media without soft magnetic underlayers have indeed shown this to be the case (Belk et al., 1985).

The shape of the hysteresis loop can give an important clue to the microscopic nature of perpendicular recording media. The hysteresis loops for Co-Cr alloys, measured perpendicular to the film plane, usually resemble rectangular loops which have been sheared into parallelogram shapes, as illustrated in Fig. 4.8. This shearing effect is directly related to micromagnetic structure, and will be addressed in the following discussion of magnetic reversal.

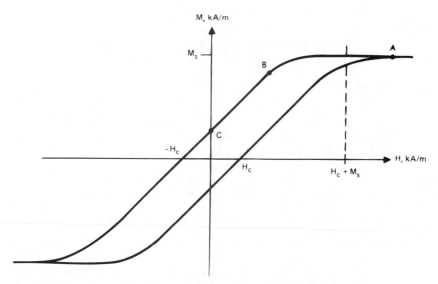

FIGURE 4.8 Hysteresis loop typical of a perpendicular medium, skewed by the aggregate perpendicular demagnetization field.

We will first consider coercivities and loop shapes expected for simple coherent rotation of magnetization. For the sake of argument, assume that the magnetic film grows such that it has a uniaxial magnetocrystalline anisotropy, with the easy axis perpendicular to the film plane. This anisotropy is characterized by an energy constant $K_\perp$. In the absence of demagnetization, the film would have a uniaxial anisotropy characterized by the energy constant $K_u = K_\perp$. The magnetocrystalline energy is a function of the angle ϕ between the magnetization vector and the perpendicular easy axis, namely $K_\perp (\sin \phi)^2$. The coercivity would be given by $H_c = H_k = 2K_u/\mu_0 M_s$, where H_k is the anisotropy field. For a Co-(23.5 at %) Cr alloy $K_\perp$ has been reported to be 9.74×10^4 J/m^3 (9.74×10^5 erg/cm^3) with $M_s = 300$ kA/m (emu/cm^3) (Fisher et al., 1984). This would give $H_c = 517$ kA/m (6460 Oe). The hysteresis loop should be perfectly square. If the grains of the film had a finite range of anisotropy constants, that is, a finite switching-field distribution, the hysteresis loop would not be perfectly square, but would have minor shearing due to these grain-to-grain variations.

An infinite-area film with its saturation magnetization perpendicular to the plane has a demagnetizing field of $-M_s$ ($-4\pi M_s$ in cgs units). When the magnetization is canted at an angle ϕ from the normal, the demagnetization energy is given by $\frac{1}{2}\mu_0 M_s^2(\cos \phi)^2$ [$2\pi M_s^2(\cos \phi)^2$]. If the inequality $K_\perp > \frac{1}{2}\mu_0 M_s^2$ holds, the uniaxial anisotropy energy constant would be $K_u = K_\perp - \frac{1}{2}\mu_0 M_s^2$ ($K_u = K_\perp - 2\pi M_s^2$). The coercivity for uniform rotation should be $H_c = H_k$ as before, but now $H_k = 2K_u/\mu_0 M_s = 2K_\perp/\mu_0 M_s - M_s$. The hysteresis loop again will be perfectly square, aside from the small effects of a finite switching-field distribution, but demagnetization lowers the coercivity by $-M_s$. For the Co-Cr parameters given above, this coercivity is 217 kA/m (2710 Oe). Both the calculations above predict nearly square hysteresis loops and coercivities far higher than the 67.2 kA/m (840 Oe) observed for this composition film (Fisher et al., 1984). In fact, coercivities calculated assuming uniform rotation are almost always higher than measured values, which are typically less than about 100 kA/m (1250 Oe) for Co-Cr alloys.

Coherent rotation is therefore unlikely to be the actual reversal mechanism, and other mechanisms, which more closely predict coercivity, will be described shortly. Nevertheless, under the assumption that a grain or grain cluster being switched sees only its local self-demagnetization field, and not demagnetization from surrounding regions, most reversal mechanisms would still predict either square hysteresis loops or no perpendicular remanence at all. If $H_{c\perp}$ denotes the intrinsic coercivity in the absence of demagnetization, then square hysteresis results when $H_{c\perp} > M_s$, with a coercivity $H_{c\perp} - M_s$. No hysteresis is expected and no perpendicular remanence can be sustained when $H_{c\perp} \leq M_s$.

The shearing of hysteresis loops which is usually observed (Fig. 4.8) is best explained by a variable aggregate demagnetization field. For a film consisting of many small, semi-independent particles (or domains), an individual particle may react to the aggregate demagnetization field of many nearby particles rather than to its own self-demagnetization only. This aggregate demagnetization field, H_d, is approximately equal to $-M$, where M is the average state of magnetization of particles in a given region. We will assume that this M is equal to the macroscopic average which is measured.

In reference to Fig. 4.8, when a positive external field is applied which is large enough to overcome the coercivity and maximum demagnetization field ($H_c + M_s$), all the particles have their magnetization aligned in the direction of the applied field (point A). The aggregate magnetization is M_s, with the demagnetization field equal to $-M_s$ ($-4\pi M_s$ in cgs units). If the applied field is decreased to just under $M_s - H_{c1}$, where H_{c1} is the demagnetization-free coercivity of the most easily switched particles, the easiest-to-switch particles reverse (point B). This lowers the average magnetization as well as the magnitude of the aggregate demagnetization. If the magnetization changes by ΔM, the demagnetization changes by $\Delta H_d \approx -\Delta M$ and the external field required to maintain that state changes by $\Delta H = -\Delta H_d = \Delta M$. As the applied field is further decreased, what would be a nearly vertical side of a hysteresis loop without aggregate variable demagnetization is mapped onto a sloped side with $dM/dH \approx 1$. When the applied field becomes zero, some remanent aggregate magnetization remains (point C), corresponding to the difference between the unswitched particles and those which have switched. As the applied field is reversed in polarity, the net magnetization becomes zero at $H = -H_c$, which is approximately the average switching field of the individual particles. The description above applies to materials whose coercivity is less than $M_s(4\pi M_s$ in cgs units), which is true for most practical perpendicular media. Under these conditions the remanent magnetization for an infinite-area film is equal to H_c ($H_c/4\pi$). If the coercivity is greater than M_s, shearing of the hysteresis loop still occurs, but the remanent magnetization is nearly equal to that for the demagnetization-free case, rather than being equal to H_c.

Both the particle and stripe-domain models are capable of explaining the sheared hysteresis loops observed, provided that the particles or domains are small enough to produce an aggregate demagnetization effect, and provided that there is a finite distribution of switching fields. For the particle model this means the "particles," or columnar grains, must be noninteracting or weakly interacting, and must have grain diameters sufficiently small so that the aggregate demagnetizing field from surrounding grains overrides an individual grain's self-demagnetizing field. For the stripe-domain model, the balance between wall energy and demagnetization energy must be favorable to the formation of a high density of small domains.

The conclusion reached above, that $dM/dH = 1$ along the side of the hysteresis loop, may be violated in certain cases. Namely, this slope may be greater than unity. This will occur in the particle model when the film thickness is small compared with the grain diameter, so that an individual grain's self-demagnetizing field is large compared with the composite effect of surrounding grains, or when the magnetization is small enough compared with the coercivity that shearing becomes a weak effect. In the domain model, a slope higher than unity can occur when the wall energy is large or the magnetization small, such that the formation of many small domains, with increased total wall length, becomes unfavorable. Decreased film thickness favors decreased wall length and therefore fewer, larger domains. Again, the effect of an aggregate demagnetizing field becomes less important and less loop shearing occurs. Although sheared hysteresis is not sought for its own sake, the fact that it represents a finer grain or domain structure (and therefore lower media noise) suggests that it may be desirable for perpendicular recording media to have loop shearing and a slope dM/dH close to unity.

Both the particle and domain models are able to account qualitatively for the relatively low coercivities observed in perpendicular film media like Co-Cr films. However, the quantitative prediction of coercivities has not been successful with any simple model. The particle models invoke more or less independent particle switching by a curling or buckling mechanism (Ohkoshi et al., 1983). Coercivity seems to be determined by a combination of mostly magnetocrystalline anisotropy and some shape anisotropy (Wuori and Judy, 1984, 1985). Ample evidence of columnar magnetic grains, isolated by nonmagnetic grain boundaries, in Co-Cr films makes this particle interpretation plausible. The domain models assume that coercivity is governed by wall motion or reverse domain nucleation. As in domain wall models for longitudinal film media, it is common to assume that the coercivity is controlled by wall energy variations due to film thickness irregularity (Wielinga, 1983). Some parameters, such as hysteresis loop shearing slope, tend to favor the wall motion model of coercivity. Microstructure (Chen and Charlan, 1983; Grundy et al., 1984) and temperature dependence of coercivity and anisotropy constant (Wuori and Judy, 1985) tend to favor the particle model. Dynamic micromagnetic computer modeling reviewed in Chap. 5 sheds important light on this controversy.

4.2 FILM MATERIALS AND PROCESSES

Many of the techniques used to deposit films for magnetic recording media are similar to those used in other film technologies. The reader will be referred to literature from these other fields for detailed treatments of standard techniques and processes whenever appropriate. Attention here will be concentrated on features which are unique or especially important to film recording media.

4.2.1 Fabrication Overview

Generally the term *media* refers to the entire recording structure, not simply the magnetic layer. This broader use of the term is especially important for film media where the substrate and any film layers beneath or on top of the magnetic layer can profoundly affect the recording properties and performance. Figure 4.9 shows the general structure of thin-film recording media, consisting of a substrate, an undercoat, a magnetic layer, and an overcoat. Usually there is an additional layer between the magnetic layer and the undercoat for the purpose of controlling the

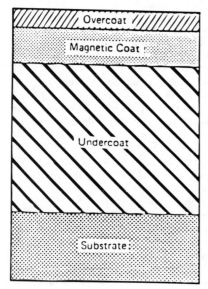

FIGURE 4.9 General structure of a film medium.

magnetic properties of the recording layer. Similarly, the overcoat has been shown as a single layer, but may consist of multiple layers and perhaps a lubricant on the surface.

The substrate may be rigid or flexible, depending on the final application. Rigid substrates are used for high-density, rapid direct-access disk files. Aluminum-magnesium alloy substrates are used for most rigid disks, whether particulate or film. Rigid aluminum alloy substrate disks require a hard undercoat when used for film media, because the Al-Mg alloy itself is too soft to provide adequate impact resistance. Glass and ceramic substrates, considered for over two decades, may have found a unique niche for portable computing applications, where diameters are less than $2\frac{1}{2}''$ and thicknesses less than 0.6 mm are sought for high disk stacking density. These substrates offer little, if any, advantage in smoothness, but have superior rigidity and impact resistance. Substrates used for tape and flexible-disk applications are generally polyethylene terephthalate (PET), with some surface treatment or thin adhesion-promoting layer (instead of a thick undercoat) required to promote strong bonding between the organic substrate and inorganic film structure.

Most magnetic films are cobalt-based metal alloys. Co-P and Co-Ni-P were the most frequently used plated alloys for longitudinal media, the phosphorus being incorporated from hypophosphite ions in the plating bath. Today plated magnetic films are no longer used commercially. Evaporated metal films have generally been elemental, such as cobalt or iron, or alloys whose constituents have similar vapor pressures, such as Co-Ni. Use of corrosion-retarding additives such as chromium or tungsten requires more sophisticated deposition rate controls to cope with their vastly different vapor pressures, but such alloys as Fe-Co-Cr have been successfully evaporated (Rossi et al., 1984; Arnoldussen et al., 1984). Only tape applications still use evaporation today. The list of metal alloys which have been rf- or dc-sputtered for use as recording films is by far the most extensive, because of the broad compositional flexibility available through this deposition technique. Cobalt, Co-Cr, Co-Ni-W, Co-Re, Co-Pt-Cr, Co-Pt-Ni, and Co-Cr-Ta are but a few of the alloys which have been sputtered for film media. Sputtering is also the preferred technique for producing nonmetal magnetic films, such as γ-Fe_2O_3. Different magnetic films usually require different substrate preparations, as is discussed below.

Finally, some means of alleviating mechanical abrasion of the magnetic film is required, because of the mechanical nature of disk and tape magnetic recording. The use of wear particles, such as Al_2O_3 in particulate media coatings, is obviously not possible for continuous films. Instead, a wear-resistant overcoat is used for virtually all forms of thin-film media. It is necessary to ensure strong bonding between layers, because mechanical wear of thin-film structures often occurs by adhesion failure. For this reason an adhesion-promoting interlayer has sometimes been used between the magnetic coating and the overcoat, or between the substrate and first deposited layer.

The film deposition processes that have been used are electroplating, electroless (autocatalytic) plating, evaporation (normal and oblique incidence), and sputtering (rf, dc, and magnetron enhancements of rf and dc). Plating and evaporation techniques are described in greater detail in a later section. Sputter deposition is depicted in Figs. 4.10 and 4.11. Sputtering is performed in a vacuum chamber which has been pumped down to a pressure of 10^{-4} to 10^{-5} Pa (0.75×10^{-6} to 0.75×10^{-7} torr), most often by means of diffusion, cryopumping, or turbopumping. The chamber is then backfilled with a sputtering gas to a pressure of 1.3×10^{-1} to 10 Pa (10^{-3} to 7.5×10^{-2} torr). In simple dc sputtering (Fig. 4.10), a dc voltage up to several thousand volts is applied between the substrate and a target of source material to be deposited, the target being biased negatively with respect to the substrate. The voltage used depends on the pressure and system geometry, but must be large enough to strike and maintain a plasma. The positively charged, sputtering-gas ions are accelerated toward the target and, upon impact, knock off atoms of target material by mechanical recoil. These atoms, on the average, move toward the substrate by their acquired momentum, and are deposited there. At higher pres-

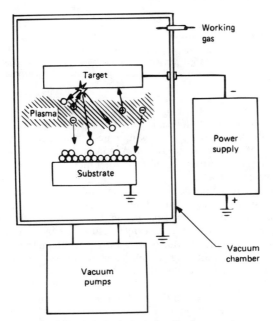

FIGURE 4.10 Schematic depiction of a dc-sputtering system. An evacuated chamber is backfilled with a working gas (usually argon). Biasing the target negatively with respect to the substrate and chamber initiates ionization of the gas. The physical arrangement of an rf-sputtering system is similar, but rf power is used instead of direct current, and the negative bias on the target is achieved by the system geometry.

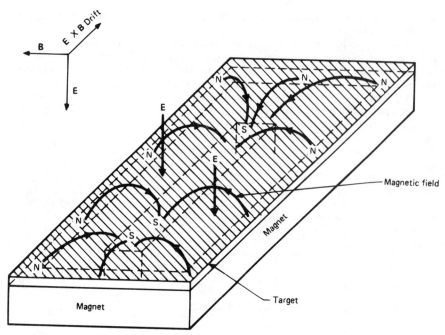

FIGURE 4.11 One type of magnetron sputtering target. The magnetic field from the permanent (or electro-) magnet behind the target penetrates the target material plate, confining most of the electrons from the plasma to a region near the target and increasing the ionization efficiency.

sures, the sputtered atoms suffer multiple collisions with the sputtering gas, arriving at the substrate with relatively low energy. At lower pressures they may reach the substrate without collision, thereby showing much adatom surface mobility due to retained energies of tens of electronvolts. Argon is generally used as the primary sputtering gas, because its mass is suitable for efficient momentum transfer and because it is chemically inert.

One disadvantage of simple dc sputtering is that fairly high pressures are needed to maintain a plasma, which, in turn, limits process versatility and the energy of deposited atoms. In addition, electrons in the plasma are accelerated toward the substrate with few collisions, thereby heating the substrate by high-energy bombardment. This makes control of substrate temperature a problem. Figure 4.11 illustrates magnetron-enhanced dc sputtering, which alleviates these problems. Electromagnets, or permanent magnets, are placed behind the target, so that the magnetic field penetrating the target causes the electrons to follow helical paths near the target surface. This accomplishes several things. First, the electron path is much longer, resulting in more ionizing collisions with gas atoms. This allows operation at lower pressures and lower voltages, while achieving high deposition rates. Lower pressures, in turn, permit higher adatom energies with consequently better adhesion. Moreover, the magnetic field near the target prevents direct acceleration of electrons toward the substrate, thereby reducing bombardment heating. Magnetic materials pose a limitation to magnetron enhancement because the target tends to shunt the field of the target magnets. This restricts the target permeability and/or thickness, or calls for high-field electromagnets or special target designs. This is less of a problem for today's disk materials which employ more easily saturated alloys.

Both dc and dc-magnetron sputtering require use of conductive target materials. To sputter insulating materials, a radio-frequency (rf) voltage is applied. Geometric asymmetry of the target, substrate holder, and chamber shielding allows a net removal of material from the target and deposition on the substrate, despite the ac field. Otherwise rf sputtering is conceptually similar to the dc methods above. This technique is used for sputtering iron oxides from an oxide target. It also permits reactive sputtering from a metal target. For example, if a partial pressure of oxygen is included in the sputtering gas while sputtering an iron target, an iron oxide film can be deposited. Oxygen can combine chemically with the iron atoms at the target surface, at the substrate, or in transit (to varying degrees). If dc sputtering were used, an insulating oxide layer could build up on the target surface, slowing or stopping the sputtering process. This is not a problem in rf sputtering, which is also a candidate for magnetron enhancement.

Commercial manufacturing of recording disk media uses two different types of sputtering systems. One configuration employs one or more sputtering stations for each layer. The targets are circular, of similar size to the substrate receiving the deposited film, and concentric with the substrate during the deposition. The substrate remains stationary during the deposition, then is transported to the next station for the next layer. To achieve high throughput, multiple lines are installed in parallel. Such an approach may be more capital intensive, in hardware if not in cost as well, but produces disks with excellent circumferential uniformity. These systems are also amenable to producing magnetic films with circumferential easy axis orientation. The other type of sputtering system employs rectangular targets much larger than the substrates. Many substrates are loaded onto a pallette which is mechanically transported past the sputtering targets in a continuous pass process. Fewer, but larger, sputtering stations are required for high throughput. If one sputtering line encounters problems, or requires routine maintenance, a large portion of the throughput is shut down. The challenge in this approach is to achieve uniform properties across the entire pallette. Disks produced by this process often exhibit a signal which shows a twice-per-revolution modulation, due to either a thickness or an orientation nonuniformity. Disks at the top or bottom of a pallette moving horizontally through the sputtering flux usually show the greatest modulation effect.

Sputtering is the dominant process used for disk technology. However, other film deposition processes are used as well. The Ni-P undercoat for disk media is plated. The magnetic layer of metal evaporated tape (MET) is obliquely evaporated. Exploratory overcoat processes use chemical vapor deposition, and exploratory recording layer depositions employ ion-beam deposition and laser ablation. For more information on film deposition processes and vacuum technology, excellent classic texts are available (Chopra, 1969; Maissel and Glang, 1970; Vossen and Kern, 1978; O'Hanlon, 1980).

4.2.2 Substrate and Undercoat Preparation

The basic requirements of the starting substrate are similar for film and particulate media. Substrate cleanliness and materials compatibility must be carefully maintained, because the mechanical nature of these storage systems demands strong adhesion between the films and between the film structure and the substrate. Film media tend to have more problems in this area than particulate media, in part because they are multilayered structures, having two to four interfaces at which adhesion failure may occur. Many of the standard thin-film techniques for controlling adhesion are used in film media (Chopra, 1969; Maissel and Glang, 1970; Vossen and Kern, 1978).

For rigid-disk systems, substrate hardness is also an important issue for film media. Although the head is usually in flight above the disk surface, it does come into contact with the disk during the starting and stopping of the file, as well as during operation when momentary contacts are possible.

In the mid 1980s head flying heights were about 200 to 300 nm. In the mid 1990s flying heights are approaching 25 to 50 nm, and even contact is being explored. The problem of wear or catastrophic crash is somewhat mitigated by using smaller sliders and lighter slider-suspension loading. The important innovation of the early 1970s, stopping and starting with the head in contact with the disk (so-called Winchester technology), is more difficult with the constraints of modern high-density media. One way around this problem is to more aggressively texture a narrow band of the disk, restricting starting and stopping in contact to this landing zone. The rest of the disk, containing data, is never intentionally contacted by the slider. Another approach is to incorporate a mechanism to load the slider after the disk has begun rotating when starting, and unload it before it slows to a stop (load/unload approach). The disk should be able to withstand a certain level of interaction without disturbing the hydrodynamic stability of the head, which can cause the head to crash into the disk. Films used for recording are generally a few tens to a few hundred nanometers thick, and do not substantially increase the composite film substrate hardness, even if the microhardness of the films themselves is high. Since the principal rigid substrate in commercial use is the aluminum-(4–5 wt %) magnesium alloy, which is too soft for film rigid-disk requirements, an undercoat is typically used to increase the composite hardness. The most commonly used undercoat is an electroless-plated layer of nickel and phosphorus, which is amorphous and contains sufficient phosphorus to make it nonmagnetic (8–12 at % P). Thicknesses from 10 to 25 μm are typical. Other undercoats that have been used include a 4-μm sputtered layer of Haynes alloy (Rossi et al., 1984), and a 3-μm layer of Al_2O_3, formed by anodization, used mainly with sputtered iron oxide and some perpendicular Co-Cr media. Table 4.1 shows the effect of undercoat thickness on the composite hardness of the undercoat and an Al-Mg substrate using electroless-plated Ni-P

TABLE 4.1 Knoop Hardness Values in kg/mm^{2†}

	Load, g		
Surface tested	25	50	200
Bare Al-Mg substrate	. . . .	92	
4-μm Haynes 188 Alloy	370	225	110
10-μm Haynes	963	. . . .	249
20-μm Haynes	939	. . . .	481
Bulk Haynes	401	. . . .	297
15-μm Ni-P	612	602	370
21-μm Ni-P	620	614	478
35-μm Ni-P	642	634	529
45-μm Ni-P	646	643	532
56-μm Ni-P	654	648	532

†For aluminum-(4%) magnesium substrates with and without various undercoats.

Source: S. Doss, Private Communication (1985).

and a harder sputtered Haynes 188 stainless alloy. Hard glass and ceramic substrates require no such undercoat.

Extremely fine surface finishes are required on substrates, especially for film media. Since read-write heads fly over the surfaces of rigid disks, the surface microtopography must be very uniform. Smoothness is not necessarily required or even desired. Controlled texturing to minimize stiction (sticking of the head to the disk) may be advantageous, although this adds to head-to-medium spacing losses. The disk must, however, be free of the occasional asperities which may disturb the head flight. Since films tend to replicate the topography on which they are deposited, elimination of asperities at the substrate level is crucial. Depressions, or pits, in the substrate are also troublesome in that a film will follow the contour of the depression. This represents a variation in the head-to-medium spacing and, consequently, a modulation of the signal amplitude such as a drop-out, as illustrated in Fig. 4.12. Particulate coatings in polymer binders, depending on their thickness, are somewhat more tolerant owing to the tendency of the liquid polymer to level by flow prior to cure.

The use of undercoats, in addition to their hardening role, can be helpful in masking such substrate defects. To do this, the undercoat must be deposited in a sufficiently thick layer that some fraction of it can be polished away. The 8–14″ diameter Al-Mg substrates of the past were normally diamond-turned on a lathe to produce a flat, nearly mirror finish with a peak-to-valley surface finish of 50 to 100 nm. Today's smaller substrates make grinding more attractive for initial surface preparation. Furthermore, today's head flying heights below 100 nm demand roughness less than about 10 nm. While very fine finishes can be achieved by

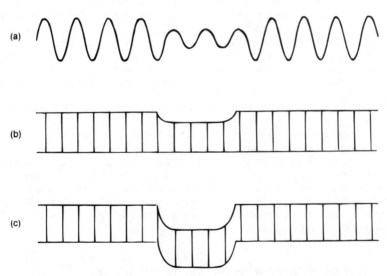

FIGURE 4.12 (*a*) A reproduced signal with a string of missing pulses, along with two types of film defects which can produce the signal decrease. (*b*) A portion of the film is missing. This could be due to a local thickness change across the entire track as depicted, or the entire magnetic film could be missing, but only from a portion of the track (e.g., delamination). (*c*) The magnetic film is present across the entire track, with no thickness variation, but the topography of a substrate pit is replicated by the film, causing a head-to-medium spacing variation.

these processes, the grinding or diamond-cutting process tends to pull out intermetallic inclusions, which are present in most Al-Mg alloys, leaving pits in the surface. If a sufficiently thick undercoat is applied to the substrate, it can then be polished back several micrometers to diminish the effect of pits or other irregularities. For such a technique to be effective, the undercoat must itself be polishable, without inclusions or nodules which might produce additional defects. While the use of film and other highly sophisticated coating techniques is often the focus of attention for advanced media, mechanical polishing and surface-finishing techniques, such as those shown in Fig. 4.13, are one of the most important factors in producing high-performance recording media. Polishing of contemporary small substrates is conceptually similar to Fig. 4.13(a), but the quill and pad are much larger than the substrates, and many disks in a retaining platen undergo a complex motion as they are simultaneously polished.

Figure 4.14 shows a relative comparison of extra and missing pulse defects on an oxide particulate and a metal-plated disk medium. Extra pulses are measured by first dc-erasing the disk. Since any data are thus erased, the head operating in the read mode should ideally register no voltage pulses. Any pulses whose amplitudes are equal to or greater than a chosen percentage of the average written pulse amplitude are recorded as extra pulses at that threshold. Missing pulses are measured by first writing a string of data pulses on the disk track. The data are then read back, and any data pulses whose amplitudes are equal to or less than a chosen percentage of the average pulse amplitude are recorded as missing pulses at that threshold.

An absence of magnetic coating can be the cause of a missing pulse because a portion of the track width is removed; or it can be the cause of an extra pulse because the coating continuity is broken, allowing flux to fringe from the surface of a dc-erased medium. Large nonmagnetic oxide wear particles in particulate media, or areas of delaminated coating in film media, can thus cause both extra and missing pulses. Substrate pits in continuous magnetic film media (Fig. 4.12c), produce missing pulses rather than extra pulses, because the coating is not broken. Thus extra pulses in film media reflect delamination-type defects and are usually far lower in number than extra pulses in particulate media. Missing pulses are important factors for both film and particulate media.

Flexible-media substrates are not inherently as prone to pits and asperities as rigid disks, which suffer from second-phase intermetallic inclusions. Moreover, since the head is usually in constant contact with the medium at slower speeds on flexible media, the catastrophic head crash is not a problem. Nevertheless, any topographic variations which do exist in the substrate, or are created in the coating process, can introduce signal amplitude variations and errors. An asperity can move a large portion of the tape or floppy disk sufficiently far away from the head to cause a significant signal decrease. A pit or depression will cause a smaller signal modulation, since it affects only a region of the physical size of the defect. Further discussion of substrate preparation is given later in Sec. 4.2.4.

4.2.3 Magnetic Film Materials, Processes and Properties

Earlier mention was made of the importance of increasing the recording layer magnetization and particle density, which allows the magnetic coating thickness to be decreased in order to achieve high-density recording with equal or better signal-to-noise ratios. This is the primary advantage of thin magnetic films for recording media. To be useful, the films should show relatively square hysteresis loops, with M_r

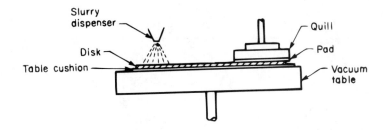

(a)

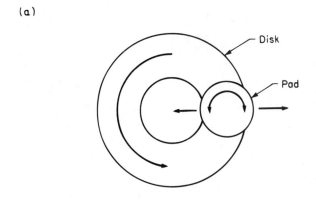

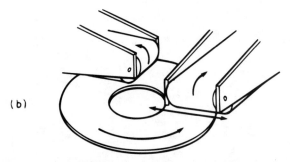

(b)

FIGURE 4.13 (a) Side and top view of a free-abrasive polishing process for rigid-disk preparation. This is a stock removal process used on the substrate and/ or the undercoat intended to produce a smooth surface for the magnetic layer. (b) Fixed-abrasive buffing of a disk, used on the substrate or undercoat to produce a desired uniform texture. A similar process may be used on the overcoat, with different pressure and buffing tape, to remove loose particles or asperities formed in the film deposition processes (*Rossi et al., 1984*).

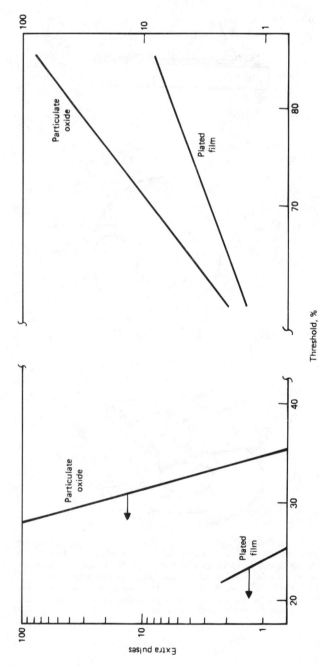

FIGURE 4.14 Extra and missing pulses as a function of threshold level (percent of average written pulse amplitude), comparing relative numbers of such defects on particulate oxide and plated-film media coercivity $H_c = 48$ kA/m (600 Oe).

at least several hundred kA/m (emu/cm^3), and H_c greater than about 80 kA/m (1000 Oe). As with particles, film media should be stable against stress, temperature, and corrosive effects. Although processes like plating and materials like Co-Ni-P are no longer used in products, they are reviewed here for historical perspective.

Metal In-Plane Isotropic Films. Plating was the first process developed for producing commercial magnetic film media, but is no longer an important approach for rigid disks. Cobalt and cobalt-nickel alloys have been electroplated from solutions containing salts of Co and Ni and hypophosphite salts (e.g., NaH$_2$PO$_2$), along with buffers to maintain the solution pH and improve film uniformity (Bonn and Wendell, 1953). Such plated films have several weight percent P incorporated in the alloy. The phosphorus is key to controlling film coercivity, although plating conditions such as pH can also dramatically affect the magnetic properties (Moradzadeh, 1965).

A similar plating bath allows autocatalytic, or electroless, deposition onto surfaces which have been prepared to initiate the reaction (Brenner and Riddell, 1946). Techniques for electroless plating onto plastic substrates, such as polyester tapes, involve soaking the substrate in hot chromic-sulfuric acid, followed by hot sodium hydroxide to render them hydrophilic (Fisher and Chilton, 1962). The substrate is then sensitized with a SnCl$_2$ solution which is thought to cause Sn^{2+} to adsorb on the substrate. Following this, immersion in a palladium chloride solution allows Sn^{2+} to reduce Pd^{2+} ions, which displace the resultant Sn^{4+} from the surface. The palladium thus deposited forms catalytic nucleation sites. After the Co(-Ni)-P plating reaction is begun, the plated transition metal itself acts as the catalyst to continue the process. The hypophosphite ion is the reducing agent for cobalt and nickel ions in the presence of a catalyst, according to the probable reaction (Pourbaix, 1974)

$$Me^{2+} + H_2PO_2^- + H_2O \rightarrow Me + H_2PO_3^- + 2H^+$$

where Me represents either Co or Ni.

To a lesser extent, phosphorus can undergo a reduction reaction. As with electroplating, the incorporation of phosphorus in the film is important to controlling coercivity. Figures 4.15 and 4.16 show coercivity dependence on phosphorus content and on film thickness. Complexing agents such as citrates, tartrates, or malonates are generally included in the plating bath to tie up some of the metal ions and release them at a controlled rate by dissociation, thereby regulating the plating rate. Solutions employing malonates codeposit virtually no phosphorus, while citrate solutions may result in as much as 6 wt % P. Films of Co-P and Co-Ni-P can be plated with coercivities from about 15 to over 130 kA/m (188 to 1625 Oe). The low-coercivity range corresponds to Co films with negligible P content, while the highest coercivities include high P content and a Co/Ni ratio of about 4:1 (Judge et al., 1965a,b). In these films high coercivity has been ascribed to (1) high (in-plane) crystalline anisotropy grains, of random orientation, decoupled from one another by nonmagnetic phosphorus-rich channels, and (2) high stacking-fault concentration resulting from a mixture of cobalt-rich hexagonal close-packed (hcp) structure and nickel-rich face-centered cubic (fcc) structure, which impedes domain nucleation and wall motion.

Phosphorus is not unique in segregating at the grain boundaries of cobalt alloys. Other additives can also decouple the magnetic grains by formation of nonmagnetic grain boundaries. When Co-X and Co-Ni-X films were plated, where X is either one of the group VA elements P, As, Sb, Bi or one of the group VIB elements W, Mo, Cr, the group VIB sequence of elements produced effects on the magnetic

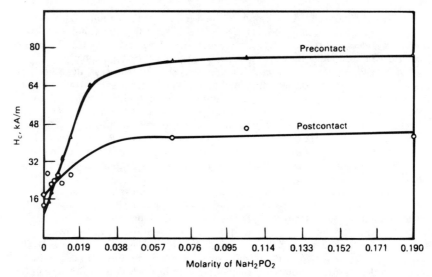

FIGURE 4.15   Coercivity of electrodeposited Co-Ni-P is seen to increase with concentration of NaH_2PO_2 in the plating bath, which also reflects the phosphorus concentration in the film. The two curves represent two different plating currents (*Judge et al., 1966*).

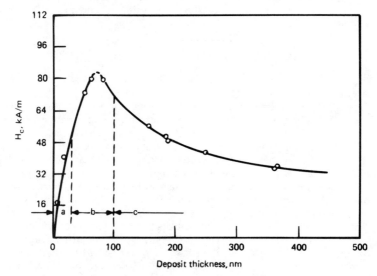

FIGURE 4.16   Coercivity of electroless-deposited Co-P versus film thickness, showing a maximum which characteristically occurs below 100 nm thickness (*Judge et al., 1965b*).

properties similar to the group VA sequence (Luborsky, 1970). In Luborsky's work, however, phosphorus still produced the highest coercivities. Tungsten was found to improve the mechanical hardness and chemical stability, suggesting it would be an advantage to incorporate W or both P and W in plated films, with some compromise on the magnetics. The most significant aspect of this work is that it links plated media to sputtered and evaporated metal films, where Cr or W are commonly used as additives or undercoats. There appears to be a great deal of commonality among the metal in-plane isotropic cobalt-based films with regard to coercivity and magnetization reversal mechanisms, whether they are plated, sputtered, or evaporated. Indeed, rf-sputtered Co-Ni-W has shown magnetic properties basically similar to the plated Co-Ni-X and Co-X alloys (Fisher et al., 1981).

Besides compositional control of magnetic properties in Co-Ni-X and Co-X films, undercoat enhancement layers such as chromium and tungsten have proved useful in vacuum deposition. For example, using normal incidence evaporation, the coercivity of pure Co films was observed to increase with increasing thickness of chromium undercoats (Daval and Randet, 1970). This effect saturates at about 400-nm Cr thickness. The observed coercivity was attributed to magnetocrystalline anisotropy at the granular level. Daval and Randet made three principal observations. (1) For high coercivity, the predominance of the hexagonal phase of cobalt is a necessary condition. (2) Coercivity increased with cobalt grain size for the samples they studied. (3) Coercivity seemed to increase with the percentage of material having the hexagonal c axis (the magnetocrystalline easy axis for cobalt) lying in the plane of the film. They speculated that the Cr underlayer, whose grain size increased with thickness and with deposition temperature, controlled the grain size of the subsequently deposited Co by means of a lattice-matching epitaxial growth process. Although they did demonstrate the ability to grow epitaxial Co with c axis in the plane using a single-crystal-(100)-oriented Cr underlayer, for polycrystalline films they only showed qualitatively that the in-plane c-axis orientation grew stronger as the evaporated Cr layer thickness increased.

Surely there exists an epitaxial relationship between Cr layers and Co alloys. In fact there are several near lattice matches, but they do not all lead to an in-plane c axis for the cobalt alloy (Ohno et al., 1987). Figure 4.17 illustrates the various Cr and hcp Co planes and potential epitaxial relationships (Laughlin and Wong, 1991). What seems more common is for sputtered Cr to orient with its (110) plane parallel to the substrate with the Co alloy orienting with substantial c axis parallel to the plane for Cr thicknesses up to 50 nm, and with substantial c axis pointing about 28° out-of-plane for thicker Cr (Yogi et al., 1988). The diffraction peak for Cr (110) in the same region as the Co (00.2) plane (Co c axis normal to the plane) makes it generally difficult to ascertain the percentage of perpendicular c-axis orientation.

Indeed, the closer the average c-axis orientation comes to lying in the plane, the higher the potential coercivity, but shape anisotropy of a planar structure usually is sufficient to force the magnetic easy axis into the film plane regardless of c-axis orientation. Although crystalline orientation can be important, it is not sufficient to produce high coercivity if the grains are strongly coupled by exchange or magnetostatic fields (Hughes, 1983; Zhu and Bertram, 1988a). To focus only on crystalline orientation obscures equally important functions of underlayers. For example, Cr underlayers have been shown to increase coercivity with moderate decrease in S^* for Fe(42.5%)-Co(42.5%)-Cr(15%) films (Arnoldussen et al., 1984). These films are body-centered cubic (Phipps et al., 1984) and do not possess a strong enough magnetocrystalline anisotropy for epitaxy to account for the enhanced coercivity, other than controlling grain size and grain isolation.

While underlayers can certainly affect the grain size and orientation of magnetic

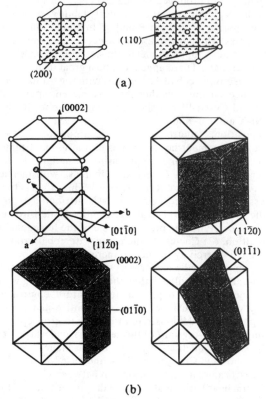

FIGURE 4.17   Schematic drawing of the low index planes and directions in (*a*) bcc and (*b*) hcp.

films, as described above, they can also affect the film roughness, the number of wall-pinning defects, and grain-to-grain decoupling. Sputtered films, especially Cr and W, tend to show increased roughness as they grow thicker, saturating at a thickness of several hundred nanometers (Thornton, 1977). Grain size increases with temperature, and so does its associated surface roughness. It follows that those conditions favoring epitaxy and grain growth also favor increased roughness, which can raise coercivity by impeding wall motion (Lloyd and Smith, 1959) or by decoupling grains. For roughness to have a strong influence on coercivity, it should be of the same order of magnitude as film thickness, grain size, or domain wall width, all of which are comparable in film media (10 to 100 nm). Various calculations of roughness effects in thin magnetic films have been made (Néel, 1956; Soohoo, 1981). Although these calculations tend to be oversimplified, they serve to demonstrate the pronounced effect film roughness can have on coercivity.

Figure 4.18 illustrates the surface morphology resulting from the columnar growth of a sputtered Cr underlayer, exhibiting surface roughness of the order of tens of nanometers (Agarwal, 1985). Cobalt-alloy films grown on such surfaces result in imperfectly oriented epitaxy. Even so, the local epitaxial relationships

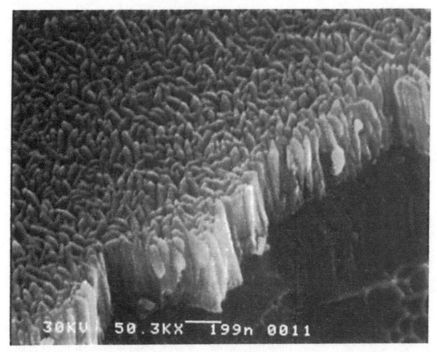

FIGURE 4.18 Electron micrograph showing the topography and columnar structure of a sputtered Cr film (*Agarwal, 1985*).

probably cause Co-alloy films to nucleate on the "elongated dome" features of the Cr, with the dome size determining the Co-alloy grain size. Elongated grains should also induce local shape anisotropy, affecting coercivity. Local stress and magnetostrictive effects should not be ignored. For magnetic layers of thickness less than or comparable to the surface roughness, the recording layer may be discontinuous or nearly so. Exchange coupling between grains is disrupted or strongly diminished. Such grain decoupling will lead to higher coercivity, lower S^*, and lower noise (Zhu & Bertram, 1988b; Sanders et al., 1989). Since the Cr roughness increases with Cr thickness up to about 400 nm, this roughness-induced grain decoupling must be a major contributor to the observed increase of coercivity and decrease of S^* with Cr thickness. Improving crystalline orientation through epitaxy might produce increasing coercivity, but should also produce increasing, not decreasing S^*. For Cr underlayers very much thinner than the magnetic layers, these morphology effects should be of diminishing importance. Barring chemical segregation effects at grain boundaries, increasing magnetic layer thickness above the roughness level should lead to strong intergranular exchange coupling, increased S^*, and a drop in coercivity.

Technological progress toward high linear recording densities has pushed the use of thinner magnetic recording layers. The use of magnetoresistive read sensors has accelerated this trend, since inductive read heads require $M_r\delta$ values of 2 to 3×10^{-3} emu/cm^2 for adequate signal amplitudes while MR heads call for values on the order of 10^{-3} or less. With thinner magnetic layers it was natural to explore thinner enhancement underlayers. Johnson et al. found that thin magnetic layers (8.5 nm) and ultrathin Cr underlayers (3 nm) exhibited media noise comparable to 120 nm Cr underlayers, although the coercivity was only about 60 kA/m (750 Oe) compared to 136 kA/m (1700 Oe) for the thicker Cr (Johnson et al., 1992). They suggested that the low noise may be due to grain lattice mismatch encouraging Cr segregation at grain boundaries of the Co-Pt-Cr alloy studied. The low noise for these ultra-thin Cr layers was intriguing, but the low coercivity would preclude use for modern high-density media. Lal et al. followed up on this study showing that thicker (60 nm) Co-Cr-Ta on 20 to 30 nm Cr could produce coercivities (128 kA/m, 1600 Oe) and signal-to-noise values (31dB), comparable to results on thick (200 nm) Cr underlayers (Lal et al., 1994). This is an important technological result because it suggests that thinner underlayers and shorter process times are possible.

Just as the above studies confound conventional wisdom about the need for thick underlayers, conventional wisdom about the desirability of perfect in-plane c-axis orientation of Co alloy media has been questioned (Shen et al., 1992). This work showed that for Co-Cr-Ta: (1) its crystallographic orientation is indeed controlled by the orientation of the Cr underlayer; but (2) the coercivity and noise are more dependent on the temperature at which the magnetic layer is sputtered than on its crystalline orientation; (3) increased substrate temperature decreases the intragranular exchange coupling which enhances coercivity and reduces noise; and (4) the (110) Cr orientation, producing a Co-Cr-Ta layer with c-axis 28° out of plane, is superior in noise to a (200) Cr underlayer producing a perfect in-plane magnetic layer c-axis, while achieving similar coercivities (144 kA/m, 1800 Oe).

In addition to the use of composition and enhancement underlayers to control coercivity, magnetic film thickness and grain size have generally been found to have a strong effect on coercivity and squareness. Many factors can influence grain size, but substrate temperature and deposition rate are two of the major process parameters. Increased temperature, adatom impingement energy, and ion bombardment or decreased deposition rate (not associated with high pressure) tend to produce a larger grain structure. Coercivity generally increases with grain size, up to a point where multidomain grains form. Similarly, and perhaps not independently, coercivity often increases with the film thickness up to a point, and then decreases with further increase in the magnetic film thickness (Fig. 4.16). To some extent this may be related to grain size effects, inasmuch as grains tend to grow and coalesce as the film grows thicker. However, superparamagnetic effects, magnetostatic coupling, and film roughness are also capable of producing this behavior. The point at which coercivity begins to decrease with thickness depends, of course, on the coercivity-controlling mechanism in a particular film, but that point is usually in the 20-nm range for sputtered or evaporated films and 40 to 80 nm for plated films.

Modern sputtered media require an ultrafine, isolated grain structure. Increasing coercivity by increasing grain size is precluded in the interest of keeping the noise low. Grains are never so large that they degrade into multidomain grains as with plated media of the past. Coercivity tends to peak and noise grows when the grains become contiguous and exchange coupling increases. Rather than forming multidomain grains, multigrain domains are formed. Combining some underlayer roughness with very thin magnetic films preserves grain isolation by physical separation or by forming voided grain boundaries. Addition of certain dopant atoms, which tend to segregate at grain boundaries, can prevent strong exchange coupling without resorting to a mechanically weaker voided structure (Christner et al., 1988).

However the ultrafine isolated grain structure is achieved, future media must cope with superparamagnetism, the term used to describe normal thermal instability of small magnetic particles. For 10 Gb/in^2 media, simple scaling suggests that independent magnetic units need to be less than about 10 nm diameter for an adequate signal-to-noise ratio (Murdock et al., 1992). For an order of magnitude magneto-crystalline anisotropy energy of 10^5 Joules/m^3, a 10 nm cube has a stabilizing energy of 0.625 eV, only 25 times the thermal energy at room temperature (kT = 0.025 eV). The combination of magnetostatic self-demagnetization and that of neighboring grains lowers the threshold of thermal instability of recorded patterns. The solution is to be found in using magnetic films with higher magneto-crystalline anisotropy.

Contemporary film media largely employ sputtered Co-Cr-Ta, Co-Ni-Cr, or Co-Cr-Pt alloys, sometimes with additives like boron for additional noise control. These are listed in the order of increasing achievable coercivity. Table 4.2 lists examples of some of the magnetic properties of alloys reported in the literature. Any given entry in the table may be a composite of many works and, since the actual values of these parameters depend on the specific process conditions, the reader is referred to the published literature for detailed results. Chromium is usually present at the 12–20 at.% level for corrosion and noise control. Cobalt is usually at the 70–85 at.% level. When present, Pt is the 12–24 at.% level; Ni at the 15–20 at.% level; and Ta at the 2–4 at.% level.

In pioneering work (Aboaf et al., 1983), sputtered Co-Pt films exhibited coercivities peaking at about 25 at % Pt with values around 160 kA/m (2000 Oe). Coercivity was found to be extremely thickness dependent. As with Co-Ni alloys, coercivity seemed to be correlated with formation of an hcp-fcc phase mixture, suggesting that coercivity was controlled by stacking faults impeding wall motion. In today's media of related compositions (achieving as high or higher coercivities), wall motion is an improbable reversal mechanism. Composition dependent anisotropy must be the critical factor. Low Pt content alloys are very susceptible to corrosion, but 28% Pt and 20% Pt–10% Ni films have been reported to show reasonable corrosion resistance (Yanagisawa et al., 1983). Today's Co-Pt media incorporate Cr to control corrosion, as well as to dilute the magnetization so that layers need not be impractically thin.

Addition of Ta to Co-Cr has been found to be an effective additive for increasing coercivity and decreasing noise (Fisher et al., 1986; Kawanabe and Naoe, 1988). It has been speculated that Ta increases coercivity and decreases noise either by enhanced grain boundary segregation or by raising the surface energy of nuclei, thereby retarding grain growth and coalescence. In either case, greater grain isolation, higher coercivity, and lower noise results.

In the late 1980s and early 1990s, much attention was directed at achieving high coercivities by combining Cr or Cr-alloy underlayers with various processing conditions to achieve epitaxial growth of a Co-alloy with its c-axis in-plane. During the same time period media noise control was understood to be every bit as important as achieving high coercivity. To this end, decoupling the magnetic layer grains was a goal. The decoupling not only lowers the noise, but it makes possible even higher coercivities. The two goals converged to produce physically separated magnetic grains by using thin magnetic films on thick Cr underlayers. This leaves a voided structure at the grain boundaries which breaks exchange coupling. One paper (Yogi et al., 1990b) of a coordinated group of papers outlined a medium which, with a magnetoresistive head, was capable of 1 Gb/in^2 areal recording density. It employed Co$_{70}$Pt$_{12}$Cr$_{18}$ over thick (> 100 nm) Cr underlayers, deposited under conditions outlined by Thornton (Thornton, 1977) to produce columnar Cr and magnetic grains decoupled by voided column boundaries (Yogi and Nguyen, 1993). This calls for low adatom mobility deposition conditions—relatively high pressure, low voltage sputtering with substrate temperatures high enough to attain high coercivity but low enough to restrict atomic surface mobility.

The desired density was demonstrated. But there was concern over use of thick

TABLE 4.2 Typical Properties of Magnetic Film Media

Material	Deposition process[a]	Orientation [b]	Dominant crystal structure[c]	M_s, kA/m	H_c, kA/m	S, S^*	K_u, 10^5 J/m^3
Co	OIE	IPA	hcp	1100–1400	60–120	. . . .	4 (bulk)
	NIE, SP	IPI	hcp	1100–1400	30–60		
Fe	OIE	IPA	bcc	1600	60–90	. . . .	0.3–3.0
	SP	IPI	bcc	1600	10		
Ni	OIE	IPA	fcc	400	20–28		
	SP	IPI	fcc	400			
Co-Ni	OIE	IPA	hcp-fcc	800–1200	30–70		
Co-Ni	SP	IPI	hcp	1000–1100	60		
Co-Fe	OIE	IPA	bcc	1400–1600	60–120	0.9, 0.9	
Co-Sm	NIE (e)	IPA	Amorphous	500–1000	33–55	1, 1	
Co-Sm	SP	IPI	hcp	650	50–250	0.8, 0.85	
Co-P	EL, EP	IPI	hcp	800–1100	36–96	0.9, 0.9	
Co-Re	SP	IPI	hcp-fcc	500–750	15–58	0.9, 0.9	
Co-Pt	SP	IPI	hcp-fcc	800–1400	60–140		
Co-Ni-P	EL, EP	IPI	hcp-fcc	600–1000	40–120	0.8, 0.8	
Co-(30 at %) Ni:N$_2$	SP	IPI	hcp-fcc	650	80	0.95	
Co-Ni:O$_2$	OIE	IPA	hcp-fcc	300–400	80	0.7–0.8	
Co-Ni-Pt	SP	IPI	hcp-fcc	800–1100	60–140	0.9, 0.97	3.8
Co-Ni-W	SP	IPI	hcp-fcc	450	30–50	0.8, 0.8	
Co-Ni-Cr	SP	IPI	hcp	950	50–60		2.1
Co-Cr-Ta	SP	IPI	hcp	420–950	55–150	0.8–0.9	1.3
Co-Cr-Pt	SP	IPI	hcp	400–800	56–160		2.2
Co-Cr-Pt-B	SP	IPI	hcp	580	110–150		
Co-Cr-Pt-P	SP	IPI	hcp	560	200		
Co-Cr-Pt-Ta	SP	IPI	hcp	500	110–175		
BaFe$_{12}$O$_{19}$: Metal	SP	IPI	hcp	350–400	250–360		0.8
Fe$_3$O$_4$	NIE, SP	IPI	I.S.	400	17–32		
γ-Fe$_2$O$_3$:Co	SP	IPI	I.S.	220–250	40–100	0.8, 0.8	
γ-Fe$_2$O$_3$:Os	SP	IPI	I.S.	240	160	0.8, 0.8	
Co-(18 at %) Cr	SP	⊥	hcp	300–550	80–100 (⊥)	. . . .	−1.0
Co-(20 at %) Cr	SP	⊥	hcp	400	65–95 (⊥)	. . . .	0.15
Co-(22 at %) Cr	SP	⊥	hcp	300–340	80–105 (⊥)	. . . .	0.4

[a]OIE = oblique incidence evaporation; NIE = normal incidence evaporation; SP = sputtered; EL = electroless-plated; EP = electroplated.

[b]IPA = in-plane anisotropic; IPI = in-plane isotropic; ⊥ = perpendicular.

[c]hcp = hexagonal close-packed; fcc = face-centered cubic; bcc = body-centered cubic; I.S. = inverse spinel.

[d]Coercivities for Co films deposited on Cr or W underlayers.

[e]Co-Sm values given for films deposited in the presence of an orienting field.

Cr (increased process time) and voided grain boundaries (mechanically weaker). The latter concern is discussed in the section on overcoats. In response, efforts were made to develop structures and compositions which would produce granular decoupling by compositional nonmagnetic grain boundary segregation. Like voided grain boundaries, compositional segregation was not a new concept. This was first hypothesised and demonstrated for Co-Cr perpendicular recording media in the 1980s. Segregation has been assumed to occur in longitudinal media (Hughes, 1983) but has only been demonstrated in recent years. Figure 4.19 illustrates intragranular Cr segregation in a Co-Cr perpendicular medium (Rogers et al., 1994). Not only can Cr segregate at grain boundaries, but segregation within a grain can produce subgrain magnetic exchange decoupling. Additives, such as Ta, can yield an even finer Cr segregation pattern.

Boron has been explored, as well, for noise and coercivity control in the Co-Pt-Cr system (Tani et al., 1991; Paik et al., 1992). Platinum increases coercivity, apparently related to lattice expansion. Cobalt has an atomic radius of 1.25 Å while Pt is 1.39 Å. The specific mechanism for increasing the coercivity is unresolved. Tantalum may play a role similar to Pt, having an atomic radius of 1.43 Å (Deng et al., 1993), although atomic size is by no means the only factor. Boron, on the other hand has a radius of 0.9 Å. Paik et al. present evidence that Pt goes into the hexagonal Co lattice substitutionally. The dilated lattice allows B to enter interstitially, but further dilating the lattice. As a result, they found that a 50-50 mix of Pt

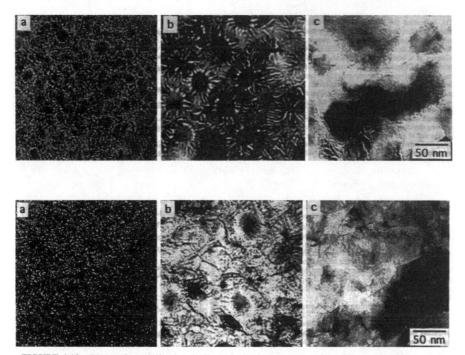

FIGURE 4.19 The preferentially chemically etched microstructure of (a) 50 nm, (b) 400 nm, and (c) 1 μm thick $Co_{86}Cr_{12}Ta_2$ thin films deposited at a T_s of 200°C. Bright regions denote those which were Co-enriched prior to etching.

and B additives could achieve comparable coercivities and lower noise. Besides the potential improvement of recording performance, this suggests that the expensive Pt content of sputtering targets can be reduced. Sohn et al. (Sohn et al., 1994) have performed a similar study of phosphourus as an additive to Co-Pt-Cr (P having an atomic radius of 1.1 Å), achieving a coercivity as high as 2600 Oe.

Another significant approach to noise control, which received a flurry of activity for a couple of years, is media lamination. This approach has not been eagerly embraced in product applications because the increased complexity and manufacturing capital costs outweigh the performance gains. Essentially the idea is to extend grain decoupling to three dimensions by splitting the recording layer into two or more layers separated by a nonmagnetic spacer layer of about 2.5 nm thickness (usually Cr). Linear modeling would expect a 3 dB gain in signal/noise ratio for a bilayer. Multiple laminations would project S/N to improve proportional to $n^{0.5}$ for n layers. For relatively thick spacer layers, this is the measured result. For very thin spacers, however, the gain is slightly greater. This additional S/N gain has been attributed to either enhanced decoupling within the individual layers or to a negative magnetostatic correlative interaction between layers (Hata et al., 1990; Lambert et al., 1990; Murdock et al., 1990; Yang et al., 1991; Duan et al., 1991; Min et al., 1991; Palmer et al., 1991). Aside from increased processing and equipment costs, lamination increases the effective recording layer thickness, and thus spacing loss, making this approach to noise control somewhat undesirable.

The following is a summary of some of the key factors which can control coercivity and noise in isotropic film media.

1. *Composition of the magnetic film.* In Co(-Ni)-X films, where X is a group VA element such as P or a group VIB element such as Cr or W, coercivity tends to increase with X to a maximum depending on the species X. This is thought to be due in large part to the formation of nonmagnetic X-rich grain boundaries, which decouple exchange interactions between grains. Increasing Ni content in such films increases the coercivity to about 20 to 25% Ni. This has been attributed to the mixture of hcp Co-rich phases and fcc Ni-rich phases causing stacking faults which impede wall motion. Platinum addition to Co behaves similarly to Ni, but achieves higher coercivities. Increasing magnetocrystalline anisotropy energy by Ni or Pt addition seems a more plausible coercivity mechanism than wall motion in contemporary media. However, it is possible that lattice dilation increases crystalline anisotropy in all films and also creates wall-impeding stacking faults in exchange coupled, large grain films.

2. *Enhancement underlayers.* Underlayers such as Cr, deposited just prior to the magnetic layer, can increase the coercivity. Coercivity increases with underlayer thickness up to about 400 nm and then saturates. Grain size and orientation control are important mechanisms, although roughness (and perhaps interdiffusion) effects on grain isolation play a key role. Recent work has shown that very thin Cr underlayers combined with comparably thin magnetic layers are also effective for coercivity and noise control.

3. *Magnetic film thickness.* Over most thicknesses of practical interest, coercivity decreases with increasing magnetic layer thickness. An initial rise produces a maximum, but this occurs at thicknesses where the film is probably still discontinuous. Nonmagnetic grain boundary segregation can affect the details of this behavior.

4. *Temperature.* Coercivity generally increases with substrate temperature during magnetic film deposition. Epitaxially oriented growth on suitable underlayers,

grain growth, interdiffusion, nonmagnetic grain boundary segregation, and roughness have all been cited as mechanisms for both coercivity and noise control.

5. *Deposition kinetics.* Low deposition rate has been cited as a condition promoting columnar growth and grain isolation, with consequent increase of coercivity and decrease of noise. The situation is actually more subtle than this. Low deposition rate combined with energetic deposited species and/or augmented ion bombardment or high temperature promotes large non-columnar epitaxial grain growth. Low sputtering pressures (as possible ion-beam deposition) are usually needed for this condition. Low deposition rates, achieved by operating conventional diode sputtering under high sputtering gas pressure, result in low adatom energy and mobility and consequent columnar structure with voided grain boundaries (Yogi et al., 1990*a*).

Metal In-Plane Anisotropic Films. Magnetic anisotropy can be induced in evaporated ferromagnetic films by controlling the angle of incidence of the vapor flux with respect to the substrate normal (Smith et al., 1960). The magnetic easy axis lies in the film plane and is perpendicular to the plane of incidence, for angles of incidence from 0° (normal) to about 60°, and this anisotropy increases with angle. Beyond 60° the easy axis rapidly becomes parallel to the plane of incidence. This behavior has been attributed primarily to shape anisotropy induced during the film growth. For angles less than 60° self-shadowing of grains occurs, resulting in formation of chains of microcrystallites perpendicular to the plane of incidence. Beyond 60° the tendency for crystallites to elongate in the direction of the incoming vapor stream induces shape anisotropy with the easy axis parallel to the plane of incidence. Substrate temperature, magnetostrictive effects, and film composition also play important roles in oblique deposition.

Oblique incidence effects such as these are not limited to evaporation, but could be produced by ion-beam sputtering, ordinary dc or rf sputtering, or ion plating. Special masks have been used in sputtering Cr underlayers to block all but a select range of incident angles, thereby causing the elongated domes of a Cr columnar structure to align in a circumferential direction on disk substrates (Abe and Nishihara, 1986). Subsequent sputtering of Co-Ni resulted in a preferred magnetic orientation of the magnetic layer. Sputtering processes employing planar targets parallel to the substrate are often termed "normal incidence" deposition, but the sputtered atoms impinge on the substrate at a distribution of angles, which depends on the pressure and target-to-substrate separation. The resultant films may be isotropic, as discussed in the previous section, due to the averaging effect of all incidence angles and adatom mobility on the surface, or they may be inadvertently anisotropic due to a predominance of certain incident angles. Low sputtering pressures can produce this if the sputtered atom mean free path is comparable to the target-to-substrate spacing. Rotation, or other complex motion, of the substrate through the sputtering flux has been employed to ensure thickness uniformity and averaging of incident angles when isotropic films are required. Sputtering systems in which the substrate and target are concentric are well suited to producing a circumferential magnetic orientation.

Early studies of oblique evaporation of Permalloy magnetic films (Smith et al., 1960) were followed by a number of similar studies of evaporated Fe, Co, Ni, and some of their alloys (Schuele, 1964; Speliotis et al., 1965) for possible recording media. Most of these showed similar results to the earlier Permalloy work. Coercivities over 80 kA/m (1000 Oe) for iron and cobalt, parallel to the plane of incidence, have been reported. Remanence squareness has also been found to be a function of deposition angle.

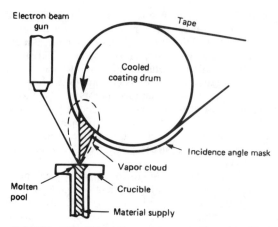

FIGURE 4.20 Schematic arrangement for depositing obliquely evaporated metal films onto a continuous web for video tape applications. The rod-fed Co-Ni source is evaporated by an electron beam. The incidence angle mask location and aperture are critical in controlling the angles at which nucleation and growth occur as the web passes around the drum (*Feuerstein and Mayr, 1984*).

Full-scale processes for fabricating tapes and disks were reported in the early 1980s (Nakamura et al., 1982; Feuerstein and Mayr, 1984; Rossi et al., 1984). Manufacturing systems for oblique deposition onto a continuous PET web recording tape substrate make use of the effect of a high angle of incidence ($> 60°$). The web is transported via rollers and drums past one or more deposition stations, as illustrated in Fig. 4.20. As the tape moves around the drum, it passes by an aperture mask which controls the range of vapor-stream incident angles seen by the tape. If the tape is moved in the direction of decreasing incident angles, higher coercivities and squareness ratios result than if the tape is run in the opposite direction. The conditions of film nucleation are apparently critical to the canted columnar-growth morphology and resulting magnetic properties. Additional stations are included within the same vacuum system for substrate cleaning, adhesion layer precoating, postdeposition glow discharge stress relief and carbon or Cr overcoats. Alloys of Co-Ni (20 to 30%) have been used to achieve coercivities as high as 64 kA/m (800 Oe) and squareness ratios > 0.8. Composition control is not a serious problem because cobalt and nickel have comparable vapor pressures. Oxygen is usually introduced during evaporation. This reduces noise and, together with the Ni content, diminishes corrosion and aging effects (Fischer et al., 1993; Fugita et al., 1982; Nouchi et al., 1993). The process was developed mainly for video and audio recording media, but could also be used for computer tape.

Oblique evaporation has also been used for rigid-disk fabrication (Rossi et al., 1984; Arnoldussen et al., 1984). In this process a magnetic layer of Fe(42.5 at %)-Co(42.5 at %)-Cr(15 at %) was evaporated at a 60° angle of incidence, while the substrate was constantly rotated to ensure circumferential uniformity (Fig. 4.21). A strong shape anisotropy was produced, with the easy axis in the plane of the film but at right angles to the plane of incidence. The self-shadowing, grain-chaining mecha-

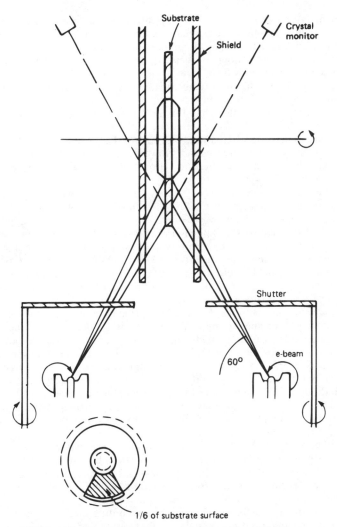

FIGURE 4.21 Schematic arrangement for depositing obliquely evaporated metal films onto a rotating Al-Mg disk substrate, from oppositely placed rod-fed, electron-beam-heated sources. The evaporant passes through an aperture mask, shown in the lower part of the figure, which controls incidence angle as well as thickness distribution (*Rossi et al., 1984*).

nism is the presumed origin of the anisotropy. Sophisticated rate control was necessary to maintain a constant composition, because the vapor pressure of chromium is significantly higher than that of iron or cobalt. A 4-μm Haynes 188 stainless alloy undercoat was first dc-magnetron-sputtered onto an Al-Mg substrate. This layer was polished with a free abrasive to remove irregularities, and then buffed with a fixed abrasive to produce a controlled circumferential texture, as described in Fig. 4.13. The texturing reduced the sticking of head to disk by reducing the contact area, but also enhanced the strong circumferential orientation of the easy axis of the magnetic layer. By controlling the deposition parameters, including the oxygen partial pressure, coercivities from 24 to over 80 kA/m (300 to 1000 Oe), remanent moments from 600 to 1000 kA/m (emu/cm^3), and squareness ratios S and S^* as high as 0.95 were reported. Chromium was used in the magnetic alloy to retard corrosion (Phipps et al., 1984) rather than for coercivity control as in Luborsky's plated films (Luborsky, 1970). The use of circumferential mechanical texture to enhance circumferential magnetic orientation, first reported for the above disk process, is often used today with sputtered media. However, unlike the Rossi/Arnoldussen et al. process which attained orientation ratios of 8 to 10, sputtered films seldom produce an orientation ratio > 2 to 3.

Magnetic field-induced anisotropy offers another approach to producing in-plane oriented films. Amorphous Co_xSm_{100-x} with $75 \leq x \leq 90$, when evaporated at normal incidence, but in the presence of a 20-kA/m (250-Oe) orienting field, shows extremely high orientation (Kullmann et al., 1984a). The coercivity increases from 20 to 88 kA/m (250 to 1100 Oe) with increasing samarium content. Magnetization varies with Sm in the opposite sense from 1000 to 350 kA/m (emu/cm^3). Both S and S^* were indistinguishable from unity. The anisotropy and hysteresis behavior in these films may be related to local ordering of the spin-orbit coupling between Co-Sm and Sm-Sm atom pairs.

Nonmetal In-Plane Isotropic Films. The primary nonmetal-film media have been iron oxide-based and isotropic. This was a natural outgrowth of the predominance of iron oxide particulate media and concern about corrosion of metal films. This technology is no longer a major commercial contender, but some interest continues in academia. The inverse spinel magnetite (Fe_3O_4) films were the first candidates investigated, in large part because they were relatively easy to prepare. In one method, pure Fe films were evaporated, and then oxidized at 450 to 500°C to nonmagnetic α-Fe_2O_3. A second layer of Fe was then deposited, which reduced the α-Fe_2O_3 to Fe_3O_4 upon heating at 350 to 400°C. Excess iron was then etched away in dilute nitric acid (Feng et al., 1972).

In another approach Fe_3O_4 was formed in situ by reactive rf sputtering from an iron target while cycling the oxygen background from high to low partial pressure. In this way a laminated structure of fully oxidized layers and iron-rich layers was formed at low substrate temperatures, while at temperatures of 200 to 250°C, homogeneous Fe_3O_4 is formed by interdiffusion (Heller, 1976).

Concern over the instability of Fe_3O_4 as a recording medium drove oxide film work toward techniques for producing γ-Fe_2O_3, as used in particulate media. Borrelli et al. (1972) chemically deposited α-Fe_2O_3 and showed that it could be completely converted to Fe_3O_4 by reduction in an H_2-H_2O atmosphere at 500°C. They then showed that the Fe_3O_4 could be converted into a solid solution of Fe_3O_4 and γ-Fe_2O_3 by heating in air or oxygen at 300°C for periods up to 1.5 h. Gamma-Fe_2O_3 is itself a defect spinel, similar in structure to Fe_3O_4; so the solid solution is more accurately written $Fe^{3+}[(Fe^{3+})_{1+2x}(Fe^{2+})_{1-3x}V_x]O_4$, where x is the defect content in the range $0 \leq x \leq \frac{1}{3}$, and V indicates a vacancy. They observed a peak coercivity of about 52 kA/m (650 Oe) for $x \approx 0.2$, attributing this to Fe^{2+}-V interactions, producing a preferred alignment of the vacancy on an octahedral site. This, in turn, was thought to yield additional magnetic anisotropy superimposed on the cubic magnetic anisotropy.

Refinements to the basic process described above were made by adding Co (2 to 3%) to increase the coercivity and comparable amounts of Ti and Cu to control grain size and the effective range of heat treatment temperatures (Terada et al., 1983). Two processes were developed for oxide films. One process involves reactive rf sputtering α-Fe$_2$O$_3$, which is then reduced to Fe$_3$O$_4$ in wet H$_2$ at about 300°C. The Fe$_3$O$_4$ is then reoxidized in air or oxygen at about 300°C to obtain γ-Fe$_2$O$_3$ (Hattori et al., 1979). In a second, similar process, Fe$_3$O$_4$ is directly sputtered, thus eliminating the reduction step (Ishii et al., 1980). This shorter process would have a manufacturing advantage. However, achieving the desired Fe$_3$O$_4$ stoichiometry and structure depends on delicate control of sputtering rate, substrate temperature, and oxygen partial pressure. Cobalt-doped Fe$_3$O$_4$ with approximately 2 at % cobalt showed M_s = 263 kA/m (emu/cm^3), H_c = 38 kA/m (470 Oe), S = 0.64, and S^* = 0.54 (Ishii et al., 1980). After oxidization to Co-modified γ-Fe$_2$O$_3$, M_s remained the same but coercivity and squareness rose to H_c = 48 kA/m (600 Oe) and $S = S^*$ = 0.85.

A much more effective dopant was found to be osmium (Ishii and Hatakeyama, 1984). Coercivity and S^* increase sharply with increasing Os content up to 2.6 at %. At that level H_c = 154 kA/m (1920 Oe) and S^* = 0.8. Annealing such a film in a 560-kA/m (7000-Oe) field further increases H_c in the direction of the applied field by about 10 percent, producing a uniaxial anisotropy constant of 4×10^6 J/m^3. More significantly, the magnetic anneal raises the S^* to 0.95 or higher. In previous Co-doped oxide films, Ti dopant served to increase S^* and Cu decreased grain size (decreasing noise), whereas Os seemed to produce the combined effects of Co, Ti, and Cu and with superior results.

Saturation magnetization in all the γ-Fe$_2$O$_3$ films is in the 240- to 260- kA/m (emu/cm^3) range, which is only about two-thirds that of the bulk value for γ-Fe$_2$O$_3$ particles. This suggests that a significant fraction of the film is nonmagnetic α-Fe$_2$O$_3$ (Kay et al., 1985). While this magnetization is about four times higher than particulate iron oxide media (20% volume packing fraction), it is only one-half to one-fourth the magnetization of metal-film media. Thus proportionately thicker oxide films must be used, compared to metals, for comparable signal amplitudes. This is a disadvantage because it represents a thickness loss of resolution. In early work this was considered to be acceptable because the γ-Fe$_2$O$_3$ films were thought not to need a wear-resistant overcoat as do metal films. However, a later study (Terada et al., 1983) showed that significant signal loss occurred when the disk was subjected to pressure and friction, such as might be exerted by a start-stop head contact. This signal loss was attributed to removal of small crystallites from the surface of the film.

Barium ferrite, BaFe$_{12}$O$_{19}$, and M-doped barium ferrite, BaFe$_{12-x}$M$_x$O$_{19}$, have been explored in the past for thin film perpendicular media because of its very high magnetocrystalline anisotropy and natural tendency to grow with its c-axis (magnetic easy axis) normal to the plane. Recent efforts to develop prototype recording systems capable of areal densities 10 Gb/in^2 (1.55 Mb/mm^2), using MR or spin-valve (giant MR) heads, has led to the search for new longitudinal thin film media materials and designs. For such high densities coercivities on the order of 240 kA/m (3000 Oe) are needed. Furthermore, the requirements of the MR heads, signal-to-noise ratios, and high linear density combine to require low M$_r$ × thickness products (ca. 0.5×10^{-5} kA, 0.5×10^{-3} emu/cm^2). Saturation magnetization for bulk material is 375 kA/m (375 emu/cm^3), and coercivities in excess of 240 kA/m (3000 Oe) are easily achieved. In fact, one of the main problems facing use of barium ferrite is maintaining a coercivity low enough for recording heads to write well. Another is keeping the easy axis predominantly in-plane for longitudinal recording.

Hylton et al. (1994) have described processes for preparing such film media using dopants to reduce grain size. A number of dopants were studied with Cr$_2$O$_3$ showing the best results. Their films were relatively isotropic, showing an orientation ratio $OR = (M_{r//}/M_{r\perp}) \approx 1.5$, due mostly to demagnetization effects. Most of their films with grains less than 200 nm had coercivities greater than 280 kA/m (3500 Oe), unsuitable for recording and noise testing with available recording heads. But based on model extrapolation of those which were testable, they projected signal-to-noise ratios of about 25 dB for 10 Gb/in^2 conditions.

In another study cobalt and titanium were used as dopants (Sui and Kryder, 1994). This dopant was extraordinarily effective in controlling coercivity, covering the range from 320 to 112 kA/m (4000 to 1400 Oe). With increased Co-Ti content, the easy c-axis moved from isotropic to predominantly in-plane. Co-Ti also reduced grain size, but not as effectively as the Hylton et al. Cr_2O_3. Taken together these two investigations suggest much promise for barium ferrite films in future media. As with most oxide media, the processes are less attractive for manufacturing than metal films and substrate choice is more constrained.

Perpendicular Anisotropy Films. All the media discussed so far have been designed for longitudinal recording, in which the magnetization vector lies predominantly in the plane of the coating and is recorded by forming magnetization reversals along the line of a recording track. A limitation of this mode of recording is demagnetization, which broadens the transitions. For perpendicular recording, the storage layer is designed so that the magnetization is oriented normal to the plane of the coating. In some designs a soft magnetic underlayer is also required.

Much like γ-Fe_2O_3 media, perpendicular recording interest and activity peaked in the late 1980s. Most recent work has been done in academia. Yet there remains sufficient merit that commercial use is still a possibility, especially in tape applications. Metal evaporated (ME) tape, after all, is partly perpendicular in nature. Aside from commercial use, perpendicular Co-Cr media is of interest as part of recording history and because of its kinship to modern commercial Co-Cr-X longitudinal media.

An infinite-area thin film with saturation magnetization normal to the plane has a demagnetization field of M_s ($4\pi M_s$ in cgs units), with associated shape anisotropy energy $\frac{1}{2}\mu_0 M_s^2$ ($2\pi M_s^2$). This shape anisotropy will force the magnetization into the plane of the film unless the film has additional anisotropy (e.g., crystalline) perpendicular to the plane with energy $K_\perp > \frac{1}{2}\mu_0 M_s^2$ ($2\pi M_s^2$). Cobalt can be made to grow with its c axis (and accompanying uniaxial anisotropy) normal to the film plane. However, $K_\perp$ for Co is only 6×10^5 J/m^3 (6×10^6 erg/cm^3), while $\frac{1}{2}\mu_0 M_s^2$ ($2\pi M_s^2$) is 12.95×10^5 J/m^3 (12.95×10^6 erg/cm^3). A solution is to dilute the Co moment with Cr, a nearly linear relation, until the required inequality is satisfied ($K_\perp$ decreasing at a less than quadratic rate) (Iwasaki and Nakamura, 1977). For an alloy with 20.5 at % Cr, $K_\perp \approx 1.15 \times 10^5$ J/m^3 (1.15×10^6 erg/cm^3), and $M_s \approx 450$ kA/m (emu/cm^3), so that the demagnetization energy is $\frac{1}{2}\mu_0 M_s^2 = 10^5$ J/m^3 (10^6 erg/cm^3) (Fisher et al., 1984). The energy requirement defined above is a necessary condition to maintain a perpendicular saturation magnetization in a uniformly magnetized infinite-area film which reverses by uniform rotation. The calculation indicates that this is satisfied for Cr content greater than about 20 at %. However, since most real films are better characterized by nonuniform reversal and aggregate demagnetizing fields, as discussed earlier, the above inequality need not be strictly met. The more appropriate inequality uses the remanent magnetization of the sheared hysteresis loop, rather than M_s, in calculating the demagnetization energy. Alloys with as low as 15 at % Cr have been used.

Without a sufficiently high coercivity, stray fields can cause data erasure even when the energy inequality above is met. Moreover, because of the loop shearing caused by demagnetization, the remanent magnetization is roughly equal to the coercivity ($H_c/4\pi$ in cgs units). Therefore the coercivity is key to achieving sufficient signal amplitude. This contrasts with longitudinal media, where M_s is the primary determinant of signal amplitude and coercivity contributes to amplitude only secondarily through transition slimming.

Dispersion of the uniaxial perpendicular orientation can cause loss of coercivity, but this cannot account for the large discrepancy between uniform rotation calculations and measured coercivities. Magnetization reversal has been attributed to single-particle (columnar grain) behavior with a curling- or buckling-type reversal (Ohkoshi et al., 1983; Wuori and Judy, 1985). This is a plausible explanation for the coercivity generally being less than 100 kA/m (1250 Oe).

Most of the experimental and theoretical investigations of perpendicular recording have focused on rf-sputtered Co-Cr alloys with Cr in the 15 to 22 at % range. Moderate substrate temperatures up to 300°C are used to facilitate growth of the proper crystal and grain structure. The desired structure is hexagonal close-packed with the c axis normal to the plane, since that is the direction of the easy axis. Moreover, these films generally grow with a columnar grain texture, due partly to the hcp crystal structure and partly to the thickness of the films (0.5 to 2.0 μm). While magnetocrystalline anisotropy is the dominant mechanism, the grain texture orientation is also important for two reasons. First, it superimposes some degree of shape anisotropy. Second, the columnar grains are often separated by nonmagnetic grain boundaries which diminish or eliminate the exchange coupling between grains (Chen and Charlan, 1983; Grundy et al., 1984). The growth of perpendicular anisotropy columnar grains depends on the substrate (or underlayer) and the process conditions. In some cases a transition layer (10 to 100 nm) forms at the early stages of film growth and has poor orientation (Wuori and Judy, 1984). Beyond this point oriented columnar growth proceeds. Films which possess such a transition layer show greater c-axis dispersion and poorer recording properties than those with little or no transition layer.

Additives other than Cr, and processes other than rf sputtering, have been explored for perpendicular media, but not as extensively. For example, substituting up to 6 at % Rh for Co in a sputtered $Co_{78-x}Cr_{22}Rh_x$ film, has been shown to improve the c-axis orientation normal to the surface without altering H_c and M_s (Kobayashi and Ishida, 1981). Chemically deposited or plated cobalt-based films (Chen and Charlan, 1983) have also been shown to produce acceptable perpendicular orientations. Sputtered barium ferrite films have been prepared with perpendicular anisotropy (Matsuoka et al., 1985); however, because of the high substrate temperatures required (400 to 650°C), they have not been widely considered for practical application.

For perpendicular recording, a single-pole head is most suitable for achieving high resolution during the writing process. But a second, return pole is required on the opposite side of the medium, and two-sided recording has practical difficulties. Some head designs have been proposed to simulate the performance of a single-pole head, without the need for a physical pole on the opposite surface, by employing a soft magnetic underlayer beneath the Co-Cr to form a magnetic image below the medium. Permalloy is usually used for such an underlayer. However, in order for a true image pole to be formed, much thicker soft underlayers are required than is practical. Instead of using a single-pole head, newer designs employ a thin primary pole for high resolution in conjunction with one or more large auxiliary poles on the same side of the recording surface (Hokkyo et al., 1984). This achieves a higher field strength and requires a soft magnetic underlayer, not to form a true image pole but simply to act as a flux return path to the large auxiliary pole. Another design uses a thin primary pole near the recording surface, and a large auxiliary pole on the opposite side of the medium, again requiring a soft magnetic underlayer to concentrate the field lines during the write process. Suitable recording head designs which can take advantage of the promised density advantage of perpendicular media are the greatest obstacle to practical use of this mode of recording. By comparison, the medium materials and process development are far more advanced.

Because most head designs require a soft magnetic underlayer, the head and medium must be considered as an integral system, more so than for longitudinal media. Not only is the permeability of the soft underlayer important, but the optimum thickness of the recording layer and the underlayer depend on the head design. For a single, thin primary pole and a large, opposite-surface auxiliary pole, the underlayer enhances write resolution and read sensitivity up to thicknesses of 0.5 to 1.0 μm. Little is gained by making it thicker. The recording layer also has an optimum thickness. Below a few hundred nanometers, read signal amplitude suffers, whereas thicker recording layers cause the soft underlayer to be spaced too far from the primary pole to achieve high resolution. This conflicts with early claimed advantages of perpendicular recording that high resolution and high signal amplitude could be simultaneously realized by using relatively thick films of 1 μm or more. Also sensitivity to substrate defects and surface abrasion were thought to be minimized by the use of thick films. If a practical recording system limits the perpendicular recording layer thickness to a few hundred nanometers, the advantage of perpendicular over longitudinal recording must be diminished.

In addition to the considerations above, the use of a soft magnetic underlayer like Permalloy poses other problems. The Permalloy underlayer has been reported to degrade the Co-Cr orientation, though the specific deposition processes used are probably as important as the materials themselves. This ranks as a practical engineering complication more than an intrinsic or insurmountable obstacle. The misorientation can be partially alleviated by inserting a Ti film about 50 nm thick to nucleate properly oriented grain growth (Kobayashi et al., 1983). Another potential problem is the formation of a corrosion couple. Corrosion has indeed been seen to increase for such a double-layer structure (Dubin and Winn, 1983). A third problem area is noise in the readback signal due to the presence of the soft magnetic underlayer (Uesaka et al., 1984). By its nature, a soft film contains domain walls which are relatively easy to move. Such walls are generally pinned, or at least their movement is impeded, by defects and inhomogeneities of any sort. As a result, walls do not all move smoothly. Rather they tend to move in jumps between pinning sites (Barkhausen noise), and local hysteresis is exhibited. It is not clear whether domain walls actually move during the read process, although this is conceivable, especially at low head-to-media spacings. Nevertheless, since the soft underlayer domains possess their own equilibrium configurations, they may randomly shift the written bit pattern to produce a modulation noise. Figure 4.22 shows the type of complex domain configuration which can occur in a soft Ni-Fe underlayer. This was observed by differential phase-contrast Lorentz microscopy of a cross-sectioned perpendicular medium.

4.2.4 Overcoats and Tribology

Small head-to-medium spacings are critical to reaching higher densities on rigid disks. This raises the risk of head-disk interactions, which can cause disk and head wear, or even a catastrophic head crash. Wear can also occur when the drive starts and stops, because the head contacts the disk at relatively high speeds. With flexible media the head is in contact continuously during read, write, and accessing operations. Particulate media have so far coped with this problem by the use of

(a)

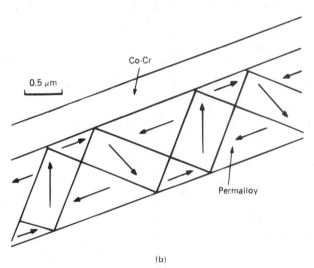

(b)

FIGURE 4.22 (*a*) Domain structure, observed by differential phase-contrast Lorentz microscopy, of a cross section of perpendicularly oriented Co-Cr on a soft Permalloy underlayer (*Courtesy of J. Chapman*). (*b*) Arrows indicate the direction of magnetization in the soft underlayer domains seen in (*a*).

hard-wear particles like Al_2O_3 or SiO_2 incorporated in the magnetic coating itself, along with the use of lubricants.

Film media require a different approach, namely, the use of wear-resistant overcoats. The film should be as thin as possible (compared with the desired head-to-medium spacing), have no asperities, resist wear by the head, and, at the same time, not inflict wear on the head. Also the film should have virtually no static or dynamic friction with the head and, as much as possible, protect against corrosion. Intuition and empiricism suggest that overcoat materials should be relatively hard and chemically inert, and should bond well to the magnetic layer but not to the head material. They should probably have high tensile strength and not be prone to brittle fracture. After some historical overcoat approaches are reviewed, modern materials and processes will be discussed.

Silicon dioxide, SiO_2, has been used with comparative success, even though it falls in the brittle category and has surface properties which are humidity-sensitive. A spin-coating technique has been used to deposit SiO_2 on plated Co-Ni-P media (Suganuma et al., 1982). A tetrahydroxy-silane and alcohol solution is spun on the disk, leaving a layer of $Si(OH)_4$ on the surface. This is then laser-irradiated, driving off water and leaving a nearly stoichiometric SiO_2 about 80 nm thick. By itself, this overcoat has shown high friction and stiction (head sticking to the disk), which varies with exposure, to the atmosphere. Suganuma et al. applied an unspecified polar solid lubricant to the surface to minimize these problems.

A plasma-polymerized fluorocarbon film has been described in a U.S. patent in which the fluorine content was varied from low values at the metal magnetic film surface to high values at the free surface (Arai and Nahara, 1983). By this, it was claimed, the smooth, lubricating properties of a fluorocarbon are achieved at the free surface with improved adhesion at the metal. This may be considered a combined overcoat and solid bonded lubricant.

A sputtered rhodium overcoat (75nm) over a Cr adhesion layer (10 nm) has also been used, in combination with a 5-nm perfluorinated polyether lubricant applied by a spray-wipe process (Rossi et al., 1984). Although rhodium is a tough metal, it is not an adequate overcoat without a lubricant on its surface. A solid lubricant is not readily bonded to metals like rhodium, and liquid lubricants tend to spin off a rotating disk. However, when a slight texture is imparted to the disk at the undercoat level, one to several molecular layers of liquid lubricant can be retained by the rhodium surface, giving moderately good wear properties. This comes at the expense of added spacing losses in the readback signal due to the texturing.

A variety of other friction-, wear-, and corrosion-resistant coatings being explored for various recording and nonrecording applications have been reviewed by Hintermann (1984). This excellent review includes TiC, TiN, SiC, Cr_2C_3, and Al_2O_3, together with the deposition processes used.

The dominant overcoat used on today's commercial media is a hard carbon. While sputtering is normally used, chemical vapor deposition (CVD) and plasma enhanced CVD (PECVD) has also been explored (King, 1981; Kolecki, 1982). Carbon films deposited by low energy processes, such as conventional diode sputtering, tend to form local atomic bonding similar to that in graphite (sp^2), rather than diamond (sp^3). They can be relatively hard and wear resistant, but not sufficient for the high reliability requirements of today's storage systems. Amorphous diamond-like carbon films, also known as I-carbon, was first studied for wear-resistant and optical coatings outside the recording industry. These terms strictly refer to films in which there is substantial tetrahedral local bonding as in crystalline diamond. Such films normally require high energy ion bombardment during growth to achieve this coordination. Films deposited using PECVD can approach diamond-like carbon, without high energy bombardment, but this has been used for recording media only in laboratory studies so far (Iechika et al., 1994).

Two basic problems are associated with graphitic (sp^2) carbon overcoats. Wear resistance and corrosion protection, though better than many alternatives, are insufficient. A primary wear mechanism was found to be tribochemical. Under the action of friction, the carbon overcoat oxidized to produce CO and CO_2 in the presence of oxygen and water vapor (Marchon et al., 1990; Pan and Novotny, 1994). In addition graphitic carbon is pervious to oxygen, allowing the cobalt alloy medium to oxidize. Cobalt oxide corrosion products diffuse through the carbon overcoat to the surface, where the head produces cobalt oxide smears leading to disastrous head-disk interactions.

The solution to this problem was to introduce dopants during the carbon deposition which saturate the carbon bonds (Howard, 1988; Yeh et al., 1991; Marchon et al., 1991). Oxygen tends to attack the double (unsaturated) carbon bonds of the sp^2 structure (Marchon et al., 1990). Saturating these bonds does not produce diamond-like carbon, but does retard oxidation and permeance to oxygen. Wear and corrosion are thereby reduced. Today commercial carbon overcoats commonly incorporate hydrogen by introducing hydrogen or a hydrocarbon gas, such as methane, into the sputtering gas. Nitrogen incorporation has also been shown to be effective but is not generally used commercially.

Without hydrogen incorporation, sputtered carbon is typically a semimetal or semiconductor. Table 4.3 (Iechika et al., 1994) compares three carbon films with regard to hydrogen content in the sputtering gas, Youngs modulus of hardness, and resistivity. The data demonstrate the usefulness of monitoring the carbon overcoat quality by resistivity. The term aC:H indicates amorphous hydrogenated carbon; DLC indicates diamond-like carbon. In contrast, Marchon et al. (1991) reported that the greatest improvement in hardness and scratch resistance was obtained with 5% H_2 in the Ar sputtering gas, and that films became soft for $H_2 > 20\%$.

Because hardness is a key durability factor, various other materials have been explored, especially oxides. Among such materials are boron (Futamoto et al., 1990), SnO_2 (Novotny and Kao, 1990), Si-N (Kovac and Novotny, 1991), yttria-stabilized zirconia and silica (Yamashita et al., 1988; Schulz and Viswanathan, 1991). Figure 4.23 shows the relationship between wear durability measured in terms of the number of frictional passes using an Al_2O_3 slider vs hardness for a variety of films (Futamoto et al., 1990). It is apparent that there is a strong correlation between hardness and durability, but that hardness alone is not sufficient. Oxides, because they contain a high density of hydroxyl groups, offer better lubricant bonding, but at the expense of requiring RF sputtering and often containing a high number of sputter defect asperities. An amorphous Fe-Mo-B nonmagnetic conductive metglass has also

TABLE 4.3

	Hydrogen %	Youngs Modulus	Resistivity
C:graphitic	8.2 %	106 GPa	10^5 ohm-cm
aC:H	33.2 %	108 GPa	10^{13} ohm-cm
DLC	30.4 %	246 GPa	10^{11} ohm-cm

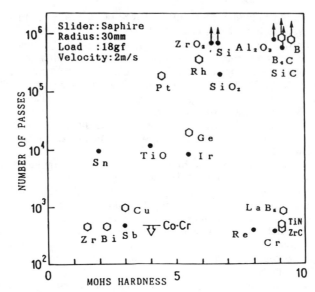

FIGURE 4.23 Relationship between hardness of protective layer material and wear durability.

been studied for tape overcoats (Akiyama et al., 1991). A conductive overcoat has the advantage of avoiding triboelectric charging and discharge.

Tribological performance is not only determined by the overcoat, but by lubricant and topography as well. The most effective lubricants have been found to have a constituent bonded to the overcoat and a somewhat mobile component. These lubricants possess a functional end group, such as COOH, which electrostatically bonds to the overcoat (Merchant et al., 1990; Schulz and Viswanathan, 1991; Sano et al., 1994; Coffey et al., 1994). Static friction, or stiction, generally increases with adsorbed water vapor. Tian and Matsudaira (1992) have reported that the thickness of adsorbed water is less for lubricated than non-lubricated surfaces. On the other hand, Smallen et al. (1994) report that the amount of lubricant has little effect on the adsorbed water layer unless the hydrogen content of the overcoat is very low.

Besides lubricant and overcoat, the tribology depends on surface topography. When undercoats are deposited such that columnar growth with voided column boundaries result, the magnetic layer and overcoat also have voided boundaries. The topography is rougher and the overcoat is weaker due to the voided structure. However, this voided structure allows greater lubricant retention (Schulz et al., 1992), which improves durability. In addition, increased topography or roughness itself improves durability. Greater roughness decreases the contact surface area between the slider and the disk. As a result, some degree of roughness is desired. Roughness has been introduced by several controlled processes. First, it may be produced by mechanical polishing and texturing as discussed earlier. Second, it may be produced by the use of thick (Cr) underlayers. Third, the overcoat itself may be patterned lithographically (Tanaka et al., 1994). Fourth, the (Cr) underlayer may be textured non-mechanically. One approach uses pulsed laser heating at the NiP level to produce controlled bumps in the underlayer which are replicated in the magnetic and overcoats (Ranjan et al., 1991; Lambeth and Ranjan, 1991; Lambeth and Ranjan, 1992), as shown in Fig. 4.24. Another approach employs a "transient

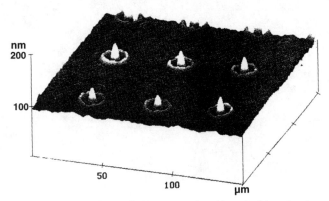

FIGURE 4.24   AFM image of controlled bumps produced by pulsed laser heating at the NiP level.

metal underlayer" (Mirzamaani et al., 1992; Teng et al., 1994). A thin nonwetting, low melting temperature metal, such as gallium, is deposited before the magnetic layer. This coating produces a uniform layer of spheroidal "droplets." When the magnetic layer is deposited, it alloys with the transient underlayer, producing a solid structure of controlled roughness of the order of 10 nm, as shown in Fig. 4.25. In a related technique, Ti/Al/Ti layers have been used to produce uniform texture bumps (Kogure et al., 1994).

In addition to the deposition of a wear-resistant overcoat, some final mechanical surface finishing is often used, especially for rigid disks where asperities can cause catastrophic head crashes. As smooth and uniform as the disk may have been at the substrate or undercoat level, asperities can form during the multiple film depositions that follow. Non-uniform nucleation and growth, spitting during evaporation, and sparking electrical discharges in sputtering are some of the possible causes of asperity formation during film deposition. Thicker films which show columnar growth, such as perpendicular magnetic films, are most prone to growth-induced roughness.

Whatever the source of process-induced asperities, a final surface buff (prior to lubrication) may be used to produce a reliable head-medium interface. One type of buffing process is illustrated in Fig 4.13. A disk is shown being buffed by a light-pressure, oscillating, fixed-abrasive polishing tape. The idea is neither to cause any stock removal nor to produce a texture as is done in the undercoat polishing process, but merely to knock off asperities. An alternative method, when few asperities are present, is to use a special burnishing head which is designed to fly lower than a recording head, clipping off asperities.

4.3 MAGNETIC AND MECHANICAL STABILITY

Practical commercial recording systems must show long-term stability of all sorts. The subject of device reliability is only sparsely treated in the literature because it falls more in the category of product engineering rather than research. Often information of a proprietary nature is involved, and long-term statistical testing of specific commercial designs is required. For such reasons, it is difficult to make strong generalizations about media stability and reliability. Nevertheless, the key

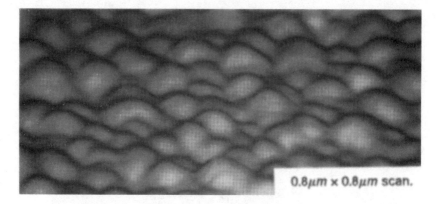

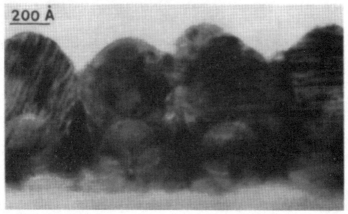

FIGURE 4.25 (*a*) AFM photograph of the surface topography of 600 Å of Co-Pt-Cr deposited onto 100 Å of Ga. (*b*) TEM micrograph of the cross section of Ga/Co-Pt-Cr deposited on SiO_2 substrate.

reliability factors can be outlined and some media comparisons made, at a qualitative level. It should also be kept in mind that film properties depend so much on the specific processes used that data on a particular type of film may vary significantly from one lab to another, even when the same nominal deposition process is used.

4.3.1 Thermal Effects

Two distinct thermal effects are of interest: reversible and irreversible. Temperature dependence of magnetization and of magnetocrystalline anisotropy constant are usually of the reversible type, at least in a temperature range below a stabilizing anneal temperature. Such dependencies stem from the energetics of ferromagnetic exchange or spin-orbit coupling. For example, saturation magnetization can be characterized by the material's Curie temperature according to

$$M_s(T) = M_{s0} \tanh \frac{M_s \theta_c}{M_{s0} \mathrm{T}} \tag{4.6}$$

where θ_c is the Curie temperature in degrees Kelvin and M_{s0} is the saturation magnetization at $0°K$.

Reversible thermal effects in films generally are related to those in bulk materials of similar composition, but the correspondence is seldom exact. Most often quantities like the Curie temperature depend on prior heat treatment of a thin film, which can affect the microstructure and microscopic composition variations. For example, a Co-(84 at %) Cr (16 at %) alloy for perpendicular media was shown to have an as-deposited Curie temperature of about 700°C compared with 355°C for the bulk alloy (Ishizuka et al., 1983); $\theta_c = 700°C$ for a bulk alloy would correspond to 9% Cr. The temperature dependence was reversible up to 400°C, but, upon annealing at 650°C, the film Curie temperature moved to even higher values. This suggests that composition may vary from grain-to-grain boundaries, and these variations may become more pronounced with heat treatment owing to diffusion processes. In the same study, perpendicular anisotropy energy was also shown to vary reversibly below a given annealing temperature, but the specific reversible temperature dependence changed character as the annealing temperature was increased. The reversible anisotropy energy temperature dependence was of the order of several hundred J/ $(m^3 \cdot °C)$. Similar studies have been reported for plated Co-Ni-P longitudinal media (Ouchi and Iwasaki, 1972) and cobalt- and copper-doped $\gamma\text{-}Fe_2O_3$-sputtered films (Nishimoto and Aoyama, 1980).

The reversible temperature variations in magnetic properties do not themselves constitute a serious stability issue. However, if a recording system must operate reliably within a broad temperature range, then even reversible changes will result in recording performance which depends on ambient conditions. If the system operates within a rather narrow range of temperatures, as in a high-performance rigid-disk computer file, such changes in performance may be small. Nevertheless it is necessary to design the media with the expected operating temperature in mind, since the magnetic properties may be significantly different than at room temperature.

In practice, media designs which have strong temperature dependencies are undesirable. Elemental magnetic materials like cobalt or iron have Curie temperatures which are so high that thermal magnetization variations are minor under practical operating conditions. In alloys, however, the addition of nonmagnetic constituents (like Cr in Co) does not simply dilute the magnetic moment, but actually lowers θ_c. If the Curie temperature is thus lowered to near the operating temperature, the saturation magnetization can change rapidly, as seen by Eq. (4.6). Bulk Co-Cr alloys with 20% Cr have Curie temperatures of only about 150°C (Bozorth, 1951). Similar considerations apply to anisotropy constants which may cause strong coercivity temperature variations.

Irreversible thermal effects pose even more hazardous stability problems. For the most part, these phenomena result from atomic diffusion, as suggested for the Co-Cr study above. Such atomic rearrangement may occur in films at temperatures above that of deposition because, during deposition, the films grow too fast for atomic arrangement to reach thermal equilibrium. Consequently, when the film is later heated, there is a driving force toward the equilibrium state. In some materials, the phase equilibrium itself may have a strong temperature dependence.

Films of Co-P and Co-Ni-P can be deposited in amorphous or crystalline form. In amorphous Co-P, magnetic properties undergo changes at low temperatures because of the relaxation of built-in stresses (Riveiro and de Frutos, 1983). As the temperature is raised, the films go through phosphorus diffusion, compositional relaxation, and finally recrystallization. Even in the crystalline state, a phosphorus-rich grain boundary continues to segregate and grow by diffusion. Similar effects have been observed in Co-Ni-P films (Maeda, 1982), Co-Pt films (Aboaf et al.,

1983), and iron oxide films (Borrelli et al., 1972). In the latter case it was vacancy defects, rather than impurity atoms, which diffused to preferred sites, causing the coercivity to increase with time.

Such relaxation phenomena often show thermally activated Arrhenius behavior, where the time constant for relaxation is inversely proportional to the relevant diffusion constant. Depending on the diffusion activation energy, the relaxation may have a strong or weak temperature dependence. For Co-P, stress relaxation has been shown to have an activation energy of about 0.2 eV, and phosphorus diffusion about 0.75 eV (Riveiro and de Frutos, 1983). Vacancy diffusion in iron oxide showed an activation energy of about 1.0 eV (Borrelli et al., 1972).

When relaxation phenomena exhibit thermally activated behavior, it is possible to make reasonable estimates of stability at recording system operating temperatures by measuring the relaxation rate at elevated temperatures. However, not all thermal behaviors possess a well-defined activation energy. Nor are the relaxation phenomena always dependent on temperature alone. Magnetic fields and chemical ambient may also play a role.

4.3.2 Stress Effects

When films are deposited they may possess built-in stresses, ranging from large tensile to large compressive stresses, depending on the process and the substrate used. These stresses can affect the magnetic properties, mechanical properties (adhesion and wear), or corrosion properties. As mentioned above, such built-in stresses may show long- or short-term relaxation, with accompanying performance instabilities. Even when the built-in stress shows little tendency to relax thermally, mechanical interaction of the head slider and the medium can induce abrupt relaxation via cracking or delaminating. Stress can also exacerbate corrosion.

In addition to stress relaxation effects, magnetic films which are sufficiently magnetostrictive may be subject to data loss caused by mechanical interaction of the head and the medium. For a material with isotropic saturation magnetostriction constant (λ_s), and saturation magnetization M_s, the magnetic field equivalent of a stress σ is

$$H_{eq} = \frac{3\lambda_s}{\mu_0 M_s} \sigma \tag{4.7}$$

To generate a field equivalent of 80 kA/m (1000 Oe) on a film with $M_s = 600$ kA/m (emu/cm^3) and $\lambda_s = 20 \times 10^{-6}$, the required stress is 10^9 N/m^2(0.1 g/μm^2). Although this is a very large stress, it is well within the realm of possibility for a corner of a head slider impacting a rigid disk. If the medium coercivity is comparable to the stress-equivalent field, written data could be partially or totally erased. Thus, even though film media are protected by an overcoat against data loss by physically wearing away the magnetic layer, erasure may still occur in highly magnetostrictive materials.

Magnetostriction is a very composition-dependent parameter. Figure 4.26 shows magnetostriction and magnetization values for chromium alloys of iron, cobalt, and nickel, as well as cobalt-platinum alloys (Aboaf and Klokholm, 1981; Aboaf et al., 1983). By using ternary alloys, magnetostriction can be made near zero over a range of Cr content, thereby allowing greater flexibility in designing for magnetization, corrosion resistance, and magnetostriction.

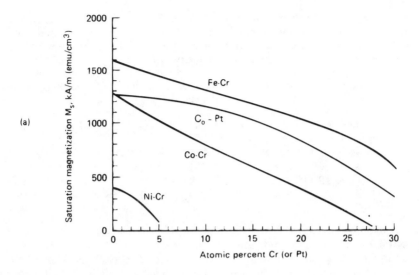

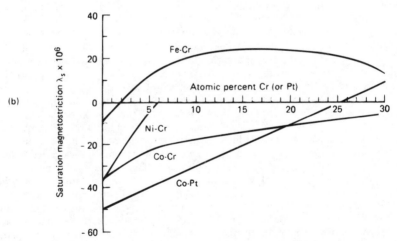

FIGURE 4.26 (*a*) Saturation magnetization and (*b*) saturation magnetostriction for various transition metals alloyed with chromium or platinum, as a function of nonmagnetic additive. The films are sputtered (*after Aboaf and Klokholm, 1981; Aboaf et al., 1983*).

4.3.3 Corrosion

Corrosion is probably the overriding stability concern for metal-film media. While gross changes in magnetic properties can occur, the more significant problems stem from microscopic corrosion sites. Such corrosion can produce magnetic defects resulting in noise or other signal aberrations, as well as mechanical defects associated with corrosion products. Conventional techniques for measuring corrosion are inadequate for evaluating recording system reliability, because most of these methods rely on macroscopic detection, such as weight gain, to quantify corrosion. Although these techniques provide useful relative information, they can be misleading. Corrosion is usually initiated at local compositional inhomogeneities, stress concentrations, or pinholes, which are statistically sparse. Such sites may become fully corroded, forming hazardous mechanical defects or signal dropouts, and yet be undetectable by macroscopic corrosion measurements. Moreover, the corrosion kinetics at these sites may be very different from those indicated by the average macroscopic rates.

In contrast to purely thermal instabilities, it is difficult to define meaningful accelerated corrosion tests. In general, corrosion depends on temperature, relative humidity, and the species of corrosive gases in the atmosphere. It is best to correlate any accelerated corrosion test with actual data under real operating conditions. Unfortunately this is often impractical because the correlation can take as long to complete as the market life of the proposed product. Just as it is difficult to define valid conditions for accelerated corrosion testing, it is also difficult to define the conditions of failure. Corrosion failure could be defined as the point at which the error rate exceeds some value, or the point at which a catastrophic head-medium crash occurs. In either case, the most suitable detector of failure is a recording head; yet to put an entire recording system in an accelerated corrosion environmental chamber could induce failure unrelated to actual corrosion. For example, high concentrations of pollutant gases, or high relative humidity, can cause adsorption or condensation on the medium, inducing mechanical failure without necessarily producing corrosion.

Corrosion studies have been made on a number of film media, including Co-P (Judge et al., 1965b); Co-Ni-P with Rh overcoat (Garrison, 1983); Co-Pt and Co-Ni-Pt (Yanagisawa et al., 1983); a variety of Co-based alloys with different undercoats and substrates (Dubin et al., 1982); Fe-Co-Cr (Phipps et al., 1984); and perpendicular Co-Cr on different substrates, with and without Ni-Fe underlayers (Dubin and Winn, 1983). The reader is referred to this and other literature for details, because the results must be evaluated within the context of the individual tests, and to specify the detailed test conditions here would be too lengthy. However, several aspects of metal-film corrosion do stand out in these studies and deserve mention: (1) Sulfur- and chlorine-containing atmospheres are the most corrosive for metal-film media. (2) Relative humidity is the single most critical factor; corrosion is relatively low even in sulfur- and chlorine-containing gases when humidity is low but proceeds rapidly when it is high. (3) Corrosion accelerates with increased temperature and constant relative humidity; however, since in most situations relative humidity decreases with increased temperature, somewhat elevated temperature operation favors decreased corrosion. (4) Pinholes in multilayered, dissimilar metal media may show enhanced corrosion due to galvanic action. (5) Applied lubricants or adsorbed organic contaminants from the atmosphere can retard corrosion.

4.3.4 Mechanical Wear

Mechanical wear has been discussed in Sec. 4.2.4 on overcoats and is further discussed in Chap. 7 on head-medium interface. Here only the instability aspect of wear is addressed. Without protective overcoats, all film media suffer signal degradation with time due to wear of the magnetic layer by the recording head, or they suffer catastrophic mechanical failure. With an overcoat, wear of the magnetic layer is not an issue but overcoat wear is of major concern.

Overcoat films which wear by delamination are undesirable, because they leave the magnetic layer exposed to damage at best, and risk a catastrophic head-medium crash at worst. Overcoats which wear by gradual loss of thickness are tolerable, provided the debris generated is not hazardous to mechanical operation and provided the overcoat is thick enough to endure the design life of the recording system. Wear of the overcoat can be virtually eliminated by the presence of a surface lubricant; however, such a lubricant itself can carry with it instabilities. For a lubricant to be useful it should be self-replenishing. For example, liquid lubricant in sufficient quantity can flow by capillary action to replenish an area depleted by rubbing contact. However, nonporous film media normally cannot retain more than a one- or two-molecule thickness of lubricant (at least on a spinning disk), and, even if more lubricant could be retained, a serious stiction problem would result. The use of carbon and oxide overcoats has made possible a new and successful method of lubrication. One component of the lube, with functional end groups, bonds to the overcoat as a monolayer. Additional lubricant layer(s) behave as a fluid with some ability to flow and replenish. These layers adhere to the bonded layer sufficiently to prevent spin-off.

Overcoats which are reasonably wear-resistant without lubricant have been sought without success. The wear properties of most overcoats, as gauged by friction and stiction measurements, are often extremely dependent on the ambient and prior history. Adsorbed organic contaminants may act as a lubricant, but, with repeated contact, such adsorbates are removed, causing friction and wear to accelerate. In other cases adsorbed water may act in just the opposite way, producing high friction and stiction values until worn away. Either of these situations represents time- and ambient-dependent wear properties and therefore a potential reliability problem.

4.4 FILM MEDIA APPLICATIONS

Although film media were studied in the laboratory since the 1960s, product applications appeared at a significant level only in the 1980s. Most of these applications are for computer data storage on rigid disks. The one exception to this is evaporated metal tape for video recording. The early-entry products often used the higher storage density capability of film media to achieve miniaturization of devices, or storage compactness, rather than higher total storage capacities. Nearly all commercially available film disks are 130 mm in diameter or smaller, compared with the older large-system disk drives which use 210 mm to 14-in-diameter disks. One reason is that small-format disks are more amenable to developing a new technology. More significantly, the personal computer market has been a major driving force in the development of film recording media as a means of maximizing storage capacity in a limited available space. Similarly, the video recording market has led to the development of metal-film tape to achieve compact portable video cameras and play-back systems. The use of miniature magnetic disks to record still images, in competition with conventional still photography, is another application. Initial video and still-photography recorders employed particulate magnetic disks, but the drive toward higher storage capacity without sacrificing compactness has inexorably led to the use of film media.

4.4.1 Film Disks

Early film-disk products were not designed to exceed the potential performance using particulate technology. This conservative approach reflects the need to prove the reliability of this new technology in products before pushing the performance levels to higher limits.

In the past decade, storage density increase has accelerated beyond the point where particulate media are competitive. This explosion of storage density was made possible by the inherent advantages of film media technology. However, it was the interaction of heightened market competition, resultant increase in demand for storage capacity, and introduction of magnetoresistive head technology (favoring film media and processing), which catapulted film media to its current dominance.

All the film-disk products introduced to date have employed longitudinal recording media, with plated Co-P or Co-Ni-P magnetic films dominating the earlier products but sputtered films now the standard. The magnetic films are typically under 50 nm thick, with coercivities in the range of 80 to 200 kA/m (1000 to 2500 Oe). Substrates of Al-Mg, usually coated with a plated Ni-P undercoat, are generally used. Most commercial film disks employ an overcoat, usually 10 to 25 nm, of sputtered carbon. Proprietary surface lubrication is used as well. Track densities of about 100 tracks per millimeter are common but two to four times that density is imminent. The technology exists to increase the track densities, but the tighter tolerance components and servo technology carry a higher cost and will be used when the market justifies it. Thus, much emphasis has been put on linear density gains for compact, low-cost system use. Linear densities on the order of 2000 fr/mm are achieved, and the use of run-length limited codes enables the bit densities to be 3000 bits per millimeter. Improved media and heads, together with PRML detection offer densities at least twice as high.

4.4.2 Film Video Tape

Compact video camera recorders have been marketed using 8-mm tapes having either metal particulate coatings or metal-evaporated films. The metal-film tapes promise potentially higher performance, but the reliability of metal-particle coatings is relatively better known, having been used in audio applications for a number of years.

The metal-film tape is fabricated by evaporation of a Co-Ni alloy onto a polyester web, such that the incident vapor stream impinging on the substrate forms a large angle (approximately 80°) relative to the substrate normal. The method of deposition was described earlier in this chapter. The oblique evaporation process is capable of high throughputs on the order of 100 m of web per minute. Magnetic layer thicknesses of 100 to 300 nm are used for this medium, with coercivities of 60 to 80 kA/m (750 to 1000 Oe). Pure Co-Ni films are corrosion-susceptible and show inadequate wear durability. Therefore an overcoat is required. However, another approach (Kunieda et al., 1984) has been outlined, in which oxygen is leaked into the vacuum chamber at a controlled rate during the Co-Ni evaporation. This has the effect of forming an oxide top layer of 10 to 30 nm, and probably introduces oxidized grain boundaries. This oxygenation improves durability and corrosion resistance and decreases noise. It also increases coercivity at the expense of saturation magnetization and hysteresis loop squareness. Such metal-film tapes are capable of recording the submicrometer wavelengths needed for video signals.

4.4.3 Perpendicular Film Media

Commercial products which use the perpendicular mode of recording have yet to emerge. Video recording seems the most likely first application of perpendicular recording, where sinusoidal recording with gapped heads does not encounter the pulse shape problems encountered in digital pulse recording. A "largely perpendicular" medium using barium ferrite particulate coatings is a more likely introduction than any purely perpendicular media like Co-Cr films.

Great advantages in linear or track density all but disappeared once practical total-system design was evaluated. A great advantage in signal-to-noise (Belk et al., 1985) also disappeared once noise mechanisms in longitudinal film media became better understood. If perpendicular recording ever gains widespread use, or even niche-applications, it will probably be for peripheral reasons, e.g., costs or simplicity of an associated technology (Tsui et al., 1985).

The most vocal arguments for and against the merits of perpendicular recording centered on linear density considerations. However, the most devastating argument against perpendicular recording was a complete surprise. After years of focus on linear density, a study of actual data error rate performance was presented (Beaulieu et al., 1989). Under conditions where longitudinal recording can typically perform adequately at an offtrack position of 20% of the trackwidth, a perpendicular media could reach only 13% offtrack for the same error rate criterion. The reason was fundamental. Longitudinal recording creates an erased band of a few tenths of a micrometer at the edge of the recorded track. This allows a read head to be mispositioned a little more off track before incurring interference from previously recorded old information. Perpendicular recording creates a sharply delineated track edge, at one time considered an advantage. But because of the absence of an edge erased band, it turned out that tolerance of head off-track mispositioning was less for perpendicular mode recording than longitudinal recording. This finding was so fundamental that research dropped abruptly from a highpoint of activity to a position of minimal interest. Nevertheless, the studies of perpendicular recording enhanced the understanding of recording physics and materials in general and, in fact, stimulated development of advanced longitudinal media.

REFERENCES

Abe, T., and T. Nishihara, "Orientation Controlled Sputtered CoNi/Cr Recording Rigid Disk," *IEEE Trans. Magn.*, **MAG-22**, 570 (1986).

Aboaf, J. A., and E. Klokholm, "Magnetic Properties of Thin Films of 3d Transition Metals Alloyed with Cr," *IEEE Trans. Magn.*, **MAG-17**, 3160 (1981).

Aboaf, J. A., S. R. Herd, and E. Klokholm, "Magnetic Properties and Structure of Cobalt-Platinum Thin Films," *IEEE Trans. Magn.*, **MAG-19**, 1514 (1983).

Agarwal, S., "Structure and Morphology of RF Sputtered Carbon Overlayer Films," *IEEE Trans. Magn.*, **MAG-21**, 1527 (1985).

Akiyama, S., S. Nakagawa, and M. Naoe, "Electrically Conductive Layer of Wear-Resistant Fe-Mo-B Alloy for Protecting Magnetic Recording Tape," *IEEE Trans. Magn.*, **MAG-27**, 5094 (1991).

Arai, Y., and A. Nahara, "Magnetic Recording Media and Process of Producing Them, Fluoropolymer Overcoating," U.S. Patent, 4,419,404, 1983.

Arnoldussen, T. C., M. A. Burleson, L. L. Nunnelley, and D. S. Parker, "Noise Distribution Measurements of Recorded Transitions in Film Media," *IEEE Trans. Magn.*, **MAG-29**, 3703 (1993).

Arnoldussen, T. C., L. L. Nunnelley, F. J. Martin, and R. P. Ferrier, "Side Writing/Reading in Magnetic Recording," *J. Appl. Phys.*, **69**, 4718 (1991).

Arnoldussen, T. C., and L. L. Nunnelley, *Noise in Digital Magnetic Recording,* World Scientific Publishing Co., Singapore (1992).

Arnoldussen, T.C., E. M. Rossi, A. Ting, A. Brunsch, J. Schneider, and G. Trippel, "Obliquely Evaporated Iron-Cobalt and Iron-Cobalt-Chromium Thin Film Recording Media," *IEEE Trans. Magn.*, **MAG-20**, 821 (1984).

Arnoldussen, T.C., and H.C. Tong, "Zigzag Transition Profiles, Noise, and Correlation Statistics in Highly Oriented Longitudinal Film Media," *IEEE Trans. Magn.*, **MAG-22**, 889 (1986).

Arnoldussen, T. C., and J. G. Zhu, "Effect of Recorded Transition Shape on Spatial Noise Distributions and Correlations," *J. Appl. Phys.*, **75**, 6773 (1994).

Barany, A. M., and H. N. Bertram, "Transition Noise Model for Longitudinal Thin-Film Media," *IEEE Trans. Magn.*, **MAG-23**, 1776 (1987).

Baugh, R. A., E. S. Murdock, and B. R. Natarajan, "Measurement of Noise in Magnetic Media," *IEEE Trans. Magn.*, **MAG-19**, 1722 (1983).

Baumgart, P., D. J. Krajnovich, T. A. Nguyen, and A. C. Tam, "A New Laser Texturing Technique for High Performance Magnetic Disk Drives," Intermag 1995, to be published in *IEEE Trans. Magn.*

Beaulieu, T. J., D. J. Seagle, M. A. Meininger, and C. J. Spector, "Track Density Limitation for Dual-Layer Perpendicular Recording in a Rigid Disk Environment," *IEEE Trans. Magn.*, **MAG-25**, 3369 (1989).

Belk, N. R., P. K. George, and G. S. Mowry, "Noise in High-Performance Thin-Film Longitudinal Magnetic Recording Media," *Trans. Magn.*, **MAG-21**, 1350 (1985).

Bonn, T. H., and D. C. Wendell, Jr., "Electrodeposition of a Magnetic Coating," U.S. Patent 2,644,787, 1953.

Borrelli, N. F., S. L. Chen, and J. A. Murphy, "Magnetic and Optical Properties of Thin Films in the System $(1-x)Fe_3O_4 \cdot xFe_{8/3}O_4$," *IEEE Trans. Magn.,* **MAG-8**, 648 (1972).

Bozorth, R. M., *Ferromagnetism,* Van Nostrand, New York, 1951, p. 289.

Brenner, A., and G. E. Riddell, "Nickel Plating on Steel by Chemical Reduction," *J. Res. Natl. Bur. Stand.*, **37**, 31 (1946).

Chen, T., "The Micromagnetic Properties of High-Coercivity Metallic Thin Films and Their Effects on the Limit of Packing Density in Digital Recording," *IEEE Trans. Magn.*, **MAG-17**, 1181 (1981).

Chen, T., and G. B. Charlan, "A Comparison of the Uniaxial Anisotropy in Sputtered Co-Re and CoCr Perpendicular Recording Media," *J. Appl. Phys.*, **54**, 5103 (1983).

Chopra, K. L., *Thin Film Phenomena,* McGraw-Hill, New York, 1969.

Christner, J. A., R. Ranjan, R. L. Peterson, and J. I. Lee, "Low-Noise Metal Medium for High-Density Longitudinal Recording," *J. Appl. Phys.*, **63**, 3260 (1988).

Coffey, K. R., V. Raman, N. Staud, and D. J. Pocker, "Vapor Lubrication of Thin Film Disks," *IEEE Trans. Magn.*, **MAG-30**, 4146 (1994).

Daval, J., and D. Randet, "Electron Microscopy on High Coercive Force CoCr Composite Films," *IEEE Trans. Magn.*, **MAG-6**, 768 (1970).

Deng, Y., and D. N. Lambeth, "Structural Characteristics of Bias Sputtered CoCrTa/Cr Films," *IEEE Trans. Magn.*, **MAG-29**, 3676 (1993).

Doss, S., Private Communication (1985).

Dressler, D. D., and J. H. Judy, "A Study of Digitally Recorded Transitions in Thin Magnetic Films," *IEEE Trans. Magn.*, **MAG-10**, 674 (1974).

Duan, S., M. R. Khan, S. Y. Lee, J. L. Pressesky, L. Tang, and G. Thomas, "Study of Multilayer Films for Magnetic Recording," *IEEE Trans. Magn.*, **MAG-27**, 5055 (1991).

Dubin, R. R., and K. D. Winn, "Behavior of Perpendicular Recording Materials in Cl and S Containing Atmospheres," *IEEE Trans. Magn.*, **MAG-19**, 1665 (1983).

Dubin, R. R., K. D. Winn, L. P. Davis, and R. A. Cutler, "Degradation of Co-based Thin-Film Recording Materials in Selected Corrosive Environments," *J. Appl. Phys.*, **53**, 2579 (1982).

Feng, J. S. Y., C. H. Bajorek, and M. A. Nicolet, "Magnetite Thin Films," *IEEE Trans. Magn.*, **MAG-8**, 277 (1972).

Ferrier, R. P., F. J. Martin, T. C. Arnoldussen, and L. L. Nunnelley, "Lorentz Image-Derived Film Media Noise," *IEEE Trans. Magn.*, **MAG-24**, 2709 (1988).

Feuerstein, A., and M. Mayr, "High Vacuum Evaporation of Ferromagnetic Materials—A New Production Technology For Magnetic Tapes," *IEEE Trans. Magn.*, **MAG-20**, 51 (1984).

Fischer, G., H. J. Richter, H. P. Schildberg, and H. Hibst, "Ageing Effects of Metal Evaporated Tapes," *IEEE Trans. Magn.*, **MAG-29**, 3757 (1993).

Fisher, R. D., and W. H. Chilton, "Preparation and Magnetic Characteristics of Chemically Deposited Cobalt for High Density Storage," *J. Electrochem. Soc.*, **109**, 485 (1962).

Fisher, R. D., L. Herte, and A. Lang, "Recording Performance and Magnetic Characteristics of Sputtered Cobalt-Nickel-Tungsten Films," *IEEE Trans. Magn.*, **MAG-17**, 3190 (1981).

Fisher, R. D., V. S. Au-Yeung, and B. B. Sabo, "Perpendicular Anisotropy Constants and Anisotropy Energy of Oriented Cobalt-Chromium Alloys," *IEEE Trans. Magn.*, **MAG-20**, 806 (1984).

Fisher, R. D., J. C. Allan, and J. L. Pressesky, "Magnetic Properties and Longitudinal Recording Performance of Corrosion-Resistant Alloy Films," *IEEE Trans. Magn.*, **MAG-22**, 352 (1986).

Freiser, M. J., "On the Zigzag Form of Charged Domain Walls," *IBM J. Res. Dev.*, **23**, 330 (1979).

Fugita, T., M. Odagiri, and K. Shinohara, "Metal Thin Film Video Tape Produced by Vacuum Deposition," *Natl. Tech. Rep. Japan*, **28**, 502 (1982).

Futamoto, M., S. Saito, T. Nishimura, Y. Honda, K. Yoshida, and T. Okuwaki, "Wear Durability and Structure of Vacuum Evaporated Boron Films," *IEEE Trans. Magn.*, **MAG-26**, 2682 (1990).

Garrison, M. C., "Effects of Absorbed Films on Galvanic Corrosion in Metallic Thin Film Media," *IEEE Trans. Magn.*, **MAG-19**, 1683 (1983).

Grundy, P. J., M. Ali, and C. A. Faunce, "Electron Microscopy of Co-Cr Films," *IEEE Trans. Magn.*, **MAG-20**, 794 (1984).

Haines, W. G., "Anisotropy in Thin-Film Media—Origins and Applications," *J. Appl. Phys.*, **61**, 3497 (1987).

Hata, H., T. Hyohno, T. Fukuichi, K. Yabushita, M. Umesaki, and H. Shibata, "Magnetic and Recording Characteristics of Multilayer CoNiCr Thin Film Media," *IEEE Trans. Magn.*, **MAG-26**, 2709 (1990).

Heller, J., "Deposition of Magnetite Films by Reactive Sputtering of Iron Oxide," *IEEE Trans. Magn.*, **MAG-12**, 396 (1976).

Hintermann, H. E., "Thin Solid Films to Combat Friction, Wear, and Corrosion," *J. Vac. Sci. Technol.*, **B2**, 816 (1984).

Hokkyo, J., K. Hayakawa, I. Saito, and K. Shirane, "A New W-Shaped Single-Pole Head and a High Density Flexible Disk Perpendicular Magnetic Recording System," *IEEE Trans. Magn.*, **MAG-20**, 72 (1984).

Howard, J. K., U.S. Patent 4,778,588 (1988).

Hsieh, E. J., R. F. Soohoo, and M. F. Kelly, "A Lorentz Microscopic Study of Head-On Domain Walls," *IEEE Trans. Magn.*, **MAG-10**, 304 (1974).

Hughes, G. F., "Magnetization Reversal in Cobalt-Phosphorus Films," *J. Appl. Phys.*, **54**, 5306 (1983).

Hylton, T. L., M. A. Parker, M. Ullah, K. R. Coffey, R. Umphress, and J. K. Howard, "Ba-ferrite Thin-Film Media for High-Density Longitudinal Recording," *J. Appl. Phys.*, **75**, 5960 (1994).

Iechika, K., Y. Kokaku, M. Ootake, K. Abe, H. Tani, and H. Inaba, "Performance of Hard DLC Protective Film Prepared by PECVD Method for Thin Film Magnetic Disk," *IEEE Trans. Magn.*, **MAG-30**, 4134 (1994).

Ishii, O., and I. Hatakeyama, "Os Doped γ-Fe$_2$O$_3$ Thin Films Having High Coercivity and Coercive Squareness," *J. Appl. Phys.*, **55**, 2269 (1984).

Ishii, Y., A. Terada, O. Ishii, S. Ohta, S. Hattori, and K. Makino, "New Preparation Process for Sputtered γ-Fe$_2$O$_3$ Thin Film Disks," *IEEE Trans. Magn.*, **MAG-16**, 1114 (1980).

Ishizuka, M., T. Komoda, T. Tsuchimoto, M. Yoshikawa, S. Ishio, and M. Takahashi, "Perpendicular Anisotropy in Co-Cr Films," *J. Magn. Magn. Mater.*, **35**, 286 (1983).

Iwasaki, S. I., and Y. Nakamura, "An Analysis for the Magnetization Mode for High Density Magnetic Recording," *IEEE Trans. Magn.*, **MAG-13**, 1272 (1977).

Johnson, K. E., M. R. Kim, and S. Guruswamy, "Dependence of Magnetic Media Noise on Ultra-Thin Cr Underlayer Thickness," *IEEE Trans. Magn.*, **MAG-28**, 3099 (1992).

Judge, J. S., J. R. Morrison, and D. E. Speliotis, "Very High Coercivity Chemically Deposited Co-Ni Films," *J. Appl. Phys.*, **36**, 948 (1965a).

Judge, J. S., J. R. Morrison, D. E. Speliotis, and G. Bate, "Magnetic Properties and Corrosion Behavior of Thin Electroless Co-P Deposits," *J. Electrochem. Soc.*, **112**, 681 (1965b).

Judge, J. S., J. R. Morrison, D. E. Speliotis, "Flexible Recording Surfaces of Electrodeposited Cobalt-Nickel-Phosphorus," *Plating*, **53**, 441 (1966).

Kawanabe, T., and M. Naoe, "Effects of Ta Addition in CoNi/Cr Double Layer Film Sputtered in Low Ar Gas Pressure," *IEEE Trans. Magn.*, **MAG-24**, 2721 (1988).

Kay, E., R. A. Sigsbee, G. L. Bona, M. Taborelli, and H. C. Siegmann, "Magnetic Depth Profiling and Characterization of Fe Oxide Films by Kerr Rotation and Spin Polarized Photoemission," *Intl. Conf. Magn., 1985 Digests*, **148** (1985).

King, F. K., "Datapoint Thin Film Media," *IEEE Trans. Magn.*, **MAG-17**, 1376 (1981).

Kobayashi, K., and G. Ishida, "Magnetic and Structural Properties of Rh Substituted Co-Cr Alloy Films with Perpendicular Magnetic Anisotropy," *J. Appl. Phys.*, **52**, 2453 (1981).

Kobayashi, K., J. Toda, and T. Yamamoto, "High Density Perpendicular Magnetic Recording on Rigid Disks," *Fujitsu Sci. Tech. J.*, **19**, 99 (1983).

Kogure, T., Y. Matsuno, T. Itoh, and C. Shima, "Isotropic Thin Film Texture for Alternative Substrates," *IEEE Trans. Magn.*, **MAG-30**, 4116 (1994).

Kojima, H., and K. Hanada, "Origin of Coercivity Changes during the Oxidation of Fe$_3$O$_4$ to γ-Fe$_2$O$_3$," *IEEE Trans. Magn.*, **MAG-16**, 11 (1980).

Kolecki, J. C., "Microhardness Studies on Thin Carbon Films Grown on P-Type 100 Silicon," NASA Technical Memorandum 82980, 1982.

Kovac, Z., and V. J. Novotny, "Silicon Nitride Overcoats for Thin Film Magnetic Recording Media," *IEEE Trans. Magn.*, **MAG-27**, 5070 (1991).

Kullmann, U., E. Köster, and C. Dorsch, "Amorphous CoSm Thin Films: A New Material for High Density Longitudinal Recording," *IEEE Trans. Magn.*, **MAG-20**, 420 (1984a).

Kunieda, T., K. Shinohara, and A. Tomago, "Metal Evaporated Videotape," *IERE Proc.*, **37** (1984).

Lal, B. B., M. Tobise, and T. Shinohara, "Effect of Very Thin Cr-Underlayer on the Magnetic and Recording Properties of CoCrTa Thin-Film Media," *IEEE Trans. Magn.*, **MAG-30**, 3954 (1994).

Lambert, S. E., J. K. Howard, and I. L. Sanders, "Reduction of Media Noise in Thin Film Metal Media by Lamination," *IEEE Trans. Magn.*, **MAG-26**, 2706 (1990).

Lambeth, D. N., and R. Ranjan, U.S. Patent 5062021 (1991).

Lambeth, D. N., and R. Ranjan, U.S. Patent 5108781 (1992).

Laughlin, D. E., and B. Y. Wong, "The Crystallography and Texture of Co-Based Thin Film Deposited on Cr Underlayers," *IEEE Trans. Magn.*, **MAG-27**, 4713 (1991).

Lloyd, J. C., and R. S. Smith, "Structural and Magnetic Properties of Permalloy Films," *J. Appl. Phys.*, **30S**, 274 (1959).

Luborsky, F. E., "High Coercive Force Films of Cobalt-Nickel with Additions of Group V*A* and VI*B* Elements," *IEEE Trans. Magn.*, **MAG-6**, 502 (1970).

Madrid, M., and R. Wood, "Transition Noise in Thin-Film Media," *IEEE Trans. Magn.*, **MAG-22**, 892 (1986).

Maeda, H., "High Coercivity Co and Co-Ni Alloy Films," *J. Appl. Phys.*, **53**, 3735 (1982).

Maissel, L. I., and R. Glang, *Handbook of Thin Film Technology,* McGraw-Hill, New York, 1970.

Mansuripur, M., and T. W. McDaniel, "Magnetization Reversal Dynamics in Magneto-Optic Media," *J. Appl. Phys.*, **63**, 3831 (1988).

Marchon, B., M. R. Khan, N. Heiman, P. Pereira, and A. Lautie, "Tribochemical Wear on Amorphous Carbon Thin Films," *IEEE Trans. Magn.*, **MAG-26**, 2670 (1990).

Marchon, B., P. N. Vo, M. R. Khan, and J. W. Ager III, "Structure and Mechanical Properties of Hydrogenated Carbon Films Prepared by Magnetron Sputtering," *IEEE Trans. Magn.*, **MAG-27**, 5160 (1991).

Matsuoka, M., M. Naoe, and Y. Hoshi, "Ba-Ferrite-Thin-Film Disk for Perpendicular Magnetic Recording," *J. Appl. Phys.*, **57**, 4040 (1985).

Merchant, K., P. Mee, M. Smallen, S. Smith, "Lubricant Bonding and Orientation on Carbon Coated Media," *IEEE Trans. Magn.*, **MAG-26**, 2688 (1990).

Middelhoek, S., "Domain Walls in Thin Ni-Fe Films," *J. Appl. Phys.*, **34**, 1054 (1963).

Min, T., J. G. Zhu, and J. H. Judy, "Effects of Inter-layer Magnetic Interactions in Multilayered CoCrTa/Cr Thin Film Media," *IEEE Trans. Magn.*, **MAG-27**, 5058 (1991).

Mirzamaani, M., C. V. Jahnes, and M. A. Russak, "Thin Film Disks with Transient Metal Underlayers," *IEEE Trans. Magn.,* **MAG-28**, 3090 (1992).

Moon, J. J., R. Carley, and R. R. Katti, "Density Dependence of Noise in Thin Metallic Longitudinal Media," *J. Appl. Phys.*, **63**, 3254 (1988).

Moradzadeh, Y., "Chemically Deposited Cobalt Phosphorus Films for Magnetic Recording," *J. Electrochem. Soc.*, **112**, 891 (1965).

Muller, M. W., and E. S. Murdock, "Williams-Comstock Type Model for Sawtooth Transitions in Thin Film Media," *IEEE Trans. Magn.*, **MAG-23**, 2368 (1987).

Murdock, E. S., B. R. Natarajan, and R. G. Walmsley, "Noise Properties of Multilayered Co-Alloy Magnetic Recording Media," *IEEE Trans. Magn.*, **MAG-26**, 2700 (1990).

Murdock, E. S., R. F. Simmons, and R. Davidson, "Roadmap for 10 Gbit/in^2 Media: Challenges," *IEEE Trans. Magn.*, **MAG-28**, 3078 (1992).

Nakamura, K., Y. Ohta, A. Itoh, and C. Hayashi, "Magnetic Properties of Thin Films Prepared by Continuous Vapor Deposition," *IEEE Trans. Magn.*, **MAG-18**, 1077 (1982).

Natarajan, B. R., and E. S. Murdock, "Magnetic and Recording Properties of Sputtered Co-P/Cr Thin Film Media," *IEEE Trans. Magn.*, **MAG-24**, 2724 (1988).

Néel, L., "Energy of Block Walls in Thin Films" (French), *C. R. Acad. Sci. Paris*, **241**, 533 (1955).

Néel, L., "Remarks on the Theory of the Magnetic Properties of Thin Films and Fine Particles" (French), *J. Phys. Radium*, **17**, 250 (1956).

Nishimoto, K., and M. Aoyama, "Preparation of γ-Fe$_2$O$_3$ Thin Film Disks by Reactive Evaporation and Their Read/Write Characteristics," *Proc. Int. Conf. Ferrites*, 588 (1980).

Nolan, T. P., R. Sinclair, R. Ranjan, and T. Yamashita, "Transmission Electron Microscopic Analysis of Microstructural Features in Magnetic Recording Media," *IEEE Trans. Magn.*, **MAG-29**, 292 (1993).

Nouchi, N., Y. Kai, Y. Maesawa, N. Nakamura, and K. Shinohara, "Corrosion Analysis for Co-Ni-O Film Adopted as the Magnetic Layer of Metal Evaporated Tape," *IEEE Transl. J. Magn. Jap.*, **29**, 21 (1993).

Novotny, V. J., and A. S. Kao, "Tin Oxide Overcoats for Thin Film Magnetic Recording Media," *IEEE Trans. Magn.*, **MAG-26**, 2499 (1990).

Nunnelley, L. L., D. E. Heim, and T. C. Arnoldussen, "Flux Noise in Particulate Media: Measurement and Interpretation," *IEEE Trans. Magn.*, **MAG-23**, 1767 (1987).

O'Hanlon, J. F., *A User's Guide to Vacuum Technology*, John Wiley and Sons, New York, 1980.

Ohkoshi, M., H. Toba, S. Honda, and T. Kusuda, "Electron Microscopy of Co-Cr Sputtered Films," *J. Magn. Magn. Mater.*, **35**, 266 (1983).

Ohno, T., V. Shiroishi, S. Hishiyama, H. Suzuki, and Y. Matsuda, "Modulation and Crystallographic Orientation of Sputtered CoNi/Cr Disks for Longitudinal Recording," *IEEE Trans. Magn.*, **MAG-23**, 2809 (1987).

Ouchi, K., and S. Iwasaki, "Thermomagnetic Behavior of Hard Magnetic Thin Films," *IEEE Trans. Magn.*, **MAG-8**, 473 (1972).

Paik, C. R., I. Suzuki, N. Tani, M. Ishikawa, Y. Ota, and K. Nakamura, "Magnetic Properties and Noise Characteristics of High Coercivity CoCrPtB/Cr Media," *IEEE Trans. Magn.*, **MAG-28**, 3084 (1992).

Palmer, D. C., K. E. Johnson, E. Y. Wu, and J. V. Peske, "Recording Properties of Multilayered Thin Film Media," *IEEE Trans. Magn.*, **MAG-27**, 5307 (1991).

Pan, X., and V. J. Novotny, "Head Material Effects on Interface Tribochemistry," *IEEE Trans. Magn.*, **MAG-30**, 433 (1994).

Phipps, P. B., S. J. Lewis, and D. W. Rice, "The Magnetic and Corrosion Properties of Iron Cobalt Chromium Films," *J. Appl. Phys.*, **55**, 2257 (1984).

Pourbaix, M., *Atlas of Electrochemical Equilibria in Aqueous Solutions*, National Association Corrosion Engineers, Houston, 1974.

Ranjan, R., D. N. Lambeth, M. Tromel, P. Goglia, and Y. Li, "Laser Texturing for Low-Flying-Height Media," *J. Appl. Phys.*, **69**, 5745 (1991).

Reimer, V., "Ein Modell aus Permanentmagneten zum Verstandnis der Ummagnetisierung in dunnen Schichten," *Z. Angew. Phys.*, **196** (1964).

Riveiro, J. M., and J. M. de Frutos, "Magnetic Annealing in Electrodeposited Co-P Amorphous Alloys," *J. Magn. Magn. Mater.*, **37**, 155 (1983).

Rogers, D. J., Y. Maeda, and K. Takei, "The Dependence of Compositional Separation on Film Thickness for Co-Cr and Co-Cr-Ta Magnetic Recording Media," *IEEE Trans. Magn.*, **MAG-30**, 3972 (1994).

Rossi, E. M., G. McDonnough, A. Tietze, T. Arnoldussen, A. Brunsch, S. Doss, M. Henneberg, F. Lin, R. Lyn, A. Ting, and G. Trippel, "Vacuum-Deposited Thin-Metal Film Disk," *J. Appl. Phys.*, **15**, 2254 (1984).

Sanders, I. L., K. Howard, S. E. Lambert, and T. Yogi, "Influence of Coercivity Squareness on Media Noise in Thin-Film Recording Media," *J. Appl. Phys.*, **65**, 1234 (1989).

Sano, K., H. Murayama, and F. Yokoyama, "Lubricant Bonding Via Hydrogen Bond Network," *IEEE Trans. Magn.*, **MAG-30**, 4140 (1994).

Schuele, W. J., "Coercive Force of Angle of Incidence Films," *J. Appl. Phys.*, **35**, 2558 (1964).

Schulz, K. J., and K. V. Viswanathan, "A Comparison of Film Structure and Surface Chemistry of Carbon and Oxide Disk Overcoats," *IEEE Trans. Magn.*, **MAG-27**, 5166 (1991).

Schulz, K. J., K. V. Viswanathan, A. C. Wall, and A. J. Bowen, "The Effect of Low Mobility Sputter Conditions on Thin-Film Disk Tribology," *IEEE Trans. Magn.*, **MAG-28**, 2527 (1992).

Seagle, D. J., N. C. Fernelius, and M. R. Khan, "Influence of Substrate Texture on Recording Parameters for CoNiCr Rigid Disk Media," *J. Appl. Phys.*, **61**, 4025 (1987).

Shen, Y., D. E. Laughlin, and D. N. Lambeth, "Effects of Substrate Temperature on Magnetic Properties of CoCrTa/Cr Films," *IEEE Trans. Magn.*, **MAG-28**, 3261 (1992).

Simpson, E. M., P. B. Narayan, G. T. K. Swami, and J. L. Chao, "Effect of Circumferential Texture on the Properties of Thin Film Rigid Recording Disks," *IEEE Trans. Magn.*, **MAG-23**, 3405 (1987).

Smallen, M., J. K. Lee, A. Chao, and J. Enguero, "The Role of Disk Carbon and Slider in Water Adsorption," *IEEE Trans. Magn.*, **MAG-30**, 4137 (1994).

Smith, D. O., M. S. Cohen, and G. P. Weiss, "Oblique Incidence Anisotropy in Evaporated Permalloy Films," *J. Appl. Phys.*, **31**, 1755 (1960).

Sohn, H. K., S. C. Seol, T. Kang, K. H. Shin, T. D. Lee, and P. W. Jang, "Magnetic Properties of $(Co_{93}Cr_7)$-P-Pt/Cr Thin Films for Longitudinal Magnetic Recording Media," *IEEE Trans. Magn.*, **MAG-30**, 4041 (1994).

Soohoo, R. F., "Influence of Particle Interaction on Coercivity and Squareness of Thin Film Recording Media," *J. Appl. Phys.*, **52**, 2459 (1981).

Speliotis, D. E., G. Bate, J. K. Alstad, and J. R. Morrison, "Hard Magnetic Films of Iron, Cobalt, and Nickel," *J. Appl. Phys.*, **36**, 972 (1965).

Suganuma, Y., H. Tanaka, M. Yanagisawa, F. Goto, and S. Hatano, "Production Process and High Density Recording Characteristics of Plated Disks," *IEEE Trans. Magn.*, **MAG-18**, 1215 (1982).

Sui, X., and M. H. Kryder, "Effects of CoTi-Doping on Longitudinal Barium Ferrite Thin Film Media," *IEEE Trans. Magn.*, **MAG-30**, 4044 (1994).

Tanaka, H., F. Ishikawa, K. Gomi, N. Yamaguchi, and Y. Miyake, "Tribological Behavior of Thin Film Rigid Disks with Regular Dot Array Texture on Carbon Overcoats," *IEEE Trans. Magn.*, **MAG-30**, 4113 (1994).

Tang, Y. S., "Noise Autocorrelation in High Density Recording on Metal Film Disks," *IEEE Trans. Magn.*, **MAG-22**, 883 (1986).

Tani, N., T. Takahashi, M. Hashimoto, M. Ishikawa, Y. Ota, and K. Nakamura, "High Coercivity Hard Disk with CoCrPtB/Cr Media," *IEEE Trans. Magn.*, **MAG-27**, 4736 (1991).

Teng, E., and N. Ballard, "Anisotropy Induced Signal Waveform Modulation of DC Magnetron Sputtered Thin Film Disks," *IEEE Trans. Magn.*, **MAG-22**, 579 (1986).

Teng, E., P. Nguyen, and A. Eltoukhy, "Sputter Induced Random Texturing on NiP Plated Aluminum and Alternate Substrates," *IEEE Trans. Magn.*, **MAG-30**, 4119 (1994).

Terada, A., O. Ishii, and K. Kobayashi, "Pressure-Induced Signal Loss in Fe_3O_4 and Gamma Fe_2O_3 Thin Film Disks," *IEEE Trans. Magn.*, **MAG-19**, 12 (1983).

Thornton, J. A., "High Rate Thick Film Growth," *Annu. Rev. Mater. Sci.*, **7**, 239 (1977).

Tian, H., and T. Matsudaira, "Effect of Relative Humidity on Friction Behavior of the Head/Disk Interface," *IEEE Trans. Magn.*, **MAG-28**, 2530 (1992).

Tong, H. C., R. Ferrier, P. Chang, J. Tzeng, and K. L. Parker, "The Micromagnetics of Thin-Film Disk Recording Tracks," *IEEE Trans. Magn.*, **MAG-20**, 1831 (1984).

Tsui, R., H. Hamilton, R. Anderson, C. Baldwin, and P. Simon, "Perpendicular Recording Performance of Thin Film Probe Heads and Double-Layer Co-Cr Media," *Digest of Intermag. Conf.*, **GA4** (1985).

Uchinami, S., F. Beppu, S. Ito, N. Tokubuchi, K. Noda, Y. Notohara, and K. Kanai, "Magnetic Anisotropies in Sputtered Thin Film Disks," *IEEE Trans. Magn.*, **MAG-23**, 3408 (1987).

Uesaka, Y., M. Koizumi, N. Tsumita, O. Kitakami, and H. Fujiwara, "Noise from Underlayer of Perpendicular Magnetic Recording Medium," *J. Appl. Phys.*, **57**, 3925 (1984).

Victora, R. H., "Micromagnetic Predictions for Magnetization Reversal in CoNi Films," *J. Appl. Phys.*, **62**, 4220 (1987).

Vossen, J. L., and W. Kern, *Thin Film Processes,* Academic Press, New York, 1978.

Wielinga, T., "Investigations on Perpendicular Magnetic Recording," Thesis, Twente University of Technology, the Netherlands, 1983.

Williams, M. L., and R. L. Comstock, "An Analytic Model of the Write Process in Digital Magnetic Recording," *AIP Conf. Proc. Magn. Magn. Mater.*, **5**, 738 (1971).

Wuori, E. R., and J. H. Judy, "Initial Layer Effects in CoCr Films," *IEEE Trans. Magn.*, **MAG-20**, 774 (1984).

Wuori, E. R., and J. H. Judy, "Particle-like Magnetic Behavior of RF-Sputtered CoCr Films," *J. Appl. Phys.*, **57**, 4010 (1985).

Yamashita, G. L., J. Chen, J. Shir, and T. Chen, "Sputtered ZrO_2 with Superior Protection and Mechanical Performance in Thin Film Rigid Disk Application," *IEEE Trans. Magn.*, **MAG-24**, 2629 (1988).

Yanagisawa, M., N. Shiota, H. Yamaguchi, and Y. Suganuma, "Corrosion-Resisting Co-Pt Thin Film Medium for High Density Recording," *IEEE Trans. Magn.*, **MAG-19**, 1638 (1983).

Yang, M. M., S. E. Lambert, J. K. Howard, and C. Hwang, "Laminated CoPtCr/Cr Films for Low Noise Longitudinal Recording," *IEEE Trans. Magn.*, **MAG-27**, 5052 (1991).

Yeh, T. A., C. L. Lin, J. M. Sivertsen, and J. H. Judy, "Durability and Structure of RF Sputtered Carbon-Nitrogen Thin Film Overcoats on Rigid Disks of Magnetic Thin Film Media," *IEEE Trans. Magn.*, **MAG-27**, 5163 (1991).

Yogi, T., G. L. Gorman, C. Hwang, M. A. Kakalec, and S. E. Lambert, "Dependence of Magnetics, Microstructures, and Recording Properties on Underlayer Thickness in CoNiCr/Cr Media," *IEEE Trans. Magn.*, **MAG-24**, 2727 (1988).

Yogi, T., T. A. Nguyen, S. E. Lambert, G. L. Gorman, and G. Castillo, "Role of Atomic Mobility in the Transition Noise of Longitudinal Media," *IEEE Trans. Magn.*, **MAG-26**, 1578 (1990).

Yogi, T., C. Tsang, T. A. Nguyen, K. Ju, G. L. Gorman, and G. Castillo, "Longitudinal Media for 1 Gb/in^2 Areal Density," *IEEE Trans. Magn.*, **MAG-26**, 2271 (1990).

Yogi, T., and T. A. Nguyen, "Ultra High Density Media: Gigabit and Beyond," *IEEE Trans. Magn.*, **MAG-29**, 307 (1993).

Zhang, X. Y., H. Suhl, and P. K. George, "Relationship between the Transition Width and the Zigzag Wavelength," *J. Appl. Phys.*, **63**, 3257 (1988).

Zhu, J-G., and H. N. Bertram, "Micromagnetic Studies of Thin Metallic Films," *J. Appl. Phys.*, **63**, 3248 (1988a).

Zhu, J-G., and H. N. Bertram, "Recording and Transition Noise Simulations in Thin Film Media," *IEEE Trans. Magn.*, **MAG-24**, 2706 (1988b).

CHAPTER 5
MICROMAGNETICS OF THIN-FILM MEDIA

Jian-Gang Zhu
Department of Electrical Engineering,
University of Minnesota

5.1 INTRODUCTION

Thin metallic films have become the recording media for rigid disk recording applications, mainly due to their spatial uniformity and high coercivity. Especially, over the past five years, longitudinal thin-film recording media have undergone significant advances in reducing medium noise and increasing film coercivity. Remarkable areal recording densities of 1 to 2 Gbits/in^2 have been achieved with high signal-to-noise ratio laboratory demonstrations and will soon be realized in products (Yogi, 1990; Futamoto, 1991). One of the main reasons for such rapid advances is the significant achievements in understanding the correlations between film microstructures, recording performance and noise, gained through extensive experimental and theoretical studies.

The most fundamental aspect of the microstructure of thin-film recording media is the granularity (Arnoldussen, 1986). These films are polycrystalline and have magnetic crystallites arranged in the film plane with nearly unity packing. Almost all the films are cobalt alloys with saturation magnetizations ranging from 300 to 800 kA/m (300 to 800 emu/cm^3). Films used as practical recording media usually have a coercivity around 120 to 200 kA/m (1500 to 2500 Oe). It has been found experimentally that by varying deposition conditions, film coercivity and other magnetic hysteresis behavior can take on a broad range of values without even varying material composition. This indicates that film magnetic hysteresis properties are strong functions of film microstructures. With a film considered as an assembly of closely packed interactive magnetic grains, the hysteresis properties depend not only on the intrinsic magnetic properties of each individual magnetic grain, but also on the magnetic interactions, including both magnetostatic and intergranular exchange interactions. Understanding the correlations of film magnetic properties and recording performance with film microstructure and material magnetic parameters has been critical for the development of advanced recording media. Computer modeling combined with experimental studies can help understanding of the underlying physics governing the magnetization processes in these films.

Magnetization reversal mechanisms of isolated single-domain magnetic particles have been studied extensively with the development of micromagnetics theory (Stoner and Wohlfarth, 1948; Brown, 1963, 1968; Shtrikman, 1960). In thin-film recording media, not only is the micromagnetic behavior of a single particle important, so are the magnetic interactions among the magnetic grains in the film. The interactions in these films are usually so significant that reversal mechanisms of isolated individual grains can be altered (Zhu and Bertram, 1989). It is often the case that in these films, collective magnetization behavior dominates during the magnetization processes.

Hughes proposed a computer simulation model for studying magnetization reversal process for CoP thin-film media (Hughes, 1983). In his model, an energy-minimization method was used to obtain magnetization configurations during magnetization processes. Using the model, Hughes studied the effects of magnetostatic interactions in the film on the hysteresis properties and collective magnetization reversals of the grains in the film. Victora studied the magnetization reversal process in obliquely evaporated CoNi films by solving the Landau-Lifshitz-Gilbert dynamic equations (Victora, 1987a, 1987b). Zhu and Bertram developed a theoretical model for studying magnetic thin films with granular structures in general (Zhu and Bertram, 1988a). In the latter model, it is assumed that each grain is always uniformly magnetized, and a film is considered as an assembly of interactive magnetic grains with inclusion of both long- range magnetostatic interaction and nearest neighbor intergranular exchange coupling. The magnetization directions of the grains during a magnetization process are determined by solving coupled Landau-Lifshitz equations. Applying the model, Zhu and Bertram went on to carry out a rather thorough study of the fundamental magnetization process in thin-film recording media, including both longitudinal and perpendicular films. Mansuripur and Giles have implemented a similar micromagnetic model on the Connection Machine to study the magnetization process in both magnetic and magnetooptical recording media (Mansuripur and Giles, 1990). Miles and Middleton also developed a similar simulation model, but added additional features such as the irregular spatial arrangement of spherical magnetic grains (Miles and Middleton, 1990).

This chapter focuses on the simulation studies of the fundamental magnetization processes, recording performance and noise properties in thin-film recording media. It is mainly based on a series of studies conducted with the model developed by Zhu and Bertram. Emphasis is placed on the effects of magnetostatic interaction and intergranular exchange coupling in the films. Description of the theoretical model for thin-film recording media is given in Sec. 5.2. In Sec. 5.3, the magnetization reversal processes and resulting hysteresis properties in longitudinal thin-film media are reviewed. The noise behavior of recorded isolated transitions and dibit transition pairs are discussed in Sec. 5.4. In Sec. 5.5, studies on the spatial correlation characteristics of the medium noise are reviewed. In Sec. 5.6, recording characteristics at the track edges are discussed. Section 5.7 presents studies on various advanced film microstructures and the related special magnetic properties and recording performance. In Sec. 5.8, perpendicular film media are discussed. A brief summary is given in Sec. 5.9.

5.2 THEORETICAL MODEL

The model considers a thin film, designed for either longitudinal or perpendicular recording, as a monolayer of closely packed magnetic grains. The main assumption in the model is that each magnetic grain is always uniformly magnetized such that during magnetization processes, only its magnetization direction is changing. Since almost all the films utilized as recording media are cobalt alloys and the sizes of the grains in a typical recording film are in the range of 100–300Å in diameter, this assumption is reasonable. Such grain sizes are well below the critical size for the existence of multidomain behavior (for Co, the critical diameter of a multidomain sphere is about 1400Å). With this assumption, the problem reduces to the modeling of an assembly of interacting Stoner-Wohlfarth particles.

5.2.1 Modeling Array

A thin film is modeled by a two dimensional array of hexagonally shaped grains arranged on a triangular lattice, as shown in Fig. 5.1. In the figure, D is the grain diameter, d is the intergranular boundary separation, and δ is the grain height which is also the film thickness. This array of hexagons was first used by Hughes to study CoP longitudinal films (Hughes, 1983). The important features of this array include the following: (1) Each hexagon has six nearest neighboring grains, closely resembling the grain arrangement in a real film. It is critical to have the number of nearest neighboring grains close to real films for obtaining correct magnetization configurations; (2) Intergranular boundary separation is uniform throughout the film; (3) Unity packing fraction can be obtained; and (4) A fast-Fourier transformation method can be utilized for the calculation of the long-range magnetostatic interactions. In the model, each grain is assumed to be a single crystal with crystalline anisotrophy dominant. In this chapter, we will consider only crystal grains with uniaxial crystalline anisotropy, although other types of crystalline anisotropy, such as cubic anisotropy, can be included in the model calculation. The crystalline anisotropy easy axis of each grain can be oriented in any desired direction.

5.2.2 Energy Consideration

The free energy considered in this model includes the uniaxial crystalline anisotropy energy, the magnetostatic energy, the intergranular exchange energy and the Zeeman energy.

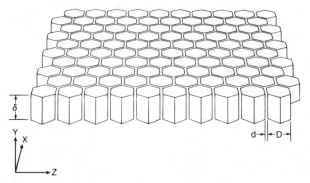

FIGURE 5.1 Illustration of 2D array of hexagons on a triangular lattice. δ is the grain height equal to the film thickness, D is the grain surface-to-surface diameter in the film plane and d is the intergranular boundary separation.

(1) *Crystalline anisotropy energy.* The uniaxial crystalline anisotropy energy density for a single crystallite (the ith grain in the array) is

$$E_{ani}(\mathbf{r}_i) = K \sin^2\theta_i, \qquad i = 1, 2, \ldots, N \tag{5.1}$$

where K is the anisotropy energy constant, θ is the angle between the easy axis orientation and the magnetization direction and N is the total number of grains in the array. In the model, it is rewritten in a vector form:

$$\begin{aligned} E_{ani}(\mathbf{r}_i) &= K \, | \, \mathbf{k}_i \times \mathbf{m}_i \, |^2 \\ &= K \, [1 - (\mathbf{k}_i \cdot \mathbf{m}_i)^2] \qquad i = 1, 2, \ldots, N \end{aligned} \tag{5.2}$$

where $\mathbf{k}$ is the unit vector along the crystalline easy axis, and $\mathbf{m}$ is the unit vector in the magnetization direction.

(2) *Magnetostatic interaction energy.* In the array, each grain interacts with all the other grains through magnetostatic interactions. For the ith grain, the magnetostatic interaction energy density averaged over the grain volume is written as:

$$E_{mag}(\mathbf{r}_i) = -\mathbf{M}_i \cdot \left[\sum_{j \neq i} D_{ij} \cdot \mathbf{M}_j + \frac{1}{2} D_{ii} \cdot M_i \right] \qquad i = 1, 2, \ldots, N \tag{5.3}$$

where the summation is over all the grains in the entire array and D_{ij} is the 3×3 interaction matrix. The matrix D_{ij} depends only on the geometric parameters of the array and is derived by integrating the magnetic poles on the surfaces of the jth grain and averaging over the volume of the ith grain, given as

$$D_{ij} = \frac{1}{v_i} \int_{v_i} d\mathbf{r}^3 \int_{s_j} d\mathbf{r}'^2 \frac{(\mathbf{r} - \mathbf{r}')\hat{n}'}{|\mathbf{r} - \mathbf{r}'|^3}. \tag{5.4}$$

where $\mathbf{r}'$ is the position vector of the position within the jth grain and $\mathbf{r}$ is the position vector within the ith grain. The self-demagnetization energy is included in the D_{ii} term. Since only the magnetization directions are to be determined, the self-demagnetization energy only gives the shape anisotropy. To avoid possible instability in the calculations caused by the component of the self-demagnetization field opposite to the magnetization direction, the term D_{ii} should be rewritten in a proper shape anisotropy form (Zhu, 1989).

(3) *Intergranular exchange coupling.* In order to describe possible exchange coupling between nearest neighboring grains through grain boundaries, an intergranular exchange coupling was introduced in a form analogous to the spin exchange energy:

$$E_{exc}(\mathbf{r}_i) = -\frac{2A^*}{M^2 a^2} \mathbf{M}_i \cdot \sum_{n.n.} \mathbf{M}_j, \qquad i = 1, 2, \ldots, N \tag{5.5}$$

where A^* is an effective exchange energy constant, M is the magnetization of each individual grain and a is the center-to-center distance between adjacent grains. The summation is over all the nearest-neighbor grains. The effective exchange energy constant A^* measures the exchange coupling between the adjacent grains and Eq. 2.5 should be considered as a phenomenological approximation.

(4) *Zeeman energy.* This energy term is due to an externally applied field and is often referred to as magnetic potential energy:

$$E_{ext}(\mathbf{r}_i) = -\mathbf{H} \cdot \mathbf{M}_i, \qquad i = 1, 2, \ldots, N \tag{5.6}$$

The total energy density of the ith grain is

$$E_{tot}(\mathbf{r}_i) = E_{ani}(\mathbf{r}_i) + E_{mag}(\mathbf{r}_i) + E_{exc}(\mathbf{r}_i) + E_{ext}(\mathbf{r}_i). \tag{5.7}$$

The effective magnetic field on the ith grain is defined as the differentiation of the energy density with respect to the magnetization:

$$\mathbf{H}_i = -\frac{\partial E_{tot}(\mathbf{r}_i)}{\partial \mathbf{M}_i}$$

$$= -\frac{\partial E_{tot}(\mathbf{r}_i)}{\partial M_i^x}\,\mathbf{e}_x + \frac{\partial E_{tot}(\mathbf{r}_i)}{\partial M_i^y}\,\mathbf{e}_y + \frac{\partial E_{tot}(\mathbf{r}_i)}{\partial M_i^z}\,\mathbf{e}_z. \tag{5.8}$$

where $\mathbf{e}_x$, $\mathbf{e}_y$, and $\mathbf{e}_z$ are unit vectors along three axes of the coordinates x, y, and z. Since the crystalline anisotropy field effectively acts like a local constraint of the magnetization orientation against the interaction fields and the external fields, it is natural to normalize the effective magnetic fields by the crystalline anisotropy field $H_k = 2K/M$ where M is the magnetization of each grain. The normalized effective field becomes

$$\mathbf{h}_i = \mathbf{H}_i/H_k$$

$$= (\mathbf{k}_i \cdot \mathbf{m}_i)\mathbf{k}_i + h_m \sum_{j=1}^{N} D_{ij} \cdot \mathbf{m}_j + h_e \sum_{n.n.} \mathbf{m}_j + \mathbf{h}_a \tag{5.9}$$

where the last term $\mathbf{h}_a = \mathbf{H}_{app}/H_k$ is the normalized external applied field. In Eq. (5.9),

$$h_m = \frac{M}{H_k} \quad \text{(cgs units)} \tag{5.10}$$

is the magnetostatic interaction field constant, measuring the magnetostatic interaction strength relative to the crystalline anisotropy constraint, and the coefficient

$$h_e = \frac{A^*}{Ka^2} \tag{5.11}$$

is the intergranular exchange coupling constant, measuring the intergranular exchange interaction strength relative to the crystalline anisotropy constraint. The symbol a is the center-to-center distance between adjacent grains, and h_e has the same form as the exchange field form used in classic micromagnetic theory (Brown, 1963) and should be considered as a first-order approximation to the exact intergranular exchange field. It is also important to point out that h_e is inversely proportional to the square of the grain diameter for zero intergranular boundary separation, so that a large grain diameter will yield a smaller intergranular exchange coupling constant with the same A^*.

5.2.3 Equation of Motion for Magnetization Orientations

The magnetization direction of a magnetic grain in the array follows the Landau-Lifshitz gyromagnetic equation of motion. The field each grain experiences is the effective magnetic field defined in Eq. (5.8). For an array with a total of N grains, there are N vectorial first-order differential equations coupled by the magnetostatic interaction field and the intergranular exchange field. The time integration of coupled equations

$$\frac{d\mathbf{M}_i}{dt} = \gamma \mathbf{M}_i \times \mathbf{H}_i - \frac{\lambda}{M} \mathbf{M}_i \times (\mathbf{M}_i \times \mathbf{H}), \quad i = 1, 2, \ldots, N \qquad (5.12)$$

gives magnetization configurations during a magnetization process. For simplicity, we can write this set of equations in a reduced form by introducing a reduced time $\tau = t\gamma H_k$ and a reduced damping constant $\alpha = \lambda/\gamma$:

$$\frac{d\mathbf{m}_i}{dt} = \mathbf{m}_i \times \mathbf{h}_i - \alpha \mathbf{m}_i \times (\mathbf{m}_i \times \mathbf{h}_i), \quad i = 1, 2, \ldots, N \qquad (5.13)$$

In some other similar models introduced previously, the Gilbert form is utilized instead (Victora, 1987a, 1987b; Mansuripur and McDaniel, 1988). It is easy to show that the Gilbert equation and Landau-Lifshtz equation are mathematically identical. The difference is that, in the Gilbert equation, the gyromagnetic motion correlates with the damping motion of the magnetization direction and the damping rate becomes limited (Hass and Callen, 1963).

Equation (5.13) is a dissipative equation and the energy dissipation rate is proportional to α. In a static external field, the stable static solutions of Eq. (5.13) are local energy minima. The main essence of this modeling study is to find the path, or paths, taken to reach some of these energy minima, i.e., to identify the physical transient magnetization processes from an initial static state to a new static state, as the external field varies. It has been found that for an infinitely slowly changing external field, suitable to simulations of hysteresis loops, calculated results are relatively insensitive to the change of the reduced damping constant α (Victora, 1987b; Zhu and Bertram, 1988a). However, if the applied field changes rapidly, the reduced damping constant could be important to the outcome. For all the calculation results presented here, the reduced damping constant was chosen in the range of $\alpha = 0.1$ to $\alpha = 1$.

5.3 MAGNETIZATION PROCESSES AND HYSTERESIS PROPERTIES

In this section, the fundamental magnetization process and resulting hysteresis properties of the films are discussed. Most of the longitudinal thin-film media are planar isotropic: i.e., the macroscopic magnetic properties are isotropic in the film plane. The discussion will be limited to two types of planar isotropic films in which the crystalline easy axes of the grains are randomly oriented either (a) in three dimensions (3D-random) or (b) in the film plane (2D-random). The calculation array contains 64×64 grains, corresponding to an approximate $2 \ \mu m \times 1.7 \ \mu m$ area with $D = 300 \text{Å}$ assumed.

Figure 5.2 shows two calculated hysteresis loops for a 3D-random film. With $h_m = 0$ and $h_e = 0$, the hysteresis loop (dashed curve) corresponds to an assembly of noninteracting Stoner-Wohlfarth particles with the coercivity around $0.48H_k$. Introduction of magnetostatic interaction with $h_m = 0.3$ and $h_e = 0$, yields an increase of the saturation remanence and a reduction of coercivity. The hysteresis loop becomes "squared-up".

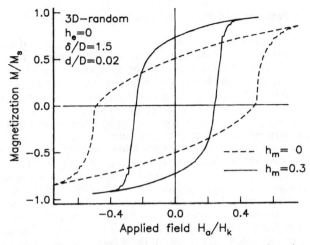

FIGURE 5.2 Calculated hysteresis loops for 3D-random planar isotropic films. The dashed curve represents result with no interactions: $h_m = 0$ and $h_e = 0$; the solid curve represents the result with only magnetostatic interaction: $h_m = 0.3$ and $h_e = 0$.

Figure 5.3 shows the effect of intergranular exchange coupling by showing hysteresis loops with (solid) and without (dashed) intergranular exchange coupling. The intergranular exchange coupling yields a further increase of the remanence and a further reduction of the coercivity and also causes much higher coercive squareness S^*.

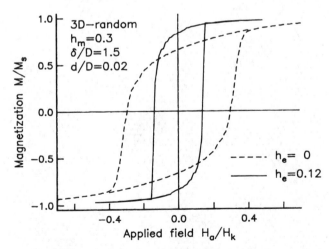

FIGURE 5.3 Calculated hysteresis loops for 3D-random planar isotropic films. The dashed curve represents the case with only magnetostatic interaction: $h_m = 0.3$ and $h_e = 0$; the solid curve represents the result with both types of interactions: $h_m = 0.3$ and $h_e = 0.1$.

5.3.1 Ripple Patterns and Magnetization Remanence

In planar isotropic thin films, even though the orientations of crystalline anisotropy easy axes are random, at the saturation remanent state the magnetizations of grains usually deviate from the local anisotropy easy axes due to the interactions in the film. The magnetization of the film forms a ripple-cluster pattern. A typical magnetization configuration at the saturation remanent state is shown in Fig. 5.4, simulated with $h_m = 0.4$ and $h_e = 0.1$. The local coherence of the magnetization orientation is apparent: a cluster of grains has a common magnetization orientation and large changes of the magnetization direction occur between adjacent clusters. Along the initial saturation direction, cluster magnetization directions alternate signs in the transverse direction with apparent quasi-periodicity: the magnetization "ripples" in the film. This cluster-ripple structure characterizes the saturation remanent state in the planar isotropic films and produces a "feather-like" Fresnel-mode Lorentz electron-microscope image (Chen, 1981; Zhu, 1989). The ripple pattern is the net result of both the randomly oriented crystalline easy axes and magnetostatic interactions among the grains. The intergranular exchange coupling results in an increase of the cluster size as well as an increase of the wavelengths in the quasi-periodicity along the initial saturation direction (Zhu, 1989; Beardsley et al., 1990; Duan et al., 1990). The resulting saturation squareness as a function of h_m and a function of h_e is plotted in Fig. 5.5 and Fig. 5.6, respectively. An initial increase of h_m results in an increase of the squareness for both 2D-random and 3D-random cases. However, if the magnetostatic interaction strength is much stronger than the local crystalline anisotropy field, large angles occur between the magnetizations of adjacent clusters, resulting in the local closure of magnetization flux which, in turn, could lead to

FIGURE 5.4 A typical magnetization pattern at the saturation remanent state for a 3D-random planar isotropic film with $h_m = 0.4$ and $h_e = 0.1$ (*Zhu and Bertram 1991c*).

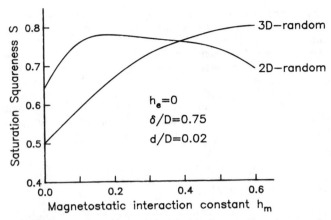

FIGURE 5.5 Squareness vs. magnetostatic interaction field constant h_m for the 3D-random case.

the formation of magnetization vortices at the saturation remanent state. By comparison, increasing the intergranular exchange coupling only yields a monotonic increase of the saturation squareness along with a decrease of the angles between the magnetization directions of adjacent clusters.

5.3.2 Magnetization Process

Through a series of simulation studies (Zhu and Bertram, 1988a, 1991b, and 1991c; Zhu, 1989), it was found that a magnetization reversal process in planar isotropic longitudinal thin films can be characterized by the formation of magnetization vortices at the beginning of the reversal, followed by vortex motion and the expansion of

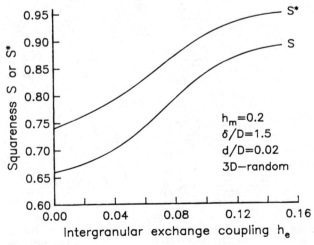

FIGURE 5.6 Squareness vs. intergranular exchange coupling constant h_e for the 3D-random case.

reversed regions, and ending with annihilations of the magnetization vortices. The formation and motion of the vortices lead to the formation and expansion of reverse domains.

(1) *Vortex formation and motion and elongated reverse domains.* The ripple structure at the saturation remanent state not only leads to the formation of a single vortex but also leads to a collective formation of a series of vortices along the applied reverse field direction and results in an elongated reverse domain. (The term "domain" here is loosely defined as compared with the concept of domains in soft magnetic films.) Figure 5.7 demonstrates a typical formation process of an elongated reversed domain for a film with zero intergranular exchange coupling: h_m

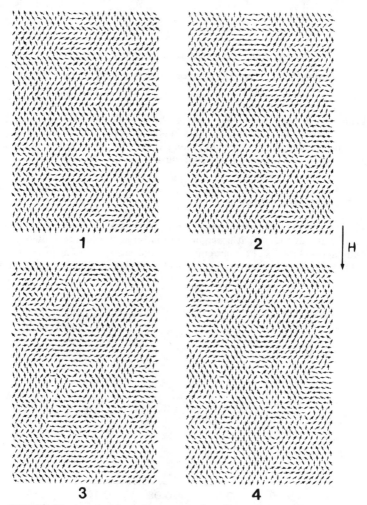

FIGURE 5.7   A typical formation process of an elongated reverse domain for a nonexchange coupled case, $h_e = 0$ and $h_m = 0.6$. The magnetization configurations 1–4 correspond to four static states along a major hysteresis loop at increasing external reversal field values (*Zhu and Bertram, 1991b*).

= 0.6 and h_e = 0. At a small applied reverse field, the ripple structure develops into a series of alternating "⊂" and "⊃" patterns (picture 1–2). At a larger field value, the "⊂" and "⊃" series evolves to a series of vortices along the field direction, with adjacent vortices having opposite senses of rotation (picture 3). Further increasing the reversal field results in transverse motion of the vortices. Vortices with opposite sense of rotation move in opposite directions and the reversed region in between expands, resulting in the reverse domain being elongated along the field direction (picture 4). Each side boundary of the reversed domain contains a series of vortices having the same sense of rotation. Since in the films with zero intergranular exchange coupling vortex motion distance is always very limited, the elongated reverse domains are narrow (only slightly larger than vortex diameters) and densely formed, narrow, elongated domains characterize the magnetization pattern around the coercive state. A reversal process calculated with h_m = 0.3 and h_e = 0 is shown in Fig. 5.8, with the gray scale representing the magnetization component in the direction of the external field. Elongation of the reverse domains (dark regions) along the field direction can be clearly seen and, near the coercive state, the magnetization pattern shows densely distributed elongated domains, characteristic of nonexchange coupled films.

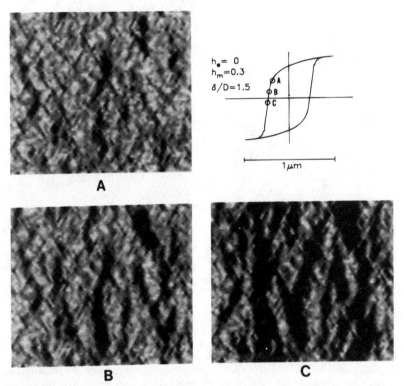

FIGURE 5.8 Magnetization patterns of three static states along a major hysteresis loop for h_e = 0 and h_m = 0.3. The gray scale represents the magnetization component along the external field direction with *full bright* for the magnetization in the initial saturation direction and *full dark* for the direction parallel to the external reversal field (*Zhu and Bertram, 1991b*).

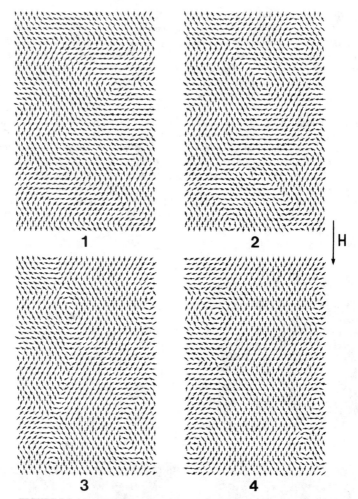

FIGURE 5.9   A typical formation process of an elongated reverse domain for a strongly exchange coupled case, $h_e = 0.2$ and $h_m = 0.3$. Pictures 1–4 represent a single transient process during a magnetization reversal with the external reversal field remaining constant (*Zhu and Bertram 1991b*).

For films with intergranular exchange coupling, the essential features in the formation of an elongated reverse domain remain the same as in the case of zero intergranular exchange coupling. However, the separation of the vortices in the domain boundaries significantly increases with an increase of the intergranular exchange coupling strength, which is a natural consequence of increased wavelengths in the ripple structure due to the exchange coupling. In between the adjacent vortices along each boundary of the domain, magnetization cross-tie structure becomes evident, similar to the cross-tie structure observed in soft films but with much smaller scale (Methfessel et al., 1960). In films with relatively strong intergranular exchange coupling ($h_e > 0.15$), vortex motion usually follows the formation of an elongated domain without increasing the external reversal field and the motion of the vortices in a domain boundary becomes collective, leading to the significant expansion of a reversed domain. The domain expansion through the collective motion of the vortices in the domain boundaries dominates the reversal process and large areas of the film reverse by the expansion. A typical formation-expansion process for a strongly exchange coupled film ($h_e = 0.2$ and $h_m = 0.3$) is shown in Fig. 5.9. However, the collective vortex motion in the domain boundaries are not as coherent as the wall motion in soft magnetic films since the spatial variation of the local crystalline anisotropy field is still comparable to both the magnetostatic and the intergranular exchange interaction fields. Magnetization reversal by domain expansion in exchange-coupled films results in high (nearly unity) coercive squareness and relatively low coercivity (as compared with the crystalline anisotropy field H_k).

The collective magnetization process resulting from magnetostatic and intergranular exchange interactions significantly changes the hysteresis properties in comparison with the behavior of non-interacting Stoner-Wohlfarth particles. An increase of the magnetostatic interaction strength results in a decrease of film coercivity as shown in Fig. 5.10 for both 2D-random and 3D-random cases. The formation of magnetization vortices driven by magnetostatic interactions causes local irreversible magnetization reversals to occur at a smaller external reversal field compared with the case without magnetostatic interaction. In exchange-coupled films, magnetization reversal in large areas in the film is realized through the expansion of reversed domains by vortex motion. Coercivity significantly decreases with increasing intergranular exchange coupling (Fig. 5.11); at the same time, the coercive squareness significantly increases.

5.3.3 Hysteresis Properties and Film Microstructures

The change of microstructural parameters, such as intergranular boundary separation and film thickness, alters the magnetostatic interaction strength, thereby chang-

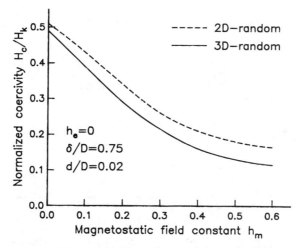

FIGURE 5.10 Coercivity vs. magnetostatic interaction field constant h_m for nonexchange coupled 2D-random (dashed curve) and 3D-random (solid curve) films ($h_e = 0$) (*Bertram and Zhu, 1992*).

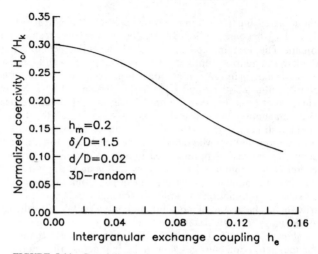

FIGURE 5.11 Coercivity vs. intergranular exchange coupling constant h_e for the 3D-random case. Similar behavior is also obtained for the 2D-random case (*Bertram and Zhu, 1992*).

ing the hysteresis behavior. In general, coercivity decreases with increasing film thickness, as shown in Fig. 5.12, which has been observed in experimental studies (Arnoldussen, 1986). It is important to emphasize here that the coercivity decreases with increasing film thickness are the result of increasing magnetostatic interaction in the film, comparable to the effect of increasing film saturation magnetization. The magnetization processes in the film become more collective with increasing film thickness, thereby reducing film coercivity.

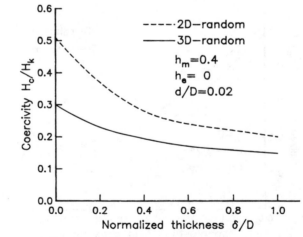

FIGURE 5.12 Calculated coercivity vs. normalized film thickness δ/D for zero intergranular exchange coupling with $h_m = 0.4$ and $d/D = 0.02$ are used in the calculation. Exchange coupled films also show similar trend (*Zhu and Bertram, 1988a*).

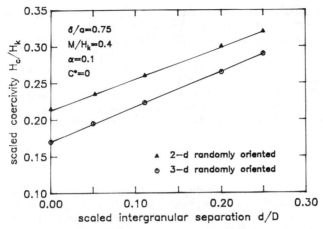

FIGURE 5.13 Coercivity as a function of scaled intergranular boundary separation d/D for 2D-random and 3D-random cases with zero intergranular exchange coupling. The grain height-to-diameter ratio is kept at a constant: $\delta/D = 0.75$ (*Zhu and Bertram, 1988a*).

Figure 5.13 shows the calculated coercivity as a function of intergranular boundary separation while keeping the intergranular exchange coupling zero at all time. With increasing separation, the film coercivity increases due to the reduction of magnetostatic interaction strength in the film.

Because of the microstructure dependence of film coercivity, spatial variation of either film thickness, or intergranular boundary separation will modulate the coercivity in a film disk, and consequently yields modulation noise of recorded transitions.

For films with zero intergranular exchange coupling, the hysteresis properties depend only on the ratio of the film thickness to grain diameter δ/D and the ratio of intergranular boundary separation to grain diameter d/D. The hysteresis properties are independent of the actual value of grain diameter D, provided that D is not so small that superparamagnetic behavior occurs and not so large that the grain becomes multidomain. However, if the intergranular exchange coupling is non-zero, the hysteresis properties would depend on the actual value of grain diameter D since, to the first order approximation, the intergranular exchange coupling constant h_e is inversely proportional to the square of grain diameter D (as discussed in Sec. 2) and changing h_e significantly changes hysteresis properties. Because the coercivity increases with decreasing the intergranular exchange coupling constant h_e, increasing grain diameter D yields an increase of film coercivity. Such coercivity behavior has been observed experimentally (Arnoldussen, 1986; Johnson et al., 1990).

5.4 TRANSITION NOISE AND FILM MICROSTRUCTURE

Transition noise is a major factor limiting recording densities, and the micromagnetic simulation model has been utilized to study this phenomenon. In this section, we review the noise properties in longitudinal thin-film media and their correlations with film microstructure. Medium noise in perpendicular thin-film media will be discussed separately in Sec. 8 of this chapter.

In micromagnetic modeling, transition noise is analyzed through the simulation of multiple transitions, each with a different spatial arrangement of the grain crystalline easy axes, mimicking recording at different locations of a medium. The simulated transitions form an assembly, usually consisting of a number of transitions, $N \geq 80$, for statistical analysis of their properties, i.e., medium noise properties. The cross-track averaged magnetization is calculated by averaging the calculated magnetization pattern $M(x, z)$ in the cross-track direction:

$$M(x) = \frac{1}{W} \int_{W/2}^{W/2} M(x, z)dz \qquad (5.14)$$

where the x-axis is along the recording track direction and the z-axis is in the cross-track direction. For the transition profile $M(x)$, only the magnetization component along the track direction (x component) is analyzed. The simulation array contains 64×128 grains, equivalent to a 3.6 μm long and 2 μm wide recording track with $D = 300\overset{\circ}{A}$. The mean transition profile of the transition assembly is

$$<M(x)> = \frac{1}{n} \sum_{i=1}^{n} M_i(x), \qquad (5.15)$$

and the variance of the transition profile ensemble is

$$<\Delta M^2>(x) = \frac{1}{(n-1)} \sum_{i=1}^{n} [M_i - <M(x)>]^2 \qquad (5.16)$$

The ensemble variance of the transition profiles gives the nonstationary spatial distribution of the medium noise. Averaging the variance over the distance of a bit length gives the total noise power, corresponding to the measured integrated noise power, as follows:

$$NP = \frac{1}{M_s^2 B} \int_{x_c - B/2}^{x_c + B/2} <\Delta M^2(x)>dx \qquad (5.17)$$

where x_c is the mean transition center position. The integrated variance of the transition profiles resembles the total noise power as measured on a spectrum analyzer since

$$\int_{-\infty}^{+\infty} |\Delta M(x)|^2 dx = \int_{-\infty}^{+\infty} |\Delta \hat{M}(k)|^2 dk. \qquad (5.18)$$

5.4.1 Reverse DC-Erase Noise and the Basis of Transition Noise Nonstationarity

Medium noise arises from spatial magnetization fluctuations. In longitudinal thin-film media, the medium noise is always the lowest at the saturation state due to good uniformity of the films. Away from saturation, the noise is a function of the magnetization level as well as the magnetization process by which the state is reached. For a reverse dc-erase process with a spatially uniform external field (a process that follows the remanent hysteresis loop), theoretical analyses (Silva and Bertram, 1990; Zhu, 1992a) show that medium noise power as defined in Eq. (5.17), follows a parabolic relation with the magnetization level:

$$NP(<m>) = \frac{s}{WM_s^2} (M_s^2 - M^2)$$

$$= \frac{s}{W} (1 - <m>^2) + \frac{s}{WM_r^2} (M_s^2 - M_r^2) \qquad (5.19)$$

where $<m> = <M>/M_r$ is the normalized mean magnetization and s is the cross-track correlation length which measures the fundamental scale of the spatial magnetization fluctuation in the cross-track direction (Silva and Bertram, 1990). The first term in Eq. (5.19) describes the parabolic dependence of the medium noise as a function of the magnetization level and the second term is the noise level at the saturation remanent state.

At the remanent coercive state, where the mean magnetization becomes zero, after subtracting the noise level at the saturation remanent state, the normalized noise power is equal to the ratio between the cross-track correlation length and track width. The cross-track correlation length characterizes the effective width of the reverse domains elongated in the applied field direction (Sec. 5.3.3). The wider the elongated domains are in the reverse dc-erased state, the larger the noise value for a given head track width. Figure 5.14 shows the micromagnetic simulation results for films with three different intergranular exchange-coupling strengths. The curves in the figure are the parabolic fits with s as a fitting parameter. Increasing the intergranular exchange coupling yields a significant increase of medium noise, due to the width increase of the reverse domains (Zhu, 1991).

The cross-track correlation length s can be experimentally measured on a spin-

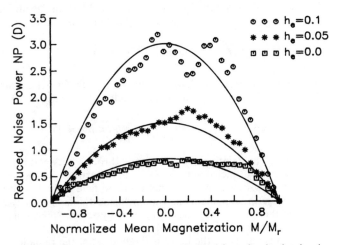

FIGURE 5.14 Medium noise power calculated from the simulated series of magnetization states along a reversed dc erase process for three films with different intergranular exchange coupling strengths. The solid curves are fitting parabolas, approximately matching the calculation data (symbols) for each case.

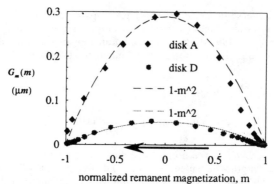

FIGURE 5.15 Experimentally measured noise power for a series of magnetization states along a reversed dc erase process for two typical film disks with very different noise behavior. The dashed curves are fitting parabolas, well matching measurement data (symbols) in each case (*Hsu et al., 1992b*).

stand tester (Silva and Bertram, 1991; Tarnopolsky et al., 1991; Hsu et al., 1992*b*; Lin and Bertram, 1993). The carefully designed measurement of the reverse dc-erase noise, performed by Hsu et al., 1992*a*, confirms the parabolic noise dependence given by Eq. (5.19). Figure 5.15 shows the measured reverse dc-erase noise power as a function of the magnetization. Two film media with different noise behavior were used in the measurement. As shown in Fig. 5.15, the results for both media well fit the parabolic dependence, although the cross-track correlation lengths of the two media shown in the figure are very different.

In a reverse dc-erase noise measurement, since the magnetization level is a function of the field in the medium given by the remanent hysteresis loop, the noise power can be expressed as a function of the total field in the medium. If the remanent hysteresis loop can be expressed as a hyperbolic tangent function:

$$M(H) = M_r \tanh \left(\frac{H \pm H_{c,r}}{\Delta H_c} \right) \tag{5.20}$$

where $H_{c,r}$ is the remanent coercivity, ΔH_c is equivalent to the switching-field distribution and the choice of + or − sign depends on field polarity, Eq. (5.19) becomes

$$NP(<m>) = C \, \frac{d < M(H)>}{dH} + NP(<m> = 1) \tag{5.21}$$

where C is a constant. This relation has been found through both cellular automata modeling and experimental measurements (Zhu and Bertram, 1991*a*; Hsu et al., 1992*a*). Figure 5.16 shows the comparison between the field derivative of the measured remanent hysteresis loop dM/dH and the measured noise power $G(H)$. They fit excellently, even though the measured remanent hysteresis loops only approximately follow a hyperbolic tangent function.

In a reverse dc-erase process, the noise is the highest at the remanent coercive state ($<m> = 0$), since the oppositely magnetized "domains" yield spatial fluctuations of magnetic flux density. The magnetization level dependence of the medium noise is the basis for the nonstationarity of the transition noise. For an isolated transition, the noise is the lowest away from the transition since the magnetization

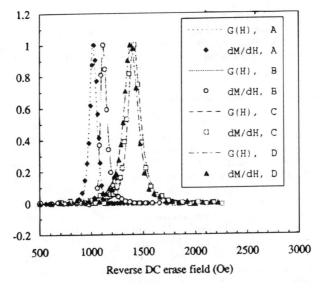

FIGURE 5.16 Comparison between field derivative of the measured remanent hysteresis loop and measured medium noise power for four different film disks. The excellent agreement for each disk confirms Eq. 5.21 (*Hsu et al., 1992a*).

level is near the saturation magnetization and is highest at the transition center where the cross-track averaged magnetization is zero, or near zero (Zhu and Bertram, 1988a; Zhu, 1992b; Bertram and Che, 1993; Arnoldussen and Zhu, 1994). However, the exact noise distribution within an isolated transition could differ from Eq. (5.19) since, within the transition, the magnetization changes rapidly over a very short distance and magnetic interactions within the transition could very well modify the magnetization dependence of the noise-power distribution (Zhu and Wang, 1995).

The noise in thin-film media depends on magnetization level, but also on the magnetization process, since different magnetization processes yield different magnetization configurations. For example, the medium noise at the remanent coercive state is usually higher than that of the ac-demagnetized state even though the mean magnetization is zero for both states. This is due to the fact that the oppositely magnetized "domains" in the film are usually much narrower or finer in the ac-demagnetized state than in the remanent coercive state (Zhu and Bertram, 1991a; Tarnopolsky et al., 1991). Here the ac-demagnetized state is defined as the medium being demagnetized with a damped ac field.

Surface roughness of film disks, such as textured grooves, can result in modulation noise (Bertram et al., 1986). The modulation noise has different properties from the noise resulting from the medium micromagnetic fluctuations discussed above. The noise power of the magnetization variation due to the surface roughness has the following dependence for the reverse dc-erase process (Bertram et al., 1986):

$$NP(<m>) \propto \left[\frac{d < M(H) >}{dH} \right]^2 \tag{5.22}$$

which is quadratic rather than linear as in the case of noise by intrinsic micromagnetic fluctuations (Eq. 5.21). If the modulation noise is comparable to the medium noise in a disk, one can obtain the weighting of each type of noise by measuring reverse dc-erase noise and fitting with Eqs. (5.21) and (5.22).

5.4.2 Noise of Recorded Transitions

Since the medium noise concentrates at the transition region where magnetization is far lower than saturation, it is referred to as *transition noise*. Using micromagnetic modeling, recorded transitions were calculated by simulating the actual recording process with the head field applied. Figure 5.17 shows a vector magnetization pattern of a recorded transition in a highly oriented film. Each vector in the figure represents the magnetization orientation of a single magnetic grain in the film. As shown in the figure, the magnetization is rather uniform away from the transition while magnetization in the transition center is characterized by a zig-zag pattern mainly resulting from minimizing the magnetostatic energy. This zig-zag transition pattern has been observed in many highly oriented thin-film media, such as highly oriented CoSm media (Kullmann, 1984) and obliquely evaporated FeCoCr films (Arnoldussen and Tong, 1986). Figure 5.18 shows a simulated transition pattern in a typical planar isotropic thin-film media. Away from the transition center, the magnetization exhibits a ripple pattern. At the center of the transition, the magnetization vectors form vortices, characteristic for the planar isotropic films. The vortex pattern at transition centers was first observed in CoRm films (Chen, 1981).

The zig-zag patterns in oriented films and vortex patterns in planar isotropic films yield fluctuations around transition centers. Since the track width is always finite, the ratio of the cross-track scale of each zig or zag width, or the diameter of the magnetization vortices, to the track width determines the transition noise in reproduce voltage pulses. The cross-track correlation length s in Eq. (5.19) becomes a statistical measure of the zig-zag cross-track scale or the diameter of the magnetization vortices (Zhu, 1989; Che and Bertram, 1993).

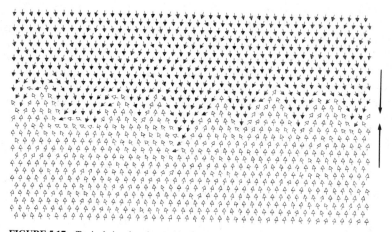

FIGURE 5.17 Typical simulated transition pattern in a highly oriented longitudinal film media. The transition boundary shows the well-known zig-zag structure.

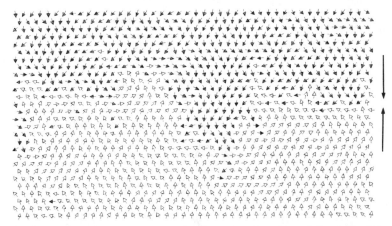

FIGURE 5.18 Typical simulated transition pattern in a planar isotropic longitudinal film media. The transition boundary consists of magnetization vortices.

5.4.3 Effect of Out-of-Plane Easy Axes Orientation

It has been suggested that out-of-plane easy axes orientation could yield a reduction of transition noise. However, micromagnetic modeling analysis shows that there is little difference in the transition noise properties between the case in which the crystalline easy axes of the grains in the film are randomly oriented in three dimensions (3D random), and the case in which the easy axes are randomly oriented only within the film plane (2D random). (The 2D random easy axes orientation can be achieved in disks by means of epitaxial growth of a magnetic film on a properly deposited polycrystalline underlayer.) The simulation study demonstrates that what really affects transition noise is the intergranular exchange coupling in the films (Bertram and Zhu, 1992). Figure 5.19 shows the calculated mean transition profiles and corresponding ensemble variance for the 2D and 3D cases with and without intergranular exchange coupling. The perpendicular component of the crystalline easy axes does not seem to affect the transition noise behavior while the reduction of intergranular exchange coupling significantly reduces the transition noise.

5.4.4 Effect of Intergranular Exchange Coupling

As shown in Fig. 5.19, intergranular exchange coupling significantly enhances the transition noise. In oriented thin-film media, the intergranular exchange coupling significantly increases the cross-track scale of the zig-zag patterns and, in planar isotropic films, the intergranular exchange coupling yields vortices with much larger diameters. Figures 5.20 (*a*) and (*b*) show the magnetization vector patterns for transitions in planar isotropic films with and without intergranular exchange coupling respectively; the h_m values have been adjusted for each case so that the transition lengths are similar. The effect of intergranular exchange coupling is very pronounced. The larger size vortices at the transition center in the exchange-coupled case yield a substantial increase of the transition noise. Figure 5.21 shows the integrated noise power as a function of intergranular exchange coupling

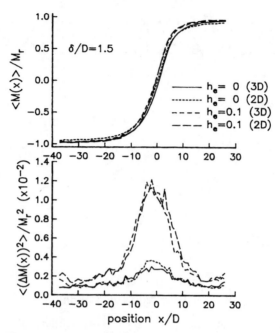

FIGURE 5.19 Ensemble mean and variance of the transition profiles for planar isotropic longitudinal thin films for different intergranular exchange coupling and both 2D and 3D random easy axis orientations (*Bertram and Zhu, 1991*).

strength h_e. Increasing intergranular exchange coupling yields a significant increase of the transition noise.

In planar isotropic films, the effect of intergranular exchange coupling can be more clearly seen if the magnetization component along the recording direction is shown. Figures 5.22(*a*) and (*b*) show two gray scale plots of typical transition patterns for the exchange-coupled case, and the case with zero intergranular exchange coupling, respectively. The gray scale here represents the magnetization component in the recording direction with full bright for $+M_s$ and full dark for $-M_s$. In the exchange-coupled case, the cross-track scale of irregular transition boundaries is large, thereby producing high transition noise. In the nonexchange-coupled case, the transition boundary is formed by narrow fingers which yield many small fluctuations in the cross-track averaged magnetization profiles.

The intergranular exchange coupling enhances the collectiveness of the magnetic moments of the grains in the film during a magnetization process. It resists rapid spatial variation of the magnetization orientations, thereby resulting in large-scale zig-zag transition boundaries in highly oriented thin-films, or large magnetization vortices at the transitions in planar isotropic films.

5.4.5 Noise of Interacting Transitions at High Recording Densities

Since the medium noise mainly concentrates at transitions, the integrated noise power, a measure of the noise power averaged over a unit distance, increases

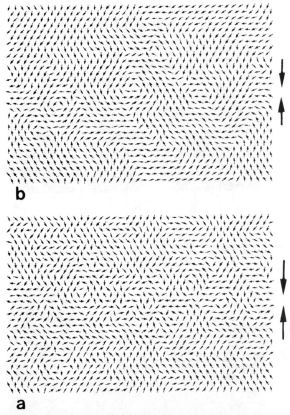

FIGURE 5.20 Typical simulated transition magnetization configurations for (a) the nonexchange coupled case: $h_e = 0$ and $h_m = 0.52$ and (b) the exchange coupled case: $h_e = 0.1$ and $h_m = 0.4$.

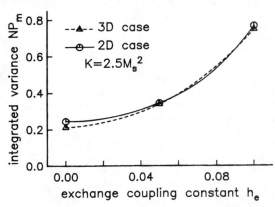

FIGURE 5.21 Integrated noise power as a function of intergranular exchange coupling for both 2D and 3D cases (*Zhu, 1992*).

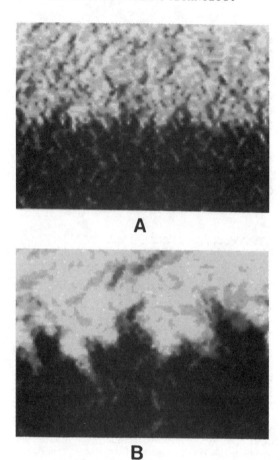

FIGURE 5.22 Typical simulated transition patterns in planar isotropic films for the exchange coupled case (A) $h_e = 0.1$ and the non-exchange coupled case (B) $h_e = 0$. The gray scale represents the magnetization component in the recording direction.

linearly with increasing recording density when the bit length is much longer than the transition length. However, for most longitudinal thin-film media, at high densities where adjacent transitions become interactive the noise power increases more rapidly than the initial noise increase at low densities. Such noise increase at high recording densities is often referred to as *supralinear.* Recent experimental measurements show that the onset of supralinear noise increase coincides with the onset of nonlinear bit shift and nonlinear partial erasure (Zhu et al., 1995).

Micromagnetic modeling studies have shown that the supralinear noise increase at high recording densities results from microscopic magnetic interactions between adjacent transitions during the recording process. It has been found that in planar isotropic films, the intergranular exchange coupling is the most important parameter in the medium resulting in the supralinear noise increase, although other medium microstructure parameters also affect the noise behavior at high recording densities. In the micromagnetic modeling study, the noise of interacting transitions has been studied through simulation of the recording of dibit transition pairs, since a dibit represents the most basic form of interacting transitions. The interbit interval B was varied to study the noise dependence on the recording density. Figure 5.23 shows the calculated ensemble mean and variance of the simulated dibit transition pairs for films with and without intergranular exchange coupling at a small bit interval. In all cases, the noise is highest at the center of the transitions, but the transition noise in the exchange-coupled case is substantially higher than in the nonexchange-coupled case. Furthermore, for the exchange-coupled film, the variance at the second transition, recorded in the presence of the first, is significantly higher than that at the first one. The magnetic interaction arising from the first transition results in the second transition becoming much more noisy. However, such noise enhancement does not occur in the case of zero intergranular exchange coupling. Figure 5.24 plots the integrated noise power for the second transition (the variance averaged over the bit interval B around the second transition) as a function of the inverse interbit interval. For the exchange coupled case ($h_e = 0.1$) at large bit intervals, the variance of the second transition is similar to that of the first one and is essentially independent of interbit interval. At small bit intervals, the noise of the second transition significantly increases, yielding the supralinear increase of the transition noise. For the nonexchange-coupled case, the supralinear noise increase at small bit intervals is virtually absent.

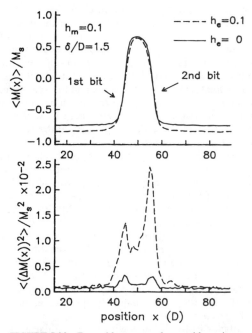

FIGURE 5.23 Ensemble mean and ensemble variance of simulated dibit transition profiles for $h_e = 0.1$ (dashed curve) and $h_e = 0$ (solid curve). The dibit transition interval is $B/D = 11$ where D is the diameter of each grain in the film.

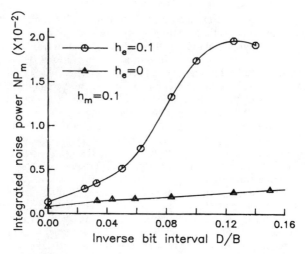

FIGURE 5.24 Variance integrated over the second transition in the dibit transition pair vs. normalized inverse bit interval. For the exchange coupled case, the supralinear increase of the integrated variance at small bit intervals is evident (*Zhu, 1991*).

The effect of intertransition interactions on transition noise can be understood by analyzing the simulated micromagnetic patterns for the dibit transitions. Figure 5.25(*a*) shows the gray-scale plot of a typical simulated dibit-transition pattern of an exchange-coupled film. In this case, the transition boundaries are irregular and the scale in the cross-track direction is large. Considering the recording of the second transition in the presence of the first, the demagnetization field arising from the first transition significantly fluctuates across the track and the spatial scale of the fluctuation follows the spatial scale of the irregular transition boundary of the first transition. The cross-track fluctuating demagnetizing field as well as the intergranular exchange field significantly enhances the irregularity of the second transition. Consequently, the second transition becomes noisier.

Figure 5.25(*b*) shows the gray-scale plot of a dibit transition for the nonexchange-coupled film. In this case, the transition boundaries are characterized by a narrow fingered structure. The demagnetization field arising from the first transition does not fluctuate in the cross-track direction due to the narrowness of the fingers, thus it does not enlarge the irregularity of the second transition and yields no noise enhancement.

At small bit intervals, the transition boundaries percolate due to the overlapping of adjacent transitions. Figures 5.26(*a*) and (*b*) show the dibit transitions at a small bit interval for the exchange-coupled and nonexchange-coupled cases respectively. In both cases, the transition boundaries are percolated. For the exchange-coupled case, the percolated region shows wide irregular percolation channels and large island domains while, for the nonexchange-coupled case, the percolated region remains a narrow-fingered structure.

In summary, in planar isotropic films with intergranular exchange coupling not only is the noise of isolated transitions high, but noise is significantly enhanced at small bit intervals due to intertransition interactions. Reducing the intergranular exchange coupling will substantially decrease the transition noise at high recording densities.

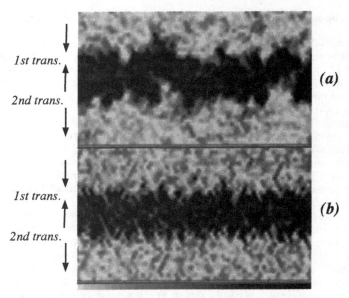

1st trans.

2nd trans.

(a)

1st trans.

2nd trans.

(b)

FIGURE 5.25 Gray scale plot of the simulated magnetization patterns of dibit transition pair at bit interval $B \approx 6a_o$ (a_o is the transition length) for (a) $h_e = 0.1$ and (b) $h_e = 0$ (*Zhu, 1991*).

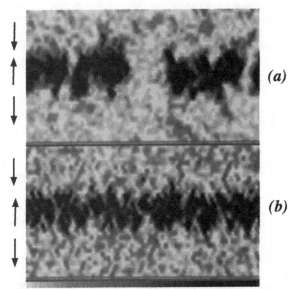

(a)

(b)

FIGURE 5.26 Gray scale plot of the simulated magnetization patterns of dibit transition pair at bit interval $B \approx 4a_o$ (a_o is the transition length) for (a) $h_e = 0.1$ and (b) $h_e = 0$ (*Zhu, 1991*).

5.4.6 Dependence on Film Saturation Magnetization and Thickness

Since the thickness of practical longitudinal thin-film media is usually smaller than 50 nm, the magnetization can be considered uniform through the film depth. The product of saturation magnetization M_s and film thickness δ measures the surface-area magnetic-moment density of the medium. The higher the $M_s\delta$ value, the stronger is the magnetostatic interaction among the grains in a medium. Therefore, transition noise is a strong function of both M_s and δ.

Figure 5.27 shows the calculated integrated noise power as a function of reverse interbit interval for films with three different saturation magnetizations while keeping other medium parameters the same (Zhu, 1993). Reducing film saturation magnetization yields a reduction of transition noise at low densities (the initial slope of the curve is smaller) and shifts the onset of the supralinear noise increase to smaller bit intervals (higher recording densities). In this calculation, a small intergranular exchange-coupling value is assumed for all three films, since practical thin film-media always have a certain degree of intergranular exchange coupling.

Analysis of the corresponding simulated transition magnetization patterns provides a physical explanation for the effect of film saturation magnetization. For the films with higher M_s, not only does the transition region become broader (i.e., the transition length increases) but the spatial scale of the irregularities of the transition boundaries in the cross-track direction become greater as well. Namely the cross-track correlation length becomes larger, and the noise power integrated over as transition increases with increasing M_s. In addition, since the magnetostatic interaction strength is proportional to M_s, at higher M_s, adjacent transitions will start to interact at a longer bit interval, giving rise to supralinear noise.

Reducing film thickness while keeping other medium intrinsic parameters unchanged has a similar effect to reducing film saturation magnetization. Figure 5.28 shows the calculated noise power as a function of inverse bit interval for two film thickness values. The thinner film exhibits smaller transition noise and the onset of the supralinear noise occurs at a smaller bit interval compared with the thicker film. In addition, reducing film thickness results in an effective reduction in head-

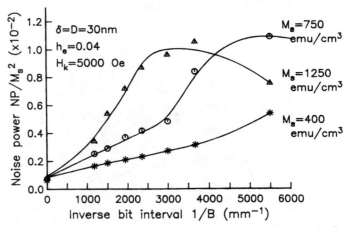

FIGURE 5.27 Calculated integrated noise power vs. recording density for three different film saturation magnetization values. The symbols are calculation results with the curves guiding the eye (*Zhu, 1993*).

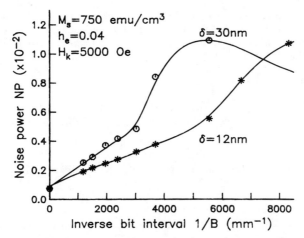

FIGURE 5.28 Calculated integrated noise power vs. recording density for two different film thicknesses (*Zhu, 1993*).

medium spacing. If the flying height is small, this effective spacing reduction can lead to a higher field gradient, leading to sharper transitions and lower medium noise (see a later subsection).

In summary, reducing either the film saturation magnetization or film thickness should yield reduction of medium noise and shift the onset of superlinear noise to higher densities. These predictions have been confirmed by various experiments (Johnson et al., 1993; Doerner et al., 1993; Zhu et al., 1995). With the introduction of magnetoresistive heads, the $M_r\delta$ product of the film media can be reduced, thanks to the high sensitivity of the MR heads. If the other intrinsic medium parameters can be kept the same, the low $M_r\delta$ media will have lower medium noise, enabling higher recording densities to be achieved.

5.4.7 Effect of Magnetic Orientation Along the Recording Direction

Mainly for tribological reasons, film disk substrates usually are textured. Magnetic films deposited on circumferentially textured substrates often become anisotropic: the hysteresis loops of the films along the texturing direction exhibit higher saturation squareness and coercive squareness as well as higher coercivity. The ratio of saturation squareness along the disk circumferential direction to that along the radius direction is often referred to as the orientation ratio (O.R.). Several physical mechanisms have been suggested for the induced orientation. It has been found that films with texturing-induced orientation also exhibit anisotropic change in the lattice constant of the magnetic film (Nishikawa et al., 1989). From electron-microscopy analysis, it also has been suggested that the grains seem to line up with texture grooves (Kawamoto and Hikami, 1991). It was speculated that depositing magnetic films on the textured substrates under certain conditions results in anisotropic strain in the magnetic films, producing stress-induced anisotropy (Doerner et al., 1991). Based on some detailed electron-microscopy analysis, it was also proposed that the surface curvature resulting from the grooves can yield an effective anisotropic orientation of the crystal-line easy axes along the direction of the grooves (Nolan et al., 1993a). In this section, we review micromagnetic studies of the effect of orientation induced by (A) preferred easy axes distribution, and (B) anisotropic stress, on transition noise properties and edge-overwrite characteristics.

A. Stress-induced orientation

(1) Modeling of the magnetoelastic effect
For a single crystallite, the magnetoelastic energy due to the net stress σ is

$$E_{ms} = -\sigma \times \lambda$$

where λ is the magnetostriction for a hcp single crystal (Bozorth, 1954) and can be written as:

$$\lambda = (\lambda_A - \lambda_B)[\hat{m} \cdot \hat{\sigma} - (\hat{k} \cdot \hat{m})(\hat{k} \cdot \hat{\sigma})]^2$$
$$+ (4\lambda_D - \lambda_A - \lambda_B) [\hat{m} \cdot \hat{\sigma} - (\hat{k} \cdot \hat{m})(\hat{k} \cdot \hat{\sigma})] (\hat{k} \cdot \hat{m})(\hat{k} \cdot \hat{\sigma})$$
$$+ [\lambda_B + (\lambda_C - \lambda_B)(\hat{k} \cdot \hat{\sigma})^2] [1 - (\hat{k} \cdot \hat{m})^2]$$

where λ_A, λ_B, λ_C, and λ_D are the magnetostriction constants (Bozorth, 1954) and $\hat{\sigma}$, $\hat{k}$ and $\hat{m}$ are the unit vectors along the directions of the stress, the crystalline easy axis, and the magnetization respectively. The effective magnetic field due to the magnetoelastic energy is:

$$H_{me} = \frac{\partial E_{me}}{\partial M} = \frac{\sigma}{M} \frac{\partial \lambda}{\partial \hat{m}}$$

(2) Hysteresis properties
Modeling results show that net compressive stress increases the saturation squareness in the direction of the stress and reduces the squareness in the transverse direction. The loop in the orientation direction is much squarer than that in the transverse direction (Zhu, 1993). It is also found that films with intergranular exchange coupling would have larger orientation ratio than the films without intergranular exchange coupling under the same magnitude compressive stress. Figure 5.29 shows the calculated orientation ratio as a function of the compressive stress magnitude. The film orientation ratio increases linearly with the stress magnitude and the exchange-coupled film shows greater dependence.

(3) Transition noise
Thin-film media with a higher orientation ratio resulting from net compressive stress have a narrower transition length parameter a due to both higher saturation squareness and higher coercive squareness. The noise level away from a transition (dc-saturated noise) and the noise of isolated transitions is lower than that for a planar isotropic film with the same other medium parameters. However, at small bit intervals, where adjacent transitions overlap, the transition noise significantly increases and becomes higher than that of the planar isotropic film.

Figure 5.30 shows the calculated integrated noise power vs. inverse interbit interval for three films with different orientation ratios. Zero intergranular exchange coupling was assumed for all three films (Zhu, 1993). For the planar isotropic film with zero net stress, the noise power shows only a slight supralinear increase at small bit intervals. For the film with an orientation ratio $O.R. = 1.3$, the noise is the lowest at low recording densities but exhibits pronounced supralinear increase and becomes the highest at high recording densities.

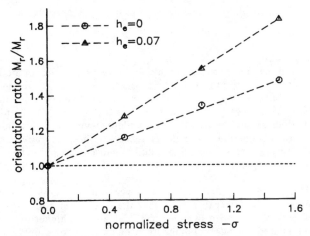

FIGURE 5.29 Calculated orientation ratio as a function of compressive stress for a non-exchange coupled film, $h_e = 0$ (circles) and an exchange coupled film, $h_e = 0.07$ (triangles) (*Zhu, 1993*).

The supralinear noise increase at high recording densities for the oriented thin-films results from severe transition boundary percolation in between adjacent transitions (Zhu, 1993). When the distance between adjacent transition boundaries is decreased, the noise distribution within a transition remains unchanged until percolation between adjacent transition boundaries occurs. In highly oriented films, the magnetization process during percolation is more collective spatially; this yields much wider percolation channels and larger island domains compared with those in

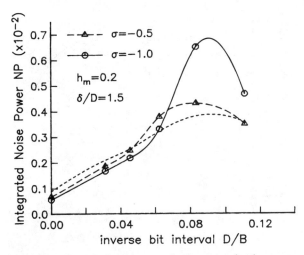

FIGURE 5.30 Calculated integrated noise power for three non-exchange coupled films with different magnitude of compressive stress (*Zhu, 1993*).

planar isotropic films with the same degree of intergranular exchange coupling and $M_s\delta$ value.

B. Preferred crystalline easy axes orientation

The preferred magnetic orientation along the recording direction could also be produced by preferred orientation of the crystalline easy axes of the grains. In the micromagnetic study, this type of oriented film was modeled by assuming the angle between the crystalline easy axis of a grain and the recording direction follows a Gaussian distribution probability with a standard deviation determining the film orientation ratio. Transition noise dependence on the orientation ratio is very similar to that for the stress-induced oriented film discussed previously. Figure 5.31 shows the integrated noise power as a function of inverse bit interval. All three films have zero intergranular-exchange coupling. The films with higher orientation ratio exhibit lower dc-saturated noise and lower transition noise at low recording densities. At small bit intervals, the higher the orientation ratio of the film, the more pronounced the supralinear noise increases and the higher the noise. Figure 5.32 shows simulated typical dibit magnetization patterns for a highly oriented film and a planar isotropic film. The wide percolation channel in the oriented film presents a contrast to the narrow fingered channels in the planar-isotropic film, indicating that the collective magnetization process in the highly oriented film is much more pronounced.

Both the stress-induced oriented film and the film having preferred crystalline easy axes orientation exhibit similar transition noise behavior. For the same orientation ratio, however, the stress-induced film exhibits more pronounced supralinear noise enhancement than that of the film with preferred crystalline easy axes orientation. In both cases, a high orientation ratio yields significant supralinear noise increase at high recording densities. Recent experimental studies have confirmed this conclusion of micromagnetic modeling analysis (Zhu et al., 1995).

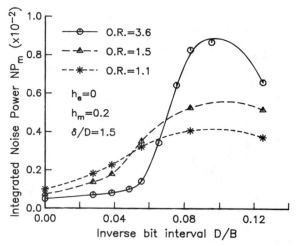

FIGURE 5.31 Calculated integrated noise power for three non-exchange coupled films with different orientation ratios.

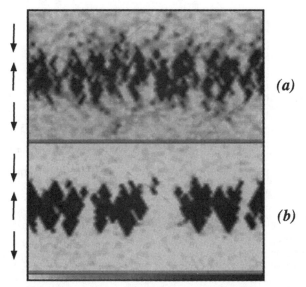

FIGURE 5.32   Typical simulated dibit transition patterns at a small bit interval, $B \approx 0.3$ μm, for two films with different orientation ratios: (*a*) *O.R.* = 1 and (*b*) *O.R.* = 3.6.

5.4.8   Effect of Head Medium Spacing and Recording Current Optimization

The head-field gradient can be improved by reducing the head-medium separation during the recording process, thereby creating sharper transitions. For a given film medium, the sharper the transition, the lower the transition noise. Reducing head-medium spacing along with optimizing writing current yields a reduction of transition noise at all densities and pushes the onset of the supralinear noise increase to higher recording densities. Figure 5.33 shows the experimental data (symbols) and micromagnetic modeling results (curves) for different head-medium spacings. The noise of isolated transitions is lower for a smaller head-medium spacing, as indicated by the initial slope of the curves, and also the onset of the supralinear noise increase occurs at a higher density.

Optimizing writing current has a similar effect to reducing head-medium spacing in terms of lowering the transition noise (Zhu et al., 1995). Figure 5.34 shows measurements of medium noise as a function of recording density on a typical thin-film longitudinal disk, with $H_c = 135$ kA/m (1650 O_e) and $M_r\delta = 25$ mA (2.5 memu/cm²) with a regular thin film inductive head. The two curves corresponding to two different writing currents. For optimized current (solid curve), the initial slope of the noise curve is much smaller and the onset of supralinear noise increase is at a significantly higher density than for a higher writing current (dashed curve).

The reduction of transition noise via either reduction of head-medium spacing or optimization of write current mainly results from the reduction of transition length. At extremely small head-medium spacing, the imaging effect of the head during the recording process could also yield further reduction of the transition length. However, the extent of the imaging effect is not clear since the head surface near the writing zone is likely partially saturated.

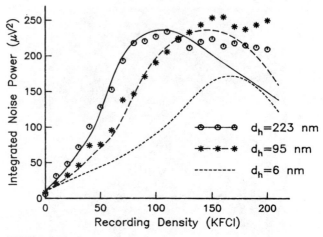

FIGURE 5.33 Integrated noise power vs. recording density for three different recording head-media spacing. The symbols are experimental data while the curves are simulation results (*Johnson et al., 1992*).

5.5 SPATIAL CORRELATION OF TRANSITION NOISE

Not only is transition noise non-stationary, it is also spatially correlated in the track direction. Such spatial noise correlation could have significant impact on data recovery channels, especially advanced data channels, such as PRML in which the channel has memory and decision making depends on sampled data

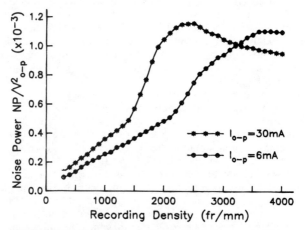

FIGURE 5.34 Measured integrated noise power at two different writing currents as a function of recording density. The recordings are performed on the same thin film disk on exactly the same recording conditions except the writing current (*Zhu et al., 1995*).

sequences: (e.g.: Moon and Carley, 1990; Fitzpatrick et al., 1994; Ye and Zhu, 1995).

Suppose that we have an assembly of medium noise corrupted voltage waveforms

$$\{V_k(x), k = 1, 2, \ldots, N\} \tag{5.23}$$

where N is a large number. (The waveforms in the assembly $\{V_k(x)s\}$ would have been identical if they were noise free.) By subtracting the ensemble mean waveform from each individual waveform, we obtain an assembly of voltage noise waveforms

$$\{\Delta V_k(x), k = 1, 2, \ldots, N\}. \tag{5.24}$$

Since the relation between the voltage waveform and the transition magnetization profile is

$$V(x) = CM_r \delta \int dx' \; \frac{dH(x + x')}{dx} \; m(x'), \tag{5.25}$$

for an assembly of noise voltage waveforms, we have a corresponding assembly of noise magnetization profiles

$$\{\Delta m_k(x), k = 1, 2, \ldots, N\}. \tag{5.26}$$

Here, $m(x)$ is defined as

$$m(x) = \frac{1}{WM_r} \int_{-W/2}^{+W/2} dz M(x) \tag{5.27}$$

The noise covariance matrix

$$A_v(x_1, x_2) = \frac{1}{N} \sum_{i=1}^{N} \Delta V_k(x_1) \Delta V_k(x_2) \tag{5.28}$$

gives the spatial correlation of the voltage noise, and

$$A_m(x_1, x_2) = \frac{1}{N} \sum_{i=1}^{N} \Delta m_k(x_1) \Delta m_k(x_2), \tag{5.29}$$

gives the spatial correlation of the magnetization noise. The values along the diagonal of the covariance matrices, i.e., $x_1 = x_2$, gives the spatial distribution of the noise power.

5.5.1 Noise Correlation within Isolated Transitions

An analytical form of the noise correlation within an isolated transition has been derived with certain assumptions (Bertram and Che, 1993):

$$A_m(x_>, x_<) \approx \frac{s}{W} (1 - <m(x_>) >)(1 + <m(x_<) >) \tag{5.30}$$

where s is the cross-track correlation length, $< m(x) >$ is the mean magnetization at position x and $x_>$ and $x_<$ are the spatial positions along the transition with $x_> \geq x_<$.

In Eq. (5.30), the noise power distribution given by the values along the diagonal $x_> = x_<$ becomes

$$A_m(x, x) = \frac{s}{W} (1 - < m >^2) \tag{5.31}$$

which exactly follows Eq. (5.19). In addition, the derived covariance Eq. (5.30) is positive definite, meaning that the transition noise is essentially position jitter-like (Fitzpatrick et al., 1994). Experimental measurements have shown that Eq. (5.27) can describe well the correlation within isolated transitions (Bertram and Che, 1993; Lin and Bertram, 1993) and it has been incorporated into models for estimating the impact of correlated medium noise on the error rate performance of various advanced channels (Che et al., 1993; Fiztpatrick et al., 1994; Fitzpatrick and Che, 1995).

For media in which the transition noise is dominated by the slope variation of the transitions, Eq. (5.30) may no longer be valid since in this case the off-diagonal values of the covariance matrix becomes negative and the noise is negatively correlated within the transition (Moon et al., 1988; Zhu and Wang, 1995).

5.5.2 Karhunen-Loeve Expansion

One of the methods used for characterizing the spatial (or time) domain correlation of non-stationary noise is the Karhunen-Loeve (K-L) expansion. Initially, it was applied to study the noise correlation of isolated transitions (Yuan and Bertram, 1989; Lin and Bertram, 1993) and then dibit and tribit transitions in thin film media (Lin et al., 1994; Zhu et al., 1994c; Zhu and Wang, 1995).

For the noise voltage waveform ensemble, Eq. (5.24), the K-L expansion method states that for any individual noise waveform in the assembly, such as the $k-th$ voltage noise waveform ΔV_k, can be expressed as

$$\Delta V_k(x) = \sum_i \alpha_i(k) \phi_i(x) \tag{5.32}$$

and for the magnetization profile ensemble, Eq. (5.4), we have

$$\Delta m_k(x) = \sum_i \beta_i(k) \psi_i(x) \tag{5.33}$$

where ϕ_i and ψ_i are the deterministic functions characterizing the spatial correlation of the noise for the voltage waveforms and magnetization profiles respectively. The K-L expansion theorem also states that ϕ_i and ψ_i are the eigenfunctions of the voltage and magnetization noise covariance matrices, $A_v(x_1, x_2)$ and $A_m(x_1, x_2)$, respectively. Also, $\alpha_i(k)$ and $\beta_i(k)$ are random variables with zero mean. The variances of the random variables, α_i and β_i, are the corresponding eigenvalues of the covariance matrices. The different correlation modes are statistically independent in the following sense:

$$\frac{1}{N} \sum_{k=1}^{N} \alpha_i(k) \alpha_j(k) = \lambda_i \delta_{ij} \tag{5.34}$$

where λ_i are the eigenvalue of the i–th eigenfunction (correlation mode) of the covariance matrix. The sum of all the eigenvalues is the total noise power.

The K-L expansion method allows us to identify the dominant noise correlation modes, the ϕ_i's and ψ_i's, and their corresponding weightings, the ratio $\lambda_i/\Sigma\lambda_j$ in the total noise power. In this section, noise correlation obtained by the K-L expansion analysis of micromagnetic modeling results on the transition noise will be reviewed and related experimental measurements will be discussed.

5.5.3 Noise Correlation of Dibit Transitions

Noise correlation of consecutive multiple transitions is of great interest since, at high recording densities, the noise of adjacent transitions becomes correlated due to intertransition interactions. The spatial scale of such intertransition correlation is much longer than that of the correlation within an isolated transition. The intertransition correlated medium noise is thought to have significant impact on the error rate performance of advanced data recovery channels.

A dibit transition pair is the most basic form of interacting transitions. Micromagnetic simulations have been performed to study the spatial correlation of the dibit transition noise (Zhu et al., 1994c). Figure 5.35 shows the noise covariance matrix of the voltage dipulse assembly with the insert figure showing the ensemble mean dipulse voltage waveform. The dipulse assembly was calculated by applying the reciprocity theorem on an assembly of simulated dibit transition pairs assuming a medium with $O.R. = 0.36$. The values along the diagonal represent the distribu-

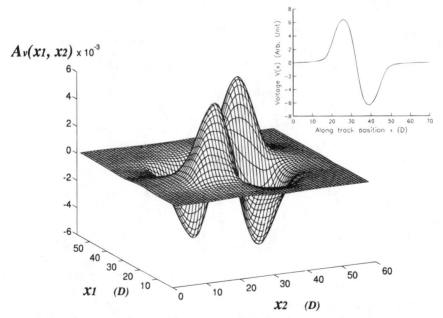

FIGURE 5.35 Noise covariance matrix of simulated voltage dipulse assembly. The insert figure shows the corresponding ensemble mean voltage dipulse. The unit in the x axes is the diameter of a grain in the film, assumed to be 30 nm. The intended writing bit interval is $B = 0.36$ μm (*Zhu et al., 1994c*).

tion of the noise power. As shown in the figure, the noise peaks at the positions of the dipulse voltage peaks. Off the diagonal line, the covariance shows two well-pronounced negative peaks, indicating that the two voltage dipulse peaks are negatively correlated, i.e., the amplitude of the two voltage peaks essentially fluctuate coherently.

Using the K-L expansion method, the noise correlation in the dibits can be characterized (Zhu et al., 1994c). It has been found that only very few eigen functions, or eigen modes, of the noise covariance matrix have significant eigen values. In other words, the spatial noise correlation can be adequately characterized by only a few dominated correlation modes. Figure 5.36 shows the three most significant correlation modes for the noise of the dipulse voltage waveforms, and Fig. 5.3 shows the corresponding noise correlation modes in the corresponding magnetization transition profiles. The bit interval is $B = 0.36$ μm where the supralinear noise enhancement is already pronounced for this medium.

In Fig. 5.36, the eigen modes of the voltage noise correlation are referred to as 1-node, 2-node or 3-node modes according to the number of zero crossings in the middle. The dominant voltage noise correlation mode is the 1-node mode which weights 80% of the total noise power. The eigen function, ω_1 (solid curve of the top figure in the left column of Fig. 5.36), has a similar shape to the dipulse itself (dashed curve in the left column). This dominant correlation mode represents the coherent amplitude variation of the two peaks in the dipulse: the two peaks of the

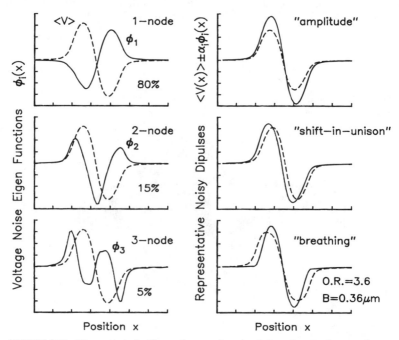

FIGURE 5.36   Three most significant eigen modes, ϕ_i, of the voltage noise covariance matrix (shown in Fig. 5.1). In the left column, the dashed curve shows the mean voltage dipulse and the solid curves show the eigen modes. In the right column, the corresponding representative noisy dipulses $< V(x) \pm \alpha_i\phi_i(x)$ are plotted. The percentage number represents weightings of each noise mode over the total noise power (*Zhu et al., 1994c*).

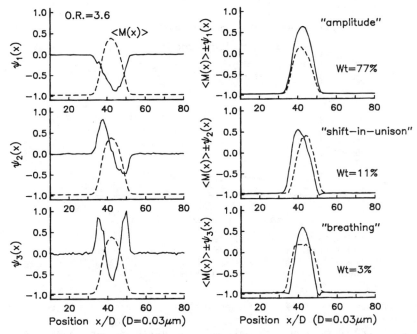

FIGURE 5.37 The eigen modes, ψ_i, of the corresponding transition profile covariance matrix. In the left column, the dashed curve shows the mean dibit transition profile and the solid curves show the noise eigen modes of the transition profiles. In the right column, the corresponding representative noisy dibit profile: $< m(x) \pm \alpha_i\psi_i(x)$ are plotted. The percentage number represents weightings of each noise mode over the total noise power (*Zhu et al., 1994c*).

dipulse decrease (or increase) their amplitude together. The noise correlation mode is referred to as the "amplitude variation" mode. Such noise correlation arises from the fluctuation of the magnetization in the region between the dibit transitions, as shown by ψ_1 in Fig. 5.37. For a highly oriented film, such magnetization fluctuations are mainly responsible for the supralinear noise increase at small bit intervals.

The second main noise correlation mode in the dibit is the "shift-in-unison" mode that the dipulse and the corresponding position shift of the dibit transition profile virtually without changing their shapes. This noise correlation mode is likely due to the local variation of the film coercivity. The third main noise correlation mode is the so-called "breathing" mode and always weighs well below 10% of the total noise power in most cases.

Studies have shown that the supralinear noise enhancement at high recording densities is mainly caused by the increase of the coherent amplitude variation noise. Figure 5.38 plots one set of representative experimental measurement data which shows the contributions of the coherent amplitude variation mode and the shift-in-unison mode for recorded dibits to the total noise power as a function of recording density (Ye and Zhu, 1995). As shown in the figure, at small bit intervals, the evident supralinear noise power increase correlates with the increase of the noise associated with the coherent amplitude variation mode. The contribution of the shift-in-unison mode essentially remains the same with decreasing bit interval.

The impact of correlated noise for dibit data pattern to the error-rate perfor-

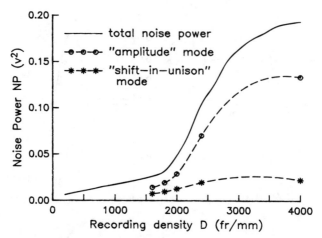

FIGURE 5.38 Experimentally measured total noise power and contributions of the dipulse "amplitude variation" mode and the "shift-in-unison" mode. The measured film disk has H_c = 140 kA/m (1800 Oe) and $M_r\delta$ = 23 mA (2.3 memu/cm^2) (*Zhu and Ye, 1995*).

mance of various advanced partial response channels has been investigated through combined experimental measurements and channel modeling (Zhu and Ye, 1995). It was found that the "amplitude variation" correlation mode significantly enhances the dibit drop-out errors for the PR-4 channel with (0,k) code constraint while the impact of the correlated noise is much smaller for the EPR-4 and EEPR-4 with (1,7) code constraint at the same user bit density. The analysis showed that if the noise in the channel is dominated by the correlated noise of the "amplitude variation" mode, using EEPR-4 channel (1,7) code constraint instead of PR-4 with (0,k) code constraint, gives a gain of as much as 5 dB SNR for the same error-rate performance.

5.6   RECORDING AT TRACK EDGES AND TRACK-EDGE NOISE

Track width in current disk drives has rapidly decreased, and the recording characteristics at track edges have become more and more important. In this section, we discuss micromagnetic modeling investigations on the track-edge recording characteristics in longitudinal thin-film media. Edge-recording properties in perpendicular thin-film media will be discussed separately in Sec. 5.8.

Edge-recording properties were studied by simulating recording of a dibit with a recording head of narrow track width. The dimension of the simulation array is significantly wider than that of the recording head track so that edge-recording properties could be properly studied. Since the head-edge field changes direction across the head gap, it is important for the simulation to mimic the realistic recording process by moving the head in very small steps. Figure 5.39 shows a gray-scale graph of the magnetization curl of a simulated dibit magnetization pattern. The dibit is calculated with a recording head of a 2μm wide track width and 0.3μm gap length. The medium was initially dc saturated with a spatial uniform field. The

FIGURE 5.39 Calculated magnetization curl image of simulated dibit transitions with a 2 μm track width ring head. The graph size is 4 $\mu\mu$ $\times$ 4 μm. The gray scale represents normal component of the magnetization curl, which essentially mimicks the Fresnel image of Lorentz electron microscopy.

recording head is moved from bottom to top. The features at the transition centers as well as at the track edges remarkably resemble the features in typical TEM Fresnel images of the recording patterns on realistic thin-film media. (The TEM Lorentz micrograph essentially images the curl of the magnetization pattern (Ferrier, 1992; Mallinson, 1994)). Note that the bright and dark star-like features indicate magnetization vortices at the centers of the transitions, exactly the same as shown in many TEM observations (Chen, 1981; Arnoldussen et al., 1991).

In the rest of this section, we will discuss the effect of film orientation on the edge-recording patterns, track-edge noise properties and edge overwrite characteristics.

5.6.1 Oriented and Planar Isotropic Film Media

The orientation ratio of a film medium is an important factor affecting track-edge recording characteristics. In a highly oriented medium, edge-recording properties are very different than in a planar isotropic film. Figure 5.40 shows a calculated dibit magnetization pattern, obtained by micromagnetic simulation, with gray scale representing the magnetization component along the recording direction (Zhu et al., 1992). In this case, the film is a highly oriented film with an orientation ratio of $O.R. = 3.6$. As shown in the figure, the recording is wider than the width of the recording head. The head-edge field produces a V-shape magnetization pattern in the side-written band. Since the film is highly oriented, there is little transverse magnetization component and the head-edge field generates a V-shape magnetization head-on transition in the side-written band.

In a planar isotropic film medium, however, the head-edge field yields a signifi-

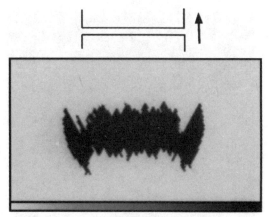

FIGURE 5.40   A simulated dibit magnetization pattern in a highly oriented film medium. The array size is 3.84 μm and the recording head width is 1.5 μm. The gray scale represents the magnetization component in the recording direction, which is indicated by the arrow (*Zhu et al., 1992*).

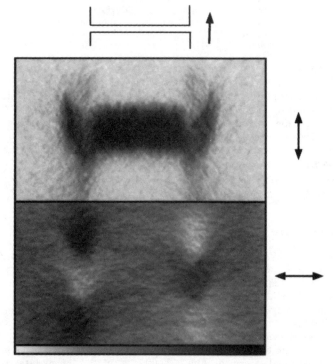

FIGURE 5.41   Gray scale plot of simulated recorded dibit in a planar isotropic film media: magnetization component along recording direction (top) and magnetization component in the cross-track direction (bottom) (*Zhu et al., 1992*).

cant transverse magnetization component in the side-written band. Figures 5.41(*a*) and (*b*) show the magnetization components in the track and cross-track directions respectively for a simulated dibit transition pair. Even though the writing is as wide as that in the oriented film case, no edge transitions are produced in the side-written band due to magnetization flux closure by the transverse magnetization component. Therefore, in this case, the side-written band essentially is an erase band. For comparison, Figs. 5.42(*a*) and (*b*) show the average magnetic pole density of a dibit transition for the planar isotropic film and the highly oriented film respectively. The V-shaped edge transitions in the side written band is apparent in the oriented film. No edge transition appears in the planar isotropic films and the transition cross-track width is essentially the same as the width of the recording head trailing pole, even though the actual writing is as wide as that in the oriented medium. The side-written band in the planar isotropic film is a transition-free erase band for recording on a previously dc-erased state.

In the planar isotropic film, the transverse magnetization component in the side-written band along the entire length of a bit cell creates dipolar pole density stripes along the edges of the side-written band. Since the transverse field has a sharper gradient at the inner edge of the side-written band than that at the outer edge, the pole density is greater at the inner than that at the outer edge. Figure 5.43 shows the calculated pole densities for the on-track, at the inner, and outer edges of the side-

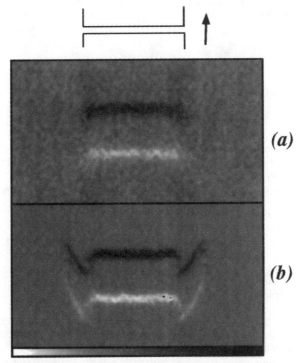

(a)

(b)

FIGURE 5.42 Calculated magnetic pole distribution of dibit transitions in (*a*) a planar isotropic film and (*b*) a highly oriented film. The writing track width in both cases are the same (*Zhu et al., 1992*).

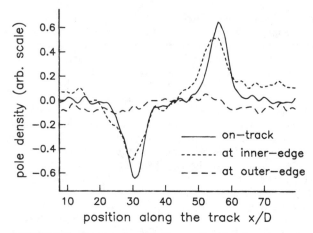

FIGURE 5.43 Calculated profile of magnetic poles along the center (solid curve), the inner edge (short dashed curve), and the outer edge (long dashed curve) in a planar isotropic film (*Zhu et al., 1992*).

written band for a typical planar isotropic film. The magnetic pole stripes at the inner edges of the side-written bands often result in base line shift in magnetoresistive head readback if the write/read margin is not sufficient (Su and Ju, 1989).

5.6.2 Edge Overwrite in Oriented Thin-Film Media

Overwrite properties at track edges are important for the following factors: (1) the off-track data error-rate performance capability of the playback heads and (2) linearity of the position error signal (PES). The off-track performance capability is usually defined as the off-track displacement of the readback head that is allowed under a given error rate. The PES linearity is critical for track servoing. In most hard-disk drives, position error signals are written on the disk using overlapped tracks with a residual track width of a fraction of the head width. Edge-overwrite properties become critically important in such cases.

Figure 5.44 shows a magnetic force microscopy (MFM) image of the edge-overwrite pattern in an oriented film with an orientation ratio $O.R. = 2.0$. The recording head used here is a regular thin-film head with the leading pole track width 1 μm wider than that of the trailing pole at each side. The edge-overwrite pattern contains two overlapping tracks with the newer recorded track overwriting half of the old track. The V-shape transitions at the track edges are apparent. At the interfacing edges of the old and the new tracks, the edge transitions of the new track are connected to those of the old track. At low recording densities, the slanted transitions in the side written band could yield phase shift of the readback voltage pulse and cause pulse broadening.

At high recording densities, edge-overwrite patterns are different. Figure 5.45 shows an MFM image of an overwrite pattern at higher recording densities. The edge transitions in the side-written bands becomes significantly weaker than those on the track since the field gradient at the edges is much poorer than that in the

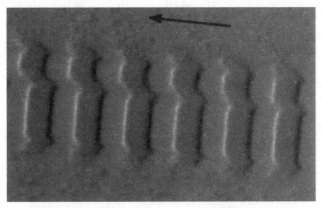

FIGURE 5.44 Magnetic force microscopy image of two partially overlapping recorded tracks in an oriented film disk (*O.R.* = 2.0), recorded with a regular thin-film head of 5 μm track width. The bit length is B = 2.5 μm. The size of the image is 30 $\times$ 30 μm.

center of the track. Partial erasure at the track edges becomes significantly more severe than on track and the playback signal from the side-written band is much weaker.

Trimming the head poles at the track edge so that both pole-tips (P_1 and P_2) have the same width at the gap results in much narrower side-written bands as compared with a head with unequal pole widths and the same gap length. Figure 5.46 shows a MFM image of the overlapping tracks in the oriented film at a relatively high recording density, $B \approx 0.5$ μm. In this case, the side-written band is significantly narrower than the band with the head with unequal pole widths. However, the essential features remain the same as in the case of writing with an untrimmed thin-film head.

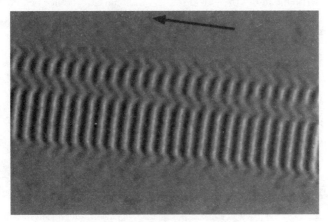

FIGURE 5.45 Magnetic force microscopy image of two partially overlapping recorded tracks in the oriented film disk, recorded with a regular thin-film head of 5 μm track width. The bit length is $B \approx 0.5$ μm.

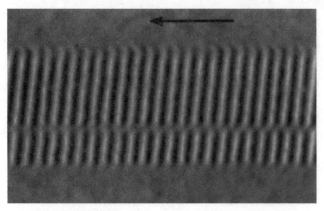

FIGURE 5.46 Magnetic force microscopy image of two partially overlapping recorded tracks in the oriented film disk, recorded with a trimmed thin-film head of 6.5 μm track width. The bit length is $B \approx 0.5$ μm.

5.6.3 Phase Dependence of Edge Erasure in Planar Isotropic Film

In planar isotropic film media, no slanted edge transitions occur in the side-written band. However, a systematic study has found that when the new track overlaps the old track, the erasure at the common edge depends on the along-track phase difference between the transitions in the two tracks (Zhu et al., 1994b). Figure 5.47 shows the MFM image of the two overlapping tracks which have slightly different recording wavelengths. On the right of the image, the transitions in the two tracks are essentially in-phase, meaning that the transitions in the two tracks with the same polarity are aligned in position along the tracks. On the left, the transitions in the two tracks are 180 degrees out-of-phase, meaning that the transitions with opposite polarity are aligned. In the in-phase case, transitions of the old track remain effectively unerased in the side-written band of the new track. As the phase difference becomes greater,

transitions out-of-phase

transitions in-phase

FIGURE 5.47 A MFM image of two partially overlapping tracks, with slightly different recording wavelengths, in a planar isotropic film medium. The bit lengths for the old (upper) and the new (lower) tracks are $B = 0.5$ μm and $B = 0.49$ μm respectively. Transitions in the two tracks are out-of-phase at the left side of the image and in-phase at the right side of the image. The arrow indicates the relative head motion (*Zhu et al., 1994*).

the erase band becomes more apparent, better defined, and wider. The erase band is the widest for the 180 degree out-of-phase situation.

At very high recording densities, the residual in-phase transitions in the side-written band for edge overwrite are much weaker due to the fact that the head edge-field gradient is much poorer than that of the field on track. Partial erasure of the previous residual edge transitions occurs at much lower densities compared with on track. It is more so using an MR head since the leading pole of the write head in most of the current magnetoresistive heads is essentially infinitely wide compared with the width of the trailing pole (Luo et al., 1995). Figure 5.48 shows the measured edge-erase band between the two overlapping recording tracks. For the out-of-phase transitions, the width of the edge-erase band increases linearly with increasing recording density. For the in-phase transitions, at low recording densities the edge erase band is essentially missing, while at high recording densities it is as wide as that for the out-of-phase transitions, even though the on-track transitions still remain well-defined.

5.6.4 Track-Edge Noise

Although the side-written band in planar isotropic films essentially behaves as an erase band, random magnetic poles with either polarity could be created during the recording process. Magnetic flux arising from the random magnetic poles in the side-written band yield noise on readback, which is referred to as track-edge noise

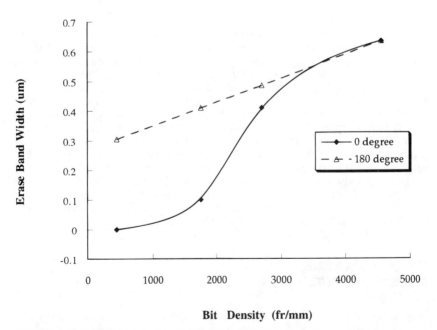

FIGURE 5.48 Measured erase band width of two partially overlapping recording tracks as a function of recording density at zero and 180° transition phase differences in a planar isotropic film medium. A MR/thin-film head with 5 μm trailing pole width is used for recording (*Luo et al., 1995*).

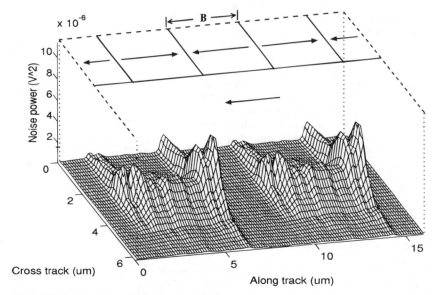

FIGURE 5.49 Two dimensional mapping of medium noise power in an isolated recording track on a previously dc saturated film medium. Zero in the cross track position indicates the readback head is exactly at the center of the track (*Lam et al., 1994*).

(Yarmchuk, 1986; Martin and Lambeth, 1992). Edge noise mainly occurs along the bit cell whose magnetization is reversed with respect to the magnetization direction in the region beyond the track edges, and the noise is highest beyond the ends of the on-track transitions in the side-written band (Zhu et al., 1992; Zhu et al., 1993).

An experimental method has been developed to obtain two-dimensional spatial distributions of medium noise for recorded tracks on a precision spin stand tester (Lam and Zhu, 1994; Lam and Zhu, 1995). Figure 5.49 shows a measured two-dimensional mapping of the noise power of a single recorded track on a previously dc-erased longitudinal thin-film media. As shown in the figure, the edge noise mainly occurs along the edges of the bit cell where the magnetization is reversed with respect to the prior dc-erase direction. The transverse edge field during recording yields no edge noise along the side of the bit cell whose magnetization has the same direction as that in the region beyond the track edge. The noise correlation analysis also showed that the noise along the edges of the bit cell is virtually non-correlated, confirming the results of the micromagnetic simulation.

5.7 MORE ADVANCED THIN-FILM MICROSTRUCTURES

To generate sharp transitions, high coercive squareness is needed. However, as discussed in Secs. 5.3 and 5.4, the high coercive squareness of conventional thin-film media is always associated with high transition noise at high recording densities. To be able to increase recording density while maintaining high signal-to-noise ratio, more advanced film microstructures need to be identified so that high coercive squareness and low medium noise can be achieved at the same time. In this section, we will discuss three types of advanced film microstructures which have significant advantages in terms of reducing medium noise.

5.7.1 Multilayer Thin-Film Media

Multilayer thin films are potential media for future ultra-high density recording applications because of their low medium noise, especially at high recording densities. Laminating a film to a multilayer structure, with adjacent magnetic layers completely decoupled, increases the number of grains per unit film surface area. If we assume that the grains are not interactive, the medium noise power would be reduced in proportion to the increased grain number (Murdock et al., 1990). However, both experimental and micromagnetic analyses have shown that reducing the separation-layer thickness yields a significant additional noise reduction, as well as changes of hysteresis loop properties, as long as the interlayer is continuous (Min et al., 1991; Zhu, 1992c). The interlayer magnetostatic interaction has been suggested as being responsible for the additional noise reduction.

One method to characterize the effect of magnetic interaction is to measure the Wohlfarth relation, often referred as the ΔM curve (Mayo et al., 1991), defined as:

$$\Delta M(H) = \frac{1}{M_r} \{2I(H) - [M_r + M(H)]\} \tag{5.35}$$

where H is the external applied field, $I(H)$ is the initial remanent magnetization curve which starts from the ac-erased state, and $M(H)$ is the remanent hysteresis curve from $-M_r$ to $+M_r$. If the grains in the film are noninteracting, ΔM vanishes at all fields. Thus, ΔM is one way of measuring the interactive effect in the film.

Figure 5.50 shows measured ΔM curves for three multilayer thin films (Min et

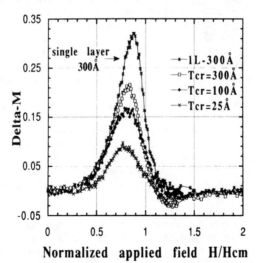

FIGURE 5.50 Measured δM curves of double magnetic layer films (CoCrTa/Cr/CoCrTa/Cr) with various non-magnetic interlayer thicknesses. Reducing the interlayer thickness while keeping the two magnetic layers non-exchange coupled results in a reduction of the peak values (*Min et al., 1991*).

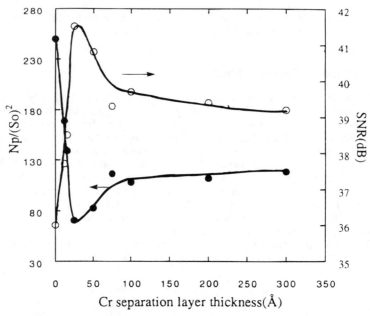

FIGURE 5.51 Normalized medium noise power and SNR as functions of Cr interlayer thickness for CoCrTa/Cr/CoCrTa/Cr double magnetic layer films (*Min et al., 1991*).

al., 1991). The magnetic layers are CoCrTa alloy and the interlayer is CR. The three films have three different interlayer thicknesses. As the interlayer thickness decreases from 30 nm to 2.5 nm, the peaks in the ΔM curve are significantly reduced. This indicates that the interlayer magnetostatic interaction results in a more localized magnetization reversal process, as shown by the diminishing of the positive peak in the ΔM curve. Medium noise measurements on these three multilayer thin films are shown in Fig. 5.51. A noise minimum occurs with a 2.5 nm interlayer thickness, coinciding with the case with small peaks in the ΔM curve measurements (Murdock et al., 1990; Min et al., 1991; Lambert et al., 1993; Teng and Eltoukhy, 1993).

The micromagnetic modeling study has provided much improved understanding of the interlayer magnetostatic interactions (Zhu, 1992c). Figure 5.52 shows the model geometry for the multilayer films with two magnetic layers separated by a non-magnetic interlayer. The simulation studies on the magnetization processes, transition noise behavior and edge noise properties will now be described.

Magnetization reversal process

The effect of interlayer magnetostatic interaction during the magnetization reversal processes has been studied for a dual-magnetic-layer film with two different interlayer thicknesses, $t = 30$ nm and $t = 0.6$ nm, assuming no interlayer exchange coupling for both cases. The interlayer magnetostatic interaction for the thin interlayer case is significantly stronger than that for the thick interlayer case. Figures 5.53 and 5.54 show the magnetization patterns during magnetization reversal for the thick and the thin interlayer cases respectively (only one of the two magnetic layers are shown here). In each case, zero interlayer exchange coupling is assumed.

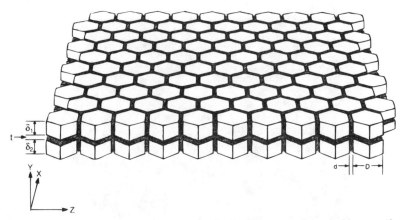

FIGURE 5.52 Illustration of the micromagnetic simulation array for a double-magnetic-layer thin film.

In the thick interlayer case, the two magnetic layers in the multilayer film behave essentially independent of each other. The reversal process starts by forming a few sparsely located narrow reverse domains, elongated in the applied field direction. The entire film reverses largely through the expansion of the reversed domains. In the case of a thin interlayer, the reverse domains nucleate densely and evenly in the film. The expansion of the reverse domains becomes very limited and the domain width near the coercive state becomes much narrower than that in the thick in-

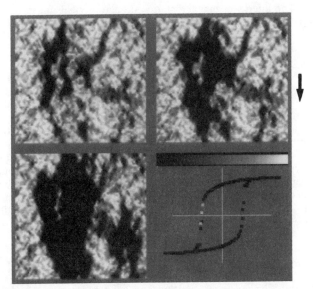

FIGURE 5.53 Magnetization patterns during a reversal process for the case of thick interlayer: $t = 30$ nm. The gray scale represents the magnetization component along the external field direction indicated by the arrow (*Zhu, 1992c*).

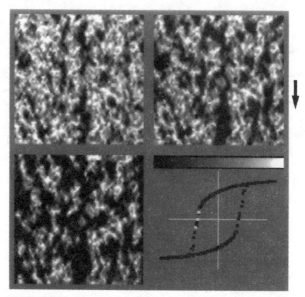

FIGURE 5.54 Magnetization patterns during a reversal process for
the case of thin interlayer: $t = 0.6$ nm. The gray scale represents the
magnetization component along the external field direction indicated
by the arrow (*Zhu, 1992c*).

terlayer case. The interlayer magnetostatic interaction yields much more localized
reversals in the thin interlayer case.

Reduction of transition and track-edge noise

Interlayer magnetostatic interaction in multilayer thin-film media yields narrower and smaller domains in the coercive state as well as narrower zig-zag boundaries in recorded transitions. Thus, additional medium noise reduction can be
achieved with minimizing interlayer thickness without introducing interlayer exchange coupling. This noise reduction mechanism has particularly significant impact on the track-edge noise (Murdock et al., 1990). As discussed in the previous
section, the edge noise arises from random magnetic poles in the side-written band
generated by the head edge field. In a multilayer structured medium with thin
separation layers (uniform enough to disrupt interlayer exchange coupling), the
interlayer magnetostatic interaction results in magnetic flux closure between the
adjacent layers in the side-written band: i.e., a positive pole is always matched by a
negative pole in the adjacent layer for magnetic flux closure. Such flux closure
yields significant edge-noise reduction (Ye et al., 1994).

5.7.2 Bicrystal Thin-Film Media

The bicrystal thin film represents another advanced microstructure which can provide significantly improved hysteresis properties and much reduced transition noise.
In the bicrystal film, the crystalline easy axes of the magnetic grains are oriented in
either one of two orthogonal directions in the film plane (Wong et al., 1991;

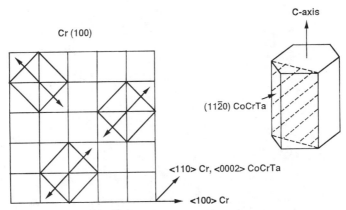

FIGURE 5.55 Epitaxy relation between (100) textured Cr single crystal and (11$\bar{2}$0) textured Co-alloy. The epitaxy causes the c-axis<0002> of the Co-alloy grain to become parallel to <110> directions of the Cr.

Mirzamaani et al., 1991). Therefore, this structure is referred to as a bicrystal structure (Fig. 5.55). In practice, this film microstructure has been realized by epitaxial growth of the magnetic layer with a proper underlayer on cubic single-crystal substrates, such as Cr (Wong et al., 1989), NaCl (Mirzamaani et al., 1991), LiF (Min and Zhu, 1994), MgO (Futamoto et al., 1994), and GaAs (Ding and Zhu, 1994). By depositing a Cr underlayer with (100) texture on the single-crystal substrate with epitaxial growth, the Cr crystallites have a single orientation. The magnetic layer usually is Co-alloy with hcp crystal structure. Under appropriate deposition conditions, the magnetic layer has (11$\bar{2}$0) texture with the c-axis of a magnetic grain oriented along either the <110> or the <$\bar{1}$10> direction of the Cr underlayer grain, usually with equal probability.

A. Hysteresis properties

The bicrystal film is modeled with the crystalline easy axes of the grains constrained only along two specific orthogonal directions in the film plane. The hysteresis is anisotropic but with four-fold symmetry. The hysteresis calculations show that the saturation squareness is the highest in the diagonal directions in between the two orthogonal c-axis orientations (45° with respect to one of the c-axis orientations) and is the smallest in the direction along either one of the c-axis directions. Figure 5.56 shows the calculated hysteresis loops along the effective easy axis and the effective hard axis respectively. The loop along the effective easy axis has a saturation squareness $S = 0.93$ and a coercive squareness $S^* = 0.91$. Note that the intergranular exchange coupling is zero.

In comparison with a planar isotropic film with the same material parameters, the easy-axis loop of the bicrystal film exhibits not only higher saturation squareness and higher coercive squareness, but also a squarer loop shoulder which is also an important property for sharp transitions (Zhu et al., 1993).

The high saturation squareness and coercive squareness in bicrystal films result from the combined effect of the easy axes orientation and magnetostatic interactions in the film. The orthogonally oriented crystalline easy axes also tend to suppress the local collective switching during magnetization processes. Figure 5.57 shows the simulated magnetization domain pattern near the coercive state for a

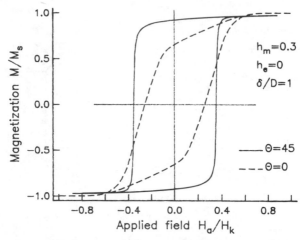

FIGURE 5.56 Calculated hysteresis loops for the bicrystal film with zero intergranular exchange coupling. θ is the angle between the direction of applied field and one of the crystallites' c-axis directions (*Zhu et al., 1993*).

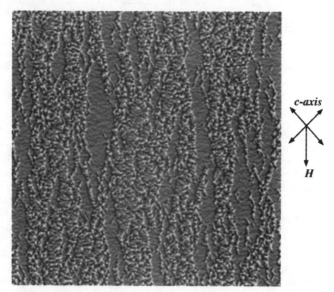

FIGURE 5.57 Calculated normal component of magnetization curl, similar to the Fresnel image of Lorentz electron microscopy, of the simulated magnetization pattern near the coercive state where array-averaged magnetization is zero. The size of the simulated image is 7.6×7.6 μm. Zero intergranular exchange coupling is assumed (*Zhu et al., 1993*).

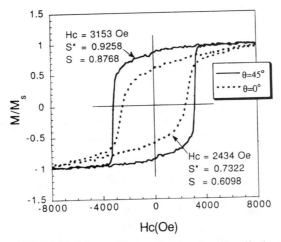

FIGURE 5.58 Measured hysteresis loops along the effective easy ($\theta = 45°$) and hard ($\theta = 0°$) axes for a CoCrTa/Cr bicrystal film deposited on LiF single crystal substrate (*Min and Zhu, 1994*).

bicrystal film with zero intergranular exchange coupling and $S^* = 0.92$. The gray scale in the figure represents the normal component of the curl of the magnetization, mimicking the Fresnel Lorentz electron microscopy image. Narrow domains, elongated along the field direction, characterize the feature of the magnetization reversal process.

Simulated hysteresis properties of bicrystal films have been confirmed by recent experimental studies with excellent agreement between the calculation results and experimental measurements. Figure 5.58 shows measured hysteresis loops in both the effective easy and hard axes of a bicrystal film deposited on a single crystal LiF substrate (Min and Zhu, 1994).

B. Transition noise property

Figure 5.59 shows the calculated integrated noise power as a function of inverse bit interval for the bicrystal film. The results of oriented films and planar isotropic films, calculated with the same material parameters except for the easy axes orientation, are plotted for comparison. All films have zero intergranular exchange coupling. The highly oriented film exhibits low transition noise at low recording densities, but the noise at high recording densities becomes extremely high. The planar isotropic film exhibits relatively high noise at high recording densities, but the supralinear noise enhancement at high recording densities is only very slight. The bicrystal film has the advantages of both these films. The noise is low at low recording densities and it also only shows a slight supralinear enhancement at high recording densities. The noise power is significantly lower than that of the planar isotropic film. The transition boundary in the bicrystal film exhibits the same narrow fingering structure as in the planar isotropic film, but with less irregularity and at very small bit intervals. Also the percolated adjacent transition boundaries show narrow fingered channels and narrow fingered domains with irregularity much less pronounced than that in the planar isotropic film.

CoCrTa bicrystal film disks have been successfully fabricated on 3 in. diameter

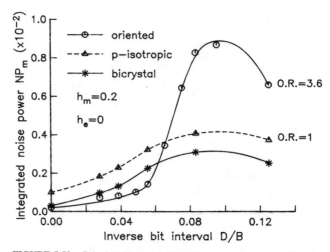

FIGURE 5.59 Calculated integrated medium noise power as a function of inverse bit length for oriented films (circles), a planar isotropic film (triangles) and the bicrystal film (stars). The smooth curves are the fitting curves for guiding the eye (*Zhu et al., 1993*).

single-crystal GaAs wafers and recording measurements have been performed on a spin stand tester under realistic recording conditions (Ding and Zhu, 1994). Figure 5.60 shows the noise power of the bicrystal film medium along with noise of a typical conventional film medium and a state-of-the-art low $M_r\delta$ medium for MR reading application. At low recording densities, the bicrystal film medium noise is comparable to that of the low $M_r\delta$ medium and at high recording densities, the medium noise of the bicrystal film is the lowest.

The reason that the bicrystal film exhibits low medium noise, especially at high recording densities, is due to the fact that half of the adjacent magnetic grains have their crystalline easy axes orthogonal to each other. This film microstructure effectively suppresses the collective behavior during magnetization processes that is mainly responsible for the medium noise, especially at high recording densities.

C. Recording characteristics at track edges

Another advantage of the bicrystal film medium is its recording properties at track edges. If the recording is along one of the effective easy axes of the film, the direction transverse to the recording track in the film is along another effective easy axis due to the four-fold symmetry of the bicrystal film. Figure 5.61 shows the simulated magnetization recording pattern at a track edge for the bicrystal film along with those for oriented and planar isotropic films. The magnetization direction is along the transverse direction beyond the edge of a transition in the side-written band. The side-written band thus becomes essentially an erased band with no edge transitions and the transitions along the track have sharply defined edges (Zhu et al., 1993).

Recording properties along the effective hard axis direction are degraded compared with the properties along the effective easy axis. To orient bicrystal thin film in a practical disk so that the effective easy axis is always along the circumferential direction exhibits significant difficulties at the present. More research is needed. Nevertheless, the understanding from the bicrystal films will certainly help in

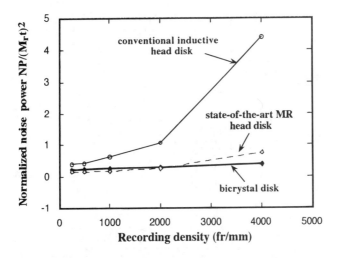

Media	Hc (Oe)	$M_r t$ (memu/cm^2)
conventional disk	1800	2.0
bicrystal disk	2000	1.4
state-of-the-art MR head disk	2100	0.9

FIGURE 5.60 Measured integrated medium noise as a function of recording density for the bicrystal disk with GaAs single crystal wafer substrate. Noise of two other conventional film disks are plotted for comparison (*Ding and Zhu, 1994*).

searching for practical optimum film microstructures. The next subsection is an excellent example.

D. Magnetization reversal processes

Magnetization reversal processes in bicrystal films are very fascinating (Ye, 1995). Figures 5.62, 5.63, and 5.64 show the reversal processes for an external field applied in the film at angles 45°, 25°, and 0° with respect to one of the crystalline easy axes. The gray scale in the figures represents the normal component of the magnetization curl. For better illustration, the intergranular exchange coupling in the film is assumed to be $h_e = 0.2$, a relatively large value.

Figure 5.62 shows the magnetization reversal with the field along the effective magnetic easy axis. At the saturation remanent state (a), the ripple pattern is not very pronounced compared with that in the planar isotropic film medium since, along the effective easy axis, the bicrystal film has nearly unity saturation squareness. The reversal starts as a small domain nucleates with magnetization rotated by 90°, parallel to the other effective easy axis direction as shown in (b). This transverse domain expands as reversal progresses and a reverse domain then nucleates within the transverse domain. Both the reverse domain and the transverse domain expand as other transverse domains continue to nucleate in the film. As shown in (c), the reverse domain nucleated inside the transverse domain has expanded through nearly half of the entire simulation area. Most of the regions in the film are reversed by expansion of the reverse domains, while the expansion and the elongation of the transverse domains is always very limited and the size of these domains is always small.

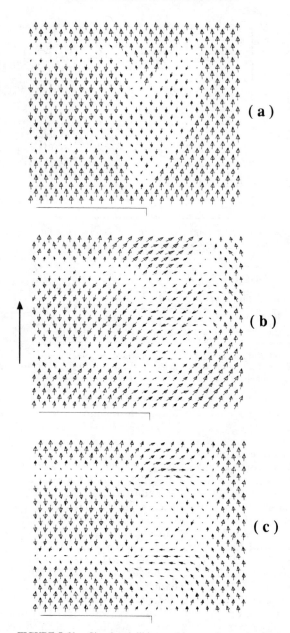

FIGURE 5.61. Simulated dibit transitions at the track edge for (*a*) a highly oriented film, (*b*) a planar isotropic film, and (*c*) the bicrystal film. The long arrow on the left indicates the head motion and the corner of the head edge indicates the track edge (*Zhu et al., 1993*).

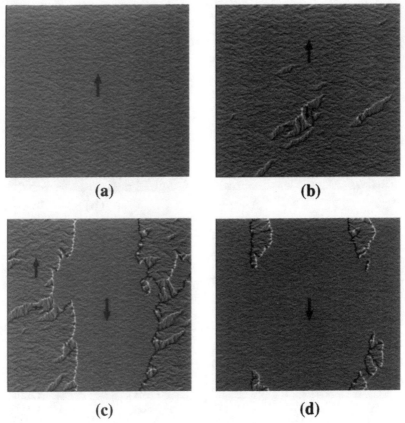

(a) **(b)**

(c) **(d)**

FIGURE 5.62 Calculated normal component of magnetization curl for simulated magnetization configurations during a magnetization reversal. The field is applied downward in the field along an effective easy axis (*Ye and Zhu, 1992*).

Figure 5.63 shows the reversal when a field is applied at an angle of 25° to one of the crystalline easy axis directions. At the saturation remanent state, the film is essentially magnetized along the nearest effective easy axis. The reversal starts by the nucleation of transverse domains with the magnetization rotated by 90° and becoming parallel to the other effective easy axis as shown in (*a*). These nucleated transverse domains elongate along the diagonal direction in between the two effective easy axes so that no magnetic poles result on the domain boundaries. Reverse domains then nucleate within the transverse domains and expand through both transverse and unreversed domains while some of the transverse domains are continuing to expand.

Figure 5.64 shows the reversal when the field is applied along the effective hard axis, i.e., parallel to one of the crystalline easy axes. Prior to the reversal, at the saturation remanent state, the magnetization is virtually along one of the effective easy axes, yielding the squareness $S = \cos 45°$. The reversal starts by nucleating transverse domains. These transverse domains elongate along the reverse field direction and expand through the initial unreversed regions by transverse motion of the domain boundaries. The domain boundary contains a series of half-formed magnetiza-

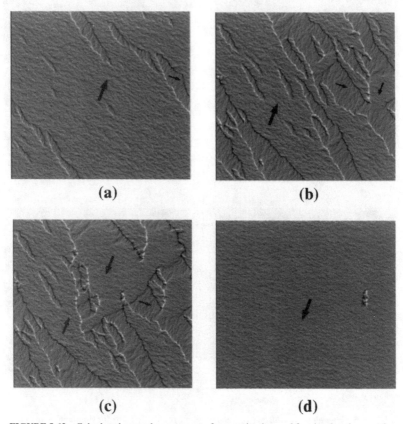

FIGURE 5.63 Calculated normal component of magnetization curl for simulated magnetization configurations during a magnetization reversal. The field is applied downward in the film with a 25° angle with respect to one of the c-axes of the crystalline grains (*Ye and Zhu, 1992*).

tion vortices. After the transverse domains expand through the entire array, further increasing the reverse field yields gradual rotation of the film magnetization towards the field direction and this portion of the reversal process is completely reversible.

5.7.3 Nano-Crystalline Thin-Film Media

High-resolution transmission electron microscopy (TEM) study has shown nano-crystalline subgrain structure in Co-alloy magnetic thin films grown on a (001) textured Cr underlayer (Nolan et al., 1993*b*). The hcp Co-alloy nanocrystallites are epitaxially grown on the underlayer with the (1120) plane matching the (001) plane of the Cr. Multiple nanocrystallites are formed on each chromium grain. The c-axis of the Co-alloy subgrains within one Cr grain can be either in Cr $<110>$ or $<\bar{1}10>$ directions, forming a bicrystal structure within each Cr grain. Clear physical separation between subgrain nanocrystallite boundaries on top of a single Cr grain has been

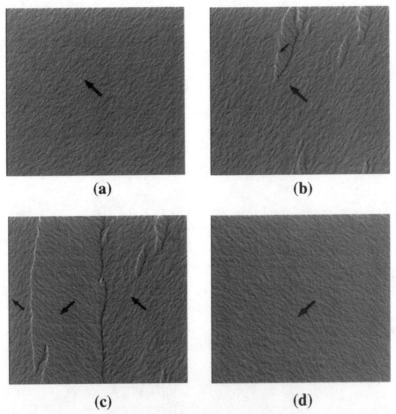

(a)　　　　　　(b)

(c)　　　　　　(d)

FIGURE 5.64 Calculated normal component of magnetization curl for simulated magnetization configurations during a magnetization reversal. The field is applied downward in the film with a 0° angle with respect to one of the *c*-axes of the crystalline grains (*Ye and Zhu, 1992*).

observed for CoCrTa magnetic film. It has been speculated that Cr segregation at subgrain boundaries may weaken the exchange coupling between the nanocrystallites within a normal grain and could reduce medium noise.

Such observed nanocrystalline structure has been modeled by micromagnetic modeling (Ye and Zhu, 1994). In the model, a nanocrystalline magnetic film is represented by a 2D array of hexagons closely packed on a triangular lattice. Each hexagon represents a subgrain, i.e., a nanocrystallite. A cluster of seven subgrains form a single normal grain, as shown in Fig. 5.65. Each cluster corresponds to the size of a grain of Cr underlayer, which was assumed to be 20 nm in the micromagnetic calculations. The crystalline easy axes of the subgrains in a cluster are oriented in either one of the two orthogonal directions mimicking the epitaxy on a single-crystal Cr grain. However, the in-plane orientation of each Cr grain is assumed to be random, therefore the principle direction of each bicrystal cluster is completely random in the film plane.

In the nanocrystalline thin films, two of the important parameters are the exchange coupling between the subgrains in the same cluster, h_{e-in}, and the exchange

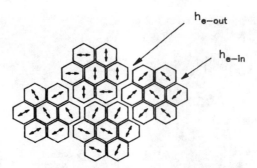

FIGURE 5.65 Modeling of nanocrystalline thin films (*Ye and Zhu, 1994*).

coupling between the subgrains in different clusters, h_{e-out}. In the micromagnetic study, these two parameters were varied independently. Weak exchange coupling between the subgrains in the same normal grain can lead to low medium noise and an appropriate amount of exchange coupling between adjacent normal grain boundaries can result in high coercive squareness, S^*. Figure 5.66 shows a calculated hysteresis loop with $h_{e-in} = 0.1$ and $h_{e-out} = 0.05$, giving a value of $S^* = 0.94$. Figure 5.67 shows the effect of h_{e-in} and h_{e-out} on S^*. An appropriate exchange coupling between the normal grain boundaries, h_{e-out}, is necessary for achieving high coercive squareness. If h_{e-out} becomes too small, a high S^* can not be achieved.

With adjusted h_{e-out} to achieve a high S^* value, reducing h_{e-in} can significantly reduce transition noise at high recording densities. Figure 5.68 shows the calculated

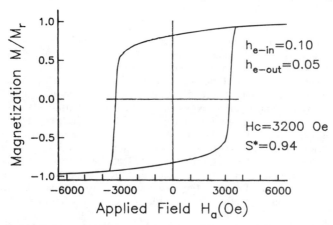

FIGURE 5.66 Calculated hysteresis loop for the nanocrystalline film with $h_{e-in} = 0.1$ and $h_{e-out} = 0.05$ (*Ye and Zhu, 1994*).

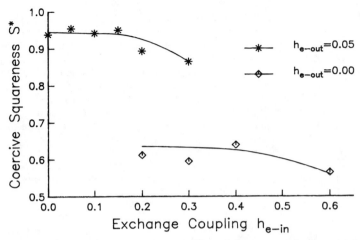

FIGURE 5.67 Effect of exchange coupling within the normal grain (among the subgrains) on the coercive squareness of nanocrystalline films (*Ye and Zhu, 1994*).

noise power as a function of inverse bit interval for various h_{e-in} values while keeping $h_{e-out} = 0.05$ for $S^* > 0.92$. As shown in the figure, a high h_{e-in} value yields well-pronounced supralinear noise increase while, for small h_{e-in} values, the noise power at high recording densities becomes significantly lower.

Planar isotropic nanocrystalline films with bicrystal subgrain structures may enable us to achieve low noise media with high coercive squareness if the exchange coupling in the film can be controlled. The bicrystal structure of subgrains within a

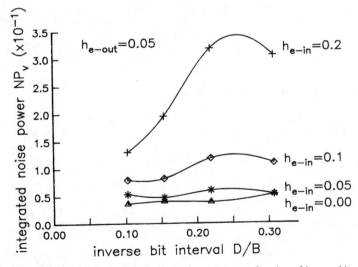

FIGURE 5.68 Calculated integrated noise power as a function of inverse bit interval for the nanocrystalline films with different sets of exchange coupling constants h_{e-in} and h_{e-out} (*Ye and Zhu, 1994*).

normal grain tends to break the collective behavior during magnetization processes, thereby yielding low medium noise. The calculated cross-track correlation length in a low h_{e-in} film is essentially the same as the diameter of a subgrain. This result provides an explanation for the low noise behavior of CoCrTa film media since the subgrain boundaries in CoCrTa film exhibit well-defined "channels" observed from high resolution TEM, thereby weakening the exchange coupling. These "channels" between the subgrain boundaries are missing in CoCrPt films (Nolan, 1993b). The possible high exchange coupling between the subgrains within a normal grain in the CoCrPt films will cause magnetization within a normal grain to be rather uniform, and the effective crystalline anisotropy of the normal grain will be significantly lower than that of a subgrain due to the orthogonal arrangement of the easy axes of the subgrains. The bicrystalline structure of the subgrains is only beneficial when the exchange coupling between the subgrains within a normal grain becomes sufficiently small.

5.8 PERPENDICULAR THIN-FILM RECORDING MEDIA

Perpendicular thin-film recording media have been considered for future ultra-high recording density applications (Iwasaki, 1984; Yamamoto et al., 1987). Recently, recording at a linear density of 1,000 kfci has been demonstrated (Ouchi, 1994). The most often used alloy for perpendicular thin-film media is CoCr. Compared with longitudinal thin-film media, the perpendicular medium is relatively thick, ranging from 50 nm to 1 μm. The film consists of columnar CoCr grains with uniaxial crystalline anisotropy perpendicular to the film plane. In this section, micromagnetic studies on the magnetization reversal processes, noise properties and recording characteristics at track edges will be discussed.

The micromagnetic modeling of CoCr perpendicular film uses the model described in Sec. 2, except that the crystalline anisotropy easy axes are assumed to be normal to the film plane. The aspect ratio between grain height and grain diameter is $\delta/D = 5$ for all the results presented in the following subsections.

5.8.1 Magnetization Reversal Processes

Micromagnetic modeling study on CoCr perpendicular films have shown that the magnetization processes are dominated by collective behavior through magnetostatic and possibly ferromagnetic exchange coupling. Figure 5.69 shows a calculated hysteresis loop for a film without intergranular exchange coupling. In this case, the coercivity is virtually equal to the crystalline anisotropy field independent of film saturation magnetization. The hysteresis loop consists of discrete small jumps. The loop is smoothly sheared because of the perpendicular demagnetizing field. For most CoCr perpendicular films reported in the literature, the value of $4\pi M_s$ is always significantly greater than the film coercivity H_c, which leads to the film remanence being significantly below the saturation magnetization value.

Each finite jump in the hysteresis loop corresponds to a single nucleation process. Figure 5.70 shows a set of transient states during such a process, starting from a state in which the magnetizations of the columnar grains in the film are virtually all in the normal direction. Nucleation begins by collective rotation of the magneti-

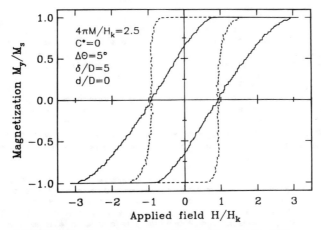

FIGURE 5.69 Simulated hysteresis loop (solid curve) for CoCr perpendicular thin film with $h_m = 0.2$ and $h_e = 0$. The dashed curve is a desheared loop using an array size average demagnetizing factor. The fine jumps in the hysteresis loop correspond to discrete nucleation processes (*Zhu and Bertram, 1989*).

zation of a chain of grains into the film plane. The magnetization of neighboring grains in the chain form a head-to-tail configuration. The nucleation chain is basically one grain wide. As time progresses, large dispersions develop in the magnetization orientation angles so that magnetization rotation is most pronounced in the centers of the chain segments. As the magnetizations of the center grains rotate beyond the film plane toward the reverse film normal direction, the magnetizations of the neighboring grains rotate back into their original film normal direction. In this example, only a total of five grains have reversed their magnetization, although many more grains participated in the nucleation process.

In the nucleation process, initial coherent rotation of chain magnetizations removes the shape anisotropy of each grain; thus, the nucleation field for closely packed grains simply equals the crystalline anisotropy field H_k. Dispersion of local magnetic properties as well as the local demagnetization field leads to subsequent reversal of only a few grains. The chain nucleation mode occurs at each nucleation process during the entire magnetization reversal.

It has been long argued that curling is the nucleation mode for magnetization reversal in CoCr perpendicular films. Thus it is of interest to compare this nucleation mode with the curling mode. For isolated columnar grains with large aspect ratio, the curling mechanism is more energetically favorable than uniform rotation due to the large shape anisotropy energy involved in the uniform rotation mechanism. However, in CoCr perpendicular films, where the columnar grains are close-packed, the chain nucleation mode described above yields essentially no shape anisotropy energy during the magnetization nucleation process. In addition, no ferromagnetic exchange energy is induced since the magnetization within each grain is uniform. Therefore, the uniform magnetization rotation becomes more energetically favorable for the closely-packed columnar grains and results in the chain nucleation mode. Figure 5.71 shows the calculated coercivity of the film as a function of inter-columnar boundary separation.

The very limited number of grains having their magnetization reversed in a single nucleation process leads to relatively homogeneous distribution of reversed

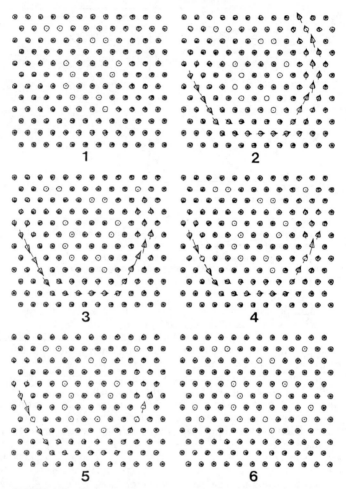

FIGURE 5.70 Transient magnetization configurations during a chain nucleation process at $M \approx 0.8 M_s$ as viewed in the film normal direction. The
pictures are time ordered and each arrow represents the magnetization of a
columnar grain. Only a portion of the simulation array is shown (*Zhu and
Bertram, 1989*).

grains in the film under a spatially uniform external field, because of the nature of
perpendicular demagnetization fields in the film. Figure 5.72 shows magnetization
patterns at various static states during reversal with the gray scale representing the
perpendicular magnetization component of the grains. The domain patterns can be
characterized as dots and single column-wide chains and are similar to those observed by Lorentz microscopy (Grundy et al., 1984). Note that noninteracting
grains would yield a random distribution of spacings between reversed grains.

If the grains in the film are weakly exchange coupled, the chain nucleation mode
still is the reversal mechanism but with wider chains and greater number of grains
reversing in each nucleation which results in wider chain reverse domains. The

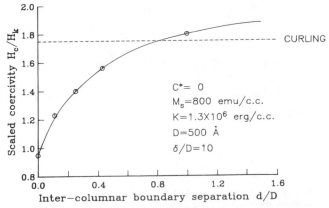

FIGURE 5.71 Calculated coercivity versus intergranular boundary separation d/D with fixed columnar aspect ratio $\delta/D = 10$. The coercive field corresponding to the curling mode is plotted as a dashed line and is independent of d/D. In practice, the system will follow the nucleation mode with the lowest nucleation field (*Bertram and Zhu, 1992*).

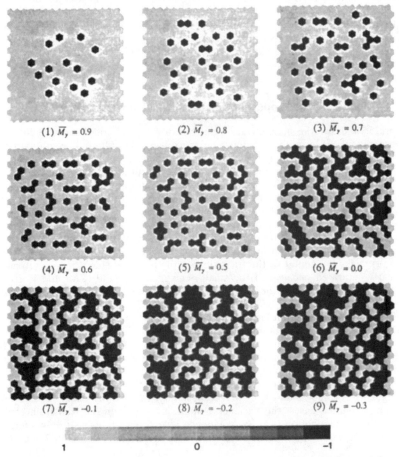

FIGURE 5.72 Static magnetization patterns at various states along a major hysteresis loop for a non-exchange coupled perpendicular film. The gray scale represents the perpendicular component of magnetization (*Zhu and Bertram, 1989*).

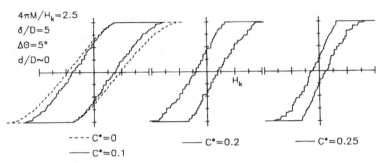

FIGURE 5.73   Calculated hysteresis loops for various values of intergranular exchange coupling constants ($C^* = h_e$) (*Zhu and Bertram, 1989*).

hysteresis loop changes its shape as well. Shown in Fig. 5.73 are calculated hysteresis loops for various values of intergranular exchange coupling constant. The film coercivity significantly decreases with increasing exchange coupling constant. In addition, the loop for high exchange coupling shows a well-defined loop shoulder at the beginning of the hysteresis loop.

If the grains are strongly exchange coupled, domain nucleation and domain wall motion become the reversal mechanism and the hysteresis loop exhibits a well-defined loop shoulder. The film no longer can be called "granular" or "particulate" but should be referred to as "continuous."

5.8.2   Medium Noise Properties and Nonlinear Transition Shift

Figure 5.74 shows the magnetization pattern of a typical simulated transition for a perpendicular film with no intergranular exchange coupling. The gray scale in the figure represents the perpendicular component of the magnetization, with white for initial saturation direction. Below the pattern, the cross-track averaged perpendicular magnetization profile (Eq. 4.2) is plotted in the figure. As indicated by the contrast in the figure, the magnetizations of the grains are all virtually perpendicular to the film plane, even in the transition region. Away from the transition, oppositely magnetized isolated columns and single-column-wide narrow chains are characteristic of the saturation remanent state, with average magnetization level determined by the film coercivity ($H_c = M_s$ in SI units ($H_c = 4\pi M_s$ in emu). Near the center of the transition on the reversed side, the magnetization is nearly saturated because of the small demagnetizing field (Zhu and Bertram, 1989). This overshoot in the transition profile is characteristic of perpendicular recording.

For films with intergranular exchange coupling, the oppositely magnetized chain columns are wider than that without intergranular exchange coupling. A simulated transition pattern for a film with $h_e = 0.1$ is shown in Fig. 5.75. Away from the transition overshoot region, the "domain" widths are wider in comparison with the non-exchange coupled film.

Statistical behavior of cross-track averaged magnetization profiles are presented in Fig. 5.76 for $h_e = 0$ and $h_e = 0.1$, respectively. In both the exchange and non-exchange coupled cases, the variance is highest away from the transition center, where the magnetization is at its remanence level. Near the transition center, the variance decreases and reaches its lowest value at the transition overshoot where

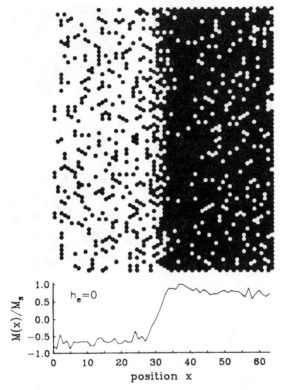

FIGURE 5.74 Magnetization pattern of a recorded transition and corresponding transition profile in a non-exchange-coupled perpendicular film ($h_e = 0$) (*Zhu and Bertram, 1991b*).

the magnetization reaches saturation. For the exchange-coupled film, the higher variance values occur away from the transition center.

The non-saturated regions away from a transition occur only through a microscopic distribution of oppositely magnetized columns. This yields fluctuations in the cross-track averaged magnetization profile for a finite track width. The variance of the transition profile (Eq. 5.16) approximately follows the equation

$$<\Delta M^2(x)> \propto \frac{s}{W} [M_s^2 - M^2(x)] \qquad (5.36)$$

with cross-track correlation length, s, on the order of the width of the chain domains, which could be as narrow as the column width.

In contrast to the noise distribution in longitudinal films, the noise in perpendicular films with $4\pi M_s > H_c$ is the lowest at transitions and highest in the regions away from transitions. In a perpendicular film, the rising portion of the transition profile essentially follows the head-field profile at the top surface of the film media due to the nature of the perpendicular demagnetizing field (Lopez and Clark, 1985; Bertram, 1994). Thus, the head-field gradient becomes critical for generating sharp transitions. Since the demagnetizing field is virtually zero at the transition, the

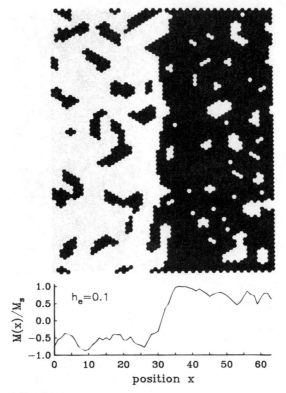

FIGURE 5.75   Magnetization pattern of a recorded transition and corresponding transition profile in an exchange-coupled perpendicular film ($h_e = 0.1$) (*Zhu and Bertram, 1991b*).

magnetization level near the transition center is no longer limited by the film coercivity, leading to transition overshoot (Zhu and Bertram, 1986). If the head-field gradient is large enough to create a sufficiently sharp transition, the magnetization level at the overshoot can be at saturation, therefore, the variance at the overshoot becomes zero according to Eq. (5.36).

This discussion of the noise distribution in perpendicular film media yields a very different density dependence of the medium noise power compared with longitudinal thin-film media (Belk et al., 1986; Zhu and Bertram, 1989). The noise decreases with increasing recording density as long as adjacent transitions are not overlapping. At the density where adjacent transitions start to overlap, the noise will increase with increasing recording density and will reach the highest noise level when the medium becomes effectively ac-erased at sufficiently high recording densities.

Not only is the noise dependence different from that of longitudinal thin film media, the nonlinear transition shift behaves in an opposite way as well. In longitudinal films, the demagnetizing field causes the nonlinear transition shift to be attractive in nature. However, in perpendicular films, the nonlinear transition shift is repulsive in nature (Zhu and Bertram, 1987). This is because the demagnetizing field in a perpendicular film decreases with decreasing inter-transition distance

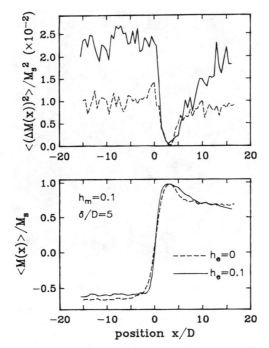

FIGURE 5.76 Mean and variance of transition profile ensembles for CoCr perpendicular films with different exchange coupling constants: $h_e = 0$ (dashed curves) and $h_e = 0.1$ (solid curves). Note that the noise is the highest away from the transition (*Zhu and Bertram, 1991b*).

while in longitudinal films, the demagnetizing field increases with decreasing inter-transition distance.

5.8.3 Recording Properties at Track Edges

As shown above, in perpendicular film media, the magnetizations of the columnar grains are essentially normal to the film. This characteristic nature yields sharp recording track edges with transition overshoot along the track edge. Figure 5.77 shows a magnetic force microscopy (MFM) picture of two recorded tracks with one partially overlapping the other (Zhu et al., 1994a). The perpendicular film medium with a soft magnetic keeper layer was recorded with a thin pole-tip head in contact. In the figure, the new track (wider one) is directly connected to the old one at the track edge without any side erase band previously seen in the planar isotropic longitudinal thin film media. The on-track transition overshoot is evident in the figure. On the outer edges, transition overshoot along the track edge is apparent since the recording is performed on the film in its as-grown state. At the inner edge, the edge transition overshoot of the new recording track varies depending on the relative magnetization polarity between the two tracks.

The lack of a side erase band was also suggested based on recording spin-stand tester measurements (Beaulieu et al., 1989). This property could be advantageous

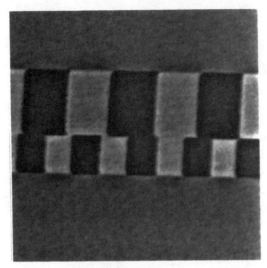

FIGURE 5.77   MFM image of an edge overwrite pattern. The track partially overwritten was recorded at a wavelength $\lambda = 6$ μm and the overwriting new track was recorded at $\lambda = 11$ μm. The new track was shifted by approximately 3.5 μm with respect to the old track in cross-track position.

in terms of more efficient use of disk storage surface for achieving high recording densities and well-defined position error signal for accurate head servo. But it also could be seriously disadvantageous in terms of more strict requirements for spindle nonrepeatable run-out or sufficient read/write track width margin. Figure 5.78 shows a MFM image of a single track recorded over and over again with various recording wavelengths. The final recording wavelength was $\lambda = 10$ μm. With the

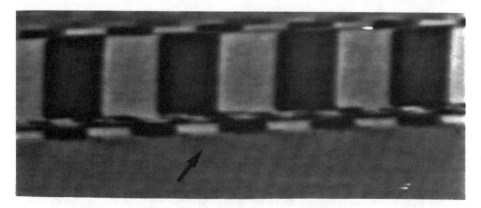

FIGURE 5.78   MFM image of a recording track (pointed by the arrow) recorded over many times with various recording wavelengths. The recording wavelength for the last time is $\lambda = 10$ μm. Due to the nonrepeatable spindle run-out and lack of an erase band, the residual of the previously recorded pattern can be clearly seen along the track edges (*Zhu et al., 1994a*).

presence of non-repeatable run-out of the spindle used, the effect of lacking an edge-erase band is well demonstrated. The residual recorded transition pattern is clearly shown at the track edges. In this case, a guard band is not sufficient to eliminate residual interference and the write-wide and read-narrow technique is probably necessary for achieving acceptable off-track performance.

The experimental study using MFM imaging technique directly on the recorded perpendicular film medium has confirmed the micromagnetic simulation predictions which demonstrated very much the same edge-recording characteristics (Zhu and Ye, 1993), although the MFM images do not have the resolution on grain size scale to resolve narrow chain domains in the film.

5.9 SUMMARY

Extensive and systematic micromagnetic modeling studies over the past decade have provided significant understanding of the micromagnetic properties and recording and noise performance of film media. One of the important factors which made the model relatively successful is the hexagonal grain geometry used, since it is based on the granular nature of realistic film microstructure. Since the magnetization states in ferromagnetic systems are always history dependent, following the correct physical path during a magnetization process by solving the Landau-Lifshitz-Gilbert dynamic gyromagnetic equation is also critical. The phenomenological inclusion of the intergranular exchange coupling in the model describes an important interaction effect which could dominate the micromagnetic properties and hysteresis behavior. Over the past eight years, extensive simulation studies have demonstrated that the model not only is useful for obtaining physical insights, but also can be used as a powerful tool in engineering more advanced film microstructures to develop future thin film recording media.

ACKNOWLEDGEMENTS

The author would like to thank Xiao-Guang Ye, Tai Min, Haiyun Wang, Terence Lam, Juren Ding, and Yansheng Luo for their contributions to this chapter.

REFERENCES

Aoi, H., M. Saitoh, N. Nishiyama, R. Tsuchiya, and T. Tamura, "Noise Characteristics in Longitudinal Thin Film Media," *IEEE Trans. Magn.*, **MAG-22**, 895 (1986).

Arnoldussen, T. C., "Thin-Film Recording Media," *Proc. IEEE*, **74**, 1526 (1986).

Arnoldussen, T. C., and H. C. Tong, "Zigzag Transition Profiles, Noise and Correlations and Statistics in Highly Longitudinal Thin Film Media," *IEEE Trans. Magn.*, **MAG-22**, 889 (1986).

Arnoldussen, T. C., L. L. Nunnelley, F. J. Martin, and R. P. Ferrier, "Side Writing/Reading in Magnetic Recording," *J. Appl. Phys.*, **69**, 4718 (1991).

Arnoldussen, T. C., and J.-G. Zhu, "Effect of Recorded Transition Shape on Spatial Noise Distributions and Correlations," *J. Appl. Phys.*, **75**, 6774 (1994).

Barany, A. M., and H. N. Bertram, "Transition Noise Model for Longitudinal Thin-Film Media," *IEEE Trans. Magn.*, **MAG-23**, 1776 (1987).

Baugh, R. A., E. S. Murdock, and B. R. Natarajan, "Measurement of Noise in Magnetic Media," *IEEE Trans. Magn.*, **MAG-19**, 1722 (1983).

Beardsley, I. A., and V. S. Speriosu, "Determination of Thin Film Media Model Parameters Using DPC Imaging and Torque Measurements," *IEEE Trans. Magn.*, **MAG-26**, 2718 (1990).

Beardsley, I. A., and J.-G. Zhu, "DC-Erase Edge Noise Simulations in Thin Film Media," *J. Appl. Phys.*, **67**, 5352 (1990).

Beaulieu, T. J., D. J. Seagle, M. A. Meininger, and C. J. Spector, "Track Density Limitation for Dual-Layer Perpendicular Recording in Rigid Disk Environment," *IEEE Trans. Magn.*, **MAG-25**, 3369 (1989).

Belk, N. R., P. K. George, and G. S. Mowry, "Measurement of the Intrinsic Signal-to-noise Ratio for High Performance Rigid Recording Media," *J. Appl. Phys.*, **59**, 557 (1986).

Bertram, H. N., *Theory of Magnetic Recording*, Cambridge, p. 237 (1994).

Bertram, N. H., and X. Che, "General Analysis of Noise in Recorded Transitions in Thin Film Recording Media," *IEEE Trans. Magn.*, **MAG-29**, 201 (1993).

Bertram, H. N., and J. C. Mallinson, "Theoretical Coercive Field for an Interacting Anisotropic Dipole Pair of Arbitrary Bond Angle," *J. Appl. Phys.*, **33**, 1308 (1969).

Bertram, H. N., K. Hallemasek, and M. Madrid, "DC Modulation Noise in Thin Metallic Media and Its Application for Head Efficiency Measurements," *IEEE Trans. Magn.*, **MAG-22**, 247 (1986).

Bertram, H. N., and J.-G. Zhu, "Simulations of Torque Measurements and Noise in Thin-Film Magnetic Recording Media," *IEEE Trans. Magn.*, **MAG-27**, 5043 (1991).

Bertram, H. N., and J.-G. Zhu, "Fundamental Magnetization Processes in Thin-Film Recording Media," *Solid State Physics*, ed. Ehrenreich and Turnbull, **46**, 271 (1992).

Bozorth, R. M., "Magnetostriction and Crystal Anisotropy of Single Crystals of Hexagonal Cobalt," *Phys. Rev.*, **96**, 311 (1954).

Brown Jr., W. F., "Micromagnetics," New York: Interscience (1963).

Brown Jr., W. F., "The Fundamental Theorem of Fine Ferromagnetic Particle Theory," *J. Appl. Phys.*, **39**, 993 (1968).

Che, X., and H. N. Bertram, "Dynamics of Nonlinearities in High Density Recording," *IEEE Trans. Magn.*, **MAG-29**, 317 (1993).

Che, X., L. Barbosa, and H. N. Bertram, "PRML Performance Estimation Considering Medium Noise Down Track Correlations," *IEEE Trans. Magn.*, **MAG-29**, 4062 (1993).

Chen, T., "The Micromagnetic Properties of High-Coercivity Metallic Thin Films and Their Effects on the Limit of Packing Density in Digital Recording," *IEEE Trans. Magn.*, **MAG-17**, 1181 (1981).

Ding, J., and J.-G. Zhu, "Microstructure and Recording Properties of Bicrystal Disks with GaAs Substrates," *IEEE Trans. Magn.*, **MAG-30**, 3978 (1994).

Duan, S. L., J. O. Artman, K. Hono, and D. E. Laughlin, "Improvement of the Magnetic Properties of CoNiCr Thin Films by Annealing," *J. Appl. Phys.*, **67**, 4704 (1990).

Doerner, M. F., P. W. Wang, M. Mirzamaani, D. S. Parker, and A. C. Wall, "Cr Underlayer Effects in Longitudinal Magnetic Recording," *Mater. Res. Soc. Proc.*, **232**, 27 (1991).

Doerner, M. F., T. Yogi, D. S. Parker, and T. Nguyen, "Composition Effects in High Density CoPtCr Media," *IEEE Trans. Magn.*, **MAG-29**, 3666 (1993).

Ferrier, R. P., "Imaging Methods for the Study of Micromagnetic Structure," *Noise in Digital Magnetic Recording*, ed. T. C. Arnoldussen and L. L. Nunnelley, World Scientific, 141 (1992).

Fitzpatrick, J., H. N. Bertram, X. Che, L. C. Barbosa, and G. H. Lin, "The Relationship of Medium Noise to System Error Rate in a PRML Channel," *IEEE Trans. Magn.*, **MAG-30**, 3990 (1994).

Fitzpatrick, J., and X. Che, "An Evaluation of Partial Polynomials for Magnetic Recording Systems," *IEEE Trans. Magn.*, **MAG-31**, 1095 (1995).

Futamoto, M., F. Kugiya, M. Suzuki, H. Takano, H. Fukuoka, Y. Matsuda, N. Inaba, T. Takagaki, Y. Miyamura, K. Akagi, T. Nakao, H. Sawagucho, and T. Munemoto, "Demonstration of 2 *Gb/in²* Magnetic Recording at a Track Density of 17 kTPI," *IEEE Trans. Magn.*, **MAG-27**, 5280 (1991).

Futamoto, M., M. Suzuki, N. Inaba, A. Nakamura, and Y. Honda, "Magnetic and Recording Characteristics of Bicrystalline Longitudinal Recording Medium Formed on an MgO Single Crystal Disk Substrate," *IEEE Trans. Magn.*, **MAG-30**, 3975 (1994).

Grundy, P. J., M. Ali, and C. A. Faunce, "Electron Microscopy of Co-Cr Films," *IEEE Trans. Magn.*, **MAG-20**, 794 (1984).

Haas, C. W., and H. B. Callen, "Ferromagnetic Relaxation and Resonance Line Widths, Magnetism," ed. Rado and Suhl, **I**, 449 (1963).

Hughes, G. F., "Magnetization Reversal in Cobalt-Phosphorus Films," *J. Appl. Phys.*, **54**, 5306 (1983).

Hsu, Y., J.-G. Zhu, J. M. Sivertsen, and J. M. Judy, "Mechanism of Reverse DC Erase Noise in Thin Film Media," *J. Magn. Magn. Matl.*, **114**, 207 (1992*a*).

Hsu, Y., J.-G. Zhu, J. M. Sivertsen, and J. M. Judy, "Magnetization Cross-track Correlations and Transition Noise of Longitudinal Thin Film Media," *IEEE Trans. Magn.*, **MAG-28**, 3138 (1992*b*).

Iwasaki, S., "Perpendicular Magnetic Recording—Evolution and Future," *IEEE Trans. Magn.*, **MAG-20**, 657 (1984).

Johnson, K. E., P. R. Ivett, D. R. Timmons, M. Mirzamaani, S. E. Lambert, and T. Yogi, "The Effect of Cr Underlayer Thickness on Magnetic and Structural Properties of CoPtCr Thin Films," *J. Appl. Phys.*, **67**, 4686 (1990).

Johnson, K. E., E. Wu, J.-G. Zhu, and D. Palmer, "Media Noise Improvement Through Head-Disk Spacing Reduction," *IEEE Trans. Magn.*, **MAG-28**, 2713 (1992).

Johnson, K. E., K. J. Schulz, and J. M. Severtson, "Composition Properties of CoPtCr Thin-Film Media," *IEEE Trans. Magn.*, **MAG-29**, 3670 (1993).

Kawamoto, A., and F. Hikami, "Magnetic Anisotropy of Sputtered Media Induced by Textured Substrate," *J. Appl. Phys.*, **69**, 5151 (1991).

Kullmann, U., E. Koester, and C. Dorsch, "Amorphous CoSm Thin Films: A New Material for High Density Longitudinal Recording," *IEEE Trans. Magn.*, **MAG-20**, 420 (1984).

Lam, T. T., and J.-G. Zhu, "Experimental Study of Track Edge Noise Distribution in Narrow Track Recording," *IEEE Trans. Magn.*, **MAG-30**, 4245 (1994).

Lam, T. T., and J.-G. Zhu, "Phase Dependence of Track Edge Noise in MR Head Written Overlapping Tracks," *IEEE Trans. Magn.*, **MAG-31**, (1995).

Lam, T. T., J-G Zhu, and T. C. Arnoldussen, "Experimental Study of Track Edge Distribution in Narrow Track Recording," *IEEE Trans. Magn.*, **MAG-30**, 4245 (1994).

Lambert, S. E., J. K. Howard, I. L. Sanders, and O. C. Allegranza, "Laminated Media for High Density Recording," *IEEE Trans. Magn.*, **MAG-29**, 223 (1993).

Lin, G. H., and H. N. Bertram, "Experimental Studies of Noise Autocorrelation in Thin Film Media," *IEEE Trans. Magn.*, **MAG-29**, 3697 (1993).

Lin, G. H., H. N. Bertram, and R. Simmons, "Noise Correlation in Dibit Recording," *J. Appl. Phys.*, **75**, 5765 (1994).

Lopez, O., and D.A. Clark, "On the Perpendicular Recording Process," *J. Appl. Phys.*, **57**, 3943 (1985).

Luo, Y., T. T. Lam, and J.-G. Zhu, "Density and Phrase Dependence of Edge Erase Band in MR/Thin Film Recording Head," *IEEE Trans. Magn.*, **MAG-31**, (1995).

Madrid, M., and R. Wood, "Transition Noise in Thin Film Media," *IEEE Trans. Magn.*, **MAG-22**, 889 (1986).

Mallinson, J. C., and K. V. Rao, "On Electron-Beam Lorentz Microscopy," *IEEE Trans. Magn.*, **MAG-30**, 1369 (1994).

Mansuripur, M., and T. W. McDaniel, "Magnetization Reversal Dynamics in Magneto-Optic Media," *J. Appl. Phys.*, **63**, 3831 (1988).

Mansuripur, M., and R. Giles, "Simulation of Magnetization Reversal Dynamics on the Connection Machine," *J. Appl. Phys.*, **67**, 5555 (1990).

Martin, B., and D. N. Lambeth, "Track-Edge Noise versus Erasure State," *IEEE Trans. Magn.*, **MAG-28**, 3286 (1992).

Mayo, P. I., K. O'Grady, P. E. Kelly, J. Cambridge, I. L. Sanders, T. Yogi, and R. W. Chantrell, "A Magnetic Evaluation of Interaction and Noise Characteristics of CoNiCr Thin Films," *J. Appl. Phys.*, **69**, 4733 (1991).

Methfessel, S., S. Middelhoek, and H. Thomas, "Domain Walls in Thin Ni-Fe Films," *IBM J. Res. Dev.*, **4**, 96 (1960).

Miles, J. J., and B. Middleton, "The Role of Microstructure in Micromagnetic Models of Longitudinal Thin Film Magnetic Media," *IEEE Trans. Magn.*, **MAG-26**, 2137 (1990).

Min, T., and J.-G. Zhu, "Effect of Grain Size Dispersion on Noise in Longitudinal Thin Film Recording Media," *J. Appl. Phys.*, **73**, 5548 (1993).

Min, T., and J.-G. Zhu, "Grain Height Fluctuation and Medium Noise in Longitudinal Thin Film Recording Media," *IEEE Trans. Magn.*, **MAG-29**, 3706 (1993).

Min, T., and J.-G. Zhu, "Bicrystal Advanced Thin Film Media for High Density Recording," *J. Appl. Phys.*, **75**, 6129 (1994).

Min, T., J.-G. Zhu, and J. Judy, "Effects of Interlayer Magnetic Interactions in Multilayer CoCrTa/Cr Thin Film Media," *IEEE Trans. Magn.*, **MAG-27**, 5058 (1991).

Mirzamaani, M., C. V. Jahanes, and M. A. Russak, "Magnetic Properties of CoPtCr Thin Films with <1120> Crystal Orientation," *J. Appl. Phys.*, **69**, 5169 (1991).

Moon, J. J., "Density Dependence of Noise in Thin Metallic Longitudinal Media," *J. Appl. Phys.*, **63**(8), 3254 (1988).

Moon, J. J., and L. R. Carley, "Detection Performance in the Presence of Transition Noise," *IEEE Trans. Magn.*, **MAG-26**, 2172 (1990).

Murdock, E. S., B. R. Natarajan, and R. G. Walmsley, "Noise Properties of Multilayered Co-Alloy Magnetic Recording Media," *IEEE Trans. Magn.*, **MAG-26**, 2700 (1990).

Nishikawa, R., T. Hikosaka, K. Igarashi, and M. Kanamaru, "Texture-Induced Magnetic Anisotropy of CoPt Films," *IEEE Trans. Magn.*, **MAG-25**, 3890 (1989).

Nguyen, T. A., I. R. McFadyen, and P. S. Alexopoulos, "Microscopic Studies of the Magnetization-Reversal Process in Co-Alloy Thin Films," *J. Appl. Phys.*, **67**, 4713 (1990).

Nolan, T., R. Sinclair, R. Ranjan, and T. Yamashita, "Crystallographic Orientation of Textured CoCrTa/Cr Sputtered Thin Film Media for Longitudinal Recording," *J. Appl. Phys.*, **73**, 5117 (1993*a*).

Nolan, T., R. Sinclair, R. Ranjan, and T. Yamashita, "Effect of Microstructure Features on Media Noise in Longitudinal Recording Media," *J. Appl. Phys.*, **73**, 5566 (1993*b*).

Ouchi, K., "Past and Future of CoCr Perpendicular Thin Films," Presentation at Workshop on CoCr System Alloy Films, (PMRC '94 Extended Workshop in Akita) (1994).

Shtrikman, S., and D. Treves, *Micromagnetics,* Magnetism, ed. Rado and Suhl, **III**, 395 (1963).

Silva, T. J., and H. N. Bertram, "Magnetization Fluctuations in Uniformly Magnetized Thin-film Recording Media," *IEEE Trans. Magn.*, **MAG-26**, 3129 (1990).

Stoner, E. C., and E. P. Wohlfarth, "A Mechanism of Magnetic Hysteresis in Heterogeneous Alloys," *Phil. Trans. Roy. Soc.*, **A240**, 599 (1948).

Su, J. L., and K. Ju, "Track Edge Phenomena in Thin Film Longitudinal Media," *IEEE Trans. Magn.*, **MAG-25**, 3384 (1989).

Takano, H., T. T. Lam, J.-G. Zhu, and J. M. Judy, "Effect of Orientation Ratio on the Recording Characteristics of Longitudinal Thin Film Media," *IEEE Trans. Magn.*, **MAG-29**, 3709 (1993).

Tarnopolsky, G. L., H. N. Bertram, and L. T. Tran, "Magnetization Fluctuations and Characteristic Lengths for Sputtered CoP/Cr Thin-Film Media," *J. Appl. Phys.*, **69**, 4730 (1991).

Teng, E., and A. Eltoukhy, "Flash Chromium Interlayer for High Performance Disks with Superior Noise and Coercivity Squareness," *IEEE Trans. Magn.*, **MAG-29**, 2679 (1993).

Victora, R. H., "Quantitative Theory for Hysteretic Phenomena in CoNi Magnetic Thin Films," *Phys. Rev. Lett.*, **58**, 1788 (1987*a*).

Victora, R. H., "Micromagnetic Predictions for Magnetization Reversal in CoNi Films," *J. Appl. Phys.*, **62**, 4220 (1987*b*).

Wong, B. Y., D. E. Laughlin, and D. N. Lambeth, "Investigation of CoNiCr Thin Films Deposited on [100] and [110] Cr Single Crystals," *IEEE Trans. Magn.*, **MAG-27**, 4733 (1991).

Yamamoto, S., Y. Nakamura, and S. Iwasaki, "Extremely High Bit Density Recording with Single-Pole Perpendicular Head," *IEEE Trans. Magn.*, **MAG-23**, 2070 (1987).

Yarmchuk, E. J., "Spatial Structure of Media Noise in Film Disks," *IEEE Trans. Magn.*, **MAG-22**, 877 (1986).

Ye, X.-G., "Study of Advanced Thin Film Media for High Density Magnetic Recording," Ph.D. Thesis in Electrical Engineering, University of Minnesota (1995).

Ye, X.-G., T. Lam, and J.-G. Zhu, "Experimental and Micromagnetic Study of Track Edge Noise Reduction Effect in Multilayer Thin Film Media," *IEEE Trans. Magn.*, **MAG-30**, 3999 (1994).

Ye, X.-G., and J.-G. Zhu, "Micromagnetic Study of Magnetization Process in Bicrystal Thin Films," *IEEE Trans. Magn.*, **MAG-28**, 3087 (1992).

Ye, X.-G., and J.-G. Zhu, "Modeling of Thin Film Media with Advanced Microstructures for Ultra-high Density Recording," *J. Appl. Phys.*, **75**, 6135 (1994).

Ye, X.-G., J.-G. Zhu, and T. Arnoldussen, "Track Edge Overwrite and Easy Axis Orientation in Narrow Track Recording," *IEEE Trans. Magn.*, **MAG-29**, 3978 (1993).

Yogi, T., G. L. Gorman, C. Hwang, M. A. Kakalec, and S. E. Lambert, "Dependence of Magnetics, Microstructures and Recording Properties on Underlayer Thickness in *CoNiCr/Cr* Media," *IEEE Trans. Magn.*, **MAG-24**, 2727 (1988).

Yogi, T., C. Tsang, T. A. Nguye, K. Ju, G. L. Gorman, and G. Gastillo, "Longitudinal Media for 1 *Gb/in²* Areal Density," *IEEE Trans. Magn.*, **MAG-26**, 2271 (1990).

Yuan, S. W., H. N. Bertram, "Statistical Data Analysis of Magnetic Recording Noise Mechanisms," *IEEE Trans. Magn.*, **MAG-28**, 201 (1992).

Zhu, J.-G., *Interactive Phenomena in Magnetic Thin Films,* Ph.D. thesis in physics, University of California at San Diego (1989).

Zhu, J.-G., "Noise of Interacting Transitions in Thin Film Recording Media," *IEEE Trans. Magn.*, **MAG-27**, 5040 (1991).

Zhu, J.-G., "Micromagnetic Modeling of Thin Film Recording Media," *Noise in Digital Magnetic Recording,* ed. T. C. Arnoldussen and L. L. Nunnelley, World Scientific, 181 (1992*a*).

Zhu, J.-G., "Coercivity Angular Dependence in Longitudinal Thin Film Media," *Journal of Magnetism and Magnetic Materials,* **109**, 367 (1992*b*).

Zhu, J.-G., "Modeling of Multilayer Thin Film Recording Media," *IEEE Trans. Magn.*, **MAG-28**, 3267 (1992*c*).

Zhu, J.-G., "Transition Noise in Longitudinal Thin Film Media," *IEEE Trans. Magn.*, **MAG-29**, 195 (1993).

Zhu, J.-G., and H. N. Bertram, "Computer Modeling of the Write Process in Perpendicular Recording," *IEEE Trans. Magn.*, **MAG-22**, 379 (1986).

Zhu, J.-G., and H. N. Bertram, "Computer Simulation of Nonlinear Bit Shift in Perpendicular Recording," *IEEE Trans. Magn.*, **MAG-23**, 2862 (1987).

Zhu, J.-G., and H. N. Bertram, "Micromagnetic Studies of Thin Metallic Films", *J. Appl. Phys.*, **63**, 3248 (1988*a*).

Zhu, J.-G., and H. N. Bertram, "Recording and Transition Noise Simulations in Thin Film Media," *IEEE Trans. Magn.*, **MAG-24**, 2706 (1988*b*).

Zhu, J.-G., and H. N. Bertram, "Magnetization Reversal in CoCr Perpendicular Thin Films," *J. Appl. Phys.*, **66**, 1291 (1989).

Zhu, J.-G., and H. N. Bertram, "Study of Noise Sources in Thin Film Media," *IEEE Trans. Magn.*, **MAG-26**, 2140 (1990).

Zhu, J.-G., and H. N. Bertram, "Self-Organized Behavior in Thin Film Recording Media," *J. Appl. Phys.*, **69**, 4709 (1991*a*).

Zhu, J.-G., and H. N. Bertram, "Magnetization Reversal and Domain Structures in Thin Film Recording Media," *J. Appl. Phys.*, **69**, 6084 (1991*b*).

Zhu, J.-G., and H. N. Bertram, "Magnetization Structures in Thin Film Recording Media," *IEEE Trans. Magn.*, **MAG-27**, 3553 (1991*c*).

Zhu, J.-G., T. T. Lam, X.-G. Ye, and Y. Luo, "Nonlinear Partial Erasure in Thin Film Media," *J. Appl. Phys.*, (1996).

Zhu, J.-G., Y. Luo, J. Ding, X.-G. Ye, and E. A. Louis, "MFM Study of Edge Overwrite in Perpendicular Thin Film Recording Media," *IEEE Trans. Magn.*, **MAG-30**, 2755 (1994*a*).

Zhu, J.-G., Y. Luo, and J. Ding, "Magnetic Force Microscopy Study of Edge Overwrite Characteristics in Thin Film Medium," *IEEE Trans. Magn.*, **MAG-30**, 4242 (1994*b*).

Zhu, J.-G., H. Wang, and T. Arnoldussen, "Micromagnetic Modeling and Experimental Study of Transition Noise Correlation in Thin Film Medium," *J. Appl. Phy.*, **75**, 5762 (1994*c*).

Zhu, J.-G., and H. Wang, "Noise Characteristics of Interacting Transitions in Longitudinal Thin Film Media," *IEEE Trans. Magn.*, **MAG-31**, 1065 (1995).

Zhu, J.-G., and X.-G. Ye, "Impact of Medium Noise Correlation on Various PRML Channels," *IEEE Trans. Magn.*, **MAG-31**, (1995).

Zhu, J.-G., X.-G. Ye, and T. C. Arnoldussen, "Side Writing Phenomena in Narrow Track Recording," *IEEE Trans. Magn.*, **MAG-28**, 2716 (1992).

Zhu, J.-G., and X.-G. Ye, "Narrow Track Recording in Perpendicular Thin Film Media," *IEEE Trans. Magn.*, **MAG-29**, 2716 (1993).

Zhu, J.-G., X.-G. Ye, and T. C. Arnoldussen, "Effect of In-Plane Easy Axis Orientation in Narrow Track Recording," *IEEE Trans. Magn.*, **MAG-29**, 324 (1993).

CHAPTER 6
RECORDING HEADS

Robert E. Jones, Jr.
Carnegie Mellon University, Pittsburgh, Pennsylvania

C. Denis Mee
Los Gatos, California

C. Tsang
IBM Corporation, San Jose, California

6.1 TYPES OF RECORDING HEADS

Until recently, the heads for virtually all audio, video, instrumentation and data recording products were based on the familiar inductive coil and magnetic core design. The demands for higher recording densities and wider bandwidths have generally been met by developing the means of achieving smaller dimensions in gap length, track width, and core volume of inductive heads. The evolution of materials for head cores from alloy laminations to ferrites and thin films has had a significant effect on the fabrication processes for head structures and on achieving the required dimensions precisely and economically.

Inductive heads can be designed to perform all three major functions in magnetic recording: recording (writing) reproducing (reading), and erasing. Whether separate heads are provided for each function, or whether a head performs multiple functions, is dictated by the application—and sometimes by cost. For stationary-head applications, such as tape drives, separate heads are usually provided for reading and writing, and often for erasing. However, in moving-head applications, such as disk files and helical-scan video recorders, the requirements for low head mass and simple connection technology have emphasized designs with single inductive elements performing all functions, although this may require some compromise in performance optimization. Normally, in disk files the function of erasing is achieved by overwriting the previous information.

Recording densities have increased dramatically in all applications of magnetic recording, and the read signal has been correspondingly reduced. This, in combination with requirements for wider bandwidths, means that the inductive head will eventually be the limiting factor in recording performance, even though the introduction of high-magnetization film media has delayed this situation in some applications.

As a result, there is a trend towards using separate heads for reading and writing even in some disk applications. Once this change can be accepted, then heads can be designed either for optimum reading or for optimum writing. In particular, reading heads using magnetoresistive transducers have significantly improved performance over inductive reading heads. Recently, magnetoresistive heads have been introduced into disk and tape data storage devices with considerable success and represent the major development in head design of recent years. For this reason, the subject of magnetoresistive heads is given extensive treatment in Sec. 6.5 of this revised edition.

6.1.1 Inductive Recording Heads

The gap in the pole pieces of a recording head is designed to produce a field amplitude capable of recording the storage medium to a sufficient depth, normally considered to be equal to or greater than the reading depth corresponding to the recorded wavelength. The pole geometry and materials are designed to provide adequate field strength at the signal frequency, and a rapid decrement of the writing field along the direction of the medium motion in order to maximize the short-wavelength recording efficiency. Normally, the optimum writing-head gap is longer than the optimum reading-head gap. A limiting factor, as writing track widths become narrower, is the relative increase in side writing that occurs for long-gap heads.

Magnetic flux is delivered to the writing poles by a magnetic yoke that normally has a greater cross-sectional area than the poles in order to avoid saturation of the yoke region. The writing coil around the yoke is usually designed to be close to the poles to improve the efficiency of the inductive coupling between the coil and the poles.

6.1.2 Inductive Reproducing Heads

Although basically identical in design to inductive recording heads, inductive reproducing heads are inherently low-flux-density devices and, therefore, can use lower-flux-density and higher-permeability core and pole materials. At low flux densities, uncontrolled domain switching in a reproducing head can add detectable noise, and this effect becomes more noticeable as the magnetic volume of the head core is reduced. The design trend in inductive reproducing heads is to maximize the reproduced voltage by using as many turns as possible. Restriction on turns occurs due to lowering of the head resonance frequency and less efficient coupling of the larger volume coils. In very high-track-density applications the uncertainty of head positioning can cause reading of the adjacent track. Head designs with separate recording and reproducing heads can reduce this sensitivity through the use of a reduced reading-head track width and, in the case of sequential track recording, through use of heads with different gap azimuth alignment for adjacent tracks.

6.1.3 Erase Heads

Erase heads have the least critical design requirements since they require high field amplitude but not high spatial resolution. For very low-cost erasing, static-field heads have been designed using a permanent magnet or an inductive head with direct current. Usually, alternating fields are applied and produce lower-noise erased media than dc-field erasing. High-magnetization materials and very long gaps are used in inductive ring-head designs to produce large erasing fields. However, even when the recorded medium experiences many field reversals during its passage close to a ring-head erasing field, the noise level achievable is not as low as can be achieved with bulk erasure of the recorded medium by a separate large ac-field electromagnet. This incomplete erasing achieved by a single-gap erase head has been explained as a re-recording effect due to the magnetic fields from the recorded medium combining with the erasing field to produce a low-level recording as the medium leaves the erasing field. This effect has been reduced by providing multiple-gap erase heads which spread the erasing field along the recording medium (Sawada and Yoneda, 1985).

6.1.4 Flux-Sensitive Heads

Flux-sensitive reproducing heads depend on flux rather than the rate of change of flux as is the case with inductive heads. The most highly developed flux-sensitive reproducing head uses the change in resistance of a magnetic material that accompanies a change in magnetization direction. To satisfy the requirement for maximum resistance change while using narrow tracks and closely packed bits, the magnetoresistive sensing element is designed as a narrow thin-film stripe perpendicular to the plane of the recorded medium with its length equal to the track width. When this element is located at the head surface, the wavelength response can be enhanced by placing magnetic shields close and parallel to the element. Since these shields short-circuit the long-wavelength recorded flux away from the sensing element, this design does not have a wide-wavelength response. Other designs, of somewhat reduced sensitivity, use conventional soft magnetic poles and a ring core with the element placed in series with the core. The core-flux response to the recorded wavelength is now similar to that of the ring head. If linear amplitude response is required, it is then necessary to apply a bias field transverse to the resistance measurement direction, and techniques for doing this are discussed in Sec. 6.5. Magnetoresistive reproducing heads using nickel-iron film elements are inherently wideband, and their low impedance matches well to low-noise preamplifiers.

Nickel-iron and other alloy films may also be used in flux-sensitive reading heads by measuring the Hall voltage along a current-carrying stripe of similar dimensions to the magnetoresistive stripe. For example, a "one-sided" design is feasible in which current enters the middle of the stripe and flows in opposite directions to each end. The output voltage is lower than that obtained in the magnetoresistive head, but it is linear with amplitude (Fluitman and Groenland, 1981). Nonmagnetic semiconductors such as indium-antimonide, with high electron mobility, have been designed as Hall effect field detectors. Films of about 1-μm thickness are sandwiched between two ferrite poles which guide the flux from the recording medium to the sensing element. In this design, current, field, and Hall voltage are orthogonal. Two-channel audio heads have been designed with the Hall elements in the rear gap of a ring-head structure (Kotera et al., 1979).

6.2 INDUCTIVE HEAD PERFORMANCE

The subject of recording head performance starts with a description of the physics of the head recording and reproducing mechanisms and the models which describe head performance.

6.2.1 Head Fields and Sensitivity Functions

6.2.1.1 Infinite-Pole-Length Inductive Heads.   A conventional inductive recording head roughly consists of a slit toroid of high-permeability magnetic material wound by several conductor turns as shown schematically in Fig. 6.1. Any treatment of recording head performance necessarily begins with a discussion of the fields in the vicinity of the recording gap. These fields determine the nature of written transitions, although a full treatment of the writing process must involve many other factors, such as the media and the recording electronics, as well as spacing between the head and media. The relationship of the head fields to output voltage is less obvious; however, the powerful reciprocity theorem states that the output voltage e is related to the field produced by a current i passing through the head windings, $\mathbf{H}(x, y, z)$, by the integral over all space:

$$e = -\frac{\mu_0}{i} \int_v \mathbf{H}(x, y, z) \cdot \frac{\partial \mathbf{M}(x, y, z)}{\partial t} \, dv \quad (6.1)$$

$$= \frac{\mu_0 V}{i} \int_v \mathbf{H}(x, y, z) \cdot \frac{\partial \mathbf{M}(x, y, z)}{\partial x} \, dv$$

where $\mathbf{M}(x, y, z)$ is the magnetization of the medium, μ_0 is the permeability of space, and V is the medium velocity in the x direction. A more complete discussion of the principle of reciprocity may be found in Chap. 2.

If it is assumed that head and media are of infinite width, techniques for solving two-dimensional potential problems can be used. The two-dimensional problem for the case of an infinite-permeability head with pole tips that extend to infinity can be solved by using a conformal mapping Schwarz-Christoffel transformation (Westmijze, 1953). These results are shown in Fig. 6.2. The fields at pole-tip corners approach infinity according to this model, a result which cannot hold for real heads whose materials have neither infinite permeability nor infinite saturation magnetization. However, fields higher than the average field in the deep-gap region ($x = 0$, $y = -\infty$) can be found at distances less than about one-tenth of the gap dimension away from the corners. This concentration of high fields is of importance only in the case of wide gaps reading thin media at a very close spacing.

The results of the Schwarz-Christoffel transformation do not permit a closed-form evaluation of the integral in Eq. (6.1) since neither the magnetic potential nor the field can be written as an explicit function of the coordinates (x, y). Thus fields at a given position can be found only by interpolation, and the integral for the output can be evaluated only by numerical methods.

Expressions for the magnetic potential U and fields in the upper half plane, $y \geq 0$, can be found if the potentials along the line $y = 0$ and at $x^2 + y^2 = \infty$ are known (and if proper mathematical constraints on that boundary potential are obeyed):

$$U(x, y) = \frac{1}{\pi} \int_{-\infty}^{\infty} \frac{U(x', 0)y}{(x - x')^2 + y^2} \, dx' \quad (6.2)$$

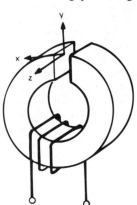

FIGURE   6.1 Approximate configuration of a conventional inductive recording head.

Useful expressions (Karlqvist, 1954) for the magnetic fields can be obtained by assuming a constant potential (implied by an infinite permeability) on each pole, and a constant field H_g between them at $y = 0$. The results for the longitudinal and perpendicular field components of a ring head are

$$H_x = \frac{H_g}{\pi} \left(\arctan \frac{g/2 + x}{y} + \arctan \frac{g/2 - x}{y} \right) \tag{6.3}$$

and

$$H_y = -\frac{H_g}{2\pi} \ln \frac{(x + g/2)^2 + y^2}{(x - g/2)^2 + y^2} \tag{6.4}$$

The limiting equations for the Karlqvist expressions and the conformal mapping result are the same at great distances from the pole corners (Westmijze, 1953). The maximum longitudinal recording field, at distances y greater than about $y = 0.2g$, is then for both models given approximately by the result

$$H_x(0, y) = \frac{2H_g}{\pi} \arctan \frac{g}{2y} \tag{6.5}$$

This field dependence, which is important in characterizing the head's ability to saturate longitudinally oriented media, is shown in Fig. 6.3.

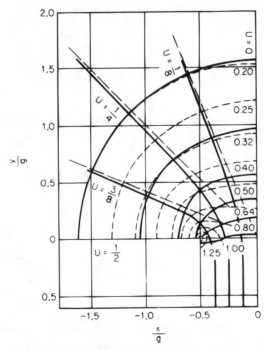

FIGURE 6.2 Equipotentials, lines of force, and lines of constant field strength (dashed curves). The center of the gap is at $x/g = 0$ and the potentials on the poles are $\pm\frac{1}{2}$ (*Westmijze, 1953*).

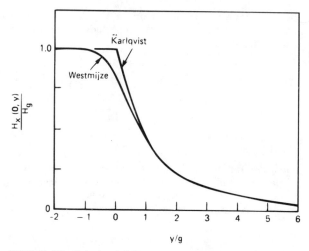

FIGURE 6.3 Calculated field strength $H_x(0, y)$ for the Karlqvist expression, Eq. (6.5), compared with Westmijze's result (*Westmijze, 1953*).

An exact two-dimensional description of the fields around an infinite-permeability head has been developed using a Fourier method (Fan, 1961). The results are in the form of a summation of an infinite series of integral terms. These results have been compared with the Karlqvist expressions, and the conditions in which the two results are in good agreement have been established (Baird, 1980). Figure 6.4 shows a comparison of computed perpendicular field components for $y = 0.4\ \mu$m and $g = 2.0\ \mu$m. The agreement between the two expressions improves as the ratio y/g increases.

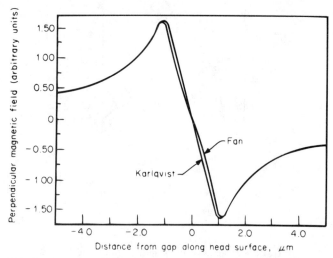

FIGURE 6.4 Calculated magnetic field H_y near the gap for a gap length of $2\ \mu$m and $y = 0.4\ \mu$m (*Baird, 1980*).

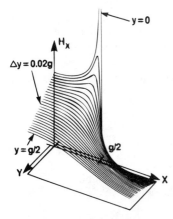

FIGURE 6.5 Three-dimensional plot of H_x for various y values using the field expression of Szczech (*Szczech et al., 1983*).

Semiempirical analytical expressions for the fields outside an infinite-pole-tip head have been derived (Szczech et al., 1983). The longitudinal field in the gap of a large-scale model was measured and the results fitted to a function of the form

$$H_x(x, 0) = H_s \left[A + \frac{Bg^2}{(Cg)^2 - x^2} \right] \quad (6.6)$$

with $H_s = H(0, 0)$ and the coefficients given by $A = 0.835$, $B = 0.0433$, and $C = 0.512$. The fields above the pole tips were then found from integrals

$$H_x(x, y) = \frac{1}{\pi} \int_{-\infty}^{\infty} H_x(x', 0) \frac{y}{(x - x')^2 + y^2} \, dx' \quad (6.7)$$

and

$$H_y(x, y) = -\frac{1}{\pi} \int_{-\infty}^{\infty} H_x(x', 0) \frac{x - x'}{(x - x')^2 + y^2} \, dx' \quad (6.8)$$

The resulting expressions, although more complex than Karlqvist's equations, reproduce many of the features of the conformal mapping solution fields, as shown in Fig. 6.5 (Szczech et al., 1983).

6.2.1.2 Finite-Width Inductive Heads. The limits to obtaining high track densities with narrow recording heads are determined by, among other things, the effects of side-fringing fields. These fields, which affect the written track width, can partially erase adjacent tracks, and, as can be shown by the reciprocity theorem, increase the reading width of the head and the pickup of signals from adjacent tracks.

The potential of an infinite-permeability head with a wedge-shaped side geometry shown in Fig. 6.6 has been derived by several workers (van Herk, 1977; Lindholm, 1977; Hughes and Bloomberg, 1977; Ichiyama, 1977). In the initial instance

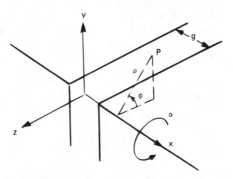

FIGURE 6.6 Polar and rectangular coordinate systems at the side of a semi-infinite head (*after Lindholm, 1977*).

the head is assumed to be one-sided, extending to infinity in the $-z$ direction. The calculation of the potential outside the head represents a three-dimensional boundary-value problem, the solution of which can be written as

$$U(\mathbf{R}) = \int\int_S U(\mathbf{R}') \, \nabla' G(\mathbf{R}, \mathbf{R}') \cdot \mathbf{n} \, dS \tag{6.9}$$

where $G(\mathbf{R}, \mathbf{R}')$ = Green's function for configuration used
$\mathbf{R}, \mathbf{R}'$ = position vectors
S = surface on which potential $U(\mathbf{R}')$ is given
$\mathbf{n}$ = unit vector normal to surface pointing outside head

For a zero gap length and the two poles at magnetostatic potentials $\pm U_0/2$, the potential $\bar{U}$ at any point outside the wedge-shaped head is given in the cylindrical coordinates shown in Fig. 6.6 by

$$\bar{U}(\rho, \phi, x) = -\frac{U_0}{\pi} \arctan\left[\csc \frac{\pi\phi}{\alpha} \sinh\left(\frac{\pi}{\alpha} \sinh^{-1} \frac{x}{\rho} \right) \right] \tag{6.10}$$

This solution for zero gap length can be extended to a finite gap length g if the potential in the gap at the head surfaces has a linear dependence on x, and only on x, as with the two-dimensional Karlqvist approximation. The finite gap potential U is then related to the potential given in Eq. (6.10) by an integral

$$U(\rho, \phi, x) = \frac{1}{g} \int_{-g/2}^{g/2} \bar{U}(\rho, \phi, x - x') \, dx' \tag{6.11}$$

The magnetic field is obtained from this equation by taking the gradient of the potential

$$\mathbf{H} = -\nabla U \tag{6.12}$$

Calculated fields in the vicinity of the head edge are shown in Fig. 6.7 (Lindholm, 1977) for the case $\alpha = 3\pi/2$. The importance of the three field components cannot be stated without knowing the magnetomotive potential difference between the pole tips, the hysteresis loops of the media in all directions, the positions of adjacent tracks, and so on. However, several general features can be noted in comparing these results with those of the two-dimensional head. In addition to the usual longitudinal and perpendicular fields H_x and H_y, there is a cross-track component H_z whose direction is in the same sense as that of the perpendicular field. That is, H_z is directed outward from the head surface on the same surface where H_y is directed outward. This field is concentrated at the edges of the head. The longitudinal field H_x begins a modest drop off inside the physical width of the poles. Outside the poles the half width of the H_x peak increases approximately in proportion to distance z to the side of the head, indicating a lower resolution in reading off-track recorded information. The peak amplitude of the longitudinal field decreases approximately in inverse proportion to the same distance. The results for a head with a one-sided, semi-finite width can be used to construct good approximations to the field for heads of finite width for which no analytical solution is available. The side effects are localized near the head edges. If the width w of a perpendicular-sided head ($\alpha = 3\pi/2$) is greater than six times the spacing y to the media, the fields on both edges are within 1 percent of the results calculated for the semi-infinite-width case. For

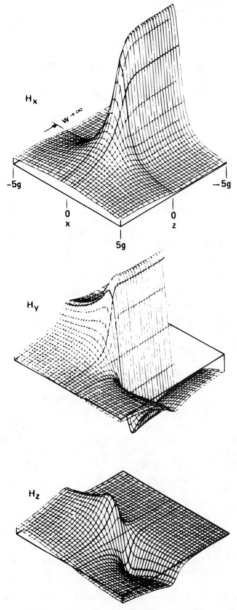

FIGURE 6.7 Magnetic fields at $y = g/2$ for a semi-infinite-width head. Components are longitudinal (H_x), vertical (H_y), and transverse (H_z). The side of the head is at $z = 0$. Projected onto each field surface are outlines of the top of the head (*Lindholm, 1977*).

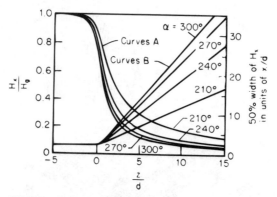

FIGURE 6.8   Maximum value of H_x (curves A) and half-width of H_x (curves B) with the head side angle as a parameter, versus z/d, where $y = d$ is the vertical spacing from the head (*van Herk, 1977*). The side of the head is at $z/d = 0$ and H_g is the deep gap field.

heads with sloping sides, $\pi < \alpha < 3\pi/2$, which are of considerable technological importance, H_x drops off less rapidly with z (Fig. 6.8), causing these heads to write and read wider than perpendicular-sided heads of the same width (van Herk, 1977). For high track densities, this generally leads to a preference for perpendicular-sided head configurations.

The effects of shields on potentials at the side of a head are illustrated in Fig. 6.9 for the rectangular head geometry shown in Fig. 6.10 (Lindholm, 1980). The potentials were computed numerically using a summation equivalent to the integration of Eq. (6.9) over the surface of the head. The shield is assumed to be at zero potential, halfway between the potentials of the two poles. In general, the effects of the side shields are to limit the lateral extent of the x and z field components, as shown in Fig. 6.9. At the same time the z component of fields in the region between the head and the shields becomes more intense. The rapid descent of the potential toward the shield intensifies the longitudinal field component near the leading and trailing edges relative to the fields present when the head is unshielded. The net effect of such shields depends on the mode of recording and the properties of the media.

Recently, commercial software packages have become available for three-dimensional analysis of head fields and are in common usage. These programs can cope with complex geometries, solving for the side-fringing fields using either finite element or boundary element numerical techniques (see, for example, Iwakura et al., 1989 or Cain et al., 1994).

6.2.1.3   *Finite-Pole-Length Heads.*

The models considered to this point have been for pole tips of infinite extent in the track direction. In practice, these models will not hold, and local fields near the leading and trailing edges must be taken into account. A first approximation to these edge fields for a two-dimensional infinite-permeability head, with a zero gap dimension, was obtained from a Schwarz-Christoffel conformal mapping (Westmijze, 1953). The potential along the line $y = 0$ is shown schematically in Fig. 6.11. At the corners the gradient of this potential, the longitudinal field H_x, is directed in the opposite sense from the gap field and goes to infinity at the corner

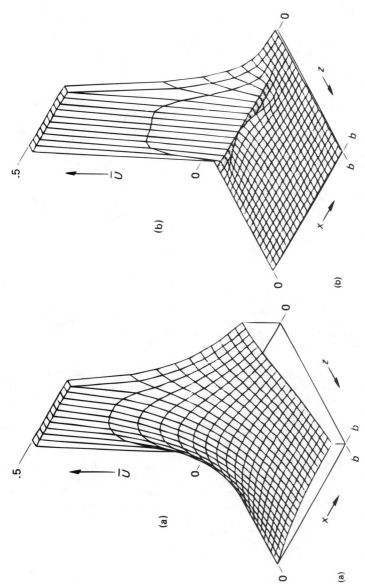

FIGURE 6.9 Potential at $y = 0$, $U(x, 0, z)$, versus x and z over a quarter of the geometry of a rectangular head, $d/b = 1$, $w/b = 0.1$. (a) Unshielded; (b) with side shields; $b_s/b = 1.5$, $c_s/b = 0.1$, $w_s/b = 0.05$ (shaded region is portion where $U = 0$ on top of the shield) (*Lindholm, 1980*).

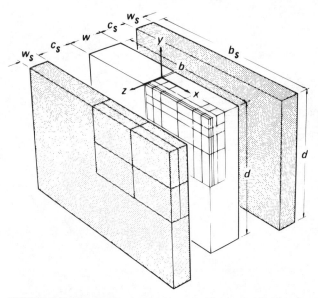

FIGURE 6.10 Rectangular head with optional side shields (shaded). Nomenclature: head length, b; head width, w; shield length, b_s; shield width, w_s; shield clearance, c_s; and depth, d (same for both head and shields) (*Lindholm, 1980*).

approximately as $(L/2 - x)^{-1/3}$, where $L/2$ is the distance from the center of the gap to the leading or trailing edge. At a fixed distance, $x - L/2$, from the pole edge the amplitude of the field is approximately inversely proportional to $L^{2/3}$, indicating that these fields diminish for large poles. The fields near the corner are shown schematically in Fig. 6.12 (van Herk, 1980b). When this type of sensitivity function is correlated with a sinusoidally recorded magnetization using Eq. (6.1), the negative portions of the sensitivity function at the edges can either add or subtract from the output associated with the gap, depending on whether the magnetization at the edge is in phase or out of phase with the magnetization at the gap. These wavelength-dependent oscillations in head output can be decreased by guiding flexible media away from the edges of the head (Westmijze, 1953) or by beveling the head edges

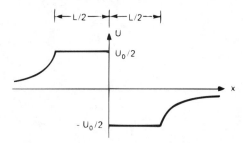

FIGURE 6.11 Distribution of the potential along the x axis for a head with $g = 0$ and a total length L (*Westmijze, 1953*).

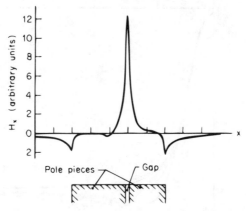

FIGURE 6.12 Schematic plot of the longitudinal field component, H_x, versus x for a head with finite pole tips (*Van Herk, 1980b*).

(Lindholm, 1979). In these ways the fields associated with the edges are made less intense either by increasing the distance to the media or by reducing the high concentration of flux associated with a corner.

The fields around three-dimensional heads have been computed using a surface-integral technique, and it has been shown (Fig. 6.13) that the x field components associated with the leading and trailing edges of heads are accentuated as the width of the head is diminished (Lindholm, 1980). Apparently the fields associated with a corner in three dimensions are even stronger than those associated with a corner in two dimensions.

With the film head, the total length of the head may be only a few times larger than the gap dimension, as shown in Fig. 6.14. In this case, the reverse fields associated with the leading and trailing edges cut into the extent of the fields

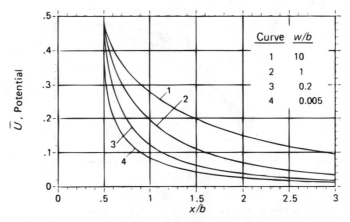

FIGURE 6.13 Magnetic potential at $y = 0$ for an unshielded head versus x/b, where b represents the length of the head, for various widths w. The head geometry is shown in Fig. 6.10 (*Lindholm, 1980*).

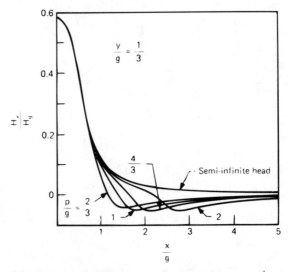

FIGURE 6.14   The effect of the ratio p/g on H_x/H_g for $y/g = \frac{1}{3}$; p is the pole-tip dimension from the edge of the gap to the corner of the pole tip, and H_g is the average longitudinal field in the gap at $y = 0$ (*Potter et al., 1971*).

associated with the gap. In this way the gap field is narrowed and gradient of the field made sharper, significantly affecting resolution in both reading and writing. Using the Schwarz-Christoffel transformation solution for fields around infinite-permeability, infinite-width heads with a finite gap dimension g and a finite pole length p (Elabd, 1963), the x and y fields have been computed, and the results for several p/g ratios are shown in Figs. 6.14 and 6.15 (Potter et al., 1971).

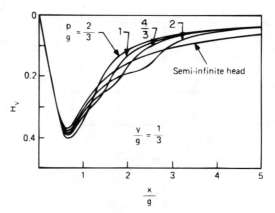

FIGURE 6.15   The effect of the ratio p/g on H_y/H_g for $y/g = \frac{1}{3}$; H_g is the average longitudinal field in the gap at $y = 0$ (*Potter et al., 1971*).

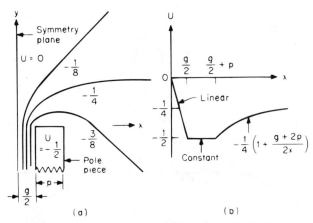

FIGURE 6.16 (*a*) Cross section of finite-pole-tip head with several equipotential lines schematically shown; (*b*) assumed magnetic potential at $y = 0$ (*Potter, 1975*).

As with most conformal mapping solutions, the field results are not closed-form analytic expressions which can be used to evaluate the integral expression for output given by Eq. (6.1). Such expressions for infinite-permeability heads have been obtained by approximating the potential at $y = 0$ outside the pole tips, $|x| \geq g/2 + p$, by

$$U(x, 0) = \pm \frac{1}{4} \left(1 + \frac{g + 2\rho}{2x} \right) \qquad (6.13)$$

and assuming a constant field between the pole tips at $y = 0$ (Potter, 1975). A constant potential will exist at the pole surface, and the potential at the pole tip is taken to be $-\frac{1}{2}$ on the positive x axis ($x > 0$, $y = 0$) and $+\frac{1}{2}$ on the negative x axis. The potential along the line $y = 0$ is then completely described as shown in Fig. 6.16, and Eq. (6.2) can be used to find closed-form expressions for the potential and its associated fields.

An improved closed-form analytical approximation to the Schwarz-Christoffel solution potential is obtained by using expressions of the form

$$U(x, 0) = \pm \frac{1}{2(1 + \gamma)} \left[\exp \frac{-\alpha(x - g/2 - p)}{g/2 - p} \right.$$

$$\left. + \gamma \exp \frac{-\beta(x - g/2 - p)}{g/2 + p} \right] \qquad (6.14)$$

for $|x| \geq g/2 + p$. The parameters α, β, and γ are chosen to optimize the fit to the conformal mapping fields. Asymmetric structures with different pole-tip thicknesses are accommodated by using different p parameters for the two sides of the head (Ichiyama, 1975).

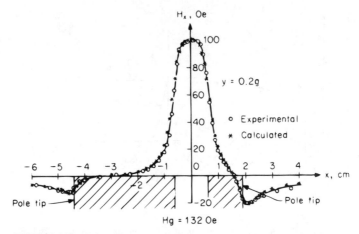

FIGURE 6.17 Comparison of calculated and experimental horizontal field components at $y = 0.2g$ for an asymmetrical scale model with one pole tip three times larger than the other (*Szczech, 1979*).

An empirical potential has been deduced based on agreement with measured values of H_x outside the pole tips of a large-scale model head (Szczech, 1979). The potential is found by integration and fitting the form

$$U(x,0) = \pm \frac{\Delta U_0}{2} \left(\frac{C_1}{x - C_2} + C_0 \right) \quad \text{for } |x| > \frac{g}{2} + p \tag{6.15}$$

where $C_1 = p/2$, $C_2 = 1.1g/2$, and $C_0 = 0.41$. Unlike the previous potential curves, the potential immediately beyond the pole tip does not equal $-U_0/2$, providing a discontinuity in potential at the pole-tip surface. As might be expected, the resulting closed-form expressions for H_y and H_x are somewhat lengthier than the Karlqvist equations, but still require only a modest computational power. The agreement between calculated and measured values of the horizontal field component H_x is shown in Fig. 6.17 for an asymmetrical head with one pole tip three times the thickness of the other.

With a properly chosen recording medium, recording mode, and head-to-medium spacing, the finite-pole-head waveform can give rise to small peak shifts in digital recording. Assuming that peak shift is due entirely to the superposition of adjacent pulses, the dibit peak shift τ can be approximated by

$$V\tau \approx \frac{de/dx|_{x = -S}}{d^2e/dx^2|_{x=0}} \tag{6.16}$$

where V is the velocity of the medium, e is the output voltage, $x = 0$ corresponds to the position of a peak, and the two symmetrical dibits are spaced a nominal distance S apart. When the peaks are widely spread out, with the adjacent peak lying outside the negative minimum in the pulse forms, the peak shift will be negative and the peaks are shifted closer together. If the peak in one pulse coincides exactly with the minimum in the adjacent pulse, there is no peak shift. Finally, if the peaks approach more closely, peak shift rises rapidly, exceeding the bit shift for an infinite-pole-tip head because of the greater derivative of pulse amplitude.

Analytical expressions for the vector two-dimensional magnetic fields and Fourier transforms associated with asymmetrical film heads have been derived (Bertero et al., 1993) from expressions for the surface field, $H_x(x', 0)$, determined from conformal mapping solutions. $H_x(x', 0)$ is assumed to be a superposition of the fields for (1) a finite gap, infinitesimally thin head of infinite length and (2) a finite length, infinitely deep head with an infinitesimally small gap (Westmijze, 1953). The field at the outer edges of the finite length head is taken to be the first expansion term for the conformal mapping solution. Since an infinitely permeable head is assumed, $H_x(x', 0)$ vanishes at the head surface over the poles. An approximation (Ruigrok, 1990) to the conformal mapping solution for the gap field is also used. Equations (6.7) and (6.8) are utilized to find the fields at any point above the head. The surface field also can be Fourier transformed exactly to yield the spectrum of each field component.

6.2.1.4 Perpendicular Recording Inductive Heads.
Numerous studies have been conducted using conventional ring heads and finite-pole-tip heads with perpendicular recording media (for example, Iwasaki et al., 1979; Iwasaki, 1980; Potter and Beardsley, 1980). However, the more extensive theoretical and experimental efforts have been directed toward the use of a single-pole head (Iwasaki and Nakamura, 1977) to accentuate the perpendicular field component. Much of this work has been done using a relatively large auxiliary pole, or a deposited high-permeability layer, beneath the recording layer. This auxiliary pole or deposited underlayer, in a sense, is part of the head structure. It modifies the head-field configurations and intensifies the perpendicular field by providing a return path for flux linking the pickup coils.

The exact solution for the fields from a single-pole head of arbitrary dimensions in proximity to an infinitely permeable layer has been derived using a Schwarz-Christoffel conformal mapping (Steinback et al., 1981). The calculated results with the geometry shown in Fig. 6.18 are displayed in Fig. 6.19 for the case $y/s = 0.001$ and $T/s = 0.28$. The presence of the infinite-permeability layer is taken into account by introducing an image pole at a spacing $2s$ from the single reference pole. As with

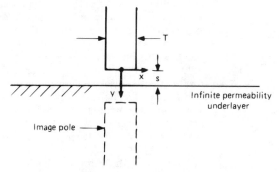

FIGURE 6.18 Geometry for a single-pole head over an infinite-permeability underlayer.

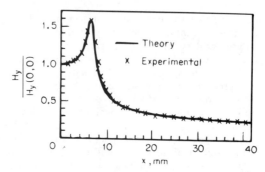

FIGURE 6.19 Comparison of measured and calculated H_y field components for a scale model; $T = 7.15$ mm, $T/s = 0.28$, $y/s = 0.001$ (*Steinback et al., 1981*).

previous Schwarz-Christoffel mappings, the vertical fields rise sharply to infinity at the corners of the probe. Such a result is physically unrealistic, arising from the assumptions of infinite permeability and infinite saturation magnetization; however, there is ample experimental evidence from scale models of field maxima near those corners (Steinback et al., 1981).

Approximate expressions for $H_y(x, y)$ and $H_x(x, y)$ in the region $0 \leq y \leq s$ can be found from the mapping solution by fitting the results for field along the line $y = 0$ to appropriate simple forms with adjustable coefficients. The approximations are then made by evaluating definite integrals involving these forms from $x = -\infty$ to $x = +\infty$ over this line. The results, although complex and tedious to write out, are closed-form expressions which are convenient for computations. A comparison of the conformal mapping and calculated y components of field is shown in Fig. 6.20 (Szczech et al., 1982). These results are compared with field measurements near a large-scale model as shown in Fig. 6.21.

In regions in which there are no magnetic poles, the potential U is a solution of Laplace's equation, $\nabla^2 U = 0$. Numerical solutions can be found for the potential in the vicinity of a single-pole head by iterating finite-difference expressions for $\nabla^2 U = 0$, subject to the approximate fixed boundary conditions (Szczech and Palmquist, 1984). Results are obtained both with and without an infinitely permeable magnetic sublayer. A potential of 1 is assumed for the single pole, and zero potential is assigned either to the surface of the infinitely permeable sublayer or at great distances from the pole, taken in this instance to be a distance of $5T$ from the pole. After iteration to a convergent solution, the resulting potential is numerically differentiated to obtain H_x and H_y. The results for H_y in the region $0 \leq y \leq \frac{1}{2}T$, with and without an infinitely permeable magnetic sublayer, are shown in Figs. 6.22 and 6.23. The infinitely permeable layer in this instance was assumed to be at $y = \frac{1}{2}T$.

Comparing these results shows that H_y fields are significantly stronger for the single-pole head with an

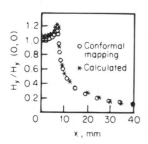

FIGURE 6.20 Comparison of conformal mapping and calculated H_y field components for a scale model; $T = 7.15$ mm, $T/s = 2.5$, $y/s = 0.35$ (*Szczech et al., 1982*).

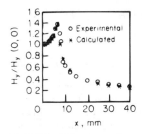

FIGURE 6.21 Comparison of experimental and calculated H_y field components for a scale model; $T = 7.15$ mm. $T/s = 0.28$, $y/s = 0.04$ (*Szczech et al., 1982*).

underlayer. The singularity at the corner $(x, y) = (T/2, 0)$ is again present, but the field maxima associated with this corner appear to vanish at about $y = 0.15T$.

These results can be compared with the H_x and H_y fields computed by the same methods for an infinite-pole-tip ring head and a finite-pole-tip film head. The perpendicular field component, with and without an infinitely permeable magnetic sublayer, for a finite-pole-tip head is shown in Figs. 6.24 and 6.25 (Szczech and Palmquist, 1984).

A complementary relationship between the fields from an infinite-pole-tip ring head with a gap dimension $g = T$ and a single-pole head of thickness T was recognized with the initial revival of interest in perpendicular recording (Iwasaki and Nakamura, 1977). It was then proposed that the H_y fields from the single-pole head would have the form of the H_x fields for the Karlqvist head model, at least as a first approximation. Later (Iwasaki et al., 1981) it was assumed the H_y field of a single probe would have the same form as the H_x field calculated by Fan (Fan, 1961).

It can be shown that a uniformly perpendicularly magnetized single-pole head gives rise to fields which can be simply related to the fields of a ring-head model in which the gap region is uniformly longitudinally magnetized. The fields H_{px} and H_{py} from the uniformly perpendicularly magnetized single-pole head without an infinite sublayer are given by

$$H_{px}(x, y) = -H_{ry}(x, y) \tag{6.17}$$

and

$$H_{py}(x, y) = H_{rx}(x, y) \tag{6.18}$$

where it is to be understood that the pole thickness T is substituted for the gap dimension g in H_{rx} and H_{ry}, which are the longitudinal and perpendicular field components given by Eqs. (6.3) and (6.4) (Mallinson and Bertram, 1984).

These expressions, which probably represent good approximations for y values greater than a few tenths of the pole thickness, can be equally well viewed as resulting from a uniform magnetic pole density at the top of the pole, uniform magnetization in the pole, or uniform magnetic electric current sheets on the sides of the pole (Mallinson, 1981; Mallinson and Bertram, 1984). The magnetic poles on the opposite end of the probe can be assumed to be at a great distance L', and hence give rise to broad field distributions H'_{px} and H'_{py} whose features are not important in the short range:

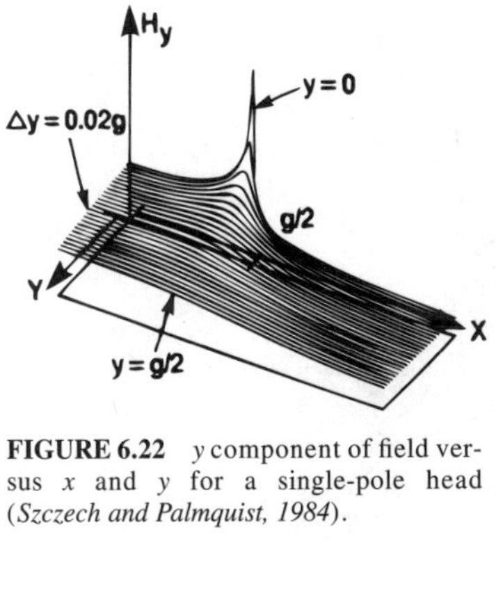

FIGURE 6.22 y component of field versus x and y for a single-pole head (*Szczech and Palmquist, 1984*).

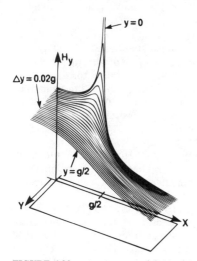

FIGURE 6.23 y component of field versus x and y for a single-pole head with a high-permeability underlayer at $y = T/2$ (*Sczcech and Palmquist, 1984*).

$$H'_{px}(x, y) = H_{ry}(x, y + L') \qquad (6.19)$$

and

$$H'_{py}(x, y) = -H_{rx}(x, y + L') \qquad (6.20)$$

Similarly, if the pole is positioned opposite an infinitely permeable layer at a spacing s, the total field in the region $0 \leq y \leq s$ will be a result of the fields given above and two other expressions representing the pole's image on the other side of the infinite-permeability layer.

The degree to which an assumption of uniform magnetization is valid will naturally depend on how uniformly fields from current sources are applied to the probe. For example, for a very thin infinite-permeability probe, only partially covered by coil turns, the field distribution will depend not only on the thickness of the pole tip but on the extent of the vertical region not covered by turns. In this case magnetic poles are distributed over the uncovered region of the probe (Minuhin, 1984).

Computations using a magnetic field surface-integral equation method (van Herk, 1980*a*, 1980*b*; Luitjens and van Herk, 1982) have been carried out for three-dimensional models of the single-pole head with and without the infinitely permeable underlayer. The single pole in this case consists of a thin slab of infinite-permeability magnetic material with $T = 0.1$ and height and width equal to 1.0. The

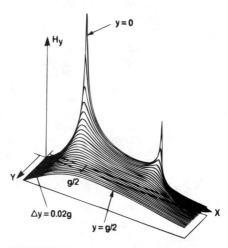

FIGURE 6.24 y component of field versus x and y for a thin-film head with $p = g$ (*Sczcech and Palmquist, 1984*).

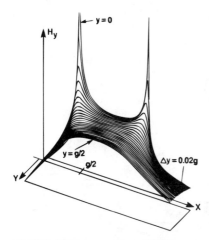

FIGURE 6.25 y component of field versus x and y for a thin-film head with $p = g$ and a high-permeability underlayer at $y = g/2$ (*Sczcech and Palmquist, 1984*).

head is excited by a homogenous magnetic field in the y direction which is not included in the calculated results. Figure 6.26 shows the resultant H_y fields. As with two-dimensional models, there are pronounced singularities at the leading and trailing edges of the pole which become less pronounced with increasing y, and finally vanish. Even more pronounced field maxima exist near the side edges of the head ($z = 0.49$). However, H_y drops off rapidly to the side of the track ($z = 0.55$), suggesting favorable side writing and reading characteristics.

Figure 6.26 also shows a feature reminiscent of the finite-pole-tip head: a region surrounding the sides and edges of the head in which the H_y fields are of opposite sign. These areas represent the return paths of flux lines from the vicinity of the pole face to the remote end of the head. This feature, which contributes to the steep field gradients near the probe edges, may, however, be significantly modified by other return paths for flux provided by permeable underlayers or second poles.

As with two-dimensional models, the y component of field is strongly enhanced by the presence of an infinite-permeability layer near the pole, as shown in Fig. 6.27. This is true both at the center of the head, $z = 0$, and at the side, $z = 0.7$. Computations also show that the y component of field varies less rapidly with y in the presence of an infinitely permeable underlayer.

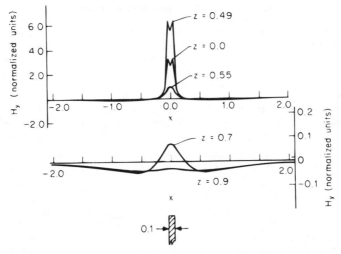

FIGURE 6.26 Perpendicular component of a magnetic field for a single-pole head. Center of the head is at $z = 0$, the geometrical edge is at $z = 0.5$, and the field is shown for $y = 0.01$ (*Luitjens and van Herk, 1982*).

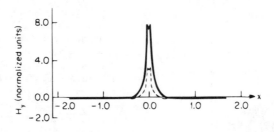

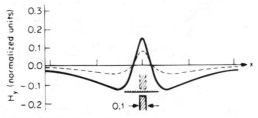

FIGURE 6.27 Perpendicular component of magnetic field for a single-pole head with an infinite-permeability underlayer at $y = 0.05$ (solid line) and without such an underlayer (dashed line). Center of the head is at $z = 0$, the geometrical edge is at $z = 0.5$, and the field is shown for $y = 0.01$ (*Luitjens and van Herk, 1982*).

6.3 INDUCTIVE HEAD MATERIALS

6.3.1 Magnetic, Electrical, and Mechanical Properties

The importance of many properties of head materials, for example, permeability and saturation magnetization, is clear from discussions of head function. Other properties can be appreciated only with a knowledge of fabrication techniques and the recording environment. A number of head core material properties which must be taken in account are as follows:

1. Permeability $\mu\mu_0$, the ratio of magnetic induction B to field H, is a key parameter for read and write performance. The relative permeability μ is sensitive to purity, thermal history, mechanical cold working, and the wear environment.

2. Saturation magnetic induction B_s dictates the maximum flux density which can be obtained in the head poles and is important for the writing function.

3. Coercivity H_c is the field necessary to reverse the magnetization and decrease the magnetic induction to zero. It is a measure of the ease of switching the magnetization and is sensitive to the material-handling history. It is also a measure of the openness of the B-H loop and therefore of the heat generation during magnetization cycles.

4. Remanent magnetic induction B_r is the magnetic induction remaining with zero applied field. Its value is closely related to coercivity and permeability and controls the residual field in and around the head, after magnetization during writing has ceased.

5. Electrical resistivity ρ influences the high-frequency performance of a head, which is reduced by eddy currents (Cullity, 1972). Eddy currents shield the interior of the head from the penetration of applied fields, reduce the effective permeability, and modify local fields around the gap. For a semi-infinite magnetic material, the maximum field amplitude follows a decaying exponential dependence, exp $(-x/\delta)$, where δ is the "penetration depth" and x is the distance from the surface. The penetration depends on material properties through the relationship $\delta \propto \sqrt{\rho/f\mu\mu_0}$, where f is the frequency.

6. An intrinsic damping phenomenon associated with spin resonance, characterized by a frequency f_c, dictates the ability of ferrite magnetic materials to follow applied fields at high frequencies. This frequency, approximately 1 to 10 MHz for common ferrite head materials, increases as the ratio $B_s/\mu\mu_0$ increases.

7. The thermal coefficients of all the properties listed above are important because of head heating. It is generally desirable to have materials with a high Curie temperature, since properties at relatively low temperatures tend to be less sensitive to temperature excursions.

8. When magnetic head materials are in the form of films or single crystals, or have a pronounced crystalline orientation texture, for example, as a result of a rolling orientation, properties such as permeability, coercivity, and residual magnetic induction need to be specified as a function of orientation. For films with a uniaxial magnetic anisotropy, the parameter most frequently associated with this anisotropy is the anisotropy field H_k, which is the field (neglecting demagnetizing fields) at which an anisotropic film saturates in the hard-axis direction. This field is related to the saturation magnetic induction and permeability in the hard-axis direction by the relationship $H_k = B_s/\mu\mu_0$.

9. Head materials are frequently subject to strain, either during their original formation, as a result of head machining and lapping processes, or through wear, abrasion, and stress during use. This leads to a consideration of magnetostriction and the parameters which characterize changes of magnetic properties as a function of strain. The magnetostriction coefficient λ relates the magnitude and sign of strain, along a given crystalline direction or magnetic anisotropy axis, to a change in magnetic properties (see, for example, Bozorth, 1951). Since stresses are inevitable during head fabrication or in use, zero-magnetostriction materials are generally preferred.

10. Purely mechanical properties are important in forming and using the head. Hardness, measured, for example, in units of Vickers hardness, is sometimes an indication of durability. Wear is typically measured as a removal rate for head material in a particular environment with a particular medium. It depends not only on material properties, but also on wear interface characteristics such as friction, hardness of the media, and corrosive constituents of the environment. Even with the head material alone, many other aspects of material science are involved, such as the yield strength, porosity, and susceptibility to chipping. With relatively soft materials, there is the tendency for the material to distort or yield during the head manufacturing process, while for hard materials porosity and the tendency to chip are crucial.

6.3.2 Magnetic Alloys

The earliest recording heads were made with laminated magnetic alloys with perhaps the three most prominent examples being molybdenum Permalloy (4 wt % Mo, 17 wt % Fe-Ni), Alfenol (16 wt % Al-Fe), and Sendust (5.4 wt % Al, 9.6 wt % Si-Fe) (see, for example, Chin and Wernick, 1980). As shown in Table 6.1, the

TABLE 6.1   Magnetic Metallic Materials

Material	$\mu\dagger$	H_c, A/m (Oe)	B_s, T (kG)	ρ, $\mu\,\Omega \cdot$ cm	Vickers hardness
4% Mo Permalloy	11,000	2.0 (0.025)	0.8 (8)	100	120
Alfenol	4,000	3.0 (0.038)	0.8 (8)	150	290
Sendust	8,000	2.0 (0.025)	1.0 (10)	85	480

†Measured at 1 K Hz with 0.2-mm-thick material.

Source: Chin and Wernick (1980, p. 164).

initial permeabilities of these materials are high at low frequencies and their coercivities are low, although a wide range can be found, depending on thermal history and work hardening. Both molybdenum Permalloy and Sendust can be made with near zero magnetostriction, rendering them relatively insensitive to strain and with high saturation magnetization and good writing performance. The resistivity of molybdenum Permalloy is low, leading to losses of permeability due to eddy currents even at moderate frequencies unless the head is made in laminate form (Cullity, 1972). The principal advantage of Sendust is its hardness (Table 6.1). This hardness unfortunately also renders it more difficult to work, although special methods for forming ribbons of material with excellent magnetic properties have been reported (Ohmori et al., 1980; Tsuya et al., 1981).

Alfenol is an alloy with properties intermediate between those of molybdenum Permalloy and Sendust. It is somewhat easier to form than Sendust and has increased hardness and resistivity in comparison to molybdenum Permalloy. The permeability of Alfenol is somewhat lower than either of the other materials, but its magnetic performance is still adequate for many applications.

Many other alloys, such as Alperm (17 wt % Al-Fe) and Mumetal (4 wt % Mo, 5 wt % Cu, 77 wt % Ni-Fe), have been used successfully in heads, and efforts continue to develop better alloys. For example, alloys near the 4 wt % Mo, 79 wt % Ni-Fe composition with niobium and titanium additions have been shown to have an enhanced hardness (Vickers hardness, 240 to 300) while still retaining the high permeability and low magnetostriction of Permalloy (Miyazaki et al., 1972).

6.3.3   Amorphous Magnetic Alloys

Ferromagnetic amorphous alloys are a relatively new class of materials typically formed of 75 to 85 at % transition element (Fe, Co, Ni), with the balance being a glass-forming metalloid (B, C, Si, P, or Al). A thorough review of this class of materials is available (Luborsky, 1980). Like glasses, these materials have no structural order that can be detected, except that associated with near-neighbor interaction, and consequently are free of some of the characteristics of crystalline materials, such as crystalline anisotropy, porosity associated with crystal grains, and stresses associated with grain growth. Amorphous magnetic materials generally have smaller permeability losses due to eddy currents than crystalline materials, since the resistivities of these alloys are typically two to four times larger than the corresponding transition metal crystalline alloys without the metalloid glass-forming elements. Amorphous magnetic alloys have shown desirable permeabilities and saturation magnetic inductions for head applications, along with low magnetostriction, suitable hardness, and stability against recrystallization and corrosion. However, all these desirable properties may not be associated with a single composition (Mukasa, 1985).

TABLE 6.2 Vickers Hardness and Wear Rates for Various Amorphous Alloys

Composition	Vickers hardness	Relative wear rate
Fe-Si-Al	560	1
$(Co_{85.5}Nb_{14.5})_{98}B_2$	850	0.3
$(Co_{85.5}Nb_{14.5})_{95}B_5$	800	0.4
$(CO_{85.5}Nb_{14.5})_{90}B_{10}$	900	0.6
$Fe_{2.5}Co_{71.5}Mn_3Si_8B_{15}$	900	2
$Fe_{80}P_{13}C_7$	760	3
$Fe_{40}Ni_{40}P_{14}B_6$	750	4

Source: Sakakima et al. (1981).

Table 6.2 shows Vickers hardnesses and wear rates for a number of amorphous alloys in comparison with Fe-Si-Al (Sendust). For Co-Nb-B alloys it is desirable to keep the boron content below about 10% to achieve a wear rate lower than that of Sendust.

Co-Fe-Si-B amorphous alloys are potentially good materials for video heads, with a higher saturation magnetic induction than Mn-Zn ferrite heads, and a higher permeability at 5 MHz than Sendust heads (Shiiki et al., 1981; Matsuura et al., 1983). Amorphous Co-Zr alloys (10 wt % Zr) produced by magnetron sputtering have been used to fabricate film heads (Yamada et al., 1984). In sputtered form the saturated magnetic induction of these materials is higher than that of Ni-Fe Permalloy (1.4 versus 1.0 T), as is its relative permeability at 10 MHz (3500 versus 2000), and hardness (Vickers hardness of 650 versus approximately 300).

A serious concern regarding amorphous alloy heads is their stability in the presence of heat generated by tape friction. Amorphous Fe-Co-Si-B materials wear faster than either ferrite or Sendust, despite having a greater hardness.

In fact, as can be noted in Table 6.2, the wear and hardness of amorphous materials are not correlated in any simple fashion. This may be because the amorphous alloy surface is crystallized, or possibly oxidized, during wear experiments to either increase or decrease the wear rate (Ozawa et al., 1984).

6.3.4 Ferrite Materials

The resistivity of ferrite materials (Table 6.3) is at least three orders of magnitude greater than that of most metallic magnetic materials, so that eddy currents and asso-

TABLE 6.3 Ferrite Properties

Property	Hot-pressed Ni-Zn ferrite	Hot-pressed Mn-Zn ferrite	Single-crystal Mn-Zn ferrite
μ	300–1500	3000–10,000	400–1000
H_c, A/m (Oe)	11.8–27.6 (0.15–0.35)	11.8–15.8 (0.15–0.20)	3.95 (0.05)
B_s, T (kG)	0.4–0.46 (4–4.6)	0.4–0.6 (4–6)	0.4 (4)
ρ, $\Omega \cdot$ cm	~10^5	~5	>0.5
θ_c, °C	150–200	90–300	100–265
Vickers hardness	900	700	

ciated permeability losses are relatively small. As a consequence, these materials dominated the field of high-frequency head applications for years. Ferrites are also hard, with Vickers hardnesses in the range of 550 to 900, and behave well when head-media contact occurs. If properly made, ferrites can be precision-machined to close tolerances with no tendency to distort; and being oxides rather than metals, they are immune from attack by atmospheric gases, including water. Chipping in the region of the write-read gap is the most severe deterioration encountered in ferrite-head cores. This becomes relatively more serious as track widths are reduced. A description of ferrite properties and preparation techniques can be found elsewhere (Slick, 1980).

There are two categories of high-permeability ferrite of commercial interest: nickel-zinc (Ni-Zn) ferrites, whose stoichiometric composition is $(NiO)_x(ZnO)_{1-x}$ (Fe_2O_3), and manganese-zinc (Mn-Zn) ferrites, $(MnO)_x(ZnO)_{1-x}(Fe_2O_3)$, both with the spinel crystal structure. Compositions of Mn-Zn ferrite, optimized for high permeability, may also contain additional ferrous (Fe^{2+}) ions replacing divalent, manganese or zinc. These ferrous ions further increase electrical resistivity and decrease eddy-current losses relative to the stoichiometric material. The properties of both materials are influenced by the nickel-to-zinc and manganese-to-zinc ratios. For small additions of zinc, permeabilities and saturation magnetic induction are increased and coercivities and Curie temperatures decreased until optimum magnetic properties are obtained in the range $x = 0.3$ to 0.7.

Although there can be advantages to porosity, for example, to provide voids in the ferrite body that inhibit domain wall motion and decrease losses, every other consideration favors the lowest porosity that can be provided practically. Wear and chipping are diminished with low porosity, and it is easier to hold precise head geometries. Toward this end, dense hot-pressed ferrites were developed (Sugaya, 1968). These materials are sintered under uniaxial compression and, as a result, can have grain sizes in the order of 70 μm and porosities of 0.1 percent or less. Hot isostatic pressing is another technique recently developed to further decrease porosity (Takama and Ito, 1979).

Ni-Zn ferrite is to be preferred over Mn-Zn ferrite for very high-frequency operation because its relatively high resistivity suppresses permeability losses due to eddy currents (Table 6.3). On the other hand, Mn-Zn ferrite is generally preferred at frequencies below a few megahertz because it has a lower coercivity, higher permeability, and higher saturation induction. Despite the fact that Ni-Zn ferrite is a harder material, it tends to have a thicker "dead layer" (or nonmagnetic layer) due to lapping or wear damage. The dead layer increases the effective flying height in the order of tens of nanometers.

Single-crystal Mn-Zn ferrites were developed to improve the porosity still further, and in several ways they represent an ideal magnetic and mechanical material. The microcracking problem of polycrystalline ferrite is largely avoided, and residual stresses and dead layers from machining can be removed by annealing. If specified crystal orientations are used, single-crystal heads also exhibit excellent wear characteristics. However, magnetostriction-induced noise due to media contact can be a problem with single-crystal heads. With certain polycrystalline ferrites, the existence of many grains and grain boundaries suppresses magnetostriction noise. Compositions can be chosen to minimize the magnetostriction coefficient, but it is difficult to achieve a zero value along with a high saturation magnetic induction. The choice of single-crystal orientation is a compromise between permeability, wear rate, and magnetostriction noise (Hirota et al., 1980). Permeabilities may vary as much as 2 to 1 and wear rates 3 to 1 with different orientations.

With regard to magnetic properties, the most serious problem with ferrites is their inherently low values of saturation magnetic induction. There is a theoretical upper limit for ferrite of 0.6 T (6 kG), which is significantly lower than that for metallic magnetic materials. Sendust, for example, has a saturation magnetic induction of 1.0 T (10 kG), approximately twice that of any currently available ferrite. Another limitation, which is not nearly so obvious, is associated with the manufacturing techniques that must be used in making ferrite heads. The precision grinding and lapping processes used tend to impose a scale and associated geometry which restrict design options. New techniques such as ion milling can effectively offset these limitations (Toshima et al., 1979).

6.3.5 Film-Head Materials

Film heads contain a variety of materials formed by techniques that are extensions of the thin-film technology of earlier magnetic microelectronic devices (Maissel and Glang, 1970; Cullity, 1972). The properties of these materials are frequently sensitive to their method of deposition, and the reader should consult the original papers cited below for descriptions of those methods and properties.

6.3.5.1 Magnetic Films. With a few exceptions, film heads have been made of approximately 80 wt % Ni with 20 wt % Fe, the material used for magnetic film devices over the past 40 years. The nature of film Ni-Fe is significantly different from bulk Ni-Fe because of its thickness, the techniques used to form it, and limitations on annealing and heat treatment. It is deposited by evaporation, sputtering, or plating (see Table 6.4) with impurities due to residual gases, the sputtering gas, or the plating bath. Because of constraints of the film substrate and other film constituents, high-temperature heat treatments and outgassing that might be used with bulk metals are not possible. As a result, very high permeabilities are rarely possible. Furthermore, because of these constraints it has not been possible to employ ferrites in thin-film form. Anisotropy fields H_k, for Ni-Fe films deposited under optimal conditions, fall in the range 200 to 400 A/m (2.5 to 5.0 Oe) and saturation inductions are near 1.0 T (10 kG), implying low-frequency relative permeabilities of 2000 to 4000. Eddy-current losses, which limit the useful frequency range of bulk Permalloy, are diminished in the film form so film heads can still operate at a frequency of 10 MHz and beyond (Calcagno and Thompson, 1975).

A tabulation of other magnetic film-head materials is given in Table 6.4, along

TABLE 6.4. Film-Head Magnetic Materials

Material	Reference
Ni-Fe, evaporated	Kaske et al., 1971; Lazzari, 1978
Ni-Fe, sputtered	Hanazono et al., 1982; Potzlberger, 1984
Ni-Fe, plated	Bischoff, 1990; Poupon et al., 1990; Wong et al., 1990; Harris et al., 1994
Ni-Fe-Cr/SiO_2, evaporated	Lazzari and Melnick, 1971
CoFeCu, plated	Chang et al., 1992
CoZrNb, sputtered	Louis and Walser, 1992
CoZrRe, sputtered	Guzman and Kryder, 1987
Fe (N)/SiO_2, sputtered	Hu et al., 1994
Fe(N)/NiFeCo(N), sputtered	Jones et al., 1993
FeAlN, sputtered	Wang et al., 1994

TABLE 6.5   Film-Head Conductors

Material	References
Copper, evaporated	Lazzari and Melnick, 1971
Copper, sputtered	Berghof and Gatzen, 1980
Copper, plated	Romankiw and Simon, 1975; Jones, 1980
Gold, plated	Jones, 1980
Mo-Au-Mo, sputtered	Hanazono et al., 1979
Aluminum, 4% copper	Miura et al., 1980

with examples of references describing their use. Laminated Ni-Fe-Cr/SiO_2 offers the advantage of suppressing edge domains which can give rise to irreproducible head response pulse shapes. Sputtered amorphous Co-Zr, annealed in a rotating field to provide a low anisotropy, has a higher saturation magnetic induction, 1.4 T, and relative permeability (3500, at 10 MHz) than Ni-Fe. Other alternatives to Ni-Fe offer, in some combination, an improved high-frequency permeability associated with a higher resistivity, greater hardness, or a higher saturation magnetic induction.

High saturation induction alloys offer potential advantages for inductive film heads of increased writing field, increased throat height and, with thinner pole tips, increased reading resolution. Candidate materials that can be deposited in film form include zero magnetostriction amorphous cobalt-based alloys, such as Co-Zr-Nb (Shimada, 1984), Co-Zr-Ta (Hoshi et al., 1983) and Co-Zr-Re (Guzman and Kryder, 1987). Iron films (Nagai et al., 1987), corrosion-resistant nitrogen-doped iron films (Naoe et al., 1985) and laminated iron films (Kobayashi et al., 1987; Hu et al., 1994; Wang et al., 1994; Campbell and Lo, 1991) all exhibit soft magnetic properties with high saturation inductions. Electroplated cobalt-iron films (Liao, 1987) also have been investigated in this context.

6.3.5.2 Conductors.   With the exception of silver, most of the high-conductivity metals have been used in fabricating film heads (Table 6.5). High conductivity and ease of fabrication are the primary requirements for conductors. At very high current densities, electromigration can be important. This is particularly true for aluminum, leading to the introduction of small amounts of copper to suppress electromigration along grain boundaries.

6.3.5.3 Insulation and Gap Materials.   The most frequently used insulation and gap materials in film heads are SiO_2, SiO, and Al_2O_3 (see Table 6.6), which are

TABLE 6.6   Film-Head Insulation and Gap Materials

Material	References
SiO_2, evaporated	Lazzari and Melnick, 1971; Lazzari, 1978
SiO_2, sputtered	Macchioni, 1990
Al_2O_3, sputtered	Hsie and Bortins, 1990; Cohen, 1994; Scherer et al., 1994; Ross and Malmhall, 1994
Cured photoresist	Hanazono et al., 1982
Polyimide	Hanazono et al., 1982

TABLE 6.7 Film-Head Substrate Materials

Material	References
Ni-Zn ferrite	Druyvesteyn et al., 1983; Kanai et al., 1979
Al_2O_3-TiC	Jones, 1980; Yamada et al., 1984; Brushan et al., 1992
Si/SiO_2	Lazzari and Melnick, 1971

reasonably durable and hard, and particularly suitable for environments in which wear or corrosion is a problem. Silicon dioxide is the principal insulation for silicon-integrated circuits and has an extensive technology base associated with it; SiO can be used if evaporation is the chosen deposition technique; and Al_2O_3 may be preferred because it has the highest thermal expansion coefficient of the three, hence will have smaller thermally induced stresses.

Under some circumstances, organic insulators such as cured photoresist and polyimide can be used, although they are much softer and less thermally stable materials. Cured photoresist is particularly convenient to deposit; however, properly cured polyimide is probably a more stable material at high temperatures. Both these materials are more suitable as insulation layers than as gap materials.

6.3.5.4 Substrate Materials. Unlike conventional heads, film heads must be deposited on a substrate which must exhibit good wear characteristics, high thermal conductivity, and, in some instances, good soft magnetic characteristics. The substrate must also be capable of being precision-formed into an air-bearing or media-interface form. Several designs have been built which have a hybrid thin-film bulk magnetic material construction. In these cases, ferrite is chosen to serve as a pole or shield, and the balance of the structure is in film form. Sometimes Ni-Zn ferrite is preferred over Mn-Zn ferrite because its high resistivity does not lead to a shorting out of deposited-film conductors. The material, Al_2O_3-TiC, has been employed for heads where extraordinary wear durability is required (Table 6.7). The hardness of these substrates (Vickers hardness of ~2100) is significantly greater than that of ferrites.

6.4 MATERIALS CONSTRAINTS ON INDUCTIVE HEAD PERFORMANCE

6.4.1 Effect of Finite Permeability on Performance

For an inductive head core with infinite permeability the magnetomotive force potential drop $\int \mathbf{H} \cdot d\mathbf{l}$ between the pole tips will be equal to the product of the number of turns in the head times the current in the turns, ni. For finite permeability, however, the ratio of the potential difference to ni will be a quantity η, known as the *head efficiency*:

$$\eta = \frac{1}{ni} \int_{\text{gap}} \mathbf{H} \cdot d\mathbf{l} \qquad (6.21)$$

The efficiency is a measure of the write-field strength for a given current and, by the reciprocity theorem, a measure of signal amplitude.

In principle, the efficiency can be determined by computations of the fields inside and outside the head caused by a current in the turns. However, as shown earlier, computations of this sort are generally complex and difficult to extend from one geometry to another, and so it is often expedient to resort to simpler models in estimating the effects of head structure and permeabilities. Simple approximate expressions for the efficiency can be obtained by considering the head as a magnetic circuit and applying Ampère's law, giving

$$gH_g + \int_c \mathbf{H} \cdot d\mathbf{l} = ni \qquad (6.22)$$

where the second term corresponds to the line integral within the magnetic material and the product gH_g corresponds to the line integral in the gap region. Through use of Eqs. (6.21) and (6.22), the efficiency in this case is given by

$$\eta = \frac{gH_g}{gH_g + \int_c \mathbf{H} \cdot d\mathbf{l}} \qquad (6.23)$$

This expression shows that the efficiency is reduced by the line integral segment in the magnetic portion of the head. If a uniform cross section in the gap region, A_g, and in the magnetic portion of the circuit, A_c, is assumed, the fields are given by

$$\mu\mu_0 HA = BA = \phi \qquad (6.24)$$

where ϕ is the flux which is continuous around the magnetic circuit. Introducing this expression into Eq. (6.23) gives

$$\eta = \frac{g/\mu_0 A_g}{g/\mu_0 A_g + l_c/\mu\mu_0 A_c} \qquad (6.25)$$

where l_c is the length of the line integral in the magnetic material whose permeability is $\mu\mu_0$, and μ_0 is the permeability of space. The individual terms $g/\mu_0 A_g$ and $l_c/\mu\mu_0 A_c$ represent the magnetic reluctances of the gap region and the magnetic regions of the head, respectively. A finite reluctance in the magnetic portion of the head effectively divides the magnetomotive force created by the current in the turns, so only a fraction η of the magnetomotive force drop occurs between the pole tips of the head. This fraction can approach unity only as the product of permeability and magnetic cross section approaches infinity, or as the magnetic path length approaches zero. Since the gap dimension g and the gap field H_g are often fixed by other constraints, such as recording resolution and media coercivity, considerations of how to obtain suitable permeabilities and magnetic geometries are basic to head design.

It is evident from Eq. (6.25) that any feature which increases the reluctance associated with the magnetic portions of the head, for example, air gaps or boundary regions with low permeability (referred to as *dead layers*), will decrease head efficiency. Similarly, saturation of portions of the magnetic material will effectively increase the reluctance of the magnetic circuit and result in a low efficiency for current increments above the point of saturation.

Flux paths parallel to the gap will also decrease the efficiency. Such fringing or leakage paths can be taken to correspond to a parallel reluctance which decreases the effective reluctances of the gap region, causing an increase in the relative magnitude of the magnetomotive force drop in the magnetic portions of the head. This in turn decreases the efficiency of the head.

Several approximate expressions have been derived for the reluctances associated with flux emanating from pole tips into the media and for flux leakage to the sides and behind the gap region. These can be incorporated in more elaborate reluctance networks to predict efficiency as a function of more complex head geometrical parameters (Unger and Fritzsch, 1970; Walker, 1972; Sansom, 1976; Jorgensen, 1980).

The head inductance, which is important in characterizing its frequency response, also can be derived from magnetic circuit models. For example, by combining Eqs. (6.22) and (6.24) for the case of uniform cross sections in both the gap and magnetic regions, one finds

$$\frac{ni}{g/\mu_0 A_g + l_c/\mu\mu_0 A_c} = \phi \tag{6.26}$$

Since inductance L is defined by the relationship

$$-L\frac{di}{dt} = e = -n\frac{d\phi}{dt} \tag{6.27}$$

this leads to a simple expression

$$L = \frac{n^2}{g/\mu_0 A_g + l_c/\mu\mu_0 A_c} \tag{6.28}$$

which shows that a low inductance requires a high reluctance in the magnetic portion of the head and/or a high gap reluctance.

6.4.2 Transmission-Line Analysis of Magnetic Circuits

A special variant of the magnetic circuit analysis has been used with filmhead structures. In this case, thin planar magnetic films, with a relatively high reluctance per unit length, are in close proximity to one another, corresponding to a relatively low reluctance per unit length for flux leakage between films. This geometry suggests a treatment which has been called a *transmission-line analysis* because it results in a differential equation analogous to those governing current and voltage in transmission lines. Although generally only relatively simple geometries are treated, a complete description of the flux flow, local fields, and the efficiency of the head results (Thompson, 1974). The original analysis of a single-turn head was derived from the integral forms of Maxwell's equation with time variations of flux taken into account (Paton, 1971). However, a simpler, more frequently used, static analysis starts from Ampère's law and results in expressions valid at low frequencies. Considering the line integral of magnetic field around a portion of a current-carrying stripe, as shown in Fig. 6.28, the portions of the line integral corresponding to legs 1 and 3 are

$$H_1 \Delta l_1 = \frac{\phi \, \Delta x}{w_0 \mu_1 t_1} \tag{6.29}$$

and

$$H_3 \Delta l_3 = \frac{\phi \, \Delta x}{w_0 \mu_2 t_2} \tag{6.30}$$

where ϕ = flux
w = head width
μ_1, μ_2 = relative permeabilities of the two films
t_1, t_2 = thicknesses of the two films

The portions of the integral corresponding to leakage in legs 2 and 4 are

$$H_2\,\Delta l_2 = \frac{g_a}{\mu_0 w}\frac{d\phi}{dx}\,(x) \tag{6.31}$$

and

$$H_4\,\Delta l_4 = \frac{g_a}{\mu_0 w}\frac{d\phi}{dx}\,(x + \Delta x) \tag{6.32}$$

where g_a is the separation between magnetic layers. For a total current i, the current enclosed by the line integral is

$$i' = \frac{\Delta x i}{\delta} \tag{6.33}$$

where δ is the conductor stripe width.

Combining Eqs. (6.29) to (6.33) and taking the limit $\Delta x \rightarrow 0$ yields the governing differential equation

$$\frac{d^2\phi}{dx^2} - \frac{\phi}{\lambda_a^2} = -\frac{\alpha}{\lambda_a^2}\,i \tag{6.34}$$

where

$$\frac{1}{\lambda_a^2} = \frac{1/\mu_1 t_1 + 1/\mu_2 t_2}{g_a} \tag{6.35}$$

and

$$\frac{\alpha}{\lambda_a^2} = \frac{\mu_0 w}{\delta g_a} \tag{6.36}$$

In general, solutions of Eq. (6.34) are linear combinations of terms of the form exp $(\pm x/\lambda_a)$ with coefficients given by the boundary conditions selected (Jones, 1978).

An analysis of the flux flow in a single-turn head has been developed in which a copper conductor completely fills the area within the yoke. Eddy currents in the conductor were also taken into account in the resultant expression for head efficiency (Paton, 1971). The predicted low-frequency efficiency is shown to be in reasonable agreement with experimental results (Valstyn and Shew, 1973). This model has been extended by considering a single-turn head with four regions: a coil

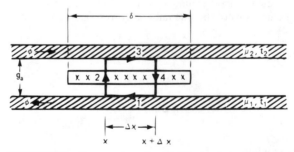

FIGURE 6.28 Cross section of a thin-film head showing a line integral enclosing a current i' (*Jones, 1978*).

region, a gap region (which has no conductor), and two permeable pole regions. Eddy currents are assumed to be in the magnetic poles as well as in the conductor. The head impedance and efficiency are modified considerably, particularly at high frequencies. The efficiency is shown first to rise with increasing frequency due to conductor eddy currents resisting flux leakage from pole to pole across the conductor. At still higher frequencies, when the pole skin depth approaches the pole thickness, the efficiency diminishes owing to a lower effective permeability caused by eddy currents in the poles (Hughes, 1983). The zero-frequency limit of this model was described earlier (Miura et al., 1978).

Equations governing the flux in multiturn film heads can be derived by extending the analysis of the single-turn head to the case where there are two regions: a thin short-gap region, where dimensions are dictated by recording performance, and a thick back region created by the combined thicknesses of multiple conductors and intervening insulation layers (Jones, 1978). The efficiency of an individual turn can be shown to depend on its proximity to the pole-tip region. It can also be shown that head performance is critically dependent on the depth ("throat height") of the pole-tip region.

The transmission-line equations have also been solved using a finite-element analysis where the differential equations are converted to difference equations and solved numerically by direct integration (Katz, 1978). Within this framework, it is possible to simulate the effects of continuous changes of pole thickness and pole width by assigning a different cross section to each serial element in the film structure. Increased widths and thicknesses in the back region of the head were shown to be effective in increasing head efficiency.

Experiments have generally shown a surprising agreement with the predictions for multiturn heads, if reasonable values of permeability are used (Anderson and Jones, 1981). More elaborate analyses involving numerical solutions of the integral form of Maxwell's equation have also generally supported the simpler transmission-line model (Kelley and Valstyn, 1980).

The transmission-line model also has been generalized by formulating two-dimensional partial differential equations which are solved by finite-element methods. Proper design of the width of the rear flux closure of film heads may greatly increase the writing current for the onset of head saturation. The case of an anisotropic permeability was also analyzed, and shown to have little effect on performance (Yeh, 1982a).

A method has been described which can combine multiple transmission line segments with fixed or varying gaps and fixed or varying widths into complex circuits (Arnoldussen, 1988). Thevenin T-reluctance circuit equivalents are obtained for each segment of the total head structure, and the magnetic flux and fields are obtained by circuit analysis. External fringe-fields at edges are also included.

6.4.3 Domains in Inductive Film Heads

In the previous analysis it was assumed that magnetic materials could be characterized by a relative permeability μ, where $\mu\mu_0 = B/H$. In fact, magnetic materials are composed of individual domains with local magnetizations equal to the saturation magnetization of the material. When a head is used for writing or reading, the rotation of magnetization within these domains, or the shift of domain walls, constitutes the head response to magnetic fields. The assumption of a constant ratio of induction to field is at best a first approximation to this response.

An example of a domain structure for an inductive film head-yoke geometry is

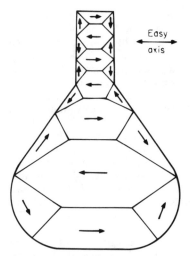

FIGURE 6.29 Domain configuration in an inductive film head.

shown in Fig. 6.29. With an easy axis in the indicated direction, most of the pattern will constitute domains with magnetizations parallel to the easy axis, but in opposite directions, separated by 180° Bloch walls. Because of the high energy associated with free poles, closure domains form at the periphery of the yoke with magnetizations parallel to the pattern edges. All domain walls are ideally positioned so the component of magnetization perpendicular to the wall is the same in adjacent domains, implying there are no magnetic poles at these walls.

In the absence of applied fields, the lowest-energy head domain pattern corresponds to the smallest sum of wall energy, anisotropy energy, and magnetostriction energy terms. Energetically favorable domain configurations representing this minimum sum have been determined for rectangular (Druyvesteyn et al., 1979; Soohoo, 1982) and trapezoidal (Narishigi et al., 1985) head patterns, and found to be in reasonably good agreement with observations. The analysis of rectangular patterns has been extended to include magnetostatic energy contributions that occur in the presence of applied fields (Druyvesteyn et al., 1981a). Analysis methods (Kishigami et al., 1986) and computer programs (Seshan and Cendes, 1985) have been written for predicting minimum energy domain patterns for more complex shapes.

With a larger anisotropy, or higher values of H_k, the energy per unit area of closure domains is larger and these domains tend to be smaller. This is illustrated by Fig. 6.30 (Narishigi et al., 1984) for materials with positive and negative values of magnetostriction. With tension applied in the hard-axis direction, the effective anisotropy energy of the positive magnetostriction material is decreased and large closure domains become energetically favorable. With a negative magnetostriction, and the same stress applied, the effective anisotropy energy increases and closure domains are small. [For a description of the relationships between tensile and compressive stresses, magnetostriction, and anisotropy energy, see Maissel and Glang (1970), Chap. 17.] In real heads, domains will not always occur in the ideal patterns shown in Figs. 6.29 and 6.30. Domain structures are often fixed by accidental features such as nicks at pattern edges and nonmagnetic inclusions and voids in the films. The magnetization pattern will also be influenced by the presence of other magnetic material, such as a second magnetic yoke layer. Domain images obtained using a scanning electron microscope (type II magnetic constrast mode) have shown a number of irregular domains originating at edge defects in head patterns, in addition to normal closure domains (Mee, 1980). More recently, a new scanning electron microscope, spin-polarized SEM, has been developed, which permits direct observation of the direction of magnetization in head domains and domain walls (Mitsuoka et al., 1987).

Inductive film heads can exhibit two types of instability or Barkhausen noise: so-called "write instability" and "read instability" (Klaassen and van Peppen, 1994). Both are associated with small irreversible jumps in domain wall positions which cause abrupt changes in the coil-linked flux, ϕ. These abrupt changes induce volt-

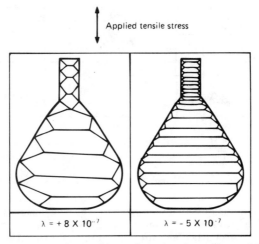

FIGURE 6.30 Domain configurations in positive and negative magnetostriction inductive film heads (*Narishigi et al., 1984*).

age transients proportional to $nd\phi/dt$, (Hempstead and Money, 1979; Klaassen and van Peppen, 1990). The complex dynamics of the demagnetization process occurring after termination of a write operation can leave the yoke in slightly different domain patterns due to irreproducible pinning.

Write instability refers to noise spikes or "popcorn noise" occurring directly after the termination of a write operation. Such noise is particularly detrimental in drives that employ sector head positioning servoing, since servoing must occur immediately after writing. Read instability is assoicated with distortions of read back pulses in the form of transient disturbances on "head wiggles" (Shi et al., 1989) located predominantly on the trailing edges of pulses (Klaassen and van Peppen, 1989; Tang, 1990) as shown in Fig. 6.31. The "ringing" of the wiggles is due to the coil's inductance and capacitance and the preamplifier capacitance (Klaassen and van Peppen, 1989). Variable pinning gives rise to variable reading response, particularly in the amplitude and timing of the wiggles.

It has long been held that read instability is associated with domain walls (Lazzari and Melnick, 1970; Hempstead and Money, 1979), but the positions of the principle offending walls have been variously placed at 180° walls transverse to the flux path (Lazzari and Melnick, 1970; Argyle et al., 1988); at 90° walls in the edge closure domains (Jones, 1979); at domain walls near the air bearing surface (Shi et al., 1994); and at 180° walls parallel to the flux path (Williams and Lambert, 1989). Extensive experimentation has lead to the conclusion that the predominant (but not necessarily exclusive) cause of instability is the last entry on this list, 180° walls oriented in the direction of flux flow located in the pole tips and lower apex region of the top pole (Klaassen and van Peppen, 1989; Kasiraj and Holmes, 1991). These are sites where the signal flux density and extent of wall motion are largest.

One-eighty degree walls parallel to the flux flow become energetically favorable in the sloping apex region of the top pole tip if the local stress-induced magnetic anisotropy is in the flux flow direction and if it outweighs the anisotropy induced

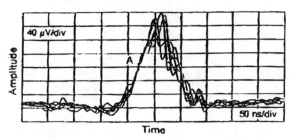

FIGURE 6.31   Read waveforms, triggered at Point A, showing read instability.

during deposition in the direction transverse to the signal flux flow. The magnitude and direction of the stress induced anisotropy is proportional to the product of the local magnetostriction constant and stress anisotropy. Stress anisotropy varies from point to point because of the local head structure and materials and the effects of disposition and machining processes (Bozorth, 1951; Ohasi et al., 1990). Modeling has shown that local stress anisotropies greater than 10^9 dynes/cm^2 are possible in the pole region (Koyanagi et al., 1990; Young, 1990), indicating a need for tight control of the local NiFe magnetostriction.

Considering the "write instability" phenomenon: the termination of a write operation is followed by a large decaying transient ("inductive kickback") caused by head demagnetization and amplifier recovery. After this transient, numerous Barkhausen noise events occur, some of which are voltage spikes in the same sense as the inductive kickback and some of which are of opposite polarity (Klaassen and van Peppen, 1994). The probability of occurrence of noise events falls off rapidly with time after writing. High noise-after-write is correlated with spike-like domains near the back gap closure of the yoke (Lin et al., 1992). The domain structure in the upper part of plated yokes is very sensitive to NiFe composition (Koeppe et al., 1992), hence it has been concluded that stress variations introduced by the cooling of non-zero magnetostriction yokes after writing are responsible for this noise (Kanda et al., 1990). The decay of noise probability is consistent with an effective thermal decay time of approximately 10 μs (Monson et al., 1984).

Generally for low write durations and low write amplitudes the probability of noise-after-write events is a complicated function of write duration and amplitude, reflecting non-uniform magnetic saturation and heating of the yoke (Klaassen and van Peppen, 1994). However, for longer ($> 10~\mu$s) durations and normal write currents the probability of Barkhausen noise events reaches a steady state value, indicative of the head reaching a constant temperature at times long compared to the thermal rise time of the head.

Domain walls are slow in responding to applied fields in comparison to magnetization rotation and, in many instances, they limit the dynamic response of film heads. It has been argued that time constants associated with closure domain wall motion are directly proportional to domain size (Jones, 1979; Soohoo, 1982), implying that large domains are particularly slow in responding. Magnetization processes associated with large closure domains also have been shown to be relatively unstable or "noisy," perhaps because of the longer distances the walls travel, or because of the larger fraction of the response controlled by domain wall motion (Narishigi et al., 1984). This has generally led to a preference for materials with small closure domains. For example, negative magnetostriction materials are better for heads with tensile stresses parallel to the hard-axis direction, since this gives smaller domain dimensions and consequently smoother head responses (Narishigi et al., 1984). Since domains can be easily reconfigured during writing, head responses in subsequent reading cycles can also be irreproducible as a result of changes in domain patterns (Jones, 1979).

Although the central portion of the yoke pattern may be free of closure domains, it has been proposed that the high-frequency magnetization rotation process in this region will still be constrained by domain wall motion. The nature of this constraint has been analyzed (Ohashi, 1985), and it has been shown that the magnetization within the 180° domains curls near the closure domain wall to prevent the occurrences of magnetic poles. The length of this constrained region was found to be comparable to the domain spacing. Since this represents a considerable portion of the track width for most film heads, much of the head response should take place with a response time associated with the closure domain wall motion. According to this model, the switching dynamics of heads with closure domains consist of two steps; a rotation of magnetization in the central 180° domains, with magnetization curling and resultant magnetic pole distribution near the closure domain walls, followed by a closure domain wall motion driven by these distributed poles. More recently a high-frequency flux conduction model has been proposed (Mallary and Smith, 1988) in which magnetization without free magnetic poles occurs in the central portions of the head not blocked by closure domains. Only a slight loss of permeability in these regions is predicted for this latest model. Observations of flux conduction in the 1- to 10-MHz range (Kasiraj et al., 1986) are in essential agreement with this picture, showing that the conduction is by magnetic rotation near the center of the head with the triangular domains at the edges having little or no magnetization rotation.

Experiments with single-pole film heads have shown that an optimum anisotropy field, H_k, exists to provide the maximum effective permeability for a given track width (Nakamura et al., 1985). This implies that there exists an optimum size for closure domains. If H_k is too small, edge domains are large and effectively block the response of the outer portions of the head pole. On the other hand, large values of H_k imply low values of hard-axis relative permeability ($\mu = B_s/H_k\mu_0$) even for the central portions of the pole. An optimum value of H_k appears to be about 480 A/m (6 Oe) for a 50-μm-wide pole corresponding to a 30 percent extension of closure domains across the pole width. Apparent permeabilities also depend on track width, a dependence evidently related to domain structure (Druyvesteyn et al., 1981a).

The local amplitude of domain wall motion in response to coil currents has been observed with a SEM lock-in technique in both the upper-pole piece of partially completed heads and the pole-tip surfaces of completed heads (Wells and Savoy, 1981). As might be expected, the amplitude of motion varied with applied current, showing the largest excursions in regions where models would indicate the greatest concentration of flux. Random changes of pole-tip magnetization were seen which were consistent with irregular domain motions in the head. Similar instabilities, particularly with positive magnetostriction (large domain) pole tips, have been observed using a Kerr magnetooptic technique (Narishigi et al., 1984).

A Kerr magnetooptic apparatus also has been used to measure local variations of magnetization as a function of frequency (Re and Kryder, 1984; Narishigi et al., 1984). Different responses are interpreted in terms of the domain structure of the yoke, and it was concluded that wall motion limits the head magnetization dynamics. At the center of the top surface of the head, the magnetization was 90° out of phase with the drive current at 8.4 MHz, while near the yoke edge this phase difference occurred at 4.7 MHz (Re and Kryder, 1984). These response frequencies, which are much lower than those associated with magnetization rotation, are at least in qualitative agreement with domain dynamics models (Jones, 1979; Soohoo, 1982; Ohashi, 1985). Magnetooptic observations of film head pole tips at the air-bearing surface have shown that eddy currents, as well as domains, are responsible for the head response (Re et al., 1985, 1986) and that the magnetization normal to the air-bearing surface is nonuniform (Re et al., 1987).

It has been appreciated for some time that closure domains in head structures can be largely eliminated by using magnetic-nonmagnetic layer laminated films (Lazzari and Melnick, 1971). Flux closure paths in these films will be provided by adjacent layers magnetized in an antiparallel arrangement, and the closure domain walls will disappear. Domains in multiple-layer pole structures have been observed to largely consist of widely spaced 180° walls (Feng and Thompson, 1977; Mee, 1980) or irregular domain patterns (Mitsuoka et al., 1987, 1988a) and edge curling walls (Mitsuoka et al., 1988b). In these films, rotation rather than wall motion should control magnetization dynamics. As an added benefit, eddy-current losses in such films can be significantly improved in the 50- to 100-MHz range if the nonmagnetic layers are an insulating material (Feng and Thompson, 1977).

6.5 MAGNETORESISTIVE HEADS

6.5.1 Flux Sensing

Magnetoresistive heads belong to a class of reproduce heads that utilizes direct magnetic flux sensing as a means of readback. An example of these flux-sensitive heads is the Hall effect head that uses the Hall voltage developed across a current carrying stripe made of either magnetic alloys (e.g., NiFe) or non-magnetic semiconductors (e.g., InSb) with high electron mobility. Another example is the fluxgate head that modulates the reluctance of an inductive head structure by a high frequency to obtain a signal larger than that from the usual induction effect. By far, the most important and highly developed flux-sensitive head is the magnetoresistive head. A magnetoresistive (MR) sensor (Hunt, 1971; Thompson, et al., 1975; Tsang, 1984; Shelledy and Nix, 1992) detects magnetic field signals through the resistance changes of a magnetoresistive material. Since the first proposal (Hunt, 1971) to use a magnetoresistive sensor as the read element in magnetic recording, there has been ever increasing activity on MR head technology. The interest in the application of MR sensors to magnetic recording comes from the signal amplitude advantage that such sensors offer. In contrast to the conventional inductive read head, the MR sensor is a parametric device (Hunt, 1971) where the signal output is proportional to the applied sense current which is limited only by thermal and electromigration considerations. Consequently, a well-designed MR head could deliver several times the signal output of a comparable inductive read head. Such a large read signal is very desirable in high-density and high-data-rate recording systems to combat head and electronic noise. Furthermore, since the MR sensors are flux sensing devices, they are even more attractive in low-velocity recording environments as in tape or small disk systems, where the inductive-head outputs will be reduced due to a slower rate of change in the magnetic induction.

In applying MR sensors to magnetic recording, however, many difficulties must be addressed. In general two types of problem exist: the first involves basic issues of designing MR sensors with magnetic behaviors that are appropriate for the recording environment. The second involves practical issues of fabricating these sensors with a reasonable yield and sufficiently good performance control. Regarding the magnetic behavior of MR sensors, linearization and noise suppression are most important (Thompson et al., 1975; Tsang, 1984; Shelledy and Nix, 1992). The magnetoresistance effect in ferromagnetic conductors is quadratic, therefore provisions (transverse biasing) must be made to linearize the sensor response for high sensitivity in small signal situations. Furthermore, small-feature MR sensors, which are desirable for high-density applications, often exhibit serious noise and instability. This so-called Barkhausen noise originates from magnetic domain activities in the sensor and must be suppressed if the sensor is to be viable.

6.5.2 Basic Principles and Configurations

The basic MR sensor is illustrated schematically in Fig. 6.32a. The read region of the sensor is made up of a magnetoresistive ferromagnetic conductor such as permalloy ($Ni_{80}Fe_{20}$) whose resistance can be modulated by the angle between its magnetic moment and the current-flow direction according to

$$\Delta R = (\Delta \rho / \rho) R \cos^2 \theta \qquad (6.37)$$

where R is resistance of the sensor when the magnetic moment is parallel to the current direction, and $\Delta \rho / \rho$ is the magnetoresistive coefficient of the sensor material. For a sensor where the rotational response of M is determined by the uniaxial anisotropy (H_k) of the material, the resultant response is parabolic, as shown by the solid curve in Fig. 6.32b. For a narrow sensor where rotational response is determined by both shape demagnetization and uniaxial anisotropy, the resultant response becomes bell shaped instead of purely parabolic, as shown by the dotted curve in Fig. 6.32b. In any case, when a magnetic field is present, rotation of the sensor magnetic moment produces a resistance change which in turn produces a voltage change across the conductor leads according to

$$\Delta V = I \Delta R \qquad (6.38)$$

where I is the sense current through the sensor. The amplitude of the voltage signal is proportional to the sense current I, which is typically limited only by thermal and electromigration considerations. With a magnetoresistance coefficient of 2–4% which is common in many alloys of Ni, Fe, and Co, a well-designed MR sensor can deliver signal outputs at least several times that of a comparable 20–30 turn inductive read head. Permalloy ($Ni_{80}Fe_{20}$) has been by far the most popular choice for the magnetoresistive layer. This is because permalloy exhibits a convergence of several desirable properties (Miyazaki et al., 1989; Valetta et al., 1991): reasonably large MR coefficient (2–4%) and resistivity (25 $\mu\Omega$-cm) for efficient conversion of magnetic into electrical excitations, as well as low uniaxial anisotropy ($H_k \sim 0.4$ kA/m or 5 Oe) and magnetostriction ($|\lambda| < 1 \times 10^{-6}$) for the retention of soft-magnetic properties even after sensor fabrication. Another candidate for the magnetoresistive layer is the NiFeCo (Tatsumi et al., 1991) alloy system around the $Ni_{82}Fe_{12}Co_6$ composition. This composition yields a higher MR

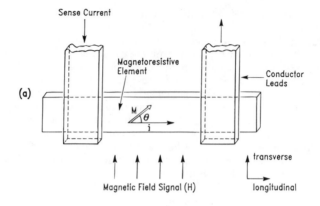

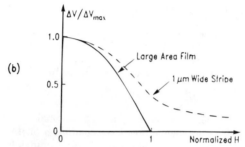

FIGURE 6.32 The basic MR sensor: (a) Schematic; (b) MR response.

coefficient (4–5%) than permalloy but it is also higher in both magnetostriction (2 $\times$ 10^{-6}) and uniaxial anisotropy ($\sim$0.7 kA/m or 9 Oe). Also, since NiFeCo is a ternary alloy, it is somewhat more difficult to synthesize and control than the binary permalloy system.

In all, Fig. 6.32 depicts an MR sensor operating in a very simple magnetic environment. This is typically not the case, however, for MR sensors operating in a magnetic recording system. To achieve linear density resolution during readback, soft-magnetic shields are often built around the MR sensor. In addition, since the MR sensor is a read-only device, an inductive write head is usually also present in its vicinity. These and other requirements (Tsang, 1984; Shelledy and Nix, 1992) in a recording system often result in a rather complicated magnetic environment in which linearization and noise-suppression schemes for the MR sensor must be made to work.

First let us examine how different MR head configurations address the linear resolution requirement. The simplest MR head configuration is the unshielded MR sensor (Fig. 6.33a), made by putting conductor leads on a rectangular piece of magnetoresistive material. The major advantage is simplicity, both in the fabrication and design of linearization and noise-suppression schemes, which might simply involve using the field from a hard magnet placed next to the unshielded sensor (Uchida et al., 1982; Doyle, 1990; Edelman et al., 1990). However, since signal flux

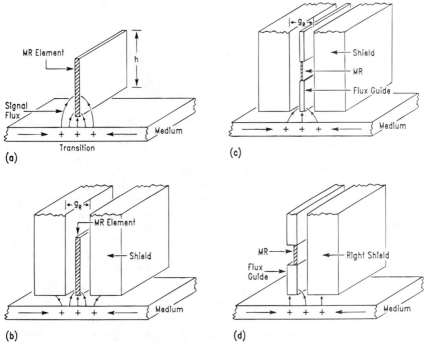

FIGURE 6.33 Various MR head configurations: (*a*) Unshielded MR; (*b*) Shielded MR; (*c*) Shielded flux-guided MR; (*d*) Half-shielded flux-guided MR.

from recorded transitions can enter the sensor from the side along its entire height, linear resolution is poor (Hunt, 1971), limited by practical lower limits to the height of the sensor. Various results (Uchida et al., 1982; Carr and Wachenschwanz, 1988; Koren, 1990; Dovek et al., 1992) have shown that it is possible to operate the unshielded sensor up to fairly high linear densities, but it would require write equalization to remove long wavelength field components from distant transitions, and extensive read equalization to reduce intersymbol interference. There have been attempts to improve the linear resolution of the unshielded sensor. A large biasing field from a permanent magnet, for example, might be used to saturate most of the unshielded sensor except for narrow regions along the top and bottom edges, thereby significantly reducing the effective height of the MR sensor (Uchida et al., 1982). However, in this scheme, the saturated portion of the sensor constitutes an electrical shunt to the narrow active part, reducing the signal output significantly. A more promising approach seems to be the dual MR scheme (Indeck et al., 1988; Smith et al., 1992; Smith et al., 1992), in which two unshielded MR sensors are placed parallel to each other at a short distance apart, and are electrically connected to produce opposite signals to the magnetic field of a transition. As a result, a transition will produce a dipolar signal response when it is close to the sensors, and a very small signal when it is far away, due to the cancellation of responses from the two sensors. The dual MR scheme can therefore exhibit good linear resolution without magnetic shields. There are, however, several limitations to this design. First, the MR sensors must be closely matched in material properties and magnetic states to eliminate response from distant transitions, creating more stringent requirements on the fabrication and material processes. Also, the distance between the two MR sensors now determines not only the linear resolution of the sensors, but also the magnitude of mutual-biasing from magnetostatic interactions between the sensors. This situation renders separate optimization of linear resolution and transverse biasing to be quite difficult. By far the most popular approach for linear density resolution is the shielded MR sensor proposed by Brock et al. (1975), which has been employed in all the MR heads in current tape and disk drives. Here the MR sensor is sandwiched between two soft magnets (Fig. 6.33) which shield the sensor from distant transitions. It has been shown (Sueoka et al., 1992) that as long as the shields are thicker than 2–3 μm, the MR readback waveform approaches that for the limiting case of infinitely thick shields except for slight broadening near the bottom of the waveform. This limiting case has in turn been shown by Potter (1974) to be roughly equivalent to a ferrite (Karlqvist) head with a gap equal to half the MR shield-to-shield spacing. This result has been improved by other models, in particular by the exact conformal mapping model of Heim (Heim, 1982). The presence of shields therefore provides good linear resolution, but it also creates a complicated magnetic environment for the MR sensor (Tsang et al., 1990). In particular, the signal flux now enters the MR sensor primarily from the lower edge, and leaks continuously to the shields as it propagates up the height of the sensor. The result is a highly non-uniform signal flux profile along the height of the sensor. Since the signal flux is concentrated near the lower edge of the sensor, this region must be well biased for efficient operation, creating difficulty for many biasing schemes, as we shall discuss later.

Next, let us examine the impact of write requirements on MR recording head configurations. For efficient read-write operations, an inductive write head must be placed in the vicinity of the MR sensor, which is accomplished in one of two ways. In the first way, the MR sensor is placed at the center of the write gap between the P1 and P2 pole-tips (Fig. 6.34) so that the pole-tips also act as shields to the MR sensor. This integrated head configuration (Lier et al., 1976; Simmons et al., 1983; Kehr et al., 1988) provides fabrication simplicity from sharing common structures between the read and the write elements. Also, since the read and write gaps are the same, read-write track alignment is made easier, and there are no skew-induced read-write track offsets in rotary-actuator systems. On the other hand, there are disadvantages to having common read and write gaps beginning with the fact that the read and write gaps cannot be separately optimized. Moreover, intense write field perturbations to the MR sensor at every write cycle may aggravate magnetic instability problems of the MR sensor (Davidson et al., 1984). The second way to provide write capability is to build a separate write head on top of the read head (Fig. 6.34b). This "piggyback" head configuration (Tsang et al., 1990; Takano et al., 1991) allows complete flexibility for separate optimization of read and write head geometries, and was employed in the IBM 0663 MR heads. The considerable distance between the read and the write gaps, however, renders read-write track alignment difficult and creates a read-write track offset when arm skew is present, as in rotary-actuator systems. The piggyback configuration may be modified by merging the write head P1 pole-piece with the read head S2 shield. This merged-head configuration was proposed in 1974 and has been employed in the IBM 0664 MR heads (Bajorek et al., 1974). This scheme not only simplifies head fabrication (Shelledy and Nix, 1992), but also reduces the read-write gap distance to diminish skew effects in rotary-actuator systems. The write field at the MR head location, however, is higher than in the piggyback case, so that better stability is required from the MR sensor.

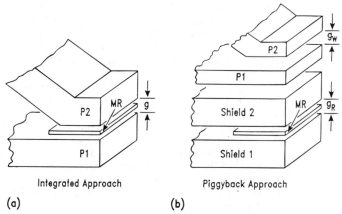

FIGURE 6.34 Various Read/Write Configurations with MR head: (*a*) Integrated head; (*b*) Piggyback head.

Reliability requirements are also very important for MR heads in magnetic recording. The lower edge of the MR sensor is typically exposed at the slider air-bearing surface (ABS) as the result of a mechanical lapping process. This exposure may cause mechanical wear and chemical corrosion problems. Electrical shorts between the sensor and the shield might also occur at the ABS due to the smearing of metallic components (Bonyhard, 1990) during the mechanical lapping process. Furthermore, contacts between the recording head and the recording medium might occasionally happen, causing a variety of undesirable events ranging from thermal disturbances (Hempstead, 1974; Hempstead, 1975; Shelledy and Cheatham, 1976; Shelledy and Nix, 1992) that might interfere with signal detection, to electrical discharges that might actually damage the sensor. One way to address these problems is to recess the MR sensor away from the edges of the shields at the ABS, but then soft-magnet flux guides (Thompson, 1974; Sawada et al., 1984; Takano et al., 1991) are often needed for bringing the signal flux to the MR sensor to maintain a reasonable read sensitivity. Figure 6.33(*c*) shows an example (Thompson, 1974; Tsang et al., 1992) where the MR sensor is situated in series with a flux guide between two shields. In this case, linear resolution might be compromised by the thickness of the flux guide. Figure 6.33(*d*) shows another example (Druvestyen et al., 1979; Druvestyen et al., 1981*b*; Ruigrok, 1982) where the MR sensor is half-shielded. In this case, the asymmetrical magnetic environment of the MR sensor creates leading-trailing edge asymmetries in the MR readback waveform (Druvestyen, 1981*b*). The half-shielded configuration can be modified by placing the MR sensor symmetrically between the flux guide and the shield, so that they now act as the pole-tips in an inductive head-like configuration (de Niet and Vreeken, 1979; Druvestyen et al., 1981*b*; Maruyama et al., 1987). This arrangement might produce more symmetrical readback waveforms with higher efficiency, but will be more complicated to fabricate. In either example, domain effects in the flux guides may create additional noise problems (Thompson, 1974; Tsang et al., 1988; Tsang et al., 1992) that may require the use of laminated flux-guide material and other solutions. An advantage, however, to the flux guide configuration is that since the MR sensor is situated in a magnetic circuit, various biasing as well as feedback schemes (de Niet and Vreeken, 1979; Druvestyen et al., 1983) can be employed to improve signal linearity and stability. In all, flux guided schemes alleviate mechanical, chemical and electrical reliability problems as well as thermal noise problems for the MR sensor, but they are usually complicated to fabricate and low in read efficiency (Tsang et al., 1992). Consequently they have found applications mostly in environments (Smith et al., 1992*a,b*) where read signal strength is not a primary issue.

Finally, track resolution is also an important requirement for the MR sensor in magnetic recording. As track density increases, the read region (Fig. 6.35*a*) of the sensor also becomes narrower, making crosstalk problems from side-track reading more serious. For shielded MR sensors, side-track reading (Seagle et al., 1990; Yeh, 1982*b*; Nix et al., 1991) is caused primarily when side-track magnetic flux incident on the end regions of the MR sensor propagates into the center read region. This flux propagation exhibits complicated dependencies on the permeabilities as well as the magnetic states (Davidson et al., 1984; Nix et al., 1991; Seagle et al., 1990) of the end and read regions. In general, a simple MR sensor with a long geometry and a narrow conductor-defined read track at the center (Fig. 6.35) would have significant crosstalk from side-tracks in narrow track environments. Crosstalk problems may be reduced to a certain extent by recessing the MR tail regions (Maruyama et al., 1990; Suzuki et al., 1991) from the air-bearing surface, or more thoroughly by using shorter MR elements. Both of these ap-

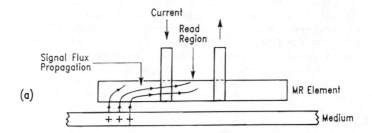

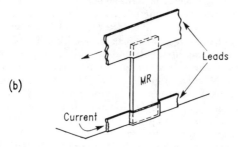

FIGURE 6.35 Track definition considerations for MR sensors: (*a*) Schematic of side-reading in typical MR head; (*b*) Orthogonal MR head for narrow track operations.

proaches are likely to result in sensor geometries that aggravate domain noise problems, which will be discussed later. Finally, for narrow track operations, orthogonal MR heads (Suyama et al., 1988; Wang et al., 1993) have also been designed with the MR sensor running orthogonally up from the air-bearing surface (Fig. 6.35b), so that the signal field now enters the sensor in the longitudinal instead of the normal transverse direction (Fig. 6.32a).

The major advantages of this sensor configuration are that the sensor resistance now actually increases as the trackwidth is reduced, and that the sensor might be safer from electrical shorting problems at the air-bearing surface. But there are also important issues (Wang et al., 1993) to be addressed, such as read-efficiency reduction due to a longer signal path through the sensor, as well as problematic magnetic behavior that might arise due to longitudinal operation of the sensor.

6.5.3 Theoretical Study of Readback Performance

The readback performance of a MR head includes primarily the signal amplitude sensitivity and the linear resolution (Potter, 1974; Davies and Middleton, 1975; Kelley and Ketcham, 1978; Middleton et al., 1979; Schwarz and Decker, 1979; Middleton, 1980; Heim, 1982) and can be studied theoretically by application of the reciprocity theorem. In this approach, the MR sensor, whose readback properties are to be investigated, is sandwiched between two imaginary current sheets with opposite currents (Fig. 6.36). The fringe magnetic field produced by the imaginary current sheet pair is then computed either analytically or numerically at the locations of the medium transitions. By the reciprocity theorem, the total magnetic flux in the MR sensor due to the transitions is then given by

$$\phi = \int_{-\infty}^{\infty} \vec{M}\,\vec{H}dx \tag{6.39}$$

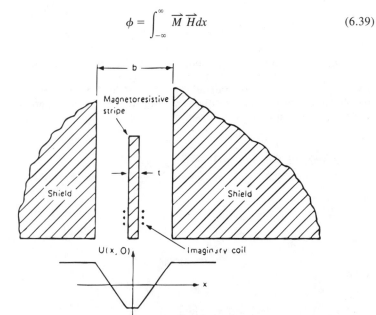

FIGURE 6.36 Imaginary coils around MR sensor for readback computations.

where $\vec{M}$ is the magnetization distribution of the transitions in the recording medium, $\vec{H}$ is the fringe field distribution due to the imaginary current sheets, and x is distance along the downtrack direction. For simplicity, Eq. (6.39) assumes a thin recording medium, but if the thickness of the medium is non-negligible, then the integral must also be carried through the thickness of the medium as well. From the total signal flux ϕ, the average angle of magnetization rotation in the MR sensor can be computed, leading to the signal amplitude through Eqs. (6.37) and (6.38). This readback computation can be repeated for transition patterns of different linear density to yield the signal amplitude rolloff behavior representing the linear density performance of the MR head. So far, our analysis has been general and the approach we outlined is applicable to various MR head configurations. We will now focus on the shielded MR sensor and discuss in detail its signal amplitude and linear resolution performance using the reciprocity approach.

The work of Potter (1974) has shown that the readback sensitivity of the shielded MR head (Fig. 6.36) can be estimated analytically by first applying the reciprocity theorem to obtain the incident flux at the exposed tip of the MR sensor, and then applying a one-dimensional transmission line model to obtain the flux distribution along the height of the MR sensor. First, to estimate the incident flux, an imaginary current loop is wrapped around the exposed tip of the MR sensor. The fringe field can then be calculated from the magnetic potential distribution along the air-bearing surface. Using the Karlqvist approximation, this potential distribution can be represented by a trapezoid (Fig. 6.36). This leads to Potter's result that the fringe field simply equals the sum of head fields from two Karlqvist heads with their gaps coincident respectively with the two half-gaps of the shielded MR head. That is,

$$H_x(x, y) = H_{Kx}\left(x + \frac{g + t}{2}, y \right) - H_{Kx}\left(x - \frac{g + t}{2}, y \right) \qquad (6.40)$$

where H_{Kx} is the longitudinal component of the Karlqvist head field, g is the half-gap of the MR head, and t is the thickness of the MR layer. The incident flux to the MR sensor is obtained by integrating this fringe field pattern with the transition magnetization pattern in the medium according to Eq. (6.39). For arctangent transition profiles, a simple analytical result is obtained,

$$\phi_i(x) = \frac{2\mu_0 M_r \delta W}{\pi} \frac{d + a}{g} \left\{ f\left(\frac{x + \frac{g + t}{2}}{d + a} \right) - f\left(\frac{\frac{x + t}{2}}{d + a} \right) \right.$$

$$\left. + f\left(\frac{x - \frac{g - t}{2}}{d + a} \right) - f\left(\frac{\frac{x - t}{2}}{d + a} \right) \right\} \qquad (6.41)$$

where

$$f(x) = x \arctan x - \frac{1}{2} \ln(1 + x^2), \qquad (6.42)$$

x is the downtrack distance of the MR sensor from the center of the transition, $M_r\delta$ is the areal magnetization density of the recording medium, W is the trackwidth of the MR head, d the head to medium distance, and a is the arctangent transition width parameter. The signal flux continually leaks into the shield as it propagates up the height of the MR sensor. This behavior can be approximated by a one-dimensional transmission line model to yield the signal flux distribution,

$$\phi_s(y) = \phi_i \sinh\left(\frac{h-y}{l_c}\right) \Big/ \sinh\left(\frac{h}{l_c}\right) \qquad (6.43)$$

where h is the height of the MR sensor, l_c is the flux decay characteristic length $\sqrt{\mu g t/2}$, and y is the distance along the height of the MR sensor. The total magnetic response of the MR sensor is the sum of the signal flux $\phi(y)$ and its own internal biasing flux $\phi_b(y)$, from which the magnetization rotation can be derived as

$$\sin\theta(y) = \frac{\phi_s(y) + \phi_b(y)}{M_s t} \qquad (6.44)$$

where M_s is the saturation moment of the MR layer. Finally, for small MR coefficients, it can be shown that the net resistance change of the MR sensor can be approximated by summing the resistance change along the height of the MR sensor. The signal response amplitude is therefore

$$\Delta V = IR \left(\frac{\Delta\rho}{\rho}\right) \int_0^h \sin^2\theta dy \qquad (6.45)$$

where I is the sense current, R is the DC resistance of the sensor, and $\Delta\rho/\rho$ is the net MR coefficient of the sensor. As an example, consider a simple shielded MR sensor 400A thick, 7.5 μm high, biased uniformly at 45°, with a resistivity of 25 μ Ohm-cm, an MR coefficient of 2% and operated at a sense current of 10mA. The recording medium has an areal moment of 2 memu/cm^2 and an arctangent transition width of 0.3 μm. The MR head reads the transitions at a head-disk separation of 0.25 μm. Application of Eq. (6.41) shows that about 25% of the flux of the transition is captured by the MR sensor as the incident flux to its exposed tip. Application of Eq. (6.43) shows the signal flux to decay exponentially up the height of the sensor with a characteristic length of 4.7 μm. Finally, application of Eq. (6.45) shows the peak-to-peak signal response amplitude is about 55 μ V/μm of read trackwidth.

    Analysis of the readback behavior reveals several important dependences of the signal amplitude on the head parameters. First, the signal amplitude depends on the MR current as a parametric scaling factor: a larger current yields more signal output. The upper limit to the MR current is usually constrained by thermal or electromigration considerations. Second, the signal amplitude is also roughly linear with the read gap. Increasing the read gap will therefore improve the sensor output, but this will be accomplished at the expense of degraded linear resolution, so that a compromise between the two goals will be necessary. Third, the signal amplitude increases significantly as the thickness of the MR sensor is reduced. This increase occurs because a thinner MR sensor not only has a higher resistance, but also concentrates the incident signal flux into a smaller cross-sectional area to increase the sensor magnetic rotation. The lower limit of the sensor thickness is usually determined by considerations related to the control of the film properties and the onset of non-linear effects when the magnetic response in the sensor becomes too large. Finally, the signal amplitude also increases significantly as the sensor height is reduced. A narrower sensor not only increases the sensor resistance, but also improves the magnetic efficiency since the signal flux tends to be concentrated near the exposed tip of the sensor. The lower limit of the sensor height is usually determined by the accuracy and consistency of the mechanical lapping process employed to form the exposed air-bearing surface of the MR sensor, and by various reliability issues.

The linear resolution of the shielded MR head can be described by its isolated transition readback waveform and its signal amplitude rolloff with linear density. As discussed in the previous paragraph, the incident flux to the shielded MR head can be calculated via the reciprocity theorem using the fringe-field distribution of Eq. (6.40), which can be approximated as the sum of two Karlqvist head fields each with a gap equal to the half-gap of the MR head, but shifted relative to each other. This relationship leads to the simple picture that the linear resolution of the shielded MR head is roughly equivalent to that of a Karlqvist head with a gap equal to the MR head half-gap. Fig. 6.37(a) shows the isolated transition readback waveform of the shielded MR head computed using the fringe field of Eq. (6.40), along with waveforms from a ferrite head and a thin-film head. The MR-head and the ferrite-head waveforms are quite similar, while the thin-film head waveform is distinctly different with the pronounced undershoots in its baseline. The effects of finite MR shield thicknesses and permeabilities have been investigated in detail using the finite element method (Middleton, 1980) and a large-scale model (Middleton et al., 1979). Results show a progressive rise in the slow varying tails of the readback waveform as the shields become thinner, suggesting a minimum shield thickness of at least 1 μm for most applications. In contrast, a progressive broadening of the entire readback waveform is observed when the shield permeability is reduced, suggesting a minimum permeability of ~500 for most applications.

After computation of the isolated transition readback waveform, the amplitude rolloff behavior with density can be computed by superposition of these waveforms at varying transition densities. The results are shown for a shielded MR head as well as a ferrite (Karlqvist) head and a thin-film head in Fig. 6.37(b). The ferrite-head rolloff is smooth and monotonic due to the absence of undershoots in the waveform from the macroscopically thick pole-tips. In contrast, the thin-film head rolloff exhibits pronounced rippling behavior due to the undershoots from the micron thick pole-tips, while the shielded MR head rolloff exhibits a slight rippling behavior as a result of its finite shield thickness. The rippling effect of the finite shield thickness has been studied in detail by a rigorous computation of the MR head fringe field using a conformal mapping approach (Heim, 1982) assuming an infinitely thin MR sensor. In addition, the conformal mapping result also indicates that the linear resolution of a shielded MR head with total gap g is more similar to a Karlqvist head of 0.7 g rather than 0.5 g from the simple approximation.

6.5.4 Linearization of the MR Response

We now explore the first basic issue for the MR sensor, namely that of sensor response linearization. As described earlier, the fundamental MR effect is quadratic (Eq. 6.37), resulting in a bell-shaped response (Fig. 6.32b) to the magnetic field signals. Such a response is maximally flat at zero field, which is not very useful for small signal operations. Consequently, transverse biasing must be provided to

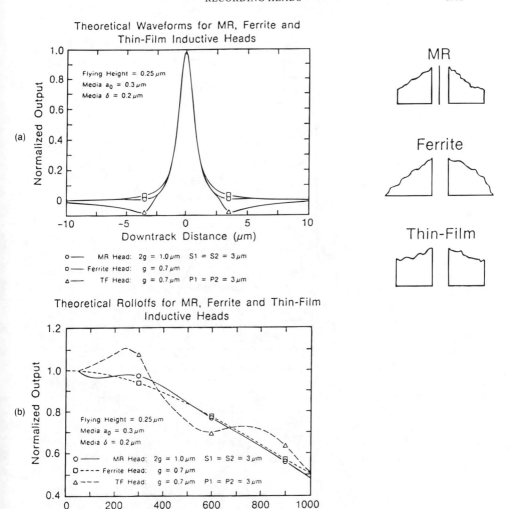

FIGURE 6.37 Linear resolution comparisons of ferrite, thin-film and MR heads; (*a*) Waveforms; (*b*) Rolloffs.

linearize the operating point about zero field. In the first approach to transverse biasing, a bias field is applied to rotate the magnetic moment to form an appropriate angle with the current path (Fig. 6.38*a*) (Thompson et al., 1975; Tsang, 1984). This moves the quiescent state operating point from the top of the response curve down to one side for better small signal response (Fig. 6.38*b*). The second approach to transverse biasing consists of canting the current path by special "barberpole" conductor patterns (Kuijk et al., 1975; Tsang, 1984) as shown in Fig. 6.38(*c*), while the magnetic moment is left along the longitudinal sensor direction. The resultant response curve, as shown in Fig. 6.38(*d*), exhibits good linearity performance with very small even harmonics. Let us now examine the more common techniques for implementing these two biasing approaches.

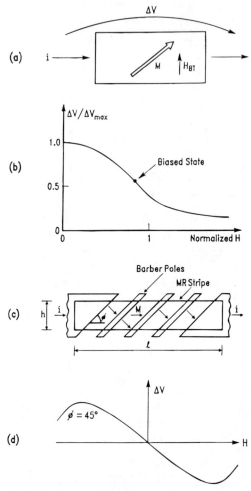

FIGURE 6.38   Basic transverse biasing approaches: (*a*) Bias field approach; (*b*) MR response for bias field approach; (*c*) Canted current approach; (*d*) MR response for canted current approach.

6.5.4.1   Bias Field Approach.   All bias field techniques involve the generation of a sufficiently strong transverse field for proper orientation of the magnetic moment of the sensor. For the shielded sensors, this requirement is complicated by the close proximity of magnetic shields around the sensor, and the concentration of signal flux around the lower edge of the sensor.

The shunt biasing technique (Shelledy and Brock, 1975; Kamo and Kitada, 1985; O'Connor et al., 1985; Tsang, 1990; Takano et al., 1991), produces a transverse bias field by passing current through a conductor stripe adjacent to the MR sensor (Fig. 6.39*a*). Typical candidates for the conductor layer, like Ti (O'Connor et al., 1985) or Nb (Takano et al., 1991), have resistivities comparable to that of the

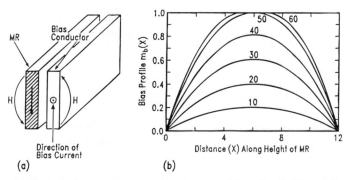

FIGURE 6.39 The shunt biasing technique: (*a*) Schematic; (*b*) Bias profile along a 12 μm high MR sensor.

MR layer so that they result in conductor thicknesses also comparable to that of the MR layer. The principal advantage of this technique is its simplicity, involving no additional magnetic components to further complicate the Barkhausen noise problems. However, due to the close proximity between conductor and the MR layer in a shielded head, electrical insulation between the two layers is often difficult. As a result, the conductor layer is usually designed in electrical shunt with the MR layer, thereby causing significant signal reduction. Another drawback to the shunt bias scheme is the weak and non-uniform biasing effect (O'Connor et al., 1985; Tsang, 1990) of a current-carrying conductor. As shown in Fig. 6.39(*b*), the shunt bias field is quite non-uniform across the height of the MR sensor, diminishing rapidly near the upper and lower sensor edges. The edge regions are therefore usually underbiased even when the center region might be overbiased. There are, however, ways (Shelledy and Brock, 1975; Kamo and Kitada, 1985) to enhance the shunt bias effect, one of which is to situate the MR sensor closer to one shield than the other. The asymmetrical image effects of the shields on the conductor current enhances the bias field by a factor of up to two. This method was indeed adopted in the MR head for the IBM 3480 tape drive.

The soft-film biasing technique (Beaulieu and Nepala, 1975; Tsang, 1984; Jeffers et al., 1985; Toussaint et al., 1986; Maruyama et al., 1987; Kehr et al., 1988; Yamada et al., 1988; Maruyama et al., 1990; Fuchigami et al., 1991; Tsang et al., 1990) also known as the soft-adjacent-layer (SAL) technique, was first proposed by Beaulieu et al. It has been the most popular biasing technique for implementation in MR recording head studies (Kehr et al., 1988; Maruyama et al., 1990; Tsang et al., 1990; Fuchigami et al., 1991), and was employed in the MR heads for the IBM 0663 and 0664 disk drives. This scheme may be regarded as shunt biasing of the MR sensor in a flux-closure environment: a soft-magnet film is placed adjacent to the MR layer and a bias current is applied along one or both of the layers (Fig. 6.40*a*). Magnetic moments of both films rotate in opposite directions in response to the current biasing effect, and in doing so they cancel each other's shape demagnetization effects. As a result, large rotations of magnetic moment can be produced, limited only by the permeabilities of the magnetic films. In addition, if the spacer layer between the two magnetic films is thin, very uniform bias profiles along the sensor height (Fig. 6.40*b*) may be obtained. Also, to minimize magnetic shunting of signal flux in the MR layer, the soft-film layer is usually designed so that it is biased well into magnetic saturation while the MR layer remains active for signal detection. In this case, the bias angle of the MR layer is roughly determined simply by

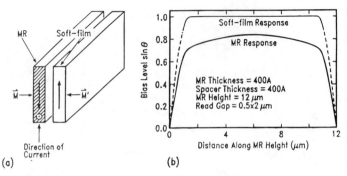

FIGURE 6.40 The soft-film (SAL) biasing technique: (a) Schematic; (b) Bias profile along a 12 μm high MR sensor.

the moment-thickness product of the soft-film layer relative to that of the MR layer, and remains fairly insensitive to the amount of current applied to the sensor. An important issue in soft-film biasing is the selection of the soft-film material. Such a material must exhibit high permeabilities ($>$ 1000) to produce good biasing efficiency, and high resistivity to minimize electrical shunting effects, since electrical insulation of the MR and soft-film layers are difficult at such a small distance apart (Toussaint et al., 1986). To avoid spurious signal response from the soft-film layer in case it departs from magnetic saturation, it is also desirable to have negligible magnetoresistive effect for the soft-film layer. Next, regarding the choice of the soft film layer, two types of material systems have been studied intensively. The first is the NiFeX ternary alloys with X = Cr, Ir, Ti, Rh (Klokholm and Aboaf, 1981) or X = Al, Au, Nb, Pd, Pt, Zr (Chen et al., 1991) and the second is the amorphous CoZrX system with X = Nb, NbTa, Mo (Jeffers, 1979; Suyama et al., 1988). For the NiFeX system, optimization efforts have yielded soft-film candidates with high resistivity ($>$ 40 $\mu\Omega$-cm), low magnetostriction ($< 1 \times 10^{-6}$) and low MR coefficient ($<$ 0.5%). In comparison with the NiFeX systems, the CoZrMo system can yield a higher resistivity ($>$ 100 $\mu\Omega$-cm), comparable magnetostriction ($< 1 \times 10^{-6}$) and a vanishing MR coefficient ($<$ 0.1%). An issue for the CoZrX system, however, is the large magnitude of the uniaxial anisotropy ($H_k >$ 1.2 kA/m or 15 Oe) for as-deposited films. As a result, post deposition anneals are usually required to reduce H_k to around 0.8 kA/m (10 Oe) or below to recover magnetic softness. Finally, variations from the classic soft-film biasing scheme are found in the unshielded dual MR sensor (Indeck et al., 1988; Smith et al., 1992a; Smith et al., 1992b) and the shielded differential MR sensor (Voegeli 1975; Jeffers 1979; Kelley et al., 1981; Bhattacharyya et al., 1987). Both schemes employ two MR layers that are biased equal and opposite to each other through the soft-film biasing effect. The dual MR sensor has been discussed earlier in connection with unshielded sensors, and the differential MR sensor is similar to the dual MR sensor except that the MR layers are much closer to each other. The MR layers are also electrically insulated from each other and connected so that their signal responses add differentially. The differential MR sensor therefore had the advantage of large signal outputs with superior linearity characteristics through the cancellation of even harmonics.

The hard-magnet biasing technique first proposed by Bajorek et al., places a hard magnet layer next to the MR sensor (Fig. 6.4a) for bias field generation (Bajorek et al., 1974; Thompson, 1974; Bajorek and Thompson, 1975; Uchida et al., 1982; Tsang, 1984; Hill et al., 1986; Edelman et al., 1990; Suzuki et al., 1991).

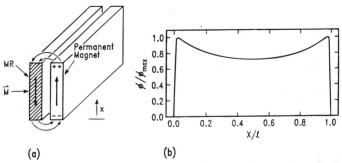

FIGURE 6.41 The hard-magnet biasing technique: (a) Schematic; (b) Bias profile along MR sensor height (1) (*after Thompson, 1974*).

Typical candidates for the hard magnet layer are the Co-RE (Uchida et al., 1982) or the CoPt (Hill et al., 1986; Edelman et al., 1990) type high-coercivity alloys. From biasing uniformity considerations, the hard-magnet biasing scheme performs well for narrow MR sensors. This is because the bias flux from the hard magnet is typically injected into the MR sensor at the upper and the lower edges, resulting in a bias profile (Fig. 6.41b) (Thompson, 1974) that is effective in linearizing the MR output. The principal issue for this biasing scheme is the degradation effects of the hard-magnets on the softness of the MR layer when they are close to each other. This happens because hard-magnet films typically derive their high coercivity from the segregation of magnetic material into small weakly-interacting granular units. Such a granular system is prolific in localized stray fields due to highly non-uniform micromagnetic behaviors. An MR layer in the vicinity therefore experiences local pinning from the stray fields, resulting in a degradation of its soft-magnet properties. To avoid such effects, it has been shown (Bajorek and Thompson, 1975; Hill et al., 1986) that the MR layer must be separated quite far away ($>$ 1000 A) from the hard-magnet layer. But then the bias field from the hard-magnet might be reduced due to bias flux capture by the shields. As a result, the hard-magnet biasing scheme has found applications mainly in the unshielded MR heads (Uchida et al., 1982; Edelman et al., 1990), where the hard-magnet can be placed far away from the MR sensor to avoid the softness degradation problem.

6.5.4.2 Canted Current Approach. The barberpole biasing technique first proposed by Kuijk (Kuijk, 1975), is the complement of the bias field techniques in that it slants the current path instead of the magnetic moment (Fig. 6.38c) (Feng et al., 1975; Kuijk et al., 1975; Lier et al., 1976; Tsang and Fontana, 1982; Simmons et al., 1983; Tsang, 1984; Mowry et al., 1986). As mentioned earlier, if the current path is properly slanted from the magnetic moment, this scheme actually produces linearity (Fig. 6.38a) that is superior to those from the common bias-field techniques. There is, however, a sizeable reduction in signal amplitude (Tsang, 1984), due to a modified MR response behavior in the canted current path environment, and a partial shorting of the read region by the conductor stripes. Also, the complexities in film deposition and properties control of other bias field methods are now replaced by issues in lithographic definition and alignment of the barberpole pattern. An important concern here is the uniformity of the current path under the barberpole pattern: despite the slanted conductor pattern, current close to the upper and lower edges of the sensor tends to flow with little or no canting. This problem might be partially offset by overdesigning the slant angle of the barberpole pattern (Tsang and Fontana, 1982), or by packing the conductor stripes closer together until lithographic limits are reached. A second concern is a broadening of the read sensitivity trackprofile on each side of the track due to the slanted conductor contacts (Tsang, 1984), thereby degrading read trackwidth definition. Consequently, the barberpole-biased recording heads have been studied mainly in the wide trackwidth environments (Lier et al., 1976; Mowry et al., 1986), and a flux-guided version has been successfully employed in analog and digital audio recording systems by Philips (Lier, 1976).

6.5.5 Suppression of Barkhausen Noise

Serious magnetic instability and noise have been reported on small trackwidth MR sensors, and they have for many years constituted the primary obstacle towards applying MR sensors to the disk-drive recording environment (Thompson, 1974; Decker et al., 1981; Davidson et al., 1984; Tsang, 1984; Shelledy and Nix, 1992). An example of magnetic instability is shown in Figure 6.42a, which is the MR response of a 60 μm long by 40 μm high permalloy element. The Barkhausen noise originates mainly from multidomain activities in the small-feature MR element. To address the noise problem, the domain behavior of small unshielded permalloy elements has been systematically studied using Bitter pattern domain observation techniques (Decker and Tsang, 1980; Decker et al., 1981; Tsang and Decker, 1981; Tsang and Decker, 1982). Results indicate, for example, that the response of a small rectangular permalloy element to a large cyclical transverse H field typically involves the systematic creation and annihilation of well-defined buckling domain structures (Fig. 6.42b). Furthermore, the principal irreversible domain process in the magnetization reversal does not involve translation of domain walls as might be expected from the classic Barkhausen noise mechanism, but instead conversions of Néel wall segments between states of different magnetization polarities. These so-called wall-state transitions (Decker and Tsang, 1980; Tsang and Decker, 1981) involve sporadic nucleations and propagations of localized micromagnetic structures called Bloch lines along the Néel walls. Indeed, the activities of these Bloch

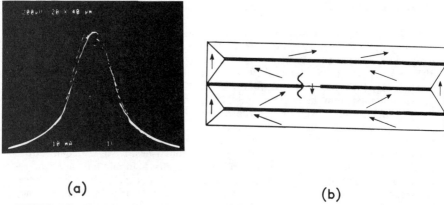

(a)   (b)

FIGURE 6.42   The Barkhausen noise problem: (a) Transverse field MR response of a 20 μm high by 60 μm long element; (b) Typical domain pattern at zero field.

lines might be regarded as the activities of lower-dimension "domain-walls" inside the actual Néel walls themselves. Besides the wall-state transitions, to a lesser extent there are also the mutual annihilations of adjacent Néel walls. They constitute another irreversible component of the magnetization process. To elucidate the impacts of these domain processes to the Barkhausen noise problem, simultaneous observations (Tsang and Decker, 1981) of domain behavior and MR response have been conducted. Results indeed confirmed the wall-state transitions to be a prolific generator of noise in the MR response. More recently, these experimental findings have been replicated theoretically with micromagnetic models of MR elements using finite-element techniques (Smith, 1988; Gao and Zhu, 1993).

Next, the causes for the formation of the buckling domain walls must be investigated. The first cause is the well-known hard-axis dispersion effect of the permalloy material, first proposed by Middelhoek (1961) to explain stripe domain formation in large-area permalloy films. The second cause is the longitudinal demagnetization effect (Tsang and Decker, 1982), a consequence of MR element geometry, where the buckling domains are created to minimize magnetostatic energies due to magnetic charges at the ends of the MR element. Experiments (Klokholm and Aboaf, 1981) have been carried out to differentiate between these two effects in small unshielded MR elements. Results suggest that the longitudinal demagnetization effect is typically dominant in buckling domain formation. Exceptions might arise, however, if magnetostrictive MR materials were used, resulting in large and improperly oriented stressed-induced uniaxial anisotropies after sensor fabrication (Shiroishi et al., 1984; Simmons et al., 1989). For the purpose of our discussion, therefore, we will assume that proper control of uniaxial anisotropy has already been accomplished through correct MR material selection and deposition processes.

The understanding obtained from these systematic studies leads to a general strategy (Tsang, 1984) for Barkhausen noise suppression, through the elimination of buckling multidomain patterns in the MR element. Since these buckling domains are typically caused by longitudinal demagnetization effects, domain suppression techniques are primarily involved with the reduction of longitudinal demagnetization and the active stabilization of the single domain state. The longitudinal demagnetization field H_{DL} can be reduced by either geometric or magnetic means. First, H_{DL} can be reduced geometrically by increasing the length-to-height aspect ratio of the MR elements. MR elements with high aspect ratios are therefore more likely to exhibit quiet MR responses. Long MR elements, however, might degrade track density resolution performance through increased side-track reading. A solution to this dilemma is found in the patterned exchange scheme of domain stabilization which will be discussed later. Next, H_{DL} can also be reduced magnetically by flux closure schemes. One method (Kamo and Kitada, 1985) is to put a soft-magnetic film next to the MR element and prepare the two layers so that they have equal but opposite magnetic moments in the longitudinal direction. Another method (Nagata et al., 1987) is to shape the MR element into a "picture-frame" geometry and orient the magnetic moments along each leg of the sensor into a flux-close state by such means as barberpole conductor patterns. We note, however, that reduction of longitudinal demagnetization effects only diminish the likelihood of domain occurrence, but does not guarantee the single-domain state. To actively maintain the single-domain state against conversion into various multidomain states, a longitudinal bias field H_{BL} is also needed (Tsang, 1984). Moreover, to be effective, H_{BL} must at least exceed the longitudinal demagnetization field (Tsang and Fontana, 1982; Corb, 1988) of the MR element in the single-domain state. There are two main approaches for generating this longitudinal bias field. The first is the exchange biasing (Hempstead et al., 1978) of the MR layer by a magnetically "hard" stabilization layer through interfacial exchange coupling. For example, deposition of an antiferromagnetic FeMn layer (Hempstead et al., 1978; Tsang et al., 1981; Tsang and Lee, 1982) next to a 400Å thick permalloy MR layer creates an effective bias field as large as 4 kA/m (50 Oe) which can be oriented longitudinally for domain suppression (Hempstead et al., 1978; Tsang and Fontana, 1982; Takano et al., 1991). Figure 6.43 shows the effects of exchange-bias stabilization for a 15 μm wide by 10 μm high MR element. The MR response is extremely noisy without any H_{BL} (Fig. 6.43a), but becomes mostly quiet with 2 kA/m (25 Oe) of H_{BL} (Fig. 6.43b) from FeMn exchange biasing (Tsang and Fontana, 1982). In general, the stabilization layer can be antiferromagnetic, ferromagnetic or ferrimagnetic, as long as it is strongly coupled to the MR layer through interfacial exchange and exhibits a high enough coercivity to be stable in the magnetic environments of interest. A TbCo ferrimagnetic stabilization layer (Cain et al., 1988; Cain et al., 1989), for example, was found to produce over 8 kA/m (100 Oe) of exchange bias field with a 400Å thick permalloy layer. The use of a ferromagnetic stabilization layer (permanent magnet) with permalloy, however, might lead to problems concerning mutual degradation of MR softness and permanent magnet hardness, as discussed earlier. The

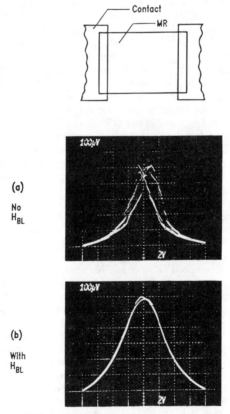

FIGURE 6.43   MR response of a 10 μm high by 15 μm long MR element: (a) No H_{BL}; (b) 25 Oe H_{BL} from FeMn exchange-biasing.

second approach for generating the longitudinal bias field is to use barberpole conductor patterns. Feng et al. (1975) have shown that current along the barberpole pattern (Fig. 6.38c) produces a small longitudinal bias field. By using a large but short current pulse through the sensor, the transient H_{BL} might be strong enough to initialize the MR sensor into a single-domain state. This method is useful only if the single-domain state is relatively stable after removal of the large initialization field. It is therefore not applicable to small-feature MR elements, where the single-domain state would spontaneously break up into multidomain states.

Our discussion so far has indicated that for proper operation of a MR sensor, a transverse bias field may be needed for response linearization, and a longitudinal bias field may be needed for single-domain stabilization. We have also discussed the various techniques of generating these two bias fields. An important issue (Tsang, 1989) arises, however, when we consider applications of both bias fields on a MR sensor: namely, that these two bias fields are perpendicular to each other and tend to compete with each other for the net magnetic behavior. In particular, a longitudinal bias field reduces the transverse permeability of the sensor, thereby reducing the transverse bias angle needed for linearization and decreasing the sensor response to magnetic signal fields. This difficulty might be solved by accurate adjustment of the longitudinal bias magnitude to be just large enough to balance out longitudinal demagnetization effects, but not large enough to cause undue loss of transverse permeability. However, the magnitude of the applied longitudinal bias may not be easily tunable to fit the demagnetization requirements of various MR sensor geometries. This is especially true for the exchange-bias technique, where the bias field magnitude is a result of the quality of the ferromagnetic-antiferromagnetic film interface. This difficulty is overcome by the concept of patterned longitudinal biasing first proposed by Tsang (Tsang 1989). In this concept, external longitudinal bias is applied not to the entire MR sensor, but only to its end regions (Fig. 6.44), to keep them in well-behaved, single-domain states. Magnetostatic and exchange coupling between the single-domain end regions and the center read region then create an effective longitudinal bias field at the read region. It has been shown that for small trackwidth MR sensors, the internal longitudinal biasing effects from the end regions are sufficient to keep the center read region in a stable single-domain state. One important advantage of this approach is that the magnitude of the internal H_{BL} can be tuned by adjusting the MR layer thicknesses in the read and the end regions to maintain a high permeability in the read region. Meanwhile, the only requirement to the external longitudinal bias at the end regions is that it exceeds certain minimum requirements. The patterned longitudinal biasing concept can be easily implemented using the exchange-biasing technique. An example is shown in Fig. 6.45 for MR sensors 10 μm high by 100 μm long, with a 10 μm wide read track at the center. If no longitudinal bias is present, then the MR response is very noisy (Fig. 6.45a). If a uniform longitudinal exchange bias of 2 kA/m (25 Oe) is present, then the MR

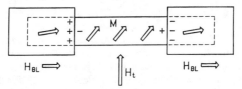

FIGURE 6.44 Schematic for the patterned longitudinal biasing concept: H_{BL} is longitudinal bias; H_t is signal field.

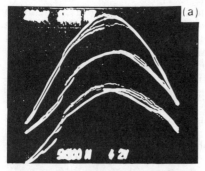

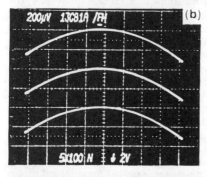

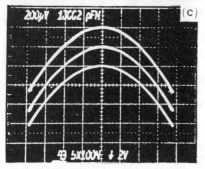

FIGURE 6.45 MR response of a 10 μm high by 100 μm long MR element with 10 μm read region: (a) No H_{BL}; (b) Uniform H_{BL} of 25 Oe; (c) Patterned (H_{BL}) of 25 Oe at the end regions only.

response is quiet but small (Fig. 6.45b), due to low transverse permeability in the read region. If, however, the longitudinal exchange bias is present only at the end regions, the MR response is both quiet and large (Fig. 6.45c), showing both suppression of Barkhausen noise and maintenance of high permeability in the read region. Another important advantage of the patterned longitudinal bias concept is that while the center read region can have a high permeability to maintain good signal sensitivity, the tail regions can have a low permeability to prohibit side-track reading by applying a large external longitudinal bias there. As a result, the MR sensor can have long geometries to lower the longitudinal bias requirements for domain suppression without sacrificing track density resolution. The patterned longitudinal bias concept was employed in the IBM 0663 MR heads as well as the IBM MR heads used in the gigabit density recording demonstration (Tsang et al., 1990; Tsang et al., 1993). Furthermore, since the basic principle here is domain suppression of the center read region by preparing proper magnetic states in the end regions at the boundary, it has also been termed, in a more generalized context, as the boundary magnetics control approach.

Finally, we note that while the foregoing discussion has been focused on the magnetics of the MR layer as the primary source of Barkhausen noise, there can also be secondary sources of noise beside the MR layer itself. In general, any magnetic structure in the vicinity of the MR sensor can be a source of noise if it is magnetically noisy and is coupled tightly to the MR sensor. In this light, efforts for Barkhausen noise suppression must be pursued with a more globalized perspective to consider the effects of all magnetic structures as well as all field generating structures in close interaction with the MR sensor (Thompson, 1974; Bonyhard, 1990; Brug et al., 1990; Feng et al., 1991; Shelledy and Nix, 1992; Tsang et al., 1992). It follows, for example, that proper magnetic behavior must be ascertained for the magnetic shields in a shielded MR sensor (Feng et al., 1991), for the flux-guides in a flux-guided MR sensor (Tsang et al., 1992), and for the soft-film in a soft-film biased MR sensor (Toussaint et al., 1986; Bonyhard, 1990; Shelledy and Nix, 1992).

6.5.6 Giant Magnetoresistance Heads

Since the early nineties, the limits of MR sensor performance have been drastically expanded by the discovery of the giant magnetoresistance effect (GMR) which is also called the spin-valve effect for a particular class of sensor configurations (Baibich et al., 1988; Dieny et al., 1991; Parkin, 1991; White, 1992; Daughton et al., 1992; Berkowitz et al., 1992; Hylton et al., 1992; Heim et al., 1994; Tsang et al., 1994). In contrast to the conventional MR effect, which is present in homogeneous ferromagnetic metals or alloys, the GMR effect is present only in heterogeneous magnetic systems with two or more ferromagnetic components. The spin-dependent scattering of current carriers by the ferromagnetic components results in a modulation of the total resistance by the angles between the magnetizations of the ferromagnetic components. An example is the trilayer permalloy/copper/permalloy system (Dieny et al., 1991), where the GMR effect operates to produce a minimum resistance for parallel alignment of the permalloy magnetizations, and a maximum resistance for anti-parallel alignment of the permalloy magnetizations. By far, the most popular configuration has been multilayer systems because of their well-defined geometry, although multigranular systems (Berkowitz et al., 1992) have also received a fair amount of attention. The first and most attractive feature of the effect for recording head applications is a large increase in the available sensor output, made possible by the largeness of the GMR coefficient. The coefficient for a multilayer system may be defined as the fractional resistance change between parallel and anti-parallel alignment of the adjacent layers. This coefficient can be as high as $\sim 10\%$ (Dieny et al., 1991) for trilayer systems and over 20% (Parkin, 1991) for multilayer systems, in comparison with conventional MR coefficients of only 2–4%. Secondly, the GMR systems are usually optimal at very small magnetic layer thicknesses ($< 100\text{Å}$), resulting in enhancements of magnetic sensitivity from flux concentration effects as discussed earlier. Thirdly, in contrast to the quadratic nature of the conventional MR effect, the GMR effect is intrinsically linear. This in principle simplifies sensor designs in the area of transverse biasing considerations. Finally, in the GMR sensors, the direction of the sense current is unimportant to the operation of the effect. This new feature gives the sensors additional design flexibilities and options. There are, however, also serious technical challenges in applying these sensors to the recording environment. Most of the high GMR coefficient systems have to date exhibited low permeabilities due to strong coupling between the magnetic layers. Until this coupling is significantly reduced, these systems would not be attractive for head applications despite the large size of the coefficients. Also, the magnitude of the GMR effect depends critically on the thicknesses of the thin ($< 100\text{Å}$) magnetic layers and the even thinner ($< 30\text{Å}$) spacer layers. This dependence escalates quality control requirements of thin-film deposition processes to an unprecedented level. The thinness of the multilayer components also renders the system especially vulnerable to thermal degradation effects caused by interdiffusion. Last but not least, since a GMR sensor comprises two or more magnetic layers, magnetic noise issues must be solved for each of the magnetic layers for the entire sensor to be viable.

As an example of a system, let us consider the popularly studied Spin-Valve configuration (Dieny et al., 1991) as shown schematically in Fig. 6.46. It consists of a ferromagnetic free layer and a ferromagnetic pinned layer separated from each other by a thin spacer layer. The magnetic moment of the pinned layer is typically fixed along the transverse direction by exchange coupling with an antiferromagnetic layer (e.g., FeMn), while the magnetic moment of the free

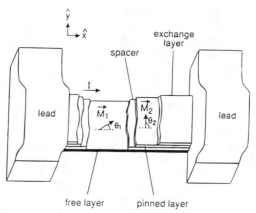

FIGURE 6.46   Schematic of a spin-valve sensor.

layer is allowed to rotate in response to signal fields. The resultant spin-valve response is given by

$$\Delta R \propto \cos(\theta_1 - \theta_2) \qquad (6.46)$$

$$\propto \sin \theta_1$$

where θ_1 and $\theta_2(= \pi/2)$ represent the directions of free and pinned layer magnetic moments respectively (Fig. 6.46). If the uniaxial anisotropy hard-axis of the free layer is oriented along the transverse signal field direction, then the magnetic signal response is linear ($\sin \theta_1 \propto H$), yielding in turn a linear spin-valve sensor response through Eq. (6.46). This linear spin-valve sensor response is in contrast to the parabolic signal response of conventional MR sensors (Hunt, 1971; Tsang, 1984).

The linear operation of the spin-valve sensor terminates when the free-layer magnetic moment becomes saturated along either the up or the down transverse direction. To maximize the signal range capability, it is therefore important to design the spin-valve sensor with the free-layer magnetic moment along the "unbiased" longitudinal direction in the quiescent state. This requirement is in practice as challenging an issue as the transverse biasing issue for the conventional MR sensors because, for small sensors, strong forces are at work to induce transverse orientations of the free layer. For example, the magnetostatic coupling between the free and the pinned layer along the upper and lower edges of the sensor favor antiparallel alignment of the two layers, while a ferromagnetic interlayer coupling between the two layers is usually also present, favoring parallel alignment. In addition to these two forces, there is the biasing field from the sense current which may favor parallel or antiparallel alignments depending on its polarity. This rather complicated situation has been analyzed by detailed micromagnetic modeling (Heim et al., 1994). Such a model uses as its inputs the resistivities, anisotropies, coupling fields and thicknesses of the pinned and the free magnetic layers as well as the height of the sensor. It then employs a finite-element algorithm to determine the biasing profile and the transfer curve response to magnetic flux excitations as from transitions in recording. Results show that longitudinal alignment of the free layer could be achieved when antiparallel tendencies from the magnetostatic edge

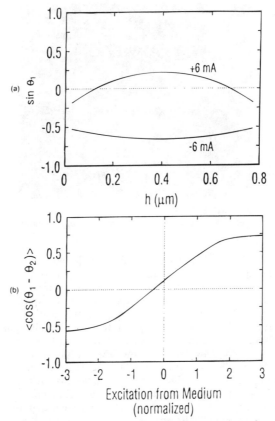

FIGURE 6.47 Micromagnetic model computation of spin-valve head: (*a*) free layer bias profiles; (*b*) transfer curves.

coupling is on the average cancelled by parallel tendencies from the sum of the interlayer coupling and the sense-current biasing effect. Figure 6.47(*a*) shows the magnetic bias profile of the free layer for such an optimized spin-valve sensor design (50Å Ta/100Å NiFe/25Å Cu/22Å Co/110Å FeMn) (Tsang et al., 1994). For a positive sense current of 6 mA, the free-layer magnetic moment is seen to be roughly longitudinal ($\theta_1 \sim 0$). The non-uniformity of the magnetostatic coupling effects, however, precludes its perfect cancellation by the ferromagnetic coupling and the current biasing effects, so that the free-layer magnetic moment actually varies by up to $\pm 20°$ about the longitudinal direction along the height of the sensor. Figure 6.47(*b*) shows the theoretical transfer curve of the optimized design, with a linear response region terminated at both ends by magnetic saturation effects. The quiescent state of the sensor is around the middle of the linear response region, yielding maximum signal dynamic range for linear operation.

Finally, Fig. 6.48 shows the actual transfer curve of a read head that incorporates the optimized spin-valve sensor as discussed earlier (Tsang et al., 1994). The read

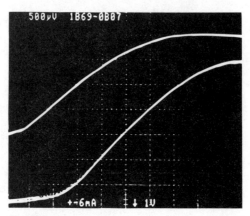

FIGURE 6.48 Experimental transfer curve (± 300 Oe) of spin-valve head (top: −6 mA; bottom: +6 mA).

trackwidth is 2 μm, the total read gap (shield-to-shield) is 0.25 μm, and the sensor is stabilized by the application of a longitudinal bias field from the tail regions as discussed in a previous section. The transfer curves for the two opposite sense current polarities are indeed quite different, reflecting the different quiescent bias states as illustrated in Fig. 6.47(a). The design current polarity (positive) is obviously desirable over the reverse polarity as it corresponds to a larger small-signal sensitivity and a larger signal range by having the quiescent state closer to the center of the linear operating region. Figure 6.48 also shows the GMR response of such a narrow track spin-valve read head to be quiet and non-hysteretic for field excitations (± 24 A/m or ± 300 Oe) strong enough to induce free layer saturation at the ABS. This result indicates that the application of a longitudinal bias field from the tail regions is as effective in inducing quiet and single-domain behavior in the spin-valve sensors as in the case of the conventional MR sensors.

6.6   HEAD APPLICATIONS

The wide scope of applications for magnetic recording systems has generated the need for a range of head designs covering signal bandwidths from the audio-frequency band up to very high data recording bandwidths. Head designs have also been influenced by the correspondingly large range of head-medium velocities, and by the different requirements for materials compatibility between head cores and the recording medium. The evolution of head designs is considered from the point of view of advances in head core materials. Initially, magnetic alloy laminations were used for head cores. Ferrite-head cores, with high-frequency capability, were introduced in the 1960s and have coexisted with alloy laminations. Alloy film heads have been introduced during the last decade, allowing heads to be fabricated by using processes similar to those developed in the semiconductor industry. Head designs have emerged which combine high-magnetization alloy film pole tips with bulk ferrite cores. Films have also enabled the introduction of galvomagnetic reproducing head designs, using magnetoresistance or Hall effect detection, with higher sensitivities than inductive reproducing heads.

6.6.1 Laminated Alloy Core Heads

High-magnetization magnetic alloys have been preferred for head core materials since large recording fields can be generated without limitations due to magnetic saturation effects. However, since these alloys are good conductors, it is sometimes necessary to laminate the head core structure to minimize losses due to eddy currents.

Design considerations involve not only electrical and mechanical performance but simplicity for manufacturing. Laminated cores are usually designed as ringlike structures, in which the rear gap is made as short as possible (Fig. 6.49). The front gap length is determined by the functional requirements (write, read, erase, or combination) and by the mechanical and electrical constraints on the gap depth, which should be sufficient for adequate wear life but small enough to provide the required gap reluctance. Laminations with a thickness as low as 25 μm have been used to reduce high-frequency eddy-current losses. The laminations are glued together and coils are wound on the bonded stacks. The stacks are then assembled with a nonmagnetic spacer in the front gap, and subsequently the top surface is lapped and polished to the desired contour.

Lamination heads have been used for many years for audio recording applications. Nickel-iron (Ni-Fe) alloy laminations (with additions of Mo, Cu, Cr) and nonmagnetic spacer shims (e.g., Cu-Be) satisfied the mechanical and electrical requirements. As shorter gaps were required for short-wavelength recording and reproducing, other gap-spacer materials were used which could be deposited by evaporation or sputtering. Typical examples of deposited gap materials are glass and silica. The shorter gap lengths ($<$ 1 μm), required to resolve very short wavelengths, are inefficient in recording head designs when wideband recording is used.

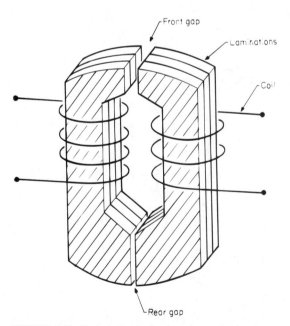

FIGURE 6.49   Basic design for laminated core ring head.

As a consequence, high flux densities in the pole-tip region are required to produce sufficient recording field throughout the coating thickness, leading to the possibility of pole-tip saturation. Under such conditions, alloy heads are preferred to ferrite heads because of their higher saturation magnetization, and are more suitable to record the higher coercivities of modern oxide and metal particle tapes and disks.

6.6.1.1 *Application of Laminated Heads in Digital Recording.* Digital tape recording heads are designed to handle high-frequency signals and operate at relatively high tape speeds. The head core efficiency is determined by the ratio of the reluctance of the flux path across the gap to the reluctance around the coil-carrying core at the signal frequency. For frequencies around 10 MHz, a lamination thickness of 8 μm or less is required to achieve permeabilities of 1000 in nickel-iron alloys. The head contour for the tape path is designed to minimize head-to-medium spacing and head wear. The airfoil between the head and tape is reduced by providing slots in the magnetic pole surface parallel to the direction of tape motion.

Multitrack laminated heads are used in high-density digital recording on tape. Reduction of cross-talk between tracks and collinearity of recording gaps are important design requirements. The design approach for multitrack laminated heads is to build the head stacks in two halves separately (Fig. 6.50). These stacks include laminations, coils, and magnetic shields between adjacent tracks. The shields are required to attenuate a range of field frequencies and amplitudes, and normally are built up with laminated structures of soft ferromagnetic sheets and good electrical conductors. Cross-talk can be reduced further by adjusting the head coil locations and the winding sense of adjacent coils. Sometimes this approach has been extended to providing bucking coils on adjacent core halves. There is a further possible cross-talk mechanism during recording which is not addressed by these changes.

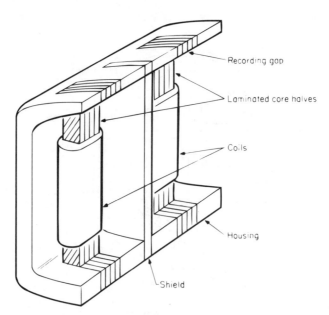

FIGURE 6.50 Multitrack laminated core ring heads with interelement shield.

This effect amounts to an anhysteretic magnetization of the tape by the cross-talk signal from adjacent tracks, when the signal on the measured track is of higher frequency (e.g., all 1s) and thereby acts as a bias. This effect can cause the recording cross-talk to be substantially higher than the playback cross-talk. Most of this cross-talk can be removed by a suitable electronic canceling circuit in the record or playback circuit. The lowest-power approach is to place the cancellation circuit in the playback channel (Tanaka, 1982).

Combined dual-element recording and reproducing heads have also found application in high-performance tape recorders. A special requirement in the case of digital tape recording is the function of read checking immediately after writing. Preferably this would be done on a bit-by-bit basis, but this would require the read and write gaps to be less than one bit length apart, and still have sufficient feed-through reduction to allow the reading of a low-level bit field immediately after writing a high-field transition. In practice, laminated read and write heads have been designed using a single C-shape lamination stack with a coil wound on it. The flux closure paths for the heads are provided by laminated stacks without coils. In this design, the read and write gaps have been placed in line along the tape path and are separated by a few millimeters. The center head section also acts as a shield to minimize feedthrough, and further reduction is sometimes obtained by using a high-permeability shield on the remote side of the tape, opposite the read and write gaps.

6.6.1.2 Applications of Laminated Heads in Analog Recording.

Probably the most challenging application for multitrack laminated head designs is the need to record more tracks in parallel, and at shorter recording wavelengths, as required for instrumentation recording. Since relatively high tape velocities are used, the wearing of Permalloy laminations by the tape places additional limitations on the efficiency of laminated read heads. To achieve reading efficiency at short wavelengths requires submicrometer gap lengths and reduced gap depth. Magnetic ferrite is a suitable core material which provides improved wearing capability, along with dimensional tolerance control and high-frequency performance. Ferrite-head designs have dominated the high-frequency applications, but laminated core heads have maintained large-volume usage in lower-frequency (and lower-tape-speed) applications such as audio recording.

The performance of laminated heads is limited by their frequency response and the read-head gap lengths achievable with adequate tolerance control. Furthermore, for very high track densities with multitrack heads, the tolerances on positioning stacks of laminations in mechanical housings become tighter, along with the tolerances on track widths for both the writing and the reading tracks. As an example of the state of the art, techniques have been developed for assembling multitrack heads with more than one track per millimeter (Cullum and Dorreboom, 1982).

Numerous attempts have been made to simplify the construction of laminated recording heads, and, for very narrow tracks, the single-lamination design is eventually feasible. Such a simplified design approach is appropriate for future high-track-density video recording. On the other hand, digital data tape recording still uses a relatively wide track, and simplification of head design has taken a different course. Laminated head designs for wide-track data recording have evolved into ferrite core designs and, more recently, into dual-element thin-film designs.

Despite the earlier trend to displace alloy laminated heads with higher-frequency ferrites, the trend to short-wavelength recording has turned attention back to high-magnetization alloys to provide sufficiently high recording fields from narrow-gap head designs (Mukasa, 1985). This is due to the increase in recording media coercivities required to support very short wavelengths. Such is the case in 8-mm video recording applications which have spurred the development of high-magnetization soft magnetic materials such as amorphous alloys. For instance, ribbons of amorphous metallic glasses [$M_s \approx 700$ to 1000 kA/m (emu/cm^3)] have been produced, by rapid quenching, with thicknesses intermediate between deposited thin films and the rolled alloy laminations described earlier. High permeabilities have been obtained in ribbons 10 to 24 μm thick, and this has led to single-lamination designs for narrow-track applications where the track width is determined by the lamination thickness (Matsuura et al., 1983). Figure 6.51 shows the design of a video recording head using a single lamination of amorphous $Fe_{4.7}Co_{70.3}Si_{15}B_{10}$. The performance of this head is superior to that of a ferrite video head in its ability to record on high-coercivity media. Although superior to nickel-iron alloys, amorphous alloys are inferior to crystalline alloys such as Sendust in their resistance to media wear. This drawback has been reduced by additions of Nb and Cr which have doubled the wear resistance of amorphous alloys and improved the corrosion resistance. The main objective of the additional components in the alloys is to improve the durability and environmental stability without compromising the high magnetization; in this regard, an amorphous alloy of Co-Ni-B has been developed (Sakakima et al., 1981). Zero magnetostriction has been obtained in these alloys by further small additions of iron or manganese.

Crystalline alloys, in thin sheet form, have also been developed for use as single-lamination video heads. With somewhat lower saturation magnetizations than the amorphous alloys [that is, $M_s \approx 580$ to 750 kA/m (emu/cm^3)], the alloys of Fe-Si-Al (Sendust) are also capable of recording beyond the capability of ferrite heads on high-coercivity media. Techniques for producing Sendust by squeeze casting have been developed which allow head cores to be fabricated with little final mechanical working. Through use of this fabrication method, head wear has been substantially reduced and approaches that of ferrite heads. Since the fabrication method is

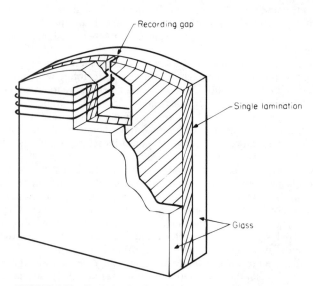

FIGURE 6.51   Single-lamination video recording head.

inexpensive, it has been applied to audio compact-cassette heads as well as video heads. It is also observed that the noise level of Sendust heads is similar to that of Permalloy heads and lower than that of ferrite heads (Senno et al., 1977).

High definition digital video recorders require heads with good high frequency response beyond 10 MHz. Compositionally modulated amorphous alloy films have been developed which combine high magnetization, 1.3T, ($4\pi M_s = 13$ kG) with high permeability. These films are thermally stable at high temperatures and are readily usable in laminated VCR heads with glass bonded structures (Kaminaka, et al., 1990).

6.6.2 Ferrite Heads

6.6.2.1 Applications. As magnetic ferrites were developed in the 1960s, the combined requirements of wide electrical bandwidth and improved head-wearing characteristics promoted a change from earlier laminated alloy cores to high-resistivity ferrite cores. In particular, the growth of instrumentation, video, and data recording applications stressed the need for durable, inexpensive heads capable of handling signals in the 10- to 100-MHz range. Improvements in heads and media have led to substantial reductions in recording and reproducing losses, and the opportunity to record even shorter wavelengths. This trend has stressed a limitation in magnetic ferrites, that is, the inherently low saturation magnetization. This limitation has been alleviated through the use of magnetic alloy pole tips, either on the head-tape surface or on the pole-gap surface. With some attendant processing complications, such pole tips have extended the ability of ferrite core heads to record on higher-coercivity media.

The high-frequency responses required by most applications are satisfied by head designs using manganese-zinc and nickel-zinc ferrite cores. Other applications, such as high-density 8-mm video tapes, high-performance rigid-disk files, high-performance audio recorders, and some instrumentation recorders, require a combination of high fields and high frequencies which pose more difficult design challenges. Not only have these requirements prompted the development of ferrite heads with alloy pole tips, but also designs which use metal alloy films for both pole tips and cores. The evolution to thin-film head designs will be described in subsequent sections of this chapter.

6.6.2.2 Rigid-Disk File Applications. The application of ferrite-head designs to rigid-disk files began in the mid-1960s as data rates rose to above 2 Mb/s. Initially, ferrite was used to replace Permalloy lamination heads in a self-acting, stainless-steel slider, and subsequently was mounted in a mechanically similar ceramic material, alumina, to provide an improved head-medium interface. Next, in the early 1970s nickel-zinc ferrite sliders were developed and provided a low-cost ferrite-head design which has been used to the present day. This slider design, Fig. 6.52 (Warner, 1974), was machined from a single block of ferrite and comprised a flat air-bearing surface with a taper on the leading edge. The magnetic element, with its coil, was mounted on the trailing edge of a center rail in the slider block. Two wider outer rails provided the bearing surface, which enabled the slider to rest on a stationary disk surface and then adopt a stable flying position when the disk was spinning. Also, during the 1970s, hot-pressed manganese-zinc ferrite material was developed for head applications; it offered higher saturation magnetization, which improves the capability of the head to overwrite the previously recorded informa-

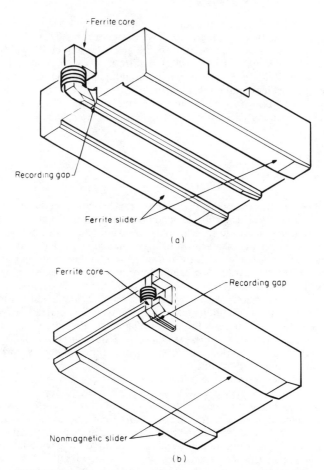

FIGURE 6.52 Ferrite slider with inductive write-read element for rigid-disk recording. (*a*) Ferrite slider design; (*b*) composite design with nonmagnetic slider.

tion (Kanai et al., 1973). This ferrite has been developed in a small-grain structure to allow narrow-track heads (less than 20 μm) to be produced without grain chipping occurring in the gap region. At the same time, low coercivity, high permeability, and high saturation magnetization have been maintained (Hirota et al., 1980). More recent designs of ferrite heads for rigid-disk applications have used a nonmagnetic slider with a small ferrite head inserted into the trailing edge of a two-rail slider design, Fig. 6.52(*b*). This approach has reduced the sensitivity of the head to external fields.

As track width is reduced, the mechanical cutting and grinding techniques become too coarse and damaging to maintain sufficient control on tolerances. Ion-beam milling is used with some success to provide shallow but accurately defined slider rails. Since no mechanical stresses are involved, the remaining track has unspoiled magnetic properties (Nakanishi et al., 1979). Auxiliary slots were required in the slider surface, away from the gap region, to adjust the flying height. These were produced mechanically or by laser-beam machining. Furthermore, in order to define the track width for long-wavelength recording, the head magnetic material at the side of the track was removed to a greater depth than can be achieved with ion-beam etching. In this case, further material may also be removed with the laser-beam machining tool. With the use of ion-beam etching technology, it is now possible to etch complex air-bearing surfaces, defined by photolithography. For instance, slider cavities with negative air-bearing force may be designed; these lead to improved takeoff performance when the start-stop, in-contact mode of operation is used (Suzuki et al., 1981). Finally, the ion-beam etching technique produced a bevel of about 70° at the edge of the ferrite poles. This was superior to mechanical grinding of the track edges, where 60° in a 30-μm track width were achieved with difficulty.

Further advances occurred with improvements in the ferrite core material to extend the frequency range of ferrite heads. To improve the high-frequency permeability of ferrite materials having high saturation magnetization requires increases in the material resistivity. Further developments in ferrite magnetic heads for application in rigid-disk files have introduced magnetic film poles with ferrite cores (MIG head design). Using this approach, the performance of ferrite heads with an Fe-Si-Al trailing pole-tip has extended their application to disk files using high-coercivity sputtered-film disks (Nishiyama et al., 1987). The larger recording fields produce improved overwrite characteristics even with small gap lengths which, in turn, increase the recording density. In the case of the trailing Fe-Si-Al pole design, the problem of a pseudo gap between the alloy pole and the ferrite core has been observed to be due to lapping damage of the ferrite at the interface and degradation of the initial layer of sputtered Fe-Si-Al. Interposing a layer of Ni-Fe and improved ferrite polishing have succeeded in suppressing the head performance degradation due to the alloy-ferrite interface (Tomiyasu et al., 1988). Continued development of MIG heads, using the double-sided film design with Fe-Ta-N films with 1.6T saturation magnetization, has evolved into nano slides with 250 Mb/in^2 density capability (Goto et al., 1994).

6.6.2.3 Flexible-Disk File Applications.

Ferrite heads have been designed for application in flexible-disk drives since the early development of such files in the 1970s. As flexible-disk drive technology has evolved from 200-mm-diameter disks to those of diameter less than 100 mm, the head-disk velocity and the head output have correspondingly been reduced. Linear recording densities have also advanced, requiring gap lengths to be reduced to around 1 μm. The result is that polycrystalline ferrite core materials have sufficed to date, but these will give way to higher magnetization pole-tip materials as shorter wavelengths are required. In parallel with these advances, the development of heads for flexible-disk applications is following video recorder head evolution, and manganese-zinc ferrite single-crystal heads are being applied.

Flexible-media head designs are heavily influenced by the cost of the design. Multigap structures have evolved due to the requirement to erase previously recorded information in adjacent track regions. Although relatively low track densities are used, it is advantageous to erase previously recorded information, since reducing the interference from adjacent tracks is more important than suffering a noise increase due to reducing the track width by the erase heads. Two dc-erase heads are provided to erase the zones to the side of the read-write tracks. A typical design for a read-write ferrite head with separate trailing "tunnel erase" heads is shown in Fig. 6.53. This head element is mounted in a slider button having a

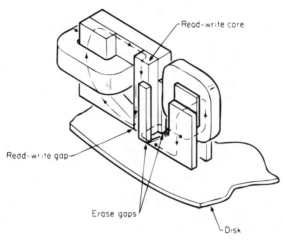

FIGURE 6.53 Write-read and tunnel erase head for flexible disk (*Baasch and Luecke, 1981*).

spherical contour, and is held in contact with the flexible recording medium by means of a pressure pad on the opposite side of the recording medium. Later designs of flexible-disk files record on both sides of the flexible disk, and the head design combines two read-write elements and two pressure pads. The overall design has to provide sufficient separation between the head units, and between the erase and read-write elements, to avoid track-to-track cross-talk and erase-write head cross-talk.

Improved ferrite heads, using the metal-in-gap design approach, have been produced for high-density flexible-disk applications. In this application, relatively thick recording media are used and special designs have evolved to increase the recording field amplitude for high-coercivity particulate disks. At the same time, there is a requirement to increase the reading resolution of the head. The conflicting requirement of a wide writing gap and a narrow reading gap has been solved in a MIG head design by using a low-saturation magnetization film for one pole and a high-saturation film for the other. In this arrangement, the low-magnetization pole is saturated during writing but has high permeability during reading (Goto et al., 1987; Abe et al., 1987).

6.6.2.4 Ferrite Video Heads. Over the last 20 years or so, the dramatic increases in recording density for video recording have been due, in part, to improvements in ferrite-head technology for producing narrow gaps and narrow tracks. Gap lengths have been reduced by nearly an order of magnitude from the 2-μm gap heads fabricated in the mid-1960s. Track widths have been reduced even more, from 180 to 10 μm, during the same period. The need for high-saturation magnetization ferrites to record very short wavelengths on high-coercivity media has spurred the evolution to manganese-zinc ferrite cores in either sintered polycrystalline or single-crystal form. To date, the mechanical and magnetic requirements for ferrite video recording heads have been met best by single-crystal cores, although fine-grain polycrystalline cores have also been used. Polycrystalline cores suffered from gap crumbling caused by microcracks in the cores. Hot-pressed ferrites were developed to improve the mechanical properties, but the most durable head poles have been produced in single-crystal cores. Single-crystal ferrite-head cores are lapped with abrasives that produce a surface-modified layer with deteriorated magnetic properties. This layer of reduced permeability is usually less than 1 μm after lapping and 0.05 μm after subsequent polishing. In video heads, noise is generated on playback by the rubbing of the tape against the head, and this is caused by magnetization fluctuations due to magnetostrictive effects, and by local heating due to contact friction. The noise in single-crystal ferrite heads due to tape rubbing has been minimized by suitable choice of crystal orientation. Using sputtered-film gaps and a specified core crystal orientation, single-crystal heads exhibit long-wearing characteristics and provide at least 1000 h playing time in home video cassette recorders. Under clean conditions, with unworn tapes, this lifetime can be substantially extended. Improved consistency of head performance has been obtained by using polycrystalline cores with single-crystal pole tips.

A typical design for a home video recorder head is shown in Fig. 6.54. The single-crystal ferrite core is narrowed in the region of the read-write gap to provide

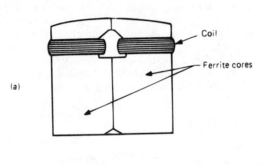

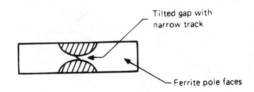

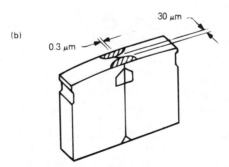

FIGURE 6.54 (*a*) Video head design for consumer tape recorder; (*b*) tilted recording gap design.

the narrow track (Fig. 6.54). An important feature of the high track density of a home video head is the tilting of the read-write gap with respect to the transverse direction of the track. As shown in Fig. 6.54, the gap is aligned at an angle of about 7° to the transverse direction. In most helical-scan recorders, two heads are provided on the rotating drum, and they record alternate tracks. Since the gap alignment of the second head is −7°, there is a 14° difference in the magnetization directions between adjacent tracks; this leads to a reduction in the signal picked up by the heads from adjacent tracks, and allows the guard band between tracks to be eliminated.

The evolution of video heads for miniaturized 8-mm video tape recorders, along with the trend to improve picture resolution, has maintained the need for reductions in the track width and gap length and therefore in the core size of video heads. It has also focused attention on higher-coercivity media. At this point, the saturation magnetization limitations of ferrite pole tips have been extended through the use of high-magnetization hard alloy pole pieces. The first approach to a solution was to use pole tips of iron-aluminum-silicon which were glued to the surface of the ferrite core material (Fig. 6.55). For a number of years in the early development of video recording, this type of recording head was in use. Nevertheless, the pole tips exhibited shorter life than the ferrite they replaced and required replacement after a few hundred hours of operation. Subsequently, sputtered alloy films have been deposited on ferrite gap faces to produce a high-magnetization recording gap region as shown in Fig. 6.55 (Jeffers et al., 1982). With this approach, both the pole tips and the

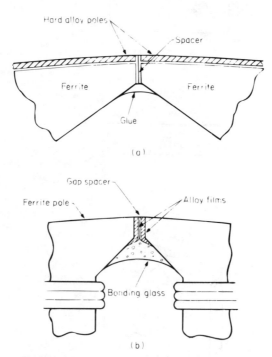

FIGURE 6.55 Video recording head pole designs. (*a*) Alloy pole-tipped ferrite head; (*b*) alloy film pole tips on gap faces.

nonmagnetic gap material are sputtered onto the gap faces. This advance has allowed the reduction of the gap length without a corresponding reduction in recording field, leading to a significant increase in the short-wavelength recording amplitude. While the deposited-film head design has the advantages of low cost and mechanical stability, it is necessary to ensure that good magnetic contact occurs between the alloy pole tips and the ferrite core. Otherwise, undesirable secondary pole effects occur if the additional gaps are of comparable magnitude to the main reproducing gap. Some of these problems can be designed out by making the alloy poles of different thicknesses, but the effect is best reduced by ensuring good magnetic contact (Ruigrok, 1984). Finally, designs using a single-alloy pole tip on one of the ferrite poles can make use of the resulting asymmetrical field pattern. If the trailing pole is alloy, the advantages are a higher recording field and a reduction of the reading interference (Ruigrok, 1984). On the other hand, if the leading-edge pole is alloy, a high field with reduced trailing-edge gradient results, and such designs have been proposed for erase heads for high-coercivity recording media (Yamashita et al., 1984). The secondary gap in the MIG design (Fig. 6.55) can result in an undulating frequency response if the boundaries between the metal poles and the ferrite cores are not magnetically uniform. One approach to avoid this problem has evolved in which the film ferrite boundaries are at a different azimuth angle to the read-write gap (Kobayashi et al., 1985). Alternatively, the poor magnetic match between Fe-Si-Al (Sendust) poles and the ferrite core may be improved by interposing a film of Permalloy. In this way, the undulating frequency response is minimized while retaining the good wear characteristics of hard Sendust poles (Sillen et al., 1988). For high-bandwidth video heads, as required for digital and high-definition VTRs, amorphous metal films have been developed to replace lower-magnetization ferrite cores. Multilayer films, a few microns thick, are laminated with nonmagnetic insulating layers to provide superior high-frequency response (Arai et al., 1988). In one example of this type of head, six layers of Co-Nb-Ta-Zr were laminated with five layers of SiO_2 onto a substrate of NiO-MgO-TiO_2. This video head gave better high-frequency output than an equivalent design Sendust or ferrite head without exhibiting the rubbing noise commonly experienced with ferrite tape heads (Takahashi et al., 1987). Very narrow track heads (5 μm) have also been developed using sputtered isotropic Fe-Si-Al laminations separated by SiO_2 films (Saito et al., 1987).

6.6.2.5 Ferrite Heads for Audio Recording.

Ferrite-head cores offer a low-cost design for audio tape recording. Unfortunately, the noise level of early polycrystalline manganese-zinc ferrite heads was substantially higher than in heads made with Permalloy laminations. As mentioned earlier, some ferrites are sensitive to the small mechanical shocks generated when a tape is run in contact with the head pole surface. Magnetostrictive coupling of these mechanical disturbances to the magnetization structure in the core is probably the source of noise in some ferrite heads (Watanabe, 1974). The noise has been reduced by optimizing both the ferrite composition and the grain size with the result that acceptable noise levels are obtained. Hot-pressed ferrite heads have been applied extensively to multitrack audio cassette designs (Nomura et al., 1973). In these designs for stereo recording and reproducing, four tracks are required with very low cross-talk between the pairs of stereo heads. Achievement of cross-talk below 45 dB was possible due to reduction of the face-to-face area of adjacent cores and by the provision of high-permeability shields between cores. Probably the greatest drawback with ferrite-head cores has been the development of reduced permeability in the surface layer after repeated playback of tapes. Furthermore, high-coercivity tapes have been introduced into audio recording applications; metal particle tapes, for instance, produce increased playback signal but require larger recording fields. All-metal heads or the combination of high-magnetization alloy pole tips and ferrite cores can produce larger recording fields and are applicable for audio recording heads.

6.6.3 Film Heads

The trend to film-head designs has been driven by the desire to capitalize on semiconductor-like processing technology with the aim of reducing the customized fabrication steps for individual heads. Batch fabrication techniques have also been developed for bulk core materials with the same objective in mind. Film heads have the combined advantages of close control of pole-piece dimensions and extended frequency response.

Applications for film heads have occurred where high-precision multitrack designs are required, such as in digital audio recording and in digital data recording. As the trend continues toward high bit density and high track density, the desire for high-magnetization head cores increases, and thin-film designs become more attractive.

6.6.3.1 Film Heads for Rigid-Disk Applications. In advancing the design of rigid-disk recording components, the requirements on the magnetic head have stressed combined improvements toward narrower track widths, reduced flying heights, wider frequency response, increased writing fields, narrower gaps for improved reading resolution, and improved side-reading response. These combined requirements have emphasized the development of film-head designs for disk file applications. Film heads can take advantage of the high-magnetization alloy poles, high-frequency response of thin films, the reduced inductance due to a small volume of magnetic core material, and the improved wavelength response due to the use of finite pole lengths.

Early film-head designs used a single-turn coil with Permalloy film cores. Two major design approaches were developed, one using films in the same plane as the recording medium, and the other using films perpendicular to it, as shown in Fig. 6.56. The earliest thin film heads were called "horizontal" heads (Fig. 6.56a) because the plane of the film structure was parallel to the air bearing surface. The later construction, which has become conventional, with the film plane perpendicular to the air bearing, is known as the "vertical" configuration (Fig. 6.56b). With horizontal heads the recording gap must be formed by a precisely controlled, narrow, non-magnetic strip that is generally several times higher than its width. In the earliest horizontal head, this gap was formed of electron beam exposed resist (Romankiw et al., 1970).

More recently there has been a revival of interest in this approach, the principle impetus being the desire to eliminate the costly precision lapping required to provide throat heights in the order of 1 μm. New processes and materials also have tended to make this approach more viable. A cross-section of a horizontal head which has been deposited in an etched recess in a silicon wafer is shown in Fig. 6.57 (Lazzari and Deroux-Dauphin, 1989). Hole connections to the back of the wafer, which are necessary to make contact to the head coils, are provided by laser drilling and chemical vapor deposition of conductors. Air bearing rails are defined by silicon etching before dicing the wafer into separate sliders. A somewhat similar fabrication scheme using crystalline glass substrates rather than silicon also has been implemented (Umesaki, 1991). In this case electrical connections from the head structure on the surface of the substrate to the back were made through vias filled with conductive material.

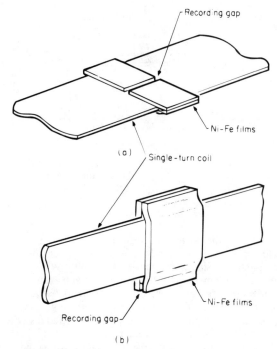

FIGURE 6.56 Single-turn film head. (*a*) Horizontal design; (*b*) Vertical design.

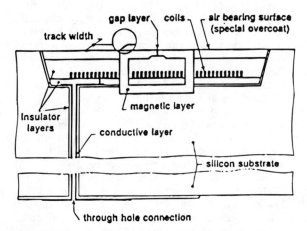

FIGURE 6.57 Schematic view of thin film silicon head.

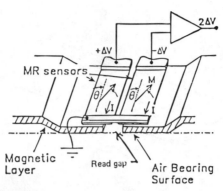

FIGURE 6.58   Geometry of the horizontal magnetoresistive head.

In another version of the horizontal head, a dual-element structure is proposed with a planar inductive write head and a novel planar magnetoresistive read head (Fig. 6.58) (Chapman, 1989; Chapman et al., 1989). With this scheme the air bearing layer and head elements are deposited on a substrate, and finally a slider-body wafer is attached to the overcoated head-elements by field-assisted bonding. Electrical contacts are made to the head elements through preformed vias in the slider-body wafer and the original substrate wafer is etched away to expose the air bearing surface. This composite is then diced into individual sliders.

Because of the small coil geometry of the single-turn design, it is natural that applications to fixed-head multitrack disk files were produced first. Multitrack single-turn read-write head designs, with high positional accuracy of the track locations, were obtained by depositing the film-head structures on the trailing edge of silicon sliders (Chynoweth et al., 1973). The track density achieved at that time was 4 tracks per millimeter and a recording density of 173 fr/mm (4400 fr/in) at a flying height of 2 μm. Four sliders, each with 29 read-write transducers, were mounted on each disk surface. Some of the early designs of single-turn read-write heads required a matching transformer for each head element.

As described extensively in Sec. 6.5, dual-element thin-film heads, using an inductive head for writing and a magnetoresistive head for reading, have been developed for narrow-track rigid-disk files. This type of head design becomes more attractive for small-disk-diameter drives where the medium surface velocity is low. The combination of high signal output, efficient writing head design, and wider tracks for writing than for reading has been demonstrated to produce high areal density disk drives. The use of magnetoresistive heads in disk files in 1991 has accelerated the increase of storage densities (Bajorek and Mee, 1994). The design of the first dual element magnetoresistive read head for disk files included two shields for the MR element. The inductive film write head gap was separated from the MR read element by about 10 μm. The second generation product head used a simplified merged structure in which a single film acts as the upper MR shield and the lower pole of the write head.

Furthermore, the first generation head used a soft adjacent bias (SAL) scheme for the transverse bias and a patterned exchange longitudinal bias. In the second-generation head, the patterned exchange bias was replaced with a permanent magnet bias film (Hannon et al., 1994).

The primary application area for recording heads for rigid-disk files has occurred in designs using a single vertical element per slider. Here, space for the head element is less constrained than in multitrack head applications, and designs using multiple turns have predominated. Although the fabrication process is more complicated than with the single-turn design, insulated single-layer multiturn coils have been developed with many turns. An example of a multiturn head design is shown in Fig. 6.59(a).

As magnetic recording progresses toward higher areal densities and track widths become smaller, there is a need to increase the number of turns in thin-film inductive heads to maintain former signal levels. The most efficient designs for adding turns provide multiple levels of turns, maintaining about the same yoke length between the recording gap and the back gap closure. In fact, multi-layer heads may have increased efficiencies since the height of the multi-layer stack increases the

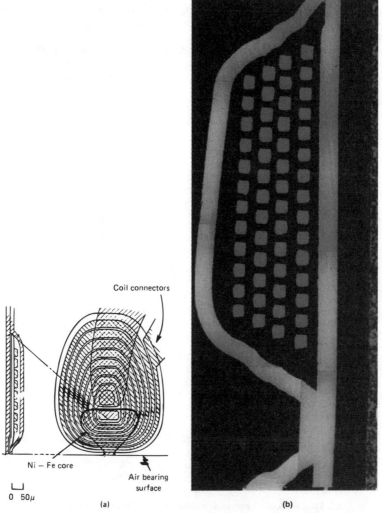

FIGURE 6.59 Multiturn film head. (*a*) Eight-turn design (*Jones, 1980*); (*b*) Four layer coil (*Courtesy E. Williams, Read-Rite Corporation*).

separation between the upper and lower yokes, decreasing the flux leakage between these layers. An example of a 4-layer coil construction is shown in cross
section in Fig. 6.59(*b*). The price paid for this improved efficiency is greater difficulty in controlling the second magnetic layer photolithographic image dimensions
over a more uneven surface topology and increased difficulty in maintaining thickness and compositional uniformity in this layer.

An ingenious means has been found for doubling the number of effective turns
in an inductive film head without increasing the number of physical turns. This is
accomplished with the "Diamond Head" design by weaving the magnetic yoke
through the coil twice, as shown schematically in Fig. 6.60 (Mallary and Ramaswamy, 1990). Since the resistance (and noise) of the head is largely dictated by
the geometry of the physical turns, this design also results in nearly a factor-of-two
improvement in signal-to-noise ratio relative to conventional heads. Furthermore,
the inductance-per-effective-turn-squared, an important figure of merit for high-
frequency operation, is also small compared with this same parameter for conventional inductive film heads. Using this means of increasing the effective number of
turns, there is no increase in the inductance due to flux closing through air around
additional coil turns. Furthermore, because the top and bottom portions of the
yoke in this design are necessarily laterally displaced, flux leakage between the two

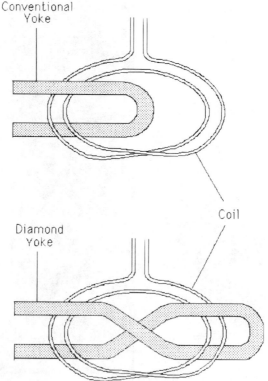

FIGURE 6.60 Cross section schematic of multi-via and conventional heads.

FIGURE 6.61 SEM micrograph of 120 turn head with helical coils and a planar yoke with two easy axes.

is minimized, diminishing this contribution to the inductance. In more advanced versions of this idea (Mallary et al., 1994) the flux path makes multiple passes through the coils, providing additional improvements in signal-to-noise ratio and inductance per turn squared.

The thin-film inductive head with the greatest number of coil turns reported to date is the planar 120-turn "Omega" head (Fig. 6.61) (Tang, 1994). In a planar head the first and second portions of the magnetic circuit are separated in the plane and only overlap in a small area near the gap. Each leg of the circuit is plated separately with a magnetic easy axis perpendicular to the direction of flux flow. Helical coils around each leg provide a tight inductive coupling to the magnetic circuit and therefore a lower inductance-per-turn-squared than conventional pancake-coil film heads.

Future advances in film-head design will require further miniaturizing of the head dimensions. The frequency response of heads of the design type shown in Fig. 6.59 shows that performance degradation is small up to 50 MHz. Thus, for immediate future applications, frequency response is not a limiting factor, but film thickness could be reduced by lamination where extended responses are required. On the other hand, smaller gap lengths, as required for short-wavelength recording, will limit the writing-field magnitude. In the future, the gap will need to be increased to write the higher-coercivity media required for very short-wavelength recording. Fortunately, materials with a higher magnetization than Permalloy have been developed in film form and may be used to increase the writing field, and also the ability of the head to write over previously recorded information. For instance, sputtered amorphous films of cobalt-zirconium (10 wt %Zr) have been applied to a film head for rigid-disk application, resulting in an improvement in overwrite capability of about 14 dB (Yamada et al., 1984).

Design optimization of the pole lengths for future high-density recording will favor relatively longer pole lengths in order to increase the recording field for high-

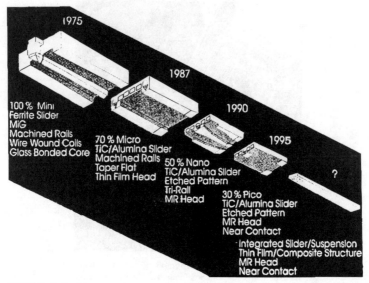

FIGURE 6.62 The evolution towards smaller sliders. Slider masses relative to the mini slider are: 35% (micro), 13% (nano), and 3% (pico).

coercivity media. As the pole length is increased relative to the bit length, both resolution and peak shift are reduced, and overwrite capability is improved. A compromise pole length is usually chosen which favors peak-shift reduction (Kakehi et al., 1982).

After the film constituents of the heads are formed and before the completion of individual sliders, head substrates are cut into row form and then lapped to a final throat height. Air bearings to provide controlled head-media spacings are then fabricated with the heads in row form. The evolution of the fabrication techniques and structure of film head sliders is shown in Fig. 6.62 (Grochowski and Thompson, 1994).

The "Winchester" ferrite "mini" slider (see Section 6.6.2.2) was fabricated by machining straight rails and lapping a taper flat at the leading edge. Substantially the same machining operations were adapted for the inductive thin film head "micro" slider (4.0 mm × 3.2 mm × 0.85 mm), omitting the thin center rail which defined the track width of the ferrite head. Since the slider was no longer a part of the film head's magnetic circuit, the slider material could be chosen on the basis of wear characteristics and the ability to hold close mechanical tolerances. A two phase Al_2O_3/TiC ceramic is widely used for this purpose.

One of the constraints in air bearing design is the minimum rail width necessary to fit the magnetic element on the rail. The machined air bearing is severely limited in this respect due to the rails being straight. As flying heights are reduced the rail widths must be reduced. At the same time the trend to narrow track widths calls for increasing the number of inductive head coil turns. Increased turns with a constrained element width can only be accomplished by resorting to complex multilayer coil structures. These problems are relieved by adopting etched, rather than machined, air bearings.

Etched air bearings were put into volume production with the IBM 3380K thin-film head (Nishihira et al., 1988) and subsequently used with the MR head tri-rail 50% "nanoslider" (2.5 mm × 1.6 mm × 0.425 mm). In this case the heads in row form are first lapped to final throat height and air bearings are then etched into the slider surface. The etching can be done by ion milling through masks (Nakanishi et al., 1980), reactive ion etching through masks (Bianchi et al., 1986), laser induced chemical etching (Von Gutfeld and Hodgson, 1982) and direct laser etching (ablation) (Khan, 1992). Etch depths are generally 10 μm or less. With some designs multiple etching operations are required (White, 1987).

The advantages of etched air bearings arise from the wide latitude in air bearing configurations available to the designer. Layouts can be used which make the rails wide at the element and narrow elsewhere. It is also possible to modify the locations and magnitude of regions of positive air bearing pressure (Nishihira et al., 1988), to form regions of negative (sub-ambient) pressure (Garnier et al., 1974), and to optimize pressure profiles for transverse motion (White, 1987). Such designs have significantly improved fly height profiles versus velocity, skew sensitivity and accessing performance compared to the machined taper flat design (Chhabra et al., 1994).

The transverse pressure contour (TPC) air bearing (White, 1987) can be designed for near constant flying height under a wide range of flying conditions, including those associated with cross-track actuating and the range of skew associated with swing-arm actuator operation. With the TPC design, each of the rails is provided with an edge contour such that one edge serves for pressurization and the other for depressurization when the slider is skewed and/or during access.

Future trends for slider and air bearings are illustrated in Fig. 6.62. Sliders undoubtedly will become smaller and lighter, perhaps evolving to being composed only of materials deposited by thin film techniques, such as proposed with the Censtor Flexhead™ (Hamilton et al., 1991). Air bearings will decrease in area as the head-media spacing diminishes to near-contact conditions.

6.6.3.2 Film Heads for Tape Applications.

Many directions have been pursued for designing high-track-density heads with accurate positional control of the tracks, adequate reading and writing sensitivity, and, in some cases, separate read and write capability. A leading application for such high-track-density heads occurs in digital audio recording where track densities of about 12 tracks per millimeter have been developed in 20-track heads (Yohda et al., 1985). Designs of film heads for high-density tape recording seek to minimize recording currents to levels handled by large-scale integration write drivers, by providing multiple turns. Offsetting this is the need to place the tracks as close together as possible, and this limits the spread of the head coil in the plane of the films. Consequently, multilayer, multiturn coil structures have been developed for digital audio heads.

Another possibility for film technology in tape heads is to combine the batch fabrication of deposited coils with ferrite yokes. Separate read- and write-head assemblies can be obtained by using two coil structures on their ferrite substrates, with a common ferrite yoke to form the closure paths as already described for earlier ferrite-head designs (Brock and Shelledy, 1975). Relatively low track densities are achieved, using a single spiral coil, and multilayer coils have been designed to increase track density while maintaining sufficient turns in the read-write coil.

The use of magnetic ferrite, rather than nonmagnetic substrate materials (such as Al_2O_3-TiC), allows the substrate to become a part of the head core and thus simplifies the design of the film-head element. Ferrites have well-proven wear characteristics and are available in large-area substrates. A significant improvement in the recording efficiency of a combined film-ferrite head core can be obtained by removing the ferrite core material in the vicinity of the head turns. As shown in Fig.

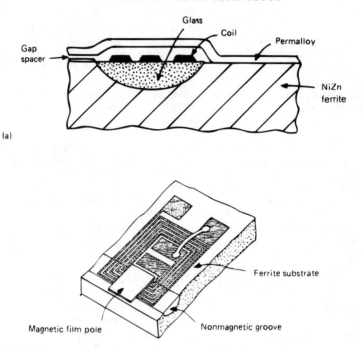

(a)

(b)

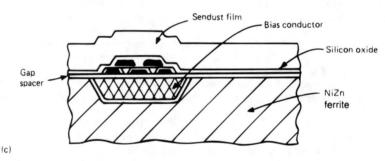

(c)

FIGURE 6.63 Head design with grooved ferrite pole piece. (*a*) Single-layer coil grooved substrate design; (*b*) head element design example; (*c*) two-layer coil grooved substrate design.

6.63(*a*) and (*b*), a semicircular groove is etched in the ferrite core and subsequently filled with glass. The deposited coil structure is close to the overlying Permalloy film, but is separated by about 50 μm from the underlying ferrite core. The improvement in head writing efficiency, resulting from the avoidance of saturation of the head core, is about a factor of 2 for the grooved ferrite design (Kanai et al., 1979).

In a further development of the grooved ferrite film-head design for digital audio recording, a high-saturation magnetization sputtered Sendust film is used to complete the head circuit. In addition, the signal-writing circuit is reduced by providing a bias field from a separate bias conductor in the groove (Fig. 6.63c) (Wakabayashi et al., 1982). The temperature sensitivity of the Sendust film is lower than that of Permalloy and, with bias recording, it was possible to design a 37-track head of this design without excessive heating.

Film heads with magnetoresistive reading elements now find major application in multitrack tape recorders for data storage (Bajorek and Mee, 1994). In addition, similar designs of multitrack magnetoresistive heads are being introduced into digital audio recorders. The main attribute of film magnetoresistive elements for reading recording fields is that the reading voltage is larger than that obtained in a film head with a few turns, especially for low-frequency signals. Compared with inductive film heads, the flux-sensing elements are compact, since no turns are required. Therefore these elements are becoming preferred as track widths are reduced, and are especially suited for multitrack designs. Even in single-track heads, the combination of relatively large signals and a low-impedance source (10 to 100 Ω) is an advantageous combination. Furthermore, the very thin layers used in magnetoresistive elements allow the design of a combination of an inductive writing and magnetoresistive reading head, in which the write and read elements can be physically close together.

The use of magnetoresistive elements has been applied to digital audio systems. For a typical 2-Mb/s data rate, multitrack heads have been designed with a range of track and bit densities. For a 32-track recording and a bit rate of 62.5 kb/s per track, the shortest recorded wavelength is 6 and 1.5 μm for tape speeds of 190 and 47.5 mm/s, respectively. Adequate response has been obtained from a magnetoresistive reading element with a reading gap length of 0.25 μm and a tape speed of 47.5 mm/s (Druyvesteyn et al., 1981b).

Multitrack magnetoresistive heads have also been applied to low-speed audio recorders and data cassettes. In one design, a symmetrical barberpole structure is used with the read current flowing in opposite directions for adjacent halves of the track (Metzdorf et al., 1982). This technique produces a linear reading characteristic across the whole track. Multitrack configurations of the element can be produced with high track density (10 tracks per millimeter) by allowing neighboring sensors to use one conductor in common. For increased reading resolution, soft magnetic film shields are deposited on each side of the sensor element. Another approach to increasing the reading resolution, without using shields, is to select the biasing level of the element to be optimum at the edge adjacent to the recording medium; spacing loss is thereby minimized (Uchida et al., 1982).

The earliest application of a multitrack magnetoresistive head for data recording was an 18-track head which used ferrite shields on either side of the MR reading elements (Cannon, et al., 1986). A shunt bias technique was used to linearize the MR element response.

Magnetoresistive reading heads have been developed further in multitrack tape recording applications. Reduction of Barkhausen noise has been achieved by stabilizing the single-domain state of the magnetoresistive element using high-coercivity film positioned at both ends of the element (Shiiba, 1987). Another approach has been demonstrated to increase the aspect ratio of the element, and thereby decrease the demagnetization fields without increasing the track width; in this design the long magnetoresistive element is shaped into a rectangle with a small gap remote from the active region. This design has been applied to an 18-track head for a tape mass-storage system (Nagata et al., 1987).

Multitrack magnetic data tape recorders requiring bidirectional operation use a combination of write-read-write heads. Thin-film heads have been developed in which two inductive write heads sandwich a central magnetoresistive read head. Multitrack versions of this three-head combination have been developed for high density data tape recorders (Edelman et al., 1990).

Thin-film magnetoresistive heads have been developed for data tape recorders in which a thin-film inductive writing head is deposited directly on top of a shielded MR element, in a similar design to the merged MR disk-drive heads. Biasing is achieved with a soft adjacent magnetic film (O'Kane and Kroes, 1994).

Ferrite substrates have been used as the starting point for combined multitrack dual-element heads for digital audio recording. In these designs, the inductive writing head is first deposited on the ferrite substrate. As described earlier (Fig. 6.63), a grooved ferrite substrate produces an efficient first pole on which to deposit the write-head windings and the second Permalloy pole. The magnetoresistive reading head can then be deposited on top of the writing head, with a suitable nonconducting smoothing layer interposed.

Another approach to combining a film magnetoresistive reading head and a film inductive writing head is to place the reading element in the gap of the writing-head yoke. This approach is feasible with the barberpole configuration for biasing since no external bias field is required. Experimental heads of this design use the perpendicular core arrangement with single or multiple write-element turns and the magnetoresistive element in the gap. Heads of this type have been applied to both tape and rigid-disk recording.

Yet another approach to a combined inductive writing head and magneto-resistive reading head places the writing turn or turns in the gap region of the head core, and the magnetoresistive element in the core circuit remote from the gap, as shown in Fig. 6.64 (Koel et al., 1981). In this design, the role of the head poles

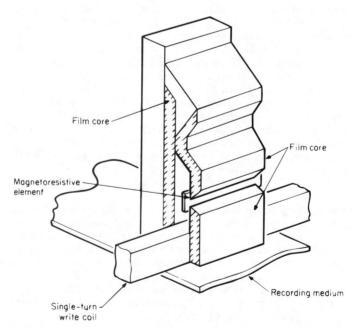

FIGURE 6.64   Inductive write and magnetoresistive read dual-element head (*Koel et al., 1981*).

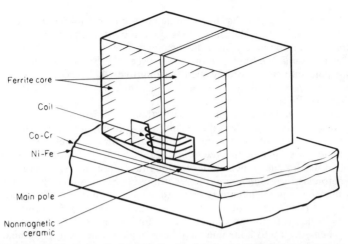

FIGURE 6.65   Perpendicular recording head design for single-sided operation.

during reading is to guide the read-head flux to the magnetoresistive element. Thus, in contrast to the previous magnetoresistive reading element, the long-wavelength recording of an audio signal is read with high efficiency.

A barber-pole head has been developed for a digital audio cassette system as an inexpensive solution for an 18-channel multitrack head. In this design, the film writing element is deposited directly on to the barber-pole element which is provided with fluxguides (Zieren et al., 1993).

6.6.3.3   *Perpendicular Recording Heads.*

Applications of perpendicular recording heads are under development for both rigid and flexible recording media. The early design for a read-write perpendicular recording head used a single pole which is attached to a W-shaped ferrite core as shown in Fig. 6.65, with an energizing coil wound on the center leg of this core. Thus, the main pole is magnetized from its end remote from the head-medium interface, as distinct from the previous design where the pole is magnetized from the end in contact with the recording medium. In this W-shaped head design, the function of the soft Permalloy underlayer is to complete the magnetic circuit from the tip of the main pole, through the recording medium, along the soft magnetic backing layer to the outer legs of the W-shaped core, via the recording medium ahead and behind the main pole. The large area of the outer legs of the head ensures that the flux density through the recording medium is low enough not to disturb any recorded signal.

The sensitivity of the W-shaped head depends on the choice of head dimensions and film permeabilities to achieve low reluctance in the film sections of the magnetic circuit. Thus the length of the main pole is made as short as possible, consistent with avoiding recording from the surrounding ferrite poles in the center leg of the W-shaped core. Also, the reluctance of the Permalloy return path through the soft film in the recording medium has to be controlled to be as low as possible. In some designs, a soft ferrite shunt is also placed on the remote side of the recording medium. This has some beneficial effect magnetically, but destroys the ease-of-operation advantage of the single-sided head. A correctly designed W-shaped head gives a similar recording sensitivity and a 3- to 6-dB improvement in reading sensitivity compared with a typical ring-type video head (Hokkyo et al, 1984).

The W-shaped pole head has been applied to digital recording on a flexible disk. For equivalent peak shift, the linear density recorded on a perpendicular medium was increased approximately an order of magnitude over the capability of a ring head with the same medium. At the same time, the greater penetration of the recording field into the recording medium improves the overwrite capability; for example, the overwrite of a 2.6-kb/mm signal on a 1.3-kb/mm original signal is better than 30 dB (Hokkyo et al., 1984).

The idea of a single-sided head may be further simplified by using a single ferrite return path for the reading-head flux, rather than the double return path of the W-shaped core. An example of this approach is shown for a magnetoresistive element reading head for perpendicular recording in Fig. 6.66. In this design, a flux guide main pole is used, as described earlier for longitudinal recording, in order to isolate the magnetoresistive element and the recording medium. Again, the soft magnetic backing film to the perpendicularly oriented cobalt-chromium recording medium is an integral part of the head magnetic circuit, and therefore uniform magnetic properties in this soft film are important for low-noise head operation. Very high recording densities up to 8 kfr/mm have been achieved in this type of head design (Takahashi et al., 1983).

Finally, inductive hybrid pole heads have also been designed for perpendicular recording (Shinagawa et al., 1982). The general design is similar to the hybrid longitudinal recording head described in Fig. 6.63, but with a much larger recording gap of the order of 10 to 30 μm. This design, in combination with a dual-layer perpendicular recording medium, has been applied to rigid-disk recording systems (Tsui et al., 1985), and to digital audio tape recording as shown in Fig. 6.67 (Yohda et al., 1985). Compared with the more open magnetic path, when auxiliary pole recording without a soft magnetic backing layer is used, these designs show high efficiency recording (~0.3 to 0.4 ampere-turns) and low cross-talk between adjacent elements.

For perpendicular recording on flexible disks, low-cost components are favored,

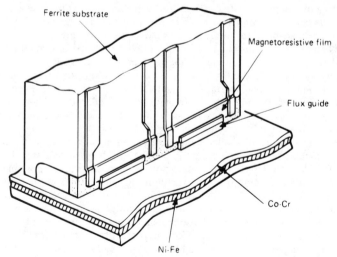

FIGURE 6.66 Composite pole head for perpendicular recording with magnetoresistive reproducing element. (*after Yohda et al., 1985*).

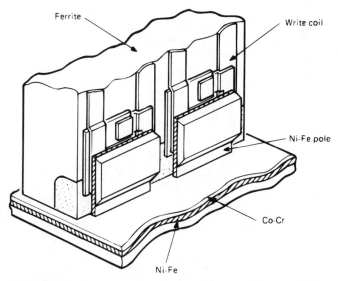

FIGURE 6.67 Composite pole inductive writing head for perpendicular recording (*after Yohda et al., 1985*).

and single-layer Co-Cr recording media have been developed. Adequate writing on a single-layer medium of coercivity about 820 Oe has been achieved with a simple film ring-head design using high-saturation magnetization Co-Zr-Nb films for the head poles. The efficiency of the head is improved by depositing the film structure onto ferrite substrates that form part of the ultimate head structure, as shown in Fig. 6.68 (Okuwaki et al., 1985).

Limited development of pole-heads for perpendicular recording continues, especially in conjunction with film media comprising a perpendicularly oriented recording layer and a soft magnetic film underlayer (Hamilton et al., 1994). Better coupling between the auxiliary pole and the underlayer also increases head efficiency. This has been achieved in the case of a ferrite auxiliary pole by providing multiple return poles for the probe flux to the surface of the recording medium (Yamamoto et al., 1988). High-density recording head designs require very narrow pole structures. Improved magnetic stability of narrow, high-magnetization alloy poles has been obtained by laminating with a nonmagnetic film to reduce the unstable closure domain structure (Iwasaki et al., 1987).

Significant enhancement of recording performance in rigid disk drives can be achieved by reducing the head-media separation to that provided by continuous sliding contact. A version of an integrated head/flexure (Hamilton et al., 1994), which promises to provide this mode of operation is shown in Fig. 6.69. To reduce wear the head/flexure is made with a very low load and a very low mass, about 300 μg versus about 30 mg for conventional thin-film head sliders. A wear resistant material provides the greater part of the contact pad.

The magnetically active portion of the head is a laminated FeAlN/NiFe pole optimized for high resolution perpendicular recording. This pole is connected to a NiFe yoke which is coupled to a multiturn spiral coil. The upper yoke extends to a pole providing a closure path for flux to the media high permeability undercoat. This head structure is embedded within a dielectric beam which serves as the

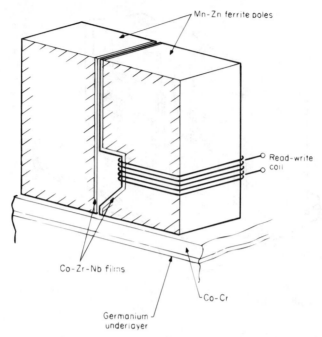

FIGURE 6.68 Composite ring head for perpendicular recording on flexible disks.

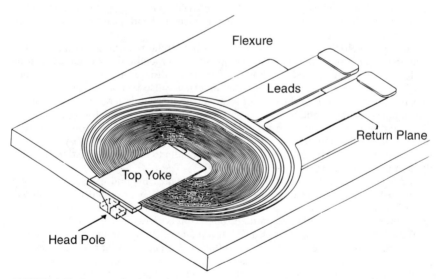

FIGURE 6.69 Integrated pole head.

flexure. Leads extend the length of the beam from the coils to external contacts. In fabricating the head/flexure, the film structure is deposited on a carrier wafer which is then sliced into the form of rows. The ends of the rows of beams are then polished and, in a departure from conventional practice, vertical poles are formed on the ends of the beams using thin-film deposition and photolithography techniques. Finally, the finished structures in beam form are chemically released from the carrier bars. Almost all conventional processes used to fabricate air bearing are eliminated.

REFERENCES

Abe, H., Y. Nose, and T. Goto, "Reproducing Analysis of Hybrid Heads," *IEEE Transl. J. Magn. Jap.*, **TJMJ-2**, 668 (1987).

Anderson, N.C., and R.E. Jones, Jr., "Substrate Testing of Film Heads," *IEEE Trans. Magn.*, **MAG-17**, 2896 (1981).

Arai, N., H. Ono, T. Morii, and K. Kishimoto, "Properties of Monolithic Gap Heads for High-Frequency Recording," *IEEE Transl. J. Magn. Jap.*, **TJMJ-3**, 407 (1988).

Argyle, B. E. , B. Petek, M. E. Re, F. Suits, and D. A. Herman, "Bloch Line Influence on Wall Motion Response in Thin-Film Heads," *J. Appl. Phys.*, **63**, 4033 (1988).

Arnoldussen, T. C., "A Modular Transmission Line/Reluctance Head Model," *IEEE Trans. Magn.*, **MAG-24**, 2482 (1988).

Baibich, M., J. Broto, A. Fert, F. Nguyen Van Dau, and F. Petroff, "Giant Magnetoresistance of (001)Fe/(001)Cr Magnetic Superlattices," *Phys. Rev. Lett.*, **61**, 2472 (1988).

Baird, A. W., "An Evaluation and Approximation of the Fan Equation Describing Magnetic Fields Near Recording Heads," *IEEE Trans. Magn.*, **MAG-16**, 1350 (1980).

Bajorek, C. H., S. Krongelb, L. Romankiw, and D. A. Thompson, "An Integrated Magnetoresistive Read, Inductive Write High Density Recording Head," *AIP Conf. Proc.*, **24**, 548 (1974).

Bajorek, C. H., and D. A. Thompson, "Permanent Magnet Films for Biasing of Magnetoresistive Transducers," *IEEE Trans. Magn.*, **MAG-11**, 1209 (1975).

Bajorek, C. H., and C. D. Mee, "Trends in Storage Technology Through the Year 2000," *Data Storage*, **1**, 23 (1994).

Beaulieu, T., and D. Nepala, "Induced Bias Magnetoresistive Read Transducers," U.S. Patent 3,864,751, February 4, 1975.

Berghof, W., and H. H. Gatzen, "Sputter Deposited Thin-Film Multilayer Head," *IEEE Trans. Magn.*, **MAG-16**, 782 (1980).

Berkowitz, A., J. Mitchell, M. Corey, and A. Young, "Giant Magnetoresistance in Heterogeneous Cu-Co Alloys," *Phys. Rev. Lett.*, **68**, 3745 (1992).

Bertero, G. A., H. N. Bertram, and D. M. Barnett, "Fields and Transforms for Thin Film Heads," *IEEE Trans. Magn.*, **MAG-29**, 67 (1993). For Erratum see *IEEE Trans. Magn.*, **MAG-30**, 159 (1994).

Bhattacharyya, M., R. Davidson, and H. Gill, "Bias Scheme Analysis of Shielded MR Heads for Rigid Disk Recording," *J. Appl. Phys.*, **61**, 4167 (1987).

Bianchi, J. K., R. A. Gdula, and D. J. Lange, "Reactive Ion Etching Process," U. S. Patent 4,601,782 (1986).

Bischoff, P. G., "Electrochemical Deposition Requirements for Fabricating Thin Film Recording Heads," *Proceedings Symp. on Magn. Mater., Proc. and Devices,* vol. 90–8, Electrochemical Society, Inc., Pennington, NJ, p. 221 (1990).

Bonyhard, P., "Design Issues for Practical Rigid Disk Magnetoresistive Heads," *IEEE Trans. Magn.*, **MAG-26**, 3001 (1990).

Bozorth, R. M., *Ferromagnetism*, D. Van Nostrand Co., Inc., New York, p. 612 (1951).

Brock, G., F. Shelledy, S. Smith, and A. Wills, "Shielded Magnetoresistive Magnetic Transducer and Method of Manufacture Thereof," U. S. Patent 3,881,190, April 29 (1975).

Brug, J., T. Anthony, and H. Gill, "Effect of Sense Current on Barkhausen Noise in Magnetoresistive Recording Heads," *J. Appl. Phys.*, **67**, 4851 (1990).

Brushan, B., M. Dominick, and J. P. Lazzari, "Contact Start-stop Studies With Silicon Planar Head Sliders Against Thin Film Disks," IEEE *Trans. Magn.*, **MAG-28**, 2874 (1992).

Cain, W. C., J. Lee, P. Koeppe, and M. H. Kryder, "Exchange Coupled NiFe-TbCo Thin Films for Use in Self-biased Magnetoresistive Heads," *IEEE Trans. Magn.*, **MAG-24**, 2609 (1988).

Cain, W. C., D. Markham, and M. H. Kryder, "Dual Exchange Biased NiFe-TbCo Unshielded MR Heads for High Density Recording," *IEEE Trans. Magn.*, **MAG-25**, 3695 (1989).

Cain, W. C., P. K. Thayamballi, and M. P. Vea, "The Effects of Pole Geometry on Recording Performance of Narrow Track Thin Film Heads," *IEEE Trans. Magn.*, **MAG-30**, 275 (1994).

Calcagno, P. A., and D. A. Thompson, "Semiautomatic Permeance Tester for Thick Magnetic-Films," *Rev. Sci. Instrum.*, **46**, 904 (1975).

Campbell, R. T., and J. S. J. Lo, "Multilayer Ferromagnetic Film, Its Preparation and a Magnetic Head Using It," U.S. Patent 5,264,981 (1991).

Cannon, D., W. Dempwolf, J. Schmalhorst, F. Shelledy, and R. Silkensen, "Design and Performance of a Magnetic Head for a High-Density Tape Drive," *IBM J. Res. Develop.*, **30**, 270 (1986).

Carr, T., and D. Wachenschwanz, "A 107-kbpi, 16-μm Track Width Recording Channel," *IEEE Trans. Magn.*, **MAG-24**, 2961 (1988).

Chang, J. W., P. C. Andricacos, B. Petek, and L. T. Romankiw, "Electrodeposition of High Ms CoFeCu Alloys for Recording Heads," *Proceedings Symp. on Magn. Mater., Proc. and Devices*, vol. 92–10, Electrochemical Society, Pennington, NJ, p. 275 (1992).

Chapman, D. W., "A New Approach to Making Thin Film Head-Slider Devices," *IEEE Trans. Magn.*, **MAG-25**, 3686 (1989).

Chapman, D. W., D. E. Heim, and M. L. Williams, "A New, Horizontal MR Head Structure," *IEEE Trans. Magn.*, **MAG-25**, 3689 (1989).

Chen, M., N. Gharsallah, G. Gorman, and J. Latimer, "Ternary NiFeX As Soft Film Biasing Film in a Magnetoresistive Sensor," *J. Appl. Phys.*, **69**, 5631 (1991).

Chhabra, D. S., S. A. Bolasna, L. K. Dorius, and L. S. Samuelson, "Air Bearing Design Consideration for Constant Fly Height Application," *IEEE Trans. Magn.*, **MAG-30**, 417 (1994).

Chin, G. Y., and J. H. Wernick, "Soft Magnet Metallic Materials," *Ferromagnetic Materials*, North-Holland, Amsterdam, 1980, vol. 2.

Chynoweth, W., J. Jordan, and W. Kayser, "A Transducer-Per-Track Recording System with Batch-Fabricated Magnetic Film Read/Write Transducers," *Honeywell Comp. J.*, **7**, 103 (1973).

Cohen, U., "A Studless Thin Film Head Produced by Deep Alumina Etching," *Proceedings Symp. on Magn. Mater., Proc. and Devices,* vol. 94–6, Electrochemical Society, Pennington, NJ, p. 45 (1994).

Corb, B., "Charging on the Metastable Domain States of Small NiFe Rectangle," *IEEE Trans. Magn.*, **MAG-24**, 2386 (1988).

Corcoran, J., and N. Pope, "Transmission Line Model for Magnetic Heads Including Complex Permeability," Pap. 4D8, *Int. Conf. Magn.*, San Francisco, 1985.

Cullity, R. D., *Introduction to Magnetic Materials*, Addison-Wesley, Reading, Mass., 1972.

Cullum, D. F., and J. Dorreboom, "High-Density Multitrack Magnetic Head," U.S. Patent 4,346,418, 1982.

Daughton, J., P. Bade, M. Jenson, and M. Rahmati, "Giant Magnetoresistance in Narrow Stripes," *IEEE Trans. Magn.*, **MAG-28**, 2488 (1992).

Davidson, B., R. Simmons, and M. Covault, "The Effect of Stripe Domains on the Displacement Curve of an MR Head," *IEEE Trans. Magn.*, **MAG-20**, 860 (1984).

Davies, A., and B. Middleton, "The Resolution of Vertical Magneto-resistive Readout Heads," *IEEE Trans. Magn.*, **MAG-11**, 1689 (1975).

Decker, S., and C. Tsang, "Magnetoresistive Response of Small Permalloy Features," *IEEE Trans. Magn.*, **MAG-16**, 643 (1980).

Decker, S., J. Dittmar, and C. Tsang, "Barkhausen Noise Characteristics of Magnetoresistive Sensors of Different Thicknesses," *IEEE Trans. Magn.*, **MAG-17**, 2662 (1981).

De Niet, E., and R. Vreeken, "A Magnetoresistive Head with Feedback," *IEEE Trans. Magn.*, **MAG-15**, 1625 (1979).

Dieny, B., V. Speriousu, S. Parkin, P. Baumgart, and D. Wilhoit, "Magnetotransport Properties of Magnetically Soft Spin-valve Structure," *J. Appl. Phys.*, **69**, 4774 (1991).

Dovek, M., D. Seagle, T. Beaulieu, E. Christensen, and R. Fontana, "Performance Comparison of Unshielded and Shielded MR Read Heads for Digital Tape Recording," *IEEE Trans. Magn.*, **MAG-28**, 2301 (1992).

Doyle, W., "A High Capacity, High Performance, Small Form Factor Magnetic Tape Storage System," *IEEE Trans. Magn.*, **MAG-26**, 2152 (1990).

Druyvesteyn, W., L. Postma, and G. Somers, "Wafer Testing of Thin Film Record and Reproduce Heads," *IEEE Trans. Magn.*, **MAG-15**, 1613 (1979).

Druyvesteyn, W. F., E. L. M. Raemaekers, R. D. J. Verhaar, J. de Wilde, J. H. J. Fluitman, and J. P. J. Groenland, "Magnetic Behavior of Narrow Track Thin-Film Heads," *J. Appl. Phys.*, **52**, 2462 (1981*a*).

Druyvesteyn, W., J. Van Ooyen, and L. Postma, "Magnetoresistive Heads," *IEEE Trans. Magn.*, **MAG-17**, 2884 (1981*b*).

Druyvesteyn, W. F., L. Postma, G. H. J. Somers, and J. de Wilde, "Thin-Film Read Head for Analog Audio Application," *IEEE Trans. Magn.*, **MAG-19**, 1748 (1983).

Elabd, L., "A Study of the Field Around Magnetic Heads of Finite Length" *IEEE Trans. Audio*, **AU-11**, 21 (1963).

Edelman, H., G. W. Brock, T. Carr, J. Freeman, and N. Smith, "A New High Density Magnetoresistive Tape Head," *IEEE Trans. Magn.*, **MAG-26**, 3004 (1990).

Fan, G. J., "A Study of the Playback Process of a Magnetic Ring Head," *IBM J. Res. Dev.*, **5**, 321 (1961).

Feng, J. S. Y., and D. A. Thompson, "Permeability of Narrow Permalloy Stripes," *IEEE Trans. Magn.*, **MAG-13**, 1521 (1977).

Feng, J., L. Romankiw, and D. Thompson, "Magnetic Self-bias in the Barber Pole MR Structure," *IEEE Trans. Magn.*, **MAG-13**, 1466 (1975).

Feng, J., J. Tippner, B. Kinney, J. Lee, R. Smith, and C. Chue, "Effects of Uniform Magnetic Fields on Shielded MR Sensors," *IEEE Trans. Magn.*, **MAG-27**, 4701 (1991).

Fluitman, J. H. J., and J. P. J. Groenland, "Comparison of a Shielded 'One-Sided' Planar Hall-Transducer with an MR Head," *IEEE Trans. Magn.*, **MAG-17**, 2893 (1981).

Fuchigami, S., H. Hata, and R. Sasaki, "MR/Inductive Head for Hard Disk Drive," *IEEE Trans. Magn.*, **MAG-27**, 4684 (1991).

Gao, Y., and J. Zhu, "Micromagnetic Study of Barkhausen Jumps in Small Magnetoresistive Sensor," *Digest for INTERMAG 1993*, Paper CA-03 (1993).

Garnier, M., T. Tang, and J. White, "Magnetic Head Slider Assembly," U. S. Patent 3,855,625 (1974)

Goto, T., T. Kabashima, Y. Nose, and S. Osada, "Hybrid Heads and Recording Analysis," *IEEE Transl. J. Magn. Jap.*, **TJMJ-2**, 665 (1987).

Goto, R., T. Kawai, M. Yamazaki, F. Tsuneda, S. Suwabe, I. Sakaguchi, and A. Iwama, "Low Inductance Double-sided Metal-in-Gap Nano Composite Sliders using Fe-Ta-N Magnetic Film System for 250 Mb/in Recording," *IEEE Trans. Magn.*, **MAG-30**, 3909 (1994).

Grochowski, E., and D. A. Thompson, "Outlook for Maintaining Areal Density Growth in Magnetic Recording," *IEEE Trans. Magn.*, **MAG-30**, 3797–3800 (1994).

Guzman, J. I., and M. H. Kryder, "Effect of Deposition Parameters on RF Sputtered CoZr and CoZrRe Thin Films for Magnetic Recording Heads," *J. Appl. Phys.*, **61**, 3240 (1987).

Hamilton, H., R. Anderson, and K. Goodson, "Contact Perpendicular Recording on Rigid Media," *IEEE Trans. Magn.*, **MAG-27**, 4921 (1991).

Hamilton, H. "Status Report: Perpendicular Contact Recording on Rigid Media," *J. Magn. Soc. Japan*, **18**, Suppl. S1 171 (1994).

Hanazono, M., K. Kawakami, S. Narishige, O. Asai, E. Kaneko, K. Okuda, K. Ono, H. Tsuchiya, and W. Hayakawa, "Fabrication of 8 Turn Multitrack Thin Film Heads," *IEEE Trans. Magn.*, **MAG-15**, 1616 (1979).

Hanazono, M., S. Narishige, K. Kawakami, N. Saito, and M. Takagi, "Fabrication of a Thin Film Head Using Polyimide Resin and Sputtered NiFe Film," *J. Appl. Phys.*, **53**, 2608 (1982).

Hannon, D., M. Krounbi, and J. Christnen, "Allicat Magnetoresistive Head Design and Performance," *IEEE Trans. Magn.*, **MAG-30**, 298 (1994).

Harris, T. M., G. M. Whitney, and I. M. Croll, "Boric Acid Complexation in the Electrodeposition of Nickel-Iron Alloys," *Proceedings Symp. Magn. Mater., Proc. and Devices*, Electrochemical Society, Pennington, NJ, vol. 94–6, p. 119 (1994).

Heim, D., "The Sensitivity Function for Shielded Magnetoresistive Heads by Conformal Mapping," *IEEE Trans. Magn.*, **MAG-19**, 1620 (1982).

Heim, D., R. Fontana, C. Tsang, V. Speriosu, B. Gurney, and M. Williams, "Design and Operation of Spin Valve Sensors," *IEEE Trans. Magn.*, **MAG-30**, 316 (1994).

Hempstead, R., "Thermally Induced Pulses in Magnetoresistive Heads," *IBM J. Res. Develop.*, **18**, 547 (1974).

Hempstead, R., "Analysis of Thermal Noise Spike Cancellation," *IEEE Trans. Magn.*, **MAG-11**, 1224 (1975)

Hempstead, R. D., and J. B. Money, U. S. Patent 4,242,710 (1979).

Hempstead, R., S. Krongelb, and D. Thompson, "Unidirectional Anisotropy in Nickel-Iron Films by Exchange Coupling With Antiferromagnetic Films," *IEEE Trans. Magn.*, **MAG-14**, 521 (1978).

Hill, E., A. McCullough, and G. Hoffman, "Analysis of Magnetoresistors with High Coercivity Biasing Films," *IEEE Trans. Magn.*, **MAG-23**, 683 (1986).

Hirota, E., K. Hirota, and K. Kugimiya, "Recent Development of Ferrite Heads and Their Materials," *Proc. Int. Conf. Ferrites*, **667** (1980).

Hokkyo, J., K. Hayakawa, I. Saito, and K. Shirane, "A New W-Shaped Single-Pole Head and a High Density Flexible Disk Perpendicular Magnetic Recording System," *IEEE Trans. Magn.*, **MAG-20**, 72 (1984).

Hoshi, Y., H. Kazama, M. Naoe, and S. Yamanaka, "Magnetic Properties of Zero Magnetorestriction Co-Ta-Zr Alloy Films Deposited by RF Sputtering," *IEEE Trans. Magn.*, **MAG-19**, 1958 (1983).

Hsie, W. C., and J. Bortens, "Production Control of Removal of Gap Alumina," *Proceedings Symp. on Magn. Mater., Proc. and Devices*, vol. 90-8, Electrochemical Society, Pennington, N.J., p. 313 (1990).

Hu, H. L., L. Vo, T. Nguyen, N. Robertson, M. Re, and C. Jahnes, "Writing Performance of Narrow Gap Heads Made with Sputtered Laminated FeN Materials on 3800 Oe Coercivity Media," *IEEE Trans. Magn.*, **MAG-30**, 3870 (1994).

Hughes, G. F., "Thin-Film Recording Head Efficiency and Noise," *J. Appl. Phys.*, **54**, 4168 (1983).

Hughes, G. F., and D. S. Bloomberg, "Recording Head Side Read/Write Effects," *IEEE Trans. Mag.*, **MAG-13**, 1457 (1977).

Hunt, R., "A Magnetoresistive Readout Transducer," *IEEE Trans. Magn.*, **MAG-7**, 150 (1971).

Hylton, T., K. Coffey, M. Parker, and J. Howard, "Giant Magnetoresistance at Low Fields in Discontinuous NiFe-Ag Multilayer Thin Films," *Science*, **261**, 1021 (1992).

Ichiyama, Y., "Reproducing Characteristics of Thin Film Heads," *IEEE Trans. Magn.*, **MAG-11**, 1203 (1975).

Ichiyama, Y., "Analytic Expressions for the Side Fringe Field of Narrow Track Heads," *IEEE Trans. Magn.*, **MAG-13**, 1688 (1977).

Indeck, R., J. Judy, and S. Iwasaki, "A Magnetoresistive Gradiometer," *IEEE Trans. Magn.*, **MAG-24**, 2617 (1988).

Iwasaki, S., "Perpendicular Magnetic Recording," *IEEE Trans. Magn.*, **MAG-16**, 71 (1980).

Iwasaki, S., and Y. Nakamura, "An Analysis for the Magnetization Mode for High Density Magnetic Recording," *IEEE Trans. Magn.*, **MAG-13**, 1272 (1977).

Iwasaki, S., Y. Nakamura, and K. Ouchi, "Perpendicular Magnetic Recording with a Composite Anisotropy Film," *IEEE Trans. Magn.*, **MAG-15**, 1456 (1979).

Iwasaki, S., Y. Nakamura, and H. Muraoka, "Wavelength Response of Perpendicular Magnetic Recording," *IEEE Trans. Magn.*, **MAG-17**, 2535 (1981).

Iwasaki, S., Y. Nakamura, I. Watanabe, K. Yamakawa, and H. Hasegawa, "Reproducing Sensitivity of Single-Pole-Type Heads with Co-Zr-Nb/SiO$_2$ Multilayered Films," *IEEE Transl. J. Magn. Jap.*, **TJMJ-2**, 386 (1987).

Iwakura T., M. Aihara, H. Fukui, and Y. Sugita, "Three Dimensional Simulation of Side-Writing and Crosstalk for Thin Film Heads with Various Pole Shapes," *IEEE Trans. Magn.*, **25,** 3197 (1989).

Jeffers, F., "Magnetoresistive Transducers with Canted Easy Axis," *IEEE Trans. Magn.*, **MAG-15**, 1628 (1979).

Jeffers, F. J., R. J. McClure, W. W. French, and N. J. Griffith, "Metal-In-Gap Record Head," *IEEE Trans. Magn.*, **MAG-18**, 1146 (1982).

Jeffers, F., J. Freeman, R. Toussaint, N. Smith, D. Wachenschwanz, S. Shtrikman, and W. Doyle, "Soft-adjacent-layer Self-biased Magnetoresistive Heads in High-density Recording," *IEEE Trans. Magn.*, **MAG-21**, 1563 (1985).

Jones, R. E., Jr., "Analysis of the Efficiency and Inductance of Multiturn Thin Film Magnetic Recording Heads," *IEEE Trans. Magn.*, **MAG-14**, 509 (1978).

Jones, R. E., Jr., "Domain Effects in the Thin Film Head," *IEEE Trans. Magn.*, **MAG-15**, 1619 (1979).

Jones, R. E., Jr., "IBM 3370 Film Head Design and Fabrication," *IBM Disk Storage Technol.*, **GA 26–1665-0**, 6 (1980).

Jones, R. E., Jr., J. Lo, and J. L. Williams, "Magnetic Properties of RF Sputtered Fe(N)/NiFeCo(N) Films," *IEEE Trans. Magn.*, **MAG-29**, 3072 (1993).

Jorgensen, F., *The Complete Handbook of Magnetic Recording*, TAB Books, Blue Ridge Summit, Penn., 1980.

Kakehi, A., M. Oshiki, T. Aikawa, M. Sasaki, and T. Kozai, "A Thin Film Head for High Density Recording," *IEEE Trans. Magn*, **MAG-18**, 1131 (1982).

Kaminaka, N., H. Sakakima, K. Takahashi, K. Osano, and H. Hasegawa, "Co-Based Super-structured Nitride Alloy Films: Characteristics and Applications for High Frequency Heads," *IEEE Trans. Magn.*, **MAG-26**, 2936 (1990).

Kamo, Y., and M. Kitada, "A New Biasing Method for Shielded MR Head," *J. Appl. Phys.*, **57**, 3979 (1985).

Kanai, K., R. Sasaki, and H. Sugaya, "Type 3330 Flying Head Using HPF," *Natl. Tech. Rep.*, **19**, 578 (1973).

Kanai, K., N. Kaminaka, N. Nouchi, N. Nomura, and E. Hirota, "High Track Density Thin-Film Tape Heads," *IEEE Trans. Magn.*, **MAG-15**, 1130 (1979).

Kanda et al., "Study of Popcorn Noise in Thin Film Heads," *Digest 14th Ann. Conf. on Magn. in Japan,* Oct. 8–11, p. 163 (1990).

Karlqvist, O., "Calculation of the Magnetic Field in the Ferromagnetic Layer of a Magnetic Drum," *Trans. R. Inst. Technol. (Stockholm),* 1 (1954).

Kasiraj, P., and R. D. Holmes, "Effect of Magnetic Domain Configuration on Readback Amplitude Variations in Inductive Film Heads," *J. Appl. Phys.,* **69,** 5423 (1991).

Kasiraj, P., R. M. Shelby, J. S. Best, and D. E. Horne, "Magnetic Domain Imaging with a Scanning Kerr Effect Microscope," *IEEE Trans. Magn,* **MAG-22,** 837 (1986).

Kaske, A. D., P. E. Oberg, M. C. Paul, and G. F. Sauter, "Vapor-Deposited Thin-Film Recording Heads," *IEEE Trans. Magn.,* **MAG-7,** 675 (1971).

Katz, E. R., "Finite Element Analysis of the Vertical Multi-turn Thin-Film Head," *IEEE Trans. Magn.,* **MAG-14,** 506 (1978).

Keel, G. J., F. W. Gorter, and J. T. Gerkema, "Thin Film Magnetic Head for Reading and Writing Information,"U. S. Patent 4,300,177 (1981).

Kehr, W., J. Nix, and D. Camps, "Integrated Thin-film Head for Flexible Disks," *IEEE Trans. Magn.,* **MAG-24,** 2615 (1988).

Kelley, G., and R. Ketcham, "An Analysis of the Effect of Shield Length on the Performance of Magnetoresistive Heads," *IEEE Trans. Magn.,* **MAG-14,** 515 (1978).

Kelley, G. V., and E. P. Valstyn, "Numerical Analysis of Writing and Reading with Multiturn Film Heads," *IEEE Trans. Magn.,* **MAG-16,** 788 (1980).

Kelley, G., J. Freeman, H. Copenhaver, R. Ketcham, and E. Valtstyn, "High-track-density, Coupled-film Magnetoresistive Head," *IEEE Trans. Magn.,* **MAG-17,** 2890 (1981).

Khan, J., "Laser Etching of Ceramics for Defining Slider Air Bearing Surfaces for Magnetic Recording Heads," *Mater. Res. Soc. Photons and Low Energy Particles in Surface Processing Symposium,* 33–8 (1992).

Kishigami, J., T. Mikazuki, and Y. Koshimoto, "Analysis of Magnetic Domains in a Film Head," *IEEE Trans. Magn.,* **MAG-22,** 1840 (1986).

Klaassen, K. B., and J. C. L. van Peppen, "Irreversible Wall Motion in Inductive Recording Heads," *IEEE Trans. Magn.,* **MAG-25,** 3209 (1989).

Klaassen, K. B., and J. C. L. van Peppen, "Barkhausen Noise in Thin-Film Recording Heads," *IEEE Trans. Magn.,* **MAG-26,** 1697 (1990).

Klaassen, K. B., and J. C. L. van Peppen, "Magnetic Instability of Thin-Film Recording Heads," *IEEE Trans. Magn.,* **MAG-30,** 375 (1994).

Klokholm, E., and J. Aboaf, "The Saturation Magnetostriction of Permalloy Films," *J. Appl. Phys.,* **52,** 2474 (1981).

Kobayashi, T., M. Kubota, H. Satoh, T. Kumura, K. Yamauchi, and S. Takahashi, "A Tilted Sendust Sputtered Ferrite Video Head," *IEEE Trans. Magn.,* **MAG-21,** 1536 (1985).

Kobayashi, T., R. Naktani, S. Ootomo, and N. Kumsaka, "Magnetic Properties of Multilayer Fe-C Film Formed by Dual Ion Beam Sputtering." *IEEE Trans. Magn.,* **MAG-23,** 2746 (1987).

Koeppe, P. V., M. E. Re, and M. H. Kryder, "Thin Film Head Domain Structures versus Permalloy Composition," *IEEE Trans. Magn.,* **MAG-28,** 71 (1992).

Koren, N., "Signal Processing in Recording Channels Utilizing Unshielded Magnetoresistive Heads," *IEEE Trans. Magn.,* **MAG-26,** 2166 (1990).

Kotera, N., J. Shigeta, K. Naria, T. Oi, K. Hayashi, and K. Sato, "A Low-Noise InSb Thin Film Hall Element: Fabrication, Device Modeling, and Audio Application," *IEEE Trans. Magn.,* **MAG-15,** 1946 (1979).

Koyanagi, H., E. Arai, K. Mitsuoka, H. Fukui, S. Narishigi, and Y. Sugita, "Three-dimensional Stress and Magnetic Anisotropy Analyses for Thin Film Heads," *IEEE Trans. J. Magn. Jap.,* **TJMJ-5,** 185 (1990).

Kuijk, K., W. Gestel, and F. Gorter, "The Barber Pole, a Linear Magnetoresistive Head," *IEEE Trans. Magn.,* **MAG-11,** 1215 (1975).

Lazzari, J. P., "Integrated Head Concepts," *IEEE Trans. Magn.*, **MAG-14**, 503 (1978).

Lazzari, J. P., and I. Melnick, "Integrated Magnetic Recording Heads," *IEEE Trans. Magn.,* **MAG-7**, 146 (1971).

Lazzari, J. P., and P. Deroux-Dauphin, "A New Thin Film Head Generation," *IEEE Trans. Magn.,* **MAG-25**, 3190 (1989).

Liao, S., "High Moment CoFe Thin Films by Electrodeposition," *IEEE Trans. Magn.,* **MAG-23**, 2981 (1987).

Lin, F. H., P Ryan, X. Shi, and M. H. Kryder, "Correlation between Noise-After-Write and Magnetization Dynamics in Thin-Film Heads," *IEEE Trans. Magn.,* **MAG-28**, 2100 (1992).

Lindholm, D. A., "Magnetic Fields of Finite Track Width Heads," *IEEE Trans. Magn.,* **MAG-13**, 1460 (1977).

Lindholm, D. A., "Long-Wavelength Response of Magnetic Heads with Beveled Outer Edges," *J. Audio Eng. Soc.*, **27**, 542 (1979).

Lindholm, D. A. "Effect of Track Width and Side Shields on the Long Wavelength Response of Rectangular Magnetic Heads," *IEEE Trans. Magn.,* **MAG-16**, 430 (1980).

Louis, E., and R. M. Walser, "Comparison of Experimental and Theoretical Permeability Spectra of CoZrNb Amorphous Thin Magnetic Films," *Proceedings Symp. on Magn. Mater., Proc. and Devices,* vol. 92-10, Electrochemical Society, Pennington, NJ, p. 289 (1992).

Luborksy, F. E., "Amorphous Ferromagnets," *Ferromagnetic Materials*, North-Holland, Amsterdam, 1980, vol. 1.

Luitjens, S. B., and A. van Herk, "A Discussion on the Crosstalk in Longitudinal and Perpendicular Recording," *IEEE Trans. Magn.,* **MAG-18**, 1804 (1982).

Macchioni, C. V., "Reactive Ion Etching of SiO_2 in the Record Gap of Inductive Thin Film Heads," *Proceedings Symp. on Magn. Mater., Proc. and Devices,* vol. 90-8, Electrochemical Society, Pennington, N.J., p. 301 (1990).

Maissel, L. I., and R. Glang, *Handbook of Thin Film Technology*, McGraw-Hill, New York, 1970.

Mallary, M., and A. B. Smith, "Conduction of Flux at High Frequencies by a Charge-free Magnetization Distribution," *IEEE Trans. Magn.,* **MAG-24**, 2374 (1988).

Mallary, M. L., and S. Ramaswamy, "A New Thin Film Head which Doubles the Flux through the Coil," *IEEE Trans. Magn.,* **MAG-29**, 3832 (1990).

Mallary, M. L., L. Dipalma, K. Gyasi, A. L. Sidman, and A. Wu, "Advanced Multi–via Heads," *IEEE Trans. Magn.,* **MAG-30**, 287 (1994).

Mallinson, J. C., "On the Properties of Two-Dimensional Dipoles and Magnetized Bodies," *IEEE Trans. Magn.,* **MAG-17**, 2453 (1981).

Mallinson, J. C., and N. H. Bertram, "A Theoretical and Experimental Comparison of the Longitudinal and Vertical Modes of Magnetic Recording," *IEEE Trans. Magn.,* **MAG-20**, 461 (1984).

Maruyama, T., K. Yamada, H. Tanank, S. Ito, H. Urai, and H. Kaneko, "A Yoke Magnetoresistive Head for High Track Density Recording," *IEEE Trans. Magn.,* **MAG-23**, 2503 (1987).

Maruyama, T., T. Suzuki, and K. Yamada, "Shielded MR Head for High-density Magnetic Recording," *J. Appl. Phys.*, **67**, 4847 (1990).

Matsuura, K., K. Oyamada, and T. Yazaki, "Amorphous Video Head for High Coercive Tape," *IEEE Trans. Magn.,* **MAG-19**, 1623 (1983).

Mee, P. B., "SEM Observations of Domain Configurations in Thin Film Head Pole Structures," *J. Appl. Phys.*, **51**, 861 (1980).

Metzdorf, W., M. Beehner, and H. Haudek, "The Design of Magnetoresistive Multitrack Read Heads for Magnetic Tapes," *IEEE Trans. Magn.,* **MAG-18**, 763 (1982).

Middelhoek, S., "Ferromagnetic Domains in Thin NiFe Films," Thesis, Drukkerij Wed. G. Van Soest N. V., Amsterdam, pp. 57–63, 1961.

Middleton, B., "Modelling the Digital Magnetic Recording Behavior of Shielded Magneto-resistive Replay Heads with Displace Elements," *R. and E. Engr.*, **50**, 419 (1980).

Middleton, B. K., A. K. Davis, and D. J. Sansom, "The Modelling of Shielded Magnetoresistive Replay Head Performance," *IERE Conf. Proc.*, **43**, 353 (1979).

Minuhin, V. B., "Comparison of Sensitivity Functions for Ideal Probe and Ring-Type Heads," *IEEE Trans. Magn.*, **MAG-20**, 488 (1984).

Mitsuoka, K., S. Sudo, N. Narishigi, M. Hanazono, Y. Sugita, K. Koike, M. Matsuyama, and K. Hayakawa, "Magnetic Domains of Permalloy Films for Magnetic RecordingThin-Film Heads Observed by the Spin-polarized SEM," *IEEE Trans. Magn.*, **MAG-23**, 2155 (1987).

Mitsuoka, K., S. Narishigi, M. Hanazono, and Y. Sugita, "Magnetic Domain Structures of Multilayer Permalloy Films for Magnetic Recording Thin Film Heads," *IEEE Transl. J. Magn. Jap.* **TJMJ-3**, 42 (1988a).

Mitsuoka, K., S. Sudo, M. Sano, K. Nishioka, S. Narishigi, and Y. Sugita, "Domain Structures in Multi-Layered Co-Ni-Fe-Pd Films Observed by the Spin-polarized SEM," *IEEE Trans. Magn.*, **MAG-24**, 2823 (1988b).

Miura, Y., A. Kawakami, and S. Sakai, "An Analysis of the Write Performance on Thin Film Head," *IEEE Trans. Magn.*, **MAG-14**, 512 (1978).

Miura, Y., Y. Takahaski, F. Kume, J. Toda, S. Tsutsumi, and S. Kawakami, "Fabrication of Multi-Turn Thin Film Head," *IEEE Trans. Magn.*, **MAG-16**, 779 (1980).

Miyazaki, T., R. Sawada, and Y. Ishijima, "New Magnetic Alloys for Magnetic Recording Heads," *IEEE Trans Magn.*, **MAG-8**, 501 (1972).

Miyazaki, T., T. Ajima, and F. Sato, "Dependence of Magnetoresistance on Thickness and Substrate Temperature for NiFe Alloy Films," *J. Magn. Mag. Mat.*, **81**, 86 (1989).

Monson, J. E., K. P. Ash, R. E. Jones, Jr., and D. E. Heim, "Self Healing Effects in Thin Film Heads," *IEEE Trans. Magn.*, **20**, 845 (1984).

Mowry, G., P. George, K. Loeffler, and N. Belk, "Thin-film Magnetoresistive Heads for Narrow-track Winchester Applications," *IEEE Trans. Magn.*, **MAG-22**, 671 (1986).

Mukasa, K., "Recent Magnetic Recording Technology II–Magnetic Heads," *J. Inst. Telev. Eng-Japan*, **39**, 295 (1985).

Nagai, Y., A. Tago, K. Yamagisama, and T. Toshima, "Well-Defined Uniaxial Anisotropy in Iron Film Formed by Ion Beam Sputtering," *J. Appl. Phys.*, **61**, 3841(1987).

Nagata, Y., T. Fukazawa, K. Wada, Y. Tosaki, and T. Aoi, "Yoke-Type Magnetoresistive Heads with Suppressed Barkhausen Noise," *IEEE Trans. Magn.*, **MAG-23**, 2500 (1987).

Nakamura Y., K. Yamakawa, and S. Iwasaki, "Analysis of Domain Structure of Single Pole Perpendicular Head," *IEEE Trans. Magn.*, **MAG-21**, 1578 (1985).

Nakanishi, T., K. Kogure, T. Toshima, and K. Yanagisawa, "Floating Thin Film Head Fabricated by Ion Etching Method," *IEEE Trans. Magn.*, **MAG-16**, 785 (1980).

Nakanishi, T., T. Toshima, K. Yanagisawa, and N. Tsuzuki, "Narrow Track Magnetic Head Fabricated by Ion-Etching Method," *IEEE Trans. Magn.*, **MAG-15**, 1060 (1979).

Naoe, M., M. Yamaga, and N. Tereda, "Deposition of Rust Proof Iron Thin Films with Soft Magnetic Properties by Dual Ion Beam Sputtering," *IEEE Trans. Magn.*, **MAG-21**, 1900 (1985).

Narishigi, S., M. Hanazono, M. Tokagi, and S. Kuwatsuka, "Measurements of the Magnetic Characteristics of Thin Film Heads Using Magneto-Optic Method," *IEEE Trans. Magn.*, **MAG-20**, 848 (1984).

Narishigi, S., T. Imagawa, and M. Hanazono, "Thin Film Heads for Hard Disk Drive–Magnetic Domain Structure of Magnetic Core" (Japanese), *39th Conf. Magn. Soc. Jpn.*, **39-5**, 1 (1985).

Nishihira, H., L. Dorius, S. Bolasna, and G. Best, "Performance Characteristics of the IBM 3380K Air Bearing Design," *Tribiology and Mechanics of Magnetic Storage Systems*, **5**, 117–123 (1988).

Nishiyama, T., K. Noguchi, K. Mouri, H. Iwata, and T. Shinohara, "Recording Characteristics of Metal-In-Gap Mini Composite Head," *IEEE Trans. Magn.*, **MAG-23**, 2931 (1987).

Nix, L., C. Helms, and D. O'Connor, "Magnetic Track Profile Asymmetries in Dual MR Heads," *IEEE Trans. Magn.*, **MAG-27**, 4693 (1991).

Nomura, Y., T. Tanaka, H. Chiba, and E. Hirota, "Development of 4-Track 4-Channel Cassette Head Made of Hot-Pressed Ferrite," *Electron. Commun. Jpn.*, **56-C**, 86 (1973).

O'Connor, D., F. Shelledy, and D. Heim, "Mathematical Model of a Magnetoresistive Read Head for a Magnetic Tape Drive," *IEEE Trans. Magn.*, **MAG-21**, 1560 (1985).

Ohashi, K., "Mechanism of 90° Wall Motion in Thin Film Heads," *IEEE Trans. Magn.*, **MAG-21**, 1581 (1985).

Ohashi, K., M. Ito, and T. Maruyama, "Effect of Plated NiFe Composition on Domain Configuration," *Proceedings of Symposium on Magnetic Materials*, **PV90-8**, Electrochemical Society, Pennington, N.J., p. 247 (1990).

Ohmori, K., K. Arai, and N. Tsuya, "Ribbon-Form Sendust Alloy Made by Rapid Quenching," *Appl. Phys.*, **21**, 335 (1980).

O'Kane, D. F., and D. J. Kroes, "A Thin Film Magnetoresistive Head for Quarter-Inch Tape Applications," *IEEE Trans. Magn.*, **MAG-30**, 322 (1994).

Okuwaki, T., F. Kugiya, N. Kumasaka, K. Yoshida, N. Tsumita, and T. Tamura, "5.25 Inch Floppy Disk Drive Using Perpendicular Magnetic Recording," *IEEE Trans. Magn.*, **MAG-21**, 1365 (1985).

Ozawa, K., H. Wakasugi, and K. Tanaka, "Friction and Wear of Magnetic Heads and Amorphous Metal Sliding Against Magnetic Tapes," *IEEE Trans. Magn.*, **MAG-20**, 425 (1984).

Parkin, S., "Dramatic Enhancement of Interlayer Exchange Coupling and Giant Magnetoresistance in $Ni_{81}Fe_{19}$/Cu by Addition of Thin Co Interface Layers," *Appl. Phys. Lett.*, **61**, 1358 (1991).

Paton, A., "Analysis of the Efficiency of Thin-Film Magnetic Recording Heads," *J. Appl. Phys.*, **42**, 5868 (1971).

Potter, R., "Digital Magnetic Recording Theory," *IEEE Trans. Magn.*, **MAG-10**, 502 (1974).

Potter, R. I., "Analytic Expressions for the Fringe Field of Finite Pole-Tip Length Recording Heads," *IEEE Trans. Magn.*, **MAG-11**, 80 (1975).

Potter, R. I., and I. A. Beardsley, "Self-Consistent Computer Calculations for Perpendicular Magnetic Recording," *IEEE Trans. Magn.*, **MAG-16**, 967 (1980).

Potter, R. I., R. J. Schmulian, and K. Hartman, "Self-Consistently Computed Magnetization Patterns in Thin Magnetic Recording Media," *IEEE Trans. Magn.*, **MAG-7**, 689 (1971).

Potzlberger, H. W., "Magnetron Sputtering of Permalloy for Thin Film Heads," *IEEE Trans. Magn.*, **MAG-20**, 851 (1984).

Poupon, G., T. Braisaz, and P. Deroux-Dauphin, "Microelectrodeposition and Domain Structure of NiFe Alloys in I. C. Head," *Proceedings Symp. on Magn. Mater., Proc. and Devices*, vol. 90-8, Electrochemical Society, Pennington, N.J., p. 267 (1990).

Re, M. E., and M. H. Kryder, "Magneto-Optic Investigation of Thin-Film Recording Heads," *J. Appl. Phys.*, **55**, 2245 (1984).

Re, M. E., D. N. Shenton, and M. H. Kryder, "Magnetic Switching Characteristics at the Pole Tips of Thin-Film Heads," *IEEE Trans. Magn.*, **MAG-21**, 1575 (1985).

Re, M. E., R. R. Katti, W. Rave, and M. H. Kryder, "Non-Uniform Response in the Pole Tips of Thin-Film Recording Heads," *IEEE Trans. Magn.*, **MAG-23**, 3161 (1987).

Romankiw, L. T., and P. Simon, "Batch Fabrication of Thin Film Magnetic Recording Heads: A Literature Review and Process Description for Vertical Single Turn Heads," *IEEE Trans. Magn.*, **MAG-11**, 50 (1975).

Romankiw, L. T., I. M. Croll, and M. Hatzakis, "Batch Fabricated Thin-Film Magnetic Recording Heads," *IEEE Trans. Magn.*, **MAG-6**, 597 (1970).

Ross, C. A., and R. Malmhall, "Properties of Sputtered Alumina Overcoats for Inductive Thin Film Heads," *Proceedings Symp. on Magn. Mater., Proc. and Devices*, vol. 94-6, Electrochemical Society, Pennington, N.J., p. 165 (1994).

Ruigrok, J., "Analytic Description of Magnetoresistive Heads," *J. Appl. Phys.*, **53**, 2599 (1982).

Ruigrok, J. M., "Analysis of Metal-In-Gap Heads," *IEEE Trans. Magn.*, **MAG-20**, 872 (1984).

Ruigrok, J. J. M., *Short-Wavelength Magnetic Recording: New Methods and Analyses*, Philips Res. Laboratories, Eindhoven, The Netherlands (1990).

Saito, K., T. Shimizu, and H. Ishida, "Wide-Band Read/Write Characteristics of an Ultra-Narrow Track Width Video Head Using Sputtered Fe-Si-Al Alloy Film," *IEEE Trans. Magn.*, **MAG-23**, 2925 (1987).

Sakakima, H., Y. Yanagiuchi, M. Satomi, H. Senno, and E. Hirota, "Improvement in Amorphous Magnetic Alloys for Magnetic Head Core," *Proc. Conf. Rapidly Quenched Metals*, Sendai, Japan, 1981, p. 941.

Sansom, D. J., "Recording Head Design Calculations," *IEEE Trans. Magn.*, **MAG-12**, 230 (1976).

Sawada, T., and K. Yoneda, "AC Erase Head for Cassette Recorder," *IEEE Trans. Magn.*, **MAG-21**, 2104 (1985).

Sawada, T., T. Sakuma, and K. Yoneda, "Yoke Type MR Head on Perpendicular Double Layer Media," *IEEE Trans. Magn.*, **MAG-20**, 857 (1984).

Scherer, M., W. Maass, and R. Stahl, "Large Area Production of Alumina Films by Reactive AC Magnetron Sputtering," *Proceedings Symp. on Magn. Mater., Proc. and Devices*, vol. 94-6, Electrochemical Society, Pennington, N.J., p. 151 (1994).

Schwartz, T. A., and S. Decker, "Comparison of Calculated and Actual Density Responses of a Magnetoresistive Head," *IEEE Trans. Magn.*, **MAG-15**, 1622 (1979).

Seagle, D., M. Meininger, T. Beaulieu, and C. Spector, "Recording Performance of an Inductive-write, Wide-shielded MR Readback Head with a Dual Layer Perpendicular Disk," *IEEE Trans. Magn.*, **MAG-26**, 2160 (1990).

Senno, H., Y. Yanagiuchi, M. Satomi, E. Hirota, and S. Hayakawa, "Newly Developed Fe-Si-Al Alloy Heads by Squeeze Casting," *IEEE Trans. Magn*, **MAG-13**, 1475 (1977).

Seshan, C., and Z. Cendes, "Computing Magnetic Domain Patterns in Thin Film Soft Magnetic Materials," *IEEE Trans. Magn.*, **MAG-21**, 2378 (1985).

Shelledy, F., and G. Brock, "A Linear Self-biased Magnetoresistive Head," *IEEE Trans. Magn.*, **MAG-11**, 1206 (1975).

Shelledy, F., and S. Cheatham, "Suppression of Thermally Induced Pulses in Magnetoresistive Heads," *Proc. IERE*, **35**, 251 (1976).

Shelledy, F., and J. Nix, "Magnetoresistive Heads for Magnetic Tape and Disk Recording," *IEEE Trans. Magn.*, **MAG-28**, 2283 (1992).

Shi, X., M. H. Kryder, and L. J. Shrinkle, "Wiggles in the Transition Response of MIG-Ferrite Heads," *IEEE Trans. Magn.*, **MAG-25**, 2638 (1989).

Shi, X., F. H. Liu, Y. Li, and M. H. Kryder, "Dynamic Response of Domain Walls on the Air-bearing Surface of Thin-film Heads," *J. Appl. Phys.*, **75**, 8394 (1994).

Shiiba, K., T. Kine, T. Miyauchi, N. Nakai, and M. Yoshikawa, "Barkhausen Noise in Yoke-Type MR Heads (I), *IEEE Transl. J. Magn. Jap.*, **TJMJ-2**, 596 (1987).

Shiiki, K., S. Otomo, and M. Kudo, "Magnetic Properties, Aging Effects and Application Potential for Magnetic-Heads of Co-Fe-Si-B Amorphous Alloys," *J. Appl. Phys.*, **52**, 2483 (1981).

Shimada, Y., "Amorphous Co-Metal Films Prepared by Sputtering," *Phys. Stat. Sol. (a)*, **83**, 255 (1984).

Shinagawa, K., H. Fujiwara, F. Kugiya, T. Okuwaki, and M. Kudo, "Simulation of Perpendicular Recording on Co-Cr Media with a Thin Permalloy Film-Ferrite Composite Head," *J. Appl. Phys.*, **53**, 2585 (1982).

Shiroishi, Y., K. Shiki, I. Yuitoo, H. Tanabe, H. Fujiwara, and M. Kudo, "Patterning Effect on Easy Axis Alignment in Permalloy Thin Film," *IEEE Trans. Magn.*, **MAG-20**, 485 (1984).

Sillen, C. W. M. P., J. J. M. Ruigrok, A. Broese van Groenon, and U. Enz, "Permalloy/Sendust Metal-in-Gap Head," *IEEE Trans. Magn*, **MAG-24**, 1802 (1988).

Simmons, R., B. Jackson, M. Covault, C. Wacken, and J. Rausch, "Design and Peak Shift Characterization of a Magnetoresistive Head Thin Film Media System," *IEEE Trans. Magn.*, **MAG-19**, 1737 (1983).

Simmons, R., R. Davidson, and H. Gill, "Anisotropy Changes in Magnetoresistive Heads Due to Lapping and Annealing," *IEEE Trans. Magn.*, **MAG-25**, 3200 (1989).

Slick, P. I., "Ferrites for Non-Microwave Applications," *Ferromagnetic Materials*, North-Holland, Amsterdam, 1980, vol. 2.

Smith, N., "Domain Theory Model for Magnetic Thin Films," *IEEE Trans. Magn.*, **MAG-24**, 2380 (1988).

Smith, N., J. Freeman, P. Koeppe, and T. Carr, "Dual Magnetoresistive Head for Very High Density Recording," *IEEE Trans. Magn.*, **MAG-28**, 2292 (1992*a*).

Smith, N., D. Smith, and S. Shtrikman, "Analysis of a Dual Magnetoresistive Head," *IEEE Trans. Magn.*, **MAG-28**, 2295 (1992*b*).

Soohoo, R. F., "Switching Dynamics in a Thin-Film Recording Head," *IEEE Trans. Magn.*, **MAG-18**, 1128 (1982).

Steinback, M., J. A. Gerber, and T. J. Szczech, "Exact Solution for the Field of a Perpendicular Head," *IEEE Trans. Magn.*, **MAG-17**, 3117 (1981).

Sueoka, K., K. Wago, and F. Sai, "Direct Measurement of the Sensitivity Distribution of Magnetoresistive Heads by the SXM Technique," *IEEE Trans. Magn.*, **MAG-28**, 2307 (1992).

Sugaya, H., "Newly Developed Hot-Pressed Ferrite Head," *IEEE Trans. Magn.*, **MAG-4**, 295 (1968).

Suyama, H., K. Tsunewaki, M. Fukuyama, N. Saito, T. Yamada, and H. Karamon, "Thin Film MR Head for High Density Rigid Disk Drive," *IEEE Trans. Magn*, **MAG-24**, 2612 (1988).

Suzuki, S., J. Toriu, C. Fukao, and H. Oda, "High Density Magnetic Recording Heads for Disk," *IEEE Trans. Magn.*, **MAG-17**, 2899 (1981).

Suzuki, T., Y. Motomura, and K. Tagami, "Offtrack Characteristics of Shielded Magnetoresistive Head," *IEEE Trans. Magn.*, **MAG-27**, 4690 (1991).

Szczech, T. J., "Analytic Expressions for Field Components of Nonsymmetrical Finite Pole Tip Length Magnetic Head Based on Measurements on Large-Scale Models," *IEEE Trans. Magn.*, **MAG-15**, 1319 (1979).

Szczech, T. J., and K. E. Palmquist, "A 3-D Comparison of the Fields from Six Basic Head Configurations," *Video and Data Recording Conference,* Southhampton, England, 1984.

Szczech, T. J., M. Steinback, and M. Jodeit, "Equations for the Field Components of a Perpendicular Magnetic Head," *IEEE Trans. Magn.*, **MAG-18**, 229 (1982).

Szczech, T. J., D. M. Perry, and K. E. Palmquist, "Improved Field Equations for Ring Heads," *IEEE Trans. Magn.*, **MAG-19**, 1740 (1983).

Takahashi, K., S. Sasaki, K. Kanai, F. Kobayashi, "A Method of Reproduction in Perpendicular Magnetic Recording," *Inst. Electr. Commun. Eng., Jpn.*, **199**, (1983).

Takahashi, K., K. Ihara, S. Muraoka, H. Yohda, E. Sawai, and N. Kaminaka, "A High Performance Video Head with Co-based Alloy Laminated Films," *IEEE Trans. Magn.*, **MAG-23**, 2928 (1987).

Takama, E., and M. Ito, "New Mn-Zn Ferrite Fabricated by Hot Isostatic Pressing," *IEEE Trans. Magn.*, **MAG-15**, 1858 (1979).

Takano, H., H. Fukuoka, M. Suzuki, K. Shiiki, and M. Kitada, "Submicron-trackwidth Inductive/MR Composite Head," *IEEE Trans. Magn.*, **MAG-27**, 4678 (1991).

Tanaka, Y., "Multitrack Magnetic Head for a Tape Player," U.S. Patent 4,322,764, 1982.

Tang, Y. S., "Characterization of Head Stability Induced Signal Fluctuations," *IEEE Trans. Magn.*, **MAG-26**, 2466 (1990).

Tang, D. D., R. E. Lee, J. L. Su, F. Chu, J. Lo, H. Santini, L. Lane, N. Robertson, M. Ponce, P. Cisneroz, and G. Guthmiller, "Omega Head—An Experimental 120-turn Inductive Head," *J. Appl. Phys.*, **75**, 6397 (1994).

Tatsumi, T., Y. Tsukamoto, K. Yamada, Y. Motomura, and M. Aoyama, "Inverse Magnetostriction Effect on Magnetoresistive Response for Evaporated NiFe and NiFeCo Films," *J. Appl. Phys.*, **69**, 4671 (1991).

Thompson, D. A., "Magnetoresistive Transducers in High-Density Magnetic Recording," *AIP Conf. Proc., Magn. Mater.*, **24**, 528 (1974).

Thompson, D. A., L. T. Romankiw, and A. F. Mayadas, "Thin Film Magnetoresistors in Memory, Storage, and Related Applications," *IEEE Trans. Magn.*, **MAG-11**, 1039 (1975).

Tomiyasu, H., K. Sato, and K. Kanai, "Characteristics of Metal Magnetic Thin Film in MIG Head and Head Performance," *IEEE Transl. J. Jap.*, **TJMJ-3**, 49 (1988).

Toshima, T., T. Nakanishi, and K. Yanagisawa, "Magnetic Head Fabricated by Improved Ion Etching Method," *IEEE Trans. Magn.*, **MAG-15**, 1637 (1979).

Toussaint, R., D. Markham, and W. Doyle, "Static Characteristics of Soft-adjacent-layer Self-biased Magnetoresistive Heads," *IEEE Trans. Magn.*, **MAG-22**, 677 (1986).

Tsang, C., "Magnetics of Small Magnetoresistive Sensors," *J. Appl. Phys.*, **55**, 2226 (1984).

Tsang, C., "Unshielded MR Elements with Patterned Exchange-biasing," *IEEE Trans. Magn.*, **MAG-25**, 3692 (1989).

Tsang, C., "A Theoretical Study of the Signal-response of a Shielded MR Sensor," *IEEE Trans. Magn.*, **MAG-26**, 3016 (1990).

Tsang, C., and S. Decker, "The Origin of Barkhausen Noise in Small Permalloy Magnetoresistive Sensors," *J. Appl. Phys.*, **52**, 2465 (1981).

Tsang, C., N. Heiman, and K. Lee, "Exchange Induced Unidirectional Anisotropy at FeMn-NiFe Interfaces," *J. Appl. Phys.*, **52**, 2471 (1981).

Tsang, C., and S. Decker, "Study of Domain Formation in Small Permalloy MR Elements," *J. Appl. Phys.*, **53**, 2602 (1982).

Tsang, C., and R. Fontana, Jr., "Fabrication and Wafer Testing of Barber-pole and Exchange-biased Narrow-track MR Sensors," *IEEE Trans. Magn.*, **MAG-18**, 1149 (1982).

Tsang, C., and K. Lee, "Temperature Dependence of Unidirectional Anisotropy Effects in the NiFe-FeMn Systems," *J. Appl. Phys.*, **53**, 2605 (1982).

Tsang, C., P. Kasiraj, and M. Krounbi, "Magnetics of Nonlaminated, Bilaminated and Multilaminated Permalloy Stripes," *J. Appl. Phys.*, **63**, 2938 (1988).

Tsang, C., M. Chen, T. Yogi, and K. Ju, "Gigabit Density Recording Using Dual-element MR/Inductive Heads on Thin-film Disks," *IEEE Trans. Magn.*, **MAG-26**, 1689 (1990).

Tsang, C., M. Krounbi, and R. Lee, "Study of Recessed MR Sensors with Unlaminated and Multi-laminated Flux-guides," *IEEE Trans. Magn.*, **MAG-28**, 2289 (1992).

Tsang, C., M. Chen, and T. Yogi, "Gigabit-density Magnetic Recording," *IEEE Proceedings*, **81**, 1344 (1993).

Tsang, C., R. Fontana, T. Lin, D. Heim, V. Speriosu, B. Gurney, and M. Williams, "Design and Fabrication, and Testing of Spin-valve Read Heads for High Density Recording," *IEEE Trans. Magn.*, **MAG-30**, 3801 (1994).

Tsui, R., H. Hamilton, R. Anderson, C. Baldwin, and P. Simon, "Perpendicular Recording Performance of Thin Film Probe Heads and Double-Layer Co-Cr Media," *Dig. Intermag. Conf.*, **GA4** (1985).

Tsuya, N., T. Tsukagoshi, K. Arai, K. Ogasawara, K. Ohmori, and S. Yosuda, "Magnetic Recording Head Using Ribbon-Sendust," *IEEE Trans. Magn.*, **MAG-17**, 3111 (1981).

Uchida, H., S. Imakoshi, Y. Soda, T. Sekiya, and H. Takino, "A Non-shielded MR Head with Improved Resolution," *IEEE Trans. Magn.*, **MAG-18**, 1152 (1982).

Umesaki, M., Y. Ohdoi, H. Hata, K. Yabushita, K. Morikawa, H. Kishi, S. Horibata, and H. Shibata, "A New Horizontal Thin Film Head," *IEEE Trans. Magn.*, **MAG-27**, 4933 (1991).

Unger, E., and K. Fritzsch, "Calculation of the Stray Reluctance of Gaps in Magnetic Circuits," *J. Audio. Eng. Soc.*, **18**, 641 (1970).

Valleta, R., G. Guthmiller, and G. Gorman, "Relation of Thickness and Some Physical Properties of NiFe Films," *J. Vac. Sci. & Technol.*, **A9**, 2093 (1991).

Valstyn, E. P., and L. F. Shew, "Performance of Single-Turn Film Heads," *IEEE Trans. Magn.*, **MAG-9**, 317 (1973).

van Herk, A., "Side Fringing Fields and Write and Read Crosstalk of Narrow Magnetic Recording Heads," *IEEE Trans. Magn.*, **MAG-13**, 1021 (1977).

van Herk, A., "Three Dimensional Analysis of Magnetic Fields in Recording-Head Configurations," Thesis, Delft University of Technology, The Netherlands, 1980a.

van Herk, A., "Three-dimensional Computation of the Field of Magnetic Recording Heads," *IEEE Trans. Magn.*, **MAG-16**, 890 (1980b).

van Lier, J., G. Koel, W. Gestel, L. Postma, J. Gerkema, F. Gorter, and W. Druyvesteyn, "Combined Thin Film Magnetoresistive Read, Inductive Write Heads," *IEEE Trans. Magn.*, **MAG-12**, 716 (1976).

Voegeli, O., "Magnetoresistive Read Head Assembly Having Matched Elements for Common Mode Rejection," U.S. Patent 3,860,965, January 14, 1975.

Von Gutfeld, R. J., and R. T. Hodgson, "Laser Enhanced Etching in KOH," *Appl. Phys. Lett.* **40**, 352 (1982).

Wakabayashi, N., I. Abe, and H. Miyairi, "A Thin Film Multi-Track Recording Head," *IEEE Trans. Magn.*, **MAG-18**, 1140 (1982).

Walker, P. A., "A Systems Overview of Transducers," *Ann. N.Y. Acad. Sci.*, **189**, 144 (1972).

Wang, P., M. Krounbi, D. Heim, and R. Lee, "Sensitivity of Orthogonal Magnetoresistive Heads," *Digest of 1993 INTERMAG*, Paper CA-05 (1993).

Wang, S., F., Liu, K. D. Maranowski, and M. H. Kryder, "Fabrication and Performance of High Moment Laminated FeAlN Thin Film Inductive Recording Heads," *IEEE Trans. Magn.*, **30**, 281 (1994).

Wang, S., F. H. Liu, K. D. Maranowski, J. A. Bain, and M. H. Kryder, "Material and Processing Aspects of Fe Al N High Moment Thin Film Heads," *Proceedings Symp. Magn. Mater., Proc. and Devices, Electrochemical Society*, Pennington, NJ, vol. 94-6, p. 25 (1994).

Warner, M. W., "Flying Magnetic Transducer Assembly Having Three Rails," U.S. Patent 3,823,416, 1974.

Watanabe, H., "Noise Analysis of Ferrite Head in Audio Tape Recording." *IEEE Trans. Magn.*, **MAG-10**, 903 (1974).

Wells, O. C., and R. J. Savoy, "Magnetic Domains in Thin-Film Recording Heads as Observed in the SEM by a Lock-In Technique," *IEEE Trans. Magn.*, **MAG-17**, 1253 (1981).

Westmijze, W. K., "Studies on Magnetic Recording," *Philips Res. Rep.*, **8**, 148 (1953).

White, J., "Magnetic Head Air Bearing Assembly Transverse Pressure Contour," U.S. Patent 4,673,996 (1987).

White, R., "Giant Magnetoresistance: A Primer," *IEEE Trans. Magn.*, **MAG-28**, 2482 (1992).

Williams, M. L., and Lambert, S. E., "Film Head Pulse Distortion due to Microvariation of Domain Wall Energy," *IEEE Trans. Magn.*, **MAG-25**, 3206 (1989).

Wong, K. H., P. C. Andricacos, and L. T. Romankiw, "Effect of Fe(II) Concentration on the Electrodeposition of Nickel-Iron Alloys," *Proceedings Symp. on Magn. Mater., Proc. and Devices*, vol. 90-8, Electrochemical Society, Pennington, N.J., p. 387 (1990).

Yamada, K., T. Maruyama, H. Tanaka, H. Kaneko, I Kagaya, and S. Ito, "A Thin Film Head for High Density Magnetic Recording Using CoZr Amorphous Films," *J. Appl. Phys.*, **55**, 2235 (1984).

Yamada, K., T. Matuyama, M. Ohmukai, T. Tatsumi, and H. Utai, "Co2+ Mo Amorphous Films as a Soft Adjacent Layer for Biasing Magnetoresistive Elements with a Currant Shunt Layer," *J. Appl. Phys.*, **63**, 4023 (1988).

Yamamoto, S., Y. Nakamura, and S. Iwasaki, "High-Density Recording with Single Pole Heads," *IEEE Transl. J. Magn. Jap.*, **TJMJ-3**, 56 (1988).

Yamashita, K., G. Takeuchi, K. Iwabuchi, Y. Kubota, and H. Miyairi, "Sendust Sputtered Flying Erase Head," *IEEE Trans. Magn.*, **MAG-20**, 869 (1984).

Yeh, N. H., "Analysis of Thin Film Heads with A Generalized Transmission Line Model," *IEEE Trans. Magn.*, **MAG-18**, 233 (1982*a*).

Yeh, N., "Asymmetric Crosstalk of Magnetoresistive Head," *IEEE Trans. Magn.*, **MAG-18**, 1155 (1982*b*).

Yohda, H., K. Takahashi, S. Sasaki, and N. Kaminaka, "Multi-Channel Thin Film Head for Perpendicular Magnetic Recording," *Natl. Tech. Rep.*, **31**, 136 (1985).

Young, K. F., "Stress in Thin Film Heads: Calculation by the Finite Element Method," *Proceedings of Symposium on Magnetic Materials*, PV90–8, Electrochemical Society, Pennington, N.J., 137 (1990).

Zieren, V., G. Somers, J. Ruigrok, M. deJongh, A. van Straalen, and W. Folkerts, "Design and Fabrication of Thin Film Heads for the Digital Compact Cassette Audio System," *IEEE Trans. Magn.*, **MAG-29**, 3064 (1993).

CHAPTER 7

TRIBOLOGY OF THE HEAD-MEDIUM INTERFACE

Bharat Bhushan

Computer Microtribology and Contamination Laboratory
The Ohio State University
Columbus, Ohio

7.1 INTRODUCTION

Magnetic recording is accomplished by relative motion between a magnetic medium (tape or disk) against a stationary or rotating (audio, video or data processing) read/write head. For high areal recording density, the linear flux density (number of flux reversals per unit distance) and the track density (number of tracks per unit distance) should be as high as possible. Reproduced (read back) signal amplitude decreases with head-to-medium spacing (clearance or flying height). In order to minimize damage of the interface, the head-medium interface is designed such that under steady operating conditions, a load-carrying air film is formed at the interface. A physical contact occurs between the medium and the head during starting and stopping. The developed air film at the operating conditions must be thick enough to mitigate any asperity contacts, yet it must be thin enough to give a large read-back magnetic signal. It is known that the signal loss as a result of spacing can be reduced exponentially by reducing the separation between the head and the medium (Wallace, 1951). However, tribological issues prevent zero spacing (or intimate contact). In modern tape and flexible and rigid disk drives, the head-to-medium separation ranges from about 50 nm to 0.3 μm, and the roughness of the head and medium surfaces ranges from 1.5 to 10 nm rms. In some of the consumer tape drives, negligible separation may occur.

The achievement of higher recording densities requires that surfaces should be as smooth as possible and flying height (physical separation or clearance between a head and a medium) be as low as possible. The ultimate objective is to run two surfaces in contact (with practically zero physical separation) if the tribological issues can be resolved. Smooth surfaces lead to an increase in adhesion, friction and interface temperatures, and closer flying heights lead to occasional rubbing of high asperities and increased wear. Friction and wear issues are resolved by appropriate selection of interface materials and lubricants, by controlling the dynamics of the head and medium, and the environment (Bhushan et al., 1984–1990; Bhushan,

1990, 1991–1995, 1992a, 1993a, 1994a, 1995). A fundamental understanding of the tribology (friction, wear and lubrication) of the magnetic head-medium interface, both on macro- and micro/nanoscales, becomes crucial for the continued growth of the magnetic storage industry.

In this chapter, initially, the construction and materials used in magnetic head and medium components are described. Then, the status of understanding of friction and adhesion, interface temperatures, wear, and solid-liquid lubrication relevant to magnetic storage systems is presented. Macrotribological studies are followed by a brief overview of the micro/nanotribological and micro/nanomechanics studies.

7.2   MAGNETIC STORAGE COMPONENTS

Magnetic storage devices used for information storage and retrieval include tape, flexible disk and rigid disk drives. In this section, construction and materials used in magnetic media and heads in various drives are described.

7.2.1 Magnetic Media

Magnetic media fall into two categories: (a) particulate media, where magnetic particles are dispersed in a polymeric matrix and coated onto a polymeric substrate for flexible media (tape and flexible disks) or onto a rigid substrate such as aluminum or on the more recently introduced glass and glass ceramics (Bhushan, 1993b) for rigid-disks; (b) thin-film media, where continuous films of magnetic materials are deposited onto the substrate by vacuum techniques. Requirements of higher recording densities with low error rates have resulted in increased use of thin-film media which are smoother and considerably thinner than the particulate media. Thin-film media are almost exclusively used for rigid disks and are beginning to be used for high-density audio/video and data processing tapes.

7.2.1.1 Flexible Media. Cross sectional views of a particulate and a thin-film (evaporated) metal tape are shown in Fig. 7.1a. Flexible disks are similar to tapes in construction except these have magnetic coating on both sides and the substrate is generally about 76 μm in thickness. The base film for flexible media is almost exclusively polyethylene terephthalate (PET) film, and recently polyethylene napthalate (PEN) polymers have been used for better dimensional stability of thinner tapes (Weick and Bhushan, 1995a,b,c,d). Typically tapes use 6.35 to 36.07-μm thick PET substrate with rms roughness of about 2 to 5 nm and peak-to-valley (P-V) distance of 50–100 nm for particulate media and 1.5 to 2 nm rms for the recording side of thin-film media. Flexible disks use a 76-μm thick PET substrate. Particulates such as silica or titania with a bimodal distribution of sizes with mean diameters on the order of 0.5 μm and 2 μm, are added in the substrate as anti-slip agents (Bhushan, 1992a).

The base film is coated on one side of a tape and both sides of a flexible disk with a magnetic coating, typically 1 to 4 μm thick and containing 70–80% by weight (or 43–50% by volume) of sub-micron and acicular magnetic particles [such as γ-Fe_2O_3, Co-modified γ-Fe_2O_3, CrO_2 (only for tapes), and metal particles for longitudinal recording or hexagonal platelets of barium ferrite for both longitudinal and perpendicular recording]. These magnetic particles are held in polymeric binders such as

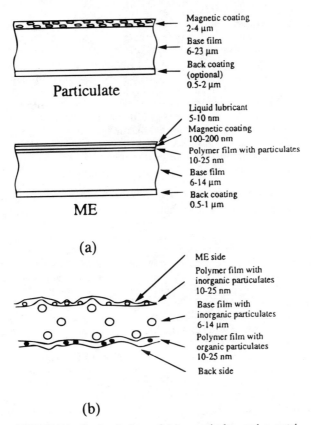

Particulate

Magnetic coating
2-4 μm

Base film
6-23 μm

Back coating
(optional)
0.5-2 μm

ME

Liquid lubricant
5-10 nm

Magnetic coating
100-200 nm

Polymer film with particulates
10-25 nm

Base film
6-14 μm

Back coating
0.5-1 μm

(a)

ME side

Polymer film with
inorganic particulates
10-25 nm

Base film with
inorganic particulates
6-14 μm

Polymer film with
organic particulates
10-25 nm

Back side

(b)

FIGURE 7.1 Sectional views of (a) a particulate and a metal-evaporated magnetic tape, and (b) coated PET substrate for ME tapes.

polyester-polyurethane, polyether-polyurethane, nitrocellulose, poly(vinyl chloride), poly(vinyl alcohol-vinyl acetate), poly(vinylidene chloride), VAGH, phenoxy, and epoxy. To reduce friction, the coating consists of 1–7% by weight of lubricants (mostly fatty acid esters, e.g., tridecyl stearate, butyl stearate, butyl palmitate, butyl myristate, stearic acid, myrstic acid). Finally, the coating contains a cross linker or curing agent (such as functional isocyanates); a dispersant or wetting agent (such as lecithin); and solvents (such as tetrahydrofuran and methyl isobutyl-ketone). In some media, carbon black is added for antistatic protection if the magnetic particles are highly insulating and abrasive particles (such as Al_2O_3 and Cr_2O_3) are added as a head cleaning agent and to improve wear resistance. The coating is calendered to a surface roughness of 8 to 15 nm rms.

For antistatic protection and for improved tracking, most magnetic tapes have a 1- to 3-μm thick backcoating of polyester-polyurethane binder containing a conductive carbon black and TiO_2, typically 10% and 50% by weight, respectively.

Flexible disks are packaged inside a soft polyvinyl chloride (PVC) jacket or a acrylonitrile-butadiene-styrene (ABS) hard jacket (for the smaller 90-mm form). Inside the jacket, a protective fabric liner is used to minimize wear or abrasion of the media. Wiping action of the liner on the medium coating removes and entraps particulate contaminants which may originate from diskette manufacturing, the jacket, head-disk contact (wear debris), or the external environment. The liner is made of nonwoven fibers of polyester (PET), rayon, polypropylene, or nylon which are thermally or fusion bonded to the plastic jacket at spots. In manufacturing of the fabric, the fibers are lubricated with lubricants such as 2 wt % oleic acid. The soft jacket near the data window is pressed against the disk with a spring-loaded lifter, to create slight friction and hence stabilize disk motion under the heads. The hard cartridge is provided with an internal plastic leaf spring for the same purpose.

Thin-film (also called metal-film or ME) flexible media consist of a polymer substrate (PET or polyimide) with an evaporated film of Co-Ni (with about 18% Ni) and experimental evaporated/sputtered Co-Cr (with about 17% Cr) (for perpendicular recording, which is typically 100–200 nm thick. Electroplated Co and electroless-plated Co-P, Co-Ni-P and Co-Ni-Re-P have also been explored but are not commercially used. Since the magnetic layer is very thin, the surface of the thin-film medium is greatly influenced by the surface of the substrate film. Therefore, an ultra-smooth PET substrate film (rms roughness ~ 1.5–2 nm) is used to obtain a smooth tape surface. A 10–25 nm thick precoat composed of polymer film with additives is generally applied to both sides of the PET substrate to provide controlled topography, Fig. 7.1b. The film on the ME treated side generally contains inorganic particulates (typically SiO_2 with a particle size of 100–200 nm diameter and areal density of typically $10,000/mm^2$). The film on the back side generally contains organic (typically cross-linked polystyrene) particles. The rms and P-V distances of the ME treated side and the backside typically are 1.5–2 nm and 15–20 nm, and 3–5 nm and 50–75 nm, respectively. The polymer precoat is applied to reduce the roughness (mostly P-V distance) in a controlled manner from that of the PET surface, and to provide good adhesion with the ME films. Particles are added to the precoat to control the real area of contact and consequently the friction. A continuous magnetic coating is deposited on the polymer film. The polymer film is wrapped on a chill roll during deposition, which keeps the film at a temperature of 0 to $-20°C$. $Co_{80}Ni_{20}$ material is deposited on the film by a reactive evaporation process in the presence of oxygen; oxygen increases the hardness and corrosion resistance of the ME film. The deposited film, with a mean composition of $(C_{80}Ni_{20})_{80}O_{20}$ consists of very small Co and Co-Ni crystallites which are primarily intermixed with oxides of Co and Ni (Feurstein and Mayr, 1984; Harth et al., 1989). (Various inorganic overcoats such as diamondlike carbon in about 10–20 nm thickness have been proposed to protect against corrosion and wear.) A topical liquid lubricant (typically perfluoropolyether with reactive polar ends) is then applied to the magnetic coating by rolling. The topical lubricant enhances the durability of the magnetic coating, and also inhibits the highly reactive metal coating from reacting with ambient air and water vapor. A backcoating is also applied to balance stresses in the tape, and for anti-static protection.

7.2.1.2 Rigid Disks. Figure 7.2 shows sectional views of two types of rigid disks—a particulate disk and a thin-film disk. The substrate for rigid disks is generally non-heat-treatable aluminum-magnesium alloy AISI 5086 (95.4% Al, 4% Mg, 0.4% Mn, and 0.15% Cr) with an rms surface roughness of about 15–25 nm rms and a Vickers hardness of about 90 kg/mm^2. For particulate disks, the Al-Mg substrate is sometimes passivated with a very thin (< 100 nm) conversion coating based on chromium phosphate. The finished substrate is spin coated with the magnetic coating and burnished to a surface roughness of about 7.5 to 15 nm rms. The binder is generally made of a hard copolymer of epoxy, phenolic and polyurethane constitu-

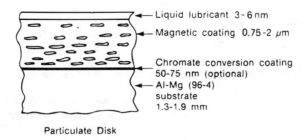

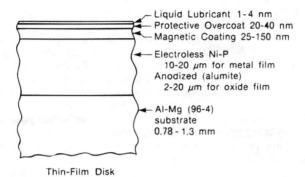

FIGURE 7.2 Sectional views of a particulate and a thin-film magnetic rigid disk.

ents. About 30 to 35% by volume of acicular magnetic particles of γ-Fe$_2$O$_3$ are interdispersed in the binder. A small percentage of Al$_2$O$_3$ particles 0.2–0.5 μm in size (2 to 8% by volume) are added to improve wear resistance. A thin film of perfluoropolyether lubricants is applied topically. The magnetic coating is made porous for lubricant retention.

For high-density recording there is a trend to use thin-film disks, with the typical construction shown in Fig. 7.2. For thin-film disks with metallic magnetic layers, the Al-Mg substrate is electroless plated with nickel-phosphorus (90–10 wt %) layer to improve its surface hardness to 600–800 kg/mm^2 (Knoop) and smoothness. The coated surface is polished with an abrasive slurry to a surface roughness of about 0.5 to 2 nm rms. For a thin-film disk with an oxide magnetic layer, a 2- to 20-μm thick alumite layer is formed on the Al-Mg substrate through anodic oxidation in a CrO$_3$ bath. Ni-P cannot be used because it becomes magnetic when exposed to high temperatures during the preparation of a γ-Fe$_2$O$_3$ film. To minimize static friction at the head-disk interface, the start-stop zone of substrates for thin-film disks needs to be textured in the circumferential or random orientation to a typical rms roughness of 4–8 nm. For convenience, the entire disk is generally textured. Disks are mostly textured by mechanical texturing techniques using either free or fixed abrasives (Bhushan, 1993b). Recently, a laser texturing technique has been used for the texturing of start-stop zone (Baumgart et al., 1995). Circumferential direction of texturing in the data zone (if textured) is preferred in order to keep the magnetic orientation ratio as high as possible. The finished substrate is coated with a magnetic film 25–150 nm thick. Some metal films require a Cr undercoat (10–50 nm thick) as a nucleation layer to improve magnetic properties, such as coercivity. Typically, magnetic films that have been explored are metal films of cobalt-based alloys (e.g., Co-Pt-Cr, Co-Pt-Ni), with sputtered iron oxide being the principal exception. Magnetic films that are used to achieve high recording density have weak durability and poor corrosion resistance. Protective overcoats with a liquid lubricant overlay are generally used to provide low friction, low wear, and corrosion resistance. Protective coatings are typically sputtered diamondlike carbon (DLC) or sputtered SiO_2. In most cases, a thin layer of perfluoropolyether lubricant with reactive polar ends is used. The trend is to use partially bonded lubricant film consisting of an unbonded or mobile film over a bonded lubricant film. The unbonded top layer would heal any worn areas on the disk surface where the lubricant may have been removed, and the bonded underlayer provides lubricant persistence. Furthermore, the bonded layer does not contribute to meniscus effects in stiction (Bhushan, 1990).

For high volumetric density, thinner disk substrates are used. As the substrates get thinner than about 0.635 mm, traditionally used Al-Mg substrates warp (curl on the edges) during disk manufacturing and assembly. Furthermore, in a drop test, sliders can dent the Al-Mg disk surfaces. Therefore, the new substrate should have high yield strength with little plastic deformation. For contact and near-contact recording applications, one would like to have the substrate as flat and smooth as possible with asperities and defects as few as possible. Al-Mg alloy disks can only be used for flying heights of about 50 nm or greater. Two other materials, chemically-strengthened glass and glass ceramics have begun to be used (Bhushan, 1993*b*; Bhushan and Gupta, 1995*a*; Gao and Bhushan, 1995*a*). Thinner substrates of glass or glass ceramic can be processed without warpage during disk manufacturing, and exhibit high dent (shock) resistance (because of their high yield strength, deformation occurs without much plastic deformation). Texture on the glass-ceramic substrates is obtained by selected crystallization and mechanical polishing. In the case of glass disks, a smooth substrate is used and texture on the entire disk surface is obtained by either controlling the grain size of a chromium underlayer deposited for film texturing purposes (Kawai et al., 1992), or by deposition of a low melting point metal as an underlayer to form isolated spherical features (Mirzamaani et al., 1992).

7.2.2 Magnetic Heads

Magnetic heads used to-date consist either of conventional inductive or of thin-film inductive and magnetoresistive (MR) devices (Bhushan, 1990, 1992*a*, 1993*b*). Film-head design capitalizes on semiconductor-like processing technology to reduce fabrication costs, and thin-film technology allows production of high-track density heads with accurate track positioning control and high reading sensitivity. If a MR head design is used, it is only for read purposes. Inductive heads consist of a body forming the air bearing (referred to as the air bearing surface or ABS) and a magnetic ring core carrying the wound coil with a read-write gap. In film heads, the core and coils or MR stripes are deposited by thin-film technology. The body of a thin-film head is made of magnetic ferrites or nonmagnetic Al_2O_3-TiC and the head construction includes coatings of soft magnetic alloys, insulating oxides and bonding adhesives.

Air-bearing surfaces of tape heads are cylindrical in shape. The tape is slightly underwrapped over the head surface to generate hydrodynamic lift during read-write operations. For inductive-coil tape heads, the core materials have been typi-

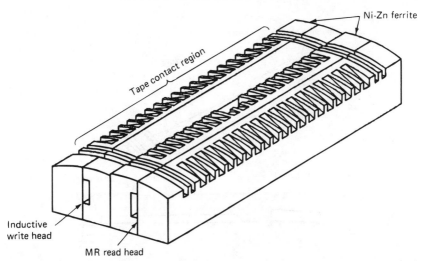

FIGURE 7.3 Schematic of an inductive/MR thin-film head (with a radius of cylindrical contour of about 20 mm) in an IBM 3480/3490 data-processing tape drive.

cally Permalloy and Sendust. However, since these alloys are good conductors, it is sometimes necessary to laminate the core structure to minimize losses due to eddy currents. The air-bearing surfaces of most inductive-coil type heads consist of plasma sprayed coatings of hard materials such as Al_2O_3-TiO_2 and ZrO_2. MR read and inductive write heads in modern tape drives (such as IBM 3480/3490) are miniaturized using thin-film technology, Fig. 7.3. Film heads are generally deposited on Ni-Zn ferrite (11 wt % NiO, 22 wt % ZnO, 67 wt % Fe_2O_3) substrates. Flexible-disk heads are inductive-coil type composite devices which are either spherically contoured or flat. Mn-Zn ferrite (30 wt % MnO, 17 wt % ZnO, 53 wt % Fe_2O_3) is generally used for head cores and barium titanate for the magnetically inert support structures.

The head sliders used in rigid disk drives are either the two- or three-rail, taper-flat design supported by a nonmagnetic steel leaf spring (flexure) suspension to allow motion along the vertical, pitch and roll axes, Fig. 7.4a. The front taper pressurizes the air lubricant, while some air leaking over the side boundaries of the rail results in a pitch angle. In a shaped-rail design, the leading-edge rail width is greater than that of the trailing end, to attain increased pitch angles, independent of air-film thickness, Fig. 7.4b. The inductive-type or inductive/MR type thin-film read-write elements used in high-end disk drives (e.g., IBM 3380/3390) are integrated in the Al_2O_3-TiC (70-30 wt %) slider at the trailing edge of each rail for the two-rail and at the center rail in the three-rail design where the lowest flying height occurs, Fig. 7.4b. The suspension supplies a vertical load ranging from 30 mN (3g) to 100 mN (10g) dependent upon the size of the slider (see discussion later), which is balanced by the hydrodynamic load when the disk is spinning. The stiffness of the suspension ($\sim$25 mN mm^{-1}) is several orders of magnitude lower than that of the air bearing ($\sim$0.5 kN mm^{-1}) so that most dynamic variations are taken up by the suspension without degrading the air bearing.

Small disk drives commonly use inductive-coil type heads of one or two types: minimonolithic (mini-Winchester) and minicomposite (Bhushan, 1990, 1993b). A minimonolithic head slider consists of a slider body and a core piece carrying the

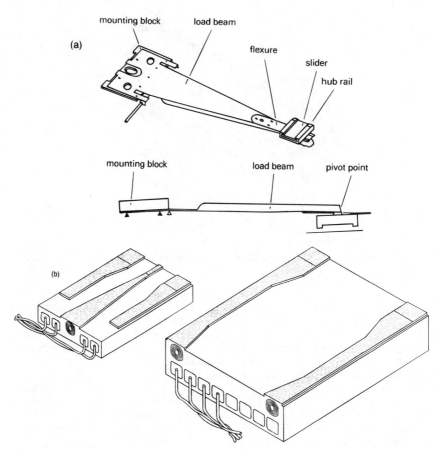

FIGURE 7.4   Schematic of (*a*) an IBM 3370/3380/3390 type suspension-slider assembly, and (*b*) an IBM shaped rail (two-rail) inductive thin-film slider (full length) and an IBM tri-rail thin-film nanoslider (U.S. Patent 4,894,740).

coil, both consisting of monolithic magnetic material (typically Mn-Zn ferrite). The taper-flat bearing area is provided by the outer rails of a tri-rail design. The center rail defines the width of the magnetic element in the trailing edge where a ferrite core is formed. A minimonolithic head slider consists of a Mn-Zn ferrite core and read-write gap, glass bonded into the air-bearing surface of a nonmagnetic, wear-resistant slider (typically calcium titanate).

The 3380-type suspensions normally used for heads in small drives apply a 95 mN (9.5-g) load onto the slider. The 3380-K/3390 type sliders are 4.045-mm long by 3.200-mm wide by 0.850-mm high with a mass of 0.45 mN (45 mg), as opposed to about 4.1 mm long by 3.1-mm wide by 1.4-mm high and 0.7 mN (70 mg) for the mini-Winchester. As the drives get smaller and flying height decreases, the size and mass of the sliders and their gram load decreases. Lower mass results in higher air-bearing frequency, which reduces dynamic impact. Smaller size and required lower gram load results in the improvement in stiction and start-stop and flyability lives.

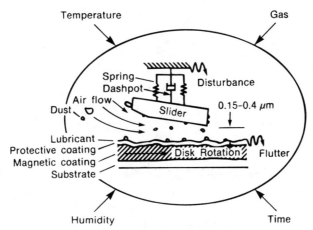

FIGURE 7.5 Schematic diagram of the head-rigid disk interface.

More recently, micro- and nanosliders with a three-rail design using thin-film induc-tive and MR heads, and Al_2O_3-TiC as a substrate material, have been introduced both for large and small drives. The sliders are about 70% and 50% of the regular sizes, respectively and vertical loads on the sliders are 50 mN (5g) and 30 mN (3g), respectively. The surface roughness of the air-bearing rails is typically 1.5-2 nm rms.

A schematic representation of the head-disk interface is shown in Fig. 7.5. Environment, usage time, and contamination (external and wear debris) play a significant role in the reliability and usable lifetime of the interface.

7.3 FRICTION AND ADHESION

When two surfaces come in contact, the load is supported by the deformation at the tips of the contacting asperities, Fig. 7.6. The proximity of the asperities results in adhesive contacts caused by interatomic attractions. In a broad sense, adhesion is considered to be either physical or chemical in nature. Experimental data suggest that adhesion is primarily due to weak van der Waals forces (Bhushan et al., 1984*b*; Bhushan, 1990). When two surfaces (in contact) move relative to each other, fric-tional force, commonly referred to as "intrinsic" or "conventional" frictional force, is contributed by adhesion and deformation (or hysteresis) of these asperities, Fig. 7.7*a*. For most practical cases, adhesional friction is the primary contributor (Bhushan, 1990). Figure 7.7*b* shows the friction force versus time or displacement. In some cases, the static friction force required to initiate sliding is larger than the kinetic friction force required to sustain sliding.

In addition, "stiction" (or high static friction), can occur due to meniscus/viscous effects, microcapillary evacuation, and changes in surface chemistry (Bhushan et al., 1984*a*, 1984*b*; Bradshaw and Bhushan, 1984; Bradshaw et al., 1986). Here we will concentrate on the meniscus/viscous effects only, Fig. 7.8. Generally, any liquid that wets or has a small contact angle on surfaces will condense from vapor in the form of an annular-shaped capillary condensate in the contact zone. The pressure of the liquid films of the capillary condensates or a preexisting film of lubricant can

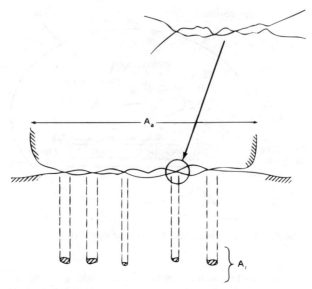

FIGURE 7.6 Schematic of two rough surfaces in contact and the corresponding contact areas.

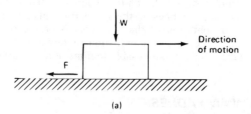

(a)

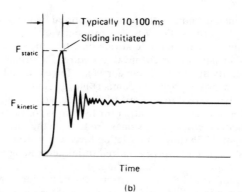

(b)

FIGURE 7.7 Schematic illustration of (*a*) a body sliding on a horizontal surface, where W is the normal load (force) and F is the friction force, and (*b*) Friction force versus time or displacement. F_{static} is the force required to initiate sliding and $F_{kinetic}$ is the force required to maintain sliding.

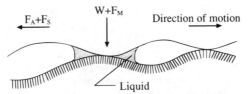

FIGURE 7.8 Schematic of a wet interface with meniscus formation, showing, various forces being applied during sliding. F_M is the meniscus force, W is the normal force, and F_A and F_S are the intrinsic friction force and the stiction force, respectively.

significantly increase the adhesion between solid bodies. Liquid-mediated adhesive forces can be divided into two components: meniscus force (F_M) due to surface tension and a rate-dependent viscous force (F_V). The total tangential force F required to separate the surfaces by sliding is equal to an intrinsic friction force (F_A) and a stiction force F_S (a combination of friction force due to the meniscus effect and the peak viscous force)

$$F = F_A + F_S = f_r(W + F_M) + F_V \qquad (7.1)$$

where f_r is the "true" static coefficient of friction and W is the normal load.

The normal force required to move two flat, well-polished surfaces (such as magnetic head and medium surfaces) in the presence of a liquid medium and/or a sticky substance can be large (up to several newtons in extreme cases). Therefore, we define the difference between stiction and conventional static and kinetic friction as being that stiction requires a measurable normal force (normally several mN or higher) to pull the two surfaces apart from the static conditions.

7.3.1 Conventional Friction

From Tabor's classical theory of adhesion (Bowden and Tabor, 1950, 1964), the frictional force due to adhesion (F_A) in dry contact is:

$$F_A = A_r \tau_a, \qquad (7.2a)$$

and for lubricated contact

$$F_A = A_r[a\tau_a + (1 - \alpha)\tau_l] \qquad (7.2b)$$

where,

$$\tau_l = \eta_l V/h \qquad (7.3)$$

A_r is the real area of contact, α is the fraction of unlubricated area, τ_a and τ_l are the shear strengths of the dry contact and the lubricant film, respectively, η_l is the absolute viscosity of the lubricant, V is the relative sliding velocity, and h is the lubricant film thickness. In the following, discussion is limited to static contact models.

7.3.1.1 *Greenwood and Williamson Contact Model.* The contacts can be either elastic or plastic which primarily depend on the surface topography and the mechani-

cal properties of the mating surfaces. The classical model for a combination of elastic and plastic contacts between rough surfaces, that of Greenwood and Williamson (G&W model), assumes the surface is composed of hemispherically-tipped asperities of uniform size with their heights following a Gaussian distribution about a mean plane (Greenwood and Williamson, 1966). The radius of these asperities is assumed equal to the mean radius of curvature obtained from roughness measurements. The real area of contact for elastic (e) and plastic (p) contacts is (Bhushan, 1984)

$$A_{re}/A_a P_a \sim 3.2/E_c(\sigma_p/R_p)^{1/2}$$

$$\text{for } \psi_p < 1.8 \text{ or } \psi < 0.6, \text{ elastic contact,} \tag{7.3a}$$

$$A_{rp}/A_a P_a = 1/H$$

$$\text{for } \psi_p > 2.6 \text{ or } \psi > 1, \text{ plastic contact,} \tag{7.3b}$$

and

$$\psi_p = (E_c/Y)\,(\sigma_p/R_p)^{1/2}, \text{ for polymers} \tag{7.3c}$$
$$\psi = (E_c/H)\,(\sigma_p/R_p)^{1/2}, \text{ for metals/ceramics} \tag{7.3d}$$

where A_a is the apparent area of contact; p_a is the apparent pressure (W/A_a); E_c is the composite modulus of elasticity, H and Y are the hardness and yield strength of the softer material, σ_p and R_p are the composite standard deviation and radius of curvature of the surface summits, and ψ and ψ_p are the plasticity indices for metals/ceramics and polymers, respectively.

Equation 7.3 for elastic and plastic contacts in the case of metals/ceramics is plotted in Fig. 7.9 for better visualization of the dependence of A_r on ψ. We note that the plastic contact results in minimum contact area. However, repeated plastic contact would lead through undesirable permanent deformation and smoothening to a higher real area of contact and elastic contacts. Since wear is more probable when asperities touch plastically than in elastic contacts, it is desirable to design components in the elastic regime with ψ close to the elastic contact limit ($\psi \sim 0.6$, or $E_c/(\sigma_p/R_p)^{1/2}$ as high as possible).

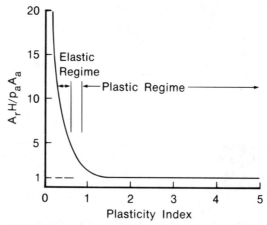

FIGURE 7.9   Influence of plasticity index on the real area of contact in metals/ceramics (*Bhushan, 1984*).

In order to use the G&W model, the modulus of elasticity and hardness of the magnetic coatings of tapes were measured by dynamic mechanical analysis (DMA) (Bhushan, 1984, 1985*a*) and those of rigid disks by nanoindentation hardness apparatus (Bhushan and Doerner, 1989). Surface roughness parameters of tapes and disks were measured using a noncontact optical profiler (NOP) with a lateral resolution in the 1 μm range, and down to atomic scale with an atomic force microscope (AFM) (Bhushan et al., 1988; Bhushan and Blackman, 1991*a*; Oden et al., 1992). AFM can measure topographic features which cannot be measured with conventional profilers. Table 7.1 shows that topography and contact statistics predictions are a strong function of the lateral resolution of the roughness measurement tool (Bhushan and Blackman, 1991*a*; Oden et al., 1992). Here η is the density of summits per unit area, n is the number of contact spots, and p_r is the real pressure. Surface topography statistics show that the average summit radius (R_p) for the AFM data is two to four orders of magnitude smaller than that for the NOP data, whereas summit density for the AFM data is two to four orders of magnitude larger than for the NOP data. The plasticity index (ψ) calculated using the AFM data suggests that all contacts made of nanoasperities are plastic; NOP data suggest that all contacts made of microasperities are elastic.

The question remains as to how do large spots become elastic when they must have initially been small plastic spots. The possible explanation is graphically shown in Fig. 7.10. As two surfaces touch, the nanoasperities (detected by AFM-type instruments) first coming into contact have smaller radii of curvature and are therefore plastically deformed instantly and the contact area increases. When the load is increased, nanoasperities in the contact zone merge and the load is supported by elastic deformation of the larger-scale asperities or microasperities (detected by NOP-type instruments).

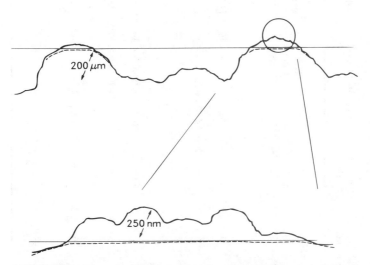

FIGURE 7.10   Schematic of local asperity deformation during contact of a rough surface against a flat surface (upper profile measured by NOP and lower profile measured by AFM, typical dimensions shown for a polished thin-film disk). The vertical axis is magnified for clarity. Firm lines show the surfaces before contact and dotted lines show surfaces after contact (*Bhushan and Blackman, 1991a*).

TABLE 7.1 Real Area of Contact Calculations for Magnetic Tape A Against Ni-Zn Ferrite Head and Rigid Disks Against Al_2O_3-TiC Slider (Bhushan and Blackman, 1991a and Oden et al., 1992)

Component Designation	E, GPa	H, GPa	σ, nm		σ_p, nm		$1/R_p$, 1/mm		η, 1/mm²		Ψ		A_r/A_aP_a, GPa		n/A_aP_a, 1/mN		A_r/n, μm²		P_r, GPa	
			NOP	AFM	NOP	AFM	NOP	AFM	NOP	AFM	NOP	AFM	NOP	AFM	NOP	AFM	NOP	AFM	NOP	AFM
Head-Tape Interface																				
Particulate tape A	1.75	0.25	19.5	36.3	19.0	45.4	2.20	1.4×10^5	5.7×10^3	8.0×10^6	0.05	50.17	241.6	4.0	9.6	4.1×10^{-2}	25.3	97.6	4.23	0.25×10^{-3}
Mn-Zn ferrite head	122	6.9	2.15	3.61	2.51	5.47	0.23	7.8×10^3	1.2×10^3	6.2×10^6										
Head-Disk Interface																				
Particulate disk A	9.4	0.53	9.39	13.6	9	10.5	4.79	6.0×10^3	5.9×10^3	2.4×10^6	0.27	5.6	22.6	1.9	9.9	0.13	2.3	14.2	0.05	0.53
Textured thin-film disk B	113	6.0	7.33	6.33	7	6.7	4.90	4.0×10^3	732	9.1×10^6	0.12	3.4	4.3	0.17	2.5	4.8×10^{-3}	1.7	28.2	0.24	6.0
Polished thin-film disk C	107	6.2	2.11	3.37	2	8.8	2.24	6.1×10^3	911	3.5×10^6	0.05	4.4	9.6	0.16	8.8	1.2×10^{-2}	1.1	13.9	0.11	6.2
Al_2O_3-TiC Slider	450	22.6	1.63	1.55	2	1.4	0.53	1.2×10^3	2.4×10^3	13.3×10^6										

7.3.1.2   Fractal Model of Elastic-Plastic Contact.   The contact analyses developed over the last quarter century consider only an averaged surface with a single scale of roughness to be in contact with another surface. However, due to the multiscale nature of surfaces it is found that the surface roughness parameters depend strongly on the resolution of the roughness measuring instrument, or any other form of filter, and hence are not unique for a surface (Bhushan et al., 1988*b*; Poon and Bhushan, 1995*a*, 1995*b*). As an example, Fig. 7.11 shows the surface profiles of a thin-film magnetic disk obtained using a stylus profiler (lateral resolution $\sim$ 2.5 μm), noncontact optical profiler (lateral resolution $\sim$ 1 μm) and AFM (lateral resolution $\sim$ 10 nm). The figure shows that roughness is found ranging from millimeter to nanometer scales. A measured roughness profile is dependent on the lateral and normal resolutions of the measuring instrument. Instruments with different lateral resolutions measure features with different scale lengths. It can be concluded that a surface is composed of a large number of length scales of roughness that are superimposed on each other.

Surface roughness is generally characterized by the standard deviation of surface heights, which is the square root of the arithmetic average of squares of the vertical deviation of a surface profile from its mean plane. However, due to the multiscale nature of surfaces, it is found that the variances of surface height and its derivatives and other roughness parameters strongly depend on the lateral resolution of the roughness measuring instrument (Bhushan, 1990), Fig. 7.12. The scale dependence in Fig. 7.12 suggests that instruments with different resolutions and scan lengths yield different values of these statistical parameters for the same surface. In order to use the roughness parameters for the prediction of real area of contact, friction, and wear, it is first necessary to quantify the multiscale nature of surface roughness.

The multiscale nature of surface roughness can be characterized by fractal modelling. The fractal characterization of surface roughness is scale independent and provides information of the roughness structure at all length scales that exhibit the fractal behavior, called here the M-B model (Majumdar and Bhushan, 1990, 1991*a*); and the G-B model (Ganti and Bhushan, 1995). The fractal model of elastic-plastic contact has been developed by Majumdar and Bhushan (1991*b*) and Bhushan and Majumdar (1992*c*). They reported relationships for the cumulative size distribution of the contact spots, the portion of the real area of contact in elastic and plastic deformation modes, and the load-area relationships (Bhushan, 1994*a*, 1995).

7.3.1.3   Numerical 3-D Models of Elastic-Plastic Contact and Computer Simulations.   With the application of computer technology, a measured surface profile can be digitized and be used for computer simulation. Over the last few years, several numerical techniques have been developed and used to solve contact problems of rough surfaces. Poon and Sayles (1994), Bhushan (1994*b*), and Tian and Bhushan (1995*a*) developed a 3-D contact numerical model which allows analysis of a large number of contact spots which go through elastic and elastic-plastic deformations. The numerical model does not require an asperity model and makes no probabilistic assumptions such as the distribution of asperity heights, slopes and curvatures. It provides useful information on the number of contact spots, their sizes and distributions, and the spacing between contacts. The model can be used to develop optimum surface roughness distributions for the head and medium surfaces.

Figure 7.13 shows the computed results of real area of contact at two nominal pressures for two scan sizes. Note that the number and total area of contact in-

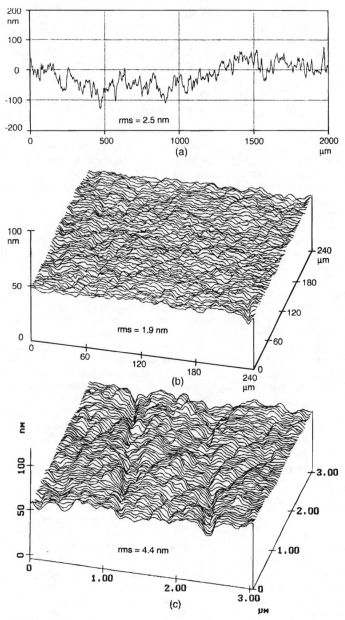

FIGURE 7.11 Surface roughness profiles of an as-polished magnetic thin-film rigid disk measured using (*a*) stylus profiler (lateral resolution ~ 2.5 μm) (*b*) noncontact optical profiler (lateral resolution ~ 1 μm), and (*c*) atomic force microscope (lateral resolution ~ 10 nm). Note that rms roughness measured using AFM is the highest followed by the stylus profiler and the noncontact optical profiler.

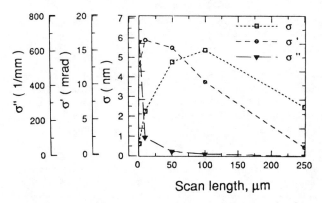

FIGURE 7.12 Scale dependence of the standard deviation of surface height (σ), σ' and σ'' for a polished thin-film rigid disk, measured using an atomic force microscope and a noncontact optical profiler.

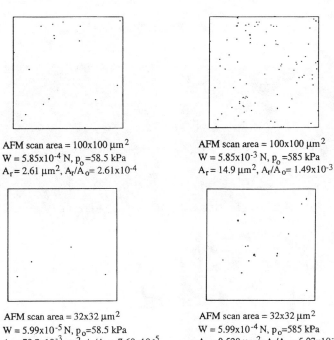

AFM scan area = 100x100 μm^2
W = 5.85x10^{-4} N, p_o =58.5 kPa
A_r= 2.61 μm^2, A_r/A_o= 2.61x10^{-4}

AFM scan area = 100x100 μm^2
W = 5.85x10^{-3} N, p_o=585 kPa
A_r = 14.9 μm^2, A_r/A_o= 1.49x10^{-3}

AFM scan area = 32x32 μm^2
W = 5.99x10^{-5} N, p_o=58.5 kPa
A_r = 78.7x10$^{-3}\mu m^2$, A_r/A_o= 7.69x10^{-5}

AFM scan area = 32x32 μm^2
W = 5.99x10^{-4} N, p_o=585 kPa
A_r = 0.520 μm^2, A_r/A_o= 5.07x10^{-4}

FIGURE 7.13 Computed real area of contact (A_r) for a given nominal pressure p_o of 58.5 kPa (typical pressure at the head-disk interface) and a larger pressure of 585 kPa for two scan sizes of $100 \times 100\ \mu m^2$ and $32 \times 32\ \mu m^2$. In this figure, A_o is the apparent area of contact and W is the normal load. Calculations were made for glass-ceramic disks in contact with an Al_2O_3-TiC slider (composite modulus of elasticity = 100 GPa, disk hardness = 5.5 GPa) (*Tian and Bhushan, 1995b*).

creases with load. Further note that a smaller scan area leads to a smaller fractional real area of contact because the small scan area reveals finer details of roughness which are analyzed in the numerical computation (Bhushan and Blackman, 1991*a*).

7.3.1.4 Measurement of Contact Area.   The real area of contact of magnetic tapes and rigid disks has been measured using the optical-interference technique (Bhushan, 1985*a*; Bhushan and Dugger, 1990*a*). A loading-unloading experiment was conducted to determine if most contacts in the range above 0.7 μm in diameter were elastic (Bhushan, 1984). Photographs of tape contacts were taken at 28 kPa; then higher pressure (1.38 MPa) was applied for short durations and the tape contact was brought back to 28 kPa and rephotographed, Fig. 7.14. Lack of changes in the real area of contact before loading to 1.38 MPa and after unloading to 28 kPa suggests that the contacts were elastic, an observation in agreement with fractal model predictions.

If the contacts are elastic, then the real area of contact and friction are governed by the values of E_c and σ_p/R_p of the magnetic medium surface. Figure 7.15*a* shows an example that the friction of various magnetic tapes depend significantly upon the complex modulus and the surface roughness (Bhushan et al., 1984*a*). Stable frictional behavior was exhibited only by those tapes which displayed a complex modulus of greater than 1.2 to 1.5 GPa. Figure 7.15*b* shows examples in which the

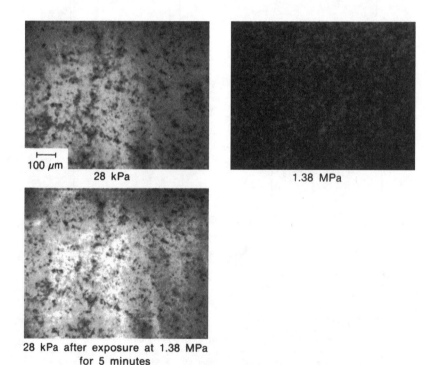

FIGURE 7.14   Optical interference photographs of tapes taken at 28 kPa; then subjected to higher pressure (1.38 MPa) for about 5 minutes and brought back to 28 kPa and rephotographed. We see no change in the real area of contact, implying an elastic contact (*Bhushan, 1984*).

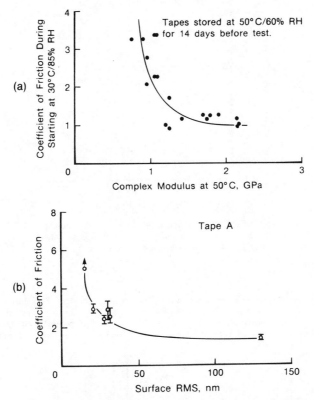

FIGURE 7.15 (*a*) Coefficient of friction during start at 30°C/85% RH measured on a commercial tape drive versus the complex modulus at 50°C. The CrO_2 tapes were stored at 50°C/60% RH for 14 days before the tests. (*b*) Effect of surface roughness on coefficient of friction for CrO_2 particulate tapes (*Bhushan et al., 1984a*).

coefficient friction also strongly depends on the surface roughness and doubles for CrO_2 particulate tape for rms surface roughness below about 50 nm. Figure 7.16 shows an example of surface roughness dependence on the coefficient of friction for a thin-film rigid disk (Bhushan, 1990). Typical contact diameters for tapes and rigid disks were found to be about 6 μm and 1.5 μm, respectively.

Bhushan and Dugger (1990a) reported a significant increase in the contact diameter, number of contacts and total real area of contact of the thin-film rigid disk as a function of loading time, Fig. 7.17. Viscoelastic and viscoplastic deformations not only increase the size of existing asperities but also bring the two surfaces closer to allow the contact of additional asperities. To minimize the rate of increase in the real area of contact as a function of loading time, attempts should be made to select materials for disk coatings having low creep compliance, to reduce normal stress at the head-disk interface, and to use methods (such as load/unload mechanisms) to minimize or avoid the storage of the head in contact with the disk. In the case of magnetic tapes, creep compliance and hydrolytic degradation of the binder also

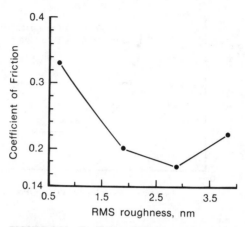

FIGURE 7.16 Coefficient of friction as a function of the degree of disk texturing for a thin-film (metal) rigid disk with sputtered carbon overcoat, against a ferrite slider.

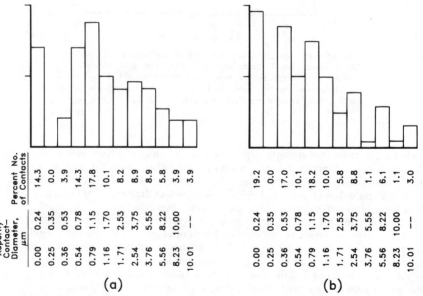

FIGURE 7.17 Log normal distribution of asperity contact diameters for a thin-film disk loaded by 500 mN (9.27 MPa) at two loading durations (*a*) initial and (*b*) after being loaded for 60 hours (*Bhushan and Dugger, 1990a*).

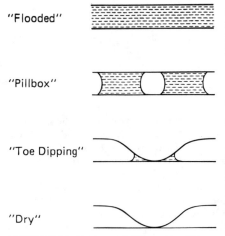

"Flooded"

"Pillbox"

"Toe Dipping"

"Dry"

FIGURE 7.18 Regimes of different liquid levels in the head-medium interface.

need to be optimized for sustained low friction after storage at high pressure (e.g., near end-of-tape on a reel) and high temperature/humidity (Bhushan, 1990).

7.3.2 Liquid-Mediated Adhesion (Stiction)

A smooth magnetic medium (especially a thin-film disk) tends to adhere or stick strongly to a smooth magnetic head. Liquid-mediated adhesion, commonly referred to as "stiction" in the computer industry, is especially pronounced when a partial film of liquid lubricants and/or adsorbed moisture is present at the interface. Liquid-mediated adhesion can be divided into two significant components: a meniscus term, which depends on the surface tension of the liquid, and a viscous term. The viscous term does not depend on surface tension and may be observed even when the surfaces are completely surrounded by the liquid. If the surfaces are submerged in the liquid they may be separated easily, provided the separation is carried out very slowly. However, if the rate of separation is rapid when the surfaces are pulled apart, liquid must flow into the space between them and the viscosity of the liquid will be the determining factor in stiction.

7.3.2.1 Stiction Modelling. To analyze a single-asperity contact, we consider a model of the contact region between smooth surfaces with different levels of "fill" of the interface depending upon the mean interplanar separation and the liquid levels, Fig. 7.18. In two extreme regimes, either a small quantity of liquid bridges the surfaces around the tip of a contacting asperity (the "toe-dipping" regime), or the liquid bridges the entire surface (the "flooded" regime); in a third intermediate "pillbox" regime, the liquid bridges a significant fraction of the apparent area. The different regimes can be modelled and the expression for F_M and F_V can be obtained (Matthewson and Mamin, 1988, Bhushan, 1990).

In the toe-dipping regime, the liquid adhesion force between a single asperity and a surface can be modelled by a sphere of composite radius of curvature in contact with a flat surface with a liquid bridge in between. The total meniscus and viscous forces of all wetted asperity contact can be calculated by multiplying the number of contacts by meniscus and viscous forces at a typical contact. The flooded regime can be modelled by a liquid bridge between two flat surfaces. The pillbox regime can be modelled by two flat surfaces. If we assume that surface asperity radii are constant and their heights follow a Gaussian distribution, the true coefficient of friction f_r can be obtained from the following expressions:

For the toe-dipping regime:

$$F \sim \frac{f_r W}{1 - 16.6\gamma_l(cos\theta_1 + cos\theta_2)/E'_c\sigma_p(\sigma_p/R_p)^{1/2}} \tag{7.4}$$

For the flooded regime:

$$F = f_r \left[W + \frac{A_a \gamma_l}{h} (cos\theta_1 + cos\theta_2) \right] + \frac{\eta_l A_a}{h} (L\alpha)^{1/2} e^{-1/2} \qquad (7.5a)$$

where

$$h/\sigma_p \sim 1.4 \left\{ log \left[0.57 \eta R_p \sigma_p E_c (\sigma_p/R_p)^{1/2}/p_a \right] \right\}^{0.65} \qquad (7.5b)$$

F is the friction force, γ_l and η_l are the surface tension and viscosity of the liquid, θ_1 and θ_2 are the contact angles of the liquid on the two surfaces, h is the average thickness of the liquid bridge, L is the distance surfaces need to slide to become unstuck, α is the start-up linear acceleration, and A_a is the apparent area.

In the toe-dipping regime, the adhesion force is independent of the apparent area and proportional to the normal load (ie., the number of asperity contacts). However, the flooded regime shows the opposite tendencies. The pillbox regime is intermediate and can exhibit either behavior at the extremes. In all three regimes, adhesion force decreases with an increase in σ_p and a decrease in R_p, and is independent of η.

For the first time, Gao and Bhushan (1995a) have developed a kinetic meniscus model to account for time and viscosity dependence of meniscus formation, which explains the experimental trends. Based on their model, the meniscus force between a spherical asperity of radius R_p in contact with a liquid film of thickness h at time t after contact is

$$f_M(t) = - 2\pi R_p \gamma_l (1 + Cos\theta) \left[1 - e \left(\frac{-C_0 h^3}{v_m \eta_l} t \right) \right]^{1/2} \qquad (7.6)$$

where η_l is the viscosity of the liquid, C_0 is a constant with the dimension of pressure, and v_m is the final meniscus volume. From Eq. (7.6) it is clear that the meniscus force increases with rest time and at a given rest time, the meniscus force is smaller for a more viscous liquid.

Analytical models for multi-asperity contacts in the presence of liquid film have been developed to quantify the effect of roughness and liquid film on stiction (Li and Talke, 1990; Tian and Matsudaira, 1993; Gao et al., 1995b). In these models, contact statistics are predicted using the Greenwood-Williamson model. Tian and Bhushan (1995b) developed a numerical meniscus model to predict the effect of multiple menisci of arbitrary geometry on stiction. This model adequately predicts the effect of liquid film and the relative humidity on the stiction.

Bhushan and Tian (1995j) carried out a contact analysis of regularly patterned rough surfaces to develop design criterion for size, shape and number of asperities for minimum real area of contact, plastic deformation, and meniscus contribution. To control the meniscus force, the number of asperities must be below a certain value. On the other hand, to prevent plastic deformation occurring at the interface, the number of asperities must be greater than a certain number. For a given radius of asperity, there is a range of asperity numbers within which neither plastic deformation nor severe stiction problem will occur. The optimum number of asperities is the situation where the contacting materials will be allowed to deform to their elastic limit within an upper limit on the meniscus force. Figure 7.19 shows an example of the number of asperities, relative meniscus force and contact area as a function of the radius of spherical asperities. The contact area starts to increase at smaller radii because the meniscus force exceeds the upper limit. In this example, the asperity radius for optimum number of asperities should range from about 1 μm

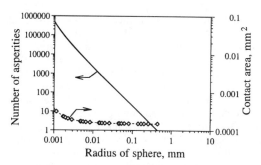

FIGURE 7.19 An optimum number of spherical asperities of constant height in the contact region, relative meniscus force and the contact area as a function of the radius of spherical asperities. Composite modulus of elasticity = 100 GPa, hardness of the softer material = 6 GPa (*Bhushan and Tian, 1995j*).

to 450 μm with a preference for the larger radius (for lower meniscus force). For the smallest radius of 1 μm and an asperity base radius of 200 nm, the optimum number of asperities is of the order of 3×10^5 over the nominal contact area of the slider which translates to about $1.8 \times 10^5/mm^2$ for a nominal contact area of 1.71 mm^2 or a pitch of about 2.4 μm or a percent occupation of 2.2 percent.

7.3.2.2 Experimental Observations. The relative humidity of the environment, the rest period, the ABS area, the surface roughness, the lubricant viscosity and its thickness and relative velocity all affect the liquid-mediated adhesion (Liu and Mee, 1983; Bradshaw and Bhushan, 1984; Bhushan, 1990; Bhushan and Dugger, 1990*b*; Li and Talke, 1990; Streator et al., 1991*a*, 1991*b*; Gitis and Sonnenfeld, 1993; Tian and Matsudaira, 1993; Gao and Bhushan, 1995*a*; Gerber et al., 1996). Miyoshi et al. (1988) found that the adhesive force (normal pull-off force) of a Ni-Zn ferrite pin in contact with a flat of Ni-Zn ferrite or of magnetic tape A, Fig. 7.20, remained low below 40% RH, but nearly doubled with increasing relative humidity, to 80%. Changes in the adhesion of contacts were reversible on humidifying and dehumidifying. The adhesive forces for a liquid bridge between a spherical surface with a radius

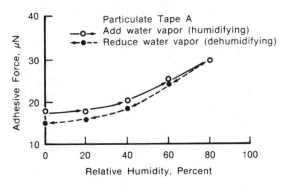

FIGURE 7.20 Effect of humidity on adhesion of CrO_2 tape A in contact with a Ni-Zn ferrite pin (*Miyoshi et al., 1988*).

the same as that of the pin and a flat surface, calculated using surface tension and contact angle values for water, compared well with measured values. They concluded that ferrites adhere to ferrites or tapes in a saturated atmosphere primarily from the meniscus effects of a thin-film of water adsorbed on the interface.

Bhushan and Dugger (1990b), Tian and Matsudaira (1993), Gitis and Sonnenfeld (1993) and Gerber et al. (1996) studied the effect of environment and operating conditions on static friction. Figure 7.21a shows the coefficient of static friction as a function of relative humidity. Static friction increases rapidly at high humidities and becomes higher for disks lubricated with thicker films. Figure 7.21b shows that the coefficient of static friction correlates well with the total thickness of liquid (liquid and adsorbed water) at the head-disk interface. Figure 9.21a shows that the coefficient of static friction increases with head rest time particularly for the smoother disk A. In Fig. 7.21a, note that the static friction of a lubricated disk increases more rapidly than that of an unlubricated disk. While the hydrophobic PFPE lubricant repels some of the water condensation, water can replace some PFPE at concentrated asperity contacts either during long exposures or if the lubricant is displaced by high pressures or by sliding of the two surfaces. Studies of penetration of lubricant layers by water (Baker et al., 1962) suggest that water may diffuse through the lubricant and condense into droplets around nuclei on the solid surfaces. Spreading of the water droplets will be controlled by the energy difference between water-disk and lubricant-disk interfaces. Water, with a surface tension on the order of 3 to 4 times that of typical magnetic medium lubricants, wets the magnetic-medium surface creating a meniscus at the asperity contacts.

Lubricant and surface roughness effects on static and kinetic coefficients of friction in thin-film disks have been studied by several authors (Yanagisawa, 1985a; Streator et al., 1991a; Gao and Bhushan, 1995a). Figure 7.22 systematically shows the lubricant and roughness effects for three glass disks and four perfluoropolyether lubricants. Variation in surface roughness was accomplished by controlling the grain size of a chromium underlayer (Kawai et al., 1992). Lubricants labeled L1, L2 and L3 are nonpolar liquid lubricants, while F is polar with dihydroxyl functional end groups. Carbon atoms form a branched structure in L3, while lubricants L1, L2 and F contain carbon atoms in linear arrangements. For all disks, coefficient of static friction starts to increase rapidly above a "critical" lubricant film thickness. The buildup of the friction at high film thicknesses is believed to be governed by microflow capabilities of the liquid on the disk. Gao and Bhushan (1995a) noted that the critical film thickness is approximately proportional to disk RMS roughness. As expected, a less viscous lubricant (say, L1) gives a smaller critical film thickness because it is relatively easier for the lubricant to migrate to form menisci. Polar lubricants appear to have no beneficial effect compared with a nonpolar lubricant. In this study, no attempts were made to bond these lubricants. The increase in friction with increasing lubricant film thickness above the critical thickness can be attributed to strong adhesive forces in the interface (Bhushan, 1990). Comparing the data for four disks, we also note that for a given lubricant thickness above the critical film thickness, the coefficient of static friction progressively decreases as the disk roughness increases. Trends observed for the kinetic friction data are similar to that for static friction data.

The critical thickness increases with disk surface roughness, with a larger mean separation of the surface involving a thicker lubricant film when the menisci are formed. The trend toward higher friction for smoother disks with above critical-film thickness is only applicable to short contact times on the order of seconds or minutes. With longer rest times (hours or days), adhesion usually reaches much higher values even if the lubricant thickness is well below the critical value. This

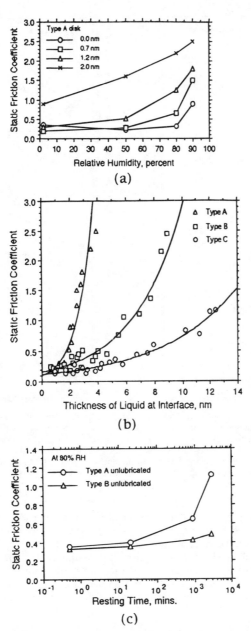

FIGURE 7.21 Coefficient of static friction as a function of (a) relative humidity, (b) thickness of liquid at interface, and (c) rest time. Rms roughnesses of tapes A, B and C were 0.84, 7.76 and 15.37 nm, respectively (*Tian and Matsudaira, 1993*).

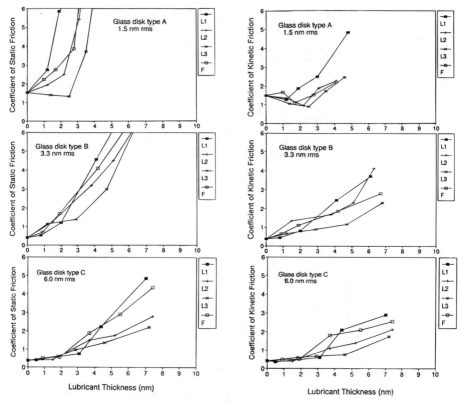

FIGURE 7.22   Coefficients of static and kinetic friction for three thin-film disks with carbon overcoat and different roughnesses sliding against Al_2O_3-TiC slider, as a function of lubricant film thickness for four lubricants. Lubricant L1-Z03 (viscosity = 30 cSt, molecular weight = 3600, density = 1.82 g/cc), lubricant L2-Z15 (viscosity = 150 cSt, molecular weight = 9100, density = 1.85 g/cc), lubricant L3 = YR (viscosity = 1600 cSt, molecular weight = 6800, density = 1.91 g/cc), and lubricant F-Z-Dol (viscosity = 80 cSt, molecular weight = 2000, density = 1.81 g/cc) (*Gao and Bhushan, 1995a*).

time effect can be explained by the slow diffusion of the lubricant molecules toward contact points driven by the Laplace pressure and the deformation of interacting asperities to increase the real area of contact.

Gao and Bhushan (1995a) also reported that the coefficient of static friction increases with start-up acceleration and the rate of increase is faster for thicker lubricants. The coefficient of kinetic friction decreases with sliding speed and the rate of decrease is faster for thicker lubricants. This is attributed to viscous effects.

7.4   INTERFACE TEMPERATURES

During sliding, almost all frictional energy is converted to heat in the material close to the interface and asperity interactions produce numerous high temperature flashes. To predict head-medium interface temperature, the contact can be modelled as a series of spherically-topped asperities (Bhushan, 1987*b*; 1992*b*). The interaction problem at an asperity contact reduces to a sphere against another sphere, assuming the distance to the center of the two spheres is fixed. When one sphere comes in contact with the other, the real area of contact starts to grow; when one sphere is directly above the other, the area is at maximum; as one sphere moves away, that area starts to get smaller. The real area of contact is a source of frictional heat and the heat intensity is proportional to the real area. The total flash temperature consists of temperature rise of an individual asperity contact supplemented by the related influence of other nearby asperity contacts (Cook and Bhushan, 1973).

Relevant equations for the average and maximum asperity temperature rise of the interface are given by (Bhushan, 1987*a*)

$$\bar{\theta} = r_1[0.65\,fp_a(A_d/A_r)(Vd_{max}/\kappa_1)^{1/2}/\,\rho_1 C_{p1} + fp_a(Vl/\kappa_1)^{1/2\,/}\rho_1 C_{p1}] \tag{7.7}$$

$$\theta_{max} = r_1[0.95\,fp_a(A_d/A_r)\,(Vd_{max}/\kappa_1)^{1/2}/\,\rho_1 Cp_1 + 1.5\,fp_a(Vl/\kappa_1)^{1/2}/\,\rho_1 Cp_1] \tag{7.7b}$$

and

$$r_1 \sim 1/[1 + (k_2\rho_2 Cp_2/k_1\rho_1 Cp_1)^{1/2}] \tag{7.7c}$$

where f is the coefficient of friction, p_a is the apparent pressure, ρC_p is the volumetric heat capacity, κ is the thermal diffusivity, k is the thermal conductivity, d_{max} is the maximum contact diameter, and l is the half length of the slider.

The average and maximum transient temperatures predicted for a typical particulate tape-head interface are 7° and 10°C, respectively (Bhushan, 1987*b*). These predictions compared reasonably well with infrared measurements (Gulino et al., 1986). Asperity contact temperatures at a head-tape interface are relatively low because of its high area of contact, compared with that of metal-metal or ceramic-ceramic contacts. The transient temperature rise of 7–10°C rise can lead to high friction in some tapes because the transition of some tape mechanical properties occurs within 5°C above ambient temperature. In isolated cases of high-speed contact of magnetic particles with the head surface, the average and maximum transient temperature rise could be about 600°C and 900°C, respectively. These temperatures would cause breakdown of the medium lubricant and degradation of the medium binder to give excessive friction and even seizure.

The average and maximum transient temperatures predicted for a typical particulate rigid-disk-slider interface are 34 and 44°C, respectively (Bhushan, 1992*b*). If exposed magnetic or alumina particles contact the slider surface, the transient rise could be more than 1000°C. The predicted average and maximum transient temperature rises for a typical thin-film disk-slider interface are 56° and 81°C, respectively, for an Al_2O_3-TiC slider, and 77 and 110°C for a Mn-Zn ferrite slider; these match reasonably well with the infrared measurements by Bair et al. (1991) and Suzuki and Kennedy (1991). The size of an asperity contact is on the order of 1.5 μm. Since the duration of an asperity contact at full operating speed is less than 1 ms, the thermal gradients perpendicular to the sliding surfaces are very large (a temperature drop of 90% in a depth typically less than a micron).

Bhushan et al. (1994*b*) used thermal analysis to predict the temperature rise at the tape edge-guide interface. They reported even at tape speeds as high as 8 m/s, the temperature rise at the tape edge-guide interface with guides made of metallic or ceramic materials is only a few degrees centigrade. They noted, however, that at high tape speeds, edge-guiding surfaces get coated with a hard-to-remove polymeric layer of about 1 μm in thickness. Thus, it becomes the case of PET polymer sliding against itself. The temperature rise in these situations can be on the order of a few hundred degrees centigrade. In fact, these authors have reported the melting of the tape edge against alumina guides because of polymeric coating on the guiding surfaces at tape speeds of 8 m/s.

7.5 WEAR

7.5.1 Head-Tape Interface

Studies to understand the failure mechanisms at the head-tape interface have been conducted by several authors (e.g., Potgiesser and Koorneef, 1974; Hahn, 1984b; Bhushan, 1985b, 1990; Bhushan et al., 1986a; Calabrese et al., 1989). Bhushan and Lowry (1994f, 1995g) ran various particulate (Co-γFe$_2$O$_3$, CrO$_2$, metal particle or MP and barium ferrite or BaFe$_{12}$O$_{19}$) and metal evaporated (ME) tapes in an accelerated wear test against Mn-Zn ferrite simulated heads. The head wear rates for various tapes are summarized in Fig. 7.23 and the optical micrographs of the worn head surfaces are shown in Fig. 7.24. Note that the head wear rate decreases with an increase in the sliding distance because of the blunting of tape asperities. The head wear rate with the CrO$_2$ tapes is highest, followed by Co-γFe$_2$O$_3$ and MP/ BaFe$_{12}$O$_{19}$ tapes, with nearly zero wear rate with the ME tape. Because the magnetic layer of the CrO$_2$ tape had no head-cleaning agents, abrasive wear of the ferrite head surface was dominated by the hard magnetic particles (Bhushan, 1985b). This tape wore a coarse polish into the head surface, Fig. 7.24. Co-γFe$_2$O$_3$ particles are known to be less abrasive than CrO$_2$ particles (Bhushan and Martin, 1988a). Because of the higher ductility of the metal particles and the relatively small size of the BaFe$_{12}$O$_{19}$ particles, abrasive wear of the ferrite surface was probably dominated by the head-cleaning agents for these tapes. The MP and BaFe$_{12}$O$_{19}$ tapes wore a smooth polish onto the ferrite head surface at lower wear rates relative to the Co-γFe$_2$O$_3$ and CrO$_2$ tapes, Fig. 7.24. The ME tapes showed some wear, however, and some transfer debris could be observed on the head surface, Fig. 7.24. The debris was a combination of an agglomeration of small ferrite wear particles and lubricant transfer.

   The first signs of ferrite-head wear with a particulate tape are very fine scratches as small as 25 nm on the head surface. The ferrite surface is microscopically removed in a brittle manner as strips or islands, depending on the tape smoothness.

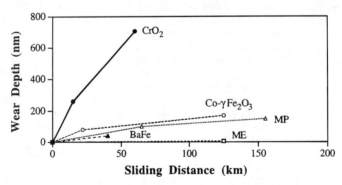

FIGURE 7.23   Wear of a Mn-Zn ferrite head as a function of sliding distance for various magnetic tapes (*Bhushan and Lowry, 1995g*).

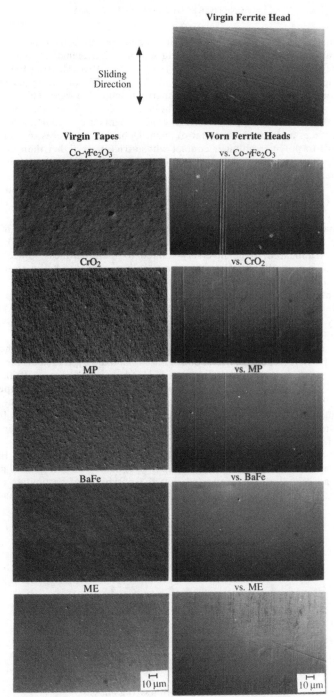

FIGURE 7.24 Optical micrographs of a worn Mn-Zn ferrite head after sliding against various tapes (*Bhushan and Lowry, 1994f*).

The worn ferrite-head surface is work hardened (resulting from plastic deformation) with a large compressive stress field which is detrimental to magnetic signal amplitude (Chandrasekar et al., 1987a, 1987b, 1988, 1990). During the contact of particulate tape with the head in contact start/stops (CSS) or during partial contact in streaming, tape debris is generated primarily by adhesive wear. The debris can be either loose or adherent (Bhushan and Phelan, 1986b). Tape debris, loose magnetic particles, worn head material or foreign contaminants are introduced between the sliding surfaces and abrade material of each. Debris that adheres to drive components leads to polymer-polymer contact whose friction is higher than that of rigid material-polymer contact and can lead to magnetic errors and sometimes catastrophic failures (Bhushan, 1990). With ME tapes, the wear mode is primarily adhesive. Debris is initially generated from the ME film and the topical lubricant acts as a cementing agent which holds the debris on the head surface. The debris then sometimes results in a three-body abrasion.

Bhushan and Lowry (1995g) ran various head materials against the most abrasive tape sample, CrO_2, for evaluation of their wear characteristics (Fig. 7.25). Wear rates appeared to be inversely related to their hardness. Since the wear mechanism is primarily abrasive, the wear rate is expected to be inversely proportional to the head material hardness (Bhushan, 1990). Bhushan and Monahan (1995i) conducted accelerated tests of various magnetic tapes ran against various tape path materials—acetal plastic, aluminum, 303 stainless steel, and Mn-Zn ferrite. They reported that the friction and wear characteristics of the Mn-Zn ferrite appeared to be superior to those of the other mating materials.

Head wear also depends on the grain size of the head material, the kind of magnetic particles, the tape surface roughness, isolated asperities on the tape surface, tape tension and tape sliding speed. Head wear increases with the surface roughness of tapes and the existence of isolated asperities on the tape surface (Hahn, 1984a; Bhushan, 1990). Wear rate also increases above about 40–60% relative humidity, Fig. 7.26 (Kelly, 1982). This increase is believed to be due to moisture-assisted fracture (or static fatigue) of the grains to yield finer particles (Bhushan, 1990).

Patton and Bhushan (1995a, b) studied the failure mechanisms of MP, $BaFe_{12}O_{19}$ and ME tapes in contact with metal-in-gap (MIG) heads in a still (pause) mode of a rotary head recorder. They reported that the durability of particulate tapes was superior to that of ME tape, Fig. 7.27. They reported that the cleaner head-to-tape

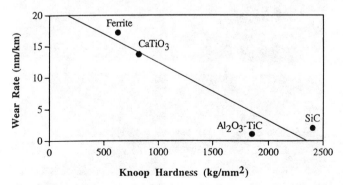

FIGURE 7.25 Wear rates of various head materials sliding against CrO_2 tape as a function of material hardness (*Bhushan and Lowry, 1995f*).

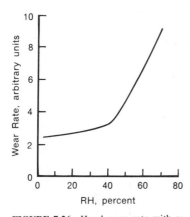

FIGURE 7.26 Head wear rate with γ-Fe_2O_3 tape as a function of relative humidity (*Kelly, 1982*).

contact interface for the particulate tapes appeared to be responsible for the better durability of particulate tapes, as compared to that of ME tapes. The major difference between the particulate and ME tapes was that signal dropouts concurrent with increases in friction, which resulted from debris accumulation on the video head, preceded catastrophic failure in the case of ME tapes. They further investigated the running-in process. They found that the durability of a tape and the initial head output increased as the head ran-in with the tape. They attributed this observation to the tape forming a favorable contour on the head rubbing surface. Patton and Bhushan (1995*b*) studied the effect of interchanging tapes and head contour on the durability of particulate and ME tapes. They reported that interchanging ME and particulate tapes caused excessive head and tape wear while a tape formed its preferred head shape in these experiments. The fundamental cause of this phenomenon was that the tapes formed different head shapes during tape recorder operation.

Tsuchiya and Bhushan (1994) studied the effect of environment on the durability of various tapes. They conducted tests at humidities ranging from 15 to 70% RH and temperatures ranging from 4 to 35°C. They reported that the durabilities of MP and $BaFe_{12}O_{19}$ tapes were insensitive to the environment, whereas ME tapes exhibited signal degradation at 15% RH. The better longevity of ME tapes at higher humidities is believed to be because of the presence of water between mating surfaces which acts as an additional lubricant.

Thin, adherent head deposits called "stains" are encountered intermittently when used with particulate tapes (Lemke, 1972; Ota et al., 1991; Stahle and Lee, 1992; Bhushan and Hahn, 1995*c*; Gupta et al., 1995*c*; Tsuchiya and Bhushan, 1995). These deposits are not the same as common, readily removable tape debris. Stains are sometimes transparent but usually have an intrinsic blue or brown coloring. Coverage of the head surface varies from spotty to continuous with thicknesses ranging from 10 to 30 nm. Stains are generally insoluble in most common solvents and require abrasive cleaning tapes for removal. These stains can be organic or metallo-organic friction polymers; however, most stains consist of both organic and iron and oxygen (inorganic) constituents. The additional head to tape separation caused by staining is undesirable.

In the case of thin-film heads, pole tip/gap recession and damage to the MR stripe is a major concern. This subject will be addressed later in the section on Head-(Thin-Film) Rigid Disk Interface.

7.5.2 Head-(Particulate) Rigid Disk Interface

During asperity contacts, disk debris can be generated by adhesive, abrasive and impact wear. Wear debris generated during disk manufacture (burnishing or buffing) and foreign contaminants can result in three-body abrasive wear and in perfor-

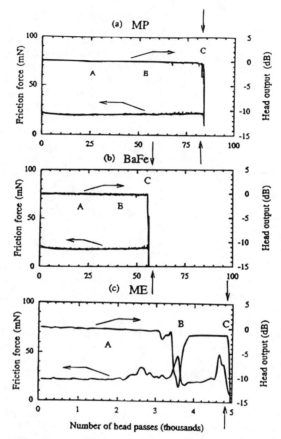

FIGURE 7.27 Friction force and head output during still mode testing at the beginning of the run-in process of virgin heads for ME, MP, and BaFe$_{12}$O$_{14}$ magnetic tapes [note different horizontal scale in (*a*)]. The X's indicate tape failure (*Patton and Bhushan, 1995b*).

mance degradation of the slider air bearing. Flash temperatures generated at asperity contacts can render boundary lubricants ineffective and degrade the disk binder to cause high friction and high disk wear. Any of these mechanisms can lead to a head crash. Humidity and temperature also significantly affect head-disk friction and wear or debris generation (Bhushan, 1990).

Disk and head surfaces after a head crash in a CSS test show microscopic circumferential wear grooves in either two-body or three-body abrasive wear (Bhushan, 1990). Karis et al. (1990) and Novotny et al. (1991, 1992) reported that the removal of lubricant from portions of the start-stop track, and the degradation of lubricant preceded the final disk failure. Lubrication of the disks increased the disk wear life up to 1000 times the number of cycles until the coating began to wear through. Cycles until frictional failure was proportional to the areal density of the lubricant. Scarati and Caporiccio (1987) found that the relative wear life of particulate disks increases with an increase in the lubricant thickness, and that polar PFPE lubricants give a longer wear life than nonpolar lubricants.

7.5.3　Head-(Thin-Film) Rigid Disk Interface

Magnetic films used for disks are soft and have poorer wear resistance than particulate disks loaded with hard magnetic particles and load-bearing alumina particles. The smoother surfaces and lower flying height of thin-film disks also result in higher friction and an increased potential of head-to-disk interactions. During normal drive operation, the isolated contacts of asperities on the head slider and disk surfaces result in adhesive and impact wear and generate debris. In addition, any asperity contacts introduce maximum shear stress at the disk subsurface, which may initiate a crack. Repeated contacts would result in crack propagation (subsurface fatigue) leading to delamination of the overcoat and magnetic layer. Isolated contacts in a clean environment generate very fine wear debris which results in rather uniform disk wear from light burnishing. This wear eventually results in high friction and head crashes (Bhushan, 1990).

External contamination readily abrades the overcoat and results in localized damage of the disk surface by three-body abrasion. Wear debris invades the spacing between the head slider and the disk and/or transfers to the head slider making it unstable. This leads to additional debris and head crashes both in the start/stop and flyability modes. With alumina contaminant particles, Koka and Kumaran (1991) observed build up in the leading-edge taper of the slider, which degraded the flyability of the slider and caused abrasive wear on the disk.

Calabrese and Bhushan (1990) conducted in-situ experiments of various head/thin-film disk (95-mm dia.) combinations in the scanning-electron microscope (see also Hedenqvist et al., 1992) to identify the initiation of particle removal. After sliding Al_2O_3-TiC at 500 mm/min. for a few minutes on a thin-film disk with a zirconia overcoat and perfluoropolyether topical lubricant (disk B_2), microscopic particles were removed from the rail edges of the head and deposited on the disk. A little disk debris was also deposited on the rail edges. After 20 minutes there was some damage to the slider edges and disk surface was very lightly burnished with only one scratch. Minute disk debris was found on the rail edges and rail surfaces including the leading taper of the head slider. Continued sliding led to increased surface change of the disk, followed by catastrophic failure. The most significant parameter that influences the initiation of particle removal is the condition of the rail edges which contact the disk. During the start of motion, the head moves with the disk until the spring suspension overcomes adhesion between the head and disk. The head then springs back in an unstable manner, causing the rail edges to contact the disk which results in transfer of material from the disk or chipping of the rail edge. Calabrese and Bhushan reported head slider and disk wear is strongly dependent on the slider and the disk overcoat materials. A zirconia overcoat generally exhibited less wear than the carbon overcoat. The Mn-Zn ferrite slider was less aggressive to the disk than the Al_2O_3-TiC slider. The calcium titanate slider cracked early on in a sliding test; hot processing of this material appears to be a problem.

Engel and Bhushan (1990) developed a head-disk interface failure model for thin-film disks based on the topography of the wearing surfaces. The principal variables include sliding speed, surface topography, mechanical properties, coefficient of friction and wear rate. Surface asperities and debris particles induce impact

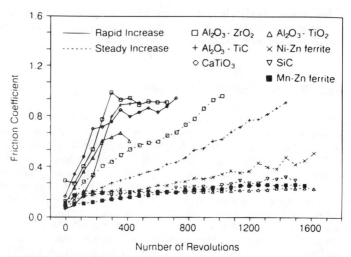

FIGURE 7.28 Coefficient of friction as a function of the number of revolutions for sliders of various materials on unlubricated disks. Solid lines represent sliders with a rapid increase in wear and dotted lines represent sliders with a slow increase in wear (*Chu et al., 1992*).

and sliding encounters, which represent a damage rate. Failure occurs when a specific damage rate, a characteristic for the system, is reached.

7.5.3.1 Role of Slider and Overcoat Materials.

Chandrasekar and Bhushan (1991), Chu et al. (1992) and Koka (1994) studied the effect of slider material on the durability of the head-disk interface. Figure 7.28 shows the representative profiles of the coefficient of friction as a function of the number of passes for an unlubricated thin-film disk with a carbon overcoat sliding against various slider materials (Chu et al., 1992). The slider materials that exhibited a slow and steady increase in friction include Mn-Zn ferrite, Ni-Zn ferrite and SiC. The slider materials that exhibited a slow as well as rapid increase in friction include Al_2O_3-ZrO_2, Al_2O_3-TiC, and Al_2O_3-TiO_2; $CaTiO_3$ exhibited a rapid increase in friction. It appears that single-phase slider materials are more consistent in wear behavior than multi-phase slider materials; all multi-phase materials showed both slow and rapid increases in friction. In general, the single-phase slider materials showed lower wear than multi-phase materials with an exception of $CaTiO_3$. The poor behavior of $CaTiO_3$ may be attributed to poor processing conditions of the material. In-situ SEM studies showed that $CaTiO_3$ disintegrated easily during sliding (Calabrese and Bhushan, 1990). The differences in the wear behavior of materials are attributed to microstructural flaws present in the multi-phase system. In addition, differences in thermal and mechanical properties between the two phases may lead to cracking during processing and machining.

Chandrasekar and Bhushan (1991) conducted tests on various slider materials in contact with lubricated thin-film disks with a carbon overcoat. Among the ceramics tested, single-crystal diamond had the lowest coefficient of friction ($\sim$0.12) followed by partially-stabilized zirconia ($\sim$0.15); the remaining ceramics -Mn-Zn ferrite, Al_2O_3-iC and $CaTiO_3$ all had an initial coefficient of friction of about 0.2.

Although the coefficient of friction increased with the number of passes, this increase was small for single-crystal diamond even after 5500 passes. The rate of increase in the coefficient of friction was highest for calcium titanate and Al_2O_3-TiC sliders; Mn-Zn ferrite and ZrO_2-Y_2O_3 sliders exhibited a smaller increase. Calcium titanate (1200 kg/mm^2) showed poor durability because it cracks readily. Al_2O_3-TiC is hardest (2300 kg/mm^2) and burnished the disk more than Mn-Zn ferrite (600 kg/mm^2) and ZrO_2-Y_2O_3 (1300 kg/mm^2). The air-bearing surface of the Mn-Zn ferrite slider was scratched which suggests that Mn-Zn ferrite is slightly softer than the disk and is gentle to the disk surface. Matching the ceramic slider and disk hardnesses is essential for low wear.

Chu et al. (1992) studied the effect of slider curvature on the interface durability. They reported that sliders with a positive crown were superior in performance to those with a negative crown. The sharp edges in the negative crown sliders scrape and damage the disk surface.

There is an interest in horizontal, thin-film head designs in which the plane of the read/write magnetic films is parallel to the ABS (Bhushan et al., 1992a). Horizontal head-sliders can be mass produced inexpensively by using integrated circuit (IC) technology and labor intensive slicing and precision lapping of the rows can be eliminated. There is a concern of head wear in horizontal heads that can be minimized by the use of wear resistant films. Bhushan et al. (1992a, 1993) have shown that the horizontal slider with about a 3-μm thick PECVD SiO_2 coating, performs as well as or better than a conventional thin-film head with an ABS made of Al_2O_3-TiC material. Since SiO_2 is transparent, it prevents the use of commonly used optical interference techniques for flying height measurements and thus is undesirable. More recently a 0.5-μm thick sputtered DLC coating has been successfully used.

The structure and properties of the overcoat play an important role in its durability. Increase in the overcoat hardness of baked SiO_2 has been reported to improve the wear resistance of thin-film disks (Yanagisawa, 1985b). Khan et al. (1988) reported that hard-carbon overcoats with better wear performance consist of homogeneous grain size, uniform grain distribution and higher percentage of sp^3 bonded carbon atoms (diamond structure). Bhushan and Gupta (1994a) reported that ion implantation improved the wear resistance of hard carbon. Cho et al. (1990) and Bhushan et al. (1992b) have shown that the deposition conditions of carbon need to be optimized to produce the best mechanical and tribological properties. Ceramic overcoats with low porosity and high electrical resistivity offer better electrochemical corrosion resistance (Bhushan, 1990).

In the case of thin-film heads, pole tip/gap recession (relative wear of the pole tip and gap materials with respect to the ABS) in inductive heads and scratching/smearing, electrical shorting electrostatic change build up, and corrosion of the MR stripe in MR heads are important problems. In composite inductive heads with nonmagnetic cores, the pole tips are wider, and gap recession becomes even a bigger problem. Wear of the head structure can be minimized by the application of a wear-resistant coating over the entire ABS including the head structure. Most MR heads with Al_2O_3-TiC substrates are coated with amorphous hydrogenated-carbon coatings deposited by dc or rf magnetron sputtering with a thickness ranging from 5 to 15 nm (Chang et al., 1992; Grill et al., 1992), together with an adhesion layer of about 5-nm thick amorphous sputtered silicon. The mechanical and tribological performance of hard coatings is dependent upon the deposition process (Bhushan and Gupta, 1991b). It has been reported that carbon coatings deposited by cathodic arc and direct ion beam deposition processes are superior to commonly used sputtered coatings (Gupta and Bhushan 1995a, 1995b).

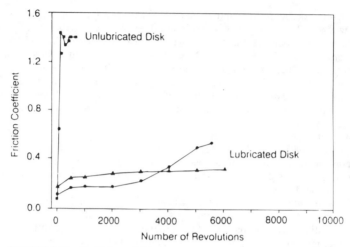

FIGURE 7.29 Coefficient of friction as a function of the number of revolutions for an Al_2O_3-TiC slider on unlubricated and lubricated disks (*Chu et al., 1992*).

7.5.3.2 Role of Lubricant Film. A lubricant film on the disk surface is essential for acceptable disk life. Figure 7.29 shows the friction behavior of an Al_2O_3-TiC slider on unlubricated and lubricated disk surfaces (Chu et al., 1992). It is observed that the coefficient of friction increases much more rapidly for the unlubricated disk than for the lubricated disk.

The effects of lubricant viscosity, thickness and functionality, and of disk surface roughness on the durability were studied by Miyamoto et al. (1988), Streator et al. (1991*b*) and Gao and Bhushan (1995*a*). Figure 7.30 shows the friction histories of unlubricated and lubricated disks with disk failure defined by a relatively sharp rise

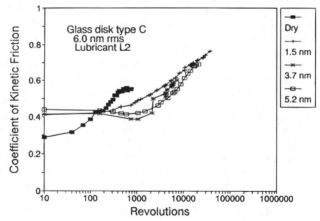

FIGURE 7.30 Friction histories during durability tests for unlubricated and lubricated thin-film disks with carbon overcoats sliding against an Al_2O_3-TiC slider (*Gao and Bhushan, 1995a*).

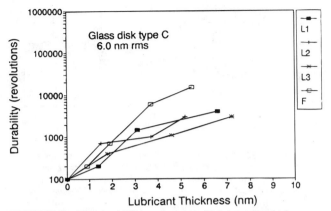

FIGURE 7.31   Disk durability as a function of lubricant film thickness on glass disk type C (roughness = 6 nm rms) for four lubricants. Data point at 0 nm is the durability for dry sliding (*Gao and Bhushan, 1995a*).

in the friction. The effect of the lubricant film thickness on durability for a glass disk (Type C) with four lubricants is shown in Fig. 7.31. We note that durability increases more or less logarithmically with lubricant film thickness. Presence of the lubricant improved the disk durability over that of dry sliding in all cases. The polar lubricant produced significantly higher durability than the nonpolar lubricant with comparable viscosity. A trend toward greater durability with the less viscous lubricants can be attributed to their greater mobility on the disk surface. The effect of surface roughness on disk durability is summarized in Fig. 7.32 for three glass disks with four lubricants. The disk durability increases with a decrease in the surface roughness. Note that the disk durability is greater for a less viscous lubricant.

Hoshino et al (1988) studied the effect of 40-days storage time on static friction for disks with a nonpolar PFPE lubricant film and disks with a dual lubricant consisting of polar (aminosilane) and nonpolar (PFPE) fractions. The increase in

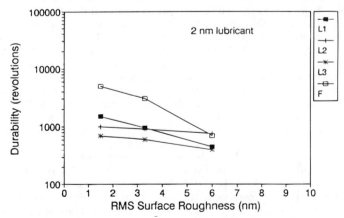

FIGURE 7.32   Disk durabilities for three glass disks as a function of surface roughness for four lubricants (*Gao and Bhushan, 1995a*).

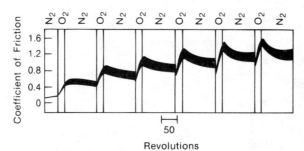

FIGURE 7.33 Coefficient of friction as a function of the number of revolutions during sliding of a Mn-Zn ferrite slider against an unlubricated thin-film disk at a normal load of 100 mN and a sliding speed of 60 mm/s in various dry gases (*Marchon et al., 1990*).

friction from aging disks with the dual-lubricant film was found to be less than that for a disk with only nonpolar lubricant. Lubricant is also spun off with disk rotation during use. Yanagisawa (1985*a*) and others have shown that polar lubricants spin off less than nonpolar lubricants with disk notation (Bhushan, 1990). The dual-layer concept with an unbonded layer over a bonded layer is very useful because the unbonded (mobile) top layer would heal any worn areas on the disk surface where lubricant may have been removed, and the bonded layer provides lubricant persistence.

7.5.3.3   Role of Environment.   Marchon et al. (1990) and Strom et al (1991) studied the wear behavior of an unlubricated thin-film disk with a DLC overcoat sliding against ceramic sliders in various environments. In sliding experiments with Mn-Zn ferrite or calcium titanate sliders, they reported that there is a gradual increase in the coefficient of friction with repeated sliding contacts performed in air; however, in pure nitrogen, no friction increase is observed, the coefficient of friction remaining constant at 0.2. The alternate introduction of oxygen and nitrogen elegantly showed the role of these gases, Fig. 7.33. Contact start/stop tests exhibited the same effect. Marchon et al. suggested that the wear process in the oxygen environment involved oxygen chemisorption on the DLC surface and a gradual loss of DLC through the formation of CO/CO_2 due to the action of the slider.

Bhushan and Ruan (1994*h*) and Bhushan et al. (1995*k*) studied the effect of environment on lubricated disks made with Ni-P coated Al-Mg, glass and glass-ceramic substrates. The Al-Mg and glass-ceramic disks had DLC overcoats, whereas the glass disks had a sputtered SiO_2 overcoat. Data on the wear lives of various disks in different environments are summarized in Fig. 7.34. For disks with DLC overcoats, wear lives are the shortest in an ultra-high vacuum (UHV) and the longest in inert atmospheres of nitrogen and argon. The wear lives of DLC-coated disks are in the following order (from best to worst): argon or nitrogen, Ar + H_2O, ambient, Ar + O_2, vacuum. These data show that oxygen and water in an operating environment worsen wear performance of the disks, but no gaseous environment (vacuum) is the worst of all. In UHV, intimate contact between disk and slider surfaces results in significant wear. In ambient air, Ar + O_2, and Ar + H_2O, tribochemical oxidation of the DLC overcoat was responsible for shorter durability. Figure 7.35 shows optical micrographs of the wear tracks of the Al-Mg disks with carbon overcoat after completion of the tests (left, unlubricated; right, lubricated).

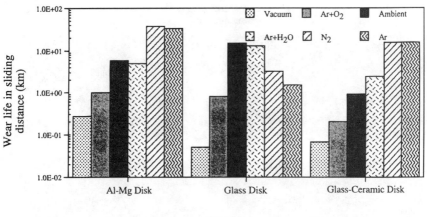

Disk Type

FIGURE 7.34 Comparison of wear lives for three types of lubricated disks in various environments (*Bhushan et al., 1995k*).

Note that the wear tracks are extremely mild for dry nitrogen and dry argon environments and the major features of these tracks are minor scratch marks. These scratch marks are probably due to the presence of debris at the interface. In argon with oxygen, and in ambient air, the wear tracks also have scratch marks, and the track is a "white" band. The wear tracks generated in vacuum are marked by severe ploughing damage to the disk surfaces. Damage to the unlubricated disks, in general, is more than that to the lubricated disks.

For the glass disks with a SiO_2 overcoat, life in vacuum was the shortest. The life of the glass disk was highest in humid atmospheres (ambient and Ar + H_2O) followed by N_2, Ar, and Ar + O_2. Humidity plays a beneficial role in the durability of SiO_2 overcoats. The environment has been known to affect friction and the wear of oxide and non-oxide ceramics (Fischer, 1988). Tribochemical reaction of oxide and non-oxide ceramics, with water present as liquid or vapor in a humid environment, form amorphous hydrated surface layers [$Si(OH)_4$] which in many interfaces reduce friction and prolong wear life at high humidities. Tribochemical reaction of a SiO_2 overcoat with the ambient humidity is believed to be responsible for longer life in an ambient and humid environment compared with a non-humid environment.

Pan and Prime (1993) reported that outgassing products in a drive affect lubricant degradation. They reported that during the sliding of a silicone seal, siloxanes start to desorb due to tribochemical degradation. The outgassing products degrade the lubricant on the disk surface and result in higher stiction/friction and shorter interface durability.

7.5.3.4 Precursors to Failure.   Strom et al. (1993), Pan and Novotny (1994), and Novotny et al. (1994) studied the wear mechanisms of sliders made of different materials sliding against unlubricated and lubricated thin-film disks with hydrogenated diamond-like carbon. In a study reported by Pan and Novotny (1994) the disks were lubricated with Fomblin Z-Dol with a thickness of 10 nm. Sliding tests were conducted in vacuum and degradation products were monitored in-situ by mass spectrometry. Quadrupole mass spectra of gaseous species generated at the

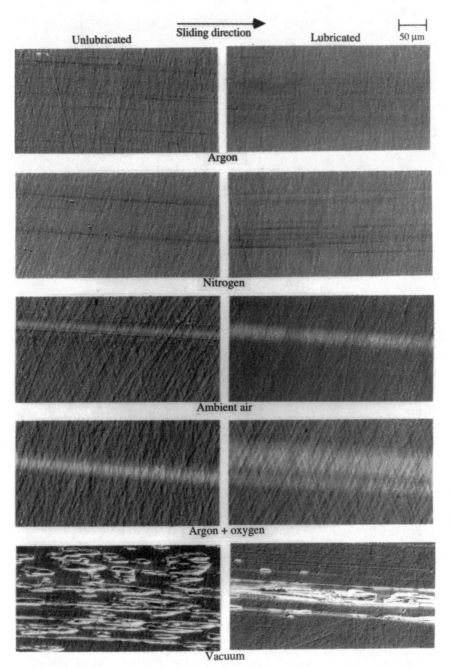

FIGURE 7.35 Optical micrographs of Al-Mg disks with DLC overcoat and with and without a lubricant film, after sliding against Al_2O_3-TiC sliders in various environments after onset of the disk failure (*Bhushan and Ruan, 1994h*).

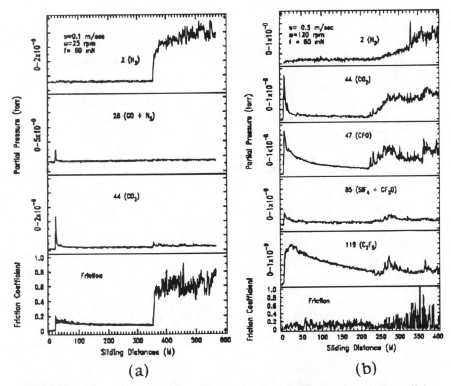

(a)   (b)

FIGURE 7.36 Mass spectra of gaseous species generated at the sliding interface and the coefficient of friction as a function of sliding distance taken during a sliding test of an Al_2O_3-TiC slider on (a) unlubricated and (b) lubricated thin-film disks with carbon overcoats in a vacuum environment (*Pan and Novotny, 1994*).

sliding interface between an Al_2O_3-TiC slider and the unlubricated carbon over-coated disk are shown in Fig. 7.36a. In addition, the coefficient of friction as a function of sliding distance is also presented. Transient evolution of C, Co + N_2 and CO_2 is observed at the beginning of the sliding experiment. Later, the coefficient of friction increases suddenly to between 0.5 and 1.0 with an accompanied rise of hydrogen evolution to a high level. Generally, at this stage, a wear track was also observed. The desorption of hydrogen from the carbon overcoat is used as a wear indicator of carbon. Mass spectra of gaseous species generated at the sliding inter-face of an Al_2O_3-TiC slider against a lubricated carbon-overcoated disk are shown in Fig. 7.36b. All of the lubricant signals and the CO_2 signal go through maxima at the beginning of sliding, then decay with sliding distance until a sudden increase occurs, accompanied by large variations of friction. Subsequently, the evolution of H_2 is detectable and, after some distance, an optically detectable wear track is observed.

Based on this study, Pan and Novotny concluded that degradation mechanisms are dominated by the removal of surface groups and adsorbates from solid surfaces and by tribochemical scission, losses and alteration of perfluoropolyether lubricant.

7.6 LUBRICATION

Mechanical interaction between the head and the medium is minimized by the lubrication of the magnetic medium. The primary function of the lubricant is to reduce the wear of the magnetic medium and to ensure that friction remains low throughout the operation of the drive. The main challenge, though, in selecting the best candidate for a specific surface is to find a material that provides acceptable wear protection for the entire life of the product, which can be several years. There are many requirements that a lubricant must satisfy in order to guarantee an acceptable life performance. An optimum lubricant thickness is one of these requirements. If the lubricant film is too thick, excessive stiction and mechanical failure of the head/disk is observed. On the other hand, if the film is too thin, protection of the interface is compromised and high friction and excessive wear will result in catastrophic failure. An acceptable lubricant must exhibit properties such as chemical inertness, low volatility, high thermal, oxidative and hydrolytic stability, shear stability, and good affinity to the magnetic medium surface.

Fatty acid esters are excellent boundary lubricants, and the esters such as tridecyl stearate, butyl stearate, butyl palmitate, butyl myristate, stearic acid, and myrstic acid, are commonly used as internal lubricants, at roughly 1 to 7% by weight of the magnetic coating, in tapes and flexible disks. The fatty acids involved include those with acid groups with an even number between C_{12} and C_{22} with alcohols ranging from C_3 to C_{13}. These acids are all solids with melting points above the normal surface operating temperature of the magnetic media. This suggests that the decomposition products of the ester via lubrication chemistry during the head-flexible medium contact may be the key to lubrication. Silicone oils are also used in the construction of some magnetic tapes.

Topical lubrication is used to reduce the wear of rigid disks. Perfluoropolyethers (PFPEs) are chemically very stable lubricants with some boundary lubrication capability, and are most commonly used for topical lubrication of rigid disks (Bhushan, 1990). PFPEs commonly used include Fomblin Z and Y lubricant (made by Ausimont, Italy), Krytox 143 AD (Dupont, U.S.A.), and Demnum (Diakin, Japan). Difunctional derivatives containing various reactive end groups, e.g., hydroxyl (Fomblin Z-Dol), piperonyl (Fomblin AM 2001), and isocyanate (Fomblin Z-Disoc) are also used. The difunctional derivatives are referred to as reactive (polar) fluoroether lubricants. We note that the rheological properties of thin films of lubricants, particularly at high shear rates during take-off and touch-down, are expected to be different from their bulk properties. Fomblin Z is a linear PFPE, while Fomblin Y and Krytox 143 AD are branched PFPEs in which the regularity of the chain is perturbed by $-CF_3$ side groups. The bulk viscosity of Fomblin Y and Krytox 143 AD is almost an order of magnitude higher than that of the Z type. The molecular coil thickness is about 0.8 nm for these lubricant molecules, and the monolayer thickness depends on the molecular conformations of the polymer chain on the surface.

Fomblin Y and Z are most commonly used for particulate and thin-film rigid disks. Usually, lubricants with lower viscosity (such as Fomblin Z types) are used in thin-film disks in order to minimize stiction.

7.6.1 Measurement of Viscosity at High Shear Rates

In a conventional air bearing design, during initial take-off and landing of the slider, or during flying when the slider comes close enough to the disk surface to touch the

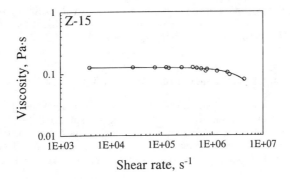

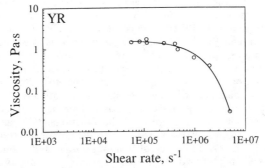

FIGURE 7.37 Measured absolute viscosity as a function of shear rate for a disk lubricated with (*a*) about 50-nm thick Z-15, and (*b*) 60-nm thick YR (*Jonsson and Bhushan, 1995*).

disk lubricant, the shearing of the lubricant occurs at high shear rates, on the order of $10^9 s^{-1}$ near ambient pressure. The viscosity of the lubricants Fomblin Z-15 and YR at shear rates up to about $10^7 s^{-1}$ were measured by Jonsson and Bhushan (1995). A special rheometer with a head-disk interface configuration was designed to allow viscosity measurements to be made using thin films at low sliding velocities so that viscous heating effects can be minimized. The viscosity data at different shear rates is presented in Fig. 7.37. We note that lubricants show non-Newtonian behavior above about $10^6 s^{-1}$. The viscosity of YR shows a stronger non-Newtonian behavior than Z-15, which may be caused by the branched structure of YR.

7.6.2 Measurement of Localized Lubricant-Film Thickness in Rigid Disks

The local lubricant thickness is measured by Fourier-transform infrared spectroscopy (FTIR), ellipsometry, angle-resolved X-ray photon spectroscopy (XPS), scanning tunneling microscopy (STM), and atomic force microscopy (AFM) (Kimachi et al., 1987; Mate et al., 1990; Bhushan and Blackman, 1991a). Ellipsometry and angle-resolved XPS have excellent vertical resolution on the order of 0.1 nm, but lateral resolution is on the order of 1 μm and 0.2 mm, respectively. STM and AFM can measure the thickness of the liquid film with a lateral resolution on the order of their tip radius of about 100 nm which is not possible to achieve by other techniques (Mate et al., 1990; Bhushan and Blackman, 1991a).

7.6.3 Lubricant-Disk Surface Interactions in Rigid Disks

The adsorption of the lubricant molecules is due to van der Waals forces, which are too weak to offset the spin-off losses or to arrest displacement of the lubricant by water or other ambient contaminants. Considering that these lubricating films are on the order of a monolayer thick and are required to function satisfactorily for the duration of several years, the task of developing a workable interface is quite formidable.

An approach aiming at alleviating the above shortcomings is to enhance the attachment of the molecules to the overcoat which, for most cases, is sputtered carbon. There are basically two approaches which have been shown to be successful in bonding the monolayer to the carbon. The first relies on exposure of the disk lubricated with neutral PFPE to various forms of radiation, such as low-energy X-ray (Heidemann and Wirth, 1984), nitrogen plasma (Homola et al., 1990), or far ultraviolet (e.g., 185 nm) (Saperstein and Lin, 1990). Another approach is to use chemically-active PFPE molecules, where the various functional (reactive) end groups offer the opportunity of strong attachments to a specific interface. These functional groups can react with the disk surface and bond the lubricant to it which reduces its loss due to spin off and evaporation. Because of the lack of cleanliness of the disk surface, chemically bonding of the functional lubricants is enhanced by thermal treatment (e.g., at 150°C for 30 min.); the thermal treatment can be adjusted to provide a desired degree of bonding. For a 100% bonding, the thermal-treated film is washed off with a solvent to remove any unbonded fractions. The main advantage of bonded lubricants, however, is their ability to enhance durability without the problem of stiction usually associated with weakly bonded lubricants.

7.6.4 Lubricant Degradation in Rigid Disks

Contacts between the slider and the lubricated disk lead to lubricant loss, Fig. 7.38 (Novotny and Karis, 1991; Novotny et al., 1992). The lubricant polymer chain is scissioned during slider-disk contacts (Novotny et al., 1994). The transient interface temperatures may be high enough (Bhushan, 1992b) to lead to the direct evaporation or desorption of the original lubricant molecules.

Novotny and Karis (1991) studied the difference between mechanisms by comparing the Fomblin Y and Z lubricants, which have different chemical structure but approximately the same molecular weight:

1. In sliding, Y is removed from the surface more rapidly than Z.
2. During flying, Z is removed more rapidly from the surface than Y.
3. Z is thermally decomposed more rapidly than Y (Kasai et al., 1991).
4. Migration rates of Z are faster than Y.

Polymer chain scission can be driven by mechanical, triboelectric, or thermal mechanisms (Kasai et al., 1991, 1992). The lubricant thickness is typically 1 to 5 nm and at 1 to 5 m/s sliding velocity, the shear rate is $0.2 \times 10^9 \text{s}^{-1}$ to $5 \times 10^9 \text{s}^{-1}$. At such

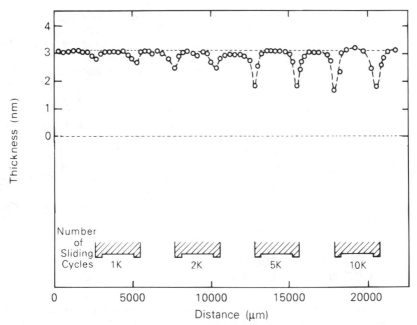

FIGURE 7.38 XPS cross-sectional profiles of lubricant thickness immediately after sliding of an Al_2O_3-TiC slider on a carbon-coated thin-film disk lubricated with 3 nm of Fomblin Y, using a load of 150 mN and a sliding velocity of 1 m/s (*Novotny and Karis, 1991*).

high shear rates, there can be much energy imparted to the polymer chain, inducing the chains to slide over one another. If the molecules are strongly interacting with the surface, the sliding may be hindered. Additional hindrance to interchain sliding can be the presence of a bulky side group such as the $-CF_3$ group on the Y lubricant. The additional intermolecular friction of the chains with the side group can hinder the rapid configurational adjustments required to support such high shear rates. The chains can be broken by tearing bonds apart along the polymer backbone and reduced to volatile products which provide the route for the observed lubricant loss when contacts occur in sliding or flying. It also follows that the loss of Y with the side group should be more rapid than that of the linear Z lubricant.

Moreover, potential differences up to 0.1 V and 0.5 V are measured on thin-film and particulate media surfaces, respectively, between areas on and off the sliding tracks. Corresponding electric fields across the slider-disk interface lead to the alteration of organic materials when the localized currents pass between the disk and slider asperities.

Thermal decomposition of perfluoropolyethers can proceed by a free-radical mechanism which involves initiation, propagation, and termination. The relative rates of initiation and propagation should be different for the two lubricants because of their chemical structure. From thermogravimetric analysis, for an equivalent rate of thermal decomposition on iron oxide, the temperature of Y must be held about 100°C higher than that of Z. However, the loss of lubricant by thermal decomposition may also depend on the relative displacement and migration rates. Thus, the higher loss rate of Y than Z in sliding can also be consistent with the thermal decomposition pathway. Faster degradation of Z than Y lubricants is believed to be due to the catalytic effect of a high concentration of acetal units (CF_2-O) in Z lubricants which results in chain scission (Kasai et al., 1991, 1992).

In flying, there is a displacement of lubricant to the outside of the track and a decrease of lubricant in the track. The displacement can be attributed to the repetitive application of pressure in the slider air bearing and intermittent contacts between the slider rails and the disk. Taking into account both the displacement and decrease in the lubricant level during flying, there is a net loss of lubricant from the disk surface. One possible mechanism for the loss is by aerosol droplet formation. This mechanism is reasonable given the tremendous negative pressure gradient at the trailing edge of the slider. The typical pressure increase under the air bearing rail is about 10^5 Pa, and this pressure drop occurs over about 10 μm, yielding a trailing edge pressure gradient of 10^{10} Pa/m. The rate of aerosol generation can depend on the lubricant surface tension (which is about the same for Z and Y) and the lubricant molecular configuration (effectively a flow property). The -CF_3 side group can act to hinder chain slippage (flow) required for efficient aerosol generation, lowering the loss rate of Y below that of Z in flying.

7.7 MICRO/NANOTRIBOLOGY AND MICRO/NANOMECHANICS

At most interfaces of technological relevance, multiple-asperity contacts occur. However, the importance of investigating single-asperity contacts in studies of the fundamental micromechanical and tribological properties of surfaces and interfaces has long been recognized. The recent emergence and proliferation of proximal probes, in particular tip-based microscopies (the atomic force microscope/friction microscope or AFM/FFM) and of computer simulations of tip-surface interactions and interfacial properties, provide nano-scale realizations of single-asperity contacts, and allow the systematic investigation of the interfacial problems of materials with high resolution, as well as ways and means for the modification and manipulation of nano-scale structures. These advances provide the impetus for intensive research endeavors aimed at reaching a fundamental understanding of the nature and consequences of the interactions between materials on the atomic scale, and guide the "rational" design of materials for technological applications. The advent of these new techniques and methodologies has led to the development of the new field of micro/nanotribology and micro/nanomechanics (Bhushan, 1995; Bhushan et al., 1995b). This field pertains to experimental and theoretical investigations of processes, ranging from the atomic and molecular scales to the microscale, that arise as a consequence of interfacial interactions.

7.7.1 Description of AFM/FFM

AFM/FFMs used in the tribological studies have been described in several papers (e.g., Bhushan, 1995). Briefly, the sample is mounted on a PZT tube scanner to scan the sample in the x-y plane and to move the sample in the vertical (z) direction. A sharp tip at the end of a flexible cantilever is brought in contact with the sample. Normal and frictional forces being applied at the tip-sample interface are measured using a laser beam deflection technique. Simultaneous measurements of friction force and surface roughness can be made with most instruments. For surface roughness and friction measurements, a microfabricated square pyramidal Si_3N_4 tip with a tip radius of about 30 nm on a cantilever beam (with a normal beam stiffness of about 0.58 N/m) is generally used at normal loads ranging from 10 to 150 nN. A preferred method of measuring friction and calibration procedures for conversion of voltages corresponding to normal and friction forces to force units, are described by Ruan and Bhushan (1994). The samples are typically scanned over areas ranging from 50 nm $\times$ 50 nm to 10 μm $\times$ 10 μm, in a direction orthogonal to the long axis of the cantilever beam (Ruan and Bhushan, 1994). The samples are generally scanned with a scan rate of 1 Hz and a sample scanning speed of 1 μm/s over, for example, a 500 nm $\times$ 500 nm scan area.

In nano-scale wear studies, the sample is initially scanned twice typically at 10 nN to obtain the surface profile, then scanned twice at a higher load of typically 100 nN to wear and to image the surface simultaneously, and then rescanned twice at 10 nN to obtain the profile of the worn surface. For magnetic media studied by Bhushan and Ruan (1994g), no noticeable change in the roughness profiles was observed between the initial two scans at 10 nN and between profiles scanned at 100 nN and the final scans at 10 nN. Therefore any changes in the topography between the initial scans at 10 nN and the scans at 100 nN (or the final scans at 10 nN) are believed to occur as a result of local deformation of the sample surface. In picoindentation studies, the sample is loaded in contact with the tip. During loading, the tip deflection (normal force) is measured as a function of vertical position of the sample. For a rigid sample, the tip deflection and the sample traveling distance (when the tip and sample come into contact) equal each other. Any decrease in the tip deflection with respect to the vertical position of the sample represents indentation. To ensure that the curvature in the tip deflection-sample traveling distance curve does not arise from PZT hysteresis, measurements on several rigid samples including a single-crystal natural diamond (IIa) were made. No curvature was noticed for the case of rigid samples. This suggests that any curvature for other samples should arise from the indentation of the sample.

For micro-scale scratching, micro-scale wear, and nano-scale indentation hardness measurements, a three-sided pyramidal single-crystal natural diamond tip with an apex angle of 80° and a tip radius of about 100 nm (determined by scanning-electron-microscopy imaging) is used at relatively higher loads (1 μN–150 μN). The diamond tip is mounted on a stainless steel cantilever beam with normal stiffness of about 30 N/m (Bhushan et al., 1994c,d). For scratching and wear studies, the sample is generally scanned in a direction orthogonal to the long axis of the cantilever beam (typically at a rate of 0.5 Hz). For wear studies, typically an area of 2 μm $\times$ 2 μm is scanned at various normal loads (ranging from 1 to 100 μN) for selected numbers of cycles. For nanoindentation hardness measurements, the scan size is set to zero, and then normal load is applied to make the indents. During this procedure the diamond tip is continuously pressed against the sample surface for about two seconds at various indentation loads. The sample surface is scanned before and after the scratching, wear, or nanoindentation, to obtain the initial and the final surface topography, using the same diamond tip at a low normal load of about 0.3 μN. An area larger than the scratched, worn, or indented region is scanned to observe the scratch or wear scars or indentation marks. Nanohardness is calculated by dividing the indentation load by the projected residual area of the indents (Bhushan et al., 1994e).

Boundary lubrication studies are conducted using either Si_3N_4 or diamond tips (Bhushan et al., 1995h; Koinkar and Bhushan, 1995).

7.7.2 Friction

Bhushan et al. (1994c, 1994d, 1994g, 1995d, 1995e, 1995f), Ruan and Bhushan (1994), and Bhushan et al. (1995b) measured friction on a microscale. They reported that the coefficient of friction on a microscale is lower than the macrofriction. For typical values of coefficients of friction of MP, barium ferrite, and ME tapes, PET tape substrate, and polished and textured, thin-film rigid disks, see Table 7.2. Friction values on the microscale are much lower than those on the macroscale, which is believed to be because of less ploughing contribution (almost no damage on the disk surface as measured). When measured for the small contact areas and very low loads used in microscale studies, mechanical properties are higher than at the macroscale (to be discussed later). This reduces the degree of wear. In addition, the smaller apparent area of contact reduces the number of particles trapped at the interface, and thus minimizes the ploughing contribution to the friction.

Next, we examine the relationship between local variations in microscale friction and surface roughness profiles. Figure 7.39 shows the surface profile, the slopes of the surface profile taken along the sliding direction, and the friction profile for a textured and lubricated disk (Bhushan and Ruan, 1994g). We note that there is no resemblance between the coefficient of friction profiles and the corresponding

TABLE 7.2   Surface Roughness (rms), Micro-Scale and Macro-Scale Friction, and Nanohardness Data of Thin-Film Magnetic Rigid Disk, Magnetic Tape and Magnetic Tape Substrate (PET) Samples

Sample	rms(nm)			Micro-scale coefficient of friction		Macro-scale coefficient of friction		Nano-hardness (GPa)/
	NOP 250 μm $\times$ 250 μm[†]	AFM 1 μm $\times$ 1μm[†]	10 μm $\times$ 10μm[†]	1 μm $\times$ 1μm[†]	10 μm $\times$ 10 μm[†]	Mn-Zn ferrite	Al$_2$O$_3$-TiC	Normal load (μN)
Polished, unlubricated disk	2.2	3.3	4.5	0.05	0.06	—	0.26	21/100
Polished, lubricated disk	2.3	2.3	4.1	0.04	0.05	—	0.19	—
Textured, lubricated disk	4.6	5.4	8.7	0.04	0.05	—	0.16	—
Metal-particle tape	6.0	5.1	12.5	0.08	0.06	0.19	—	0.30/50
Barium-ferrite tape	12.3	7.0	7.9	0.07	0.03	0.18	—	0.25/25
Metal-evaporated tape	9.3	4.7	5.1	0.05	0.03	0.18	—	0.7 to 4.3/75
PET tape substrate	33	5.8	7.0	0.05	0.04	0.55	—	0.3/20 and 1.4/20[‡]

[†]Scan area; NOP - Noncontact optical profiler; AFM - Atomic force microscope.

[‡]Numbers are for polymer and particulate regions, respectively.

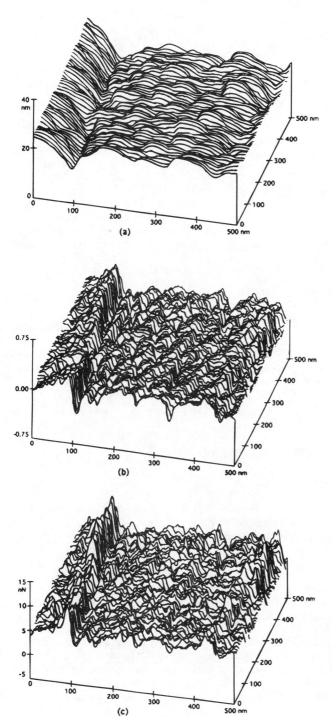

FIGURE 7.39 (*a*) Surface roughness profile ($\sigma = 4.4$ nm), (*b*) slope of the roughness profile taken in the sample sliding direction (the horizontal axis) (mean $= 0.023$, $\sigma = 0.197$), and (*c*) friction force profile (mean $= 6.2$ nN, $\sigma = 2.1$ nN) for a textured and lubricated disk for a normal load of 160 nN (*Bhushan et al., 1994c*).

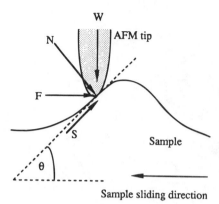

FIGURE 7.40 Schematic illustration showing the effect of an asperity (making an angle θ with the horizontal plain) on the surface in contact with the tip on local friction in the presence of "adhesive" friction mechanism (*Bhushan and Ruan, 1994g*). W and F are the normal and friction forces, respectively. S and N are the force components along and perpendicular to the local surface of the sample at the contact point, respectively.

roughness profiles, e.g., high or low points on the friction profile do not correspond to high or low points on the roughness profiles. By comparing the slope and friction profiles, we observe a strong correlation between the two. (For a clearer correlation, see the gray-scale plots of slope and friction profiles shown in Fig. 7.41, to be presented later). We have shown this correlation holds for various magnetic tapes, silicon, diamond, and other materials, and it can be explained by a "ratchet" mechanism, Fig. 7.40. Based on this mechanism, the local friction is a function of the local slope of the sample surface (Makinson, 1948). The local coefficient of friction in the ascending part (left hand side) of the asperity (in the absence of ploughing) is

$$\mu_1 \sim \mu_0 + \tan \theta \qquad (7.8)$$

where μ_0 is the coefficient of friction of a smooth surface as a result of adhesive friction mechanism and θ is the asperity slope. Equation 7.8 indicates that, in the ascending part of the asperity, one may simply add the asperity slope to the adhesion. Similarly, on the descending part of the asperity,

$$\mu_2 \sim \mu_0 - \tan \theta \qquad (7.9)$$

For a symmetrical asperity, the average coefficient of friction experienced by the AFM tip in traveling across the whole asperity is

$$\mu_{\text{ave}} \sim \mu_0 (1 + \tan^2 \theta) \qquad (7.10)$$

if $\mu_0 \tan \theta$ is small. Thus, friction is high at the leading edge of asperities and low at the trailing edge. The ratchet mechanism thus explains the correlation between the slopes of the roughness profiles and friction profiles observed in Fig. 7.39.

Gray scale plots of local coefficients of friction of the textured and lubricated disk as the FFM tip is scanned in either direction are shown in Fig. 7.41, together with gray scale plots of the slope of roughness profiles. The left figures correspond to the sample sliding from left to right, the middle figures correspond to the sample sliding from right to left, and the right figures correspond to the first set with the sign of the friction values reversed. We again note a general correspondence between the slope and friction profiles. We note that generally the points which have high friction in the left-to-right scan have low friction as the sliding direction is reversed. This relationship is not true at some locations. On the right, the sign of the friction profile is the reverse of the left-hand profile, but we still observe some differences in the two right friction profiles which may result from the asymmetrical asperities and/or asymmetrical transfer of wipe material during manufacturing of

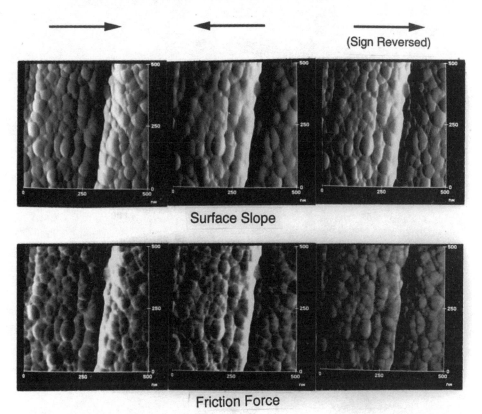

(Sign Reversed)

Surface Slope

Friction Force

FIGURE 7.41 Gray-scale plots of the slope of the surface roughness and the friction profiles for a textured and lubricated disk with FFM tip sliding in different directions. Higher points are shown by lighter color.

the disk. The directionality effect in friction on a macroscale is observed in some magnetic tapes (Bhushan, 1995).

7.7.3 Scratching and Wear

Bhushan and Ruan (1994g) conducted nanoscale wear tests on metal particle (MP) tapes at a normal load of 100 nN. Figure 7.42 shows the topography of the MP tape obtained at two different loads. For a given normal load, measurements were made twice. There was no discernible difference between consecutive measurements for a given normal load. However, as the load increased from 10 to 100 nN, material (indicated by an arrow) was pushed toward the right side in the sliding direction of the AFM tip relative to the sample. The material movement is believed to occur as a result of plastic deformation of the tape surface. Similar behavior was observed on all tapes. With disks, we did not notice any deformation under a 100 nN normal load.

Microscratches made on the MP tape and an unlubricated polished thin-film rigid disk at various loads are shown in Fig. 7.43. All scratches were made with 10 cycles. We notice that the scratch depth increases with an increase in the normal

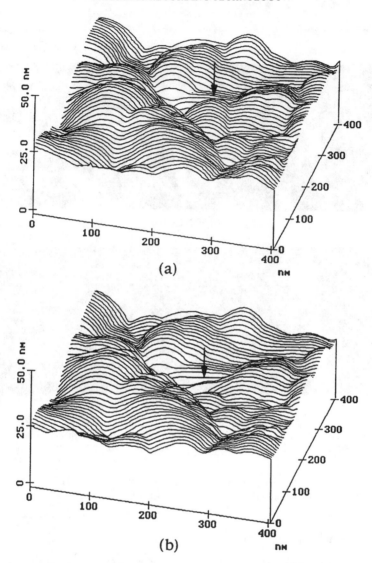

FIGURE 7.42 Surface roughness profiles of a calendered metal-particle magnetic tape. The applied normal force was (*a*) 10 nN and (*b*) 100 nN. Location of the change in surface topography as a result of microwear is indicated by arrows (*Bhushan and Ruan, 1994g*).

load. Figure 7.44 shows the micro-wear profiles at 20 μN load and at various cycles of an unlubricated polished thin-film disk. We note that the wear is not uniform and is largely initiated at the texture marks present on the disk surface. This suggests that surface defects act as initiation sites for wear. Figure 7.45*a* shows the wear depth as a function of number of cycles for an unlubricated and a lubricated thin-film disk at 10 and 20 μN loads. Wear initially takes place slowly with a sudden

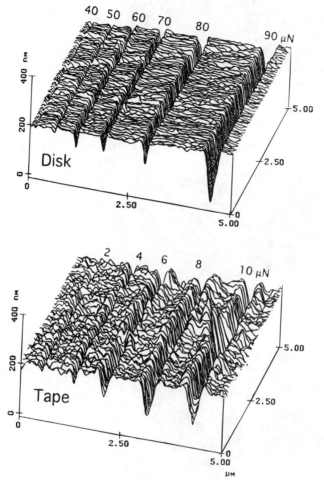

FIGURE 7.43 Surface profiles for a scratched unlubricated polished thin-film rigid disk and a MP tape (*Bhushan et al., 1994c*).

increase after about 40 cycles at 10 μN and after about 10 cycles at 20 μN. The rapid increase is associated with the breakdown of the carbon coating. Similar behavior has been reported by Bhushan et al. (1995*f*) for ME tapes. Wear rates for particulate tapes (Fig. 7.45*b*) and PET tape substrates are approximately constant for various loads and number of cycles.

PET tape substrate contains particles sticking out of its surface to facilitate winding. Figure 7.46 shows the wear profiles as a function of time at 1 μN load on the PET film in the nonparticulate and particulate regions (Bhushan et al., 1995*d*). We note that polymeric materials tear in microwear tests. The particles do not wear readily at 1 μN. Polymer around the particles is removed but the particles remain intact. Wear in the particulate region is much smaller than that in the polymer region. Nanohardness of the particulate region is about 1.4 GPa compared to 0.3 GPa in the nonparticulate region.

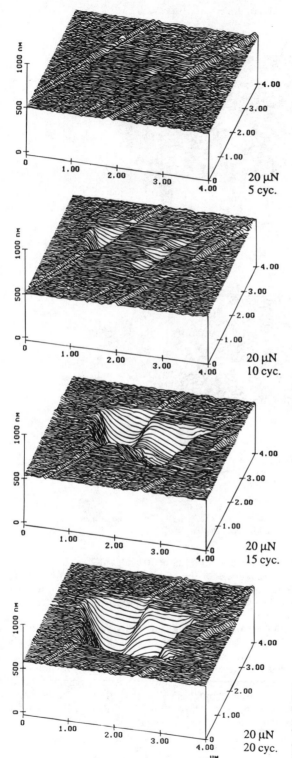

FIGURE 7.44 Surface profiles of an unlubricated polished thin-film rigid disk showing the worn region (center 2 μm $\times$ 2 μm). The normal load and the number of test cycles are indicated in the figure (*Bhushan et al., 1994c*).

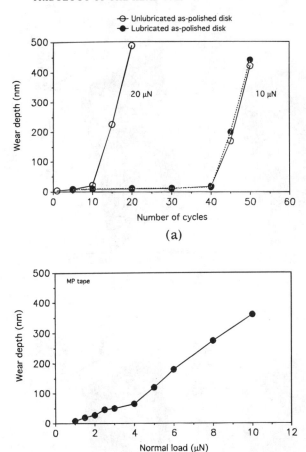

FIGURE 7.45 Wear depth as a function of the number of cycles for (*a*) unlubricated and lubricated polished, thin-film rigid disks at 10 μN and 20 μN loads, and (*b*) MP tape at a normal load of 2 μN (*Bhushan et al., 1994c, 1995f*).

We note that scratches and wear profiles can be produced with very shallow depths, thus the AFM technique can be used to measure scratch resistance and wear resistance of ultra thin films.

7.7.4 Indentation

The mechanical properties of materials can be measured using AFM (Bhushan et al., 1994c, 1994d, 1994e, 1995d, 1995e, 1995f). Bhushan and Ruan (1994g) measured indentability of magnetic tapes at increasing loads on a picoscale, Fig. 7.47. In the figure, the vertical axis represents the cantilever deflection and the horizontal axis represents the vertical position (z) of the sample. The "extending" and "retract-

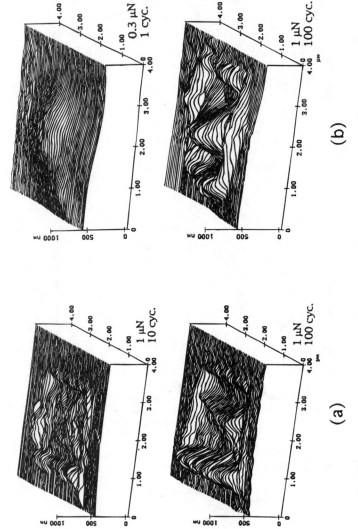

FIGURE 7.46 Surface profiles of a PET film showing the worn regions (center $2 \mu m \times 2 \mu m$) in the (*a*) nonparticulate and (*b*) particulate regions. The normal load and the number of test cycles are indicated in the figure (*Bhushan et al., 1995d*).

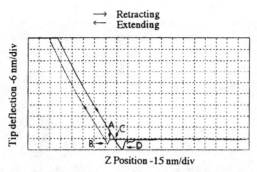

FIGURE 7.47   Indentation curve for an MP tape. The spring constant of the cantilever used was 0.4 N/m (*Bhushan and Ruan, 1994g*).

ing" curves correspond to the sample being moved toward or away from the cantilever tip, respectively. The left portion of the curve shows the tip deflection as a function of the sample traveling distance during sample-tip contact, which would be equal to each other for a rigid sample. However, if the tip indents into the sample, the tip deflection would be less than the sample traveling distance, or in other words, the slope of the line would be less than 1. In Fig. 7.47, we note that the line in the left portion of the figure is curved with a slope of less than 1 shortly after the sample touches the tip, which suggests that the tip has indented the sample. Later, the slope is equal to 1, suggesting that the tip no longer indents the sample. Since the curves in extending and retracting modes are identical, the indentation is elastic up to a maximum load of about 22 nN used in the measurements.

Bhushan et al (1994*e*) have reported that indentation hardness with a penetration depth as low as 1 nm can be measured using AFM. Bhushan et al. (1994*c*) measured the hardness of polished thin-film disks at loads of 80, 100, and 140 μN loads. Hardness values were 21 GPa (10 nm), 21 GPa (15 nm) and 9 GPa (40 nm); the depths of indentation are shown in parenthesis. The hardness value at 100 μN is much higher than at 140 μN. This is expected since the indentation depth is only about 15 nm at 100 μN, which is smaller than the thickness of the carbon coating ($\sim$30 nm). The hardness value at lower loads is primarily the value of the carbon coating. The hardness value at higher loads is primarily the value of the magnetic film, which is softer than the carbon coating (Bhushan, 1990). This result is consistent with the scratch and wear data discussed previously.

For the case of hardness measurements made on a magnetic thin-film rigid disk at low loads, the indentation depth is on the same order as the variation in the surface roughness. For accurate measurements of indentation size and depth, it is desirable to subtract the original (unindented) profile from the indented profile. We developed an algorithm for this purpose. Because of hysteresis, a translational shift in the sample plane occurs during the scanning period, resulting in a shift between the images captured before and after indentation. Therefore, the image for perfect overlap needs to be shifted before subtraction can be performed. To accomplish this objective, a small region on the original image was selected and the corresponding region in the indented image was found by maximizing the correlation between the two regions. (Profiles were plane-fitted before subtraction). Once two regions were identified, overlapped areas between the two images were determined and the original image was shifted with the required translational shift and then subtracted

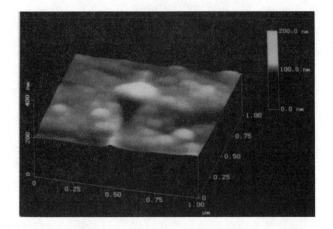

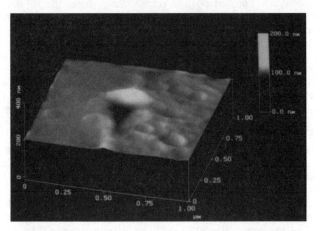

FIGURE 7.48 Images with nanoindentation marks generated on an unlubricated polished thin-film disk at normal loads of 140 μN with an indentation depth of 40 nm (*a*) before and (*b*) after subtraction (*Bhushan et al., 1994c*).

from the indented image. An example of profiles before and after subtraction is shown in Fig. 7.48. It is easier to measure the indent on the subtracted image. At a normal load of 140 μN the hardness value of an unlubricated, as-polished magnetic thin-film rigid disk (rms roughness = 3.3 nm) is 9.0 GPa and the indentation depth is 40 nm.

7.7.5 Lubrication

AFMs have been used to measure the film thickness of ultra-thin (2 nm) lubricant films with a lateral resolution on the order of the AFM tip radius (100 nm or less),

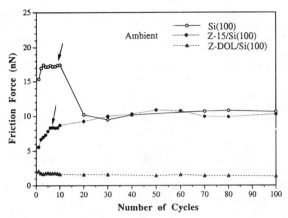

FIGURE 7.49   Friction force as a function of number of cycles for the unlubricated and lubricated silicon samples (*Koinkar and Bhushan, 1996a*).

which is not possible by other techniques (Mate et al., 1989, 1990; Bhushan and Blackman, 1991*a*).

Bonded lubricants are commonly used to reduce the friction and wear of sliding surfaces such as in thin-film rigid disks (Bhushan, 1990). Blackman et al. (1990) and Mate (1992) studied the deformation of bonded lubricant using AFM. They reported that the bonded lubricants behave as a soft polymeric solid while in contact with an asperity.

To study lubricant depletion during micro-scale measurements, Koinkar and Bhushan (1996a, 1996b) measured micro-scale friction as a function of the number of cycles of a virgin Si (100) surface, and a silicon surface lubricated with about 2-nm thick Z-15 and Z-Dol PFPE lubricants, Fig. 7.49. These experiments were conducted in an AFM/FFM by sliding a Si_3N_4 tip against the samples. Z-Dol is PFPE lubricant with hydroxyl end groups. Its lubricant film was thermally bonded at 150°C for 30 minutes and washed off with a solvent to provide a chemically bonded layer of the lubricant film. From Fig. 7.49, we note that the friction force in a virgin silicon surface decreases a few cycles after the natural oxide film present on the silicon surface gets removed. In the case of the Z-15 coated silicon sample, the friction force starts out to be low and then approaches that of the unlubricated silicon surface after a few cycles. The increase in friction of the lubricated sample suggests that the lubricant film gets worn and the silicon underneath is exposed. In the case of the Z-Dol coated silicon sample, the friction force starts out to be low and remains low during the 100 cycles test. It suggests that Z-Dol does not get displaced/depleted as readily as Z-15. Thus, AFM studies can be used to study the performance of lubricants in simulated single-asperity contact.

REFERENCES

Bair, S., I. Green, and B. Bhushan, "Measurements of Asperity Temperatures of a Read/Write Head Slider Bearing in Hard Magnetic Recording Disks," *ASME Journal of Tribology,* **113**, 547–554 (1991).

Baker, H. R., W. D. Bascom and C. R. Singleterry, "The Adhesion of Ice to Lubricated Surfaces," *J. Collo. Sci.,* **17,** 447–491 (1962).

Baumgart, P., T. Nguyen, and A. Tam, "Laser Texture: A New Solution for Stiction and Durability in Disk Drives," *IEEE Trans. Magn.* (1995).

Bhushan, B., "Analysis of the Real Area of Contact Between a Polymeric Magnetic Medium and a Rigid Surface," *J. Lub. Tech.,* Trans. ASME, **106,** 26–34 (1984).

Bhushan, B., "The Real Area of Contact in Polymeric Magnetic Media—II: Experimental Data and Analysis," *ASLE Trans.,* **28,** 181–197 (1985a).

Bhushan, B., "Assessment of Accelerated Head-Wear Test Methods and Wear Mechanisms," *Tribology and Mechanics of Magnetic Storage Systems,* **2,** eds. B. Bhushan and N. S. Eiss, SP-19, pp. 101–111, ASLE, Park Ridge, Illinois (1985b).

Bhushan, B., "Magnetic Head-Media Interface Temperatures, Part I—Analysis," *ASME Journal of Tribology,* **109,** 243–251 (1987a).

Bhushan, B., "Magnetic Head-Media Interface Temperatures, Part II—Application to Magnetic Tapes," *ASME Journal of Tribology,* **109,** 252–256 (1987b).

Bhushan, B., *Tribology and Mechanics of Magnetic Storage Devices,* Springer-Verlag, New York (1990).

Bhushan, B., ed. *Advances in Information Storage Systems,* vol. 1–5, ASME, New York; vol. 6, World Scientific, River Edge, NJ (1991–1995).

Bhushan, B., *Mechanics and Reliability of Flexible Magnetic Media,* Springer-Verlag, New York (1992a).

Bhushan, B., "Magnetic Head-Media Interface Temperatures—Part 3: Application to Rigid Disks," *ASME Journal of Tribology,* **114,** 420–430 (1992b).

Bhushan, B., "Magnetic Recording Surfaces," *Characterization of Tribological Materials,* ed. W. A. Glaeser, Butterworth-Heineman, Boston, 116–133 (1993a).

Bhushan, B., "Magnetic Slider/Rigid Disk Substrate Materials and Disk Texturing Techniques—Status and Future Outlook," *Adv. Info. Storage Syst.,* **5,** 175–209 (1993b).

Bhushan, B., "Tribology of Magnetic Storage Systems," *Handbook of Lubrication and Tribology,* **3,** CRC Press, Boca Raton, FL, 325–374 (1994a).

Bhushan, B., "Tribology of Solid Contacts in Magnetic Recording Devices," *App. Mech. Rev.,* **47** (6), Part 2, S199–S203 (1994b).

Bhushan, B., ed. *Handbook of Micro/Nanotribology,* CRC Press, Boca Raton, FL (1995).

Bhushan, B., and R. M. Phelan, "Frictional Properties as a Function of Physical and Chemical Changes in Magnetic Tapes During Wear," *ASLE Trans.,* **20,** 402–413. (1986b).

Bhushan, B., and R. J. Martin, "Accelerated Wear Test Using Magnetic-Particle Slurries," *Tribol. Trans.,* **31,** 228–238 (1988a).

Bhushan, B., and M. F. Doerner, "Role of Mechanical Properties and Surface Texture in the Real Area of Contact of Magnetic Rigid Disks," *ASME Journal of Tribology,* **111,** 452–458 (1989).

Bhushan, B., and M. T. Dugger, "Real Contact Area Measurements on Magnetic Rigid Disks," *Wear,* **137,** 41–50 (1990a).

Bhushan, B., and M. T. Dugger, "Liquid-Mediated Adhesion Measurements at the Thin-Film Magnetic Disk/Head Slider Interface," *ASME Journal of Tribology,* **112,** 217–223 (1990b).

Bhushan, B., and G. S. Blackman, "Atomic Force Microscopy of Magnetic Rigid Disks and Sliders and Its Applications to Tribology," *ASME Journal of Tribology,* **113,** 452–457 (1991a).

Bhushan, B., and B. K. Gupta, *Handbook of Tribology: Materials, Coatings and Surface Treatments,* McGraw-Hill, New York (1991b).

Bhushan, B., and A. Majumdar, "Elastic-Plastic Contact Model of Bifractal Surfaces," *Wear,* **153,** 53–64 (1992c).

Bhushan, B., and S. Venkatesan, "Friction and Wear Studies of Silicon in Sliding Contact with Thin-Film Magnetic Rigid Disks," *J. Mater. Res.,* **8,** 1611–1628 (1993).

Bhushan, B., and B. K. Gupta, "Friction and Wear of Ion Implanted Diamondlike Carbon and Fullerene Films for Thin-Film Rigid Disk," *J. Appl. Phys.*, **75**, 6156–6158 (1994a).

Bhushan, B., and V. N. Koinkar, "Tribological Studies of Silicon for Magnetic Recording Applications," *J. Appl. Phys.*, **75**, 5741–5746 (1994d).

Bhushan, B., and V. N. Koinkar, "Nanoindentation Hardness Measurements Using Atomic Force Microscopy," *App. Phys. Lett.*, **64**, 1653–1655 (1994e).

Bhushan, B., and J. A. Lowry, "Friction and Wear of Particulate and ME Magnetic Tapes Sliding Against a Mn-Zn Ferrite Head in a Linear Mode," *IEEE Trans. Magn.*, **MAG-30**, 4182–4184 (1994f).

Bhushan, B., and J. Ruan, "Atomic-Scale Friction Measurements Using Friction Force Microscopy: Part II—Application to Magnetic Media," *ASME Journal of Tribology*, **116**, 389–396 (1994g).

Bhushan, B., and J. Ruan, "Tribological Performance of Thin Film Amorphous Carbon Overcoats for Magnetic Recording Disks in Various Environments," *Surface and Coatings Technology*, **68/69**, 644–650 (1994h).

Bhushan, B., and B. K. Gupta, "Micromechanical Characterization of Ni-P Coated Aluminum-Magnesium, Glass, and Glass-Ceramic Substrates and Finished Magnetic Thin-Film Rigid Disks," *Adv. Info. Storage Syst.*, **6**, 193–208 (1995a).

Bhushan, B., and F. W. Hahn, "Stains on Magnetic Tape Heads," *Wear*, **184**, 193–202, (1995c).

Bhushan, B., and V. N. Koinkar, "Microtribology of PET Polymeric Films," *Tribol. Trans.*, **38**, 119–127 (1995d).

Bhushan, B., and V. N. Koinkar, "Macro and Microtribological Studies of CrO_2 Video Tapes," *Wear*, **180**, 9–16 (1995e).

Bhushan, B., and V. N. Koinkar, "Microtribology of Metal Particle, Barium Ferrite and Metal Evaporated Magnetic Tapes," *Wear*, **183**, 360–370 (1995f).

Bhushan, B., and J. A. Lowry, "Friction and Wear Studies of Various Head Materials and Magnetic Tapes in a Linear Mode Accelerated Test Using a New Nano-Scratch Wear Measurement Technique," *Wear* (1995g) (in press).

Bhushan, B., and J. A. Monahan, "Accelerated Friction and Wear Studies of Various Particulate and Thin-Film Magnetic Tapes Against Tape Path Materials in Pure Sliding and Rotary Sliding Modes," *Tribol. Trans.*, **38**, 329–341 (1995i).

Bhushan, B., and X. Tian, "Contact Analysis of Regular Patterned Rough Surfaces in Magnetic Recording, *ASME J. Electronic Packaging*, **117**, 26–33 (1995j).

Bhushan, B., R. L. Bradshaw, and B. S. Sharma, "Friction in Magnetic Tapes II: Role of Physical Properties," *ASLE Trans.*, **27**, 89–100 (1984a).

Bhushan, B., B. S. Sharma, and R. L. Bradshaw, "Friction in Magnetic Tapes I: Assessment of Relevant Theory," *ASLE Trans.*, **27**, 33–44 (1984b).

Bhushan, B., et al. ed. *Tribology and Mechanics of Magnetic Storage Systems*, vol. 1–7, STLE, Park Ridge, Ill. (1984–90).

Bhushan, B., G. W. Nelson, and M. E. Wacks, "Head-Wear Measurements by Autoradiography of the Worn Magnetic Tapes," *ASME Journal of Tribology*, **108**, 241–255 (1986a).

Bhushan, B., J. C. Wyant, and J. Meiling, "A New Three-Dimensional Digital Optical Profiler," *Wear*, **122**, 301–312 (1988).

Bhushan, B., M. Dominiak, and J. P. Lazzari, "Contact-Start-Stop Studies with Silicon Planar Head Sliders Against Thin-Film Disks," *IEEE Trans. Magn.*, **MAG-28**, 2874–2876 (1992a).

Bhushan, B., A. J. Kellock, N. H. Cho, and J. W. Ager, "Characterization of Chemical Bonding and Physical Characteristics of Diamond-like Amorphous Carbon and Diamond Films," *J. Mater. Res.*, **7**, 404–410 (1992b).

Bhushan, B., H. F. Hintaregger, and A. E. E. Rogers, "Thermal Considerations for the Edge Guiding of Thin Magnetic Tape in a Longitudinal Tape Transport," *Wear*, **171**, 179–193 (1994b).

Bhushan, B., V. N. Koinkar, and J. Ruan, "Microtribology of Magnetic Media," *Proc. Instn. Mech. Engrs., Part J: J. Eng. Tribol.,* **208,** 17–29 (1994c).

Bhushan, B., J. N. Israelachvili, and U. Landman, "Nanotribology: Friction, Wear and Lubrication at the Atomic Scale," *Nature,* **374,** 607–616 (1995b).

Bhushan, B., T. Miyamoto, and V. N. Koinkar, "Microscopic Friction Between a Sharp Tip and Thin-Film Magnetic Rigid Disks by Friction Force Microscopy," *Adv. Info. Storage Syst.,* **6,** 151–161 (1995h).

Bhushan, B., L. Yang, C. Gao, S. Suri, R. A. Miller, and B. Marchon, "Friction and Wear Studies of Magnetic Thin-Film Rigid Disks with Glass-Ceramic, Glass and Aluminum-Magnesium Substrates," *Wear* (1995k).

Blackman, G. S., C. M. Mate, and M. R. Philpott, "Interaction Forces of a Sharp Tungsten Tip with Molecular Films on Silicon Surface," *Phys. Rev. Lett.,* **65,** 2270–2273 (1990).

Bowden, F. P., and D. Tabor, *The Friction and Lubrication of Solids,* Clarendon Press, Oxford, U.K. Part I (1950), Part II (1964).

Bradshaw, R. L., and B. Bhushan, "Friction in Magnetic Tapes Part III: Role of Chemical Properties," *ASLE Trans.,* **27,** 207–219 (1984).

Bradshaw, R. L., B. Bhushan, C. Kalthoff, and M. Warne, "Chemical and Mechanical Performance of Flexible Magnetic Media Containing Chromium Dioxide," *IBM J. Res. Develop.,* **30,** 203–216 (1986).

Calabrese, S. J., and B. Bhushan, "A Study by Scanning Electron Microscopy of Magnetic Head-Disk Interface Sliding," *Wear,* **139,** 367–381 (1990).

Calabrese, S. J., B. Bhushan, and R. E. Davis, "A Study by Scanning Electron Microscopy of Magnetic Head-Tape Interface Sliding," *Wear,* **131,** 123–133 (1989).

Chandrasekar, S., and B. Bhushan, "Control of Surface Finishing Residual Stresses in Magnetic Recording Head Materials," *ASME Journal of Tribology,* **110,** 87–92 (1988).

Chandrasekar, S., and B. Bhushan, "Friction and Wear of Ceramics for Magnetic Recording Applications—Part II: Friction Measurement," *ASME Journal of Tribology,* **113,** 313–317 (1991).

Chandrasekar, S., M. C. Shaw, and B. Bhushan, "Comparison of Grinding and Lapping of Ferrites and Metals," *ASME J. Eng. for Indus.,* **109,** 76–82 (1987a).

Chandrasekar, S., M. C. Shaw, and B. Bhushan, "Morphology of Ground and Lapped Surfaces of Ferrite and Metal," *ASME J. Eng. for Indus.,* **109,** 83–86 (1987b).

Chandrasekar, S., K. Kokini, and B. Bhushan, "Influence of Abrasive Properties on Residual Stresses in Lapped Ferrite and Alumina," *J. Amer. Ceramic Soc.,* **73,** 1907–1911 (1990).

Chang, H. C., M. M. Chen, C. T. Horng, and R. O. Schwenker, "Thin Film Magnetic Head Having a Protective Coating and Method for Making Same," U.S. Patent 5,175,658, Dec. 29 (1992).

Cho, N. H., K. M. Krishnan, D. K. Veirs, M. D. Rubin, C. B. Hopper, B. Bhushan, and D. B. Bogy, "Chemical Structure and Physical Properties of Diamond-Like Amorphous Carbon Films Prepared by Magnetron Sputtering," *J. Mater. Res.,* **5,** 2543–2554 (1990).

Chu, M. Y., B. Bhushan, and L. De Jonghe, "Wear Behavior of Ceramic Sliders in Sliding Contact with Rigid Magnetic Thin-Film Disks," *Tribol. Trans.,* **35,** 603–610 (1992).

Cook, N. H., and B. Bhushan, "Sliding Surface Interface Temperatures," *J. Lub. Tech.,* Trans. ASME, **95,** 59–64 (1973).

Engel, P. A., and B. Bhushan, "Sliding Failure Model for Magnetic Head-Disk Interface," *ASME Journal of Tribology,* **112,** 299–303 (1990).

Feurstein, A., and M. Mayr, "High Vacuum Evaporation of Ferromagnetic Materials—A New Production Technology for Magnetic Tapes," *IEEE Trans. Magn.,* **MAG-20,** 51–56 (1984).

Fischer, T. E., "Tribochemistry," *Ann. Rev. Mater. Sci.,* **18,** 303–323 (1988).

Ganti, S., and B. Bhushan, "Generalized Fractal Analysis and its Applications to Engineering Surfaces," *Wear,* **180,** 17–34 (1995).

Gao, C., and B. Bhushan, "Tribological Performance of Magnetic Thin-Film Glass Disks: Its Relation to Surface Roughness and Lubricant Structure and its Thickness," *Wear*, in press (1995a).

Gao, C., X. Tian, and B. Bhushan, "A Meniscus Model for Optimizing of Texturing and Liquid Lubrication of Magnetic Thin-Film Rigid Disks," *Tribol. Trans.*, **38**, 201–212 (1995b).

Gerber, C. T., B. Bhushan, and N. V. Gitis, "Experimental Study of Long-term Static Friction and Magnetic Slider/Disk Interplanar Separation," *ASME Journal of Tribology*, in press (1995).

Gitis, N., and R. Sonnenfeld, "Long-term Stiction at the Magnetic Thin-Film Disk-Slider Interface," *ASME Journal of Tribology*, **115**, 214–218 (1993).

Greenwood, J. A., and J. B. P. Williamson, "Contact of Nominally Flat Surfaces," *Proc. Roy. Soc. (Lond.)*, **A295**, 300–319 (1966).

Grill, A., C. T. Horng, B. S. Meyerson, V. V. Patel, and M. A. Russak, "Magnetic Head Slider Having a Protective Coating Thereon," U.S. Patent 5,159,508, Oct. 27 (1992).

Gulino, R., S. Bair, W. O. Winer, and B. Bhushan, "Temperature Measurement of Microscopic Areas within a Simulated Head/Tape Interface Using Infrared Radiometric Technique," *ASME Journal of Tribology*, **108**, 29–34 (1986).

Gupta, B. K., and B. Bhushan, "Mechanical and Tribological Properties of Hard Carbon Coatings for Magnetic Recording Heads," *Wear*, in press (1995a).

Gupta, B. K., and B. Bhushan, "Micromechanical Properties of Amorphous Carbon Coatings Deposited by Different Techniques," *Thin Solid Films*, in press (1995b).

Gupta, B. K., B. Bhushan, Y. Zhou, N. Winograd, and K. Krishnan, "Chemical Analysis of Stains Formed on Co-Nb-Zr Heads Sliding Against Oxide and MP Magnetic Tapes," *J. Mater. Res.*, **10**, 1795–1810 (1995c).

Hahn, F. W., "Head Wear as a Function of Isolated Asperities on the Surface of Magnetic Tape," *IEEE Trans. Magn.*, **MAG-20**, 918–920 (1984a).

Hahn, F. W., "Wear of Recording Heads by Magnetic Tape," *Tribology and Mechanics of Magnetic Storage Systems*, SP-16, pp. 41–48, ASLE, Park Ridge, Ill. (1984b).

Harth, K., H. Hibst, H. Mannsperger, H. P. Schildberg, and A. Werner, *J. Magn. Soc. Jap.*, **13, S-1,** 69–72 (1989).

Hedenqvist, P., M. Olsson, S. Hogmark, and B. Bhushan, "Tribological Studies of Various Magnetic Heads and Thin-Film Rigid Disks," *Wear*, **153**, 65–78 (1992).

Heidemann, R., and M. Wirth, "Transforming the Lubricant on a Magnetic Disk into a Solid Fluorine Compound," *IBM Tech. Disclosure Bull.*, **27**, 3199–3205 (1984).

Homola, A. M., L. J. Lin and D. D. Saperstein, "Process for Bonding Lubricant to a Thin Film Magnetic Recording Disk," U.S. Patent 4,960,609, October 2 (1990).

Hoshino, M., Y. Kimachi, F. Yoshimura, and A. Terada, "Lubrication Layer Using Perfluoropolyether and Aminosilane for Magnetic Recording Media," *Tribology and Mechanics of Magnetic Storage Systems*, **5,** eds. B. Bhushan and N. S. Eiss, SP-25, pp. 37–42, STLE, Park Ridge, Illinois (1988).

Jonsson, U., and B. Bhushan, "Measurement of Rheological Properties of Ultrathin Lubricant Films at Very High Shear Rates and Near-Ambient Pressure," *J. Appl. Phys.*, **78**, 3107–3114 (1995).

Karis, T. E., V. J. Novotny, and R. M. Crone, "Sliding Wear Mechanism of Particulate Magnetic Recording Media," *Tribology and Mechanics of Magnetic Storage Systems*, **7,** ed. B. Bhushan, SP-29, pp. 35–42, STLE, Park Ridge, Illinois (1990).

Kasai, P. H., "Degradation of Perfluoropolyethers Catalyzed by Lewis Acids," *Adv. Info. Storage Syst.*, **4,** 291–314 (1992).

Kasai, P. H., W. T. Tang, and P. Wheeler, "Degradation of Perfluoropolyethers Catalyzed by Aluminum Chloride," *Appl. Surf. Sci.*, **51**, 201 (1991).

Kawai, H., A. Kurikawa, and H. Suzuki, "Method of Manufacturing Magnetic Recording Medium Capable of Recording Information at a High Recording Density," U.S. Patent 5,087,482, Feb. 11 (1992).

Kelly, J., "Tape and Head Wear," *Magnetic Tape Recording for the Eighties,* NASA Ref. Publ. 1075, 7–22 (1982).

Khan, M. R., N. Heiman, R. D. Fisher, S. Smith, M. Smallen, G. F. Hughes, K. Veirs, B. Marchon, D. F. Ogletree, M. Salmeron, and W. Siekhaus, "Carbon Overcoat and the Process Dependence on its Microstructure and Wear Characteristics," *IEEE Trans. Magn.,* **MAG-24,** 2647–2649 (1988).

Kimachi, Y., F. Yoshimura, M. Hoshino, and A. Terada, "Uniformity Quantification of Lubricant Layer on Magnetic Recording Media," *IEEE Trans. Magn.,* **MAG-23,** 2392–2394 (1987).

Koinkar, V. N., and B. Bhushan, "Microtribological Studies of Unlubricated and Lubricated Surfaces Using Atomic Force/Friction Force Microscopy," *J Vac. Sci. Technol. A,* in press (1996a).

Koinkar, V. N., and B. Bhushan, "Micro/nanoscale Studies of Boundary Layers of Liquid Lubricants for Magnetic Disks," *J. Appl. Phys.,* in press (1996b).

Koka, R., "Wear of Silicon Carbide in Sliding Contact with Lubricated Thin-Film Rigid Disk," *Tribology and Mechanics of Magnetic Storage Systems,* **9,** SP-36, pp. 46–52, STLE, Park Ridge, Illinois (1994).

Koka, R., and A. R. Kumaran, "Visualization and Analysis of Particulate Buildup on the Leading Edge Tapers on Sliders," *Adv. Info. Storage Syst.,* **2,** 161–171 (1991).

Lemke, J. U., "Ferrite Transducers," *Annals N.Y. Academy of Sciences—The Advances in Magnetic Recording,* eds. D. E. Speliotis and C. E. Johnson, **189,** Jan., 171–190 (1972).

Li, Y., and F. E. Talke, "A Model for the Effect of Humidity on Stiction of the Head/Disk Interface," *Tribology and Mechanics of Magnetic Storage Systems,* **7,** eds. B. Bhushan and N. S. Eiss, SP-29, pp. 79–84, STLE, Park Ridge, Ill. (1990).

Liu, C. C., and P. B. Mee, "Stiction at the Winchester Head-Disk Interface," *IEEE Trans. Magn.,* **MAG-19,** 1659–1661 (1983).

Majumdar, A., and B. Bhushan, "Role of Fractal Geometry in Roughness Characterization and Contact Mechanics of Surfaces," *ASME Journal of Tribology,* **112,** 205–216 (1990).

Majumdar, A., and B. Bhushan, "Fractal Model of Elastic-Plastic Contact Between Rough Surfaces," *ASME Journal of Tribology,* **113,** 1–11 (1991b).

Majumdar, A., B. Bhushan, and C. L. Tien, "Role of Fractal Geometry in Tribology," *Adv. Info. Storage Syst.,* **1,** 231–266 (1991a).

Makinson, K. R., "On the Cause of the Frictional Difference of the Wool Fiber," *Trans. Faraday Soc.,* **44,** 279–282 (1948).

Marchon, B., N. Heiman, and M. R. Khan, "Evidence for Tribochemical Wear on Amorphous Carbon Thin Films," *IEEE Trans. Magn.,* **MAG-26,** 168–170 (1990).

Mate, C. M., "Atomic-Force-Microscope Study of Polymer Lubricants on Silicon Surface," *Phys. Rev. Lett.,* **68,** 3323–3326 (1992).

Mate, C. M., M. R. Lorenz, and V. J. Novotny, "Atomic Force Microscopy of Polymeric Liquid Films," *J. Chem. Phys.,* **90**(12), 7550–7555 (1989).

Mate, C. M., M. R. Lorenz, and V. J. Novotny, "Determination of Lubricant Film Thickness on a Particulate Disk Surface by Atomic Force Microscopy," *IEEE Trans. Mag.,* **MAG-26,** 1225–1228 (1990).

Matthewson, M. J., and H. J. Mamin, "Liquid-Mediated Adhesion of Ultra-Flat Solid Surfaces," *Proc. Mat. Res. Soc. Symp.,* **119,** 87–92 (1988).

Mirzamaani, M., C. V. Jahnes, and M. A. Russak, "Thin Film Disks with Transient Metal Underlayers," *IEEE Trans. Magn.,* **MAG-28,** 3090–3092 (1992).

Miyamoto, T., I. Sato, and Y. Ando, "Friction and Wear Characteristics of Thin-Film Disk Media in Boundary Lubrication," *Tribology and Mechanics of Magnetic Storage Systems,* **5,** eds. B. Bhushan and N. S. Eiss, SP-25, pp. 55–61, STLE, Park Ridge, Illinois (1988).

Miyoshi, K., D. H. Buckley, T. Kusaka, C. Maeda, and B. Bhushan, "Effect of Water Vapor on Adhesion of Ceramic Oxide in Contact with Polymeric Magnetic Medium and Itself,"

Tribology and Mechanics of Magnetic Storage Systems, **5,** eds. B. Bhushan and N. S. Eiss, SP-25, pp. 12–16, STLE, Park Ridge, Illinois (1988).

Novotny, V. J., and T. E. Karis, "Sensitive Tribological Studies on Magnetic Recording Disks," *Adv. Info. Storage Syst.,* **2,** 137–152 (1991).

Novotny, V. J., T. E. Karis, and N. W. Johnson, "Lubricant Removal, Degradation, and Recovery on Particulate Magnetic Recording Media," *ASME Journal of Tribology,* **114,** 61–67 (1992).

Novotny, V. J., X. Pan, and C. S. Bhatia, "Tribochemistry at Lubricated Interfaces," *J. Vac. Sci. Technol. A,* **12,** 2879–2886 (1994).

Oden, P. I., A. Majumdar, B. Bhushan, A. Padmanabhan, and J. J. Graham, "AFM Imaging, Roughness Analysis and Contact Mechanics of Magnetic Tape and Head Surfaces," *ASME Journal of Tribology,* **114,** 666–674 (1992).

Ota, H., K. Namura, and N. Ohmae, "Brown Stain on VCR Head Surface Through Contact with Magnetic Tape," *Adv. Info. Storage Syst.,* **2,** 85–96 (1991).

Pan, X., and V. J. Novotny, "Head Material Effects on Interfacial Chemistry," *IEEE Trans. Magn.,* **MAG-30,** 433–439 (1994).

Pan, X., and R. B. Prime, "Tribologically Induced Outgassing and its Effects on the Mechanical Performance of Rigid-Disk File," unpublished (1993).

Patton, S. T., and B. Bhushan, "Friction and Wear of Metal Particle, Barium Ferrite and Metal Evaporated Tapes in Rotary Head Recorders," *ASME Journal of Tribology,* in press (1995a).

Patton, S. T., and B. Bhushan, "Effect of Interchanging Tapes and Head Contours on the Durability of Metal Evaporated, Metal Particle and Barium Ferrite Magnetic Tapes," *Tribol. Trans.,* **38,** 801–810 (1995b).

Poon, C. Y., and R. S. Sayles, "Numerical Contact Model of a Smooth Ball on an Anisotropic Rough Surface," *ASME Journal of Tribology,* **116,** 194–201 (1994).

Poon, C. Y., and B. Bhushan, "Comparison of Surface Roughness Measurements by Stylus Profiler, AFM and Noncontact Optical Profiler," *Wear* (1995a).

Poon, C. Y., and B. Bhushan, "Surface Roughness Analysis of Glass-Ceramic Substrates and Finished Magnetic Disks, and Ni-P Coated Al-Mg and Glass Substrates," *Wear* (1995b).

Potgiesser, J. A. I., and J. Koorneef, "Mechanical Wear and Degeneration of the Magnetic Properties of Magnetic Heads Caused by the Tape," *The Radio and Electronic Engineer,* **44,** 313–318 (1974).

Ruan, J., and B. Bhushan, "Atomic-Scale Friction Measurements Using Friction Force Microscopy: Part I—General Principles and New Measurement Techniques," *ASME Journal of Tribology,* **116,** 378–388 (1994).

Saperstein, D. D., and L. J. Lin, "Improved Surface Adhesion and Coverage of Perfluoropolyether Lubricants Following Far-UV Radiation," *Langmuir,* **6,** 1522–1524 (1990).

Scarati, A. M., and G. Caporiccio, "Frictional Behavior and Wear Resistance of Rigid Disks Lubricated with Neutral and Functional Perfluoropolyethers," *IEEE Trans. Magn.,* **MAG-23,** 106–108 (1987).

Stahle, C. M., and T. D. Lee, "Characterization of the Deposits on Helical Scan Heads," *Adv. Info. Storage Syst.,* **4,** 79–86 (1992).

Streator, J. L., B. Bhushan, and D. B. Bogy, "Lubricant Performance in Magnetic Thin Film Disks with Carbon Overcoat—Part I: Dynamic and Static Friction," *ASME Journal of Tribology,* **113,** 22–31 (1991a).

Streator, J. L., B. Bhushan, and D. B. Bogy, "Liquid Performance in Magnetic Thin Film Disks with Carbon Overcoat—Part II: Durability," *ASME Journal of Tribology,* **113,** 32–37 (1991b).

Strom, B. D., D. B. Bogy, C. S. Bhatia, and B. Bhushan, "Tribochemical Effects of Various Gases and Water Vapor on Thin Film Magnetic Disks with Carbon Overcoats," *ASME Journal of Tribology,* **113,** 689–693 (1991).

Strom, B. D., D. B. Bogy, R. G. Walmsley, J. Brandt, and C. S. Bhatia, "Gaseous Wear Products from Perfluoropolyether Lubricant Films," *Wear*, **168**, 31–36 (1993).

Suzuki, S., and F. E. Kennedy, "The Detection of Flash Temperatures in a Sliding Contact by the Method of Tribo-Induced Thermoluminescence," *ASME Journal of Tribology*, **113**, 120–127 (1991).

Tian, H., and T. Matsudaira, "The Role of Relative Humidity, Surface Roughness and Liquid Build-up on Static Friction Behavior of the Head/Disk Interface," *ASME Journal of Tribology*, **115**, 28–35 (1993).

Tian, X., and B. Bhushan, "A Numerical Three-Dimensional Model for the Contact of Rough Surfaces by Variational Principle," *ASME Journal of Tribology*, **117**, in press (1995*a*).

Tian, X., and B. Bhushan, "Micro-Meniscus Effect of Thin Liquid Film on Static Friction of Rough Surface Contact," *J. Phys. D: Appl. Phys.*, in press (1995*b*).

Tsuchiya, T., and B. Bhushan, "Running Characteristics of MIG Heads Against MP, Barium Ferrite and ME Tapes," *IEEE Trans. Magn.*, **MAG-30**, 4176–4178 (1994).

Tsuchiya, T., and B. Bhushan, "Metal Core Recession and Head Stain Studies of MIG Heads Sliding Against Cobalt-Doped Gamma Iron Oxide and Metal Partical Tapes," *Tribol. Trans.*, **38**, 941–949 (1995).

Wallace, R. L., "The Reproduction of Magnetically Recorded Signal," *Bell Syst. Tech. J.*, **30**, 1145–1173 (1951).

Weick, B. L., and B. Bhushan, "Shrinkage and Viscoelastic Behavior of Alternative Substrates for Magnetic Tapes," *IEEE Trans. Magn.*, in press (1995*a*).

Weick, B. L., and B. Bhushan, "Characterization of Magnetic Tapes and Substrates," *IEEE Trans. Magn.*, in press (1995*b*).

Weick, B. L., and B. Bhushan, "Viscoelastic and Shrinkage Behavior of Ultra-thin Polymeric Films," *Jour. App. Poly. Sci.*, in press (1995*c*).

Weick, B. L., and B. Bhushan, "Tribological and Dynamic Behavior of Alternative Magnetic Tape Substrates," *Wear*, in press, (1995*d*).

Yanagisawa, M., "Lubricants on Plated Magnetic Recording Disks," *Tribology and Mechanics of Magnetic Storage Systems*, **2**, eds. B. Bhushan and N. S. Eiss, SP-19, pp. 7–15, ASLE, Park Ridge, Illinois (1985*a*).

Yanagisawa, M., "Tribological Properties of Spin-Coated SiO_2 Protective Film on Plated Magnetic Recording Disks," *Tribology and Mechanics of Magnetic Storage Systems*, **2**, eds. B. Bhushan and N. S. Eiss, SP-19, pp. 16–20, ASLE, Park Ridge, Illinois (1985*b*).

CHAPTER 8
RECORDING LIMITATIONS

John C. Mallinson
Mallinson Magnetics Inc.
Belmont, California

8.1 DISTINCTION BETWEEN NOISE, INTERFERENCE, AND DISTORTION

The output signal of a magnetic recorder is not perfect but is accompanied to some extent by three faults: noise, interference, and distortion. To understand the limitations of a recording channel, it is essential to distinguish clearly between these phenomena.

Noise is due to an uncertainty in some phenomenon and is, therefore, treated statistically. Thus magnetic medium noise arises from a lack of knowledge of, or randomness in, the positions of or directions of magnetization of the individual magnetic sources. Head and electronics noises arise from fluctuations of magnetic domain walls or electric charge carriers. Medium noise is fixed spatially, and, consequently, given a precision transport, each replay of a recorded medium produces exactly the same noise waveform. The head-medium motion transforms the spatial randomness into a pseudo-temporal effect. Head and electronics noises are, on the other hand, purely temporal; these noises never repeat exactly.

Interference is frequently confused with noise even though it is of completely different origin. Interference is due to the reception or reproduction of signals other than those intended. Several examples are discussed in this chapter: crosstalk, incomplete erasure, feedthrough, misregistration, sidefringing, and print-through. Interference is completely deterministic and may, in principle, be calculated exactly.

Distortion is also frequently confused with noise although it, too, is deterministic. Recording channels and systems show distortion because they are not ideal linear channels. There are two ways that the inevitable distortion is minimized in recording systems. For a linear, ac-biased recording system, such as that shown in Fig. 8.1, ac bias makes the magnetic recording channel itself almost linear and distortionless for small signals. In a nonlinear, unbiased recording system, such as that shown in Fig. 8.2, modulation schemes, for example, frequency or pulse-code (digital) modulation, are used to make the system almost distortionless for particular signals. In unbiased recording the channel is highly nonlinear, but is required to preserve exactly only a specific feature of the recorded waveform, for example

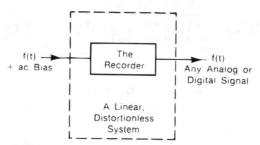

FIGURE 8.1   A linear, distortionless, ac-biased recording system.

zero crossing positions in frequency modulated video or peak positions in binary digital, rather than the complete waveform.

Noise, interference, and distortion all combine to render the output signal an imperfect replica of the input signal. It is for this reason that the phenomena are often confused. The task of the recording system designer is to reduce these faults to tolerable levels so that some predetermined criteria of performance are met. Common criteria are signal-to-noise ratio (SNR), third harmonic distortion (THD), and bit error rate (BER). In this context, it is important to realize that there are no truly digital or binary devices; at the device level, the performance is always governed by a number of analog considerations. These considerations are virtually indistinguishable in, for example, a frequency-modulated analog video cassette recorder and a run-length coded digital disk recorder.

In linear recorders, the input signal current and ac bias are applied directly to the write head. The magnitudes of the noise, interference, and distortion are controlled solely by the parameters of the recording channel. In nonlinear recorders using modulation schemes, the effects of the noise, interference, and distortion in the recording channel are additionally controlled by the parameters of the modulation scheme used. In all modulation schemes, a trade-off is made between bandwidth and immunity to channel faults. By recording a greater bandwidth than that of the input signal, the signal-to-noise ratio may be increased. In professional frequency-modulated video recorders, for example, almost three times the video bandwidth is recorded on tape. To reduce the quantizing errors inherent in analog-

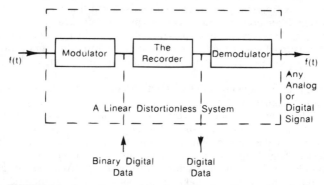

FIGURE 8.2   A nonlinear, unbiased recorder in a linear, distortionless system.

to-binary digital conversion, digital recorders employ the greatest increase in bandwidth. Thus the 16-bit resolution of a digital audio recorder requires approximately a 16-fold increase in bandwidth.

In analog-modulation schemes, the system signal-to-noise ratio bears a direct relationship to the medium noise. With digital modulation, however, the cumulative effect of noise, interference, and distortion leads only to bit errors. In a binary digital system, corruption of the output signal can only confuse 1s with 0s. The limited lexicon (two states only) of binary systems makes the implementation of error detection and correction (EDAC) coding as simple as is possible. Since error detection and correction is a purely logical or mathematical procedure, it is possible, in principle, to achieve perfect correction of bit errors. Thus, apart from quantizing errors, digital recording systems can be made to operate virtually perfectly, notwithstanding the recording channel faults.

In Sec. 8.5, a forecast is made for the future of magnetic recording. Binary digital recording will be used almost universally because of its ability to achieve near-perfect operation. The increasing ease with which error correction can be implemented will lead systems designers to considerably higher areal densities with concomitantly higher raw bit error rates. At least a 10-fold increase in areal density is forecast in the next decade.

8.2 NOISE

There are three principal contributors to the noise power of a recording channel: the electronic noise, the reproduce-head noise, and the recording medium noise. The noise power spectra of these noises for a 2-MHz-band-width instrumentation recorder are sketched in Fig. 8.3. The electronic noise is generally negligible at medium and high frequencies, but increases at $1/f$ at very low frequencies. The head noise behaves conversely; at low frequencies, it is usually negligible but increases to be significant at higher frequencies. In most analog recorders (audio, instrumentation, video), the recording medium noise is, by design, dominant over most of the band. Thus, all analog recorders are medium-noise-limited. Since in reality similar analog considerations govern the operation of digital recorders, it follows that most of them (digital audio, digital video, computer flexible and rigid disk) are, or should be, medium-noise-dominated.

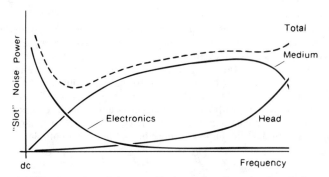

FIGURE 8.3 The relative contributions of medium, head, and electronic noise in a 2-MHz instrumentation recorder.

8.2.1 Electronic Noise

Electronic noise is caused by random fluctuations in time of the electric charge carriers. Essentially all the electronics noise is generated by the first-stage amplifier in the reproduce circuitry. Textbooks and semiconductor manufacturers' handbooks cover the basic principles and give equivalent circuit diagrams. Since these equivalent diagrams have both voltage and current noise power generators, it follows that the best performance (lowest noise figure) is obtained when the amplifier is driven by a source (the read head) of optimum impedance. The noise figure is the decibel ratio of the integrated wideband output noise power to that of an ideal, noiseless amplifier and, in well-designed systems, is 1 to 2 dB only. For amplifiers designed to operate at frequencies of around 10 MHz, a typical optimum source impedance is 50 Ω, and, further, it matters little whether the source impedance is real (dissipative) or imaginary (inductive). Electronic noise is well understood, is not unique to magnetic recording, and can be made almost negligible; therefore, the subject is not pursued further here.

8.2.2 Head Noise

The magnetic flux in both write and read heads is subject to thermally induced fluctuations in time. Because the flux densities are high ($>$ 100) mWb/m^2, or 1000 G) in write heads, the resultant noise is negligible. In read heads, however, the flux densities are low ($<$ 1 mWb/m^2, or 10 G), and read-head noise is often appreciable. The key to understanding read-head noise is the Nyquist noise theorem, which states that "any device, which dissipates energy when connected to a power source, will generate noise power as a passive device." The magnitude of the noise power is

$$e_N^2 = 4kT \, \text{Re} \, (Z)\Delta f \qquad \text{watts into a hypothetical 1-}\Omega \text{ load} \qquad (8.1)$$

where k = Boltzmann's constant
        T = absolute temperature
Re (Z) = real part of the impedance, Ω
     Δf = band width, Hz

A familiar example is the Johnson noise power of a resistor, given by

$$e_N^2 = 4kTR \, \Delta f \qquad (8.2)$$

where R is the resistance (ohms).

     The crucial factor about the Nyquist theorem is that only the dissipative part of the impedance generates noise. Accordingly, only the dissipative part of the read-head impedance generates noise. In any system where the response is not precisely in phase with the driving function, there is dissipation or heat generation. This includes all systems which display hysteresis, for example, magnetic materials.

     Consider the initial (i.e., low-level) hysteresis loops shown in Fig. 8.4. The loss, or heat generated per unit volume per cycle, is equal to the area enclosed by the loop. In the interests of mathematical simplicity, it is usual to assume that these initial loops are elliptical in shape and may be defined by a complex permeability

$$\mu^* = \mu' - j\mu'' \qquad (8.3)$$

having two parts: μ', the real part, which is exactly in phase, and μ'', the imaginary part, which is exactly 90° out of phase. The complex notation serves solely to keep track of the phase in subsequent algebraic manipulations.

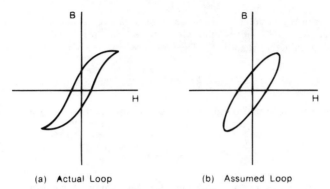

(a) Actual Loop (b) Assumed Loop

FIGURE 8.4 (a) The actual low-level hysteresis loop and (b) the assumed elliptical Lissajous loop of the head core.

Because physical systems are causal, that is, they cannot respond before being driven, certain relationships linking μ' and μ'' exist; they are known as Kramers-Kronig, Bode, and Hilbert transforms to physicists, electrical engineers and mathematicians, respectively. Only the Hilbert transform formalism is given here:

$$\mu'(\omega) = \frac{1}{\pi} \int_{-\infty}^{\infty} \frac{\mu''(\omega')\, d\omega'}{\omega - \omega'} \tag{8.4a}$$

and

$$\mu''(\omega) = \frac{1}{\pi} \int_{-\infty}^{\infty} \frac{\mu'(\omega')\, d\omega'}{\omega - \omega'} \tag{8.4b}$$

where $\mu'(\omega)$ and $\mu''(\omega)$ are the real and imaginary parts of the permeability spectrum. Typical μ' and μ'' spectra are shown in Fig. 8.5. Note that if either part is known at every frequency, then the other part is completely determined. This fact holds whatever the origin (domain wall damping, eddy currents, etc.) of the hysteresis or losses.

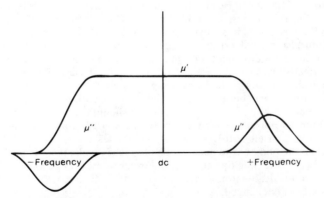

FIGURE 8.5 The magnitude of the real (μ') and imaginary (μ'') parts of the permeability.

Consider now a circular toroid made of a lossy material with cross-sectional area A and circumference l, and wound with N turns. This toroid will serve as a simple model for an inductive read head. The complex inductance is

$$L* = C \frac{N^2 A \mu^*}{l} \tag{8.5}$$

where C is a proportionality constant, and the impedance $Z* = j\omega L*$ is, dropping the proportionality constant,

$$Z* = \frac{j\omega N^2 A \mu'}{l} + \frac{\omega N^2 A \mu''}{l} \tag{8.6}$$

The first term represents an ideal inductor. Such inductors merely store energy when excited; they are dissipationless and, therefore, noiseless. The second term, the real part of the impedance, represents a dissipator and generates noise according to the Nyquist theorem. At frequencies well below that where $\mu''(\omega)$ peaks, the real part of the impedance, and therefore the noise power spectrum, increases with increasing frequency. This explains why inductive head noise becomes of increasing importance at high frequencies.

In general, the dissipative impedance of a head has two parts: the hysteretic loss term discussed above and the resistance of the coil. In manganese-zinc ferrite video heads, the coil resistance is almost negligible ($< 1 \ \Omega$), and the noise is generated principally by the hysteresis losses. With a complex inductance of several microhenries, the dissipative impedance at 10 MHz is usually of the order of 10 Ω. The efficiency of a head is independent of scale, but from Eq. (8.6), the impedance is proportional to the scale; therefore, improvements in heads attend reductions in size. Thus a half-scale head would have one-half the impedance and noise power. To retain the optimum impedance match to the preamplifier, the designer might then choose to increase the number of turns by $\sqrt{2}$, which returns the impedance and noise power to their full-scale values. Either choice (N or $\sqrt{2}$ N) yields a twofold increase in signal-to-head-noise power ratio, with the latter choice giving the better signal-to-electronic-noise power ratio. Factors which limit such size reductions include the reduced bandwidth due to long-wavelength head "bumps" caused by finite pole lengths, the increased mechanical fragility, and the difficulties of fabrication of smaller heads.

The converse situation exists in inductive film heads. Here the inductance is negligible ($< 10^{-8}$ H), but the coil resistance is in the range of 10 to 20 Ω. Thus, at frequencies of 10 to 20 MHz, the noise power of film and ferrite video heads is comparable. Since the scaling rule for resistors is the opposite of inductors, namely, doubling the size halves the resistance, it is clear that improved film heads need larger coils.

In the future, as areal densities and data rates increase, it is anticipated that head noise will become the dominant form of noise when inductive read heads are used. The most effective way to increase areal density is, as discussed below, to increase the track density. Narrower tracks, which generate less medium noise, and higher frequencies or data rates both make the relative contribution of head noise greater. It may be argued that narrower-track recording should use narrower heads, which also have reduced noise. For a wide variety of mechanical and magnetic reasons, however, the region close to the gap, which defines the track width, is usually narrower than the body of the head. In ferrite video heads, the cores are notched, and in film heads, the pole tips are often an order of magnitude narrower than the coil area. As a practical matter then, as track width is changed, the head width and noise stays almost unchanged.

In the case of magnetoresistive read heads, the read head noise power is determined almost solely by the electrical resistance of the magnetoresistive sensor because the dissipative inductive part of the impedance is negligible. For a typical high performance disk file magnetoresistive head of trackwidth 5 μm, the permalloy sensor resistance is about 10 ohms and thus the noise power produced is comparable to that of inductive read heads. However, magnetoresistive heads have extremely high sensitivity and thus the reproduce signal and medium noise power levels are high. A well-designed permalloy magnetoresistive head produces output levels (both signal and noise) which are equivalent to those of an inductive head with an NV product of about 50,000 cm/sec. It follows that in low speed applications, for example in tape and small diameter rigid disk drives, the reproduced medium noise greatly exceeds the magnetoresistive head noise. It is expected, therefore, that such recording systems will remain medium-noise dominated in the foreseeable future even at extremely high densities and data rates.

Two other forms of head noise occur in some circumstances. In ferrite heads, rubbing noise is generated if the material has nonzero magnetostriction. The acoustic waves generated by the head-tape rubbing contact cause fluctuations in the magnetic flux threading the head coil. While the excitation of the acoustic waves is thought to be random, thus injecting white noise, the properties of the head (size, elastic constants) often cause the rubbing noise to peak at certain mechanical frequencies. Rubbing noise is, however, reduced when polycrystalline materials are used, because the random orientations of the crystallites permits some cancellation of the magnetostrictive effect. In both inductive and magnetoresistive film heads, Barkhausen noise can be observed. This is caused by large changes in the domain wall structure in the thin films in response to magnetic fields or mechanical stresses. The distinction between Barkhausen and the normal hysteretic noise discussed above is not well defined and is simply one of magnitude: many small domain wall jumps give normal hysteresis. Barkhausen noise is reduced by careful micromagnetic design; the use of multilayer film structures and the application of easy-axis magnetic fields have been explored (Decker and Tsang, 1980). This topic is discussed in detail in Chapter 6.

8.2.3 Additive Medium Noise

Recording medium noise is due to the uncertainty or randomness of some property of the medium. Any variation or fluctuation from point to point will produce medium noise. The two most basic random processes are the uncertainty in the physical positions of and the directions of magnetization of the magnetic sources in the medium. In tapes, where the volumetric packing fraction of the magnetic particles, p, is less than 0.5, the magnetic sources are the individual particles themselves in well-dispersed media, or the clusters chains or ropes of particles seen in poorly dispersed media. In thin film disks, where the packing fraction is close to unity and there is no possibility of the grains clustering physically, the sources can be either the individual grains or groups of grains. When the coercive force, H_c, or anisotropy field, H_k, is high relative to the magnetostatic and exchange interaction fields, the magnetization of each grain is almost independent of that of its neighboring grains. Conversely, when the coercive force is low or inter-grain exchange coupling exists, the magnetization in adjacent grains becomes correlated, forming the swirls and vortices which appear so prominently in micromagnetic computations (Zhu and Bertram, 1991). Whereas clusters are correlated groups of particles, vortices are correlated magnetization patterns. Although physical clumping of particles is magnetization independent, micromagnetic vortices must vary with the magnetic state of the medium. For example, vortices almost disappear in the maximum remanent magnetization state.

When the size of the sources is very small compared with the trackwidth and wavelength of the recording and the sources are distributed according to Poisson's statistics, that is equal probabilities in equal volumes, then the medium noise is additive. Additive noise is simply added to the signal and exists, of course, even in the absence of a recorded signal. On the other hand, when the size of the sources is comparable with or larger than the trackwidth and wavelength so that Poisson statistics no longer hold over such dimensions, then the noise becomes multiplicative. Multiplicative noise power is proportional to the signal power and is, therefore, zero in the absence of a recorded signal. Obviously intermediate cases exist where the size of the sources is such that both additive and multiplicative noise coexist.

In this section, the theory of additive noise will be developed and applied to the problems of calculating the signal-to-noise ratio of audio, instrumentation and video recorders. The effect of additive noise on the detection process in digital recorders will be reviewed. Because the larger scale non-Poisson phenomena which give rise to modulation noise cannot be predicted, a priori, no useful general theory exists.

Consider the algebraic manipulation

$$\overline{(e_1 + e_2)^2} = \overline{e_1^2} + \overline{e_2^2} + \overline{2e_1e_2} \tag{8.7}$$

where e_1 and e_2 are voltage waveforms in time and the bar indicates time averaging. If e_1 and e_2 are not correlated, that is, they bear no fixed relationship to each other, then the cross-term $\overline{2e_1e_2}$ is equal to zero, and the square of the sum is equal to the sum of the squares. With correlated or coherent signals, the average power is obtained by adding the voltages and then squaring. With uncorrelated sources, the total noise power is obtained by adding the individual noise powers. This rule finds application, for example, in assessing the total noise power in a recording channel: the medium-noise power plus the head-noise power plus the electronic-noise power equals the total-noise power.

Figure 8.6 shows a single magnetic particle passing a reproduce head. A fraction of its flux threads the coil producing the voltage and power waveforms shown. When the recording medium is ac erased and thus has zero remanence, the total noise power is simply the sum or integral of all these individual source power pulses. If the sources are small and identical and are packed as a Poisson process, the noise power P at any magnetization may be calculated by simple binomial statistical arguments (Mallinson, 1991). Assuming that the read head has 100 percent efficiency, one turn, and no gap loss, the result is

$$P = \left[1 - p \left(\frac{M}{M_r} \right)^2 \right] \mu_0 m^2 N w V^2 \frac{\delta(d + \delta/2)}{d^2(d + \delta)^2} \tag{8.8}$$

where

  p = average volumetric packing factor
  M/M_r = average magnetization of the medium divided by the maximum remanent magnetization.
  m = the dipole moment of the identical magnetic sources
  N = number of sources per unit volume
  w = track width

V = head-medium relative velocity
δ = coating thickness
d = head-to-medium spacing

The power P is given in watts into a hypothetical 1-Ω load (Mee, 1964). Equation (8.8) shows that the noise power increases with the dipole moment and the average number of sources; thus the more magnetic the medium, the greater the noise. The power also increases as w and V^2, which illustrates the difference between a coherent and an incoherent process; the sources across the width are uncorrelated, whereas all the sources are subject to the same velocity. The noise power decreases with increasing head-to-medium spacing, as it must. Finally, the power is almost independent of the coating thickness because only the near layers contribute significantly to the head flux.

The noise power also varies as $(1 - p(M/M_r)^2$. Thus, when the average magnetization of the medium is zero the noise power is maximum. Conversely, when the magnetization is saturated the noise power is minimum. It follows that when a varying signal is recorded, the noise power is, in statistical terms, "non-stationary," that is it varies at different parts of the waveform. On the other hand, when a non-varying or constant waveform is recorded the noise power is "stationary".

When varying signals are recorded, the "nonstationary" noise in the magnetization of the medium is high at those positions where M is low and low at those locations where M is high. On the other hand, the changing noise level seen in the

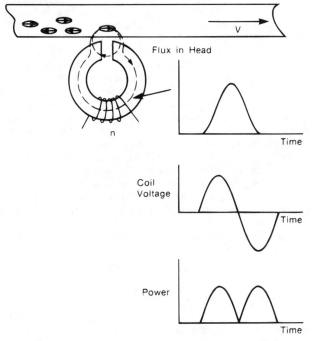

FIGURE 8.6 The flux induced in the reproduce head, and the voltage and power in the coil of the head, as a single magnetic particle passes the gap.

read head flux or output voltage may no longer coincide spatially with the written magnetization due to the dispersive nature of the reading processes. For example, the read process transfer function makes the magnetization noise of an isolated transition spread and cause output pulse amplitude and width variations (Wallace, 1951; Slutsky, 1994). The non-stationary media magnetization noise has been previously called media flux noise (Nunnelley, 1987). However, this is misleading because it ignores the fact that a flux has two parts: magnetic field and magnetization.

In audio and instrumentation analog tape recorders where $p < 0.5$ and the maximum signal level M is usually held below 0.2 of the remanence in order to limit distortion, the difference between the maximum and minimum noise power is quite small (about 2% only) and the distinction between stationary and non-stationary noise is not significant. In such recorders it is easy, for example by using a spectrum analyzer, to measure the additive medium noise and deduce a meaningful signal-to-noise power ratio.

In video tape recorders, both analog and digital, and in digital tape recorders the packing fraction is low but the maximum signal level is close to the maximum remanence and, accordingly, a considerable difference (about two to one) exists between the maximum and minimum noise powers. In these cases, a meaningful measurement of noise becomes more difficult because a spectrum analyzer simply averages the varying noise power over many hundreds or thousands of cycles of the complete waveform. A more useful approach is to capture many examples of the complete reproduced waveform, using perhaps a digitizing oscilloscope with memory, in order to determine the noise power at the critical points of the waveform where the frequency demodulator or binary bit detector operates. Examples of such critical points include the zero-crossings used in analog frequency demodulators, the peak positions used in differentiating peak detectors, and the amplitude sampling points in partial response detection schemes.

In thin film disk digital recorders, the packing fraction is close to unity and, again, the maximum signal levels recorded are close to the maximum remanence of the medium. In this case, the minimum noise, which occurs when the magnetization of the media is at maximum, may be less than 10% of the maximum noise on the zero magnetization parts of the recorded waveform. Since most of the noise occurs at the recorded waveform zero crossings or magnetization transitions, it is indeed found that a spectrum analyzer measures a noise power which is proportional to the number of magnetization transitions per unit time or the flux reversal linear density (Baugh et al., 1983). In order to obtain useful noise data which is of relevance to the digital detection process two options exist. The simpler is merely to measure the noise power at non-varying constant magnetization levels of particular interest, for example, at zero magnetization. The more difficult alternative is to perform time domain analysis upon complete noisy waveforms captured on a suitable storage oscilloscope as discussed above.

Unfortunately, knowing the total noise power does not reveal the noise power spectral density $e^2(k)$, where

$$P = \int_{-\infty}^{\infty} e^2(k)\, dk \qquad (8.9)$$

To deduce the noise power spectral density, the most direct analysis uses the Wiener autocorrelation theorem. This theorem states that the noise power spectral density is the Fourier cosine transform of the autocorrelation function $F(x)$; thus

$$e^2(k) = \int_{-\infty}^{\infty} F(x) \cos kx \, dx \qquad (8.10)$$

where

$$F(x) = \frac{1}{L} \int_{-L/2}^{L/2} e(x')e(x - x') \, dx' \qquad (8.11)$$

Completion of these operations results in

$$e^2(k) = \left[1 - p \left(\frac{M}{M_r} \right)^2 \right] \mu_0 m^2 Nw V^2 |k| (1 - e^{-2|k|\delta}) e^{-2|k|d} \, \Delta k \qquad (8.12)$$

where Δk is the wave number interval (or slot) over which the power spectrum is measured (Mann, 1957; Mallinson, 1969, 1991).

It is instructive, at this point, to compare the noise power spectrum with the maximum possible signal power spectrum $E^2(k)$. The signal power spectrum is, for a 100 percent efficient, one-turn, zero-gap approximation head, simply one-quarter the square value of the spectrum corresponding to uniform, sinusoidal magnetization (Wallace, 1951). Thus

$$E^2(k) = \tfrac{1}{4} [\mu_0 m Nw V (1 - e^{-|k|\delta})]^2 \qquad (8.13)$$

with units, again, watts into a hypothetical 1-Ω load. The signal and noise power spectra are plotted versus frequency ($f = Vk/2\pi$) in Fig. 8.7. Both the signal and noise power spectra increase at 6 dB, or a factor of 4, per octave at the longer wavelengths; but at wavelengths comparable with the coating thickness, differences in slope occur. The signal power spectrum becomes flat due to the onset of the thickness loss term. The noise power spectrum, on the other hand, now slopes at 3 dB, or a factor of 2, per octave. This difference has had a profound influence upon

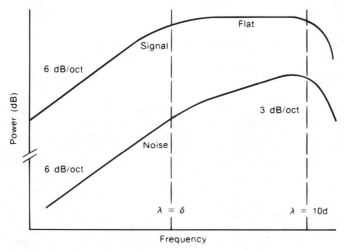

FIGURE 8.7 The signal and medium-noise power spectra for an ideal medium.

the optimal design of tape recorders as is discussed below. At small wavelengths at which appreciable spacing loss is suffered, say $\lambda < 10d$, both spectra roll over according to the same exponential spacing loss term.

At this point, we can obtain, by division, the narrow-band, or slot, signal-to-noise ratio (SNR). This is the signal power divided by the noise power, in a slot Δk, at the same wave number k:

$$(\text{SNR})_{\text{slot}} = \left[1 - p \left(\frac{M}{M_r} \right)^2 \right] \frac{\pi Nw(1 - e^{-|k|\delta})^2}{|k|(1 - e^{-2|k|\delta})\Delta k} \tag{8.14}$$

Several interesting facts now appear. The slot signal-to-noise ratio is independent of the source's moment, because all signal-to-medium-noise ratios essentially involve statistics only and, as such, are merely noise source counting exercises. The ratio is independent of head-to-medium velocity and head-to-medium spacing for the same reason; while these changes may alter the absolute values of the signal and the noise powers, they do not affect the underlying statistics.

In order to have a nearly distortionless output signal, all recorders must be equalized; that is, electrical filter or compensation networks are employed to correct the signal spectrum. For audio and instrumentation analog tape recorders, which are linearized by using ac bias, it is necessary to make the overall channel amplitude transfer function flat, that is, constant, between some lower and upper frequency limits. The required equalization is the reciprocal of the signal spectrum, so that the overall transfer function is given by $E(k)[E(k)]^{-1} = 1$, a constant. The resulting expression for the wideband signal-to-noise ratio is

$$(\text{SNR})_{\text{wide}} = \left[1 - p \left(\frac{M}{M_r} \right)^2 \right] \pi Nw \left(\int_{k_{\min}}^{k_{\max}} |k| \coth \frac{|k|\delta}{2} \, dk \right)^{-1} \tag{8.15}$$

which at short wavelengths, $kd > 1$, reduces to

$$(\text{SNR})_{\text{wide}} \approx \left[1 - p \left(\frac{M}{M_r} \right)^2 \right] 2\pi Nw(k_{\max}^2 - k_{\min}^2) \tag{8.16}$$

and for large-bandwidth systems, $k_{\max} >> k_{\min}$, becomes

$$(\text{SNR})_{\text{wide}} \approx \left[1 - p \left(\frac{M}{M_r} \right)^2 \right] 2\pi Nwk_{\max}^2 = \left[1 - p \left(\frac{M}{M_r} \right)^2 \right] \frac{Nw\lambda_{\min}^2}{2\pi} \tag{8.17}$$

The underlying reason for the simplicity of this result is shown in Fig. 8.8. The volume of medium effectively sensed by the reproduce head is strictly limited; in the longitudinal direction, it is only the half wavelength that actually spans the reproduce-head gap which is sensed. In the perpendicular direction, the thickness loss limits contributions to a depth equal to a small fraction (say one third) of a wavelength. Thus the volume, shown shaded, of medium sensed at any instant is proportional to $(\lambda/2)(\lambda/3)w$, or $w\lambda^2/6$, and the number of sources sensed is proportional to $Nw\lambda^2/6$. The signal-to-medium-noise ratio involves a statistical calculation in which the mean signal power is analogous to the square of the mean value of the distribution, and the noise power is analogous to the mean-square deviation or variance. The wideband signal-to-noise ratio is therefore determined by the number of sources being sensed at any instant by the read head. If the ratio is, say, 40 dB, that means 10,000 sources are being sensed in the shaded volume; 30 dB corresponds to 1000, 20 dB to 100, and so on.

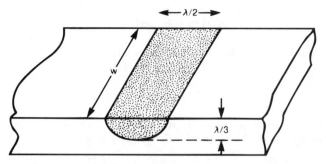

FIGURE 8.8 The volume sensed by the read head with particulate recording media is $\lambda/2$ long, $\lambda/3$ deep, and w wide.

Another important conclusion to be drawn from Fig. 8.8 and Eq. (8.17) is that it is in principle better, when seeking higher areal densities on tape media which are relatively thick, to use higher track densities than it is to use shorter wavelengths. Halving the track width costs 3 dB in wideband signal-to-noise ratio, whereas halving the wavelength costs 6 dB. In many recorders, halving the wavelength will cost more than 6 dB because it may no longer be possible to keep the channel signal-to-medium-noise limited. This conclusion is unfortunate because reducing the head-medium velocity is always the easiest thing to do in the quest for higher areal densities. Reengineering the whole machine to utilize narrower track-width heads is a considerably more difficult undertaking.

A similar analysis may be conducted in order to determine the SNR when recording digital transitions for thin film disk media. It is, of course, understood that the noise is, in a strict sense, "non-stationary" because the noise varies as $1 - p(M/M_r)^2$. However, at high linear densities, where the written magnetization transitions overlap appreciably, the noise may be approximated as a stationary phenomenon. Indeed, the noise when measured on a spectrum analyzer is but a single averaged "stationary" value.

Suppose that the recording is made at the Nyquist rate of two digital bits per cycle of bandwidth. This rate is closely approached in carefully equalized class IV partial response channels. The SNR analysis follows that given earlier for thick media with the single change that now the depth or thickness of the medium sensed by the read head is the thin film thickness, δ, itself as seen in Fig. 8.9. Accordingly, the wide band signal power-to-medium noise ratio becomes,

$$(\text{SNR})_{\text{WIDE}} \approx \left[\, 1 - p \left(\frac{M}{M_r} \right)^2 \right] \frac{Nw\delta\lambda}{2} \tag{8.18}$$

The signal power is proportional to the square of the mean number of sources in a single digital bit cell. The noise power is proportional to the mean number. The SNR is equal to the mean number. Again, the reason for the simplicity of this result is that signal-to-medium noise ratios are nothing more than statistical counting exercises over the sources. This extremely simple idea will be used in Sec. 8.5 on future areal densities.

Another interesting way to assess the noise in binary recording on thin film media is to calculate the noise power integrated over the length of the magnetization transition, see Fig. 8.10. In the Williams and Comstock analysis, the magnetization transition is assumed to have the form

$$M(x) = \frac{2}{\pi} M_r \tan^{-1}\left(\frac{x}{a}\right) \tag{8.19}$$

where a is called the transition slope parameter and is given by,

$$a = 2\sqrt{\frac{M_r}{H_c} \delta\left(d + \frac{\delta}{2}\right)} \tag{8.20}$$

The straight line approximation of this transition has a length of πa. The integrated noise power, that is the noise energy, E, over this length is, from equation, 8.8,

$$E \propto \int_{-\frac{\pi a}{2}}^{\frac{\pi a}{2}}\left[1 - \left(\frac{2}{\pi}\tan^{-1}\left(\frac{x}{a}\right)\right)^2\right] dx$$

$$\propto 0.82\ \pi a \tag{8.21}$$

It will be noted that, as expected, the noise energy, E, is proportional to the transition slope parameter, a. It is also seen that the average of the integrated noise power is just 0.82 of the instantaneous maximum, noise power. A similar calculation assuming a hyperbolic tangent transition yields a similar result (0.75). It is clear that, at high linear densities, where adjacent transitions overlap, the noise power and SNR are well-approximated by merely counting the number of sources in each bit cell. In cases where "zig-zag" or "sawtooth" transitions occur, it is similarly expected that E is proportional to the zig-zag or sawtooth length, because these lengths must be approximately equal to πa. An important conclusion is that the noise energy decreases with sharper transitions.

This leads directly to the question of how the transition noise, whether it be the instantaneous maximum value at the transition center or the average power just discussed, affects the binary bit detection process. In the case of the ubiquitous, but old-fashioned, differentiating peak detector, the answer is both obvious and simple because the principal effect of the noise is to introduce timing or phase margin errors which are usually called transition jitter (Katz, 1979). The transition jitter introduced is proportional to the noise voltage divided by the slope of the differentiated output signal. When more sophisticated detection schemes are used, such as those used with the many partial response post-equalizations, the analysis becomes, of course, more complicated in detail but it nevertheless remains simple in principle.

Given a particular recording format, the track width and minimum wavelength are fixed. Thus, the only improvement possible is in the medium, and, according to

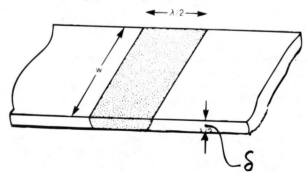

FIGURE 8.9   The volume sensed by the read head with thin film recording media: it is $\lambda/2$ long, δ deep, and w wide.

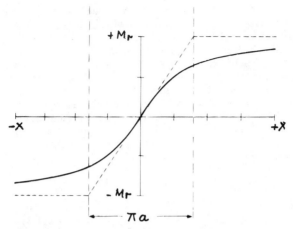

FIGURE 8.10   An arctangent transition of magnetization showing the straight line approximation of length πa.

the analysis above, the only parameter of consequence in well-dispersed tapes is the number of particles per unit volume. A change from $\gamma\text{-Fe}_2\text{O}_3$ to metallic iron particles will not change the signal-to-noise ratio if the particle density remains unchanged. It follows that the correct way to exploit metallic iron, or other higher-energy particles, is to use smaller particles which are equally stable against superparamagnetic decay. Thus, for metallic iron particles of one-sixteenth the volume, with 16 times the particle density may be used and thus a 12 dB-higher signal-to-noise ratio is achieved in medium-noise-limited recorders.

In thin film disks it is clear that higher signal-to-noise ratios, lower transition noise energies, and smaller noise-induced timing errors can be obtained by using smaller grains because this increases the all-important number of sources per unit volume, N. Concomitantly, of course, smaller grains lead to media with a higher coercive force, H_c, which in turn reduces the magnetization transition length, a. The higher the coercive force, the greater the ratio H_c/M_r. The higher this ratio becomes, the less important are the magneto-static interactions which cause the magnetization vortices and swirls discussed earlier and, therefore, the smaller the number of grains in these vortices. Thus smaller grains have many beneficial effects: higher coercive forces, smaller noise sources, higher signal-to-medium noise ratios and, finally, sharper magnetization transitions. The evolution of thin film media over the last 35 years since its introduction by Ampex in 1958 in "stop-motion" video disk recorders may be understood in this context.

It is of interest to compare the calculated signal-to-noise ratios with measurements made on various tape recorders. In linear recorders using ac bias, a maximum signal level of only 20 percent of the maximum is allowed in order to limit the third harmonic distortion (THD) to 1 percent. This means that only one source out of five in the coating is used to record the signal, which imposes a factor of 25, or a 14-dB penalty, on the attainable ratio because all the particles still contribute to the noise. A professional audio recorder has a bandwidth of 40 Hz to 15 kHz, a track width of approximately 2 mm, and a tape speed of 190 mm/s (7.5 in/s). Using cobalt-$\gamma\text{-Fe}_2\text{O}_3$ tape with 10^{12} particles per cubic millimeter, the measured wideband ratio is 75 dB; Eq. (8.17) yields 76 dB. An instrumentation recorder has a 400-Hz to 2-MHz bandwidth, 1.25-mm track width, 3-m/s (120-in/s) speed, and a measured

34-dB ratio versus the computed value of 36 dB. It may be concluded that in cobalt-γFe_2O_3 tape, the sources are, in fact, the individual particles.

Frequency-modulated (FM) video recorders are nonlinear machines where distortion is controlled by using a modulation scheme. Detection of the FM waveform is performed on the zero crossings, and it is critical that every zero crossing be detected with its correct timing. This is achieved by ensuring that the overall transfer function of the channel has "straight-line" amplitude and phase characteristics. Because the FM signal is analog, with an infinitude of permitted zero-crossings, equalizing an FM channel is a considerably more demanding task than that of equalizing a digital channel where only a finite, and usually small, number of pulse positions can occur. With the requisite straight-line equalization, the video baseband signal-to-noise ratio is

$$(\text{SNR})_{\text{video}} \approx \left[1 - p \left(\frac{M}{M_r} \right)^2 \right] \frac{3NwV^2(\Delta f)^2}{8\pi f_c f_s^3} \tag{8.22}$$

where f_c is the carrier frequency, Δf is the change in f_c for a 1-volt video input, and f_s is the video bandwidth (Mallinson, 1975). For a type C professional video recorder, f_c is 9 MHz, Δf is 3 MHz, f_s is 4.5 MHz, w is 200 μm, and V is 25 m/s (1000 in/s), and approximately 4 dB of video preemphasis is used. The computed signal-to-noise ratio is 38 dB when normal γ-Fe_2O_3 tape is used. To this figure, 4 dB is to be added for video preemphasis and 9 dB (i.e., 20 log $2\sqrt{2}$) to convert from the mean signal power used above to the peak-to-peak signal power customarily used in the video industry. The net figure calculated is then 51 dB, which concurs well with the 50 to 52-dB values measured on such recorders.

The good agreement between the calculated and measured ratios is to some degree fortuitous. The signal power spectrum measured is always considerably different from that given by Eq. (8.13) (Smaller, 1969). Specifically, the short-wavelength signal power is smaller because of the existence of writing-process losses which increase at shorter wavelengths. Similarly, the measured noise power spectrum does not follow that given by Eq. (8.12), but, at long and short wavelengths, the actual noise power is larger and smaller respectively than is expected (Thurlings, 1983; Denteneer, 1990). The origin of this discrepancy is explored below. At medium wavelengths, both signal and noise spectra are as expected; at short wavelengths, the lower-than-predicted signal and the lower-than-predicted noise fortuitously compensate nearly exactly.

Much better agreement between theoretical and experimental noise power spectra is obtained by applying second order statistics to the noise problem. Here it is assumed that rather than having a multitude of identical noise sources, there exists a statistical distribution of the sizes of noise sources. For example, the lengths of the sources, measured in the head-media relative motion direction, x, can be assumed to have a Lorentzian distribution of the form $(1 + (x/l)^2)^{-1}$ were l is termed the along-track correlation length. Recall that the auto-correlation function, given in the spatial domain in equation 5.11, becomes a product of spectra in the frequency domain. Thus a Lorentzian distribution of particle lengths yields an exponential noise power spectrum, because the Fourier transform of a Lorentzian is an exponential. Experimentally, many noise power spectra are found, indeed, to be approximately exponential. Conversely, of course, the accurate measurement of the noise power spectral shape may be considered to be a measurement of the (cross track averaged) along-track correlation function since they are but a Fourier transform pair.

Additionally, the width of the sources, measured in the cross-track direction, z, can be considered to be a statistical variable. Again it is common to assume that the width or cross sectional area (y, z) of the sources have a Lorentzian distribution with an associated "cross-track correlation length."

Recall, however, that all read heads, both inductive and magnetoresistive, operate by first summing, which is equivalent to averaging, the flux of the sources across the track and then performing the auto-correlations of Eq. 8.11. It is not possible, therefore, from noise power spectral measurements alone, to determine the actual form of a cross-track correlation function. All that may be obtained is the cross-track average of the correlation length. An infinitude of physically possible cross-track correlation functions can have the same cross-track average correlation length.

Due to this indeterminancy, it is, perhaps, best to regard these second order statistical concepts as being merely curve fitting exercises. They are just a way to fit experimental noise power spectra to theory (Nunnelley, 1987; Denteneer, 1990; Bertram, 1994). The shape of the noise power spectrum may be adjusted by a suitable choice of the average along-track correlation function. The spectral magnitude or power level may then be adjusted by a suitable choice of the average cross-track correlation length.

In the interest of completeness, a brief discussion of quantizing noise in digital systems is given. Digital systems can never be absolutely accurate when an analog signal is to be recorded. An analog-to-digital converter tests the analog signal against a number of preset digital levels and chooses the digital level which is closest. The inevitable error may, in principle, be made arbitrarily small by increasing the resolution, that is, the number of levels, of the analog-to-digital converter. Practical engineering factors limit the number of levels to approximately 10^5 corresponding to the number of 16-bit words. The error is called *quantizing noise,* although it is not really a noise but is rather an instrumentation error or distortion inherent in the digitization of the analog signal. When the source data are already digital as in computers, then, of course, no apparent quantizing error occurs.

Suppose there are N bits corresponding to 2^N quantizing levels. The mean-square quantizing error for equally probable input signals is one-twelfth of the interval. It follows that the signal power to quantizing-noise power ratio is

$$(SNR)_{quant} = (6N + 7.8) \quad dB \tag{5.23}$$

Thus, for $N = 8$, the standard for digital video recorders, the ratio is 56 dB. For $N = 16$, as in digital audio tape recorders (and optical compact disks), the ratio is 104 dB, a figure that could be achieved with an analog recorder of the type discussed above only if, for example, the track width were to be increased by a factor of about 1,000! For a discussion of the relative merits of the various modulation schemes, the reader is referred to the standard textbooks. The concepts are not unique to magnetic recording and are not pursued further here.

8.2.4 Multiplicative (or Modulation) Noise

As stated previously, modulation noise becomes appreciable when the physical size of the noise sources becomes comparable with the trackwidth. In this case, the usual averaging of the noise sources across the track width which occurs in all read heads is no longer appropriate. When there are many sources across the trackwidth, the noise power is their statistical variance. When there is only one noise source across the track width, the concept of cross track statistical averaging becomes meaningless and Poisson statistics become irrelevant. The result is that the signal

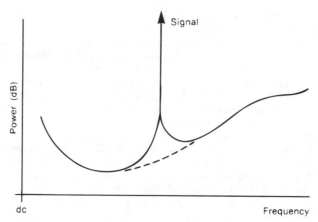

FIGURE 8.11   The total noise spectrum showing the modulation noise "skirts" around the signal.

waveform itself is multiplied by the noise. For example, gross variations in the medium maximum remanence, due to gross clumping of particles causes modulation noise. Accordingly, the output power spectrum of a recorder has the typical features shown in Fig. 8.11. Note how the convolution has caused the appearance of characteristic modulation noise sidebands, or skirts, around the signal.

There are, of course, many other sources of modulation noise other than those attributable to the magnetic noise sources themselves. Among the most important media effects are variations in coating thickness, packing fraction, surface roughness and substrate roughness which are coherent across the track. Variations in packing fraction due to the gravure coating process are a frequent source of modulation noise in video tapes. Other sources of modulation noise are not even directly associated with the recording medium itself such as head-to-medium spacing variations and relative velocity variations (wow and flutter) both of which are inherently coherent across the trackwidth. Because modulation noise comes from phenomena which are coherent across the trackwidth it follows that, in every case, the modulation noise power is proportional to the trackwidth squared and consequently signal-to-modulation noise ratios are independent of trackwidth.

8.3   INTERFERENCE

Interference is the reception or reproduction of signals other than those intended. It is deterministic and thus may be measured and, in principle, calculated exactly. It may be reduced to arbitrarily small magnitude by proper design. In this section, the principal interferences encountered in recorders are discussed.

8.3.1   Crosstalk

Crosstalk is due to the unintentional leakage of flux from one channel to another in a multichannel read or write head stack. The leakage flux may have either polarity and is generally of the order of 1 percent ($-$ 40 dB) in immediately adjacent heads.

Although the leakage flux may be calculated by using, for example, the finite-element method, considerable sophistication is required in the analysis to achieve the necessary accuracy.

Consider a multichannel head stack with only the center channel excited with write current. Because the leakage fluxes fall off approximately geometrically (-40, -80, -120 dB, etc.), crosstalk is essentially limited to the immediately adjacent tracks. When the adjacent heads carry write current, the flux in these gaps adds linearly to the leakage fluxes. Consequently, the writing field and the written magnetization pattern are corrupted by a small fraction of the signal from the adjacent track. Suppose that the leakage flux is -40 dB. With ac bias, the writing process is virtually linear, and, accordingly, the written magnetization will contain a -40-dB component of the adjacent track signal. When ac bias is not used, somewhat surprisingly, the written crosstalk magnetization is even higher; the crosstalk has been measured to be approximately a factor of 4 ($+12$ dB) higher (Tanaka, 1984). The origin of the apparent gain is not understood. Presumably a very similar effect occurs in consumer video recorders, where (in the color-under system) the color chrominance signals are recorded linearly at a low level relative to the frequency-modulated luminance signal.

In multi-channel digital recorders, the effects of writing cross-talk can be eliminated entirely at the expense of increased write electronics complexity. Suppose that there are 10 adjacent tracks and that a virtually perfect write process can be obtained with a mere 5% duty cycle of the write current. This condition obtains when the combination of data rate and head-medium speed is such that the diameter of the "writing field bubble," which is governed by the write gap-length and the magnitude of the write current, is greater than the digital bit length. By arranging for the write electronics to provide 5% bit length pulses asynchronously to the 10 adjacent write heads, writing cross talk vanishes because now only head is active at any instant in time (Lokhoff, 1991).

By reciprocity, the writing and reading crosstalk performances of a given multichannel head are identical. If the writing current in a coil engenders -40-dB leakage flux in an adjacent head gap, then, during reproducing, flux will appear in the same head coil which is -40 dB below that entering the channel. If ac bias is used, the total (write plus read) system crosstalk is doubled to -34 dB. Without ac bias, the total system crosstalk becomes -26 dB. It should be noted that the phenomenon of concern in crosstalk is not the coupling from coil to coil in the multichannel head stack. The important aspects of crosstalk arise from coil to adjacent gap in writing and gap to adjacent coil in reading. Coil-to-coil phenomena involve entirely different flux paths and are more properly categorized as an example of feedthrough.

The measures taken to minimize crosstalk include adding magnetic shields, increasing the distance between the heads, and reducing the side areas of the heads. In this regard, film heads, with their extremely small side areas, have very low crosstalk without resorting to magnetic shields. Because crosstalk is a diminished version of the adjacent track signal with the same spectral properties as the signal, signal processing techniques cannot be applied to reduce crosstalk. In this sense, crosstalk is more troublesome than noise.

8.3.2 Incomplete erasure

There are several methods of erasing previously recorded information. The most effective is bulk erasure in which the complete tape reel or disk is subjected to an ac field of decreasing magnitude. If the initial field magnitude is great enough to switch even the hardest (highest-nucleation-field) particles, very nearly perfect erasure can be achieved. Typically, the initial field magnitudes needed are about five times the coercive force. Instrumentation and professional video recorders use bulk erasure.

A less effective erasure method is the use of erase heads. These are generally similar in construction to read-write heads, but have a gap (or double gaps) of greater gap length. The longer gap lengths permit higher-magnitude erase fields at the far side of thick media. Wherever erase heads are used, only a very small length of tape is subjected to the erasing field at any instant. The erasure is, therefore, less effective than that achieved with bulk erasure because the regions just downstream of the erase-head gap can be re-recorded by the magnetic field arising from the unerased tape upstream of the gap (McKnight, 1963). The re-recording effect is expected to be greatest at relatively long wavelengths because then the upstream magnetic field is highest.

The erasure technique used in digital tape and disk recorders is much less effective. In these machines, there is no specific erase process; the new data are simply written over the old data. In longitudinal recording, it is found that overwriting a low-density recording with a high-density recording results in the least complete erasure; accordingly, most overwrite tests use two square waves, $f_2 > f_1$, with f_2 erasing the f_1 recording. Typically, f_1 is incompletely erased to about -30 dB only. When perfect square waves of writing-head flux are used, the field history of any point in the medium is a succession of fields having opposite polarities but the same magnitude. The magnitude differs, of course, at different depths in the medium. According to the Preisach formalism, the application of alternating-polarity fields of fixed magnitude causes the remanence to alternate between two levels, implying that perfect erasure of digital data should be possible.

It seems likely, that several explanations of the incomplete erasure are possible. The first is that the write head deep-gap flux and fringing field has a finite rise-time (of the order 10^{-8} seconds) and thus not all the length of the old record is properly over-written. The second is that a re-recording phenomenon similar to that occurring with erase heads is happening (Fayling et al., 1984; Wachenschwantz and Jeffers, 1985). The third is the usual reduction of head efficiency at higher frequencies; long wavelengths are written deeper than short. These reasons explain why it is more difficult to overwrite the low-frequency, long-wavelength data.

In order to record optimally short-wavelength, high-bit-density data, it is necessary to use lower record currents and writing-field magnitudes. In turn it is thus found that satisfactory overwrite performance can be obtained only with thinner media. This had led to the widespread adoption of a scaling rule that the medium thickness and the bit interval should remain in the same ratio; higher linear densities necessitate thinner coatings.

8.3.3 Feedthrough

Feedthrough refers to any unintentional coupling of signals which does not involve the recording medium. Thus there may be feedthrough from the write to the read electronics within a channel. Signals from one channel can leak in the adjacent channels, as in the misnamed transformer crosstalk between head coils. Feedthrough can occur via electromagnetic, inductive, capacitive, and resistive coupling. Feedthrough is mentioned here only in the interest of completeness. The methods used to reduce or eliminate feedthrough, such as shielding and grounding, are well known in electrical engineering and are not unique to magnetic recorders.

8.3.4 Misregistration

Misregistration interference is due to the inability of a recording system to maintain the relative positions of the heads and media exactly. In a fixed-head tape recorder, misregistration is principally associated with interchange, that is, playing a recorded tape upon other machines. In disk recorders, the imperfect reproducibility of the moving-head positioning system and differential thermal expansion are the principal causes of misregistration.

In longitudinal-track, fixed-head tape machines (audio, instrumentation, and digital), maximum peak-to-peak tracking errors of approximately 10 μm are typical; this strictly limits the minimum track widths usable. With moving-head tape machines (professional and consumer video recorders and serpentine track data cartridge recorders), the relative position of the heads to the tracks can be servoed continuously, and maximum tracking errors of perhaps 1 μm occur. In rigid-disk recorders, the maximum head positioning error can be reduced to less than 0.1 μm by "sector servo" systems.

When an erase head and guard bands are employed, the initial effect of misregistration is simply to reduce the true signal-to-noise ratio. If, however, the mistracking is severe enough to permit the reproduce head to cover the adjacent track, interference occurs because the signal is contaminated by another signal. At short wavelengths, the magnitudes of interfering signals are proportional to track widths covered by the reproduce head. At long wavelengths, an additional effect occurs which is included in the discussion on side fringing below.

When an erase head is not used, as in digital disk recorders, even seemingly small misregistrations can cause serious interference. Suppose that a new data track is overwritten with a mere 0.3-μm tracking error with a 5-μm-wide track width. Suppose that subsequently, perhaps after large-amplitude excursions of the head, the reproduce head is repositioned with a 0.3-μm error of the opposite sense. In the worst case, the reproduce head may now cover only 4.4 μm of the new overwritten data and 0.6 μm of old data. Thus the ratio of new data to old data is only 7 (17 dB), which is sufficiently low to have a serious impact on the channel performance.

In the interests of achieving extremely high areal recording densities, digital and analog video recorders do not use guard bands. In order to combat the effects of the inevitable misregistration, use is made of slant azimuth recording. In this technique, two record-reproduce heads are used alternately. The gap azimuth angles of the heads are set at positive and negative angles. Typically, angles of ±5 to 10° are employed. This results in recordings where the angle of the phase fronts of the recorded signal slants alternately from track to track. When reproducing such a recording, the head with matching azimuth angle reproduces without incurring any loss in performance. If, however, this reproduce head is misregistered and partially covers an adjacent track, the azimuth angle of the head and the recorded phase fronts are misaligned by twice the slant angle. If the maximum phase error thus incurred is a multiple of 2π radians, complete cancellations of the adjacent track reproduce signal occurs. In consumer video recorders, the design is such that this phase error occurs at the most probable tracking error with the FM luminance signal of maximum energy. Thus, the objectionable effects of misregistration are greatly reduced.

8.3.5 Side Fringing

Side-fringing interference occurs increasingly at longer wavelengths because a reproduce head can sense the fringing field which exists to the side, that is, not directly above, a recorded track. Consequently, a side-fringing signal is reproduced even when the head is not physically positioned above the track.

The side-fringing effect can best be understood with the aid of the reciprocity theorem. When the head is excited by a current in the coil, a fringing field exists, not only above the gap but also from the sides of the head. Essentially perfect but very complicated mathematical analyses of the three-dimensional fields around the gap sides are available (Lindholm, 1978). For our purposes, however, it is sufficient to regard the gap when viewed from the side as being virtually equivalent to a half head. The relevant half lies underneath the plane of the head surface; the missing half lies above the plane. To a good approximation, the side-fringing field is, therefore, one-half that in the usually considered xy plane. Upon Fourier transformation, the side-reading differential sensitivity is, by reciprocity, equal to $\frac{1}{2}e^{-kz}$, or $(55z/\lambda - 6)$dB, where z is the off-track distance. Upon integration, the side-fringing reproduce voltage spectrum from an adjacent track of width w with a guard bandwidth of b is

$$e(k) \approx \tfrac{1}{2}(1 - e^{-|k|w})e^{|k|b} \tag{8.24}$$

The similarity to the well-known thickness and spacing loss spectrum is obvious.

An interesting consequence of side fringing is that, when the reproduce spectrum of a head with a width much less than the track width of the recorded track (write wide, read narrow) is measured, the long-wavelength spectral slope turns out to be 3 dB per octave and not the usual 6 dB per octave. While the side-fringing interference is potentially worse than true noise, it is generally of lesser consequence than other interferences because the spectrum is weighted; negligible side-fringing effects occur at short wavelengths.

8.3.6 Print-through

Print-through occurs when the magnetic field from a layer of recorded tape magnetizes the layers of tape above and below it in a reel of tape. The basic physical process is closely related to superparamagnetism where thermal energy is sufficient to cause individual particles to switch (Tochihara et al., 1970; Bertram et al., 1980). Only a very small fraction (0.3 percent or − 50 dB) of the tape particles contributes to print-through in most tapes. Print-through is principally a long-wavelength phenomenon; the maximum effect occurs when the wavelength is 2π times the distance between the layers of tape (i.e., the total tape thickness) (Daniel and Axon, 1950). Negligible print-through occurs in FM video tape recorders where short wavelengths ($< 12 \; \mu$m) are used; in disk recorders the effect is absent because the disks are never closely packed.

Superparamagnetism occurs when the thermal energy kT is of the order of the energy required to switch a particle, $\Delta E = \frac{1}{2}M_s H_c (1 - H/H_c)^2 v$. The relaxation time of the process is given by

$$\tau = \frac{1}{f_0} \exp \frac{\Delta E}{kT} \tag{8.25}$$

where f_0 is a frequency factor of about 10^9 Hz. When $\Delta E = 25kT$, $\tau = 76$ s; when $\Delta E = 40kT$ (corresponding to a 20 percent increase in particle linear dimensions), $\tau > 100$ years. Thus, a very sharp division separates the thermally stable from the thermally unstable particles.

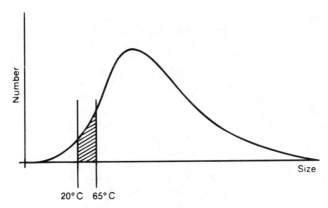

FIGURE 8.12 The particle-size distribution function, showing the superparamagnetic stability limits at 20 and 65°C.

In the measurement of print-through, a reel of tape is stored at elevated temperature; a standard industry test is 4 h at +65°C. The distribution function of particle sizes together with the effective superparamagnetism limiting volumes for both +65°C and room temperature is shown in Fig. 8.12. At +65°C, essentially all the particles with sizes below the +65°C limit will become magnetized by the fields from adjacent tape layers. Upon cooling back to room temperature, most of the particles between the two temperature limits will retain their print-through signal when the tape is unreeled and the printing fields vanish. Thus we see that the magnitude of the print-through signal depends critically upon the distribution function of particle sizes, a property that is not easy to manipulate. This presents the tape designer with a difficult problem. If the particle size of a given magnetic material is reduced in order to increase the signal-to-noise ratio, then print-through will increase. Thus the wideband signal-to-noise ratio and the print-through levels of gamma ferric oxide professional audio tapes have remained essentially unchanged at 75 and 65 respectively for many years.

An interesting phenomenon with regard to print-through is that, depending upon whether the tape is wound with magnetic coating inside or outside, differences in print-through level occur between the "preprints" and "postprints." The preprints occur outboard in the tape pack and vice versa for the postprints. The larger print-through always occurs in the layer of tape whose magnetic coating contacts the base film side of the printing layer. This has been explained in terms of the spatially rotating or Hilbert transform properties of the fringing-field outside tapes (Daniel, 1972; Mallinson, 1973).

8.4 NONLINEARITY AND DISTORTION

In linear recorders, ac bias makes the writing process linear for small signals. Since the reproduce process is linear, the complete recording channel is linear, and it has a well-defined, mathematically rigorous transfer function. When suitable equalization is added to linear recorders, the channel becomes almost distortionless, and the output signal is a noisy replica of the input signal. Analog audio and instrumentation recorders are such linear recorders. In nonlinear recorders, no attempt is made to linearize the channel with ac bias; accordingly, the channel does not have a single-valued transfer function. In order to make the complete recording system distortionless for particular input signals, use is made of some form of modulation scheme; in analog video recorders this is frequency modulation, while in digital audio and video recorders pulse-code modulation (binary digital) is used. In all nonlinear machines, including digital data recorders, the output signal is highly distorted, but, given particular postequalization, certain features of the waveform can be recovered precisely. In FM video it is usual to recover the zero-crossing positions, whereas in digital recording the positions of waveform peaks are recovered. The system's output signal is then reconstituted from these samples, and, subject to certain constraints, a noisy but distortion-free replica of the input signal is produced. Thus, in a nonlinear recorder, only certain features of the waveform after the equalizer are distortion-free, with the remainder of the waveform highly distorted.

8.4.1 A Linear, Distortionless System

A linear system has certain specific input-output characteristics. Mathematically, if

$$L[ax_1(t) + bx_2(t)] = aL[x_1(t)] + bL[x_2(t)] \tag{8.26}$$

the system is said to be linear. Here L is a time-domain operator such that the output for a signal input, $x(t)$, is $y(t) = L[x(t)]$, a and b are arbitrary scaling constants, and $x(t)$ and $y(t)$ are independent input signals. In a linear system, the output has no cross-modulation terms of the form $x(t)y(t)$; different input signals do not become mixed together. In reality, of course, systems approach linearity only for small signals. An example of this limitation is seen in the anhysteretic curve shown in Fig. 8.13. This curve, frequently approximated by the error-function curve, introduces 1 and 3 percent third harmonic distortion (a measure of nonlinearity) at about 20 and 30 percent of maximum remanence levels, respectively (Fujiwara, 1979).

In order that the output of a linear system be distortionless, further conditions must be met. It is required that the linear operator L change in a specific way only

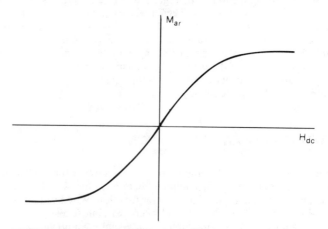

FIGURE 8.13   The anhysteretic curve, M_{ar} versus H_{dc}.

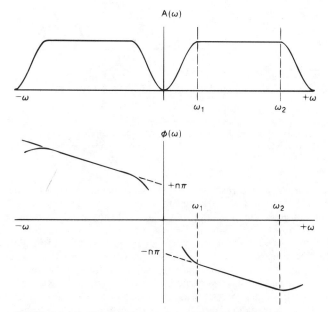

FIGURE 8.14 The amplitude A (ω) and phase $\phi(\omega)$ transfer functions required for the distortionless transmission of signals.

for different frequency input signals. Suppose that the frequency-domain transfer function of the linear system is

$$L(\omega) = A(\omega)e^{-j\phi(\omega)} \tag{5.27}$$

where $A(\omega)$ and $\phi(\omega)$ are the amplitude and phase transfer functions, respectively. For an input signal, band-limited between ω_1 and ω_2, distortion-free transmission through the linear system occurs if $A(\omega)$ is constant for $\omega_1 < \omega < \omega_2$, and $\phi(\omega)$ is a linear function of ω for $\omega_1 < \omega < \omega_2$, as shown in Fig. 8.14. The condition for $A(\omega)$ is usually called *flat amplitude response,* and that for $\phi(\omega)$ is called *constant group delay,* because all symbols are simply delayed by an equal time. The $\phi(\omega)$ condition is also, and most confusingly, called *linear phase* simply because it has a straight-line plot. The phase response, $\phi(\omega)$, must also have an intercept equal to an integer multiple of π when it is extrapolated to zero frequency. Inductive reproductive heads produce their output voltage by Faraday's law, that is, by differentiating the head flux in time. Shielded magnetoresistive heads effectively differentiate in space. Differentiation introduces a $\pi/2$ phase shift; for sine-wave inputs, the output voltage is a cosine, that is, a sine wave lagging in phase angle by $\pi/2$. This phase distortion must be corrected in both linear and nonlinear recorders. In all linear recorders, the correction is made by integration. In nonlinear machines, integration is also used except in digital disk recorders where differentiation is employed as in the differentiating peak detection. This introduces a further $\pi/2$ phase shift making π in total, which is equivalent to a mere polarity reversal.

In nonlinear recorders, mathematically rigorous transfer functions do not exist because the system is nonlinear in the sense discussed above. Nevertheless, it is found that, provided the input signal to the write head is limited to sequences of alternating-polarity step functions, the reproduce-head output voltage can be the

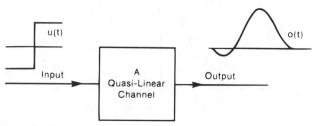

FIGURE 8.15 A quasi-linear channel displays linear superposition if the input and output are related by the following expressions. Input: Σ_j $(-1)^j u(t - j\Delta)$; output: $\Sigma_j (-1)^j o(t - j\Delta)$.

linear superposition of the response to the individual input step functions. This is shown in Fig. 8.15. Requirements are that (1) the steps must alternate in polarity, (2) they must all be of the same amplitude, and (3) they must not come closer than some minimum bit interval. One of the reasons for the minimum bit-length limit is that the writing field adjacent to the write-head gap must rise to its full value within the minimum bit interval (Mallinson and Steele, 1969). At high frequencies or data rates, this implies that a specific analog preequalization operation must be performed, without which linear superposition would not hold. Of course, in true linear systems, the signal output waveform is, apart from noise, unchanged by varying the pre- and postequalizers as long as the product of their transfer functions remains constant.

Given the correct conditions for linear superposition, a nonlinear recorder displays a pseudo-transfer function. This pseudo-transfer function fails the test of linearity because, for example, different input step-function amplitudes yield different output spectra; nevertheless, it is an extremely useful aid in understanding the system's behavior. It may be measured by (1) Fourier transformation of the isolated pulse response, (2) noting the amplitude of the fundamental of a varying-frequency square wave, and (3) noting the envelope of a pseudo-random square-wave sequence.

8.4.2 Amplitude Response

The amplitude response spectrum is essentially given by calculations based upon the output expected from a medium magnetized sinusoidally along its length and

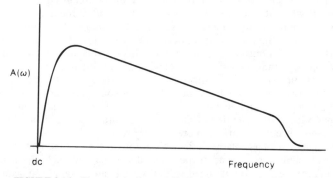

FIGURE 8.16 The straight-line amplitude response required to preserve FM signal zero crossings.

uniformly through its depth (Wallace, 1951). In order to obtain a flat amplitude response in linear recorders, the required equalization is the inverse of this spectrum. Thus the output is boosted at both low and high frequencies.

In frequency-modulated video recorders, the overall pseudo-transfer function of the cascade, write process, reproduce process, and reproduce head must be postequalized to obtain the straight-line characteristic shown in Fig. 8.16 (Felix and Walsh, 1965). In this highly nonlinear system, the transfer functions of the preequalizer and the record head have already been accounted for as prerequisites for pseudolinearity. The straight-line equalization then ensures that the output waveform zero-crossing positions occur with the right timing.

In nonlinear digital recorders, which include digital audio, digital data tape, and digital data disk recorders, the task of the postequalizer is easier than in video recorders. In frequency modulation, the analog waveform has a continuum of zero-crossing positions to be preserved, whereas a binary digital channel has zero crossings allowed only at certain well-defined positions. These positions are determined by the channel code being used and are often specified in $[d, k]$ notation, where d is the minimum string or run of zeros allowed, and k is the maximum run allowed. It follows that many different postequalizers are acceptable in digital recording. Often, the transfer function of the cascade, write process, reproduce process, reproduce head, and postequalizer has one of the (infinite) set of Nyquist amplitude responses shown in Fig. 8.17 (Gibby and Smith, 1965). More recently, partial response equalization is being utilized. Whereas Nyquist equalization completely eliminates intersymbol interference between adjacent bits, partial response equalization permits specific intersymbol interference to exist. Although an infinite set of partial response equalizations may be imagined, practical interest centers upon the so-called Class IV partial response. Because Class IV does not require dc response, it is particularly suited to the magnetic recording channel. The overall transfer function sought in Class IV is shown in Fig. 8.18. Signal-to-noise ratio and circuit complexity criteria govern the actual choices used in practical hardware.

8.4.3 Phase response

As discussed above, the standard output spectrum includes the phase shift due to Faraday's law. In complex notation, the voltage spectrum is preceded by the factor j ($= \sqrt{-1}$); in the signal power spectrum, of course, phase information is sup-

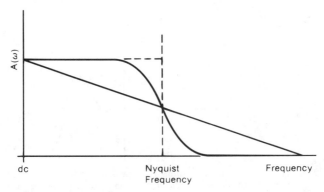

FIGURE 8.17 Examples of the infinite set of Nyquist amplitude responses which yield zero intersymbol interference.

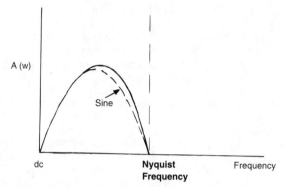

FIGURE 8.18 The amplitude response required for Class IV partial response.

pressed. In all recorders, it is necessary to correct for the phase distortion introduced by the j factor. As mentioned earlier, this is usually done by integration but, exceptionally, in digital disk recording, differentiation is employed. Since integrating pulses yields steps and differentiating pulses yields dipulses, as shown in Fig. 8.19, in both cases the subsequent (nonlinear) detector has to identify zero crossings which are now coincident in time (or phase) with the written magnetization transition.

There are other sources of phase distortion in magnetic recording. If the direction of magnetization in the recording medium is changed by an angle θ, the phase

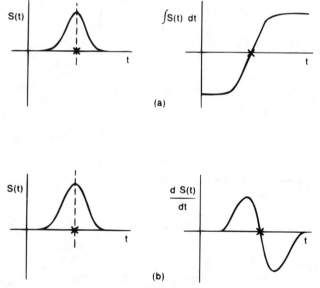

FIGURE 8.19 Finding the position of the peak of a pulse, $S(t)$, by (a) integration and (b) differentiation involves, in both cases, finding the position of zero crossings.

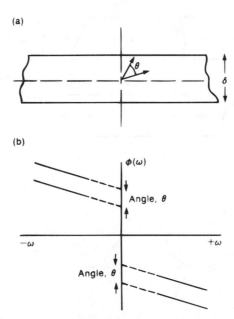

FIGURE 8.20 (*a*) The medium magnetization rotated by an angle θ and (*b*) the dc-extrapolated phase response, $\phi(\omega)$, changed by the same angle.

response changes by the same angle, as shown in Fig. 8.20 (Mallinson, 1981). Thus, when going from purely longitudinal recording to purely perpendicular recording, a phase shift of 90° occurs, and the corresponding isolated step-function output pulses are the Hilbert transform pair shown in Fig. 8.21. In distinction to the operations of integration and differentiation, the Hilbert transformation involves only a 90° phase change with no amplitude change. The transfer functions of differentiation, integration, and Hilbert transformation are $j\omega$, $(j\omega)^{-1}$, and $j\omega(|\omega|)^{-1}$, respectively.

Merely changing the phase response does not alter the energy in a pulse or signal. Phase-shifting equalizers can, therefore, be made and used for phase correction, and they have, in principle, no effect upon the signal-to-noise ratio. Accordingly, the odd-and-even symmetry Hilbert pair of pulses shown in Fig. 8.21 have identical information content, and preferences between the two must depend solely on considerations of circuit realization or complexity. When a nonlinear recorder is not properly equalized in both amplitude and phase, the pulse responses to step-function inputs overlap each other as shown in Fig. 8.22. The peak positions of the summed waveforms are displaced outward. The phenomenon is called *linear peak shift*. As long as the peak shift is caused solely by linear superposition, it is, in principle, correctable by proper postequalization, but with an inevitable reduction in signal-to-noise ratio.

At higher densities, when the minimum-bit-cell rule for linear super-position is violated, additional peak shifts of nonlinear origin arise which cannot be corrected completely by linear postequalizers. The origin of this nonlinear peak (or bit) shift is the demagnetizing field from the previously recorded bit (Mallinson and Steele, 1969). In order for linear superposition to hold, the magnetic field writing the nth transition must be solely the write-head field corresponding to the nth transition. At

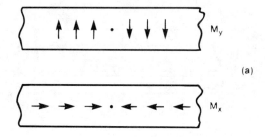

(a)

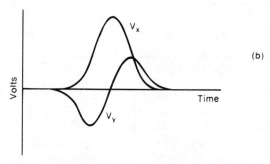

(b)

FIGURE 8.21 (*a*) Transitions of perpendicular and longitudinal magnetization. (*b*) Corresponding Hilbert pair of output voltage pulses.

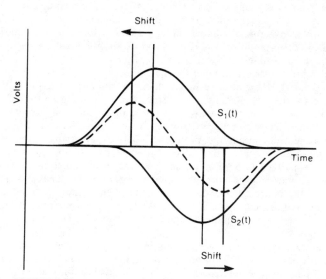

FIGURE 8.22 The peaks of the summed curve (dashed) are shifted outward: the peaks appear to repel each other.

higher linear densities, the demagnetizing field from the $(n - 1)$th transition causes the total field writing the nth transition to be changed. In longitudinal recording, the total field is increased by the $(n - 1)$th transition demagnetizing field. In perpendicular recording, the total field is decreased below the value it would have in the absence of the $(n - 1)$th transition. It follows that, in longitudinal and perpendicular recording, nonlinear bit shifts of opposite sense are incurred. The actual recorded transition position, determined by the point where the total field equals the medium's coercivity, is recorded early in longitudinal and late in perpendicular recording. Thus, nonlinear effects push longitudinal transitions together and pull perpendicular transitions apart. It is found, therefore, that the total peak shift in longitudinal recording is, at high linear densities, less than that expected by linear superposition alone; the converse is expected for perpendicular recording (Bertram and Fielder, 1983).

In general, a linear or nonlinear peak shift of either polarity is undesirable because the peak positions become dependent on previous data. Many digital data disk recorders employ "prewrite compensation" in which the timing of each write-current step function is adjusted, early or late, depending upon the data pattern to be recorded. This is usually implemented with a read-only memory look-up table and is a rare example of the application of nonlinear equalization to a communications channel.

Finally, in audio tape duplication operations, considerable increases in production can be realized if it is possible to play the master tape both forward and backward and so eliminate the rewinding operation. Similarly, in computer tape drive operations, significant increases in data throughput occur if it is possible to read the data equally well in both directions of tape movement. In order to have a perfect, but time-reversed, output signal in the reverse direction, it is necessary that the reproduce head and postequalizer cascade have a linear phase transfer function which intercepts zero frequency at an integer multiple of π; this makes the reproduce cascade impulse response an even function of time and thus indistinguishable from its reverse (Mallinson and Ferrier, 1974). It follows that the preequalizer used in recording the master must have a zero-frequency phase intercept which corrects any other phase factor, so that no phase distortion occurs for the overall system.

8.5 FUTURE AREAL DENSITIES

In the future it is expected that essentially all magnetic recorders will operate digitally. The only likely exceptions, consumer analog audio cassette and analog video cassette recorders, may well persist for a number of years, but even they will eventually be replaced with their digital counterparts. Indeed the digital compact cassette (DCC) and the digital VCR are already announced products.

One of the most important reasons for digital recording is the relative ease with which error detection and correction can be performed in binary digital systems. This not only permits indefinitely repeated error-free duplication of the recording, but it encourages the development of digital recording systems with considerably higher areal densities. Today, most digital recorders employ tape or disk formats which provide analog wide-band signal-to-noise ratios of approximately 30 dB. Concurrently, interferences, for example, overwrite, are held at the -30-dB level. These figures permit the nonlinear digital detector a sufficient margin for the effects of mistracking and tape or disk defects, so that raw (uncorrected) bit error rates in the range 10^{-6} to 10^{-9} are achieved. With advances in integrated-circuit technology (photolithography, large-scale integration, etc.), it seems inevitable that recording system designers will move to much higher digital areal densities and concomittant raw error rates; an analog signal-to-noise ratio of 20 dB and a raw bit error rate of 10^{-3} to 10^{-4} appear to be reasonable design goals for the next decade. Error detection and correction will then operate to yield the final error rate required for the particular application. For video, audio, and data recorders, the final error rates sought are of the order 10^{-6}, 10^{-9}, and 10^{-12}, respectively.

In the quest for higher areal densities, both linear and track densities will be increased. Both actions reduce the signal level, and the latter the noise level, from the recording medium.

At narrower trackwidths, it is desirable to reduce the read head impedance so that the read head noise decreases in proportion with the decreased medium noise. With inductive read heads, however, fabrication problems render this not possible. In ferrite heads, the core width or thickness cannot be made less than, say, 5 μm. In thin film inductive heads, the coil size cannot be increased substantially. It therefore seems likely that, in these cases, read head noise will become the dominant source of noise and this will limit the areal densities attainable.

On the other hand, magneto-resistive (MR) heads need not suffer a similar limitation. This enormously important difference arises because the magneto-resistive element width is limited only by photo-lithography and it is the magneto-resistive element which determines both the reproduced trackwidth and the head noise. In narrow trackwidth MR heads, the resistance and thermal noise power are proportional to the trackwidth. The reproduced signal power is, of course, proportional to the square of the trackwidth. Thus the signal-to-MR head noise power is proportional to the trackwidth just as is the signal power-to-medium noise ratio.

The fact that inductive read head systems will become signal-to-read head noise limited at lower areal densities than MR head systems is expected to have far reaching consequences in the evolution of high areal density recorders.

8.5.1 Head-Noise-Limited Areal Densities

In recording systems where the reproduce-head noise is dominant and of known magnitude, it is possible to estimate the wide band signal-to-noise ratio whenever absolutely calibrated data are available. In the data to be discussed, 0 dB corresponds to 1 nV rms per turn for each 1 μm of track width and 1 m/s of relative head-to-media velocity (Bertram and Fielder, 1983).

Figure 8.23 shows the signal level, which is required to attain a 20 dB (a factor of 10 in voltage) signal-to-head noise ratio in a 10 MHz channel, that could support a 20×10^6 b/s data rate, when a 10-turn, 10 ohm, 100 percent efficient inductive head is used, versus linear density. It may be shown that this signal level is directly proportional to areal density (Mallinson, 1985). The five parametric curves show the absolute signal levels needed for operation on various track widths. The curves are 6 dB apart and rise at 6 dB per octave because, when the data rate is held constant, higher densities force lower speeds.

The choice of a 20-Mb/s data rate has been made because it is representative of many different digital recording applications. Typical requirements are computer rigid disk, 10 to 50 Mb/s; digital audio, 1 to 2 Mb/s; digital instrumentation, 4 to 400 Mb/s; digital consumer video, 10 to 100 Mb/s; and digital professional video, 100 to 250 Mb/s. The highest published data rates in a single write-read channel, for ferrite, thin film and film heads are 117 Mbs, 160 Mbs and 300 Mbs respectively

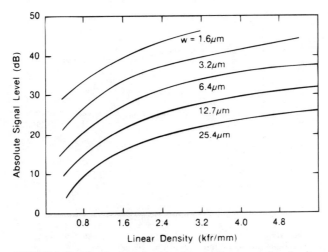

FIGURE 8.23 The absolute signal level versus linear recording density, with track width as a parameter (*Mallinson, 1985*).

(Coleman, 1984; Ash, 1990; Hong, 1991). In higher-rate applications, such as in HDTV and intelligence satellite recorders, multiple parallel channels are used.

Figure 8.24 shows the signal level, required to attain a 20 dB signal-to-head noise ratio in a 20 Mb/s, 10 MHz channel when a magnetoresistive head with 10 ohm resistance is used, versus linear density. The absolute signal level is, in this case, proportional to the track density and the parametric curves show the signal level required for differing areal densities (Mallinson, 1993).

8.5.1.1. Absolute Signal Data. Absolutely calibrated, measured output voltage versus linear density data taken on two media are shown in Fig. 8.25. The two

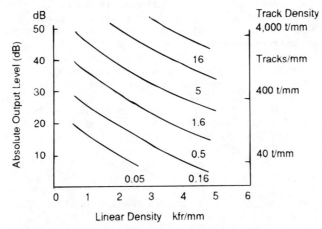

FIGURE 8.24 Absolute output and track density versus linear density, with areal density as a parameter, for magnetoresistive heads. The areal density is shown in *fr/mm²* × 10^6.

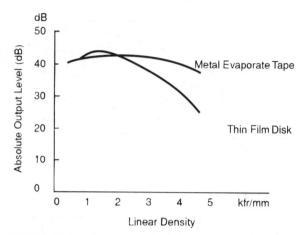

FIGURE 8.25　Absolutely calibrated output signals from metal-evaporated tape and thin-film disk versus linear density.

media are a metal thin film disk with 72 kA/m coercivity and a 30 nm coating thickness and a cobalt-nickel metallic evaporated (ME) film tape with an 80 kA/m (1000 Oe) coercivity and 75 nm coating. The thin film rigid disk was operated with an estimated physical head-disk spacing of 0.1 μm. The ME tape was run with no deliberate physical head-tape spacing; the spectral shape, however, indicates an effective magnetic spacing for the complete write and read process of approximately 0.03 μm. The ME tape has exceptional performance, yielding over 4.8 kfr/mm potential linear density on a 12.5μm track width; accordingly the Hi-8 VCRs operate at a maximum density of 4.3 kfr/mm.

It can be shown that 0 dB on this absolutely calibrated scale is equivalent to a sinusoidal peak magnetic flux density of 0.56 kA/m (7.07 Oe) entering the reproduce head; 50 dB thus corresponds to approximately 80 kA/m (1,000 Oe). Since the fields emanating from a recording medium cannot exceed the coercivity, and the two media have coercivities in the range 70–80 kA/m, it appears that signal levels very close to the maximum possible are being observed. The attainment of higher signal levels would necessitate media of higher coercivity. In the cobalt alloys used in these media, the maximum coercivity attainable is closely related to the magneto-crystalline anisotropy field of cobalt (2K/M = 500 kA/m [6,000 Oe]). Media with coercivities exceeding 320 kA/m (4,000 Oe) will undoubtedly appear, which will have the potential of producing fourfold higher (+12 dB) absolute output signals.

Both media shown in Fig. 8.25 have their maximum outputs at linear density of approximately 1.6 kfr/mm (40,000 frpi). When the inductive head is used, this corresponds to 20 dB SNR, 20 Mb/s operation with a 1.5 μm trackwidth head or an areal density of 10^6 fc/mm^2 (625 10^6 fr/in^2).

In the magneto-resistive head case, the maximum possible areal density occurs at approximately 3.2 kfr/mm (80,000 frpi), 10^3 tp/mm (25,000 tpi) and 3 10^6 fr/mm^2 (2000 10^6 fr/in^2).

This comparison makes clear yet another advantage of MRHs. The high signal sensitivity, about 2 volt/cm of trackwidth independent of head-medium relative velocity, permits narrower trackwidth operations and makes possible higher areal densities than with an inductive read head of the same thermal noise. With the advent of MR heads which use the giant magneto-resistive effect (GMR), this advantage will become greater because the signal sensitivity of a GMR head is expected to be significantly (a factor of 10 perhaps) higher.

The thin magnetic films used in both rigid disk and tape media produce extremely high head output voltages. It has been found, both theoretically and experimentally, that this is true regardless of the orientation (horizontal, oblique or vertical) of the magnetization in the metallic film (Mallinson and Bertram, 1984). It is expected, moreover, that, in applications limited by reproduce-head noise, the system performance will be very nearly the same regardless of how a metallic film has been produced. Second-order differences due to differing deposition techniques (evaporation, plating or sputtering) are expected to affect only the medium noise, which is of little consequence in head noise limited systems.

8.5.2 Media Noise Limited Areal Densities

Most high areal density recording systems in use today are, by design, media noise limited. It is expected that this condition will continue to prevail even at the much higher areal densities anticipated in the future because magneto-resistive heads will be used.

A convenient example for a discussion of a media noise limited high area density recording system is the 1989 IBM Gigabit per square inch (1.5 Mb/mm^2) demonstration. It is to be noted, moreover, that in 1995, several mass-produced high end disk drives enjoy very similar performance and specifications.

Figure 8.26 shows an electron micrograph of the media used in the 1989 IBM Gigabit demonstration (Yogi, 1990). It can be seen that the individual grains of the Co-Cr alloy a) are about 30–40 nm in size, b) form a mono-layer and c) are well-separated from each other. Taking the average grain-to-grain spacing to be 40 nm, the area density of the grains is about 6.25 10^8 grains per square millimeter.

According to Eq. (8.18) and the subsequent discussion, the media limited SNR is just the mean number of magnetic sources being read in a single digital bit cell. At the actual areal density of 1.78 Mb/mm^2 (1.15 Gb/in^2), the area of a single written bit cell is 5.62 10^{-7} mm^2. With the write wide (4 μm), read narrow (2 μm)

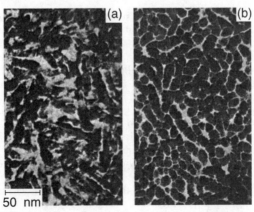

FIGURE 8.26 Electron micrograph showing the IBM Gigabit per inch^2 recording medium *(from Yogi et al., 1990)*.

system used, the area of the playback bit cell is 2.81 10^{-7} mm^2. There are, therefore, approximately 175 grains in each bit cell on playback.

If the grains in the Gigabit medium were statistically independent, or uncorrelated, from each other, the number of grains per bit cell is, of course, equal to the number of magnetic sources per bit cell. The expectation then is that the signal-to-medium limited noise ratio would be about 175 or 22.4 dB.

In fact, the measured SNR (about 19 dB) was within a factor of three of this expectation (Howell, 1990). This concordance leads to the important conclusion that the magnetic sources in the Gigabit media consist, on the average, of two or three grains only. The grains were only slightly coupled, or correlated. Thus, the pronounced inter-particle gap precluded inter-particle exchange coupling and the relatively high coercive force (136 kA/m, 1700 Oe) inhibited magnetostatic coupling.

Indeed, with regard to the minimal magnetostatic coupling, it may be recalled that the magnetization to coercivity ratio, $H_c/4\pi M_R$, of the Gigabit medium (136kA/m/1T = 136) is almost identical to that of ordinary γFe_2O_3 tape (24kA/m/0.16T = 150). To the extent that the magnetic sources in ordinary tape are the individual particles, so it is that the magnetic sources in high coercivity thin film disks are the individual grains seen by electron microscopy. As coercive forces continue to rise in the future it thus appears that the computationally intensive micromagnetic simulations of vortices and other interactive phenomena will become less rather than more necessary. Simple grain or particle counting exercises will suffice for SNR estimations.

8.5.3 The Next Decade

Areal densities are more difficult to forecast than linear densities because there is more uncertainty concerning the track widths and track densities which will be used. Current consumer video cassette recorders and computer rigid-disk recorders have approximately 10 μm minimum track widths. In the video recorders, no guard band is needed, and the maximum track densities are over 100 tracks per millimeter (2500 tracks per inch). It seems certain that substantial increases will be achieved through fuller exploitation of embedded servo techniques. A track width of 6 μm with 160 tracks per millimeter (4000 tracks per inch) is a reasonable expectation in several years.

With computer rigid-disk systems, a substantial guard band, equal to half the track width, is the norm. Positioning and servoing systems are improving rapidly, and track densities seem likely to reach 400 tracks per millimeter (10,000 tracks per inch) in the short term.

There is, nevertheless, a general belief that 16 Mb/mm^2 (10 Gb/in^2) will be achieved within several years in rigid disk recorders. Presently, areal densities of approximately 1.6 Mb/mm^2 (1 Gb/in^2) are entering production. The compound growth rate of areal density in small high end drives over the last five years, a period coincident with the use of magneto-resistive read heads, has been about 50–60% per year. If this rate can be maintained, as seems to be very likely, 10 Gb/in^2 will be achieved by the end of the millenium!

This chapter concludes with a brief review of current ideas concerning the future attainment of 10 Gb/in^2 recording.

First, it is clear that the coercivity of the thin film media will increase substantially. Whilst staying within the present Cobalt alloy system, coercive forces in the range 320–480 kA/m (4,000–6,000 Oe) will be developed. Part of this increase will be due to alloy compositional changes and part due to smaller grain sizes. One of the advantages of higher coercive force media is the attendant reduction (proportional to $1/\sqrt{H_c}$) of the written digital transition width. This, in turn, permits high linear recording densities. Increases from the current 5 kb/mm (125,000 bpi) to perhaps 16 kb/mm (400,000 bpi) are expected.

In order to write and read properly such high linear densities it will be necessary to reduce, concomitantly, the head-disk spacing. Currently, this spacing is as small as 50 nm (2 microinches). It seems likely that operation with zero deliberate head-disk spacing will be shown to be possible. Profound difficulties attend the measurement of, and even the definition of, "in contact" operation. It is anticipated, however, that effective magnetic spacings, such as those measured from output spectral slopes, of approximately 10 nm will be achieved with satisfactory durability and reliability.

In order to reach 10 Gb/in^2, it is assumed that the trackpitch will be reduced to about 1 μm, so that the track density approaches 800 t/mm (20,000 tpi). The resistance of the magnetoresistive read head permalloy sensor, of dimensions close to 0.5 μm width, 0.5 μm depth and 10 nm thickness will be about 20 ohms. The thermal noise in a 10 MHz, 20 Mb/s channel will be about 2 μV. With the usual anisotropic magnetoresistive effect type of MRHs the output voltage is of the order 2 volt/cm of trackwidth (Mallinson, 1995). It follows that the MRH limited SNR will be about 20 dB. With MRHs using the giant magnetoresistive effect the GMRH limited SNR will be even higher.

The system SNR will be dominated by the media noise. If the grain sizes used in the 1989 Gigabit demonstration media were to be reduced by a factor of three, say from 30 nm to 10 nm, the same SNR would be achieved at $3^2 \approx 10$ the areal density. A channel SNR of about 100 or 20 dB is expected even at 10 GB/in^2.

The final question to be answered concerns the thermal stability of a cobalt alloy with 10 nm grain size. For cobalt metal, the conventional 25 kT (50 times thermal energy) criterion of 100 second relaxation time super-paramagnetic behavior gives a grain size of about 5 nm. Thus, media with the proposed grain size of 10 nm would be adequately stable against thermal decay.

In summary, the proposed system will use a cobalt alloy medium with a monolayer of 10 nm well-separated grains and a coercivity of about 400 kA/m (5,000 Oe). The write head will be of the usual thin film inductive type but with high magnetic moment (Co-Zr, Fr-N) pole tips. The read head will be of the shielded anisotropic magnetoresistive type with a 20 ohms resistance permalloy sensor of dimensions 0.5 $\times$ 0.5 $\times$ 0.01 μm. The half-gaps will be approximately 0.05 μm in order to provide the necessary 16 kb/mm (400,000 bpi) linear resolution. The effective write and read head to disk spacing will be about 10 nm (0.4 microinch). The track pitch will be about 1 μm using the same write wide (1 μm), read narrow (0.5 μm) philosophy which is found in today's high end drives.

REFERENCES

Ash, K. P., D. Wachenschwanz, C. Brucker, J. Olson, M. Treka, and T. Jagielinski, "A Magnetic Head for 150 MHz High Density Recording," *IEEE Trans Magn.,* **MAG-26,** 2960 (1990).

Baugh, R. A., E. S. Murdock, and B. R. Najarajan, "Measurements of Noise in Magnetic Media," *IEEE Trans. Magn.,* **MAG-19,** 1722 (1983).

Bertram, H. N., *Theory of Magnetic Recording,* Cambridge University Press (1994).

Bertram, H. N., and L. D. Fielder, "Amplitude and Bit Shift Comparisons in Thin Metallic Media," *IEEE Trans. Magn.,* **MAG-19,** 1605 (1983).

Bertram, H. N., M. Stafford, and D. Mills, "The Print-Through Phenomenon and Its Practical Consequences," *J. Audio Eng. Soc.,* **28,** 690 (1980).

Coleman, C., D. Lindholm, D. Petersen, and R. Wood, "High Data Rate Recording in a Single Channel," *Int. Conf. Video Data Recording, IERE Proc.,* **59,** 151 (1984).

Daniel, E. D., "Tape Noise in Audio Recording," *J. Audio Eng. Soc.,* **20,** 92 (1972).

Daniel, E. D., and P. E. Axon, "Accidental Printing in Magnetic Recording," *BBC Q.,* **4,** 241 (1950).

Decker, S. K., and C. Tsang, "Magneto-Resistive Response of Small Permalloy Features," *IEEE Trans. Magn.,* **MAG-16,** 643 (1980).

Denteneer, D., and H. Cramer, "Correlation of Particle Length and Radius; A New Model for Flux Noise in Particulate Media," *IEEE Trans. Magn.,* **MAG-26,** 2110 (1990).

Fayling, R. F., T. J. Szczech, and E. F. Wollack, "A Model for Overwrite Modulation in Longitudinal Recording," *IEEE Trans. Magn.,* **MAG-20,** 718 (1984).

Felix, M. O., and H. Walsh, "F.M. Systems of Exceptional Bandwidth," *Proc. Inst. Electr. Eng.,* **112,** 1659 (1965).

Fujiwara, T., "Nonlinear Distortion in Long-Wavelength AC Bias Recording," *IEEE Trans. Magn.,* **MAG-15,** 894 (1979).

Gibby, R. A., and J. W. Smith, "Some Extensions of Nyquist's Telegraph Transmission Theory," *Bell Syst. Tech. J.,* **44,** 1487 (1965).

Hong, J., R. Wood, and D. Chan, "An Experimental 180 mb/sec PRML Channel, *IEEE Trans. Magn.,* **MAG-27,** 4532 (1991).

Howell, T. D., D. P. McCown, T. A. Diola, T. Yow-Shing, K. R. Hense, and R. L. Gee, "Error Rate Performance of Experimental Gigabit per Square Inch Recording Components," *IEEE Trans. Magn.,* **MAG-26,** 2298 (1990).

Katz, E. R., and T. G. Campbell, "Effect of Bit-Shift Distribution on Error Rate in Magnetic Recording, *IEEE Trans. Magn.,* **MAG-15,** 1050 (1979).

Lokhoff, G., "DCC-Digital Compact Cassette," *IEEE Trans. Consumer Electronics,* **37,** 702 (1991).

Mallinson, J. C., "Maximum Signal-to-Noise Ratio of a Tape Recorder," *IEEE Trans. Magn.,* **MAG-5,** 182 (1969).

Mallinson, J. C., "One-Sided Fluxes—A Magnetic Curiosity?" *IEEE Trans. Magn.,* **MAG-9,** 678 (1973).

Mallinson, J. C., "The Signal-to-Noise Ratio of a Frequency Modulated Video Recorder," *EBU Rev. Tech.,* **153,** 241 (1975).

Mallinson, J. C., "On the Properties of Two-Dimensional Dipoles and Magnetized Bodies," *IEEE Trans. Magn.,* **MAG-17,** 2453 (1981).

Mallinson, J. C., "The Next Decade in Magnetic Recording," *IEEE Trans. Magn.,* **MAG-21,** 1217 (1985).

Mallinson, J. C., "A New Theory of Recording Media Noise," *IEEE Trans. Magn.,* **MAG-27,** 3519 (1991).

Mallinson, J. C., *The Foundations of Magnetic Recording,* Academic Press (1993).

Mallinson, J. C., *Magnetoresistive Heads: Fundamentals and Applications,* Academic Press (1995).

Mallinson, J. C., and H. Ferrier, "Motion Reversal Invariance in Tape Recorders," *IEEE Trans. Magn.,* **MAG-10,** 1084 (1974).

Mallinson, J. C., and C. W. Steele, "Theory of Linear Superposition in Tape Recording," *IEEE Trans. Magn.,* **MAG-5,** 886 (1969).

Mann, P. A., "Das Rauschen eines Magnettonbandes," *Arch. Electr. Ubertragung,* **11,** 97 (1957).

McKnight, J. G., "Erasure of Magnetic Tape," *J. Audio Eng. Soc.*, **11**, 223 (1963).

Nunnelley, L. L., D. E. Heim, and T. C. Arnoldussen, "Flux Noise in Particulate Media: Measurement and Interpretation," *IEEE Trans. Magn.*, **MAG-23**, 1767 (1987).

Slutsky, B., and H. N. Bertram, "Transition Noise Analysis of Thin Film Magnetic Recording Media," *IEEE Trans. Magn.*, **MAG-30**, 2808 (1994).

Smaller, P., "Reproduce System Noise in Wide-Band Magnetic Recording Systems," *IEEE Trans. Magn.*, **MAG-1**, 357 (1969).

Tanaka, K., "Some Considerations on Crosstalk in Multihead Magnetic Digital Recording," *IEEE Trans. Magn.*, **MAG-20**, 160 (1984).

Thurlings, L. F. G., "On the Noise Power Spectral Density of Particulate Recording Media," *IEEE Trans Magn.*, **MAG-19**, 84 (1983).

Tochihara, S., Y. Imaoka, and M. Namikawa, "Accidental Printing Effect of Magnetic Recording Tapes Using Ultra-Fine Particles of Acicular γFe_2O_3," *IEEE Trans. Magn.*, **MAG-6**, 808 (1970).

Wachenschwanz, D., and F. Jeffers, "Overwrite as a Function of Record Gap Length," *IEEE Trans. Magn.*, **MAG-21**, 1380 (1985).

Wallace, R. L., "The Reproduction of Magnetically Recorded Signals," *Bell Syst. Tech. J.*, **30**, 1145 (1951).

Yogi, T., C. Tsang, T. A. Nguyen, K. Ju, G. L. Gorman, and G. Castillo, "Longitudinal Media for 1 Gb/in^2 Areal Density," *IEEE Trans Magn.*, **MAG-26**, 1578 (1990).

Zhu, J- G., and H. N. Bertram, "Magnetization Structures in Thin Film Recording Media," *IEEE Trans. Mag.*, **MAG-27**, 3553 (1991).

CHAPTER 9
RECORDING MEASUREMENTS

James E. Monson
Harvey Mudd College, Claremont, California

This chapter treats various aspects of magnetic measurements and evaluation of system performance in relation to magnetic recording. It is assumed that the reader already has some familiarity with basic magnetic measurement techniques. Excellent texts are available which describe these techniques (Cullity, 1972; Zijlstra, 1967). Other useful sources include a brief review of measurements for digital recording media (Newman, 1978), a text describing the principles and applications of scanning electron microscopy (Wells, 1974), and a review of imaging methods for micromagnetic structure (Ferrier, 1992).

9.1 MEDIA PROPERTIES

9.1.1 Hysteresis Loop Parameters

Chapter 3 on particulate recording media presents definitions of the important hysteresis loop parameters and their relation to recording performance. These parameters are reviewed here in the context of how they are measured. Figure 9.1 shows a typical hysteresis loop measured quasi-statically with a maximum applied field of H_m. It is important to note the value of H_m because loop parameters are functions of the maximum applied field. $M(H_m)$ is the maximum magnetization observed on the loop. The saturation magnetization M_s is the limiting value $M(\infty)$ of $M(H_m)$ approached as the peak applied field is made higher and higher. The remanent magnetization $M_r(H_m)$ is the magnetization remaining when the applied field is reduced from H_{i_m} to zero. The retentivity $M_r(\infty)$ is the remanent magnetization which would be observed as the peak applied field is made infinitely large. The coercivity H_c is the field required to reduce the magnetization to zero; its measured value, $H_c(H_m)$, also depends upon H_m.

The remanence squareness $S(H_m)$ is the ratio of remanent magnetization $M_r(H_m)$ to maximum magnetization $M(H_m)$. Another characterization of squareness, the coercivity squareness S^*, is also illustrated in Fig. 9.1 (Williams and Comstock,

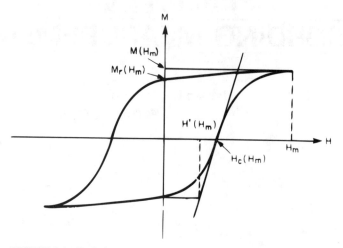

FIGURE 9.1 Typical measured hysteresis loop of magnetization versus applied field with peak value H_m. Graphical determination of remanence squareness, $S = M_r(H_m)/M(H_m)$, and coercivity squareness, $S^* = H'(H_m)/H_c(H_m)$, is shown.

1971). The coercivity squareness is related to the slope of the M versus H curve at $H = H_c$ and is given by

$$S^* = 1 - \frac{M_r(H_m)/H_c(H_m)}{dM/dH} \qquad (9.1)$$

The coercivity squareness approaches unity as dM/dH becomes infinitely large.

In addition to conventional hysteresis loops, remanence curves are measured to characterize recording media. The virgin remanence curve is measured by first erasing the medium in an ac field. In this condition of zero magnetization, 50 percent of the particles are magnetized in the opposite sense to the remaining 50 percent. A small dc field is applied and then removed. The remanent magnetization $M_r(H)$ is measured and plotted versus H as the process is repeated and H increased. $H_{0.5}$ is the field at which 25 percent of the particles have switched. The virgin remanence curve is also known as the isothermal remanent magnetization curve.

$$\frac{M_r(H_{0.5})}{M_r(\infty)} = 0.50 \qquad (9.2)$$

The reverse, or dc demagnetization, remanence curve is measured by saturating the sample and then applying a reverse field $-H$. The magnetization remaining after the reverse field is removed is plotted versus H. Figure 9.2 illustrates the measurement of both the virgin (Fig. 9.2a) and reverse remanence curves (Fig. 9.2b). The remanence coercivity H_r is the field which must be applied to a saturated sample to bring its remanent magnetization to zero.

Hysteresis measurements may be used to characterize the distribution of switching fields. A commonly used technique is to plot the derivative of the M-H loop versus the applied field H. The width ΔH between the half-amplitude points is normalized by H_c to give an estimate of the switching-field distribution suitable for comparing different media. This method is not sensitive to irreversible switching

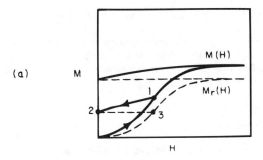

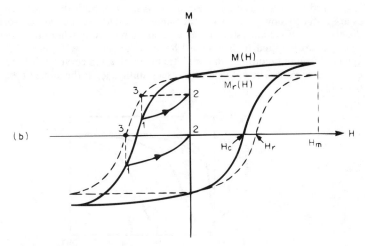

FIGURE 9.2 Measurement of (*a*) virgin and (*b*) reverse remanence curves (dashed). Magnetization paths from hysteresis loop to remanence curve are shown.

processes and may be very misleading when these are important. It is much better to define switching-field distribution in terms of the reverse remanence curve, M_r versus H, which measures irreversible magnetization changes. The parameter corresponding to the normalized half width of the dM/dH curve is

$$\Delta h_r = \frac{H_{0.75} - H_{0.25}}{H_r} \tag{9.3}$$

where $H_{0.25}$ and $H_{0.75}$ are the fields corresponding to 75 and 25 percent of the particles having been switched. These conditions are observed when the magnitudes of the reduced remanent magnetizations are equal to one-half.

$$\left| \frac{M_r(H_{0.25})}{M_r(\infty)} \right| = \left| \frac{M_r(H_{0.75})}{M_r(\infty)} \right| = 0.5 \tag{9.4}$$

The quantity $1 - S^*$, which can be obtained from the *M-H* loops, is a good estimate of Δh_r (Köster, 1984).

The virgin and reverse remanence characterizations may be used to study particle or grain interaction effects. Henkel plots for this purpose show reverse remanent magnetization as a function of virgin remanent magnetization for the range of applied field values (Henkel, 1974).

9.1.2 Anhysteretic Parameters

Anhysteretic magnetization results when an alternating field is applied along with a dc field. There are two modes of applying the fields to a sample of recording medium. In the first, the alternating field is reduced slowly to zero while the dc field is held constant. This process is often called *ideal anhysteretic magnetization.* In the second, referred to as *modified anhysteretic magnetization,* both the alternating and dc fields are reduced slowly to zero at the same rate. The second case corresponds more closely to practical anhysteretic, or ac-biased, recording where both bias and signal currents are applied to the record head simultaneously. Figure 9.3*a* and *b* shows typical ideal and modified anhysteretic magnetization curves as a function of H_{dc}, the applied dc field. The anhysteretic susceptibility, χ_{ar}, is the slope of the curve $dM_{ar}(H_{dc})/dH_{dc}$.

(a)

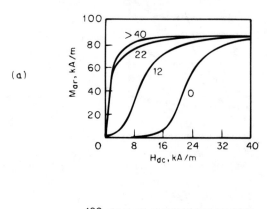

(b)

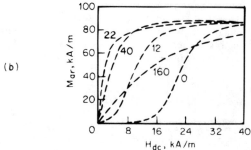

FIGURE 9.3 Plots of (*a*) ideal and (*b*) modified anhysteretic magnetization curves for various ac-bias levels in kiloamperes per meter (*Daniel and Levine, 1960*).

The ac demagnetization curve may be measured by using the ideal anhysteretic mode (with $H_{dc} = 0$) initiated from the negative saturation state instead of the ac-demagnetized state. The parameter H_{ac} is the peak applied ac field at which 25 percent of the particles have switched:

$$\frac{M_r(H_{ac})}{M_r(\infty)} = -0.5 \tag{9.5}$$

9.1.3 Anisotropy Parameters

The most commonly measured anisotropy parameter is the orientation ratio, which is the ratio between the remanent magnetizations measured in two orthogonal directions. For conventional longitudinal media, the directions are chosen to be longitudinal, that is, along the direction of writing, and transverse to that direction but in the plane of the medium. For perpendicular media, the directions are taken to be in plane and perpendicular to the plane of the medium. The anisotropy constant K and anisotropy field H_k also characterize the anisotropic behavior of the material.

9.1.4 Instruments

9.1.4.1 Vibrating Sample Magnetometer. The vibrating sample magnetometer (VSM) is the instrument most often used for accurately measuring the magnetic properties of recording media. Figure 9.4 shows a diagram of a typical apparatus. A large electromagnet applies a uniform dc field to the sample. The resulting magneti-

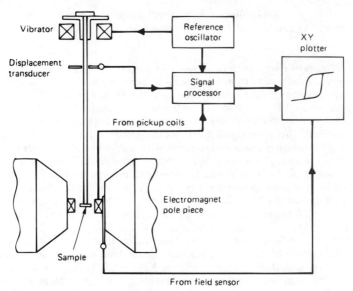

FIGURE 9.4   Diagram of vibrating sample magnetometer.

zation induced in the sample is then measured by vibrating the sample to produce a voltage in a pair of pickup coils. The coil output voltage is combined with the output from the displacement transducer to produce a magnetization signal. Variations in vibration amplitude and frequency are canceled out. The signal is then detected, usually by a lock-in amplifier, and fed along with the applied field signal to an *xy* plotter to generate a hysteresis loop.

Some care must be taken in the design of the instrument to ensure the uniformity of the fields and field gradients involved and to calibrate the measurements properly (Foner, 1959). Design of the pickup coils is simplified by the application of the reciprocity theorem (Mallinson, 1966), and detailed analyses of various configurations have been made (Pacyna and Ruebenbauer, 1984).

Commercially available vibrating sample magnetometers have many special features, such as computer control and automatic data acquisition, temperature control of the sample, and rotational positioning of the sample. The vibrating sample magnetometer is well suited for measuring major and minor hysteresis loops, initial magnetization curves, and remanent magnetization curves.

9.1.4.2 *Alternating Gradient Magnetometer.*

In the alternating gradient magnetometer (AGM), the sample is mounted on the end of a rod and placed in a uniform dc field as in a VSM. Instead of vibrating the rod, the instrument uses a pair of coils to produce a uniform field gradient over the region of the sample. Exciting these coils with an ac current produces a force on the sample which is proportional to its magnetic moment. The vibrating rod is part of a resonant mechanical system containing a piezoelectric element to provide a voltage output proportional to the force. By operating near the mechanical resonant frequency, the signal can be amplified, and very high sensitivity achieved. Unlike the sense coils in a VSM, the piezoelectric elements are not sensitive to changing magnetic fields, but careful attention must be paid to mechanical and acoustic noise sources (Flanders, 1988).

Commercially available alternating gradient magnetometers have the same convenient computer control and data acquisition features of VSMs.

9.1.4.3 *Hysteresis Loop Tracers.*

Hysteresis loop tracers, also known as *B-H* meters, measure steady-state hysteresis loops by applying an ac field, usually at the power-line frequency, to the sample. The induction is then measured by integrating the voltage across the sense coil. Figure 9.5 shows a schematic diagram of a representative loop tracer. With no sample present, the applied field will induce a voltage in the sense coil. This error signal must be canceled out, and usually this is done by a balancing coil which is connected in series with the sense coil. In order to obtain a correct measurement of the loop, a number of other errors must be eliminated, such as phase errors between applied current and integrator output, noise pickup, and zero drift. The reduction of these errors in the design of a 450-kA/m loop tracer has been described (Manly, 1971). Development of low noise electronic components has enabled the construction of a new version of the classic loop tracer with ultra-high sensitivity (Slade and Berkowitz, 1992).

In contrast to conventional hysteresis loop tracers that average magnetic behavior over the volume of the sample, magnetooptical loop tracers based on the Kerr effect have high spatial resolution (Shieh and Kryder, 1988). A swept magnetic field is applied to the sample, as in the conventional loop tracer, but the magnetization is sensed by the Kerr rotation of the polarized light incident on the sample. Spatial resolution, determined by the spot size of the incident light, can be on the order of

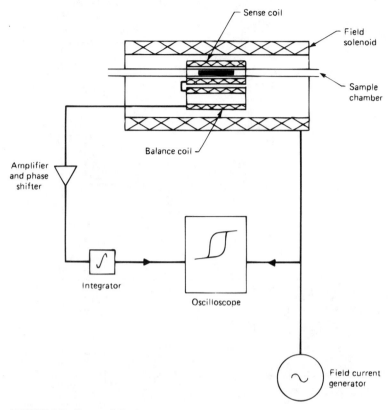

FIGURE 9.5   Hysteresis loop tracer.

0.5 μm, a useful feature for characterizing both magnetooptical and conventional film media. A rapid scanning Kerr loop tracer has the magnetic mapping capabilities required for high volume disk manufacturing development and process control (Gudeman et al., 1990). Loop testers are very convenient for rapid testing of media parameters.

9.1.4.4 Torque Magnetometer.   In the classical torque magnetometer, the sample is suspended from a support by a torsion wire and placed in a uniform applied field. The torque on the sample is measured by the angular twist of the torsion wire. Figure 9.6a shows an instrument which uses electrical feedback to drive the net torque to zero in the suspension (Penoyer, 1959). This technique makes it possible to automate the measurement of torque as a function of the angle of sample orientation in the applied field. A typical torque curve measured for a sample of perpendicular recording medium is shown in Fig. 9.6b (Iwasaki and Ouchi, 1978). From interpretation of torque curves, anisotropy behavior of the sample material can be determined. Most torque magnetometers have been homemade in individual laboratories. A number of these instruments covering a wide range of torques and sensitivities have been described (Pearson, 1979).

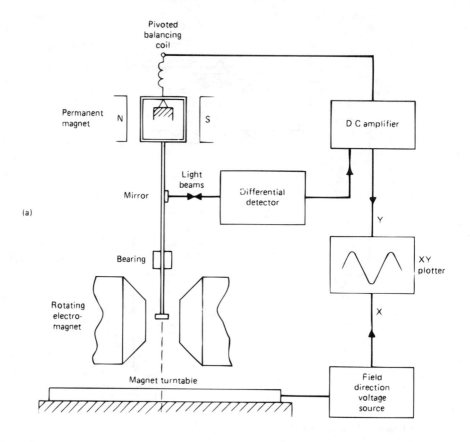

(a)

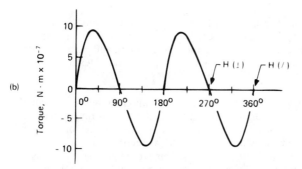

(b)

FIGURE 9.6 (a) Torque magnetometer (*after Penoyer, 1959*) and (b) torque curve measured for sample of perpendicular recording medium (*Iwasaki and Ouchi, 1978*).

9.1.5 Measurement Techniques

9.1.5.1 Differences Between Particulate and Film Media.

Sample Preparation. Particulate media on flexible substrates can be measured in a number of configurations. Magnetic coating thicknesses may range from 1 to 20 μm. For the remanent magnetizations usually encountered, one thickness of material suffices for the sensitivity of most instruments. If more output signal is required, several thicknesses may be laminated together. For in-plane measurements in a loop tracer, the samples may be made long and rolled up into a tube so that skewing of the hysteresis loop by demagnetizing effects is minimized.

Particular care must be taken in preparing samples for measurement of anhysteretic remanence. In the course of this measurement, demagnetizing fields caused by the shape of the sample can mask the effects of small interaction fields to produce erroneous results. It is good practice to use a sample shape with a demagnetizing factor in the applied field direction of less than 0.0001. Effects of internal demagnetizing fields, caused by voids and particle clusters in the sample, must also be considered.

To take account of various particle loadings of the coatings, it is useful to determine the specific magnetic moment σ_s, defined as the saturation magnetization divided by the bulk material density.

Samples for the vibrating sample magnetometer must be small enough to fit within the uniform field working volume of the instrument. The shape of the sample may then require deskewing of the measured hysteresis loops to remove demagnetizing field effects. Because the samples are rarely ellipsoids with uniform demagnetizing field, care must be taken to determine an appropriate average demagnetizing factor over the entire sample. This choice is particularly important for measurements perpendicular to the plane of the medium, for which an inappropriate demagnetizing factor can result in false reentrant loops.

Figure 9.7 shows a typical hysteresis loop of magnetization versus applied field for a sample of film perpendicular recording media measured in a vibrating sample magnetometer. The measured loop must be deskewed using the relationship

$$H = H_{\text{appl}} - NM \tag{9.6}$$

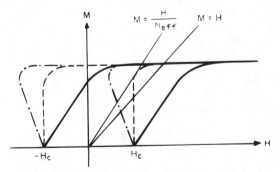

FIGURE 9.7 Deskewing of hysteresis loop measured for sample of film perpendicular recording media (—). Deskewing with a demagnetizing factor $N = 1$ gives reentrant loop (— • —). Deskewing with N_{eff} determined from slope of measured loop at $-H_c$ gives well-behaved loop (— — —).

where H_{appl} is the field applied in the vibrating sample magnetometer. For a thin sample shape, N approaches a limiting value of 1. However, when $N = 1$ is used to deskew the loop, the resulting loop is a reentrant loop, as shown in Fig. 9.7. A better estimate for the effective demagnetizing factor N_{eff} can be derived from the slope of the M versus H_{appl} loop at the coercivity point, $H_{appl} = -H_c$ (Chu, 1984). In the neighborhood of this point, the magnetization of the *deskewed* loop is approximately

$$M = \chi_c(H + H_c) \tag{9.7}$$

Substituting for H from Eq. (9.6) and rearranging gives

$$M = \frac{\chi_c}{1 + \chi_c N_{eff}}(H_{appl} + H_c) \tag{9.8}$$

Differentiating with respect to H_{appl} gives the slope of the M versus H_{appl} loop

$$\left[\frac{dM}{dH_{appl}}\right]_{-H_c} = \frac{\chi_c}{1 + \chi_c N_{eff}} \tag{9.9}$$

For large χ_c, corresponding to high-coercivity squareness,

$$\left[\frac{dM}{dH_{appl}}\right]_{-H_c} \approx \frac{1}{N_{eff}} \tag{9.10}$$

Loops deskewed using N_{eff} determined from Eq. (9.10) are well behaved, as shown in Fig. 9.7. It should be noted, however, that the analysis assumes that N_{eff} is not a function of applied field.

Special measurement apparatus has been developed to study the properties of individual particles. Knowles (1978, 1980) describes sample preparation and special measurement techniques required for this work. A very dilute suspension of particles is made in a transparent viscous lacquer. Ultrasonic vibration produces wide dispersion of the particles so that interactions between individual particles or small agglomerates of particles are small. The solution is sucked into a small, flat capillary tube which is placed in a region of uniform, controllable magnetic field. By observing the particles on a television display of the image of a 10^4 magnification optical microscope, it is possible to observe single particles as distinct from small agglomerates. By aligning a particle in a field and then applying a pulsed field in the reverse direction of sufficient amplitude to rotate the particle by 180°, the remanence coercive force of the particle can be readily obtained. A remanent loop may be drawn by observing the time for the particle to rotate 90° as a function of the pulsed field amplitude.

Most film media are deposited on rigid, conducting substrates. The conducting substrate complicates the measurements with the ac field used in hysteresis loop plotters; thus the vibrating sample magnetometer is more commonly used. Although film media often have higher retentivity than particulate media, the recording layers are much thinner so that the magnetization in samples with the same area may differ by as much as a factor of 20. Samples are cut out of the medium and are typically 10-mm squares or disks. These sizes require instrument sensitivities on the order of 0.1 μm$A \cdot m^2$ (0.0001 emu) or better. Demagnetizing effects must also be taken into account for out-of-plane measurements.

Anisotropy Characterization. Anisotropy is often characterized by measuring hysteresis loops in two, sometimes three, orthogonal directions. For isotropic media, such curves should be identical. The anisotropy magnitude can be inferred from the shapes and parameters of the loops. Often, a simple characterization is made in terms of a single parameter, for example, remanent magnetization M_r. This parameter leads to the orientation ratio defined earlier. Sometimes, remanence squareness is used as the single parameter.

The anisotropy constants are usually more important for describing film media performance. This is particularly so for perpendicular film media, for which torque magnetometer measurements can be used to obtain K and the anisotropy field H_k. By placing a sample in a rotating field produced by two orthogonal sets of Helmholtz coils, H_k can be determined by finding the elliptical applied field pattern that causes the sample magnetization vector to rotate uniformly in time with no phase modulation (Harlee et al., 1994). H_k is the difference between the peak values of the fields produced by the orthogonal coil pairs.

Anisotropy field characterization of particulate media is also possible. A method for obtaining the anisotropy field from measurement of initial reversible susceptibility of ac-erased particulate media samples has been reported (Köster, 1970; Kullmann et al., 1984). H_k can also be obtained from hysteresis loop data. Plotting the second derivative of M with respect to H gives a curve exhibiting a small cusp. The H field corresponding to this cusp is the anisotropy field H_k (Asti and Rinaldi, 1974; O'Grady, 1990).

Amplitude Effects. For particulate media, hysteresis loop shapes can change significantly as a function of the peak amplitude of the field, even for fields 10 times the coercivity. Figure 9.8 shows typical variations of maximum magnetization and remanent magnetization versus maximum applied field. All variables are normalized with respect to their values as $H_m \to \infty$. It is seen that $M_r(H_m)$ approaches its

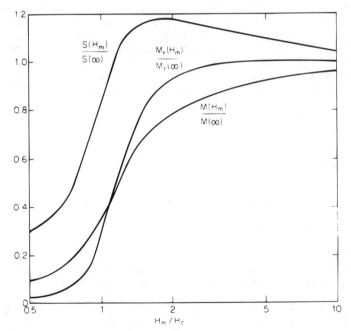

FIGURE 9.8 Variation of hysteresis loop parameters with maximum applied field strength.

final value fairly rapidly, while $M(H_m)$ approaches the final saturation value more slowly. This behavior causes a wide variation in the apparent remanence squareness of the material as seen in the plot of $S(H_m)/S(\infty)$. Fortunately, the approach of $M(H_m)$ to saturation is predictable for most particulates and follows closely a $1/H$ law:

$$M(H_m) = M_s - \frac{a}{H_m} \tag{9.11}$$

where a is a constant. This behavior has several important practical consequences. The saturation magnetization can be accurately estimated by plotting $M(H_m)$ as a function of $1/H_m$ and making a linear extrapolation to $1/H_m = 0$ to obtain M_s. Using this method avoids the need to produce the very high fields required to saturate the samples completely. Field values of roughly 10 times the coercivity are adequate.

To eliminate the large variations in apparent squareness as a function of the peak applied field H_m, M_s determined from the extrapolation method should be used to obtain the squareness of a particulate sample.

Film media do not appear to approach saturation in a simply predictable way. In most cases, they approach saturation faster than a $1/H$ law, and so that peak applied fields of 10 times the coercivity are adequate for characterization of saturation behavior. Because of the relatively rapid approach to saturation, squareness is not so variable with applied field as for particulate media.

9.1.5.2 Preisach Diagram Measurement.

The Preisach diagram, treated in Chap. 2, is a useful way of depicting the distribution of interaction fields in recording media. Figure 9.9 shows a Preisach diagram in terms of interaction fields H_1 and H_2. The relative number of particles in the shaded region with area $\Delta H_1 \, \Delta H_2$ can be determined from magnetization measurements. Define the magnetization $M(H_1, -H_2)$ as that resulting from applying to the sample a field sequence of negative saturation, positive field of amplitude H_1, and negative field of amplitude H_2. The saturation magnetization $M(\infty)$ may be expressed in terms of a particle-interaction-field distribution function, $K(H_1, H_2)$, as

$$M(\infty) = 2 \int_{-\infty}^{0} \int_{0}^{\infty} K(H_1, H_2) \, dH_1 \, dH_2 \tag{9.12}$$

The distribution function $K(H_1, H_2)$ may then be obtained from

$$K(H_1, H_2) = \frac{1}{2 \, \Delta H_1 \, \Delta H_2} \{ M[(H_1 + \Delta H_1), -H_2] + M[H_1, -(H_2 + \Delta H_2)]$$
$$- M(H_1, -H_2) - M[(H_1 + \Delta H_1), -(H_2 + \Delta H_2)] \} \tag{9.13}$$

A number of workers have used experimentally determined Preisach diagrams to characterize particulate media. Using an automatic measurement of the Preisach diagram, magnetization measurements for the field sequences shown in Fig. 9.9 are made to determine the relative number of particles in the hatched area on the diagram (Völz, 1971). In general, the measured Preisach distribution depends upon the field history used to obtain it. By measuring minor hysteresis loops of the sample, it is possible to evaluate the extent of dependence of the distribution on field history (Salling and Schultz, 1988). The degree of non-congruence of minor

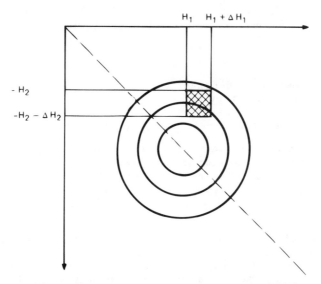

FIGURE 9.9 Preisach distribution contours in interaction-field plane (H_1, H_2). Particle density in shaded area can be determined from magnetization measurements.

loops measured at different values of remanence, but with constant field excursion, indicates the sensitivity of the Preisach distribution to field history.

9.1.5.3 Vector Magnetization Measurements. In magnetic recording, the field experienced by the recording medium as it passes the head is a time-varying vector field. Consequently, scalar M versus H curves, even three curves for orthogonal components, can only coarsely predict recording performance. A true vector magnetization characterization would be superior. Several approaches to vector magnetization measurements have been made in which programmable currents were applied to two orthogonal sets of Helmholtz coils which magnetized a sample placed at their center (Lemke and McClure, 1966; Clark and Finegan, 1985). The sample experienced a rotating field history similar to what it would experience if passed under a recording head. After the completion of the vector-field program, the vector magnetization was measured by spinning the sample in the sense coils.

Vector vibrating sample magnetometers have been developed and applied to three-dimensional anisotropy measurements (Josephs et al., 1987) and vector Preisach characterizations of recording media (Wiesen and Charap, 1990).

9.1.5.4 Measurement of Time-Scale Effects. In measuring hysteresis loops, the time dependence of switching mechanisms can influence the experimental results significantly. For example, the measured values of coercivity from a relatively long time-scale vibrating sample magnetometer may differ from the results of a 60- or 50-Hz hysteresis loop tester by as much as 10 percent. This behavior is caused by the temperature dependence of the energy barrier which must be overcome for the domains to switch.

Assuming that the magnetization reversal of an ensemble of identical, noninteracting, single-domain particles follows first-order kinetics, the rate constant r is given by

$$r = Ae^{-\Delta E/kT} \tag{9.14}$$

where A = frequency of approach to the barrier
ΔE = height of the energy barrier
k = Boltzmann's constant
T = absolute temperature

For particles of uniaxial anisotropy, an expression for the coercivity as a function of the measurement time scale t can be derived (Kneller and Luborsky, 1963; Sharrock, 1984):

$$H_c(t) = H_k \left[1 - \left(\frac{kT}{K_u v} \ln \frac{At}{0.69} \right)^{1/2} \right] \tag{9.15}$$

K_u is the uniaxial anisotropy constant, and v is the volume of each particle. By making measurements of H_c on two different time scales, it is possible to determine H_k and the $K_u v$ product. From these, the coercivity on any time scale may be predicted, and such a characterization is very useful for evaluating high-frequency writing performance, long-term storage stability, and print-through.

Very short switching times for particulate recording media have been measured by discharging a charged transmission line into a microstrip line to produce a pulsed magnetic field on a sample of the medium (Thornley, 1975; Doyle et al., 1993). The switching speeds of metal particle media indicate that recording should be frequency independent up to frequencies of at least 250 MHz. The slower switching speeds of Co-γ Fe$_2$O$_3$ and barium ferrite media will cause frequency dependent effects at 100 MHz and above.

9.2 RECORDED MAGNETIZATION

Measurement of recorded magnetization patterns can provide valuable information about the recording process. Most magnetization measurement techniques are indirect and measure the external fields produced by the magnetization pattern. It is not possible to infer uniquely the magnetization distribution from field measurements, no matter how accurate or complete (Mallinson, 1981). The field can be represented in terms of net dipole, quadrupole, and higher-order moments of the magnetization through a multipole expansion. The difficulty is that many magnetization distributions have the same moments. In spite of this basic limitation, field measurements on recorded media are very useful and plausible, though not unique, and magnetization distributions may be inferred using additional knowledge of media and head-field properties.

9.2.1 Bitter Pattern Techniques

Magnetized media are coated with a suspension of very fine magnetic particles which are attracted to regions of nonuniform field produced by the magnetization pattern in the medium. The resulting patterns of particles are then viewed under a microscope. This technique was first used to observe domain walls in ferromagnetic metals (Bitter, 1931). Several methods of preparing the colloidal magnetic suspension have been developed (Bozorth, 1951; Chikazumi, 1964). Another approach has been to use a magnetic viewer (Youngquist and Hanes, 1961) containing an aqueous dispersion of Fe_2O_3 platelets. In regions of high field normal to the medium, the platelets stand on edge and reflect less light, causing a longitudinally recorded transition to appear dark. Figure 9.10 shows a typical pattern seen using the Bitter method to observe the magnetization recorded. Bitter methods are widely used because of their convenience. Although they give a useful qualitative picture of magnetization patterns, quantitative information is lacking. Resolution is limited by the particle size, which may be as small as 0.1 μm.

9.2.2 Fringing-Field Measurement

To obtain a quantitative description of the magnetization, the stray or fringing fields produced by the recorded magnetization may be measured directly. One high-resolution system uses a Hall probe (Lustig et al., 1979). The active area of the Hall probe is 2 by 2 μm, and it can be accurately positioned to a minimum separation of 1 μm from the surface of the medium. In principle, finite separation from the surface of a single-layer medium is not a problem because the Fourier transforms of the fields at any two separations are related by the exponential spacing-loss formula. Measurement accuracy imposes a practical limit on transferring field measurements from one spacing to another. High-resolution piezoelectric positioners and electronic position sensors are used to achieve 0.1-μm resolution under computer control, and the minimum detectable fields are 200 to 300 A/m (3 to 4 Oe). The system has been used to study transitions recorded on longitudinal and perpendicular media (Baird et al., 1984).

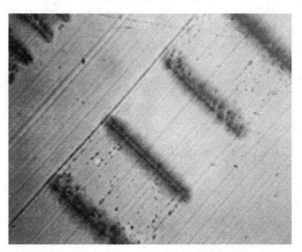

FIGURE 9.10 Bitter pattern of recorded magnetization transitions (*Tong et al., 1984*).

9.2.3 Lorentz Microscopy

In Lorentz microscopy, electrons in a beam directed at the medium sample are deflected by the Lorentz force, $\mathbf{F} = q\mathbf{V} \times \mathbf{B}$, which is produced by the magnetization in the medium. The deflection of the electrons is measured, and the magnetization M and fringing field H are inferred. Experiments are generally performed in commercially available scanning electron microscopes (SEM) or transmission electron microscopes (TEM).

Several techniques have been used to measure the fringing field above the surface of the medium with a scanning electron microscope. Figure 9.11 shows the electron beam directed parallel to the medium surface and normal to a magnetized track. The deflection of the beam is sensed below the recording by use of a microchannel plate as a two-dimensional detector of the beam's deflection (Elsbrock and Balk, 1984). The two components of stray field can be determined from the displacement in two dimensions. The deflection of the beam can also be determined by observing how the image of a reference grid is distorted (Thornley and Hutchison, 1969).

When the electron beam is directed so as to strike the medium sample, fringing fields or magnetization can be measured by using the SEM type 1 or type 2 methods. In the type 1 method, low-energy secondary electrons are produced when the primary electrons hit the medium surface. The detector is a collector of these secondary electrons and is sensitive to the direction from which they leave the surface (Banbury and Nixon, 1967; Joy and Jakubovics, 1968). The direction of the secondary electrons is dependent on the surface magnetic field and topography. The image produced from the collected electrons has both magnetic and topographic contrast. For a smooth, thin-film medium, the topographic contrast is small. For inhomogeneous specimens, there may be additional contrast caused by variation in the secondary emission coefficient along the surface. Several methods have been used to reduce these effects (Cort and Steeds, 1972; Griffiths et al., 1972).

In the type 2 method, higher-energy incident electrons are used, and the image is formed by detecting the number of electrons which are back-scattered from inside the medium (Fathers et al., 1973). The beam strikes the specimen at an oblique

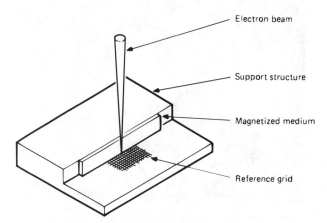

Electron beam

Support structure

Magnetized medium

Reference grid

FIGURE 9.11 Measurement of fringing field by deflection of electron beams (*Thornley and Hutchison, 1969*).

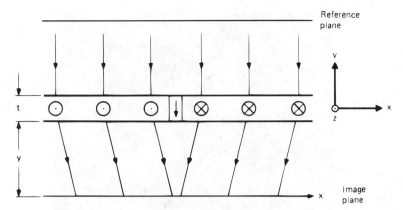

FIGURE 9.12 Deflection of electrons around a domain wall in a thin magnetized sample placed in a transmission electron microscope.

angle and penetrates inside. Depending upon the sense of the B field tangent to the surfaces of the medium, the electrons are forced toward or away from the surface. The electrons with shallower trajectories are more likely to be backscattered. Consequently, the detected intensity of backscattered electrons can be related to the B field inside the medium. Both magnetization and fields inside the medium contribute to this effect. Because the effect occurs inside the specimen, the image is relatively insensitive to the surface topography, in contrast to the type 1 method.

Magnetization microstructure can also be observed in thin samples (less than 1 μm) by passing high-energy electrons through them in a transmission electron microscope. Figure 9.12 shows a beam of electrons with intensity I_0 being deflected as they pass through a medium sample of thickness t. The magnetization is normal to the plane of the paper and has a reversal in the domain wall shown. This picture might represent a section cut normal to the domain wall of a sawtooth domain typically observed in transitions written on film media. The beam is focused on a plane which is a distance y below the surface of the medium. This method is referred to as the *defocused,* or *Fresnel,* mode. The relative intensity of the electrons striking the image plane is given by

$$\frac{I(x')}{I_0} = \left[1 + by \frac{dB_z(x)}{dx} \right]^{-1} \tag{9.16}$$

where $b = (|e|/m)(t/V)$, $|e|/m$ is the electron charge-to-mass ratio and V is the electron velocity in the y direction. Note that there is no variation in intensity when $y = 0$. This is why the beam must be defocused. The intensity is proportional to the derivative of the B field so that image contrast appears in regions of changing magnetization such as domain walls. Figure 9.13a and c shows typical Fresnel mode electron micrographs of a recording track region exhibiting irregular transition domain walls.

A novel method has been used to obtain both magnetization gradient and fringing-field measurements on the same magnetized sample (Chen, 1981). The sample is examined in the transmission electron microscope using the defocused mode and is then folded back on itself. At the fold, the plane of the surface fields becomes normal to the direction of the incident electron beam, and the deflection of the beam indicates the field distribution.

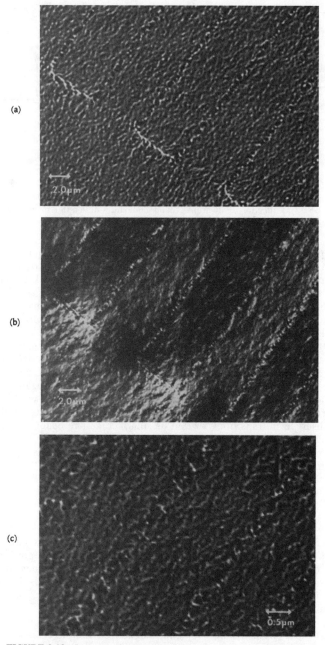

(a)

(b)

(c)

FIGURE 9.13 Lorentz micrographs of a portion of a recorded track on an isotropic sputtered Co-Pt alloy film medium (*Alexopoulos and Geiss, 1985*). (*a*) Fresnel mode showing contrast in regions of magnetization changes, such as domain walls. (*b*) Foucault mode showing contrast between domains of a different orientation or magnitude of magnetization. (*c*) Enlarged Fresnel micrograph showing irregular zigzag domain wall.

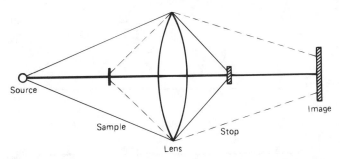

FIGURE 9.14 Optical magnification using the Foucault mode (*after Marton, 1948*).

The transmission electron microscope may also be operated in the Foucault mode (Marton, 1948). The principle is illustrated in Fig. 9.14 in its optical version. The source illuminates the object and is focused by an objective lens onto a stop which blocks all direct rays from the source. If now some inhomogeneity is introduced in the index of refraction, some rays will miss the stop and form an image of the inhomogeneity in the image space beyond the stop. In the transmission electron microscope, inhomogeneities are produced by the magnetization in the sample, and the stopping action is achieved by a knife edge. The Foucault mode is similar to the optical schlieren method for showing shock waves in air (Wells et al., 1983). Figure 9.13*b* shows a Foucault image Lorentz micrograph of a recording track. Magnetization, rather than its derivative, produces contrast in this mode.

All the Lorentz microscopy techniques are labor-intensive and time-consuming in the sense that they require very careful sample preparation and adjustment of complex equipment. There is always a chance that the magnetization on the medium may change during the course of the experiments.

This treatment of Lorentz microscopy has been based upon geometric optics. Application of geometric optics has a fundamental limit (Wohlleben, 1966). The smallest detectable flux change $\Delta\phi$ between two ray paths separated by Δx is given by $h/2e$, $\frac{1}{2}$ fluxon. To go beyond this limit, wave optics must be used (Cohen, 1967). In wave optics, the magnetization in the medium sample changes the phase of the incident electron waves, but not their amplitude. One method recently demonstrated for observing the phase change is electron holography.

9.2.4 Electron Holography

The idea of holography was first proposed for electron microscopy (Gabor, 1949), but with the invention of the laser, much more work has been done with optical holography. Figure 9.15 shows the phase shift occurring when an electron wave front is incident on a magnetized medium. The difference in phase between rays 2 and 1 at a plane below the medium is given by (Aharonov and Bohm, 1959)

$$\phi_2 - \phi_1 = \frac{2\pi e}{h} \int \mathbf{A} \cdot d\mathbf{l} = \frac{2\pi e}{h} \int_s \mathbf{B} \cdot d\mathbf{s} \qquad (9.17)$$

where $\mathbf{A}$ is the vector potential.

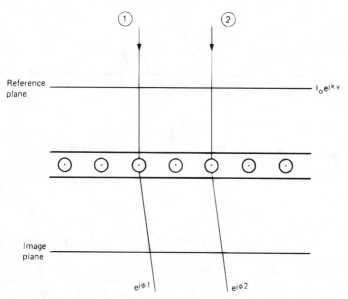

FIGURE 9.15   Aharonov-Bohm phase shift produced in electron wave front passing through magnetized sample. Complex representation of wave is $I_o e^{jky}$ at reference plane y. Phase shift $\phi_2 - \phi_1$ between points 2 and 1 on the image plane is proportional to flux enclosed by ray paths.

This phase difference is equal to 2π when

$$\int_s \mathbf{B} \cdot d\mathbf{s} = \frac{h}{e} \tag{9.18}$$

which is 1 fluxon, approximately 4 mT · μm^2 (40 G · μm^2). Suppose that lines of constant phase spaced apart at a constant phase interval $\Delta\phi$ were drawn on the image plane. Between any two adjacent phase contours, a tube of constant flux between the reference plane and image plane would have been enclosed by the rays which produced the contours. For thin media magnetized in plane, the **B** field may be considered to be localized within the thickness of the medium. Consequently, the equal phase contours coincide with **B** field lines.

In order to display equal phase contours, a hologram is made by superimposing a reference wave on the wave which contains the phase information from the image plane. Figure 9.16 shows the production of the hologram by using an electron biprism to superpose the two waves (Yoshida et al., 1983). The two waves interfere to produce an intensity given by

$$I = A \cos \frac{\phi(x, z)}{2} \tag{9.19}$$

where $\phi(x, z)$ is the phase shift in the image plane. This intensity variation is recorded on the hologram, which is removed from the vacuum chamber.

Reconstruction from the hologram is accomplished by uniform laser light as shown in Fig. 9.17. The light is diffracted upon passing through the hologram and

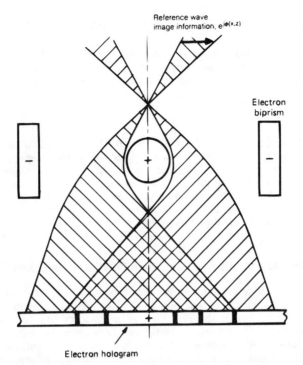

FIGURE 9.16 Hologram formation by superposing electron wave containing image phase information $\phi(x, z)$ on reference wave in an electron biprism (*after Tonomura et al., 1980*).

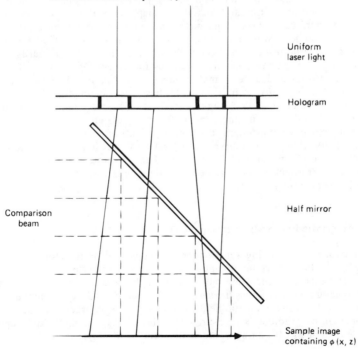

FIGURE 9.17 Optical reconstruction of electron hologram by superposing coherent light diffracted by hologram and uniform comparison beam to produce sample image.

acquires the phase information $\phi(x, z)$. A comparison wave superimposed upon the diffracted wave reconstructs the $\cos(\phi/2)$ variation in intensity which produced the hologram in the vacuum chamber originally. Interference fringes appear when $\phi/2 = 0, \pi, 2\pi, \ldots$, corresponding to

$$\phi = 0, 2\pi, 4\pi, \ldots$$

Two adjacent fringes enclose a flux of h/e, which is just twice the limit of detectable flux using geometric optics. In the reconstructed hologram, intensity can be measured between fringes to obtain higher resolution. By more complicated optical signal processing using multiple conjugate images, it is possible to obtain phase amplification to increase the resolution between fringes (Tonomura et al., 1980). The ability to do signal processing on the hologram outside the vacuum chamber is an important feature of electron holography.

9.2.5 Magnetization Imaging Using Spin-Polarized Secondary Electrons

Measurement of magnetization in media samples or film head structures by Lorentz microscopy in a scanning electron microscope using the type 1 method is subject to distortion caused by topographic roughness of the samples. In spite of clever methods used to reduce these effects, the image generated from the collected secondary electrons exhibits both magnetic and topographic contrast. Analysis using spin-polarized secondary electrons allows the magnetic contrast to be separated from the topographic. The method relies upon the property that secondary electrons are emitted from a magnetized surface with spins antiparallel to the magnetization (Unguris et al., 1982; Celotta and Pierce, 1986). Hence, analysis of components of the spin-polarization vector can give a direct mapping of the magnetization vector in the sample surface. The technique has been demonstrated in a conventional SEM modified to include a Mott detector for electron spin analysis (Koike and Hayakawa, 1985). Spatial resolution of the technique is high, limited primarily by beam diameters for which quantum noise becomes too large. Operation with a beam diameter of 10 nm and an extremely compact polarization detector using spin-dependent absorbed current in a gold film has given an improved measurement capability (Pierce et al., 1981; Unguris et al., 1985). In a comparison study with Bitter fluid, longitudinal magnetooptical Kerr effect, and Lorentz transmission electron microscopy, spin-polarized secondary electron analysis produced very favorable results, giving quantitative magnetization vector images with intermediate difficulty of use (Cameron and Judy, 1988). The technique is similar to the magnetooptical Kerr effect in that surface magnetization is sensed rather than the total field as in Lorentz microscopy.

9.2.6 Magnetic Force Microscopy (MFM)

The techniques of scanning tunneling microscopy and atomic force microscopy (Binnig et al., 1986) have been applied to the measurement of magnetic forces to investigate fields from recorded patterns on media and recording heads. A very small magnetic tip scans across the surface to be studied and experiences a spatially varying force from the magnetic field produced by the recorded medium or head. The force or its gradient is measured and the corresponding field components calculated. Figure 9.18 shows a block diagram of a magnetic force microscope

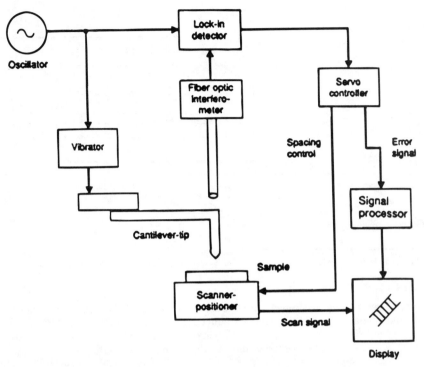

FIGURE 9.18 Block diagram of magnetic force microscope (*after Rugar et al., 1988*).

(Rugar et al., 1988). The magnetic tip, which has a typical diameter of 50 nm, is formed on the end of a cantilever with a mechanical resonance in the kilohertz range. A piezoelectric transducer oscillates the cantilever-tip near resonance and the motion is sensed by a fiber optic interferometer. The changing force gradient experienced by the tip as it scans across the sample is equivalent to a changing spring constant, shifting the cantilever resonant frequency, which produces variations in the detected amplitude of oscillation. A servo loop controls the distance between tip and sample so that the oscillation amplitude is maintained constant throughout the scan. Signal processing of the servo error signal gives the desired force gradient information.

The magnetic tip is the critical component of the technique. Tip fabrication methods include etching nickel wire (Rugar et al., 1990) and sputtering thin Co-Cr films onto etched silicon cantilever tips (Grütter et al., 1991; Babcock et al., 1994). Small tip diameter and cone angle as well as the magnetic structure are important in determining measurement resolution. 50 nm resolution is routinely achievable at present (Grütter, 1994). Interpretation of results can involve careful treatment of all force interactions between tip and sample (Saenz et al., 1988). One approach is to iterate realistic model simulations of tip and sample magnetization until good agreement with the observed MFM images is obtained (Rugar et al., 1990). Alternatively, the tip response can be determined experimentally. A high-sensitivity AGM has found use in calibrating the response of MFM tips to known magnetic fields and field gradients (Gibson and Schultz, 1991). The response of an MFM to a

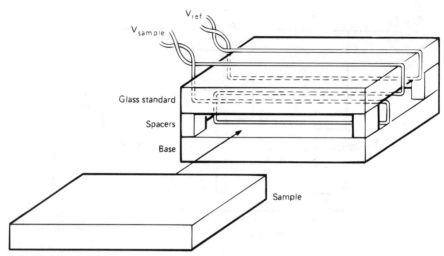

FIGURE 9.19 Permeance measuring jig for film samples (*after Calcagno and Thompson, 1975*).

point magnetic charge can be used to deconvolve an MFM image to obtain the magnetic charge distribution which produced it (Chang et al., 1992). A 90 nm wide, 1 μm long Ni strip produced the point charge in this study, but 10 nm wide strips have been fabricated and should improve the resolution accordingly.

Several methods can remove topographic effects from MFM images. By placing a dc voltage on the cantilever tip and measuring the Coulomb force interaction between tip and sample, topographic information can be obtained independently from the magnetic interaction (Schönenberger et al., 1990). A tunneling stabilization method maintains a constant tunnel current and hence spacing between tip and sample as the tip is scanned over the sample (Gomez et al., 1992). A third approach uses two scans over each raster line. In the first, the topography is recorded as the tip is scanned in contact with the sample. This information is used on the second scan to maintain the tip at a constant separation from the sample as the magnetic image is taken (Babcock et al., 1994).

In a relatively short time, magnetic force microscopy has found wide application. Images of domains in a Tb-Fe thin film (Martin et al., 1988), written magnetization patterns on longitudinal recording media (Mamin et al., 1988), and studies of fields from a thin-film recording head (Martin and Wickramasinghe, 1987) are but a few of the earliest examples. MFM has also been used to study particle switching effects (Chang et al., 1993) and to provide a highly resolved local field source for studying the spatial response of both inductive and magneto-resistive heads (Gibson et al., 1992).

9.3   HEAD MEASUREMENTS

Many types of head measurements are useful in characterizing head performance. These include measurements of impedance, frequency response, noise, saturation effects, and field distributions. This section will describe several measurements developed especially for magnetic recording heads.

9.3.1 Material Properties

One of the most important material properties of the soft magnetic materials used in magnetic recording heads is permeability. For conventional isotropic head materials, measurement of toroidal samples is adequate. For anisotropic films used in film ring heads or magnetoresistive heads, special permeance meters have been developed.

Calcagno and Thompson (1975) developed a permeance meter capable of measuring permeance of films with uniaxial anisotropy at frequencies up to 100 MHz. The measured permeance is the average permeability over the film cross section times its thickness. Figure 9.19 shows the permeance measuring jig into which the samples are inserted. Mutually perpendicular Helmholtz coils apply any desired preconditioning fields to the sample, for example, saturation in the easy axis. A drive strap supplies sinusoidal drive fields to the sample, inducing a voltage in the figure-eight sense coil. The coil is wound so that its induced voltage is zero with no sample inserted. An absolute permeance value is obtained by comparing the sense voltage with the voltage from the reference coil which surrounds a glass substrate of precisely known dimensions. An important feature of the technique is that the field linking the reference coil is not the applied field but the total field, which includes the demagnetizing field from the sample. The geometry has been carefully designed so that the total field in the reference coil agrees with that in the sample coil within 2 percent. This results in high accuracy and great simplification in the measurement. A number of automated procedures and data reduction techniques were designed into the apparatus.

A similar permeance meter capable of operation to 100 MHz has been reported (Kawakami et al., 1973). In addition, this meter can be used for magnetostriction measurements. The glass substrate upon which the magnetic film has been deposited is subjected to stress by means of a weighted fixture using the four-point wedge method. Magnetostriction constants as small as 0.05×10^{-6} can be measured with this meter. Use of transmission line techniques and scattering parameter measurements using a network analyzer have extended complex permeability measurements to frequencies beyond 200 MHz (Grimes et al., 1988).

9.3.2 Head Fields

Many of the same techniques used to measure fringing fields from recorded magnetization patterns on media are also applicable to measuring head fields. Direct measurement of head fields is possible using miniaturized Hall probes (Lustig et al., 1979) and magnetoresistive probes (Fluitman, 1978). Lustig's apparatus is described in Sec. 9.2.2. Fluitman was able to use a relatively wide (3-μm) transducer to obtain useful results by shifting the position of the transducer over very small increments and processing the gathered data. He used a computer simulation which included demagnetizing effects in the magnetoresistive film to obtain the relation between the transducer output and a given applied field variation. With this approach and an air-bearing traversing table for positioning, he was able to achieve a resolution of 0.4 μm.

Another approach for measuring head fields directly is to sense the fields with an inductive pickup loop. The head gap dimensions currently used in high-density recording make it very difficult to build a pickup loop with adequate spatial resolution to resolve the head-field variations. Hoyt et al. (1984) have used a high-resolution "microloop" to measure fields from both ferrite and film heads. The

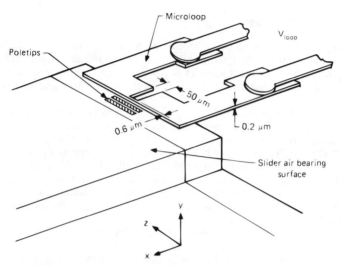

FIGURE 9.20 Microloop positioned for inductive sensing of fields from film head (*Hoyt et al., 1984*).

microloop was fabricated using advanced processing techniques. Masks were produced by electron beam lithography. After a film of Au-Ti was deposited on a glass substrate, the final dimensions of the microloop were obtained by ion milling. The high-resolution side of the loop, which is shown in Fig. 9.20, measures 0.6 μm wide by 50 μm long by 0.2 μm thick. The loop is accurately positioned vertically using optical interferometry and then moved along the track to obtain the voltage readings of the surface flux. The macroscopic portions of the loop, including the leads, sense fields from portions of the head structure which are far from the pole tips. Because these fields are much more slowly varying than those emanating from the pole tips, they are easily subtracted out. Direct measurement of the efficiency of Permalloy film heads gave values of 75 percent at low frequencies, decreasing slowly to 60 percent at 50 MHz. The inductive microloop technique has also been used to study head saturation (Hoyt, 1985).

Several techniques have been developed to measure recording head fields by Lorentz microscopy. Some of these are also applicable to measurement of fringing fields from recorded media and have already been described. Some additional methods include the stroboscopic electron mirror microscope (Spivak et al., 1971) and field plotting in the scanning electron microscope (Thornley and Hutchison, 1969; Ishiba and Suzuki, 1974; Rau and Spivak, 1980; Wells and Brunner, 1983; Wells et al., 1983).

For field plotting in the scanning electron microscope, the electron beam passes through the head field and strikes a reference grid placed below. The beam will be deflected by the head field and cross the plane of the reference grid at a spot displaced from the position of incidence with no field present. This displacement of the beam will cause the image of the reference grid to appear distorted. Figure 9.21 shows the two modes commonly used to scan the beam in the *xy* plane to determine head-field patterns. In the normal scanning mode, Fig. 9.21*a*, the grid distortion vector is measured at points in the *xy* plane and the corresponding head-field vector is calculated.

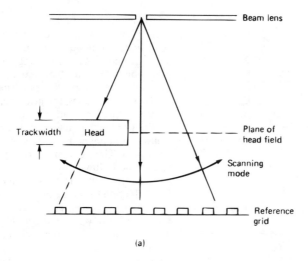

(a)

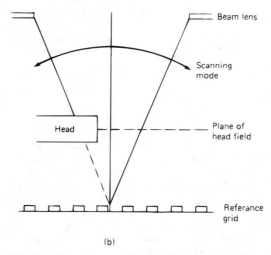

(b)

FIGURE 9.21 Measurement of head fields in a scanning electron microscope using (*a*) normal mode and (*b*) rocking mode (*Wells and Brunner, 1983*).

In the rocking mode, shown in Fig. 9.21*b*, scanning is done by rocking the beam about a fixed point in the reference grid plane, for example, the intersection of two grid conductors. In the absence of any head field, the beam will strike the conductors in the same spot during the whole scanning cycle, giving an image with constant intensity over its entire area. With field present, the image shows a distorted picture of the reference grid with the interesting and useful property that the distorted

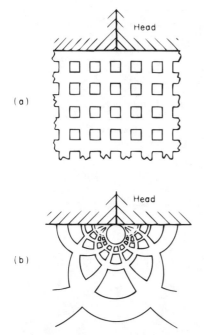

FIGURE 9.22 Distortion of (*a*) reference grid to produce (*b*) contours of constant *x* and *y* head-field components (*after Wells et al., 1983*).

reference grid conductors now lie along contours of equal magnitude of the respective head-field components in the *xy* plane. Figure 9.22 shows how a rectangular reference grid would appear distorted to show contours of constant *x* and *y* head-field components. Other shapes for grids may be used. For example, a grid of concentric rings would produce a distorted image showing contours of constant vector magnitude of the head field. The field contouring property occurs in the following way. The condition that a contour will appear in the image is just that the deflection of the beam from its fixed, no-field position in the reference grid plane is sufficient for it to strike the neighboring conductor in the grid. In the rocking mode, this condition is determined only by the head-field component experienced by the beam and not by the position in the scanning cycle. Hence, as the scan is carried out, contours are mapped as the beam is deflected to strike successive conductors. Note that the mapping is inverse in that the conductor closest to the origin is mapped the farthest away in the *xy* image plane because that is where the head fields are weakest.

Camarota and Thompson (1983) made a novel measurement of recording head frequency response in a standard scanning electron microscope. They recognized that a broadband detector is not necessary because the electrons, even in a low-voltage beam of 5 kV, traverse the track of a typical high-density recording head in a very short time, on the order of a picosecond. Consequently, transit-time effects can be ignored at frequencies up to a gigahertz. A head was placed so that the electron beam passed across the head in the center of the gap and continued on to a reference grid below. The beam was then scanned in a line outwardly normal to the head. With no current applied to the head, the microscope detector current is a square wave with transitions corresponding to the edges of the reference grid conductors. When a sinusoidal current is applied to the head coil, the ac head field causes a time-varying deflection of the electron beam which shears the sharp edges of the detected square wave. The amount of shear is proportional to the peak ac field. The head coil is switched on successive line scans between a low-frequency reference current and a test current source variable in both frequency and amplitude. Response at a particular test frequency is measured by adjusting the test current amplitude to match the detector waveforms on successive line scans. The ratio of test current to reference current is the frequency response. The frequency response of film heads measured in this way was lowered by 3 dB at 100 MHz.

Electron-beam tomography is a useful tool for measuring the full three-dimensional fringing fields from a recording head (Elsbrock et al., 1985). The deflection of an electron beam passed over the head surface is measured as the head is rotated about an axis normal to its surface. This procedure is repeated as the beam is scanned across the head surface. Because the head fields being measured are in a source free region, the complexity of the calculations to reconstruct the full three-dimensional vector tomography of the head field is significantly reduced. By pulsing the electron beam and synchronizing the deflection measurements to the head current waveform, it is possible to measure stroboscopically the dynamics of the head field (Shinada et al., 1992).

Each technique for head-field measurements has its particular requirements for success. Resolution problems manifest themselves in requirements for micro-fabrication, micromanipulation, and background cancellation for direct methods such as Hall probe or inductive sensors. Lorentz microscopy methods require careful control of head positioning and beam and detector control, alignment, and sensitivity. The experimenter has a number of attractive alternatives, but must choose carefully, consistent with requirements and resources.

9.3.3 Domain Observation

The increasing interest in using film heads has led to the need for observing domain and domain wall structure in heads under both static and dynamic conditions. Bitter techniques are useful for showing static domain wall structure over reasonably large areas.

Wells and Savoy (1981) have used a scanning electron microscope to observe domains in film heads. Except for regions near the pole tips and localized regions around domain walls, the magnetic fields of a film head are largely inside the films. For an undriven head, the fringing fields near the pole tips are zero except for any residual remanent magnetization in the tips. For this reason, the type 2 magnetic contrast using backscattered electrons from the interior of the films is the most effective method for the study of domains. The nature of the film surfaces, particularly the last surface to be deposited, is such that, even after conventional techniques have been used to remove the topographic contrasts, it is still difficult to observe domain structure using type 2 magnetic contrast. Wells and Savoy overcame this problem by using a lock-in image processing technique. In this technique, a small alternating current is applied to the head coil along with a direct drive current. This results in a modulated output from the backscattered electron detector which is demodulated in a lock-in amplifier. In this way, the topographic contrast is greatly reduced. For proper signal processing, the frequency of the applied ac current must be greater than 10 times the frequency at which the picture elements are being generated in the scanning electron microscope.

Magnetooptic techniques have also been used to investigate domain behavior in film heads. Detection of the Kerr magnetooptic effect caused by the reflection of a scanned laser beam from a magnetized head characterizes the local domain behavior. Spot sizes are on the order of 0.3 μm. Both magnetization curves and frequency responses have been measured (Narishige et al., 1984; Re and Kryder, 1984). Through the use of lock-in amplifier techniques, frequency responses up to 50 MHz have been measured. Magnetic activity is observable at frequencies up to 250 MHz, indicating the large bandwidths of magnetooptic instruments. By pulsing the laser and using stroboscopic techniques similar to flash photography it is possible to image high speed, time-resolved, domain dynamics (Kryder et al., 1990; Petek et al., 1990). Because of the small values of the Kerr component of reflected light, extensive digital image processing is used to separate magnetic effects from surface topography and background light fluctuations (Argyle et al., 1987; Trouilloud et al., 1994). Use of near-field optics offers the possibility of higher resolution, as low as 10 nm (Silva and Schultz, 1993). The depth of penetration of light into common head materials is very small, and consequently, Kerr images depict surface magnetization behavior.

Irreversible domain wall movements in thin-film heads produce Barkhausen noise pulses. These have been studied by sensing the head output voltage in a carefully designed measuring apparatus that can capture isolated pulses (Klaassen and van Peppen, 1990). Barkhausen noise has also been studied with Kerr-effect microscopes, and the noise probabilities found correlate with those determined from direct measurement of the head voltage (Liu and Kryder, 1994).

9.4 LARGE-SCALE MODELING

Large-scale modeling is an attractive measurement technique for studying many recording phenomena. It serves as a useful link between highly complex computer simulations of recording using self-consistent mathematical models of media and very demanding measurements in real time and space.

9.4.1 Scaling Laws

Under certain conditions, behavior of magnetic devices can be determined from scale models having the same magnetic properties as those in the modeled device (Valstyn et al., 1971). Consider Maxwell's equations:

$$\nabla \times \mathbf{E} = -\frac{\partial \mathbf{B}}{\partial t} \tag{9.20}$$

$$\nabla \times \mathbf{H} = \sigma \mathbf{E} + \frac{\partial \mathbf{D}}{\partial t} \tag{9.21}$$

The left-hand side of each equation contains first derivatives with respect to the space variables. Expanding the spatial scale by a factor of n amounts to multiplying the left-hand side by n. If the time scale is also expanded by a factor of n, the Faraday's law equation remains unchanged. In the Ampére's law equation, if the conductivity is decreased by the factor n, the equation will remain the same. Hence, the amplitudes and spatial variations of all of the vectors $\mathbf{E}$, $\mathbf{B}$, $\mathbf{H}$, and $\mathbf{D}$ will remain unchanged. If displacement current can be neglected, which is a good assumption for magnetic recording applications, then the conductivity may remain the same. That is, it is possible to use exactly the same materials in the scale model as in the simulated devices. The time scale must be expanded by the factor n^2, $\mathbf{B}$ and $\mathbf{H}$ remain the same, but $\mathbf{E}$ must be divided by the factor n.

In summary, if both space and time variables are scaled by the same factor, the scale model will faithfully simulate actual devices in both static and dynamic behavior if all electrical and magnetic material properties are identical except for conductivity, which must be reduced by the factor n in the scale model. When only static and quasi-static behavior are required, all material properties are the same, time is scaled by n^2, and the electric field is divided by n. There is no other restraint on the bulk material properties. They may be linear or nonlinear, magnetically soft or hard, and so on.

9.4.2 Large-Scale Modeling Applications

Workers in several laboratories have built large-scale models for a number of applications. These include measurement of head fields and study of both read and write processes.

Scale models of simple head geometries have given head fields in close agreement with those calculated by numerical methods. The increasing availability of both hardware and software for head-field calculations is reducing the attractiveness of scale models for simply measuring head fields. Nonetheless, in applications where numerical studies are still difficult or time-consuming, scale models may be useful. Applications have included complex geometries (Fluitman and Marchal, 1973; Iwasaki et al., 1983; Chi and Szczech, 1984), and saturation effects (Nakagawa et al., 1972).

A scale model head can be used to study the read process (Monson et al., 1975). In this application, the recorded magnetization is simulated by a "magnetization generator" consisting of a rectangular loop of very fine wire whose plane is perpendicular to the surface of the recording medium. The outline of the loop surrounds the track width to the desired depth of recording, and its magnetic shell equivalent is an impulse of longitudinal magnetization. Exciting the loop with alternating current induces a voltage in the head which is identical, as a function of position, to that produced by a step transition in a real recording system. This approach is very useful for the study of three-dimensional effects.

Several large-scale models have been built for the study of the recording process (Tjaden and Leyten, 1964; Hersener, 1973). The scale factors used in these models ranged from 2000 to 10,000. Tjaden and Leyten used a scale factor of 5000 in constructing a medium 50 mm thick. The medium was composed of 50 mm-wide lamina of gamma ferric oxide particles which were dispersed in plastic and longitudinally oriented. The plastic strips were then tightly stacked in a tray to form the medium. After recording with a large-scale ring head with a 20 mm gap length, the middle strip was removed from the medium to measure the recorded magnetization. This was done by punching out small disks 3 mm in diameter and measuring their remanent magnetization vectors in a specially constructed magnetometer. In this way, the vector magnetization along the track and through the thickness of the medium was determined. Experiments with both biased sine-wave recording and digital recording of isolated transitions were performed. The power line at 50 Hz provided the bias for a signal frequency of 0.1 Hz. The power dissipated in the recording head was 2.5 kW! The experiments showed significant components of perpendicular magnetization in the recorded medium. Another interesting result was the existence of a circular magnetization mode at very short wavelengths.

Hersener's model is very similar to that of Tjaden and Leyten, except for the method of determining the recorded magnetization in the medium. Hersener's medium contained slots designed so that a Hall probe could be inserted into the medium to measure internal fields. The magnetization distribution was then inferred from the field measurements. His experiments also confirmed the existence of a circular magnetization mode at short wavelengths.

Iwasaki and his coworkers built a model at 10,000 times actual scale to study perpendicular recording (Nakamura and Iwasaki, 1983). They used an array of slender cylinders of hard magnetic material to simulate the columnar structure of a Co-Cr perpendicular recording medium. Recording performance was determined from field measurements made just above the medium surface. Measurements could be made both during and after the recording process. Extensive experimenta-

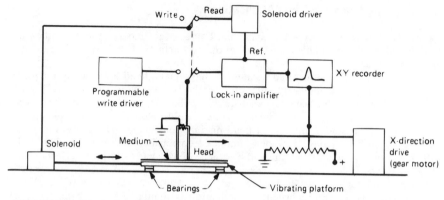

FIGURE 9.23 Block diagram of large-scale model apparatus. Platform is vibrated to produce readback of written magnetization transitions (*Valstyn et al., 1979*).

tion and modification of this apparatus led to the development of Iwasaki's purely perpendicular recording system.

Further improvement of scale-model studies was achieved by providing capability for both recording and reproducing (Monson et al., 1978). A 5000-times scale model of a film head was used to write and read scaled-up particulate and film media. Figure 9.23 shows a block diagram of the apparatus. Writing is carried out by slowly moving the head over the stationary medium and energizing it with a programmable write-current driver. During the read operation the head again sweeps slowly over the recorded medium, but now the medium vibrates sinusoidally with an amplitude small compared with the gap length. The voltage induced in the head coil by this vibration is detected by a lock-in amplifier and plotted as a function of head position on an *xy* recorder.

An expression for the head voltage can be derived as follows. The position of the head with respect to the medium is

$$x = Vt + \Delta x \cos \omega t$$

where V is the head velocity and Δx is the peak vibration amplitude at radian frequency ω. The readback voltage from the changing flux ϕ is

$$E = -\frac{d\phi}{dt} = -\frac{d\phi}{dx}\frac{dx}{dt} \tag{9.22}$$

$$= (\omega \, \Delta x \sin \omega t - V)\frac{d\phi}{dx}$$

The lock-in amplifier detects the peak value of the ac component, giving

$$E_{\text{det}} = \omega \, \Delta x \frac{d\phi}{dx} \tag{9.23}$$

which is of the same form as that which would result from flying the head over the medium in an actual disk drive. The vibrational frequency must be chosen small enough to avoid eddy-current effects in the large-scale Ni-Fe head (Monson et al., 1975). This scale model has been used to study transition density effects and side writing (Monson et al., 1978). On scale models it is easy to measure stray fields on both sides of a recorded medium. From such measurements it was shown (Valstyn and Monson, 1979) that flux from an isolated magnetization transition written on an isotropic particulate medium tended to concentrate on one side as predicted (Mallinson, 1973). Studies of perpendicular recording were carried out using the model with a film ring head and single-layer medium. By using the same scaled-up film medium in two configurations, it was possible to obtain a direct comparison between longitudinal and perpendicular recording modes (Monson et al., 1981).

The main limitation of scale modeling is that of simulating micromagnetic effects. In principle, it ought to be possible to make scaled-up particles and construct media with controlled switching-field distributions. Care would have to be taken to ensure that the multidomain scaled-up particles accurately simulate single-domain particle behavior. The simulation of domain behavior in film media offers additional challenges.

9.5 RECORDING SYSTEM PERFORMANCE

Measurement of recording system performance requires careful instrumentation techniques over many disciplines. The task is further complicated by the wide range of parameters used in magnetic recording systems. The head-to-medium velocities of rigid and flexible disks may range from 1.2 to 50 m/s. Data frequencies range from 100 kHz to 20 MHz, while wavelengths span 500 μm to about 1 μm. In some tape systems, frequencies as low as 1 Hz combined with a velocity of 25 mm/s produce wavelengths up to 25 mm long. High-density digital tape recorders and video recorders operate at wavelengths as short as 500 nm.

Measurement systems for evaluating recording performance should have precise speed and position control. They should be isolated from unwanted environmental disturbances. It is desirable to have separate fixtures for record and reproduce heads so that these two processes may be evaluated separately. Provision for various modes of erasure should also be made. The reproduce amplifier following the head should have a frequency response which is flat in gain and linear in phase over the required bandwidth. The amplifier should also have a noise level which is lower than the other noises in the system. Amplifier input impedance should be carefully designed for the reproduce head to optimize frequency response and noise.

9.5.1 Absolute Head Efficiency

Head efficiency should be measured in a low-frequency range where it is independent of frequency. Head efficiency may be defined as

$$\eta = \frac{R_g}{R_g + R_c} \tag{9.24}$$

Where R_g and R_c are the gap and core reluctances, respectively. Frequency dependence of the efficiency is caused by eddy currents and other mechanisms in the core which result in a complex, frequency-dependent core reluctance.

9.5.1.1 Input. The input to the head should be a calibrated square wave of flux recorded on a medium. Calibrated recorded media are commercially available.

They may be produced on longitudinal media by recording square waves of low density at saturation so that the remanent magnetization is known approximately. To calibrate the flux precisely requires careful consideration of a number of effects (McKnight, 1970). These include fringing effects to the side of the track, head efficiency, and frequency and wavelength response factors. By using a large-gap, high-efficiency head operating at medium wavelengths of 0.25 to 2.0 mm, it is possible to achieve a flux calibration accuracy of better than 3 percent.

9.5.1.2 Output. The output voltage from the head has a fundamental component whose root-mean-square value is given by

$$e = 4 \sqrt{2}\, nf\mu_0 M_r w_{\text{eff}} \delta \eta \qquad (9.25)$$

where n = number of turns
   f = frequency
   M_r = remanent magnetization
   w_{eff} = effective track width
   δ = medium thickness
   η = head efficiency.

From the measured voltage, the efficiency may be determined. Best accuracy is obtained by having the recorded track much wider than the head. An effective track width is then used, which takes into account flux induced in the head from its sides (Bertram, 1985):

$$w_{\text{eff}} = w + \frac{3\lambda}{4\pi} (1 - e^{-\pi \Delta w/\lambda}) \qquad (9.26)$$

where Δw is the difference between the recorded track width and the head width.

As an alternative, or a check to the efficiency determined from Eq. (9.25), the isolated pulse waveform may be integrated to obtain the total flux sensed by the head:

$$\int e\, dt = n\mu_0 (2M_r w_{\text{eff}} \delta \eta) \qquad (9.27)$$

in which w_{eff} should be chosen to account for flux sensed at the sides of the head. If the observed pulse shape closely resembles a standard form such as a Lorentzian or Gaussian form, then the area under the pulse may be obtained from measurement of its peak amplitude and width.

9.5.2 Nonlinear Recording

Much useful information for characterizing a recording system can be obtained from nonlinear recording measurements.

9.5.2.1 Output Voltage Versus Write Current. Measurement of the output voltage versus write current provides information for setting system write-current levels. Square waves are recorded at the highest recording density to be used. The peak output voltage is then measured as a function of write current. Figure 9.24 shows the shape of curve which is typically found for longitudinal particulate media. The output voltage increases with increasing current and then drops, often exhibiting several sharp nulls. These can be caused by a circular magnetization mode pro-

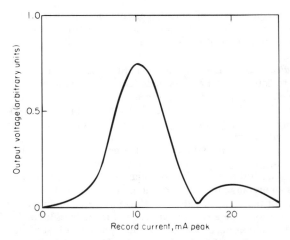

FIGURE 9.24 Output voltage as a function of record current for square-wave recording on a γ-Fe$_2$O$_3$ medium. Observed null can be caused by circular magnetization mode (*after Bertram and Niedermeyer, 1978*).

duced at high current levels (Iwasaki and Takemura, 1975). The current for maximum peak output voltage is designated I_{opt}.

9.5.2.2. *Roll-Off Curve.* To measure a roll-off curve, the write current is set to I_{opt} and square waves are written at various densities. Both the peak voltage and the rms amplitude of the fundamental component are plotted as a function of recording density, as shown in Fig. 9.25. The density at which the peak voltage falls to 50 percent of its low density limit is labeled D_{50}. At very high densities one or more read-head gap nulls are seen, and their locations may be correlated with the gap length observed optically. Also at high densities, only the fundamental component of the square wave is recorded, so the peak voltage approaches 1.414 times the fundamental rms component.

Roll-off curves can exhibit several interesting effects. When a film head is used to read a longitudinal medium, the negative undershoots of the isolated pulse

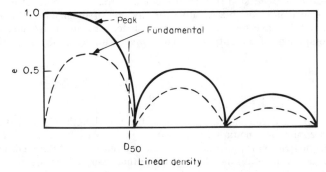

FIGURE 9.25 Output voltage as a function of recording density for recorded square waves. Both peak amplitude and rms amplitude of fundamental component of reproduced waveform are shown.

interfere with the pulse peaks from adjacent magnetization transitions to produce a peaking of the roll-off curve. A similar, more pronounced effect is seen when a perpendicular recording medium is read with a ring head.

9.5.2.3 Isolated Pulse Shape.

At low recording density, the isolated pulse shape from a single transition may be measured. As far as the read portion of the system is concerned, the isolated pulse shape is the step response of the system. By taking the Fourier transform of the isolated pulse, the system gain and phase response can be found. This information, particularly the phase portion, is very useful for designing linear post-equalization.

Under some simplifying assumptions, it is possible to obtain information about head-to-medium spacing and transition width from a measurement of the width of the isolated pulse. If the magnetization is purely longitudinal and varies only in the x direction as an arctangent function with parameter a, then it is possible to obtain an expression for the isolated pulse waveform by performing a correlation integral of the magnetization with a simple expression for the longitudinal field component of a ring head (Middleton, 1966). The isolated pulse width at 50 percent amplitude is given by

$$p_{50} = [g^2 + 4(a + d)(a + d + \delta)]^{1/2} \qquad (9.28)$$

If the gap length and medium thickness are known, then $a + d$ may be found from Eq. (9.28). Note that a and d have the same effect on the pulse width as a result of the arctangent transition assumption.

The amplitude of the isolated pulse is proportional to the product of medium remanent magnetization and thickness ($M_r\delta$). This property has been used to make a transfer curve magnetometer for rapid characterization of the magnetic properties of rigid disks (Johnson and Kerr, 1990). Two medium scale heads—track width 19 mm and gap length 300 μm—write a magnetization step of variable amplitude. A third head then reads the isolated pulse to find the $M_r\delta$ product. A capacitance probe senses head to medium spacing, which is carefully controlled to maintain calibration. The instrument can rapidly and nondestructively map the magnetic properties, including remanent coercivity and coercive squareness, of a disk over its area.

9.5.2.4 Fundamental Amplitude Versus Wave Number Analysis.

Although the isolated pulse width expression [Eq. (9.28)] contains four important recording system parameters, it is not possible to solve for any one of them without knowing the other three. If a wave number analysis is carried out on an isolated pulse, the Fourier component of the output voltage at wave number k may be approximated by

$$e(k) = 2\,nV\mu_0 M\eta w\delta \,\frac{1 - e^{-k\delta}}{k\delta}\, e^{-k(d+a)} \frac{\sin{(kg_{eff}/2)}}{kg_{eff}/2} \qquad (9.29)$$

where the effective gap length $g_{eff} = \lambda_{null}$, the wavelength of the first null. This expression applies for media with no soft magnetic back layer, and it is assumed that the magnetization is uniform throughout the thickness of the medium.

The form of Eq. (9.29) has the advantage that many of the system parameters are separated in product form so that they may be determined from measurement of output voltage as a function of wavelength. The measurements are carried out by recording square waves at low density and observing the output voltage on a spec-

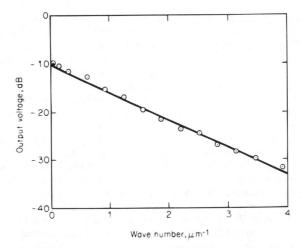

FIGURE 9.26 Output voltage as a function of wave number, corrected for thickness and gap effects. Slope is proportional to $a + d$. Voltage intercept is $2nV\mu_0 M\eta w\delta$ (*after Bertram and Niedermeyer, 1978*).

trum analyzer or by varying the recording density and measuring the rms value of the fundamental component at the wavelength corresponding to each density. The methods give the same result within the assumptions of Eq. (9.29), but the latter is equivalent to multiplying (9.29) by $\sqrt{2}k/\pi$, giving higher signals at short wavelengths. At long wavelengths, or small k, the thickness loss term $(1 - e^{-k\delta})/k\delta$ may be approximated as unity. In the long-wavelength region, the other terms are essentially constant. By measuring the slope of the fundamental curve, the thickness δ may be obtained.

After the gap length and thickness are known, their wave number effects can be removed from the measured output voltage curve. Figure 9.26 shows a plot of the relative output voltage in decibels which has been corrected for medium thickness and gap loss effects. By measuring the slope of the curve, which is linear, the combined arctangent parameter and head-to-medium spacing may be determined. It is important to note the conditions for which this method is valid. The magnetization transition must be of arctangent form, and the medium must be single-layer. Some measurements have been made which indicate negative transition widths for perpendicular recording, but these have been attributed to magnetization transitions which are not arctangent in form (Yeh, 1985).

Equation (9.29) is not valid for double-layer media except in the limit of very short wavelengths. At long wavelengths, the slope of the output voltage curve can greatly exceed that shown in Fig. 9.25 (Yamamoto et al., 1984). Also it must be remembered that Eq. (9.29) is based upon a Fourier or sine-wave analysis of the output voltage. Applying Eq. (9.29) to plots of the peak of the voltage waveform instead of its sine-wave components could give misleading results.

9.5.2.5 Overwrite.

Overwrite is defined and measured in several different ways depending upon the recording system application. The highest square-wave frequency used in the system is denoted as f_2, the frequency corresponding to an all-1s data pattern. At a particular write-current level, square waves are written at the frequency f_1, which is half of f_2. The amplitude of the readback voltage at f_1 is measured on a spectrum analyzer. Square waves at f_2 are then written at the same current level, and the voltages at both f_1 and f_2 are measured. *Overwrite* is most often defined as the ratio of the two f_1 voltages measured before and after overwriting with f_2. Overwrite performance is usually measured as a function of write current. This definition represents a worst case for longitudinal recording, where transitions recorded at lower frequencies are most difficult to overwrite. In perpendicular recording, the opposite seems to hold, and a more appropriate test is to record f_2 first and then overwrite with f_1 (Langland and Albert, 1981).

An overwrite measurement which emphasizes the phase modulation produced by the residual f_1 signal after overwriting with f_2 is made by measuring the peak-to-peak time jitter, or bit shift, between transitions recorded at f_2. Amplitude effects can be measured by first dc erasing the medium and then writing a low-frequency square wave to produce isolated transitions. The positive- and negative-going peak amplitudes of the readback pulses are measured separately and their ratio defined as a pulse asymmetry. When measurements are carried out as a function of write current, it is usually found that minimum pulse asymmetry and minimum bit shift do not occur at the same current level.

Care must be taken in making and interpreting overwrite measurements. Large variations in overwrite performance have been observed which depend upon gap length, write current, and transition density (Wachenschwanz and Jeffers, 1985). These appear to be related to interference effects between residual overwritten data and data which are re-recorded with the overwriting signal acting as bias. Similar effects have been observed in ac-erasure studies (McKnight, 1963).

By successively displacing the readback head from the track centerline and making a series of overwrite measurements, it is possible to obtain a plot of overwrite as a function of offtrack position. Depending upon the writing conditions, overwrite performance may be uniform across track or degrade at the track edges (Palmer and Peske, 1990).

9.5.2.6 *Bit Shift.*

Bit shift, also referred to as *peak shift,* is defined as the normalized shift in detected positions of readback bits with respect to the positions where they were written. The simplest measurement of bit shift is made by recording a dibit pattern, namely, two magnetization transitions spaced apart by the bit cell length. The distance between the two peaks of the readback pulses is the detected bit cell length. The bit shift is given by the difference between the detected and recorded bit cell lengths, normalized to the recorded bit cell length. Bit shift is sensitive to the recorded pattern, and the measurement is readily extended to tribit and higher order patterns of recorded transitions.

Bit shift has both linear and nonlinear components. The linear component results from superposition of isolated pulse waveforms which interfere to produce peak shift as they are spaced closer and closer together. Because it results from superposition, linear bit shift may be equalized by linear networks in the read circuits. Nonlinear bit shift arises from interbit interactions occurring in the nonlinear write process. Although nonlinear bit shift may be partially canceled by predistorting the write-current waveform, it cannot be postequalized by linear networks. Consequently, the measurement of the nonlinear component of bit shift is a very important one for evaluating high-density recording system performance.

In many applications, nonlinear writing effects extend over only a few bit cells so that nonlinear bit shift can be determined from measurements on tribit patterns (Koren, 1981). An alternative approach is to write a maximal-length pseudorandom sequence of data and observe the spectrum of the readback signal (Haynes,

1977; Wood and Donaldson, 1979). The envelope of the spectral lines follows the linear recording channel response, while nonlinearities are indicated by ripples and irregularities in the spectrum. By adjusting the predistortion of the write-current waveform to minimize the rippling in the read spectrum, nonlinear bit shift can be minimized (Coleman et al., 1984). A quantitative measure of nonlinear bit shift can be obtained by expressing the distorted readback waveform in a Volterra series expansion. The coefficients of this expansion are obtained from the measured cross-correlation function between the input pseudo-random sequence and the readback waveform (Wood and Donaldson, 1979). An alternative approach is to find the impulse response of the channel from signal processing of the pseudo-random input and output waveforms by Fourier transformation. For a linear channel, the impulse response would be a simple dipulse. The channel nonlinearities appear in the form of distorted echoes of the dipulse. The nature and amplitudes of these echoes characterize the physical mechanisms introducing the nonlinearities in a fundamental way (Palmer et al., 1987). Pseudo-random sequences are also useful in overwrite measurements (Palmer et al., 1988).

9.5.3 Linear Recording

Linearization of the recording process is achieved by using an ac bias whose frequency is more than three times the highest signal frequency to be recorded. Adjustment of the bias amplitude is very important for optimizing system performance with respect to frequency response, harmonic distortion, and output at short wavelengths.

To evaluate the frequency response, the output voltage is measured as a function of wave number with bias amplitude as a parameter. The signal level is kept at a low, constant level. Typical results are shown in Fig. 9.27. At bias levels under the optimum, short-wavelength response is improved at the expense of long wavelengths. Overbiasing gives good long-wavelength response but poor performance at short wavelengths.

The effects of bias amplitude on signal output level and distortion are measured at long wavelengths. The signal input level is held constant as bias amplitude is varied. The output level and third harmonic distortion are plotted as a function of bias level as shown in Fig. 9.28 (Mee, 1964). The long-wavelength output signal saturates and decreases as the bias field penetrates into and through the medium

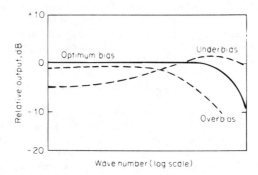

FIGURE 9.27 Wavelength response for ac-bias recording, showing effect of bias amplitude.

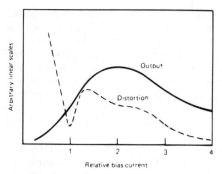

FIGURE 9.28 Output and distortion versus bias amplitude for long-wavelength recording (*after Mee, 1964*).

with increasing bias amplitude. Third harmonic distortion has a minimum value associated with the shapes of the signal output versus input curves as bias level is increased. The initial portion of these curves changes shape from concave upward to concave downward with increasing bias amplitude (Daniel and Levine, 1960). The curve is most nearly linear at the bias setting where the change occurs, giving minimum distortion (Westmijze, 1953; Fujiwara, 1979). The bias value for minimum distortion is less than that for maximum output level.

Another commonly measured curve is the peak output level at short wavelengths as a function of bias amplitude. The bias amplitude for peak output level at short wavelengths is less than that for maximum output level at long wavelengths. Consequently, the choice of bias level in a recording system must be a compromise among the various performance curves obtained from the measurements.

The linear recording counterpart to overwrite measurement in nonlinear recording is the measurement of signals remaining after ac erasure. Erasure is usually done by a separate erase head. To measure the effectiveness of erasure, signals are recorded at various wavelengths and levels and reproduced after erasure. Both frequency and wavelength effects have been observed along with interference phenomena which are caused by re-recording by the erase head (McKnight, 1963).

Gain and phase measurements on linear recorders are important for systems implementation. Gain measurements as a function of frequency or wave number are readily performed, but phase measurements using conventional methods are more difficult because of the long delays between recording and reproducing. One approach is to record long-wavelength square waves and analyze the reproduce waveforms using Fourier transform techniques to obtain the phase response. Some care must be taken in this measurement to ensure that the square-wave amplitude is small enough that the recording channel is linear, yet large enough that there is enough signal strength at short wavelengths compared with noise to give valid results.

An alternative approach which overcomes these problems is to use a very long pseudo-random binary sequence as input (Haynes, 1977). Such an input signal has a favorable spectral density for testing the channel at amplitudes which produce negligible harmonic distortion. By digitizing the output voltage and carrying out a fast Fourier transform for comparison with the Fourier transform of the input, the system transfer function, both gain and phase, is determined. Accuracy may be improved by averaging repeated measurements. Generating an accurate time base is important for sampling of the output waveform, and this can be accomplished by generating a stable trigger from a preset data pattern occurring in the input sequence.

In instrumentation recording applications, which often use several subcarriers for transmitting data, the group or envelope delay performance is more important than the overall phase function (Starr, 1965). Measurement of group delay is carried out by using sets of reference signals (IRIG standard, 1979).

9.5.4 Noise Measurements

9.5.4.1 Noise Spectrum Measurements. Noise arises from several sources in a magnetic recording system, and these may be isolated by careful measurement of the noise spectra under different conditions. The rms noise voltage in a very narrow bandwidth is measured, and the noise voltage density, in $V/(Hz)^{1/2}$, is plotted as a function of frequency. This measurement is sometimes referred to as a slot signal-to-noise ratio, for which the bandwidth of the frequency slot and a reference signal level are specified. For conversion to absolute noise amplitudes, spectrum analyzer readings must be corrected for several filtering and other signal processing operations carried out in the spectrum analyzer (Nunnelley, 1992). The net correction is on the order of 2 dB.

Measurements are first carried out with the medium stopped. Under this condition, the equipment, including amplifiers and other circuitry, and head produce the measured noise. This is the condition for lowest noise, as shown in Fig. 9.29. Motion of the medium induces several kinds of nonmagnetic noise. Variations in heat transfer across the head-to-medium interface can cause noise voltage spikes in magnetoresistive heads (Hempstead, 1974). In perpendicular recording, mechanically induced noise mechanisms in the permeable back layer have been observed to produce noise voltage spikes (Ouchi and Iwasaki, 1985). Magnetostrictive effects can produce noise in heads which can be measured by using a mechanically equivalent nonmagnetic medium such as one made of α-Fe_2O_3.

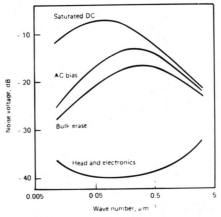

FIGURE 9.29 Slot noise spectrum as a function of wave number, showing noise contributions from head and equipment, bulk-erased medium, ac-biased medium, and dc-saturated medium.

In addition to providing information about system noise performance, noise measurement is a useful tool for analyzing the quality of recording media. In such an application, it is helpful to subtract out on a power basis the equipment and head noise. Measurement of noise from bulk-erased media gives the spectral density of the additive noise caused by granularity of the medium. For proper interpretation of media noise, it is essential to correct the observed voltage spectrum for the effects of the channel frequency response, including the head transfer function. What is desired is the noise spectral density of the medium's magnetization. Ac-biased noise is measured after passing a record head energized with an ac-bias current over the bulk-erased medium. The noise voltage will increase over that for the bulk-erased medium. Noise from the bulk-erased medium is re-recorded by the bias field to produce additional noise.

Bulk modulation effects such as packing and coating thickness variations may be observed by measuring the noise from the medium after it has been recorded to saturation by a dc field. Usually, the applied field is made strong enough to saturate the medium through its entire thickness. Finer spatial resolution of the noise measurement may be achieved by measuring the noise using a very narrow gap head which is excited with direct current. By varying the amplitude of the current, the zone of medium saturation can be controlled to explore regions very close to the surface of the medium. The measured noise characterizes the surface asperities of the medium (Daniel, 1964; Eldridge, 1964).

Recording a signal such as a single-tone sine wave, or a square wave corresponding to an all-1s data pattern, causes some interesting changes in the observed noise spectrum. In the neighborhood of the recorded signal frequency, a sideband structure caused by noise amplitude and phase modulation is seen on a spectrum analyzer. For some particulate media, the wideband dc-noise spectrum is not greatly changed in amplitude in the presence of a recorded signal, as shown in Fig. 9.30. Changing the frequency of the recorded signal does not appreciably change the wide-band noise spectrum for particulate media, and, if anything, the noise decreases with increasing signal frequency.

For film media, on the other hand, the amplitude of the noise spectrum varies significantly with the frequency of the recorded signal. Figure 9.31 shows typical

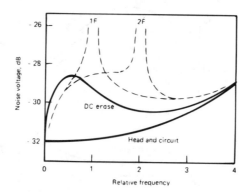

FIGURE 9.30 Noise spectra from particulate medium under dc-erased condition and recorded signal conditions of 1*F* and 2*F*. Noise spectrum is nearly independent of recorded frequency (*after Stefanelli and Lelarge, 1984*).

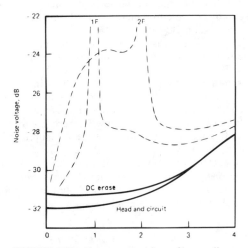

FIGURE 9.31 Noise spectra from film medium. Spectra vary markedly with recorded frequency (*after Stefanelli and Lelarge, 1984*).

measured spectra which indicate that the noise amplitude increases with the frequency of the recorded signal. Experimental results indicate that the noise observed in film media is localized in the magnetization transition regions (Tanaka et al., 1982; Baugh et al., 1983). Measurements and analyses by a number of workers have led to increased understanding of noise mechanisms in film media (Murdock, 1992).

9.5.4.2 Time-Domain Noise Measurements. The apparent nonuniform spatial distribution of noise in film media with recorded signals has motivated the development of several techniques for measuring media noise in the time domain.

One method obtains the time jitter of the transition locations of a recorded square wave (Baugh et al., 1983). The times between successive transitions are measured using a time interval meter. The root-mean-square time jitter is then calculated. The jitter caused by only the medium noise may be obtained by subtracting on a mean-square basis the jitter from many repeated measurements on a single pair of adjacent transitions. The time jitter, Δt, of a transition detected by a zero-crossing detector may be expressed as

$$\Delta t = -e_n(t_0) \left[\frac{de_s(t_0)}{dt} \right]^{-1} \tag{9.30}$$

where e_n and e_s are the noise and signal voltages, respectively. When the noise is a stationary process and the signal is a square wave whose transition density is greater than $1/3D_{50}$, Eq. (9.30) gives for the rms jitter

$$\Delta t_{\text{rms}} = \frac{1}{2\pi f(\text{SNR})} \tag{9.31}$$

where f is the frequency of the recorded square wave, and SNR is the broadband signal-to-noise ratio expressed as a voltage ratio. Equation (9.31) holds well for particulate media, indicating that the noise is stationary. When the noise is not stationary, as observed for some film media, transition-time jitter and noise power are not simply related (Nunnelley et al., 1987).

Two commercially available instruments for application to time-domain noise measurements are the digitized sampling oscilloscope and the time interval analyzer. Sampling oscilloscopes can sample at a rate of $2\ (10)^9$ samples per second, convert samples from analog to digital, and store them in fast memory for subsequent processing. These features allow separation of stationary from non-stationary processes and other measurement possibilities. Time interval analyzers can measure time intervals between events, such as the zero crossings of differentiated readback pulses, and generate distributions of the measured intervals. In addition to studies of noise, time interval analyzers are useful to characterize interferences such as adjacent track effects, overwrite, and bit shift.

A powerful approach to time-domain noise measurement is to use autocorrelation to characterize both stationary and nonstationary noise in media (Tang, 1985). The autocorrelation function is given by

$$R_n(t_1,\ t_2) = \frac{1}{m} \sum_{i=1}^{m} e_{ni}(t_1)e_{ni}(t_2) \tag{9.32}$$

Noise voltages are obtained by subtracting from each measured noise-contaminated signal the average signal waveform. For stationary noise process, the autocorrelation function depends only on the difference between t_2 and t_1 and not on their values, so a measurement and plot of Eq. (9.32) will clearly distinguish between stationary and nonstationary processes. Tang observed significant differences in shape between the measured autocorrelation functions of particulate and film media.

One of the main problems in performing generalized autocorrelation in a magnetic recording system is to develop a timing technique which can be corrected for jitter. This is especially difficult because much of the jitter is caused by the noise which is to be autocorrelated. Noise-independent jitter correction may be accomplished by generating a reference timing signal which is insensitive to amplitude-modulation noise, and then delaying the beginning of waveform timing by a fixed time. If this time delay is long enough, the additive noise at that point is uncorrelated with the noise at the reference time.

REFERENCES

Aharonov, Y., and D. Bohm, "Significance of Electromagnetic Potentials in the Quantum Theory," *Phys. Rev.,* **115**, 485 (1959).

Alexopoulos, P. S., and R. H. Geiss, Private Communication (1985).

Argyle, B. E., B Petek, and D A. Herman, Jr., "Optical Imaging of Magnetic Domains in Motion," *J. Appl. Phys.,* **61**, 4303 (1987).

Asti, G., and S. Rinaldi, "Singular Points in the Magnetization Curve of a Polycrystalline Ferromagnet," *J. Appl. Phys.,* **45**, 3600 (1974).

Babcock, K., V. Elings, M. Dugas, and S. Loper, "Optimization of Thin-Film Tips for Magnetic Force Microscopy," *IEEE Trans. Magn.,* **MAG-30**, 4503 (1994).

Baird, A. W., R. A. Johnson, W. F. Chaurette, and W. T. Maloney, "Measurements and Self-Consistent Calculations of the Magnetic Fields near a Perpendicular Medium," *IEEE Trans. Magn.,* **MAG-20**, 479 (1984).

Banbury, J. R., and W. C. Nixon, "The Direct Observation of Domain Structure and Magnetic Fields in the Scanning Electron Microscope," *J. Sci. Instrum.*, **44**, 889 (1967).

Baugh, R. A., E. S. Murdock, and B. R. Natarajan, "Measurement of Noise in Magnetic Media," *IEEE Trans. Magn.*, **MAG-19**, 1722 (1983).

Bertram, H. N., Private Communication (1985).

Bertram, H. N., and R. Niedermeyer, "The Effect of Demagnetization Fields on Recording Spectra," *IEEE Trans. Magn.*, **MAG-14**, 743 (1978).

Binnig, C., C. F. Quate, and Ch. Gerber, "Atomic Force Microscope," *Phys. Rev. Lett.*, **56**, 930 (1986).

Bitter, F., "On Inhomogeneities in the Magnetization of Ferromagnetic Materials," *Phys. Rev.*, **38**, 1903 (1931).

Bozorth, R. M., *Ferromagnetism,* Van Nostrand, New York, 1951, p. 533.

Calcagno, P. A., and D. A. Thompson, "Semiautomatic Permeance Tester for Thick Magnetic Films," *Rev. Sci. Instrum.*, **46**, 904 (1975).

Camarota, R. C., and D. A. Thompson, "Measurement of Recording Head Frequency Response Using a Scanning Electron Microscope," *3M Conf.*, Pittsburgh, 1983.

Cameron, G. P., and J. H. Judy, "SEMPA Domain Observation Compared to Three Other Methods," *IEEE Trans. Magn.*, **MAG-24**, 3063 (1988).

Celotta, R. J., and D. T. Pierce, "Polarized Electron Probes of Magnetic Surfaces," *Science*, **234**, 333 (1986).

Chang, T., M. Lagerquist, J.-G. Zhu, J. H. Judy, P. B. Fischer, and S. Y. Chou, "Deconvolution of Magnetic Force Images by Fourier Analysis," *IEEE Trans. Magn.*, **MAG-28**, 3138 (1992).

Chang, T., J.-G. Zhu, and J. H. Judy, "Method for Investigating the Reversal Properties of Isolated Barium Ferrite Fine Particles Utilizing Magnetic Force Microscopy (MFM)," *J. Appl. Phys.*, **73**, 6716 (1993).

Chen, T., "The Micromagnetic Properties of High-Coercivity Metallic Thin Films and Their Effects on the Limit of Packing Density in Digital Recording," *IEEE Trans. Magn.*, **MAG-17**, 1181 (1981).

Chi, C. S., and T. S. Szczech, "A Write-Head Design with Improved Field Profile for Perpendicular Recording," *IEEE Trans. Magn,* **MAG-20**, 836 (1984).

Chikazumi, S., *Physics of Magnetism,* Wiley, New York, 1964.

Chu, Y., Private Communication (1984).

Clark, B. K., and J. D. Finegan, "Rotational Magnetic Measurements on Recording Media," *IEEE Trans. Magn.*, **MAG-21**, 1456 (1985).

Cohen, M. S., "Wave-Optical Aspects of Lorentz Microscopy," *J. Appl. Phys.*, **38**, 4966 (1967).

Coleman, C., D. Lindholm, D. Petersen, and R. Wood, "High Data Rate Magnetic Recording in a Single Channel," *IERE Conf. Proc.*, **59** (1984).

Cort, D. M., and J. W. Steeds, "A Liquid Helium Cooled Stage for the Scanning Electron Microscope," *Proc. Fifth Eur. Congr. Electron Micros.*, 376 (1972).

Cullity, B. D., *Introduction to Magnetic Materials,* Addison-Wesley, Reading, Mass., 1972.

Daniel, E. D., "A Preliminary Analysis of Surface-Induced Noise," *IEEE Trans. Comm. Electron.*, **83**, 250 (1964).

Daniel, E. D., and I. Levine, "Experimental and Theoretical Investigation of the Magnetic Properties of Iron Oxide Recording Tape," *J. Acoust. Soc. Am.*, **32**, 1 (1960).

Doyle, W. D., L. He, and P. J. Flanders, "Measurement of the Switching Speed Limit in High Coercivity Magnetic Media," *IEEE Trans. Magn.*, **MAG-29**, 3634 (1993).

Eldridge, D. F., "D-C and Modulation Noise in Magnetic Tape," *IEEE Trans. Comm. Electron.*, **83**, 585 (1964).

Elsbrock, J. B., and L. J. Balk, "Profiling of Micromagnetic Stray Fields in Front of Magnetic Recording Media and Heads by Means of a SEM," *IEEE Trans. Magn.,* **MAG-20,** 866 (1984).

Elsbrock, J. B., W. Schroeder, and E. Kubalek, "Evaluation of Three-Dimensional Micromagnetic Stray Fields by Means of Electron-Beam Tomography," *IEEE Trans. Magn.,* **MAG-21,** 1593 (1985).

Fathers, D. J., J. P. Jakubovics, D. C. Joy, D. E. Newbury, and H. Yakowitz, "A New Method of Observing Magnetic Domains by Scanning Electron Microscopy," *Phys. Status Solidi (a),* **20,** 535 (1973).

Ferrier, R. P., "Imaging Methods for the Study of Micromagnetic Structure," *Noise in Digital Magnetic Recording,* ed. T. C. Arnoldussen and L. L. Nunnelley, World Scientific Publishing Co., Singapore, 1992.

Flanders, P. J., "An Alternating-gradient Magnetometer," *J. Appl. Phys.,* **63,** 3940 (1988).

Fluitman, J. H. J., "Recording Head Field Measurement with a Magnetoresistive Transducer," *IEEE Trans. Magn.,* **MAG-14,** 433 (1978).

Fluitman, J. H. J., and J. Marchal, "Head Fields of Asymmetric Recording Heads," *IEEE Trans. Magn.,* **MAG-9,** 139 (1973).

Foner, S., "Versatile and Sensitive Vibrating-Sample Magnetometer," *Rev. Sci. Instrum.,* **30,** 548 (1959).

Fujiwara, T., "Nonlinear Distortion in Long Wavelength AC Bias Recording," *IEEE Trans. Magn.,* **MAG-15,** 894 (1979).

Gabor, D., "Microscopy by Reconstructed Wavefronts," *Proc. R. Soc. London, Ser. A,* **197,** 454 (1949).

Gibson, G. A., and S. Schultz, "A High-Sensitivity Alternating-Gradient Magnetometer for Use in Quantifying Magnetic Force Microscopy," *J. Appl. Phys.,* **69,** 5880 (1991).

Gibson, G. A., S. Schultz, T. Carr, and T. Jagielinski, "Spatial Mapping of the Sensitivity Function of Magnetic Recording Heads Using a Magnetic Force Microscope as a Local Flux Applicator," *IEEE Trans. Magn.,* **MAG-28,** 2310 (1992).

Gomez, R. D., A. A. Adly, I. D. Mayergoyz, and E. R. Burke, "Magnetic Force Scanning Tunneling Microscope Imaging of Overwritten Data," *IEEE Trans. Magn.,* **MAG-28,** 3141 (1992).

Griffiths, B. W., P. Pollard, and J. W. Venables, "A Channel Plate Detector for the Scanning Electron Microscope," *Proc. Fifth Eur. Congr. Electron Micros.,* 176 (1972).

Grimes, C. A., P. L. Trouilloud, and R. M. Walser, "A New Swept-Frequency Permeameter for Measuring the Complex Permeability of Thin Magnetic Films," *IEEE Trans. Magn.,* **MAG-24,** 603 (1988).

Grütter, P., "An Introduction to Magnetic Force Microscopy," *MSA Bull.,* **24,** 416 (1994).

Gudeman, C. S., M. V. Mitchell, and D. E. Peter, "A Fast Scanning Magneto-Optic Kerr M-H Hysteresigraph for Thin Film Media," *IEEE Trans. Magn.,* **MAG-26,** 2568 (1990).

Harlee, P. S., G. H. Bellesis, and D. N. Lambeth, "Anisotropy and Magnetostriction Measurement by Interferometry," *J. Appl. Phys.,* **75,** 6884 (1994).

Haynes, M. K, "Experimental Determination of the Loss and Phase Transfer Functions of a Magnetic Recording Channel," *IEEE Trans., Magn.,* **MAG-13,** 1284 (1977).

Hempstead, R. D., "Thermally Induced Pulses in Magnetoresistive Heads," *IBM J. Res. Dev.,* **18,** 547 (1974).

Henkel, O., "Remanence Reduction and Exchange Effects in Collections of Hard Magnetic Particles" (German), *Phys. Stat. Sol.,* **7,** 919 (1974).

Hersener, J., "Model Investigation of the Magnetization Distribution of Sinusoidal Recordings in Magnetic Tape" (German), *Wiss. Ber. AEG TELEFUNKEN,* **46,** 15 (1973).

Hoyt, R. F., "Microloop Measurements of Recording Head Fields versus Current," *J. Appl. Phys.,* **56,** 3947 (1985).

Hoyt, R. F., D. E. Heim, J. S. Best, C. T. Horng, and D. E. Horne, "Direct Measurement of Recording Head Fields Using a High-Resolution Inductive Loop," *J. Appl. Phys.,* **55,** 2241 (1984).

IRIG Document 118-79, *Test Methods for Recorder/Reproducer Systems and Magnetic Tape,* 1979, vol. III.

Ishiba, T., and H. Suzuki, "Measurements of Magnetic Field of Magnetic Recording Head by a Scanning Electron Microscope," *Jpn. J. Appl. Phys.,* **13,** 457 (1974).

Iwasaki, S., and K. Ouchi, "Co-Cr Recording Films with Perpendicular Magnetic Anisotropy," *IEEE Trans. Magn.,* **MAG-14,** 849 (1978).

Iwasaki, S., and K. Takemura, "An Analysis for the Circular Mode of Magnetization in Short Wavelength Recording," *IEEE Trans. Magn.,* **MAG-11,** 1173 (1975).

Iwasaki, S., Y. Nakamura, S. Yamamoto, and K. Yamakawa, "Perpendicular Recording by a Narrow Track Single Pole Head," *IEEE Trans. Magn.,* **MAG-19,** 1713 (1983).

Johnson, K. E., and M. G. Kerr, "A Magnetometer for the Rapid and Nondestructive Measurement of Magnetic Properties on Rigid Disk Media," *IEEE Trans. Magn.,* **MAG-26,** 2565 (1990).

Josephs, R. M., D. S. Crompton, and C. S. Krafft, "Vector Vibrating Sample Magnetometry—A Technique for Three Dimensional Magnetic Anisotropy Measurements," *Intermag Conf. Dig.,* CF-05 (1987).

Joy, D. C., and J. P. Jakubovics, "Direct Observation of Magnetic Domains by Scanning Electron Microscopy," *Phil. Mag.,* **17,** 61 (1968).

Kawakami, K., S. Narishige, and M. Takagi, "A High Frequency Permeance Meter for Anisotropic Films and Its Application in the Determination of Magnetostriction Constants," *IEEE Trans. Magn,* **MAG-19,** 2154 (1973).

Klaassen, K. B., and J. C. L. van Peppen, "Barkhausen Noise in Thin-Film Recording Heads," *IEEE Trans. Magn.,* **MAG-26,** 1697 (1990).

Kneller, E., and F. E. Luborsky, "Particle Size Dependence of Coercivity and Remanence of Single-Domain Particles," *J. Appl. Phys.,* **34,** 656 (1963).

Knowles, J. E., "Measurements on Single Magnetic Particles," *IEEE Trans. Magn.,* **MAG-14,** 858 (1978).

Knowles, J. E., "Magnetic Measurements on Single Acicular Particles of gamma Fe_2O_3," *IEEE Trans. Magn.,* **MAG-16,** 62 (1980).

Koike, K., and K. Hayakawa, "Domain Observation with Spin-Polarized Secondary Electrons," *J. Appl. Phys.,* **57** (1), **4244** (1985).

Koren, N. L., "A Simplified Model of Nonlinear Bit Shift in Digital Magnetic Recording," *Intermag Conf. Dig.,* **2–9** (1981).

Köster, E., "Reversible Susceptibility of an Assembly of Single-Domain Particles and Their Magnetic Anisotropy," *J. Appl. Phys.,* **41,** 3332 (1970).

Köster, E., "Recommendation of a Simple and Universally Applicable Method for Measuring the Switching Field Distribution of Magnetic Recording Media," *IEEE Trans. Magn.,* **MAG-20,** 881 (1984).

Kryder, M. H., P. V. Koeppe, and F. H. Liu, "Kerr Effect Imaging of Dynamic Processes in Magnetic Recording Heads," *IEEE Trans. Magn.,* **MAG-26,** 2995 (1990).

Kullmann, U., E. Köster, and B. Meyer, "Magnetic Anisotropy of Ir-doped CrO_2," *IEEE Trans. Magn.,* **MAG-20,** 742 (1984).

Langland, B. J., and P. A. Albert, "Recording on Perpendicular Anisotropy Media with Ring Heads," *IEEE Trans. Magn.,* **MAG-17,** 2547 (1981).

Lemke, J. U., and R. J. McClure, "The Effect of Vector Field History on the Remanence of Magnetic Tape," *IEEE Trans. Magn.,* **MAG-2,** 230 (1966).

Liu, F. H., and M. H. Kryder, "Inductance Fluctuation, Domain Instability and Popcorn Noise in Thin Film Heads," *IEEE Trans. Magn.,* **MAG-30,** 3885 (1994).

Lustig, C. D., A. W. Baird, W. F. Chaurette, H. Minden, W. T. Maloney, and A. J. Kurtzig, "High-Resolution Magnetic Field Measurement System for Recording Heads and Disks," *Rev. Sci. Instrum.,* **50,** 321 (1979).

Mallinson, J. C., "Magnetometer Coils and Reciprocity," *J. Appl. Phys.,* **37,** 2514 (1966).

Mallinson, J. C., "One-Sided Fluxes—A Magnetic Curiosity," *IEEE Trans. Magn.*, **MAG-9**, 678 (1973).

Mallinson, J. C., "On the Properties of Two-Dimensional Dipoles and Magnetized Bodies," *IEEE Trans. Magn.*, **MAG-17**, 2453 (1981).

Mamin, H. J., D. Rugar, J. E. Stern, B. D. Terris, and S. E. Lambert, "Force Microscopy of Magnetization Patterns in Longitudinal Recording Media," *Appl. Phys. Lett.*, **53**, 1563 (1988).

Manly, W. A., Jr., "A 5.5-kOe 60-Hz Magnetic Hysteresis Loop Tracer with Precise Digital Readout," *IEEE Trans. Magn.*, **MAG-7**, 442 (1971).

Martin, Y., and H. K. Wickramasinghe, "Magnetic Imaging by 'Force Microscopy' with 1000 Å Resolution," *Appl. Phys. Lett.*, **50**, 1455 (1987).

Martin, Y., D. Rugar, and H. K. Wickramasinghe, "High-Resolution Magnetic Imaging of Domains in TbFe by Force Microscopy," *Appl. Phys. Lett.*, **52**, 244 (1988).

Marton, L., "Electron Optical Schlieren Effect," *J. Appl. Phys.*, **19**, 687 (1948).

McKnight, J. G., "Erasure of Magnetic Tape," *J. Audio Eng. Soc.*, **11**, 223 (1963).

McKnight, J. G., "Tape Flux Measurement Theory and Verification," *J. Audio Eng. Soc.*, **18**, 250 (1970).

Mee, C. D., *The Physics of Magnetic Recording*, North-Holland, Amsterdam, 1964.

Middleton, B. K., "The Dependence of Recording Characteristics of Thin Metal Tapes on their Magnetic Properties and on the Replay Head," *IEEE Trans. Magn.*, **MAG-2**, 225 (1966).

Monson, J. E., D. J. Olson, and E. P. Valstyn, "Scale-Modeling the Read Process for a Film Head," *IEEE Trans. Magn.*, **MAG-11**, 1182 (1975).

Monson, J. E., M. A. Barker, S. T. Ritchie, and E. P. Valstyn, "Scale-Modeling the Write and Read Processes in Digital Magnetic Recording," *Intermag Conf. Dig.*, 26-5 (1978).

Monson, J. E., R. Fung, and A. S. Hoagland, "Large Scale Model Studies of Vertical Recording" *IEEE Trans. Magn.*, **MAG-17**, 2541 (1981).

Murdock, E. S., "Measured Noise in Thin Film Media," *Noise in Digital Magnetic Recording*, ed. T. C. Arnoldussen and L. L. Nunnelley, World Scientific Publishing Co., Singapore, 1992.

Nakagawa, S., K. Kanai, and F. Kobayashi, "Investigation of Head Saturation Using a Large-Scale Ferrite Model Head," *IEEE Trans. Magn.* **MAG-8**, 538 (1972).

Nakamura, Y., and S. Iwasaki, "Perpendicular Magnetic Recording Characteristics," *Bull. Magn. Soc. Japan*, **32-2**, 7 (1983).

Narishige, S., M. Nanazono, M. Takagi, and S. Kuwatsuka, "Measurements of Magnetization Processes of Thin Film Heads Using Micro-Kerr Method," *J. Appl. Phys.*, **8**, 2 (1984).

Newman, J. J., "Magnetic Measurements for Digital Magnetic Recording," *IEEE Trans. Magn.*, **MAG-14**, 154 (1978).

Nunnelley, L. L., "Practical Noise Measurements," *Noise in Digital Magnetic Recording*, ed. T. C. Arnoldussen and L. L. Nunnelley, World Scientific Publishing Co., Singapore, 1992.

Nunnelley, L. L., R. D. Harper, and M. Burleson, "Time Domain Noise-Induced Jitter: Theory and Precise Measurement," *IEEE Trans. Magn.*, **MAG-23**, 2383 (1987).

O'Grady, K., "Magnetic Characterization of Recording Media," *IEEE Trans. Magn.*, **MAG-26**, 1870 (1990).

Ouchi, K., and S. Iwasaki, "Properties of High Rate Sputtered Perpendicular Recording Media," *J. Appl. Phys.*, **57**, 4013 (1985).

Pacyna, A. W., and K. Ruebenbauer, "General Theory of a Vibrating Magnetometer with Extended Coils," *J. Phys. E: Sci. Instrum.*, **17**, 141 (1984).

Palmer, D., P. Ziperovich, and R. Wood, "Identification of Nonlinear Write Effects Using Pseudorandom Sequences," *IEEE Trans. Magn.*, **MAG-23**, 2377 (1987).

Palmer, D., J. Coker, M. Meyer, and P. Ziperovich, "Overwrite in Thin Media Measured by the Method of Pseudorandom Sequences," *IEEE Trans. Magn.*, **MAG-24**, 3096 (1988).

Palmer, D., and J. V. Peske, "Spatial distribution of Overwrite Interference on Film Disks," *IEEE Trans. Magn.,* **MAG-26,** 2451 (1990).

Pearson, R. F., "Magnetic Anisotropy," in *Experimental Magnetism,* G. M. Kalvius and R. S. Tebble (eds.), Vol. I, Wiley, Chichester, England, 1979.

Penoyer, R. F., "Automatic Torque Balance for Magnetic Anisotropy Measurements," *Rev. Sci. Instrum.,* **30,** 711 (1959).

Petek, B., P. L. Trouilloud, and B. E. Argyle, "Time-Resolved Domain Dynamics in Thin-Film Heads," *IEEE Trans. Magn.,* **MAG-26,** 1328 (1990).

Pierce, D. T., S. M. Girvin, J. Unguris, and R. J. Celotta, "Absorbed Current Electron Spin Polarization Detector," *Rev. Sci. Instrum.,* **52,** 1437 (1981).

Rau, E. I., and G. V. Spivak, "Scanning Electron Microscopy of Two-Dimensional Magnetic Stray Fields," *Scanning,* **3,** 27 (1980).

Re, M. E., and M. H. Kryder, "Magneto-Optic Investigation of Thin-Film Recording Heads," *J Appl. Phys.,* **55,** 2245 (1984).

Re, M. E., R. R. Katti, S. L. Zeder, and M. H. Kryder, "Magneto-Optic Determination of Magnetic Recording Head Fields," *IEEE Trans. Magn.,* **MAG-22,** 840 (1986).

Rugar, D., H. J. Mamin, R. Erlandsson, J. E. Stern, and B. D. Terris, "Force Microscope Using a Fiber-Optic Displacement Sensor," *Rev. Sci. Instrum.,* **59,** 2337 (1988).

Rugar, D., H. J. Mamin, P. Guethner, S. E. Lambert, J. E. Stern, I. McFadyen, and T. Yogi, "Magnetic Force Microscopy: General Principles and Application to Longitudinal Recording Media," *J. Appl. Phys.,* **68,** 1169 (1990).

Saenz, J. J., N. Garcia, and J. C. Slonczewski, "Theory of Magnetic Imaging by Force Microscopy," *Appl. Phys. Lett.,* **53,** 1449 (1988).

Salling, C. T., and S. Schultz, "Using Minor Loop Behavior to Investigate the Preisach Distribution for Particulate Media," *IEEE Trans. Magn.,* **MAG-24,** 2877 (1988).

Schönenberger, C., S. F. Alvarado, S. E. Lambert, and I. L. Sanders, "Separation of Magnetic and Topographic Effects in Force Microscopy," *J. Appl. Phys.,* **67,** 7278 (1990).

Sharrock, M. P., "Particle-Size Effects on the Switching Behavior of Uniaxial and Multiaxial Magnetic Recording Materials," *IEEE Trans. Magn.,* **MAG-20,** 754 (1984).

Shieh, H.-P. D., and M. H. Kryder, "High Resolution Measurement of Coercivity Variations in Magneto-Optical Recording Media," *IEEE Trans. Magn.,* **MAG-24,** 2464 (1988).

Shinada, H., H. Suzuki, S. Sasaki, H. Todokoro, H. Takano, and K. Shiiki, "Time-resolved Measurement of Micro-magnetic Field by Stroboscopic Electron Beam Tomography," *IEEE Trans. Magn.,* **MAG-28,** 3117 (1992).

Silva, T. J., and S. Schultz, "Further Development of a Scanned Near-field Optical Microscope for Magneto-Optic Kerr Imaging of Magnetic Domains with 10nm Resolution," *Optical Engineering, SPIE, Scanning Probe Microscopies,* **1855,** 180 (1993).

Slade, S. B., and A. E. Berkowitz, "Ultra-High Sensitivity B-H Looper/AC Susceptometer," *IEEE Trans. Magn.,* **MAG-28,** 3132 (1992).

Spivak, G. V., A. E. Lukianov, E. I. Rau, and R. S. Gvosdover, "Electron Mirror Measurements of Magnetic Fields Over Audio and Video Heads and Tapes," *IEEE Trans. Magn.,* **MAG-7,** 684 (1971).

Starr, J., "Envelope Delay in a Tape Recorder System," *Proc. Int. Telem. Conf.,* **1,** 595 (1965).

Stefannelli, P., and J. L. LeLarge, "Signal-to-Noise Ratio Measurement in Digital Recording," Paper BP-21, *Intermag Conf. Dig.* (1984).

Tanaka, H., H. Goto, N. Shiota, and M. Yanagisawa, "Noise Characteristics in Plated Co-Ni-P Film For High Density Recording Medium," *J. Appl. Phys.,* **53,** 2576 (1982).

Tang, Y. S., "Noise Autocorrelation in Magnetic Recording Systems," *IEEE Trans. Magn.,* **MAG-21,** 1389 (1985).

Thornley, R. F. M., "Pulse Response of Recording Media," *IEEE Trans. Magn.,* **MAG-11,** 1197 (1975).

Thornley, R. F. M., and J. D. Hutchison, "Magnetic Field Measurements in the Scanning Electron Microscope," *IEEE Trans. Magn.*, **MAG-5,** 271 (1969).

Tjaden, D. L. A., and J. Leyten, "A 5000 : 1 Scale Model of the Magnetic Recording Process," *Philips Tech. Rev.,* **25,** 319 (1964).

Tong, H. C., R. Ferrier, P. Chang, J. Tzeng, and K. L. Parker, "The Micromagnetics of Thin-Film Disk Recording Tracks," *IEEE Trans. Magn.,* **MAG-20,** 1831 (1984).

Tonomura, A., T. Matsuda, J. Endo, T. Arii, and K. Mihama, "Direct Observation of Fine Structure of Magnetic Domain Walls by Electron Holography," *Phys. Rev. Lett.,* **44,** 1430 (1980).

Trouilloud, P. L., B. Petek, and B. E. Argyle, "Methods for Wide-Field Kerr Imaging of Small Magnetic Devices," *IEEE Trans. Magn.,* **MAG-30,** 4494 (1994).

Tsang, C., and Y. Tang, "An Experimental Study of Hard-Transition Peakshifts through the Overwrite Spectra," *IEEE Trans. Magn.,* **MAG-24,** 3087 (1988).

Unguris, J., D. T. Pierce, A. Galejs, and R. J. Celotta, "Spin and Energy Analyzed Secondary Electron Emission from a Ferromagnet," *Phys. Rev. Lett.,* **49,** 72 (1982).

Unguris, J., G. G. Hembree, R. J. Cellotta, and D. T. Pierce, "High Resolution Magnetic Microstructure Imaging Using Secondary Electron Spin Polarization Analysis in a Scanning Electron Microscope," *J. Micros.,* **139,** RP1 (1985).

Valstyn, E. P., and J. E. Monson, "Magnetization Distribution in an Isolated Transition," *IEEE Trans. Magn.,* **MAG-15,** 1453 (1979).

Valstyn, E. P., R. I. Potter, and A. Paton, "Validity of Scale Models in Magnetics," *Comput. Dis.,* **9,** 94 (1971).

Valstyn, E. P., J. E. Monson, R. W. Akeo, and R. K. Moloney, "A Study of Transition-Density Effects with Film Heads," *Int. Conf. Video Data Recording,* **27** (1979).

Völz, H., "Device for Semi-Automatic Measurement of Preisach Values of Magnetic Tape," *Hochfrequenztech. U. Electakust.,* **79,** 101 (1971).

Wachenschwanz, D., and F. Jeffers, "Overwrite as a Function of Record Gap Length," *IEEE Trans. Magn.,* **MAG-21,** 1380 (1985).

Watanuki, O., K. Sueoka, and K. G. Ashar, "Direct Measurement of Side Fringe Field and Two-Dimensional Head Field Using High-Resolution Inductive Loop," *IEEE Trans. Magn.,* **MAG-23,** 3164 (1987).

Wiesen, K. C., and S. H. Charap, "A Rotational Vector Preisach Model for Unoriented Media," *J. Appl. Phys.,* **67,** 5367 (1990).

Wells, O. C., *Scanning Electron Microscopy,* McGraw-Hill, New York, 1974.

Wells, O. C., and M. Brunner, "Schlieren Method as Applied to Magnetic Recording Heads in the Scanning Electron Microscope," *Appl. Phys. Lett.,* **42,** 114 (1983).

Wells, O. C., and R. J. Savoy, "Magnetic Domains in Thin-Film Recording Heads as Observed in the SEM by a Lock-in Technique," *IEEE Trans. Magn.,* **MAG-17,** 1253 (1981).

Wells, O. C., P. J. Coane, and C. F. Aliotta, "Measuring the Field From a Magnetic Recording Head in the Scanning Electron Microscope," *Proc. 18th Annu. Conf. MAS,* Phoenix, 1983.

Westmijze, W. K., "Studies on Magnetic Recording," *Philips Res. Rep.,* **8,** 343 (1953).

Williams, M. L., and R. L. Comstock, "An Analytic Model of the Write Process in Digital Magnetic Recording," *AIP Conf. Proc.,* **5,** 738 (1971).

Wohlleben, D., "On the Detection of Magnetic Microstructures with Charged Particles," *Phys. Lett.,* **22,** 564 (1966).

Wood, R. W., and R. W. Donaldson, "The Helical-Scan Magnetic Tape Recorder on a Digital Communication Channel," *IEEE Trans. Magn.,* **MAG-15,** 935 (1979).

Yamamoto, S., Y. Nakamura, and S. Iwasaki, "Spacing Loss in Perpendicular Magnetic Recording," *Rep. TGMR IECE Jpn.,* **84,** 27 (1984) (in Japanese).

Yeh, N. H., "A Negative Transition Width in Perpendicular Recording?" *J. Appl. Phys.,* **57,** 3940 (1985).

Yoshida, K., T. Okuwaki, N. Osakabe, H. Tanabe, Y. Horiuchi, T. Matsuda, K. Shinagawa, A. Tonomura, and H. Fujiwara, "Observation of Recorded Magnetization Patterns by Electron Holography," *IEEE Trans. Magn.,* **MAG-19,** 1600 (1983).

Youngquist, R. J., and R. H. Hanes, "Magnetic Reader," U.S. Patent 3,013,206, 1961.

Zijlstra, H., *Experimental Methods in Magnetism,* Wiley, New York, 1967, vol. 2.

CHAPTER 10
MAGNETOOPTICAL RECORDING

Dan S. Bloomberg

Xerox Palo Alto Research Center, Palo Alto, California

G. A. Neville Connell

Xerox Palo Alto Research Center, Palo Alto, California

Masud Mansuripur

University of Arizona, Tucson, Arizona

10.1 OVERVIEW OF MAGNETOOPTICAL DATA STORAGE

High-density optical recording became a reality in a number of write-once products introduced in the mid-1980s. These drives offer about 2 GB of storage per disk at an areal density of about 4×10^5 b/mm^2 and data rates of about 5 Mb/s. The average access time was about 100 ms, but 20 adjacent tracks that contain about 1 MB of information could be accessed in about 1 ms. The disks themselves were removable. While there continue to be many opportunities for further innovations in this area, there is now keen competition to build systems that add erasability to this list of features. One approach, magnetooptical recording, is the subject of this chapter.

The principle of magnetooptical recording is as follows. A focused laser beam, pulsed to high power for a short time, raises the temperature of a perpendicularly magnetized medium sufficiently for an externally applied magnetic field to reverse the direction of magnetization in the heated region. When the medium returns to a lower temperature for readout, the reverse-magnetized domain persists. Erasure of domains is accomplished by the same thermal process, now aided by an oppositely directed magnetic field. At this fundamental level, there is one important difference between magnetooptical and magnetic recording; that is, the switching rate of the magnetic field may be much lower than the data rate. The latter is determined by the pulse rate of the laser and, therefore, very high-frequency recording should be possible. The price paid is that the write process must first be preceded by a separate erase step when a single magnetooptical layer is used, and unless this is compensated by the disk controller and operating system software, there will be a write delay of one revolution. Alternatively, a complex magnetic structure, consisting of a magnetooptical memory layer supported on a field-controlling magnetic underlayer, may be used to provide a direct overwrite capability (Saito et al., 1987).

Readout of information employs the polar Kerr effect. Linearly polarized light, reflected from a perpendicularly magnetized medium, is rotated to the left or right, according to the direction of magnetization. (Some ellipticity is also introduced into the reflected light, but it may be ignored for now.) By checking the direction of the plane of polarization of the reflected light, magnetization transitions along a recorded track can be read out by the same focused laser beam that was used for recording information. Reading has no influence on the recorded information because the read laser power is low and causes little temperature rise.

The essential features of a magnetooptical recording system are shown in Fig. 10.1a. In this system, collimated linearly polarized light from a Ga-As laser passes through a slightly rotated polarizing beam splitter and is focused on a magnetooptical medium. The reflected light is then guided to the detection system by the same polarizing beam splitter. The detection system consists of a second polarizing beam splitter rotated by 45° about the optical axis so that the incident light is split between photodiodes 1 and 2. The detection system itself has three purposes: to sense the magnetic transitions and to provide focusing and tracking signals that maintain the laser spot in precise position relative to the disk surface and data tracks. The performance of each of these features will determine the eventual system performance. Currently, either the laser power and medium sensitivity or the focus and tracking servos impose an upper limit on the disk rotation rate; the signal-to-noise ratio imposes a limit on the minimum bit size; and tracking servo accuracy and read spot size determine the minimum track spacing. It will be seen later that these constraints suggest that, with currently available technology, removable 90 mm-diameter disks will contain 500 MB in systems maintaining a data rate of 5 Mb/s.

The first suggestion of thermomagnetic writing (Mayer, 1958) apparently came from the observation that when thin perpendicularly magnetized films of Mn-Bi were heated by the point of a needle, magnetization reversal occurred in the heated region. Called *Curie-point writing,* this phenomenon occurred because the heated region had cooled from above the Curie temperature in the demagnetizing field created by the surrounding sample. A potential benefit of some ferrimagnetic materials for thermomagnetic recording (Chang et al., 1965) is that the rapid decrease of coercivity above the compensation temperature (at which the net magnetization on both sublattices is zero) permits recording to occur with a relatively small temperature rise. This recording process is known as *compensation point writing.* The writing and erasing processes can therefore, in principle at least, be achieved without thermal degradation of the sample, a problem that plagued much of the later work with Mn-Bi.

The principles for recording were thus established, but practical means for the subsequent readout of the recorded information were absent. The important events that changed this situation were the availability of solid-state lasers, the use of multilayer interference structures to improve the magnetooptical conversivity (Smith, 1965a; 1965b), the understanding and optimization of the system-medium performance (Goldberg, 1967; Mansuripur et al., 1982; Mansuripur and Connell, 1983a; Connell et al., 1983), and the discovery of the amorphous rare-earth transition-metal alloys (Chaudhari et al., 1973; Sunago et al., 1976; Mimura et al., 1976, 1978).

Lasers provide a simple means of delivering to a 1-μm-sized area the thermal energy needed for the writing and erasing processes (Smith, 1967). They therefore

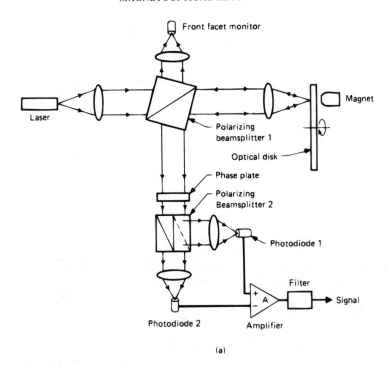

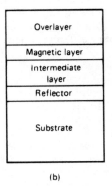

(b)

FIGURE 10.1 (a) Schematic representation of the layout of a magnetooptical recording system; and (b) a section of a magnetooptical quadrilayer medium (*after Connell et al., 1983*).

offer the potential to record at the densities that are now available in the commercial nonerasable optical recording products. They also make the readout process more amenable to drive integration. Nevertheless, readout with adequate signal-to-noise ratio was, until recently, a major problem. The primary issue is the minuscule size of the polar Kerr effect. When plane-polarized light is normally incident on a magnetooptical medium, a small fraction of the light reflected is polarized at right angles

TABLE 10.1 Comparison of the Magnetooptical Effect in Amorphous and Crystalline Alloys

Material	r_y†
$Tb_{0.2}Fe_{0.8}$	3.0×10^{-3}
Mn-Bi	1.0×10^{-2}
Pt-Mn-Sb	1.3×10^{-2}
$Tb_{0.2}Fe_{0.8}$‡	8.0×10^{-3}

†Data at 633 nm.
‡30-nm layer in a quadrilayer.

to the incident polarization. We denote the reflectivity of the medium by $R = r_x^2 + r_y^2$, where r_x and r_y are the unconverted (ordinary) and converted (magnetooptical) amplitudes, respectively, and $r_y \ll r_x$. In Sec. 10.3, it will be shown that the signal-to-shot-noise voltage ratio in the photodetectors is proportional to r_y, and Table 10.1 shows that the value of r_y in typical amorphous and polycrystalline materials is between 3×10^{-3} and 10^{-2}. Methods to enhance the signal-to-noise ratio by improving signal delivery, material selection, or medium design are essential for the success of the technology.

In early work, an intensity beam splitter was placed in the main beam, and one-half of both the incident laser light and the reflected magnetooptical signal were lost (by reflection and transmission, respectively). Improvement in the signal delivery system was achieved by using instead a polarizing beam splitter, which transmitted a large fraction of the incident laser light and reflected all of the magnetooptical signal (Connell et al., 1983). Further improvement was achieved by using a second polarizing beam splitter with a differential detection scheme in the detector module (Goldberg, 1967), instead of a simple analyzer and detector.

Incorporation of the magnetic layer in multilayer interference structures improves the magnetooptical conversivity. These structures couple more incident light into the magnetic layer and couple more of the magnetooptically induced light back out. The quadrilayer structure shown in Fig. 10.1(b) is inverted in newer designs so that the substrate is at the top of the structure. However, the use of amorphous rare-earth transition-metal alloys has probably been the most important advancement. The alloy composition and multilayer design can be selected to withstand the maximum read power and therefore allow for maximum signal size. This is accomplished by minimizing the writing sensitivity, subject to thermomagnetic recording remaining possible in the system at hand. The method involves the careful adjustment of the Curie and compensation temperatures of the alloy and the heat-flow characteristics of the medium. This is possible only because in amorphous alloys, the Curie and compensation temperatures can be controlled independently and continuously by alloying. Although the magnitude of the polar Kerr effect is smaller in these alloys than in some polycrystalline compounds, as shown in Table 10.1, the magnetic media noise on readout is negligible. This is in contrast with the performance of polycrystalline media in which the noise proved to be unacceptable. The difference occurs because the domain walls can be pinned intrinsically in the best amorphous alloys, rather than on grain boundaries or defects as in polycrystalline material. As a result, bit-to-bit fluctuations in the location of the transitions are minimal in the amorphous media. In well-designed systems, shot-noise-limited performance can be approached.

There have also been important advances in noise suppression by both optical and electronic means. The differential detection scheme in Fig. 10.1a reduces medium noise associated with substrate and medium inhomogeneities (Goldberg, 1967), while laser noise can be reduced to acceptable levels by rf drive techniques (Ohishi et al., 1984). Finally, the substrate quality itself has improved through the earlier development of write-once commercial products.

Several review articles are recommended for further information on magnetooptical recording. There is an excellent introduction to the physics of magnetooptical effects (Freiser, 1968), and there are several historical reviews with expositions of thermomagnetic processes, optical properties, and the micromagnetics of magnetooptical recording (Smith, 1967; Hunt, 1969; Dekker, 1976). Other reviewers compare magnetooptical and magnetic recording, as they were envisioned to develop during the 1980s (Bell, 1983) and summarize the status of magnetooptical technology with rare-earth transition-metal films (Kryder, 1985). For an introduction to the technology of read-only and nonerasable optical memories, which have many features in common with erasable magnetooptical systems, there is a set of review articles on digital audio (Carasso et al., 1982; Heemskerk and Immink, 1982; Hoeve et al., 1982) and books on optical-disk systems (Bouwhuis et al., 1985; Marchant, 1990; Mansuripur, 1995).

The primary technical problems in the construction of an erasable magnetooptical system have historically been, and continue to be, in the development of a suitable storage medium. For this reason, the physical properties of the magnetooptical materials (Sec. 10.2) and the enhancement and optimization of the optical and thermal response of structures fabricated from these materials (Sec. 10.3) occupy a central position in this chapter. Section 10.2 covers the magnetic, optical, and electronic properties of the rare-earth transition-metal films, including film preparation and chemical stability. Section 10.3 describes the use of multilayered structures both to enhance the magnetooptical signal and to protect the magnetooptical film. Additionally, some problems associated with fabricating and preformatting the substrate are discussed. The other components of the magnetooptical system—the optics, laser, detectors, servos, and magnet—are described in Sec. 10.4. System performance is given in Sec. 10.5 in terms of the various noise sources, signal-to-noise ratio, modulation transfer function, areal data density and data rate, data encoding, error rate, and error correction. Finally, Sec. 10.6 describes the position of magnetooptical memories in the evolution of both digital recording systems and digital computers.

10.2 PHYSICAL CHARACTERISTICS OF MAGNETOOPTICAL MATERIALS

10.2.1 Basic Properties

The alloys currently of most interest for magnetooptical recording are based on the amorphous $(Tb, Gd)_x (Fe, Co)_{1-x}$ system with $0.2 \leq x \leq 0.3$. While the actual structural topology of these materials is unknown (Cargill, 1975; Rhyne, 1977), measurements on $TbFe_2$, $GdFe_2$, and $SmFe_2$ (D'Antonio et al., 1982) show some distinct differences between the coordination of the rare-earth atoms in the amorphous and corresponding crystalline Laves phase. For example, the tetrahedral Tb-

Tb coordination of the crystal is approximately doubled in the amorphous phase, an effect that is accompanied by a 10 percent increase in the Tb-Tb distance. In contrast, the Fe-Fe coordination shells and distances are not very much changed. There are therefore both qualitative and quantitative differences between many properties of the amorphous and crystalline phases. This is exemplified by the diverse trends for the Curie temperatures of amorphous alloys and crystalline compounds (Heiman et al., 1975). Understanding the structural origin of these differences is of paramount importance when devising high-performance magnetooptical media.

As far as the magnetic properties are concerned, the key intrinsic structural feature of the amorphous phase is that no two atomic sites are equivalent (Coey, 1978). Three effects can result: a distribution in magnitude of the atomic moments, a distribution in the magnitude and sign of the exchange interaction, and the possibility of local anisotropy dominating the magnetic behavior in alloys containing highly anisotropic rare-earth ions. Some important cases are sketched in Fig. 10.2. In the simplest case, represented by Gd-Co, the local anisotropy is zero at the rare-earth site because Gd is an S-state ion. Thus, because the Co subnetwork is strongly ferromagnetic and the coupling between the Gd and Co spin angular momenta is weakly antiferromagnetic, simple ferrimagnetic behavior occurs. In the two other cases, the random anisotropy at the non-S-state rare-earth site competes with exchange to determine the orientation of the rare-earth moment. Moreover, according to Hund's rule, $J = L + S$ for the heavy elements and $J = L - S$ for the light elements. Thus, while both Nd-Co and Tb-Co are sperimagnetic (Coey, 1978), only the latter will show ferrimagnetic-like behavior. Figure 10.2 also shows one final complication, namely the scatter in the orientation of the iron moments in Tb-Fe alloys that arises either through the distribution in the exchange interaction between iron atoms (see Sec. 10.2.3) or through the effect of local anisotropy at the rare-earth sites on the iron subnetwork.

The resulting magnetic behavior of the heavy rare-earth alloys is indicated in Fig. 10.3 (Connell et al., 1982). With a suitable choice of composition, the saturation magnetization M_s will be close to zero over a wide temperature range and exactly zero at the compensation temperature. In contrast, the magnetization of each subnetwork is large at temperatures reasonably below the Curie temperature. For example, low-temperature magnetization measurements suggest that the mag-

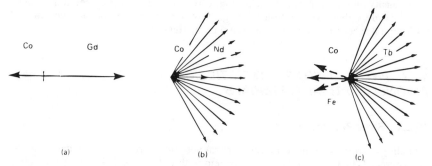

FIGURE 10.2 Competition between exchange and anisotropy in determining magnetism in amorphous rare-earth transition-metal materials. (*a*) S-state ion (Gd); (*b*) non-S-state ion (light rare earth); (*c*) non-S-state ion (heavy rare earth). In (*a*) there is no local anisotropy. In (*b*) and (*c*), a large local anisotropy results in either ferromagnetic (for light rare-earth elements) or ferrimagnetic (for heavy rare-earth elements) alignment. Sperimagnetic distribution of resulting moments is also shown (*after Coey, 1978*).

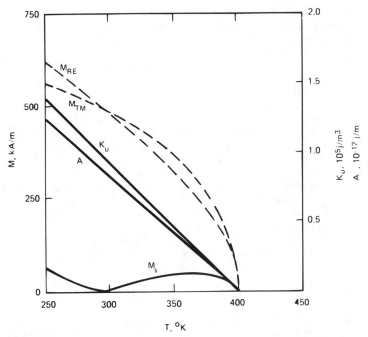

FIGURE 10.3 Mean-field model of magnetization versus temperature for a ferrimagnetic alloy with compensation point near room temperature. M_{RE} and M_{TM} are the magnetization of the rare-earth and transition-metal sublattices, respectively, and M_s is the net magnetization. The temperature dependencies of the exchange stiffness A and anisotropy energy density K_u are also shown (*after Mansuripur and Connell, 1984*).

netic moment per Fe atom approaches two Bohr magnetons at compositions of interest, while the magnetic moment per rare-earth atom, after accounting for sperimagnetic scatter, takes on its normal ionic value (Rhyne, 1977). The magnetooptical effect, which is found to depend almost entirely on the magnetic moment of the transition metal (Argyle et al., 1974; Connell and Allen, 1983), has the important property of being finite and smoothly varying with temperature at the compensation temperature.

There is also a key extrinsic feature in the structure of these alloys that arises from the deposition process itself. Namely, a uniaxial anisotropy develops in the growth direction that ranges from columnar microstructure in poor material to more subtle pair-ordering effects (Mizoguchi and Cargill, 1979; van Dover et al., 1985) in the best material. The latter establish a uniaxial anisotropy in the averaged local order around each atomic site. Alloys containing non-S-state rare-earth ions, whose moments are directed by the local order through single-ion anisotropy, thus have a mechanism not present in S-state alloys for developing a large macroscopic uniaxial magnetic anisotropy ($K_u > 0$) in the growth direction. (This mechanism could also operate through the local anisotropy of transition metal ions and could be responsible for the weak magnetic anisotropy in S-state alloys.) The temperature variation of K_u in these alloys is sketched in Fig. 10.3. As mentioned earlier, the exact orientation of each non-S-state rare-earth moment is set by the competition between single-ion anisotropy and exchange, and this leads to a scatter of the moments about the growth direction from site to site. The ensuing fluctuations can stabilize domains at submicrometer dimensions by providing an intrinsic mechanism for the pinning of walls (Gambino et al., 1974). This important interplay between structural and magnetic anisotropy, which occurs in alloys containing non-S-state ions, is absent in the S-state systems, such as Gd-Co.

The final key structural feature that affects many aspects of the media performance is the flexibility inherent in the amorphous structure itself. For example, the Curie temperature can be increased linearly by substituting Co for Fe (Tsunashima et al., 1982; Connell and Allen, 1983) or Gd for Tb (Imamura et al., 1985) in Tb-Fe alloys, or the compensation temperature can be varied by changing the alloy composition (Chaudhari et al., 1973; Rhyne, 1977). Other elements that may be added, such as Al, Cr, and Pt, have very little effect on the magnetic properties but significantly improve the corrosion resistance (Imamura et al., 1985).

Along with these advantages of the amorphous phase, there is the possibility that crystallization may limit its performance and life in a recording system. While there are currently no general arguments to provide a priori rules for stable alloy design, empirical evidence has shown that crystallization is not likely to occur either at the high temperatures present during the recording and erasure cycles or at the lower ambient temperatures present in a drive or storage environment (Luborsky et al., 1985).

10.2.2 Preparation

Rare-earth transition-metal alloys can be made in the amorphous state by a large variety of vacuum-deposition processes. In the time since their discovery, thermal (Biesterbos et al., 1979) and electron-beam (Hasegawa and Taylor, 1975; Hansen and Urner-Wille, 1979) evaporation, rf-diode sputtering (Chaudhari et al., 1973; Mimura et al., 1976), magnetron sputtering (van Dover et al., 1986), and ion-beam sputtering (Harper and Gambino, 1979) have all been used successfully to make amorphous specimens. Some of the properties of the resulting material are influenced by the character of the deposition process itself rather than by the alloy composition (Heitmann et al., 1985), including, in some cases, the ability of the material to maintain perpendicular domains (Sakurai and Onishi, 1983) and to resist corrosion (Imamura et al., 1985). Of the various evaporation and sputtering methods available, magnetron sputtering, with its ability to coat thermally fragile substrates, is most favored for disk production. The remainder of this section therefore is addressed to the problems encountered when sputtering these materials.

Various forms of sputtering targets have been used. In early work, mosaic targets (Mimura et al., 1978) were often employed. In this case, the composition of the alloy is controlled by selecting the number and location of rare-earth platelets on a transition-metal base target. Small samples with a fixed or uniformly varying composition are readily obtained for study (Connell and Allen, 1983), an approach that has been particularly valuable for developing the ternary and quaternary alloys. Scaled-up production can follow two routes: the use of alloy or sintered powder targets that produce the required alloy film directly, or the use of multiple targets whose flux is mixed at the substrate.

Whichever method is selected, the problem of film contamination, particularly through rare-earth oxidation, must be faced both at the stage of target fabrication and particularly during film growth. Since adequate, multicomponent alloys are now becoming available from a number of target manufacturers, only the prevention of oxidation and contamination are significant barriers for successful production. Three important techniques have been used: a high vacuum with base pressures of 10^{-7} torr or less (Biesterbos et al., 1979); high-purity sputtering gases, often stripped of oxygen just prior to entering the chamber (Connell et al., 1982); and a gettering geometry in the system design (Theuerer et al., 1969). One example of the latter employs dual magnetron sputtering targets to prepare Tb-Fe alloys (van Dover et al., 1986). In this case, the magnetron guns and substrates are surrounded by a liquid nitrogen-cooled copper Meissner trap to getter both residual gases in the system and impurities introduced with the sputtering gas. The effective pressure of reactive gases inside the trap during sputtering is estimated to be in the vicinity of 5 $\times$ 10^{-10} torr. For production, a similar method using either an ambient or water-cooled trap is sufficient.

It is also necessary to control the composition of the alloys to a few tenths of an atomic percent over the entire surface of the disk to ensure uniform performance. This in fact is one of the most difficult requirements to meet under production conditions, requiring both system stability and reproducible target material. Full servo controls on the gas pressure, gas flow, and target voltage are needed, and stringent quality control on target material must be exercised.

The final essential component of a magnetooptical medium, required both for environmental stability and optical performance, is provided by dielectric overlayer and underlayer materials. These materials are again frequently deposited by rf-magnetron sputtering, and often reactively sputtered. The material chosen must prevent chemical reactions with the rare-earth transition-metal alloy from destroying the magnetooptical performance. It must therefore be a diffusion barrier to oxygen and water vapor and must itself not react with either rare-earth or transition metals. The search for such materials has been empirical, and to date some attractive candidates appear to be SiO (Nagao et al., 1986), AlN (Deguchi et al., 1984), SiN (Anthony et al., 1986; Ichihara et al., 1986), and TiO_2 (Fukunishi et al., 1985). More information is provided on this in Sec. 10.2.6.

10.2.3 Magnetic Properties

This section will present the phenomenology of the magnetic properties of the amorphous rare-earth transition-metal alloys. The major topics are the dependence of the magnetization, exchange, anisotropy, and coercivity on alloy composition and temperature and the dependence of the Curie and compensation temperatures on alloy composition. The relationship between the magnetooptical properties and these magnetic properties will be described in Sec. 10.2.4.

The typical behavior of the magnetization is shown in Fig. 10.4 for three Fe-based alloys (Mimura et al., 1978). In each case, the composition is chosen such that a compensation temperature exists. Under these conditions, the magnetization is less than 100 kA/m (100 emu/cm^3) at any temperature of interest for system operation, and each alloy, when prepared in thin-film form, will have only a small demagnetizing field to compete with perpendicular anisotropy (Chaudhari et al., 1973). The condition $K_{eff} = K_u - \frac{1}{2}\mu_0 M_s^2 > 0$ ($K_{eff} = K_u - 2\pi M_s^2 > 0$), required to obtain perpendicular magnetization, can therefore be readily achieved in each case over a useful temperature range. Figure 10.5 demonstrates, however, that this feature is not without cost. Namely, the compensation temperature varies rapidly with composition, at a rate of about 50°K/at %, implying that compositional and batch-to-batch uniformity must be high to provide reliable system performance. The degree of uniformity required depends on a complicated interplay of system read and write parameters.

Figure 10.5 shows that the Curie temperature is much less sensitive to alloy composition and, to a first approximation, may be regarded as constant over the range of perpendicular anisotropy. However, it can be altered deliberately to advan-

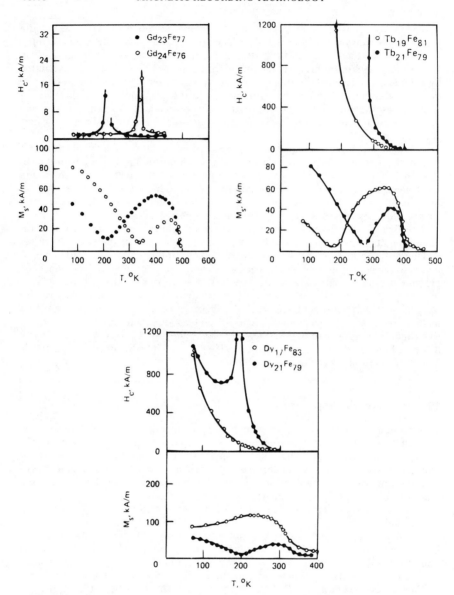

FIGURE 10.4 Magnetization and coercivity of various rare-earth-Fe films versus temperature. Each film shows a compensation temperature characterized by zero net moment and infinite coercivity (*after Mimura et al., 1978*).

tage in ternary and quaternary alloys by substituting for the base rare-earth and transition-metal elements. Figure 10.6 shows the result of substituting transition metals T at levels up to about 10 at % in $Tb_{0.2} (Fe_{1-x}T_x)_{0.8}$ alloys. There is some uncertainty in the exact values of dT_c/dx because of difficulties in measuring x, but a value of about 10°K/at % Co seems reasonable from the published data and the

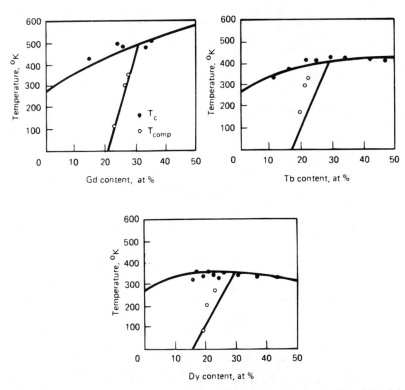

FIGURE 10.5 Variation of Curie and compensation temperatures for the films of Fig. 6.4, versus rare-earth content (*after Mimura et al., 1978*).

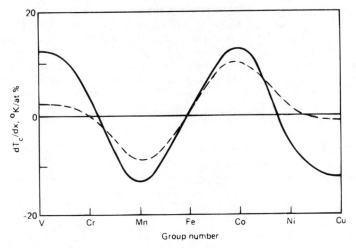

FIGURE 10.6 Variation of Curie temperature with substitution of small amounts of various transition metals in amorphous $Tb_{0.2}(Fe_{1-x}T_x)_{0.8}$ (dashed) and in crystalline $Fe_{1-x}T_x$ (solid line) materials.

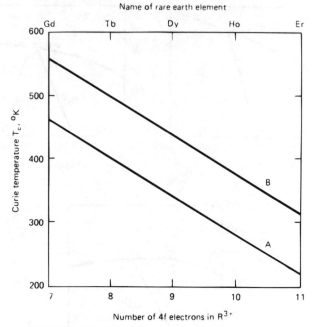

FIGURE 10.7   Variation of Curie temperature with substitution of various rare earths for Tb in (curve A) $(Tb_{1-x}R_x)_{0.2}Fe_{0.8}$ and (curve B) $(Tb_{1-x}R_x)_{0.2}(Fe_{0.9}Co_{0.1})_{0.8}$ where x is determined from the average number of $4f$ electrons in the alloy (*after Uchiyama, 1986*).

corresponding result for crystalline $Fe_{1-x}T$ alloys. Figure 10.7 shows the equivalent results of substituting heavy rare earths R for Tb in $(Tb_{1-x}R_x)_{0.2} Fe_{0.8}$ and $(Tb_{1-x}R_x)_{0.2} (Fe_{0.9} Co_{0.1})_{0.8}$ alloys (Uchiyama, 1986). In this case, the Curie temperature is found empirically to vary linearly with the average number of $4f$ electrons for the full range of x, when R is Gd, Tb, Dy, Ho, and Er. (To the accuracy of the measurements, the Curie temperature could possibly vary linearly with the deGennes factor rather than the number of $4f$ electrons.) There have been many attempts to derive mean-field parameters from these results (Gangulee and Kobliska, 1978). While there are numerous intricacies involved in obtaining reliable parameters, the values for the magnetic moment and exchange integrals in Table 10.2 express the observed trends.

TABLE 10.2   The Magnetic Moment of the Transition Metal and Exchange Integrals for Amorphous Gd-Co, Gd-Fe, and Tb-Fe Alloys

Material	TM moment, m_B	Exchange Integral, J		
		J_{TM-TM}	J_{RE-TM}	J_{RE-RE}
Gd-Co	1.2	25×10^{-22}	-2.5×10^{-22}	0.3×10^{-22}
Gd-Fe	1.9	$\approx 10 \times 10^{-22}$	-1.7×10^{-22}	0.3×10^{-22}
Tb-Fe	1.9	$\approx 10 \times 10^{-22}$	-1.0×10^{-22}	0.3×10^{-22}

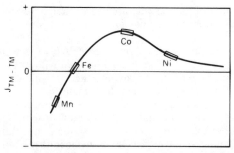

FIGURE 10.8 Bethe curve for the dependence of the exchange integral $J_{TM\text{-}TM}$ on the normalized interatomic spacing r. The boxes indicate the expected variation in spacing for each amorphous metal. A negative exchange integral results in antiferromagnetic ordering (*after Taylor and Gangulee, 1982*).

There are several features to note. First, the magnetic moment of the transition metal is independent of the rare-earth element. In contrast, the transition metal moment decreases rapidly on going from Fe-based to Co-based alloys (Masui et al., 1984). While this parallels the trend in the corresponding crystalline alloys, the moments themselves are smaller in the amorphous phase. There are both qualitative similarities and quantitative differences in these results that relate to the electronic density of states of the two phases, a topic that will be pursued further in Sec. 10.2.4.

Second, while $J_{TM\text{-}TM}$ dominates the other exchange forces in all the alloys, its value in Fe-based alloys is considerably smaller than in Co-based alloys. One explanation (Taylor and Gangulee, 1982; Mansuripur et al., 1985) is based on the Bethe curve for the variation of $J_{TM\text{-}TM}$ with normalized interatomic distance, shown in Fig. 10.8 (Bozorth, 1951). Owing to the reduction with separation for distances below the Goldschmidt radius and the range of interatomic distances that occur in these amorphous alloys, the average $J_{Fe\text{-}Fe}$ experiences a large downward displacement from its value in crystalline Fe. Indeed, it is conceivable that a fraction of the iron subnetwork might be antiferromagnetically coupled. It follows that a simple two-subnetwork mean-field theory cannot be expected to provide a detailed description of the Fe-based alloys. In contrast, $J_{Co\text{-}Co}$ is not similarly sensitive to interatomic separation, and neither downward displacement of $J_{Co\text{-}Co}$ nor significant deviations from the mean-field theory are to be expected.

Finally, the mean-field parameters themselves provide an estimate of the exchange stiffness $A(T)$. For nearest-neighbor exchange, it has been shown (Gangulee and Kobliska, 1978) that

$$A(T) = \tfrac{1}{6}N \sum_{i=1}^{n} B_i(T)X_i \sum_{j=1}^{n} B_j(T)J_{ij}Z_{ij}r_{ij}^2 \qquad (10.1)$$

where $B_i(T)$ = Brillouin function that represents the total angular momentum of atom i

X_i = atomic fraction of atom i

r_{ij}, J_{ij} = interatomic distance and exchange interaction between nearest neighbor atoms i and j

Z_{ij} = number of j atoms that are nearest neighbors of atom i
N = total number of atoms per unit volume

Figure 10.3 shows the result for the simple two-network mean-field model for a Tb-Fe alloy. The exact quantitative value must be used with caution, but the order of magnitude of $A(T)$ and its temperature dependence are vital to both the understanding of domain stability and wall width in these materials.

Figure 10.4 also shows how the coercivity varies with temperature in Fe-based alloys. The Gd alloys are qualitatively different from the others in that the coercivity is highly peaked around the compensation temperature but falls precipitously to values less than 4 kA/m [50 Oe] over most of the temperature range. In principle, this material is suited for compensation-point writing, but its small coercive energy density ($(\mu_0/2)M_sH_c \sim 10^2$ J/m^3 ($M_sH_c \sim 10^3$ erg/cm^3) precludes the formation of stable submicrometer domains (Kryder et al., 1983). The coercivity of both the Tb and Dy alloys has a different character. While still peaked around the compensation temperature, the coercivity falls much more slowly, and the coercive energy density [$\sim 10^4$ J/m^3 ($\sim 10^5$ erg/cm^3)] is several orders of magnitude larger. Submicrometer-sized domains are therefore stable throughout the system operation range.

A clue to the origin of this behavior is provided by Fig. 10.9, in which the anisotropy constant K_u is plotted versus rare-earth content x in $(Gd_{1-x}R_x)_{0.3}Co_{0.7}$ alloys (Sato et al., 1985). Upon substitution of non-S-state ions, changes are induced in K_u, the magnitude and direction of which are proportional to the magnitude and sign of the local anisotropy effects of the rare-earth ion in corresponding crystalline alloys. For Tb-substitution in particular, the result is an increase of K_u by over an order of magnitude at the point at which the Gd has been completely replaced. The conclusion is that the magnetic anisotropy of Tb-based alloys is dominated by local forces at each Tb site that arise from pair ordering of Fe atoms in the plane of the film (Nishihara et al., 1978). On average, these forces align each $4f$ electron cloud in the plane of the film, with its electron spin perpendicular to the plane, in analogy with the crystal-field effects that occur in the corresponding crystalline alloys. This mechanism is crucial for obtaining materials with large magnetic anisotropy and, as a consequence, with small wall widths that allow high-density recording.

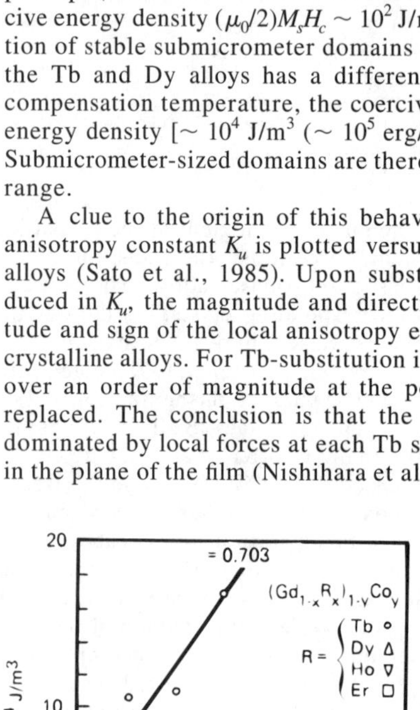

Numerous mechanisms have been proposed for the origin of the alignment forces. Of these, pair ordering (Mizoguchi and Cargill, 1979) and internal planar stress due to substrate constraint (Takagi et al., 1979) are most significant in good-quality material. Since both are subject to variation and control by adjustments to the deposition process, the deposition conditions are generally chosen to minimize the internal planar stress near room temperature. The value of K_u in stress-free Tb-Fe alloys made by magnetron sputtering has a peak anisotropy

FIGURE 10.9 Variation of anisotropy constant K_u in $(Gd_{1-x}R_x)_{1-y}Co_y$ versus amount x of substituted rare earth, for R = (Tb, Dy, Ho, and Er) and for alloys with $y \simeq 0.7$ (*after R. Sato et al., 1985*).

of about 3×10^5 J/m^3 [3×10^6 erg/cm^3] (van Dover et al., 1985), although variations in K_u by a factor of about 2 to 4 can be induced by modifying the degree of resputtering during growth (Okamine et al., 1985). Conveniently, the peak values occur across the region of most interest for recording media, namely, between 15 and 25 at % Tb.

Armed with this information for the Tb-based alloys, it is reasonable to write (Alben et al., 1978)

$$K_u(T) \simeq NW_{Tb} \, X_{Tb} \, B_{Tb}^2(T) \tag{10.2}$$

where W_{Tb} is a phenomenological parameter that expresses the strength of the single-ion anisotropy at each Tb site, and the other parameters are taken from the mean-field theory. While W_{Tb} must depend implicitly on the degree of pair ordering, and therefore on alloy composition, the expression itself is quite different qualitatively and quantitatively from that for S-state ions (Mansuripur et al., 1985), where dipolar interactions are assumed to lead to the anisotropy (Gangulee and Kobliska, 1978; Mizoguchi and Cargill, 1979). A typical result is shown in Fig. 10.3 for the simple two-network model for a Tb-Fe alloy. Again the precise values must be used with caution, but the order of magnitude and temperature dependence are vital for the studies of domain recording and stability.

There is as yet no detailed argument for the relationship between magnetic anisotropy and the wall coercivity in these non-S-state rare-earth alloys. However, since the exact orientation of each non-S-state rare-earth moment is set by the competition between single-ion anisotropy and exchange (Harris et al., 1978), there will be a scatter of the moments about the easy axis from site to site. The ensuing fluctuations can stabilize domains because the wall energy can be minimized by deforming the wall so that it passes through regions of lower-than-average anisotropy (Alben et al., 1978). Movement of the wall away from this optimized location can then be achieved only by thermal activation over a magnetic field-dependent energy barrier. The correlation length of the fluctuations will be comparable with the wall width, unlike the situation in crystalline materials where wall pinning is infrequent and defect related. The result is an intrinsic mechanism for the wall coercivity, in that it is a feature of the natural fluctuations of the amorphous state of non-S-state alloys and does not occur in Gd-based alloys.

Intrinsic coercivities of this type are not observed as a static coercive force (Egami, 1973). Rather, the process should be treated statistically as wall diffusion that is accelerated both by temperature and applied field. Studies of the characteristic time for magnetization reversal at various temperatures versus inverse magnetic field for a Tb$_{0.21}$Fe$_{0.79}$ alloy have been made (Connell and Allen, 1981). The conclusion is that any finite field is sufficient to cause wall movement, but for well-chosen medium and system parameters, data recorded in micrometer-sized domains will not be endangered in 10 years of exposure to magnetic fields and temperatures that might be expected to occur under normal operating conditions.

The initial stage of the magnetization reversal process in a uniformly magnetized film appears to occur by the growth of a small number of nuclei that form soon after the reversal field is applied (Connell and Allen, 1981). The number of these nuclei varies inversely with the size of the magnetizing field (Ohashi et al., 1979), but the origin and number of nuclei in well-magnetized films present interesting but unanswered questions (Harris, 1980). For magnetooptical recording, however, the nucleation process during field-driven magnetization reversal is not of great concern. Instead domain nucleation is achieved thermomagnetically by cooling the medium

TABLE 10.3 Magnetic Properties of Various Amorphous Rare-Earth Transition-Metal Alloys (*After Heltmann et al., 1986*).

Material	Curie temp. T_c, °K	Compensation temp. T_{comp}, °K	Coercive energy density M_sH_c, 10^4 j/m^3	Anisotropy constant K_u, 10^4 j/m^3	Kerr† rotation θ_K, deg.
$Tb_{23}Fe_{77}$	400	300	4	30	0.23
$Tb_{21}Co_{79}$	. . .	300	4	14	0.33
$Gd_{26}Fe_{74}$	480	300	0.02	2.5	0.29
$Gd_{21}Co_{79}$	. . .	300	0.02	1	0.33
$Tb_{22}Fe_{66}Co_{12}$	~500	<300	8	10	0.38
$Gd_{22}Tb_4Fe_{74}$	450	300	1.5	4	0.30
$Gd_{16}Tb_6Co_{78}$	. . .	280	1 .1	4	0.32

†Measured second surface at 633 nm.

through the Curie temperature in a reverse field. The ensuing stability is then determined by the wall coercivity described earlier.

Table 10.3 summarizes the properties of the alloys that have been discussed. The polar Kerr rotation θ_K has been measured at 633 nm through the supporting glass substrate, and a reflectivity of about 0.45 is typical of all the alloys. The relation between θ_K and the magnetooptical component r_y is given in Sec. 10.3.4. The Tb-Fe-Co alloys are presently favored for their combination of high magnetic anisotropy, high coercive-energy density, and optimized Curie temperature. The addition of a fourth element to improve corrosion resistance will be discussed in Sec. 10.2.6.

10.2.4 Magnetooptical Effect and Electronic Properties

Many empirical efforts have been made to increase the magnetooptical effect of amorphous rare-earth transition-metal alloys. These efforts have been retarded by the lack of any workable model for the relation between the electronic structure and the optical properties of highly disordered metals. Recently, ideas that were originally proposed for the optical properties of amorphous semiconductors (Hindley, 1970) have been extended (Connell and Bloomberg, 1985; Connell, 1986) to develop a model that, as a minimum, provides useful guidelines for materials engineering. It recognizes that the usual free-electron model of optical conductivity fails when the structural disorder is large, because the uncertainty in the wavevector becomes comparable to the wavevector itself. Under these conditions, the optical absorption can be described by a convolution of filled and empty states that are separated by the photon energy, together with a weakly energy-dependent matrix element. The magnetooptical properties then follow in the same manner from the difference between the optical absorption of left and right circularly polarized light (Bennett and Stern, 1965).

In this approach, the frequency dependence of the conductivity, $\sigma^{xx} = \sigma_1^{xx} + j\sigma_2^{xx}$, can be described solely in terms of transitions between filled and empty states separated by energy ω and occurring with a dipole matrix element $|x|^2$. When spin-flip contributions that occur through spin-orbit interaction are treated as negligible in comparison with spin-conserving transitions, the absorptive component of the conductivity, σ_1^{xx}, becomes a sum of separate contributions from spin-up and spin-down electron states. Thus the contribution from spin-up states is

$$\sigma_{1,u}^{xy}(\omega) \sim \omega^2 |x|^2 \int_{E_f - \omega}^{E_f} \frac{N_u(E_f - E)N_u(E_f + \omega - E)dE}{\omega} \tag{10.3}$$

The contribution from spin-down states is formally identical but, because of exchange splitting in magnetic materials, the two contributions must be evaluated separately. It has been found empirically that the dipole matrix element for the classical oscillator provides a good estimate of $|x|^2$ in amorphous Ge and Si (Jackson et al., 1985). Therefore, with this approximation,

$$\sigma_{1,u}^{xy}(\omega) \sim \frac{1}{\omega^2 + \Delta^2} \int_{E_f - \omega}^{E_f} \frac{N_u(E_f - E)N_u(E_f + \omega - E)dE}{\omega} \tag{10.4}$$

where Δ is a fitting parameter of the order of the bandwidth. The frequency dependence of σ^{xx} can therefore be derived directly from the electronic density of states. From an expansion of the density of states near E_f, it can be shown that the frequency dependence of the conductivity is Drude-like, but the parameter formerly interpreted as a relaxation time is now proportional to the logarithmic derivative of the density of states at the Fermi energy (Connell and Bloomberg, 1985).

The polar Kerr effect is determined by the off-diagonal conductivity, $\sigma^{xy} = \sigma_1^{xy} + j\sigma_2^{xy}$, and results from the difference between the absorption of left and right circularly polarized light. When spin-flip processes are again neglected, the off-diagonal absorptive component of the conductivity, σ_2^{xy}, is the sum of separate contributions from spin-up and spin-down electron states. For spin-up states it is

$$\sigma_{2,u}^{xy}(\omega) \sim \omega^2 (|r_-|^2 - |r_+|^2) \int_{E_f - \omega}^{E_f} \frac{N_u(E_f - E)N_u(E_f + \omega - E)dE}{\omega} \tag{10.5}$$

where $|r_-^2|$ and $|r_+^2|$ are the dipole matrix elements for left and right circularly polarized light, respectively. Making the harmonic oscillator approximation for the matrix elements as before

$$\sigma_{2,u}^{xy}(\omega) \sim \frac{\omega}{(\omega^2 + \Delta^2)^2} H_u \int_{E_f - \omega}^{E_f} \frac{N_u(E_f - E)N_u(E_f + \omega - E)\,dE}{\omega} \tag{10.6}$$

where H_u is an effective field seen by the spin-up electrons as the result of the spin-orbit interaction and is of opposite sign for transitions between spin-down states. Therefore, above the Curie temperature, where the spin polarization is zero, $\sigma_2^{xy} = 0$. On the other hand, σ_2^{xy} depends on both the spin-orbit interaction and the spin polarization at low temperature, and specific information about the density of states is needed for a discussion of its behavior.

Theoretical work (Malozemoff et al., 1983) provides important insights into the development of the electronic density of states in amorphous transition metal alloys and, in particular, into the role that is played by the rare earth in developing the magnetism in amorphous 12-coordinated iron. Hybridization between the rare-earth and Fe d states leads to a strong depression of the density of states at the top of the Fe d band and an accompanying accumulation of states at lower energy, sufficient to satisfy the Stoner criterion. A clear gap also separates the Fe-dominated low-lying band from the higher-lying rare-earth band. The location of the Fermi level and the net moment per Fe atom are found to be very sensitive to the Fe-Fe distance. However, the minority spin density is always much greater than the majority spin density at the Fermi energy, and optical effects for photon energies less than 2 to 3 eV should be dominated by transitions within the minority states. Experimental photoemission and inverse photoemission measurements on amorphous $Tb_{0.25}Fe_{0.75}$ (Connell et al., 1984) appear to confirm these views.

Figure 10.10 summarizes the results. The parts of the density of states represented by solid lines are derived directly from the experimental measurements, while those represented by broken lines are estimated using the hybridization scheme proposed. These data provide the basis for the comparison of the measured and calculated magnetooptical properties of Tb-Fe-based alloys. The measured conductivity $\sigma_1^{xx}(\omega)$ is nearly frequency-independent between 0 and 3 eV, with a value of about 5×10^5 $(\Omega \cdot m)^{-1}$ (5×10^{15} sec^{-1}). This is consistent with the conductivity calculated from Eq. (10.4) using $\Delta = 10$ eV. The contributions to the conductivity from transitions within the nearly full Fe majority spin band can be neglected. The calculation shows that the Fe d states dominate the conductivity

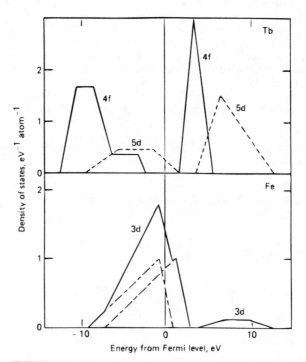

FIGURE 10.10   The local electronic density of states at Fe and Tb sites versus energy relative to the Fermi level. Solid lines are derived from experimental measurements; dashed lines for Tb are estimates for the hybridized bonding and antibonding states; dashed lines for Fe are estimates for the spin-up and spin-down bands (*after Connell, 1986*).

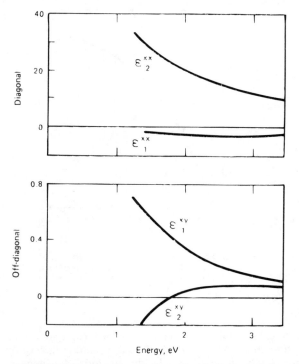

FIGURE 10.11 Experimental diagonal and off-diagonal elements of the complex dielectric tensor $\varepsilon = \varepsilon_1 + j\varepsilon_2$ versus photon energy (*after Connell, 1986*).

behavior below 3 eV, although transitions between Tb d and f states begin to occur at about 1.5 eV and provide a significant contribution by 3 eV.

The experimental diagonal and off-diagonal elements of the dielectric tensor, shown in Fig. 10.11, suggest that

$$\frac{\varepsilon_1^{xy}(\omega)}{\varepsilon_2^{xx}(\omega)} = \frac{\sigma_2^{xy}(\omega)}{\sigma_1^{xx}(\omega)} \approx \text{const} \tag{10.7}$$

to within a factor of 2 for the range $1 \le \hbar\omega \le 3$ eV. This is qualitatively similar to the simple prediction of Eqs. (10.4) and (10.6) for $\Delta \approx 10$ eV and $H_u = \text{constant}$. Quantitative agreement will require better approximations for both the matrix element and density of states used in Eqs. (10.4) and (10.6), and the inclusion of the contribution of the Tb d-to-f transitions to $\sigma_2^{xy}(\omega)$ in the range $2 \le \hbar\omega \le 3$ eV. Nevertheless, there is an indication that contributions to $\sigma_2^{xy}(\omega)$ from d-to-f transitions in light rare earths that occur near 1 eV should enhance r_y.

There are a number of major points that come out of this. First, the Fe d states dominate the magnetooptical properties, as they do the conductivity at energies below 3 eV, explaining the long-known relation between the polar Kerr and extraordinary Hall effects. The similarity of the temperature dependences of the magnetization of the Fe subnetwork and the polar Kerr effect is also rationalized.

Second, variations of $\sigma_2^{xy}(\omega)$ at low temperatures in $\text{Tb}_x(\text{Fe}_{1-y}\text{T}_y)_{1-x}$ alloys,

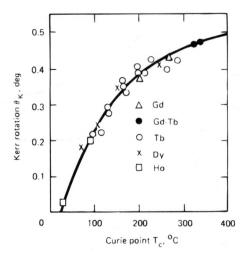

FIGURE 10.12 Kerr rotation angle θ_K versus Curie temperature for various rare-earth-substituted Fe-Co alloy films (*after Uchiyama, 1986*).

where T is a transition metal that replaces Fe in small amounts $y \leq 0.1$, should occur largely through changes within the Fe d states rather than through changes in the spin-orbit interaction. For example, the measured dependence of σ_2^{xy} at low temperatures on Co, Mn, V, or Cu substitution can all be explained in this way (Connell et al., 1982). The increase that is found at 300°K with Co substitution then derives almost entirely from the increase in Curie temperature. Figure 10.12, which shows the polar Kerr rotation at 300°K versus Curie temperature for numerous rare-earth Fe-Co alloys, confirms this viewpoint (Uchiyama, 1986). While this is extremely significant for magnetooptical recording, there is no intrinsic enhancement of σ_2^{xy}. Figure 10.6 shows that some substitutions cause very little change of the Curie temperature, and there is only a small reduction of the magnetooptical conversivity (Smith, 1965a). Therefore, these substitutions can improve the oxidation or corrosion resistance of the alloy, the price paid in magnetooptical performance is small.

The third and final point is that, while Tb d-to-f transitions do not contribute to σ_2^{xy} at energies of interest for magnetooptical recording, the results obtained suggest that enhancements of $\sigma_2^{xy}(\omega)$ over its value in Tb-Fe should be possible in $(Tb_{1-y}R_y)_xFe_{1-x}$ alloys when R is a suitable light rare earth. Photoemission and inverse photoemission data for Tb, Gd, Sm, and Nd metals (Lang et al., 1981) suggest that both Nd and Sm substitution should produce useful enhancements in the low-temperature value of σ_2^{xy}, because transitions between their d and f states are possible at energies between 1 and 2 eV. There should be no such contribution upon substituting Gd.

Figure 10.13 shows the change in the low temperature value of the polar Kerr rotation, measured at 2 eV, versus Nd and Sm substitution. As expected $\Delta\theta_K(0)$ is positive, with Sm substitution being especially effective. This is consistent with work on Nd and Pr alloys with iron and cobalt (Gambino and McGuire, 1986). The maximum improvement obtained, however, still leaves the value of r_y much below

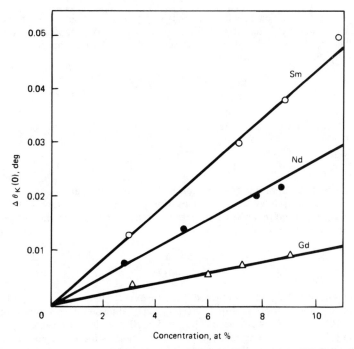

FIGURE 10.13 Measured change of the low temperature value of the polar Kerr rotation of $Tb_{0.2}(Fe_{1-y}R_y)_{0.8}$ alloys versus concentration of substituted rare-earth element R, where R is Gd, Nd, or Sm (*after Connell, 1986*).

those shown in Table 10.1 for crystalline Mn-Bi and Pt-Mn-Sb. Figure 10.13 also shows that $\Delta\theta_K(0)$ for Gd substitution is small.

10.2.5 Domain Formation and Stability

The process of thermomagnetic recording involves the formation of a reverse-magnetized domain in the region of the hot spot produced by a focused laser beam and the ensuing growth or contraction of this domain as the heating and subsequent cooling progresses. The approach used to assess the stability of the domain at any point during the recording process follows the analysis established for magnetic bubble domains (Thiele, 1970), in which a cylindrical domain is assumed to be already present in the film, and its wall is subject in general to a contracting or expanding radial force. In bubble materials, a domain is stable when this force is exactly zero. In magnetooptical materials, the condition for domain stability is less stringent, because a force on the domain wall must overcome the large wall coercivity of these materials for domain collapse or expansion to occur (Huth, 1974).

This principle is most readily used to obtain the conditions for domain stability when the temperature distribution in the film is uniform (Kryder et al., 1983). There are four contributions to the energy formation of the domain (Mansuripur and Connell, 1984): the external field energy, the anisotropy energy, the exchange energy, and the self (demagnetizing) energy. The force on the domain wall may then be calculated by differentiating the total energy E_t with respect to the domain radius. The minimum stable domain diameter, obtained when this force is exactly balanced by the coercive force, is

$$d_0 = \frac{4\,(AK_u)^{1/2}}{\mu_0 M_s (H_c - H)} + \frac{M_s L_f}{2\,(H_c - H)}\, Q\left(\frac{r}{L_f}\right) \tag{10.8}$$

where H_c = coercivity
   r = domain radius
   L_f = film thickness
   Q = complicated function of r/L_f

Typical amorphous rare-earth transition-metal materials that are used for magnetooptical recording have their compensation point near room temperature; thus $M_s \approx 0$ and the applied recording fields are much less than H_c. Consequently, a good estimate of the minimum domain size is

$$d_0 \approx \frac{4(AK_u)^{1/2}}{\mu_0 M_s H_c} \tag{10.9}$$

The magnitude of d_0 can be obtained from the experimental data in Table 10.3 and the mean field value for A in Eq. (10.1). Typical values at room temperature are $\mu_0 M_s H_c = 10^4$ J/m^3 [$M_s H_c = 10^5$ erg/cm^3], $K_u \approx 5 \times 10^5$ J/m^3 [5×10^6 erg/cm^3] and $A \approx 10^{-12}$ J/m [10^{-7} erg/cm]. The minimum domain size d_0 is therefore about 50 nm at room temperature. For small excursions about room temperature, the coercive energy density decreases slowly with temperature, indicating that variations of d_0 will be controlled by the temperature dependence of the wall energy. Since this decreases with temperature, as shown by the mean field results in Fig. 10.3, domains stable at room temperature will remain stable over a reasonable system operating range. The currently available magnetooptical media can therefore be pushed to much higher recording densities when the optical-head technology is improved.

Equation (10.9) provides an important design rule for the preferred magnetic characteristics of the magnetooptical media. At first examination, it might appear that the requirement is for materials with low wall energy and high coercive-energy density. However, these are mutually exclusive for the following reason: in the non-S-state rare-earth alloys, the wall coercivity derives from fluctuations in the anisotropy constant, as explained earlier, and these fluctuations are greater in materials with larger K_u. It is therefore reasonable to write

$$H_c \approx \chi\, \frac{K_u}{\mu_0 M_s} \tag{10.10}$$

where $\chi \approx 10^{-2}$ is the ratio of the average fluctuation in K_u to the mean value of K_u. It follows that

$$d_0 \approx \frac{1}{\chi}\left(\frac{A}{K_u}\right)^{1/2} = \frac{\delta_w}{\chi} \tag{10.11}$$

where δ_w is the domain-wall width parameter. The minimum domain diameter thus scales with the wall width.

The appropriate design rule therefore is to engineer materials with small exchange stiffness and large magnetic anisotropy. Since the magnitude of A is almost

TABLE 10.4 Thermal and Optical Properties of Materials Used in Media Engineering

Layer	Complex refractive index	Specific heat J/cm³/°K	Thermal conductivity, J/cm/°K/s	Diffusivity, cm²/s
Substrate	1.46	1.7	0.002	0.0012
Aluminum	$2 + 7.1i$	2.7	2.4	0.89
Quartz	1.5	2.0	0.015	0.0075
Tb-Fe	$3.6 + 3.7i$	2.6	0.16	0.062

entirely determined by J_{TM-TM} and J_{TM-RE} in Eq. (10.1), it follows from the earlier discussion of the mean-field data that the first requirement, small exchange stiffness, is best met in Fe-based alloys. The second requirement, large magnetic anisotropy, requires the presence of a non-S-state rare earth that has a large single-ion anisotropy term W_{RE} in Eq. (10.2), and this is best met in Tb-based alloys. It therefore appears that Tb-Fe-based alloys provide the best prospect for high density recording.

The behavior of the spin system under conditions of thermomagnetic writing can be investigated only by intensive computer simulations (Mansuripur and Connell, 1984). There are no simple expressions for the contributions to the total energy because the radial changes in the magnetic film temperature during the recording process make each individual energy contribution a complicated integral of radius and time. Nevertheless, the evolution of the domain energetics can be followed, and considerable insight into the process can be gained from numerical results.

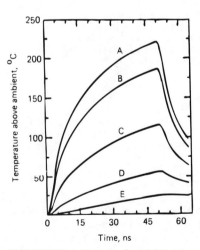

FIGURE 10.14 Increase in temperature within the magnetic film of a quadrilayer (described in the text) versus time, generated by a 5-mW, 50-ns pulse from a beam with full-width-at-half-maximum $W = 0.83$ μm. Curves are for different radii: (curve A) 0, (curve B) 250 nm, (curve C) 500 nm, (curve D) 750 nm, and (curve E) 1000 nm (*after Mansuripur and Connell, 1984*).

As an example, consider the simulated recording of a quadrilayer medium (see Fig. 10.1b) consisting of a 50-nm-thick aluminum layer, an 80-nm-thick quartz intermediate layer, a 15-nm-thick magnetic layer, and a 120-nm-thick quartz overlayer. (The thermal and optical parameters used in the calculation are given in Table 10.4.) The procedure is as follows: first, calculations are made of the temperature profiles that develop in the magnetic material when a 5-mW, 50-ns pulse from a Ga-As laser is focused to a Gaussian spot of 1-μm diameter at the e^{-1} point. These are shown in Fig. 10.14 for different radii and times. Second, the total magnetic energy E_t for domain formation is calculated versus domain radius at different times during the heating and cooling cycle, using the magnetic properties represented by Fig. 10.3 and Eq. (10.10) and assuming an applied field of 32 kA/m [400 Oe]. (These properties are typical of good magnetooptical materials and system operating conditions.) The results are shown in Fig. 10.15. At $r = 0$, before the laser is switched on, the total energy is an increasing function of radius, and therefore no re-

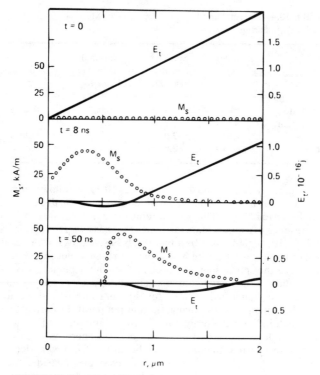

FIGURE 10.15 Magnetization M_s and net magnetic energy E_t produced on formation of a domain in the quadrilayer of Fig. 10.14 versus domain radius r. The magnetization M_s is given by the dotted curve. Three graphs are shown: at $t = 0$ (just before heating), and at times $t = 8$ and 50 ns during heating (*after Mansuripur and Connell, 1984*).

versed domain of any radius can be formed. At $t = 8$ nS, there is a minimum of energy around 500 nm, and the coercivity at $r = 0$ is less than the applied field. Domain nucleation therefore occurs, and the domain expands until the force on the wall is balanced by the wall coercivity. This condition is met when

$$\left(\frac{\partial E_t}{\partial r} \right)_{r_c} = 4\pi\mu_0 r_c L_f M_s (r_c) H_c(r_c) \tag{10.12}$$

which will occur at some radius r_c less than 500 nm. At $t = 50$ nS, the end of the heating period, points at $r \leqq 520$ nm are above the Curie temperature, and the minimum of energy has moved to $r = 1200$ nm. The domain wall itself, however, will not progress beyond $r = 1000$ nm because of the effect of the wall coercivity.

The calculations also demonstrate the relative importance of the different contributions to the total energy. In this example, the self-energy is much smaller than the other terms. This is a feature of the magnetic characteristics and medium design chosen. Were the magnetic film greater than 100 nm thick or had it a much lower compensation temperature, the self-energy could no longer be ignored. For system optimization, such a situation might be an advantage since recording could then be achieved with lower applied fields. The disadvantage is that erasure would require relatively greater applied fields to overcome the larger demagnetizing field.

The total energy curves for the cooling period can also be calculated. It is found that depending on the position of the wall at a given instant, the forces on the domain wall can be contractive or expansive. Just after the end of the laser pulse, when coercivities are low and the wall is between the center of the beam and the radius of minimum energy, the forces tend to be expansive and prevent the written spot from collapsing. By the time the temperature drops back to room temperature, the coercivities have increased drastically, and despite the presence of contractive forces, there is no longer any danger of domain collapse.

Similar considerations apply to the erasure process. It is found that if the demagnetizing energy is negligible, it is possible to erase the recorded spots without an external field or in the presence of only a small reverse field by raising the local temperature until the coercivity drops below the contractive forces that act on the domain wall. If the demagnetizing energy is large, however, an appreciable external field in the reverse direction together with local heating is needed to achieve erasure. The erasure process in this case is likely to be a combination of two processes: nucleation of a new domain within the recorded spot and the destabilization and contraction of the recorded spot itself. If the reverse field is not large enough, the process could lead to partial erasure and the creation of ring-like domains.

10.2.6 Exchange-Coupled Magnetic Multilayers

Up to this point we have considered "simple" media structures only; the word simple in this context implies that although the medium might contain a stack of dielectric and metallic layers, its magnetic constituent is a single, uniform film with a fixed chemical composition. Such media designs are highly practical and, in fact, single-magnetic-layer constructs are the only type of media that are commercially available at the time of writing. For the purpose of studying the physics of thermomagnetic recording, we have relied on single-magnetic-layer media to the exclusion of all others, since these simplest of structures exhibit the most essential features of the recording and erasure processes. There exist, however, more complex media designs with two or more magnetic layers in contact with each other. Such designs provide additional degrees of freedom and create possibilities for enhancing performance or introducing new features to the media. In this section we shall describe three types of exchange-coupled magnetic multilayers, and discuss the specific improvements and new modes of operation that these designs engender.

10.2.6.1 Magnetic Capping Layer for Lowering the Write/Erase Field. A double-layer magnetic structure has been proposed for reducing the required external field for writing and erasure (Yamada et al., 1991). This double-layer design, shown in Fig. 10.16a, consists of the usual Tb-Fe-Co layer with perpendicular magnetization, and a second layer consisting of either CoPt alloy or amorphous RE–TM alloy with in-plane magnetization. The two layers are coupled by mutual exchange interaction at the interface. During writing and erasure, the external field lifts the magnetization of the in-plane layer, which in turn will pull or push the magnetization of the perpendicular layer in the desired direction (Fig. 10.16b). This assistance from the forces of exchange helps reduce the external field required for recording and erasure. Accordingly, it has been reported that optimum recording by magnetic field modulation can in this case be achieved with as little as ± 50 Oe of external field. Figure 10.16c shows measured data of carrier and noise in readout versus the

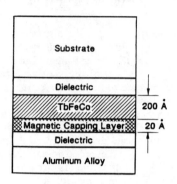

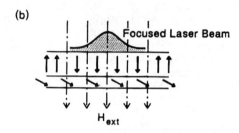

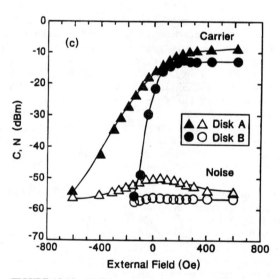

FIGURE 10.16 (*a*) Schematic diagram of a multilayer magneto-optical disk incorporating a magnetic capping layer in conjunction with the regular MO layer. The capping layer has in-plane magnetization. (*b*) During thermomagnetic recording the applied field forces the magnetization of the capping layer out of the plane, which pulls the magnetization of the MO layer along, thus facilitating the reversal process. (*c*) Measured carrier and noise levels as functions of the write field for two disks, one without the capping layer (disk A) and one with the capping layer (disk B). The disk with the capping layer has a sharper threshold and can operate with smaller magnetic fields (*after Yamada et al., 1991*).

applied magnetic field for writing for two disks referred to as A and B. The disks were identical except for a 20 Å capping layer deposited on the MO layer of disk B. The transition region between fully recorded and fully erased states is much narrower in disk B, a characteristic that enables magnetic-field-modulation recording on this disk to be achieved with a small, low-power magnetic head and at a high recording frequency.

10.2.6.2 Direct Overwrite in Exchange-Coupled Multilayer. Direct overwrite (DOW) has been the subject of extensive research over the past few years. Aside from recording by magnetic field modulation, the most promising solutions have originated from the concept of exchange-coupled magnetic multilayers (Saito et al., 1987; Aratani et al., 1989; Tsutsumi et al., 1991). Figure 10.17 shows the essential features of one such scheme based on a triple-magnetic-layer MO disk structure. In this configuration, one magnetic layer is the storage layer, another is the "assist" layer, and a third is simply there to facilitate magnetic transitions between the other

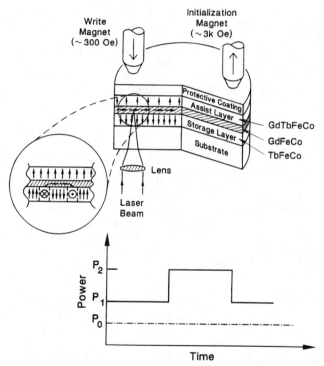

FIGURE 10.17 Direct overwrite in exchange-coupled triple-layer MO media. The initialization magnet can erase only the assist layer, since its field is weaker than the coercivity of the storage layer. The write magnet works in conjunction with high-power laser pulses, magnetizing both the assist layer and the storage layer in the "down" direction. The inset shows a recorded "down" domain in the storage layer, after the assist layer has been erased. In this case, a 180° wall between the two layers creates a quasi-stable state, which responds to a medium-power laser pulse by annihilating the "down" domain (*after Aratani et al., 1989*).

two layers. The recording scheme requires two permanent magnets, one for erasing (or initializing) the assist layer, and the other for writing. In every pass under the initializing magnet the assist layer is fully erased, but the storage layer, thanks to its high coercivity, retains its pattern of recorded domains.

For readout, the laser power is set at a low level, causing negligible heating of the magnetic layers. For writing, the laser is pulsed, either with moderate or high peak power, depending on whether the intended domain's magnetization is up ($\uparrow$) or down ($\downarrow$). The high-power pulses heat all three magnetic layers and create $\downarrow$ domains in both the storage layer and the assist layer; (the $\downarrow$ direction being set by the write magnet). Subsequent to formation of these domains, the track passes under the initializing magnet, which erases the assist layer but leaves the $\downarrow$ domain in the storage layer intact. This creates a 180° magnetic wall between the two layers, an energetically unfavorable configuration (see the inset to Fig. 10.17). Now, when a moderate pulse raises the temperature of the storage layer (but not the assist layer), this interlayer magnetic wall provides a destabilizing force and pushes the $\downarrow$ domain to annihilation. In the only other possible situation where both layers are $\uparrow$, the moderate pulse is too weak to cause any magnetization reversals. Thus the moderate-power and high-power pulses create in the storage layer the desired $\uparrow$ and $\downarrow$ domains, regardless of any previously recorded data. This is the essence of direct overwrite.

The above scheme requires a complex media-fabrication process, and perhaps the sacrifice of a few dB of CNR in exchange for DOW. There are other, more complex exchange-coupled designs for direct overwrite with certain additional advantages (such as elimination of the initializing magnet); these designs will not be reviewed here but the reader is encouraged to consult the literature (Tsutsumi et al., 1991).

10.2.6.3 Magnetically Induced Super Resolution (MSR). The MSR scheme, first proposed by researchers at Sony Corporation, arose in the course of investigations involving exchange-coupled structures for DOW (Aratani et al., 1991). There are two slightly different ways of achieving MSR, known as front-aperture detection, FAD, and rear-aperture detection, RAD. Both FAD and RAD require trilayer exchange-coupled magnetic media similar to those used for direct overwrite. As before, the role of the intermediate layer is to make the magnetic transition between the other two layers smooth. The storage layer is written onto at the time of writing, and maintains a faithful copy of the recorded data at all times. The read layer, on the other hand, receives a copy of "selected" domains from the storage layer and presents this modified version to the readout beam. It is this selective presentation of recorded domains to the read beam that achieves super-resolution, since it removes the adjacent domains at the time of reading and essentially allows the read beam to "see" one domain at a time. Selective copying is activated by the rise in media temperature induced by the read beam itself. Details of operation of the two MSR methods will now be given separately.

MSR by Front-Aperture Detection. In this method, shown schematically in Fig. 10.18a, both the storage layer and the read layer normally contain identical copies of the recorded domains. Within a small area in the rear side of the focused spot, however, the rise of temperature weakens the coupling between the layers. At this point the magnetization of the read layer in the rear aperture aligns itself with the applied field $\mathbf{H}_r$, which is always in the same direction during readout; the beam thus sees the magnetization pattern in the front aperture only. Super-resolution is achieved by virtue of the fact that intersymbol interference from the domains in the rear aperture has been eliminated. Once the disk moves away and the temperatures

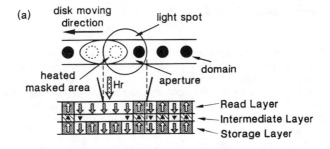

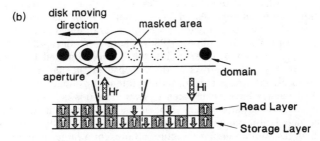

FIGURE 10.18   The principle of magnetic super-resolution (MSR) in exchange-coupled triple-layer structures. (*a*) MSR by front-aperture detection. (*b*) MSR by rear-aperture detection (*after Aratani et al., 1991*).

return to normal, interlayer exchange regains its strength and the magnetization of the read layer reverts to its original orientation.

MSR by Rear-Aperture Detection. Figure 10.18*b* shows the schematic diagram of MSR by RAD. Initially the data are recorded on both the storage layer and the read layer, but the latter is erased prior to readout by the initialization field $\mathbf{H}_i$. During readout, thermal effects of the read beam reduce the coercivity of the read layer within the rear aperture. As a result the underlying domains in the storage layer copy themselves onto the hot area of the read layer by the force of interlayer exchange (and, if necessary, by assistance from an applied $\mathbf{H}_r$). Thus super-resolution is achieved because the front aperture is erased and the only domain that is being read is within the rear aperture. When the disk moves away and the temperatures return to normal, the transferred domains persist in the read layer until such time as they are erased again by the initializing field $\mathbf{H}_i$.

Needless to say, for the above readout mechanisms to succeed, the coercivities of the read and storage layers, the read field $\mathbf{H}_r$, the initialization field $\mathbf{H}_i$, the various wall energies σ_w, and the temperature-dependence of several magnetic parameters involved must all be carefully selected. With MSR it has been possible to increase the recording densities beyond the cutoff frequency normally allowed by an objective lens. For instance, recorded mark lengths of 0.4 μm have been read with good CNR at $\lambda = 780$ nm with an objective lens having NA = 0.53 (M. Ohta et al., 1991). The drawbacks to MSR, aside from the complexity of media manufacture, are the inevitable sacrifices one will have to make in desirable media characteristics such as minimum jitter, maximum noise immunity, environmental stability, and so forth. The systems demonstrated in the laboratories to date, however, seem quite promising.

10.2.7 Chemical Stability and Aging

The stability and aging characteristics of the rare-earth transition-metal alloys have received much attention (Luborsky et al., 1985). Two independent and equally important issues have been addressed: first, the intrinsic stability of the magnetic and magnetooptical properties, and second, the stability of the magnetic information after thermomagnetic write-erase cycling. The purpose of this section is to distill some general principles from the large body of experimental work and, in so doing, expose the areas of concern.

Many studies agree that the principal mechanism of degradation of rare-earth transition-metal alloys is oxidation, particularly by OH^- species. In general, the rare-earth element has a stronger affinity for oxygen than the transition metal and tends to oxidize preferentially (Allen and Connell, 1982). The complex oxidation profile that results when unprotected Tb-Fe films are annealed in air at 200°C is shown in Fig. 10.19 (van Dover et al., 1986). There is first a rapid formation of an outer Fe_2O_3 layer on a Tb_2O_3 layer. Below these layers a mixed Tb-deficient alloy and Tb-suboxide layer then grows at the expense of the underlying unoxidized region. The process continues until the whole film is consumed.

Several approaches have been taken to overcome this potentially catastrophic failure mechanism. First, attempts have been made to reduce the oxidation rate by selecting the deposition parameters that minimize the microstructure of the film; voids, residual gas, and columnar structure all present a larger reaction surface by which oxidation can progress. As an example of what is possible, the perpendicular anisotropy of smooth, dense, magnetron-sputtered Tb-Fe-Co films changes very little on air exposure at 300°K, in contrast to similar data taken on gas-containing diode-sputtered samples (Hong et al., 1985). This result should not necessarily be taken as indicating a limitation on the diode method but rather the significant effects of microstructure on the corrosion properties.

Second, while Co-containing alloys are chemically more stable than Fe-containing alloys (Ichihara et al., 1985), the addition of a component chosen to passivate the surface of the alloy upon its first exposure to air is necessary in both cases for the best stability. It is found that the addition of small amounts of Cr to Tb-Fe alloys is most effective in this regard. Recently, it has been shown that a few atomic % of Pt, Al, or Ti also greatly improve the corrosion resistance and suppress the generation and growth of pinholes (Imamura et al., 1985). Furthermore, the addition of Pt slightly increases the polar Kerr rotation. The quaternary alloys of Tb-Fe-Co-Pt, therefore, appear to offer the best total performance characteristics.

Finally, there has been much work done to find effective protection layers between which to sandwich magnetooptical media to prevent both the direct exposure of the medium to air and the occurrence of substrate-medium interfacial reactions. The latter is a particular problem when using plastic substrates. For example, Gd-Tb-Fe films deteriorate rapidly both on polymethyl methacrylate (PMMA) substrates (M. Sato et al., 1985) and in humid conditions on 2P-coated glass substrates (Hartmann et al., 1984; Jacobs et al., 1984). As one response to this, techniques for directly formatting glass substrates have been developed (Deguchi et al., 1984), but most of the effort has been expended in finding suitable dielectric protection layers. Of those examined to date, it appears that SiO (Nagao et al., 1986), SiN (Anthony et al., 1986; Ichihara et al., 1986), AlN (Deguchi et al., 1984), ZnS (Togami et al., 1985), Al_2O_3 (Bernstein and Gueugnon, 1985), and TiO_2 (Fukunishi et al., 1985) have been used with some success. It is apparent, however, that much effort will be required in this area to find an optimum solution.

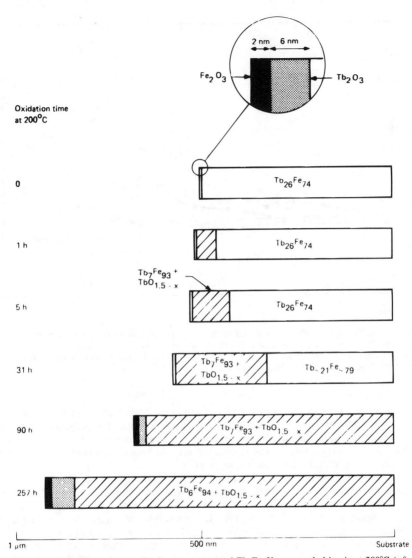

FIGURE 10.19 Oxidation profile in an unprotected Tb-Fe film, annealed in air at 200°C (*after von Dover et al., 1986*).

The preceding focus on the macroscopic magnetic and chemical properties provides an indication of both the intrinsic stability of the magnetooptical material and the stability issues in medium design. It is now possible to understand how these observed limitations affect the stored data integrity. For a multielement alloy, it was concluded that the rate-limiting factor in the life of the data is the change of K_u that occurs with thermal annealing (Luborsky et al., 1985). This is not surprising given that the magnetic anisotropy derives almost entirely from the single-ion anisotropy

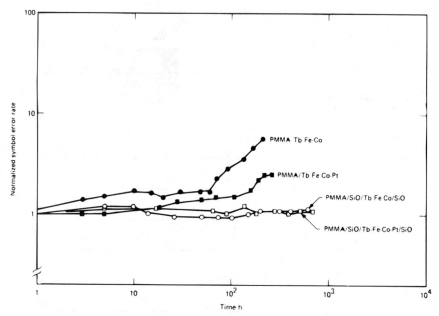

FIGURE 10.20 Symbol (8-bit) error rate on magnetooptical disk versus time, with accelerated aging at 55°C and 60% relative humidity. Results are shown for ternary and quaternary Tb-Fe alloys, with and without SiO overcoat and undercoat protection. The absence of degradation in films with SiO protection is notable (*after Nagao et al., 1986*).

of non-S-state rare earths, and the rare-earth constituents are oxidized in preference to the transition metals. Then from Arrhenius plots, it is projected that the shelf life of recorded data at 20°C is 3000 years and the number of write-erase cycles is 2×10^{11}. Actual real-time experimental results put lower bounds of greater than 5 years and 10^6 cycles on the same parameters.

While these estimates are encouraging, they completely ignore extrinsic effects, such as the existence and growth of microscopic defects that can destroy the integrity of the recorded information. These are best studied by bit error rate measurements. Figure 10.20 shows bit error rate data on various magnetooptical media that have been exposed at 55°C and 60 percent RH for different times (Nagao et al., 1986). For Tb-Fe-Co–based films with an SiO overcoat, there is no apparent increase in error rate in 1000 hours of exposure. Error maps produced during other accelerated aging experiments (Freese et al., 1985) show that observed increases in bit error rate are caused primarily by the growth of preexisting defects, rather than the nucleation of new defects. These results demonstrate that the medium design itself and the cleanliness of the preparation conditions, rather than the alloy composition, can determine the data life. Since thin films are more susceptible to pinhole formation and local crystallization during growth than thick films, the trade-off to be made between the ultimate magnetooptical performance available from a quadrilayer structure (Sec. 10.3.1) and the data integrity is a major issue for study. Finally, estimates of the aging factor for the accelerated test data in Fig. 10.20 suggest that data written on films protected by SiO will not experience degradation for many years under normal operating conditions.

10.3 MEDIA DESIGN AND OPTIMIZATION

There are many properties of magnetooptical media that must be considered in the design of practical films for storage and retrieval. The basic design goals are to maximize the signal-to-noise ratio, achieve archival stability and high write-erase cyclability, achieve a low medium modulation noise with small bit shift and low defect (error) rates, and work in a reflectivity range that is sufficient for reliable servo operation but not high enough to cause problems with laser noise.

In this section, some of these problems are described, and the methods that have been devised to solve them are explored. These involve the nature and preparation of the substrate; the material properties and dimensions of the magnetooptical and adjacent films; and the optical, thermal, and protection characteristics provided by the medium design. As expected, multiple trade-offs occur. For example, the use of second-surface recording potentially gives greater protection to the magnetic layer and reduces errors due to surface contaminants. However, the substrate and optics birefringence must be limited, and it is more difficult to achieve a low reflectivity. As another example, the use of a quadrilayer structure for interference enhancement of the readout signal allows a greater choice of materials for the protection layers but at the cost of fabrication complexity and expense.

The first step in media design is to calculate the magnetooptical response of multilayer media. As shown in Fig. 10.21, normally incident plane-polarized light, when reflected from a perpendicularly magnetized specimen, becomes in general elliptically polarized with magnetooptical (polar Kerr) amplitude r_y and unrotated amplitude r_x. Because the magnetooptical signal is weak, $r_y \ll r_x$ and

$$r_x = \sqrt{R} \qquad (10.13)$$

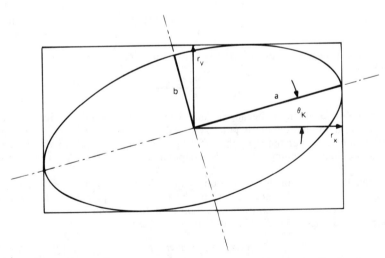

FIGURE 10.21 Schematic of elliptical polarization resulting from reflection from a magnetooptical medium of incident linearly polarized (along x axis) light. The magnetooptical component r_y is much smaller than the unrotated component r_x. The Kerr rotation angle is θ_K, and the ellipticity is $\eta_K = \pm b/a$, where a and b are the major and minor ellipse axes.

where R is the reflectivity. For the present purpose, it is sufficient to understand that in the shot noise limit

$$\text{SNR} \sim \sqrt{P_i} r_y \qquad (10.14)$$

where P_i is the power incident on the medium during readout. The optical goal for a multilayer design therefore is to increase r_y through interference enhancement without decreasing R so much that servo control is made difficult. Typical results of this step, using the techniques described in Sec. 10.3.1, are given in Sec. 10.3.2.

The second step is to select those designs that can withstand large incident laser power during readout, without any degradation of r_y occurring through an increase in the temperature of the magnetic film. One of these will provide the maximum signal-to-noise ratio. The physical basis of this thermal engineering process is described in Sec. 10.3.3, and the different roles of the various thermal time constants are pointed out. In Sec. 10.3.4, two figures of merit for media performance in the shot noise limit are derived, and several media designs are compared. The final step is to make the trade-off between maximum signal performance and data and system integrity. The decisions that must be taken and the areas of concern are reviewed in Sec. 10.3.5.

10.3.1 Magnetooptics of Multilayer Media

A general method for calculating the magnetooptical response of any multilayer media has been described (Smith, 1965a, 1965b). The polar Kerr effect, however, can be treated in a much simpler way. The starting point is the dielectric tensor that describes the magnetooptical response of a perpendicularly magnetized medium (Landau and Lifshitz, 1958):

$$\varepsilon = \begin{bmatrix} \varepsilon^{xx} & \varepsilon^{xy} & 0 \\ -\varepsilon^{xy} & \varepsilon^{xx} & 0 \\ 0 & 0 & \varepsilon^{zz} \end{bmatrix} \qquad \mathbf{M}_s \parallel z \qquad (10.15)$$

It follows that the normal modes of propagation are circularly polarized with refractive indices

$$n_\pm = \sqrt{(\epsilon^{xx} \pm j\epsilon^{xy})} \qquad (10.16)$$

The polar Kerr effect arises because of the difference between the optical constants for these right and left circularly polarized modes (Jackson, 1967) and is controlled by the magnetic dependence of the off-diagonal component ε^{xy} of the dielectric tensor. The diagonal component ε^{xx} is independent of magnetic effects to the first order.

To calculate the polar Kerr rotation θ_K and ellipticity η_K of the elliptically reflected light in Fig. 11.21, let $\mathbf{r}_+$ and $\mathbf{r}_-$ be the external complex Fresnel coefficients that correspond to the amplitude and phase of the reflected circular modes of propagation (Jackson, 1967). Then defining Ψ and Δ from

$$\mathbf{r}_-/\mathbf{r}_+ = \tan \Psi \exp j\Delta \qquad (10.17)$$

allows θ_K and η_K to be expressed as

$$\theta_K = \frac{\Delta}{2} \qquad (10.18)$$

and

$$\tan \eta_K = \frac{1 - \tan \Psi}{1 + \tan \Psi} \tag{10.19}$$

It is therefore sufficient to calculate $\mathbf{r}_+$ and $\mathbf{r}_-$ independently, using the optical constants and thicknesses of the layers that constitute the multilayer structure, and then combine them in Eq. (10.17). The values of $\mathbf{r}_+$ and $\mathbf{r}_-$ also give the reflectivity, since

$$R = \tfrac{1}{2}(r_+^2 + r_-^2) \tag{10.20}$$

where $r_+ = |\mathbf{r}_+|$ and $r_- = |\mathbf{r}_-|$. The complex Fresnel coefficients themselves can be calculated by a number of simple iterative schemes that were originally proposed for the calculation of the Fresnel coefficients for plane polarized light (Heavens, 1965). They apply equally to this case when the refractive indices for circular polarization replace those for plane polarization in the formalism.

For completeness, it should be noted that the polar Kerr rotation and ellipticity can also be expressed in terms of the external complex Fresnel coefficients for linearly polarized light $\mathbf{r}_x$ and $\mathbf{r}_y$ since

$$\mathbf{r}_x = \tfrac{1}{2}(\mathbf{r}_+ + \mathbf{r}_-) \tag{10.21}$$

and

$$\mathbf{r}_y = \tfrac{1}{2}(\mathbf{r}_+ - \mathbf{r}_-) \tag{10.22}$$

The reflectivity amplitudes used elsewhere in this chapter are then

$$r_x = |\mathbf{r}_x| \tag{10.23}$$

and

$$r_y = |\mathbf{r}_y| \tag{10.24}$$

In terms of the polar Kerr rotation and ellipticity, these are

$$r_x^2 = R(\sin^2 \theta_K \sin^2 \eta_K + \cos^2 \theta_K \cos^2 \eta_K) \tag{10.25}$$

and

$$r_y^2 = R(\sin^2 \theta_K \cos^2 \eta_K + \cos^2 \theta_K \sin^2 \eta_K) \tag{10.26}$$

where the reflectivity expressed in these terms is

$$R = r_x^2 + r_y^2 \tag{10.27}$$

10.3.2 Interference Enhancement

The tools of the previous section can now be used to evaluate the effectiveness of multilayer interference structures for increasing the magnetooptical component r_y. The design goals are twofold: first, to provide an antireflective coating to couple the incident radiation into the medium, and second, to provide interference conditions that will capture all of the converted magnetooptical radiation and emit it in phase from the medium with the normally reflected light. In the following, the type of medium (e.g., bilayer, trilayer, quadrilayer) is defined from the number of layers deposited on the substrate. In a completed assembly, it is conceivable that other layers would be added to provide further protection, but it is assumed that these would not affect the optical performance.

Bilayer, trilayer, and quadrilayer media can be constructed for both first-surface and second-surface recording. In Figs. 10.22 and 10.23, the bilayer and quadrilayer cases are shown. In both cases, the dielectric overlayer must act both as an antireflection layer and as a protection layer against chemical attack from either the atmosphere or substrate. A trilayer medium for magnetooptical recording differs from a quadrilayer medium by the removal of either the intermediate dielectric layer or the metallic reflecting layer, such that the magnetic layer remains protected by under- and overlayers in either situation. This contrasts with the accepted definition of a trilayer in nonerasable recording (Bell and Spong, 1978), where the ablative recording material is the uppermost, unprotected layer.

To establish a baseline, Figs. 10.24 and 10.25 show the reflectivity, rotation, ellipticity, and r_y of bare Tb-Fe: first, as an optically thick film versus wavelength, and second, as a thin film on a glass substrate versus film thickness for a wavelength of 840 nm. The components of the dielectric tensor from which these results are derived (Connell, 1983) were already presented in Fig. 10.11. There are several points to notice. First, the optical and magnetooptical parameters are all weakly dependent on wavelength, and Eq. (10.14) indicates that only a small decrease of

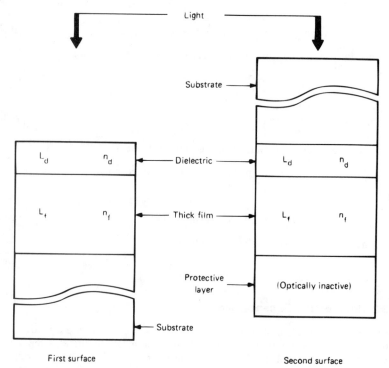

FIGURE 10.22 First- and second-surface bilayer media. Layer thickness and index of refraction are L and n, respectively. The magnetooptical film, labeled by L_f and n_f, is sufficiently thick that no light penetrates.

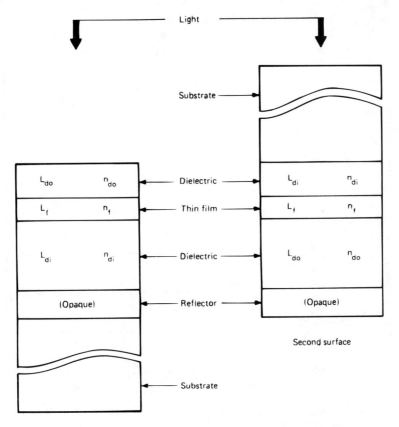

FIGURE 10.23 First- and second-surface quadrilayer media with two dielectric layers: an intermediate layer near the substrate and an outer layer deposited on top of the thin magnetooptical film.

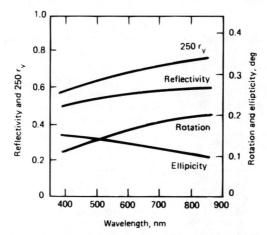

FIGURE 10.24 Reflectivity, rotation, ellipticity, and 250 r_y from a thick bare Tb-Fe film versus wavelength (*after Allen and Connell, 1982*).

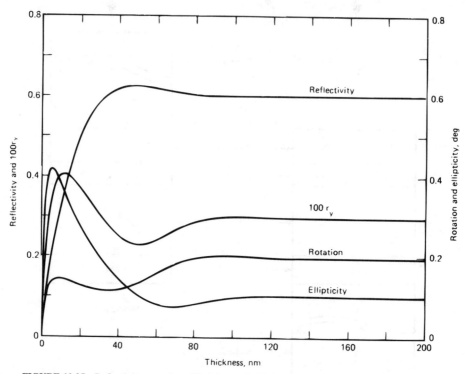

FIGURE 10.25   Reflectivity, rotation, ellipticity, and 100 r_y from a thin bare Tb-Fe film versus film thickness for a fixed wavelength $\lambda = 840$ nm.

signal-to-noise ratio will occur with decreasing wavelength. Therefore, the media will remain useful as solid-state lasers with high-output power become available at shorter wavelengths. Second, the optical and magnetooptical parameters all vary rapidly with thickness below about 80 nm. In particular, r_y rises strongly to a peak near 10 nm, and Eq. (10.14) shows that this leads to an increase of signal-to-noise ratio. The object of the multilayer designs is to make further improvements of this kind and provide protection to the magnetic film at the same time. A simple argument can be made for the degree of improvement that is possible (Connell et al., 1980; Connell, 1982). Consider a thick magnetooptical film of reflectivity R that is illuminated with plane-polarized light. From the light that penetrates the surface of incidence, a perpendicularly polarized component is created by the magnetooptical interaction. The intensity of this converted radiation, which is emitted from the surface of incidence I_s is then (Loudon, 1965)

$$I_s \sim \frac{(1 - R)^2}{2\alpha} \tag{10.28}$$

where α is the absorption coefficient of the magnetic film.

This equation also holds for an overcoated thick magnetic film. In this case, a proper choice of the thickness and refractive index of the overcoating material will cause the reflectivity of the specimen to be reduced considerably. The maximum

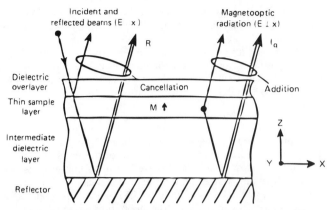

FIGURE 10.26 Schematic representation of reflection from a quadrilayer. The reflected component R consists of the superposition of a beam reflected from the magnetooptical film and all beams having at least one bounce from the reflector. Similarly the rotated component I_q consists of the back emitted radiation from the magnetooptical film plus radiation having at least one bounce from the reflector (*after Connell and Allen, 1981*).

intensity enhancement of the bilayer signal over that from the bare thick sample is therefore

$$G_b \approx \frac{1}{(1 - R)^2} \tag{10.29}$$

Now consider the quadrilayer configuration shown in Fig. 10.26. For very thin magnetic films ($\alpha L_f \ll 1$), the light reflected from the sample can be nearly cancelled by light that has suffered at least one reflection from the back reflector, when both the overlayer thickness is about one-half wavelength and the intermediate layer thickness is about one-quarter wavelength. As a result, most of the light is absorbed by the magnetic film. Furthermore, the converted radiation suffers relatively little reabsorption in the film, and the interference conditions that have been set up to create total absorption of the incident beam are exactly those required to maximize the exiting radiation I_q by in-phase addition. (The difference between the behavior of R and I_q stems from a 180° phase shift experienced by R at the top surface of the film, that is absent for I_q). It follows that the intensity of converted radiation I_q emitted by the ideal quadrilayer film from its surface of incidence is

$$I_q \sim 4L_f \tag{10.30}$$

where the factor of 4 results from the assumption that the converted radiation is emitted equally in the forward and backward directions, and that the two components exit the film in phase. The intensity enhancement of the quadrilayer signal over that from the bare thick film is then

$$G_q \sim \frac{8\alpha L_f}{(1 - R)^2} \tag{10.31}$$

This holds for $\alpha L_f \leq 0.2$, beyond which an exact calculation indicates that G_q rapidly approaches a maximum value. Consequently, using $R \approx 0.6$, $\alpha \approx 10^8 \mathrm{m}^{-1}$ and $L_f \approx 3\,\mathrm{nm}$, it is estimated that $G_b \leq 8$ and $G_q \approx 15$.

Figure 10.27 shows exact calculations of the reflectivity, rotation, ellipticity, and r_y of a first-surface bilayer versus overcoat thickness. The refractive index of the overlayer n_0 was chosen to be 2.0, a value typical of several of the dielectric materials currently used and close to the condition

$$n_0 = (n_i |\mathbf{n}|)^{1/2} \tag{10.32}$$

at which a minimum reflectivity occurs at the antireflection thickness. In this equation, n_i and $\mathbf{n}$ ($= n + jk$) are the refractive indices of the incident medium and the magnetic material. It follows that r_y and therefore the signal-to-noise ratio in Eq. (10.14) reach a maximum value at an overlayer thickness of about 85 nm. This is close to the quarter-wave thickness of $\lambda/4n_0 = 105$ nm but is different because of the large absorptive component in $\mathbf{n}$. From the maximum value of r_y and that of the bare thick film in Fig. 10.25, it is seen that $G_b \approx 4.9$, in reasonable agreement with the earlier estimate. It should also be noted that the rotation is peaked at the maximum of r_y, having a value of $1.0°$, while the ellipticity drops to near $0.1°$. The ellipticity therefore makes a negligible contribution to r_y in Eq. (10.26), which can be of some significant value for efficient system design.

Finally, Fig. 10.28 shows the reflectivity and r_y versus magnetic film thickness for numerous second-surface quadrilayer designs. The dielectric overlayer and intermediate layer again have refractive indices of 2.0, but now their thicknesses have been allowed to vary between 150 and 350 nm at each magnetic layer thickness, so that r_y is maximized. While the value of the refractive index is no longer of such great consequence for establishing a large r_y, in this second-surface configuration it is still necessary for n_0 to meet the condition (10.32) to obtain low reflectivities. It is then found that the maximum of r_y is broad, being close to 9×10^{-3} for thicknesses between 5 and 20 nm. Its value together with that for the thick film data in Fig. 10.25 indicates that $G_q = 10.2$. This is again in reasonable agreement with an earlier estimate. The breadth of this maximum provides wide latitude in which to optimize other features: the protection provided by the dielectric stacks, the integrity of the media, the balance between rotation and ellipticity in r_y, and the thermal response of the medium. This flexibility is of great importance in the final stages of system engineering.

10.3.3 Thermal Engineering

From the media designs available with high magnetooptical component r_y, it is now necessary to select those which can withstand large readout powers such that the signal-to-noise ratio is maximized. There are two approaches that can be taken. First, the Curie point can be raised by alloying, such as by substituting Co for Fe in iron-based alloys (see Sec. 10.2.3). Second, and of concern here, the stack can be arranged to increase heat flow out of the magnetic film, typically into an underlying conducting layer, thus reducing the temperature rise for a given incident optical power. This method is particularly useful for recording at high density in that the lateral heat spreading is reduced and very small domains can be written given sufficient laser power (Mansuripur and Connell, 1983b).

In this thermal engineering problem, the maximum temperatures reached during recording or erasing are low enough that radiation can be ignored. There are

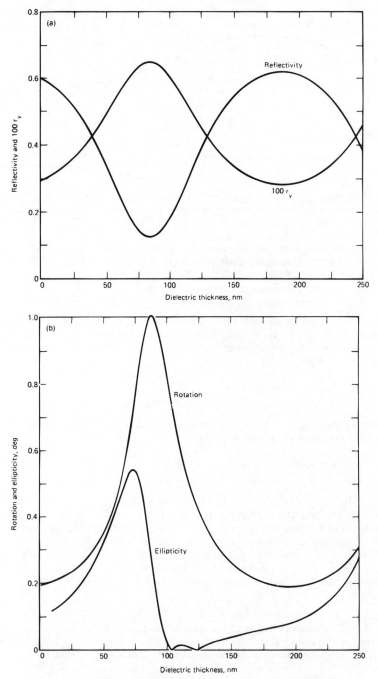

FIGURE 10.27 Optical parameters at $\lambda = 840$ nm from a first-surface Tb-Fe bilayer versus overcoat thickness. (*a*) Reflectivity and 100 r_y (*b*) ellipticity and rotation. The Tb-Fe layer thickness is 200 nm, and the overcoat dielectric has an index of refraction $n_0 = 2.0$.

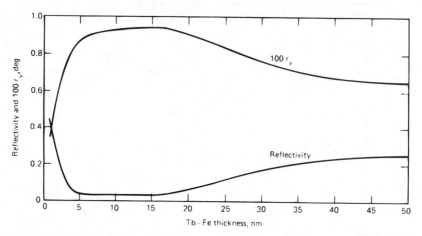

FIGURE 10.28   Reflectivity and 100 r_y from a second-surface quadrilayer versus Tb-Fe thickness. The thicknesses of dielectric overlayer ($n_0 = 2.0$) and intermediate layer ($n_i = 2.0$) have been allowed to vary to maximize r_y at each value of Tb-Fe thickness.

then three characteristic thermal time constants for the magnetooptical media that determine the dynamic response and equilibrium conditions (Corcoran and Ferrier, 1977). First, for a magnetic film of thickness L_f, thermal conductivity κ, specific heat (per unit volume) C_f, and diffusivity

$$D_f = \frac{\kappa}{C_f} \tag{10.33}$$

the time constant τ_{eq} that determines when a uniform temperature is established through the thickness of the film is given by

$$\tau_{eq} \simeq \frac{L_f^2}{D_f} \tag{10.34}$$

With $L_f \simeq 10^{-5}$ cm and $D_f \simeq 10^{-1}$ cm²/s from Table 10.4, $\tau_{eq} \simeq 10^{-9}$ s. This is much shorter than any practical laser pulse time, and as a result the temperature through the thickness of the magnetic layer may be treated as uniform. Second, there is the penetration diffusion time constant τ_d, which determines the characteristic time for loss of energy to a conducting layer through an intervening dielectric layer. This can be approximated using a one-dimensional analysis (Kivits et al., 1981) in which the adiabatically heated volume is proportional to the diffusion length

$$L_{dif}(t) = \sqrt{D_d t} \tag{10.35}$$

where D_d is the diffusivity of the adjacent dielectric layers. Then as time proceeds, a thickness L_{dif} of each adjacent layer is heated in addition to the magnetic film, and the fraction of energy deposited into the magnetic film is approximately

$$\zeta = \frac{C_f L_f}{C_f L_f + 2 C_d L_{dif}} \tag{10.36}$$

where C_d is the specific heat per unit volume of the adjacent layers. For a laser pulse time of 10^{-7} s, a bilayer with the thermal parameters in Table 10.4 and $L_f \simeq 10^{-5}$ cm has $\zeta \simeq 0.2$. There is therefore a great gain in energy efficiency to be made by shortening the laser pulse time to the order of 10^{-8} s. This provides other advantages for system operation, which are discussed in Sec. 10.5.2. In a quadrilayer, one of the dielectric layers, of thickness L_d, separates the magnetic film from a conducting layer, so that at a time

$$\tau_d \simeq \frac{L_d^2}{D_d} \tag{10.37}$$

the further rate of heating is considerably slowed. The laser therefore should apply sufficient power to heat these layers close to the required temperature in a time τ_d, because for times longer than τ_d, the temperature will not rise appreciably further. For typical quadrilayer designs, $L_d \simeq 10^{-5}$ cm, and from Table 10.4, $D_d \simeq 10^{-2}$ cm^2/s, giving $\tau_d \simeq 10^{-8}$ s. Therefore, in both bilayer and quadrilayer designs, the same limit on laser pulse time is obtained.

Finally, there is a characteristic lateral diffusion time within the film, found from a two-dimensional solution to the diffusion equation (Carslaw and Jaeger, 1959),

$$\tau_{\text{lat}} \simeq \frac{r_b^2}{4D_f} = \frac{0.09W^2}{D_f} \tag{10.38}$$

where r_b and W are the e^{-1} intensity radius and full-width-at-half-maximum of the Gaussian beam, respectively. After the pulse is turned off, the temperature of the medium at a radius greater than $r_c \simeq r_b$ from the beam center continues to rise because of lateral heat diffusion and can cause domain spreading. This must be inhibited, for example, by thermal diffusion into the substrate, if the minimum size of the written bit is to be limited by the optics.

Figure 10.14 shows an exact calculation for the increase of temperature of a magnetic layer in a quadrilayer structure versus time at different radii (Mansuripur and Connell, 1983b). Over two-thirds of the temperature rise occurs in the first 15 ns, and thereafter only a small rate of increase is achieved by the incident radiation. The magnetic media could therefore be heated to the same final temperature by a 15 ns pulse of 50 percent more power than was used in the original 50-ns pulse of the calculation. This confirms the simple arguments that follow from Eq. (10.37).

These exact calculations also provide a detailed appreciation of the balance between axial and radial heat flow and the effects of the motion of the media during writing and readout (Mansuripur and Connell, 1983c). The calculations show that films with poor heat sinking exhibit lateral spread, both in the cross-track and down-track directions, whereas the heated area for films with good heat sinking approaches the shape of the writing beam. The central temperature increase also differs considerably in the two cases. The conclusion is that structures designed to withstand the greatest incident laser power during readout and requiring the highest write power provide the potential for the highest-density recording.

In selecting the media design, therefore, from the group of high r_y candidates, the system designer should first consider the least thermally sensitive design, because of its highest signal-to-noise ratio in Eq. (10.14) and ability to achieve the highest recording densities. If lack of writing sensitivity cannot be compensated with a larger applied magnetic field, then the search for the appropriate media structure can be systematically pursued by increasing the thermal sensitivity to obtain a structure that provides the best compromise between the writing and reading constraints of the magnetooptical system.

10.3.4 Magnetooptical Signal and Figures of Merit

It is now necessary to establish figures of merit for the medium, and two such figures of merit are derived in this section. Consider the simplest detection scheme, a single analyzer oriented at an angle α to the unrotated direction r_x, as shown in Fig. 10.29. Assume that all of r_y and a fraction ξ of r_x is reflected toward the detectors by the first polarizing beam splitter (PBS) in Fig. 10.1a. (This is approximately correct if ξ is small, but the detailed operation of the polarizing beam splitter is given in Sec. 10.4.) After compensating for the phase difference between r_x and r_y (i.e., removing the ellipticity), the polarization is linear and makes an angle $\pm \theta_s$ for the two directions of magnetization in the film, where

$$\theta_s = \tan^{-1} \frac{r_y}{\xi r_x} \simeq \frac{r_y}{\xi r_x} \ll 1 \tag{10.39}$$

Because θ_s is small, the optical power P transmitted through the analyzer is approximately

$$P \simeq P_i R \xi^2 \cos^2 \alpha \tag{10.40}$$

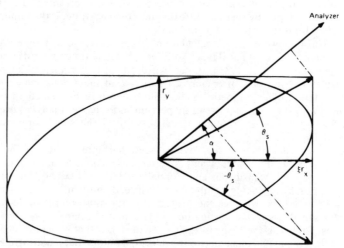

FIGURE 10.29 Ordinary r_x and magnetooptical r_y components, after attenuation of r_x by the factor ξ in the polarizing beam splitter and compensation to bring them into phase. The resulting linear polarization can have two directions, represented by angles θ_s and $-\theta_s$, depending on the magnetization direction. Maximum projections on an analyzer at angle α are also shown for the two magnetization directions.

where P_i is the incident power on the medium, and $R \simeq r_x^2$.

The magnetooptical signal P_s is the change in optical power transmitted through the analyzer to the detector when the magnetization state is reversed:

$$P_s = P_i R \xi^2 [\cos^2(\alpha - \theta_s) - \cos^2(\alpha + \theta_s)] \qquad (10.41)$$

$$= P_i R \xi^2 \sin 2\alpha \sin 2\theta_s$$

This is maximized by placing the analyzer at $\alpha = 45°$, so that

$$P_s = P_i R \xi^2 \sin 2\theta_s \simeq 2 P_i R \xi^2 \theta_s \simeq 2 P_i \xi r_x r_y \qquad (10.42)$$

and the magnetooptical signal is proportional to the product P_i and r_y and to a fraction of the unrotated component ξr_x that must be coherently added to r_y.

The first figure of merit K_r that represents the rotating power of the film is defined by (see Fig. 10.21)

$$K_r \equiv r_y \simeq r_x \sin \theta_K \simeq \sqrt{R} \sin \theta_K \simeq \theta_K \sqrt{R} \qquad (10.43)$$

where Eq. (10.26) is used with the assumption of small ellipticity, $\eta_K \ll 1$, and the last approximation holds for small Kerr rotation. Table 10.1 gives values of 3.0×10^{-3} for K_r for a Tb-Fe bilayer and 8.0×10^{-3} for a Tb-Fe quadrilayer.

Because K_r does not take into account the increase in signal with incident read power P_i, a second figure of merit K_p is required that incorporates P_i and the limit on P_i set by the reduction of r_y at elevated temperatures. The shot-noise power on the detector is proportional to $\sqrt{P_i}$, and under the best circumstances, the signal is shot-noise limited. Hence, K_p is defined to be proportional to the signal to shot-noise ratio

$$K_p \equiv K_r \sqrt{P_i} = r_y \sqrt{} P_i \sim \frac{P_s}{P_{shot}} \qquad (10.44)$$

Although K_p is not dimensionless, it provides a better measure of the obtainable signal-to-noise ratio than K_r under shot-noise limited conditions. Both figures of merit are of significant value at the early stages of media design.

10.3.5. Plastic Substrates and the Effects of Birefringence

In this section we examine the effects of substrate birefringence on the focused spot as well as on the quality of the read signal. Plastic disk substrates used in practice typically have three different refractive indices n_r, n_t, n_z along the radial, tangential, and vertical directions (Marchant, 1988; Takahashi et al., 1988; Fu et al., 1994). These differences are caused in the injection molding process where preferential alignment of polymer molecules occurs in the plane of the substrate. Observed values of birefringence for polycarbonate substrates are on the order of $n_r - n_t \simeq 10^{-5}$, and $n_r - n_z \simeq 10^{-4}$. Substrate birefringence introduces astigmatism on the focused spot and affects the polarization state of the beam, both of which cause performance degradations in the optical disk system (Prikryl, 1992; Bernacki and Mansuripur, 1993; Mansuripur and Hsieh, 1994; Sugaya and Mansuripur, 1994).

For technical reasons having to do with the computational procedure, we must treat the substrate as an isotropic, semi-infinite medium in contact with a birefringent layer of finite thickness, as indicated in Fig. 10.30a. In the figure a thin metallic film is shown supported by a substrate whose birefringence is concentrated within a 20 μm-thick layer having $n_x = 1.5$, $n_y = 1.50$, and $n_z = 1.47$. The direction of beam propagation, Z, is perpendicular to the plane of the substrate, and the state of incident polarization is linear along the X-axis. The beam is focused on the metallic film through the substrate by a lens of NA = 0.55 and $f = 3.76$ mm. (In order to compensate the spherical aberration caused by the 20 μm-thick birefringent layer, it is necessary to place its interface with the substrate at 13 μm before the focus.) The beam reaching the metallic layer is very close to the ideal Airy pattern, as can be seen from its intensity profile in Fig. 10.30b.

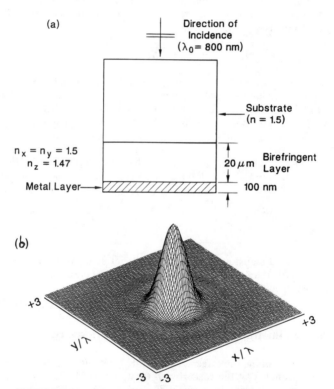

FIGURE 10.30 (a) Substrate birefringence is concentrated in the 20 μm-thick layer between the metallic film and the isotropic part of the substrate. The assumed vertical birefringence, $n_r - n_z$, is 60 times greater than that of typical polycarbonate substrates, since the layer's thickness is 60 times smaller than the standard thickness. (b) Intensity distribution at the interface of the metallic and birefringent layers. (The assumed objective lens has NA = 0.55 and $f = 3.76$ mm.) The spherical aberrations induced by the 20 μm-thick layer have been compensated by the addition of defocus. The optimum amount of defocus is found by maximizing the peak intensity at the metallic layer.

Let us first assume that the metallic layer is a perfect, non-magnetic reflector. Figure 10.31a shows the computed phase distribution at the exit pupil of the objective; its cross-sections along X and Y are shown in Fig. 10.31b. The peaks and valleys of the curves in Fig. 10.31b are produced by the residual amounts of spherical aberration and defocus, but the astigmatism, amounting to nearly $0.2\lambda_0$, is a direct consequence of birefringence. In essence, s-polarized rays within the focused cone, which are not affected by the n_z of the birefringent layer, suffer a greater phase shift than the p-polarized rays, which do have a component of **E** in the Z-direction. Note that the astigmatism of $0.2\lambda_0$ is twice the amount produced in each passage through the substrate. Figure 10.32 shows contour plots of intensity at the metallic layer for three values of disk defocus: $-2\lambda_0$, 0 and $+2\lambda_0$. At best focus the

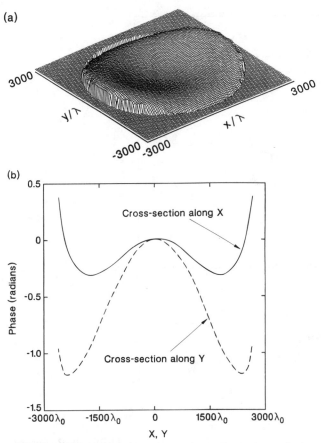

FIGURE 10.31 (a) Distribution of phase for the X-component of polarization at the exit pupil of the objective. The assumed disk structure is that of Fig. 10.30a, with the metal layer acting as a perfect reflector. (b) Cross-sections of the phase plot in (a) along the X-direction and the Y-direction. The phase difference of 1.3 radians at the edge of the pupil corresponds to $0.2\lambda_0$ of astigmatism.

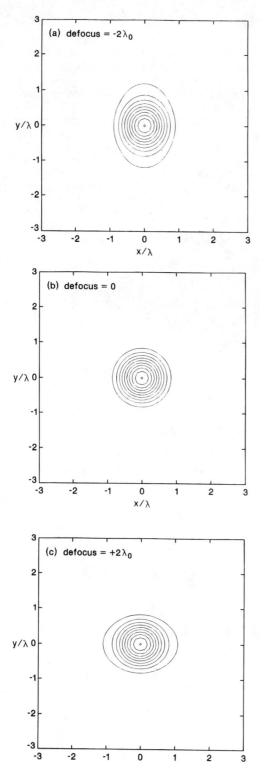

FIGURE 10.32 Contour plots of intensity, I_x, at the metallic layer for the disk structure of Fig. 10.30a. The plots in (a)–(c) correspond, respectively, to a defocus of $-2\lambda_0$, best focus, and a defocus of $+2\lambda_0$. In each case the distribution is normalized to unity at the peak, and the individual contours range from 0.1 to 1 in steps of 0.1. Peak intensities are in the ratio of 0.67:1:0.74.

spot is circularly symmetric, but at either side of focus it is elongated along X or Y. This elongation is another manifestation of the astigmatism produced by vertical birefringence. In a disk drive, if the polarization happens to be parallel to the tracks (tangential) or perpendicular to the tracks (radial), then birefringence of the type described here will enlarge the focused spot either along the track or perpendicular to it, depending on the sign of defocus. Tangential elongation will degrade the resolution of MO readout, while radial elongation will reduce the magnitude of the push–pull track-crossing signal.

Next we assume that the metallic layer is magnetooptical, with diagonal and off-diagonal elements $\epsilon_{xx} = -5 + 20i$ and $\epsilon_{xy} = 0.5 + 0.005i$ respectively. Figure 10.33 shows plots of polarization rotation angle Θ and ellipticity ϵ at the exit pupil of the objective lens after reflection from the disk. Despite the nonuniform distributions across the aperture, the differential signal will not suffer excessively from birefringence, provided that a phase plate is used to convert ellipticity into rotation. In this case, the maximum signal obtained is $S_1 - S_2 \simeq \pm 0.0059$, while, in the absence of the birefringent layer, the maximum signal is found to be $S_1 - S_2 \simeq \pm 0.0063$. (In both cases, an optimally oriented quarter-wave plate is assumed to be present before the differential detector.) Similar conclusions are reached when the disk substrate, in addition to having vertical birefringence, is assumed to have a small amount of in-plane (or lateral) birefringence. In general, substrate birefringence in itself does not appear to cause a perceptible degradation of the differential MO signal. However, when the distribution of birefringence over the surface area of the disk is nonuniform, or when the birefringence is combined with residual aberrations of the optical system, its negative effects could become significant (Bernacki and Mansuripur, 1993; Sugaya and Mansuripur, 1994).

10.3.6 Disk Integration and Design Compromises

There is a continuing effort, through the use of new materials, to (1) improve the optical, mechanical, and chemical properties of the substrate to ensure the integrity of the written data; (2) reduce the cost of the substrate, preformatting, and disk assembly; and (3) improve the packaging of the disk. These goals often compete with each other and with the media design itself. In this section, some of these conflicts will be addressed. We will look at construction of the multilayer stack, choice of substrate, substrate preformatting, and packaging of nonerasable and magnetooptical disks.

In comparison with a bilayer, the quadrilayer stack has an improved signal-to-noise ratio from optical and thermal construction, and it has improved flexibility in the choice of dielectric layers. This comes at a price: a more expensive and complex medium construction and, because the magnetic film must be thin in the quadrilayer, potentially a larger defect density.

Metal substrates are not practical for magnetooptical recording because the large inhomogeneous magnetic field that is applied during erase and write cycles induces eddy currents within the substrate. The Lorentz force, which increases with conductivity and thickness, would create a drag on an aluminum substrate that is roughly a million times greater than that on the RE-TM layer, and is of a magnitude that is unacceptable for practical applications. Of the possible nonconducting substrates, glass provides the smoothest and most inert surface on which to deposit magnetooptical media. Medium noise and defects increase with surface roughness, and it is critical to prevent chemical attack on the magnetic film from the substrate. A glass substrate with etched preformatted information would require the least protec-

(a)

(b)

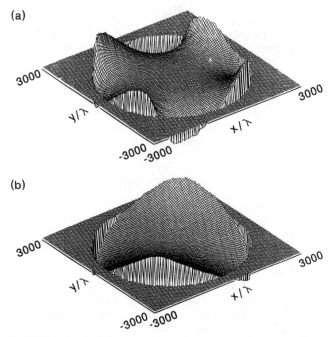

FIGURE 10.33 Distributions of the polarization rotation angle Θ and ellipticity ϵ at the exit pupil of the objective, corresponding to the disk structure of Fig. 10.30a with a magnetooptical metallic layer. In (a) $\Theta_{min} = 118.2°$, $\Theta_{max} = +19.7°$. In (b) $\epsilon_{min} = -36.3°$, $\epsilon_{max} = +35.9°$.

tion, but it represents the most difficult preformatting process (Deguchi et al., 1984). Further, when glass is coated with the photopolymer 2P process (van Rijsewijk et al., 1982; Kloosterboer et al., 1982), it loses the advantage of chemical neutrality, and undercoats must be used to protect the magnetooptical film from the 2P layer (Hartmann et al., 1984). Plastic substrates engender a variety of problems, such as increased surface roughness, lack of rigidity (especially at elevated temperatures), birefringence, and retention of water. The advantages relative to glass are that plastic substrates are less fragile and less expensive. Additionally, the preformatting may be molded during the substrate manufacturing process itself.

Birefringence can cause serious problems in second-surface recording systems (Treves and Bloomberg, 1986a). With substrate birefringence typical of the in-plane polycarbonate, the substrate principal birefringence axis will rotate with the disk, causing a low-frequency oscillation (four times the rotation rate) in both the sum and difference channels of a magnetooptical system. With additional birefringence in the system optics, the variation has in general a twofold rotational symmetry. The substrate birefringence effects add on each pass through the substrate, and for a one-way phase lag of 5°, the modulation of the difference channel signal is of the same order of magnitude as the magnetooptical signal itself. This modulation increases as the square of the birefringence and degrades system performance primarily through an amplification of laser and medium noise due to a large unbalance in the difference channel. The constraint of a 5° one-way phase lag is equivalent to an in-plane (lateral) substrate birefringence

$$\frac{\Delta n}{n} \leq 10^{-5} \qquad (10.45)$$

There remains much activity in the search for suitable transparent and inexpensive substrate materials.

Preformatted grooves are favored for nonerasable, write once, disks because they can increase contrast by interference effects, help confine the written (ablated) marks, and improve track-seeking performance by providing a continuous-tracking servo signal. Grooved disks, however, are disadvantageous for magnetooptical media. They can potentially lower medium quality because of the difficulty in coating over groove edges without losing the integrity of the protection layer. Medium noise is increased due to groove nonuniformities and the magnetooptical signal can be reduced through complex interference effects at the groove edges. Loss of signal-to-noise ratio is much more critical with magnetooptical media than with nonerasable media because the magnetooptical signal is relatively small. Some compromises in media design will have to be made in order to use both types of media on the same drive.

Nonerasable media are typically packaged into a sandwich composed of two disks with data on facing surfaces, separated by ring spacers at the hub and outer edges. Second-surface recording is used on each disk. This configuration has two disadvantages. First, the data surfaces are not well protected from gases and ions inside the air space. Second, the total package is relatively thick (about 3.5 mm). A preferable configuration for magnetooptical media is to cement the two disks together with the films facing each other, again using second-surface recording. The advantages are maximum protection of the data layer and a more compact packaging arrangement. As yet, this construction cannot be used with ablative nonerasable media because the constraint that the underlayer places on material movement pushes the recording threshold to unacceptably high energies. Nonerasable phase change or dye media would not suffer from this limitation and would provide a better match with magnetooptical media.

10.4 COMPONENTS AND SYSTEM DESIGN

Erasable magnetooptical systems differ from nonerasable write-once systems in several respects that make design of the former more difficult. The signal is smaller by more than one order of magnitude when using the Kerr effect for readout, and a large amount of light is necessarily reflected back into the laser. Also, a magnet is required in magnetooptical systems for writing and erasure. In this section, the operation of the optical, mechanical, electrical, and magnetic components are discussed, and those system design issues that relate directly to the functioning of these components are addressed.

Figure 10.1a shows the optical path for a typical magnetooptical system. The laser light is initially polarized in the x direction (perpendicular to the figure) and is collimated and made of circular cross section with a Gaussian intensity distribution by a lens and two prisms (not shown). After transmission through a leaky polarizing beam splitter, the light is focused by the objective lens onto the medium, achieving a theoretical minimum spot size with a full-width-at-half-maximum intensity

$$W = \frac{0.56\,\lambda}{N_A} \tag{10.46}$$

where λ is the wavelength, and N_A, the numerical aperture of the objective lens of diameter d_l and focal length f, is defined by

$$N_A = \sin(\tan^{-1} d_l/2f) = \sin\theta_h. \tag{10.47}$$

The half-angle of the lens, as viewed from the focal plane, is θ_h. The depth of focus δ for Gaussian optics varies inversely with the square of the numerical aperture

$$\delta = \frac{\pm\lambda}{2N_A^2} \tag{10.48}$$

Thus, whereas use of a large numerical aperture reduces the spot size, the objective lens is expensive and the reduction in depth of field makes focus servoing much more difficult. A reasonable compromise is to use an objective with $N_A \simeq 0.5$. For $\lambda = 0.82\ \mu$m, the spot size is then 0.9 μm and the depth of focus is 1.6 μm.

The light returning from the magnetooptical medium is incident on the leaky polarizing beam splitter, which is constructed to reflect almost all of the r_y component and a fraction of ξ of the r_x component. Such a beam splitter can be visualized as a perfect one that transmits all of r_x and reflects all of r_y, but is rotated about the x axis by an angle $\phi = \sin^{-1}\xi$, as shown in Fig. 10.34. This rotation causes the fraction ξ of r_x and $\sqrt{(1 - \xi^2)}$ of r_y to be reflected by the beam splitter. The magnetooptical signal is proportional to the product of x and y amplitudes reflected to the detectors. Consequently, when using a rotated beam splitter, the magnetooptical signal from a single detector [Eq. (10.42)] is more accurately given by

$$P_s = 2P_i\xi r_x \sqrt{(1 - \xi^2)}\ r_y = 2P_i r_x r_y \sin\phi\cos\phi \tag{10.49}$$

But for a small beam splitter rotation ϕ, essentially all of the magnetooptical signal r_y goes to the detector, so that Eq. (10.42) is a satisfactory approximation. The beam splitter therefore optimizes the detection of the magnetooptical signal.

The rotation of the polarizing beam splitter also provides a useful side benefit: no light is directly reflected back to the laser from either its front or back face, and laser mode instabilities that could so result are prevented. In contrast, most of the light reflected from the medium returns to the laser, and noise control techniques must be used (see Sec. 10.4.2). In nonerasable and read-only systems, such light feedback is almost entirely eliminated by inserting a quarter waveplate between the beam splitter and the medium at 45° to the incident polarization direction. The polarization of the incident beam is therefore converted from linear to circular, and upon reflection the handedness is reversed. Traversing the quarter waveplate again, the light becomes polarized perpendicular to the incident direction and is reflected by the polarizing beam splitter toward the detector. Unfortunately, this scheme does not work for a magnetooptical system, because the light incident on the medium must be linearly polarized, and no analogous practical method to rotate the polarization has yet been devised. (A Faraday rotator can be used, but it is necessarily large and expensive.)

The light reflected into the detection module is linearized by a phase plate that brings r_y into phase with r_x. A second polarizing beam splitter then divides the light into two components polarized along orthogonal directions for differential detection. Thus, upon reversal of the film magnetization, the phase of r_y changes by 180°, and the change in the difference signal (i.e., the magnetooptical signal) is $2P_s$. The

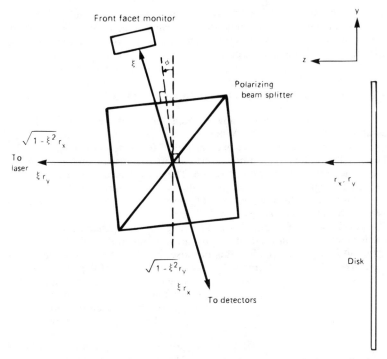

FIGURE 10.34 Operation of a polarizing beam splitter in the main beam, showing amplitude r_x and r_y upon reflection from the disk. The relation between ξ and the physical rotation angle ϕ of the polarizing beam splitter is $\xi = \sin \phi$. A front surface monitor is conveniently placed as shown.

differential scheme therefore doubles the signal and, at the same time, eliminates the common mode noise.

The mass of the moving components should be minimized to achieve fast track-seeking performance. This is accomplished by splitting the optical system into two parts: a stationary laser, magnet, and detector and a moving objective lens. Focus is maintained with a small actuator attached to the objective lens. This is necessary because the optical path length between the lens and the magnetic film is not constant because of variations in lens-disk spacing and, for second-surface recording, variations in substrate thickness as well. In the latter case, the lens-disk spacing averages about 1.5 mm, and the substrate thickness is typically 1.2 mm. The objective lens can be mounted on either a moving carriage or a rotating arm, but the linear motion of the latter simplifies the design if the optical system is split.

Coarse and fine tracking positioners are also required. Coarse tracking may be accomplished by either using a stationary actuator attached by bands to a moving objective carriage or allowing a coil on the carriage to move between stationary permanent magnets. Fine tracking can be accomplished by either attaching a small radial actuator to the objective lens or using a mirror mounted on a high-speed galvanometer. The fine-tracking actuator or galvanometer typically adjusts the radial tracking position by ± 30 μm. Thus, with a track spacing of 1.5 μm, about 40 tracks are accessible with an access time of a few milliseconds. Use of a fine-tracking positioner can thus mimic the performance of a cylinder in a multihead multidisk magnetic recording system. The necessity for a separate fine-tracking positioner will be discussed in Sec. 10.4.3.

10.4.1 Semiconductor Laser Operation and Collimation

Semiconductor diode lasers can now be made and packaged in small, low-power, efficient, and inexpensive units. Whereas the efficiency of gas lasers is about 10^{-3}, efficiencies near 50 percent have been achieved for semiconductor lasers. Because of their small size, however, diode lasers exhibit a relatively large amount of beam spread, which requires optical correction. They also typically excite several widely spaced modes, and exhibit mode instabilities when pumped with reflected light. These instabilities in turn create intensity modulations (laser noise), which, if not prevented, can significantly degrade the signal.

The beam emitted from the laser has a range of divergence angles. It must both be collimated and given a circular cross section, and the resulting beam must be directed along a given axis. For this purpose, a collimating lens followed by two prisms is used. The lens is arranged to collimate the rays. However, because of the different divergence angles parallel and perpendicular to the plane of the laser, the beam is elliptical in cross section after collimation. The purpose of the prism pair is to provide an anamorphic correction for this ellipticity without rotating the optic axis.

The optical power from a semiconductor laser is zero below a threshold current of about 20-50 mA and rises linearly with current thereafter. For a typical 820-nm infrared laser, the gain envelope is positive for about 15 modes. The mode separation is determined by the length of the lasing cavity and is typically about 0.4 nm. Redistribution of the energy between different modes results in laser noise, a variation in output light intensity. This variation is strongly affected by light reflected back into the laser from optical components or the disk. The physics of the effect is not completely understood. In the absence of reflected light, the laser usually oscillates in a single longitudinal mode (Stubkjaer and Small, 1984). Figure 10.35 shows the variation of laser noise with the logarithm of light intensity reflected back into the laser (Biesterbos et al., 1983). Very low levels (less than 0.1 percent) of reflected light cause the laser to oscillate noisily in a single mode. The noise is a maximum for a reflected light level of about 0.3 percent, where two modes share the energy. For re-

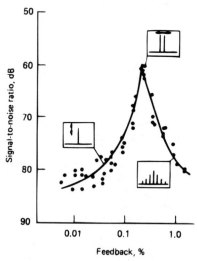

FIGURE 10.35 Variation of laser noise with light reflected back into the laser. Three types of excited mode structures are indicated. The signal-to-noise ratio is measured in a 10-kHz bandwidth (*after Biesterbos et al., 1983*).

flected light levels above this, many modes are typically excited, and the noise monotonically decreases with light level. Above 10 percent and especially at higher laser power, it is observed that the laser can operate between two metastable states, of which one typically has large non-Gaussian noise spikes.

Three approaches must be taken to reduce laser noise. First, direct reflections from optical elements back into the laser should be minimized. This light is highly coherent and can stimulate rapid fluctuations in both the coherency and intensity of the light (Arimoto and Ojima, 1984). Second, stray light that reaches the detectors after reflection from optical elements should be minimized to reduce coherent interference effects. Finally, superposition of a high-frequency (300 to 700 MHz) current on the (essentially) dc current driving the laser has been shown to reduce the laser noise to an acceptable level (Ohishi et al., 1984; Kanada, 1985). Recent developments in self-pulsating diode lasers promise to reduce the complexity of future optical disk systems by incorporating high-frequency modulation of the laser output directly into the structure of the laser (Takayama et al., 1994).

In nonerasable systems, a diode near the back facet of the laser can be used to monitor laser power. This is useful for two reasons: it may be desired to control the write and read power at different levels for the inner and outer tracks, and a gradual increase in injection current is necessary to compensate for a decrease in laser power with aging. This arrangement is not satisfactory for magnetooptics, because the dc output from front and back facets of the laser varies oppositely with light feedback. Therefore, it is preferable to use a front facet monitor to maintain constant or desired output. The signal can be obtained from a small amount of the laser light that is diverted from the main beam by the polarizing beam splitter (see Fig. 10.34), and a feedback loop is closed through a several-megahertz servo to adjust the laser driving current.

Use of feedback to correct for the slow decrease in light output due to aging cannot continue indefinitely. The rate of aging depends on the operating temperature through an Arrhenius relation with an activation energy of about 0.8 eV. The useful life is reduced by a factor of 10 for each 25°C temperature increase (Tsunoda et al., 1983). Commercially available diode lasers give stable operation for 10^4 h at a continuous output power of 15 to 30 mW.

10.4.2. Properties of the Focused Spot

In this section we examine the properties of the focused spot obtained at and near the focal plane of a high-NA objective lens. This examination entails a comparison of the intensity profiles at different positions relative to the optimal focus, the effects of various primary aberrations on the focused spot, and the conversion of polarization caused by the bending of the various rays within the aperture of the lens.

Figure 10.36 shows plots of the intensity distribution in the vicinity of the focal plane of an aberration-free lens with NA = 0.5 and $f_0 = 4000\lambda$. The assumed incident beam is a uniform plane wave propagating along Z, and the numerical computations are performed with the method of fast Fourier transforms on a discrete 512 × 512 mesh. Panels (a) to (d) of this figure correspond, respectively, to defocus distances of 0, 3λ, 5λ, and 20λ. For the numerical values employed in this example, there is symmetry with respect to the focal plane and the results, therefore, apply to either side of focus. We note that even 3λ of defocus can cause a substantial enlargement of the focused spot, causing a loss of resolution both in readout and in tracking. In practice, the focus must be maintained to better than a fraction of the wavelength.

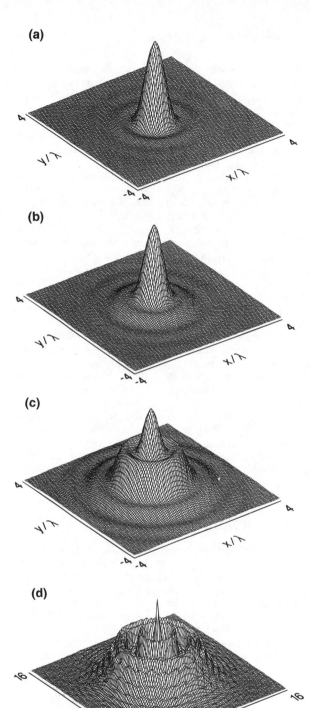

(a)

(b)

(c)

(d)

FIGURE 10.36 Patterns of intensity distribution in the vicinity of the focal plane of a lens with NA = 0.5 and $f_0 = 4000\lambda$. (a) shows the distribution in the focal plane, while (b), (c), and (d) correspond to defocus distances of 3, 5, and 20 wavelengths respectively. The vertical scale varies among the plots and the actual peak intensities in (a)–(d) are in the ratio of 1:0.57:0.17:0.01.

The effects of various primary aberrations on the focused spot are shown in Fig. 10.37. (a) shows the intensity pattern in the focal plane of the lens in the presence of 0.5λ of spherical aberration. The ratio of the peak intensity to that in the absence of aberrations is known as the *Strehl ratio,* and is found in this case to be 0.39. (b) shows the effect of 0.75λ of primary coma; the Strehl ratio in this case is 0.72. The effect of 0.7λ of astigmatism on the focal plane intensity pattern is shown in (c); the Strehl ratio here is 0.44. (d) corresponds to a value of 0.5λ of primary curvature, and its computed Strehl ratio is 0.4. To a good approximation, primary curvature is the same as defocus. Finally, (e) shows the effect of 1λ of primary distortion on the focal plane distribution. This kind of aberration results in a simple shift of the spot in the focal plane. Again, it is clear that small amounts of aberrations can deteriorate the quality of the focused spot; in practice, these aberrations must be kept below a tenth of a wavelength.

The effects of polarization on the focused spot are shown in Fig. 10.38 (Richards and Wolf, 1959; Wolf, 1959; Mansuripur, 1989). The assumed incident plane wave is linearly polarized in the X-direction, and the incident power (integrated intensity) in the aperture of the lens has been set equal to unity. The intensity plots for the X-, Y-, and Z-components of polarization at the focal plane are shown in frames (a), (b), and (c) respectively. Note that the vertical scale, which has been adjusted for the best display, varies significantly from one plot to another. The integrated intensity (area under the curve) for the X-component of polarization in (a) is 0.9361. The same quantity for the Y-component in (b) is 0.0007, and for the Z-component in (c) is 0.0627. Note that the Y-component is concentrated equally in the four quadrants of the XY-plane, whereas the Z-component is mainly in two lobes, split along the Y-axis. These observations are also consistent with geometric-optical arguments based on ray bending.

10.4.3 Detection Methods

In the best detection method, the signal is derived differentially from a detector module containing a polarizing beam splitter and two photodiode detectors (Fig. 10.1a). This method has two advantages over the single-analyzer scheme described in Sec. 10.3.4. First, with a single analyzer, half the signal is lost, whereas the polarizing beam splitter divides the signal essentially without loss. Second, differential detection allows common mode rejection of additive noise, and if the detection threshold is correctly placed, it can also reduce the zero-crossing shift from multiplicative (e.g., laser) noise.

Using Eq. (10.40) with $\alpha = 45°$, the optical power on each detector is

$$P = 0.5\, P_i R \xi^2 \tag{10.50}$$

As in Eq. (10.42), when the magnetic state of the storage medium is reversed, the power on each detector changes by

$$P_s = 2P_i r_y \xi r_x = 2P_i K_r \xi \sqrt{R} \tag{10.51}$$

and the peak-to-peak differentially detected signal is twice this. Reduction of the component of r_x that is reflected by the beam splitter in the main beam improves the contrast

$$\frac{P_s}{P} = \frac{4K_r}{\xi \sqrt{R}} \tag{10.52}$$

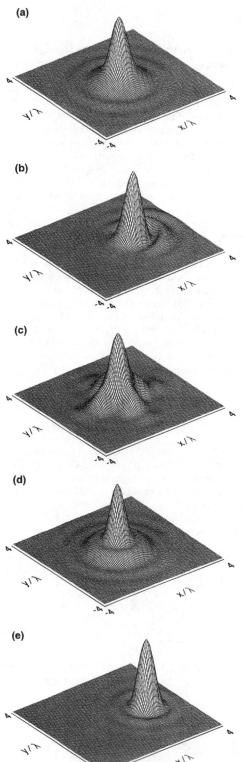

(a)

(b)

(c)

(d)

(e)

FIGURE 10.37 Effects of the various primary (Seidel) aberrations on the intensity distribution in the focal plane of a lens with NA = 0.5 and f_0 = 4000. (*a*) Spherical aberration; (*b*) coma; (*c*) astigmatism; (*d*) curvature; (*e*) distortion.

(a)

(b)

(c)

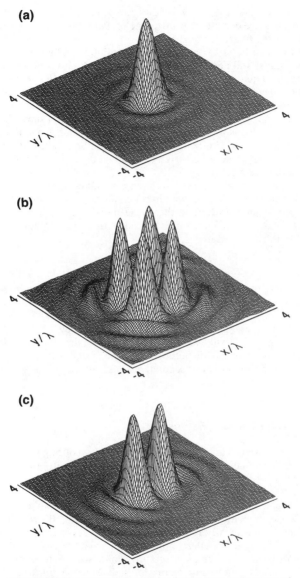

FIGURE 10.38 Intensity distribution for the three components of polarization in the focal plane of a lens with NA = 0.5 and f_0 = 4000. The incident beam has been assumed uniform and linearly polarized along the X-axis. The vertical scale varies among the plots and the actual peak intensities in (a)–(c) are in the ratio of 10000:2.3:341 respectively.

The contrast is readily measured by dividing the peak-to-peak signal by the average power that reaches the detectors. Knowledge of ξ and the reflectivity then allows a determination of the figure of merit K_r.

The detectors can be either avalanche photodiodes (APD) or PIN diodes. An analysis of the signal and noise from APDs and PIN diodes is given in Secs. 10.5.1 and 10.5.2. Here, a qualitative comparison is given. Avalanche photodiodes have a built-in gain factor $G \simeq 20$, which is typically sufficient for the shot noise from the source to be greater than the electronic noise of the detector. The signal-to-noise ratio is then shot-noise limited, and the results of Sec. 10.3.4 show that it depends only on P_i and r_y. Because APDs can handle only a small dynamic range of light power and require a large contrast, $\xi = \sin \phi$ should be small, and a beam splitter with $\xi^2 = 0.1$ is a good choice. The primary disadvantages of APDs are that they are expensive and require high voltages.

PIN diodes are inexpensive and can handle a higher light level. There are two reasons for increasing the light on the photodetectors. First, without the added gain of the APD, the signal is lower and the output noise is typically dominated by the electronics of the amplifier. Thus for PIN diodes, the signal-to-noise ratio (SNR) is proportional to the signal itself

$$\text{SNR} \sim P_i r_x r_y \sin \phi \cos \phi \qquad (10.53)$$

For constant laser power, the power P_i incident on the disk is proportional to $1 - \xi^2$ $= \cos^2 \phi$ of the incident laser power. Maximization of Eq. (10.53) then occurs for $\phi = 30°$, whence a polarizing beam splitter with $\xi^2 = \sin^2 \phi = 0.25$ is more appropriate. A second advantage is that by increasing the light level on the detectors, the focus and tracking signals will be larger. There are two disadvantages incurred with increasing ξ: first, the contrast is reduced, and the system will be more sensitive to alignment error and to laser noise; second, less laser power will arrive at the disk for writing.

10.4.4   Focus and Tracking Servos

Focus and tracking servos are required in all optical recording systems to compensate for the variation in optical path length and radial runout. For a 13-cm disk, the optical path length will typically vary by up to ± 200 μm as the disk rotates, and a focus servo is therefore required to maintain focus within about ± 1 μm that is set by the depth of field. Likewise, because the disks are removable, a typical radial runout of ± 20 μm must be reduced by a tracking servo to ± 0.1 μm. The extremely high track density additionally requires that tracking servo information be embedded in the disk. The servos can derive information from the disk either continuously or at specified times. In either case, this information is preformatted on the disk substrate during fabrication. For example, a continuous tracking signal can be derived from grooves between tracks. Alternatively, a sample and hold servo can receive updates periodically, at equally spaced intervals around the track, from a preformatted header that has focus, timing, track-following, and sector identification data. In both cases, the focus and tracking methods must provide feedback signals that are linear in the error.

Several focus methods have been used, and the obscuration, knife-edge, biprism, and astigmatic methods are illustrated here (Bouwhuis and Braat, 1983). They all rely on the divergence of the reflected rays increasing (decreasing) near the detector as the disk approaches (moves away from) the objective lens. This change in divergence is then translated into a change in differential output from two or more photodiodes. The better techniques combine a large slope of the error signal near focus with an acquisition range that is 100 times the depth of focus.

In the knife-edge or Foucault approach (Kocher, 1983), a one-sided obstruction is placed at the nominal focal point of the detector lens, as in Fig. 10.39, and the focus-error signal is derived differentially from the split diode. A disadvantage with this method is the loss of half the signal by the obstruction.

A biprism method which retains the full signal and requires two pairs of diode detectors is shown in Fig. 10.40. A double wedge splits the beam in two parts, each of which is detected by a split diode. The focus error signal is derived from $(S_1 + S_4) - (S_2 + S_3)$.

In the astigmatic method (Cohen et al., 1984), a cylindrical lens is placed within the detector module. If the beam is out of focus on the disk, its image on the quadrant photodetector will be elliptical, with the major axis orientation dependent on the out-of-focus direction, as shown in Fig. 10.41. The error signal can then be constructed from the differential output $S_1 + S_3 - (S_2 + S_4)$.

All tracking-servo methods work by diffracting light out of the optical path to the detector. In a sample and hold system, alternate off-track pits are used with precise timing to develop an error signal. The pit depth is $\lambda/4$ to diffract light as efficiently as possible. When the beam is in the center of the track, the light reflected to the detector is the same for each pit. When the beam is off-center, the

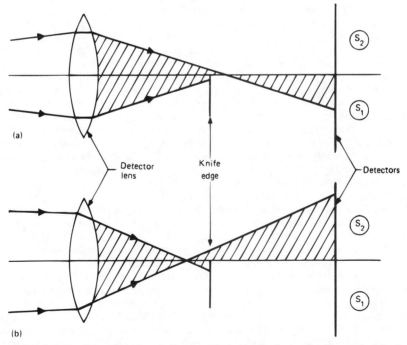

FIGURE 10.39 Focus signal from knife edge. The knife edge is placed at the nominal focal plane of the detector lens. When the disk is (*a*) too close to, or (*b*) too far from the objective lens, the differential signal $S_1 - S_2 > 0$ and $S_1 - S_2 < 0$, respectively (*after Bouwhuis and Braat, 1983*).

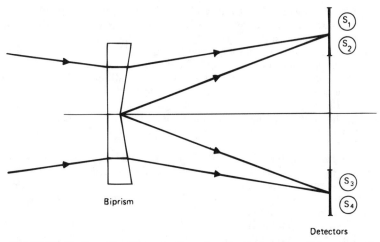

FIGURE 10.40 Focus signal from double wedge. The biprism directs light to two split photodiodes. As the disk moves out of focus, the beam-splitting angle changes, and the focus error signal is $S_1 + S_4 - (S_2 + S_3)$ (*after Bouwhuis and Braat, 1983*).

light reflected to the detector differs for each pit, and an error signal can be developed. This is fed back into the track-following servo.

For continuous far-field tracking, an error signal is derived from preformatted grooves. The objective lens must then capture the zeroth- and first-order diffraction beams, shown in Fig. 10.42 imaged in the far-field on a detector, that these grooves produce. The tracking signal is developed from a split detector, which covers the zeroth-order beam and part of the first-order beam, as shown. When the read beam is centered on or between grooves, the first-order diffraction beams are symmetrical, and the differential signal is zero. However, when the beam is not centered on or between grooves, the two first-order beams are no longer identical, and they will interfere differently in the region of overlap with the zeroth-order beam. The differential signal from the split detector can then be used to center the beam on the track. It has been shown that rectangular phase grooves with a depth of about $\lambda/8$ provide an adequate tracking signal (Jipson and Williams, 1983), and optimal readout is obtained from grooves that are half the width of the track pitch (Pasman et al., 1985).

Among other suggested tracking methods, the three-spot approach (Kryder, 1985) has been used effectively in read-only systems like the digital audio disk, but the use of laser power is too inefficient for writeable systems. It has also been shown that the far-field diffraction pattern from the data itself (a phase grating) can be used to develop both focus and tracking servo signals (Braat and Bouwhuis, 1978), but this too is probably restricted to a read-only system.

In summary, all of the tracking techniques have advantages and disadvantages. The sample and hold technique works well with short sectors of a few hundred bits, but for larger sectors it is necessary to use updates which are more frequent than once per sector. This method therefore is implemented at the cost of formatted data density. The continuous far-field tracking technique provides the ability to count tracks during track seeking, which can shorten access time. Moreover, for some write-once systems, the data written in the grooves are physically contained by the groove walls, thus enhancing readback uniformity and reducing crosstalk from adjacent tracks. In contrast, for magnetooptical media, data in the grooves can

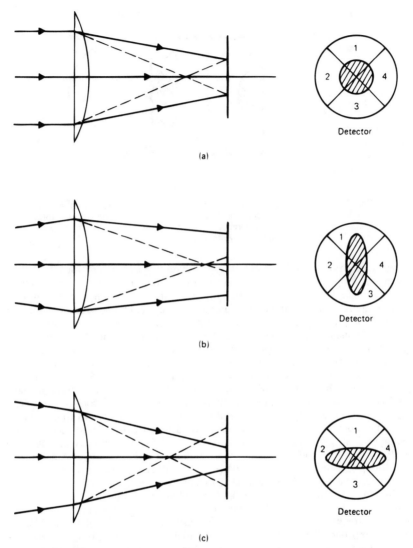

FIGURE 10.41 Focus signal from astigmatic lens. (*a*) The quadrant detector is placed equidistant between focal planes for the two orthogonal axes, when the beam is focused on the disk. Out-of-focus conditions are shown in (*b*) and (*c*). Dashed rays are in the perpendicular plane (*after Bouwhuis and Braat, 1983*).

have significant additional amplitude modulation (medium noise) due to groove irregularities, as well as loss of signal due to interference. If the data are written on wide "land" areas between grooves, it is difficult to acquire enough tracking signal. It would appear, therefore, that sample and hold techniques for tracking might be better suited to magnetooptical recording at present data densities.

In write-once systems, the data, focus, and tracking signals can all be generated

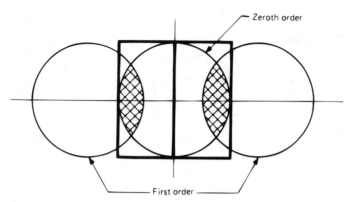

FIGURE 10.42 Diffraction pattern produced at the detector by the groove structure on the disk. The detector (heavy outline) is split and covers the zeroth order diffraction beam. Interference of zeroth- and first-order beams occurs at the overlap (crosshatched) (*after Braat and Bouwhuis, 1978*).

from a quadrant PIN diode, by taking appropriate output combinations (Bell, 1983). In a magnetooptical system, there are many options. One simple approach is to generate the servo signals in separate arms of the data detection module. For example, astigmatic focusing can be implemented in one arm by placing a cylindrical lens in front of a quadrant detector. Far-field tracking can then be implemented in the other arm by using a split detector placed beyond the focal plane of the lens. Another method is to use a separate optical arm for the servo signals (Imamura et al., 1985).

The necessity for a separate fine-tracking actuator can be seen from the following considerations. Suppose it is desired to operate the disk at a 50-Hz rotation rate. To prevent instability, the closed-loop gain of the servo is constrained to have a slope of approximately -1 near the unity gain point. (Away from this point, the slope can be increased to -2.) With this constraint, a bandwidth (unity-gain frequency) of about 2 kHz is required for a closed-loop track servo to follow a 20-μm runout with an error of not more than 0.1 μm. To avoid positive feedback, no poorly damped mechanical resonances should exist below about ten times the closed-loop unity-gain frequency (20 kHz). A small galvanometer or transverse lens actuator can be designed without sharp resonances below 20 kHz, but this is not possible for a 10- to 50-gm carriage and optical head assembly.

It is beyond the scope of this chapter to give details of the large number of lens focus and tracking actuators that can be built into the optical head. The most common approach is to combine focus and tracking into two orthogonal actuators, typically using a voice-coil arrangement for focus motion. For radial track-following motion, there are several possibilities. The optical system can be mounted off-center with respect to a rotated shaft (Okada et al., 1980); a voice coil or variable reluctance structure can be used to translate the lens (Bouwhuis et al., 1985), or the beam can be shifted by a mirror on a stationary galvanometer which is not on the moving head.

10.4.5 Magnet Design

As described in the introduction, erasure and writing in currently practical systems occur in two passes with an oppositely directed magnetic field. That this will remain a requirement of magnetooptical recording can be seen from an order-of-magnitude calculation for the time required to switch a several-hundred-oersted field from an air coil. The time constant

$$\tau_m = \frac{L}{R} \tag{10.54}$$

of a coil with inductance L and resistance R must be comparable with or less than the inverse of the data rate. No specific assumptions are made about the coil shape, other than it has n turns of average radius r, and the n turns have a total cross-sectional area $A \simeq r^2$. The coil inductance is

$$L = q\mu_0 rn^2 \tag{10.55}$$

where q is a factor on the order of unity that depends on the coil shape. The coil resistance is

$$R \simeq \frac{\kappa 2\pi rn}{A/n} \simeq \frac{2\pi\kappa n^2}{r} \tag{10.56}$$

where the resistivity of copper is $\kappa = 1.7 \times 10^{-8} \ \Omega \cdot \text{m}$. For a given cross-sectional area, the time constant is thus independent of n

$$\tau_m = \frac{q\mu_0 r^2}{2\pi\kappa} \tag{10.57}$$

The coil radius and number of turns are determined by requirements on the field and coil resistance. When energized with a current i, the magnetic field near the coil center is

$$H \simeq \frac{ni}{2r} \tag{10.58}$$

and the coil resistance is designed to match the power supply. For example, suppose the power supply can deliver 1 A at 5 V. Using $i = 1$ A, $r = 5 \ \Omega$, and $H = 40$ kA/m [500 Oe] in Eqs. (10.56), (10.58), and (10.57) gives

$$n \simeq 600 \text{ turns} \tag{10.59}$$

$$r \simeq 7 \times 10^{-3} \text{ m} \tag{10.60}$$

$$\tau_m \simeq 10^{-3} \text{ s} \tag{10.61}$$

This time constant is four orders of magnitude too great to operate at a data rate of 10 Mb/s. The problem with the air coil is that it is too large: the inductance is about 1 mH. Some improvement can be achieved by designing a smaller coil, but the coil radius cannot be made less than a few millimeters, which is the spacing between the coil and the medium. This relatively large separation prevents a low-inductance structure from focusing the magnetic field on the small region where thermomagnetic writing is occurring. It is possible to use a one-sided disk, with a flying magnetic recording head on the side opposite to the optics, to build a system which uses the magnetic field to switch the heated medium at the data rate. However, mechanical complications, including alignment and co-tracking of the flying head with the laser beam, make this an unattractive alternative. Therefore, should direct overwrite become an important system requirement, it must be accomplished through medium engineering, such as the use of multiple magnetic layers to obviate the need for a separate erase cycle (Saito et al., 1987).

The requirements on a practical (two-pass system) magnet are that it (1) generates a field of several hundred oersteds at the medium, (2) switches direction in a few milliseconds (a fraction of a disk rotation period), (3) does not interfere with the tracking and focus actuators on the optical head, (4) causes no problems with heat dissipation, (5) does not substantially increase the seek time, and (6) fits into the packaging constraints, which are particularly severe in small drives.

These requirements can be met by several designs. An electromagnet can be placed on either the front (optics) or the back side of the disk. An electromagnet on the front side must be designed around the objective lens, but its size should be minimized for maximum field generation from the ampere-turns. A greater magnetic efficiency can be achieved by winding a coil around a soft-iron pole on the back side, and then shimming with soft iron to reduce both the magnetic circuit reluctance and the demagnetization near the pole tip. Removal of joule heating is simpler for this back-side geometry, because the magnet can be thermally tied to a structure not directly attached to the optical path. Alternatively, a high-energy permanent magnet on the back side can be physically rotated to reverse the field direction. With either front or back (electro-) magnets, it is best if the magnet covers all useful tracks on the medium and hence does not move during track seeking. The substrate must be nonconducting because of eddy-current drag induced in conductors that move in an inhomogeneous magnetic field.

The power dissipated by the magnet depends on the coil shape and ampere-turns. If no portion of the electromagnet saturates during writing or erasure, the field is proportional to the ampere-turns. The power is then given by

$$ P = \frac{\kappa c}{FA} \left(\frac{H}{h} \right)^2 \tag{10.62} $$

where c = average length per turn in the coil
F = coil filling factor (typically $F \approx 0.6$)
h = efficiency (in A/m of field per ampere-turn of current)

Because the power varies directly as the square of the field to be attained and inversely as the square of the coil efficiency, the requirement on the former should be minimized and the efficiency should be maximized, subject to packaging constraints. Efficiencies of 60 A/m per ampere-turn and time constants of a few milliseconds can be achieved in low-power backside designs.

10.5 SYSTEM PERFORMANCE CHARACTERISTICS

System performance is ultimately characterized by data rate and by corrected bit error rate as a function of track density and linear bit density. Internal performance measures that are crucial for design are the signal-to-noise ratio and the uncorrected bit error rate. Adequate signal-to-noise ratio is required to guarantee that the error-correction circuitry is not overwhelmed by soft errors due to Gaussian noise, and an uncorrected bit error rate of less than 10^{-4} is needed to allow a corrected bit error rate of better than 10^{-12}. Consequently, the emphasis in this section is on the signal and noise in magnetooptical systems and on encoding and error-correction techniques designed to maximize areal bit density while maintaining the required corrected error rate.

The magnetooptical signal depends on the medium, the optics, the size and spacing of the written marks, the detectors and electronics, and the signal processing for removing intersymbol interference. The noise originates in the electronics, the quantized nature of light, the intensity modulations of the laser output, and the medium. Some of the noise components, like the electronic and shot noise, have a Gaussian amplitude distribution. Others, like the laser noise and the noise due to previously written data, are non-Gaussian, with negligible tails, and act to narrow the timing window. The hard medium errors are also non-Gaussian, but they have a large probability in the tail region and cannot be treated analytically. All of these noise sources ultimately cause errors in the interpretation of the digital message. For example, when the message is encoded by the presence or absence of a pulse at a specified time, noise can cause errors by shifting the signal amplitude across the detection threshold. Or when the message is encoded by zero crossings, the noise can move the zero-crossing position out of the timing window.

The magnetooptical signal and the shot, electronic, and thermal Gaussian noise sources in APD and PIN detectors are presented in Sec. 10.5.1. The signal-to-noise ratio in typical magnetooptical systems and medium noise are then discussed in Sec. 10.5.2. Additional loss of signal-to-noise ratio, due to the modulation transfer function of the optical system and the loss of timing window through run-length-limited encoding, is described in Secs. 10.5.3 and 10.5.4, respectively. Finally, error-correction methods are briefly described in Sec. 10.5.5.

10.5.1 Magnetooptical Signal and Noise

The photodetector converts optical power (watts) to electrical current, with a quantum efficiency $\eta \simeq 0.5$ A/W

$$i = \eta P \tag{10.63}$$

An avalanche photodiode (APD) has a built-in current gain G, so that in general, the detector current is

$$i = G\eta P \tag{10.64}$$

A transimpedance amplifier can be used to convert the current generated by an APD or a PIN diode into a voltage signal. The amplifier holds the diode collector at ground and forces all current through the feedback resistor R, producing an output voltage

$$V = GR\eta P \tag{10.65}$$

A 10 kΩ resistor allows operation up to 20 MHz, a reasonable bandwidth for the passage of the signals through the electronics.

The peak-to-peak differentially detected magnetooptical signal on each diode is given by Eq. (10.49)

$$P_s = 2P_i r_x r_y \sin \phi \cos \phi \tag{10.66}$$

and the average power on each detector is

$$P = 0.5P_i(r_x^2 \sin^2 \phi + r_y^2 \cos^2 \phi) \simeq 0.5P_i r_x^2 \sin^2\phi \tag{10.67}$$

The rms shot noise current from each detector is then (Horowitz and Hill, 1980)

$$i_{shot} = G \sqrt{2e\eta\beta P} \simeq G \sqrt{e\eta\beta P_i}\, r_x \sin \phi \tag{10.68}$$

where $e = 1.6 \times 10^{-19}$ C, and β is the amplifier bandwidth. There will also be some electronic and thermal noise current in the amplifiers, denoted by

$$i_n = \sqrt{i_{ne}^2 + i_{nt}^2} \tag{10.69}$$

A good amplifier has an equivalent noise input current of about 3 pA/$\sqrt{\text{Hz}}$. Thus,

$$i_{ne} = 3 \times 10^{-12} \sqrt{\beta} = 0.013 \ \mu\text{A} \tag{10.70}$$

with the bandwidth $\beta = 20$ MHz. The rms thermal noise current from the feedback resistor is (Horowitz and Hill, 1980)

$$i_{nt} = \sqrt{4kT\beta/R} = 0.006 \ \mu\text{A} \tag{10.71}$$

for $k = 1.38 \times 10^{-23}$ J/°K, $T = 300$°K, and a nominal value of $R = 10$ kΩ.

Electrical power out of the amplifiers is proportional to the square of these currents (and also to the square of the input optical power). Because the three noise contributions are uncorrelated, the total noise current is the sum of squares of individual currents. From Eqs. (10.64), (10.66), and (10.68), the signal-power-to-noise-power ratio is (Mansuripur et al., 1982)

$$\text{SNR} = \frac{4G^2\eta^2 P_i^2 \, r_x^2 r_y^2 \sin^2 \phi \cos^2 \phi}{e\eta\beta G^2 P_i r_x^2 \sin^2 \phi + i_n^2} \tag{10.72}$$

Due to the high internal gain of APDs, the shot-noise dominates the electronic and thermal noise, and

$$\text{SNR} = \frac{4\eta P_i}{e\beta} r_y^2 \cos^2 \phi \tag{10.73}$$

Note that the gain G does not appear in this equation; the system is limited by the signal-to-shot-noise ratio. However, with PIN diodes ($G = 1$), the electronic and thermal noise together are typically larger than the shot noise, and

$$\text{SNR} \simeq \frac{4\eta^2}{i_n^2} P_i^2 r_x^2 r_y^2 \sin^2 \phi \cos^2 \phi \tag{10.74}$$

10.5.2   Signal-to-Noise Ratio in Magnetooptical Systems

It is useful to represent the detector currents by an equivalent input optical power, the noise equivalent power (NEP). This is found, using Eq. (10.64), by dividing the detector current by $G\eta$. For illustration, the optical power and noise equivalent powers for practical systems constructed with APD and PIN diode detectors are given in Table 10.5. Both systems use a magnetooptical medium with parameters $R = 0.2$, $r_x = \sqrt{R} = 0.45$, and $r_y = 5 \times 10^{-3}$. For APD detectors, the power on each detector should not exceed about 10 μW, and we choose $P_i = 2$ mW, $\xi^2 = 0.05$, and

TABLE 10.5 Power and Noise-Equivalent Powers on APD and PIN Detectors

Quantity	Formula	APD	PIN
P_s (peak-to-peak)	$2P_i r_x r_y \sin\phi\cos\phi$	2.0 μW	4.0 μW
P (average)	$0.5\,P_i r_x^2 \sin^2\phi$	10 μW	50 μW
Contrast	P_s/P	0.20	0.08
NEP_{shot} (rms)	$\sqrt{(e\beta P/\eta)}\,r_x\sin\phi$	0.011 μW	0.025 μW
NEP_e (rms)	$3\times 10^{-12}\sqrt{\beta}/\eta G$	0.001 μW	0.027 μW
NEP_t (rms)	$\sqrt{(4kT\beta/R)}/\eta G$	0.001 μW	0.012 μW
$\text{NEP}_{\text{total}}$ (rms)	$\sqrt{\begin{array}{c}(\text{NEP}_{\text{shot}})^2 + \\ (\text{NEP}_e)^2 + (\text{NEP}_t)^2\end{array}}$	0.011 μW	0.039 μW

$G = 20$. For PIN diodes, the parameters $P_i = 2$ mW, $\xi^2 = 0.25$, and $G = 1$ are more appropriate. It is seen that the contrast P_s/P for the PIN system is quite low, and any increase obtained by reducing ξ is accompanied by a loss of signal.

The signal-to-noise ratio can be calculated from the shot, thermal, and electronics noise equivalent powers, using

$$\text{SNR} = 10\log\frac{P_s^2}{NEP_{\text{shot}}^2 + NEP_t^2 + NEP_e^2}\ \text{dB} \tag{10.75}$$

and the results are given in Table 10.6 for both the APD and PIN detector systems. The APD will actually perform a few dB worse than shown because of extra noise generated with the gain (Mansuripur et al., 1982). The two systems show similar performance, because the extra electronic noise of the PIN is partly compensated by the larger magnetooptical signal that it can detect, because of its greater dynamic range.

TABLE 10.6 Representative Signal-to-Noise Ratio in Magnetooptical Systems with APD and PIN Detectors

System configuration	Correction to SNR, dB	SNR, dB	
		APD	PIN
One-detector[†]	0	45	40
One-detector[‡]	-9	36	31
Two-detectors[‡]	+3	39	34
At moderate data density[‡]	-6	33	28
With enhanced NRZ [≈0.9][§]	0	33	28
With 1,3 code [1.0]	-3	30	25
With 1,7 code [1.33]	-3	30	25
With 2,7 code [1.5]	-6	27	22

[†]Ratio (signal, peak-to-peak)/(total noise-equivalent power, rms), from Table 10.5.

[‡]rms/rms.

[§]The figures in brackets are the changes in data density achieved with RLL encoding.

The signal-to-noise ratios calculated above are for a single detector with the signal given by the peak-to-peak change when the magnetization reverses in a saturated region of magnetooptical film. The signal-to-noise ratios from data in a system with differential detection differ from this in several ways, as is also shown in Table 10.6. The corrections to the signal-to-noise ratio are +3 dB from using two detectors, −9 dB for converting the signal from peak-to-peak to rms, about −6 dB for loss of readback signal due to the modulation transfer function (see Sec. 10.5.3), and various effective losses in signal-to-noise ratio due to narrower timing margins with RLL encoding (see Sec. 10.5.4).

Because the PIN detector system is not shot-noise limited at 2 mW incident read power, an increase in power delivered to the disk causes a proportional increase in signal-to-noise ratio. This trend is being followed, with the availability of higher power lasers to write on media designed to be less thermally sensitive. In a reasonably designed system, a 25 mW laser can deliver about 12 mW to the disk during writing. With a 4:1 ratio of write-read power, this allows 3 mW of read power to be used.

The various noise sources are shown in Fig. 10.43, in which the signal power and the various noise equivalent powers in a 20-MHz bandwidth are plotted as a function of read power. With increasing read power, the shot-noise contribution overtakes the fixed electronic noise, and for higher read powers where the PIN response is shot-noise limited, there is no signal-to-noise ratio advantage to using APD detectors rather than PIN diodes. Above some value of read power, the medium noise overtakes the other noise sources and provides the ultimate limitation. The medium noise line given in Fig. 10.33 is from the best available film deposited on a glass substrate, and has a signal-to-noise ratio of about 42 dB in a 20-MHz bandwidth. Thus, at the nominal power $P_i = 2$ mW at the disk, the medium noise is only slightly greater than the shot noise. From these curves, the typical dependence of the signal-to-noise ratio on read power can be derived. At very low read powers where thermal and electronic noise are dominant, the ratio is proportional to the incident power; at intermediate powers where shot noise is dominant, the ratio is proportional to the square root of the read power; and at higher powers where medium noise limits the performance, the ratio becomes independent of power.

In addition to electronic and shot noise, two other sources of noise, the laser and the medium, adversely affect system performance. Laser noise has been discussed in Sec. 10.4.1. When rf driving is used on the laser, and back-reflection to the laser and extra internal reflection to the photodetectors are minimized, the noise from commercial diode lasers can be reduced to acceptable levels.

Medium noise is usually multiplicative (proportional to the incident power) and has several sources. First, there are microscopic substrate imperfections, including surface roughness and wobble in the preformatted grooves. Flat glass substrates offer the lowest variation in medium reflectivity. If preformatted grooves are used to generate a continuous tracking signal, medium noise is reduced if the magnetooptical data are written on a wide "land" area rather than in the grooves. Second, there are magnetooptical film imperfections, including voids resulting from contaminants and other process problems, that result in hard repeatable errors. These hard errors must be corrected through redundancy of information (see Sec. 10.5.5). Third, there is modulation noise due to a scatter in the shape and position of the recorded transitions. For stable systems in which focus and tracking fluctuations can be ignored, modulation noise is related to the domain-wall pinning mechanisms in the thermomagnetic process described in Sec. 10.2.5. It is very small in amorphous Tb-transition-metal alloys, often significant in ablative nonerasable materials, and usually unacceptably large in polycrystalline magnetooptical materials such as Mn-Bi.

Those aspects of medium noise exclusive of hard errors are most easily character-

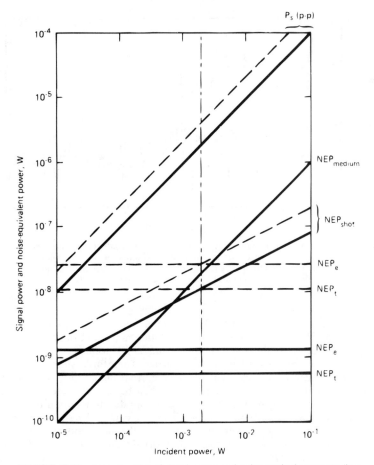

FIGURE 10.43 A log-log plot of signal power and noise-equivalent power (in a 20-MHz bandwidth) versus incident power for the PIN (dashed line) and APD (full line) systems described in the text. The signal power is peak-to-peak, and all noise-equivalent powers are rms. The vertical line is the assumed operating point $P_i = 2$ mW of Tables 10.5 and 10.6. For the APD system with P_i near 2 mW, the total noise-equivalent power (neglecting medium noise) is given by NEP_{shot}.

ized experimentally from a power spectrum—the readback spectrum of a single-frequency low-density pattern on an optimized system with shot-noise limited detectors. The carrier-to-noise ratio, defined as the signal-to-noise ratio in a 30 kHz bandwidth from such a data pattern, is commonly used to compare performance from different systems. Without medium noise, the carrier-to-noise ratio from a shot-noise limited system is about 61 dB (add 28 dB for bandwidth correction to the 33-dB value in Table 10.6). The modulation component of the medium noise can be found by comparing the noise when the medium is saturated (erased) with the noise after the pattern is written. The signal is a series of spikes at multiples of the fundamental, and the modulation noise is seen as an elevation of the noise baseline after writing the low-frequency pattern. Figure 10.44 shows typical results from a spectrum analyzer with 200-kHz bandwidth, for a 2.5 μm bit length 101010 . . .

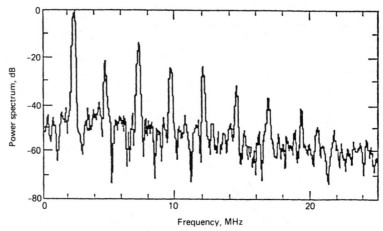

FIGURE 10.44 Readback power spectrum in a 200-kHz bandwidth for data written at 2.5 MHz. (The carrier-to-noise ratio in a 30-kHz bandwidth is obtained by adding 8 dB.) The signal-to-noise ratio is limited by the medium noise. In this case the shot noise power is about 6 dB below the medium noise (*after Bloomberg and Connell, 1985*).

pattern recorded at 5 Mb/s with 10 mW incident power (50 percent duty cycle) on a preerased area. There is no evidence of modulation noise, but the carrier-to-noise ratio (add 8 dB for bandwidth correction) is about 55 dB, which is slightly below the shot-noise limit of about 61 dB mentioned earlier. Therefore, while the measured carrier-to-noise ratio compares favorably with current nonerasable recording systems, further improvements will be possible when better substrate materials become available. It should be noted that hard errors due to medium defects have little rms noise power, and their presence is not detectable by spectrum analysis.

As the read power (and temperature) increases, the magnetooptical component r_y decreases. Consequently, the signal is not strictly proportional to P_i, and the carrier-to-noise ratio, when limited by medium noise, will decrease at higher read power. For example, a broad maximum in the carrier-to-noise ratio of 52 dB was obtained near $P_i \simeq 1$ mW on a Tb-Fe-Co disk deposited on a plastic substrate (Aoki et al., 1985).

The signal-to-noise ratio required for a reliable system may be estimated in the following way: considering only noise fluctuations with a Gaussian amplitude distribution, an rms ratio of 17 dB has a probability of 10^{-12} for a noise fluctuation to exceed the signal, and a probability of 10^{-4} corresponds to 12 dB. A soft-error rate below 10^{-12} is clearly satisfactory, whereas an error rate of 10^{-4} would not be sufficiently correctable. To guarantee a worst-case signal-to-noise ratio greater than 17 dB (after corrections such as in Table 10.6), margins must be built in to anticipate signal loss through (1) reflection, absorption, and diffraction in the optics; (2) variations in medium quality; and (3) inadequate performance of various components (laser, detectors, electronics). Considering that halving the signal-to-noise ratio corresponds to a drop of 6 dB, the nominal corrected value should be at least 25 dB. Table 10.6 indicates that this is presently achievable with both APD and PIN detectors at moderate bit densities and with an enhanced NRZ code that does not reduce the timing window. Performance of PIN detectors with codes that reduce the timing window may be marginal at high density.

10.5.3 Areal Bit Density and Data Rate

10.5.3.1 Modulation Transfer Function. The magnetooptical signal given in Eq. (10.66) assumes that the entire read beam illuminates regions that are uniformly magnetized in both the written and erased states. However, for actual written data, the mark size is smaller than the Gaussian beam. Consequently, the maximum signal amplitude is found to decrease as the written bits get smaller. The signal decreases rapidly below a characteristic bit length that depends on the wavelength, numerical aperture of the objective lens, and shape of the written bits.

This is best summarized by the modulation transfer function S_{MTF} that gives the zero-to-peak amplitude of the output for a repeated pattern of magnetization reversals. For convenience, all such outputs are normalized to half the change in output when a uniformly magnetized region is reversed. As will be shown later, S_{MTF} depends on three properties of the recorded pattern: the repeat distance (recorded "wavelength"), the mark width, and the actual placement of the upward- and downward-going transitions within the repeated pattern.

At the very high data density for which a full recorded wavelength is incorporated within W, the full-width-at-half-maximum of the optical read beam, the modulation transfer function is small. In fact, at such short recorded wavelengths, the signal is limited by diffraction, and for Gaussian optics, the transfer function from a coherent source vanishes for recorded wavelengths smaller than (Goodman, 1968)

$$\lambda_{cutoff} = \frac{0.5\,\lambda}{N_A} \simeq W \tag{10.76}$$

As expected from the geometrical (as opposed to diffraction) argument given above, the cutoff wavelength is comparable to W, given in Eq. (10.46). For typical values of $\lambda = 0.83$ μm and $N_A = 0.5$, $\lambda_{cutoff} = 0.83$ μm. Therefore, the average distance between flux reversals at cutoff is only 0.415 μm and is far smaller than any useful bit size.

In a proper treatment of the magnetooptical signal, the film acts as a 180° phase grating on the small signal component r_y, and the signal is determined from the light coherently diffracted into the objective lens. In a simpler geometrical model, the signal is assumed to be proportional to a convolution of the reversed magnetization in the written pattern with the Gaussian read spot intensity

$$I(r) = I(0)e^{-2.77\,(r/W)^2} \tag{10.77}$$

and results from this model are in good agreement with data from magnetooptical systems (Bloomberg and Connell, 1985). When calculating the normalized signal $S(t)$, it is not necessary to subtract the convolution of $I(r)$ with the unreversed background, because this would merely double the dynamic range and cause a level shift.

The convolution can also be performed as a superposition of responses from properly positioned $+ \rightarrow -$ and $- \rightarrow +$ transitions. The response from one such transition is shown in Fig. 10.45, with the level adjusted so that $S(-x) = -S(x)$. The normalized signal from such an isolated transition has a long linear portion and attains a maximum value S_{trans}. The tangent at the zero crossing equals this maximum at a characteristic distance Λ_{trans} from the zero crossing, given by

$$\Lambda_{trans} \equiv \frac{S_{trans}}{dS/dx} \simeq 1.1\,W = \frac{0.62\,\lambda}{N_A} \tag{10.78}$$

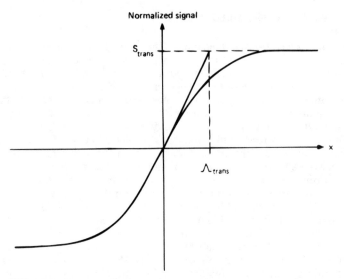

FIGURE 10.45   Normalized signal from an isolated transition, showing definition of S_{trans} and Λ_{trans}.

where dS/dx is the slope at the zero crossing (Bouwhuis et al., 1985). The maximum signal S_{trans} depends on the ratio w/W of the written mark width to the read beam full-width-at-half-maximum, as shown in Fig. 10.46. Several points should be noted about Λ_{trans}. First, it gives the approximate location of the knee of S_{MTF}: the modulation transfer function drops precipitously when the distance between transitions is reduced below Λ_{trans}. Second, Λ_{trans} is determined entirely by W. Third, it is essentially independent of either the written mark width w or the relative curvature of the written mark and the read beam.

The modulation transfer function is then derived by superposition of a pattern of isolated transitions, each with a magnitude given by $S_{\text{trans}}(w/W)$, that repeats every two transitions. The location of the transitions depends on the mark shape and the average distance between transitions ("bit length" b). For a typical bit length $b \simeq 1.5\ W$, the waveform thus composed is nearly sinusoidal, with magnitude S_{MTF}.

In addition to spatial frequency and the ratio w/W, the S_{MTF} for actual written patterns depends on the duty cycle of the write laser. Consider the simplest encoding method, NRZ level detection, in which a region of reversed magnetization (mark) is written in the data cell for a 1 and is not written for a 0. The mark shape is then determined by the write power, size of the write spot, and the pulse time. It ranges between two extremes; namely, from nearly circular marks for pulse times much less than the inverse data rate to elongated marks, with rounded ends which protrude from data = 1 cells into adjacent data = 0 cells, for the maximum pulse time (equal to the inverse data rate).

Two examples of written bits are given in Fig. 10.47 for 50 percent and 5 percent duty cycles. The parameters in the model are the bit length b, the skid length l, the written mark width w, and the full-width-at-half-maximum of the read beam W. At high bit density, the modulation transfer function falls off most rapidly for the 50 percent duty cycle written marks because the space between the marks is sharply reduced. This is seen in Fig. 10.48, where a 5 Mb/s 101010 . . . pattern was written with 5 mW. Both b and l are 0.92 μm, $\lambda = 0.82$ μm, $N_A = 0.61$, and W is 0.75 μm. It

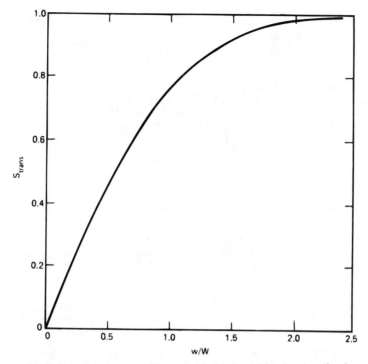

FIGURE 10.46 Maximum amplitude of an isolated transition S_{trans} (as a fraction of saturation amplitude), as a function of the ratio of mark width w to the read beam full-width-at-half-maximum W.

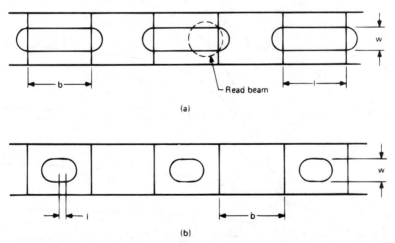

FIGURE 10.47 Assumed written mark shape for 101010 . . . NRZ pattern, where w is the mark width, b is the bit length, and l is the skid length. (a) $l = b$ (50 percent duty cycle); (b) $l = b/10$ (5 percent duty cycle).

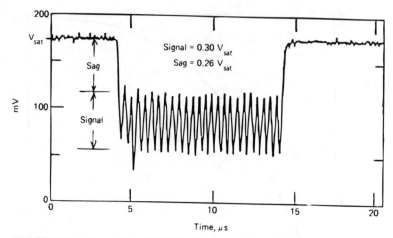

FIGURE 10.48 Output from 101010 . . . pattern written at high density with $b = l = 0.92$ μm, $W = 0.75$ μm, and data-rate $D = 5$ Mb/s. Because of the large sag, the modulation transfer function for this pattern is only 0.30 (*after Bloomberg and Connell, 1985*).

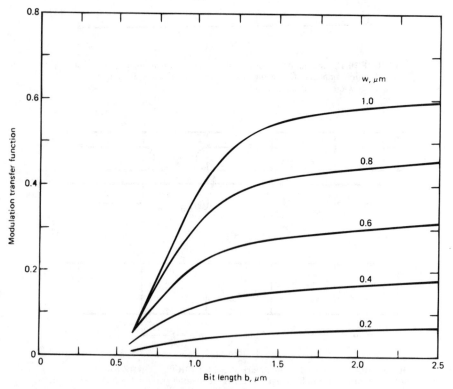

FIGURE 10.49 Computed modulation transfer function versus bit length b, for $l = b/10$, $W = 1.0$ μm, and various mark widths. The theoretical cutoff is at $b = 0.45$ μm.

is seen that the (peak-to-peak) signal amplitude is 0.30 of saturation. Furthermore, the encroachment of the marks into the 0 bit cells produces a loss or "sag" equal to 0.26 of the saturation signal. The data can be fit to the model with one adjustable parameter, $w = 0.5$ μm. At other write powers, equally good fits are obtained with different values of write power.

The modulation transfer function is constructed by taking such 101010 . . . data patterns at different bit lengths. Calculated transfer functions are shown in Fig. 10.49 for a series of mark widths and for $l/b = 0.1$ and $W = 1.0$ μm. The written mark width will have the least sensitivity to laser power if the mark extends to the maximum slope of the Gaussian write beam, which occurs at

$$w = 0.85\ W \tag{10.79}$$

Therefore, for a practical case of $b = 1.5$ μm and $w = 0.8$ μm, the signal is reduced to about 0.41 of the saturated value (nearly -8-dB loss).

Two modulation transfer functions are shown in Fig. 10.50, with $W = 0.75$ μm.

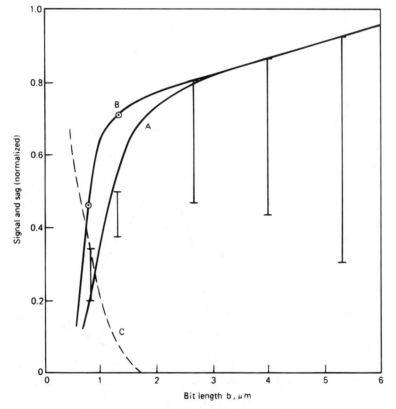

FIGURE 10.50 Comparison of calculated modulation transfer function (solid lines) with observed values versus bit length. Data are read from an NRZ 101010 . . . pattern with $W = 0.75$ μm. The vertical lines show the range of measured values of the transfer function for different write powers for $l = b$, and their envelope should be compared with curve A. The circles are measured for $l = b/10$ and fall on the theoretical curve B. Curve C is normalized sag for $l = b$ (*after Bloomberg and Connell, 1985*).

Curves *A* and *B* show the calculated fractional signal versus bit length *b*, maximized with respect to mark width, for $l = b/10$ and $l = b$, respectively. The vertical lines show the range of experimental values obtained using different write powers and $l = b$. The two data points are the measured signal for $l = b/10$, and the dashed curve *C* is the observed sag for $l = b$. Note that the sag rises steeply as the bit length is decreased below the knee of the transfer function curve.

Figure 10.51 compares theory (solid lines) and experiment for signal and sag

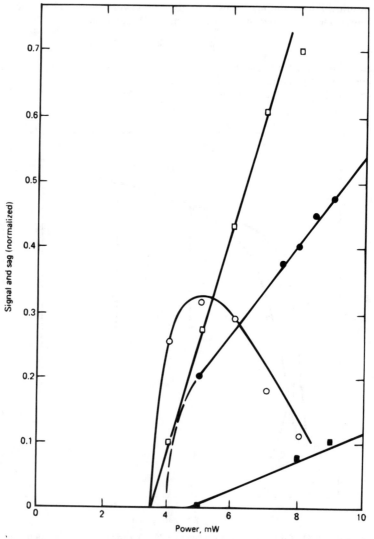

FIGURE 10.51 Modulation transfer function (circles) and normalized sag (squares) for NRZ 101010 . . . pattern with $b = 0.92$ μm, for $l = b$ (open symbols) and $l = b/10$ (filled symbols). Theoretical predictions are given by solid lines; measured values are given by symbols. Read beam $W = 0.75$ μm (*after Bloomberg and Connell, 1985*).

versus write power at the disk. When the bit length is 0.92 μm and $l = b$ (50 percent duty cycle), the signal attains a maximum over a narrow range of write power, and then rapidly decreases because of sag as the written marks become larger. In contrast, when $l = b/10$ (5 percent duty cycle), the sag remains small and the signal increases monotonically with write power. Essentially the same power is required to write the bits with either 200-ns pulses or 20-ns pulses, indicating that the thermal time constant τ_d for heat to flow into the adjacent dielectric layers is short compared with 200 ns. This is a demonstration of the argument presented in Sec. 10.3.3 on thermal engineering. The maximum signal amplitude is obtained when the transitions in a 101010 . . . NRZ pattern are equally spaced, so that the mark and space are of equal length. This criterion can be approached at high density by use of very short duration pulses.

As noted earlier, there is an optimum mark width w for writing information. Figure 10.52 shows how w varies as a function of the incident laser power and the disk speed. In the figure, w is inferred by comparing the signal amplitude from 101010 . . . NRZ data with the prediction of the readback model. The dashed curves are smooth fits to the experimental points, and w is given in units of W (= 0.75 μm). At low linear velocities, the optimum mark width is readily achieved, but at higher velocities the required power rises rapidly and may not be attainable.

Thus, choice of the mark width depends on several factors. When sag is minimized through short pulses, the signal increases with the mark width, as shown indirectly in Fig. 10.51. It is feasible therefore to approach the criterion given by Eq. (10.79), subject to medium sensitivity and available laser power. When long pulses are used, the signal at high data densities may be reduced by sag before the

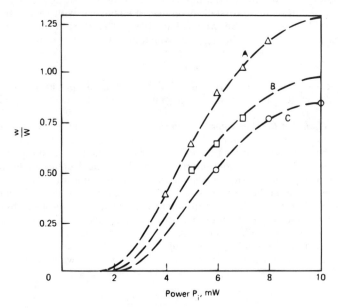

FIGURE 10.52 Ratio of mark width w to read beam full-width-at-half-maximum W versus laser power P_i incident on the disk, for three disk speeds: (curve A) 4.6 m/s, (curve B) 8.9 m/s, and (curve C) curve 26.3 m/s. Data are written as NRZ 1010 . . . pattern at 5 Mb/s, with 200 ns pulse time for the written marks. Read beam $W = 0.75$ μm.

condition in Eq. (10.79) is reached. The mark width is also constrained by erasure requirements. That is, the erase width must be sufficiently larger than the written mark width to allow for worst-case tracking errors during writing and erasure. This is best achieved through higher laser power during erasure, rather than higher bias field, so that if laser power is limited, the written mark width may be less than the value given by Eq. (10.79).

In summary, media can be designed so that extremely short pulses can be used to write data. The knee of the modulation transfer function sets a practical upper limit on useful flux-reversal densities. For example, from Fig. 10.50, the -6-dB point for the short pulse transfer function at $W = 0.75$ μm occurs at $b \approx 1.0$ μm. For an NRZ code, this corresponds to a linear data bit density $D_l = 10^3$ bits per millimeter. In Sec. 10.5.5, the possibility of further increasing this linear data density without decreasing the minimum distance between transitions through run-length-limited encoding will be discussed.

10.5.3.2 Limitations on Track Density.

When marks are present on adjacent tracks, the tail of the Gaussian read beam will always generate cross-track interference. Figure 10.53 shows the crosstalk that occurs in the carrier-to-noise ratio as the read beam is moved between two adjacent tracks separated by $t = 2.0$ W and written with 2.5- and 3.5-MHz signals. When the beam is centered on one track, the carrier-to-noise ratio from the adjacent track is reduced by more than 40 dB. With perfect tracking and with an ideal optical system, crosstalk from adjacent tracks is thus negligible at this track spacing. However, in a practical system, tracking errors are about ± 0.1 μm, effectively moving the tracks together by 0.2 μm in the worst case. A second major contribution to crosstalk is the expansion of the spot size because of focus error. Additionally, crosstalk is increased somewhat with spatial frequency, owing to diffraction effects (Bouwhuis et al., 1985). Therefore, a conservative value for the minimum track spacing t_{min}, for which crosstalk will not be a problem, is

$$t_{min} = 2.0 \ W \tag{10.80}$$

For a typical $W = 0.75$ μm, a track density $D_t = 670$ tracks per millimeter is easily attained. As the technology evolves, t_{min} can be expected to decrease significantly.

10.5.3.3 Trade-Off Between Capacity and Data Rate.

There are several constraints between the system parameters (disk size, rotation rate, data capacity, and data rate) and the underlying bit length and track spacing. The focus and tracking servos impose an upper limit on the rotation rate of the disk. The decrease in the signal-to-noise ratio at high bit density, as shown by the modulation transfer function, imposes a lower limit on the bit length at the inner track, for a system with a constant number of sectors per track. The minimum track spacing is determined by tracking servo accuracy and the read optics. The data rate is constrained by the inner-track bit length, inner-track radius, and rotation rate. And the data capacity is determined by the disk size, track spacing, and minimum bit length.

The interplay of all these factors can be described by two equations, one for capacity

$$8 \times 10^6 C = \frac{(2\pi r_i/b)(r_o - r_i)}{t} \tag{10.81}$$

and one for data rate

$$10^6 D = \frac{2\pi r_i}{b} \frac{\Omega}{60} \tag{10.82}$$

where C = unformatted capacity in MB
  b = inner track bit length
  r_i, r_o = inner and outer track radii
  t = track spacing
  D = data rate in Mb/s
  Ω = rotation rate in rpm.

Substitution of Eq. (10.82) into Eq. (10.81) leads to an equation for inner track radius

$$r_i = r_o - 0.1333 \, \frac{\Omega C t}{D} \qquad (10.83)$$

and this value can be used in Eq. (10.82) to find the minimum bit length b.

For example, with a rate $D = 5$ Mb/s, outer radius $r_o = 6$ cm and track spacing t

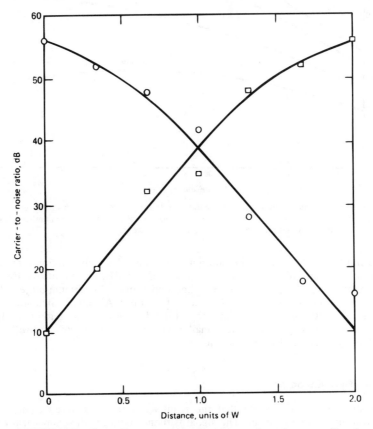

FIGURE 10.53 Crosstalk measurement of carrier-to-noise ratio versus off-track position of read beam center, in units of W. Tracks written at 2.5 and 3.5 MHz are centered at $x = 0$ and $x = 2W$, respectively. Circles and squares give carrier-to-noise ratios for the 2.5 and 3.5 MHz signals, respectively. For these measurements, $W = 0.75$ μm, and the mark width $w \simeq 0.85$ W.

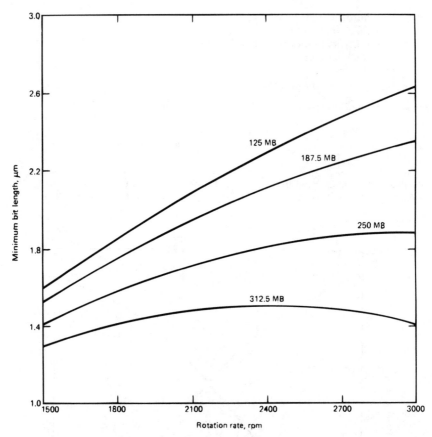

FIGURE 10.54 Minimum bit length versus rotation rate for a 13-cm disk with various unformatted capacities and with data rate $D = 5$ Mb/s. The track spacing $t = 1.5$ μm, and the number of bits per track is assumed to be constant (*after Bloomberg and Connell, 1985*).

$= 1.5$ μm, Fig. 10.54 shows the minimum bit length b versus rotation rate Ω, for different data capacities. For capacities less than 250 MB, there is a clear trade-off between the servo-limited rotation rate and optics-limited minimum bit length. At higher capacities, an increase in Ω has less effect on b. A similar calculation, for a data rate $D = 10$ Mb/s, demonstrates that if the data rate is chosen to be too large, the minimum bit length will be too small at practical rotation rates and will not be significantly increased by lowering the capacity C.

10.5.4 Data Encoding

For simplicity, let us assume that the readback signal is derived from a well-balanced differential channel. The signal is then bipolar, with symmetrical excursions in both directions from the zero level, and a clock defines the channel bit cells. There are two ways to encode and detect message bits. In the first method, known as pulse-position-modulation encoding, the message bit is determined from the signal polarity at the center of the bit cell. The value of the message bit is most easily found by comparing the signal with a threshold voltage level (which is set to zero for this ideal situation). In the second method, known as pulse-duration-modulation encoding, the message bit is determined from the existence (or absence) of a zero-crossing of the signal within the bit cell. This is most directly found by comparing the signal polarities at the cell boundaries. Either encoding method unambiguously determines the message bit to be a 0 or a 1.

In the general encoding process, m data bits are encoded as n message bits. The simplest encodings are NRZ and NRZI, where the data and message bits are identical. NRZ is a pulse-position encoding, where 1s and 0s are encoded into regions of opposite magnetization direction. NRZI is a pulse-duration encoding, where 1s and 0s are encoded into the presence or absence of a transition between magnetization directions. Because the domains in (two-pass) magnetooptical recording are always written with the same polarity, opposite to a preerased state (unlike conventional magnetic recording), it is easier to implement a simple polarity detection scheme using NRZ. Thus, a region of reversed magnetization is written to store a 1 message bit, and the erased state is left undisturbed for a 0. Implementation of an NRZI encoding with zero crossing detection is more difficult, because two zero crossings will be detected from each isolated region of reversed magnetization. The length of the reversed region must be adjusted so that the detected crossings of a 111 . . . message pattern are equally spaced. Local changes in medium write sensitivity will alter the length of the reversed regions, shifting adjacent zero crossings in the opposite direction. Such shifts cannot be compensated by self-clocking techniques.

Run-length-limited codes with (d,k) constraints are useful both for self-clocking and for packing data at a higher density on the disk. The (d,k) constraints apply to the message bits, which are encoded on the disk as if they were NRZ. The d and k constraints specify that there be at least d and not more than k 0s between adjacent 1s in the message bit stream. The k constraint allows self-clocking, whereas the d constraint can be used to increase the minimum distance between 1s. The penalty for using constraints on the message bits is that each message bit is not entirely random and thus contains less information than a (random) input data bit. Consequently, the m data bits must be encoded into $n > m$ message bits, and the message bit cell is therefore smaller than the data bit cell. Now by definition, for RLL codes there are $d + 1$ message bits within each minimum flux reversal interval. The timing window is always the size of the message bit cell, and for NRZ ($d = 0$), the timing window is also equal to the minimum distance between flux reversals. Therefore, for the same minimum distance between flux reversals, the d constraint reduces the RLL timing window from the NRZ value by

$$T_{RLL} = \frac{T_{NRZ}}{d + 1} \tag{10.84}$$

At high density, when the message bit cell is smaller than the optically constrained minimum feature size, regions of reversed magnetization centered on one bit cell will extend into the adjacent bit cells. Under such conditions, which are exacerbated when a $d \geq 1$ RLL code is used, pulse-position encoding may give errors when decoding the adjacent message bits. In contrast, pulse-duration encoding can be used as long as the minimum distance between flux reversals is larger than the optically determined minimum feature size. Thus, pulse-duration encoding must be used at sufficiently high density.

The reduction of the timing window for RLL codes has a significant effect on the required signal-to-noise ratio for magnetooptical systems. Suppose first that additive electronic noise is the only source of noise or timing error. From Eq. (10.84), when using pulse duration modulation encoding, the window around the zero crossing is narrowed to 0.5 of the NRZ window for $d = 1$ codes and 0.33 for $d = 2$ codes. For a sinusoidal waveform

$$S(t) = S_{\text{MTF}} \sin \frac{\pi t}{T_{\text{NRZ}}} \tag{10.85}$$

shown in Fig. 10.55, the amount of noise that will cause an error is then reduced for these codes from the NRZ value by factors of $\sqrt{2}$ and 2, respectively. Hence, the signal-to-noise requirement is 3 dB (for $d = 1$) and 6 dB (for $d = 2$) greater than when using NRZ with the same minimum feature size.

However, in addition to Gaussian noise there are invariably other sources of noise and timing error that can degrade performance by further reducing the timing window (Treves and Bloomberg, 1986b). The effect of timing jitter is to decrease the window size. Non-Gaussian noise sources (such as laser noise, medium noise, crosstalk from adjacent tracks, and noise from data not entirely overwritten on the same track) typically have an amplitude spectrum without long Gaussian tails, and each acts to decrease the timing window by a fixed amount. Because these amounts are independent of the total window, they will occupy a larger fraction of the window budget for encoding methods with small windows. Consequently, the effective loss of signal-to-noise due to RLL encoding will be larger than the estimate given above.

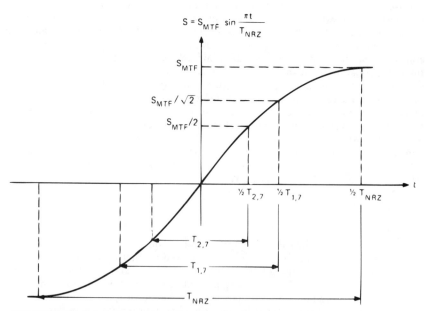

FIGURE 10.55   Relation between relative allowable signal-to-noise ratio and window width for various pulse duration modulation encodings of a sinusoidal waveform. For a (2,7) code, the window is reduced to one-third that for NRZ encoding, with an effective loss of signal-to-noise-ratio of at least 6 dB and a gain in data density of 50 percent.

These losses in signal-to-noise ratio can be semiquantitatively expressed as follows. Let the time T_{fixed} budgeted to the non-Gaussian noise sources be a fraction γ of the NRZ window:

$$T_{fixed} = \gamma\, T_{NRZ} \tag{10.86}$$

Then, again referring to the sinusoidal waveform of Fig. 10.45, the effective fractional loss ΔSNR of signal-to-noise ratio due to window narrowing from both the encoding method and T_{fixed} is

$$\Delta SNR = \sin \frac{(\pi/2)T_{RLL} - 2T_{fixed})}{T_{NRZ}} \tag{10.87}$$

$$= \sin \left[\frac{\pi}{2} \left(\frac{1}{d+1} - 2\gamma \right) \right]$$

When this is combined with the loss from the modulation transfer function, the normalized effective signal amplitude is

$$S = S_{MTF} \sin \left[\frac{\pi}{2} \left(\frac{1}{d+1} - 2\gamma \right) \right] \tag{10.88}$$

RLL encoding enables both self-clocking and, in some cases, data compression. For example, use of 1,7 codes gives a 1.33 increase in data density between flux reversals. Likewise, 2,7 codes give a 1.5 increase in data density. However, as shown by Eq. (10.87), the price in window loss (and, equivalently, loss in signal-to-noise ratio) can be high.

An understanding of intersymbol interference is essential to evaluate the tradeoffs involved with the use of RLL codes. At high flux-reversal density, the lowering of the modulation transfer function is accompanied by intersymbol interference, whereby the zero-crossing position of a particular transition depends on adjacent transitions. There are two components to intersymbol interference: a nonlinear effect introduced during writing and a linear part that occurs in readback and is also responsible for the sag effect described earlier. Because the intersymbol interference in readback is linear, it can be greatly reduced, with some loss of signal-to-noise ratio, through equalization of the read channel. The choice between using a $d \geq 1$ RLL code or an enhanced NRZ (with, for example, an extra 1 message bit added after every n data bits for self-clocking) at a higher flux-reversal density depends in part on the ability to remove intersymbol interference with channel equalization. The relatively low signal-to-noise ratio and the absence of high-frequency components because of the sharp cutoff in the optical modulation transfer function, however, will make channel equalization more difficult.

In flying-head conventional magnetic recording, there is a large nonlinear component to intersymbol interference, introduced in the write process by both hysteresis and demagnetization effects, that cannot be equalized. This nonlinear bit shift increases rapidly when adjacent transitions crowd together. Consequently, RLL codes can provide a slight improvement in data bit density for conventional recording by spreading the closest transitions farther apart. In contrast, hysteresis and demagnetizing effects are negligible in magnetooptical recording, and as a result there is minimal nonlinear bit shift. If good channel equalization is achieved, an enhanced NRZ code may be preferable to $d \geq 1$ RLL codes at moderate flux-reversal densities.

In summary, the choice of a particular code depends on available signal-to-noise ratio, the timing window, the degree of intersymbol interference, the ability to equalize the read channel, and ease of encoding/decoding. Methods can be altered at will. For example, the $(d,k = 2,10)$ EFM code used in digital audio uses an extra "merging" bit that improves the channel by suppressing low frequencies, at a cost of 6 percent overhead (Heemskerk and Immink, 1982). There are multiple trade-offs for any decision, and while designers may agree that several approaches are good, few will agree on a best design.

10.5.5   Error Correction and Hard Errors

Because of the extremely high areal densities attained in optical recording, media currently produced, even under clean room conditions, can be expected to have an uncorrected bit-error rate of up to 10^{-4} associated with disk surface defects. While there will certainly be reductions of the bit-error rate with time, particularly as the substrate technology improves, error correction will always be required to provide a corrected bit-error rate of less than 10^{-12}, as demanded for digital data storage.

To obtain high-bandwidth, real-time operation, the error-correction method chosen must be designed for the expected distribution of hard errors on the disk. An example of the distribution of errors that occurs in optical systems is shown in Fig. 10.56. Fortunately, very long burst errors, which can cause loss of clocking in self-clocked systems, are rare. Most of the errors are in the one- to three-bit range, but approximately 10 percent are larger. Thus, the error-correction method must

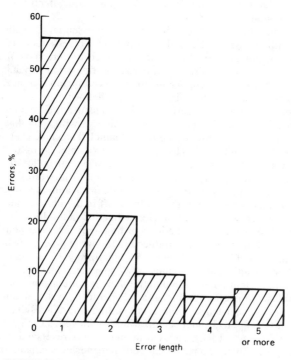

FIGURE 10.56 Distribution of the size of uncorrectable medium errors for a magnetooptical disk.

primarily be designed to handle the relatively large number of short-length errors, but must also be capable of correcting the less frequent longer bursts.

Linear block codes, such as Reed-Solomon codes are used because they both meet these requirements and are easily implemented in hardware. In a block code, s message bits form a message symbol, and k message symbols are combined with $p = n - k$ parity symbols to form encoded blocks of n symbols. It can be shown (Clark and Cain, 1981) that using a symbol length $s > 1$ and a block length $n \leq 2^s - 1$, a Reed-Solomon code can be constructed that will correct $t = p/2$ symbols. Further, if the errors occur at not more than p "erasure" positions, all of which are known by some method (e.g., a loss of signal amplitude) external to the decoder, then the code can correct up to $t = p$ errors. Note that error correction applies equally to message and parity symbols.

Theoretically, a Reed-Solomon code with $s = 8$ bits per symbol (i.e., 1 byte symbols), block length $n = 255$ symbols per block, $k = 223$ message symbols per block, and $p = 32$ parity symbols per block, can correct any 16 incorrect symbols. In practice, decoding of such efficient codes has not yet been implemented in hardware. Instead, the relatively easy correction of up to two symbols in each block is made at the data rate. When more than two symbols are in error, decoding is delayed, and correction is performed in software.

Interleaving, whereby consecutive bits are placed in different blocks, can, in two ways, reduce delays in the processing of error-correction algorithms. First, two-way interleaving is particularly useful because of the high probability that a two-bit error will fall across an eight-bit symbol boundary, thus corrupting two symbols in one block. Partitioning such an error into different blocks will decrease the likelihood that it must be decoded in software. Second, for error-correcting architectures that allow decoding of the interleaved blocks in parallel, N-way interleaving will increase the computation time allocated to correction of each block by a factor of N. Therefore it will be possible to implement the efficient codes required for correction of a larger number of incorrect symbols at the data rate. Finally, interleaving also provides the capability to correct the small number of long burst errors that are found in magnetooptical recording media.

These methods of error correction are currently in use in the compact disk read-only memory, digital audio, and write-once systems. The industrywide standard of the digital audio disk industry uses two crosswise interleaved Reed-Solomon codes, with $s = 8$ bits per symbol and $p = 4$ parity symbols per block in each block of $n = 32$ symbols (Hoeve et al., 1982). As presently implemented, it can correct errors in any two symbols and up to four errors if the erasure positions are known. Uncorrected error bursts are hidden by interpolation schemes. This is sufficient because the demands of audio technology are met without extremely low corrected error rates. MO standards (through 4X systems) specify $s = 8$ bits per symbol Reed-Solomon codes with $n = 120$ and $p = 16$ interleaved to depth 10 in disks with 1024 bytes per sector ($n = 22$; $p = 16$ interleaved to depth 5 in disks with 512 bytes per sector).

There is no theoretical impediment to high-data-rate, efficient, real-time error correction. It can be expected that VLSI implementations of interleaved Reed-Solomon codes, capable of correcting worst-case errors at the full data rate, will be operating on magnetooptical systems with corrected error rates well below 10^{-12}.

10.6 OPPORTUNITIES AND LIMITATIONS

Magnetooptical recording combines very high storage density, low cost, random access, erasability, and removability. The areal storage densities of 0.5×10^6 b/mm^2

that are easily attainable with magnetooptical recording remain greater than those in currently available magnetic recording products in spite of impressive progress.

The ability to read and write small bits with a large mechanical clearance leads to many favorable attributes of magnetooptical systems. First, it enables second-surface operation, which greatly improves immunity to surface dirt and scratches, and allows good isolation of the active film from the atmosphere. This in turn permits the removal of media, consequently enabling the drive to be used with any medium (erasable, nonerasable, and read-only). Removability requires little additional servo performance, because embedded servos are in any event required at high track densities. Second, there is no possibility of data-destroying head "crashes," and magnetooptical drives should be relatively immune to shock and vibration. A shock large enough to cause loss of focus would only delay disk I/O by a fraction of a second.

The success of magnetooptical recording technology hinges on the ability to make archival-quality erasable media. The primary concern is to protect the magnetooptical thin film from chemical degradation. The problem is particularly severe with the amorphous rare-earth transition-metal films, in which the rare-earth atoms are highly reactive. Nevertheless, such archival-quality films are in commercial production.

A present and continuing limitation of small magnetooptical drives is a relatively low data rate when compared to high performance Winchester drives. This is required because close tracking tolerances and small servo bandwidth limit the rotation rate, and the minimum bit length is limited by the optics.

Agreement on format standards, which are necessary for interchangeability, may take several years because of competing interests. For example, grooves are favored for nonerasable disks because they both help confine the written (ablated) marks and improve track-seeking performance by providing a continuous servo signal. Grooves in magnetooptics, however, are disadvantageous because they lower the medium quality and increase medium noise. A compromise, perhaps made at the expense of continuous tracking, might be to use grooves for both but to write in the (narrow) grooves for nonerasable and on the (wide) lands for magnetooptical media.

The technological push for magnetooptics comes currently from digital audio players (Compact Discs). The commercial success of these drives requires the development of inexpensive diode lasers, optics, actuators, servos, photodiodes, VLSI error correction, and preformatted substrates. Many of these components can be incorporated in magnetooptical systems with small changes. These drives also provide the incentive for investment in manufacturing technology for low-cost components, such as 30-mW lasers, low-noise photodiodes, VLSI circuitry for efficient real-time error correction, high-quality substrates, and preformatting techniques. As a consequence, the cost and performance of magnetooptical media and drives continues to improve.

An important aspect of magnetooptical systems is that their capabilities span many applications. At the low end (single-user workstations), they provide inexpensive, random-access replacement and backup for Winchester drives. On multifunctional drives, archival nonerasable and read-only media can also be used.

Magnetooptical drives can also be used with large general-purpose computers. To compensate for the relatively low data rate, two options are possible. For applications where files are being stored or retrieved, an I/O processor (buffer) can match the data rate of the drive to that of the mainframe. For virtual memory systems, the processor needs rapid access to disk memory. To achieve this, the data rate can be improved by using either several magnetooptical drives in parallel through a single data channel, or multiple read beams and read circuitry in one drive. The former has the advantage of simplicity and retains cylinderlike access, whereby the fine tracking actuator gives rapid access to several nearby tracks. With proper staggering of data on adjacent tracks, there should be little loss in peak data rate due to track-seeking or latency. Such a buffered multiple disk configuration will provide tremendous data rates and should be an inexpensive replacement for large magnetic disk drives. Smart controllers will shield the computer from delays due to the two-pass erase-write cycle.

Magnetooptics can also be used to build an on-line mass storage system, which combines removability with random access and terabyte capacity. There are interesting problems relating to the architectural organization of such a system, especially if it is composed of hundreds or thousands of single-disk magnetooptical drives.

Perhaps most important, magnetooptical technology will enable a significant class of new computer-based applications. The processing of graphics, image, video, and audio data makes enormous demands on the storage requirements of computer systems. Computer workstations of the 1990s will enable such applications by using a matched combination of powerful processors, high resolution color monitors, large semiconductor random-access memory, high-bandwidth network communications, and inexpensive random-access magnetic and magnetooptical storage.

10.7 RECENT DEVELOPMENTS

10.7.1 Direct Overwrite Techniques

The thermomagnetic recording process, as envisaged in this chapter, requires the erasure of an already recorded track before rewriting can occur. Without using sophisticated device drivers that physically erase deleted files at convenient times, the effective data recording rate will be impaired, falling to less than one half of the actual record and erase rates. This penalty has spurred the invention of numerous single-head, direct overwrite techniques that require either the modulation of the applied magnetic field (Tanaka et al., 1987; Nakao et al., 1987), the modulation of the laser intensity (Sun and Laumann, 1987; Hansen, 1987; Saito et al., 1987; Shieh and Kryder, 1987; Shultz et al., 1988) or both (Rugar, 1988; Rugar and Siegel, 1989). Currently, each technique has its advantages and drawbacks, and work continues to establish if any method provides a viable approach.

10.7.1.1 Direct Overwrite by Magnetic Field Modulation.
Figure 10.57 shows a typical system for magnetooptical recording by magnetic field modulation (Nakao et al., 1987). A track is continuously illuminated through the disk substrate by a focused laser beam, and a magnetic field, applied close to the recording surface, is switched in direction according to the bit stream received. Thus, depending on the direction of the field during cooling, magnetic domains of both orientations can be written. Figure 10.58 shows the carrier-to-noise ratio versus recording frequency obtained with a Tb-Fe-Co recording medium. Using a recording laser power of 10 mW and a magnetic field modulation amplitude of 24 kA/m (300 Oe), the carrier-to-noise ratio is greater than 50 dB for recording frequencies up to about 5 MHz.

While promising results such as the above have been obtained, there are a number of issues that remain unresolved. In particular, to overwrite at high data rate, the magnetic head must be placed very close to the recording surface in order that a coil with the small inductance needed for high-speed switching can produce a

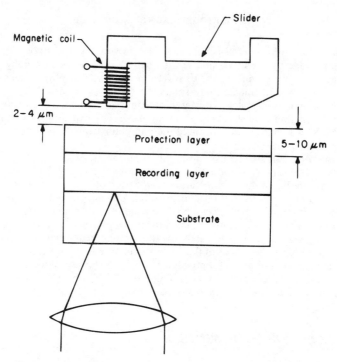

FIGURE 10.57 Schematic design of a magnetic coil used for direct overwrite by the magnetic modulation methods (*Nakao et al., 1987*).

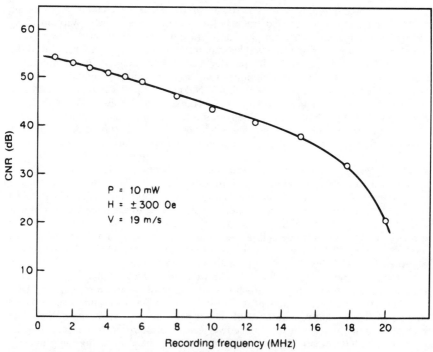

FIGURE 10.58 Carrier-to-noise ratio versus recording frequency obtained in direct overwrite using the magnetic field modulation method (*Nakao et al., 1987*).

sufficient field. From Sec. 10.4.4 on magnet design, the time constant varies as the square of the head-disk spacing. Consequently, the spacing must be reduced by a factor of 100 to decrease the time constant to 10^{-7} s. With the floating-head design shown in Fig. 10.57, a head-disk spacing of about 50 μm is required for a field of 24 kA/m (300 Oe) to be generated. While this allows the magnetic film to be coated with a thick protection layer that both insures the data against head-crashes and allows the disk to be removed, it nevertheless limits a disk to single-side operation.

A method that addresses this particular problem is the resonant-bias-coil overwrite technique (Rugar, 1988; Rugar and Siegel 1989), in which a sufficiently large field amplitude is obtained at frequencies up to about 10 MHz with coil-to-media spacings of about 1 mm. In this method, a coil wound on a ferrite rod is part of a resonant circuit that is driven sinusoidally at a frequency that is higher than the required data rate, as shown in Fig. 10.59. The magnetization along the track is then controlled by short laser pulses which are fired at either the positive or negative peaks of the applied magnetic field. Thus, at each pulse a circular magnetic domain is produced with an orientation determined by the instantaneous direction of the magnetic field. When the disk velocity is set so that there is considerable overlap between the successive circular domains, any pattern of magnetization orientation can be overwritten into a track with a resolution set by the magnetic field modulation frequency. The data stream can therefore be encoded using a pulse width modulation code, where the positions of the domain transitions signify binary 1s, and the clock frequency is twice the frequency of the applied magnetic field.

One major issue is the power requirement for effective operation of the resonant coil. When a field H is produced in a volume V at frequency f using a circuit with quality factor Q, the power needed is

$$P = \mu_0 H^2 V f \left(\frac{\pi}{Q} \right) \quad \left[10^{-7} \left(\frac{H^2}{4\pi} \right) V f \frac{\pi}{Q} \right]$$

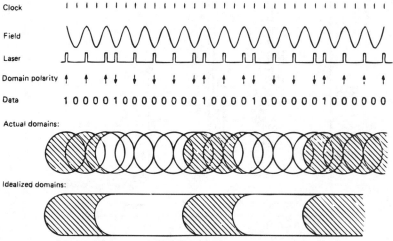

FIGURE 10.59 Timing diagram and the resulting mark shapes for the resonant coil direct overwrite technique. The laser is pulsed at either positive or negative field peaks to produce circular domains that then add to continuous marks of controllable length (*Rugar and Siegel, 1989*).

Therefore, in a typical, two-sided disk system, for which $H = 24\,\text{kA/m}$ (300 Oe), $V = 200\,\text{mm}^3$, $f = 5$ MHz, and $Q = 50$, power of 45 W would be required. This is an order of magnitude too large for many applications.

10.7.1.2 *Direct Overwrite by Laser Intensity Modulation.* Direct overwriting of a previously recorded track by laser intensity modulation has been demonstrated using the domain nucleation and erasure properties of Tb-Fe-Co alloys which have compensation temperatures in the vicinity of 80°C (Shieh and Kryder, 1987). In this technique, domains are written and erased in zero applied field by selecting the power and duration of the laser pulse. Figure 10.60 shows the laser pulse duration and amplitude margins at different temperatures for nucleation and erasure for a Tb-Fe-Co alloy (Shieh and Kryder, 1987). Typically, the erase pulse is significantly

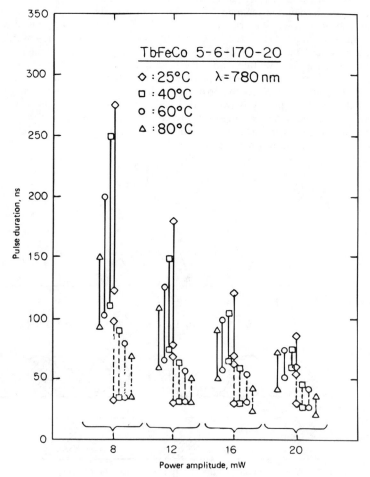

FIGURE 10.60. The laser pulse duration and amplitude margins at different temperatures for nucleation and erasure of domains in the absence of an applied magnetic field in Tb-Fe-Co films (*Shieh and Kryder, 1987*).

shorter than the write pulse. For example, at a power level of 12 mW at an ambient temperature of 25°C, a domain written by a pulse with a duration of 80 ns can be erased by a subsequent pulse of 30-to 70-ns duration.

Two mechanisms for domain nucleation and erasure have been suggested. In one of them erasure is accomplished by the nucleation of a reverse domain at the center of the domain to be erased (Shieh and Kryder, 1987). However, stringent constraints are placed on the recording medium for this process to occur successfully (Hansen, 1987). Specifically, the medium composition and the laser pulse characteristics must be chosen, on the one hand, to avoid ring domain formation during the writing process, and on the other hand, to create a ring domain formation during the erasure process. These constraints are very difficult to satisfy practically. The more probable erasure mechanism is the thermal destabilization of a domain under the influence of a low-power laser pulse that results in the inward collapse of the domain wall (Savage et al., 1988). This destabilization may be achieved without approaching the Curie temperature so that the erasure pulse will not create domains in an unwritten, uniformly magnetized region. The specific details of the collapse depend on the relative sizes of the wall and demagnetizing energies, consistent with observations.

An alternative technique for direct overwrite using exchange-coupled magnetic multilayers has been developed recently and was described in Sec. 10.2.6.

10.7.2 Cross-Talk Cancellation

Using three beams focused on three adjacent tracks during readout, it has been demonstrated that cross-talk between tracks can be reduced substantially using adaptive signal processing techniques (Kayanuma et al., 1990). The basic idea is to have two side-rigger beams read the adjacent tracks at low power, then subtract their signals from the signal coming from the main track. This technique has been successful in effectively eliminating the cross-talk. New algorithms are presently under development to optimize the performance of the three-beam cross-talk canceller.

10.7.3 Land/Groove Recording

This scheme utilizes both the land and the groove for recording of the user data. Typically, the width of the land equals that of the groove, and the groove depth is optimized for cross-track cross-talk cancellation using only one focused spot (Fukumoto et al., 1994). It turns out that at a groove depth close to $0.15\lambda_0$, where λ_0 is the vacuum wavelength of the light, cross-talk from adjacent tracks disappears.[†] Unfortunately, this interesting phenomenon is very sensitive to variations of the various parameters of the system. In particular, substrate birefringence causes the optimum groove depth for land-reading to differ from that for the groove-reading. To remedy this situation one must either use substrates with little or no birefringence (e.g., glass or amorphous polyolephine), or use substrates whose birefringence is uniform across the disk (and invariant from disk to disk), or use a dynamic servo that senses and automatically compensates for the effects of birefringence during readout (Goodman and Mansuripur, 1995).

[†]The exact groove depth depends on a number of factors, including the numerical aperture of the objective lens, the track pitch of the disk, and the truncation radius of the incident beam.

10.7.4 Blue/Green Lasers for Optical Recording

Recent developments in the II-VI class of semiconductor materials for blue/green lasers have been encouraging and show a promising path for the evolution towards future generations of optical recording systems. Unfortunately, at present, these lasers have a very short lifetime at room temperature, especially when operated in CW mode. GaN is another interesting material system, in which LED operation has been demonstrated, and laser operation is expected in the near future. Another possibility for obtaining short-wavelength light is frequency doubling using nonlinear optical materials. Although high efficiency and reliable operation has been demonstrated in this area (Hurst et al., 1993), the light sources thus obtained are expensive, sensitive to temperature fluctuations, and, generally speaking, not suitable for low cost optical storage applications.

10.7.5 Partial Response Signalling

Partial response signalling in conjunction with maximum likelihood detection (PRML) is a technique that has been discussed recently in relation to optical recording systems (Tobita et al., 1992; Honma et al., 1994). In this scheme a certain amount of intersymbol interference (ISI) is deliberately introduced into the read signal in order to reduce constraints on the bandwidth of the electronic circuitry. The ISI is then removed using the maximum likelihood detection scheme (based on the Viterbi algorithm) or otherwise. Assuming that the intrinsic jitter of the recorded marks can be brought sufficiently under control, PRML can be very useful in permitting high-density recording at a given wavelength. The minimum mark length Δ_{min} that can be resolved is determined by the cutoff frequency of the objective lens and is given by

$$\Delta_{min} = \frac{\lambda_0}{4\,\mathrm{NA}}$$

where NA is the numerical aperture of the objective lens. One advantage of PRML is that, given a sufficient amount of signal-to-noise ratio (SNR), it can resolve mark lengths down to Δ_{min}, thus obviating the need for (d,k) modulation codes having $d \neq 0$ (Cheng et al., 1995).

10.7.6 Solid Immersion Lens (SIL)

By placing a hemispherical glass lens in contact or near-contact with the optical disk surface, it is possible to reduce the diameter of the focused spot substantially (Mansfield and Kino, 1990). In one proposed version of this scheme, the spot diameter is reduced by a factor of n, where n is the refractive index of the glass material of the hemisphere. Another variation on the same theme involves a SIL that is slightly greater than a hemisphere, and yields a spot size reduction by a factor of n^2. Using a glass of refractive index close to 2 as the SIL material, a fourfold reduction in the spot size is therefore feasible. The flying height of the SIL over the disk surface is critical and must remain within a fraction of the wavelength of the laser beam. Laboratory demonstrations of this technique have been quite impressive (Terris et al., 1995), but its potential for application in commercial drives depends on the ability to maintain disk removability in the presence of a flying head.

REFERENCES

Alben, R., J. J. Becker, and M. C. Chi, "Random Anisotropy in Amorphous Ferromagnets," *J. Appl. Phys.,* **49,** 1653 (1978).

Allen, R., and G. A. N. Connell, "Magneto-optic Properties of Amorphous Terbium-Iron," *J. Appl. Phys.,* **53,** 2353 (1982).

Anthony, T. C., J. Brug, S. Naberhuis, and H. Birecki, "Thermal Stability of Magnetooptical Quadrilayers," *J. Appl. Phys.,* **59,** 213 (1986).

Aoki, Y., T. Ihashi, N. Sato, and S. Miyaoka, "A Magneto-optic Recording System Using TbFeCo," *IEEE Trans. Magn.,* **MAG-21,** 1624 (1985).

Aratani, K., T. Kobayashi, S. Tsunashima, and S. Uchiyama, "Magnetic and Magnetooptic Properties of Tb-Fe-Co-Al Films," *J. Appl. Phys.,* **57,** 3903 (1985).

Aratani, K., M. Kaneko, Y. Mutoh, K. Watanabe, and H. Makino, "Overwriting on a Magnetooptical Disk with Magnetic Triple Layers by Means of the Light Intensity Modulation Method," *Proc. SPIE,* **1078,** 258 (1989).

Aratani K., A. Fukumoto, M. Ohta, M. Kaneko, and K. Watanabe, "Magnetically Induced Super Resolution in Novel Magnetoopitical Disks," Proc. SPIE, **1499,** 209 (1991).

Argyle, B. E., R. J. Gambino, and K. Y. Ahn, "Polar Kerr Rotation and Sublattice Magnetization in GdCoMo Bubble Films," *AIP Conf. Proc.,* **24,** 564 (1974).

Arimoto, A., and M. Ojima, "Diode Laser Noise at Control Frequencies in Optical Videodisc Players," *Appl. Optics,* **23,** 2913 (1984).

Bell, A. E., "Critical Issues in High Density Magnetic and Optical Data Stoarge," *Proc. SPIE,* **382,** 2 (1983).

Bell, A. E., and F. W. Spong, "Antireflection Structures for Optical Recording," *IEEE J. Quantum Electr.,* **QE-14,** 487 (1978).

Bennett, H. S., and E. A. Stern, "Faraday Effect in Solids," *Phys. Rev. A.,* **137,** 448 (1965).

Bernacki, B. E., and M. Mansuripur, "Investigation of Substrate Birefringence Effects on Optical-Disk Performance," *Applied Optics,* **32,** 6555 (1993).

Bernstein, P., and C. Gueugnon, "Properties of Amorphous Rare-Earth Transition Metal-Thin Films for Magnetooptical Recording," *IEEE Trans. Magn.,* **MAG-21,** 1613 (1985).

Biesterbos, J. W. M., A. G. Dirks, M. A. J. P. Farla, and P. J. Grundy, "Microstructure and Magnetic Properties of Amorphous Tb-Fe(O_2) Thin Films," *Thin Sol. Films,* **58,** 259 (1979).

Biesterbos, J. W. M., A. J. D. Boef, W. Linders, and G. A. Acket, "Low-Frequency Mode-Hopping Optical Noise in AlGaAs Channeled Substrate Lasers Induced by Optical Feedback," *IEEE J. Quantum Elect.,* **OE-19,** 986 (1983).

Bloomberg, D. S., and G. A. N. Connell, "Prospects for Magnetooptic Recording," *Proc. IEEE Compcon Spring,* 32 (1985).

Bouwhuis, G., and J. Braat, "Recording and Reading of Information on Optical Disks," in R. R. Shannon and J. C. Wyant (eds.), *Applied Optics and Optical Engineering,* vol. 9, Academic Press, New York, 1983.

Bouwhuis, G., J. Braat, A. Huijser, J. Pasman, G. van Rosmalen, and K. Immink, *Principles of Optical Disk Systems,* Adam Hilger Ltd., Bristol, England, 1985, p. 49*ff.*

Bozorth, R. M., *Ferromagnetism,* van Nostrand, Princeton, N.J., 1951.

Braat, J. J. M., and G. Bouwhuis, "Position Sensing in Video Disk Readout," *Applied Optics,* **17,** 2013 (1978).

Carasso, M. G., J. B. H. Peek, and J. P. Sinjou, "The Compact Disc Digital Audio System," *Philips Tech. Rev.,* **40**(6), 151 (1982).

Cargill, G. S., "Structure of Metallic Alloy Glasses," in H. Ehrenreich, F. Seitz, and D. Turnbull (eds.), *Solid State Physics*, vol. 30, Academic Press, New York, 1975.

Carslaw, H. S., and J. C. Jaeger, *Conduction of Heat in Solids,* Clarendon, Oxford, 1959.

Chang, J. T., J. F. Dillon, and U. F. Gianola, "Magnetooptical Variable Memory Based upon the Properties of a Transparent Ferrimagnetic Garnet at its Compensation Temperature," *J. Appl. Phys., 36,* 1110 (1965).

Chaudhari, P., J. J. Cuomo, and R. J. Gambino, "Amorphous Metallic Films for Magneto-optical Applications," *Appl. Phys. Lett., 22,* 337 (1973).

Cheng, L., M. Mansuripur, and D. G. Howe, "Partial Response Equalization in Magnetooptical Disk Readout: A Theoretical Investigation," to appear in *Applied Optics, 34,* 5153 1995.

Clark, G. C., and J. B. Cain, *Error-Correction Coding for Digital Communications,* Plenum, New York, 1981.

Coey, J. M. D., "Amorphous Magnetic Order," *J. Appl. Phys., 49,* 1646 (1978).

Cohen, D. K., W. H. Gee, M. Ludeke, and J. Lewkowics, "Automatic Focus Control: The Astigmatic Lens Approach," *Appl. Optics, 23,* 565 (1984).

Connell, G. A. N., "Interference Enhanced Kerr Spectroscopy for Very Thin Absorbing Films," *Appl. Phys. Lett., 40,* 212 (1982).

Connell, G. A. N., "Measurement of the Magneto-optical Constants of Reactive Metals," *Appl. Opt., 22,* 3155 (1983).

Connell, G. A. N., "Magneto-optics and Amorphous Metals: An Optical Storage Revolution," *J. Magn. and Mag. Mat., 54-57,* 1561 (1986).

Connell, G. A. N., R. J. Nemanich, and C. C. Tsai, "Interference Enhanced Raman Scattering from Very Thin Absorbing Films," *Appl. Phys. Lett., 36,* 31 (1980).

Connell, G. A. N., and R. Allen, "Magnetization Reversal in Amorphous Rare-Earth Transition-Metal Alloys: TbFe," *Proc. 4th Int. Conf. on Rapidly Quenched Metals, 1981,* Sendai, Japan, 1981.

Connell, G. A. N., R. Allen, and M. Mansuripur, "Magneto-optical Properties of Amorphous Terbium-Iron Alloys," *J. Appl. Phys., 53,* 7759 (1982).

Connell, G. A. N., and R. Allen, "Amorphous Terbium-Iron Based Alloys," *J. Magn. and Mag. Mat., 31–34,* 1516 (1983).

Connell, G. A. N., D. Treves, R. Allen, and M. Mansuripur, "Signal-to-Noise Ratio for Magneto-optic Readout from Quadrilayer Structures," *Appl. Phys. Lett., 42,* 742 (1983).

Connell, G. A. N., S. J. Oh, J. Allen, and R. Allen, "The Electronic Density of States of Amorphous Y-Fe and Tb-Fe Alloys," *J. Non-Cryst. Solids, 61 & 62,* 1061 (1984).

Connell, G. A. N., and D. S. Bloomberg, "Amorphous Rare-Earth Transition-Metal Alloys," in D. Adler, H. Fritzsche, and S. R. Ovshinsky (eds.), *Physics of Disordered Materials,* Plenum, New York, 1985, p. 739.

Corcoran, J., and H. Ferrier, "Melting Holes in Metal Films for Real-Time High-Density Permanent Digital Data Storage," *Proc. SPIE, 123,* 17 (1977).

D'Antonio, P., J. H. Konnert, J. J. Rhyne, and C. R. Hubbard, "Structural Ordering in Amorphous $TbFe_2$ and YFe_2," *J. Appl. Cryst., 15,* 452 (1982).

Deguchi, T., H. Katayama, A. Takahashi, K. Ohta, S. Kobayashi, and T. Okamoto, "Digital Magneto-optic Disk Drive," *Appl. Optics, 23,* 3972 (1984).

Dekker, P., "Manganese Bismuth and Other Magnetic Materials for Beam Addressable Memories," *IEEE Trans. Magn.,* **MAG-12,** 311 (1976).

Egami, T., "Theory of Intrinsic Magnetic After-Effect," *Phys. Stat. Sol., (a) 19,* 747 (1973).

Freese, R. P., R. N. Gardner, T. A. Rinehart, D. W. Siitari, and L. H. Johnson, "An Environmentally Stable, High Performance, High Data Rate Magneto-optic Media," *Proc. SPIE,* **529,** 6 (1985).

Freiser, M. J., "A Survey of Magneto-optic Effects," *IEEE Trans. Magn.,* **MAG-4,** 152 (1968).

Fu, H., S. Sugaya, J. K. Erwin, and M. Mansuripur, "Measurement of Birefringence for Optical Recording Disk Substrates," *Applied Optics,* **33,** 1949 (1994).

Fukumoto, A., S. Masuhara, and K. Aratani, "Crosstalk Analysis of Land/groove Magnetooptical Recording," *Symposium on Optical Memory,* 1994, Technical Digest, paper TuA4.

Fukunishi, S., M. Miyagi, and N. Funakoshi, "Amorphous Magneto-optical Disk with Multilayered Structure," *Conf. Lasers and Electro-Optics,* 132 (1985).

Gambino, R. J., P. Chaudhari, and J. J. Cuomo, "Amorphous Magnetic Materials," *AIP Conf. Proc.,* **18,** 578 (1974).

Gambino, R. J., and T. R. McGuire "Enhanced Magneto-optic Properties of Light Rare-Earth Transition-Metal Amorphous Alloys," *J. Magn. and Mag. Mat.,* **54–57,** 1365 (1986).

Gangulee, A., and R. J. Kobliska, "Mean Field Analysis of the Magnetic Properties of Amorphous Transition-Metal Rare-Earth Alloys," *J. Appl. Phys.,* **49,** 4896 (1978).

Goldberg, N., "A High Density Magneto-optic Memory," *IEEE Trans. Magn.,* **MAG-3,** 605 (1967).

Goodman, J. W., *Introduction to Fourier Optics,* McGraw-Hill, San Francisco, 1968, p. 120.

Goodman, T. D., and M. Mansuripur, "Optimization of Groove Depth for Cross-talk Cancellation in the Scheme of Land/Groove Recording in Magnetooptical Disk Systems," *Applied Optics,* 1995.

Hansen, P., "Direct Overwrite in Amorphous Rare-Earth Transition-Metal Alloys," *Appl. Phys. Lett.,* **50,** 356 (1987).

Hansen, P., and M. Urner-Wille, "Magnetic and Magneto-optic Properties of Amorphous GdFeBi-Films," *J. Appl. Phys.,* **50,** 7471 (1979).

Harper, J. M. E., and R. J. Gambino, "Combined Ion Beam Deposition and Etching for Thin Film Studies," *J. Vac. Sci. Tech.,* **16,** 1901 (1979).

Harris, R., "Metastable States in the Random Anisotropy Model for Amorphous Ferromagnets: The Absence of Ferromagnetism," *J. Phys. F: Metal Phys.,* **10,** 2545 (1980).

Harris, R., S. H. Sung, and M. J. Zuckermann, "Hysteresis Effects in Amorphous Magnetic Alloys Containing Rare Earths," *IEEE Trans. Magn.,* **MAG-14,** 725 (1978).

Hartman, M., J. Braat, and B. Jacobs, "Erasable Magneto-optical Recording Media," *IEEE Trans. Magn.,* **MAG-20,** 1013 (1984).

Hasegawa, R., and R. C. Taylor, "Magnetization of Amorphous Gd-Co-Ni Films," *J. Appl. Phys.,* **46,** 3606 (1975).

Heavens, O. S., *Optical Properties of Thin Films,* Dover, New York, 1965.

Heemskerk, J. P. J., and K. A. S. Immink, "Compact Disc: System Aspects and Modulation," *Philips Tech. Rev.,* **40**(6), 157 (1982).

Heiman, N., K. Lee, and R. I. Potter, "Exchange Coupling in Amorphous Rare Earth-Iron Alloys," *AIP Conf. Proc.,* **29,** 130 (1975).

Heitmann, H., M. Hartmann, M. Rosenkranz, and H. J. Tolle, "Amorphous Rare-Earth Transition-Metal Films for Magnetooptical Storage," *J. Phys. Colloq (France),* **46,** 9 (1985).

Hindley, N. K., "Random Phase Model of Amorphous Semiconductors," *J. Non-Cryst. Sol.,* **5,** 17 (1970).

Hoeve, H., J. Timmermans, and L. B. Vries, "Error Correction and Concealment in the Compact Disc System," *Philips Tech. Rev.,* **40**(6), 166 (1982).

Hong, M., D. D. Bacon, R. B. van Dover, E. M. Gyorgy, J. F. Dillon and S. D. Albiston, "Aging Effects on Amorphous Tb-Transition Metal Films Prepared by Diode and Magnetron Sputtering," *J. Appl. Phys.,* **57,** 3900 (1985).

Honma, H., T. Iwanaga, K. Kayanuma, M. Nakada, R. Katayama, S. Itoī, and H. Inada, "High Density Land/Groove Recording Using PRML Technology," *Proceedings of the Optical Data Storage Conference, SPIE,* **2338,** 314 (1994).

Horowitz, P., and W. Hill, *The Art of Electronics,* Cambridge University Press, Cambridge, 1980, pp. 288–290.

Hunt, R. P., "Magnetooptics, Lasers and Memory Systems," *IEEE Trans. Magn.,* **MAG-5,** 700 (1969).

Hurst, J. E., and W. J. Kozlovsky, "Optical recording at 2.4 Gbit/sq-in Usign a Frequency Doubled Diode Laser," *Jpn. J. Appl. Phys.,* **32,** 5301 (1993).

Huth, B. G., "Calculations of Stable Domain Radii Produced by Thermomagnetic Writing," *IBM J. Res. Dev.,* **18,** 100 (1974).

Ichihara, K., K. Taira, Y. Terashima, S. Shimanuki, and N. Yasuda, "Highly Reliable TbCo Film for Erasable Optical Disk Memory," *Proc. of Topical Meeting on Optical Data Storage,* Laser and Electro-Optic Society of IEEE, Washington, D.C., 1985, p. WAA2-1.

Ichihara, K., S. Shimanuki, and N. Yasuda, "The Underlayer Film Treatment Effect on Tb-Co Film Properties in Optical Disk Memory Structure," *IEEE Trans. Magn.,* **MAG-22,** 1331 (1986).

Imamura, N., S. Tanaka, F. Tanaka, and Y. Nagao, "Magneto-optical Recording on Amorphous Films," *IEEE Trans. Magn.,* **MAG-21,** 1607 (1985).

Jackson, J. D., *Classical Electrodynamics,* Wiley, New York, 1967.

Jackson, W. B., S. M. Kelso, C. C. Tsai, J. W. Allen, and S. J. Oh, "Energy Dependence of the Optical Matrix Element in the Hydrogenated Amorphous and Crystalline Silicon," *Phys. Rev.,* **B31,** 5187 (1985).

Jacobs, B., J. Braat, and M. Hartman, "Aging Characteristics of Amorphous Magnetooptic Recording Media," *Appl. Optics,* **23,** 3979 (1984).

Jipson, V. B., and C. C. Williams, "Two-Dimensional Modeling of an Optical Disk Readout," *Appl. Optics,* **22,** 2202 (1983).

Kanada, T., "Theoretical Study of Noise Reduction Effects by Superimposed Pulse Modulation," *Trans. IECE Japan,* **E68,** 180 (1985).

Kayanuma, K., T. Iwanaga, H. Inada, K. Okanoue, R. Katayama, K. Yoshihara, Y. Yamanaka, M. Tsunekane, and O. Okada, "High Track Density Magnetooptical Recording Using a Cross-talk Canceller," *Proc. SPIE,* **1316,** 35 (1990).

Kivits, P., R. deBont, and P. Zalm, "Superheating of Thin Films for Optical Recording," *Appl. Phys.,* **24,** 273 (1981).

Kloosterboer, J. G., G. J. M. Lippits, and H. C. Meinders, "Photopolymerizable Lacquers for LaserVision Video Disks," *Philips Tech. Rev.,* **40,** 298 (1982).

Kocher, D. G., "Automated Foucault Test for Focus Sensing," *Appl. Optics,* **22,** 1887 (1983).

Kryder, M. H., W. H. Meiklejohn, and R. E. Skoda, "Stability of Perpendicular Domains in Thermomagnetic Recording Materials," *Proc. SPIE,* **420,** 236 (1983).

Kryder, M. H., "Magnetooptic Recording Technology," *J. Appl. Phys.,* **57,** 3913 (1985).

Kryder, M. H., and W. Meiklejohn, to be published by the Cambridge University Press, 1996.

Landau, L. D., and E. M. Lifshitz, *Statistical Physics,* Pergamon, London, 1958, pp. 379–406.

Lang, J. K., Y. Baer, and P. A. Cox, "Study of 4f and Valence Density of States in Rare Earth Metals," *J. Phys. F: Metal Phys.,* **11,** 121 (1981).

Loudon, R., "Theory of Resonance Raman Effect in Crystals," *J. Physique,* **26,** 677 (1965).

Luborsky, F. E., J. T. Furey, R. E. Skoda, and B. C. Wagner, "Stability of Amorphous Transition Metal-Rare Earth Films for Magneto-optic Recording," *IEEE Trans. Magn.,* **MAG-21,** 1618 (1985).

Malozemoff, A. P., A. R. Williams, K. Terakura, V. L. Moruzzi, and K. Fukamichi, "Magnetism of Amorphous Metal-Metal Alloys," *J. Magn. and Mag. Mat.,* **35,** 192 (1983).

Mansfield, S. M., and G. S. Kino, *Appl. Phys. Lett.,* **57,** 2615 (1990).

Mansuripur, M., "Certain Computational Aspects of Vector Diffraction Problems," *J. Opt. Soc. Am. A,* **6,** 805 (1989).

Mansuripur, M., *The Physical Principles of Magnetooptical Recording,* Cambridge Univ. Press, London, 1995.

Mansuripur, M., and Y. C. Hsieh, "A Novel Method for Measuring the Vertical Birefringence of Optical Disk Substrates," *Optics and Photonics News,* Engineering Laboratory Notes S12 (May 1994).

Mansuripur, M., G. A. N. Connell, and J. W. Goodman, "Signal and Noise in Magneto-optic Readout," *J. Appl. Phys.,* **53,** 4485 (1982).

Mansuripur, M., and G. A. N. Connell, "Magneto-optical Recording," *Proc. SPIE,* **420,** 222 (1983*a*).

Mansuripur, M., and G. A. N. Connell, "Thermal Aspects of Magneto-optical Recording," *J. Appl. Phys.,* **54,** 4794 (1983*b*).

Mansuripur, M., and G. A. N. Connell, "Laser-induced Local Heating of Moving Multilayer Media," *Appl. Optics,* **21,** 666 (1983*c*).

Mansuripur, M., and G. A. N. Connell, "Energetics of Domain Formation in Thermomagnetic Recording," *J. Appl. Phys.,* **55,** 3049 (1984).

Mansuripur, M., M. F. Ruane, and M. N. Horenstein, "Magnetic Properties of Amorphous Rare-Earth Transition-Metal Alloys for Erasable Optical Storage," *Proc. SPIE,* **529,** 25 (1985).

Marchant, A. B., *Optical Recording,* Addison-Wesley, Massachusetts (1990).

Marchant, A. B. "Retardation Effects in Magnetooptic Readout," in Optical Mass Data Storage II, R. P. Freese, A. A. Janberdino, and M de Haan, eds., *Proc. Soc. Photo. Instrum. Eng.,* **695,** 270 (1986).

Masui, S., T. Kobayashi, S. Tsunashima, S. Uchiyama, K. Sumiyama, and Y. Nakamura, "Magnetic and Magneto-optic Properties of Amorphous GdFeCo and GeFeCoBi Films," *IEEE Trans. Magn.,* **MAG-20,** 1036 (1984).

Mayer, L., "Curie-Point Writing on Magnetic Films," *J. Appl. Phys.,* **29,** 1003 (1958).

McDaniel, T. W., and R. Victora, eds., to be published by the Noyes Publishers, 1995.

Mimura, Y., N. Imamura, and T. Kobayashi, "Magnetic Properties and Curie Point Writing in Amorphous Metallic Films," *IEEE Trans. Magn.,* **MAG-12,** 779 (1976).

Mimura, Y., N. Imamura, T. Kobayashi, A. Okada, and Y. Kushiro, "Magnetic Properties of Amorphous Alloy Films of Fe with Gd, Tb, Dy, Ho, or Er," *J. Appl. Phys.,* **49,** 1208 (1978).

Mizoguchi, T., and G. S. Cargill, "Magnetic Anisotropy from Dipolar Interactions in Amorphous Ferrimagnetic Alloys," *J. Appl. Phys.,* **50,** 3570 (1979).

Nagao, T., S. Tanaka, F. Tanaka, and N. Imamura, "Improvement of TbFeCo Disks for Magneto-optical Recording," *Intermag. Conf. 1986,* Paper No. FC-07, 1986.

Nakao, T., M. Ojima, Y. Miyamura, S. Okamine, H. Sukeda, N. Ohta, and Y. Takeuchi, "High Speed Overwritable Magneto-optic Recording," *Jap. J. Appl. Phys.,* **26,** 149 (1987).

Nishihara, Y., T. Katayama, Y. Yamaguchi, S. Ogawa, and T. Tsushima, "Anisotropic Distribution of Atomic Pairs Induced by Preferential Resputtering Effect in Amorphous Gd-Fe and Gd-Co Films," *Jap. J. Appl. Phys.,* **17,** 1083 (1978).

Ohashi, K., H. Takagi, S. Tsunashima, S. Uchiyama, and T. Fujii, "Magnetic Aftereffect Due to Domain Wall Motion in Amorphous TbFe Sputtered Films," *J. Appl. Phys.,* **50,** 1611 (1979).

Ohishi, A., N. Chinone, M. Ojima, and A. Arimoto, "Noise Characteristics of High Frequency Superposed Laser Diodes for Optical Disc Systems," *Elect. Lett.,* **20,** 821 (1984).

Ohta, M., A. Fukumoto, K. Aratani, M. Kaneko, and K. Watanabe, "Readout Mechanism of Magnetically Induced Super Resolution," *J. Mag. Soc. Japan,* **15,** 319 (1991).

Okada, K., T. Kubo, W. Susaki, and T. Sato, "A New PCM Audio Disk Pickup Employing a Laser Diode," *J. Audio Eng. Soc.,* **28,** 429 (1980).

Okamine, S., N. Ohta, and Y. Sugita, "Perpendicular Anisotropy in Rare-Earth Transition-Metal Amorphous Films Prepared by Dual Ion Beam Sputtering," *IEEE Trans. Magn.,* **MAG-21,** 1641 (1985).

Pasman, J. H. T., H. F. Olijhoek, and B. Verkaik, "Developments in Optical Disk Mastering," *Proc. SPIE,* **529,** 62 (1985).

Prikryl, I., "Effects of Disk Birefringence on a Differential Magnetooptic Readout," *Appl. Opt.,* **31,** 1853 (1992).

Rhyne, J. J., "Amorphous Magnetic Rare Earth Alloys," in K. A. Gschneider and L. Eyring (eds.), *Handbook on the Physics and Chemistry of Rare Earths,* North-Holland, Amsterdam, 1977.

Richards, B., and E. Wolf, "Electromagnetic Diffraction in Optical Systems: Structure of the Image Field in an Aplanatic System," *Proc. Roy. Soc. A,* **253,** 358 (1959).

Rugar, D., "Magnetooptic Direct Overwrite Using a Resonant Bias Coil," *IEEE Trans. Magn.,* **MAG-24,** 666 (1988).

Rugar, D., and P. Siegel, "Recording Results and Coding Considerations for the Resonant Bias Coil Overwrite Technique," *SPIE Tech. Dig. Opt. Data Storage,* **1,** 149 (1989).

Saito, J., M. Sato, H. Matsumoto, and H. Akasaka, "Direct Overwrite by Light Power Modulation on Magnetooptical Multilayered Media," in *Proc. Internat. Symp. on Optical Memory,* 1987, published as Supplement 26-4 in *Jpn. J. Appl. Phys.,* **26,** 155 (1987).

Sakurai, Y., and K. Onishi, "Preparation and Properties of RE-TM Amorphous Films," *J. Magn. and Mag. Mat.,* **35,** 183 (1983).

Sato, M., N. Tsukane, S. Tokuhara, and H. Toba, "Magneto-optical Memory Disk Using Plastic Substrate," *Proc. SPIE,* **529,** 33 (1985).

Sato, R., N. Saito, and Y. Togami, "Magnetic Anisotropy of Amorphous Gd-R-Co (R = Tb, Dy, Ho, Er) Films," *Jap. J. Appl. Phys.,* **24,** L266 (1985).

Savage, C. M., F. Marquis, M. Warson, and P. Meyste, "Direct Overwrite in Magnetooptical Recording," *Appl. Phys. Lett.,* **52,** 1277, (1988).

Shieh, H-P. D., and M. H. Kryder, "Operating Margins for Magneto-Optic Recording Materials with Direct Overwrite Capability," *IEEE Trans. Magn.,* **MAG-23,** 171 (1987).

Shultz, M. D., H-P. D. Shieh, and M. H. Kryder, "Performance of the Magneto-Optical Recording Media with Direct Overwrite Capability," *J. Appl. Phys.,* **63,** 3844 (1988).

Smith, D. O., "Magneto-optical Scattering from Multilayer Magnetic and Dielectric Films. Pt. I. General Theory," *Optica Acta,* **12,** 13 (1965a).

Smith, D. O., "Magneto-optical Scattering from Multilayer Magnetic and Dielectric Films. Pt. II. Applications of the General Theory," *Optica Acta,* **12,** 193 (1965b).

Smith, D. O., "Magnetic Films and Optics in Computer Memories," *IEEE Trans. Magn.,* **MAG-3,** 433 (1967).

Stubkjaer, K. E., and M. B. Small, "Noise Properties of Semiconductor Lasers Due to Optical Feedback," *IEEE J. Quantum Elect.,* **QE-20,** 472 (1984).

Sugaya, S., and M. Mansuripur, "Effects of Substrate Birefringence on Focusing and Tracking Servo Signals in Magnetooptical Disk Data Storage," *Applied Optics,* **33,** 5073 (1994).

Sugaya, S. and M. Mansuripur, "Effect of Tilted Ellipsoid of Birefringence on Readout Signal in Magnetooptical Disk Data Storage," *Applied Optics,* **33,** 5999 (1994).

Sun, S. S., and C. W. Laumann, "Self-Biasing Thermal Magneto-Optic Medium," European Patent Application 86110794.4, 1987.

Sunago, K., S. Matsushita, and Y. Sakurai, "Thermomagnetic Writing in TbFe Films," *IEEE Trans. Magn.,* **MAG-12,** 776 (1976).

Takagi, H., S. Tsunashima, S. Uchiyama, and T. Fujii, "Stress Induced Anisotropy in Amorphous Gd-Fe and Tb-Fe Sputtered Films," *J. Appl. Phys.,* **50,** 1642 (1979).

Takahashi, A., M. Mieda, Y. Murakami, K. Ohta, and H. Yamaoka, "Influence of Birefringence on the Signal Quality of Magnetooptic Disks Using Polycarbonate Substrates," *Appl. Opt.,* **27,** 2863 (1988).

Takayama, T., O. Imafuji, H. Sugiura, M. Yuri, H. Naito, M. Kume, and A. Yoshikawa, "Low Operating Current Self Sustained Pulsation Ga Al As Laser Diodes with a Real Refractive Index Guided Structure," *Appl. Phys. Lett.,* **65,** 1211 (1994).

Tanaka, F., S. Tanaka, and N. Imamura, "Magneto-Optical Recording Characteristics of TbFeCo Media by Magnetic Field Modulation Method," *Jap. J. Appl. Phys.,* **26,** 231 (1987).

Taylor, R. C., and A. Gangulee, "Magnetic Properties of Amorphous GdFeB and GdCoB Alloys," *J. Appl. Phys.*, **53**, 2341 (1982).

Terris, B. D., H. J. Mamin, and D. Rugar, "Optical Data Storage Using a Solid Immersion Lens," *Magneto-optical Recording International Symposium,* J. Mag. Soc. Japan, **19**, Suppl. S1, 409 (1995).

Theuerer, H. C., E. A. Nesbitt, and D. D. Bacon, "High Coercive Force Rare-Earth Alloy Films by Getter Sputtering," *J. Appl. Phys.*, **40**, 2994 (1969).

Thiele, A. A., "Theory of the Static Stability of Cylindrical Domains in Uniaxial Platelets," *J. Appl. Phys.*, **41**, 1139 (1970).

Tobita, M., T. Yamagami, and T. Watanabe, "Viterbi Detection of Partial Response on a Magnetooptical Recording Channel," *Proceedings of the Optical Data Storage Conference, SPIE*, **1663**, 166 (1992).

Togami, Y., R. Sato, N. Saito, and M. Shibayama, "Magneto-optical Kerr Effect in Amorphous RE-Co-Fe Films," *Jap. J. Appl. Phys.*, **24**, 106 (1985).

Treves, D., and D. S. Bloomberg, "Effect of Birefringence on Optical Memory Systems," *Proc. SPIE*, **695**, 262 (1986a).

Treves, D., and D. S. Bloomberg, "Signal, Noise and Codes in Optical Memories," *Optical Engineering*, **25**, 881 (1986b).

Tsunashima, S., S. Masui, T. Kobayashi, and S. Uchiyama, "Magneto-optic Kerr Effect of Amorphous Gd-Fe-Co Films," *J. Appl. Phys.*, **53**, 8175 (1982).

Tsunoda, Y., S. Horigome, and Z. Tsutsumi, "Optical Digital Data Storage Technologies with Semiconductor Laser Head," *Proc. SPIE*, **382**, 24 (1983).

Tsutsumi, K., Y. Nakaki, T. Fukami, and T. Tokunaga, "Directly Overwritable Magnetooptical Disk with Light Power Modulation Method Using No Initializing Magnet," in *Proc. SPIE*, **1499**, 55 (1991).

Uchiyama, S., "Magneto-optic Properties of Ternary and Quaternary Rare-Earth Transition-Metal Amorphous Films," in Y. Sakurai (ed.,) *Jap. Annu. Rev. Electron., Comput., Telecommun.: Recent Magnetics for Electronics,* N. Holland, Amsterdam, 1986.

van Dover, R. B., M. Hong, E. Gyorgy, J. F. Dillon, and S. D. Albiston, "Intrinsic Anisotropy on Tb-Fe Films Prepared by Magnetron Co Sputtering," *J. Appl. Phys.*, **57**, 3897 (1985).

van Dover, R. B., E. M. Gyorgy, R. P. Frankenthal, M. Hong, and D. J. Siconolfi, "Effect of Oxidation on the Magnetic Properties of Unprotected TbFe Thin Films," *J. Appl. Phys.*, **59**, 1291 (1986).

van Rijsewijk, H. C. H., P. E. J. Legierse, and G. E. Thomas, "Manufacture of Laser-Vision Video Discs by Photopolymerization Process," *Philips Tech. Rev.*, **40**, 287 (1982).

Wolf, E., "Electromagnetic Diffraction in Optical Systems, I. An Integral Representation of the Image Field," *Proc. Roy. Soc. A,* **253**, 349 (1959).

Yamada, Y., M. Yoshihiro, N. Ohta, H. Sukeda, T. Niihara, and H. Fujiwara, "Highly Power Sensitive and Field Sensitive MO Disk for 8 MB/s Data Transfer," *J. Mag. Soc. Japan*, **15**, Suppl. S1, 417 (1991).

APPENDIX
CONVERSION TABLE

Units for Magnetic Properties

Quantity	Symbol	Gaussian & cgs emu†	Conversion factor C‡	SI§
Magnetic flux density, magnetic induction	B	gauss (G)	10^{-4}	tesla (T), Wb/m²
Magnetic flux	Φ	maxwell (Mx), G · cm²	10^{-8}	weber (Wb)
Magnetic potential difference, magnetomotive force	U	gilbert (Gb)	$10/4\pi$	ampere (A)
Magnetic field strength, magnetizing force	H	oersted (Oe)	$10^3/4\pi$	A/m
Magnetization	M	emu/cm³	10^3	A/m
Specific saturation magnetization	σ	emu/g	1	A · m²/kg
Magnetic moment	m	emu	10^{-3}	A · m²
Susceptibility	χ	dimensionless	4π	dimensionless
Permeability of vacuum	μ_0	dimensionless	$4\pi \times 10^{-7}$	Wb/(A · m)
Permeability	μ	dimensionless	$4\pi \times 10^{-7} = \mu_0$	Wb/(A · m)
Demagnetization factor	N	dimensionless	$1/4\pi$	dimensionless

†Gaussian units and cgs emu are the same for magnetic properties. The defining relation is $B = H + 4\pi M$.

‡Multiply a number in Gaussian units by C to convert it to SI.

§SI (Système International d'Unités) has been adopted by the National Bureau of Standards and is based on the definition $B = \mu_0(H + M)$.

INDEX

Italic page numbers indicate where defining or detailed descriptions are given.

Adhesion, 7.9
Air-bearing surface:
  of rigid disk sliders, 7.7
  of tape heads, 7.6
  (*See also* Slider bearing)
Alfenol, 6.24
Alperm, 6.24
Alternating gradient magnetometer, 9.6
Amorphous magnetic alloys, 6.24
Amplitude distortion, 8.26
Amplitude equalization, 8.12, 8.26
Analog recording (*see* Linear recording)
Anhysteresis:
  as evidence of particle interactions, 3.21
  ideal, 2.53
  measurement of, 9.4
  modified, 2.59
  Monte Carlo modeling of, 2.56
  Preisach diagram representation of, 2.59
  (*See also* Linear recording)
Anhysteretic susceptibility, 2.56, 3.21
Anisotropy of films, 4.3
  in-plane, 4.39
  magnetocrystalline, 4.3
  magnetostatic (shape), 4.4
  magnetostrictive, 4.5
  perpendicular, 4.6, 4.44
Anisotropy of magnetooptical materials:
  anisotropy constant, 10.14
  change during aging, 561
  and pair ordering, 10.14
  perpendicular, 10.9
  and planar stress, 10.14
  single-ion, 10.15
  uniaxial, 10.7
Anisotropy of particulates:
  exchange, 3.8
  induced, 3.62

Anisotropy of particulates (*Cont.*):
  local, 3.7
  magnetocrystalline, 3.
  magnetostatic (interaction), 3.9
  magnetostatic (shape), 3.9
  magnetostrictive, 3.8
  mixed, 3.18
Anisotropy measurements, 9.5, 9.10
Arctangent transitions:
  longitudinal recording, 2.10, 2.35
  perpendicular recording, 2.15, 2.42
Areal density:
  head-noise limited, 8.32
  in magnetooptical recording, 10.1, 10.87
  media-noise limited, 8.35
  in next decade, 8.36
  predictions of, 8.31
Atomic force/friction microscope (AFM/
    FFM):
  description, 7.46
  use for scratching and hardness measure-
    ment, 7.47
  use for wear studies, 7.47
Audio recording, 6.70
  heads for, 6.63, 6.67, 6.73
  media for 3.65
Autocorrelation theory:
  use in analyzing noise, 8.10
  Weiner theorem of, 8.10
Azimuth recording, 8.21

Barium ferrite:
  film media, 4.43
  particles, 3.36, 3.44
Barkhausen noise:
  in high-permeability underlayer, 4.46
  in magnetoresistive heads, 6.54
  in film heads, 6.33
BH loop tracer, 9.6